Welcome to PEARSON mystratlab™

Your Strategic Management course is personalized by you, it is NOT the same as the course taught down the hall. So, shouldn't your online resources be personalized as well? MyStratLab is an easy to use on-line tool that personalizes course content and provides robust assessment and reporting to measure student and class performance.

What Is MyStratLab?

Your course can include textbook assignments, case analysis, simulations, readings, and financial analysis. Now, all the resources both professors and students need for course success are in one place — easily organized and adapted for your course. **MyStratLab** is the ONLY **Strategic Management** tool which includes: Readiness Quizzes, Cases, Case Teaching Notes, Video Cases, Case Analysis Tools, Financial Templates, Team Evaluation Tools, **InterActive** How Would You Do Thats.

Features for Instructors

- **MyStratLab** matches the organization of this textbook. Preloaded content for every chapter of this book allows instructors to use **MyStratLab** as is or to customize **MyStratLab** with their own materials

- **Strategic Management Cases**-Almost every case from the book is available online in MyStratLab

- **Case Teaching Notes** which each include: Case at a Glance, Case Learning Objectives, Case Synopsis, Case Questions and Discussion, What if Discussions

- **Financial Analysis Tools**-Generic financial statement templates and pre-loaded financials from selected cases

- **Test Item File** and TestGen Test Generating Software

- **PowerPoint™** slides: 2 Sets—Both chapter specific and case specific

- **Team** evaluation tools

- **Built-in Electronic Gradebook** to track students' progress on the assessments and remediation activities

- **Interactive How Would You Do Thats**-Using Excel, students have the chance to experience the impact of management decisions and the interdepence of formulation and implementation

Features for Students

- **Chapter Readiness Quizzes**—Give students the opportunity to make sure they understand key chapter concepts and to prepare for Case Analysis. Readiness Quizzes test students on chapter learning outcomes and create a personalized study plan based on their results. Students can track their own progress through the course and use the personalized study plan activities to help them achieve success in the classroom and in their professional lives

- **Customized Study Plan**—Based upon the results of the Readiness Quizzes, students receive a plan to help them remediate important concepts and applications where they need improvement. Study Plans correlate to the Learning Objectives from the textbook and analysis tools to help students understand and apply the concepts. Some of the tools include: **Ebook pages, Powerpoint presentations, Strategic Management videos**

- **Financial Statement Templates**-Generic Financial Statement Templates and pre-loaded financials from selected cases

- **Interactive How Would You Do Thats**-Using Excel, students have the chance to experience the impact of management decisions and the interdepence of formulation and implementation

- **Chapter Resources**—Students have access to standard reference resources throughout *MyStratLab* to use as needed including: cases from the book, case writing guidelines, team guidelines

Your Strategy. Your Course.

www.mystratlab.com

THE UNIVERSITY *of* **WISCONSIN** MADISON

BYU BRIGHAM YOUNG UNIVERSITY

We're often asked....

WHAT IS A DYNAMIC PERSPECTIVE ON STRATEGY AND WHY IS IT IMPORTANT?

Dynamic perspective on strategy gives students a means of connecting the dots between internal resources and capabilities, ever- and increasingly rapid-changing external conditions, and firm and industry survival and profitability. Taking a dynamic perspective on strategy allows students to see that change is inevitable in strategy and can occur rapidly or slowly.

WHAT IS STRATEGIC LEADERSHIP AND WHY IS IT IMPORTANT?

Strategic Leadership is the role that top and middle-managers play in strategy and formulation and implementation. Strategic Leadership is important in regards to dynamic strategy because managers are often the key sources of dynamic capabilities that allow firms to complete in rapidly changing competitive environments. Students can see how the strategic tone is set at the top but that successful implementation is dependent on individuals. Instructors have an opportunity to talk about the personalities of executives in cases they use and how these personalities play out in formulation and implementation.

WHAT IS THE INTERDEPENDENCE
OF FORMULATION AND IMPLEMENTATION AND WHY IS IT IMPORTANT?

Executives often say "I would rather have a mediocore strategy with great implementation than a great strategy with mediocore implementation." Students will have a clear understanding that formulation and implementation are interdependent and that effective formulation take implementation details into account early in the strategy process.

To sum it up....

Our treatment of the process of strategic management—managing the firm's strategy formulation and implementation over time—**allows us to bring management back into strategy**. By returning strategic leadership into the teaching strategy, we believe students at all levels can more readily see themselves as instrumental in the strategic management process.

Mason Carpenter

Wm. Gerard Sanders

Be Dynamic. Be Strategic.

The Fundamentals of Economic Logic

Ratios	How Calculated	Relevance of Concept
Profitability Indicators		
EBIT (Earnings before interest and taxes)	Net sales – operating expenses (also called operating profit)	Represents the amount of cash that such a company will be able to use to pay off creditors.
EBITDA (Earnings before interest, taxes, depreciation, and amortization)	EBIT + depreciation expenses + amortization expenses	A good way of comparing companies within and across industries. EBITDA is essentially the income that a company has free for interest payments.
Net Profit Margin	$\dfrac{\text{Profits after taxes}}{\text{Sales}}$	This number is an indication of how effective a company is at cost control. The higher the net profit margin is, the more effective the company is at converting revenue into actual profit.
Gross Profit Margin	$\dfrac{\text{Sales} - \text{Cost of goods sold}}{\text{Sales}}$	A good indication of what the company has left over to cover administrative costs after it has cover the cost of the goods sold
Return on assets	$\dfrac{\text{Return after taxes}}{\text{Total assets}}$ or $\dfrac{\text{Profits after taxes} + \text{interest}}{\text{Total Assets}}$	A measure of how effectively a firm uses its total assets.
Return on capital employed (ROCE)	$\dfrac{\text{EBIT}}{\text{Total assets} - \text{current liabilities}}$	A measure of the returns that a company is realizing from its capital employed. The ratio can also be seen as representing the efficiency with which capital is being utilized to generate revenue. It is commonly used as a measure for comparing the performance between businesses and for assessing whether a business generates enough returns to pay for its cost of capital.
Return on Equity (ROE)	$\dfrac{\text{Profits after taxes}}{\text{Total stockholders' equity}}$	A measure of how well a company has used reinvested earnings to generate additional earnings.
Return on Investment (ROI)	$\dfrac{\text{Operating income}}{\text{Total assets}}$	How effectively the firm uses its capital to generate profit; the higher the ROI, the better.
Return on Invested Capital (ROIC)	$\dfrac{\text{Profits after taxes} - \text{Preferred stock dividends}}{\text{Total stockholders' equity} + \text{total debt} - \text{par value of preferred stock}}$	How effectively a company uses the money (borrowed or owned) invested in its operations.
EBITDA margin	$\dfrac{\text{EBITDA}}{\text{Total revenue}}$	Measures the extent to which cash operating expenses use up revenue.
Operating Profit Margin	$\dfrac{\text{EBIT}}{\text{Total revenue}}$	A measure of a company's earnings power from ongoing operations. Operating profit margin indicates how effective a company is at controlling the costs and expenses associated with their normal business operations.

Retail	Mfg	Svc	Tech	COUNTRY	FIRM SIZE	Strategic Leadership	Implementation	Entrepreneurship	Joint Ventures/Alliances	International	Resource based view	Industry Change	Ethics
		x		UK	Small	x	x	x	x				
	x		x	Global	Industry Case	x	x	x			x		
		x		USA	Medium	x	x				x	x	
		x		USA	Small	x	x						x
x	x			Canada/ Japan	Small	x	x		x	x	x		
			x	Global	Large	x					x	x	
		x	x	Global	Large	x	x		x		x		
x			x	Global	Industry Case						x	x	x
			x	Global	Medium	x		x			x	x	
	x			Global	Medium			x		x	x	x	
x				Global	Large	x				x	x		
x				USA	Large	x	x				x	x	
		x		Europe/ UK	Medium	x		x			x		
	x			Global	Large		x				x	x	
	x			Global	Medium	x		x		x	x		
		x	x	Global	Large	x	x				x	x	
x		x		Global	Large		x	x	x		x		
		x		Global	Large	x				x	x	x	
	x			USA /Europe	Large	x					x	x	
	x			Global	Large		x		x	x	x		x
	x			North America	Medium		x	x	x	x	x		
		x		Global	Large	x			x	x	x		
	x			Global	Large		x		x				x
	x		x	Global	Large	x				x	x	x	
		x		Global	Large	x	x		x		x		
		x	x	Global	Large	x	x				x		
	x			Canada/ USA	Medium		x	x		x	x		
	x		x	Global	Large		x	x			x		
	x			Global	Medium		x			x	x	x	
		x	x	China/ USA	Large		x			x			x
		x	x	USA	Small		x	x			x		
		x		USA	Small	x	x	x			x		
		x	x	USA	Small	x	x	x			x	x	
		x		USA	Medium	x		x			x		
	x			Global	Large	x	x			x			x
		x		Global	Large	x	x						x
		x		Netherlands/ USA	Large	x	x				x		x

CASE	(Available in *Concepts and Cases* version only)	Book Page Number	CHAPTERS		TITLE	INDUSTRY
			Primary	Secondary	Primary Chapter	
1	Robin Hood	474	1	2, 11, 13	Strategic Management	Community Service
2	Three Dimensional Printing	476	1	2,12,4	Strategic Management	Manufacturing Design
3	Southwest Airlines	488	2	5,11	Vision and Mission	Airline
4	Pleasant Valley Elementary School: Celebrating Success One Student at a Time	497	2	11, 12	Vision and Mission	Education
5	Prince Edward Island Preserve Co.	502	3	4,5,12	Internal Environment	Specialty Food
6	ESRI: Changing World	514	3	4,6,12	Internal Environment	Software
7	Li & Fung The Global Value Chain Configurator	522	3	8, 9, 10,11	Internal Environment	Consumer Goods Distribution
8	Update: Music Industry in 2006	545	4	6,7,8	External Environment	Music Publishing
9	Razorfish	554	4	6, 11,12	External Environment	Web Technology/ Design
10	Embraer: Shaking Up the Aircraft Manufacturing Market	568	4	5,6,8	External Environment	Commercial Aircraft Manufacturing
11	Wal-Mart in the 21st Century: a Global Perspective	581	5	6,8	Creating Business Strategies	Retail
12	Home Depot's Strategy Under Bob Nardelli	593	5	3,4,12	Creating Business Strategies	Home Improvement
13	Ryan Air: The Southwest of Eurpean Airlines	602	5	3,4,12	Creating Business Strategies	Airline
14	Airbus: From Challenger to Leader	611	6	3,4,8	Bus Strat for Dynamic Context	Commercial Aircraft Manufacturing
15	Hornby PLC: Building Communities	621	6	3,8,10	Bus Strat for Dynamic Context	Toys
16	Oracle Corp.: Transformation to an E-business	630	6	4,7,11	Bus Strat for Dynamic Context	Software
17	McDonalds and the McCafe Coffee Initiative	639	7	3,4,12	Corporate Strategy	Fast Food
18	House of TATA -1995: The Next Generation (A)	645	7	8,9,11	Corporate Strategy	Consulting
19	Apple's iPod System: iPod, iTunes, and Fairplay	661	7	4, 6, 11	Corporate Strategy	Electronics
20	Coca-Cola's Reentry and Growth Strategies in China	666	8	3,4,6	International Strategies	Beverage
21	Neilson International in Mexico (A)	675	8	5, 9, 11	International Strategies	Candy
22	e-Bay International	683	8	5,9	International Strategies	Internet Auction
23	Renault-Volvo Strategic Alliance(A): March 1993	690	9	11,13	Alliances and Cooperative Strategies	Automobile Manufacturing
24	Symbian Ltd. And Nokia: Building the Smart Phone Industry	698	7	4, 6, 11	Corporate Strategies	Electronics
25	British Airways - USAir: Structuring A Global Strategic Alliance (A)	706	9	8,11	Alliances and Cooperative Strategies	Airline
26	Oracle: Growth by Acquisition	724	10	9,11	Mergers and Acquisitions	Software
27	The Expansion of Vincor	735	10	3,8,12	Mergers and Acquisitions	Wine
28	Cisco Systems, Inc.: Acqusition Integration for Manufacturing (A)	742	10	3,6,12	Mergers and Acquisitions	Communications
29	Porsche	761	11	3,4,6	Strategy Implementation Levers	Automobile Manufacturing
30	Google in China	768	11	2,8,13	Strategy Implementation Levers	Internet Services
31	Green Room Productions LLC	773	11	2,3,12	Strategy Implementation Levers	Internet Travel
32	Blue Whale Moving Company, Inc. (A)	785	12	3,5,11	New Ventures and Corporate Renewal	Moving/Relocation
33	Atomshockwave (A): A Venture Rollercoaster in the Online Entertainment Industry	795	12	5,6,10	New Ventures and Corporate Renewal	Online Entertainment
34	David Walentas' Two Trees Management Company	806	12	3,6,7	New Ventures and Corporate Renewal	Real Estate Development
35	Daimler Chrysler: Corp Governance Dynamics in a Global Co	812	13	8,10,11	Corp Governance in 21st Century	Automobile Manufacturing
36	Trouble in the Magic Kingdom: Governance Problems at Disney	828	13	2,3,11	Corp Governance in 21st Century	Entertainment
37	VNU's Strategy Derailed by Active Investors	836	13	3,7,10	Corp Governance in 21st Century	Media/ Communication

Ratios (continued)	How Calculated	Relevance of Concept
Activity Indicators		
Asset turnover	$$\frac{\text{Sales}}{\text{Total Assets}}$$	How efficiently sales are using the firm's asset base.
Inventory turnover	$$\frac{\text{Sales}}{\text{Inventory of finished goods}}$$	How efficiently a firm is able to convert inventory into sales.
Working Capital Turnover	$$\frac{\text{Sales}}{\text{Working capital}}$$	How efficiently a firm is able to convert working capital into sales.
Accounts receivable turnover	$$\frac{\text{Annual credit sales}}{\text{Accounts receivable}}$$	How quickly a firm is collecting on the monies owed it.
Accounts payable turnover	$$\frac{\text{Cost of goods sold}}{\text{Accounts payable}}$$	How quickly a firm is pay creditors.
Leverage Indicators		
Debt to equity ratio	$$\frac{\text{Total debt}}{\text{Total stockholders' equity}}$$	One measure of financial leverage. A higher debt/equity ratio may be riskier, especially in times of rising interest rates, due to the additional interest that has to be paid out for the debt.
Debt to assets	$$\frac{\text{Total debt}}{\text{Total assets}}$$	Another measure of leverage. If the ratio is greater than one, most of the company's assets are financed through debt. Companies with high debt/asset ratios are said to be "highly leveraged."
Interest coverage ratio	$$\frac{\text{Profits before interest and taxes}}{\text{Total interest charges}}$$	A calculation of a company's ability to meet its interest payments on outstanding debt. The lower the interest coverage, the larger the debt burden is on the company.
Liquidity Indicators		
Quick ratio (Acid Test Ratio)	$$\frac{\text{Current assets} - \text{Inventory}}{\text{Current liabilities}}$$	Using the firm's most liquid assets (typically cash + AR), is an "acid test" of a firm's ability to meet current financial obligations.
Current ratio	$$\frac{\text{Current assets}}{\text{Current liabilities}}$$	Using all the firm's current assets, is an indication of a firm's ability to meet current financial obligations.
Other Key Indicators		
Sustainable growth rate	ROE * (1– dividend-payout ratio)	Evaluates a firm's financial health by determining the rate of growth the company can sustain with its current capital structure.
Operating leverage	$$\frac{\text{Gross margin (or gross profit)}}{\text{Net profit margin}}$$	Indicates how sensitive a firm's profits are to small increases or decreases in revenue.
Weighted average cost of capital (WACC)	$$\frac{\text{Debt}}{\text{Cost of debt}} + \frac{\text{Equity}}{\text{Cost of equity}}$$	Represents the overall required return on the firm as a whole and is often used internally by company directors to determine the economic feasibility of expansionary opportunities and mergers.

Concepts and Cases

Strategic Management

A Dynamic Perspective

SECOND EDITION

Mason A. Carpenter
University of Wisconsin–Madison

Wm. Gerard Sanders
Brigham Young University

PEARSON

Prentice
Hall

Pearson Education International

Editor-in-Chief: David Parker
Executive Editor: Wendy Craven
Development Editor: Claire Hunter
Manager, Product Development: Ashley Santora
Project Manager, Editorial: Christina Volpe
Assistant Editor, Media: Valerie Patruno
Director of Marketing: Patrice Jones
Senior Managing Editor: Judy Leale
Project Manager, Production: Kevin H. Holm
Permissions Project Manager: Charles Morris
Senior Operations Supervisor: Arnold Vila
Operations Specialist: Arnold Vila
Creative Director: John Christiana
Interior and Cover Design: John Christiana
Cover Illustration/Photo: ©Adam Peiperl
Director, Image Resource Center: Melinda Patelli
Manager, Rights and Permissions: Zina Arabia
Manager: Visual Research: Beth Brenzel
Manager, Cover Visual Research & Permissions: Karen Sanatar
Image Permission Coordinator: Nancy Seise
Photo Researcher: Diane Austin
Composition: S4Carlisle Publishing Services
Full-Service Project Management: S4Carlisle Publishing Services
Printer/Binder: Courier/Kendallville; Coral Graphics
Typeface: Minion 10/12

Credits and acknowledgments borrowed from other sources and reproduced, with permission, in this textbook appear on appropriate page within text (or on page 885).

Pearson Education LTD.
Pearson Education Singapore, Pte. Ltd
Pearson Education Canada, Ltd
Pearson Education—Japan

Pearson Education Australia PTY, Limited
Pearson Education North Asia Ltd
Pearson Educación de Mexico, S.A. de C.V.
Pearson Education Malaysia, Pte. Ltd.

10 9 8 7 6 5 4 3 2 1
ISBN-13: 978-0-13-500934-5
ISBN-10: 0-13-500934-0

Dedication

My work on this book is dedicated to my wife Lisa , and to our boys Wesley and Zachary.

—MAC

This book is dedicated to my family—my wife Kathy, and our children Ashley, Adam, and Noelle— for providing the patience and support necessary to complete this project.

—WGS

Brief Contents

Contents

6 Crafting Business Strategy for Dynamic Contexts   204

13 Corporate Governance in the Twenty-First Century   462

PART SIX   CASE STUDIES: PULLING IT ALL TOGETHER

Preface

Intended Audience

This book is designed for undergraduate and MBA students and is most often used in strategic management or business policy courses. This book is available in two versions:

Strategic Management 2e Concepts and Cases

Strategic Management 2e Concepts

New and Enhanced in This Edition

With strategic management evolving so rapidly, textbooks and learning packages must evolve just as quickly. Here are highlights of the revisions in this edition:

- **New and Substantially Revised Chapter Opening Vignettes:** All chapter openers highlight dynamic companies and their leaders who make the strategic decisions. For example, Chapter 1 highlights UnderArmour and the decisions its founder Kevin Plank needed to make; and Chapter 2 highlights Anne Mulcahy, the first female CEO in Xerox history.

- **Interactive How Would You Do That (HWDYT) features:** We've pushed the envelope and in every chapter, students have a chance to place themselves in the role of a strategic decision maker at a well-known (and interesting) company. Using Excel, HWYDTs clearly show students the interdependence of formulation and implementation and lets them practice their decision-making skills. For example, see Mapping Your Social Network in Chapter 2 and Creating a Value Curve in Chapters 4 and 6.

- **NEW Ethical Questions in Every Chapter:** These questions require students to think about the ethical implications of strategic decision making.

- **NEW Emphasis on Financial Implications and Decision Making:** Key Economic Indicator ratios included at the front of the book AND Excel-based financial templates and selected case financials can be found at www.mystratlab.com.

Resources For Instructors

INSTRUCTOR'S RESOURCE CENTER: REGISTER. REDEEM. LOGIN.

At www.prenhall.com/irc, instructors can access a variety of print, digital, and presentation resources available with this text in downloadable format. Registration is simple and gives you immediate access to new titles and new editions. As a registered faculty member, you can download resource files and receive immediate access and instructions for installing course management content on your campus server.

The following supplements are available to adopting instructors at www.prenhall.com/irc

- www.mystratlab.com

- Instructor's Manual

- Test Item File

- TestGen Test Generating Software.

- PowerPoint Slides

- Author Podcasts

Need Help? Our dedicated Technical Support team is ready to help with the media supplements that accompany this text. Visit www.247.prenhall.com for answers to frequently asked questions and toll-free user support phone numbers.

PEARSON
mystratlab™

Welcome to MyStratLab

www.mystratlab.com

Your Strategic Management course is personalized by you and is NOT the same as the course taught down the hall. So, shouldn't your online resources be personalized as well? MyStratLab is an easy to use online tool that personalizes course content and provides robust assessment and reporting to measure student and class performance.

Your course can include textbook assignments, case analysis, simulations, readings, and financial analysis. Now, all the resources both professors and students need for course success are in one place — easily organized and adapted to your course. MyStratLab is the ONLY Strategic Management tool that includes: Readiness Quizzes, Cases, Case Teaching Notes, Case Analysis Tools, Financial Templates, Team Evaluation Tools, and InterActive How Would You Do That features.

FEATURES FOR INSTRUCTORS

- *MyStratLab* matches the organization of this textbook. Preloaded content for each chapter of this book allows instructors to use MyStratLab as-is or to customize MyStratLab with their own materials.

- Strategic Management Cases: Almost every case from the book is available online in MyStratLab.

- Case Teaching Notes that each include: Case at a Glance, Case Learning Objectives, Case Synopsis, Case Questions and Discussion, and What If Discussions

- Financial Analysis Tools: Generic financial statement templates and preloaded financials from selected cases

- Test Item File and TestGen Test Generating Software

- PowerPoint™ Slides: Two sets—both chapter and case specific

- Team Evaluation Tools

- Built-in Electronic Gradebook: Track student progress on the assessments and remediation activities.

- **Interactive How Would You Do That Features:** Using Excel, students have the chance to experience the impact of management decisions and the interdependence of formulation and implementation.

FEATURES FOR STUDENTS

- **Chapter Readiness Quizzes:** Give students the opportunity to make sure they understand key chapter concepts and prepare for Case Analysis. Readiness Quizzes test students on chapter learning outcomes and create a personalized study plan based on results. Students can track their own progress through the course and use the personalized study plan activities to help them to achieve success in the classroom and in their professional lives.

- **Customized Study Plan:** Based upon the results of the Readiness Quizzes, students receive a plan to help them remediate important concepts and applications where they need improvement. Study Plans correlate to the Learning Objectives from the textbook and analysis tools to help students understand and apply the concepts. Some of the tools include: **Ebook pages, Powerpoint presentations, Strategic Management videos**

- **Financial Statement Templates:** Generic Financial Statement Templates and preloaded financials from selected cases

- **Interactive How Would You Do That features:** Using Excel, students have the chance to experience the impact of management decisions and the interdependence of formulation and implementation

- **Chapter Resources:** Students have access to standard reference resources throughout *MyStratLab* to use as needed, including: almost all cases from the book, Case Writing Guidelines, and Team Guidelines.

CourseSmart Textbooks Online

CourseSmart Textbooks Online is an exciting new *choice* for students looking to save money. As an alternative to purchasing the print textbook, students can *subscribe* to the same content online and save up to 50% off the suggested list price of the print text. With a CourseSmart etextbook, students can search the text, make notes online, print out reading assignments that incorporate lecture notes and bookmark important passages for later review. For more information, or to subscribe to the CourseSmart eTextbook, visit www.coursesmart.com.

Acknowledgments

Many people were involved in reviewing the First Edition of the book and the Second Edition manuscript. Others were instrumental in developing MyStratLab and all of the teaching and learning material. All deserve to be recognized.

Chapter Reviewers

Robert DeFillippi *Suffolk University*
Scott Droege *Western Kentucky University*
Varghese George *University of Massachusetts Boston*
Manuela Hoehn-Weiss *University of Washington*
Necmi Karagozoglu *Sacramento State University*
Ismatilla Mardanov *Southeast Missouri State University*

Jeffrey Nystrom *University of Colorado at Denver and Health Sciences Center*
Timothy Palmer *Western Michigan University*
Abe Qastin *Lakeland College*
Steven Samaras *Longwood University*
Paul Thurston *Siena College*
Kenneth Wendeln *Indiana University*

Virtual Focus Group Attendees

Peter Antoniou *California State University*
LaKami Baker *Mississippi State University*
Greg Berezewski *Robert Morris College*
Steven Boivie *University of Arizona*
Aruna Chandra *Indiana State University*
Scott Elston *Iowa State University*
Robert DeFillippi *Suffolk University*
Betty Deiner *Barry University*
Scott Gallagher *James Madison University*

Debbie Gillard *Metropolitan State College, Denver*
Alan Miller *University of Nevada, Las Vegas*
Roman Nowacki *Northern Illinois University*
??? Phelan *University of Nevada, Las Vegas*
Douglas Polley *St. Cloud State University*
Katsu Shimizu *University of Texas, San Antonio*
John Upson *Florida State University*
Edward Ward *St. Cloud State University*
Marta White *Georgia State University*

Case Survey Respondents

Garry Adams *Auburn University*
Todd Alessandri *Syracuse University*
Errol Alexander *Menlo College*
A. Alkhafaji
Brent Allred *The College of William and Mary*
A Amason *The University of Georgia*
Clarence Anderson *Walla Walla College*
Rex Anderson *Gardner Webb University*
Steve Andersen *Black Hills State University*
Anthony Avallone *Saint Peter's College*
Warren Baker *Roanoke College*
Paul Bell *Southwest Wisconsin Technical College*
Richard Birkenbeuel *University of Dubuque*
Sylvia Black *North Carolina A & T State University*
William Boulton *Auburn University*
Thomas Box *Pittsburg State University*
Robert Brown *Idaho State University*
Scott Bryant *Montana State University*

Patricia Buhler *Goldey-Beacom College*
Thomas Butte *Humboldt State University*
Anthony Cantarella *Murray State University*
Samuel Cappel *Southeastern Louisiana University*
Steven Carr *Texas A & M University*
Tim Carroll *Georgia Tech University*
Ronald Clement *Pittsburg State University*
Robert Cline *Binghamton University*
Bob Comerford *University of Rhode Island*
Robert Corsini *Bryant University*
Peter Crowell *Fordham University*
Refik Culpan *Pennsylvania State University at Harrisburg*
Don Daake *Olivet Nazarene University*
William Davig *Eastern Kentucky University*
Peter Davis *The University of Memphis*
Rolf Dixon *Weber State University*
Bambi Douma *University of Montana*

Scott Droege *Western Kentucky University*
Robert Edelson *Wilmington College*
Cathy Enz *Hotel School*
Rangamohan Eunni *Youngstown State University*
Ronald Ferner *Philadelphia Biblical University*
Robert Ferrari *Marymount College*
Phyllis Flott *Tennessee State University*
Richard Gendreau *Bemidji State University*
Armand Gilinsky *Sonoma State University*
Bill Godair *College of Saint Joseph*
Anita Gorham *Central Michigan University*
Peter Goulet *University of Northern Iowa*
Shane Greenstein *Kellogg School of Management*
Bill Gregory *Northwestern Oklahoma State University*
Allen Harmon *University of Minnesota Duluth*
Tom Holubik *Texas Tech University*
Andrew Hoh *Creighton University*
Peter Hom *Arizona State University*
Stephen Horner *Arkansas State University*
Peter Hughes *University of New Hampshire*
Alan Jackson *College of Saint Mary*
Stuart Johnston *Texas Christian University*
Susan Anne Kadlec *Dillard University*
Rick Koza *Chadron State College*
Scott Latham *University of Massachusetts, Lowell*
Ted Legatski *Texas Christian University*
Art Lekacos *State University of New York, Stony Brook*
Annette Lohman *California State University Long Beach*
Patricia Luoma *Quinnipiac University*
Sean Lux *Florida State University*
Barbara MacLeod *Ohio Wesleyan University*
Paul Mallette *Colorado State University*
Alfred Marcus *University of Minnesota*
Theresa Marron-Grodsky *University of Maryland University College*
Richard McCabe *Graziadio School of Business and Management*
Paul McCullough *Aquinas College Primetime*
Sal Monaco *Graduate School of Management and Technology*
Ann Mooney *Wesley J. Howe School*
Rebecca Morris *University of Nebraska at Omaha*
Alisa Mosley *Jackson State University*
Robert Moussetis *North Central College*
Art Padilla *North Carolina State University*
C. Patrick Palmer *Siena Heights University*
Ralph Parrish *University of Central Oklahoma*
Sharon Peck *Capital University*

Christine Pence *California State University*
Phillip Phan *Rensselaer Polytechnic Institute*
A Pillutla *St. Ambrose University*
Carol Pope *Alverno College*
Burt Reynolds *Southern New Jersey University*
Barbara Ribbens *Western Illinois University*
Nancy Robinson *East Tennessee State University*
Charles Roe *Arkansas State University*
Marty Rogoff *Philadelphia University*
Robert Roller *LeTourneau University*
Robert Rottman *Kentucky State University*
L. Alan Schafler *Florida Atlantic University*
Randolph Schewering *Rockhurst University*
Frank Schultz *Michigan State University*
Mark Seabright *Western Oregon University*
Bob Seigel *Buena Vista University*
Matthew Semadeni *Moore School of Business/University of South Carolina*
Jeffrey Sherlock *Tri-State University*
Chris Shook *Auburn University*
Nicolaj Siggelkow *Wharton School*
Patty Silfies *Western Kentucky University*
Quentin Skrabec *University of Findlay*
Jeff Slattery *Northeastern State University*
Anne Smith *University of Tennessee*
Howard Smith *University of New Mexico*
Marion Smith *Texas Southern University*
Stephen Standifird *University of San Diego*
Paul Stepanovich *Southern Connecticut State University*
Bill Stevens *School of Business Administration*
Roy Suddaby *University of Iowa*
Mohammad Syed *Miles College*
Michael Sykuta *University of Missouri*
Qingjiu Tao *Lehigh University*
Doug Thomas *University of New Mexico*
Paul Tiffany *University of California*
Bert Turner *Arkansas State University*
Steve Varga-Sinka *Saint Leo University, Atlanta Center*
Robert Von der Ohe *Rockford College*
Alan Wallace *Mesa State College*
Peter Wallace *Stonehill College*
Rod Walter *Western Illinois University*
Al Warner *Penn State*
Morrison Webb *Manhattanville College*
Paula Weber *St. Cloud State University*
William Worthington *Texas A & M University*
Russell Wright *University of Utah*
Ray Zammuto *University of Colorado, Denver*

"Live" Focus Group Attendees

Adam Fremeth *University of Minnesota*

Cynthia Lengick-Hall *University of Texas, San Antonio*

Santo Marabella *Moravian College*

Michele Masterfano *Drexel University*

Jacquelyn Palmer *Wright State University*

Sandu Petru *Elizabethtown College*

Peter Stanwick *Auburn University*

Paul Thurston *Siena College*

Margaret White *Oklahoma State*

Douglas Ross *Towson University*

Teaching Package and MyStratLab

Cara Cantarella *Pace University*

Robert Panco *Pace University*

Noushi Rahman *Pace University*

Paul Thurston *Siena College*

Diana Wong *Eastern Michigan University*

Personal Acknowledgments from the Authors

We wrote this Second Edition to build on the success of our First Edition and further improve the student and faculty experience with learning and teaching about strategic management. We take the perspective of practicing managers, and want to acknowledge the students, faculty, and managers who were directly and indirectly engaged in developing this new edition of *Strategic Management: A Dynamic Perspective*. This includes our own students and colleagues at the University of Wisconsin–Madison and Brigham Young University, the many executives and managers we have consulted with and brought into our classes, and those we worked with in our travels as we developed this new edition.

Although we had a specific vision for the book, we cannot take full credit for all the content that supports that vision. In particular, we want to acknowledge the contributions of the many researchers whose work helps managers understand and cope with the challenges of crafting and implementing revolutionary strategies in changing times. You will see their work cited throughout the text, and we encourage you to read the original studies (including our own) upon which the content of this book is based. We also want to acknowledge the many managers whose views and daily challenges helped us develop a theoretically rigorous, yet practically relevant and readable approach to strategic management. At many points along the way these colleagues challenged us with observations like, "That's nice, but how would you do that?" and forced us to continually refine our writing to connect the dots—from concept to action—so to speak.

Out of this group, one team of researchers continues to deserve particular note: Don Hambrick at Penn State University and Jim Fredrickson at the University of Texas at Austin. These talented and prolific researchers and award-winning teachers have been leading the bandwagon to put managers back into strategy, and have been exceptional mentors to both of us. You can see their imprint in our early research, in the managerial orientation of our textbook, and in the strategy diamond that ties all the chapters together. This strategy diamond will endure long after they are done writing; it will create a rich and relevant learning environment for students of strategy, and it will provide managers a tool for thinking through and answering in the affirmative, "Yes, I really have a strategy!"

We thank our team at Pearson Prentice Hall for making the book a reality. We wanted a publishing partner that shared and supported our vision and high aspirations for the next generation of undergraduate and MBA strategy textbooks, and with Pearson Prentice Hall we got one.

Feedback The authors and the product team would appreciate hearing from you! Let us know what you think about this textbook by writing to college_marketing@prenhall.com. Please include "Feedback about Carpenter/Sanders 2e" in the subject line.

About the Authors

Mason A. Carpenter

Professor Carpenter is the M. Keith Weikel Professor of Leadership at the Wisconsin School of Business. He has a B.S. in Business Administration from California State University (Humboldt) and University of Copenhagen, Denmark, and an M.B.A. from California State University (Bakersfield). He also completed graduate studies in enology at the University of Bordeaux, France. Before obtaining his Ph.D. in strategy at the University of Texas, Austin, he worked in banking, management consulting, and software development. His research concerns corporate governance, top management teams, and the strategic management of global firms, and is published in Strategic Management Journal, Academy of Management Journal, Academy of Management Review, Academy of Management Executive, Journal of Management, and Human Resource Management. He serves on the editorial boards of the Academy of Management Journal, Academy of Management Review, Journal of Management Studies, and the Strategic Management Journal, was voted Professor of the Year by M.B.A. students, and identified as one of the most popular professors in the BusinessWeek M.B.A. poll. He recently received the Larson Excellence in Teaching award from the School of Business, and the University of Wisconsin's Emil H. Steiger Distinguished Teaching Award.

Wm. Gerard Sanders

Professor Sanders is an associate professor and the Department Chair in Organization Leadership and Strategy at the Marriott School of Management at Brigham Young University. He earned a Ph.D. in strategic management from the University of Texas at Austin. In 1996, Professor Sanders joined the faculty at BYU, where he teaches strategic management. He has also been a visiting professor at Penn State University. His research is in the area of corporate governance and its affects on firm strategy and performance. He has published extensively in the Academy of Management Journal, Strategic Management Journal, Journal of Management, Human Resource Management, among other outlets. His work on the effects of stock option pay has been featured in such outlets as the New York Times, the Economist, BusinessWeek, CFO, and on National Public Radio's Marketplace. Professor Sanders is an Associate Editor of the Academy of Management Journal. In 2001 he received the Marriott School's J. Earl Garrett Fellowship and in 2003 he was designated a University Young Scholar. Prior to entering graduate school, Dr. Sanders spent twelve years in industry managing the acquisitions and financing of large portfolios of commercial real estate.

Concepts and Cases

Strategic Management
A Dynamic Perspective

1

Introducing
Strategic Management

In This Chapter We Challenge You To >>>

1. Understand what a *strategy* is and identify the difference between business-level and corporate-level strategy.

2. Understand why we study *strategic management*.

3. Understand the relationship between *strategy formulation* and *implementation*.

4. Describe the determinants of *competitive advantage*.

5. Recognize the difference between the *fundamental* and *dynamic* views of *competitive advantage*.

Click Clack—
David Challenging Goliath

*T*welve years ago, Kevin Plank was a walk-on football player for the University of Maryland Terrapins. He hated how his cotton T-shirts became soaking wet with sweat during every practice. The wet T-shirts would cause chaffing, gain several pounds in weight, and generally just feel very uncomfortable. He wondered why, in an era of microfiber fabric with moisture-wicking properties, he and other football players had to put up with uncomfortable cotton T-shirts under their shoulder pads. Runners, bicyclists, and others were already benefiting from clothing made of advanced materials to make their workouts more comfortable. Plank, who grew up always looking for a way to make money, went to a fabric store and bought a bolt of moisture-wicking fabric and paid a tailor to make several prototype shirts. Plank's teammates envied his new shirts, so he set out to make more samples. He officially launched his company out of his grandmother's basement and called his product Under Armour®. As you can see from the snapshot in Exhibit 1.1, sales in 2006 were $430 million, and the company's equity was valued at over $1.8 billion.[1] With such dominant incumbents as Nike and adidas, how did Plank successfully enter and grow his company into one of the best performing companies on Wall Street? Apparently, at least early on, its competitors did not heed Under Armour's savvy and mega-successful advertising campaign titled "Click-Clack: I think you hear us coming!" Although Under Armour has been successful to date, surely Nike and others did not stand idly by while watching its customers migrate to the new upstart. What can Under Armour do to maintain and grow its position in the industry? Let's first look at the industry, then we'll review Under Armour's strategy for entering and competing in this dynamic industry.

Exhibit 1.1   Under Armour at a Glance

	1996	2006
Revenues	$17,000	$430,000,000
Net Income	0	57,300,000
Equity Value	0	1,800,000,000

Revenue Distribution

Apparel

men's 59.4%
women's 19.9%
youth 7.4%

footwear 6.2%
accessories 3.5%
licensing revenues 3.6%

Brands and Trademarks		Under Armour®, HeatGear®, ColdGear®, AllSeasonGear®, LooseGear®, Under Armour design mark, Protect This House™, Duplicity™, I Think You Hear Us Coming™ and Click Clack™
NYSE Ticker (Went public in August 2005)		UA
Kevin Plank's Vision		To become the #1 performance athletic brand in the world

The Performance Apparel Industry Under Armour participates in the sports apparel market, which NPD Group, a leading provider of consumer and retail market research information, estimated was a $45 billion market in 2006. Approximately 30 percent of the market is synthetic product and purchased for use in active sport or exercise. While one might assume that Nike dominates the market, in fact the active sports apparel market is fragmented—10 brands combine to comprise the top 30 percent of the market.

Historically, exercise clothing consisted of products made with relatively unsophisticated design and generic fabrics. The most common shirt used in exercise was a standard cotton T-shirt, often decorated with logos and company or team names. In segments like running and basketball, there were specialized jerseys made of synthetic fibers and tank top designs that improved performance. Lycra® revolutionized sportswear in the late twentieth century, and the microfibers revolutionized the market later. Fabrics like fleece and Sympatex® were specifically developed for fluctuations in weather conditions. It is unlikely that street fashion would have adopted them so readily if there had not been the status association of sporting prowess. When this was combined with effective functional utility, a fabric fashion was born that encompassed all ages from young skateboarders to mature golfers. Moisture-management fibers were developed to accommodate the desire for more comfortable sportswear. According to Dupont, who invented Coolmax® and Tactel®, function is paramount. These fibers are used commonly today not only in sports apparel, but in other products ranging from socks to lingerie.

The performance apparel segment of the sports apparel market is growing more rapidly than other segments. This growth is fueled by demographic trends and increased consumer awareness and participation in active lifestyles. During the past two decades, consumers have continued to spend heavily in the areas of weight loss and dieting, fitness center memberships, and sports and athletic equipment. And sports enthusiasts tend to spend more for their equipment than casual users, which translates to the possibility for higher price points and greater margins.

As upstarts like Under Armour in sports apparel and Sketchers in specialized footwear have gained strong footholds in emerging segments, industry giants like Nike and adidas have taken notice and responded in kind with their own specialized products. However, while the market is large and growing rapidly, incumbents in traditional segments of the industry have not grown as rapidly.

Under Armour's Entry The original Under Armour shirt that Kevin Plank designed was made as a form-fitting compression using microfiber that would wick perspiration away from the body and dry quickly. The shirts he shared with teammates were a big hit and this led him to believe there was a market for these "performance shirts." He guessed there would be a big market for his shirts among professional and amateur athletes who, like himself, were irritated by working out in cotton shirts but continued to do so simply because there were few alternatives. Kevin Plank figured he had a winning product that was quite different from current products. His product has three distinct features. First, the fabric wicks moisture and dries quickly (a sweat-soaked cotton T-shirt can weigh two to three pounds). Second, Plank used a compression design—tight, form-fitting cuts that reduced the amount of fabric and improved comfort when worn under a uniform (and equipment like shoulder pads). Third, Under Armour shirts were made with a tagless design; conventional tags on the collar often irritate the neck of athletes. Plank designed a way to heat-seal the tag information directly to the fabric rather than needing to sew on a separate tag.

With a superior product designed for a specific market, Plank still faced the issue of how to get his product to market. Like many entrepreneurs, he started with who he knew—former teammates from college and prep school who were now playing in the National Football League (NFL). He figured that if he could get some professional athletes to use the product, teammates would hound them for their own shirts, much like his college teammates did at Maryland. While working on getting athletes to demand his product, Plank also went about securing wholesale and retail accounts. Early NFL players who started wearing Under Armour shirts included quarterbacks Jeff George and Frank Wycheck (a former Maryland teammate) and all pro and hall of fame receiver Jerry Rice. In baseball, Roger Clemens got Under Armour rolling by being an early adopter of the new shirts. Today, Under Armour is available via the Internet, catalogs, and 12,000 sporting goods stores worldwide.

With the early success of the basic product, Under Armour set out to find natural product extensions. The first product growth came in expanding from the basic shirt, known as AllSeason Gear®, to HeatGear® and ColdGear®, products designed to be worn in hot climates or cold temperatures while still providing the basic performance technology of the original product. Later, Under Armour looked for additional growth from new geographic areas. The major targets for international expansion today are Europe and Asia. More recently, Under Armour has expanded into new product and sports segments. In 2006, Under Armour launched what has proved to be a highly successful line of footwear. The specific target area? Football and baseball cleats. Why did Under Armour pick this particular segment? Plank says that the Under Armour strategy is not to be a niche player in football (or baseball) cleats. Rather, this segment is designed to be the platform from which to launch into a broader athletic footwear position at a later time. Because so many football and baseball players were already using Under Armour performance shirts, Under Armour felt that they would be a very receptive audience for footwear. The highly successful "Click-Clack" advertising campaign propelled Under Armour to a fabulous first year in footwear; in its first year of marketing cleats, Under Armour captured 20 percent market share overall, and an amazing 40 percent of the market for cleats priced over $70! In 2007, Under Armour launched lines of performance sunglasses and sports watches, both targeted at the premium price segments.

Under Armour's targets for growth in the near future focus on three main areas. First, Plank plans to continue to reinvigorate the core products, which are men's and women's apparel. And, Under Armour is just beginning to grow in the women's market. Within the basic product segment, Under Armour sees room to expand into other sports. For instance, within the last year, Under Armour started to notice that their shirts were showing up on golf courses. Golfers who used the products in other activities saw the benefits of the product while spending hours on the golf course. That led Under Armour to start marketing a specific polo-style shirt line through golf stores and later to start a full line of golf apparel. Similarly, Under Armour now targets outdoor adventure seekers (climbers, hikers, skiers), largely because they noticed the product being used in those venues. In addition, Under Armour sees lots of growth opportunity in footwear. Football and baseball cleats are seen as a mechanism to get Under Armour into this vast and potentially lucrative market. Analysts are anxious to know when Under Armour will move into other sports shoes (e.g., running, basketball). Plank simply responds: "When the time is right." Finally, Under Armour has just begun to get serious about international expansion. Under Armour recently opened a European office to lead negotiations with local athletes and distributors.

In a recent conference call with financial analysts covering Under Armour's stock, Kevin Plank was asked how Nike and adidas could have been taken by surprise by Under Armour's entry into the performance apparel segment. Indeed, Under Armour is now credited with creating the sports performance segment because former products are seen

Exhibit 1.2   Under Armour's Cumulative Total Stock Market

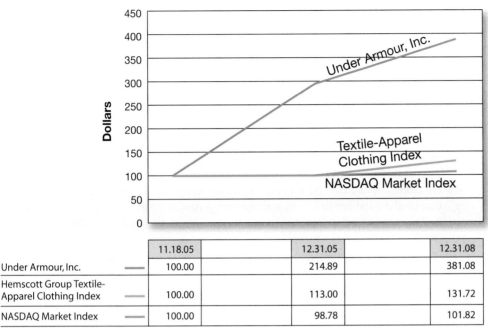

		11.18.05		12.31.05		12.31.08
Under Armour, Inc.	———	100.00		214.89		381.08
Hemscott Group Textile-Apparel Clothing Index	———	100.00		113.00		131.72
NASDAQ Market Index	———	100.00		98.78		101.82

as so technologically backwards. Analysts posed the question: "How was the door left so wide open (for your entry)?" Plank's response was telling: "I don't know, but our job is to close that door." He went on to comment that nobody thought consumers would spend $25 to $35 for a T-shirt. He concluded by noting that when you give the consumer some tangible benefit, you're able to reinvent entire product categories. Evidently, as summarized in Exhibit 1.2, in its first year of trading as a public company, Wall Street appeared to like Plank's plays as much as consumers did.[2]

Why are some firms incredibly successful while others are not? And why is it that once they're successful, so few can sustain a high level of success? We are sure that you are familiar with many once successful firms, that today no longer enjoy such success. In this text, we'll introduce you to the concepts that you'll need to answer questions about gaining and sustaining success in the world of business competition. <<<

Three Overarching Themes

As you've probably gathered from the topic of this book—*strategic management*—a firm's performance is directly related to the quality of its strategy and its competency in implementing it. You also need to understand that concerns about strategy, sometimes referred to as *business policy*, preoccupy the minds of many top executives. Their responsibility is to see that the firm's whole is ultimately greater than the sum of its parts—whether these parts are distinct business units, such as Under Armour's men's apparel and footwear, or simply the functional areas that contribute to the performance of one particular business, such as Under Armour's distribution through national sporting goods chains. Good strategies are affected by, and affect all of, the functional areas of the firm, including marketing, finance, accounting, and operations. Thus, we'll also introduce you to the concepts and tools that you'll need to analyze the conditions of a firm and its industry, to formulate appropriate strategies, and to determine how to implement a chosen strategy.

Three themes that run throughout this book are critical to developing competency in the field of strategic management:

1. **Firms and industries are *dynamic* in nature.** In recent years, theories and research have emerged on issues regarding dynamic markets and the importance of developing dynamic capabilities to create value. Our first theme, then, is the dynamic nature of both firms and their competitive environments. It's easy, for instance, to look at a financial snapshot of Under Armour and understand the competitive position that it commands in its industry. But we need to see Under Armour not as a snapshot at one particular moment in time but as an ongoing movie. Under Armour's current position isn't the result of a single strategic decision but rather the product of many decisions made over time. Under Armour's current stock of resources and capabilities weren't always available to the firm; they had to be developed dynamically. For instance, entering segments dominated by companies such as Nike and adidas required it to develop exceptional capabilities in design and marketing. And as tempting as it is to use hindsight to see some of Under Armour's competitors as inept, they didn't sit idly by while Under Armour ascended, created new market segments, and stole market share in existing segments. Indeed, Nike now has its own line of compression performance sports apparel. For pedagogical simplicity, we first introduce some fundamental concepts in strategic management and then move on to discuss the concepts and tools that managers use to think of strategy in dynamic terms.

2. **To succeed, the *formulation* of a good strategy and its *implementation* should be inextricably connected.** Unfortunately, many managers tend to focus on formulating a plan of attack and give too little thought to implementing it until it's too late. Likewise, they may similarly give short shrift to the importance of strategic leadership in effectively bridging strategy formulation and implementation. In fact, research suggests that, on average, managers are better at formulating strategies than they are at implementing them. This problem has been described as a "knowing–doing gap."[3] Effective managers realize that successfully implementing a good idea is at least as important as generating one. To implement strategies, the organization's leaders have numerous levers at their disposal. Levers such as organization structure, systems and processes, and people and rewards are tools that help strategists achieve alignment—that is, the need for all of the firm's activities to complement each other and support the strategy.

3. **Strategic leadership is essential if a firm is to both formulate and implement strategies that create value.** Strategic leaders are those responsible for formulating firms' strategies, such as Kevin Plank at Under Armour. They have this responsibility as a consequence of their hierarchical status in management. In addition, strategic leadership plays two critical roles in successful strategy implementation, and it's important to highlight them here so that you can incorporate them into your own assessment of a strategy's feasibility as well as ensure that you include these roles in your implementation plans. Specifically, strategic leadership is responsible for (1) making substantive implementation-lever and resource-allocation decisions and (2) developing support for the strategy from key stakeholders.

What Is Strategic Management?

Strategic management is the process by which a firm manages the formulation and implementation of its strategy. But we still need to ask ourselves: What is the *goal* of strategic management? What does "having a *strategy*" mean? Even if we're pretty sure that we have a strategy and a goal for it, how do we know whether we have a good strategy or a bad one?

strategic management
Process by which a firm manages the formulation and implementation of a strategy.

THE STRATEGIC LEADER'S PERSPECTIVE

The word *strategy* is derived from the Greek *strategos*. Roughly translated, it means "the general's view," and thinking about military ranks and responsibilities is one way to focus on the difference between the general's view (and the CEO's view) and that of some lower-level officer (like line or middle managers). The primary responsibility of a lower-level officer might be supply logistics, infantry, or heavy armored vehicles. Thus, lower-level officers may not be too concerned with the overall plan because of their attention to detail in specific areas of responsibility. The general, however, must not only understand how *all* of the constituent parts interrelate, but must use that understanding to draw up a plan that will lead to victory—a strategy. In the business context, the idea of strategy, therefore, suggests a big-picture perspective on the firm and its context. We call this holistic view of the organization the *strategic leader's perspective.*

The success of a military strategy depends not only on the quality of the general's planning and the vision behind it, but also on the execution of the strategy by the forces under the general's command. In business settings, likewise, a strategy is of little use if it is not well-executed by line managers. In addition, the quality of a strategy is often dependent on the leader's soliciting and utilizing the advice of other senior and midlevel leaders. In other words, a good leader can't afford to devise a strategy in isolation from the lower-level leaders who are responsible for executing it.

The ideas of strategy need not focus exclusively on military analogies just because the root of the word is from this context. You can see ideas analogous to the difference between the general's view and the lower-level officer's view in sports, education, personal life, and business. The important thing about the Greek derivation of the word *strategy* is that the big-picture perspective is fundamentally different from the detail of operational tactics.

In business, strategy requires a big-picture perspective. Up to this point, most of your business courses have probably focused on important but limited aspects of business. Indeed, most business-education classes are devoted to specialized areas of study on specific functional areas, such as finance or marketing. In strategic management, however, we're concerned with an overall, holistic view of the firm and its environment and the ways in which such a view determines the competitive decisions that businesspeople have to make. For this reason, when studying strategic management we generally take the perspective of the strategic leader. Recognize, however, that strategies often emerge from bottom-up processes and from fortuitous circumstances that the leader could not have anticipated. The strategic leader's perspective does not mean to suggest that plans are formulated in some linear fashion by a single leader. Rather, the strategic leader's perspective is the holistic consideration of the business and its environment rather than the myopic focus on a single functional area.

WHY STUDY STRATEGY?

You may wonder why it is important to study strategy when your career is unlikely to begin at the level of strategic leadership. From a practical standpoint, employers expect you to be functionally fluent in accounting, marketing, or some other specialization. They also expect that you will understand the "big picture"—strategic management gives you the tools to understand and describe the big picture. If strategy is the means by which an organization goes about pursuing its overarching objectives, then studying and gaining an understanding of the principles, theories, and tools of strategic management will be an important aid for you even early in your career. This course will help you in several areas critical to your career: you will be in a better position to understand your firm's objectives (or what they should be), you will be equipped to analyze and understand how competition will interfere with attaining your objectives and what can be done to minimize these threats, you will comprehend how effective strategy formulation and implementation requires complementary organizational resources and capabilities, and you will be able to identify which of these key factors may be missing in your organization. In addition, while the ultimate responsibility for strategy lies with senior management, the process of strategic management is one that requires the coordinated cooperation of employees at all levels of the organization. Top executives are not lone wolves when it comes to devising and implementing strategy. They rely on lower-level managers to collect and analyze data regarding competition and commercial opportunities. Consequently, the better employees understand the firm's strategy, the better they'll be able to make choices that are consistent with it. It's critical, therefore, that managers at every level understand the firm's strategy and work toward implementing its strategic initiatives.

WHAT IS STRATEGY?

The idea of "strategy" means different things to different people (and a lot of these ideas aren't particularly accurate).[4] In fact, experts in the field have formulated various definitions of *strategy*. We've adopted the simple and direct definition; **strategy** is the coordinated means by which an organization pursues its goals and objectives.[5] A strategy thus encompasses the pattern of actions that have been taken and those that are planned to be taken by an organization in pursuing its objectives.[6]

strategy The coordinated means by which an organization pursues its goals and objectives.

Because firms are attempting to sell products or services to potential customers, an implication of strategy in this context is that the firm is attempting to gain an advantage over other potential providers of those products and services. Virtually all firms face some level of competition. A strategy helps a firm accomplish its objectives in the face of competition. Strategy is not, however, necessarily a zero-sum game in which one firm wins and one loses. In many instances, firms cooperate in some aspects of business and compete in others.

Exhibit 1.3 outlines the strategic management process that you will be exploring and applying throughout this textbook.[7] From the exhibit, you can see how vision, goals and objectives, internal and external analysis, and implementation levers can be used to help formulate and implement strategy. Strategy outlines the means by which a firm intends to create unique value for customers and other important stakeholders.[8] This definition of strategy is important because, as you will see later, it forces managers to think holistically and dynamically about what the firm does and why those activities consistently lead customers to prefer the firm's products and services over those of its competitors.

BUSINESS STRATEGY VERSUS CORPORATE STRATEGY

In studying strategy, you'll find it useful to distinguish between strategic issues at the *business level* and those at the *corporate level*. Some firms are focused sharply on their *business* strategy: They compete in only one or very few industries. Other firms compete in many industries. The opening vignette on Under Armour paints a picture of a firm that has a very specific core business (athletic apparel). Some firms, such as General Electric (GE) or United Technologies, are called *conglomerates* because they're so diversified that it's difficult to pigeonhole them into any specific industry.

Consider the two largest competitors in the aircraft-engine industry. The largest is General Electric (GE), with $11 billion in aircraft-engine sales; the second largest is Rolls-Royce PLC, with approximately $8.4 billion in total sales. Rolls-Royce gets most of its revenue—approximately 74 percent—from this industry. (The firm no longer makes luxury cars; the operation was parceled off to BMW and Volkswagen in 1998.) In contrast, GE is involved in hundreds of businesses, including such diverse enterprises as manufacturing light bulbs, medical devices, and commercial jet engines; providing home mortgages; broadcasting (it

Exhibit 1.3 The Strategic Management Process

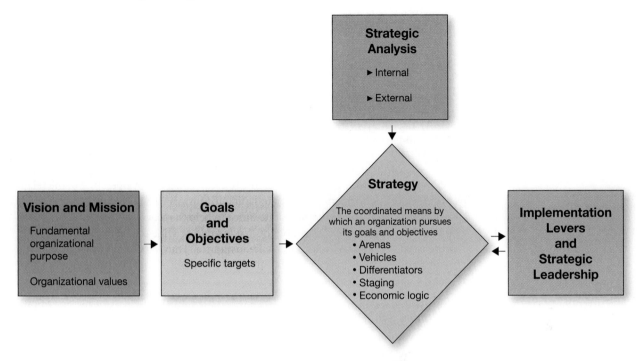

owns NBC); and operating self-storage facilities. It derives less than 10 percent of its revenue from aircraft engines. Within this industry, of course, both GE and Rolls-Royce face the same competitive pressures, such as determining how to compete against each other and such rivals as Pratt & Whitney (the third-largest firm in the industry). In managing its portfolio of businesses, GE faces strategic issues that are less relevant to Rolls-Royce.

Business Strategy   What sort of issues are these? **Business strategy** refers to the ways a firm goes about achieving its objectives within *a particular industry* or *industry segment*. In other words, one of GE's business strategies would be how it pursues its objectives within the jet engine business. This strategy may encompass such things as how it competes against Rolls-Royce for contracts from Boeing and Airbus, how it cooperates with other suppliers of technology it uses in designing its engines, and the decision to ramp up scale in an effort to reduce its costs. When Under Armour managers decide how to compete with Nike for consumer dollars, they, too, are engaged in business strategy. Business strategy, therefore, focuses on *achieving a firm's objectives within a particular business line.*

Increasingly, business strategy also takes into account the changing competitive landscape in which a firm is located. Two critical questions that business strategy must address are (1) how the firm will achieve its objectives *today,* when other companies may be competing to satisfy the same customers' needs, and (2) how the firm plans to compete *in the future.* In later chapters, we'll focus specifically on issues related to business strategy.

Corporate Strategy   Many firms are involved in more than one line of business. Large corporations like 3M and GE can be involved in dozens or hundreds of separate business activities. Under Armour started with a focus on men's performance apparel, but has expanded into other apparel like footwear. **Corporate strategy** addresses issues related to

business strategy Strategy for competing against rivals within a particular industry or industry segment.

corporate strategy Strategy for guiding a firm's entry and exit from different businesses, for determining how a parent company adds value to and manages its portfolio of businesses, and for creating value through diversification.

three fundamental questions associated with managing a company that operates in more than one business:

1. **In what businesses will we compete?** In the 1970s and 1980s, for instance, the retailer Sears chose to branch out of retailing into credit cards, stock brokerage, and real estate. Later, it decided that many of these moves were ill-advised and it divested most of these new businesses. GE managers address corporate-strategy questions when deciding whether the firm should enter a new business. All of the decisions about what businesses to compete in (including decisions to exit businesses) are issues of corporate strategy.

2. **How can we, as a corporate parent, add value to our various lines of business?** At GE, for instance, senior management might be able to orchestrate synergies and learning across its commercial- and consumer-finance groups, which are two separate business units. Under Armour sees an opportunity to create synergies by operating in the related businesses of performance apparel and athletic footwear. These synergies, if they are to materialize, will require the corporate office to help the business units to work in a co-operative manner. Sears once thought that it could provide one-stop shopping at retail outlets for everything from tools to life insurance. Thus, corporate strategy also deals with *finding ways to create value by having two or more owned businesses cooperate and share resources.*

3. **How will diversification or our entry into a new industry help us to compete in our other industries?** Under Armour thinks that by entering athletic footwear they may be better positioned to sell more performance apparel. In addition, because Nike operates in both markets, it puts them in a better competitive position in both industries relative to this large incumbent. Wal-Mart has found that diversification into the grocery business segment of retailing has increased retail foot traffic and boosted sales of non-grocery retail products.

Strategy Formulation and Implementation

strategy formulation Process of developing a strategy.

strategy implementation Process of executing a strategy.

Earlier we defined *strategy* as the means by which an organization pursues its goals and objectives. **Strategy formulation** is the process of *deciding what to do;* **strategy implementation** is the process of performing all the activities necessary *to do what has been planned.*[9] Because neither can succeed without the other, the two processes are iterative and interdependent from the standpoint that implementation should provide information that is used to periodically modify business and corporate strategy. Our opening vignette focused mostly on Under Armour's strategy. However, as the company has grown, it found that in order to implement this strategy, it had to invest heavily in organizational structure, systems, and processes.

The Under Armour example also shows how good strategies represent solutions to complex problems. They help to solve problems *external* to the firm by enabling the production of goods or services that both beat the competition and have a ready market. They solve problems *internal* to the firm by providing all employees, including top executives, with clear guidelines as to what the firm should and should not be doing.

STRATEGY FORMULATION

So now we know that strategy formulation means deciding what to do. Some strategies result from rational and methodical planning processes based on analyses of both internal resources and capabilities and the external environment. Others emerge over time and are adopted only after an unplanned pattern of decisions or actions suggests that an unfolding idea may unexpectedly lead to an effective strategy. Sometimes the recognition of a strategically good idea is accidental or "lucky," but corporate innovation and renewal are increasingly the products of controlled experiments and the opportunistic exploitation of surprise.[10] As you can see in Exhibit 1.4, these different aspects of strategy are referred to as intended, deliberate, realized, emergent, and unrealized.[11] You can think of intended strategy as the initial plan, whereas the realized strategy is what actually is put in place and succeeds. Thus, parts of the realized strategy can be credited to deliberate choices and actions (i.e., intended strategies that are realized), and parts are due to unplanned ones (i.e., realized strategies that were not deliberate but nevertheless emerged). Finally, some aspect of the initial strategic plan is not realized at all, and drops by the wayside.

You can see these various aspects of intended and realized strategy through the experience of Intel. During its early years, for instance, the chipmaker Intel was consciously focused on the design and manufacture of dynamic, random-access memory chips (DRAMs), and through the 1970s and early 1980s virtually all of the firm's revenue came from DRAMs. Intel's participation in the DRAM market was intentional and planned virtually from the moment of its founding. By 1984, however, 95 percent of the company's revenue came from the microprocessor segment of the industry. Ironically, Intel's participation in this segment of the industry was not planned by senior management. Rather, it evolved from an experimental venture to make processors for Busicom, a Japanese maker of calculators.[12] Unbeknownst and unforeseen by top management was the fact that market demand was shifting dramatically from DRAMs to microprocessors. Only through the Busicom experiment—and Intel's willingness to follow the signals this experiment sent them in terms of market-demand shifts—was the firm able to dramatically change its business strategy. To this day, Intel officials give credit for the firm's dominance in the microprocessor market to a strategy that emerged originally from a lower-level management initiative—one that, at the time, wasn't greeted with unanimous enthusiasm by senior management.[13]

Exhibit 1.4   Intended and Realized Strategies

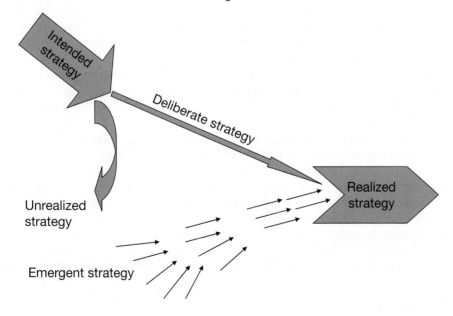

You might be more familiar with Rolls-Royce's automobiles than its jet engines. The fact is, however, that Rolls-Royce PLC no longer even makes luxury automobiles (BMW manufactures the cars). The company's core business is now jet engines. Jet engines generate 72 percent of its revenues.

Since their lucky foray into the microprocessor market, Intel managers have obviously focused on effective strategies for maintaining the firm's advantages in the segment while at the same time promoting experiments and exploiting surprises like Busicom to keep abreast of significant underlying market-demand shifts.

The Strategy Diamond and the Five Elements of Strategy

Good strategy formulation means refining the elements of the strategy.[14] Remember, first of all, not to confuse *part* of a strategy—for example, being a low-cost provider or first mover in an industry—for strategy itself. Being a low-cost provider or first mover may be part of a strategy, but it's not a complete strategy.

As we noted earlier, a strategy is the means by which a firm will achieve its goals and objectives. This is, of course, the *intended strategy* (referring back to Exhibit 1.4), although through this process managers have a good chance of shaping the *realized strategy* as well. In a for-profit firm, a business strategy will generally address how it will compete against its rivals and make a profit. For instance, if a firm has an objective to be one of the top two firms in a particular industry, this is a complex objective. As result, a strategy designed to pursue this objective will consist of an *integrated set of choices*. These choices can be categorized as five related elements of strategy based on decisions that managers make regarding *arenas, vehicles, differentiators, staging,* and *economic logic.* We refer to this constellation of elements, which are central to the strategic management process outlined in Exhibit 1.3, as the *strategy diamond.* Unfortunately, many naïve managers only focus on one or two such elements, often leaving large gaps in the overall strategy. Or, they may have all five pieces, but not understand how they need to fit together. Only when you have answers to your questions about *each of these five elements* can you determine whether your strategy is an integrated whole; you'll also have a better idea of the areas in which your strategy needs to be revised or overhauled. As Exhibit 1.5 shows, a good strategy diamond provides answers to all five questions:[15]

1. **Arenas.** Where will we be active?

2. **Vehicles.** How will we get there?

3. **Differentiators.** How will we win in the marketplace?

4. **Staging and pacing.** What will be our speed and sequence of moves?

5. **Economic logic.** How will we obtain our returns?

Let's take a closer look at each of these elements.

Arenas By **arenas**, we mean areas in which a firm will be active. Decisions about a firm's arenas may encompass its products, services, distribution channels, market segments, geographic areas, technologies, and even stages of the value-creation process. Unlike vision statements, which tend to be fairly general, the identification of arenas must be very specific: It will clearly tell managers what the firm should and should not do. In addition, because firms can contract with outside parties for everything from employees to manufacturing services, the choice of arenas can be fairly narrowly defined for some firms.

For example, Under Armour made the choice to compete in performance apparel for men, women, and children. Historically, their target market has been in the U.S., but they recently expanded into Europe. More recently, they also targeted users in new market segments and moved into athletic footwear. They sell their products primarily through sporting goods stores. In addition to these arena choices, Under Armour has entirely outsourced the production of its products to outside textile firms, mostly in Asia.

Vehicles Vehicles are the means for participating in targeted arenas. For instance, a firm that wants to go international can achieve that objective in different ways. Under Armour sent their own personnel to Europe to open those operations. Wal-Mart, in recent moves to

arena Area (product, service, distribution channels, geographic markets, technology, etc.) in which a firm participates.

Exhibit 1.5 The Business Strategy Diamond

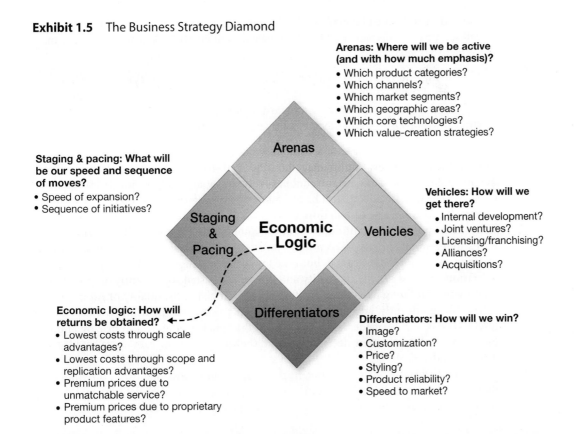

enter certain international markets (such as Argentina and China), has both acquired local retail chains and opened new stores on its own in order to gain more immediate presence. Likewise, a firm that requires a new technology could develop it through investments in R&D. Or, it could opt to form an alliance with a competitor or supplier who already possesses the technology, thereby accelerating the integration of the missing piece into its set of resources and capabilities. Finally, it could simply buy another firm that owns the technology. In this case, then, the possible vehicles for entering a new arena include acquisitions, alliances, and organic investment and growth.

Differentiators A firm that understands why its customers regularly choose its products or services over those of competitors has identified its **differentiators**. The output of differentiators can be seen in the features and attributes of a company's products or services that help it win sales. Firms can be successful in the marketplace along a number of common dimensions, including *image, customization, technical superiority, price,* and *quality and reliability*. Under Armour gains sales in the marketplace through both image and technical superiority. Toyota and Honda have done very well by providing effective combinations of differentiators. They sell both inexpensive cars and cars with high-end, high-quality features, and many consumers find the value that they provide hard to match. As you will learn later in this course, while effective strategies often combine differentiators, it is important to make very specific choices about what your product or service is and what it is not. It is impossible to be all things to all consumers. It's difficult to imagine, for instance, a single product that boasts both state-of-the-art technology and the lowest price on the market. Part of the problem is perceptual—consumers often associate low quality with low price. Part of it is practical—leading-edge technologies cost money to develop and command higher prices because of their uniqueness or quality.

There are two critical factors in selecting differentiators:

- **These decisions must be made early.** Key differentiators rarely materialize without significant up-front decisions, and without valuable differentiators, firms tend to lose marketplace battles.

- **Identifying and executing successful differentiators means making tough choices—tradeoffs.** Managers who can't make tough decisions about tradeoffs often end up trying to satisfy too broad a spectrum of customer needs; as a result, they make too many strategic compromises and execute poorly on most dimensions.

Audi provides an example of a company that has aligned these two factors successfully. In the early 1990s, Audi management realized that its cars were perceived as low-quality, high-priced German automobiles—obviously a poor position from which to compete. The firm decided that it had to move one way or another—up market or down market. It had to do one of two things: (1) lower its costs so that its pricing was consistent with customers' perceptions of product quality or (2) improve quality sufficiently to justify premium pricing. Given limited resources, the firm could not go in both directions—that is, produce cars in both the low-price and high-quality strata. Audi made a decision to invest heavily in quality and image; it invested significantly in quality programs and in refining its marketing efforts. Ten years later, the quality of Audi cars has increased significantly, and customer perception has moved them much closer to the level of BMW and Mercedes. Audi has reaped the benefits of premium pricing and improved profitability, but the decisions behind the strategic up-market move entailed significant tradeoffs.[16]

Differentiators are what drive potential customers to choose one firm's offerings over those of competitors. The earlier and more consistent the firm is at defining and driving these differentiators, the greater the likelihood that customers will recognize them.

---

differentiator Feature or attribute of a company's product or service (e.g., image, customization, technical superiority, price, quality, and reliability) that helps it beat its competitors in the marketplace.

Staging **Staging** refers to the timing and pace of strategic moves. Staging choices typically reflect available resources, including cash, human capital, and knowledge. At what point, for example, should Under Armour enter specific international markets? Perhaps if the company pursues global opportunities too early, it may redirect resources that are needed to exploit its existing opportunities in the U.S. And, when it is time to expand internationally, it is critical to decide which countries they will enter first and which will come later. Furthermore, as product lines are expanded, it is critical to decide which products make the most sense to enter next, and which should be saved for a later time. For instance, there are many possible expansion moves for Under Armour in sporting goods. They have sacrificed some of these possible opportunities for the time being (e.g., running shoes) in order to focus on other activities first (e.g., football cleats). Wal-Mart explicitly decided to delay its international moves so that it could focus first on dominating the U.S. market, which is, after all, the largest retail market in the world. Despite mixed results overseas, Wal-Mart is the undisputed leader in global retailing and has recently increased its emphasis on international markets as the basis for future growth.[17]

Staging decisions should be driven by several factors: resources, urgency, credibility, and the need for early wins. Because few firms have the resources to do everything they'd like to do immediately, they usually have to match opportunities with available resources. In addition, not all opportunities to enter new arenas are permanent; some have only brief windows. In such cases, early wins and the credibility of certain key stakeholders may be necessary to implement a strategy.

Economic Logic Most of the firms you will study in this course are likely to be for-profit firms. As such, a key objective of these firms is to earn an economic profit. The previous four elements of strategy just reviewed (arenas, vehicles, differentiators, and staging) will only make sense for a for-profit firm to the extent that they combine to earn a profit. **Economic logic** is the fifth element of strategy and it refers to *how* the firm will earn a profit—that is, how the firm will generate positive returns over and above its cost of capital. Economic logic is the "fulcrum" for profit creation. Earning normal profits, of course, requires a firm to meet all of its fixed, variable, and financing costs, and achieving desired returns over the firm's cost of capital is a tall order for any organization. In analyzing a firm's economic logic, think of both costs and revenues. Sometimes economic logic resides primarily on the *cost* side of the equation. Southwest Airlines, for example, can fly passengers for significantly lower costs per passenger mile than any major competitor. At other times, economic logic may rest on the firm's ability to increase the customer's willingness to pay premium prices for products (in other words, prices that significantly exceed the costs of providing enhanced products).

When the five elements of strategy are aligned and mutually reinforcing, the firm is generally in a position to perform well. The discussion in the box entitled "How Would *You* Do That? 1.1" demonstrates how you would apply the strategy diamond to JetBlue airlines. High performance levels, however, ultimately mean that a strategy is also being executed well, and we now turn to strategy implementation. It is important to note that you can apply the strategy diamond at multiple levels—at a product level (product strategy), business level (business strategy), corporate level (corporate strategy), and global level (international strategy). The strategy diamond will become a powerful and flexible tool in your strategic management and business policy toolkit.

STRATEGY IMPLEMENTATION LEVERS

Whatever the origin of a strategic idea, whether it was carefully planned from the outset or evolved over time by means of luck or experimentation, successful strategies are dependent on effective implementation. As discussed earlier in the chapter, *strategy implementation* is the process of executing the strategy—of taking the actions that put the strategy into effect and ensure that organizational decisions are consistent with it.[18] The

staging Timing and pace of strategic moves.

economic logic Means by which a firm will earn a profit by implementing a strategy.

The Five Elements of Strategy at JetBlue

To experience how you might apply the strategy diamond, let's consider a recent entrepreneurial success story. The major U.S. airlines lost over $7 billion between 1998 and 2002. David Neeleman, however, confounded the experts when he decided that despite the industry's horrendous performance, the time was right to step down from his executive position at Southwest Airlines to launch a new airline. JetBlue took off on February 11, 2000, with an inaugural flight between New York City's John F. Kennedy International Airport and Fort Lauderdale, Florida. Today, the airline serves more than 50 cities around the country and in the Caribbean and intends to expand further. If you follow the financial fortunes of commercial airlines you will know that JetBlue has obviously done something right. As shown in Exhibit 1.6, even after suffering some recent setbacks that have severely affected profitability, it is second only to Southwest Airlines in profitability over the past three years.[19] To begin applying the strategy diamond to JetBlue, let's quickly review JetBlue's vision, which is to "bring humanity back to air travel" through product innovation and excellent service. It intends to be a low-fare, low-cost passenger airline that provides high-quality customer service. Using the strategy diamond, and public documents posted at www.jetblue.com, we can determine what strategy JetBlue has pursued in order to meet its stated objective.

Exhibit 1.6 Performance of JetBlue

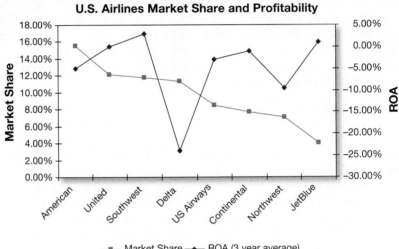

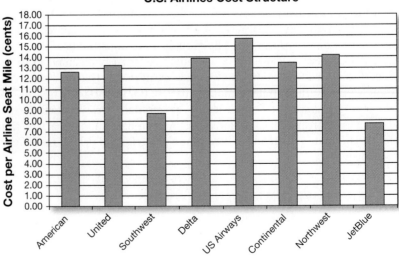

- *In what arenas does JetBlue compete?* Management states that the company competes as a low-fare commercial air carrier, and caters to underserved but overpriced U.S. cities. Its main base of operations is John F. Kennedy airport in New York City, which serves the largest travel market in the country.

- *What vehicles does JetBlue use to enter the arenas in which it competes?* JetBlue started from scratch and has achieved all of its growth in flights per day through internal growth. The firm could have grown by purchasing regional airlines, but chose not to.

- *What are its differentiators?* Price is a big part of JetBlue's strategy for winning new customers, but it also wants to develop the image that it is a low-fare airline with high-quality service. Although it offers only one class of service, the level of service is rather high for a low-fare airline. For instance, it offers leather seating and individual in-seat live satellite TV. Thus, JetBlue states that it aims to create a new segment in airline travel based on value, service, and style.

- *How does JetBlue's staging—the speed of its expansion and the sequence of its growth initiatives—reflect its timetable for achieving its objectives?* JetBlue has grown from 1 route between 2 cities to routes that serve more than 50 cities in just 7 years. At first, it limited itself to the East Coast (between its JFK home base and destinations in Florida and upstate New York), but it soon proceeded westward, establishing locations in the west. Expansion in the east has filled in many more cities, and destinations

When former Southwest Airlines employee and JetBlue founder David Neeleman (shown vacuuming a plane) announced that he was launching a new airline company, people were aghast. Although the airline industry as a whole is losing money, JetBlue has found a way to prosper by effectively aligning the five elements of its strategy that is both internally consistent and externally generates great market demand. The strategy includes low-fare but upscale service, complete with leather seats and satellite TV.

in the Caribbean were also added. JetBlue has targeted more cities for future expansion.

- *What's the economic logic of JetBlue's strategy?* JetBlue's income statements show that its costs are significantly lower than industry averages. Indeed, in 2006 JetBlue had the lowest costs per airline seat mile of any major airline (with Southwest a close second). These cost advantages appear to come from an *ability to perform key tasks in ways that are fundamentally less expensive* than those of competitors. By flying only one make of aircraft that is relatively fuel efficient, JetBlue also keeps maintenance and training costs down. By securing a home base at JFK at a time when the New York Port Authority was anxious to attract more air traffic, JetBlue secured lower airport fees. Locating in

secondary locations (Long Beach, California, instead of Los Angeles International Airport, Fort Lauderdale, Florida, instead of Miami) also means lower-than-average airport fees. On the revenue side, although JetBlue offers very low fares, it wins customers from competitors and uses its low-cost incentive as a means to convert non-fliers to JetBlue customers. It has also attracted customers by concentrating on underserved, high-priced routes. As a result, it now boasts the highest load factor of any major airline.

As you can see, walking through JetBlue's strategy diamond helps illustrate its strategy. The plan looks sound, but what is required to implement such a plan? The next sections of this chapter provide an overview of this critical issue.

process of implementation also encompasses the refinement, or change, of a strategy as more information is made available through early implementation efforts. The goal of implementation is twofold:

■ To make sure that strategy formulation is comprehensive and well informed

■ To translate good ideas into actions that can be executed (and sometimes to use execution to generate or identify good ideas)

In sports, a coach's play-calling is only as good as the excellence with which the players execute it. Likewise in business: The value of a firm's strategy is determined by its ability to carry it out. "Any strategy," says Michael Porter, one of the preeminent writers on the subject, ". . . is only as good as its execution."[20] Adds Peter Drucker, one of our most prolific writers on management: "The important decisions, the decisions that really matter, are strategic. . . . [But] more important and more difficult is to make effective the course of action decided upon."[21]

Strategy implementation is usually studied in business school graduate courses, and it's the subject of hundreds of books in business school libraries. We don't intend to supplant the results of all of this study, but we do want you to focus on the implications of a very basic fact: *The processes of strategy formulation and strategy implementation are inextricably linked.* The five elements of strategy, for instance, are related to both formulation and implementation. Good implementation means that an organization coordinates resources and capabilities and uses structure, systems, processes, and strategic leadership to translate a deliberate strategy into a realized strategy and to positive bottom-line results. Throughout the text we help you to see the relationship between formulation and implementation. Chapter 2 introduces you to the role of strategic leadership, and Chapter 11 drills down much deeper into our implementation framework. At this point, and in order to help you consider the complexity of implementing a strategy, we introduce you to just the basic ideas of strategic leadership and implementation.

To implement strategies, organization leaders have numerous levers at their disposal. The framework summarizing these levers is shown in Exhibit 1.7.[22] We categorize these levers into three broad categories: (1) *organization structure,* (2) *systems and processes,* and (3) *people and rewards.* The strategist uses these tools to test for alignment, which is the need for all of the firm's activities to complement each other and support the strategy.

Exhibit 1.7
Implementation Framework

Implementation Levers
- Organizational structure
- Systems and processes
- People and rewards

Intended Strategy

Realized Strategy

Strategic Leadership
- Lever- and resource-allocation decisions
- Develop support among stakeholders

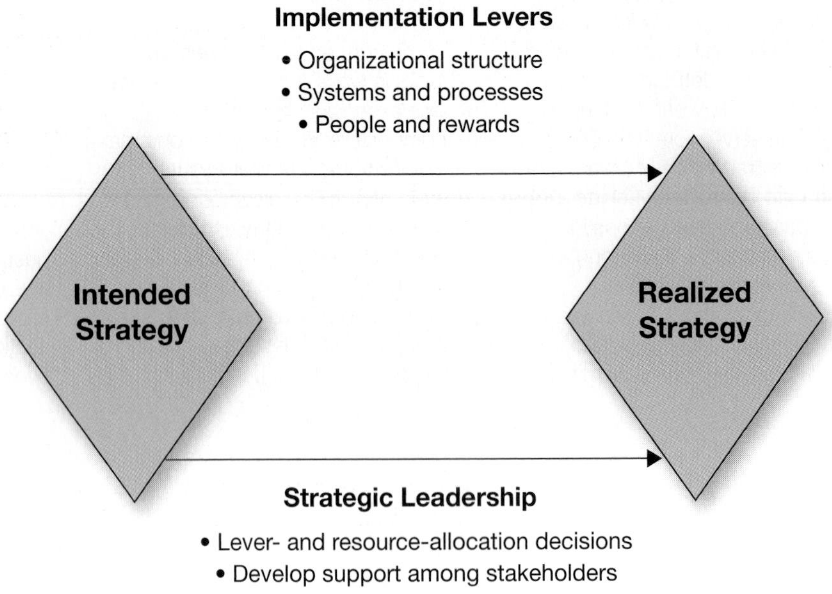

In addition, strategic leadership engages in a few activities related to implementing the strategy that are unique to their positional authority. As the exhibit suggests, implementation includes the activities carried out by the organization that are aimed at executing a particular strategy. Often, the strategy that is realized through these implementation efforts are somewhat different from the original plan. Ideally, these deviations from the original plan are a result of explicit alterations of the strategy that result from feedback during early implementation efforts as well as from the exploitation of serendipitous opportunities that were not anticipated when the strategy was formulated.

Organization Structure   Structure is the manner in which responsibilities, tasks, and people are organized. It includes the organization's authority, hierarchy, units, divisions, and coordinating mechanisms. At this point, we just need to remind ourselves of a few key questions that managers must consider when implementing a strategy:

- Is the current structure appropriate for the intended strategy?

- Are reporting relationships and the delegation of authority set up to execute the strategic plan?

- Is the organization too centralized (or decentralized) for the strategy?

Systems and Processes   Systems are all the organizational processes and procedures used in daily operations. Obviously, these include control and incentive systems, resource-allocation procedures, information systems, budgeting, distribution, and so forth.

People and Rewards   The *people and rewards* lever of the model underscores the importance of using all of the organization's members to implement a strategy. Regardless of your strategy, at the end of the day, it's your people who will have implemented it. Competitive advantage is generally tied to your human resources.[23] Successful implementation depends on having the right people and then developing and training them in ways that support the firm's strategy. In addition, rewards—how you pay your people—can accelerate the implementation of your strategy or undermine it. We have all seen instances in which unintended consequences happen because a manager rewards "A" while hoping for "B."[24]

STRATEGIC LEADERSHIP

Strategic leadership plays two critical roles in successful strategy implementation, and it is important to highlight them here so that you can incorporate them into your own assessment of a strategy's feasibility as well as ensure that you include these roles in your implementation plans. Specifically, as will be discussed in greater detail in Chapter 11, strategic leadership is responsible for (1) making substantive implementation lever and resource-allocation decisions and (2) developing support for the strategy from key stakeholders. Kevin Plank at Under Armour obviously spends a lot of time deciding what needs to be done, such as which new products to launch next, which markets to enter, and which suppliers and distributors to use. However, he also spends a significant amount of time talking to analysts at large U.S. brokerage firms, mutual funds, and pension funds. Why? Because he must keep these key financial stakeholders and shareholders abreast of what Under Armour is doing so that they retain confidence in the firm.

A successful strategy is not generally formulated just by a single person or a small group of leaders. Strategic leadership requires involving the right people in critical decisions because key information may be widely dispersed within the firm. In addition, successful strategy implementation requires active leadership to ensure that what emerges and what is realized are desirable and that needed changes of course are detected before it is too late.

What Is Competitive Advantage?

Earlier we defined *strategy* as the means by which a firm will achieve its objectives. We noted that within a firm's business operations, its objectives will generally encompass some notion of being successful at selling products or services to customers. Because virtually all firms face competition when trying to serve these customers, to achieve its objectives, a firm will have to be perceived by at least some customers as superior to its competition. Thus, the concept of strategy suggests a relationship between strategy on the one hand and performance and competitive advantage on the other. Specifically, we explained that a strategy encompasses the pattern of actions taken by a firm to achieve its objectives. These premises lead us to a logical conclusion: The activities of strategic management are based on the assumption that *firms attempt to achieve a position of competitive advantage over their rivals when serving target customers.*[25] Or, to put it another way: Firms prefer to be winners in their respective industries rather than subpar or even average performers. This leads us to define **competitive advantage** as a firm's ability to create *value* in a way that its rivals cannot.

competitive advantage A firm's ability to create value in a way that its rivals cannot.

Performance itself, however, is not competitive advantage; it's merely a result of it. A firm may achieve relatively high short-term performance levels without gaining any substantial advantage over its rivals. Maybe the company just had an unusually good year or took drastic measures to cut costs (perhaps to unsustainably low levels). By the same token, a firm may enjoy significant competitive advantage in some lines of business but still perform more poorly than its competitors because of other underperforming business units or because it chooses to keep prices lower than its competitive position would otherwise allow. For instance, a firm with a competitive advantage may desire to gain additional market share. Alternatively, it may keep prices lower than its competitive position would otherwise allow to avoid regulators' or competitors' attention.

The question that we now want to answer is: *Why are some firms able to achieve greater advantages over rivals than other firms?* All firms are not alike. For many years, Dell, for example, seemed to have some capabilities that other computer manufacturers, such as Hewlett-Packard and Acer, were unable to duplicate. Thus, for many years Dell sustained a competitive advantage which only recently may have been neutralized by Hewlett-Packard and Acer. Toyota enjoys a similar advantage in the automotive industry. In some industries, we see new entrants quickly outmaneuver incumbents. For instance, why has Under Armour been able to enter an industry with some very formidable incumbents and still be able to earn very good profits? Most industries are *not* accurately characterized by the theoretical condition of perfect competition that you likely learned about in micro econonics (i.e., in perfect competition firms can only earn "normal" profits because super normal profits will attract new entrants and this additional competition will drive profits down). In reality, many industries have one or more companies that earn more than "normal" profits for many years. In addition, some firms appear to outperform competitors consistently, which is likely an indication that they have some form of competitive advantage over their rivals. As we will see, however, it's become increasingly difficult for any one firm to sustain a competitive advantage over a long period of time.[26]

DETERMINANTS OF COMPETITIVE ADVANTAGE

The field of strategic management focuses on explanations for competitive advantage—on the reasons why companies experience above- and below-normal rates of returns. In other words, strategic management offers theories and models that help us understand why some firms perform better than others, and more to the point, offers managers tools to help their firm obtain a competitive advantage and perform better than the competition. Generally speaking, as summarized in Exhibit 1.8, there are three primary perspectives on this issue (perspectives that, as we shall see, reflect contrasting but complementary points of view):

- The *internal perspective* focuses on resources and capabilities as internal sources of uniqueness that allow firms to beat the competition.

- The *external perspective* focuses on the structure of industries and the ways in which firms can position themselves within them for competitive advantage.

- The *dynamic perspective,* which bridges the internal and external perspectives, is a third view of competitive advantage. This view helps explain why competitive advantages do not typically last over long periods of time.

Let's examine each of these perspectives, or theories, more closely.

The Internal Perspective   The first of the two fundamental perspectives on competitive advantage is an internal one. It is often called the *resource-based view of the firm.* This perspective suggests that no two firms are identical because they possess resources and capabilities of different qualities. The advantage goes to the firms with superior resources and capabilities. Proponents of this theory argue that a firm gains an advantage by obtaining valuable and rare resources and developing the capability to utilize these resources to drive customers toward their products and services at the expense of competitors. As a result, firms with superior resources and capabilities enjoy competitive advantage over other firms.[27] This advantage makes it relatively easier for these firms to achieve consistently higher levels of performance than competitors. Competitive advantage, therefore, arises when a company's resources allow its products, services, or businesses to compete

Exhibit 1.8   Three Perspectives on Competitive Advantage

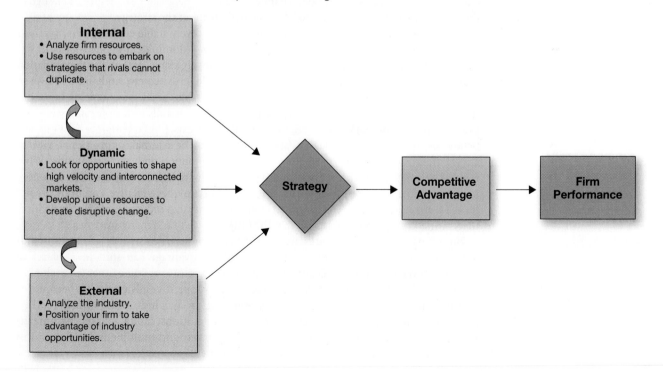

successfully against rival firms in the same industries. According to this perspective, the objective for managers is to determine what resources and capabilities offer the most potential value, to acquire them if they are lacking, and then to leverage those specific resources in executing the firm's strategy. The resource-based view also holds that a firm's bundle of resources may either hinder or help its entry into new businesses—an idea that we'll explore further in later chapters.[28]

The External Perspective The second fundamental perspective on competitive advantage contends that variations in firms' competitive advantage and performance are primarily a function of industry attractiveness and the *position* of firms within the industry relative to competitors. Thus, this external perspective suggests that competitive advantage comes from a firm's positioning within the competitive business environment.

The seminal work supporting this approach is Michael Porter's work on competitive strategy.[29] Porter's theory—sometimes called *industrial organization economics* (I/O economics)—suggests that firms should do one of two things: (1) position themselves to compete in attractive industries or (2) adopt strategies that will make their current industries more attractive. In some countries, for instance, carmakers lobby for import tariffs in order to make their domestic markets more attractive. When the strategy works, the access of foreign manufacturers to the market is limited, and the cost of participating in it is higher. (In later chapters, we'll explore in more detail the theoretical models and tools that help managers analyze, understand, and shape a firm's competitive environments.)

The Dynamic Perspective In addition, the two fundamental perspectives that focus on internal and external determinants of competitive advantage, some industries or market segments are less stable than others. Not surprisingly, competitive advantage is more likely to endure in stable markets than in unstable ones. Conversely, the competitive advantage held by one firm over another tends to change very slowly in stable markets but more quickly in unstable ones. As a result of current or possible future changes in the competitive environment, strategies need to be dynamic in nature. The greater the degree of change in the environment, the greater will need be the dynamism of the strategy.

The global chocolate industry, for example, is a relatively stable environment because a few firms—notably, M&M/Mars, Nestlé, and Hershey— dominate it in terms of both size and brands. In addition, demand for chocolate is relatively stable, growing with population growth. To stimulate growth, large companies try to formulate new candy bars. However, this type of growth is rather incremental and predictable. Smaller companies carve out niches in which to offer differentiated products, but this generally does not result in any significant upheaval of market position. In such stable contexts, fundamental theories of competitive advantage usually explain most economic facts. The external (or positional) view of strategy tends to dominate questions of strategy formulation and implementation. Why? Because a firm's current market position, as gauged by market share or some other criterion, may be a good indicator of competitive advantage and provides a relatively accurate predictor of future performance. This view also tends to assume that industries are clearly defined, that competition is predictable, and that the future doesn't hold many surprises.

But what about dynamic industries—such as computer chips or laser printers or medical products—in which it seems that competitive advantage can shift in a matter of months or even days simply because of a new product release or some other technological breakthrough?[30] A so-called *dynamic perspective* on competitive advantage has become increasingly important in explaining the economic facts in such industries in which markets converge, technologies rapidly change competitive conditions, capital markets become increasingly impatient, firms compete in multiple markets and multiple industries against common rivals, and the costs of establishing a competitive position soar (and so increase dramatically the cost of failure). The dynamic perspective suggests that a firm's current market position or competitive advantage is *not* an accurate predictor of future performance or sustainable competitive advantage. Why not? Because current market position itself is not a competitive advantage, but rather an outcome of past competitive activities. Consequently, as the competitive environment changes, new leaders may be past leaders, new entrants, or prior incumbents who are better positioned for the future state of the industry. From the dynamic perspective, we look to the past for clues about how the firm arrived at its current position and to the future in an effort to predict the look of the new competitive landscape.

The External Dimension of the Dynamic Perspective Of course, the dynamic strategy perspective has both external and internal dimensions as well. On the external side, it's useful in analyzing "high-velocity" markets—markets that are changing rapidly and unpredictably.[31] Often, such changes result from technology. For instance, the personal music player market has seen tremendous upheaval in the status quo as digital formats replaced analog devices. However, as we noted earlier, there are usually several contributing factors. The dynamic perspective is also a good tool for examining industries characterized by *multimarket competition*—those in which firms tend to encounter the same rivals in multiple markets.[32] Goodyear, Michelin, and Bridgestone, for instance, compete head-to-head in tire markets around the world. Another form of multimarket competition is illustrated by Nestlé and Mars; these companies battle it out in global industries ranging from pet foods to snack foods and will often use resources from one industry to bolster competitive position in another—say, by offering retailer discounts on pet food in exchange for shelf space for snack foods. For instance, Proctor & Gamble's entry into Vietnam appears to be less driven by the profit motive (P&G tends to lose money on Vietnamese soap sales) than by a determination to keep rival Unilever in check. If P&G had not entered the Vietnamese market, Unilever could have reaped monopoly-like profits and proceeded to use the windfall to pay for competitive efforts against P&G in other markets. By competing with Unilever in a market in which it has no competitive advantage (and may not even seek one), P&G's strategy reduces Unilever's ability to wage war on other fronts.

The Internal Dimension of the Dynamic Perspective The dynamic perspective can also help us to focus on a firm's resources and capabilities, particularly those that lead to a *continuous flow* of advantages in resources or market position and those that strengthen the firm's ability to embrace (and even foster) continuous and sometimes disruptive *change*. Risk taking, experimentation, improvisation, and continuous learning are—at least from the dynamic perspective—key features of successful firms. Later in the text, we will explore several relevant analytical tools for shaping strategy formulation. You'll also learn how to combine your analysis of an industry's cumulative technological development with your assessment of whether a firm can exploit an innovative product or disruptive technology through its entire life cycle or whether it must instead leap from product to product at strategically defined crossover points.

As suggested by our opening vignette on Under Armour, note that the dynamic perspective also provides valuable insight into the formulation and implementation of strategies at firms competing in ostensibly stable markets and industries. Few observers classified the men's athletic apparel market as a dynamic industry. While there were many competitors in various segments, Nike was viewed as the Goliath of the industry that led much of the innovation of new products. Under Armour entered the industry with an innovative product targeted at an underserved market. Under Armour's compression performance wear products were able to generate significant price premiums over incumbents' products (remember, $25 to $35 for a T-shirt). Yet, while the creation and design of the concept was proprietary to Under Armour, they used off-the-shelf technology from third-party suppliers. Consequently, in order to successfully enter and capitalize on his idea, Kevin Plank needed to be able to marshal organizational resources to implement his plan and gain market share before he awoke the giant incumbents. By the time Under Armour appeared on Nike's and adidas' radar, it had already created and was in position to defend a rather dominant position in the performance apparel segment. You will find the same theme in stories about Amazon.com versus Barnes & Noble and U.S. mini-mills versus major steel producers.[33]

Summary of Challenges

1. Understand what strategy is and identify the difference between business-level and corporate-level strategy. Strategic management is the process by which a firm manages the formulation and implementation of its strategy. A strategy is the central, integrated, externally oriented concept of how a firm will achieve its objectives. Strategies typically take one of two forms: business strategy or corporate strategy. The objective of a business strategy is to spell out how the firm plans to compete. This plan integrates choices regarding arenas (where the firm will be active), vehicles (how it will get there), differentiators (how it will win), staging (the speed and sequence of its moves), and economic logic (how it obtains its returns). The objective of corporate strategy is to spell out which businesses a firm will compete in, how ownership by the corporate parent adds value to the business, and how this particular diversification approach helps each business compete in its respective markets.

2. Understand why we study strategic management. It should be clear to you by now that strategic management is concerned with firm performance. Strategic management holds clues as to why firms survive when performance suffers. Strategy helps you to understand which activities are important and why and how a plan, absent good execution, is perhaps only as valuable as the paper it's printed on.

3. Understand the relationship between strategy formulation and implementation. Strategy formulation is the determination of what the firm is going to do; strategy implementation is how the firm goes about doing it. These two facets of strategy are linked and interdependent. This interdependence is made strikingly clear by the strategic management process (Exhibit 1.3) you are introduced to in this chapter, examples throughout the text, and the specific treatment of implementation levers in Chapter 11.

4. Describe the determinants of competitive advantage. Competitive advantage is realized when one firm creates value in ways that its competitors cannot, such that the firm clearly performs better than its competitors. Advantage is not simply higher relative performance; rather, superior performance signals the ability of a firm to do things in ways its direct competitors cannot. The two primary views of competitive advantage—internal and external—are complementary and together are used to help formulate effective strategies. The internal view portrays competitive advantage to be a function of unique, firm-specific resources and capabilities. The external view holds that a firm's performance is largely a function of its position in a particular industry or industry segment given the overall structure of the industry. Profitable industries are considered attractive, and therefore, high firm performance is attributed to a firm's position in the industry relative to the characteristics of the industry or industry segment.

5. Recognize the difference between the fundamental and dynamic views of competitive advantage. The two fundamental views of competitive advantage are characterized by a largely internal or external orientation toward competitive advantage, research shows that few firms persist in their dominance over competitors over prolonged periods of time. For most firms, therefore, competitive advantage is considered to be temporary. The dynamic perspective assumes that a firm's current market position is not an accurate predictor of future performance because position itself is not a competitive advantage. Instead, the dynamic perspective looks at the past for clues about how the firm arrived at its present position and to the future to divine what the new competitive landscape might look like. It also holds that it's possible for the firm to influence the future state of the competitive landscape.

Review Questions

1. What is strategic management?

2. What are the key components of the strategic management process?

3. How does business strategy differ from corporate strategy?

4. What is the relationship between strategy formulation and strategy implementation?

5. What five elements comprise the strategy formulation diamond?

6. What are the internal and external perspectives of competitive advantage?

7. What are the fundamental and dynamic perspectives of competitive advantage?

8. Why should you study strategic management?

Experiential Activities

Group Exercises

1. Identify the characteristics of a firm that the members of your group would like to work for and try to identify an example of this type of firm. What's the difference between business and corporate strategy at this firm? How might that affect your experiences and opportunities in that organization? Use your knowledge of the firm's strategy to construct a high-impact job application cover letter to apply for a job with this firm.

2. How is international expansion related to business and corporate strategy? Identify a firm that may be thinking of expanding into new international markets. Apply the staging element of the strategy diamond to the firm's international expansion opportunities or plans. Which markets should it target first and why?

Ethical Debates

1. Should ethics be a formal and explicit part of strategy formulation and implementation? What would you do to achieve this type of objective?

2. For many of the firms you will study in this class, competitive advantage is measured by some form of financial profitability. How should you evaluate ethical choices in terms of accounting costs and benefits?

How Would YOU DO THAT?

1. Go to Warren Buffet's *Letter to Shareholder's* page at www.berkshirehathaway.com/letters/letters.html and read the most recent letter. How many of the strategy topics covered in this chapter are referenced in the letter? Pick one of the businesses owned by Berkshire Hathaway and draft a strategy formulation diamond similar to the one outlined in the JetBlue example in the box entitled "How Would *You* Do That? 1.1."

2. Go back to the discussion of JetBlue in the box entitled "How Would *You* Do That? 1.1." Use the strategy implementation model in Exhibit 1.7 to identify what would be necessary to successfully implement JetBlue's strategy. How would the implementation levers be different for JetBlue than for some of the major airlines?

Go on to see How Would You Do That at www.prenhall.com/carpenter&sanders

Endnotes

1. Under Armour, Inc., *2006 Annual Report.*

2. Under Armour, Inc., *2006 Annual Report.*

3. J. Pfeffer and R. I. Sutton, *The Knowing-Doing Gap: How Smart Companies Turn Knowledge into Action* (Boston: Harvard Business School Press, 2000).

4. M. Porter, "What Is Strategy?" *Harvard Business Review* 74:6 (1996), 61–78.

5. D. C. Hambrick and J. W. Fredrickson, "Are You Sure You Have a Strategy?" *Academy of Management Executive* 15:4 (2001), 48–59.

6. K. R. Andrews, *The Concept of Corporate Strategy* 3rd ed. (Homewood, IL: Irwin, 1987).

7. Adapted from D. C. Hambrick and J. W. Fredrickson, "Are You Sure You Have a Strategy?" *Academy of Management Executive* 15:4 (2001), 48–59.

8. R. H. Waterman, T. J. Peters, and J. R. Phillips, "Structure Is Not Organization," *Business Horizons* 23:3 (1980), 14–26.

9. Andrews, *The Concept of Corporate Strategy* 3rd ed. (Homewood, IL: Irwin, 1987).

10. S. Brown and K. Eisenhardt, *Competing on the Edge* (Boston: Harvard Business School Press, 1998); R. A. Burgelman and L. Sayles, *Inside Corporate Innovation* (New York: Free Press, 1986).

11. Adapted from H. Mintzberg, "The Strategy Concept I: Five Ps for Strategy" *California Management Review* 30:1 (1987): 11–24.

12. R. A. Burgelman, "Fading Memories: A Process Theory of Strategic Business Exit in Dynamic Environments," *Administrative Science Quarterly* 39 (1993): 24–56.

13. Burgelman, "Fading Memories"; Grove, *Only the Paranoid Survive.*

14. This section draws extensively from Hambrick and Fredrickson, "Are You Sure You Have a Strategy?"

15. Adapted from D. C. Hambrick and J. W. Fredrickson, "Are You Sure You Have a Strategy?" *Academy of Management Executive* 15:4 (2001), 48–59.

16. Personal interviews with company executives.

17. T. Carl, "After Growing on Small Towns, Wal-Mart Looks to World for More Expansion," Associated Press Newswires, March 26, 2003.

18. *The Strategy Execution Imperative: Leading Practices for Implementing Strategic Initiative* (Washington, D.C.: Corporate Executive Board, 2001); Christensen, "Making Strategy."

19. Data obtained from *JetBlue 2006 Annual Report*, Transportation Workers Union, TWU Airline Industry Review, at www.twuatd.org; Bureau of Transportation, *TransStats Reports*, at www.transtats.bts.gov.

20. M. F. Porter, "Know Your Place: How to Assess the Attractiveness of Your Industry and Your Company's Position in It," *Inc.*, September 1991, 90.

21. P. F. Drucker, *The Practice of Management* (New York: HarperCollins, 1954), 352–353.

22. Adapted from D. Hambrick and A. Cannella, "Strategy Implementation as Substance and Selling," *Academy of Management Executive* 3:4 (1989), 278–285.

23. See J. B. Barney and P. M. Wright, "On Becoming a Strategic Partner: The Role of Human Resources in Gaining Competitive Advantage," *Human Resource Management* 37:1 (1998), 31–46; J. Pfeffer, *Competitive Advantage Through People* (Boston: HBS Press, 1994).

24. S. Kerr, "On the Folly of Rewarding A, While Hoping for B," *Academy of Management Journal* 18:4 (1975), 769–783.

25. J. B. Barney, "Firm Resources and Sustained Competitive Advantage," *Journal of Management* 17:1 (1991), 99–121; M. A. Peteraf, "The Cornerstones of Competitive Advantage: A Resource-Based View," *Strategic Management Journal* 14:3 (1993), 179–191.

26. R. R. Wiggins and T. W. Ruefli, "Sustained Competitive Advantage: Temporal Dynamics and the Incidence and Persistence of Superior Economic Performance," *Organization Science* 13:1 (2002), 82–105.

27. Barney, "Firm Resources and Sustained Competitive Advantage"; Peteraf, "The Cornerstones of Competitive Advantage"; B. Wernerfelt, "A Resource Based View of the Firm," *Strategic Management Journal* 5:2 (1984), 171–180.

28. Peteraf, "The Cornerstones of Competitive Advantage"; C. A. Montgomery and S. Hariharan, "Diversified Expansion by Large Established Firms," *Journal of Economic Behavior* 15:1 (1991), 71–99.

29. M. Porter, *Competitive Strategy* (New York: Free Press, 1980).

30. C. M. Christensen, *The Innovator's Dilemma: When New Technologies Cause Great Firms to Fail* (Boston: Harvard Business School Press, 1997).

31. Brown and Eisenhardt, *Competing on the Edge.*

32. J. Gimeno and C. Woo, "Multimarket Contact, Economies of Scope, and Firm Performance," *Academy of Management Journal* 42:3 (1999), 239–259.

33. Christensen, *The Innovator's Dilemma.*

2

Leading Strategically Through Effective
Vision and Mission

In This Chapter We Challenge You To >>>

1. Explain how strategic leadership is essential to strategy formulation and implementation.

2. Understand the relationships among vision, mission, values, and strategy.

3. Understand the roles of vision and mission in determining strategic purpose and strategic coherence.

4. Identify a firm's stakeholders and explain why such identification is critical to effective strategy formulation and implementation.

5. Explain how ethics and biases may affect strategic decision making.

The
Xerox Vision

*O*ur strategic intent is to help people find better ways to do great work—by constantly leading in document technologies, products and services that improve our customers' work processes and business results.

How to Pull a $15-Billion Cow Out of a Ditch[1] From an outsider's perspective, there was very little in Anne Mulcahy's background at Xerox to suggest that she'd be prepared for the kind of crisis management that awaited her. Most recently, she'd been vice president for human resources and chief staff officer to former chief executive officer (CEO) Paul A. Allaire. The Xerox board promoted Mulcahy to president in May 2000, ousting G. Richard Thoman after a mere 13 months and reinstalling Chairman Allaire as CEO.

When Allaire stepped down on August 1, 2001, Mulcahy became the first female CEO in Xerox history. When Mulcahy's promotion to CEO was announced, Xerox stock took a 15% nosedive. "Not a big confidence boost," Mulcahy said. She also knew that even some of her fellow senior managers did not have confidence in her leadership. So she quickly called a meeting of all senior Xerox leaders and told them point blank that if any of them wanted to leave she would help. Mulcahy did this because she needed the entire team to buy into her plan. "To my surprise, four people asked to leave from the leadership team. But those who stayed became very active. They were stretched, but I did not want armchair quarterbacks criticizing my every move. We needed to work quickly," she said.

The Fall from the Nifty 50 The Xerox story is pretty well known. Introduced in 1959, the Xerox 914 copier transformed office work and installed Xerox as a charter member of the so-called "Nifty 50"—the 50 stocks most favored by institutional investors. Since the 1970s, however, Xerox had been crippled by competition (mostly Japanese), repeated failures to capitalize on innovations coming out of its own Palo Alto Research Center (PARC), and tardiness in embracing digital imaging. After years of weak sales, the company was foundering, and employees were as disgruntled as customers. Then things went from bad to worse. In October 2001, Xerox reported its first quarterly loss in 16 years, and as debt piled up, the Securities and Exchange Commission began investigating the company's accounting practices.

Although the move from senior executive to CEO was a huge jump, Mulcahy was given the chance because she'd instilled confidence in the board. "She has the strategic mind and toughness to serve as CEO," said board member (and Johnson & Johnson CEO) Ralph Larsen.

Mulcahy was a popular manager with years of experience in dealing with customers. Granted, she'd never been involved in product development and didn't boast Allaire's financial expertise, but she'd demonstrated smart decision-making skills as head of the company's $6-billion division for small-office equipment. She'd also put together one of its biggest acquisitions—the $925-million purchase from Tektronix Inc. of a color-printing division that's now a source of fast-growing revenues (in large part because Mulcahy had preserved the division's autonomy and many of its business practices).

Running the Gamut from Enthusiasm to Pragmatism If there was ever any uncertainty about her qualifications as a CEO, they were soon dispelled. Mulcahy refined the Xerox vision and went out of her way to remind Xerox employees that the core values embedded in the company's mission statement had always been part of the firm's deep culture. More important, she moved decisively to align the firm's operations with its refined statement of mission and values.

On the less philosophical side, she sold Xerox's China and Hong Kong operations, and in March 2001 she raised $1.3 billion by selling half of its stake in a joint venture with Fuji. Mulcahy also proved willing to make other tough decisions. In June 2001, she closed down the unit that made desktop inkjet printers in Rochester, New York—a business that she'd once supported. Soon after taking the reins, she eliminated the company's stock dividend and announced that PARC would be spun off as a separate company.

Internally, she spread her message with a regular memo called "Turnaround Talk," which alternates between enthusiasm ("Together We Can Do It!") and pragmatism ("When we shut off the bottled water, it's not because we want to be mean-spirited. It's because all these little expenses can spell the difference between losing money and turning a profit"). By 2002, stressing fidelity to the Xerox mission and long-term vision, she'd cut annual expenses by $1.7 billion, sold $2.3 billion worth of noncore assets, and reduced long-term debt to $9.2 billion, down from a high of $15.6 billion in 2000. Xerox returned to full-year profitability in 2002, generating $1.9 billion in operating-cash flow and $91 million in net income on $15.8 billion in sales.

The Next Chapter In July 2003, with Xerox gaining market share in important segments with new-product introductions, Mulcahy announced that the current chapter in the Xerox "turnaround story" had been closed. Her new challenge would be reigniting growth. Even during weak sales years, she'd invested $1 billion annually in research and development. Her investment in R&D paid off. By 2006, two-thirds of Xerox revenues came from new products that had been introduced just two years prior. "I would say the most important way we foster innovation is our funding of research, which so many companies have walked away from," Mulcahy said. In 2006, the company introduced 49 new products. In the first four months of 2007, Xerox introduced 19 more new products. Mulcahy also bet big on growth through such service businesses as document-management flow and computer networking and achieved a win there as well. In the first quarter of 2007, 70 percent of revenue came from supplies and services.

The task of turning Xerox around has taken its toll on Mulcahy's personal life. Friends say that she laughs when asked about hobbies and executive-suite privileges like golf. Nowadays, reports *Business Week,* Mulcahy "only has time for work and her family, including her two teenage sons." But that, concludes the article, is "the kind of effort it takes to pull a $15-billion cow out of a ditch—and then try to make it run." **<<<**

Strategic Leadership

Imagine starting a new job and then finding out that your job description includes the following items:

■ You'll be personally responsible for the entire company's performance—success, or failure.

■ You'll be relatively powerless to control most of what goes on in the organization.

■ You'll have more authority than any other employee, but in using that authority, you'll make some people so unhappy that they'll harbor personal grudges against you.[2]

Congratulations: You're a CEO.

The basic responsibility of a CEO—*strategic leadership*—is so important that you'll find chapters on it in every management and organizational behavior book you pick up. Stories about leaders and leadership regularly command the covers and fill the pages of major business publications around the world. Some business leaders become celebrities.

What do these leaders do when they're on the job? *Leadership* is the task of exerting influence on other people's pursuit of goals in an organizational context. **Strategic leadership** is the task of managing an overall enterprise and influencing key organizational outcomes, such as company-wide performance, competitive superiority, innovation, strategic change, and survival. As the process of communicating the vision and mission that top executives espouse and model through their own actions, strategic leadership also sets the stage for strategy creation and implementation. Strategic leadership is often associated with individuals like Anne Mulcahy, but increasingly it's being exercised by teams of top executives. Given the complexity and speed of competitive change and uncertainty facing most firms today, this shift shouldn't be surprising.

strategic leadership Task of managing an overall enterprise and influencing key organizational outcomes.

WHAT THIS CHAPTER IS ABOUT

Most of this section explains why top executives, through their decisions and behavior, have both a symbolic and a substantive impact on the outcomes that concern a firm's key stakeholders. What we can tell you at this point, however, is that executives tend to be reactive and defensive in their decisions when their firms don't have clear strategies, and that is generally not a desirable situation for a manager. Thus we start by introducing the roles filled by top individual managers and management teams as they exercise strategic leadership. We'll discuss the functions of individuals and executive teams, as well as the conditions under which strategic-leadership efforts may flourish or founder. We will then discuss the ways in which vision, mission, values, and strategy relate to one another, and we'll show how vision and mission are reflected in the properties of strategy that we call *purpose* and *coherence*. Next, we'll introduce the principles of stakeholder analysis and explain why the best strategic leaders consider stakeholder interests when developing organizational vision and mission and strategies for realizing them. We conclude by showing how unethical and biased judgments can undermine even the best-laid strategic-leadership plans.

THE ROLES LEADERS FILL

What do senior managers do? What occupies their days and nights and fills up their personal digital assistants (PDAs)? As our opening vignette suggests, their jobs are complex and multifaceted, and we can understand the CEO's job only by analyzing it in some detail.[3] Let's start by dividing executive activities into the three basic roles illustrated in Exhibit 2.1: *interpersonal, informational,* and *decisional*.[4]

Exhibit 2.1   The Roles That Leaders Play

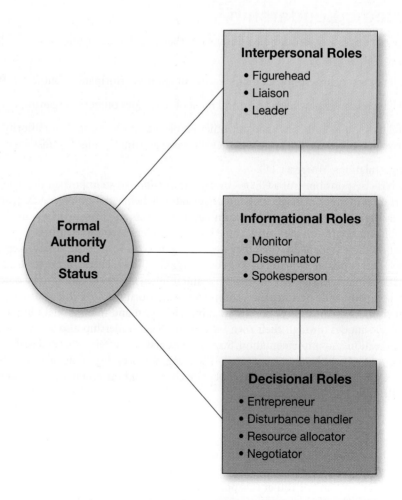

Formal Authority and Status

Interpersonal Roles
- Figurehead
- Liaison
- Leader

Informational Roles
- Monitor
- Disseminator
- Spokesperson

Decisional Roles
- Entrepreneur
- Disturbance handler
- Resource allocator
- Negotiator

Interpersonal Roles   Some executive tasks derive from the status and formal authority that come with the job. They're often interpersonal in nature and have a degree of symbolic value. Many of these roles may seem to have little to do with the practical exigencies of running a company, but they frequently occupy a great of deal of a CEO's time in all firms, from the smallest to the very largest.

Figurehead and Liaison   As *figureheads,* top executives perform various ceremonial tasks, such as breaking ground at new facilities, hosting retirement dinners, and even fielding calls from irate stakeholders. As *liaisons,* they maintain relationships with external stakeholders, thus strengthening the company's links with its external environment. In this role, they serve on the boards of other companies, meet with suppliers and customers, and participate in charities and civic organizations.

Leader   Whereas the role of liaison is horizontal in nature, leadership is a vertical relationship: Top executives are *leaders* because employees and other stakeholders who don't possess their authority look to them for motivation and direction. In this chapter, we'll focus on senior-leadership responsibilities, such as providing vision, purpose, and direction.

Informational Roles   Informational roles include those of monitor, disseminator, and spokesperson. As *monitor,* the executive taps into a larger network of contacts, colleagues, and employees to collect and collate the information needed to understand the organization and its environment. An effective monitor, says strategic-leadership expert Henry Mintzberg, "seeks information in order to detect changes, to identify problems and opportunities, to build up knowledge about his milieu, to be informed when information must be disseminated and decisions made."[5]

Sharing Information: Disseminator and Spokesperson   Not surprisingly, information is never in short supply; in fact, information overload is a common condition of executive life. Top managers are bombarded with reports, analyses, and projections and information about both internal operations and external events. Obviously, the good monitor must know what to do with all of this information. Much of it, of course, is passed on to people both inside and outside the firm who can put it to use. In passing information to internal stakeholders, executives are *disseminators;* in passing it to external stakeholders, they're *spokespersons.*

As disseminators, CEOs communicate not only factual information, such as data received from bankers and consultants, but also what's often called *value-based information.* In leading Xerox through a period of change, for example, Anne Mulcahy spent much of her time communicating value statements to both internal and external stakeholders.

As spokespersons, CEOs perform such communications tasks as lobbying, public relations, and formal reporting. CEOs communicate with both boards of directors, to whom they report, and the general public. Needless to say, being an effective spokesperson means focusing on the most current, accurate, and relevant information.

Decisional Roles   Perhaps the most obvious—some will say the most important—role of top managers is making key decisions about the company's strategy and future. In developing and implementing strategy, top executives may play any or all of four decisional roles: *entrepreneur, disturbance handler, resource allocator,* and *negotiator.*

The Entrepreneur   As entrepreneur, the CEO designs the firm's strategy. Clearly, many people are involved in the process, but the CEO must ultimately authorize major strategic initiatives and supervise their implementation.

The Disturbance Handler   Whereas the entrepreneurial role focuses on voluntary and proactive initiatives, disturbance handling deals with unforeseen situations or those in which the firm is involved involuntarily. Any number of "disturbances" can threaten the successful implementation of a strategy, including both internal and external conflicts. Internal conflicts, such as infighting by divisions or managers over responsibilities and authority, often require the CEO's arbitration. Likewise, the CEO will probably have to take action to smooth out conflicts in the distribution channel (a key supplier's announcement, for example, that it will no longer deal with the company on an exclusive basis).

The Resource Allocator The role of resource allocator is crucial both to the task of formulating strategy and to the task of executing it successfully. If resources aren't effectively allocated, even a well-formulated strategy has little chance of success. With authority over the organization's financial, material, and human resources, the CEO is the only person who can manage the tradeoffs among competing strategic projects.

The Negotiator As a negotiator, the CEO is usually concerned with nonroutine transactions involving other organizations. Such decisions as whether to acquire or merge with another firm, to sell a major division, or to renegotiate a labor contract require significant participation from the CEO.

The Surprised CEO

Obviously, then, being a CEO isn't easy.[6] What's astonishing, however, is the result of recent research showing that many new CEOs are quite surprised by many aspects of their jobs. Some report, for instance, that they're surprised at having to work with limited information and insufficient time to accomplish what they're expected to do. Others are surprised that being a CEO means that they can no longer run day-to-day operations the way they once did. As heads of divisions or small companies, managers are much more deeply involved in nuts-and-bolts operations, but when they move into the executive suite of a large organization, they no longer have the time for hands-on management.

Yet other new CEOs learn the hard way that being the most powerful person in the organization doesn't mean that that you can use power as liberally as you please; power is a privilege best indulged in moderation. Conversely, many CEOs reach the top rung on the organizational ladder only to be reminded—sometimes rudely—that they still have to answer to a board of directors. Finally, new CEOs are often surprised at how hard they have to work to make their brilliant strategies understood and get them accepted by a broad range of stakeholders.

In addition, as demonstrated by Anne Mulcahy's situation, many who rise to senior leadership positions in large organizations often pay a price—sacrificing their personal and family lives in order to meet their managerial responsibilities. Roger Deromedi, the recently appointed CEO of Kraft Foods, notes that "I travel about 40 percent of the time, so life is a balancing act. People often don't make time with their spouse that's separate from time with their kids. I prioritize my wife and family, which means I don't have as much time for outside interests."[7]

THE SKILL SET OF THE EFFECTIVE STRATEGIC LEADER: THE LEVEL 5 HIERARCHY

What does it take to be an effective organizational leader? Obviously, neither all leaders nor leadership challenges are created equal. A diverse set of skills, therefore, can come in handy. In this section, we'll discuss the development of leadership skill sets in terms of a model called the **Level 5 Hierarchy**, which was popularized by management researcher Jim Collins in the book *From Good to Great*.[8] The key to this framework is the idea that leadership requires a wide range of abilities, some of which are hierarchical in nature—in other words, that before mastering certain higher-level abilities, one must first master certain lower-level skills.[9] Collins proposes the five levels of leadership skills summarized in Exhibit 2.2.[10]

Level 5 Hierarchy Model of leadership skills calling for a wide range of abilities, some of which are hierarchical in nature.

- **Level 1.** Before becoming an effective leader, you must prove highly competent in your work. On the first level of leadership, therefore, productive contributions of your talent, knowledge, hard work, and skills must be made.

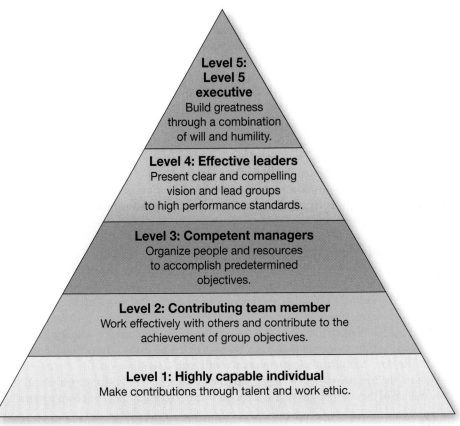

Exhibit 2.2 Level 5 Leaders: A Hierarchy of Capabilities

- **Level 2.** Senior management is often a team endeavor, and CEOs must be able to delegate major responsibilities to teams of senior executives. At level 2, therefore, you must also show the ability to work effectively as a member of a team.

- **Level 3.** After teamwork abilities have been demonstrated, you need to show the ability to manage other people—the ability to organize people and marshal resources to achieve specific objectives.

- **Level 4.** Next, you must prove capable of leading a larger organization by generating broad commitment to a clear vision of the organization's future. At level 4, you need to show the ability to lead a group to superior levels of performance. Anne Mulcahy, for example, didn't reverse Xerox's fortunes by herself. She assembled a team with diverse backgrounds and capabilities and drew upon their collective abilities.

- **Level 5.** Level 5 leadership tends to feature an unusual, even paradoxical, combination of skills. Level 5 executives not only express an unwavering resolve, or *professional will,* to achieve higher goals but demonstrate a surprising degree of *professional modesty.* Let's take a closer look at these two managerial attributes.

Professional Will   Carrying out bold strategy moves requires commitment across the entire organization. A level 5 leader can translate strategic intent into the resolve needed to pursue a strategy—and usually to make hard choices—over a period of time.

Here's a good illustration. Walgreen Company was founded in 1901 by Chicago pharmacist Charles Walgreen. Eight years later, Walgreen began serving lunch at a new soda fountain, where, by the 1920s, he was doing his part to popularize the milk shake. Although food services remained a key part of Walgreen's business, the company realized during the 1960s that its classic soda-fountain operations were draining profits from the modern self-service retail operations that generated far greater sales per square foot. Now, to many people, soda fountains were a Walgreen hallmark, and because its history of food service was part of the firm's identity, there was considerable internal resistance to the idea of closing down the soda-fountain operations. In fact, CEO Charles Walgreen III found that phasing out food-service operations was more easily said than done; simply announcing his plan by no means ensured organization-wide cooperation. Ultimately, Walgreen set a deadline of five years, admonishing senior executives that "the clock is ticking." When reminded six months later that management had only five years to get out of the restaurant business, Walgreen reasserted his resolve to stick to the schedule: "Four and a half years," he replied.[11] In the final analysis, it was largely Walgreen's resolve that transformed the old model of the drugstore chain into a new (and more profitable) retail model.

Professional Modesty Oddly, level 5 executives also tend to be modest people—a fairly rare trait among people with upward career trajectories. Most research suggests that hubris is much more common than humility in the upper echelons of Management, and given the drive that's needed to found or lead a successful firm, that fact shouldn't be surprising. And although examples abound of successful leaders who would not be described as modest, Collins' research suggests that companies that improve from average profitability and then beat the market over the long haul tend to be led by people who prefer to share credit rather than hog it. They tend to shun public attention, act with calm determination, and exercise their ambitions on the company's behalf rather than their own. They're also concerned about the future welfare of the company as well as its performance record during their own tenures.

WHAT DOES IT TAKE TO BE A CEO?

Having established the fact that senior executives influence the formation and implementation of strategy through both judgment and behavior, we know that it's worthwhile to understand what makes them think and act the way they do. We'll start by focusing on the characteristics of individual executives and the roles that they play in shaping strategic-leadership abilities.

Are you CEO material? Just what does it take? Charisma? Integrity? An Ivy League MBA? International management experience? Not surprisingly, there's no single answer to these seemingly simple questions. Although some answers involve such personality differences as charisma and emotional intelligence, others point to such demographic characteristics as gender, race, education, or work experience. There's little consensus on the issue of whether personality or background counts more, but understanding their actions is important if you want to understand successful leaders. With this fact in mind, let's take a closer look at all three perspectives on leadership characteristics: *personality differences, background and demographic differences,* and *differences in competence and actions.*

Personality Differences Largely because psychological traits can be measured through surveys and other quantitative approaches, a large amount of research has been done on the personality or psychological determinants of strategic leadership. Many of these studies focus on four personality characteristics: *locus of control, need for achievement, tolerance for risk or ambiguity,* and *charisma and emotional intelligence.*[12]

What's Your Tolerance for Ambiguity? Analyzing all of these characteristics goes beyond the purpose of this chapter, but you may find it instructive to investigate how you measure up on one key personality attribute—tolerance for ambiguity—compared to typical executives. *Tolerance for ambiguity* means that one tends to perceive situations as promising rather than threatening. If you are intolerant of ambiguity, then uncertainty or a lack of information, for example, would make you uncomfortable. Ambiguity arises from three main sources: novelty, complexity, and insolubility. You can use the ambiguity scale in Exhibit 2.3 to see how you measure up in terms of tolerance for ambiguity.[13]

Personality Traits Versus Leadership Abilities If there is indeed a correspondence between certain personality characteristics and leadership abilities, then (at least in theory) boards of directors could sift through applicant pools and choose CEOs on psychological grounds. Unfortunately, the jury is still out on the question of whether "natural" leaders can be classified according to personality differences or identified through psychological test instruments. In fact, some researchers warn against placing undue importance on trendy personality screens. In short, personality characteristics may be important in some respects, but defining and isolating effective leadership abilities is a complex task.

Background and Demographic Differences

Background differences typically refer to such factors as work experience and education, whereas *demographics* refers to such factors as gender, nationality, race, religion, network ties, and so forth.[14] Obviously, many factors of both kinds will figure prominently on your résumé.

Historically, the profile of the typical *Fortune*-500 top executive was a white male between the ages of 45 and 60 with a law, finance, or accounting degree from an Ivy League school.[15] Sociologists explain this pattern by pointing out that, for a long time, a large portion of the educated population—and thus of the managerial talent pool—consisted of white males. Moreover, white males were favored by certain structural features of the executive-employment market, including the usual prejudice of people to show favoritism toward people who are like them (in this case, white males).

Changes in demographics of business school students, as well as legal and social influence from lawsuits and legislation, have helped to diversify management ranks. Although there are significantly more female and minority managers at the start of the twenty-first century than there were just 20 years ago, few women and minorities have ascended to the level of CEO at the largest companies. For instance, as of 2007 there were only twleve female CEOs among the 500 largest U.S. companies (2.4 percent), up from nine in 2005 and more than double the number a decade ago. In addition, 16 percent of the corporate officers of these same companies are female, suggesting that change is happening, even if only gradually. It is interesting to note that the diversity of CEOs among privately owned smaller companies is much more reflective of the U.S. population. Although the diversity of large public companies has been slow to change, the diversity of leadership in smaller companies is much greater and growing.

Although there are still a lot of white males in the upper echelons of business, most of today's CEOs don't have an Ivy League pedigree, and we're now finding much greater diversity on other dimensions among top-management teams.[16] Again, however, we need to remember that boards don't rely on any single criterion when choosing a CEO. In fact, our opening vignette features a CEO who came up not by following the usual accounting or finance track but rather through strategic human resource management.

Beside the fact that it's unethical (and, in many countries, illegal) to discriminate in hiring and promotion, a number of practical explanations account for the increasing diversity in the ranks of top managers, both in the U.S. and elsewhere:

- Although an advanced degree remains a typical prerequisite for promotion, college education is now available to more people than ever before. All around the world, schools compete for the best and brightest regardless of race, gender, or religion, and employers reap the benefits of more diverse talent pools.

Exhibit 2.3 Can You Tolerate Ambiguity?

You may have taken this survey earlier in the semester in preparation for this course. By definition, ambiguity characterizes strategic management and the study of strategy through cases. Your response to the case method itself is a function of your own attitude toward ambiguity. Take the following survey and tabulate your score to find out your tolerance for ambiguous situations.

Please respond to the following statements by indicating the extent to which you agree or disagree with them. Fill in the blanks with the number from the rating scale that best represents your evaluation of the item. There's a scoring key at the end of the survey.

1	Strongly disagree	5	Slightly agree
2	Moderately disagree	6	Moderately agree
3	Slightly disagree	7	Strongly agree
4	Neither agree nor disagree		

_____ 1. An expert who doesn't come up with a definite answer probably doesn't know too much.

_____ 2. I would like to live in a foreign country for a while.

_____ 3. There is really no such thing as a problem that can't be solved.

_____ 4. People who fit their lives to a schedule probably miss most of the joy of living.

_____ 5. A good job is one where what is to be done and how it is to be done are always clear.

_____ 6. It is more fun to tackle a complicated problem than to solve a simple one.

_____ 7. In the long run it is possible to get more done by tackling small, simple problems rather than large and complicated ones.

_____ 8. Often the most interesting and stimulating people are those who don't mind being different and original.

_____ 9. What we are used to is always preferable to what is unfamiliar.

_____ 10. People who insist upon a yes or no answer just don't know how complicated things really are.

_____ 11. A person who leads an even, regular life in which few surprises or unexpected happenings arise really has a lot to be grateful for.

_____ 12. Many of our most important decisions are based upon insufficient information.

_____ 13. I like parties where I know most of the people more than ones where all or most people are complete strangers.

_____ 14. Teachers or supervisors who hand out vague assignments give one a chance to show initiative and originality.

_____ 15. The sooner we all acquire similar values and ideals, the better.

_____ 16. A good teacher is one who makes you wonder about your way of looking at things.

To score the instrument, **the even-numbered items must be reverse scored**. That is, the 7s become 1s, 6s become 2s, 5s become 3s, and 4s remain the same. After reversing the even-numbered items, sum the scores for all 16 items to get your total score. High scores indicate a greater intolerance for ambiguity. Use the comparison scores provided below to benchmark your own score, and read the following paragraphs to interpret such results.

Total Score

Subscores (follow same even/odd reverse scoring)
(N) Novelty score (sum 2, 9, 11, 13) _____
(C) Complexity score (sum 4, 5, 6, 7, 8, 10, 14, 15, 16) _____
(I) Insolubility score (sum 1, 3, 12) _____

Being intolerant of ambiguity (relatively high score) means that an individual tends to perceive situations as threatening rather than promising. Lack of information or uncertainty, for example, would make such a person uncomfortable. Ambiguity arises from three main sources: *novelty, complexity, and insolubility*. These three subscales exist within the instrument you just completed.
Comparison total scores: Senior executives 44–48, MBAs 55–60.

■ Groups tend to make better decisions when they can draw on heterogeneous perspectives, especially when facing turbulent or uncertain environments. When uncertainty makes it difficult to predict the future, top-management teams make better strategic decisions when they get input from diverse sources.[17]

■ Companies today need top managers with strong international skills gained through work experience abroad. Because these skills are still fairly rare, even among college graduates, firms must look harder and farther to find them.[18]

■ Firms increasingly seek competitive advantage through the quality of their human capital—the people who work for them. Because human capabilities are color, gender, and ethnicity blind, people with greater background and demographic diversity are rising to the ranks of upper management. Indeed, any form of bias that prevents talented employees from being promoted will put a firm at a distinct competitive disadvantage, particularly in terms of its ability to attract and retain talented people.

Competence and Actions Do actions speak louder than words (or perhaps even louder than personality, background, or demographic differences)? Among the main reasons that Anne Mulcahy rose to the top at Xerox was her experience as vice president and staff officer for customer operations in South and Central America, Europe, Asia, Africa, and China. Increasingly, the consensus on what it takes to make it to the top-executive ranks goes beyond skin color, gender, and even line items on a résumé. More companies are placing value on substantive work experience—looking as much for the knowledge gleaned from mistakes as for the successes accumulated along the way.

Mulcahy had already demonstrated courage and toughness when it came to making and sticking to decisions, and although such toughness may be a product of experience, many experts argue that superior executives are distinguished by a talent for strategic thinking. Mulcahy was promoted because of her proven strength as a business strategist as well as her decision-making toughness. What, exactly, does a "talent for strategic thinking" add to "toughness"? By *toughness,* we mean a willingness and ability to change an organization's strategic course even when that change represents a significant departure from its traditional way of doing business. Whereas the average manager emphasizes the efficient execution of a given plan, the strategic leader works not only to develop the plan in the first place, but to empower the organization to realize the vision behind it.

Strategists and nonstrategists differ in how they think about problems. Like personality differences, these differences are too broad to review in detail in this chapter. However, a few of these dimensions of strategic thinking are reviewed in the "Are You a Strategist?" exercise in Exhibit 2.4. Test yourself on a few dimensions of strategic leadership by taking the survey.[19] As you can see, strategists are characterized by having a spirit of entrepreneurship and an eye to the future.

WHAT MAKES AN EFFECTIVE EXECUTIVE TEAM?

In reality, of course, organizations need good managers as well as great leaders, just as armies need hard-working soldiers and inspirational generals. Ironically, one hallmark of great leadership is knowing when and how to follow the lead of others. In this section, we'll discuss the ways in which the interaction of members of a top-management team can influence—for better or for worse—the contributions of a strategic leader. (We'll also discuss the importance of top-management teams and teamwork in strategic leadership in later chapters as well.) At the very least, the team has the advantage of a division of labor, and in any case, no single person, regardless of talent and ability, can single-handedly attend to all the details encountered at the top of today's complex organizations.

Exhibit 2.4 Are You
a Strategist?

Answer each question with "Yes," "Mostly Yes," "Mostly No," or "No." Tally up the percentage of answers in each category.	Yes	Mostly Yes	Mostly No	No
1. Do you like to be entrepreneurial and come up with new ideas or plans but are also comfortable having others execute them? _____	☐	☐	☐	☐
2. Do you have clear guiding values for your actions (i.e., strategic intent and coherence)? _____	☐	☐	☐	☐
3. Do you think about your strengths and weaknesses before making major life choices? _____	☐	☐	☐	☐
4. Do you engage in activities that are in concert with your vision of the future and personal guiding values? _____	☐	☐	☐	☐
5. When you work with others, do you try to foster a climate where your colleagues can act freely in the interests of the objective you are seeking to achieve? _____	☐	☐	☐	☐
6. When you are working with others to achieve a certain objective, do you actively and regularly involve them in formulating the strategy to achieve that objective? _____	☐	☐	☐	☐
7. When working with others to achieve an objective do you seek harmony in matching your group's culture with your strategy? _____	☐	☐	☐	☐
8. Do you point out new directions and take novel approaches? _____	☐	☐	☐	☐
9. Have you been lucky so far (strategic leadership includes the ability to place oneself in positions that favor being lucky)? _____	☐	☐	☐	☐
10. Do you make a contribution to society and yourself (strategic leaders leave a legacy)? _____	☐	☐	☐	☐

If you answered "Yes" or "Mostly Yes" to these questions, congratulations—you have the makings of a strategic leader!

Teamwork and Diversity   What does effective teamwork mean if the team consists of top-management personnel? Basically, effective teamwork requires four criteria:

1. The team responds to a complex and changing environment.

2. The team can manage the needs of interdependent but often diverse units, arenas, or functional areas.

3. The team has a valuable and effective **social network**.

4. The team is able to develop a coherent plan for executive succession.

There's a common key to satisfying the first two criteria: A team can accommodate diverse input while acting as an integrated unit. In other words, the team is composed of people who have diverse backgrounds in terms of demographics and experience but who can nevertheless work well together as a network and take advantage of the resources and knowledge they have access to by virtue of each team member's personal and professional networks. Large firms typically can afford, and often have, larger top-management teams than do smaller firms, which also means that executives in larger firms have access to broader personal and professional networks.

Social Networks The third area, which we will call the team's social network, reflects the personal or professional set of relationships between individuals that extend beyond the management team. Social networks represent both a collection of ties between people and the strength of those ties. A related concept is **social capital**. Social capital is a core concept in business, economics, organizational behavior, political science, and sociology, defined as the advantage created by a person's location in a structure of relationships. So, when you say that a manager or management team has valuable social capital, you are actually talking about the value created by their social network. Often used as a measure of social "connectedness", recognizing the size and other characteristics of social networks assists in determining how information moves throughout groups, and how trust can be established and fostered. Just as a team can often accomplish more than a given individual, so too can network differences allow one management team to be more effective than another, by virtue of the information or other resources the network allows them to access. For instance, a firm that plans to use acquisitions as a growth vehicle is well-served when members of the management team have established good relationships with bankers and the managers of possible acquisition targets. It is possible for you to map out other important characteristics of social networks, as shown in the box entitled "How Would *You* Do That? 2.1," which is another reason that you should add social network analysis to your strategy toolkit.

Succession Planning The fourth area, succession planning, has received increased attention in recent years as turnover among upper-echelon executives has increased. This is the case even among small firms, although the process is often made more complex by the fact that potential successors may include family members, in addition to current executives and outsiders hired from other companies. As a practical matter, succession planning has become more important because the rate of CEO dismissals by relatively large public firms has increased by 170 percent from 1995 to 2004 (from 30 out of 2,500 to 75). Globally, CEO job security is declining, with average tenure decreasing by 23 percent between 1995 and 2004, to a low of 7.6 years. Twenty-eight percent of the 238 CEOs who departed in 2004 were outsiders—the highest proportion in any year since 1995.[20]

Experts agree that a well-planned and executed succession process is essential for a successful transition. **Succession planning** is typically overseen by the board, often with an outside consulting firm, and usually involves the current CEO. In most cases, succession is typically considered final only when the new CEO is in place and the old one has departed. Why? Given the power that sitting CEOs may command, it's often better that a long-term CEO leave the company entirely. Boards, says Jeffrey Sonnenfeld, an expert on CEO succession, "should recognize that creators have a strong tendency to act like monarchs or generals, and both kinds have trouble giving things up."[21]

Even with CEO succession planning becoming more established and accepted in corporations around the world, its practice is a science tempered by a strong dose of art. The science part involves the development of a methodical approach to identifying desirable CEO characteristics and then drawing out a short-list of candidates from a broad field of wanna-be

social network The collection of ties between people and the strength of those ties.

social capital The advantage created through the characteristics of a person's network.

succession planning Process of managing a well-planned and well-executed transition from one CEO to the next with positive outcomes for all key stakeholders.

Mapping Your Social Network

Social networks exist to accomplish specific tasks, manage careers, or in relation to hobbies or leisure. Obviously, social networks are not just for the workplace. For instance, you are probably familiar with popular social networking websites such as Friendster.com, MySpace.com, or Classmates.com, or perhaps you already manage a professional network through LinkedIn.com, or another business-related networking site. While you probably know that social networks are important, particularly for managers, what network characteristics should you pay attention to? Here is a step-by-step process to help you answer that question.

First, imagine a particular objective, be it getting a job or being effective in your current job. Next, make a list of the people you communicate with on a regular basis, who are also relevant to the objective you identified. These are your network ties—that is, the people who tie you into the social network. Remember, this list is based only on who you interact with, and not whether you work with them, go to school with them, and so on. If they are relevant to the objective, they should be on your list. To give you an idea of how many names you might have, a 35-year-old manager would list 10 to 20 contacts. Now that you have your list, the third step in this mapping process is to categorize your relationships. While you can use any criteria that you want, we will use "closeness" here. Very close relationships are those characterized by

high degrees of liking, trust, and mutual commitment. Distant relationships are those characterized by not knowing the person very well, or by having very little liking, trust, and mutual commitment. A problematic relationship is still a network relationship if it is related to your

objective. The fourth and final step is to calculate the density of your social network. To do this, you create a simple grid where you indicate who knows who in your network. Tally up the number of unique pairs then calculate your network density as follows:

---

a) Total number of people in your network

Pat's N = 10

N = _____

b) Maximum Density (i.e., if everyone in your network knew each other). *Pat's maximum density is (10*9) ÷ 2 = 45.*

$[N * (N - 1)] \div 2 = M$

M = _____

c) Total number of checkmarks on your network grid (i.e., the number of relationships among people in your network).

Pat's C = 19.

C = _____

d) Density of Your Network. *Pat's D = 19 ÷ 45 = .42* (will be between 0.00 and 1.00)

$C \div M = D$

D = _____

Now we are ready to talk about your social network. The number of people on your list is obviously the size of your social network. In the example shown here in Exhibit 2.5, the network is comprised of 10 people, plus you. More people means more information, and possibly access to greater resources. But notice that not all of the ties in the example are equally close. You can compare absolute numbers here, or boil these down into percentages—for instance, 20 percent of these ties are very close, and 10 percent are distant. For most people, it would be hard to

manage a huge network where all the ties are very close, just by virtue of the amount of time and energy it takes to satisfy the conditions for closeness. Moreover, there is a natural tradeoff between closeness and number of ties, or network size. Though this also means that some people in your network may be less useful than others, in terms of the resources and information they would readily and voluntarily provide you. You can use other characteristics to categorize these ties as well, such as demographics or hierarchy. For instance, what

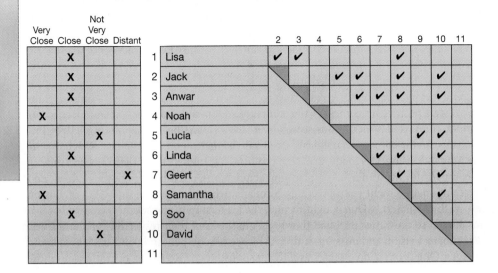

Exhibit 2.5 Sample of Pat's Social Network Grid

Very Close	Close	Not Very Close	Distant			2	3	4	5	6	7	8	9	10	11
	X			1	Lisa	✔	✔					✔			
	X			2	Jack				✔	✔		✔		✔	
	X			3	Anwar					✔	✔	✔		✔	
X				4	Noah										
		X		5	Lucia								✔	✔	
	X			6	Linda						✔	✔		✔	
			X	7	Geert							✔		✔	
X				8	Samantha									✔	
	X			9	Soo										
		X		10	David										
				11											

percentage of your network ties are the same age, gender, or nationality as you? What percentage come from the same organization, or are lower or higher than you on the organization chart?

This brings us back to the density of your network. At this point you are probably getting some idea about the nature of your social network, and how and why information and resources may flow through it. Density is important because, if it is close to 1.00, then everyone in your network knows everyone else. This is great if everyone in your network has their own network density close to 0.00, because you are very central in the network, have access to diverse information and resources, and provide a common link to the others in the network. If you were to map out the connections between network members you could clearly see examples of individuals who are more or less central in this particular network. Unfortunately though, if your network density is high, then so is theirs, and you all have access to the same information. Why is this bad? Well, if you are a team of music industry executives, and only have experience with that industry, then you might not be aware of opportunities or threats emerging in, say, a little place called the Internet! More generally, the more dense the network, the less that new information will come into it, and that is probably not a good thing in a changing world. We also know that, on average, your social network is likely to change in structure over time as a function of things like your tenure in one industry. For instance, the longer you have been in one industry, the more likely it is that you will see your network size begin to shrink and that its density increases.

Now that you understand how social networks operate and can map them, you can also begin to evaluate and manage them. With this map, identify the people on whom you are dependent. Focus your energies on cultivating relationships with those dependencies, or network ties that bypass or co-opt them. Develop strategies for networking with difficult targets—individuals who would make your network more useful. Two broad organizing principles will assure that you have a useful network— similarity and exchange. The similarity principal suggests that relationships develop spontaneously between people with common backgrounds, values, and interests; the exchange principal suggests that "difference" is what makes ties useful, in that it increases the likelihood that each party has a complementary resource. Through this exercise you should have also learned something else—your attitude toward networks and perhaps some intuition about your networking style. That knowledge alone provides you a good start.

CEOs. As you can see, the art part comes into play when making the difficult judgments about who should make the short list and then ranking those candidates realistically in terms of their ability to meet the firm's strategic needs.

When the succession process flounders, it can destroy the CEO's legacy—not to mention the company's health—by undermining investor confidence, depressing the stock price, creating dissension on the board, disrupting the continuity of ongoing initiatives, and even crippling the organization for years. Conversely, when the process goes well, a smooth transition fosters positive outcomes for the company and its stakeholders. General Electric, for example, conducted a meticulous search over several years before appointing Jeffrey Immelt, who ran the company's medical-systems division, to succeed CEO Jack Welch. By the time a final decision was made, according to insiders, Immelt had in effect been running the company for most of a year—planning acquisitions, attending employee reviews, and overseeing management team meetings. Similarly, when the founder and CEO of Boston auto-wash chain ScrubaDub sought to turn the leadership of the business over to his two sons, he did so only after they had thoroughly hashed out their respective roles and titles, the company's vision and mission, and their respective compensation and stock ownership packages. One brother now serves as CEO, responsible for R&D and operations, and the other serves as president, responsible for training, sales, and marketing.[22]

Sometimes, of course, the timing of a transition can't be predicted. In such cases, an even higher premium is placed on good managerial bench strength and prior planning. At McDonald's, for example, the promotion of Charlie Bell only hours after the sudden death of CEO Jim Cantalupo reassured employees and investors that the firm was under competent leadership. The smooth transition was possible only because the plan for Bell's succession was already in place, and a year later, when Bell himself resigned because of illness, the board already had Jim Skinner waiting in the wings. "The worst-case scenario planning of most companies," points out Jeffrey Sonnenfeld, "is only a Band-Aid transitional solution, not a strategic solution. McDonald's directors, by immediately naming a battle-tested insider, showed the wisdom of having a succession plan in place."[23]

The Imprint of Strategic Leadership: Vision and Mission

Top executives provide the context for strategy formulation and implementation through the vision and mission that they espouse and model with their own actions. Sometimes, they're the originators of the vision and mission; at other times, they're caretakers or stewards who work to sharpen employees' shared understanding of the vision and mission. In any case, the vision and mission remain central, and that's why the overarching model of strategic management that we introduced in Chapter 1 starts with vision and mission.

DEFINING *VISION* AND *MISSION*

vision Simple statement or understanding of what the firm will be in the future.

Vision is a simple statement of where a firm is going, and what the firm's leaders want it to be in the future. A statement of vision is forward-looking and identifies the firm's desired long-term status. Think of the vision statement like a car's headlights, perhaps its high beams, and the illuminating or guiding role they might play for a driver who is negotiating a curvy road on a dark, stormy night. Vision statements can be very brief, even just a couple of words or sentences. They describe what the firm wants to look like many years from now, or how the organization aims to fulfill customers' future needs and expectations. In contrast, a **mission** is a declaration of what a firm stands for in relation to key organizational stakeholders like employees, customers, investors, government, and the environment—the

mission Declaration of what a firm is and what it stands for—its fundamental values and purpose.

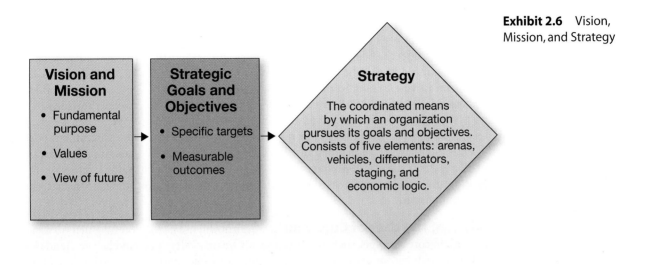

Exhibit 2.6 Vision, Mission, and Strategy

fundamental values and purpose that its leaders believe are shared and prized among those stakeholders. Because it's difficult to execute a strategy if it can't be described or understood, firms with clearly and widely understood visions and missions find it easier to make strategic decisions entailing difficult tradeoffs.

Thus, as you can see in Exhibit 2.6, vision and mission influence strategy formulation and implementation.[24] Sometimes this influence is exercised when leaders focus explicitly on defining or refining a firm's vision, as was the case with Mulcahy at Xerox. More often, however, an organization's vision and mission are well established and functional. In these cases, leaders work to formulate the firm's strategy in a manner that's consistent with the fundamental values and purpose expressed in its statements of core beliefs. Discussion of the vision and mission provides shared understanding of the firm's direction and values, and thus helps guide both executives and employees in their daily decisions and actions. Similarly, when external stakeholders like investors or customers understand the vision and mission, they may have a better understanding of why a particular strategy is pursued. Vision and mission, therefore, reinforce and support strategy; conversely, strategy provides a coherent plan for realizing vision and mission.

Once you've finished this and the next section, you should be able to identify a firm's vision and mission and understand their roles in more complex organizational activities. You'll understand how vision and mission are translated into strategic action, and you'll be able to make recommendations for improving organizational performance or competitive position. You'll see how vision and mission contribute to the organizational functions that we call *strategic purpose* and *strategic coherence*. Because strategy can be successful only to the extent that key stakeholders (customers, suppliers, government, and employees) facilitate its implementation, you'll also learn how to use the tool that we call *stakeholder analysis*.

WHAT SHOULD VISION AND MISSION STATEMENTS ENCOMPASS?

A study by the consulting firm Bain and Company reports that 90 percent of 500 firms surveyed issue some form of vision and mission statements.[25] Toward what end? Together, vision and mission statements not only express a firm's identity and describe its work but inform both managers and employees of the firm's direction. They're not strategies in and of themselves, but they convey organizational identity and purpose to critical stakeholders both inside and outside the firm.

Vision: The Uses of Ambition and Ambiguity   In the early 1950s, Sony stated its vision of "becoming the company that most changes the worldwide image of Japanese products as being of poor quality." Back in 1915, CitiBank (now CitiGroup aka Citi) announced its grandiose vision of becoming "the most powerful, the most serviceable, the most far-reaching world financial institution the world has ever seen."[26] As these two examples suggest, vision statements generally express long-term action horizons, and they're ambitious by design, because ambition forces the firm to stretch both by challenging external competitors and by questioning the internal status quo. Because they're often ambiguous, they don't inhibit the firm from reaching for the stars (or at least aspiring to reach for the stars). Ambiguity also enables flexibility for changing strategy or implementation tactics when it looks as if business as usual isn't going to realize the expressed vision.

Mission: The Uses of Core Values   A firm will use its mission statement to identify certain core concepts, such as its purpose, or *raison d'être;* values and beliefs; standards of behavior; or corporate-level aims.[27] All employees are supposed to internalize core ideals and call upon them to guide their decisions and actions. At Siemens, for example, a core value is the innovative solution of problems. Merck wants employees to preserve and improve human life, and Wal-Mart wants them to devote themselves to selling ordinary folks the same things that affluent people buy.[28]

WHY VISION AND MISSION STATEMENTS ARE NOT SUBSTITUTES FOR STRATEGY

Research suggests that the best-performing firms boast clear visions and missions.[29] However, it should be obvious by now that clearly articulated, coherent, and widely understood vision and mission statements are not substitutes for strategy. Nevertheless, we need to spend a little time on this point.

In 1993, when outsider Lou Gerstner was hired as CEO and charged with the daunting task of saving IBM from potential ruin, he announced that "the last thing IBM needs (right now) is a vision." The statement was widely circulated (although press reports usually edited out the words "right now"),[30] as was Gerstner's charge that IBM's vision was nothing but a litany of platitudes, like those of firms who declare commitment to "total quality" or "customer service." Having discovered that some divisions at IBM were busier squabbling over the distribution of revenue than responding to customer needs, Gerstner was more interested in consistent and tangible managerial action.

Likewise, vision statements don't help much if managers view them as cure-alls for organization ailments or if they paint pictures of a future that's clearly unattainable. Sometimes, a vision is so irrelevant to organizational reality that employees and customers simply reject it. Small firms, in particular, need a clear vision and mission to provide them with focus, but they also need a concrete strategy to translate concepts and resource constraints into profitable action. In the case of IBM, an enormous firm, Gerstner wanted to send a strong message to all employees that serious changes were needed if the company was to survive—changes that would extend far beyond any revamped statement of vision.

Vision and mission can be powerful tools, but because they're general and ambiguous by design, they must be realized through carefully crafted and executed strategy. Firms undergoing strategic change are especially susceptible to serious discrepancies between a new vision statement that's crafted on high and the organizational processes designed to realize it on the factory floor. As you can see from Exhibit 2.7, Gerstner did in fact have a clear vision for IBM (namely, to get it back to the top spot in its industry), but he first set out to anchor this vision in specific goals and objectives derived from a focused and clearly articulated strategy.[31] IBM's prospects were gloomy back in 1993, but thanks to Gerstner's clear-headed understanding of the relationship between strategy and vision (and his talent for leadership), IBM is once again one of America's most admired companies.

GOALS AND OBJECTIVES

If talk of visions and missions conjures up images of crystal balls and astrology, don't be too surprised. Some executives treat vision and mission statements as symbolic pronouncements, and in many organizations they exist on a different plane than actual strategy and strategic actions. Such discrepancies are symptomatic of various conditions. Perhaps the firm is floundering from a lack of clear or unique strategic direction; perhaps its strategy is too complex; maybe management has lost sight of the competitive realities facing the company.

What is one of the key determinants of whether a vision and mission are judged to be effective? The answer appears to be found when leaders have spelled out a set of clear and specific quantitative or qualitative **goals and objectives** that provide a bridge between the vision and the strategy. Progress toward a certain goal or achievement of an objective serve as indicators of how well the strategy is delivering on the aspirations laid out in the vision and mission. Employee pay can also be tied to such progress. Firms can choose from a myriad number of goals and objectives, and a subset of these are shown in Exhibit 2.7. A goal can be as simple as a single performance figure, like sales growth or **return on invested capital (ROIC)**. Single goals like this are also called **superordinate goals**, because they serve as an overarching reference point for other goals and objectives. Wal-Mart's annual report, for example, states that the company will grow sales and profits by 20 percent per year; Ryanair says that it will be Europe's largest airline in seven years; Matsushita intends to become a "Super Manufacturing Company." Ultimately, the strength with which a firm's vision and mission are anchored in relevant goals and objectives will determine which ones walk the talk and which ones just . . . talk.

Increasingly, managers track their strategic progress against goals and objectives with a tool called a **balanced scorecard**, which is a system for bridging vision and strategy. The general idea here is that shareholder value (and value created for other stakeholders) is a function of firm productivity and growth. However, because financial measures of productivity

goals and objectives
Combination of a broad indication of organizational intentions (*goals*) and specific, measurable steps (*objectives*) for reaching them.

return on invested capital (ROIC)   How effectively a company uses the money (borrowed or owned) invested in its operations.

superordinate goal
Overarching reference point for a host of hierarchical subgoals.

balanced scorecard
Strategic management support system for measuring vision and strategy against business- and operating-unit-level performance.

Exhibit 2.7   Key Elements of Gerstner's 1993 Vision for IBM

- IBM will not be split up and its many parts will be even more closely coordinated.

- IBM will reassert its identity as customers' primary computing resource.

- The company will be the dominant supplier of technology in the industry.

- PowerPC, a new microprocessor design, will be IBM's centerpiece. Built into many future computers, it will run a wide range of standard industry software. And it will steeply cut manufacturing costs.

- Mainframes are no longer central to the strategy, but IBM will still make them, now with microprocessors.

- IBM is its own worst enemy. Employees must waste fewer opportunities, minimize bureaucracy, and put the good of the company before their division's.

and growth are typically retrospective (for instance, ROIC or month-to-month sales increases, respectively), they don't readily provide managers with the information to monitor or influence their underlying determinants. If managers can map out the financial, customer, and organizational factors that feed productivity, growth, or both, then they can better measure and set goals for these finer-grained indicators of eventual performance. Typically, the best scorecards let managers know how the strategy is going before they see the financial numbers, or even provide a glimpse into the future. For example, one of GE's goals is to have better relationships with customers such that they refer more business to GE, and GE is investing in marketing and innovation skills to support that objective. GE actually measures progress on this objective by asking customers "Would GE be the first company you would refer a colleague to?" And because GE has found that this measure is an accurate predictor of business growth, it can tie it to managerial pay as well.

Strategic Purpose and Strategic Coherence

An overview of the examples presented in this chapter should tell you that it's relatively easy to compose a snappy vision statement. You should also have gathered by now that having vision and mission statements doesn't guarantee higher levels of performance. For one thing, some statements are more effective than others. How so? Research suggests the importance of the process used to develop and articulate statements. Performance, for example, is positively correlated with the integration of internal stakeholders—in other words, manager and employee satisfaction with the statement-development process.[32] This is yet one more reason why we'll focus on the stakeholder-analysis tool in the next section and why we stress the importance of considering stakeholders in the practice of strategic leadership. First, however, let's focus on the two most critical aspects of effective vision and mission statements: *strategic purpose* and *strategic coherence*.

STRATEGIC PURPOSE

Vision and mission statements are actually statements of organizational identity and purpose that can guide executives in making corporate decisions. After all, one individual—even a group of individuals—can cope with only so much complexity in a problem. Vision and mission statements provide all employees with **strategic purpose**: a simplified, widely shared model of the organization and its future, including anticipated changes in its environment.

strategic purpose Simplified, widely shared mental model of the organization and its future, including anticipated changes in its environment.

Tradeoffs, Options, and Other Decisions
Most major strategic decisions require tradeoffs—deciding on one course of action may necessarily eliminate other options. In addition, although some courses of action may satisfy the needs of some stakeholders, they may adversely affect others.

The consumer-products companies Mars Inc. and SC Johnson, for example, remain private corporations. When you visit either firm's Web site, you'll see that independence is a core value for both. Moreover, private ownership means greater flexibility in strategic choices: Because neither firm must cater to the stock market as a stakeholder, each can choose to make costly investments in the kinds of socially responsible programs that often draw fire from the shareholders of public companies. And the tradeoffs? The growth potential of each firm is limited, and it's more difficult to arrange for employee ownership, whether through direct share ownership or stock options.

Newman's Own, founded by actor Paul Newman and a partner in 1982, makes and sells salad dressing, lemonade, popcorn, salsa, steak sauce, and other food items through major grocery chains around the world. In 2003, McDonald's announced that it would use Newman's Own dressings exclusively in its new Premium Salad line. Newman expects this alliance to increase profits by 25 percent. The firm's success derives from two policies anchored in its vision: (1) It insists on top-quality products with no artificial ingredients or preservatives and (2) It donates all after-tax profits to educational and charitable organizations, including UNICEF, Habitat for Humanity, and the Hole in the Wall Gang Camp for seriously ill children. The determination to combine commerce with philanthropy underlies a fairly unique vision, but it's guided the company's strategy for more than two decades. The tradeoff? Although adhering to a strongly held corporate philosophy helps managers choose certain courses of action over others, the decision to use more expensive natural ingredients means sacrificing higher short-term profitability.

Even a company with a more traditional profit orientation can be guided by a fairly simple vision. Michael Dell founded Dell Computers in 1984 on an investment of $1,000. His vision was to sell computer systems directly to customers. The company now has more than 78,000 employees and boasted revenues in excess of $57 billion in 2006.[33] Such rapid growth, however, means that the great majority of Dell employees are relative newcomers to the corporate family, which puts pressure on the company to preserve the values that guided it in its early years. Dell training, therefore, strives to imbue all employees with the "Soul of Dell"—the set of values that guides all of the firm's business practices.

As you can see in Exhibit 2.8, Matsushita Electric, the Japanese parent company of Panasonic, is preparing to stretch by comparing what the company does today with what it will have to do to become a "Super Manufacturing Company" in the future.[34] Such a company, explains Matsushita CEO Kunio Nakamura, "must in essence be 'light and speedy.' Now when the nature of business is changing, emphasis will be placed on the maintenance, broadening and strengthening of IT, on R&D and marketing. Moreover, Matsushita at present is like a heavy lead ball loaded with assets. In the future we need to cast off superfluous assets and become a company that can move lightly like a soccer ball."[35]

The Challenge of Closing the Gap The challenge posed by a strategic purpose is to close the gap between the firm's aspirations and its current capabilities and market positions. All strategies, for example, address the tradeoff between efficiency and effectiveness, and a firm can easily fall into the trap of adhering to its current strategy (say, becoming more efficient) even though customers no longer value its products (in other words, becoming less effective). Like long-term personal goals, the forward-looking aspect of strategic purpose means more than merely setting long-term goals that require stretch. Rather, an effective strategic purpose must be tied to a coherent set of activities, near-term goals, and objectives anchored in *measurable strategic outcomes*—that is, *strategic coherence*.

Matsushita's Goal: To Become a 21st-Century "Super Manufacturing Company"		
	Today: A Conventional Manufacturing Company	**Tomorrow: A 21st-Century Super Manufacturing Company**
Role	Providing goods	Providing solutions
Investment	Principally capital investment	Expansion of R&D, marketing, and IT investment
Information	From the company	Interactive/direct contact with customers
Organization	Pyramid	Flat and web

Exhibit 2.8 Creating Strategic Purpose at Matsushita

STRATEGIC COHERENCE

An effective strategy is coherent. As we saw in Chapter 1, a firm's strategy entails an integrated set of choices regarding the five elements of the *strategy diamond.* **Strategic coherence** (versus *incoherence*) is the symmetrical coalignment of the five elements of the firm's strategy, the congruence of policies in such functional areas as finance, production, and marketing with these elements, and the overarching fit of various businesses under the corporate umbrella. Successful firms depend on dozens of critical elements operating in concert and in balance. These elements are integrated so that everyone from design to manufacturing to marketing to accounting understands them in the same way.

In practice, some firms suffer from incoherent and fragmented strategies. For instance, a firm's decision to grow rapidly through acquisitions may be out of sync with its attempts to differentiate its products on the basis of strong brand equity. Some firms lack coherence because functional areas are treated like independent domains, as if they were silos of business activity that don't need orchestrated cooperation. Finally, some firms lack a coherent strategy because they move in and out of new businesses, as AT&T has done over the past two decades.

Applying the Strategy Diamond How can firms achieve strategic coherence? The answer seems to be serious commitment to, and widespread communication of, well-understood and shared organizational vision and values. The strategy diamond framework is useful in testing the coherence of the elements of a strategy. Specifically, do the five diamond facets—arenas, differentiators, vehicles, staging, and economic logic—all add up to an internally consistent, externally-relevant set of choices that allow the firm to realize its vision and mission? From an internal perspective, a coherent strategy aligns all of the strategy's strategic, tactical, and design elements. From an external perspective, coherence is an alignment of the strategy with the industry environment and the vision of where and how the firm will be positioned in that environment in the future. Incoherence tends to plague firms that allocate resources primarily in response to competitors' strategies. That is, instead of working on an internally-consistent strategy, the firm is trying to keep up with diverse competitors by mimicking their strategies and tactics. As a result, it will appear as if their actions and functions are about average for the industry. In reality, of course, there's nothing distinctive about such a firm because it has in effect allowed its competitors to determine its strategy.

The Clear and Compelling Vision Statement In many ways, strong vision statements function as guidelines for clear and compelling strategies that distinguish a firm from its competitors. What do we mean by "compelling"? Namely, that the underlying strategy is not only coherent but is accepted as truthful and useful by employees, customers, and other key stakeholders.[36] A clear vision of what the organization wants to achieve, coupled with an unambiguous understanding of its mission, helps managers make coherent strategic decisions.

Stakeholders, Stakeholder Analysis, and Stakeholder Planning

Stakeholders are individuals or groups who have an interest in an organization's ability to deliver intended results and maintain the viability of its products and services. We've already stressed the importance of stakeholders to a firm's vision and mission. We've also explained that firms are usually accountable to a broad range of stakeholders, including shareholders, who can make it either more difficult or easier to execute a strategy. This is the main reason why strategy formulators must consider stakeholders' interests, needs, and

strategic coherence
Symmetric coalignment of the five elements of the firm's strategy, the congruence of functional-area policies with these elements, and the overarching fit of various businesses under the corporate umbrella.

stakeholder Individual or group with an interest in an organization's ability to deliver intended results and maintain the viability of its products and services.

preferences. Considering these factors in the development of a firm's vision and mission is a good place to start, but first, of course, you must identify critical stakeholders, get a handle on their short- and long-term interests, calculate their potential influence on your strategy, and take into consideration how the firm's strategy might impact stakeholders (beneficially or adversely).

As we've already seen, for instance, one key stakeholder group is composed of the CEO and the members of the top-management team. This group is important for at least three reasons:

1. Its influence as either originator or steward of the organization's vision and mission

2. Its responsibility for formulating a strategy that realizes the vision and mission

3. Its ultimate role in strategy implementation (a role that we'll discuss in more detail in Chapter 11)

Typically, stakeholder evaluation of both quantitative and qualitative performance outcomes will determine whether or not strategic leadership is effective. We summarized some relevant performance outcomes in Exhibit 2.9. Different stakeholders may place more emphasis on some outcomes than other stakeholders who have other priorities.

STAKEHOLDERS AND STRATEGY

Stakeholder analysis is the technique used to identify the key people who have to be won over. You then use stakeholder planning to build the support that helps you succeed.

The benefits of using a stakeholder-based approach are that:

■ You can use the opinions of the most powerful stakeholders to shape your strategy and tactics at an early stage. Not only does this make it more likely that they will support you, their input can also improve the quality of your strategy

■ Gaining support from powerful stakeholders can help you to win more resources—this makes it more likely that your projects will be successful

■ By communicating with stakeholders early and frequently, you can ensure that they fully understand what you are doing and understand the benefits of your project—this means they can support you actively when necessary

■ You can anticipate what people's reaction to your project may be, and build into your plan the actions that will win people's support.

Financial Performance Metrics	Nonfinancial Performance Metrics
▸ Return on sales	▸ Customer retention
▸ Return on assets	▸ Customer satisfaction
▸ Return on equity	▸ Customer complaints
▸ Return on invested capital	▸ Employee turnover
▸ Sales per employee	▸ Product returns
▸ Sales growth	▸ Product quality
▸ Inventory turn	▸ Patents
▸ Accounts receivable turn	▸ New products released
▸ Debt ratio	▸ Product development speed
▸ Current ratio	▸ Reputation
▸ Cost reduction	▸ Web traffic

Exhibit 2.9 Some Financial and Nonfinancial Performance Metrics

STAKEHOLDER ANALYSIS

The first step in stakeholder analysis is identifying major stakeholder groups. As you can imagine, the groups of stakeholders who will be affected either directly or indirectly by or have an effect on a firm's strategy and its execution can run the gamut from employees to customers to competitors to governments.

Let's pause for a moment to consider the important constituencies charted on our stakeholder map. Before we start, however, we need to remind ourselves that stakeholders can be individuals or groups—communities, social or political organizations, and so forth. In addition, we can break groups down demographically, geographically, by level and branch of government, or according to other relevant criteria. In so doing, we're more likely to identify important groups that we might otherwise overlook.

With these facts in mind, you can see that, externally, a map of stakeholders will include such diverse groups as governmental bodies, community-based organizations, social and political action groups, trade unions and guilds, and even journalists. National and regional governments and international regulatory bodies will probably be key stakeholders for global firms or those whose strategy calls for greater international presence. Internally, key stakeholders include shareholders, business units, employees, and managers.

Steps in Identifying Stakeholders

Identifying all of a firm's stakeholders can be a daunting task. In fact, as we will note again shortly, a list of stakeholders that is too long actually may reduce the effectiveness of this important tool by overwhelming decision makers with too much information. Again, the goal of stakeholder analysis is to identify the key players, not every single possible player (otherwise your list of stakeholders will begin to look like a telephone book!). To simplify the process, we suggest that you start by identifying groups that fall into one of four categories: *organizational, capital market, product market,* and *social.* Let's take a closer look at this step.

Step 1: Determining Influences on Strategy Formulation

One way to analyze the importance and roles of the individuals who comprise a stakeholder group is to identify the people and teams who should be consulted as strategy is developed or who will play some part in its eventual implementation. These are *organizational stakeholders,* and they include both high-level managers and frontline workers. *Capital-market stakeholders* are groups that affect the availability or cost of capital—shareholders, venture capitalists, banks, and other financial intermediaries. *Product-market stakeholders* include parties with whom the firm shares its industry, including suppliers and customers. *Social stakeholders* consist broadly of external groups and organizations that may be affected by or exercise influence over firm strategy and performance, such as unions, governments, and activists groups.

Step 2: Determining the Effects of Strategic Decisions on the Stakeholder

Step 2 in stakeholder analysis is to determine the nature of the effect of the firm's strategic decisions on the list of relevant stakeholders. Not all stakeholders are impacted equally by strategic decisions. Some effects may be rather mild, and any positive or negative effects may be secondary and of minimal impact. At the other end of the spectrum, some stakeholders bear the brunt of firm decisions, good or bad.

At this stage, it's critical to determine the stakeholders who are most important based on how the firm's strategy impacts the stakeholders. You must determine which of the groups still on your list have direct or indirect material claims on firm performance or which are potentially adversely impacted. For instance, it is easy to see how shareholders are affected by firm strategies—their wealth either increases or decreases in correspondence with firm actions. Other parties have economic interests in the firm as well, such as parties the firm interacts with in the marketplace, such as suppliers and customers. The effects on other parties may be much more indirect. For instance, governments have an economic interest in firms doing well—they collect tax revenue from them. However, in cities that are well diversified with many employers, a single firm has minimal economic impact on what the government collects. Alternatively, in other areas individual firms represent a significant contribution to local employment and tax revenue. In those situations, the impact of firm actions on the government would be much greater.

Step 3: Determining Stakeholders' Power and Influence over Decisions The third step of stakeholder analysis is to determine the degree to which a stakeholder group can exercise power and influence over the decisions the firm makes. Does the group have direct control over what is decided, veto power over decisions, nuisance influence, or no influence? Recognize that although the degree to which stakeholders are affected by firm decisions (i.e., step 2) is sometimes highly correlated with their power and influence over the decision, this is often not the case. For instance, in some companies, frontline employees may be directly affected by firm decisions but have no say in those decisions. Power can take the form of formal voting power (boards of directors and owners), economic power (suppliers, financial institutions, and unions), or political power (dissident stockholders, political action groups, and governmental bodies). Sometimes the parties that exercise significant power over firm decisions don't register as having a significant stake in the firm (step 2). In recent years, for example, Wal-Mart has encountered significant resistance in some communities by well-organized groups who oppose the entry of the megaretailer. Wal-Mart executives now have to anticipate whether a vocal and politically powerful community group will oppose its new stores or aim to reduce their size, which decreases Wal-Mart's per-store profitability. Indeed, in many markets, such groups have been effective at blocking new stores, reducing their size, or changing building specifications.

Once you've determined who has a stake in the outcomes of the firm's decisions as well as who has power over these decisions, you'll have a basis on which to allocate prominence in the strategy-formulation and strategy-implementation processes. The framework in Exhibit 2.10 will also help you categorize stakeholders according to their influence in determining strategy versus their importance to strategy execution.[37] For one thing, this distinction may help you identify major omissions in strategy formulation and implementation.

	Power of the Stakeholder over Strategic Decisions			
	Unknown	Little/no power	Moderate degree of power	Significant power
Effect of Strategy on the Stakeholder — Unknown				
Little/no effect				
Moderate effect				
Significant effect				

Exhibit 2.10 Mapping Stakeholder Influence and Importance

Having identified stakeholder groups and differentiated them by how they are affected by firm decisions and the power they have to influence decisions, you'll want to ask yourself some additional questions:

■ Have I identified any vulnerable points in either the strategy or its potential implementation?

■ Which groups are mobilized and active in promoting their interests?

■ Have I identified supporters and opponents of the strategy?

■ Which groups will benefit from successful execution of the strategy and which may be adversely affected?

■ Where are various groups located? Who belongs to them? Who represents them?

Although the stakeholder-analysis framework summarized in Exhibit 2.10 is a good starting point, you'll find that many of the strategic-analysis tools that we introduce in later chapters will also help you determine which stakeholders may be most critical to the success of your chosen strategy (and why). Ultimately, because vision and mission are necessarily long-term in orientation, identifying important stakeholder groups will help you to understand which constituencies stand to gain or lose the most if they're realized.

STAKEHOLDER PLANNING

Now that you have identified and analyzed your key stakeholders, you can develop your plan for managing them. Stakeholder planning involves mapping out your communications and actions so that you can win stakeholder support for your strategy. Stakeholder planning is the means by which to orchestrate this sometimes highly political process.

Steps in Stakeholder Planning   Planning builds on the analysis you have completed so far. It takes the stakeholders you have identified and asks that you develop a communication and action plan for dealing with them to gain or retain their support for your strategy. Exhibit 2.11 provides you with an excellent starting point for organizing this process.

Step 1. Fill in Names of Key Stakeholders   Based on the stakeholder map you created in your stakeholder analysis, enter the stakeholders' names, their influence and interest in your strategy, and your current assessment of where they stand with respect to it.

Step 2. Plan Your Approach to Stakeholder Management   The amount of time you should allocate to stakeholder management depends on the size and difficulty of the projects and goals related to your strategy, the time you have available for communication, and the amount of help you need to achieve the results you want. Consider the amount of time that will be taken to manage this and the time you will need for communication.

Step 3. Evaluate What You Want from Each Stakeholder   Next, work through your list of stakeholders and consider the levels of support you want from them and the roles you would like them to play (if any). Consider the actions you would like them to perform. Write this information down in the 'Desired Support', 'Desired Strategy Role', and 'Actions Desired' columns.

Step 4. Identify the Messages You Need to Convey   Next, identify the messages that you need to convey to your stakeholders to persuade them to support you and engage in your strategy or goals. Typical messages will show the benefits of your strategy or goals to the person or organization, and will focus on key performance drivers like increasing profitability or delivering real improvements relevant to that stakeholder.

Step 5. Identify Actions and Communications   Finally, work out what you need to do to win and manage the support of these stakeholders. With the time and resources you have

Exhibit 2.11   Your Stakeholder Management Plan

Stakeholder Name	Communication Approach	Key Interests and Issues	Current Status	Desired Support	Desired Role in Strategy	Actions Desired	Messages/ Actions Needed	Action and Communication

available, identify how you will manage the communication to and the input from your stakeholders. Focusing on the high-power/high-effect stakeholders first and the low-effect/low-power stakeholders last, devise a practical plan that communicates with people as effectively as possible and that communicates the right amount of information in a way that neither under- nor over-communicates. Consider what you need to do to keep your best supporters engaged and on-board. Plan how to win over or neutralize the opposition of skeptics. Where you need the active support of people who are not currently interested in what you are doing, consider how you can engage them and raise their level of interest.

The effective application of stakeholder analysis and planning for a newly appointed manager is described in the box entitled "How Would *You* Do That? 2.2." From this example, you can see why stakeholder management should be an important input into both strategy formulation and implementation and how the roles of certain stakeholders create important interdependencies between formulation and implementation.

Ethics, Biases, and Strategic Decision Making

Because the stakes are so high when executives make strategic decisions, they must do everything they can to make sure that those decisions are sound. You should thus weigh two additional factors before committing yourself to a major strategic endeavor: (1) whether the decision is ethical and (2) whether any potential biases have clouded your strategic decision-making process.

It should be obvious by now that our conception of strategy is that it is a means to accomplish organizational goals. The fact that we see numerous examples in the media of corporate scandals suggests the unfortunate observation that some people justify any means to accomplish a desired goal. Although it would be unfair to suggest that most corporations engage in

Driving Stakeholder Analysis at Tritec Motors

The first challenge in managing stakeholders is stakeholder analysis—determining how stakeholders are affected by a firm's decisions and how much influence they have over the implementation of the decisions that are made. Not all stakeholders are affected in the same way, and not all stakeholders have the same level of influence in determining what a firm does. When stakeholder analysis is executed well, as you will see from the following example of the Tritec joint venture in Curitiba, Brazil, stakeholder planning will give the resulting strategy a better chance of succeeding, because the entities you might rely on in the implementation phase also helped to formulate the strategy.

THE STALLED MOTOR MAKER

Formed in 2001, the Tritec joint venture between Daimler-Chrysler and BMW represented a $400-million state-of-the-art engine manufacturing facility in Curitiba, Brazil. From the start, however, production problems with the new motors were wreaking havoc with BMW's newly minted line of wildly successful Mini Coopers. On the Chrysler side, Daimler's acquisition of the U.S. firm resulted in the triage of the main line of vehicles that would receive engines from the Curitiba plant. In sum, the Curitiba plant was producing poor-quality engines for BMW, and Daimler was paying for half

of a factory that it was barely even using.

In stepped Bob Harbin, a 25-year employee of Chrysler. Bob was given 90 days to come up with a plan to fix Tritec's problems. This was a make-or-break assignment for Harbin. Fortunately, Harbin knew how to apply stakeholder analysis and stakeholder planning, and he knew that the key players he involved in designing the turnaround strategy would likely be instrumental in executing it as well. In some cases, even if they did not have a role in implementation, certain stakeholders, such as the Brazilian government, could actually hurt Tritec's turnaround chances.

THE DISCOVERY PROCESS

Harbin spent the first five days of his assignment meeting with top executives at Daimler and BMW, both to gain an understanding of their needs and expectations and to determine how much discretion they would afford him if drastic changes were needed. After all, the corporate partners were essentially Tritec's financial backers and its only customers. Next, he spent two weeks in Curitiba meeting with everyone from the shop-floor employees to his future management team. He also spent time with key local parts suppliers as well as members of the newly installed Brazilian government. The government was particularly important because of the

tax incentives and export credits that it had put into place to entice Tritec to Brazil; however, the change in government meant that those credits were in danger of being annulled. Throughout this discovery process, Harbin reiterated a common vision: "If we can't produce quality engines and get them to BMW on time, then the plant will likely be closed. No jobs, no tax revenues, no engines. Period." Not only did this quickly gain each stakeholder's attention, it also fostered cooperation and a sense of urgency among all the key players.

SENDING MESSAGES AND IMPLEMENTING A PLAN

After the first 30 days, Harbin assembled his leadership team based on impressions gained during his early interviews. Most of his team were Brazilians, which sent a strong message of confidence to the Brazilian workforce as well as to the Brazilian government. Together, Harbin and his team put together a rescue plan for the engine-manufacturing process; he then took this plan back to Germany for endorsement by both BMW and Daimler. With the key pieces of the plan in place and the most important stakeholders squarely behind the plan—the alliance partners, the Brazilian government, Tritec's employees, and the new Tritec management team—Harbin began the steady process of turning around Tritec.

Although there were some minor setbacks along the way, within one year the factory was a world benchmark plant in many areas for both Daimler and BMW. By 2005, Tritec's production quality and efficiency were so high that even Toyota executives considered it one of the world's best-run auto-engine plants.

PLOTTING ROLES

Although every firm has multiple stakeholders, in this particular case the major stakeholders can be identified as BMW, Daimler-Chrysler, local employees, suppliers, the Brazilian and Curitiba governments, the Tritec leadership team (including Harbin), and competitors. What roles did these stakeholders play in the tough decisions faced by Harbin? Let's take each stakeholder individually and plot them on the stakeholder-analysis grid (see Exhibit 2.12). In some cases you may find you fill in every cell, but since the goal is to narrow the set of stakeholders down to those that are key, most of the time several of the cells will be left empty. Though empty cells are also an opportunity to ask yourself whether you have identified all the relevant players.

What role does BMW play in this situation? BMW is an owner/investor in the Tritec joint venture; thus on the power dimension BMW would be plotted in the far-right column, because it has voting and veto rights over all major decisions. However, BMW plays another role as well; it is the customer buying most of the engines made in this factory. Thus, BMW simultaneously has an economic interest apart from its ownership stake. Daimler-Chrysler's position is similar; it is an equity investor in the plant—thus it has an equity interest—and it has voting rights over all major decisions. Daimler is also a customer, but buys a fraction of the production used by BMW.

What position do the suppliers have? In terms of interests, they have a nonownership economic interest in the health of the plant. If the plant were to close, they would lose a major buyer. What influence/power do they have over decisions? They do not have major decisional power.

What about employees? Employees do not directly influence factory decisions, but they do have an economic, nonequity stake in the factory. Individually, though, they are relatively powerless. What about the Brazilian or Curitiba government? The government clearly has a stake in ensuring that local businesses are prosperous. However, that stake is not as direct or significant as an equity stake or employees' or suppliers' economic interest. The national and local government can, however, dictate key issues like domestic content requirements, transfer pricing, or union and labor policies that affect the viability of Tritec's strategy. Competitors have no real power over this strategy, and at this point it is unclear of the impact of the strategy on them.

What does this analysis suggest? It suggests that if BMW does not get on board, all bets are off. Moreover, the government is a critical stakeholder; at this stage of the game Tritec should actively manage its relationship with the Brazilian government and make sure suppliers, employees, and management implement a plan that keeps BMW and Daimler-Chrysler satisfied.

Exhibit 2.12 Stakeholder-Analysis Grid for Tritec

	Power of the Stakeholder over Strategic Decisions			
	Unknown	Little/no power	Moderate degree of power	Significant power
Effect of Strategy on the Stakeholder — Unknown				
Little/no effect			Brazilian Government	
Moderate effect				Tritec Leadership Team
Significant effect		Tritec Suppliers Employees		BMW Daimler-Chrysler

deliberate acts of malfeasance to accomplish their goals, and that all executives are crooks, it would likewise be unwise to ignore such potential problems and the safeguards that can help firms avoid unethical behavior. Although there's no reason why a sound strategy has to have any hint of unethical motives or tactics, managers must take precautions to ensure that their firms don't figure in the next headline trumpeting the ethical bankruptcy of corporations.

In addition to ethical lapses, strategic decision making can be subject to a number of common decision-making biases. When executives fail to recognize and account for them, they may unwittingly pursue a course of action that they'd otherwise avoid. In this section, we'll review some of the ethics- and bias-related issues that may arise in the course of strategic decision making.

ETHICS AND STRATEGY

A quick survey of business history and recent business news will give you a good idea of the disastrous effects that questionable strategies can have on shareholders, clients, and even decision makers themselves. Enron is the most notorious recent example, but it's certainly not the only—nor even the most egregious—case. In early 2004, for example, Royal Dutch/Shell Group announced that executives had knowingly overstated oil and gas reserves by 4.5 million barrels, or 23 percent. In October of that year, Shell announced that it would have to "restate" its reserves by another million barrels. Investors were naturally unhappy at being misled about the firm's key assets, and its management ranks soon underwent a major shakeup.[38] Executives at other companies—notably Adelphia, a telecommunications provider, and Tyco, a diversified manufacturer and services provider—have been indicted (and some convicted) for diverting firm resources to private use. In other instances, misbehavior has taken the form of fraud; at the hospital chain HealthSouth, for example, no fewer than five onetime CFOs have been convicted in a $2.5-billion case of accounting fraud.[39]

Why Organizations Are Vulnerable to Ethics Violations   In some of these cases, a few key executives were responsible for the violations of legal and ethical standards. In others, the misdeeds required a larger cast of characters. So why shouldn't organizations

In February 2004, former Enron CEO Jeffrey Skilling (handcuffed) was charged with 35 counts of conspiracy, securities fraud, wire fraud, and insider trading. According to the government, Skilling presided over accounting schemes to inflate the energy-trading company's earnings, leading to its collapse (and the loss of thousands of jobs) in 2001. Some say Enron's flawed incentive system was to blame. Employees were lavishly rewarded for making the company look good, whether their actions were legal or not. He was convicted in 2006 of multiple felony charges and was sentenced to a 24-year term in a U.S. Federal Correctional Facility.

just be careful to hire principled people? For one thing, companies are often vulnerable because of organization-level conditions. In this section, we'll review two of these conditions—*authority structures* and *incentive systems*—and show how avoiding certain pitfalls can reduce a firm's risk.

Authority Structures Whereas some organizational characteristics foster potential opportunities for exploiting the system, others discourage potential whistle-blowers from alerting the proper authorities.[40] For example, because responsibility is distributed throughout an organization and tasks are specialized, there's a tendency for people to assume that someone else will blow the whistle on suspicious activity. The phenomenon, of course, can also be observed in society at large, as in cases in which bystanders will ignore an accident or criminal activity on the assumption that someone else will intervene.

The authority structure of modern organizations also inhibits lower-level employees from disclosing questionable practices. People who are relatively obedient tend to follow the directions of legitimate authorities even when they know that what they're doing is dubious.[41] And, of course, whistle-blowing is not an attractive option when those who are engaged in the questionable behavior occupy positions of authority.

Incentive Systems The larger the potential reward, the more some people are willing to compromise their standards. Research shows, for instance, that business-unit managers are more likely to defer income to subsequent accounting periods when earnings targets in their bonus plans won't be met or when they've already reached maximum payouts.[42]

More recently, some analysts have questioned whether stock-option pay induces executives to make decisions designed to improve near-term stock prices rather than to enhance the firm's long-term competitive position. Because of the potential effect that financial incentives can have on managerial behavior, firms must take stronger measures to ensure that they're not "rewarding A, while hoping for B."[43]

The Role of Corporate Governance

We'll discuss *corporate governance*—the roles of owners, directors, and managers in making corporate decisions—in more detail in Chapter 13. Here, we'll mention only that good corporate governance can reduce the risk of unethical and illegal activities. Because many unethical deeds are the work of individuals acting alone, quality governance can't guarantee ethical behavior. However, *poor* corporate governance provides a breeding ground for *un*ethical behavior. More and more firms are thus using governance mechanisms to discourage undesirable activities.

The Role of Decision Making Lapses

When managers aren't fully aware of the biases influencing their judgment and strategic decision making, lapses in the quality of strategic decision making may lead to ethical lapses. In this section, we'll sort potential biases into three sets of theories that we may hold about the conditions under which we make decisions: *theories about ourselves, theories about other people,* and *theories about the world.*[44]

Theories About Ourselves It shouldn't come as any surprise to hear that your self-perceptions influence your judgment and decisions. For instance, because strategic decision making is characterized by uncertainty and ambiguity, you'd expect that most senior executives are confident in their ability to make judgments under such conditions. When self-confidence, however, borders on the belief in one's own superiority, rational decision making may be impaired. Confidence, for example, can lead people to give themselves more credit for their successes and take less responsibility for their failures. It can also lead people to underestimate the prospect of negative future events while overestimating the prospect of positive outcomes. And when managers are confident they are more likely to believe that they are in greater control of a situation than rational analysis would support. Research, for example, shows that when people are allowed to touch a playing card before it's been reshuffled into the deck, they're more likely to believe that they can find it again on a random draw than if they hadn't touched it. In reality, of course, their odds are the same under both circumstances.

Importantly, this set of theories about ourselves also contribute to a decision-making bias called **escalation of commitment**—the willingness to commit additional resources to a failing course of action. Obviously, this particular bias might well influence an executive's decision to change a strategy, to pursue an acquisition even though the bidding has reached astronomical levels, or to continue or discontinue a particular project related to current strategy.

Similarly, research shows that a manager who initiates a project is less likely to perceive that it's failing, more likely to remain committed to it, and more likely to continue funding it than the manager who comes on board after the project is underway. People also tend toward increased commitment to innovative products than to less innovative products. Such findings suggest that simply giving managers better information won't necessarily lead to better decisions. They also indicate that escalation of commitment is a more serious problem during new-product development than after a product has been rolled out.[45] In short, escalation of commitment seems to be a particularly dangerous decision-making bias, especially when we consider the ambiguity and uncertainty inherently involved in most strategic decisions.

So, what are the potential ethical consequences of these theories about ourselves? The worst-case upshot of confidence-related biases is that some executives believe that they aren't subject to the same rules as everyone else. Top managers may delude themselves that they can get away with unethical or even felonious behavior because they believe either that they won't be caught or that, if they are, their status will protect them from the consequences. According to some researchers, executives believe that they are fair people and want to act in ways that are perceived as fair and just. Like most people, however, they usually do a better job of tracking their own contributions to a project and thus tend to take more credit for good outcomes than they give. As a result of this tendency, executives may rationalize lavish pay and perks on the grounds that they earned them because they contributed more than others.

Theories About Other People   In many ways, our theories about other people reflect our theories about ourselves:

- We give ourselves more credit than we deserve and others less.

- We expect more credit and reward and expect others to accept less.

- We view positive future outcomes as more likely than negative outcomes but believe that the outcomes achieved by others are more likely to fail.

- We think that we're better than others at judging uncertain futures and so give more credence to our plans than to those of others.

- We believe that although we're acting on the best knowledge of present and future conditions, others are acting on imperfect knowledge.

In addition to these obvious biases, our theories about other people also encompass both *ethnocentrism* and *stereotyping*. **Ethnocentrism** is a belief in the superiority of one's own ethnic group, but it can be interpreted more broadly as the conviction that one's own national, group, or cultural characteristics are "normal" and ordinary. That belief, of course, renders everyone else foreign, strange, and perhaps dangerous.

In fact, we're all ethnocentric to some degree. Your ethnocentrism accounts for your opinion of foreigners' speech patterns and favored cuisines. Being ethnocentric, then, doesn't necessarily mean that you're hostile toward other groups, but it does mean that you probably regard your group as superior. Ethnocentrism is dangerous because it's automatic and often subtle: we tend to believe that our own group has multiple dimensions, whereas other groups can be characterized according to one relatively homogeneous characteristic—say, nationality, gender, or ethnicity. When you've reached this stage, you're engaged in

---

escalation of commitment Decision-making bias under which people are willing to commit additional resources to a failing course of action.

ethnocentrism   Belief in the superiority of one's own ethnic group or, more broadly, the conviction that one's own national, group, or cultural characteristics are "normal."

stereotyping—relying on a conventional or formulaic conception of another group based on some common characteristic. The fallacy of ethnocentrism, then, is the belief in your own group's superiority; the fallacy of stereotyping lies in ascribing limiting characteristics to an entire set of people.

Stereotyping puts executives at risk of making unethical, unfair, and sometimes illegal decisions because it limits their evaluations of other people to group affiliation while ignoring individual qualities. Ethnocentrism exposes businesspeople to rationally and ethically unsound decisions because it exaggerates the differences between us and them.

In terms of strategic decision making, ethnocentrism and stereotyping can have disastrous results. U.S. automakers, for example, ignored the Japanese competitive threat for decades because of a twofold mistaken belief: (1) that American car manufacturers were the best in the world and (2) that Japanese automakers could never produce high-quality vehicles. Thus ethnocentrism and stereotypes combined to blind U.S. (and European) carmakers to the emergence of extremely formidable rivals.

Theories About the World Today's top executives must be able to understand global events—or at least know where to get the information they need. Otherwise, it's too easy to misjudge the risks and consequences of an action with international ramifications. The trick, of course, is knowing what you don't know. Granted, it's often impossible to foresee all the possible consequences of a strategic choice, but a good starting point is the premise that "you can never do just one thing."[46] All actions, in other words, have multiple consequences, some intended, some unintended.

For example, the management of Levi Straus & Co. (LS&CO.) has a firm commitment to its corporate values. LS&CO. quickly stepped in to enforce a policy of not using contractors who employ child labor. Upon finding that a subcontractor in Bangladesh was employing children younger than 14, LS&CO. made the factory rectify the situation. Levi's decision to demonstrate its commitment to ethical practices and global social responsibility by discouraging child labor had an unintended consequence: Because factory jobs were no longer available, poor families that depended on their daughters' incomes resorted to pushing them into prostitution. Where did Levi Straus go wrong? Arguably, a few fallacious theories about the world resulted in a faulty perception of certain stakeholders: LS&CO. looked initially only at the situation of the girls and inadvertently ignored the needs of their families. Once discovering the complication, LS&CO. decided to pay for the underage children to go to school and guarantee jobs in the factory once they were of age.

Similarly, imperfect theories about the world may lead executives to discount low-probability events or to underestimate the probability of certain activities becoming public. The effects of such poor judgment can snowball into strategic and ethical blunders. In the early 1970s, for example, internal safety tests on the Ford Pinto revealed that under rare rear-impact conditions the gas tank could explode. The defect could be remedied with a $10 part, but Ford opted for a less costly response and, what's worse, covered up its own test results when the fatal rear-end crash turned out to be more common and more deadly than the company had figured.[47] The more recent example of how Ford proactively responded to tire problems from its chief supplier Bridgestone/Firestone, which caused some SUVs to roll when experiencing a flat, suggests that Ford may have learned its lesson.

Related to these imperfections in strategic decision making is the fact that we tend to discount the future and to place lower values on collective outcomes. In other words, we often focus on today's problems because we believe them to be more important than those that may be encountered down the road. Similarly, because we're prone to underestimate the consequences of our actions on large groups, we tend to ignore collective outcomes. Ford's behavior in the Pinto case, for example, contributed to public perception that the auto industry couldn't, or wouldn't, police itself on the issue of safety—a reaction that, in turn, led to an unprecedented raft of auto-safety regulations.

> **stereotyping** Relying on a conventional or formulaic conception of another group based on some common characteristic.

Summary of Challenges

1. *Explain how strategic leadership is essential to strategy formulation and implementation.* **Strategic leadership** is concerned with the management of an overall enterprise and the ways in which top executives influence key organizational outcomes, such as performance, competitive superiority, innovation, strategic change, and survival. Leaders typically play three critical roles—interpersonal, informational, and decisional—all of which support the firm's vision and mission and the implementation of its strategy. The **Level 5 Hierarchy** is a model of leadership skills that calls for a wide range of abilities, some of which are hierarchical in nature. Leaders can be distinguished by personality and demographic differences, and strategic leadership can be exercised either by individuals or groups.

2. *Understand the relationships among vision, mission, values, and strategy.* An organizational **vision** is a simple forward-looking statement or understanding of what the firm will be in the future. A **mission** is a declaration of what a firm is and what it stands for—its fundamental values and purpose. Together, mission and vision statements express the identity and describe the work of a firm. They also state the firm's direction. Vision and mission statements support strategy, which provides a coherent plan for realizing the firm's vision and mission.

3. *Understand the roles of vision and mission in determining strategic purpose and strategic coherence.* Guidance in making decisions is important because there's only so much complexity in a given problem with which any individual or group can reasonably cope. Vision and mission statements are thus useful because they inform all employees of the firm's **strategic purpose**—a simplified, widely shared model of the organization and its future, including anticipated changes in its environment. The challenge posed by a defined strategic purpose is closing the gap between aspirations on the one hand and current capabilities and market positions on the other. **Strategic coherence** refers to the symmetrical coalignment of the five elements of the firm's strategy, the congruence of functional-area policies with these elements, and the overarching fit of various businesses under the corporate umbrella.

4. *Identify a firm's stakeholders and explain why such identification is critical to effective strategy formulation and implementation.* Stakeholder analysis improves the understanding of the range and variety of parties who have a vested interest in the formulation and implementation of a firm's strategy or some influence on firm performance. The first step in stakeholder analysis is identifying stakeholder groups that are affected by or that may affect the firm's strategy. The second step calls for identifying those stakeholders who are important for strategy formulation and implementation, those for whom the strategy will be important, and those who are influential in determining the strategy. The third step involves categorizing stakeholders according to their influence in determining strategy versus their importance in its execution. Stakeholder analysis also helps expose any major omissions in strategy formulation and implementation.

5. *Explain how ethics and biases may affect strategic decision making.* Strategic leadership and strategic decision making have much in common. Indeed, strategic leadership can be characterized by strategic decision making and the actions in which it results. The effectiveness of strategic decision making is threatened when managers act unethically or without being fully aware of the biases influencing their judgment. Ethical lapses may reflect an individual shortcoming, but they can often be traced to a lack of clear organizational mechanisms for making individuals accountable for their actions. Decision-making biases, or threats to rational decision making in general, result from theories about oneself, theories about other people, and theories about one's world. They may impair both rational and ethical decision making and even an organization's ability to realize its vision and mission.

Review Questions

1. Why is strategic leadership important for effective strategy formulation and implementation?

2. How do the characteristics of strategic leadership differ between individuals and teams?

3. What is a vision? A mission?

4. How are vision and mission related to strategy? What roles does strategic leadership play in realizing vision and mission?

5. How does strategy differ from vision and mission?

6. What is strategic purpose?

7. What is strategic coherence?

8. Who are a firm's stakeholders? Why are they important?

9. What tools can you use to identify the impact of various stakeholders on the firm and the impact of the firm on various stakeholders?

10. Why are ethics and biases relevant to strategic decision making and strategic leadership?

Experiential Activities

Group Exercises

1. (a) Craft a vision and mission statement for your business school and then for your college or university as a whole. How are these statements related? How are they similar? How do they differ? How are they similar or different from those that you might craft for a for-profit organization? (b) Using the vision and mission you crafted, develop a list of key stakeholders for your school and their relative power and stake in the school. Which of these stakeholder groups is accounted for in your vision and mission statement, and which ones are left out? Did you identify any stakeholder groups that could negatively affect your realization of this vision and mission?

2. What roles should strategic leadership play in the realization of the vision and mission statements that you articulated in the previous question? Whom have you identified as strategic leaders?

Ethical Debates

1. A slogan on an ethics poster for Boeing states: "Between right and wrong is a troublesome gray area." What aspects of this statement do you agree or disagree with? As a future business leader, what should you be doing to manage the "gray area"?

2. When reading the business press, it seems that leaders are regularly challenged by ethical dilemmas. Is this a function of the individual leader or the situation, or both?

How Would YOU DO THAT?

1. Building on the CEO-successor selection process described in the box entitled "How Would *You* Do That? 2.1," devise a succession plan for the dean of your business school. Be sure to include the following in your succession-planning process: (a) Translate your school's strategy into actual operating needs and key activities; (b) identify the skills needed for these operating needs and activities; (c) outline an internal and external candidate search process; and (d) develop a list of goals and milestones and a compensation structure that ties actions to the strategic drivers of success at your school.

2. Based on the framework applied to Tritec Motors in the box entitled "How Would *You* Do That? 2.2," use the opening vignette on Anne Mulcahy at Xerox to map out the key stakeholders in her turnaround effort. Which stakeholders would you expect to be most resistant? Most supportive? Create a 90-day action plan for Mulcahy, following the example laid out by Bob Harbin in "How Would *You* Do That? 2.2."

Go on to see How Would You Do That at www.prenhall.com/ carpenter&sanders

Endnotes

1. W. M. Bulkeley and J. S. Lublin, "Xerox Appoints Insider Mulcahy to Execute Turnaround as CEO," *Wall Street Journal* (Eastern edition), July 27, 2001, A3; P. Moore, "Anne Mulcahy: She's Here to Fix Xerox," *Business Week*, August 6, 2001, 47; A. Klein, "Xerox to Expand Color-Printing Business," *Wall Street Journal* (Eastern edition), September 23, 1999, B12; J. Bandler, "Xerox Profit Falls, but CEO Sees a 'Breakthrough'," *Wall Street Journal* (Eastern edition), July 29, 2003, A3; J. Bandler, "Xerox Corp.: CEO Sees Improving Finances, Broadening Product Offering," *Wall Street Journal* (Eastern edition), May 16, 2003, B6; O. Kharif, "Anne Mulcahy Has Xerox by the Horns," *Business Week Online*, May 29, 2003 (accessed June 21, 2005), at www.businessweek.com/technology/content/may2003/`tc20030529_1642_tc111.htm; Marc Ferranti, "Mulcahy: Innovation, Services Key to Xerox Future," *InfoWorld*, October 2, 2006, p3; Paolo Del Nibletto, "The Saviour," *Computer Dealer News*, September 8, 2006, p30; Claudi H. Deutsch, "Prices Are Lower, but Profit Is Up at Xerox," *New York Times*, April 21, 2007.

2. M. Porter, J. Lorsch, and N. Nohria, "Seven Surprises for New CEOs," *Harvard Business Review* 82:10 (2004), 62–72.

3. This discussion of the nature of CEO job responsibilities draws heavily from the seminal work of H. Mintzberg, *The Nature of Managerial Work* (New York: Harper and Row, 1973).

4. Exhibit is adapted from H. Mintzberg, *The Nature of Managerial Work* (New York: Harper and Row, 1973).

5. Mintzberg, *The Nature of Managerial Work*, 67.

6. Information in this paragraph is based on Porter, Lorsch, and Nohria, "Seven Surprises for New CEOs," 62–72.

7. Stanford Graduate School of Business Alumni Profiles (accessed July 12, 2005), at www.gsb.stanford.edu/news/profiles/deromedi.shtml.

8. J. Collins, *Good to Great: Why Some Companies Make the Leap . . . and Others Don't* (New York: HarperBusiness, 2001).

9. Collins, "Level 5 Leadership: The Triumph of Humility and Fierce Resolve," *Harvard Business Review* 79:1 (2001), 67–76.

10. Exhibit is adapted from Collins, "Level 5 Leadership: The Triumph of Humility and Fierce Resolve," *Harvard Business Review* 79:1 (2001), 67–76.

11. Collins, "Level 5 Leadership," 73.

12. For a review of this material, see D. Whetten and K. Cameron, *Developing Management Skills*, 5th ed. (Upper Saddle River, NJ: Prentice Hall, 2002).

13. Source: S. Budner, "Intolerance of Ambiguity as a Personality Variable," *Journal of Personality* 30 (1982), 29–50.

14. For a comprehensive review of this literature, see M. A. Carpenter, W. G. Sanders, and M. A. Geletkanycz, "The Upper Echelons Revisited: The Antecedents, Elements, and Consequences of TMT Composition," *Journal of Management* 30 (2004), 749–778.

15. M. Useem and J. Karabel, "Pathways to Corporate Management," *American Sociological Review* 51 (1986), 184–200.

16. 'Any College Will Do' Nation's Top Chief Executives Find Path to the Corner Office Usually Starts at State University, *Wall Street Journal* (2006), B1.

17. S. L. Keck, "Top Management Team Structure: Differential Effects by Environmental Context," *Organization Science* 8 (1997), 143–156.

18. M. A. Carpenter, W. G. Sanders, and H. B. Gregersen, "International Experience at the Top Makes a Bottom-Line Difference," *Human Resource Management* 39:2/3 (2000), 277–285; Carpenter, Sanders, and Gregersen, "Bundling Human Capital with Organizational Context: The Impact of

International Experience on Multinational Firm Performance and CEO Pay," *Academy of Management Journal* 44 (2001), 493–512.

19. Adapted from H. Hinterhuber and W. Popp, "Are You a Strategist or Just a Manager?" *Harvard Business Review* 70:1 (January–February 1992), 105–113.

20. C. Lucier, R. Schuyt, and J. Handa, "CEO Succession 2003: The Perils of 'Good' Governance" (accessed June 21, 2005), at www.boozallenhamilton.com.

21. S. Hamm, "Former CEOs Should Just Fade Away," *Business Week*, April 12, 2004 (Online Extra) (accessed July 12, 2005), at www.businessweek.com/magazine/content/04_15/b3878092_mz063.htm; J. Sonnenfeld, *The Hero's Farewell: What Happens when CEOs Retire* (New York: Oxford University Press, 1991).

22. P. Estess, "Twos Company," entrepreneur.com, May 1997 (accessed June 22, 2005), at www.entrepreneur.com/article/0,4621,227207,00.html.

23. C. Hymowitz and J. S. Lublin, "McDonald's CEO Tragedy Holds Lessons," *Wall Street Journal*, April 20, 2004, B1.

24. Adapted from D.C. Hambrick and J.W. Fredrickson, "Are You Sure You Have a Strategy?" *Academy of Management Executive* 15:4 (2001), 48–59.

25. C. K. Bart and M. C. Baetz, "The Relationship Between Mission Statements and Firm Performance: An Exploratory Study," *Journal of Management Studies* 35 (1998), 823–853.

26. J. C. Collins and J. I. Porras, *Build to Last* (New York: Harper Business, 1997).

27. Bart and Baetz, "The Relationship Between Mission Statements and Firm Performance"; A. Campbell and S. Yeung, "Creating a Sense of Mission," *Long Range Planning* 24:4 (1991), 10–20; P. Drucker, *Management: Tasks, Responsibilities, and Practices* (New York: Harper and Row, 1974); R. D. Ireland and M. A. Hitt, "Mission Statements: Importance, Challenge and Recommendations for Development," *Business Horizons* 35:3 (1992), 34–42.

28. Collins and Porras, *Build to Last.*

29. J. Collins and J. Porras, "Building a Visionary Company," *California Management Review* 37 (1995), 80–100; W. Kim and R. Mauborgne, "Charting Your Company's Future," *Harvard Business Review* 80:6 (2002), 5–11.

30. D. Kirkpatrick, "Gerstner's New Vision for IBM," *Fortune*, November 15, 1993, 119–124.

31. D. Kirkpatrick, "Gerstner's New Vision for IBM," *Fortune*, November 15, 1993, 119–124.

32. Bart and Baetz, "The Relationship Between Mission Statements and Firm Performance."

33. "Company Background: The History and Overview of Dell" (accessed July 12, 2005), at www1.us.dell.com/content/topics/global.aspx/corp/background/en/index?c=us&l=en&s=corp.

34. Panasonic, "In the Pursuit of a Super Manufacturing Company" (accessed July 18, 2005), at matsushita.co.jp/corp/vision/president/interview2/en/index.html.

35. Panasonic, "About Panasonic: Vision" (accessed January 11, 2005) at panasonic.co.jp/global/about/vision/index.html.

36. Kim and Mauborgne, "Charting Your Company's Future."

37. Adapted from R.E. Freeman, *Strategic Management: A Stakeholder Approach* (Boston, MA: Pitman, 1984).

38. M. Curtin, "THE SKEPTIC: Thorough Shell Revamp, But Where's the Oil?" *Dow Jones International News*, October 28, 2004.

39. B. Berkrot, "First HealthSouth Sentencing Set for Wednesday," Reuters, November 11, 2003.

40. This discussion draws heavily on R. Gandossy and J. Sonnenfeld, "I See Nothing, I Hear Nothing: Culture, Corruption, and Apathy," in Gandossy and Sonnenfeld (eds.), *Leadership and Governance from the Inside Out* (Hoboken, NJ: Wiley, 2004), 3–26.

41. S. Milgram, *Obedience to Authority* (New York: Harper, 1974).

42. P. M. Healy and J. M. Wahlen, "A Review of the Earnings Management Literature and Its Implications for Standard Setting," *Accounting Horizons* 13 (1999), 365–383.

43. S. Kerr, "On the Folly of Rewarding A, While Hoping for B," *Academy of Management Journal* 18 (1975), 769–783.

44. This material draws from behavioral decision theory. Excellent references are D. Kahneman, P. Slovic, and A. Tversky, *Judgment Under Uncertainty* (Cambridge: Cambridge University Press, 1982); M. Bazerman, *Judgment in Managerial Decision Making* (New York: John Wiley, 1994); J. Janis, *Groupthink* (Boston: Houghton-Mifflin, 1982).

45. J. Schmidt and R. Calantone, "Escalation of Commitment During New Product Development," *Journal of the Academy of Marketing Science* 30:2 (2002), 103–118.

46. G. Hardin, *Filters Against Folly* (New York: Penguin Books, 1985).

47. R. Nader, *Unsafe at Any Speed* (New York: Grossman, 1965).

3

Examining the Internal Environment

Resources, Capabilities, and Activities

In This Chapter We Challenge You To >>>

1. Explain the *internal context of strategy*.

2. Identify a firm's resources and capabilities and explain their role in firm performance.

3. Define *dynamic capabilities* and explain their role in both strategic change and firm performance.

4. Explain how value-chain activities are related to firm performance and competitive advantage.

5. Explain the role of managers with respect to resources, capabilities, and value-chain activities.

Strategy Inside Intel

*P*aul Otellini, the current CEO of the computer chipmaker Intel, joined the company right after getting his MBA in 1974. "I consider myself a product guy," Otellini said in an interview. "I've had my fingerprints on products for 20 years. I ran the microprocessor division for a decade, during the 486 [and] Pentium days. I get into products. I like them, I use them."

Intel is, at its core, an engineering company. Intel was founded in 1968 by three engineers—Robert Noyce, Gordon Moore, and Andy Grove—who left secure jobs at Fairchild Semiconductor to create a new company that would develop technology for silicon-based semiconductor chips. From that small start, Intel has gone on to become the world's largest computer chip maker. The $35 billion company's strengths lie in technology innovations and manufacturing capability. When Otellini took over as CEO, he reiterated Intel's key strengths in R&D, manufacturing and technology: "You're going to see Intel combine its R&D innovation, manufacturing and technology leadership with energy-efficient micro-architectures and powerful multicore processors to deliver unique platforms best tailored to individual needs." Otellini is only Intel's fifth CEO, and he sees a continuity of strategy across the CEOs. Intel's current chairman, Craig Barrett, summarized the strategy and each CEO's contribution: "Robert Noyce and Gordon Moore were the two founders of the company, and they founded the company on the very simple premise of doing something with integrated-circuit technology and commercializing integrated circuits. I look at their era as heavily focused on advancing technology," Barrett said. Andy Grove, CEO from 1987–1997, "took over when the PC started to build, and that's when he had the most influence on the company; he drove us hard in that direction, and we achieved a more reasonable market signature, market penetration, with the microprocessor," Barrett said. Reflecting on his own tenure as CEO from 1998–2005, Barrett said, "What did we do in the seven years I was CEO that will reap Intel benefits seven years hence? We clearly invested in basic R&D and process technology, extreme-UV lithography and all sorts of good stuff that I think will allow us to continue to be at the front of the parade in Moore's Law and driving transistors. I think we made the investments in manufacturing, and we'll continue to reap those benefits to the next decade."

A key facet of Intel's strategy is its choice to build its differentiators based on massive investments in R&D. "You have two choices with R&D, lead or be led," Barrett said. "R&D drives the next level of innovation. You can have the best business model in the world, but if it's creating last year's technology, it will not be successful." Intel starts with an innovation, gets a toehold in the new field, and then methodically exploits its financial and technical resources to gain an advantage. In server chips, for instance, Intel had a negligible market share in 1995 when the Pentium Pro, the company's first chip specifically designed for servers, debuted. Now, more than 80 percent of servers coming out of factories run on Intel chips.

Intel invests in innovation through thick and thin. Barrett often quoted Gordon Moore's adage that a chip company can't save its way out of a recession. "You invest your way out of a recession," Barrett said. Intel uses recessions and downturns to continually develop new products and better position itself for the next expansion. The 2001 U.S. recession was no exception. Barrett and Grove explained the strategy in the company's 2001 Annual Report: "[W]e know that a downturn is no time to shy away from strategic spending. Consequently, during this downturn, we did what may seem counterintuitive: We accelerated our capital investments, spending $7.3 billion in 2001, compared with approximately $10 billion in capital spending over the previous two years combined. We also invested $3.8 billion in research and development in 2001." The payoff for Intel was handsome. When the 2002–3 recovery came, Intel was able to quickly launch new products such as its Centrino mobile processor technology. Consequently, Intel had a banner year in 2003, with revenues increasing 13 percent and net income rising 81 percent over the previous year. By 2006, however, the company was again facing challenges, especially from rival chipmaker AMD. Otellini responded to the challenge in characteristic Intel fashion: "We accelerated the introduction of new products, leading the industry into an era of energy-efficient, multi-core computing and ending the year with one of the strongest product lineups in our history." The year ended on a strong note and Intel reported its 20th consecutive year of profitability.

Processing Competitive Threats   Initially, Intel (the name is a contraction of "*int*egrated *el*ectronics") made read-only memory chips for computers and experienced early success in the industry. Before long, however, Asian competitors stepped up their competitive practices, using low-cost capital financing, large advantages in economies of scale, and aggressive pricing to dominate global market share. In addition, technological improvements in new generations of memory chips continued at lightning speed. These forces converged to create an extremely volatile market. As a result, Intel and other U.S. memory-chip companies suffered financially.

Fortunately for Intel, just when competition was intensifying in the memory-chip business, a new microprocessor technology that Intel had developed earlier was paying off and picking up some of the slack. In 1971, Intel introduced the world's first commercial microprocessor, the 4004. When a subsequent generation of the chip (the 8088) was chosen for the IBM PC in 1981, Intel secured its place as the standard setter in the microprocessor business.

A Few Knowledgeable Workers Go a Long Way   Intel's transition from a memory-chip company to the leading manufacturer of microprocessors was not planned. In fact, the official corporate strategy was to compete primarily in the memory-chip market, not the microprocessor market, based on Intel's senior executives' views that the firm's historic success in memory chips could be carried into the future. Rather, the company's production managers started shifting manufacturing capacity from memory chips to microprocessors because the yields per wafer square inch were higher. They followed a rather simple managerial rule—allocate production capacity based on a "margin-per-wafer-start." Margins on memory wafers were declining and margins for microprocessor wafers were increasing. In light of this change, Intel production managers shifted production capacity toward microprocessors, and they did so rapidly, because Intel's incentive and accountability systems rewarded plant managers based on wafer yields. Moreover, the chairman and CEO of Intel, Andy Grove, had successfully nurtured a strong internal culture that encouraged open debate about strategic initiatives and discouraged the use of hierarchy or position over the power of knowledge to make key decisions. The confluence of these factors—Intel's experiment with microprocessors, IBM's selection of the Intel chip, the excessive price competition in the memory market, and Intel's organizational processes that enabled plant managers to make these changes without explicit approval from senior management—enabled Intel to change rapidly from a memory-chip company to a microprocessor company.

Taking Strategic License   An important benefit of the change to microprocessors was the evolution of Intel's capabilities beyond narrow technical design to the implementation of complex design architectures in logic products, which gave Intel a much larger market domain. As the standard setter and chief supplier for the world's largest PC maker, Intel became a formidable player in the microprocessor industry. IBM, however, was reluctant to allow a small company to be the sole supplier of such a key technology. Consequently, Intel chose to license the technology to other companies to satisfy IBM's concern. It licensed its next chip design, the 286, to other semiconductor firms, such as Advanced Micro Devices (AMD). Licensing reinforced Intel's status as an industry technology architecture leader, and it also enabled the company to supplement profits from its own sales with the healthy fees paid by licensees.

With a patent on the microprocessor design that had become the industry standard, Intel controlled a valuable intellectual property. The licensing fees paid by other firms were substantial; nevertheless, Intel moved to ease its dependence on outside manufacturers by adopting a three-pronged approach to improving its competitive position:

■ The company used revenues from licensing agreements and profits from chip sales to fund the expansion of its manufacturing capacity and manufacturing-processing capabilities. Intel realized that if it could improve the manufacturing process, it would not only control the technology that semiconductor firms used to make processors, but it might also be able to generate cost savings. With a superior manufacturing process in hand, Intel then increased manufacturing capacity by building larger fabrication plants (called "fabs"), which also resulted in superior economies of scale.

■ At the same time that Intel was building both innovation and manufacturing capability for microprocessors, the PC industry was expanding and credible threats to IBM were emerging. Compaq decided to adopt the 486 chip design after IBM decided to delay adoption of the chip, and other small PC companies soon followed Compaq's lead. The new chip proved to be a success with consumers. Because Intel had been investing in additional capacity in its fabs, it was able to exploit these new dynamics in the PC industry. Intel started revoking licensing agreements from other semiconductor companies for future generations of the Intel microprocessor. This move allowed Intel to capture a larger market share and boosted profits because canceling licenses eliminated competitors and the number of PC makers was increasing dramatically.

■ Intel set out to brand its product in order to make it the microprocessor of choice among end users, even if similar products entered the market. PC manufacturers, of course, preferred to source their technology from multiple suppliers. Thus, Intel still faced the threat that AMD or some other upstart would begin to compete aggressively and weaken its market share. Intel responded by advertising its product to end users—the individual consumers who purchase PCs from computer makers. The campaign was so successful that consumers turned out to be willing to pay higher prices for PCs with "Intel Inside." <<<

Internal Drivers of Strategy and Competitive Advantage

In this chapter, we'll introduce theories and models that explain why some firms outperform their rivals and others lag behind. You have probably been introduced to a very simple tool in other classes (such as marketing) called *SWOT analysis*. Recall that SWOT is an acronym for *s*trengths, *w*eaknesses, *o*pportunities, and *t*hreats. This chapter deals primarily with firms' strengths and weaknesses, or the resource-based inputs into the strategy process. These are internal characteristics of firms. Firms within an industry generally have different strengths and weaknesses, and those differences often have a strong bearing on which firms win competitive interactions. We will introduce you to more rigorous models that help managers diagnose their strengths and weaknesses and prescribe future actions to exploit their strengths or remedy their weaknesses. Of course, a complete understanding of a firm's strengths and weaknesses requires an understanding of competitors. Chapter 4 will introduce the basic tools for analyzing competitors, thereby enabling you to evaluate firms relative to their competitors.

This chapter focuses on firms' resources and capabilities, the choices managers make when configuring the activities they chose to perform internally (versus outsourcing), and the role of managers in allocating, reconfiguring, and exploiting firm resources and capabilities. All firms, of course, must consider the external context when formulating and implementing strategy, but focusing on the internal perspective reminds us that firms differ in terms of resources and capabilities. Indeed, the internal perspective should help you describe and understand the *differentiators* facet of the strategy diamond for a given firm. ◆ If you  can identify the key resources and capabilities that allow it to differentiate its products or services in its targeted arenas, you are well on your way to understanding its strategy and strategic opportunities. To this end, we'll examine several models and analytical tools that will help you analyze and formulate competitive strategies.

Our opening vignette has already given us some insight into the internal sources of competitive advantage. Although the microprocessor industry is extremely competitive, Intel has been able to maintain its competitive advantage over most of its rivals for an extended period of time. This fact suggests that Intel has access to internal resources and capabilities that other firms do not. Many firms in the industry, for example, are capable of making innovations in chip design. Intel, however, has always been able to get new products to market faster than its competitors and get them there in the volume necessary to achieve significant cost advantages. Speed to market is thus an Intel differentiator. It is a differentiator because Intel is relatively unique in this area, and because speed to market is highly valued by its customers. This advantage in speed to market results, in part, from Intel's ability to convince computer makers to use its products and from its ability to move new products into production in a timely manner.

However, as we also noted in the opening vignette, at one point Intel was forced to license its technology to other manufacturers because its chief customer demanded multiple sourcing options. Being forced to license the technology to other firms meant that Intel didn't have the immediate in-house capacity to manufacture chips fast enough and in large enough quantities to satisfy market demand. The firm addressed this problem by investing heavily to improve its manufacturing processes. The related judgment and willingness of management to undertake such a risk—new semiconductor plants cost over $1 billion to build and take several years to complete—may be considered another of Intel's internal strengths. This combination of speed to market and manufacturing-process capability means that Intel can charge significant price premiums during the first months following a new-product release. Competitors who get to market later must settle for lower profits because prices have fallen.

As our description of Intel's history, strategy, and performance suggests, the firm's advantage is due, in part, to its use of engineering expertise to create valuable technologies, operational efficiencies to make its new products proprietary standards in the industry, and marketing skills to exploit its ability to speed products to market. Not surprisingly, its competitive advantage translates into higher levels of performance.

Firms in many other industries have also managed to do what Intel has done—namely, to outperform major competitors for extended periods of time. As you can see in Exhibit 3.1, such firms can be found in industries ranging from semiconductors to retail grocers. Notice that the average profitability (return on sales and return on assets) for firms within these very different industries varies significantly across firms over long periods of time. Intel's average return on assets (ROA) and return on sales (ROS), which are measures of financial performance that gauge profits as a percentage of total sales and total assets, respectively, dwarf those of its nearest competitor, Texas Instruments. In the exhibit, note that the only competitors who approach Intel's average returns are much smaller companies focused on specialized niches. In the grocery industry, Publix, Whole Foods, and Weis appear to perform much better on average than other grocery chains even though they are much smaller than the largest firms in the industry. The exhibit only illustrates two industries, but these are representative of what you would generally find in most industries. Whether we look at high-tech industries, such as semiconductors or a retail business, such as grocery stores, within industries some firms perform much better than others over time.

Exhibit 3.1 Comparative Performance in Selected Industries

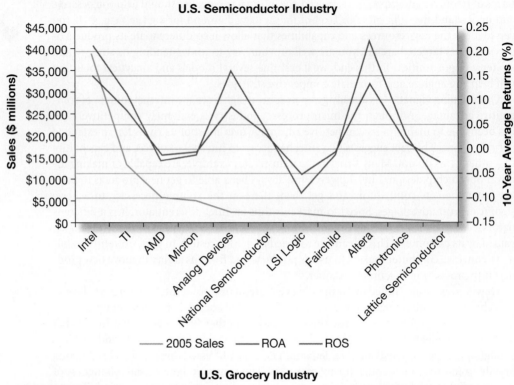

U.S. Semiconductor Industry

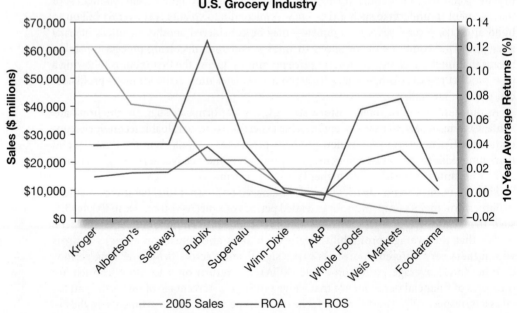

U.S. Grocery Industry

One of the primary purposes of this chapter is to help you understand how such differences in profitability materialize as a result of firms being able to use their resources and capabilities to create differentiators, and perhaps other unique choices related to facets of the strategy diamond, and what firms can do to improve their performance relative to firms in their industry.

INTERNAL MODELS OF COMPETITIVE ADVANTAGE

This chapter presents the two dominant models regarding internal sources of competitive advantage; they help to explain how and why some firms perform better than others. Recall in Chapter 1 we told you that there are three perspectives of competitive advantage: internal, external, and dynamic. The two models presented in this chapter are distinct but complementary theories that both suggest that differences in long-term-performance outcomes across firms within the same industry are derived largely from different levels of internal sources of competitive advantage. However, the source of competitive advantage differs between these theories. The first explanation as to why some firms perform better than others attributes this success to fundamental differences in the resources firms control as well as their capabilities to perform certain aspects of value creation activities. The dynamic perspective introduced in Chapter 1 is necessary to understand how these differences in resources and capabilities evolve over time. The second theory for why firms differ within industries focuses not on resources, but on *the specific value chain activities firms choose to engage in*. This activity perspective, treated toward the end of this chapter, relies heavily on the value chain and the advantages firms might gain by configuring value-chain activities in ways to add more value to their products or services than competitors. We'll explain how these two theories help to determine which firms are able to develop a competitive advantage and potentially perform above industry averages and which ones suffer from liabilities and struggle to keep up.

STRATEGIC LEADERSHIP

Finally, whether we trace a firm's competitive advantage to its resources and capabilities or to the organization of its value-chain activities, we must always consider the role played by its managers. Senior and mid-level managers make key decisions about how to acquire, allocate, and discard resources, and they're also in charge of organizing a firm's value-chain activities. This is why we include managers' strategic leadership as a potentially valuable internal input into strategy. Exhibit 3.2 provides an overview of how resources, capabilities, and managerial decision making are interdependent; all are necessary to understand how and why firms perform differently within similar industry environments. As we'll explain in more detail later, notice how the role of management is both to use the resources and capabilities to devise strategies and to make decisions about reconfiguring resources and

Exhibit 3.2 Resources, Capabilities, and Managerial Decisions

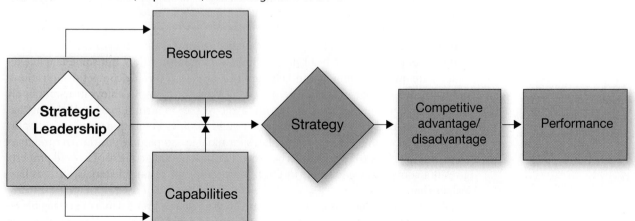

capabilities. Indeed, managers play the unique role of being a resource for the firm, having capabilities which they use to manage the firm, and making choices about the stewardship and deployment of other resources and capabilities (our opening vignette on Intel is an example here).

Resources and Capabilities

Resources and capabilities are the fundamental building blocks of a firm's strategy. The choices made by firms' managers relative to the five elements of a strategy, as organized by the strategy diamond, require resources and capabilities. For instance, if a firm wants to enter new arenas, it will need appropriate resources and capabilities in order to compete there. In addition, no matter how a firm plans to differentiate its products—whether on quality, image, or price—it needs the right resources and capabilities to make the differentiation real. Likewise, when a firm is deciding on the best way to enter a new market—whether by means of acquisition, alliance, or internal development—it has to consider its available resources and capabilities. Sometimes a firm uses a vehicle such as an acquisition or an alliance specifically for the purpose of acquiring resources or capabilities that it does not currently own.[1] Not surprisingly, successful strategies exploit the resources and capabilities that a firm enjoys and put the firm on a path to acquire missing resources and capabilities and upgrade existing ones; whereas unsuccessful strategies often reflect the fact that critical resources and capabilities are lacking.

RESOURCES

resources Inputs used by firms to create products and services.

What, exactly, do we mean by *resources?* **Resources** are the inputs that firms use to create goods or services. Some resources are rather undifferentiated inputs that any firm can acquire. For instance, land, unskilled labor, debt financing, and commodity-like inventory are inputs that are generally available to most firms. Other resources are more firm-specific in nature.[2] They are difficult to purchase through normal supply chain channels. For instance, managerial judgment, intellectual property, trade secrets, and brand equity are resources that are not easily purchased or transferred. From this description, it is clear that some resources have physical attributes; these are referred to as *tangible* resources. Other resources, such as knowledge, organizational culture, location, patents, trademarks, and reputation are *intangible* in nature. Some resources have both tangible and intangible characteristics. Land, for instance, has physical properties and satisfies certain functional needs. At the same time, some properties may have value as a resource by virtue of their location, which is an intangible benefit arising from unique proximity to customers or suppliers due to preferences or relative location.

Because tangible resources are easier to identify and value, they may be less likely to be a source of competitive advantage than intangible resources. This is because their tangible nature gives competitors a head start on imitation or substitution. But some tangible resources are quite instrumental in helping firms achieve favorable competitive positions, partly because of their intangible benefits. Wal-Mart, for example, enjoys near-monopoly status in many rural locations. As the first large retailer in a rural market, Wal-Mart has locked out potential competitors who won't build facilities in locations that can't support two stores. Thus, one reason for Wal-Mart's formidable competitive position in rural markets is its tangible real estate. Similarly, Union Pacific Railroad's control of key rail property gives it a competitive advantage in the transportation of certain materials, such as hazardous chemicals.

Likewise, McDonald's controls much more than a valuable brand name (an intangible resource that does in fact convey a significant advantage). Like Wal-Mart, it also controls a great deal of valuable real estate by virtue of its location near high-traffic centers. Indeed, without its prime real-estate locations, McDonald's would have a less valuable brand name. Obviously, the pace at which McDonald's grew required a certain capability in finding the needed real estate.

CAPABILITIES

Capabilities refer to a firm's skill in using its resources (both tangible and intangible) to create goods and services. A synonym that is often used to describe the same concept is *competences*. For simplicity, we use the term *capabilities*. Capabilities may be possessed by individuals or embedded in company-wide rules and routines.[3] In essence, they are the combination of procedures and expertise that the firm relies on to engage in distinct activities in the process of producing goods and services. Several examples of companies and their capabilities are listed in Exhibit 3.3.[4] For instance, Wal-Mart is widely regarded as having excellent capabilities related to the management of logistics, which it uses to exploit resources such as large stores, store locations, its trucking fleet, and massive distribution centers.

Capabilities span from the rather simple tasks that firms must perform to accomplish their daily business, such as taking and fulfilling orders, to more complex tasks, such as designing sophisticated systems, creative marketing, and manufacturing processes. Collectively, these capabilities are the activities that constitute a firm's **value chain**. Not all capabilities are of equal value to the firm—a fact that has, in turn, given rise to the rapid growth of **outsourcing**. Outsourcing is contracting with external suppliers to perform certain parts of a company's normal value chain of activities. Later in the chapter, you will be introduced to a special class of capabilities known as *dynamic capabilities*.

Two other special classes of capabilities with which you should be familiar, if for no other reason than that they are part of the generally used business vocabulary, are *distinctive competences* and *core competences*. **Distinctive competences** (or *distinctive capabilities*) are the capabilities that set a firm apart from other firms. They are the capabilities that are unique to the firm within its competitive landscape. **Core competences** (or *core capabilities*) are those capabilities that are central to the main business operations of the firm; they are the capabilities that are common to the principal businesses of the firm and that enable the firm to generate new products and services in these businesses. Thus, a core competence at GE, which operates in many unrelated businesses, is

capabilities A firm's skill at using its resources to create goods and services; combination of procedures and expertise on which a firm relies to produce goods and services.

value chain Total of primary and support value-adding activities by which a firm produces, distributes, and markets a product.

outsourcing Activity performed for a company by people other than its full-time employees.

distinctive competence Capability that sets a firm apart from other firms; something that a firm can do which competitors cannot.

core competence Capability which is central to a firm's main business operations and which allow it to generate new products and services.

Exhibit 3.3 A Few Extraordinary Capabilities

Company	Capability	Result
Wal-Mart	Logistics—distributing vast amounts of goods quickly and efficiently to remote locations.	200,000 percent return to shareholders during first 30 years since IPO.
The Vanguard Group	Extraordinarily frugal system using both technological leadership and economies of scale for delivering the lowest cost structure in the mutual-fund industry.	25,000 percent return to shareholders during the 30+ year tenure of CEO John Connelly. Shareholders in Vanguard equity funds pay, on average, $30 per $10,000 versus a $159 industry average. With bond funds, the bite is just $17 per $10,000.
3M	Generating new ideas and turning them into innovative and profitable products.	30 percent of revenue from products introduced within the past four years.

its general management capability; GE is able to manage a portfolio of businesses based on sound business principles when most firms cannot manage such unrelated business simultaneously.

The relationship between resources and capabilities can be further illustrated by a few more examples. Intel's manufacturing capacity (i.e., its plants, equipment, and production engineers), its patented microprocessor designs, and its well-established brand name are among its key resources. Like its capabilities in speed-to-market, these other internal factors contribute to its strategic differentiators, in terms of the strategy diamond. Intel has also demonstrated the organizational capability to design new generations of leading-edge microprocessors and to do so rapidly. In addition, Intel has demonstrated marketing adroitness by creating the "Intel Inside" campaign, which stimulated greater demand and higher switching costs among end users—the customers of Intel's customers. This clearly suggests a marketing capability. The combination of Intel's resources and capabilities collectively comprise its differentiators, and enable its managers to execute a value-creating strategy and achieve a formidable competitive advantage in the microprocessor industry.

In the oil industry, too, we can see that resources and capabilities aren't uniformly developed by all competitors. Some firms, for example, are highly integrated. These integrated firms are involved in every stage of the value chain, including risky and time-consuming oil exploration and extraction activities. BP, ChevronTexaco, ExxonMobil, and Royal Dutch/Shell all possess significant capabilities in exploration and extraction, refining, distribution, and marketing. As a result, they also own rights to significant petroleum deposits around the world, and these reserves are potentially valuable tangible resources. In contrast, other oil companies are involved primarily in "downstream activities." These companies gear their capabilities to refining, distribution, and marketing. Valero Energy and Sunoco, for instance, are the largest independent U.S. oil refiners and distributors. Neither, however, is active in exploration. Their resources include refineries, pipelines, distribution networks, and equipment, but both buy crude oil from other companies.

The important complementary relationship between one of McDonald's tangible resources (real estate) and one of its capabilities (its site-location skills) are highlighted in the following example. Few people go out for the sole purpose of buying a hamburger or a taco. Most fast-food purchases are impulse buys, and this fact points to just one reason why site location is so important in the fast-food industry. Like magazines and candies strategically placed at supermarket checkout counters, fast-food outlets are situated by design. At one time, McDonald's used helicopters to assess the growth of residential areas: Basically, planners looked for cheap land alongside thoroughfares that would one day run through well-populated suburbs.

Today, the site-location process is even more high-tech. In the 1980s, McDonald's turned to satellite photography to predict urban sprawl. The company has developed a software package called *Quintillion,* which integrates information from satellite images, detailed maps, demographic information, CAD drawings, and sales data from existing stores. With all of this information at its disposal, McDonald's has taken the strategy of site location to new heights. Prime locations, of course, command prime dollars: The difference between the cost of a prime location and a mediocre site could be three times the price per square foot.[5]

THE VRINE MODEL

In a given industry, then, all competitors do not have access to the same resources and capabilities—a fact that should have significant implications for the strategies that they develop. In addition, one firm's resources or capabilities aren't necessarily as effective as an-

Exhibit 3.4 Applying the VRINE Model

	The Test	The Competitive Implication	The Performance Implication
Is it valuable?	Does the resource or capability allow the firm to meet a market demand or protect the firm from market uncertainties?	If so, the company is able to compete in an industry, but value by itself does not convey an advantage.	Valuable resources and capabilities have the *potential* to contribute to *normal profits* (profits that cover the cost of all inputs, including capital).
Is it rare?	Assuming that the resource or capability is valuable, is it scarce relative to demand or is it widely possessed by competitors?	Valuable resources that are also rare contribute to a *competitive advantage*, but that advantage may be only temporary.	A *temporary competitive advantage* can contribute to *above-normal profits*, at least until the advantage is nullified by other firms.
Is it inimitable and/or nonsubstitutable?	Assuming that the resource is both valuable and rare, how difficult is it for competitors either to imitate it or substitute other resources and capabilities that yield similar benefits?	Valuable and rare resources and capabilities that are also difficult to imitate or substitute can contribute to *sustained competitive advantage*.	A sustained competitive advantage can contribute to *above-normal profits for extended periods of time* (until competitors find ways to imitate or substitute or environmental changes nullify the advantage).
Is it exploitable?	If the resource or capability satisfied any or all of the preceding VRINE criteria, can the firm actually exploit it?	Resources and capabilities that satisfy the first four VRINE criteria but that cannot be exploited do not convey competitive advantage. In fact, they may increase opportunity costs.	Firms that control but don't exploit their VRINE resources and capabilities (even after they satisfy the V, R, I, and N criteria) generally suffer from lower levels of financial performance and depressed market valuations *relative to what they would enjoy if they could in fact exploit them* (although they won't be in as bad a shape as competitors who don't control any VRINE-certified resources and capabilities).

other's in helping it develop or sustain a competitive advantage. Why do some resources and capabilities enable some firms to develop a competitive advantage? Exhibit 3.4 summarizes five basic characteristics that determine whether a resource or capability can help a firm compete and, indeed, achieve superior performance: (1) value, (2) rarity, (3) inimitability, (4) nonsubstitutability, and (5) exploitability.[6]

According to the **VRINE model** (for *v*alue, *r*arity, *i*nimitability, *n*onsubstitutability, and *e*xploitability), resources and capabilities contribute to competitive advantage to the extent that they satisfy the five components of the model. VRINE analysis helps managers systematically test the importance of particular resources and capabilities and the desirability of acquiring new resources and capabilities. VRINE analysis also suggest to you how a firm might use its resources and capabilities to differentiate its products or services in valuable ways that competitors cannot imitate; that is, it suggests what the firm might do in terms of the differentiator facet of the strategy diamond. In the following sections, we'll explain and provide examples of each VRINE characteristic.

VRINE model Analytical framework suggesting that a firm with resources and capabilities which are valuable, rare, inimitable, nonsubstitutable, and exploitable will gain a competitive advantage.

Value   A resource or capability is *valuable* if it enables a firm to take advantage of opportunities or to fend off threats in its environment.[7] Union Pacific (UP) Railroad, for example, maintains an extensive network of rail-line property and equipment on the U.S. Gulf Coast. It operates in the western two-thirds of the United States, serving 23 states, linking every major West Coast and Gulf Coast port and reaching east through major gateways in Chicago, St. Louis, Memphis, and New Orleans. UP also operates in key north-south corridors (see Exhibit 3.5).[8] It's the only U.S. railroad to serve all six gateways to Mexico, and it interchanges traffic with Canadian rail systems.

Its rail system is a tangible resource that enables UP to compete with other carriers in the long-haul transportation of a variety of goods. UP is, for example, the United States' largest hauler of chemicals, and much of that traffic originates along the Gulf Coast near Houston, Texas. The company enjoys this advantage because it owns the physical resources necessary to compete in this market—the railway rights of way through strategic areas—and because it has the specialized capability to transport chemicals safely and cost effectively. Government studies indicate that railroads are very efficient compared to alternative forms of transportation (such as truck and air) for the transportation of chemicals. Thus, railroad assets are valuable because they enable the company to provide a cost-effective means of transporting chemicals. In addition, because the Gulf Coast is the source for most chemical production in the United States, this network permits UP to take advantage of a market opportunity.

Alternatively, UP owns many rights of way that are no longer active. These resources would appear to convey no value to UP unless it can find a new use for these properties although UP's ownership of them is a deterrent to new railroad industry entrants. Consequently, UP frequently sells these abandoned railway rights of way to communities for such things as bike trails, and not to competing railroad operators.

Finally, it is worthwhile to remember that some resources that can be sources of value can also be abused and consequently become sources of corporate overhead. For instance,

Exhibit 3.5   The Union Pacific Right-of-Way System

Source: Union Pacific, "System Map" (accessed August 4, 2005), at www.uprr.com/aboutup/maps/sysmap/index.shtml.

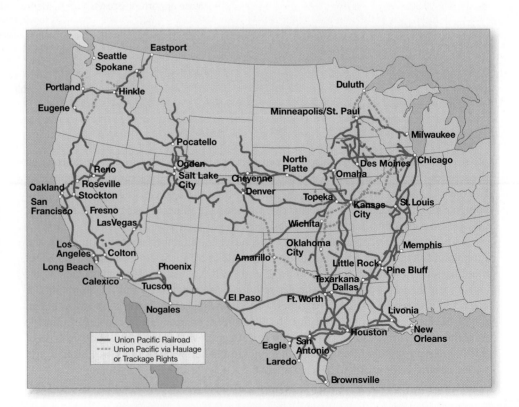

consider a small fleet of business jets owned by a company. Occasionally, the company may need to be able to get top executives in and out of remote or congested locations quickly, which would make the jets a valuable resource. However, in other situations, the jets may be a costly convenience and an example of corporate excess that provide no real economic value.

If a firm cannot use a resource to minimize threats or take advantage of opportunities, then it probably doesn't enhance its competitive position. In fact, some experts suggest that owning resources that *don't* meet the VRINE criteria for value actually puts a firm at a competitive *disadvantage*. Why? Because the capital tied up in the resource could be put to better use,[9] the capital could be reinvested in other resources that do satisfy the value requirement of VRINE, or the capital could be redistributed to shareholders.

Rarity   *Rarity* is defined as scarcity relative to demand. An otherwise valuable resource that isn't rare won't necessarily contribute to competitive advantage: Valuable resources that are available to most competitors simply enable a firm to achieve parity with everyone else. Sometimes such resources may be called *table stakes,* as in poker, because they are required to compete in the first place. But when a firm controls a valuable resource that's also rare in its industry, it's in a position to gain a competitive advantage. Such resources, for example, may enable a company to exploit opportunities or fend off threats in ways that competitors cannot. When McDonald's signs an agreement to build a restaurant inside a Wal-Mart store, it has an intangible location advantage over its competitors Burger King and Wendy's that is not only valuable but also rare because it has an exclusive right to that geographic space.

How rare does a resource have to be in order to offer potential competitive advantage? It's a difficult question to answer with any certainty. At the two extremes, of course, *only one* firm has the resource or *every* firm has it, and the answer is fairly obvious. If only one firm possesses a given resource, it has a significant advantage. Monsanto, for instance, enjoyed an advantage for many years because it owned the patent to aspartame, the chemical compound in NutraSweet. As the only legal seller of aspartame, Monsanto dominated the artificial-sweetener market. Such is typically the case in the pharmaceutical industry for those who are first or second to patent and market a therapy for a particular disease.

Satisfying the rarity condition, however, doesn't necessarily require *exclusive* ownership. When a resource is controlled by a handful of firms, those firms will have an advantage over the rest of the field. Pfizer was first to the market for a drug to treat erectile dysfunction with its Viagra product, but it was later joined by two other products offered by competitors (Levitra and Cialis). Pfizer no longer has a monopoly in the market to treat this condition, but the three firms collectively control resources that are scarce relative to demand. Thus, Pfizer's resource, the patent for Viagra, would still seem to satisfy both the value and the rarity requirements of VRINE. Consider an example from another context. Both Toyota and Honda, for example, can build high-quality cars at relatively low cost, and the products of both firms regularly beat those of rivals in both short-term and long-term quality ratings. The criterion of rarity requires only that a resource be scarce *relative to demand.* It also follows, of course, that the more exclusive the access to a valuable resource, the greater the benefit of having it.

A firm that controls a valuable and scarce resource or capability may create a competitive advantage, but there is no assurance that the advantage will persist. We now turn to the two criteria that must be satisfied if the advantage is to be sustained.

Inimitability and Nonsubstitutability   A valuable and rare resource or capability will grant an advantage only so long as competitors don't gain possession of it or find a close substitute. We review these two criteria jointly because they work in similar fashions. The criterion of *inimitability* is satisfied if competitors cannot acquire the valuable and rare resource quickly or if they face a cost disadvantage in doing so. The *nonsubstitutability* criterion is satisfied if a competitor cannot achieve the same benefit using

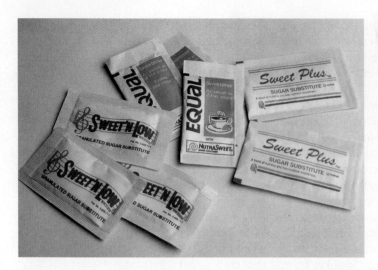

Monsanto enjoyed a competitive advantage for many years because it owned the patent to aspartame, the chemical compound in NutraSweet. The patent on aspartame ran out in 1992, and in 2000 Monsanto sold NutraSweet to private investors. NutraSweet now faces fierce competition from other aspartame-containing products, and newer and more popular nonaspartame-based sweeteners.

different combinations of resources and capabilities. When a resource or capability is valuable and rare and contributes to a firm's advantage, one can assume that competitors will do all they can to get it. Of course, firms can acquire needed resources or capabilities in a number of different ways, including internal investment, acquisitions, and alliances. They can, for instance, form alliances in order to learn from and internalize a partner's capabilities.[10]

Some firms find alternative resources or capabilities that "mimic" the benefits of the original. For several years, for example, Barnes & Noble and Borders enjoyed formidable advantages in the retail-book industry. Their sheer size gave them an immense advantage over smaller players: Because they had access to more customers, they were able to take advantage of greater buying power. Eventually, however, Amazon.com's ability to substitute online for conventional retail marketing provided a feasible substitute for geographic accessibility to consumers. Generally speaking, then, valuable and rare resources can provide competitive advantage only as long as they're difficult to imitate or substitute.

The High Cost of Imitation and Substitution Several factors can make some resources and capabilities difficult to duplicate or substitute. A rival might, for instance, try to acquire a competitor or supplier that possesses the resource it needs.[11] But acquisitions of this kind often entail large premiums that result in a buyer paying more for a resource than it cost competitors to develop the original.[12] In 1999, for example, when Cisco purchased Cerent in order to acquire fiber-optic data-transfer capabilities, it ended up paying $6.9 billion for a startup company with just $10 million in sales.[13] Cisco desperately wanted the capabilities of Cerent, but managers felt it would take too long to develop those capabilities internally. Absent Cisco's excellent capabilities in merger integration and new product distribution, therefore, the firm would be at a cost disadvantage relative to any competitor who could develop the same collective capabilities for less money.

Inimitability, Nonsubstitution, and Property Rights Perhaps the most straightforward cause of resources and capabilities being difficult to imitate or substitute is property rights. Competitors can be prevented from copying resources if they are protected by ownership rights. For instance, patented items or processes cannot be directly copied during the term of the patent without the imitator being subject to severe legal repercussions. Media companies own copyrights on titles in their libraries. Because of this, it is very difficult for competitors to substitute for Mickey Mouse. However, property rights alone do not protect all resources and capabilities from imitation or substitution.

Inimitability, Nonsubstitution, and Time Another factor that can make resources and capabilities difficult to imitate or substitute is the unique historical conditions surrounding their development or the fact that their acquisition requires the passage of time.[14] Sometimes a firm's resources and capabilities are the result of unique historical events that converged to its benefit. For instance, in order to build troop morale during World War II, U.S. General Dwight D. Eisenhower requested that Coca-Cola be available to all American servicemen and servicewomen. To ensure that GIs could buy Coke for five cents a bottle, the government and Coca-Cola cooperated to build 64 bottling plants around the world. In the long term, Coke gained the competitive advantage of instant global presence, both in bottling capacity and brand recognition.[15] At war's end, Coke ramped up its overseas production and marketing and succeeded in penetrating new markets. In effect, Coke's market entry had been subsidized by the government, and rival Pepsi faced considerable cost disadvantages in competing with Coke's international presence. Coke's global advantage over Pepsi remains even today. Of Coke's $24.1 billion sales in 2006, fully 71 percent were from outside North America; whereas just 57 percent of PepsiCo's $22.5 billion in beverage sales were from outside North America.[16]

The simple passage of time creates inimitability and nonsubstitutability as well, typically because the original owner may have built up the value of the resource or capability through a process of gradual learning and improvement that can't be matched through catch-up programs. For instance, firms that invest a given rate of R&D spending over an extended time period appear to produce larger gains in knowledge and intellectual property than firms that invest at twice the same level over half the time.[17] Thus, we can say that a resource is difficult to imitate if shorter development time results in inferior imitations.

Causal Ambiguity Another factor that makes imitation difficult is **causal ambiguity**. For a number of reasons, it may be difficult to *identify* or *understand* the causal factors of a resource or capability—the complex combination of factors that make it valuable.[18] For instance, what makes Apple, Google, 3-M, and Toyota so much more innovative than their direct competitors? There is clearly something special about these firms but you would be hard-pressed to create a carbon copy from scratch, even if you had the money to do so. Firms may enjoy resources that have resulted from a complex convergence of activities that the company itself doesn't fully understand.[19] For example, 3M enjoys an enviable capacity for innovation that, at least in part, is a function of company culture. A competitor may copy certain 3M policies—say, allowing employees to spend 10 percent of their time experimenting on potential new products—but it will be more difficult to imitate the complex culture of cooperation and rewards that facilitates innovation at 3M. The causal process, in other words, would be difficult to identify because it's *socially complex*. Products that are technologically complex are relatively easier to duplicate (say, by adopting such processes as reverse engineering) than are socially complex organizational phenomena.[20] Firms with socially complex resources and capabilities like this must strive to appreciate what contributes to them—even if they can't be fully understood or quantified—so that strategic choices continue to protect and nourish such unique underlying sources of competitive advantage.

causal ambiguity Condition whereby the difficulty of identifying or understanding a resource or capability makes it valuable, rare, and inimitable.

Exploitability The fifth and final VRINE criterion reminds us that mere possession of or control over a resource or capability is necessary but not sufficient to gain a competitive advantage: A firm must be able to *exploit* it; that is, the firm must be able to nurture and take advantage of the resources and capabilities that it possesses.

The question of exploitability is, of course, quite broad, but in this case, we're focusing on *a company's ability to get the value out of any resource or capability that it may generate*. Thus, the issue of an organization's exploitative capability incorporates all of the dimensions of a firm's value-adding processes. Although we may not deal directly with organizational processes until the final criterion in the VRINE model, bear in mind that, without this skill, a firm won't get much benefit from having met any of the first four VRINE criteria. A valuable resource or capability that is also possessed by many other competitors has the potential to give the firm competitive parity, but only if the firm also has the exploitative capabilities to implement a strategy that utilizes the resource or capability. Likewise, a firm that possesses a valuable and rare resource will not gain a competitive advantage unless it can actually put that resource to effective use.

In fact, many firms do have valuable and rare resources that they fail to exploit (in which case, by the way, their competitors aren't under much pressure to imitate them). For many years, for instance, Novell's core NetWare product gave it a significant advantage in the computer networking market. In high-tech industries, however, staying on top requires continuous innovation, and according to many observers, Novell's decline in the 1990s reflected an inability to innovate in order to meet the demands of changing markets and technology. But shortly after he was hired from Sun Microsystems to turn Novell around, new CEO Eric Schmidt (now CEO of Google) arrived at a different conclusion: "I walk down Novell hallways," he reported, "and marvel at the incredible potential for innovation here. But Novell has had a difficult time in the past turning innovation into products in the marketplace."[21] The company, Schmidt confided to a few key executives, was suffering from "organizational constipation."[22] According to its new CEO, Novell had the resources and capabilities needed to innovate, but it lacked the exploitative capability (especially in its product-development and marketing processes) to get innovative products to market in a timely manner.

Xerox, too, went through a period when it was unable to exploit its resources to innovate products. At a dedicated facility in Palo Alto, California, Xerox established a successful research team known as Xerox PARC. Scientists in this group invented an impressive list of innovative products, including laser printers, Ethernet, graphical-interface software, computers, and the computer mouse. All of these products were commercially successful, but, unfortunately for Xerox shareholders, they were commercial successes for other firms. Xerox couldn't get information about them to the right people in a timely fashion. Why? Largely because the company's bureaucracy tended to suffocate ideas before they had a chance to flow through the organization. Compensation policies ignored managers who fostered innovations and rewarded immediate profits over long-term success.[23]

The VRINE model can be used to assess any resource or capability in order to determine if it is a source or potential source of competitive advantage and, if so, whether that advantage is likely to be temporary or sustained. To illustrate how this is done, we use the VRINE model in Exhibit 3.6 to analyze Pfizer's ownership of the patents for Zoloft as a possible source of competitive advantage.[24]

Where Do Resources Come From?   Our earlier definitions of *resources* and *capabilities* describe them as something the firm may own or possess. However, we have also suggested that many resources and capabilities cannot be easily purchased. Brand equity, for example, can't be readily purchased unless a company purchases an existing brand from another company. Otherwise, a brand will need to be developed, and that takes time. The brand equity of Coke, for example, has been developed through decades of marketing efforts with investments in the hundreds of millions per year. Toyota's reputation for quality automobiles has been developed through stringent quality-control methods; Intel's R&D capability is the result of years of investment. In other words, intangible resources such as brand equity, reputation, and innovative capability result from policies and strategies that have been implemented over extended periods of time; they can't be acquired through one-time purchases.

Dynamic Capabilities

Thus far, our discussion of resources and capabilities has portrayed a rather static view. However, the process of developing, accumulating, and losing resources and capabilities is inherently dynamic. We now introduce two concepts to demonstrate the dynamic aspects of resources and capabilities. The first deals with *stocks versus flows;* the second deals with a special class of capability referred to as a *dynamic capability.*

RESOURCES AS STOCKS AND FLOWS

Resources can be thought of as both stocks and flows. A firm's stock of resources and capabilities is what it possesses at any given point in time. However, that stock of resources and

Exhibit 3.6   Putting Pfizer's Drug Patents up to the VRINE Test

Putting Pfizer's Drug Patents up to the VRINE test		Answers
	Let's walk through the VRINE model as applied to Pfizer's patents for Zoloft (sertraline HCl), an antidepressant known as a selective serotonin reuptake inhibitor (SSRI). If you were studying Pfizer and the pharmaceutical industry using the VRINE model, you would probably identify a number of resources and capabilities that may be the source of competitive advantage. You would probably identify patents, R&D capabilities, and marketing as key resources and capabilities that drive the differentiator facet of its strategy.	
Value: Do Pfizer's two patents on Zoloft provide value?	In any given year, about 7 percent of the U.S. population (approximately 20 million people) will experience a depressive disorder. Approximately 16 percent of adults will experience depression at some point in their lives. Women are twice as likely as men to experience depression. Thus, it appears that having a patent for a treatment for depression would enable a pharmaceutical company to take advantage of a large market opportunity.	Yes
Rarity: Are they rare?	Pfizer's patents on Zoloft give it the exclusive right to use the chemical compound sertraline HCl to treat depression (the patents expired in June, 2006). When the patents expire, generic drug makers will be able to sell copied versions of the drug. The patents for Zoloft are definitely rare during the term of the patents, but will not be after they expire (assuming that several generic companies make the drug, its scarcity relative to demand will decline).	Yes, but not after they expire.
Inimitability?	Pfizer is certainly not the only large pharmaceutical company that desires to profit from therapies for depression. However, a patent makes direct imitation illegal until the patent expires.	
Nonsubstitutability: Is there protection against ready substitutes?	Competitors can and do attempt to find substitute compounds that have similar effects. Indeed, Zoloft itself was a Pfizer innovation in the face of Eli Lilly's patent for Prozac. Zoloft is not the only treatment for depression; other SSRIs include Prozac, Paxil, and others. The patents for Zoloft may convey temporary advantage, but Pfizer's value from them will probably erode over time as others invent substitute compounds and as the patents expire, resulting in direct imitation.	Not completely.
Exploitability: Is there evidence these are exploitable?	To satisfy this VRINE criterion, Pfizer needs to be able to move drugs from successful clinical trial to market distribution. Fortunately for Pfizer, marketing and distribution are two of its core competences. Indeed, Pfizer has more drug representatives than any other pharmaceutical company. Pfizer also has large cash reserves that can be used to bring sufficient quantities of the product quickly to market prior to the lapsing of the patents.	Yes
The verdict?	As you may have guessed by now, Pfizer's patents on Zoloft largely stand up to the VRINE framework, suggesting that patents are a resource that can generate competitive advantage. The expiration of those patents could largely diminish the VRINE advantages they provided. Note, however, that Zoloft is such a resource not just because of patents. Pfizer also possesses the complementary VRINE resources and capabilities underlying its exploitability.	Yes

capabilities was created over time through a combination of initial endowment and accumulated investment. Consider the resource stock represented by a patent. To a large degree, the value of the patent depends on the level of innovation its original discovery represented, and that discovery was probably the result of years of investment and a process of trial and error. However, continual resource inflows may augment the value of the patent. For instance, additional R&D investments may lead to further discoveries that can be bundled with the original patent. Alternatively, investments in marketing efforts can spur demand, which leads to increased value. However, value also dissipates over time, as in the gradual expiration of the patent. The key point is that the value of resources and capabilities is a function of both the level (or stock) of resources and capabilities and the net effect of additional investment and depreciation.

This stock can be increased through development activities and sustained investment. It can be reduced through the divestiture of business units, loss of key personnel, and shifts in the competitive environment that alter the value of given resources. Remember, too, that strategic resources and capabilities are accumulated *over time*. Thus, the *process* of resource accumulation through dynamic capabilities is fundamentally different from the static possession of stocks of resources and capabilities.

REBUNDLING RESOURCES AND CAPABILITIES

Beyond making investments to augment the accumulation of resources and capabilities, firms can make decisions about how resources and capabilities are utilized and configured, and thereby change their fundamental value. And although a firm can't easily change its stock of resources and capabilities, it can reconfigure or integrate them in new ways. **Dynamic capabilities** are processes by which a firm integrates, reconfigures, acquires, or divests resources in order to achieve new configurations of resources and capabilities.[25] In fact, the term *dynamic* is added to the description of these special kinds of capabilities because it refers to a firm's ability to modify and revise its resources and capabilities to match a shifting environment. The ability to reconfigure firm resources and capabilities is especially critical in markets that move quickly, and it is typically seen in complex areas of the firm, such as its culture, knowledge base, and ability to learn.

Dynamic capabilities are manifest in several ways. The ability to integrate different resources and capabilities to create new revenue-producing products and services is a dynamic capability.[26] Disney, for instance, recently launched its "Princess Line," which brings together merchandise based on famous female Disney characters. The effort required that Disney integrate development and marketing campaigns geared toward groups of characters that had before been developed and marketed separately.[27] Reconfiguring or transferring resources and capabilities from one division to another is another form of a dynamic capability. Mail Boxes Etc. (MBE), the postal center that was recently purchased by UPS, illustrates this fact. By encoding its knowledge of how to start up a master-area franchise, MBE created "templates" for future franchisees. New master-area franchisees are required to duplicate the template exactly prior to making any adjustments to meet local market needs. This is because their internal research shows that master-area franchisees who duplicate the template significantly outperform those who first customize the model.[28] The opening vignette about Intel also illustrates how resource-allocation rules can result in a dynamic capability to reallocate resources to new uses.

The rebundling of resources and capabilities is also accomplished through alliances and acquisitions. Resources and capabilities can both be acquired and lost through these vehicles. Cisco has been able to launch many new products by strategically acquiring bits and pieces of network architecture through acquisitions.[29]

The dynamic view of resources and capabilities differs somewhat from the traditional view. It emphasizes the need to renew resources and capabilities, either in order to keep pace with a

dynamic capabilities A firm's ability to modify, reconfigure, and upgrade resources and capabilities in order to strategically respond to or generate environmental changes.

changing environment or to reconfigure the organization proactively (i.e., to change the environment). One or both of these capabilities—the ability to adapt to change or to initiate it—is particularly important in industries in which time to market is critical, technological change is rapid, and future competition is difficult to forecast.[30] When incumbent firms, even strong companies, don't have such capabilities, they're likely to be outmaneuvered by new competitors who are ready to introduce new industry standards.[31] Consequently, the value of a firm's portfolio of resources and capabilities is directly affected by its dynamic capability to reconfigure resources and capabilities to the evolving requirements of the competitive environment.

More complex forms of dynamic capabilities are typically associated with dynamic or turbulent environments. As we saw in our opening vignette, for example, Intel's internal organizational processes and organizational culture enabled it to make a dramatic change from one technological platform to another.[32] Specifically, the firm was able to shift scarce manufacturing resources from the memory-chip business to the emerging microprocessor business in a very brief period of time.

The Value Chain

Earlier in the chapter, we demonstrated that firms in the same industry differ in their resources, capabilities, and dynamic capabilities and that these differences account for much of the variance in firm performance that we see within industries. This is because such differences allow firms to create products and services with hard to imitate *differentiators* in their strategy diamond.

Firms in the same industry may also differ in the scope and type of their value-chain activities. As we saw in our discussion of the *strategy diamond* model in Chapters 1 and 2, firms can also make unique decisions about the value-chain *arenas* in which they'll participate within a given industry. ◆ So, just as firms might be making choices about what industry arenas they should compete in, so too can they make choices about what internal functions to emphasize, de-emphasize, or outsource entirely. It is the differentiators, in conjunction with the choices about value chain arenas, that further solidifies internal sources of competitive advantage. Returning to the oil industry, which we discussed earlier, Valero and Sunoco make very different choices about which value-chain activities to engage in (e.g., refining and distribution but not exploration) relative to the major integrated oil companies. Even if two firms possess similar resources and capabilities, it is still possible for one firm to gain the upper hand and achieve a competitive advantage. One way this can be done is by having a different configuration of value-adding activities.[33]

 Arenas

Firms make products or provide services by engaging in many different activities. The basic structure of these activities is embodied in the firm's value chain. Value-chain activities are of two types: primary activities and support activities. *Primary activities* include inbound logistics, operations, outbound logistics, marketing and sales, and service. *Support activities* include human resources, accounting and finance operations, technology, and procurement. The term *support activities* may seem to minimize the importance of these operations, but bear in mind that all activities—primary and support—are potential sources of competitive advantage (or disadvantage).

Exhibit 3.7 depicts the value chain for Under Armour, the performance apparel company introduced in Chapter 1.[34] Notice that the primary activities are located along the horizontal axis and represent the value-added activities that are necessary to produce and sell a product. For instance, Under Armour needs to purchase raw materials to have its apparel products manufactured. Notice, however, that a critical step in the value chain is outsourced—Under Armour outsources virtually all of its manufacturing to third party firms. To fulfill orders, the outbound logistics steps of the value chain would include matching the merchandise with the order and organizing the shipping to the customer. This is

Exhibit 3.7   The Value Chain for Under Armour

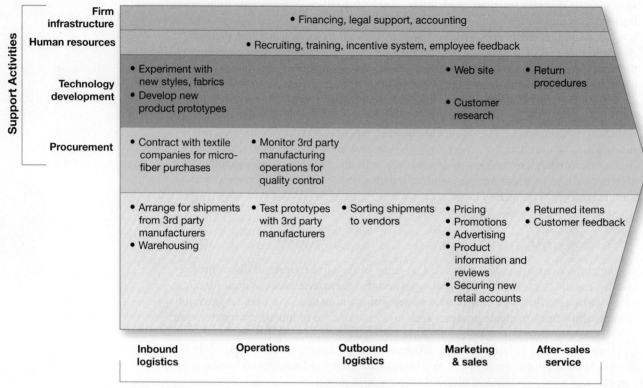

handled from one central warehouse in Maryland. Marketing and service functions are directed both at Under Armour's wholesale clients, like national sporting goods retailers, and directly at consumers through television and print advertising.

Support activities are represented on the top half of the vertical axis. Again, although these activities are generally portrayed as not being a part of the primary logistics involved in securing inputs, adding value, and fulfilling orders, when you see the types of activities performed by support functions, you begin to realize that any company would be hard-pressed to fulfill orders without these functions being performed. For instance, much of the value of Under Armour's products is a function of the advanced technological design of their performance apparel. They were the first to design tight-fitting compression athletic apparel made with moisture-wicking properties. Likewise, Under Armour's innovation of shirts with different properties for use in hot, cold, or moderate weather was a first—prior to that, athletes simply bundled on more, or removed, layers according to the temperature. So, technological design and other support activities can be sources of competitive advantage if they allow the firm to deliver products or services with unique differentiators.

Firms can use value-chain activities to create value by either finding *better* ways to perform the same activities or by finding *different* ways to perform them. However, any advantage obtained by doing the same activities but better than competitors may be short-lived. The VRINE framework that you studied earlier in this chapter should tell you that. Best practices in activities are often rapidly diffused throughout industries. Eventually, rivals improve performance in activities that they once performed less efficiently than industry leaders. For instance, a beverage distributor located in Kern County, Central California, sends its trucks to Los Angeles to pick up its products, and makes the 120-mile return trip to sell them in Bakersfield and other cities in Kern County. Obviously, transportation can be a huge cost for distributors and sending a fleet of empty trucks to Los Angeles represented a significant opportunity cost. Fortunately, this enterprising distributor found a Bakersfield manufacturing company that needed its products trucked to Los Angeles, and now the beverage company makes money as a shipper (transporting goods from Bakersfield to Los Angeles) and in its core business as a distributor in Kern County. Thus, even though shipping is not part of the beverage company's strategy, this value-chain choice directly, and positively, affects the firm's profitability and economic logic. However, logistical tactics that prove efficient at one firm often show up at rival firms through consultants or as a result of outsourcing. Thus, performing the same activities better than rivals usually results in a temporary advantage. Alternatively, configuring value-chain activities in different ways than competitors makes it harder for rivals to imitate those activities. This is due to what is known as *tradeoff protection*.

TRADEOFF PROTECTION

By organizing their value-chain activities in unique and specific ways, firms may be able to make imitation quite difficult. Gaining advantage through value-chain configuration usually involves a rather complex system of activities. When a firm reconfigures the value chain, it exercises some tradeoffs. By adding or dropping certain activities, it may necessitate the elimination or addition of other activities. Rivals find it very difficult and costly to imitate a system of interdependent activities because they have made some investments in their system of activities that may be irreversible. For example, in early competitive battles between global tractor makers Caterpillar and newcomer Komatsu, Komatsu invested in the development of tractors that required little service and easy maintenance. In contrast, industry incumbent Caterpillar made big profits in parts and service for its tractors, so was very hesitant to invest in making more reliable tractors (hence less need for parts and repairs). Generally, as shown with Caterpillar and Komatsu, companies won't imitate activities if doing so would mean abandoning one or more activities that are essential to their own strategies.[35] In other words, they'll balk at the tradeoff.

To further illustrate this point, let's consider some differences between the value-chain activities of Southwest Airlines and those of most other major U.S. airlines, which are summarized in Exhibits 3.8 and 3.9.[36] Despite the fact that other low-cost carriers have emerged,

	Southwest	Major Airlines
Technology and design	• Single aircraft	• Multiple types of aircraft
Operations	• Short-segment flights • No meals • No seat assignments • Single class of service • No baggage transfers to other airlines • Smaller markets and secondary airports in major markets	• Hub-and-spoke system • Meals • Seat assignments • Multiple classes of service • Baggage transfers to other airlines
Marketing	• Limited use of travel agents • Word of mouth	• Extensive use of travel agents

Exhibit 3.8 Key Value-Chain Activities in the U.S. Airline Industry

Exhibit 3.9 Comparative Revenues and Costs for U.S. Airlines

	2006 Revenue ($ millions)	2006 Cost of Available Seat Miles	2006 Revenue per Available Seat Miles	Difference
Low-Cost Carriers				
AirTran	1,893.40	9.80	12.9	3.10
ATA	1,160.00	9.36	13.1	3.74
Frontier	994.30	10.78	11.7	0.92
JetBlue	2,363.00	7.54	9.7	2.16
Southwest	9,086.00	8.50	12.4	3.90
Sector Average		9.40	11.8	
Major Carriers				
Alaska	3,334.40	11.70	13.9	2.20
American	22,563.00	12.50	12.8	0.30
Continental	13,128.00	13.30	12.2	−1.10
Delta	17,171.00	13.62	11.8	−1.82
Northwest	12,286.00	14.28	13.1	−1.18
United	19,340.00	13.06	12.2	−0.86
US Airways	7,117.00	15.36	13.2	−2.16
Sector Average		13.32	12.5	

Transportation Workers Union, TWU Airline Industry Review, *at www.twuatd.org; Bureau of Transportation,* TransStats Reports, *at www.transtats.bts.gov.*

Southwest has achieved unrivaled cost advantages among large airlines by radically pruning the number of activities that it performs and by undertaking others in nontraditional ways. Consequently, the configuration of its value chain is fundamentally different from those of most other airlines. Southwest, for example, uses only one type of aircraft—a strategy that reduces maintenance and training costs. In addition, the chosen aircraft is efficient for the kind of shorter flights that comprise most of Southwest's schedule. Southwest has also cut many of the services normally provided by major carriers (such as baggage transfers, meals, and assigned seats).

As a result of its unique configuration of activities, Southwest operates at a significantly lower cost than its competitors. We can confirm this conclusion by taking a look at a factor known as *CASM* (cost of available seat miles), which is a common measure of costs in the airline industry. As you can see in Exhibit 3.9, Southwest's CASM is significantly lower than that of every major competitor. Moreover, Southwest is generating greater revenue per seat mile, suggesting that many of the major airlines are trying to compete with it by lowering their prices. Why don't other major airlines imitate Southwest's value chain? Primarily because doing so would mean ceasing certain activities that are fundamental to their operations. Although many airlines have stopped serving meals to save costs, they can't stop transferring luggage, abandon the hub-and-spoke system, or convert exclusively to Boeing 737s. So many tradeoffs would mean changing their business model completely. Thus, Southwest has protected its advantage by configuring its value-chain activities in such a way that imitating them is not attractive to competitors.

Further analysis of Exhibit 3.9 reveals another important insight. The airline with the lowest CASM is actually JetBlue. This recent startup has been able to imitate much of Southwest's value chain and then make a few modifications that have further lowered costs (e.g., newer, more fuel-efficient planes, low-cost labor). This illustrates that although it may be very difficult for an established competitor to imitate the successful value-chain configuration of a leading company, a new entrant has much more flexibility to do so. A new firm that hasn't already made irreversible commitments to another value-chain configuration may be in a better position to imitate a successful value-chain configuration and even make improvements upon that model.

Innovation and Integration in the Value Chain   IKEA, the Swedish furniture company, has built a hugely successful business by almost completely reconfiguring the value-chain activities of the furniture industry by transferring delivery and assembly to the customer. IKEA's stores double as warehouses. The furniture is shipped in flat-packed boxes. Customers shop among display models, but then take the unassembled furniture off the shelves and assemble it at home. This significantly lowers the costs of production and distribution.

Similarly, Dell's success is based on an innovative reconfiguration of sales, distribution, and customer-service activities in the personal-computer industry that exploits the growing base of knowledgeable PC consumers around the world. Dell PCs use components manufactured entirely by suppliers. In addition, its distribution and marketing operations rest on a direct-sales model that avoids retailers. This combination of strategies—outsourcing component manufacturing and distributing finished products directly—was a radical departure from the business models that prevailed in the industry.

Many competitors have tried to imitate this model, but at Dell the model supports—and is integrally linked to—a *chain* of value-adding activities. Large, established PC firms have never been able to duplicate Dell's cost structure because they haven't been willing or able to make all of the tradeoffs that would be necessary to imitate its value-chain activities.

The message in each of these examples is pretty much the same: The key to the value-chain approach to competitive advantage is not only developing value-chain activities that differ from those of rivals but also configuring them so that they're integrally related and can't be imitated without significant tradeoffs. *Value-chain fit* is important, Michael Porter reminds us, because it locks out imitators by "creating a chain of activities that is as strong as its strongest link."[37] By this we mean that strong links have positive spillover effects into the costs and benefits of other activities. For instance, Southwest's use of one type of jet, gives it greater flexibility with pilots, more reliable maintenance by ground crews, and faster turnarounds (and thus happier customers) at airport gates.

SEEKING CLUES TO VALUE CHAIN ADVANTAGES THROUGH FINANCIAL ANALYSIS

How might you intuit, at least in a rough way, if a firm is exploiting value chain advantage or particular resources or capabilities to create competitive advantage? Remembering that firms compete based on lower costs, an ability to gain higher prices for comparable products, or a combination of both, one tool you can use is the basic DUPONT financial analysis. You may have encountered this analytical tool in an accounting or finance course, and it is a very useful strategic analysis tool as well. The DuPont formula helps you break down determinants of a firm's profitability based on the equation where ROA = Net Profit Margin × Asset Turnover. A more detailed version of the basic formula is presented in Exhibit 3.10, and applied in "How Would *You* Do That? 3.1".

Beyond the math part, what does the formula tell you? The DuPont formula integrates the income statement and balance sheet to show how a firm's return on assets can be disaggregated into two components—asset turnover and profit margins. Asset turnover measures the firm's efficiency at generating revenues from its assets, while profit margin measures the firm's ability to garner higher prices to generate the revenues.

Exhibit 3.10 DuPont Analysis Formula

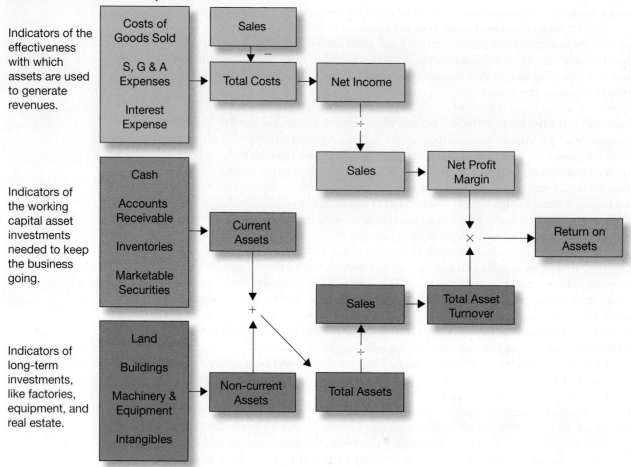

Indicators of the effectiveness with which assets are used to generate revenues.

Indicators of the working capital asset investments needed to keep the business going.

Indicators of long-term investments, like factories, equipment, and real estate.

OUTSOURCING, OFFSHORING, AND THE VALUE CHAIN

Given that strategy is about making tradeoffs, one of the most fundamental tradeoffs managers make today is whether to outsource a historically integral value-chain activity. **Outsourcing** is simply sourcing the function, product, or service of a value chain activity from another company. **Offshoring** is taking that activity from a high-cost country to a low-cost country. We often commingle the two concepts of outsourcing and offshoring but a firm can do the former, the latter, or both. Indeed, value chain analysis gives you an opportunity to identify activities and capabilities the firm must possess itself, and those that can be performed outside of the firm. Referring back to IKEA, one of IKEA's innovations was to outsource furniture assembly to the end consumer, and 70% of the inputs into Boeing's new Dreamliner are outsourced to its commercial airframe partners.

Outsourcing and offshoring are not new; it is just that they have become so prevalent, and sometimes contentious, especially when it involves the loss of domestic jobs, that they may seem relatively new. Part of this prevalence is due to the broad number of choices managers have in terms of outsourcing and offshoring; they are able to outsource or offshore nearly any activity that they please. Although outsourcing or offshoring a value-chain activity may be feasible and lower a firm's direct costs and overhead, based on what you have learned about the resource and capability perspective, you should know that caution must be exercised. For instance, if a firm outsources its marketing or distribution function, it may lose access to the knowledge of customer preferences that inspired its early product breakthroughs in the first place. This perhaps explains why brand leaders such as Nike and Pacific Cycle (Schwinn brand) have outsourced functions such as manufacturing to low-cost countries (hence, offshoring that activity) and have instead focused their efforts on activities surrounding product development, logistics, brand management, and customer retention and expansion.

While outsourcing and offshoring remain as much an art as it is a science, they are an integral part of your strategy toolkit. What functions do you outsource? Offshore? Again, there is no perfect recipe but your strategy, and the VRINE-based value chain analysis should be a good starting point in answering that question. A firm may be better served by improving technologies or shaking up existing operations, instead of outsourcing the broken parts to lower-cost overseas locales. If you give the green light to outsourcing certain activities, then you will need to decide if you run it yourself in a cheaper offshore location (offshoring) or contract for the service from an outside provider. Again, outsourcing does not always mean the latter. For instance, Boeing Co. opened its own center in Moscow, where it employs 1,100 skilled but relatively low-

Southwest Airlines founder and former CEO Herb Kelleher created a value chain for his company unlike that of any of his competitors. Using a low-fare, no-frills, no-reserved seating approach, Southwest has managed to earn a profit for 30 years straight—an astonishing feat in the airlines industry.

cost aerospace engineers on a range of projects, including the design of titanium parts for the new 787 Dreamliner jet. Likewise, Chicago-based law firm Baker & McKenzie has its own English-speaking team in Manila that drafts documents and does market research.

Whether value chain activities are outsourced or kept internally but sent offshore, three criteria appear to be common among successful outsourcing and offshoring arrangements:

Commit Time and Effort   Firms typically choose outsourcing and/or offshoring to lower their costs. However, such cost reductions are typically a one-time event. Beyond the first year, the firm must be committed to invest in quality control and training to keep the outsourced or offshored activity competitive and efficient.

Treat Outsourcing Partners as Partners   Many outsourced operations, in particular, are run by a third party. So, whereas the function was historically internally managed, the firm now contracts for that function with an external supplier. There is a temptation to treat such suppliers as order-takers, instead of taking advantage of the relationship to learn new things about product and process innovations.

Involve Middle Management   As you will learn from the following section, middle managers are the life-blood of strategy execution. Outsourcing and offshoring are undertaken to improve competitiveness in a function or set of functions, and not because the function is unimportant. For example, aerospace engineering is very important to Boeing and any other airplane manufacturer. However, the offshoring arrangement in Moscow gives Boeing access to a greater quantity of engineering expertise and at a lower cost than it could manage domestically. Middle managers play the role of bridging the offshored activities with the internal ones, and putting additional outsourcing arrangements into place as opportunities arise.

Applying DuPont Analysis to Understand Competitive Advantage in Retailing

Let's see if we can apply the DuPont tool to some "big box" retailers—Wal-Mart, Sears, and Kohl's—to better understand where they might be gaining their competitive advantage. We start by going to their company websites, or sites like Yahoo finance or Hoover's that provide balance sheet and income statement information on public firms.

In Exhibit 3.11, notice how straightforward the information-gathering is. We simply put together a small grid, and transferred a few pieces of financial information for each company. Since we were already gathering data, we decided to look at each firm's total equity as well—and we will show you how this small piece of information can add further depth to your DuPont toolkit. Also, we picked a single recent year for the data, but you

could take an average of several years, if you like. The important thing is that you have chosen a time period where you think that the differences across firms are fairly reflective of what they might be doing in the future.

When we look at the information in Exhibit 3.11, we can see that Wal-Mart is the largest firm of the three, in terms of assets and sales. They also have the greatest amount of profits. The problem, though, is that this information does not tell us much about how efficiently or effectively each firm is managing its sales or assets. For example, Wal-Mart has sales that are 23 times greater than those of Kohl's, but only 12 times greater profit. And even though Wal-Mart is so much bigger than Kohl's, it looks like Kohl's is much more profitable in terms of the returns it generates for a given asset

base. The DuPont analysis will help us understand the source of these differences.

With the data you have compiled in Exhibit 3.11, you can calculate the pieces of the DuPont formula. For instance, net profit margin is simply net profits divided by total sales, and so on. With this analysis in hand, we are now able to better understand the underlying determinants of these firms' performance. That is, you can explain why Kohl's has a higher return on assets than does Wal-Mart, despite the obvious size differences. This information, in turn, should provide you with clues as to the resources, capabilities, and value chain choices that might be part and parcel to each firm's strategy.

For instance, DuPont analysis shows that Kohl's has a very high net

Exhibit 3.11
Comparative Financial Information

Company	Total Assets ($ millions)	Total Sales ($ millions)	Net Profit ($ millions)	Total Equity ($ millions)
Wal-Mart	94,685	244,524	8,039	39,337
Sears	50,409	41,366	1,584	6,753
Kohl's	6,315	9,120	643	3,511

profit margin—7.1%, or $7.10 for every $100 of sales—relative to the others. This means that it is able to sell products for higher prices than competitors, or manage a higher priced mix of products. This suggests that one of Kohls' differentiators, in terms of the strategy diamond, might be the ability to merchandise higher-margin products. In contrast, you probably know that Wal-Mart competes with its low prices, so that it is willing to make a tradeoff between greater sales and lower relative margins. Thus, even though Kohl's and Wal-Mart are both "discount" retailers, each is using a somewhat different set of differentiators to arrive at net profits. You can further see this with asset turns, where Wal-Mart has nearly twice the asset turns as Kohl's. This difference means that Wal-Mart is very efficient with its assets, and for every $1 in assets it is generating $2.60 in sales. Indeed, Wal-Mart has made a set of very unique choices in terms of how it manages its value chain, and through DuPont analysis we can see where it is clearly the low cost leader. And what about Sears? Well, it looks like Sears is stuck in the middle—net profit margins are ok, but asset turns

are horrible.[38] The combination leaves Sears with the lowest relative ROA of the three.

Finally, recall that we jotted down total equity since we were collecting financial data on our sample of discount retailers. If you divide total assets by total equity, you arrive at an equity multiplier—in other words, for every $1 of equity, this is the dollar amount of assets it supports. You will be interested to know that you can multiply ROA by this number to arrive at a firm's return on equity, or ROE. This is called the Extended DuPont Analysis (Exhibit 3.12). Higher equity multipliers mean that a firm is using a greater amount of debt to finance its productive assets.

This can tell you that the firm's management has a greater appetite for debt, and risk, and is perhaps good at managing this type of risk. Conversely, you know that debt requires fixed payments of principle and interest. If these payments are not made, the firm can be forced into bankruptcy. Therefore, extremely high levels of debt (and a correspondingly high equity multiplier) represent poor capital structure management. Only by comparing one firm's multiplier against

others in its industry, as well as its own cash flow, can you judge whether such debt is excessive.

As with all financial analysis, you should remember that the DuPont formula only provides a snapshot of what a firm is doing. Ratios can vary from year to year as well as by industry, so it is important to calculate them across several years for each firm and compare them to other firms in the industry or industry averages to get a sense of their consistency and trends. Also, if you have applied the VRINE tool and concluded that a firm has resources and capabilities that are valuable, rare, and difficult to imitate, but the firm still is performing worse than its competitors, then you may conclude that the *exploitability* dimension is the problem. Again, the DuPont framework is a useful starting point in determining the degree to which the firm has advantages based on identifiable resources and capabilities. It also provides some indication of where the firm's resources and capabilities might be found, and can therefore help you to evaluate differentiators and their alignment with internal and external arenas.

Exhibit 3.12 Extended DuPont Analysis

Company	Net Profit Margin	×	Total Asset Turn	=	ROA	×	Equity Multiplier	=	ROE
Wal-Mart	3.3%		2.6		8.5%		241.1%		20.4%
Sears	3.8%		0.8		3.1%		175.4%		23.5%
Kohl's	7.1%		1.4		10.2%		179.4%		18.3%

Strategic Leadership: Linking Resources and Capabilities to Strategy

The opening vignette in this chapter notes the central role of leaders in managing a firm's resources and capabilities. It is important to not lose sight of the fact that it is a firm's managers who scan its external and internal environments and consequently decide how to use resources and capabilities and how to configure value-chain activities based on their assessment of those sometimes rapidly changing environments. Indeed, the role of managers is so critical that some experts include managerial human capital among a firm's resources; others include management among a company's dynamic capabilities.[39] A recent McKinsey consulting report concluded that "companies that overlook the role of leadership in the early phases of strategic planning often find themselves scrambling when it's time to execute. No matter how thorough the plan, without the right leaders it is unlikely to succeed."[40] To incorporate these views, we regard managers as *decision agents*—the people who put into motion the processes that use the firm's resources and capabilities.

SENIOR MANAGERS

In addition to deciding how to use resources and capabilities and configuring a firm's value-chain activities, senior managers also set the context that determines how frontline and middle managers can add value. Recall from the opening vignette that senior managers did not change Intel's strategy from memory chips to microprocessors—at least not until frontline managers made that change a *fait accompli*.

Strategy research has shown that senior managers in the most effective firms around the globe view their organizations as portfolios of processes—specifically, entrepreneurial, capability-building, and renewal processes—and key people, such as those who comprise the firm's middle and frontline managerial ranks.[41] Collectively, these processes may be seen as part of a firm's culture.

The *entrepreneurial process* encourages middle managers to be externally oriented—to seek out opportunities and run their part of the business as if they owned it. Senior managers who foster this process are stepping back from the notion that they are the sole visionaries and saviors of the company and instead seek to share this responsibility with the managers on the front lines. The *capability-building process* also looks to middle managers to identify, grow, and protect new ways to create value for the organization and its key stakeholders. In many ways, this process is the internal side of the externally oriented entrepreneurial process. Finally, the *renewal process* is senior managers' way of shaking up the firm and challenging its historic ways of operating; however, this process is based on information learned through current business activities performed elsewhere in the firm.

We can see all three of these processes taking place in the opening vignette about Intel. Senior management implemented processes and a culture that encouraged entrepreneurial activities. Similarly, middle management helped the firm to develop new capabilities to capitalize on the microprocessor opportunity. Finally, senior management stepped in to validate this major change in strategy, based on upgraded organizational resources and capabilities related to logic-device architecture. The only piece missing from the opening case is the role played by senior management in the selection, retention, and promotion of middle and frontline managers.

Of course, not all senior managers are equipped equally to act effectively. Obviously, basic managerial talent isn't bestowed equally on all managers, even if they have risen to the highest levels in the organization. Moreover, specific experiences and backgrounds will make some managers better qualified to work with a specific bundle of resources. Researchers have discovered, for instance, that multinational firms (those with operations in several countries) achieve higher levels of performance when their CEOs have had some experience in foreign operations.[42] In addition, entrepreneurial operations must often rely on few or no valuable or rare resources. Managers of these enterprises generally start with ideas and goals and not much more. In such situations, the positive influence of managers is even more important.[43] Likewise, in firms facing financial or competitive turmoil, the galvanizing and enabling effects of superior senior management are also more pronounced.

MIDDLE MANAGERS

From the discussion on senior managers, you should be able to see that middle managers play a key role in what the firm is doing and what it may be adept at doing in the future. The entrepreneurial, capability-building, and renewal processes all require the involvement, choices, and actions of middle and frontline managers. Executives must consider their leadership pool as they shape strategy and align their leadership-development programs with long-term aspirations. Particularly in large firms, the effect of senior executives on firm performance is a function of the choices they have made about the context in which frontline managers work and the appointment of particular managers themselves.

Strategic leadership researcher Quy Nguyen Huy has identified four areas where middle managers are better positioned to contribute to competitive advantage and corporate success than are senior executives:[44]

- **Entrepreneur.** Middle managers are close enough to the front lines to spot fires, yet far enough away to understand the bigger picture. Because middle management ranks are typically more diverse in terms of ethnicity, gender, experience, and geography, this group has the potential to contribute richer ideas than the senior management team.

- **Communicator.** Middle managers are typically long tenured and have very broad social networks. This gives them great credibility with employees, and they are therefore better able to move change initiatives in nonthreatening ways. Their tenure also gives them deep knowledge about how to get things done in the organization.

- **Psychoanalyst.** Internal credibility also enables middle managers to be more effective in quelling alienation and chaos, as seen by high productivity among anxious employees during times of great change. Because they know their troops, frontline managers also know when and how to provide one-on-one support and problem solving.

- **Tightrope walker.** Particularly in the case of dynamic capabilities and dynamic environments, firms are faced with the need to balance continuity and radical change. Middle managers are well poised to accomplish this balancing act. With the right process in place courtesy of senior executives, middle managers can help the firm avoid inertia and too little change or slow change and also avoid the paralyzing chaos accompanying too much change too quickly.

In many ways, it's the central role of upper and middle management that distinguishes the internal perspective on strategy from the external perspective that we'll discuss in Chapter 4. After all, if competitive advantage results from the different characteristics of firms, then the key task in the role of management is to identify resources and capabilities, specify the resources that will create competitive advantage, locate an attractive industry in which to deploy them, and then select the strategy to get the most out of them. Finally, it's the job of managers to choose *when* to change a firm's mix of resources, capabilities, and targeted markets. As you learned in Chapter 2, the managements of smaller firms typically differ from those of larger firms in terms of their overall number, not the roles that they play. This means that in smaller firms, senior leaders—often the owners or company founders—may wear many, if not all, of the middle and frontline manager hats described.

Summary of Challenges

1. *Explain the internal context of strategy.* Firms facing similar industry conditions achieve different levels of competitive advantage and performance based on their internal characteristics and managerial choices. Although firms must always take the external context into account when formulating and implementing strategy, the internal perspectives stress the differences among firms in terms of the unique resources and capabilities that they own or control. These perspectives offer important models and analytical tools that will help you to analyze and formulate competitive strategies.

2. *Identify a firm's resources and capabilities and explain their role in its performance.* Resources are either tangible or intangible. Resources and capabilities that help firms establish a competitive advantage and secure higher levels of performance are those that are valuable, rare, and costly to imitate. The VRINE model helps you analyze resources and capabilities. A resource or capability is said to be valuable if it enables the firm to exploit opportunities or negate threats in the environment. In addition, the firm must have complementary organizational capabilities to exploit resources and capabilities that meet these three conditions. Rare resources enable firms to exploit opportunities or negate threats in ways that those lacking the resource cannot. Competitors will try to find ways to imitate valuable and rare resources; a firm can generate an enduring competitive advantage if competitors face a *cost disadvantage* in acquiring or substituting the resource that is lacking. Unique historical conditions that have led to resource or capability development, time-compression diseconomies, and causal ambiguity all make imitation more difficult. Firms often use alliances, acquisitions, and substitution with less costly resources as mechanisms to gain access to difficult-to-imitate resources.

3. *Define* dynamic capabilities *and explain their role in both strategic change and a firm's performance.* The process of development, accumulation, and possible loss of resources and capabilities is inherently dynamic. The resource-accumulation process and dynamic capabilities are fundamentally different from the static pos-

session of a stock of resources and capabilities. Dynamic capabilities are processes that integrate, reconfigure, acquire, or divest resources in order to use the firms' stocks of resources and capabilities in new ways. The ability to adapt to changing conditions or to proactively initiate a change in the competitive environment is particularly important in industries in which time-to-market is critical, technological change is rapid, and future competition is difficult to forecast.

4. *Explain how value-chain activities are related to firm performance and competitive advantage.* Firms produce products or offer services by engaging in many activities. The basic structure of firm activities is illustrated by the firm's value chain. The value chain is divided into primary and support activities. One way a company can outperform rivals is to find ways to perform some value-chain activities better than its rivals or to find different ways to perform the activities altogether. Selective outsourcing of some value-chain activities is one way to perform activities differently. Competitive advantage through strategic configuration of value-chain activities only comes about if the firm can either deliver greater value than rivals or deliver comparable value at lower cost. The essence of the activity-based value-chain perspective of competitive advantage is to choose value-chain activities that are different from those of rivals and to configure these activities in a way that are internally consistent and that requires significant tradeoffs should a competitor want to imitate them.

5. *Explain the role of managers with respect to resources, capabilities, and value-chain activities.* Managers make decisions about how to employ resources in the formulation and implementation of strategy. Managers are the decision agents who put into motion the use of all other firm resources and capabilities; they are key to the success of a firm's strategy. Managers with specific experiences and backgrounds may be more qualified to work with a specific bundle of resources owned by a firm. The influence of managers is more pronounced in contexts such as entrepreneurial phases, turnarounds, and competitive turmoil.

Review Questions

1. What are resources? How do different types of resources differ?

2. What is a capability?

3. What are the five components of the VRINE model?

4. How do time and causal ambiguity relate to the value, rarity, and inimitability of a resource or capability?

5. What is the difference between a stock of resources and capabilities and a flow of resources and capabilities?

6. What are dynamic capabilities? How do they differ from general capabilities?

7. What is a firm's value chain? How does it figure into a firm's competitive advantage?

8. What is your role as a manager in linking resources and capabilities to strategy and competitive advantage?

Experiential Activities

Group Exercises

1. What is the role of luck in gaining possession of a particular resource or capability? Can a firm manage luck? Give an example of a resource or capability that a firm garnered through luck and determine whether it was subsequently well-managed.

2. Some firms' products are so well known that the entire category of products offered in the industry (including rivals' products) is often referred to by the leading firm's brand name (which is called an *eponym*). Identify one such product and discuss whether its brand recognition gives the leading firm a competitive advantage. Why or why not?

Ethical Debates

1. Companies are increasingly looking to India for outsourced IT and knowledge work. To attract and accommodate an even greater influx of foreign firms, the government has given a contract to Reliance, a local company, to turn a vast area of farmland near Mumbai into a new high-tech city. And, in the process, the government has given Reliant essentially the powers of eminent domain and the power to evict farmers whose families have worked the land for generations. Does this pose a problem for foreign firms looking to India for outsourcing opportunities?

2. What are some of the ethical issues that seem to accompany discussions of outsourcing or offshoring? What tradeoffs might a management team be weighing with a particular outsourcing or offshoring option?

How Would YOU DO THAT?

1. In the box entitled "How Would *You* Do That? 3.1," we walked through how to apply the DuPont analysis to better understand the value chain choices, and possibly resources and capabilities, that support a firm's strategy. Pick two competing firms, and develop a DuPont analysis on both of them. What conclusions do you draw from this analysis and comparison?

2. Based on your analysis, are there activities that this organization performs differently than its rival? Start by looking at the firm's products, services, or target markets. Do any of the rival firm's value-chain activities give them a competitive advantage? If so, why don't others imitate these activities? What resources and capabilities does your focal organization possess? What are the resources and capabilities possessed by the rival? How do your focal organization's resources and capabilities fare relative to those of the rivals' when you apply the VRINE model to them?

Go on to see How Would You Do That at www.prenhall.com/ carpenter&sanders

Endnotes

1. J. Haleblian and S. Finkelstein, "The Influence of Organizational Acquisition Experience on Acquisition Performance: A Behavioral Learning Perspective," *Administrative Science Quarterly* 44:1 (1999), 29–56; F. Vermeulen and H. Barkema, "Learning Through Acquisitions," *Academy of Management Journal* 44:3 (2001), 457–476.

2. D. J. Teece, G. Pisano, and A. Shuen, "Dynamic Capabilities and Strategic Management," *Strategic Management Journal* 18 (1997), 509–529.

3. R. R. Nelson and S. G. Winter, *An Evolutionary Theory of Economic Change* (Cambridge, MA: Belknap Press of Harvard University Press, 1982).

4. G. Stalk, P. Evans, and L. E. Shulman, "Competing on Capabilities: The New Rules of Corporate Strategy," *Harvard Business Review* 70:2 (1992), 54–65; R. Makadok, "Doing the Right Thing and Knowing the Right Thing to Do: Why the Whole Is Greater Than the Sum of the Parts," *Strategic Management Journal* 24:10 (2003), 1043–1054.

5. english.pravda.ru/usa/2001/11/03/20045.html and www.restaurantreport.com/qa/location.html (accessed June 28, 2005).

6. This framework is consistent with the larger literature on the resource-based view of the firm. For another helpful discussion, see J. B. Barney, "Looking Inside for Competitive Advantage," *Academy of Management Executive* 9:4 (1995), 49–61.

7. J. B. Barney, "Firm Resources and Sustained Competitive Advantage," *Journal of Management* 17:1 (1991), 99–120.

8. Union Pacific, "System Map" (accessed August 4, 2005), at www.uprr.com/aboutup/maps/sysmap/index.shtml.

9. Barney, "Firm Resources and Sustained Competitive Advantage."

10. C. K. Prahalad and G. Hamel, "The Core Competence of the Corporation," *Harvard Business Review* 68:3 (1990), 79–92.

11. L. Capron and W. Mitchell, "The Role of Acquisitions in Reshaping Business Capabilities in the International Telecommunications Industry," *Industrial and Corporate Change* 7:4 (1998), 715–730.

12. P. R. Haunschild, "How Much Is That Company Worth? Interorganizational Relationships, Uncertainty, and Acquisition Premiums," *Administrative Science Quarterly* 39:3 (1994), 391–414.

13. B. Labaris, "Has Your Vendor Gone Buyout Crazy?" *Computerworld* 33:36 (1999), 34–35.

14. J. B. Barney, "Looking Inside for Competitive Advantage," *Academy of Management Executive* 9:4 (1995), 49–61; I. Dierickx and K. Cool, "Asset Stock Accumulation and Sustainability of Competitive Advantage," *Management Science* 35:12 (1989), 1504–1511.

15. M. Pendergrast, *For God, Country and Coca-Cola* (New York: Basic Books, 1993).

16. Coca-Cola, *2006 Annual Report*; PepsiCo, *2006 Annual Report*.

17. Dierickx and Cool, "Asset Stock Accumulation and Sustainability of Competitive Advantage."

18. Dierickx and Cool, "Asset Stock Accumulation and Sustainability of Competitive Advantage."

19. Nelson and Winter, *An Evolutionary Theory of Economic Change.*

20. Barney, "Looking Inside for Competitive Advantage"; Dierickx and Cool, "Asset Stock Accumulation and Sustainability of Competitive Advantage."

21. Author's personal communication with Margaret Haddox, Novell Corporate Librarian, October 2003.

22. Author's personal communication with former Novell executives, September 2003.

23. D. T. Kearns and D. A. Nadler, *Prophets in the Dark* (New York: HarperCollins, 1992); Barney, "Looking Inside for Competitive Advantage."

24. "Could Cymbalta Bring Cheer for Lilly?" *IMS Health.com*, August 23, 2004 (accessed August 4, 2005), at open.imshealth.com; C. Baysden, "Report: Blockbuster Drug Marketing Costs Average $239M," *Triangle Business Journal*, February 24, 2005 (accessed August 4, 2005), at triangle.bizjournals.com; "Medication for Depression: Antidepressant Medications," *Psychology Information Online* (accessed August 4, 2005), at www.psychologyinfo.com.

25. Eisenhardt and Martin, "Dynamic Capabilities."

26. Eisenhardt and Martin, "Dynamic Capabilities."

27. B. Orwall, "In Disney Row, an Aging Heir Who's Won Boardroom Bouts," *Wall Street Journal*, December 5, 2003, A1.

28. G. Szulanski and R. J. Jensen, "Overcoming Stickiness: An Empirical Investigation of the Role of the Template," *Managerial Decision Economics*, 25: 6–7 (2004:) 347–363.

29. Eisenhardt and Martin, "Dynamic Capabilities."

30. Teece, Pisano, and Shuen, "Dynamic Capabilities and Strategic Management."

31. C. Christensen, *The Innovator's Dilemma* (New York: Harper Business Press, 1997).

32. R. Burgelman, "Fading Memories: A Process Theory of Strategic Business Exit in Dynamic Environments," *Administrative Science Quarterly* 39:1 (1994), 24–56.

33. M. E. Porter, "What Is Strategy?" *Harvard Business Review* 74:6 (1996), 61–78.

34. The generic value chain model was developed by M. E. Porter, *Competitive Advantage: Creating and Sustaining Superior Performance* (New York: The Free Press, 1985), p. 47.

35. Porter, "What Is Strategy?"

36. Transportation Workers Union, TWU Airline Industry Review, at www.twuatd.org; Bureau of Transportation, *TransStats Reports*, at www.transtats.bts.gov.

37. Porter, "What Is Strategy?"

38. Sears' and Kohls' asset turns and return on assets are much more similar when you capitalize Kohls' leases as part of its asset figure, though Kohl's still outperforms Sears after this adjustment.

39. Barney, "Firm Resources and Sustained Competitive Advantage."

40. T. Hseih and S. Yik, "Leadership as the Starting Point of Strategy," *McKinsey Quarterly* 1 (2005), 11–26.

41. S. Ghoshal and C. A. Bartlett, "Changing the Role of Top Management: Beyond Structure to Processes," *Harvard Business Review* 73:3 (1995), 86–96; C. A. Bartlett and S. Ghoshal, "Changing the Role of Top Management: Beyond Systems to People," *Harvard Business Review* 73:3 (1995), 132–134.

42. M. A. Carpenter, W. Sanders, and H. Garegersen, "Bundling Human Capital with Organizational Context: The Impact of International Assignment Experience on Multinational Firm Performance and CEO Pay," *Academy of Management Journal* 44:3 (2001), 493–512.

43. M. A. Carpenter, T. G. Pollock, and M. M. Leary, "Testing a Model of Reasoned Risk-Taking: Governance, the Experience of Principals and Agents, and Global Strategy in High-Technology IPO Firms," *Strategic Management Journal* 24:9 (2003), 803–820.

44. Q. Huy, "In Praise of Middle Managers," *Harvard Business Review* 79:8 (2001), 72–79.

Exploring the External Environment

Macro and Industry Dynamics

In This Chapter We Challenge You To >>>

1. Explain the importance of the external context for strategy and firm performance.

2. Use PESTEL to identify the macro characteristics of the external context.

3. Identify the major features of an industry and the forces that affect industry profitability.

4. Understand the dynamic characteristics of the external context.

5. Show how industry dynamics may redefine industries.

A Chronicle
of the Cola War

Coca Cola sells a billion servings—in cans, bottles, and glasses—every day. You can grab a Coke in almost 200 countries. Its archrival, Pepsi, isn't too far behind. Like Ford versus Chevy, theirs is a battle not just for customer dollars, but for their hearts and minds as well.

—The History Channel, "Empires of Industry: Cola Wars"

As the environment changes, companies are forced to change as well. Often, the change is challenging. PepsiCo, for example, saw its sales drop from $31 billion in 1999 to $25 billion in 2002. Pepsi's leaders needed to transform the company to meet the new industry realities. As Indra Nooyi, Pepsi's President and CEO said, "In a perfect world, I'd be able to tell you we executed this restructuring flawlessly. Naturally, that's not the case. The process was neither smooth nor seamless. Many times it felt like baptism by fire."

For generations, the soft drink industry has been one of the most profitable industries. Experts estimate that gross margins in soft drink concentrate are approximately 83 percent and net margins about 35 percent. Coke had long been the dominant player while Pepsi fought hard to win market share. The "Cola Wars" between the two giants defined the industry, as we'll see in more detail below. But as the two companies battled intently with each other, the battleground around them was changing.

"Some dark clouds moved in," Nooyi recalls. "After years of investing aggressively, too aggressively in retrospect, our international beverage businesses suffered dramatic losses." During the battle, Pepsi had also entered the restaurant business—buying Taco Bell, Pizza Hut, and KFC—to block Coke from further gains in the fountain market. Coke dominated the fountain market with a strategic partnership with McDonalds, which accounted for 75–100 million gallons of Coke sold each year in the U.S. alone. Pepsi bought the three chains to ensure that those restaurants sold only Pepsi products.

Although buying the restaurants seemed a good strategic move, it brought Pepsi into an unfamiliar industry, and the venture started sapping Pepsi's profits. Nooyi and her colleagues realized that the restaurant business had to go. As Nooyi's then-boss Roger Enrico explained, "The central part of her proposition was that we weren't retailers ourselves, and we didn't have the expertise to run them the way they could and should be run." Nooyi therefore created a new company, Yum Brands, that consisted of the three restaurant chains, and sold it off. "You have to think of a business like any investment. You have to know when to get in, but more important, when to get out. Getting out can be a lot tougher, especially if you develop an emotional tie to the business. But the world changes, and so should the models we apply to our businesses."

The core carbonated soft drinks business started changing, too. Both Coke and Pepsi face challenges as consumers become more health conscious and start to substitute juice and water for soda. In order to appeal to investors and stay relevant, Coca-Cola's Chairman-CEO Neville Isdell switched from using the word "carbonated" to using the term "sparkling," and using the word "still" in place of "noncarbonated." "Sparkling beverages," he said, "are what we simply define as nonalcoholic, ready-to-drink consumer beverages with carbonation." Coke's press releases have been changed so say that Coke "markets four of the world's top five nonalcoholic sparkling brands." Industry expert Gary Hemphill, managing director of the Beverage Marketing Group, sees the change in nomenclature as a shift: "It signals a changing marketplace," he said. "'Sparkling' spans multiple categories like carbonated soft drinks, energy drinks, sparkling water, and sparkling juice; whereas the term 'carbonated' is mostly associated solely with carbonated soft drinks." In fact, Pepsi recently acquired Izze Beverage, known for its all-natural, sparkling fruit juices, and both Coke and Pepsi have begun marketing some sodas as sparkling, including Coke's Fresca and Enviga and Pepsi's Tava.

In another move to stay relevant, Pepsi's Nooyi is shifting Pepsi's strategy to address health issues. Born in India, Nooyi understands the concerns over nutrition, and she has promised that at least half of all new Pepsi products will now be comprised of "essentially healthy" ingredients or offer "improved health benefits". Under her new strategy, Pepsi's North American drinks business is now led by noncarbonated, "healthier" options: waters, "enhanced" waters, and teas and energy drinks, which all show double-digit growth. PepsiCo's Aquafina brand is the number-one bottled water in the U.S. and has so-called functional variants that include B-Power, Calcium+, Daily C, and Multi-V in 20-ounce bottles.

Despite the new strategy, Nooyi is aware that strategic wins are a moving target. "The minute you've developed a new business model, it's extinct, because somebody is going to copy it," she said.

And indeed, in classic cola-war fashion, Coke vowed to invest an additional $400 million annually in 2005 on innovation and is trademarking a fortified fruit drink and energy-enhanced diet drink.

Let's take a look at the history of cola wars. Its roots can be traced back to 1886, when a pharmacist in Atlanta, Georgia, concocted a headache tonic that he sold for five cents a glass. His bookkeeper named the remedy "Coca-Cola" and committed its secret formula to writing. About a decade later, and just a few hundred miles away in New Bern, North Carolina, another pharmacist created Pepsi Cola.

Over a century later, the stakes in the soft-drink industry are enormous. The average American consumes 53 gallons of carbonated beverages per year—about 29 percent of the total consumption of all liquids! Given gross margins on soft drink concentrate that can be as high as 83 percent, enormous profit is potentially at stake. It's no wonder that Coke and Pepsi go to great lengths to defend their turf.

Trading Punches Although Coke has long been dominant, Pepsi has worked hard to weaken its enemy's position. In 1950, for example, Pepsi recruited a former Coke marketing manager and proclaimed the battle cry "Beat Coke." In the 1960s, Pepsi launched its "Pepsi Generation" campaign to target younger buyers. In the mid-1970s, spurred by the success of blind taste tests in Texas, Pepsi launched a nationwide offensive called the "Pepsi Challenge." Coke, however, refused to retreat, countering with such tactics as retail price cuts and aggressive advertising.

Coke's tactics intensified after Roberto Goizueta became CEO in 1981. Once in command, Goizueta more than doubled advertising, switched to lower-priced sweeteners, sold off noncarbonated beverage businesses, and introduced new flavors and diet versions of existing brands. Coke's victories included Diet Coke, the most successful new product introduction of the 1980s. Then, however, Coke made a serious tactical error: It tried to reformulate the 100-year-old recipe for Coke. When consumers rebelled, Coke was forced to retreat to the original formula. Pepsi proclaimed the effort to reformulate Coke as an admission that Pepsi had a superior taste.

The value-chain activities that bring carbonated beverages to market are centered on four functions: production (producing concentrate), marketing (managing a portfolio of brands), packaging (bottling finished products), and distribution (distributing products for resale). Concentrate is the syrup that provides the distinctive flavor to soft drinks. Historically, the major beverage companies focused on the production of concentrate and marketing, and independent regional bottlers were tasked with packaging and distribution. Bottlers mixed the soft drink concentrate with sweetener and carbonated water and then packaged and distributed the finished product in cans, bottles, or bulk (for restaurant and other on-premises sales). In the early years, both Coke and Pepsi expanded rapidly by granting franchises to independent bottlers around the country. This strategy avoided huge investments in capital-intensive bottling operations.

Bottling Operations However, as the industry matured, the economics of bottling operations changed. Two trends resulted in a change in the bottling industry. First, a few bottling companies saw an opportunity to buy up local franchises in contiguous markets and restructure local operations by building large plants with greater economies of scale designed to serve multiple markets. As these bottling operations began to grow in size, they also grew in power relative to Coke and Pepsi, which posed a legitimate threat to Coke and Pepsi. This threat led to the second trend in the bottling industry. Even though bottling operations generated much less than half the operating margins of concentrate production, both Coke and Pepsi entered the bottling industry. They began buying up independent bottling operations, consolidating territories, and building newer, more efficient facilities.

Although entering the bottling industry could have diluted Coke's and Pepsi's earnings, they actually were able to use this move to improve their overall performance. They did this in two ways. First, by purchasing the bottling operations based on existing profitability, they were able to buy these strategic operations cheaply relative to their value once they restructured operations and made them more efficient. Second, both Coke and Pepsi later divested part of their holdings by spinning off bottling subsidiaries (based on higher profitability) but retaining significant holdings in these now partially owned subsidiaries. These ownership positions enabled them to counteract any power that these operations may have had in negotiations were they to be completely independently owned and operated.

A New Age An outside observer might think that such a fierce battle for market share would gradually erode the combatants' profitability. Since the mid-1960s, however, both Coke and Pepsi have increased market share by about 11 percent, and both enjoy healthy profits. Entry barriers created by large market shares, tremendous brand equity, and ownership or control of regional bottlers explain much of this profitability. Of course, that increased market share had to be captured from weaker rivals, although competitors like Cadbury Schweppes and private label suppliers are making up ground as well. Perhaps the only thing that is certain at this point is that the global hostilities between the two cola superpowers are far from over. <<<

The External Context of Strategy

To formulate an effective strategy—one that has a good chance of helping you achieve your objectives—it is crucial that you understand the external environment. In the broadest sense, the external environment consists of a wide array of economic and sociopolitical factors. In the narrowest sense, the external environment is the specific market arenas that the firm has chosen in its strategy. It is the external environment that provides the business opportunities—ultimately in the form of its chosen arenas—to the firm. ◆ However, the external environment is also a source of threats—forces that may impede the successful implementation of a strategy. The external environment in which firms compete exerts a strong influence on firms' profitability.

 Arenas

As we noted at the start of Chapter 3, where we discussed some tools for identifying the internal determinants of a firm's strengths and weaknesses, you should think of the chapters on the internal and external contexts of strategy as related sections of a single unit. Individually, each discussion provides you with only half of the information you need to analyze a firm's strategy.

In this chapter, you'll learn how to identify the external opportunities and threats that affect every firm's strategy. Taken together, these two chapters provide the tools that will enable you to perform a rigorous analysis of the firm's competitive environment and its capabilities to implement a strategy. In previous coursework, you probably approached these issues with a *SWOT analysis,* which is a relatively simple tool. The tools provided in Chapters 3 and 4 will help you systematically analyze what you could only do intuitively with the SWOT tool.

The long-term profitability of both Coke and Pepsi has probably been influenced by the structure of the soft drink industry. Many enterprising entrepreneurs have seen this long-term propensity to make lots of money in the soft drink industry and have desired to share in that wealth. Many small, profitable companies have emerged; yet, none has succeeded in becoming a major player alongside Coke and Pepsi. In this chapter, you will begin to understand why some industries are more profitable than others, why some industries are easier to enter than others, and what firms can do to influence these environmental factors in their favor.

Exhibit 4.1 Comparative Industrywide Levels of Profitability, 1996–2006

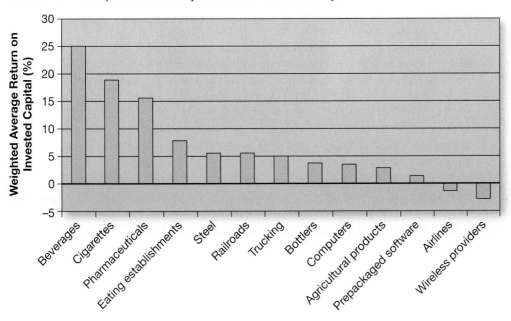

INDUSTRY- AND FIRM-SPECIFIC FACTORS

Knowing what industry- and firm-specific factors affect a firm is critical to understanding its competitive position and determining what strategies are viable. We can examine the complementary roles of industry- and firm-specific factors on firm performance in many different industries. For instance, consider the venerable position of Coca-Cola in the soft drink industry. Clearly, Coca-Cola has some firm-level advantages over its competitors. However, what happened when Coca-Cola entered the wine industry? The entry of Coca-Cola into the wine industry won't change at least two fundamental facts; namely, there is relatively little brand loyalty in wine, and the sale and distribution of the product is heavily regulated in most parts of the world. In 1977, Coke swallowed up industry giants Taylor Wine and Sterling Vineyard. As a beverage, wine is not entirely unrelated to Coke's core products, but unfortunately, Coke never mastered the complexities of a production and distribution process that's often as much an art as a science. After ringing up huge losses for a few years, Coke sold off its wine businesses—for much less than it initially paid for them. Evidently, some things don't go better with Coke.

As shown in Exhibit 4.1, profitability varies widely from industry to industry.[1] Even without the analytical tools to which you'll be introduced in this chapter, you can see that there must be some things about the airline industry relative to the pharmaceutical industry that result in such drastic differences in profitability. Likewise, there are probably factors about the soft drink industry that have helped Coke and Pepsi maintain such high profits over such an extended period of time. Why *are* some industries more profitable than others? For instance, why is the beverage concentrate industry (e.g., Coke, Pepsi, and their competitors) so much more profitable than the bottling industry?

What is needed to answer these questions are tools that allow you to systematically analyze a firm's external context. In the following sections you will be introduced to these tools. The proper use of these tools will help identify some of the major reasons industries differ so much in their long-term profitability.

We'll start this chapter by introducing methods for analyzing the macro environment and firms' industries. We then draw attention to the dynamic facets of the external environment.

FUNDAMENTAL CHARACTERISTICS OF THE EXTERNAL CONTEXT

Identifying the industry in which a firm competes is a logical starting point for analyzing its external context. By the fundamental characteristics of an industry, we mean those factors that are relevant to firm performance at a given point in time—the distinct features that you'd see if you could take an industry snapshot. Remember, too, that industry analysis will include many, but not all, of a firm's key external stakeholders. Thus, in order to avoid blind spots in an industry analysis, managers should always integrate their analysis of a firm's industry with a broader stakeholder analysis like that discussed in Chapter 2.

KEY QUESTIONS

Managers should ask the following questions when analyzing the firm's external context: "What is the firm's industry?" "What macro environmental conditions will have a material effect on our ability to implement our strategy successfully?" "What appear to be unstoppable trends?" "What are the characteristics of the industry?" and "How stable are these characteristics?" By addressing such questions, managers can gain a better sense of a firm's strategic options and challenges. Managers must remain focused on the industry, not on a particular firm operating within it. Focusing on Coca-Cola alone will not provide much information on the general characteristics of the soft drink industry, especially given the fact that Coke is far from average in terms of resources and capabilities. In addition, an industry analysis examines much more than simply the competitors in the industry. Our goal throughout this chapter is to present a deeper understanding of the external context in which *all* firms in an industry operate.

The external environment has two major components: the macro environment and the industry environment. The industry environment is composed of strategic groups—groupings of firms that seem to be more similar in certain ways than other members of the larger industry. The various levels of analysis necessary to examine a firm's external context are summarized in Exhibit 4.2. We will start with the macro environment most removed from the firm and work our way toward more micro analysis.

Exhibit 4.2   The External Environment of the Organization

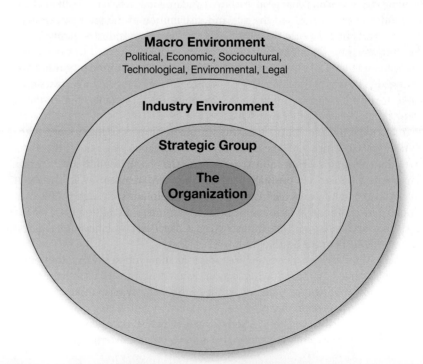

Macro Environment

The macro environment refers to the larger political, economic, social, technical, environmental, and legal issues that confront the firm. To analyze the macro environment, we introduce the PESTEL model and present the determinants and consequences of globalization.

PESTEL ANALYSIS

A simple but important and widely used tool that can be used to develop an understanding of the big picture of a firm's external environment is **PESTEL analysis**. PESTEL is an acronym for the *p*olitical, *e*conomic, *s*ociocultural, *t*echnological, *e*nvironmental, and *l*egal context(s) in which a firm operates. It provides a nonexhaustive list of potential influences of the environment on the organization. It helps managers gain a better understanding of the opportunities and threats they face and consequently aids them in building a better vision of the future business landscape and how the firm might compete profitably. The PESTEL analysis is a useful tool for understanding market growth or decline. Its primary focus is on the future impact of macro environmental factors.

> **PESTEL analysis** Tool for assessing the political, economic, sociocultural, technological, environmental, and legal contexts in which a firm operates.

Firms need to understand the macro environment to ensure that their strategy is aligned with the powerful forces of change that are affecting their business landscape. When firms exploit changes in the environment, they are more likely to be successful than when they simply try to survive or oppose change. A good understanding of PESTEL also helps managers avoid strategies that may be doomed to failure for reasons beyond their control. Finally, understanding PESTEL is a good starting point for entering into a new country or region.

The fact that a strategy is congruent with PESTEL in the home environment gives no assurance that it will be so aligned in new geographic arenas. For example, when the online clothier Lands' End sought to expand its operations from the United States to Germany in 1996 it ran into local laws prohibiting Lands' End from offering unconditional guarantees on its products. In the United States, Lands' End had built its reputation for quality on its no-questions-asked money-back guarantee. However, this practice was considered illegal under Germany's regulations governing incentive offers and price discounts. The political skirmish between Lands' End and the German government finally came to an end in 2001, when the regulations were abolished. Although the regulations did not put Lands' End out of business in Germany, they did slow its growth there until the laws against advertising unconditional guarantees were abolished.

A PESTEL analysis involves three steps. First, you should consider the relevance of each of the PESTEL factors to your particular context. Second, you identify and categorize the information that applies to these factors. Third, you analyze the data and draw conclusions. A mistake too many students make is to stop after the second step. A second common mistake is to assume that your initial analysis and conclusions are correct without testing your assumptions and investigating alternative scenarios.

The PESTEL analysis framework is detailed in Exhibit 4.3. It has six sections, one for each of the PESTEL headings. The table includes sample questions or prompts, the answers to which will help you determine the nature of opportunities and threats in the macro environment. The questions are not meant to be exhaustive; rather, they are merely examples of the types of issues that you should be concerned about in the macro environment.

Political Factors   The political environment can have a significant influence on businesses as well as affect consumer confidence and consumer and business spending. Managers need to consider numerous types of political factors. For instance, the stability of the political environment is particularly important for companies entering new markets. In addition, government policies with respect to regulation and taxation vary from state to state and across national boundaries. Political considerations also encompass trade treaties, such

Exhibit 4.3 The Dimensions of PESTEL Analysis

Political
- How stable is the political environment?
- What are local taxation policies and how do these affect your business?
- Is the government involved in trading agreements such as those adopted by the EU, the ASEAN, and North America (NAFTA, e.g.)?
- What are the foreign-trade regulations?
- What are the social-welfare policies?

Economic
- What are current and projected interest rates?
- What is the level of inflation, what is it projected to be, and how does this projection reflect the growth of your market?
- What are local employment levels per capita and how are they changing?
- What are the long-term prospects for gross domestic product (GDP) per capita and so on?
- What are exchange rates between critical markets and how will they affect production and distribution of your goods?

Sociocultural
- What are local lifestyle trends?
- What are the current demographics and how are they changing?
- What is the level and distribution of education and income?
- What are the dominant local religions and what influence do they have on consumer attitudes and opinions?
- What is the level of consumerism and what are popular attitudes toward it?
- What pending legislation affects corporate social policies (e.g., domestic-partner benefits or maternity/paternity leave)?
- What are the attitudes toward work and leisure?

Technological
- What is the level of research funding in government and industry and are those levels changing?
- What is the government and industry's level of interest and focus on technology?
- How mature is the technology?
- What is the status of intellectual-property issues in the local environment?
- Are potentially disruptive technologies in adjacent industries creeping in at the edges of the focal industry?

Environmental
- What are local environmental issues?
- Are there any pending ecological or environmental issues relevant to your industry?
- How do the activities of international pressure groups (e.g., Greenpeace, Earth First, PETA) affect your business?
- Are there environmental-protection laws?
- What are the regulations regarding waste disposal and energy consumption?

Legal
- What are the regulations regarding monopolies and private property?
- Does intellectual property have legal protections?
- Are there relevant consumer laws?
- What is the status of employment, health-and-safety, and product-safety laws?

as NAFTA, and regional trading blocks, such as ASEAN and the European Union (EU). Such treaties and trading blocks tend to favor trade among the member countries and to impose penalties or less favorable trade terms on nonmembers.

Economic Factors   Managers also need to consider the macroeconomic factors that will have near- and long-term effects on the success of their strategies. Factors such as inflation rates, interest rates, tariffs, the growth of the local and foreign national economies, and exchange rates are critical. Unemployment rates, the availability of critical labor, and the local labor costs also have a strong bearing on strategy, particularly as it relates to where to locate disparate business functions and facilities.

Sociocultural Factors   The social and cultural influences on business vary from country to country. Depending on the type of business the firm operates, factors such as the local languages, the dominant religions, leisure time, and age and lifespan demographics may be critical. Local sociocultural characteristics also vary on such things as attitudes toward consumerism, environmentalism, and the roles of men and women in local society. Making assumptions about local sociocultural norms derived from your experience in your home market is a common cause of early failure when entering new markets. However, even home-market norms can change over time, often caused by shifting demographics due to immigration or aging populations. For example, Coca-Cola and Pepsi have grown in international markets due to increasing levels of consumerism around the world.

Technological Factors   The critical role of technology will be discussed in more detail later in the chapter. For now, suffice it to say that technological factors have a major bearing on the threats and opportunities firms encounter. Does technology enable products and services to be made more cheaply and to a better standard of quality? Do technologies provide the opportunity for more innovative products and services, such as online stock trading, reduction in communications costs, and increased remote working? How might distribution of products or services be affected by new technologies? All of these factors have the potential to change the face of the business landscape.

Environmental Factors   The environment has long been a factor in firm strategy, primarily from the standpoint of access to raw materials. Increasingly, however, this factor is best viewed as a direct- and indirect-operating cost for the firm, as well as from the lens of the footprint left by a firm on its respective environments in terms of waste, pollution, and so on. For consumer products companies such as Pepsi, for example, this can mean waste management and organic farming practices in the countries from which raw materials are obtained. Similarly, in consumer markets it may refer to the degree to which packaging is biodegradable or recyclable.

Legal Factors   Finally, legal factors reflect the laws and regulations relevant to the region and the organization. Legal factors may include whether the rule of law is well established and how easily or quickly laws and regulations may change. It may also include the costs of regulatory compliance. For instance, Coca-Cola's market share in Europe is greater than 50 percent, and as a result, regulators have asked that Coke give up shelf space to competitors' products in order to provide greater consumer choice.

As you can see, many of the PESTEL factors are interrelated. For instance, the legal environment is often related to the political environment in that laws and regulations will change only when politicians decide that such changes are needed.

GLOBALIZATION

Over the past decade, as new markets have been opened to foreign competitors, whole industries have been deregulated and state-run enterprises have been privatized; globalization has become a fact of life in almost every industry.[2] Because of this, the topic of globalization spans both the subjects of PESTEL analysis and industry analysis in both relatively stable and dynamic contexts. We define **globalization** as the evolution of distinct geographic product markets into a state of globally interdependent product markets.

globalization   Evolution of distinct geographic product markets into a state of globally interdependent product markets.

Exhibit 4.4 Factors in Globalization

Pressures Favoring Industry Globalization			
Markets	**Costs**	**Governments**	**Competition**
• Homogeneous customer needs • Global customer needs • Global channels • Transferable marketing approaches	• Large scale and scope economies • Learning and experience • Sourcing efficiencies • Favorable logistics • Arbitrage opportunities • High R&D costs	• Favorable trade policies • Common technological standards • Common manufacturing and marketing regulations	• Interdependent countries • Global competitors

Globalization entails much more than a company simply exporting products to another country. Some industries that aren't normally considered global do in fact have strictly domestic players, but they're often competing alongside firms with operations in many countries, and in many cases, both sets of firms are doing equally well. In contrast, in a truly global industry, the core product is standardized, the marketing approach is relatively uniform, and competitive strategies are integrated in different international markets.[3] In these industries, competitive advantage clearly belongs to the firms that can compete globally.

A number of factors reveal whether an industry has globalized or is in the process of globalizing. In Exhibit 4.4, we've grouped them into four categories: *market, cost, government,* and *competition.*[4]

Markets The more similar markets in different regions become, the greater the pressure for an industry to globalize. Coke and Pepsi, for example, are fairly uniform around the world because the demand for soft drinks is largely the same in every country. The airframe-manufacturing industry, dominated by Airbus and Boeing, also has a highly uniform market for its products because airlines all over the world have the same needs when it comes to large commercial jets. When the distribution channels used to take products to market have already globalized, an incumbent that globalizes early will gain an advantage over other competitors. Thus, if distribution channels are global in nature, waiting to become a global player will put a firm at a disadvantage that may never be overcome. Finally, when similar marketing approaches are widely transferable across geographic markets, there will be pressure to globalize in order to reap the benefits of economies in scale in advertising (i.e., spreading the fixed-cost component of the advertising campaign across more customers).

Costs Anytime fixed costs are extremely high, there will be pressure to globalize in order to spread fixed costs across more customers. In both the automobile and airframe-manufacturing industries, costs also favor globalization. For instance, Airbus and Boeing can invest millions in new-product R&D only because the global market for their products is so large. Coke and Pepsi make huge investments in marketing and promotion, and because they're promoting coherent images and brands, they can leverage their marketing dollars around the world. Pharmaceuticals spend billions of dollars researching and developing new therapies and applications. Consequently, again, there is tremendous pressure to sell products in any economy that might have demand for the drug to help recoup this investment.

Governments can have a huge impact on trade by setting industry-wide standards and regulations. In some parts of Western Europe, for example, people and freight can't travel easily from country to country without switching railroads. Because each country's rail standards and technology are different from its neighbors', rail lines are in some cases incompatible with one another.

Beyond leveraging fixed costs, there are several other cost pressures to globalize. For instance, in many industries the only way to have competitive manufacturing costs is to move these operations to locations outside the home country and into one of the emerging economies that offers significantly lower wages. Finally, the improvement in logistics and transportation capabilities within companies and in the logistics service industry generally make it very easy to enter new markets. Thus, the cost to globalize has been reduced significantly over the past several decades. This means that competitors seeking growth will globalize; failing to do so in your own company could negatively affect your competitive position.

Governments and Competition   Obviously, favorable trade policies encourage the globalization of markets and industries. Governments, however, can also play a critical role in globalization by determining and regulating technological standards. Railroad gauge—the distance between the two steel tracks—would seem to favor a simple technological standard. In Spain, however, the gauge is wider than in France. Why? Because back in the 1850s, when Spain and neighboring France were hostile to one another, the Spanish government decided that making Spanish railways incompatible with French railways would hinder a French invasion.

The cell-phone industry offers a more recent example. The EU has mobilized around one GSM standard, whereas most of the North American market adheres to another GSM standard or the CDMA standard that originally dominated most of the U.S. market. Although recent breakthroughs have made multistandard phones possible, these differences still create fragmented markets for cell-phone manufacturers, such as Nokia and Motorola. Moreover, the interdependence of the European and North American markets means that manufacturers must maintain a strong regional presence. Finally, recent entrants into the industry, including Samsung and NEC, already engage in other global operations. Thus, the problem of multiple standards and the entry of large global competitors both spur globalization in the industry.

Several of the examples reviewed above in the other categories (e.g., markets and costs) suggested that competition was a strong factor affecting globalization. With the exception of niche players, an incumbent may need to globalize simply because competitors are doing so. This will be the case when competitors' globalization gives them any form of advantage that is applicable across their markets.

Now that you understand how PESTEL analysis and an assessment of globalization can help you characterize the general conditions of the macro environment, you are prepared to delve deeply into industry analysis. The next section reviews critical information that will help you analyze the structure of an industry and better understand your competitors.

Industry Analysis

Neoclassical microeconomics has long held the position that in market economies where competition is encouraged and monopolies are not allowed, firms should be able to earn only "normal" profits—that is, enough return to cover the cost of production and the cost of capital. Why? Because of competition. When there is perfect competition, there are numerous sellers and buyers (no monopolies), perfect information, relatively homogenous products offered by different firms, and no barriers to entry or exit. What happens if firms earn greater-than-normal profits (as most managers and shareholders are trying hard to accomplish)? Competition will increase, usually through the entry of new firms into the industry, and profits will be driven back to normal levels. Conversely, if profits fall *below* normal levels, some firms will exit, easing competition and allowing profits to increase to normal levels. However, even a casual reexamination would suggest that most industries must not be held to the laws of perfect competition because we see industries with long-run average profits far exceeding normal levels and others with profits way below such levels.

In this book, however, we have asserted more than once that the strategist's goal is to develop a *competitive advantage* over rivals. When one firm enjoys an inherent advantage over other firms in its industry, above-normal returns are possible (at least for the firm with the advantage) because competition under these conditions is not perfect. In contrast to the conditions of perfect competition, imperfect competition is characterized by relatively few competitors, numerous suppliers and buyers, asymmetric information, heterogeneous products, and barriers that make entry into an industry difficult. Industry analysis helps managers determine the nature of the competition, the possible sources of imperfect competition in the industry, and the possibility of the firm earning above-normal returns.

I/O ECONOMICS AND KEY SUCCESS FACTORS

The insights that help managers analyze an industry originate in a discipline called *industrial organization (I/O) economics*. Fortunately, one does not need to be an economist to understand the basic tools of industry analysis. These tools enable managers to understand the business landscape in which the firm operates. These tools and the insights derived from their use should be used iteratively with the tools of internal analysis. However, for simplicity's sake we will hold constant the internal condition of the firm and focus on external conditions in this chapter.

One implication of industry analysis is that firms perform best when they select a strategy that fits the industry environment. Researchers often argue that the goal of managers should be to acquire the necessary skills and resources, often called the **key success factors (KSFs)**, to compete in their industry environment.[5] For example, KSFs in the soft drink industry might include (1) the ability to meet competitive pricing; (2) extensive distribution capabilities, including ownership of vending machines and cold-storage cases; (3) marketing skills to raise consumer brand awareness in a highly crowded marketplace; (4) a broad mix of products, including diet and noncaffeinated beverages; (5) global presence; and (6) well-positioned bottlers and bottling capacity.

key success factor (KSF)
Key asset or requisite skill that all firms in an industry must possess in order to be a viable competitor.

On the surface, this strategy-development process is similar to the process of strategy formulation and implementation that we discussed in Chapter 3, with one critical difference: According to the I/O approach, the appropriate strategy, key assets, and requisite skills are dictated by *industry* characteristics. Why do I/O researchers regard KSFs as a function of the industry? Simply because all firms in an industry must possess them in order to be viable. Thus, KSFs fit the definition of valuable resources as defined in Chapter 3 because they are like table stakes in a poker game: You need the stakes just to get a seat at the poker table. The soft drink example shows that these stakes actually create barriers to entry because they are complex and costly to put in place. While KSFs are resources and skills that would satisfy the *value* criteria from the VRINE model introduced in Chapter 3, by definition they will not satisfy the *rareness* criterion. Thus, possessing KSFs will not grant a firm a competitive advantage over other key players in the industry, but it will permit it to compete against such firms.

I/O researchers also argue that the analyst should focus primarily on the industry as a whole, and not on a particular firm, because KSFs are easily transferred from one firm to another. Thanks to relatively efficient markets, firms can readily buy the KSFs they need. In summary, the I/O approach suggests that managers should study an industry in order to understand which strategies are rewarded most profitably and to acquire the industry-relevant KSFs required to implement them.

WHAT IS AN INDUSTRY?

Economists define an *industry* as a firm or group of firms that produce or sell the same or similar products to the same market. Is there such a thing as a one-firm industry? If a firm holds a *monopoly*—if it's the only seller in the market—then it's the only firm in the industry. Many utilities operate as monopolies within specific geographic areas (and are typically regulated or owned outright by government bodies). Most industries have several or many competitors. But even some industries that have many competitors are dominated by a few powerful firms.

Fragmentation and Concentration   In a *duopoly* or *oligopoly*, the market is dominated by only two or a few large firms, and the industry is characterized as concentrated. In our opening vignette on the Cola War, it is clear that the soft drink industry is very concentrated. At the other end of the spectrum, industries in which there's no clear leader are characterized as fragmented.

How can we determine the extent to which an industry is concentrated or fragmented? One useful tool is the *concentration ratio,* which represents the combined revenues of the largest industry participants as a ratio of total industry sales. For manufacturing industries, the U.S. Department of Commerce calculates these ratios at different levels, according to the number of firms treated as the industry's largest—4, 8, 20, or 50. Thus, we refer to these ratios as C4, C8, C20, and C50, respectively. Industry concentration is one of several important factors in industry analysis, because concentration affects the intensity of competition in an industry. For instance, fragmented markets are believed to be more competitive than concentrated markets, whereas concentrated markets are more difficult to enter.

To determine what constitutes an industry, it is necessary to identify clear classifications of products or markets. In the case of Coke and Pepsi, for instance, the industry could be defined as the *beverage industry.* This industry would include every firm that manufactures beverages—Lipton (tea), Starbucks (coffee), Seagram's (liquor), Heineken (beer), Mondavi (wine), Ocean Spray (juice), Coke and Pepsi (soft drinks), and so on. However, such a broad definition makes analysis very difficult and probably obscures important micro-level structural features. Coke and Pepsi's industry could alternatively be defined as the *carbonated soft-drink* industry. There is no definitive rule as to where to draw the boundaries when analyzing an industry. The key is to not be so inclusive that important factors that differ across heterogeneous markets cannot be detected (e.g., Are there key differences between alcoholic beverage markets and soft drink markets?) nor so exclusive that important threats are missed (e.g., Does excluding bottled water from the carbonated soft-drink industry miss the main growth segments?).

Defining Industry Boundaries

Indeed, the answer to the question "What industry am I in?" is not as simple as it might seem, even if you're only thinking about something to drink. You'll probably be surprised by the implications of different answers that can be given to this deceptively simple question. This is because industries are typically composed of many segments with different structural characteristics. In the midst of the Cola War, both antagonists were looking for ways to grow. Hard-nosed head-to-head competition was one option, but a simpler strategy involved merely redefining what industry each company was in—say, *beverages* in general or, more particularly, *soft-drink beverages*. Toward this end, Coke bought Minute Maid in 1960, and since then Coke and Pepsi seem to have agreed that they're in the *nonalcoholic beverage* industry, which includes not only soda but also juices and teas. Pepsi purchased Tropicana (juices) in 1999 and South Beach Beverage in 2000. Coke bought Odwalla (juices) in 2001.

Today, the hottest new-product area in the nonalcoholic beverage business is water—bottled water, to be exact. Bottled water is a multibillion-dollar growth industry, and it's well on its way to becoming the most consumed beverage in America (except for soft drinks). With an active market consisting of nearly half of all Americans, bottled water is on track to surpass beer, milk, and coffee to become the second-best-selling beverage in the United States.

Although Coke is big in soda, it comes in a distant third in the global bottled water business.[6] With 70 brands in 160 countries, the Swiss company Nestlé controls nearly a third of the market, and its share is growing. In North America alone, Nestlé sells nine domestic brands, including Arrowhead, Poland Spring, and Deer Park; and five imported brands, including San Pellegrino and Perrier. Pepsi, with a nearly 10 percent share, comes in second with Aquafina, the top-selling single-serve bottled water in the United States. Coca-Cola is third (though not last) with Dasani, which has 8 percent of the market. Recently, however, Coke entered into a partnership with France's Groupe Danone that may vault it into second place once it begins producing, marketing, and distributing Danone's niche brands, which include Evian.

At least one thing should be clear by now: Before getting into an industry, the firm's managers must know the type of product and the geographic market that they're considering. Exhibit 4.5 underscores the importance of drawing industry boundaries in a way that enables managers to understand the dynamics of competition.[7] As shown in Exhibit 4.5, concentration ratios vary dramatically among segments within the same broad industry group. In comparison to other industries, for example, the food industry is relatively fragmented: The four largest manufacturers account for only 14 percent of sales. Within this broad grouping, however, some areas are highly concentrated; the four largest competitors, for instance, account for a full 83 percent of breakfast cereal sales. The apparel industry also consists of numerous segments. Concentration ratios in the men's and boys' segment are quite different from those in the women's and girls' segment: Sales are much more concentrated in the former. The differences in concentration ratios remind us that industry dynamics vary dramatically across various sectors of the same industry. As demonstrated by such differences in concentration ratios, the definition of an industry is critical to gaining an understanding of the competitive dynamics facing firms that operate in it and, ultimately, to the formulation of a strategy for competing in it.

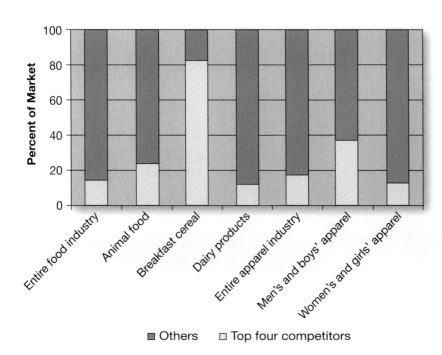

Exhibit 4.5 Concentration in Selected U.S. Industries

A MODEL OF INDUSTRY STRUCTURE

Once the boundaries of the industry to be analyzed have been identified, the next step is to examine the industry's fundamental characteristics and structure. The model shown in Exhibit 4.6 identifies five forces that determine the basic structure of an industry.[8] We've added a sixth force, complementors, to the model because it's an increasingly critical industry force, and therefore an input into your strategic analysis (you will learn more on complementors below).

These five forces were identified by Michael Porter as the industry **five-forces model**.[9] The horizontal axis is a stylized version of the industry value chain. An industry purchases inputs, or supplies, from other industries. Likewise, an industry sells its products or services to customers, which are often other businesses but may be retail consumers as well. In negotiations with suppliers and buyers, transactions are not always between parties of equal negotiating strength. The five-forces model draws attention to factors that systematically alter the negotiating strength in favor of suppliers, industry members, or buyers. Likewise, the model draws attention to threats posed by the possibility of new entrants (and conversely, the difficulty of exit) and possible substitute products from other industries or industry segments, either of which can pose threats to industry participants.

It's sometimes useful to think of these forces as countervailing sources of power all vying for a larger piece of the industry's total profits. Recall that when an industry is characterized by perfect competition, rivals in an industry will achieve normal levels of profitability—enough to pay for all factors of input, including the cost of capital. However, industries actually vary considerably in their average level of returns. A key reason for this variance in industry profitability is differences in the power of these five forces across different industries.

Rivalry   Firms can compete in an industry in many ways. The intensity of competition is known as **rivalry**. The key questions to ask when analyzing the degree of rivalry in an industry include: Who are the competitors? How do rival firms compete? Which firms will be identified as competitors? Because an understanding of the nature of rivalry is so important, we include a separate section on competitor analysis that details ways in which the future actions of competitors can be more accurately predicted.

five-forces model   Framework for evaluating industry structure according to the effects of rivalry, threat of entry, supplier power, buyer power, and the threat of substitutes.

rivalry   Intensity of competition within an industry.

Exhibit 4.6   The Five Forces of Industry Structure

Source: Adapted from M. E. Porter, Competitive Strategy: Techniques for Analyzing Industries and Competitors (New York: Free Press, 1980)

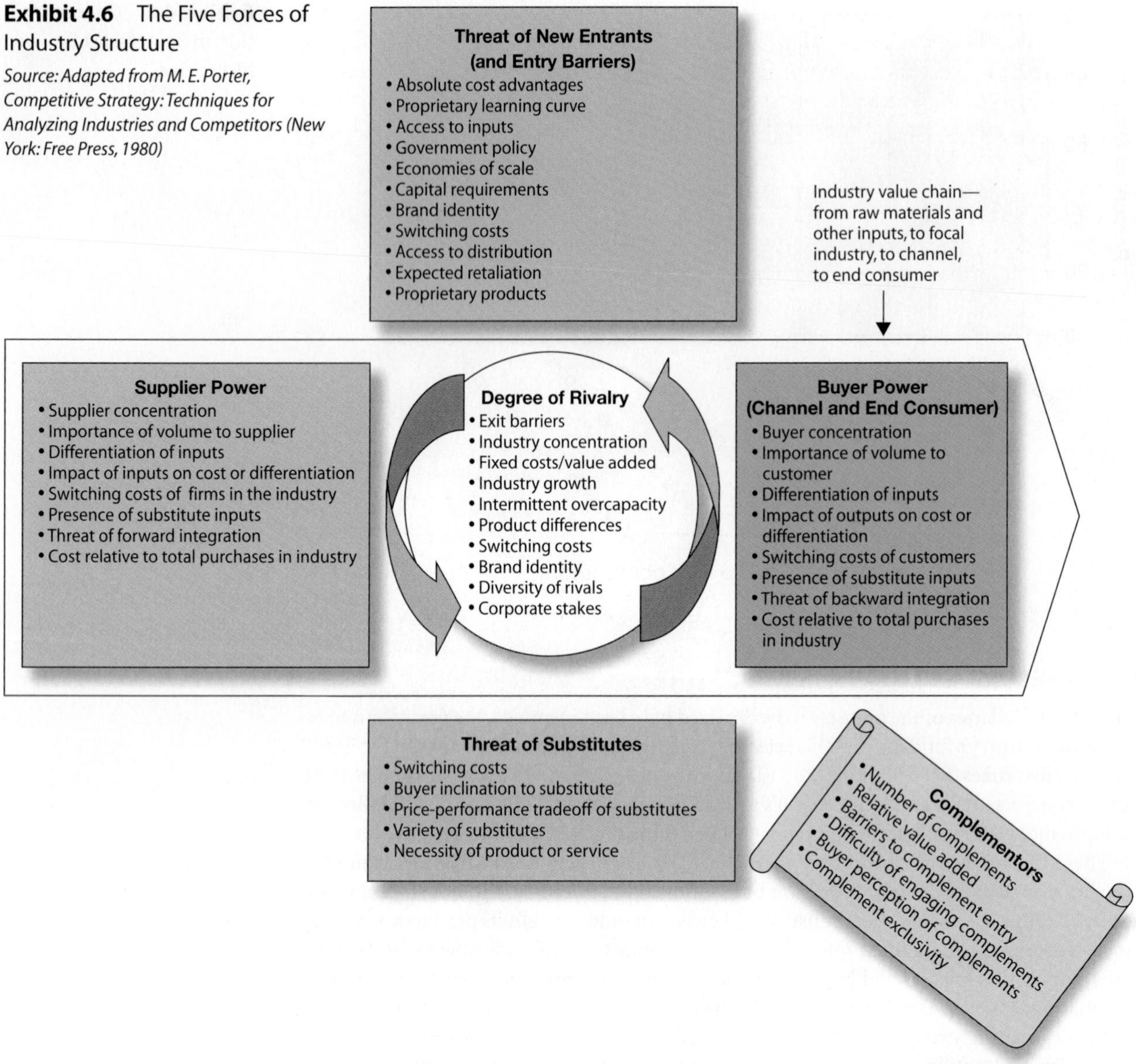

Threat of New Entrants (and Entry Barriers)
• Absolute cost advantages
• Proprietary learning curve
• Access to inputs
• Government policy
• Economies of scale
• Capital requirements
• Brand identity
• Switching costs
• Access to distribution
• Expected retaliation
• Proprietary products

Industry value chain—from raw materials and other inputs, to focal industry, to channel, to end consumer

Supplier Power
• Supplier concentration
• Importance of volume to supplier
• Differentiation of inputs
• Impact of inputs on cost or differentiation
• Switching costs of firms in the industry
• Presence of substitute inputs
• Threat of forward integration
• Cost relative to total purchases in industry

Degree of Rivalry
• Exit barriers
• Industry concentration
• Fixed costs/value added
• Industry growth
• Intermittent overcapacity
• Product differences
• Switching costs
• Brand identity
• Diversity of rivals
• Corporate stakes

Buyer Power (Channel and End Consumer)
• Buyer concentration
• Importance of volume to customer
• Differentiation of inputs
• Impact of outputs on cost or differentiation
• Switching costs of customers
• Presence of substitute inputs
• Threat of backward integration
• Cost relative to total purchases in industry

Threat of Substitutes
• Switching costs
• Buyer inclination to substitute
• Price-performance tradeoff of substitutes
• Variety of substitutes
• Necessity of product or service

Complementors
• Number of complements
• Relative value added
• Barriers to complement entry
• Difficulty of engaging complements
• Buyer perception of complements
• Complement exclusivity

At this stage of the analysis, it is important simply to come to a better sense of the overall nature of rivalry within an industry. The outcome associated with high degrees of rivalry is generally defined in terms of price competition. The most aggressive forms of competition include price wars. When firms are willing to sacrifice their margins through significantly lower prices, it can be assumed that the nature of the rivalry is very intense. This is not to say that competition isn't serious in industries in which price wars are not common. Rather, in those industries firms have found nonprice-based forms of competition. From this definition of rivalry, it is easy to see that higher degrees of rivalry result in lower levels of average industry profitability: As price competition increases, average prices decline, resulting in lower levels of profitability.

What factors tend to increase rivalry? These factors can be categorized into attributes about firms within the industry and attributes about the products or markets themselves. First we will review the attributes of firms that make them likely to compete on prices. When there are numerous competitors, price competition is typically more intense than when there are only a few competitors. Consider the Cola War reviewed in the opening vignette. As intense as that rivalry has been, competition in most periods has focused on nonprice factors. Although advertising to build brand loyalty has been very expensive for Coke and Pepsi, it has been less harmful to profits than intense price wars. More generally, recall that the definition of perfect competition assumes that there are numerous buyers and sellers. In addition, price competition increases when competitors are of relatively equal size and power. Thus, rivalry is affected not only by the number of firms competing but also by how similar those firms are. For instance, the software industry includes many competitors, but Microsoft's size relative to most firms has the effect of marginalizing the threat of price competition.

Another factor that increases the threat of price competition is the degree to which the industry is strategically important to competitors. Recall that many firms are diversified and compete in multiple industries. Price competition tends to be fiercer when the industry is a key business for the major players in that industry.

Characteristics about the products and markets within an industry can also have a strong influence on the degree of price competition. Price competition tends to be fiercer in industries that are growing slowly. When a company's products are difficult to differentiate from those of competitors, they are forced to compete on price. Price competition is reduced when firms are able to create the impression that their products are different from those of competitors. Coke and Pepsi, for example, have spent billions of dollars to build brand equity and loyalty. Likewise, when there are very low costs for buyers to switch from one firm's offerings to another's, then competitors feel compelled to motivate buyer loyalty with aggressive pricing. Conversely, when customers face high switching costs, there is less pressure to keep prices low because a firm's buyers are somewhat locked in. Industries characterized by high fixed costs, such as the airline industry, are also more prone to price wars.

Finally, recall that the concept of perfect competition suggested that if profits dropped too low, some competitors would choose to exit the industry, resulting in profits rising back to normal levels. However, in some industries firms may face high **exit barriers** when it is very costly to leave an industry or market, particularly given the opportunity set possessed by any given incumbent. Firms with high exit barriers are typically forced to compete aggressively. So, exit barriers tend to increase rivalry and price competition. For instance, the exit barriers in the airline industry are very high because air carriers have few opportunities outside of air travel, and those firms that exit the industry are likely to do so only by selling off their business or otherwise dissolving the firm.

Indeed, a firm may remain in an industry due to high exit barriers even when the business is not profitable. As an example, Litton Industries was very successful in building ships for the U.S. Navy in the 1960s. However, when the Vietnam war ended and defense spending plummeted, Litton was so heavily invested in shipbuilding that it could not feasibly exit the industry, particularly given the high specialized investment in now-unattractive shipbuilding facilities. As a result, Litton was forced to stay in the shipbuilding market even though it was unattractive and in decline.

Threat of Entry   Not surprisingly, industries that boast relatively high average profitability attract the attention of firms operating elsewhere that are looking for promising new arenas in which to compete. Paradoxically, industries with consistently high average profitability also tend to be those that are the most difficult to enter. The degree to which new competitors may enter an industry and make rivalry more intense is known as the **threat of new entry**. Conditions that make it difficult to enter an industry are known as **barriers to entry**. Note that perfect competition is characterized by the absence of barriers to entry. Several industry characteristics contribute to such barriers, including strong brands, proprietary technologies, and other bases for product differentiation. Certain technologies, for instance, give their owners cost advantages that new entrants can't readily match or compensate for. In some industries, restricted access to investment capital or distribution channels constitutes barriers. Other industries, such as computer-chip manufacturing, require large incremental

exit barriers Barriers that impose a high cost on the abandonment of a market or product.

threat of new entry Degree to which new competitors can enter an industry and intensify rivalry.

barrier to entry Condition under which it is more difficult to join or compete in an industry.

capital investments in specialized manufacturing facilities. In others, the need for location-based or preferential access to distribution networks can hinder or block entry by new players.

The concept of barriers to entry and their effect on industry structure is illustrated in Exhibit 4.7. Competitors A, B, and C are incumbents in this industry. If D were to enter, the competition in the industry would increase (each incumbent would now have three competitors instead of two). A variety of factors and associated illustrative examples are detailed in the exhibit. Some industries possess more than one of these barriers. But, the more of these barriers that exist, the harder it will be for D to enter.

Let's consider the soft drink industry from our chapter-opening vignette as an illustration. The soft drink industry is shown as an example of access to distribution as a barrier to entry in Exhibit 4.7. But this industry actually has several barriers making it difficult for new entrants to compete nationally with Coke and Pepsi. With such perennially high levels of profit experienced by Coke and Pepsi, one would expect the industry to attract envious firms and entrepreneurs. And to be certain, there have been many new entrants at the margins and in newer segments not yet dominated by Coke and Pepsi. However, there has yet to be a successful entrant to the cola segment that has been able to capture a significant share of the market. A number of brave companies have tried. For instance, Sir Richard Bransen's Virgin Group has tried twice to enter the soft drink market. In 1998, the British billionaire rode into New York's Times Square atop a tank, promising a battle with Coke and Pepsi. Virgin tried extensive hard-edge advertising to gain market awareness. However, it found it nearly impossible to secure premium shelf space in traditional retail outlets. Thus, difficulty gaining access to distribution is a major stumbling block for companies wanting to enter the industry. Branson also faced considerable brand awareness problems; he discovered that the cost and time required to create brand awareness posed another monumental problem. Indeed, the difficulty gaining shelf space and lack of brand awareness were mutually reinforcing weaknesses. Retailers didn't want to allocate much shelf space to a new brand, and Virgin couldn't succeed in making the brand more well-known without shelf space. After pulling out of the U.S. for a period, Virgin is giving it another try in America. The strategy this time is to be a niche player, having secured a deal for distribution through 7-Eleven stores.[10] Thus, entry barriers in the soft drink industry include both extreme levels of brand loyalty and virtual control of prime distribution channels. The only competitive space available for new entrants in the near term appears to be on the periphery of the market. Thus, new entry is most often seen with local brands, private label offerings, and specialty drinks.

Exhibit 4.7   Barriers to Entry

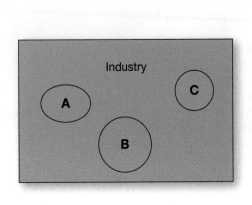

- Scale economics
  —Aerospace
- Scope economies
  —Retailing
- Capital requirements
  —Automobiles
- Switching costs
  —Computer operating systems
- Access to distribution
  —Soft drinks
- Regulation
  —Pharmaceuticals

The greater the degree of difficulty that potential entrants face in accumulating the resources necessary to compete in an industry, the higher the barriers to entry; and high barriers to entry have the effect of reducing potential competition by limiting supply and reducing rivalry. This results in higher prices and higher levels of average profitability than in industries in which there are fewer barriers to entry.

Supplier Power   In transactions between industry participants and firms in supply industries, the relative power of each party affects both the pricing of transactions and the profitability of each industry. The degree to which firms in the supply industry are able to dictate favorable contract terms and thereby extract some of the profit that would otherwise be available to competitors in the focal industry is referred to as **supplier power**. When focal-industry participants have negotiating strength, suppliers have limited bargaining power, and the focal industry acts to reduce supplier industry performance rather than the other way around. Suppliers are powerful when they control such factors as prices, delivery lead times, minimum orders, postpurchase service, and payment terms.

> **supplier power**   Degree to which firms in the supply industry are able to dictate terms to contracts and thereby extract some of the profit that would otherwise be available to competitors in the focal industry.

Supplier power arises when the suppliers are relatively concentrated, control a scarce input, or are simply bigger than their customers. In some cases, firms in a focal industry need a unique product or service and have only a few alternative suppliers to which to turn. In these instances, of course, suppliers can demand higher prices.

For instance, from the opening vignette it is easy to see that the soft drink industry is very consolidated and the two major players are very large. They purchase most of their inputs in commodity markets (e.g., sweeteners, food coloring). As a result, suppliers have no leverage over soft drink manufacturers. In contrast, consider the situation from the point of view of the bottlers, who buy soft drink concentrate from manufacturers like Coke and Pepsi and cans and bottles from canning companies. The bottling industry faces significant supplier-power problems because their concentrate suppliers are heavily consolidated. When a firm has a franchise to bottle Coke (or Pepsi), the contract is exclusive, meaning that it has agreed to let Coke or Pepsi be its supplier in perpetuity. By contract, the bottler cannot buy cola products from any other concentrate maker. Thus, soft drink bottlers face a condition of considerable supplier power.

Likewise, the jewelry business requires access to diamonds. Because South Africa's DeBeers controls over 50 percent of the world's diamond supply, it is in the position to force jewelry makers to pay high prices for its diamonds.

Even when an industry is sourcing products that may be considered commodities, such as textiles or wood, suppliers can impose payment terms that implicitly raise the cost of the resource for the focal industry. Such is the case when the supplier industry is more consolidated than the focal industry. Because the furniture industry, for example, is highly fragmented, no single manufacturer has much power when bargaining with the larger wood and fabric suppliers who provide the industry's primary raw materials. Suppliers of wood have many possible firms to which to sell.

Supplier power is also high when firms in the supply industry present a threat of forward integration—that is, if it's possible for them to manufacture finished products rather than just sell components to manufacturers. Coke and Pepsi, for example, could easily integrate forward into bottling instead of just supplying bottlers with concentrate. They have demonstrated this by purchasing bottlers in the past. This potential gives them significant power in negotiating prices with their bottling networks.

Finally, suppliers are powerful when firms in the focal industry face significant switching costs when changing suppliers. For instance, companies purchasing enterprise resource planning (ERP) software have several supplier choices, including SAP, Oracle, and PeopleSoft. However, once a firm purchases from one supplier and incurs the significant implementation costs associated with ERP, it will be very reluctant to switch to another supplier because the costs of doing so are significant. Because of the high costs involved in switching ERP systems, firms switch suppliers less frequently than one would expect in a market with many sellers.

South Africa's DeBeers controls half of the world's diamonds. As such, it wields a great deal of buyer and supplier power and controls the prices that it both pays and charges for diamonds.

In summary, in transactions between industry participants and firms in supply industries, the relative power of each party affects both the pricing and profitability of each industry. When focal-industry participants have negotiating strength, suppliers have limited bargaining power, and the focal industry acts to reduce the supplier-industry performance rather than the other way around.

Buyer Power   The mirror image of supplier power, **buyer power** is the degree to which firms in the buyers' industry are able to dictate favorable terms on purchase agreements that extract some of the profit that would otherwise be available to competitors in the focal industry. When firms in the focal industry sell to their customers (i.e., buyers), those transactions are subject to the same bargaining forces just reviewed for supplier power. Buyers, for example, whether in a business-to-business or business-to-consumer relationship, compete with sellers by trying to force prices down.

buyer power   Degree to which firms in the buying industry are able to dictate terms on purchase agreements that extract some of the profit that would otherwise go to competitors in the focal industry.

Several factors lead to buyers having high degrees of relative power over their suppliers. A buyer group has greater power in the exchange relationship with its suppliers when the buyers are prestigious and when their purchases represent a significant portion of the sellers' sales. By the same token, if a product has little value for the buyer group, buyers are more powerful negotiating with firms in the industry. A buyer group is also powerful when it has numerous choices, such as when the products and prices of multiple competitors are easy to compare. Tire makers, for instance, have little power over carmakers because their product is standardized and there are many competitors in the industry. If a tire maker tried to raise prices, large automobile manufacturers would turn to one of several other firms that could fill their needs. Conversely, when buyers have few alternatives, their power is minimal, and industry prices increase, resulting in higher-than-average industry profitability.

Consider the extreme case of the Green Bay Packers of the National Football League. The Packers have maintained a waiting list for season tickets for the past 45 years; the average wait is 30 years. Because there are few other entertainment alternatives in Green Bay, Wisconsin, there is essentially one seller and many buyers for the opportunity for professional sports entertainment. The team is certainly under no pressure to discount prices.[11]

Information also provides buyers with power, particularly when they have choices, when the products are relatively inexpensive, or when products are not heavily regulated. New-car buyers, for example, are relatively powerful not only because there are numerous makes and models in every category, but because they can now use the Internet to compare products and prices online. In contrast, dealers don't have a corresponding advantage when negotiating with carmakers because operating agreements require them to sell certain manufacturers' products.

Finally, buyers are powerful to the extent that they pose a threat of backward integration. Large brewers, for instance, could conceivably make their own beer cans (in fact, some do). The implicit threat that these buyers of aluminum cans could move backward into a supplier's industry naturally diminishes the supplier's price-setting power.

What About Retail Consumers? Let's make a final—and critical—point about the role of buyer power in any definition of an industry. Note that the industry is the unit that we're analyzing: The focal point of our assessment of rivalry in an industry is the industry segment that we've chosen to analyze. Consequently, when we talk about buyers, we don't mean end retail consumers (unless, of course, we're analyzing a retail-market segment—grocery stores, new-car dealers, department stores, etc.). Japan's Matsushita Electric Industrial, for example, markets many well-known electronics brands, including Panasonic, Quasar, and JVC. When Matsushita markets Panasonic TVs, its targeted customers are not household consumers but, rather, large retail chains and electronics wholesalers. Certainly, retail consumers are important, but they don't negotiate directly with manufacturers, and they don't wield any direct power in nonretail segments. Consumers affect industry profits indirectly when they exercise power as the last link in an industry value chain. An analysis of Panasonic's industry segment would examine the relative power of Matsushita and its rivals in negotiating with retailers, such as Best Buy and Circuit City, who carry their products.

Threat of Substitutes

Sometimes products in other industries can satisfy the same demand as the products of the focal industry (see Exhibit 4.8). The degree to which this is the case is known as the **threat of substitutes**. Recall, for example, our earlier discussion of bottled water and soft drinks. These two different types of products may be substituted for one another in satisfying the demand of some customers. If we defined Coke and Pepsi's industry as soft drinks, then bottled water would be a substitute to which we'd have to pay attention. Consider the case of the movie rental business. Blockbuster faces direct competition from Hollywood Video, Movie Gallery, Netflix, and other U.S. regional and local chains. What are substitutes for DVD and video rental services? Customers' options seem to be increasing. Cable and satellite TV would seem to be a separate industry from movie rentals. However, movie channels available through these outlets are clear substitutes for movie rentals. And, more recently, the availability of on-demand movie streaming through cable and satellite providers seems to provide an even closer substitute product. Thus, the prices that Blockbuster and other movie rental businesses can charge is held in check to some extent by the availability of these viable substitutes.

Even when market segments aren't as closely related as cable and satellite TV are to the movie rental industry, products may still be potential substitutes. In the broadest sense, a *substitute* is any product that satisfies a common need or desire. The desire for leisure, for instance, can be satisfied with both books and travel. Narrowing the classification scheme, consider substitute products between segments in the travel industry. At Southwest Airlines, for example, the primary competition for many shorter flights comes not from other airlines but, rather, from competitors in the automobile- and bus-transportation segments. Thus, within certain geographic limitations, automobiles and bus service are substitutes for airline travel.

It should be clear by now that the prevalence of viable substitute products from other industries places pressures on the prices that can be charged in the focal industry. When there are no viable substitutes, there is less pressure on price. Consequently, average industry profits tend to be lower when clear substitutes are available.

The Impact of Complementors

As we noted at the beginning of this discussion, the five forces that we've just described comprise a model of industry structure proposed by

threat of substitutes Degree to which products of one industry can satisfy the same demand as those of another.

Exhibit 4.8 Threat of Substitutes

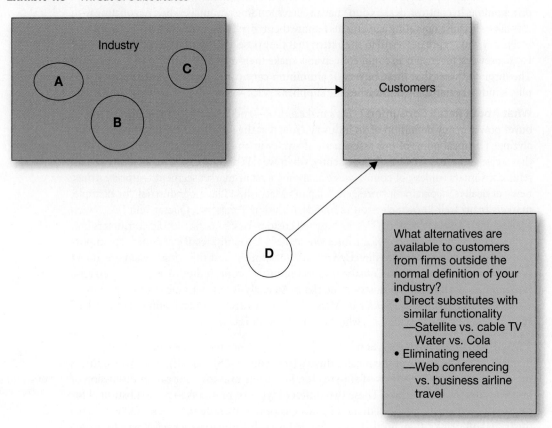

Michael Porter. When these forces are strong, industry profitability tends to be reduced. More recently, some researchers have argued that the players outlined in the five-forces model do not always compete exclusively in zero-sum games. Sometimes these players work together to create value jointly rather than competing to divide the market. **Complementors** are players who provide complementary rather than competing products and services.[12]

complementor Firm in one industry that provides products or services which tend to increase sales in another industry.

Factors affecting the importance of complementors in a given industry are shown in Exhibit 4.6. Firms in the music and electronics industries, for example, sell products that must be used together—such as Ipods, headphones, and music. Each benefits from the other's presence. Likewise, when people buy hot dogs, an increase in sales of buns, condiments, and beverages is likely. These three products are marketed by complementary industry segments (which is why grocers can sell buns below cost to stimulate sales of higher-margin hot dogs). Sometimes firms in the same industry or suppliers and buyers simultaneously play the role of complementors. For instance, United and Delta compete fiercely in trying to attract customers to fill their airline seats. However, when upgrading their fleets to a newer plane, both airlines are probably better off when they jointly order a new model from Airbus or Boeing. Because both are in the market for new planes at the same time, aircraft manufacturers are able to achieve greater economies of scale with larger orders, thereby lowering the cost of new planes.

This example helps introduce a more formal definition of *complementor:* A complementor is any factor that makes it more attractive for suppliers to supply an industry on favorable terms or that makes it more attractive for buyers to purchase products or services from an industry at prices higher than it would pay absent the complementor. However, even though a firm or industry segment fulfills a complementor role, it may still compete with firms in the focal industry. A firm or industry segment may simultaneously play the roles of complementor and competitor (as in the Delta/United example). In addition, a complementor that results in increased focal-industry sales will not necessarily share equally in the increased bounty. These relationships still have elements of bargaining power akin to supplier and buyer relationships; one party to a complementor relationship may receive more of the benefit than the other even though both are better off.

Customers, then, are likely to put a higher value on the products of one industry segment when they already have or have access to complementary products from another segment.[13] The value of computer peripherals obviously increases as the number of personal computers increases. Likewise, the value of a commercial real estate development is enhanced if there are neighboring amenities valued by business tenants, such as restaurants, entertainment venues, and transportation facilities. More new cars are sold when affordable financing is easier to get or dealers offer extended service warranties. Thus, financing and warranty arrangements can be regarded as complementors to the retail new-car market.

Finally, note one important difference between complementors and the other five forces in this model of industry analysis: Whereas the five forces typically work to *decrease* industry profitability, the presence of strong complementors may *increase* profits by increasing demand for an industry's products.

Using the Industry-Structure Model

An understanding of the five industry forces and complementors can help managers evaluate the general attractiveness of an industry as well as the specific opportunities and threats facing firms in their focal segment. An industry is most attractive—that is, has the highest profit potential—when attractive complementors create positive externalities and when the effects of the other five forces are minimal. The pressure on operating margins will be significantly lower than in industries in which suppliers or buyers exercise high levels of power, in which entry barriers are low, and in which abundant substitute products are available.

How does industry analysis affect strategy formulation? First, a good industry analysis will enable an executive to answer a few basic questions with much greater certainty than could be done before the analysis. Some of these questions include the following: Does the firm's current strategy fit with current industry conditions—specifically, the industry conditions relevant to the firm's chosen industry arenas? What changes in the industry may result in misalignment? Which elements of the firm's strategy will need to be altered to exploit future industry conditions? Second, a high quality strategy will be one that helps the firm adapt to the five forces so that they are more in the favor of the firm. Specifically, a successful strategy will help minimize buyer power, offset supplier power, avoid excessive rivalry, raise the barriers to entry, and reduce the threat of substitution. A firm might minimize buyer power by attempting to build customer loyalty through specific differentiators. Supplier power can be offset by assuring that there are multiple sources of key inputs. Excessive rivalry can be avoided by attempting to grow in emerging segments rather than attacking competitors in mature markets. Barriers to entry might be built by making preemptive investments that reduce the incentives for new entrants. Finally, the threat of substitutes can be reduced by understanding the benefits that substitutes offer and then incorporating those in your own products or services.

When using the five-forces model to formulate strategy, remember that these forces are not static. The actions of various industry players keep industry conditions in an almost constant state of flux. Consequently, unattractive industry structure isn't necessarily an omen that profitability is destined to be marginal. Wise strategists use information gleaned from the study of industry structure to formulate strategies for dealing with threats highlighted by industry analysis.

Remember, too, that this type of analysis views industry forces from an overall industry perspective and not from that of any particular firm. The industry-wide effect of these forces will determine whether an industry is attractive or not. We walk through the use of Porter's five-forces analysis in the box entitled "How Would *You* Do That? 4.1."

A Five-Forces—Plus Complementors—Analysis of the U.S. Airline Industry[14]

Let's apply the five-forces model to the U.S. airline industry to illustrate how it is used in practice. Examination of data maintained by the U.S. Department of Transportation reveals that the Department categorizes the airline industry into four groups: international, national, regional, and cargo. Let's focus on national airlines (with sales of at least $1 billion). This will include all U.S. international airlines because they are also large, national airlines.

To perform an industry analysis using the Porter model, it is often useful to translate the concepts into quantitative data. One way to do this is to assign points to each sub-factor of the 5 forces. For illustrative purposes, we will use a scale of 1–5. If the particular force is strong, meaning the threat to firms in the industry is very high on account of that particular sub-factor, we will assign it 5 points. If the particular sub-factor poses no threat to firms in the industry, we will set it equal to 0. Points in between can be used for various gradations.) After identifying each relevant sub-factor for a particular force, you will then take the *average* score for sub-factors associated with that force. So, for illustrative purposes, let's assume we're analyzing the threat of substitutes for an industry. Refer to Exhibit 4.6 and rate this industry on the five sub-factors identified on the exhibit.

A word of caution: The validity of your analysis is only as good as (1) your identification of sub-factors associated with each particular force and (2) your subjective evaluation of each sub-factor. Exhibit 4.6 is intended to be a guide for determining these sub-factors, but is not necessarily an exhaustive list (threats could be industry-specific in many cases).

RIVALRY

The first step is to identify the key players in the national passenger-airline market. Who are the rivals? You could turn to numerous available data sources to identify the key players. Using hoovers.com, we identify the top three competitors as United, American, and Delta; other competitors include AirTran, Alaska Air, America West, Continental Airlines, Hawaiian Air, JetBlue, Northwest Airlines, Southwest Airlines, and US Airways. How competitive is this industry? Is competition based on price or nonprice competition? It would not take a lot of research to discover that this is a highly competitive industry. Most airlines make extremely low returns; indeed, many are currently losing money. Let's assume that, after studying the industry data, you evaluate the sub-factors as outlined below. A score of 3.6 leads you to determine that this industry has an above average level of rivalry, which will hurt margins for most players.

Exit barriers:	4
Industry concentration:	3
Fixed costs:	5
Industry growth:	4
Overcapacity:	4
Product differences:	3
Switching costs:	3
Brand identity:	2
Diversity of rivals:	4
Corporate stakes:	3
Average:	3.6

POWER OF SUPPLIERS

Who are the suppliers to national airlines? Most, such as caterers, airports, airplane manufacturers, and security firms, are oligopolies, meaning that the airlines are in a less advantageous position. Key suppliers include makers of aircraft; two companies, Boeing and Airbus, dominate that market and are able to garner significant profits at the airlines' expense by virtue of their specialized positions and government subsidies. The other key supply for airlines is fuel. Due to oil shortages, the price of fuel is currently proving a very problematic issue for airlines. However, this is not a function of supplier power but, rather, conditions in the oil market.

After studying the industry data, you evaluate the sub-factors as outlined below. A score of 2.4 indicates that this force is relatively neutral. Airlines and their suppliers have points of bargaining power that about cancels out the other.

Supplier concentration:	5
Importance of volume:	1
Input differentiation:	3
Input effect on company differentiation:	1
Switching costs of firms in industry:	2
Presence of substitute inputs:	5
Threat of forward integration:	1
Cost relative to total purchases in supplier industry:	1
Average:	2.4

POWER OF BUYERS

To whom do national airlines sell their services? Buyers can be categorized into three primary groups: business travelers, leisure travelers, and buyers of large blocks of seats known as consolidators, who buy excess seat inventory at large discounts. What bargaining power do these customers have? Switching costs are very low, though airlines have increased them somewhat through frequent flier programs. Buyers are price sensitive, but they have very little individual buyer power.

Again, you study the industry data and you evaluate the sub-factors as outlined below. A score of 2.5 indicates that this force is neutral. Each party (firms in your industry and customers) has points of bargaining power that about cancels out the other.

Buyer concentration:	1
Importance of volume:	1
Differentiation in airline industry:	3
Switching costs of customers:	4
Presence of substitute inputs:	1
Threat of backward integration:	1
Price sensitivity:	4
Buyer information:	4
Average:	2.5

THREAT OF SUBSTITUTES

What is the likelihood that airline customers will use alternative means of transportation? When it comes to business travelers, this would seem minimal. However, communication technology has proven to be a viable substitute for some forms of business travel. For leisure travelers, the threat of substitutes is mainly for shorter flights. Thus, alternatives such as auto and bus transportation are more viable substitutes for regional airlines and national airlines that specialize in shorter flights (e.g., Southwest).

After studying the industry data and evaluating the sub-factors, you determine the ratings outlined below. A score of 1.8 indicates that this force is relatively in the industry's favor—substitutes exist, but they don't seem to be a major threat.

Switching costs:	4
Buyer inclination to substitute:	1
Price-performance tradeoff of substitute:	2
Variety of substitutes:	1
Necessity of product or service:	2
Average:	1.8

THREAT OF NEW ENTRANTS

The capital intensity of the airline industry appears to pose an entry barrier. However, JetBlue, AirTran, and other entrants have proven that financing is available when there is a convincing business plan and when economic conditions are conducive to the business model proposed. Brand name and frequent flier plans also seem to be deterrents to entry. However, JetBlue's success demonstrates that customers are willing to switch airlines if the price is right.

On balance, in this analysis you rate the threat of new entry as only moderate. The structural factors make it unlikely the industry will attract many profitable new entrants.

Average profitability of incumbents:	1
Incumbents have a cost advantage:	5
Learning curve advantage for incumbents:	3
Access to inputs:	5
Government policy (regulation):	2
Economies of scale:	3
Capital requirements:	2
Brand identity:	2
Switching costs:	3
Access to distribution (gates):	2
Expected retaliation:	1
Proprietary products:	5
Average:	2.8

THE ROLE OF COMPLEMENTORS

Your analysis of complementors suggests that there are complementors such as credit cards and rental cars, that they are unlikely to become direct competitors, but that it is hard to tie up these complementors in exclusive relationships that competitors can't duplicate with the same or comparable complementor.

Number of complementors:	2
Relative value added:	3
Barriers to complement entry:	2
Difficulty of engaging complements:	1
Buyer perception of complements:	2
Complement exclusivity:	5
Average:	2.5

In summary, it appears that supplier power, buyer power, and substitutes do not pose ominous threats to the airline industry. Complementors, while present, do not make the industry overly attractive. The only two forces that seem to account for the poor performance of the industry are moderately low entry barriers and intense competitive rivalry.

COMPETITOR ANALYSIS

The industry analysis that we've discussed so far has focused on the broad industry definition. Another purpose of an industry analysis is to develop a clear understanding of who the firm's competitors are and what their behaviors are likely to be in the future in its chosen industry arena or arenas. Consequently, after completing a five-forces analysis, it is critical to investigate the strategies and behaviors of the firm's competitors. That is, after understanding the five forces, we want to dive deeply into the study of the firm's rivals. There are many ways you might study a firm's rivals. We present a model that can be used to map out who the competitors are and the strategies they're pursuing. This type of competitor analysis will then be used when turning to the formulation of your firm's strategy, which will be discussed in detail in Chapters 5 and 6. This tool, explored in "How Would *You* Do That? 4.2," is known as the *value curve* and it offers an intuitive way to map competitors' strategies using the industry KSFs discussed earlier in the chapter.

Mapping Competitors

Mapping competitors within an industry starts by identifying who the competitors are. This is usually the easiest step. Firms generally know who they compete against for sales. It is perhaps more problematic when the firm only currently competes in a niche market and doesn't encounter all the competitors with regularity. Nevertheless, there are numerous data sources that will list the companies in specific industries. Once identifying the primary competitors, the next step is to document how these firms go about competing within the industry. What you will generally find is that specific types of competitors emerge—groups of competitors will follow similar strategies along the KSFs, and the various groups will be distinct in how they go about doing this.

The fact that we can segment market competitors into their central locations in the business landscape doesn't mean, of course, that firms with similar strategies only compete amongst themselves. However, firms with relatively similar strategies are more likely to be mutual threats than are groups with significantly different characteristics. For instance, Trek, which manufactures high-quality performance bicycles that are sold through independent dealers, faces more competition from Specialized than it does from Huffy, which makes mass market bikes with lower-end components that are sold through mass merchandisers like Wal-Mart and Target. However, for its lower-end models, Trek does experience some competition with Schwinn, who sells its bikes both in mass merchants and independent bicycle dealers. Similarly, luxury hotel chains face a greater threat from high-quality business hotels than from the economy hotel market.

We analyze competitors' strategies to get a more detailed look at the competitive environment in which firms operate. Through such an analysis as the value curve, we can more readily identify a firm's closest competitors (something that most decision makers can usually do intuitively). More importantly, however, we can also better identify any probable *future competition* that we might otherwise ignore or underestimate. Likewise, analyzing competitors like this also helps us identify growth opportunities because it makes us focus on potential competitive positions that are compatible with a firm's unique set of resources and capabilities.

THE VALUE CURVE

Now that we have described why firms need to have a deep understanding of their competitors, we'll describe the **value curve**, a convenient tool to help managers visualize their competitive landscape. An intuitive way to do this is to use the key success factors discussed earlier in this chapter and use a rating system to compare the various competitors on how they score on these dimensions. In "How Would *You* Do That? 4.2," we walk you through this exercise using the U.S. wine industry. The tool's purpose is to visually plot how major groups of firms compete. This tends to reveal the underlying assumptions firms make about the market and customers. The first step is to determine the existing key success factors as

value curve   A graphical depiction of how a firm and major groups of its competitors are competing across its industry's factors of completion.

perceived by incumbents. List these factors along the horizontal axis. The vertical axis is used to rate the level of delivery of the major groups of firms. For instance, if room comfort were one of the key success factors that you identified when evaluating the hotel industry, then you would rate establishments like Hyatt and Marriott much higher than hotels like the Sleep Inn and Best Western. The scale you use is not as important as your judgment in segregating different levels of products and services along the key success factors. For illustrative purposes, we use a scale of 1–5. Generally, you can plot firms by the central tendency of clusters of firms following similar strategies. We call these clusters **strategic groups.**

After ranking the firms or groups on each dimension, connect the points for each firm or group. Connecting the points, which is drawing the value curve for that respective company or group, reveals a visual representation of the various ways rivals compete in the industry. For instance, if you were mapping the airline industry, even without plotting them you would assume that most of the major airlines would have very similar value curves and, therefore, constitute one strategic group. Plotting Southwest Airlines, as well as Southwest's imitators, such as JetBlue or Air Tran (or Ryanair in Europe), would probably reveal a strikingly different value curve. It is often convenient to consolidate similar competitors into a single value curve. The value curves in the industry visually represent the underlying logic incumbents use in positioning their products. Being able to visualize how competitors perform along these differentiators helps reveal industry assumptions. Understanding how competitors compete and surmising their assumptions are essential steps in predicting their future behaviors.

Predicting Competitors' Behaviors   After identifying the firm's closest rivals, it is important to gain a better understanding of their likely future behaviors. The specific rivals that are most pertinent to the analysis are those in the firm's same strategic group, those likely to move into the group, and those operating in groups that the firm may enter in the future. In the opening vignette on the Cola War, it is clear that Coke and Pepsi care deeply about what the other is doing. Neither wants to be caught off guard by a move the other may make in the future. Likewise, as new strategic groups have emerged in the beverage industry, such as in the flavored ice teas or premium sodas, they have had to pay more attention to these upstarts.

Several goals can be achieved by closely analyzing the firm's closest competitors. For instance, you may gain a better understanding of the competitors' future strategies. Similarly, you may gain a better appreciation for how competitors will respond to your strategic initiatives. Finally, you may also conclude that your firm's actions may influence competitors' behaviors, and some of these reactions may be to your benefit (or detriment). Although the firm's strategy should not be *determined* by competitors' behaviors, it should be *influenced* by what you think your competitors' behaviors are likely to be.

Porter suggests a four-step approach for making predictions about competitors. The first step in predicting the behaviors of competitors is to understand their objectives. These objectives are often surprisingly easy to determine if the companies are publicly-held firms, because their objectives are usually communicated regularly to shareholders through disclosure documents. The second step is to determine the competitors' current strategies. If you have already completed a strategic-group map, you probably have a good idea of those strategies. Further insight can be gained by using the strategy diamond and using public documents to see what competitors are doing in terms of arenas, vehicles, differentiators, staging, and economic logic. The third step is a bit more difficult, but it is critical to understanding the competitors' future behaviors: What assumptions does each competitor hold about the industry and about itself? People's behaviors are strongly influenced by the assumptions they make about themselves and the world. Again, communications between top executives and shareholders often hold insights into what these assumptions may be. Finally, the competitors' future behaviors will likely be related to the resources and capabilities they possess. What are the competitors' key strengths and weaknesses?

strategic group   Subset of firms which, because of similar strategies, resources, and capabilities, compete against each other more intensely than with other firms in an industry.

Evaluating the Value Curve in the Wine Industry[15]

L et's uncork an example of the value curve in action. With over $20 billion in annual revenues, the U.S. market is the largest contiguous wine market in the world. However, the market is intensely competitive, and California wines command two-thirds of all U.S. wine sales. This intense competition is further fueled by the fact that wines are produced and imported from almost every continent on the planet, and new entrants increasingly sell their wines at very low prices.

The threat of new entrants to the wine industry is very high; suppliers (wine-grape growers) are powerful; wineries are concentrated (C8 is 75 percent); sales channels are powerful because of consolidation; consumers are powerful because of the breadth of choices; and substitutes (any beverage) are many. Moreover, complements, such as the *Wine Spectator* and wine experts such as Robert Parker, are also powerful, because they rank wines based on taste and price, potentially swaying

Exhibit 4.9 A Value Curve for the U.S. Wine Industry

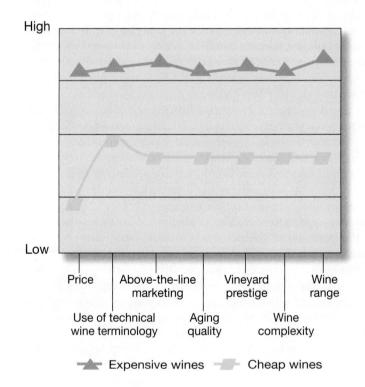

channel and consumer purchases. These factors suggest that the industry is not very attractive to new entrants. In fact, an old saying in the wine industry is that if you want to make $5 million, you need to start with $40 million!

So what does this mean with regard to the value curve and dynamic strategy? If we map the wine industry based on the characteristics of the dominant players and those factors considered essential to success, we would produce a map similar to the one in Exhibit 4.9. Notice that Exhibit 4.9 captures the dominant strategic groups—wineries competing in the budget or high-price segments. A new entrant could fight it out in the already hypercompetitive and overcapacity high-price or budget wine segments, or it could try to have a presence in both segments and use the resulting scale to its advantage.

You can use the value curve to see how incumbents are competing, map the strategic groups in an industry, and suggest how a new entrant might reconfigure the way it defines being a winery. In Chapter 6 you will learn how to use the value curve tool to craft a truly revolutionary strategy, and see such application in action by a wine company known as [yellow tail]®.

After addressing these four primary questions, you are in a position to make reasonable predictions about what your competitors are likely to do in the future. For instance, are they about to change their strategy? You may also gain insights into their likely reaction to any initiatives you are pondering.

Dynamic Characteristics of the External Context

The various models and analytical tools that we've discussed so far can provide an excellent snapshot of a firm's external context. In some industries, such a snapshot view gives a fairly accurate portrayal of the business landscape in the foreseeable future. In other cases, however, a snapshot captures little more than a first impression: The essential features of many industries are often undergoing gradual or rapid change. What's worse, snapshot views may give an overblown picture of a firm's competitive advantage: All we see may be a firm that's staked out a nice position in an attractive market, reaps enormous profits, and regularly makes large deposits in the bank. But if you reflect on the opening story of Coke and Pepsi, you know that competitors do not typically stand still and that overconfidence in the strength of one's competitive position is often a prelude to organizational decline.

Research increasingly shows that the durability of competitive advantages varies by industry or market.[16] For instance, the structural characteristics of some industries, such as utilities, will shift very little in the absence of significant regulatory changes. Other industries or markets may be undergoing gradual changes that may evolve into the kind of dramatic changes that we described in our story about Sears and Wal-Mart, where the change in market structure was dramatic but evolved over a long period of time. This is typically the case in the consumer products industry. As a rule, the relatively static analysis afforded by the five-forces model, plus the complementors dimension, applies best to industries such as these.

Industries in a third category, however, may be undergoing substantial change, whether because of the scale and scope of environmental changes, the rapid pace of such changes, or a combination of both. Dramatic change, for instance, can result from deregulation, which may bring about significant changes in key success factors and completely redesign the competitive playing field. Deregulation in the airline industry gave rise to discount carriers such as Southwest Airlines and JetBlue. Once a segment of niche players, the discount segment now poses a serious threat to the traditional hub-and-spoke segment dominated by American and United Airlines.

Changes in technology can dramatically change the business landscape and alter the nature of competitive advantage within an industry. In such cases, a relatively stable industry can be thrown into disarray until a new equilibrium is reached. Up until the mid-1980s, for example, the pineapple industry was relatively sleepy and fragmented. Then, Fresh Del Monte introduced a new variety developed by scientists at the Pineapple Research Institute. This "Extra Sweet Gold" pineapple has a bright gold color, rather than the pale yellow of the traditional pineapple; it is sweeter, less acidic, and highly resistant to parasites and rotting. Early introductions into the U.S. market were limited to a few cities on the East Coast. The pineapple was so well received that Fresh Del Monte quickly raised prices and exported the pineapple to all major U.S. markets. Despite higher prices, the Extra Sweet Gold captured 70 percent of the market.

What propelled Fresh Del Monte to the top of the market and allowed it to maintain the lion's share of what one would normally consider to be a commodity market? Fresh Del Monte successfully exploited a technological development that other firms ignored. Once it proved successful, Fresh Del Monte claimed proprietary rights to this particular strain of pineapple and was able to forestall other producers from planting the same variety. Eventually, the courts ruled that Fresh Del Monte did not have exclusive legal rights to this strain of pineapple, and companies such as Chiquita and Dole are now converting much of their production to this particular strain. Once again, dominance in the pineapple industry is up for grabs.

In this part of the chapter, we'll describe some tools for analyzing industries and formulating strategy in a dynamic context. We start by reviewing the most fundamental reason why some industries are more dynamic than others—the fact that the five forces or essential complementors are changing, not static. We then discuss two macro-level drivers of industry change: the *industry life cycle* and *discontinuities*. Although globalization itself is a profoundly important driver of change, as you read earlier in the chapter, it often goes hand-in-hand with the changes that accompany industry evolution and technological discontinuities.

DRIVERS OF CHANGE: MAKING THE FIVE-FORCES MODEL DYNAMIC

While learning to apply the various facets of industry analysis, you probably observed that some of your conclusions about industry structure would have to be modified if a given factor, such as the competitive behavior of one or more firms, altered any one of the five forces. One way to focus on the dynamic nature of the external context is to stop thinking of your analysis in terms of an industry snapshot and start thinking of it in terms of a "storybook" that shows how an industry structure is changing or may change. Any of the five forces that we have described so far can change significantly, and when that happens, the industry's structure and balance of power will probably be upset. Again, remember that some industries are dynamic simply because of the *rapid pace* of change. Think about the almost daily releases of new products in such markets as cell phone handsets, laser printers, and digital cameras.

Exhibit 4.10 lists a few potential sources of change and their effects on industry structure and profitability. Entry barriers, for instance, may be weakened, perhaps because of changes in technology.[17] The industry may be in its early stages, with many firms jockeying for position, many of whom will probably go out of business or be acquired as the industry matures. As the industry becomes more dynamic, such factors as substitutes and complementors may become more important. Finally, as an industry matures, buyers become more knowledgeable about product features and costs. We'll start our discussion of industry-change drivers by examining how industries often evolve over time.

Industry Life Cycle   Where do new industries come from? A new industry emerges when entirely new products are developed that satisfy customer demands in ways that existing products and technologies could not. The automobile industry emerged after Karl Benz developed an automobile powered by an Otto gasoline engine in 1885 and granted a patent in the following year.[18] Prior to that time, personal transportation was largely accomplished by means of horse and carriage, or trains for longer trips. Much like living organisms, industries evolve over time. The **industry life cycle** is a model that describes this evolution from inception through to its current state and possible future states. You have probably learned of a similar concept in your studies of marketing relating to the product life cycle. It so happens that competitive dynamics often follow a similar evolution at the industry level—from the point at which an industry emerges to the point at which it matures or perhaps even stagnates. The industry life cycle is a powerful driver of industry dynamics because it's a phenomenon characterized by change. Exhibit 4.11 illustrates the basic trajectory of the industry life cycle as well as numerous examples of industries at different stages of evolution.[19]

industry life cycle   Pattern of evolution followed by an industry inception to current and future states.

Evolution and Commoditization   One common result of this evolution is that an industry tends to become characterized by price competition, partly because many or most of its incumbents acquire similar resources and capabilities and so offer fairly similar products.

Exhibit 4.10 Dynamics of Industry Structure

Industry Rivalry
- *Increase in industry growth* ➜ Reduced rivalry and less pressure on prices
- *Globalization of industry* ➜ Increased rivalry as new foreign players enter the market, pressure for scale economies leading to consolidation, and market domination by fewer but larger competitors
- *Change in mix between fixed and variable costs* ➜ Shift to greater fixed costs creating more pressure to maintain sales levels and leading to greater propensity to compete on price

Threat of New Entrants
- *Decline in scale necessary to compete effectively* ➜ Increased rivalry because it's easier for start-ups to enter and effectively compete
- *Increases in customer heterogeneity* ➜ Easier entry because some customer segments are likely to be underserved plus increased ability to protect those segments that the firm serves well
- *Increased customer concentration* ➜ Reduces threat of new entry, leading to less pressure to compete on price

Bargaining Power of Suppliers
- *Increasing concentration of firms in supply industries* ➜ Greater supplier power and likelihood of reduced profitability in focal industry
- *Forward-integration by some key suppliers* ➜ Loss of power in focal industry because of reduction in number of viable suppliers
- *Emergence of substitute inputs that are good enough to satisfy basic needs* ➜ Reduction of supplier power and increased profits for focal industry

Bargaining Power of Buyers
- *Increased fragmentation of buyers' industry* ➜ Reduction in buyer power as the number of potential buyers increases and size of buyer industry declines relative to size of focal industry
- *Improvement in buyer information* ➜ Increased buyer power because of ability to compare
- *Emergence of new distribution channels* ➜ Reduction in buyer power because focal industry has more options

Threat of Substitutes
- *Emergence of a new substitute* ➜ Reduced ability to maintain high prices due to more buyer alternatives
- *Decline in the relative price performance of a substitute* ➜ Reduction in the threat of substitutes and pressure to maintain lower prices

Role of Complementors
- *Emergence of new complementors* ➜ Increased demand and less pressure on prices in focal industry
- *Higher barriers to entry in complementor industry* ➜ Greater complementor leverage and ability to profit from complementary relationship
- *Lower barriers to entry in complementor industry* ➜ Reduction in leverage of individual complementors leading to net increase of possible firms who can serve as complementors and increased demand

Source: Adapted from M. E. Porter, Competitive Strategy: Techniques for Analyzing Industries and Competitors (New York: Free Press, 1980)

commoditization Process during industry evolution by which sales eventually come to depend less on unique product features and more on price.

This trend is called **commoditization**—the process by which sales eventually come to depend less on unique product features and more on price.[20] Commoditization even affects technologically sophisticated products. Take the cell phone industry for example. Although handset sales are booming thanks to the addition of cameras, music players, and fancy software, cell phone voice services are fast becoming a basic commodity distinguished primarily by price. It is a pattern that other industries, from airlines to personal computers, have followed in recent decades as onetime technological breakthroughs became widely available.

Some cell phone service providers are introducing new services, such as picture messaging and video downloads, but the revenue they generate is minuscule alongside the

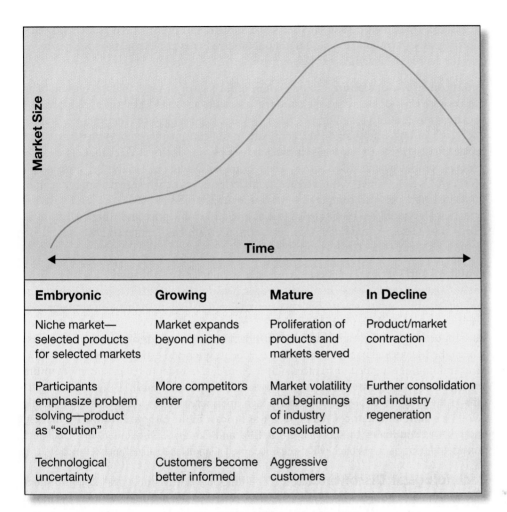

Exhibit 4.11 Industry Life Cycle Curve

Embryonic	Growing	Mature	In Decline
Niche market—selected products for selected markets	Market expands beyond niche	Proliferation of products and markets served	Product/market contraction
Participants emphasize problem solving—product as "solution"	More competitors enter	Market volatility and beginnings of industry consolidation	Further consolidation and industry regeneration
Technological uncertainty	Customers become better informed	Aggressive customers	

vast sums spent on voice calls, and their growth is expected to be slow. In Europe, there has been an influx of so-called no-frills service providers that basically use a model similar to that of low cost airlines. The U.S. market, although still growing, has already become more commoditized, with prices plunging and companies locked in fierce competition for new customers. A marked slowdown in revenue growth could exacerbate the long-running price war in the U.S., where competition has pushed the average per-minute cost of a call down more than 65 percent in the past four years, according to Yankee Group, a consulting firm.[21] One effect of the slowdown is increasing globalization and consolidation in the cell phone industry, as some of Europe's big service providers look for revenue growth by expanding outside their home markets. Demand for cell phone services is growing much faster than analysts had expected in Southeast Asia, Africa, Latin America, and other emerging markets, which tend to be dominated by a couple of local players.

Evolution and Reinvigoration As some industries mature, however, certain segments may emerge to reinvigorate them, sometimes even restoring their status as growth industries (as a matter of fact, it's hard to imagine any industry that doesn't have at least one growth segment). The bicycle industry, for example, has existed for more than 200 years, and during that time, technological advances have periodically increased the product's popularity and given rise to growth segments in an otherwise stagnant industry. In the 1960s, for instance, the emergence of children's bike designs and the 10-speed accelerated sales. More recently, the mountain bike has not only spurred sales growth but has spawned many new specialized bike manufacturing companies.

Evolution and Information Although most of the factors involved in the evolution of an industry are fairly obvious, the role of information and customer learning has only recently begun to attract the attention of researchers.[22] We're beginning to see, for example, that the effects of learning, information, and competition can conspire to enable newer entrants to replace industry leaders, especially in the later stages of industry-wide change. The emergence of computer retailer Dell is an excellent example. Originally, because Dell targeted sophisticated buyers—buyers who were technologically savvy and who needed little education on the uses of a personal computer—it was able to invest less money in pre- and postsales activities. Dell could sell leading-edge PCs at a relatively low price and still make a profit, and as the market matured and price competition became more intense, Dell was able to leapfrog IBM and other larger companies.

Evolution and Tactics The effect of customer learning and information often isn't apparent until later in the life cycle. In the early stages, because there's usually a lack of knowledge and information about new products, customers tend to look to industry incumbents not only as a source of education but as a form of insurance in the way of more extensive product support. During the transition from introduction to growth, as once-new products establish themselves and become accepted, incumbents often add extra services, such as shipping, training, or extended warrantees at little or no cost in order to retain sales momentum through the growth phase. Taken together, these factors usually mean higher *average* margins in the early stages of growth because high and increasing operating costs are usually offset by relatively high prices. Again, such was the case in the early years of the PC market, when it was dominated by such players as IBM and Compaq. Discounters like Dell were considered fringe players back when they occupied a small, specialized market niche.

Technological Discontinuities

The link between technological discontinuities and industry change should be readily apparent from our discussion of industry evolution as a driver of change.[23] Moreover, technology is one of the key factors in the PESTEL framework you learned about earlier in the chapter: Discontinuities are a special, intensive case of technological change in action. Get in the habit of thinking broadly about the nature of the changes that create technological discontinuities. Technological discontinuities are much more extreme than mere incremental technological change.

To examine these extreme forms of change, it is important to understand first that technological discontinuities include both changes in science-based technologies (such as innovations) and business-process technologies (such as new business models). The two major forms of technology are *process technology* and *product technology.* Process technology refers to the devices, tools, and knowledge used to transform inputs into outputs. Product technology creates new products.[24] Needless to say, technological changes can have traumatic effects on industries and firms.[25] Indeed, major technological changes often alter firm environments and industry structures significantly. Of course, not all technological changes affect competitors and industries equally. Some, for example, work to the advantage of incumbents, others to that of new entrants.

Disruptive Product-Related Change Patterns of technological change often reflect gradual *incremental* evolutionary change. However, other forms of episodic change are also prone to punctuate industry evolution; we characterize these forms of change as *discontinuous* change.[26] Discontinuous technological change occurs when breakthrough technologies appear, sometimes sustaining the competencies of incumbent firms and sometimes destroying them. Competency-sustaining technologies are typically introduced by incumbents.

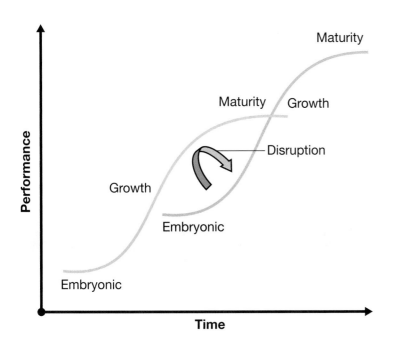

Exhibit 4.12 Discontinuity in the Industry Life Cycle

Those that destroy incumbents' competencies are called **disruptive technologies.** In many instances, these disruptions have been introduced by new firms.[27] A disruptive change introduced by a new technology also has the effect of altering the industry life cycle. The industry is reinvigorated and rather than proceeding into decline accelerates into new phases of growth, as illustrated by Exhibit 4.12.

As an illustration of this process, consider the minicomputer industry. Out of 116 major innovations introduced in the minicomputer industry (the precursor to the personal computer), 111 were incremental sustaining technological improvements and only 5 were disruptive. All 111 sustaining technologies were introduced by incumbents, whereas all 5 disruptive technologies were introduced by outsiders—firms specializing in new personal computers. In the disk drive industry, virtually every new generation of technology has led to the demise of the market leader. The arrival of the personal computer, for example, heralded the downfall of every major competitor in the minicomputer industry.[28] This process, known as the **innovator's dilemma,** unfolds in established industries when incumbents continue to develop competency-enhancing innovations, while new entrants develop disruptive innovations.[29] Specifically, the *dilemma* for incumbents is that their economic incentives are to continue developing evolutionary improvements in their existing technology and to avoid sponsoring disruptive innovations, even when the disruptive technology may eventually supplant the existing technology.

What are these incentives that usually persuade incumbents to maintain a course of incremental, sustaining innovations rather than adopting the disruptive innovation? Sustaining innovations are introduced to satisfy the needs of firms' best customers; those who demand the most from their products and who pay the highest margins to receive such service. In the case of minicomputers, firms like DEC were satisfying their largest business customers by continually improving the speed and power of their top-of-the-line minicomputers. These units would sell for tens of thousands of dollars and have margins of 25 percent or more. The new personal computers that new entrants were producing would sell for only a few thousand dollars, and the margins may have been ten percentage points or more less. Thus, you could say that DEC was being entirely rational to avoid this market. However, that calculus ignores the new business landscape that disruptive innovations will create in the not-too-distant future. ◆

disruptive technology
Breakthrough product- or process-related technology that destroys the competencies of incumbent firms in an industry.

innovator's dilemma
When incumbents avoid investing in innovative and disruptive technologies because those innovations do not satisfy the needs of their mainstream and most profitable clients.

Economic Logic

Exhibit 4.13 The Innovator's Dilemma

Adapted from C. M. Christensen, The Innovator's Dilemma *(Cambridge, MA: Harvard Business Press, 1997).*

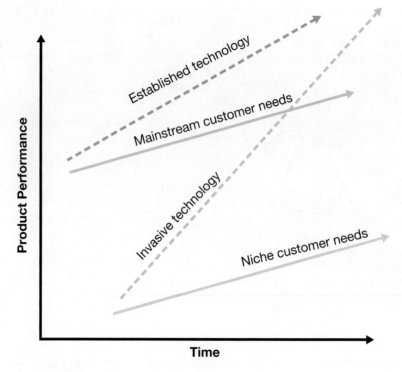

The process of disruptive change is illustrated in Exhibit 4.13. Incumbents tend to serve the needs of their best customers. Ironically, they are executing and improving upon the *economic logic* of their existing strategy, even though the other facets—*differentiators* and *arenas*—of the strategy will be made dramatically obsolete by the innovator's products or services. Consequently, over time, their products tend to migrate away from the center of the market; they out-innovate the needs of most customers. Disruptive technological innovations are often initially aimed at a small segment of the market, perhaps the lower end—those customers for whom incumbents' innovations are really more than they need. The margins for these innovations are often much lower than the margins on new, competency-enhancing innovations. It isn't until the disruptive innovation goes through several phases of refinement and improvement that it eventually migrates up the industry product hierarchy that it eventually steals more valued customers from incumbents. By this time the new entrants have improved their products sufficiently that they satisfy most of the needs of the larger market, and they do so for a fraction of the cost of incumbents.

Exhibit 4.13 demonstrates the interplay between incumbents' innovation and new entrants' innovation. Notice how established companies sometimes follow an innovation trajectory that leads them to overshoot the majority of their mainstream customers' needs. The invasive technology, however, which may be initially targeted at lower-end customers eventually migrates upstream to be good enough for the basic needs of many mainstream customers. This process, while not universally true in all industries, has been documented as the source of dynamic change in many industries. A few examples are notebook computers and handheld digital appliances, full-service stock brokerage and on-line stock brokerage, printed greeting cards and free on-line greeting cards, classroom- and campus-based higher education and distance education, offset printing and digital printing, and cardiac surgery and angioplasty, just to name a few.[30]

Disruptive Process-Related Change It's important to remember that disruptive technologies can be process-related as well as product-related. The development of manufacturing (TQM) methods, for instance, eventually elevated the Japanese auto industry to world-class status. TQM programs such as *six sigma* and *lean* are process innovations. No automaker in the world can now ignore the competitive threat posed by such firms as Toyota and Honda, and, in fact, many who once did are now struggling to emulate the TQM methods pioneered by these one-time fringe players.

Southwest Airlines radically changed the business model that had long dominated the industry, but established full-service airlines originally took little notice. Why? Because Southwest's new process couldn't help them meet the needs of their most profitable customers. In time, however, the number and length of Southwest's flights reached the point at which the services provided by its model could satisfy the demands of customers who normally used larger airlines.

Likewise, Wal-Mart's business model was originally of little threat to Sears because it focused on rural areas that Sears was happy to ignore. Eventually, Wal-Mart's model was transferable to larger markets, but it was too late for Sears to respond. A similar pattern unfolded in the steel industry. At first, large firms ignored the emergence of so-called "mini-mills" because their unsophisticated technology was efficient only in turning out the least profitable products. But as the capabilities of mini-mill technology improved, so did the ability of the new firms to enter more profitable segments of the industry.

WHEN INDUSTRIES DIVIDE

The industry life cycle model is too simplistic to describe the evolution of many industries. In some cases, one industry becomes two or more distinct but related industries. One cause of such a split is the decision by a firm to divest a once-core business that has been separated from the firm's original core because of industry changes. As a rule, the divestiture is prompted by the emergence of a new market.

Such was the case with 3Com Corporation and its Palm division. 3Com originally specialized in modems, which have both hardware and software components. In developing this interface, 3Com innovated a new product that linked the two components. It was called the PalmPilot, and it soon defined the new personal data assistant (PDA) industry. Once convinced that the PDA industry was distinct from its core business in the modem industry, 3Com sold off its Palm division in a public stock offering. New entrants into the PDA industry began to specialize in either the software or hardware side of the business, with Sony, Compaq, and Dell making hardware and Palm and Microsoft selling software. Now Palm is weighing the idea of breaking up into two smaller firms—one that specializes in software and one that develops hardware. Remember: Before 3Com's original innovation, there was no such thing as a PDA industry—let alone any subindustries.

Finally, industries may divide when the market for a particular product becomes large enough that firms can economically justify dedicating a distribution channel to it. This type of division typically results in new industry *segments* or *subindustries* rather than in new industries. A good example is the emergence of so-called *category killers* in various retail industries—industry segments composed of large, highly specialized retail chains, such as PetSmart or Home Depot and Lowe's. They're called "category killers" because they aim to dominate whatever category they participate in by offering the broadest possible assortment of goods at the lowest possible prices. The Internet has spawned a number of such segments and some well-known firms, including Amazon.com and BarnesandNoble.com in books and Travelocity.com and Zuji.com in travel.

WHEN INDUSTRIES COLLIDE

Although some changes lead to industry division, others result in new industry definitions that consolidate two or more separate industries into one. As you read this section of the chapter, note the distinction between industry *consolidation* and industry *concentration*. Whereas *concentration* results in an industry with fewer players, *consolidation* results in fewer industries. Ironically, changes in concentration can lead to either consolidation or division.[31]

Today, for example, both the global media and entertainment industries seem to be agglomerations of many once-distinct industries. The definition of the media industry now includes firms with a significant presence in both program distribution (they own or control television networks) and program content (they own or develop new shows). The largest incumbents are often called media and entertainment *conglomerates* (which suggests organizations composed of unrelated divisions), but in reality the dominant players, including VivendiUniversal, Fox, Disney, and Viacom, have consolidated a broad range of functions that were once performed by suppliers, substitutes, complementors, or even customers.

Industry division and convergence happens over time. Opportunities to create significant value tend to be greatest for firms that lead the charge in convergence and division of industries. However, when firms define their industries very broadly, performing external analysis becomes much more complicated. For instance, framing a printing company like FedEx/Kinko's as a simple printer versus a marketing-communications firm connotes a broadly different set of industry conditions.

Now that you're familiar with a few key drivers of industry change, it is important that you understand the particular implications of technological and business-model breakthroughs for both the pace and extent of industry change. The *rate* of change may vary significantly from one industry to the next. The rate of change in the computing industry, for example, has been much faster than in the steel industry. Nevertheless, changes in both industries has prompted complete reconfigurations of industry structure and the competitive positions of various players. The idea that all industries change over time and that business environments are in a constant state of flux is relatively intuitive. As a strategic decision maker, therefore, the question you need to keep asking yourself is, how accurately does current structure (which is relatively easy to identify) predict future industry conditions?

Summary of Challenges

1. *Explain the importance of the external context for strategy and firm performance.*   In order to understand the threats and opportunities facing an organization, you need a thorough understanding of its external context, including not only its industry, but the larger environment in which it operates. The proper analysis of the external context, together with the firm-level analysis you learned in Chapter 3 (e.g., VRINE, value-chain), allow you to complete a rigorous analysis of a firm and its options. You could say that with these tools you can now perform a thorough and systematic (rather than intuitive) *SWOT analysis;* that is, an assessment of a firm's strengths, weaknesses, opportunities, and threats.

2. *Use PESTEL to identify the macro characteristics of the external context.*   PESTEL analysis and an understanding of the drivers of globalization can be used to characterize the macro characteristics of the firm's external environment. PESTEL is an acronym for the political, economic, sociocultural, technological, environmental, and legal contexts in which a firm operates. Managers can use the PESTEL analysis to gain a better understanding of the opportunities and threats faced by the firm. By knowing the firm's opportunities and threats, managers can build a better vision of the future business landscape and identify how the firm may compete profitably. By examining the drivers of globalization, managers can identify how market, cost, governments, and competition work to favor the globalization of an industry.

3. *Identify the major features of an industry and the forces that affect industry profitability.*   The major factors to be analyzed when examining an industry are rivalry, the power of suppliers, the power of buyers, the threat of substitutes, and the threat of new entrants. When suppliers and buyers have significant power, they tend to be able to negotiate away some of the profit that would otherwise be available to industry rivals. Thus, profits tend to be lower than average in industries that face high levels of supplier and buyer power. Likewise, as the threat of new entrants and the availability of substitutes increases, the ability of rivals in the industry to keep prices high is reduced. Rivalry within an industry decreases profitability. High levels of rivalry result in heavy emphasis on price-based competition. Rivalry is reduced when products are differentiated. Strategic-group analysis is used to gain a better understanding of the nature of rivalry. Whereas industry profits tend to be reduced when any of the five forces are strong, the presence of complementors results in the opposite; they increase the ability of firms to generate profits. Finally, an analysis of competitors' objectives, current strategies, assumptions, and resources and capabilities can help managers predict the future behaviors of their competitors.

4. Understand the dynamic characteristics of the external context. The various models and analytical tools presented can provide an excellent snapshot of a firm's external context. In some industries, such a snapshot view gives an accurate portrayal of the look of the business landscape for the foreseeable future. The five forces of industry structure change, and very rapidly in some industries; other drivers of change to which managers must be attuned include the stage and pace of transition in the industry life cycle and technological discontinuities.

5. Show how industry dynamics may redefine industries. In some cases, one industry becomes two or more distinct, but often related, industries. Industries may also divide when the market for a particular product becomes large enough that firms can economically justify dedicating a distribution channel to it. Whereas some changes lead to industry division, others result in new industry definitions that consolidate two or more separate industries into one. Industry convergence and division happen over time, and firms that identify such changes and initiate early changes have a better opportunity to create value.

Review Questions

1. What constitutes the external context of strategy?

2. What are the five forces affecting industry structure?

3. What are complementors?

4. What is a key success factor (KSF)?

5. What are strategic groups?

6. What factors increase industry dynamics?

7. What is the industry life cycle?

8. What is a technological discontinuity?

9. What is the innovator's dilemma?

10. How does globalization affect the external context of strategy?

11. What is industry redefinition?

Experiential Activities

Group Exercises

1. Pick two of the industries listed in Exhibit 4.1, one on the high end of profitability and one on the low end. What are the boundaries of these industries? What are their market and geographic segments? Who are the key players? Draw up a five-forces model of each industry and compare and contrast their industry structure. Now shift your analysis to the dynamic five-forces model. What dimensions of the five-forces model are most likely to change in the near future? Which are most likely to stay relatively stable? Answer these questions for both 5- and 10-year windows.

Ethical Debates

1. Genetically modified organisms (GMOs) include food products in which genetics have been used to extend product shelf

life, deter pests, and other product innovations. Much of the food consumed in the U.S. is genetically modified, while many other developing countries prohibit them for ethical and other reasons. Ethical objections to GMO foods typically center on the possibility of harm to persons or other living things. What do you believe explains this striking difference in ethical views about GMO food between the U.S. and other global markets?

2. Despite the pharmaceutical industry's notable contributions to human progress, including the development of miracle drugs for treating cancer, AIDS, and heart disease, there is a growing ethical tension between the industry and the public. What are some of the key ethical questions, and how does that affect your analysis of the pharmaceutical industry?

How Would
YOU DO THAT?

1. The box entitled "How Would *You* Do That? 4.1" illustrates the five-forces model for the airline industry. Use the analysis there as an example and perform a five-forces analysis for one of the following industries: soft drinks, cable television, or cell phone service providers. What are the one or two most important issues from your analysis that managers in that industry must take into account when they revisit their strategies?

2. Using the value curve model illustrated in "How Would *You* Do That? 4.2," map the strategic groups in the soft drink industry. What groups are there other than the two dominant companies? How do they compete relative to Coke and Pepsi?

Go on to see How Would You Do That at www.prenhall.com/ carpenter&sanders

Endnotes

1. Data from Standard & Poor's Compustat.

2. G. Yip, "Global Strategy in a World of Nations," *Sloan Management Review* 31:1 (1989), 29–40.

3. M. Porter, *Competition in Global Industries* (Boston: Harvard Business School Press, 1986); Yip, "Global Strategy in a World of Nations."

4. Adapted from M. E. Porter, *Competition in Global Industries* (Boston: Harvard Business School Press, 1986); G. Yip, "Global Strategy in a World of Nations," *Sloan Management Review* 31:1 (1989), 29–40.

5. R. Amit and P. J. H. Schoemaker, "Strategic Assets and Organizational Rent," *Strategic Management Journal* 14 (1993), 33–46; J. A. Vasconcellos and D. C. Hambrick, "Key Success Factors: Test of a General Framework in the Mature Industrial-Product Sector," *Strategic Management Journal* 10 (1989), 367–382.

6. "A Fruit Revolution," *Convenience Store News* 41:4 (2005), 20; J. Cioletti, "Flavoring the Market," *Beverage World* 124:3 (2005), 6; B. Bobala, "Water Wars," March 10, 2003 (accessed July 15, 2005), www.fool.com/news/commentary/2003/commentary030310bb.htm.

7. U.S. Census Bureau, "Economic Census: Concentration Ratios," *Economic Census 2002* (accessed April 15, 2007), www.census.gov/epcd/www/concentration.html.

8. Adapted from M. E. Porter, *Competitive Strategy: Techniques for Analyzing Industries and Competitors* (New York: Free Press, 1980).

9. M. Porter, *Competitive Strategy: Techniques for Analyzing Industries and Competitors* (New York: Free Press, 1980).

10. S. Leith, "Virgin Cola Returns—but More Quietly," *Atlanta Journal Constitution*, July 1, 2004, E1.

11. www.packersnews.com/archives/news/pack_10906648.shtml (accessed July 15, 2005).

12. A. Brandenburger and B. Nalebuff, *Co-Opetition* (New York: Currency Doubleday, 1996).

13. Much of this section is adapted from important studies in the field of game theory, and we'll return to the topic when we discuss strategic alliances and other cooperative strategies. At this point, we offer merely an overview. See A. Dixit and B. Nalebuff, *Thinking Strategically: The Competitive Edge in Business and Politics and Everyday Life* (New York: W. W. Norton, 1992); and A. Brandenburger and B. Nalebuff, *Co-Opetition.*

14. J. E. Ellis, "The Law of Gravity Doesn't Apply: Inefficiency, Overcapacity, Huge Debt . . . What Keeps U.S. Carriers Up in the Air?" *BusinessWeek,* September 26, 2005, p. 49; H. Tully, "Airlines: Why the Big Boys Won't Come Back," *Fortune,* June 14, 2004, p. 101.

15. W. C. Kim and R. Mauborgne, "Blue Ocean Strategy," *California Management Review* 47:3 (2005), 105–121; Wine Institute, "Strong Sales Growth in 2004 for California Wine as Shipments Reached New High," April 5, 2005 (accessed July 12, 2005), www.wineinstitute.org; www.elitewine.com/site/index.php?lang=en&cat=news&art=159.

16. R. Wiggins and T. Ruefli, "Competitive Advantage: Temporal Dynamics and the Incidence and Persistence of Superior Economic Performance," *Organization Science* 13 (2002), 82–105.

17. Adapted from M. E. Porter, *Competitive Strategy: Techniques for Analyzing Industries and Competitors* (New York: Free Press, 1980).

18. R. Stein, *The Automobile Book* (London: Paul Hamlyn Ltd, 1967).

19. Adapted from K. Rangan and G. Bowman, "Beating the Commodity Magnet," *Industrial Marketing Management* 21 (1992), 215–224; P. Kotler, "Managing Products Through Their Product Life Cycle," in *Marketing Management: Planning, Implementation, and Control,* 7th ed. (Upper Saddle River, NJ: Prentice Hall, 1991).

20. L. Argote, *Organizational Learning: Creating, Retaining, and Transferring Knowledge* (Boston: Kluwer Academic Publishers, 1999); A. S. Miner and P. Haunschild, "Population Level Learning," *Research in Organizational Behavior* 17 (1995), 115–166.

21. D. Pringle, "Slower Growth Hits Cellphone Services Overseas in EU, Japan, Saturation Leads to Some Contraction; Looking Beyond Voice," *Wall Street Journal,* May 23, 2005, A1.

22. See G. Moore, *Crossing the Chasm* (New York: Harper Business Essentials, 2002); C. Shapiro and H. R. Varian, *Information Rules: A Strategic Guide to the Network Economy* (Boston: Harvard Business School Press, 1998).

23. N. Rosenberg, *Technology and American Economic Growth* (New York, Harper & Row, 1986); M. L. Tushman and P. Anderson, "Technological Discontinuities and Organizational Environments," *Administrative Science Quarterly* 31 (1986), 439–465.

24. W. P. Barnett, "The Organizational Ecology of a Technological System," *Administrative Science Quarterly* 35 (1990), 31–60; R. M. Henderson and K. B. Clark, "Architectural Innovation: The Reconfiguration of Exist-

ing Product Technologies and the Failure of Established Firms," *Administrative Science Quarterly* 35 (1990), 9–30.

25. Tushman and Anderson, "Technological Discontinuities and Organizational Environments."

26. Tushman and Anderson, "Technological Discontinuities and Organizational Environments."

27. C. M. Christensen, *The Innovator's Dilemma* (Cambridge, MA: Harvard Business Press, 1997).

28. Christensen, *The Innovator's Dilemma.*

29. Christensen, *The Innovator's Dilemma.*

30. Christensen, *The Innovator's Dilemma.*

31. Consolidation may result from increased concentration when bigger players in an industry absorb the functions of suppliers, substitutes, complements, or customers (a process under way in the global media and entertainment industries). By getting bigger, these firms broaden the definition of their operations, but successfully managing all the components of a broader operation is a separate matter. Concentration often results in division when players that have grown too big can no longer give adequate attention to some segment of their market or some facet of their operations. Division also occurs when, because of increased concentration, a new market emerges to attract large firms.

5 Creating Business Strategies

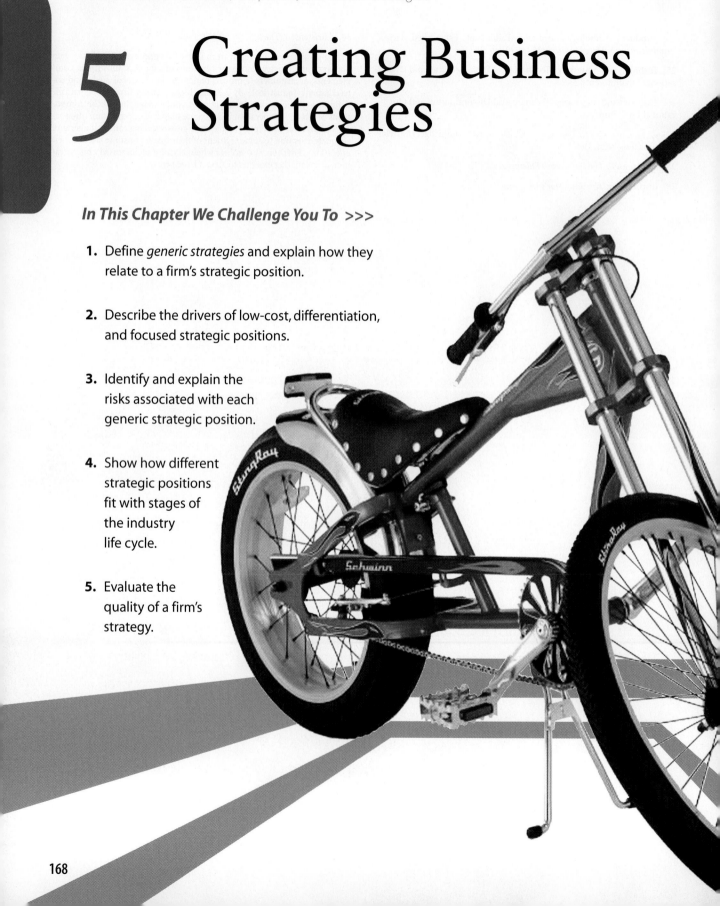

In This Chapter We Challenge You To >>>

1. Define *generic strategies* and explain how they relate to a firm's strategic position.

2. Describe the drivers of low-cost, differentiation, and focused strategic positions.

3. Identify and explain the risks associated with each generic strategic position.

4. Show how different strategic positions fit with stages of the industry life cycle.

5. Evaluate the quality of a firm's strategy.

A Tale of
Three Wheels
in the Bicycle Industry

hris Hornung, founder and first CEO of Pacific Cycle, grabbed the lion's share of the U.S. bicycle market by buying well-known brands and crafting big distribution deals with America's largest retailers. In 2005, over 19.8 million bicycles were sold in the U.S.[1] According to industry trade reports, the total retail value of bikes, parts, and accessories was more than $6 billion. Who sold all of these bicycles and bike-related products? There are literally hundreds of bicycle manufacturers in the U.S., but most are small, specialized firms.

Among them, one company—Pacific Cycle—sells more bicycles than any other company in North America. "We're interested in a high-volume business," said Hornung. "That's our business model." Pacific Cycle designs, markets, and imports a full range of bikes and recreation products under such familiar brand names as Schwinn, GT, Mongoose, Kustom Kruiser, Roadmaster, Pacific, Dyno, Powerlite, InSTEP, and Pacific Outdoors. Its powerful brand portfolio serves virtually all consumer demographics, price categories, and product categories (e.g., children's, mountain, and racing bikes).

Hornung started his company at age 22 as a modest bike import business. He pioneered the concept of sourcing bicycles from Asia for distribution in the U.S. While on a buying trip to Taiwan in 1983, Hornung met buyers from Target Corp. and Toys 'R' Us, which provided him an entryway into the mass market retailers.

Now, his company is one of the fastest-growing branded consumer-product companies in the U.S. Hornung has achieved this success by combining an aggressive acquisition of power brands with low-cost outsourcing, efficient supply-chain management, and multichannel retail distribution. In December 2000, Hornung acquired the bicycle division of Brunswick Corp. for $60 million, which included the Mongoose, Mongoose Pro, and Roadmaster brands. In the deal, Hornung got more than the brands of Brunswick, he got a very big customer. That purchase nearly doubled Pacific's sales, because Wal-Mart was Brunswick's biggest account, Hornung said. A year later, Hornung bought the assets of Schwinn/GT Corp. out of bankruptcy for $86 million, a move that added an American icon to the company portfolio.

Pacific Cycle's channels include leading mass-market retailers such as Wal-Mart, Target, and Toys 'R' Us; sporting goods chains such as Dick's, The Sports Authority, and Gart Sports; and independent dealers serving local markets. The company's brands appeal to the full spectrum of demographics, price preferences, and image and usage criteria that are critical to targeting the key consumer segments served by each channel. This broad-based marketing strategy enables Pacific to provide retailers with one-stop shopping and to respond efficiently to changes in the marketplace. For example, the Schwinn brand historically was only sold through specialty bike shops. But Hornung brought it into the mass market. "We didn't want to limit the Schwinn brand to just specialty dealers," Hornung said. "The major retailers were anxious to carry a brand that has 107 years of history behind it." The public wanted it, too: "Cycling is a family sport, and our move into the mass-market channel simply recognizes that Schwinn—the premium bike brand—must be available where most families shop today," Hornung said. Moving the brand into mass retailers broadened access to Schwinn bicycles to greater numbers of consumers and helped lower the price. The average price of a Schwinn at a mass retailer is $65, compared to $387 at a specialty store, according to the U.S. National Bicycle Dealers Association. Overall, the average retail price of bikes has declined steadily, at about 15 percent per year. That decline has made it important for Pacific to control costs, Hornung said. Hornung faces new challenges as well. Competition among distributors "is as tough now as I've ever seen it," Hornung said.

Hornung's strategy has been simple: Import quality bikes from Asia. Distribute them to mass merchants such as Wal-Mart. Keep payrolls to an absolute minimum. Since applying that strategy to Schwinn, Hornung has seen the brand lose the support of most independent dealers. But it's been a hit among mass merchants. Consumers now pay less for the new Sting Ray under Pacific's ownership. It may not be the engineering marvel that was the old Schwinn, but it retails at Wal-Mart for about a third of the original's price.

Pacific Cycle was recently acquired by Doral Inc., and now operates as an independent strategic business unit (SBU). It is now one of the most prolific bicycle suppliers in the world, selling products in more than 60 countries via more than 50 international distributors. In 2007, Pacific Cycle's President, Jeff Frehner, was promoted to President and Chief Executive Officer as Hornung ended his 30-year tenure at the company, leaving Pacific to launch NextTesting. Frehner will continue to build Pacific's international business and strengthen its brands across the globe.

Another successful bike maker, Trek Bicycle, has revenues similar to Pacific. Richard Burke and Bevill Hogg founded Trek in 1976. With $25,000 in seed money, Burke and Hogg started building bikes by hand in a Wisconsin barn. From the beginning, they targeted upper-end users, and success came quickly. Today, customers pay top dollar for smooth suspensions, custom paint jobs, and innovations in racing geometry. With annual sales of about $400 million, Trek is now the country's number-one maker of high-quality bikes and was perhaps the first U.S. bike maker to overcome European resistance to American-made cycles by focusing on quality and innovation, which have long been Trek's hallmarks. The company introduced its first mountain bike line in 1983, the first bonded-aluminum road bike in 1985, and a carbon-fiber road bike in 1986.

Although most of Trek's growth has been fueled by internally developed products, Trek has also made a few strategic acquisitions, including Gary Fisher Mountain Bike and two mountain bike competitors (Bontrager and Klein) in 1995. Trek now makes various types of bicycles, including mountain, road, children's, recumbent, police, and BMX bikes. Internationally, Trek bikes are sold through wholly owned subsidiaries in 7 countries and through distributors in 65 others. Trek designs all of its bikes at its Wisconsin headquarters and manufactures a quarter of them in the United States. Finally, the company's sponsorship of seven-time Tour de France winner Lance Armstrong has given the company tremendous exposure and the centerpiece for a marketing plan that, as one Trek executive puts it, can be summed up as "Lance, Lance, Lance."

Whereas Pacific Cycle and Trek represent the larger players in the U.S. market, Montague fits the profile of a boutique-style bike firm. Frustration prompted Harry Montague, a Washington, D.C. architect and inventor, to develop the Montague line of high-performance, travel-friendly bicycles: He was unable to find anything but small-wheeled folding bikes, and they were both uncomfortable and inefficient for serious cyclists who wanted to take their bikes in the car or on public transportation. After much trial and error, Montague succeeded in developing a full-size high-performance folding bicycle that he then custom-built and sold out of his garage for D.C.-area riders.

Montague moved out of the garage after Harry's son David was required to create an extensive business plan for a course in entrepreneurship at the Massachusetts Institute of Technology (MIT) Sloan School of Business. David designed a formal business plan around his father's bicycle, and as soon as David passed the course, he and his father formed the Montague Corp. to design and produce full-size bicycles that sacrifice little in performance while providing travel-friendly convenience for a targeted market of customers. Today, Montague is the world's leading manufacturer of folding bikes. All Montague bikes fold into a compact size in less than 30 seconds without the use of tools. They have been sold to the military for tactical use and to several car manufacturers for promotional packaging with SUVs.

Pacific Cycle, Trek, and Montague may be in the same industry, but each pursues a very different strategy in an attempt to meet the needs of customers. In this chapter, you will be introduced to the basics of business strategy—the tools and models that will help you formulate coherent strategies for competing within an industry context. **<<<**

An Introduction to Business Strategies

In this chapter, we build on Chapters 3 and 4 by discussing ways in which firms formulate business strategies that capitalize on their resources and capabilities to exploit opportunities in their competitive environments. At the same time, we set the stage for Chapter 6, which explores strategy in dynamic contexts. As we saw in Chapter 1, *business strategy* refers to the choices that a firm makes about its competitive posture within a particular line of business. These choices can be summarized by the *strategy diamond* and its *five elements of strategy.*

 **Economic Logic**

As we saw in our opening vignette about three bicycle companies, there's more than one economic logic or way to compete in an industry. ◆ Pacific Cycle, for example, markets a product for virtually every segment, offers a range of quality in its product mix, and keeps costs down by outsourcing all of its production to China and Taiwan. Trek, meanwhile, though also a large company with a broad product mix, focuses on specialized and innovative product attributes to target specific customer segments and one channel—independent bike distributors. Montague is an entirely different company, marketing a highly specialized product targeted at a narrow range of potential customers.

As a rule, competitive positions can be established in many different ways, and the task of finding the best configuration of positions is the subject of this chapter. We'll start by introducing a well-established framework for strategic positioning developed by Michael Porter and then describe the conditions under which particular strategic positions are viable. We'll also examine ways in which alternative strategic positions are compatible with different stages of the industry life cycle. Finally, because a successful strategy must be consistent with both a firm's resources and the competitive environment, we'll conclude by describing a process for testing the quality of a strategy according to this criterion.

Types of Strategies—Finding a Position That Works

When you consider all the choices that can be made relative to the strategy diamond, there are almost endless potential strategies that a firm could choose. To simplify these possible choices for managers, in this section we introduce the generic strategy typology. This typology is useful to help select a starting strategic position. **Strategic positioning** refers to the ways managers situate a firm relative to its rivals along important competitive dimensions. The strategic positioning model that we present in this chapter is a classic framework in the field of strategic management—Michael Porter's *generic strategy model*. Recall that under the industry structure model that we introduced in Chapter 4, the key force in an industry—indeed, the force around which all others revolve—is rivalry among the firms in the industry. The purpose of strategic positioning is to reduce the effects of rivalry and thereby improve profitability, and the generic strategies that derive from the strategic positioning model are related to the industry structure model: They help managers stake out a position for their firm relative to rivals *in ways that reduce the effects of intense rivalry on profitability.*

strategic positioning   Means by which managers situate a firm relative to its rivals.

The concept of strategic positioning is a useful starting point in dealing with issues deriving from the strategy diamond model that we explored in Chapter 1. The generic strategy typology has managers start by identifying the intended *economic logic* of their strategy and the *arenas* in which they will compete. Underlying the choice of economic logic is also some idea as to what *differentiators* the firm might employ. First, the model asks strategists to decide if they will compete based on the logic of being a low cost leader (e.g., a competitor that will achieve higher margins due to a lower cost basis than rivals) or as a differentiator (e.g., a competitor that will achieve higher prices and margins because of superior quality). For instance, Trek attempts to position its brands as possessing superior quality, and therefore warranting higher prices, through endorsements by industry superstars such as Lance Armstrong and exclusive distribution through independent bike dealers. Secondly, the model asks strategists to decide whether they intend to serve the broad market or more specialized niches. An automobile manufacturer, for example, must decide whether to compete in all geographic markets and all product lines (say, everything from high-performance to economy-priced cars—as you might see when contrasting Porsche with Daimler).

This model also helps decision makers deal with questions about a firm's tactics for motivating customers to choose its products over those of competitors. Consider the market for luxury cars. Will customers buy from a firm because it offers the lowest-priced luxury sedan (such as the Buick Park Avenue), because it's known for its quality (say, Lexus), or because it offers the most valuable brand image (perhaps Mercedes Benz)?

A firm's choice of position should be primarily influenced by two important factors: (1) firm resources and capabilities and (2) industry structure. Formulating a strategy means using tools such as those that we introduced in Chapters 3 and 4 to make critical decisions about how and where to compete—that is, how to position a company relative to its rivals. In addition, if a firm hopes to exploit opportunities while withstanding competitive threats from within its industry, its strategy should be built on its unique resources and capabilities.

GENERIC STRATEGIES

In this section, we'll discuss one of the most durable concepts in the field of strategic management—Michael Porter's concept of the generic strategies by which firms develop defensible strategic positions. These positions are a function of two sets of choices—economic logic (low-cost leadership versus differentiation) and scope of arenas (broad versus niche market arenas). We'll explain the logic of the resulting four positions—*low-cost leadership, differentiation, focused cost leadership,* and *focused differentiation*—and show how a successfully implemented generic strategic position can reduce the negative effects of industry rivalry.

A simple two-by-two matrix, shown in Exhibit 5.1, helps you visualize the four alternative competitive positions; the alternative positions suggested by this model are what we mean by **generic strategies**.[2] The integrated position, shown in the middle of the exhibit, is discussed at the end of the section. Bear in mind that in order to be consistent with the overall model of strategy that we presented in Chapter 1 and avoid confusing Porter's categories with the more general concept of strategy, we'll refer to Porter's generic strategies as *strategic positions*. You can see that the strategic positions are not *strategies* in the way we define them using the strategy diamond. Rather, they are configurations of several elements of a firm's strategy. Consequently, understand that any one of these strategic positions still requires a carefully formulated set of choices regarding the five elements of the strategy diamond. However, selecting an intended generic strategic position first gives you a head start and guidance on making specific choices regarding the five elements of the strategy diamond.

Cost or Differentiation   In 1980, Michael Porter introduced an integrated theory of strategy. Porter's model revised the concept of how firms achieve competitive advantage by going beyond the basic (and often wrong) notion that market share is the key to profitability. In part, Porter's theory considered the structure of an industry and its effect on the performance of firms within it (an idea that we introduced in Chapter 4). Porter also demonstrated the economic logic behind some prescriptions for choosing among viable means of gaining competitive advantage. As you see in Exhibit 5.1, the model hinges on two dimensions: the economic logic and the breadth of the target market.

According to Porter, there are two essential economic logics (or the source) of competitive advantage. These alternative sources of advantage are (1) having a lower cost structure than industry competitors or, (2) having a product or service that customers perceive as

generic strategies   Strategic position designed to reduce the effects of rivalry, including *low-cost, differentiation, focused cost leadership, focused differentiation, and integrated positions.*

Exhibit 5.1 The Strategic Positioning Model

The positioning model is adapted from M. E. Porter, Competitive Strategy *(New York: Free Press, 1980). The examples used in the model are the authors' analysis.*

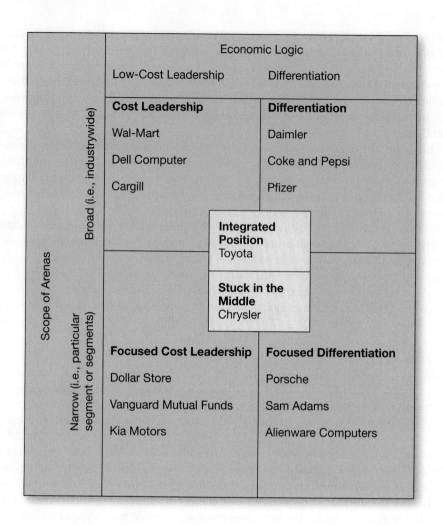

differentiated from other products in the industry—to the point that they will pay higher prices than what is charged for other products in the industry. In other words, a firm can gain a significant advantage over rivals in one of two ways:

- It can produce a product at a lower cost than its rivals.

- It can produce a differentiated product and charge sufficiently higher prices to more than offset the added costs of differentiation.

Along the horizontal dimension of Exhibit 5.1, firms choose the underlying economic logic by which they intend to establish a competitive advantage—that is, whether to compete on differentiation or cost. *Differentiation* refers to a general condition of perceived product "uniqueness" that causes customers to be willing to pay premium prices. When are customers willing to pay more for a product? Generally, premium prices for otherwise similar products are paid when a firm is able to uniquely satisfy a customer's needs. This satisfaction could be along the dimensions of quality, image, speed, access, or other identifiable dimensions of perceived need. However, firms can gain advantage in other ways as well. As shown on Exhibit 5.1, firms may decide to seek higher returns and a competitive advantage by keeping costs lower than those of competitors. This is typically done by offering a product that is good enough to meet the basic needs of many consumers, thereby allowing firms to cut down on production costs.

Scope of Arenas
Firms also make choices about the number and breadth of arenas in which they will compete when they decide how broadly they will compete for customers—a decision known as *scope of arenas*. In other words, firms make choices about which customers to pursue. Some firms compete broadly by trying to offer something for virtually everyone; others focus their efforts on narrower segments of the market. The vertical dimension in Exhibit 5.1 measures the scope of the market arenas in which a firm chooses to compete.

Importantly, even though a narrow market scope implies some form of market niche, this does not mean that every niche market is small. For example, Porsche is very focused on the high performance sports car market, a niche market in the auto industry, but Porsche still commands over $7 billion in revenues. Indeed, when you think of category killers like Staples (office supplies) or Lowe's (home and garden supplies), they have defined big and attractive market niches.

Four generic strategic positions result from the decisions measured by the model in Exhibit 5.1: *low-cost leadership, broad differentiation, focused (or niche) cost leadership,* and *focused (or niche) differentiation.* The primary classification criterion for the focused positions is that the firm targets one or a few related arenas or segments in an industry, as opposed to many industry segments. Let's look more closely at each of these positions.

Low-Cost Leadership
A strategic position that enables a firm to produce a good or offer a service while maintaining total costs that are lower than what it takes competitors to offer the same product or service is known as **low-cost leadership**. Not surprisingly, a firm that can produce substantially similar products at a lower cost has a significant competitive advantage. With a cost advantage, a firm can sell products for lower prices while still maintaining the same margins as rivals. In the process, of course, it will also gain market share. However, a low-cost leader does not necessarily pass all the cost savings onto the customer. Rather, the firm could keep its prices closer to those of competitors and reap higher margins than competitors. In this case, it will accumulate surplus resources that it can either distribute to shareholders or use to finance future strategic initiatives. Wal-Mart, for instance, attempts to share cost savings with customers—they offer lower prices than most mass merchants, but they retain a significant portion of the cost savings for their own benefit.

As a general rule, because taking a low-cost position requires sacrificing some features or services, firms that stake out this position try to satisfy basic rather than highly specialized customer needs.

The low-cost position works in many industries. In the bicycle industry, for instance, Pacific Cycle keeps manufacturing costs down by standardizing design and outsourcing production to low-cost labor markets. Unlike some low-cost leaders, Pacific also offers a wide array of products, many of which have strong brand equity, such as Schwinn and Mongoose—a strategic decision more often associated with a strategy of differentiation. Remember, however, that most of these brands came into Pacific's portfolio through acquisitions, and the company retained the brand names because they enjoy greater brand awareness than "Pacific Cycle." In the wine industry, Gallo Wines has achieved a low-cost leadership position by innovating cost-effective blending techniques, having lower costs due to scale of operations, developing efficiencies in the grape-procurement function, and generating scale economies in marketing and distribution.

In summary, with the low-cost position, firms attempt to deliver an acceptable product that satisfies basic needs at the lowest possible cost. In doing so, the firm attempts to create a sustainable cost gap over other firms. Successfully following this path results in above-industry-average profits. However, cost leaders must maintain parity or proximity in

low-cost leadership
Strategic position based on producing a good or offering a service while maintaining total costs that are lower than what it takes competitors to offer the same product or service.

To avoid head-to-head competition, Pacific Cycle positions itself differently than Trek. Pacific makes many different brands, selling them at various prices in numerous retail outlets. To keeps costs down, it manufactures its bikes exclusively in countries where costs are low.

differentiation Strategic position based on products or offers services with quality, reliability, or prestige that is discernibly higher than that of competitors and for which customers are willing to pay.

satisfying the basic needs of buyers. Doing so is a challenge, because it generally requires tradeoffs—eliminating some features or services in order to drive costs down.

Some well-known companies, including Wal-Mart and Southwest Airlines, are successful low-cost leaders. Interestingly, both of these companies started out as a focused low-cost competitor but took up a more broad-based position as they grew.

Differentiation   If a firm markets products whose quality, reliability, or prestige is discernibly higher than its competitors', and if its customers are willing to pay for this uniqueness, the firm has a competitive advantage based on **differentiation**. Successful differentiation enables firms to do one of two things:

- Set prices at the industry average (and gain market share because consumers will choose higher quality at the same price).

- Raise prices over those of competitors (and reap the benefits of higher margins).

Coca-Cola and Pepsi—which spend billions to develop brand equity, sell in most markets, and strive to win customers through brand image—are also well-known differentiators. Or consider Mercedes Benz, perhaps the world's leading manufacturer of premium passenger cars. What differentiates Mercedes' products? A reputation for innovative engineering, safety, and comfort, along with product design aimed at buyers who will pay premium prices for the image that goes along with a Mercedes.[3] Interestingly, although most Americans regard Mercedes as a focused differentiator because only affluent customers can afford its products, Europeans have a different view. In Europe, Mercedes markets a wide line of products, ranging from the tiny SmartCar to more familiar luxury sedans.

In the motorcycle market, Honda, Yamaha, and Suzuki all have something for virtually every enthusiast. Honda's lineup, for instance, starts with the entry-level XR50R, which comes with semiautomatic gears to help youngsters learn off-road riding. Honda then proceeds to appeal to almost every other segment of the market with products ranging upward to the Gold Wing ST1300, a six-cylinder touring bike equipped with a sophisticated sport-type suspension, antilock brakes, and luxury touring features.

A successful differentiation position requires that a firm satisfy a few basic criteria. First, it must uniquely satisfy one or more needs that are valued by buyers and do so in a manner superior to that available from most competitors. However, doing so will *typically* result in higher costs in some value-chain activities. Thus, the second requirement that must be satisfied is that customers must be willing to pay higher prices for the added points of differentiation. Consequently, companies successful at a differentiation position pick cost-effective forms of differentiation. The results are above-average industry profits.

An example of a successful broad differentiator is Stouffers, the frozen-food company. Stouffers spends more on high-quality inputs than its competitors, it has developed a technology to make a superior sauce, and it offers innovative menus. Stouffers combines these features with high-quality packaging, the use of food brokers to get broad distribution, and advertising that creates the perception of quality. The price premium that Stouffers is able to generate exceeds the cost to improve frozen-food entrees above industry norms.

Focused Low-Cost Leadership
A strategic position that enables a firm to be a low-cost leader in a narrow segment of the market is known as **focused cost leadership**. JetBlue, a recent entry into the commercial airline market, is a focused low-cost competitor that serves a small subset of commercial travelers who are price sensitive. Using a variation on Southwest Airline's early business model, JetBlue managed during its first few years of operation to keep its operating costs per airline seat mile lower than even Southwest's. It was the most profitable commercial U.S. airline in 2002 and 2003 and second behind only Southwest in 2004. Fuel costs and weather-related operational difficulties hurt profits in 2005 and 2006; however, JetBlue still has the lowest operating costs of the major airlines.

focused cost leadership
Strategic position based on being a low-cost leader in a narrow market segment.

Focused Differentiation
When unique products are targeted to a particular market segment or arena, the positioning strategy is called **focused differentiation**. By definition, the greater the differentiation, the smaller the market segment to which a product will appeal: As quality is continually improved or luxury features added, fewer customers can afford the higher prices. In the bicycle industry, for example, Montague focuses on a small, specialized segment of the market that demands unique product features. Trek Bicycles also started as a focused differentiator. However, it now offers products in numerous segments and is moving toward a broad-based differentiator. Trek's products boast high quality and demand price premiums over products from Pacific Cycle, and, because it only sells products through independent bicycle dealers, are still classified as a focused differentiator. You also may be familiar with Cannondale, another focused differentiator that produces high-end mountain bikes. Unfortunately for Cannondale, however, the firm sought to leverage its reputation for quality mountain bikes in the motocross motorcycle market and went bankrupt as a result. It found that the resources and capabilities required to compete in mountain bikes, such as sturdy, high-performance frames, were very different than those required for gas-engined bikes—namely high-performance engines and drivetrains. Moreover, motorcycles are not typically sold by the same dealers that sell bikes.

Likewise, Mercedes Benz imports into the U.S. only its most expensive top-of-the-line models in each product category. In the U.S., therefore, Mercedes is a focused differentiator that markets only to the most affluent customers. Even more focused are such companies as Porsche and Ferrari. In the motorcycle industry, Harley-Davidson, which makes only larger models targeted at very specific segments of the market, is a more focused differentiator than Honda. Harley's lowest-priced motorcycle begins at about $6,500. Recently, other firms have entered this market space and have tried to out-focus Harley-Davidson. For instance, Orange County Choppers, which was made famous by the *American Chopper* TV series, sells only made-to-order motorcycles. Therefore, Orange County Choppers focuses on a very small segment of the overall motorcycle market.

focused differentiation
Strategic position based on targeting products to relatively small segments.

Harley-Davidson has successfully focused its business strategy on the large high-priced end of the motorcycle market. Other manufacturers, such as Orange County Choppers, have tried to muscle into Harley's well-defined market space with bikes such as the Fire Bike shown here.

Integrated Positions

It is very difficult for any firm to initially offer both a differentiated product demanding higher prices and still maintain a lower cost structure than competitors. In fact, firms that attempt to exploit both low-cost and differentiation strategies are often described as "stuck in the middle"—meaning they aim to do both but do neither very well. Chrysler, for instance, has suffered from attempting to lower costs while simultaneously trying to deliver differentiated products. The result in recent years has been a line up of cars that does not command premium prices (because of some of the quality problems associated with cost control initiatives) and higher than average costs (because of the increased costs of design efforts to differentiate the product). It is hard to escape the fact that the tradeoffs required to achieve a superior level on one dimension make it hard to succeed on the other. However, as firms perfect their initial position, the tradeoff choices may not be as stark. Some firms are eventually able to achieve an **integrated position**—one in which elements of one position support a strong standing in the other. And while it is typically unwise for a firm to aim to excel at both low cost and differentiation, the competitive reality is that if a firm excels on one dimension it still must be really good on the other dimension. For instance, a company that sells very unique products must also have good cost controls in place. Similarly, a firm that competes on price (or low cost), should also seek attributes that differentiate its products beyond price alone.

Some elements of a differentiation position can be adopted by low-cost competitors. Some low-cost companies, for instance, develop strong brand images even though branding typically supports a differentiation strategy. Heavy reliance on branding enables McDonald's to position itself as a reliable, high-quality provider of low-cost fast food. Whether the firm has achieved an integrated position, however, is judged by whether it achieves higher prices than its competitors for similar products. Toyota, for example, is an excellent example of a company that has achieved a successful integrated position. When Toyota first entered the U.S. market, it did so as a low-cost leader. Toy-

integrated position Strategic position in which elements of one position support strong standing in another.

ota was able to manufacture small cars at a much lower cost than U.S. automobile manufacturers. Over time, however, Toyota invested heavily in quality control, design, and marketing. Toyota's cars are now consistently rated as among the highest in customer and mechanic evaluations of quality. In addition, while Toyota used to have the cheapest cars available in the U.S., their models now command premium prices compared to their American competitors' models. Consequently, Toyota is now a model of both cost control and quality; they have lower costs than competitors and higher quality products, allowing them to charge higher prices for similar models and reap much larger margins than most automobile manufacturers.

Another example is IKEA Svenska AB, which manages to remain the world's largest home furnishings retailer while specializing in stylish but inexpensive furniture. IKEA's success can be traced to its vast experience in the retail market, where it practices both product differentiation and cost leadership. IKEA outlets are essentially warehouses stacked with boxes of unassembled furniture. The company operates under a fairly unique premise: namely, that value-conscious buyers will perform some of the tasks that other retailers normally perform for them, such as transporting and assembling their own furniture. By transferring these functions to the customer, IKEA can drive costs down and, therefore, offer prices low enough to fit most budgets. Thus, IKEA targets a rather large segment of the market, ranging from young low- to middle-income families. At the same time, the company has established a highly differentiated image with its enormous selection of self-assembly home furnishings and fun in-store experiences.

Firms that have integrated low-cost and differentiation positions can be found in most industries. So can firms whose products don't seem to fall into either category. As Exhibit 5.2 shows, integrated—and enviable—positions have in fact been forged in the auto industry. Note, for instance, that Toyota, a successful firm with an integrated position, generates better profit margins on comparable models than Chevrolet, Hyundai, or Ford. Chevrolet, at least in this model class, appears to be a successful low-cost leader.

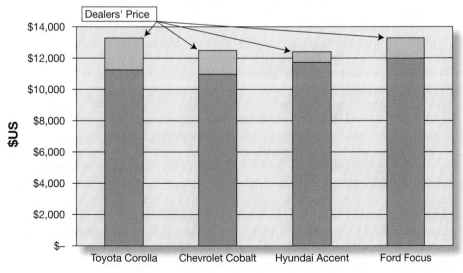

Comparative Cost and Profit of Automobile Manufacturers

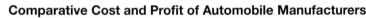

Exhibit 5.2 Integrated Positions: Low-Cost, Differentiation, Stuck-in-the-Middle

Exhibit 5.3 The Interplay Between Cost and Differentiation

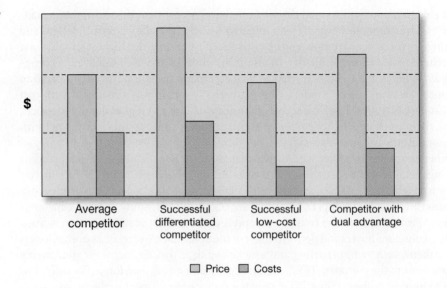

Ford is attempting to be a differentiator, yet their margins are significantly less than Toyota. Notice that Chevrolet's margins are even greater than Fords. Hyundai seems to be stuck in the middle. Their stated strategy is to be a low-cost leader. However, operational problems have resulted in costs greater than all but Ford in this example. Yet, the quality and image of the brand does not permit them to charge prices consistent with a differentiator.

The financial results of successful low-cost, differentiation, and integrated positions are illustrated in Exhibit 5.3. It is critical to remember that these successful positions are predicated on the effective implementation of the drivers of cost or differentiation advantage, or both. In the next section, we explore these drivers in detail.

Strategic Position, Firm Resources, and the Strategy Diamond As we've seen, the appropriate strategic position for any firm depends on two factors: (1) its resources and capabilities and (2) the condition of its industry environment. A firm with strong innovative capabilities, for example, will generally favor differentiation strategies. Why? Because the ability to make product improvements, whether incremental or radical, enables a firm to offer newer and more unique products directed at specific customer needs. Intel favors heavy investment in product innovation so that it can remain on the leading edge of new-product introductions in the microprocessor industry. Notice, however, that Intel's differentiators (innovation and product development speed) are particularly valuable in the arenas where computer manufacturers like Dell want to be able to provide the latest and greatest technologies to their customers. This strategy enables Intel to charge higher prices during the early stages of the product life cycle, generating increased cash flows that it can, in turn, invest in building its brand and further differentiating its products.

Alternatively, capabilities in large-scale manufacturing and distribution generally favor low-cost strategies. Cooper Industries, for example, has developed skills in acquiring and consolidating companies in mature tool, hardware, or electrical-product industries, infusing them with modern manufacturing technology and increasing supplier power over critical customer segments. In particular, the ability to modernize manufacturing processes (the company calls it Cooperizing) gives the firm a cost advantage over many competitors. Thus, Cooper uses differentiators that are cost effective and give it an advantage in arenas where customers look at price as a key decision criterion. The point we are making here with the Intel and Cooper examples is that a strategic position is valuable to the extent that it helps the firm stake out turf in a desirable market.

Economic Drivers of Strategic Positioning

In order to fully understand the logic behind different strategic positions, we need to identify the different economic drivers that support and facilitate each strategic position and foster their success. In this section, we'll describe some of the key economic drivers of both low-cost and differentiation strategies. (Remember that because *focus* strategies are special variations on these two basic types of strategy, the same economic drivers apply to them.) In order to understand how firms might be able to achieve a competitive advantage as a result of their strategic position, we need to understand economic drivers and how they function.

DRIVERS OF LOW-COST ADVANTAGE

Firms have different production costs for several reasons. Some of the more common (and important) include economies of scale, learning, production technology, product design, and location advantages for sourcing inputs. In this section, we'll review some of these more important sources of potential cost advantage. A successful low-cost strategy requires that a firm is proficient at exploiting one or more of these drivers. Conversely, of course, firms that are unable to leverage these cost drivers either need to acquire the capabilities and resources to do so or to reevaluate their strategy.

Economies of Scale **Economies of scale** exist during a given period of time *if the average total cost for a unit of production is lower at higher levels of output.* To better understand the nature and importance of economies of scale, we need to review the various types of production costs:

> **economy of scale** Condition under which average total cost for a unit of production is lower at higher levels of output.

- *Fixed costs* (such as rent and equipment) remain the same for different levels of production unless a firm expands the size of its production operations.

- *Variable costs* are the costs of variable inputs (such as raw materials and labor); they vary directly with output.

- *Marginal cost* is the cost of the last unit of production.

- *Total cost* is the sum of all production costs; it increases as output goes up.

- *Average cost* is the *mean* cost of total production (e.g., total costs/total # of units produced) during a given period (say, a year).

Economies of scale exist if *average costs* are lower at higher levels of production. Under what circumstances might it cost less to manufacture more products during one given time period than during another?

Economies of scale can result from a variety of efficiencies, all related to higher volumes of production relative to a given asset base: spreading fixed costs over greater volume, specializing in a specific production process, practicing superior inventory management, exercising purchasing power, or spending more effectively on advertising or R&D.

Economies of scale result primarily from the first reason—spreading fixed costs over greater levels of output. It stands to reason that within the feasible range of production at a given facility, increasing output will enable the firm to spread its fixed costs over greater levels of production. If, for example, R&D costs account for a significant portion of the firm's total cost, larger scale production enables the firm to cut average cost by spreading R&D costs over more units of production.

Often, greater economies of scale are only available if the firm expands its operations or consolidates several disparate operating facilities into a single, larger, and more efficient operation. For example, Coca-Cola bought back many bottling operations from individual franchisees during the 1980s and 1990s. These facilities were optimal for the exclusive geographic territory controlled by franchisees, but not as optimal as they could have been if they had served a larger area. But, individual franchisees had no incentive to expand their operation because they were limited by contract to being able to sell in a defined geographic territory. To solve this problem, Coca-Cola bought back many franchises, then consolidated into larger, more efficient geographic territories and built large and efficient bottling plants that had much greater economies of scale.

In addition, greater scale often encourages the use of more sophisticated inventory management systems. Some of these systems, though not cost-effective at lower volumes, bring significant rewards at sufficiently large scales of production. Audi, for instance, persuaded suppliers to locate operations in facilities adjacent to its newly centralized facilities in Ingoldstadt, Germany. In turn, the carmaker was able to implement just-in-time inventory techniques that didn't work when smaller-scale manufacturing operations were more widely dispersed.[4] Similarly, when numerous inputs are involved, the price depends, in part, on the volume purchased. That's why large buyers often have more leverage in negotiating price. Wal-Mart, for example, is renowned (even notorious) for exercising its buying power to hold down input costs.

If branding plays a key role in the firm's strategy, larger scale often provides a significant advertising advantage. In order to influence consumer decisions, advertising must first reach a certain "threshold" at which it creates awareness. If two firms of significantly different size allocate the same *proportion* of revenues to advertising, they'll achieve significantly different levels of awareness. Thus, large firms allocate more total dollars for advertising and reap the benefit of greater awareness. In addition, large firms can bargain for price discounts in various media that aren't extended to smaller accounts.

Diseconomies of Scale　Do not, however, make the mistake of assuming that size automatically ensures economies of scale. In reality, almost all operations processes are subject to the **diseconomies of scale** that occur when average total cost *increases* at higher levels of output.

Diseconomies of scale can result from bureaucracy, high labor costs, and differences in efficiency between interdependent operations. Moreover, a firm may have economies of scale in some value-chain activities that result in diseconomies of scale on other dimensions. For instance, consider the world of institutional fund management. The 20 largest fund managers control over 40 percent of professionally managed money in the world. According to research by a large consulting practice specializing in financial services, Mercer Oliver Wyman, fund management is a very scale-sensitive business. A fund manager with a $10,000,000 portfolio incurs the same costs as a manager with a $100,000,000 portfolio. The scale economies in the fund management industry are evidenced in the profitability of fund management companies. Profits for fund management companies are typically a function of scale—larger firms are more profitable. However, Mercer notes that while smaller firms are at a cost disadvantage, the funds that deliver the higher returns to investors in the fund (i.e., customers, not shareholders) tend to be smaller boutique firms.[5] They suggest that this might be due to some form of diseconomy of scale that manifests itself in fund performance, not firm profits.

Greater production volume may lead to greater sales revenues, but those added sales may have greater transportation or service costs or lower price structures. For instance, Microsoft is finding that it has saturated developed country markets with its Windows operating systems, and the entry into emerging economies like India and China will require very, very deep discounts on its traditional pricing. Large-scale operations can also lead to inflexibility—and increased costs—in the face of changing needs.[6] This is what happened to General Motors in the early 1990s. After spending billions to complement its massive scale with an appropriate level of automation, GM discovered that its technological upgrade didn't allow it to switch platforms fast enough to respond to shifts in the market. Inflexibility in the face of changing consumer preferences and new-model intro-

---

diseconomy of scale
Condition under which average total costs per unit of production increases at higher levels of input.

ductions by competitors actually caused costs at GM's newly automated plants to go up, not down.

Minimum Efficient Scale   How, then, can a firm achieve optimal performance? Ultimately, the objective is to find the scale necessary to achieve the lowest possible average cost. Let's examine this concept in more detail.

As we've just seen, costs may decline at some ranges of production but increase at others. This fact suggests that *total average cost* can be represented by a *U*-shaped curve that has a minimum point. The output level that delivers the lowest possible costs is the **minimum efficient scale (MES)**. Often, firms operating below or above MES suffer from a cost disadvantage. Generally, there is a range of scale—or of output levels—at which costs will be minimized. MES is the smallest scale necessary to achieve maximum economies of scale. It's critical to decisions about a firm's scale of operations because it targets the level of production needed to enjoy all the benefits made possible by large scale. It also establishes the size that a new entrant must achieve in order to match the scale advantages enjoyed by incumbents. Exhibit 5.4 illustrates some possible relationships between economies of scale, diseconomies of scale, and minimum efficient scale, along with examples of these types of economies and diseconomies. Exhibit 5.5 gives you some examples of the ways in which scale may result in lower costs. Although MES understandably varies by industry and market segment, the exhibit generally conveys the idea that managers must take into account economy-of-scale tradeoffs when making investments in service or production capacity.

> **minimum efficient scale (MES)**   The output level that delivers the lowest total average cost.

MES and Technology   Not surprisingly, MES is also a function of technology. Obviously, an industry may employ more than one type of technology. In the steel industry, for example, some plants—so-called minimills—use electric-arc furnaces; whereas old-line integrated steel companies continue to use blast-arc furnaces. Minimills are designed to make steel in a simple three-stage process that starts with scrap metal; whereas integrated steel manufacturing requires investments in equipment that start earlier in the value chain with iron ore and coal. Consequently, the scale requirements of the two technologies are quite different, and minimills can achieve MES at roughly one-tenth the scale required for efficient operation at an integrated mill. However, the large integrated mills can have a cost advantage over the minimills when they are able to operate at full capacity.

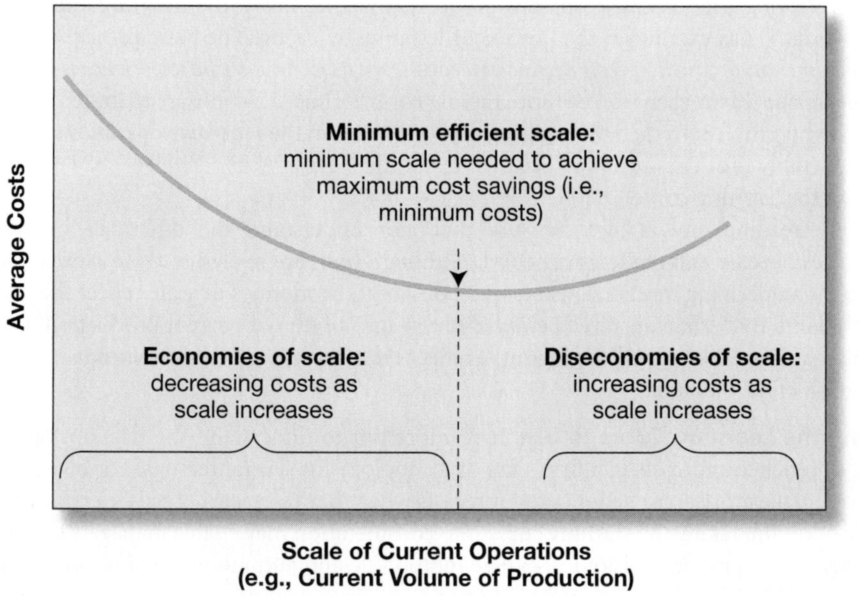

Exhibit 5.4   Scale and Cost

Exhibit 5.5   Examples of Scale Economies

Examples of Economies and Diseconomies of Scale	
Economies of Scale	**Diseconomies of Scale**
"Because we are producing and selling more, we can run our factories at full capacity." "Greater sales volume lets us deliver full truckloads instead of partial loads." "We have greater purchasing power with our suppliers." "Now our advertising costs in a region are spread over a larger number of retail outlets."	"Selling more products has required loosening production standards, which results in higher service and warranty work." "Higher production volumes has required more or larger suppliers of raw materials, who may be in a better bargaining position." "No distribution company is big enough to handle our increased volume, which means we have to build and manage the logistics capability ourselves." "Now that we are bigger, we have a bigger regulatory burden."

With some technologies, MES is reached only at relatively low levels of production, and although there's no scale advantage at higher levels, neither is there any disadvantage. Some technologies result quite quickly in a disadvantage at a scale larger than MES; whereas still others support wide ranges of scale without generating any real cost differences.

The Learning Curve   In addition to scale economies, other factors can contribute to lower operating costs. Two firms of the same size, for example, may have significantly different operating costs because one has progressed farther down the **learning curve**—in other words, it has excelled at the process of learning by doing. The basic principle holds that *incremental production costs decline at a constant rate as production experience is gained;* the steeper the learning curve, the more rapidly costs decline. This idea is attributed to T. P. Wright, who proposed a theory for basing cost estimates on the repetitive operations of airplane assembly processes in 1936.[7] See the box entitled "How Would *You* Do That? 5.1" for more on the learning curve.

Before reading any farther, be sure that you understand the difference between economies of scale and the learning curve. Although both are related to the quantity produced, the underlying mechanisms are quite different. Economies of scale reflect the scale of the operation *during any given period of time*—the volume of current production. Cost decreases attributable to the learning curve reflect *the cumulative level of production since the production of the first unit.*

Putting the Learning Curve to Use   It is important to understand the relationship between experience and costs in a firm's use of technology for several reasons. For one, managers can make more accurate total-cost forecasts when they're preparing bids for large projects. In addition, taking the learning curve into consideration may enable managers to make more aggressive pricing decisions. Japanese motorcycle and automobile manufacturers, for

learning curve   Incremental production costs decline at a constant rate as production experience is gained; the steeper the learning curve, the more rapidly costs decline.

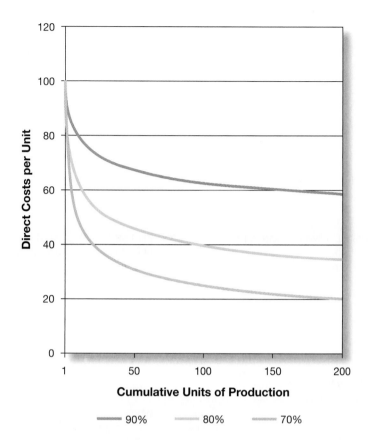

Exhibit 5.6 Pricing, Profitability, and the Learning Curve

example, considered the expected future costs savings associated with the learning curve when setting entry prices for the U.S. market. Although initial prices may actually have been below *current* production costs, they were set to reflect *future* cost estimates. The low prices also enabled the Japanese to make rapid gains in market share. Resulting higher volumes not only contributed to economies of scale, but also reduced costs due to learning. Later, Asian computer-chip manufacturers adopted the same strategy for entering the U.S. market.[8] This basic logic is summarized in Exhibit 5.6, where you can see how the price set for the product generates profits after a certain amount of cumulative volume-based learning has been accumulated. The intuition of the learning curve is that direct costs decline as a function of cumulative units of production. But different companies and different industries are likely to have different learning curves. So, in the second graph of Exhibit 5.6, you see three different learning curves compared. For instance, a 90% learning curve means that every time cumulative production doubles, direct costs are only 90% of what they were at prior levels. What else can you apply the learning curve to? Here are a few more questions that could help you answer:

■ A new bank clerk needed an hour to encode his first 500 checks, 50 minutes for the second 500, and 42 for the fourth 500. When will he be able to work at the standard rate of 1,000 checks per hour?

■ An electrical contracting firm wired a home in two hours. The same team took 90 minutes to wire an identical second home. The fourth home only took 70 minutes. How long will it take it to wire the tenth home?

How to Take the Learning Curve on Two Wheels

How can the learning curve actually help a company? To consider this question, let's review a problem faced by Montague, the maker of full-size, high performance bicycles that fold. Montague's latest innovation is the Paratrooper™ bike—a full-sized bike that is strong enough to drop from a plane, durable enough to traverse any terrain, and moves at high speeds with minimal maintenance. Montague actually developed this novel bike in partnership with the U.S. government's Defense Advanced Research Projects Agency (DARPA) to bridge the gap between heavy military vehicles and walking soldiers. Up to this point, the Paratrooper™ has only been in prototype form for evaluation by Montague and DARPA. However, after several tradeshows, it appears that there may be heavy commercial demand for the bike from military groups, emergency, police, and rescue patrols, and many civilians. Of course, now the challenge for Montague is to set a price for the Paratrooper™ that customers are willing to pay, and at which it is likely to make a good profit. How can Montague take the principle of the learning curve into consideration in forecasting its cost and offering the most attractive price?

Let's assume that Montague has already made four prototypes and that it cost the firm $300 in direct costs to make the first bike, $270 for the second, and $243 for the last (fourth) bike made. (Fortunately, there were four prototypes; it's never wise to estimate trends with only two data points.) Using the concept of the learning curve, Montague can systematically use historical data to estimate future costs. Montague can do this in several ways. (Bear in mind, by the way, that we could measure either in terms of costs or hours; for the sake of simplicity, we'll use costs throughout this exercise.)

One way to estimate future costs is simply to calculate projected values using some basic math. To do this, we need to know a fundamental rule for quantifying the learning curve: For every *doubling* of *cumulative* production levels, costs decline at a constant rate. In our example, cumulative production has reached four bikes. In other words, it's doubled twice—once from one to two, and again from two to four. If we calculate the percentages for each doubling, we see that (conveniently enough) we have a 90-percent learning curve: The direct costs to make the second bike were 90 percent of the first, and the fourth was 90 percent of the second. Now we just repeat the process to estimate future costs: In other words, we take 90 percent of current production as our estimate for costs *once cumulative production doubles again,* repeating the process until we've reached our target level of production (100 bikes). Using this quick and dirty method, we see that the cost per bike falls to approximately $150 by the time we've reached 100 bikes. Our findings are summarized in Exhibit 5.7.

This procedure works fine for small batches, but it could become quite cumbersome for large production runs.

In more complicated situations, we need the actual *learning-curve formula*. With this formula and a good calculator or spreadsheet, we can project costs for a specific estimated number of units rather than having to interpolate from a table of values that increase at doubling rates.

Here's the formula for estimating learning curves:

$$y = ax^{-b}$$

where *y* is the cost per unit for the *xth* unit produced; *a* is the cost of the first unit produced; *x* is the cumulative number of products produced (or desired level if the rate of learning, *b*, is already determined); and *b* is the *rate* at which costs are reduced every time cumulative production doubles (always a negative number calculated from other known quantities). Using this formula and a spreadsheet, we can project future costs for any level of production and thus make a more informed decision about our costs. Our new findings are summarized in Exhibit 5.8.

If you're averse to math, you may prefer to resort to one of several aids. First, we could create a table in which we plug in the *rates* for several common learning curves (i.e., the figures needed to plug *b* into the previous formula). Then we can find our solutions by combining these rates with our spreadsheet capabilities, as shown in Exhibit 5.9.

If you want things even simpler, you could visit a Web site that contains a "learning-curve calculator" at

Number of Bikes Produced	Cost per Bike
1st	$300 actual
2nd	$270 actual
4th	$243 actual
8th	$218.70 estimate
16th	$196.83 estimate
32nd	$177.15 estimate
64th	$159.43 estimate
100th	$148.98 estimate
128th	$143.49 estimate

Exhibit 5.7 Cost per Bike and the Learning Curve

www.jsc.nasa.gov/bu2/learn.html. Using this handy device, you can plug in a few basic data and wait for it to solve the problem for you. (*Hint:* Use the Crawford version of the calculator, which corresponds to the current formulation used in business.)

So, back to our question: At what price should Montague offer the Paratrooper™? Well, average gross margins (i.e., sales minus cost-of-goods-sold, as a percentage of sales) in the bike industry are 37 percent, and Montague aims to sell unique products,

so its margins should be better than this.[14] If Montague is confident that it can sell more than 100 Paratroopers™, then a price of $300 per bike would provide it with a $151.02 gross margin, or approximately 50 percent, per bike once it reaches the 100 unit sale mark.

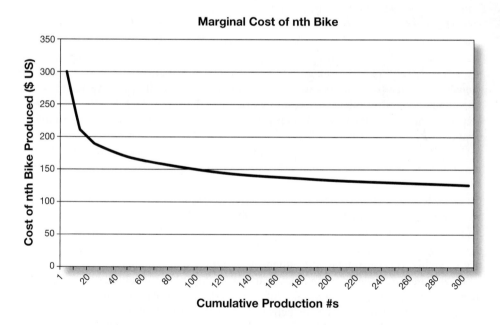

Marginal Cost of nth Bike

Cost of nth Bike Produced ($ US) vs *Cumulative Production #s*

Exhibit 5.8 Marginal Costs for Montague

Learning Curve	80%	85%	90%	95%
Rate of Learning	−.322	−.234	−.152	−.074

Exhibit 5.9 Spreadsheet for Montague

- A fast-food trainee takes an hour to prepare her first 20 sandwiches, 45 minutes for the second 20, and her fourth batch of 20 sandwiches only took 34. What will her production rate be after 24 hours of experience?

- A custom boat builder built a prototype of a new sailboat. From past experience, he knows the learning curve rate for similar boats. What are the labor requirements for the second and third boats?

These questions may seem on the surface to be overly operational to be considered strategic. However, understanding the learning curve and how it works in your specific business helps a strategic manager forecast future costs, and develop an optimal strategic position for the firm given its cost structure. Cost structure is, after all, one of the key factors underlying your strategy's economic logic.

Multiunit Organizations and the Learning Curve A related effect of the learning curve occurs when a multiunit organization transfers learning from one unit to another.[9] Franchise systems, for instance, can codify their knowledge about the most effective way to operate a store. Technically, therefore, each new franchise doesn't have to start from scratch. Rather, every unit benefits from corporate training programs that give new franchisees a head start at tackling the learning curve. Because units can share new knowledge about effective practices, multiunit firms can make faster progress in mastering learning curves than single-unit operations.

Other Sources of Cost Advantage Other potential sources of cost advantage include *economies of scope, production technology,* and *product design.*

Economies of Scope   As the term suggests, *economies of scope* are similar to economies of scale. They refer, however, to potential cost savings associated with *multiproduct* production. When a firm produces two or more products, it has greater scope of operations than a firm that produces only one. If such a firm can share a resource among one or more of its products—thereby lowering the costs of each product—it benefits from **economies of scope**.[10] We discuss this concept more fully in Chapter 7 because it's fundamental to diversification as a corporate strategy. Economies of scope, however, are available not only to large diversified firms but also to small privately held enterprises that are just beginning to expand their product offerings.

Here we offer a simple example to help you understand economies of scope.[11] The multipurpose table and furniture industry is made up of a fragmented group of about 60 major manufacturers who share a $1-billion market. One of these companies, Mity-Lite, was formed in 1987 by Gregory Wilson when he was in the institutional furniture business. The company's original product line consisted of folding tables targeted at such institutional users as schools, churches, civic organizations, and hospitals. From the outset, Mity-Lite used a heat- and vacuum-thermoforming process to mold engineering-grade plastics, and combined this process with durable folding-metal frames to build tables that are both much lighter and more durable than competing particleboard or plywood tables. As the company grew, it learned to implement a number of changes in both its manufacturing process and product designs—changes that have increased production volumes, improved quality, and lowered costs.

After a decade of successful market penetration, Mity-Lite developed a reputation as a leading designer, manufacturer, and marketer of folding-leg tables. With excess capacity in one of his plants, Wilson began to study possible growth options. Because customers of folding-leg tables often buy folding or stacking chairs at the same time, Wilson saw at least one opportunity to expand into complementary products. He soon discovered that the same technology he used to form durable tables could be used to manufacture chairs. Moreover, because expansion into chair production didn't require a new plant, the cost of the manufacturing facility could be shared in the production of both tables and chairs. These

economy of scope Condition under which lower total average costs result from sharing resources to produce more than one product or service.

cost savings reflect economies of scope. From its small beginnings as a supplier of church furniture, Mity-Lite has grown an average of 35 percent per year and has become an international player in the institutional furniture industry.

Production Technology   Naturally, different production technologies entail different costs. Often, a new entrant who wants to compete against industry incumbents with significant scale and experience advantages tries to match or beat incumbents' costs by introducing a production technology that's subject to different economics. JetBlue, for instance, has the lowest operating costs of all major U.S. airlines, and the source of its successful strategy—its production technology—compares quite favorably with the technologies used by other airlines.

Similarly, Nucor Steel originally entered an industry that wasn't particularly attractive from a traditional point of view. Profits were low, capital intensity was high, and the bargaining power of buyers was strong (i.e., steel is a commodity, which means that buyers make purchase decisions primarily on price if all other factors are equal). In addition, most incumbents had the advantage of a century's worth of experience. Nucor, however, didn't use the same technology as its incumbent competitors. Rather than building an integrated mill with blast-arc furnaces, Nucor opted for the lower-cost electric-arc technology favored by minimills.[12]

Product Design   Similarly, product design can sometimes be altered to lower a firm's production costs.[13] When Canon, for example, decided to enter the photocopier industry, incumbents such as Xerox had formidable advantages in scale and experience. Canon, however, redesigned the photocopier so that it required fewer parts and allowed for simpler assembly. The new design dropped Canon's costs below those of Xerox and enabled the new entrant to gain significant market share at Xerox's expense.

Finally, different sourcing practices result in different cost structures. Some firms try to attain lower production costs by locating their operations in cheaper labor markets. Others outsource manufacturing altogether. Pacific Cycle, for instance, makes bikes for less than Trek, whose operations are in the U.S., by outsourcing much of its production to China and Taiwan.

Drivers of Differentiation Advantages
In order to sell products at premium prices, firms must make their uniqueness and value apparent to customers. In this section, we'll review the economic logic and some of the common drivers of a successful differentiation strategy. While firms that pursue differentiation advantages must still be cost conscious and good at managing tangible aspects of their products and services, they must typically also excel at managing the intangibles. As a rule, differentiation involves one or more of the following differentiators among product offerings: *premium brand image, customization and convenience, unique styling, speed,* and *unusually high quality.* And though these differentiators have much about them that is intangible, these intangibles were nonetheless expressly managed and developed.

Premium Brand Image   When Toyota introduced its premium Lexus line in 1989, its strategy was based on extensive market analysis and product development efforts. Relying on its ability to manufacture high-quality automobiles, Toyota was confident that it could penetrate the highly profitable luxury car segment. In fact, managers regarded the whole idea as quite logical, given the brand image already enjoyed by Toyota. Consequently, the company launched and developed an entirely new brand with a separate dealer network. High quality was a Lexus trademark from the beginning, with the new luxury car winning its first J.D. Power and Associates number-one ranking in the 1990 Initial Quality Study. Being named one of *Car & Driver* magazine's 10 best and the Motoring Press Association's Best Imported Car of the Year also bolstered the Lexus image.

Bear in mind, however, that although quality earned a slew of technical awards for Lexus, targeted marketing created something even more important—customer awareness. In practice, a differentiation strategy means that marketers understand how to *segment* the market in which they intend to compete—a process known as *market segmentation*. They must identify specific subgroups of buyers who have distinguishable needs, select one or more of these unique buyer needs, and satisfy them in ways that competitors don't or can't.

Customization and Convenience   Curves International, for instance, saw a unique opportunity to segment the fitness-club industry by targeting women who desired a nonintimidating environment. Curves' equipment is different from that of competitors, not only because it's designed for women but because it uses hydraulic-resistance equipment that eliminates the need to worry about weight stacks. In addition, the Curves program features a convenient 30-minute exercise routine and small, local neighborhood gyms. Since its founding in 1992, Curves has opened more than 10,000 locations, and the company's success suggests that the segment it targeted was indeed overlooked or underserved by industry incumbents.

Similarly, customization and convenience are a theme evident at Swiss Colony. In case you have not heard of it before, Swiss Colony is a successful, privately-held direct-mail company with over $600 million in sales. If you have heard of it, you may think of this catalog sales company only as a purveyor of fine holiday cheese, sausage, and cracker gift baskets. However, then you would be overlooking the many other catalog brands that bring in the lion's share of the revenues per year for this profitable catalog and online retailer. Some of its many catalogs include Durdy Looks (apparel, furniture, and accessories), Room for Color (furnishings organized by color coordination), and Ashro Lifestyle (fashionable clothing for African American women).

Unique Styling   Some firms use style, fashion, and design as key ingredients in a differentiation advantage. Ironically, this can result in premium prices even when product quality is not particularly high. For instance, Harley-Davidson generates prices for motorcycles that exceed that of the competition even though its quality is measurably lower. Why would a potential motorcycle customer pay more for a Harley when it breaks down more often and requires more regular trips to the repair shop? Because many customers for large motorcycles are looking for the image that a Harley-Davidson motorcycle portrays. At a technical level, Honda motorcycles are superior and their quality is higher. Yet, for many enthusiasts, the styling, sound, and image offered by a Harley is worth every penny (or every $7,000–$20,000, as the case may be) that they cost.

Speed   You have probably heard of Moore's Law, the prediction attributed to Intel cofounder Gordon Moore that the number of transistors on an integrated circuit (a microchip) would double every 18 to 24 months. Although Moore's Law was initially made in the form of an observation and forecast, the more widely it became accepted, the more it served as a goal for an entire industry. This drove both marketing and engineering departments of semiconductor manufacturers to focus enormous energy aiming for the specified increase in processing power that it was presumed one or more of their competitors would soon actually attain. Intel is a great case in point. It uses its need for speed to remain in high demand among customers and well ahead of competitors. Ironically, not only are its products getting physically faster (i.e., the processing capacity and speed of its computer chips), but it is also getting faster at developing them and introducing them to the market. The strategic advantages created by Intel's speed are many. Most important perhaps is the fact that the people who buy computers also want to have very fast ones, which means that customers as well as suppliers are keeping fast chips in high demand. Moreover, since Intel is able to deliver on this promise of speed, its customers (like Dell and Apple) and related product developers (like Microsoft) are able to engineer their leading-edge products around Intel chips.

Unusually High Quality   Apple's computers cost, on average, ten percent more than comparably equipped Dell computers. There may be several reasons customers are willing to pay this premium, but the one most often cited by Apple users is the quality of the hardware and software. Apple's operating system is demonstrably more reliable and less susceptible to crashing than the Windows operating system included on Dell computers. In the fast food industry, it is easy to see that hamburgers (or any other genre of food) cost more at restaurant chains like Fuddruckers than they do at McDonald's. The main reason a customer would pay four times more for a hamburger than they could at a more convenient location is because the product is of significantly higher quality.

Creating Value and Promoting Willingness to Pay   The goal of differentiation is to be able to demand a price sufficient to do two things: (1) recoup the added costs of delivering the value-added feature and (2) generate enough profit to make the strategy worthwhile. The point of differentiation is to drive up the customer's **willingness to pay**—that is, to induce customers to pay more for the firm's products or services than a competitors'. The producer wants to drive a wedge between what customers are willing to pay and the costs of producing the product or service.

willingness to pay   Principle of differentiation strategy by which customers are willing to pay more for certain product features.

Threats to Successful Competitive Positioning

For a firm using any of the generic strategies that we've discussed in this chapter, success hinges on a number of factors. Does the firm have the right resources, such as those that may accrue from scale or learning, for implementing a low-cost strategy? Will the marketplace reward a differentiation strategy? In some markets (those which, like steel, are more commodity-like), customers' purchase decisions are driven much more strongly by price than by product features, and in these cases there's not much that firms can do to justify higher prices. A summary of the common drivers of differentiation and low-cost advantage, along with the threats to those positions, is listed in Exhibit 5.10. Under most circumstances, a successful strategic position must satisfy two requirements: (1) It must be based on the firm's resources and capabilities, and (2) it must achieve some level of consistency with the conditions that prevail in the industry.

	Drivers	Threats
Low Cost	• Economies of scale • Learning • Economies of scope • Superior technology • Superior product design	• New technology • Inferior quality • Social, political, and economic risk of outsourcing
Differentiation	• Premium brand image • Customization • Unique styling • Speed • Convenient access • Unusually high quality	• Failing to increase buyers' willingness to pay higher prices • Underestimating costs of differentiation • Overfulfilling buyers' needs • Lower-cost imitation

Exhibit 5.10   Low Cost and Differentiation: Drivers and Threats

THREATS TO LOW-COST POSITIONS

In terms of these two critical requirements, let's look first at the numerous threats facing firms aiming for a low-cost competitive position. First, the firm may face threats on the technological front. In particular, the resource that makes it possible for a firm to compete on the basis of cost—often a certain technology—can be imitated. Efficient production and process technologies can move from firm to firm by any number of means, such as consultants with clients throughout the industry and the movement of key personnel from company to company.

Granted, even though an imitator may acquire comparable technology, the original firm may still enjoy the benefits of greater experience and the learning curve. A more serious threat to low-cost competitors is the possibility that another firm may introduce a new technology—one which, like minimill technology in the steel industry, supports a different scale and a more efficient learning process. In such cases, even small latecomers can establish cost positions significantly lower than those of larger, more experienced low-cost leaders.

Second, low-cost leadership means offering an acceptable combination of price and quality. A real threat to an intended low-cost position is the failure to offer sufficient quality to satisfy buyers' basic needs. Over the past decade, for example, Kmart's experiments in low-cost positioning have been thwarted not only by Wal-Mart's ability to stake out an even lower-cost position, but by Kmart's own inability to offer a retail experience of comparable quality (customers complain of empty shelves, uninviting environments, and less helpful staff).

Recently, another serious threat has arisen to low-cost competitors in labor-intensive industries: increased public awareness of questionable labor practices in developing countries. Struggling to keep wage costs as low as possible, many companies (some unwittingly) have entered into agreements with suppliers who enforce excessive work hours, deny basic employee services, employ children, and violate what are considered acceptable working conditions. Watchdog groups regularly publicize such cases, and reforms push up costs.[15] Many multinational companies have established codes of ethical conduct for suppliers, but enforcing these standards—inspecting and auditing overseas suppliers—also increases costs. Managers must be certain that their foreign sourcing arrangements are in compliance with their corporate values.

THREATS TO DIFFERENTIATION POSITIONS

Needless to say, the intent to provide a differentiated product doesn't necessarily result in competitive advantage and enhanced profitability. A number of factors can sabotage a differentiation strategy. Obviously, a differentiating feature that buyers don't care about merely increases costs without increasing willingness to pay, which cuts into profit margins. Until recently, for example, Audi suffered from the fact that although its manufacturing costs were comparable to those of BMW and Mercedes, it couldn't get customers to pay comparable prices. In effect, Audi was either overfulfilling the needs of buyers who were in the market for well-made but more modestly priced cars or underfulfilling the needs of customers in the market for high-image, high-quality cars.

In addition, failing to understand the total costs entailed by differentiation can derail a differentiation position. The cost of differentiation has no direct effect on customers' willingness to pay, and in most industries, cost-plus pricing is not an option. Jaguar, for example, found itself in an apparently enviable position in the early 1980s: It had a highly differentiated product with good brand recognition and strong customer appeal, and unlike Audi's targeted customers, car buyers were willing to pay premium prices for Jaguars. Unfortunately, antiquated manufacturing processes drove costs so high that, even with products selling in the top price range, the company lost money. Many of its operations weren't even automated, but ironically, Jaguar took pride in its traditional hands-on methods—in part because managers believed that brand recognition and customer loyalty were tied to an appreciation of the individualized manufacturing process. Ford purchased Jaguar in 1990 and, after studying the company's operations, revamped assembly plants in an effort to combine the best aspects of both traditional and modern methods. Ford, for instance, retained the practice of installing hand-sewn leather interiors and natural wood inlays but significantly modernized the processes for assembling bodies and power trains.[16]

Two additional reasons differentiation can fail are overfulfillment and ease of imitation. When product features exceed buyer needs, the added costs to provide these unwanted features, coupled with customers' lack of willingness to pay for this differentiation, results in significantly lower margins. For instance, several years ago John Deere invested significant resources in the technologies that went into their farm equipment. The company was able to produce some of the most technologically sophisticated tractors on the market. Unfortunately, Deere's customers were unwilling to pay for them. They liked the technology, just not the price that went with the technology. Today, Deere gradually introduces new features at a pace that keeps them ahead of competitors, but only as quickly as customers demonstrate their willingness to pay. Finally, as the Deere example suggests, creating differentiation that competitors can emulate quickly or cheaply undermines any advantage that it might afford. Naturally, once competitors have matched a product's unique feature, it's no longer unique and will probably lose its ability to command premium prices. In some industries, patents provide short-term protection for innovative products. In others, companies must seek alternative means of protection. In the soft drink industry, where products are easily imitated (they are, after all, simple combinations of water, sugar, color, and flavoring), Coke and Pepsi discourage imitation by exercising power of scale over suppliers and buyers and conducting aggressive marketing campaigns to sustain brand image.

THREATS TO FOCUS POSITIONS

Although focused low-cost or focused differentiation positions are specialized cases of low-cost leadership and broad differentiation and thus subject to all the same threats as those just reviewed, they face one additional threat that deserves mention. Firms that implement focus positions face the threat of being out-focused by competitors. A firm relying on a focus strategy may lose its advantage by attempting to grow and consequently attempt to meet the needs of too many customers. If that happens, a competitor or new entrant may then more successfully target the needs of the original focused group of customers. As existing or new competitors identify new or previously unexploited needs of the segment, they may be in a better position to uniquely satisfy the needs of that segment. For instance, Harley-Davidson faces the threat that custom chopper shops will pull away customers because they can more uniquely satisfy the needs of a segment of Harley's market.

THREATS TO INTEGRATED POSITIONS

In his original analysis of generic strategic positions, Porter, arguing that they were mutually exclusive, warned against the temptation to straddle positions: Firms that try both to differentiate and to achieve a low-cost position will end up **straddling** two inconsistent positions.

All firms, Porter suggested, must make decisions about positioning their products and will consequently choose one strategy over the other. Developing a low-cost strategy means that a firm must forgo subsequent opportunities to enhance product uniqueness or quality (that is, to develop a position based on differentiation). In this respect, selected strategies and forgone opportunities must be regarded as tradeoffs. The tax preparation firm H&R Block, for example, can't enter the field of high-level estate and tax planning because such services require the kind of high-cost specialists that a low-cost competitor can't

straddling Unsuccessful attempt to integrate both low-cost and differentiation positions.

afford. Thus, Block trades off the advantages of high-margin services for the advantages of a low-cost tax preparation business. By the same token, a "pure" differentiator trades off the cost-saving advantages of producing standardized products for the advantages of satisfying a demand for customized products.

Although many firms have succeeded in pursuing integrated strategies, it's still critical for managers to understand the tradeoffs they make when they opt for one position over the other. Virtually no firm can succeed in being all things to all customers. For one, firms need to know exactly what opportunities they're forgoing.

Second, knowing what tradeoffs can be made in an industry helps managers recognize what competitors can and can't do in attempts to juggle strategies. Why, for instance, can't other airlines lower their costs to match those of Southwest Airlines? Many of the specific practices by which Southwest maintains its lower-cost position entail tradeoffs that the other carriers can't make. Other airlines don't have the option of flying just one type of aircraft, even if it would save on training and maintenance costs. Nor can they abandon their expensive hub facilities, which are integral to the logistics of their flight systems, even though the hub system and its accompanying gate fees are much more costly than Southwest's reliance on secondary airports and smaller destination cities.

Strategy and Fit with Industry Conditions

In Chapter 1, we introduced the strategy-diamond model of strategy formulation. Recall that an important input into this model is a firm's objectives. Earlier in the chapter we detailed generic strategies *by type*, but in order to show how the strategy-diamond and generic-strategy models are compatible, we need to remind ourselves that when managers decide on generic competitive positions, they aren't deciding on strategies themselves: ◆ Rather, they're stating *objectives* with respect to several elements of their overall strategy—indicating precisely how they intend the firm to systematically deal with differentiators, economic logic, and certain aspects of arenas.

We know, too, that industry conditions have an important effect on strategy formulation. One way to illustrate this effect is to examine the threats and opportunities presented to a company during different phases of the industry life cycle. In this section, we'll treat each phase of the life cycle as if conditions are not likely to change in the short term. In other words, in order to show how alternative strategies function under different life-cycle conditions, we'll take advantage of the fact that industry analysis gives us a "snapshot" view of an industry at a particular point in its life cycle. In reality, of course, many industries are changing rapidly, and in Chapter 6, we'll turn our attention to strategies that take advantage of changes, such as the rapid and sometimes managed evolution of an industry from one stage in its life cycle to the next.

STRATEGIES FOR DIFFERENT INDUSTRY LIFE CYCLE CONDITIONS

Industry conditions should inform strategic leaders and have an influence on the strategies their firms formulate. Of course, not all firms will respond similarly to different industry conditions, but conditions at different phases of an industry life cycle provide differential opportunities and constraints. Consequently, firms' strategies tend to vary across these different phases. Exhibit 5.11 summarizes some of the more common effects of the industry life cycle on the elements of firms' strategies.

Embryonic Stage During an industry's *embryonic* phase, when business models are unproven, no standardized technology has been established, capital needs generally outstrip the resources and capabilities of startups, and uncertainty is high. Early movers—those who

Exhibit 5.11 Strategies Tailored to Industry Life Cycle

Phase of Industry Life Cycle	Arenas	Vehicles	Differentiators	Staging	Economic Logic
Embryonic	Staying local	Internal development Alliances to secure missing inputs or distribution access	Target basic needs, minimal differentiation	Tactics to gain early footholds	Prices tend to be high Costs are high; focus is on securing additional capital to fund growth phase
Growth	Penetrating adjacent markets	Alliances for cooperation Acquisitions in targeted markets	Increase efforts toward differentiation Low-cost leaders emerge through experience and scale advantages	Integrated positions require choice of focusing first on cost or differentiation	Margins can improve rapidly because of experience and scale Price premiums accrue to successful differentiators
Mature	Globalizing Diversifying	Mergers and acquisitions for consolidation	More stable positions emerge across competitors	Choices of international markets and new industry diversification need rational sequencing	Consolidation results in fewer competitors (favoring higher margins), but declining growth demands cost containment and rationalization of operations
Decline	Abandoning some arenas if decline is severe Focusing on segments that provide the most profitability	Acquisitions for diversifying Divestitures enable some competitors to exit and others to consolidate larger shares of the market	Fewer competitors result in less pressure for differentiation, but declining sales results in greater pressure for cost savings	Timing of exit from selected segments or businesses	Rationalizing cost

succeed in establishing solid competitive positions during this stage—can set themselves up to be in a strong position during later phases of the industry life cycle.[17] Because primary demand is just being established and customers lack good information on the relative quality of products, successful tactics during this phase include getting a strong foothold and building capacity to meet growing demand.

Growth Stage As industries enter periods of rapid growth, incumbent firms increase market share by taking advantage of footholds established earlier. Rapid growth increases speed down the learning curve and presents leaders with an opportunity to establish low-cost positions that are difficult to imitate, at least in the short term. During this phase, however, technologies can change as new entrants learn from and improve on the work of early movers.

After introducing the PalmPilot, for example, Palm enjoyed an apparently formidable advantage in the PDA industry. The PalmPilot was hailed as the most successful consumer-product launch in history, reaching sales of 2 million units within three years and surpassing the adoption rates of camcorders, color TVs, VCRs, and cell phones.[18] Although it considered itself primarily a hardware device company, Palm developed its own operating system because it was dissatisfied with Microsoft's system for handheld devices. But as the PDA industry grew in size, it caught Microsoft's attention. Before long, Microsoft had renewed interest in its own operating system, and other new competitors, some of whom already had complementary relationships with Microsoft, entered the PDA software industry.[19] There's obviously an advantage in moving early, gaining a foothold that supports quick growth, and reaping cost advantages by moving quickly along the learning curve, but it doesn't necessarily constitute an impenetrable competitive barrier. New technologies and changing industry competitive structure remain threats.[20]

During the growth phase of an industry, firms make important decisions about how they intend to grow: They determine the strategic vehicles that they'll use to implement their preferred strategies. High-tech companies, for example, may seek alliances with established firms in adjacent industries, similar to the embryonic stage, in order to fill in gaps in their own range of competencies. Such is the case in the biotechnology industry; virtually all of the pure biotech companies have established alliances with large pharmaceutical companies in order to access clinical trial expertise and marketing capabilities.[21] During the growth stage, too, firms with desirable resources become attractive acquisition targets, both for incumbents wanting to grow rapidly and for firms in related industries seeking to enter the market.

Maturity Stage   As industries mature and growth slows, products become more familiar to the vast majority of potential customers. Product information is more widely available, and quality becomes a more important factor in consumer choice. A mature market, therefore, increases the ability of firms to reap premium prices from differentiation strategies.

Mature industries often undergo *consolidation*—the combination of competitors through merger or acquisition. Consolidation is often motivated by the twofold objective of exploiting economies of scale and increasing market power. The U.S. bicycle industry profiled through the examples of Pacific Cycle, Trek, and Montague, for instance, has experienced a virtual cascade of mergers and acquisitions for the better part of a decade. Although each new combination promises cost saving through greater economies of scale, evidence of significant savings remains inconclusive at best. Market power is a factor because many bicycle companies want to stay large enough to serve the needs of high-volume distribution channels such as Wal-Mart.

Decline Stage   In declining industries, products can take on the attributes of quasi commodities. Because price competition can be intense, containing costs is critical, and firms with low-cost positions have an advantage. Although customers don't entirely ignore differentiated products, declining sales discourage firms from investing in significant innovations.

During this stage, many firms consider the strategy of exiting the industry. Generally, the decision to exit means selling the company or certain divisions to competing firms. Because demand is declining, the industry probably suffers from overcapacity. Thus, reducing the number of competitors can enhance the profitability of those firms that remain. But this fact doesn't mean that exit signifies failure. In many cases, exit can be the best use of shareholders' resources.

A short case study about General Dynamics (GD) drawn from the defense industry demonstrates the potential benefits of exiting an industry during its decline stage.[22] GD was founded in 1899 as the Electric Boat Co. and a year later produced the first workable submarine, which it sold to the U.S. Navy. By the 1950s, GD was a full-fledged defense contractor, producing missiles, rockets, nuclear-powered submarines, and military air-craft. In the mid-1950s, due to the wide range of its defense-industry operations, the company changed its name to General Dynamics Corp. During the 1970s and 1980s, GD emerged as the only defense contractor to supply major systems to all branches of the U.S. military.

Despite many successful weapons programs, however, GD's profitability dropped during the late 1980s, largely because of changes in government procurement processes. In addition, the Cold War thawed rapidly in 1989 and 1990, with the Soviet withdrawal from Afghanistan, the fall of the Berlin Wall, and the collapse of Communist governments across Eastern Europe. Needless to say, the proliferation of arms treaties dampened the demand for weapons systems. GD was particularly hard-hit because it was the least diversified of all defense contractors, with a full 87 percent of its revenue tied to defense system sales.

In 1989, GD hired William Anders as chairman and CEO. His specific charge was to turn the floundering company around. Motivated by lucrative contracts that included generous incentives tied to stock-price performance, Anders and his top management team set about implementing a radical new strategy. Anders' team made immediate changes, cutting capital spending to 20 percent of the level just two years earlier (saving $337 million). They lost over $1 billion in sales and slashed R&D spending targets by 50 percent. Spending cuts were followed by massive layoffs. Anders was quite public in his pronouncements that the defense industry suffered from overcapacity, too many competitors, and dwindling demand. He publicly urged the industry to consolidate.

Over a two-year period beginning in late 1991, GD sold seven defense businesses for more than $3 billion, emerging as a much smaller and more focused company. Revenues for the new GD were a mere 34 percent of levels of two years earlier, but exiting from so many markets enabled GD to eliminate 94 percent of its outstanding debt, repurchase over 13 million shares of stock, increase dividends by 140 percent, and issue special dividends totaling $50 per share. At the end of this massive downsizing and business-exit campaign, GD had returned $3.4 billion to shareholders and debt holders. Moreover, despite the massive reduction in size, GD's market capitalization increased from about $1 billion in January 1991 to almost $2.9 billion by the end of 1993. Shareholders who held their stock during the three-year restructuring campaign realized a return of over 550 percent.

Testing the Quality of a Strategy

Now that you have command of an adequate repertory of strategy formulation tools—namely, the strategy diamond, VRINE, industry structure, and the strategic positioning models—you should be able to use them to test the quality of a firm's strategy. Clearly, developing a successful business strategy is a complex task. Although we've focused in this chapter on decisions regarding competitive position and strategic interactions, we must also stress that evaluating the effectiveness of a strategy requires that you apply all the tools and models that we've discussed in the first four chapters of this book. In this section, we'll lay out a simple five-step process that makes use of all of these tools and models to evaluate the quality of a firm's strategy. These steps are summarized in Exhibit 5.12.[23]

DOES YOUR STRATEGY EXPLOIT YOUR FIRM'S RESOURCES AND CAPABILITIES?

Your first step in testing the quality of a strategy is determining whether your strategy and competitive position exploit your firm's resources and capabilities. Low-cost strategic positions require manufacturing resources and capabilities that are likely to contribute to a cost

Exhibit 5.12   Testing the Quality of Your Strategy

Adapted from D. C. Hambrick and J. W. Fredrickson, "Are You Sure You Have a Strategy?" Academy of Management Executive 15:4 (2001), 48–59.

Key Evaluation Criteria	
1. Does your strategy exploit your key resources?	With your particular mix of resources, does this strategy give you an advantageous position relative to your competitors?
	Can you pursue this strategy more economically than your competitors?
	Do you have the capital and managerial talent to do all you plan to do?
	Are you spread too thin?
2. Does your strategy fit with current industry conditions?	Is there healthy profit potential where you're headed?
	Are you aligned with the key success factors of your industry?
3. Will your differentiators be sustainable?	Will competitors have difficulty imitating you?
	If imitation can't be foreclosed, does your strategy include a ceaseless regimen of innovation and opportunity creation to keep distance between you and the competition?
4. Are the elements of your strategy consistent and aligned with your strategic position?	Have you made choices of arenas, vehicles, differentiators, staging, and economic logic?
	Do they all fit and mutually reinforce each other?
5. Can your strategy be implemented?	Will your stakeholders allow you to pursue this strategy?
	Do you have the proper complement of implementation levers in place?
	Is the management team able and willing to lead the required changes?

advantage. For instance, Pacific Cycle is the lowest-cost bike distributor in the U.S. by virtue of its lean operations and the complete outsourcing of bike manufacturing to Taiwan and China. Likewise, a differentiation position depends on your ability to produce quality products and to project the necessary image of quality. In Trek's case, it has been careful to cultivate its high-performance image by sponsoring bike luminaries such as Lance Armstrong and selling only through the exclusive independent dealer channel. When two firms follow similar strategies, you must determine whether you can use your resources to implement your strategy more economically than your competitors can. Finally, you need to be sure that you have the capital resources—both financial and human—necessary to pull off your strategy.

DOES YOUR STRATEGY FIT WITH CURRENT INDUSTRY CONDITIONS?

Next, you must ask whether your strategy fits with the current conditions in your competitive environment. You need to know whether that environment is hostile, benign, or somewhere in between. Essentially, you want to be sure that you understand the profit *potential* of both your current position and the position toward which your strategy is taking you. Pacific Cycle viewed the big-box retailers and consolidation of the bike industry as opportunities for profitable growth. Ironically, Trek viewed the same environment with an eye toward shoring up relationships with independent bike dealers as a way to combat the influx of sales through low-cost, big-box retail channels. Thus, you need to determine whether your strategy aligns with the key success factors favored by your competitive environment.

ARE YOUR DIFFERENTIATORS SUSTAINABLE?

If competitors can imitate your differentiators, can you protect your current relationship with your customers? Imitation can erode competitive advantage, but some forms of imitation can reinforce brand loyalty to individual firms. Frequent flier programs, for example, are very easy to imitate, but customers who have accumulated many miles with one carrier are harder to steal than those who don't have very many miles. Ironically, then, imitation in this case actually serves to increase existing brand loyalty and, potentially, to benefit both firms. Frequent flier programs put up barriers to customer mobility, and without some kind of barrier that increases the cost of switching brands, a firm with easily imitated differentiators will have to rely on a continual stream of innovative offerings in order to sustain revenues.

ARE THE ELEMENTS OF YOUR STRATEGY CONSISTENT AND ALIGNED WITH YOUR STRATEGIC POSITION?

Your next step in testing the quality of a strategy is determining whether all of the elements of your strategy diamond are not only internally consistent but that they are also aligned with your strategic position, whether it is the one you occupy currently or the one toward which your strategy may direct you in the future. The challenge is to ensure that your choices of arenas, vehicles, differentiators, staging, and economic logic are mutually reinforcing and consistent with your objective, whether it's to be a low-cost leader, a differentiator, or a focused firm. For instance, to be poised for the growth phase, your strategy will need to accommodate rapid growth through the use of acquisitions or significant internal development of additional products and services. If you do not do so, your firm will be marginalized. This may be an acceptable outcome if the intended strategic position is one of focus. Alternatively, if your industry is approaching the end of the growth phase, have you implemented appropriate cost containment measures that will be required when additional price competition increases? The key is to make clear and explicit links between the vision of the firm, your strategy, and industry conditions. When these factors are aligned, the likelihood of achieving your objectives is maximized. When one of these features is not in alignment with the others, lack of coherence almost always causes the firm to slip behind competitors.

CAN YOUR STRATEGY BE IMPLEMENTED?

It does no good to concoct a brilliant strategy within the safe confines of your office at headquarters if your firm can't implement it. To test whether your strategy can be implemented, you need to make sure that it's aligned with the appropriate implementation levers. For instance, do you have the appropriate people, the necessary systems and processes, and incentives that are congruent with your objectives? If not, can you make these modifications within the organization in time to execute the strategy? Do you have the sufficient managerial talent and interest to pursue the strategy? One of the biggest obstacles to firm growth is insufficient managerial resources (e.g., time, people, interests) to focus on the details of execution. As a startup, for instance, JetBlue has set aggressive objectives for financial returns, growth, and a focused low-cost leadership position. Among other things, executing this strategy will mean continually hiring new employees who fit the company culture—people who share the core values of the firm. Otherwise, it will be vulnerable to the sort of labor problems that have beset other low-cost airlines. The most successful firms routinely discuss the integration of strategy and leadership. For instance, all discussions of new strategic initiatives will include answers to the question of "who exactly will get this done?" If there is no clear answer to this question, or if those individuals are likely to be spread too thin as a consequence, even attractive plans should not be given a green light.

Summary of Challenges

1. *Define* generic strategies *and explain how they relate to a firm's strategic position.* Strategic positioning is the concept of how executives situate or locate their firm relative to rivals along important competitive dimensions. The strategic positioning model—Porter's generic strategy model—is an enduring classic in the field of strategic management. Porter's strategy model uses two dimensions: the potential source of strategic advantage and the breadth of the strategic target market. The four generic strategies are low-cost leader, differentiation, focused low-cost, and focused differentiation.

2. *Describe the drivers of low-cost, differentiation, and focused strategic positions.* Low-cost leaders must have resources or capabilities that enable them to produce a product at a significantly lower cost than rivals. Successful low-cost leaders generally have superior economies of scale, are farther down the learning curve, or have superior production or process technologies than their rivals. However, to substantially reduce costs over rivals, low-cost leaders generally have to be willing to make tradeoffs—they cannot offer all the features, attributes, and quality that a successful differentiator can. Likewise, successful differentiators will normally have to accept higher costs than low-cost leaders. To make a differentiation strategy pay off, firms must segment the market so that customer needs are well understood, products are designed to uniquely satisfy those needs, and the products offered increase a customer's willingness to pay. Firms that attempt to straddle both positions generally do not perform well along either dimension. However, some firms have been successful at integrating basic features of both low-cost and differentiation. Those that do, typically perfect one set of economic drivers before trying to complement those with the seemingly inconsistent drivers associated with the other economic logic. A focused strategy is generally the application of a low-cost or differentiation approach to a narrowly defined arena.

3. *Identify and explain the risks associated with each generic strategic position.* Successful strategic positions are still vulnerable. Threats to low-cost leadership include not having the resources necessary to implement the position, having low-cost drivers imitated by firms with better products, and not having sufficient quality to attract buyers. Threats to a differentiation strategy include increasing costs significantly to differentiate a product only to misperceive customer preferences, excessive cost to provide the targeted differentiation, and differentiating in ways that are easily imitated. A firm relying on a focus strategy risks growing too large, trying to meet too many needs, and then being outfocused by a more specialized company. An integrated position runs the risk of unsuccessfully straddling the logic of seemingly inconsistent economic drivers, resulting in neither a low cost position nor a differentiated one.

4. *Show how different strategic positions fit with stages of the industry life cycle.* During embryonic stages, primary demand is just beginning, and customers lack good information on the relative quality of products. Thus, building a strong foothold and the capacity to meet growing demand are more important than aggressively differentiating products. During growth stages, building on early footholds provides incumbents with an opportunity to gain market share and move down the learning curve and establish low-cost positions. Maturity stages bring lower levels of growth, and information is widely available to customers. Differentiation can reduce competitive threats and result in higher prices. During industry decline, price competition intensifies and cost containment becomes more important.

5. *Evaluate the quality of the firm's strategy.* The quality of a firm's strategy can be assessed by answering a few questions that can be answered by the basic tools of strategy, including the strategy diamond, VRINE, industry structure, and the strategic positioning models. First, you must determine whether the strategy and competitive position exploit the firm's resources and capabilities. Strategic positions such as low-cost leadership and differentiation have economic assumptions that cannot be satisfied in the absence of complementary resources and capabilities. Second, a quality strategy will also fit with the external environment—the current environment and the anticipated environment in dynamic contexts. Third, a firm's differentiators must be sustainable. Fourth, all of the elements of the strategy diamond must be inter-

nally consistent and aligned with the current or desired strategic position. Finally, a quality strategy is one that can be implemented by the firm. Brilliant plans are of little value if the firm is unable to execute them.

Review Questions

1. What do we mean by *generic strategies?*

2. What criteria must be met in order for differentiators and low-cost leaders to be successful?

3. What is the relationship between economies of scale and minimum efficient scale?

4. What are economies of scope?

5. How does the learning curve work?

6. What is market segmentation? What role does it play in strategic positioning?

7. What is willingness to pay? How does it relate to strategic positioning?

8. How does the industry life cycle affect business strategy?

9. What are the steps in testing the quality of a strategy?

Experiential Activities

Group Exercises

1. Review the opening vignette about the three bicycle manufacturers. Use the strategy-diamond and the generic strategy model to describe the positioning strategy of each firm. Based on what you know about the bicycle industry, can you identify any underserved (or overserved) segments?

2. Go back to Exhibit 4.1 in Chapter 4. Identify low-cost leaders from two of these industries. What seem to be the drivers of their cost-leadership positioning strategies? Are they the same? If not, why?

Ethical Debates

1. Among the global trends facing business, it is increasingly unclear who should provide basic social services (e.g., pensions, public health services, school infrastructure), regulate business and personal behavior (eg, self-regulation vs. government oversight), and be accountable for protecting rights, public goods, and resources. In developing a business strategy, where should a company's leaders draw the line between what is acceptable from a purely legal standpoint and what would be dictated by the ethics of different generations or demographic segments of consumers?

2. Environmental issues, including climate change, are increasingly discussed in the executive suite as it relates to strategy formulation and implementation. How "green" should a company be that is pursuing a low-cost strategy in an increasingly environmentally conscious society? And if following a differentiation strategy, would customers pay extra for being "green?" Is "green" a viable differentiator in either low cost or differentiation?

How Would YOU DO THAT?

1. Let's revisit the learning curve and change some of the assumptions made in the box entitled "How Would *You* Do That? 5.1." Assume that the first bike took 100 hours, the second 85, and the fourth 72.25. What would the incremental "cost" in hours be for the 16th bike? For the 124th? For the 1,000th? Try to find these numbers using both the formula presented in the feature and the learning curve calculator located at www.jsc.nasa.gov/bu2/learn.html.

2. Based on the information in the box entitled "How Would *You* Do That? 5.1," assume that you have determined that established leaders have such an experience advantage that you'll never catch their cost position. Devise a realistic strategy for entering and competing against an established player that has a significant low-cost leadership position.

Go on to see How Would You Do That at www.prenhall.com/carpenter&sanders

Endnotes

1. Personal interview with Trek executives, fall 2004; "Trek Bicycle Corporation Hoover's Company In-Depth Records," *Hoover's,* www.hoovers.com (accessed September 28, 2005); S. Silcoff, "Dorel Buys Biggest U.S. Cycle Maker: Gains 27% of U.S. Market Share with US$310M Purchase of Schwinn, GT Brands," *Financial Post,* January 14, 2004, p.1; www.montagueco.com/aboutusourhistory.html (accessed October 20, 2005). Statistics are from National Bicycle Dealers Association http://nbda.com/page.cfm?PageID=34 (accessed April 27, 2007); Becca Mader, "Shifting into High Gear," *The Business Journal of Milwaukee,* May 16, 2003; Becca Mader, "Firm to Launch Schwinn Line for Mass Retailers," *The Business Journal of Milwaukee,* August 7, 2002; Griff Witte, "Schwinn's Bard Bump in the Road," *The Washington Post,* December 9, 2004; http://www.pacific-cycle.com/ourstory/timeline.php (accessed on April 27, 2007).

2. Exhibit adapted from M. E. Porter, *Competitive Strategy* (New York: Free Press, 1980).

3. http://www.autointell.net (accessed July 15, 2005).

4. Personal interview with Audi senior management, May 2003.

5. S. Targett, "U.S. Companies Win at the Scale Game," *Financial Times,* February 16, 2004, p. 9.

6. R. Sanchez, "Strategic Flexibility in Product Competition," *Strategic Management Journal* 16 (1995), 135–149.

7. See S. S. Liao, "The Learning Curve: Wright's Model vs. Crawford's Model," *Issues in Accounting Education* 3 (1988), 302–315.

8. A. S. Grove, *Only the Paranoid Survey: How to Exploit the Crisis Points That Challenge Every Company* (New York: Currency, 1996).

9. E. D. Darr, L. Argote, and D. Epple, "The Acquisition, Transfer, and Depreciation of Knowledge in Service Organizations: Productivity in Franchises," *Management Science* 41 (1995), 1750–1762.

10. D. Teece, "Economies of Scope and the Scope of the Enterprise," *Journal of Economic Behavior and Organization* 1 (1980), 223–247.

11. Interview with Mity-Lite corporate officers, November 2004. See also www.mity-lite.com.

12. C. Christensen, *The Innovator's Dilemma* (New York: Harper Business Press, 2000).

13. C. K. Prahalad and G. Hamel, "The Core Competence of the Corporation," *Harvard Business Review* 68:3 (1990), 79–91.

14. Estimates of margins from the National Bicycle Dealers Association, nbda.com.

15. See www.sweatshops.org/; www.uniteunion.org/sweatshops/sweatshop.html; and www.business-humanrights.org/home.

16. Personal interview with Jaguar executives, June 2003.

17. D. C. Hambrick, I. A. MacMillan, and D. L. Day, "Strategic Attributes and Performance in the BCG Matrix: A PIMS-Based Analysis of Industrial Product Businesses," *Academy of Management Journal* 25 (1982), 510–531.

18. D. B. Yoffie and M. Kwak, "Mastering Strategic Movement at Palm," *Sloan Management Review* 43:1 (2001), 55–63.

19. Yoffie and Kwak, "Mastering Strategic Movement at Palm."

20. Hambrick, MacMillan, and Day, "Strategic Attributes and Performance in the BCG Matrix."

21. F. T. Rothaermel and D. L. Deeds, "Exploration and Exploitation Alliances in Biotechnology: A System of New Product Development," *Strategic Management Journal* 25:3 (2004), 201–221.

22. J. Dial and K. B. Murphy, "Incentives, Downsizing, and Value Creation at General Dynamics," *Journal of Financial Economics* 37 (1990), 261–314; company annual reports, hoovers.com (accessed September 28, 2005).

23. This adapted exhibit and section draws heavily on D. C. Hambrick and J. W. Fredrickson, "Are You Sure You Have a Strategy?" *Academy of Management Executive* 15:4 (2001), 48–59.

6 Crafting Business Strategy for Dynamic Contexts

In This Chapter We Challenge You To >>>

1. Distinguish the ways in which firms' strategies are related to dynamic contexts.

2. Identify, compare, and contrast the various routes to revolutionary strategies.

3. Evaluate the advantages and disadvantages of choosing a first-mover strategy.

4. Recognize when an incumbent is caught off guard by a revolutionary strategy and identify defensive tactics to reduce the effects of this competition.

5. Explain the difficulties and solutions to implementing revolutionary strategies.

Roxio *and the* Resurrection *of* Napster

"Napster concludes our fiscal year 2007 with over 830,000 paid subscribers, which we believe makes us the largest on demand music subscription service in the industry," said Chris Gorog, Napster's chairman and chief executive officer.[1] "We have a paid subscriber base that is both larger than Rhapsody, as well as larger than all of the remaining subscription competitors combined." Napster was riding high again in April 2007, under the leadership of Chris Gorog, whose career spans virtually all aspects of the media and entertainment industry and its convergence with technology. In this dynamic industry, Gorog was the one to lead Napster, given his background. Gorog had been Chairman and CEO of Napster, the leader in CD recording and digital media, which he took public under the corporate name of Roxio in 2001. Before that, Gorog served as President of New Business Development and Executive Vice President of Group Operations for Universal Studios Recreations Group. Prior to Universal, Gorog was President and CEO of ITC Entertainment Group, a leading motion picture and television producer, and led a management buy-out of the group's global business. Before joining ITC, Gorog served as Vice President of Business Affairs for Motion Pictures and Television at The Walt Disney Company. Gorog was also a director of House of Blues, a leading North American concert producer and The Guitar Center, a large musical instrument retailer.

When someone draws up a conclusive list of the software that made the Internet what it is, somewhere among e-mail and Web browsers there will be a spot for Napster. Napster was really two pieces of software: freely available "client" software that ran on home computers, enabling individuals to copy music to their PCs and play it for free, and a central Napster-run server that dispensed information about music. When it arrived in late 1999, Napster showed how easily music could be distributed without a costly infrastructure (namely, recording-artist royalties, CD manufacturers, record distribution, and record stores). The timing was also right as consumer preferences were shifting to entertainment-on-demand, big players such as Sony and Samsung were providing stylish, miniaturized portable music systems, and there was little in terms of clear legal precedent against music sharing. By facilitating music sharing, Napster sent ripples of panic through the music industry, which depended on the traditional music-industry infrastructure to generate a considerable amount of revenue. In June 2002, after four years of legal battles with the Recording Industry Association of America (RIAA), which represents every major U.S. music label, Napster filed for bankruptcy. At the time, Napster had listed assets of $7.9 million and liabilities of more than $101 million.

Gorog led the acquisition of Napster after its bankruptcy through his software company, Roxio. This illustrates a common pattern in which a new CEO, such as Gorog, remakes his company to fit his prior experience. Under Gorog, with his media background, Roxio morphed from software company to a media company. In 2003, Gorog relaunched Napster as a legal download music provider site and took over as its CEO. Roxio itself had gone public in 2001 as a software-only firm specializing in the development and sale of CD-recording products to both original-equipment manufacturers (OEMs) of PCs and CD-recordable-drive manufacturers, integrators, and distributors. In preparation for the Napster launch, Roxio courted two tech-industry players once spurned by Napster—Microsoft and music producers. Why Microsoft? Roxio supplied the CD-burning software bundled with all new PCs operated by Microsoft XP. As for music producers, Roxio, unlike the original Napster, intended to keep them happy by abandoning the idea of free music sharing.

The question for Roxio was whether it would still be around in five years, after the online-music business had shaken out. It faced competition not only in its original software business, but in its new online-music business as well. Approaches to providing online music included the following:

■ The à la carte approach (employed by Roxio and Apple's iTunes). For 79 cents to $1.20, customers can buy any number of individual tracks (or albums for $9.99 and up). After downloading music onto their hard drives, they can burn it onto CDs, copy it to portable music players, or stream it through home-entertainment centers.

■ The subscription model (used by emusic). Customers pay a monthly fee to download a specified number of songs. For $9.99 a month, emusic lets customers download 40 songs (65 for $14.99) and use them any way they want.

■ The streaming model (favored by RealNetwork's Rhapsody). Music lovers pay a monthly fee to listen to as many songs as they can stand and, for a little extra (usually under a dollar a track), download their favorites.

The uncertainty created by the availability of competing technological standards was heightened by the fact that the idea of online-music consumption had only just begun to catch on.

Going forward, Roxio aimed to compete by keeping its hand in the turbulent online-music business while keeping a firm grip on its position as the number-one seller of CD- and DVD-burning software. This strategy meant that the company had to maintain strong ties with Microsoft as well as with other tech-industry heavyweights, such as RealNetworks, and the music industry—an array of stakeholders who view Roxio as everything from a partner to competitor. Moreover, Roxio would also need to keep close tabs on firms that manufacture CD and DVD burner/players. Why? Because they may enter the software business as a means of differentiating increasingly commoditized hardware products.

Perhaps the most telling factor in this story of dynamic strategy in dynamic contexts is the sale of Roxio's software business to competitor Sonic Solutions in January 2004 and the subsequent renaming of the surviving online-music company to Napster. This completed the remaking of the company to fit Gorog's background in media. In May 2005, Yahoo! entered the online-music fray with a service priced at half that of Napster's—now that's a dynamic context!

The dynamic nature of the Internet has made it challenging for Gorog to find a workable (that is, a legal and profitable) business model for Napster. Even as late as September 2006, Gorog was struggling. "Napster's still trying to find a working business model, which is bad from an operating standpoint," said Kit Spring, analyst with Stifel Nicolaus & Co Inc. Spring thought that Gorog would put Napster up for sale, based on Gorog's hints that "We do not have our heads in the sand regarding an M&A (merger and acquisition) transaction," In a call to analysts in September 2006, Gorog left all options on the table. "We continue to receive a lot of interest in the company. We will always carefully weigh any valuation alternative against the opportunity and risk associated with continuing as a stand-alone company," Gorog said.

In 2006, Napster was facing stiff competition from iTunes, which is not a subscription-based service. Gorog decided to go back to a model that had worked before: free. Gorog created a Web site where consumers could listen to as many as five tracks for free while watching ads. This time, though, the free music would be legal because Napster would pay the record labels from the ad revenues. New subscriber growth on Napster fell as Gorog focused on the new site, but Gorog believed that the new site would improve conversion from free users to paid users. In addition, Napster would get a new revenue stream from ads. Gorog's ad sales team worked with advertisers to create custom playlists to accompany the ads. Analysts remained skeptical, however. "It will be interesting to see how much revenue they can get from advertising," said Jupiter Research analyst David Card. "But they're still going to live and die by subscriptions."

Perhaps the greatest testimony to the competitiveness and dynamism of this market space is Napster's profitability: From the date of its spinoff from Adaptec through April 2007, Napster has never shown a profit. **<<<**

Strategy and Dynamic Contexts

In this chapter, we build on Chapter 5 by showing you how firms can develop competitive advantage in the face of dynamic competition. Although the notion of the industry life cycle you studied in Chapter 5 suggests that strategy should always be dynamic, because it must be externally oriented to be effective, the dynamic competition we refer to here requires that strategies also be dynamic by virtue of the rapid and sometimes unpredictable changes taking place in the firm's external environment. For most industries, certain features of the industry are dynamic. In some industries, these features are central to success in the largest and most lucrative parts of the industry. So, at a minimum, firms must know how to respond to dynamic competition. More important is figuring out how to be the instigator of successful and dynamic change; being an industry revolutionary can be the path to improved and dynamic competitive advantage. As you can see from our opening vignette about the on-line music business, dynamic strategies still require firms to make coherent tradeoffs between the economic logic of low cost and differentiation as the primary factors in any strategy for getting customers to buy their products. Dynamic competition, however, challenges a firm to improve its game continuously, and maybe even figure out how to rewrite the rules of competition.

This challenge is what differentiates the relatively stable context of strategy explored in Chapter 5—even for strategies that address one stage of the industry life cycle—from the *dynamic* context of strategy. Moreover, successful strategies increasingly require that they be revolutionary—that they change the rules of the game. These strategies, however, also necessitate the nearly seamless integration of formulation and implementation and tend to reward an appetite for experimentation and risk taking. This is why, after understanding what constitutes a dynamic context, you will also learn how to conceive of a revolutionary strategy and use tools designed to help formulate revolutionary strategies, such as the value-curve and real-options analysis.

Before introducing the strategies and tools for dealing with dynamic markets, let's start by reviewing the specific ways in which dynamic contexts can undermine competitive advantage.

THE CHALLENGES TO SUSTAINABLE COMPETITIVE ADVANTAGE

It's important to understand why dynamic conditions can undermine competitive advantage, whether with blinding speed or over an extended period of time. Indeed, as we saw in the opening vignette, even though it may seem that an industry has changed overnight, many of the seeds of that apparently dramatic change may have been sown and nourished over a fairly long period. For instance, changes in consumer preferences and portable music technologies evolved over an extended period of time. In addition, change often results from a combination of drivers, several of which you learned about in earlier chapters and which are reviewed further in this chapter.

Recall from prior chapters that competitive advantage is developed when a firm can create value in ways that rivals cannot. And the likelihood of developing a competitive advantage is facilitated by possessing resources and capabilities that fulfill the VRINE criteria. Firms with VRINE resources and capabilities are much more likely to be able to create strategic positions of low cost and differentiation than firms that lack such resources and capabilities. Challenges to sustained competitive advantage include anything that threatens VRINE resources and capabilities. Consequently, we need to examine the types of change that make valuable resources and capabilities lose their value; that make valuable and rare resources and capabilities become common; that make valuable and rare resources and capabilities easy to imitate or substitute; and that weaken a firm's ability to exploit resources and capabilities that satisfy the value, rarity, inimitability, and nonsubstitutability criteria of the VRINE model.

In addition, formulating strategies either to protect against threats from or to exploit the opportunities associated with dynamic environments generally encompass special cases of finding new ways to generate a low-cost or differentiation advantage. Because dynamic markets move at a much faster pace than stable markets, strategies for dealing with dynamic markets involve special attention to the *arenas* and *staging* elements of the strategy diamond.

Three dimensions of dynamic change are explored in this chapter: *Competitive interactions, industry evolution,* and *technological disruptions* (global issues, the other cause of dynamic contexts, will be discussed separately in Chapter 8). These categories are interrelated and are intended to help you think about the different facets of a changing competitive landscape. The relative speed of changes in these categories further complicates strategy in dynamic contexts.

Competitive Interaction

How do principles of dynamic context and change complement the principles of strategic decision making that we've already discussed in prior chapters? We know that managers can use tools such as the strategy diamond, the VRINE model, and industry structure analysis to formulate a strategy and hammer out a strategic position. We know, too, that the firm's strategy and strategic position should be consistent with its strengths and its ability to seize opportunities presented by its competitive environment. Finally, we know that strategic positioning decisions are supported by a wealth of tactical decisions made to implement and reinforce the firm's strategy.

Now consider the possible effects of all this decision making in a context of interactive competition. Competitive interactions are composed of two related factors: the interactions between incumbents and the interactions of new entrants and incumbents. The interactions caused by new entrants are a particularly severe source of dynamism when the entrants introduce a new business model—that is, a strategy that varies significantly from those used by incumbents. Research on competitive interaction has identified four underlying phases, summarized in Exhibit 6.1.[2]

To examine these phases, let's say that a regional title insurance company developed a strategy designed to help it grow into a premier national company. That strategy involves a sequence of activities: entry into adjacent regional markets, followed by increased focus on differentiators designed to build brand awareness, followed by more rapid expansion through acquisitions funded by an increasingly valuable stock price.[3] In its first phase, such an aggressive series of tactical moves may go unnoticed or ignored by competitors. Eventually, however, if customer reactions in phase 2 appear to be, or are anticipated to be, positive, then other firms will formulate responses to the first firm's competitive behavior, as shown in phase 3. In phase 4, competitors evaluate the results of their interactions, and the cycle may then recommence.

Competitive actions can generate a wide range of competitive responses.[4] *Competitive interaction theory* suggests that because competitive actions will generate reactions, a firm's managers should predict reactions to its actions and use that information to determine what would be the best course of action given competitors' likely reactions.[5] Competitive action can be initiated in phase 1 in essentially four ways: aggressiveness, complexity of the competitive action repertoire, unpredictability, and tactics that delay the leaders' competitive reaction. The responses to those various actions have been shown to play out differently in terms of the competitive advantage of the challenger and the challenged.

With regard to competitive aggressiveness, strategy research has shown that a challenger can erode the leadership position of another firm by rapidly launching many assaults on the leader in a short period of time. Such interaction explains how Nike overtook Reebok's dominant sports shoe position in the late 1980s and how, in 2005, SABMiller regained market-share-growth leadership from Anheuser Busch in the light beer segment. SABMiller did so through a combination of aggressive advertising that suggested that Anheuser Busch's beers lacked flavor and backed it up with consumer surveys saying that the SABMiller's beers had more and better taste.

Exhibit 6.1 Phases of Competitive Interaction

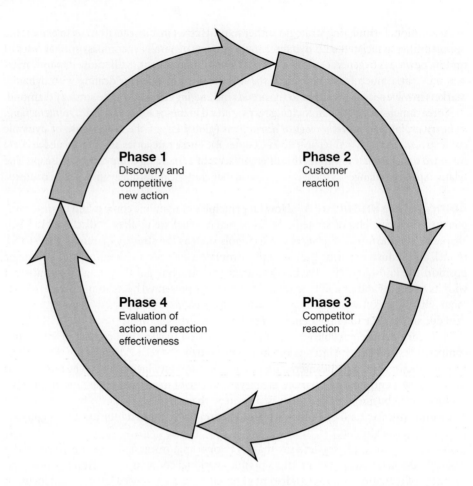

Phase 1
Discovery and competitive new action

Phase 2
Customer reaction

Phase 4
Evaluation of action and reaction effectiveness

Phase 3
Competitor reaction

Similarly, the more complexity and unpredictability inherent in these aggressive moves, the more likely the attacker will succeed in improving its market position. Complexity and unpredictability play to the attacker's advantage by confusing the industry leader and putting it on the defensive. As a result, the leader may also lose focus on the coherent execution of its strategy, as seen by the fragmentation of scarce resources to defending multiple competitive fronts. For example, Anheuser Busch was so thrown off by SABMiller's aggressive tactics that it responded by launching a new beer, Budweiser Select, and advertising it as a flavorful, high-quality beer. SABMiller turned around and pointed to the new product as further evidence that Anheuser Busch's products did not have taste.

Finally, to the extent that the challenger can engage in competitive moves that are difficult to respond to quickly or simply catch the leader unaware, the attacker can gain competitive market position. Strategy research has shown, for instance, that Nike's competitive success can be partially attributed to the fact that Nike initiated new competitive moves (e.g., promotions, new product launches, endorsements) and responded to Reebok's actions much faster than Reebok responded to Nike's.[6] This same research has shown such tactics to hold true in industries ranging from telecommunications and personal computers to airlines and brewing.

When leading companies face new competitors who utilize new business models that are disruptive—strategies that are both different from and in conflict with those of incumbents—they face vexing dilemmas. Should they respond to these new entrants with disruptive strategies and, if so, how? These types of innovations essentially result in a possible change in the rules of competition within the industry. Such disruptions have several common characteristics. First, compared to incumbents, these firms typically emphasize different product attributes. Second, they generally start out as rather low-margin businesses. Third, they can grow into significant companies that take away market share. However, because of tradeoffs with value-chain activities that are essential to the incumbents, these new firms' business models cannot be imitated in short order by incumbents. Examples of these types of disruptive entrants are found in many industries, such as rental cars (Enterprise), retailing (Amazon.com), retail brokerage (E*Trade and Charles Schwab), steel (Nucor), and airlines (Southwest, JetBlue, and RyanAir). Your opening vignette on the new Napster is another good example of a new business model. Devising appropriate strategies to deal with these types of competitive interactions is particularly difficult.

Industry Evolution Rivalry and the nature of competition, as we pointed out in Chapter 4, often change as a function of industry evolution—from differentiation to cost, or vice versa. Because a successful low-cost strategy requires different resources and capabilities than a differentiation strategy, a change in the basis of competitive advantage will cause advantage to shift over time from firms with the obsolete resources and capabilities to those favored by industry conditions. Because all industries evolve and mature, a firm's strategy must always anticipate the repercussions of change. Of course, the best case is where the firms can both be the cause of such change, and be positioned to benefit from it. As we saw in Chapter 5, for example, strategies may differ from one stage of the industry life cycle to another. The strategic management of industry evolution involves not only dealing with the industry life cycle but also strategies for changing arenas and strategies for responding to changes in a firm's environment. One particular challenge associated with industry evolution that goes beyond the industry life cycle challenges outlined in Chapter 5 is the pressures of commoditization.

The Pressures of Commoditization Managers must consider the pressure for change exerted by *commoditization,* which we defined in Chapter 4 as the process by which industry-wide sales come to depend less on unique product features and more on price. As industry products become perceived as undifferentiated, the ability of firms to generate premium pricing diminishes. Consequently, differentiation strategies are vulnerable to the pressures of commoditization.

Research suggests that firms can choose from among different tactics to deal with the pressures of commoditization.[7] The manager, however, must make difficult choices in terms of timing—for instance, if the firm changes its strategy too soon, it risks losing extra profits, but if it moves too late, it may never be able to regain the market lost to newcomers or incumbents who moved sooner. As you will see, all the tactics have clear implications for the five elements in the strategy diamond—namely, arenas, differentiators, vehicles, pacing, and economic logic.

Technological Change Chapter 4 introduced you to the concept of *technological disruptions*, which can cause leading firms to fall by the wayside. Industry decline is often forestalled by the introduction of a new technology that propels the industry into another growth phase. A *technological discontinuity* is an innovation that dramatically advances an industry's price-versus-performance frontier; it generally triggers a period of ferment that is closed by the emergence of a dominant design. A period of incremental technical change then follows, which is, in turn, broken by the next technological discontinuity.[8]

Keep in mind that *technology* is a very broad term. We tend to think of technology rather myopically, focusing only on pure technological innovations. However, technological disruptions may also be *process innovations* (such as Charles Schwab's migration to on-line trading or Toyota's adaptation of lean manufacturing), *application innovations* (such as GM's integration of Global Positioning Systems into vehicles through the OnStar system), and *business model innovations* (such as Amazon.com's move from online bookselling to becoming a logistics provider for countless retailers).[9]

Technological change is particularly disruptive when change is discontinuous, so that it does not sustain existing leaders' advantage. Additionally, technological change is particularly risky when it primarily affects business *processes*. The Progressive Direct on-line insurance market is an example of this. Progressive bypasses traditional and costly insurance agents and relies instead on direct sales through the Internet. In doing so, Progressive is able to offer some of the lowest-priced insurance products on the market. And to ensure that customers shop with Progressive first, the company provides quotes for competitors' policies, and will even sell them instead if a consumer prefers that. Progressive makes money both ways, through the sale of its own policies and through the commissions it receives from the sale of competitors' policies. Discontinuities that affect *product* technology often favor differentiation strategies. In the moderate to high-end segment of the photo industry, for instance, the current technological shift from chemical film to digital photography gives firms like Sony an opportunity to establish a competitive stronghold based on their electronic miniaturization capabilities in an industry that it might never have entered prior to the digital age. Similarly, Apple's pricey iPod portable music device takes advantage of the technological shift reviewed in the opening vignette on Napster.

If the new technology is introduced by an incumbent firm, it stands a good chance to continue its dominance. For instance, in the aircraft manufacture business, Boeing has long been an innovator in the development of new airframes and has persisted as a leading firm, though the technology of the most efficient design has changed numerous times. Some discontinuous technologies are introduced by new entrants, and because they change the face of the business landscape by altering who the leaders are, they are often referred to as *disruptive technologies*. When the new technology is developed by new entrants, incumbent firms face the very real possibility that they will be marginalized or eliminated. For instance, every leading firm in the minicomputer business was wiped out by firms that innovated and marketed the PC.

What can firms do to avoid or withstand a technological discontinuity? Research suggests that to withstand such technological changes, firms must either proactively create new opportunities for themselves or react defensively in ways to counteract the powerful forces of change.

Speed of Change Over and above any particular change driver, the speed of change is a critical factor in keeping up with the basis of competition in an industry. Speed tends to compound the effects of every change driver, whether industry evolution, technological discontinuities, or other causes. As the pace of change increases, so, too, must a firm's ability to react swiftly to (and even anticipate) changes in the basis of competitive advantage. In many cases, the most profitable avenue is availed to firms that have the ability to *lead* industry change.[10] *Reacting to change* means detecting and responding quickly to unexpected customer demands, new government regulations, or competitor's actions. *Anticipating change* means foreseeing the appearance of global markets, the development of new market segments, and emergence of the complementary or conflicting technologies.

Then we'll discuss the development of revolutionary strategies designed to help firms thrive in dynamic environments. We then examine when and why firms would want to be firm movers in introducing new strategies. Finally, we conclude by applying the five elements of the strategy diamond to strategies in dynamic contexts. When you're finished with this chapter, you should be able to formulate a strategy for managing the dynamic context and prepare a plan for implementing it.

Revolutionary Strategies That Lead Industry Change

In Chapters 4 and 5 we needed to walk a bit of a pedagogical tightrope. We presented you with some fundamental theories and models of strategic management, like the model of industry structure and generic strategies. These tools are frequently used in industry and have enormous analytical power. However, if used naively, they present a static picture of the world and suggest that there is a strategic position that a firm can assume to assure high levels of profitability. If you correctly identify the factors affecting industry profitability, and zero in on the key success factors in the industry, you can then use your resources and capabilities to position your firm with a well-developed strategy that results in a cost or differentiation advantage. But, as we noted in those chapters, industry contexts are not usually stable; they are always changing (slowly or quickly, but inevitably) and this makes formulating a strategy that will have enduring profitable returns very problematic.

Consider a few industries that you are very familiar with; you will see several types of competitors. First, there are the large incumbents, usually some of the earliest and most successful entrants. Companies such as McDonald's in fast food, Hertz in rental cars, and Blockbuster in movie rentals are firms that originally established the "rules" of the industry; these "rules" are the norms that most firms follow in carving out their strategy. Each of these industries has a group of other firms that have imitated the leader and tried to carve out a subsistence through a similar, if somewhat differentiated, strategy. These are firms like Burger King, Avis, and Hollywood Video that all compete directly with the major leaders using strategies that are only slightly differentiated from their rival—they implicitly seem to follow the rules laid down by the market leaders. But, then there are the rule breakers. These are firms like Subway, Enterprise, and NetFlix. Each of these firms made fundamentally different assumptions about what consumers would pay for and introduced strategies that differed in some radical ways from the industry leaders.

In this section we outline five types of revolutionary strategies that can introduce dynamic change into an industry. Successfully implemented, such strategies can overturn an established industrial structure and rewrite the rules of competition. Research suggests that these five revolutionary strategies tend to fall into one of three categories: high-end disruptions, low-end disruptions, or hybrid.

High-End Disruption A new-market disruption that significantly changes the industry value curve by disrupting the expectations of customers by vastly improving product performance is referred to as **high-end disruption**. High-end disruption often results in huge new markets in which new players unseat the largest incumbents. Incumbents can also use new-market disruption strategies. To do so, they need to shift competitive focus from head-to-head competition to the task of redefining the business model for at least a part of the existing market. A new-market-creation strategy, for example, may enable a firm to avoid the pitfalls of commoditization and evolution, but pursuing it doesn't necessarily mean that the same firm will become, or even intends to become, the industry leader. Cirque du Soleil significantly disrupted the circus industry by incorporating many features more common in Broadway theater than in traditional circuses, generating significant new growth and higher profits than any other traditional circus.

high-end disruption Strategy that may result in huge new markets in which new players redefine industry rules to unseat the largest incumbents.

Low-End Disruption Recall the concept of *disruptive technologies*. Some disruptive technologies appear at the low end of industry offerings and are referred to as **low-end disruptions**. Incumbents tend to ignore such new entrants because they target the incumbents' least valuable customers. These low-end disruptions rarely offer features that satisfy the best customers in the industry. However, these low-end entrants often use such footholds as platforms to migrate into the more attractive space once their products or services improve. Indeed, by the time they do improve, these low-end disruptions often satisfy the needs of the center of the market better than incumbents' products do because incumbents have been busily making incremental improvements to satisfy their best clients' demands even while these improvements cause the firms to outshoot the needs of the center of the market. Southwest Airlines has been a very successful low-end disrupter, satisfying only the most basic travel needs and eliminating many services that had been taken for granted by established airlines.

low-end disruption Strategy that appears at the low end of industry offerings, targeting the least desirable of incumbents' customers.

Hybrid Disruption Strategies   As you might expect, most newcomers adopt some combination of new-market and low-end disruption strategies. Today, it may look as if Amazon.com has pursued a single-minded low-end disruption strategy, but along the way, it also has created some new markets, mainly by bringing more buyers into the market for books. Many Amazon customers buy in the quantities they do because of the information that the Amazon site makes available. The strategies of such companies as JetBlue, the brokerage firm Charles Schwab, and the University of Phoenix are also hybrids of new-market and low-cost disruption strategies.[11] JetBlue's focused low-cost strategy, for instance, has been able to achieve the lowest-cost position in the industry by eliminating many services (a business model it borrowed from Southwest) but also adding services that increased customer loyalty. In addition, they targeted overpriced but underserved markets, thereby stimulating new demand—both taking a portion of the existing market from incumbent competitors *and* creating a new market by attracting consumers who couldn't ordinarily afford air travel. Schwab pioneered discount brokerage as a new market but has since enticed legions of clients from full-service brokers such as Merrill-Lynch. The University of Phoenix, which offers low-cost distance learning degrees, is taking a strategic path much like the one blazed by Schwab.

We now turn to the five types of revolutionary strategies that can introduce major disruption into an industry by changing the rules of the game. In Exhibit 6.2, we categorize these five types as: *reconceiving a product/service, reconfiguring the value chain, redefining the arenas, rescaling the industry, and reconsidering the competitive mindset.*

Exhibit 6.2   Revolutionary Strategies

Type of Industry Disruption	Reconceiving a Product/Service	Reconfiguring the Value Chain	Redefining the Arenas	Rescaling the Industry	Reconsidering the Competitive Mindset
Definition	Breaking away from existing industry conceptions of what products and services look like	Changing elements of the industry value chain	Changing when and where you compete	Using a business model that relies on different economics relative to scale	Avoid direct competition
Example	• Creating a new value curve (e.g., Cirque du Soleil) • Separate function from form (e.g., electronic hotel keys)	• Use a new value chain (e.g., Amazon) • Compress the value chain (e.g., IKEA)	• Changing temporal and geographical availability (e.g., Redbox) • Total imagined market versus served market (e.g., disposable cameras)	• Increase scale for greater economies of scale (e.g., waste disposal) • Downscale in search of higher prices in niche markets (e.g., microbreweries)	• Look to make competitors complementors (e.g., American and Delta defraying costs from Boeing) • Avoid head-to-head competition by moving into areas where there is little competition (e.g., [yellow tail]®)

RECONCEIVE A PRODUCT OR SERVICE

Creating a New Value Curve You are probably already familiar with the Montreal-based entertainment group Cirque du Soleil, a recent example of how a new value curve is created. Exhibit 6.3 summarizes Cirque's novelty. Cirque's value curve demonstrates that they dropped a number of features common in other circuses, but they added features completely unheard of before in the circus industry. Where did these ideas come from? They appear to have been borrowed from another form of entertainment—Broadway theatre.

Most companies have no trouble focusing on their existing rivals and actively trying to match or beat their rivals' customer offerings. However, as a result of this focus on rivals' behaviors, strategies often converge. This convergence grows stronger according to the amount of conventional industry wisdom about how to compete. This type of convergence is often associated with incremental innovation. It will rarely result in breakthroughs that create new markets.

One way to create a revolutionary strategy that avoids the pitfall of strategic incrementalism is the creation of a new value curve (a model introduced in Chapter 4). Creating a new value curve requires a different approach and a different way of thinking about innovation. Instead of looking for the next incremental improvement, new markets are often created when managers create innovations that build on the best of the existing industry, import ideas from other industries, and eliminate some features that industry incumbents take for granted but that are not critical to key customers. This style of new-market creation has been shown to work in both fast-paced industries and those that are seemingly stagnant—both conditions that are ripe for significant changes. Fast-paced industries are dynamic by definition. Stagnant industries are often ripe for change—through new technologies that will send the industry on a new growth trajectory, or through shakeout, which is a dynamic process but usually in a very negative sense for many incumbents.

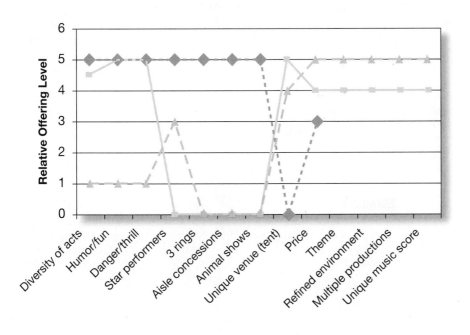

Exhibit 6.3 Cirque du Soleil at the Nexus of Circus and Broadway

The key to discovering a new-market space lies in asking four basic questions. These questions are illustrated in the Four-Actions Framework shown in Exhibit 6.4.[12] By answering these questions, you will be able to define a new value curve for an industry, or at least a segment of an industry.

First, what product or service attributes that rivals take for granted should be *reduced* well below the industry standard? Second, what factors that the industry has taken for granted should be *eliminated*? Third, what product or service attributes should be *raised* well above the industry standard? And fourth, are there any factors that the industry has never offered that should be *created*? By finding answers to these questions, managers could modify a firm's strategy either so that its products are further differentiated from competitors', so that its cost structure is driven significantly below that of competitors or, conceivably, both. In addition, by following this path, firms often generate new customers for the industry or industry segment; they actually grow the business by means other than, or in addition to, stealing customers from competitors. And while we introduce the four-actions framework in the context of new value curve creation, you will likely find that the framework translates well to all the revolutionary strategies covered in this section.

"How Would *You* Do That? 6.1" illustrates the application of the value-curve tool, in conjunction with the four-actions framework, to the wine industry using [yellow tail]®.[13] In Chapter 4 you learned how to apply the value curve to help map existing competitors. Here, the purpose of the tool is extended to reveal how a firm might create a new value curve in ways that separate its strategy from those of incumbents.

As you will recall from the earlier definition of strategic groups in Chapter 4, a strategic group is a cluster of firms that pursue similar strategies within an industry. The curve for each strategic group visually represents how those firms present their products to customers along key buying criteria. It conceptually represents the underlying logic incumbents use in positioning their products. Being able to visualize how competitors perform along these differentiators helps reveal the assumptions being made by the industry. It also helps you to determine which assumptions might be tested. Along these dimensions, question whether some levels of delivery on the key success factors can be reduced or eliminated; likewise, question whether some can be increased or whether new points of differentiation can be added. As a result of using the

Exhibit 6.4 The Four-Actions Framework of New Market Creation

The key to discovering a new value curve lies in answering four basic questions.

Reduce
What factors should be reduced *well below* the industry standard?

Eliminate
What factors that the industry has taken for granted should be eliminated?

Creating New Markets: A new value curve

Create/Add
What factors that the industry has never offered should be created or added?

Raise
What factors should be raised *well above* the industry standard?

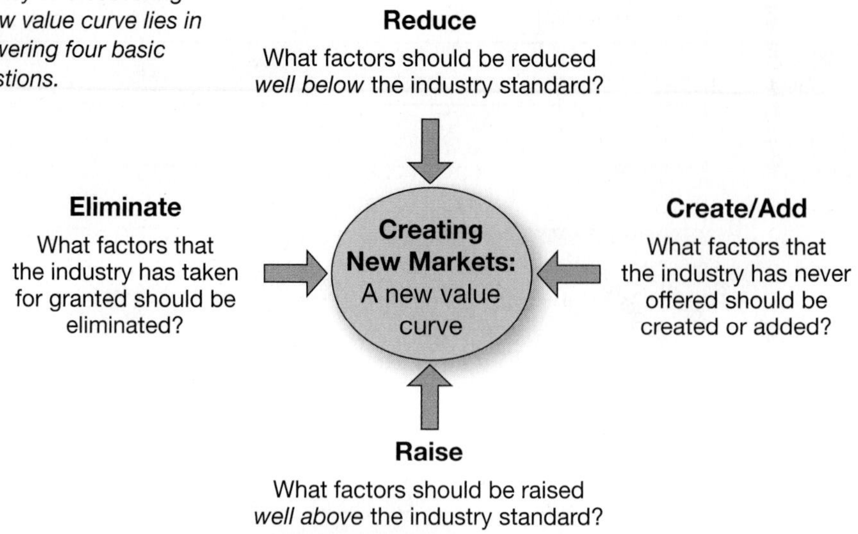

value-curve tool, firms can develop strategies that challenge and change the rules of competition.

Separating Function and Form   Another way to create a revolutionary strategy is to look for ways to separate function and form. *Function* is the benefits of the product; *form* is the embodied product. Let's consider credit cards as an example. Credit cards first emerged at the beginning of the 20th century. Toward the end of the century, magnetic storage technology was used to make credit cards more secure and speed the payment to merchants by encoding cards with data about the customer and their account. When swiping the card through a reader, the transfer of funds from the purchaser to the merchant could be significantly accelerated.

So, let's think about the function and the form of the credit card. The function includes the identification of the cardholder and their account along with permission to charge a purchase. The form is a slim piece of plastic. How can permission and identification be used in ways other than the specific case of permission to make a charge at a merchant? Several uses have emerged: employment identification badges, which allow access to secured areas; hotel keys, which grant access to your hotel room but no others; student identification cards, which allow everything from library checkout privileges to payment for lunch; and membership and discount cards for establishments ranging from grocery stores to athletic gyms. In all of these cases, the credit card companies did not see the opportunity to apply the form of the encoded card to a new or related function—rather it was new entrants attempting to solve problems for customers that used existing technology from other industries to do so.

RECONFIGURE THE VALUE CHAIN

Recall that a value chain is the sequential steps of value-added activities that are necessary to create a product or service that is used by the end consumer. Some revolutionary strategies were created while reconfiguring the value chain in ways that others never thought of, or tried to do, before. Two related ways this can be done are to improve the customer's value equation by using a *new* value chain, and *compressing* the value chain.

Radically New Value Chain   Sometimes an industry can be revolutionized by making completely new assumptions about the value chain. When Jeff Bezos started Amazon.com as the world's largest bookstore, he actually started with the concept that the Internet would provide an opportunity to bring a radically new value chain to a number of industries. He settled on the book industry, but Amazon has now taken their radically new value chain into many products. Beyond eliminating the costly physical infrastructure of retail stores, the Amazon model also cuts other significant costs from the value chain. For instance, large book retailers return on average about 30 percent of their orders each year to wholesalers and publishers, but at Amazon, returns are a slim 3 percent.

Skype Technologies' popular Web-based phone service is another example of a radically new value chain. Indeed, there was virtually no overlap in Skype's value chain and that of traditional telephone companies. Skype uses software to allow users to make phone calls using the Internet. Initially, all calls had to be made PC-to-PC, but a new SkypeOut service allows PC-to-phone calling, and these calls are still at much lower rates than traditional phone service. After eBay purchased Skype in 2005, Skype added new services, including content distribution (users can send and receive pictures and ringtones, for example) and a call-forwarding service. To use Skype, customers download free software, and must have a PC with a microphone and speakers, or a USB phone. So, the only portion of the traditional telecommunications value chain that Skype kept was the local land line for customers who use dial-up Internet access.

Compress the Value Chain   A more conventional way to reconfigure the value chain is to simply compress it. Wal-Mart, Dell, and IKEA are all good examples of this. The typical compression involves eliminating a middle-man in the value chain. Often, the

[yellow tail]® Creates a New Value Curve in the Wine Industry[14]

You learned a bit about the intensely competitive wine industry in Chapter 4. When we mapped the industry in "How Would *You* Do That 4.1," based on the characteristics of the key players, you saw that the industry was comprised of two dominant strategic groups—wineries competing in the budget segment or high-price segments, or both.

So what is a new entrant to do? [yellow tail]® arrived at its new value curve through a process of strategic steps taken over many years. It all began back in the 1820s, when the first Casellas began crafting wine in Italy, then moved to Australia in 1951 to pursue their hopes and dreams of a better life. After years of growing and selling grapes to local wineries in 1969, the Casellas decided it was time to put their own winemaking skills to use, and the Casella winery was born. A new generation of Casellas entered the family business in 1994 and embarked on an ambitious

expansion to build a new winery with a vision of blending Old World heritage with New World technology. Today, Casella Wines is run by fifth- and sixth-generation Casella family members. In 2000, Casella Wines joined forces with another family-run company, W. J. Deutsch & Sons, to bring Casella wines and [yellow tail]® to the United States.

As shown in Exhibits 6.5 and 6.6, you can use the value-curve and four-actions framework to see how [yellow tail]® reconfigured the way it defined being a winery: offering wines at a moderate price; avoiding wine lingo; encouraging impulse purchases with its catchy labels; and targeting only two high-demand wines, Chardonnay and Shiraz. It also added new features that incumbents did not offer—easy drinking, ease of selection (again, only two varieties), and a spirit of fun and adventure.[15] [yellow tail]® used the four-actions framework to create a new value curve. It created alternatives instead of competing head-on with the

major players. It converted noncustomers to customers by luring traditional beer and cocktail drinkers with its catchy labels and easy-drinking wines. Sold around $7 a bottle, the [yellow tail]® Shiraz is the top-selling imported red wine in the U.S., while the [yellow tail]® Merlot and Chardonnay are both number two in their respective categories. This year, the Australian brand could sell 15 million cases in the U.S., and [yellow tail]® accounted for 39 percent of the total imported Australian wine market in the U.S. food store segment in 2006.

Ultimately, the choice between new-market and low-end disruption strategies depends on a firm's resources and capabilities, and the ability to then execute the chosen strategy. [yellow tail]® conceived of a new way to approach the wine industry, but it did so with the knowledge that it possessed the resources and capabilities to do so.

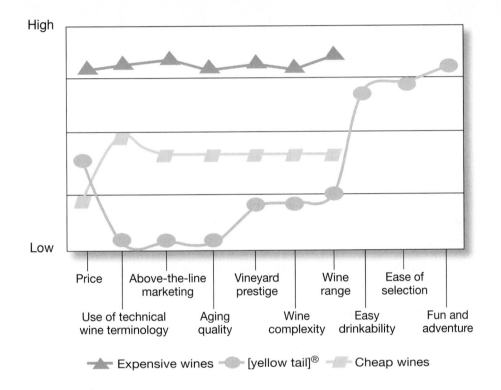

Exhibit 6.5 A Value Curve for [yellowtail]®

Labels along horizontal axis: Price, Use of technical wine terminology, Above-the-line marketing, Aging quality, Vineyard prestige, Wine complexity, Wine range, Easy drinkability, Ease of selection, Fun and adventure

Vertical axis: High, Low

Legend: Expensive wines, [yellow tail]®, Cheap wines

Exhibit 6.6 The Four-Actions Framework and [yellowtail]®

Reduce	Eliminate	Create/Add	Raise
Wine complexity Wine range Vineyard prestige	Enological terminology and distinctions Aging qualities Above-the-line marketing	Easy drinking Ease of selection Fun and adventure	Price versus budget wines Retail store involvement

wholesaler or distributor is removed, though the compression need not be at this link in the value chain. Dell eliminated retail stores and manufacturing components (choosing to outsource all parts and simply oversee the assembly of computers). IKEA, one of the world's top furniture retailers, sells Scandinavian-style home furnishings and other housewares. IKEA lowers cost significantly by compressing several value chain activities. First, it cuts transportation costs by shipping unassembled furniture to its retail stores in flat packaging, allowing it to ship more product in much smaller spaces. But, it doesn't stop there; rather than incur the cost of assembly at the retail site, it shifts this step of the value chain to customers because customers buy the product in the box and assemble it at home. So, by designing furniture in pieces that can be easily assembled, it eliminates two costly steps from the value chain. This allows IKEA to pass some of the savings on to customers and keep some of the savings in the form of higher margins.

REDEFINE YOUR ARENAS

Managers generally have an idea of who their customers are and in what arenas they compete. Sometimes these conceptions act as blinders; they can obscure the vision of potential customers that don't traditionally purchase the company's products.

Changing the Temporal or Geographic Availability

New customers are often available at different times or places than those conventionally served. Fast food outlets inside large retailers like Wal-Mart and Target are obvious examples of finding new geographic availability without venturing into far-flung foreign markets. Similarly, many grocery stores now have bank branches located on the premises. Airlines, too, have a captive shopping audience during the flight. Of course, the Internet has opened up temporal and geographic accessibility for many businesses. McDonald's and Coinstar are partners in a radical innovation to the DVD rental industry by making DVDs available in vending machines located at McDonald's restaurants. After initial market tests were successful in the Denver, Colorado, market, the Red-Box concept was quickly rolled out. Customers can select from a selection of recent releases and popular titles and rent a DVD for one night for one dollar. The concept was so popular, that it quickly expanded into other non-McDonald's locations such as grocery stores.

Imagining the Total Possible Market Rather than the Served Market

One way to redefine your arenas is to imagine the *possible* market rather than focusing on the *served* market. Consider the market for cameras. Today you can find inexpensive disposable cameras available at the grocery store checkout stand. These relatively new products opened up an entirely new market for filmmakers—children. Prior to these disposable cameras, no child was viewed as a likely customer for film.

New technologies can enable this reconceptualization of the total possible market as well. For instance, Copeland Corporation was considering the introduction of a new scroll compressor for residential air conditioning units. The compressor is to an air conditioner, what a computer processing chip is to a PC (the analogy would be "Intel Inside"). At low production volumes, this new and highly efficient and quiet scroll technology would cost too much for the average homeowner, and would therefore be attractive only to a small niche market. However, with higher production volumes, Copeland's costs for the scroll compressor dropped dramatically, to the point where it could actually be price-competitive with low-cost units. Copeland opted for the volume option, and actually helped move the technological standard in the industry to scroll.

Spearheading Industry Convergence

Industry convergence occurs when two distinct industries evolve toward a single point where old industry boundaries no longer exist. As you learned in Chapter 4, convergence examples are numerous. Computing and entertainment have come together in the TiVo video digital recorder, which allows users to time-shift their TV viewing. The convergence of entertainment and communications have created a mobile music revolution—the distribution of digital music over wireless networks. Your cell phone is a tangible illustration of multiple industries converging in a single product; at one moment you use it as a phone, later you click a photograph, it serves as your music and video player, and it may also be your personal organizer all rolled into one. For example, the PlayStation 2 is not only a games console, but also a CD player, DVD player, and Internet connector. Broadband Internet access, television, telephone, and mobile phone service by firms that traditionally only offered one or two of these services, is another example of leading industry convergence.

Industries will converge over time. A revolutionary firm is one that discovers and leads convergence. Opportunities to create significant value are often found at the convergence of two or more industries. For instance, Napster and Swedish telecommunications company Ericsson teamed up to offer a new digital music service aimed at mobile phone customers around the world. Ericsson's long-established relationships with carriers could help Napster gain ground in what is new territory for a primarily PC-focused company. As this example illustrates, convergence can be the driver behind bundling multiple products into a single offering, or it may lay the groundwork for entirely new products.

RESCALE THE INDUSTRY

Significant economic opportunities can be found by exploring whether industry conventions about minimum efficient scale are correct. Revolutionary strategies can be created by searching for industries that have opportunities to benefit from increases in economies of scale. However, there are also many opportunities available to create value by downscaling.

Increase Scale   The financial services industry is currently in the middle of a major rescaling from local and regional, to national. Historically, regulation kept banks from seeking national economies of scale but deregulation opened the door for new business models. In this industry, rescaling has been accomplished mostly through mergers and acquisitions.

Service Corporation International (SCI) is a company whose strategy was almost entirely developed around the economic logic of seeking economies of scale through consolidating an industry. SCI is to death what McDonald's is to hamburgers; it is the largest funeral, cremation, and cemetery services company in the world. Historically, the funeral business was a local business with most operations owned and operated by local families. When SCI founder Robert Waltrip was 20 years old in the early 1950s, he inherited the Heights Funeral Home in Houston, Texas, which his father and aunt founded in 1926. Waltrip noticed that national chains were emerging in several industries such as hotels (Holiday Inn) and fast food (McDonald's). As he examined the economics of running a funeral business, he determined that several of the cost drivers would indeed be sensitive to scale increases. Thus, Waltrip began his quest to achieve cost advantages through scale. SCI went public in 1969, and by 1975 it was the largest provider of funeral services in the United States.

Some revolutionary strategies used increases in scale that were unconventional at the time in their industries; examples include such disparate industries as waste management services and adult education. Many firms attempting to rescale an industry toward larger economies of scale do so through acquisitions (e.g., SCI, Waste Management), but others, such as the University of Phoenix in adult education, have done so primarily through internal growth.

Downscaling to Serve Narrow or Local Customers   In some industries, there is an opportunity to generate significant margins by downscaling. Downscaling necessarily implies going after a smaller segment of the market. But, rather than just going after a small market, downscaling also implies attempting to add significant value to a niche of the market that is underserved.

Take the example of local microbreweries. The minimum efficient scale for breweries necessitates broad-based, national marketing. However, significantly smaller scale can be efficient if the market is local and the quality offered justifies a significant price premium. Examples of successful microbreweries can be found in almost every major city. Bed and breakfast inns (B&Bs) are another example of how one can compete against large national chains in the lodging industry. Bed and breakfast inns typically have only a few to a dozen rooms. At one level of analysis, the cost structure would seem very inefficient compared to the scale economies available to national chains. However, because the level of service is so personal at B&Bs, and because the properties are generally very unique and charming, B&Bs can charge prices that far exceed that of the chain hotel.

RECONSIDERING THE COMPETITIVE MINDSET

Creating Complementors Out of Suppliers, Buyers, and Competitors Recall that in Chapter 4 you learned about industry structure and Porter's Five-Forces model which suggests that the attractiveness of an industry is a function of the power of *suppliers, buyers,* and *substitutes,* the *barriers to entry,* and the degree of *rivalry.* In essence, each of these forces competes for a share of industry profitability.

We noted that a new factor is often added to that model, the idea of *complementors.* Rather than compete for industry profitability, a complementor helps to increase the total profits that can be made in an industry. How does the idea of complementors relate to reconsidering the competitive mindset? Research suggests that most managers tend to view the parties they interact with as competitive threats. As summarized in Exhibit 6.7, the value net model is a framework that represents all the players in the market and the interdependencies between them.[16] It will help you think about how the competitive mindset might be changed.

Here is how you use the value net. Identify a player as a complementor if customers value your product more when they have the other player's product than when they have your product alone. Alternatively, identify them as a competitor if customers value your product

Exhibit 6.7
The Value Net

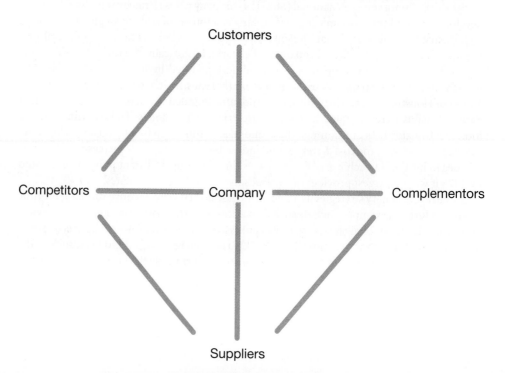

less when they have the other player's product than when they have your product alone. One complementor for GM would be any company providing auto loans. Most customers cannot afford to pay cash for a new car. Thus, more GM cars are sold when there are more firms involved in automobile financing. Similarly, FedEx and UPS are complementors for Land's End catalog. The ability to ship product quickly and reliably increases catalog sales, so they are complementors. Of course, novel software that is available to run on computers will increase PC sales.

An important insight from the value net model is that the same player might be a competitor in some interactions but a complementor in others. Let's illustrate this through a few simple relationships. British Airways and Lufthansa are fierce competitors in the airline business. Do they ever act as complementors? The answer is *yes*. Consider who the suppliers to British Airways and Lufthansa are. Both airlines buy many planes from Airbus, but they also have the option of buying from Boeing. In order for Airbus to make money on a new plane, they need many orders. If only Lufthansa orders planes from Airbus, the costs must all be passed on to Lufthansa. Alternatively, if British Airways also places an order for an Airbus plane, then Airbus can amortize its fixed costs of product development over a greater number of sales, which results in the ability to lower the price for both airlines. Airbus also will benefit from greater production scale economies, and some of the benefits of these economies will likely be passed on to buyers like British Airways and Lufthansa in the form of lower prices. Consequently, in trying to persuade travelers to fly on their airlines, British Airways and Lufthansa are competitors, but in dealing with one of their key suppliers, they are complementors.

This insight leads us to four observations about competitors and complementors.

■ A firm is your *competitor* if customers value your product *less* when they have the other firm's product than when they have your product alone (e.g., British Airways and Lufthansa).

■ A firm is your *complementor* if customers value your product *more* when they have the other firm's product than when they have your product alone (e.g., British Airways and American Express).

■ A firm is your *competitor* if it's *less* attractive for a supplier to provide resources to you when it's also supplying the other firm than when it's supplying you alone (e.g., Micron and Apple bidding for flash memory from Lexar when Lexar has capacity constraints).

■ A firm is your *complementor* if it's *more* attractive for a supplier to provide resources to you when it's also supplying the other firm than when it's supplying you alone (e.g., British Airways and Lufthansa).

The opportunity to use this insight to create value, then, is to avoid the bias of looking at other players in your industry strictly from a competitive mindset; hunt for opportunities to cooperate as complementors as well. As the value net framework suggests, turning parties who compete with you for profits into partners who help you create value increases the size of the economic pie available in the industry.

A Shift in the Focus of Strategic Thinking   Several of the revolutionary strategies just reviewed suggest a shift in focus from conventional head-to-head rivalry to a different strategic mindset. Some of the fundamental differences in assumptions between viewing strategy as head-to-head competition and thinking instead about creating new markets through revolutionary strategies are summarized in Exhibit 6.8. Whereas the traditional view emphasizes actions and capabilities that are determined by competitors' moves, new-market creation emphasizes *actions and capabilities that eclipse the competition rather than meet it head-on* [yellow tail]®, the company discussed in the box entitled "How Would *You* Do That? 6.1," provides a nice example of such a strategy in dynamic contexts.

Exhibit 6.8 Creation of New Markets through Revolutionary Strategies

Dimensions of Competition	Head-to-Head Competition	New-Market Creation
Industry	Emphasizes rivalry	Emphasizes substitutes across industries
Strategic group and industry segments	Emphasizes competitive position within group and segments	Looks across groups and segments
Buyers	Emphasizes better buyer service	Emphasizes redefinition of the buyer and buyer's preferences
Product and service offerings	Emphasizes product or service value and offerings within industry definition	Emphasizes complementary products and services within and across industries and segments
Business model	Emphasizes efficient operation of the model	Emphasizes rethinking of the industry business model
Time	Emphasizes adaptation and capabilities that support competitive retaliation	Emphasizes strategic intent—seeking to shape the external environment over time

First Movers, Second Movers, and Fast Followers

First- versus second-mover categories are related to the principles of competitive interaction that we discussed in Chapter 5. In this chapter, we focus on the relative magnitude of the firm's actions. Specifically, here we are talking about the introduction of a new product or service that defines or redefines a new market segment; whereas in Chapter 5, competitive interaction involved actions taken within a preexisting market segment. In particular, we need to know how each approach to technological discontinuities depends on a firm's resources and capabilities. The principle of dynamic strategy suggests that firms consider the relative strength of their resources and capabilities when they determine whether to lead or to respond to change.

First movers are firms that choose to initiate a strategic action. This action may be the introduction of a new product or service or the development of a new process that improves quality, lowers price, or both. Consequently, you may see firms pursuing either differentiation or low-cost strategies here. **Second movers** are simply firms that aren't first movers, but their actions are important nonetheless.[17] A second mover, for instance, may simply imitate a first mover—that is, those aspects of its new product, service, or strategy that meet its needs—or it may introduce its own innovation.[18]

FIRST-MOVER STRATEGY AND THE INDUSTRY LIFE CYCLE

Being a second mover doesn't necessarily mean that a firm is a *late* mover; in fact, many effective second movers can legitimately be characterized as *fast followers*—even if the elapsed time between first and second moves is several years. Why isn't the lag necessarily detrimental? For one, new products don't always catch on right away. They may eventually generate rapid growth and huge sales increases, but this period—widely known as the

first mover The firm that is first to offer a new product or service in a market.

second mover (often *fast follower*) Second significant company to move into a market, quickly following the first mover.

takeoff period—starts, *on average,* at some point within six years of the new-product introduction.[19] Although the industry life cycle suggests that the drivers of industry demand evolve over time, it doesn't predict how *quickly* they'll evolve. Indeed, it may take some new products a decade or more to reach the growth stage, and only then will they attract competitors.

takeoff period Period during which a new product generates rapid growth and huge sales increases.

By the same token, of course, *habitually* late movers will eventually fall by the wayside. Typically, survivors are either first movers or relatively fast followers. Late movers usually survive only if they're protected by government regulation, monopolistic or oligopolistic industry positions, or extensive cash reserves. Increasingly, however, competitive advantage results from the ability to manage change and harness the resources and capabilities consistent with first- or second-mover strategies.

THE PROS AND CONS OF FIRST-MOVER POSITIONING

Intuitively, we tend to think of first movers as having a distinct advantage: After all, many races are won by the first contestant out of the starting blocks. The history of the Internet offers a wealth of first-mover success stories. The market dominance of Amazon.com, for instance, reflects a first-mover advantage—namely, the firm's ability to charge higher prices for books. According to a recent study, a 1-percent price increase reduced Amazon.com sales by 0.5 percent; at BarnesandNoble.com, however, the same price hike cut sales by a relatively whopping 4 percent.[20]

However, if you take a close look at Exhibit 6.9, you'll see that first-movers don't always attain dominant positions.[21] For instance, you are probably familiar with the Microsoft XBox, the Palm Pilot PDA, and the Airbus A380, but did you know that the first electronic games, PDA, and commercial jets were released by Atari, Apple (the Newton in 1993), and deHaviland, respectively? In some cases, a first-mover strategy can even be a liability, and in many others, the first mover isn't necessarily in a position to exploit the advantages of being first.

A first-mover advantage is valuable only under certain conditions:

■ A firm achieves an absolute cost advantage in terms of scale or scope.

■ A firm's image and reputation advantages are hard to imitate at a later date.

■ First-time customers are locked into a firm's products or services because of preferences or design characteristics.

■ The scale of a firm's first move makes imitation unlikely.[22]

First movers also bear significant risks, including the costs not only of designing, producing, and distributing new products, but of educating customers about them. Let's say, for example, that you're a midsized consumer products company with a promising new product. When you stop to consider the immense power wielded by a certain member of your distribution channel—say, Wal-Mart—you'll recall how dependent you are on one giant retailer to help you attract a market large enough to make your product profitable. Meanwhile, certain second movers (say, Unilever or Procter & Gamble) may take the time to evaluate your new product and decide to compete with it only when it's developed some traction in the market (at some point during the takeoff period). Sometimes, a patient (and sufficiently powerful) second mover simply acquires the first mover; sometimes, a second mover introduces a similar product, perhaps of higher quality or with added features.

In short, first-mover advantages diminish—and fast-follower advantages increase—under a variety of conditions, including the following:

■ Rapid technological advances enable a second mover to leapfrog a first mover's new product or service.

Exhibit 6.9 A Gallery of First Movers and Fast Followers

Product	Pioneer(s)	Imitators/Fast Followers	Comments
Automated teller machines (ATMs)	DeLaRue (1967) Docutel (1969)	Diebold (1971) IBM (1973) NCR (1974)	The first movers were small entrepreneurial upstarts that faced two types of competitors: (1) larger firms with experience selling to banks and (2) the computer giants. The first movers did not survive.
Ballpoint pens	Reynolds (1945) Eversharp (1946)	Parker (1954) Bic (1960)	The pioneers disappeared when the fad first ended in the late 1940s. Parker entered 8 years later. Bic entered last and sold pens as cheap disposables.
Commercial jets	deHaviland (1952)	Boeing (1958) Douglas (1958)	The pioneer rushed to market with a jet that crashed frequently. Boeing and Douglas (later known as McDonnel-Douglas) followed with safer, larger, and more powerful jets unsullied by tragic crashes.
Credit cards	Diners Club (1950)	Visa/Mastercard (1966) American Express (1968)	The first mover was undercapitalized in a business in which money is the key resource. American Express entered last with funds and name recognition from its traveler's check business.
Diet soda	Kirsch's No-Cal (1952) Royal Crown's Diet Rite Cola (1962)	Pepsi's Patio Cola (1963) Coke's Tab (1964) Diet Pepsi (1964) Diet Coke (1982)	The first mover could not match the distribution advantages of Coke and Pepsi. Nor did it have the money or marketing expertise needed for massive promotional campaigns.
Light beer	Rheingold's & Gablinger's (1968) Meister Brau Lite (1967)	Miller Lite (1975) Natural Light (1977) Coors Light (1978) Bud Light (1982)	The first movers entered 9 years before Miller and 16 years before Budweiser, but financial problems drove both out of business. Marketing and distribution determined the outcome. Costly legal battles, again requiring access to capital, were commonplace.
PC operating systems	CP/M (1974)	Microsoft DOS (1981) Microsoft Windows (1985)	The first mover set the early industry standard but did not upgrade for the IBM PC. Microsoft bought an imitative upgrade and became the new standard. Windows entered later and borrowed heavily from predecessors (and competitor Apple), then emerged as the leading interface.
Video games	Magnavox's Odyssey (1972) Atari's Pong (1972)	Nintendo (1985) Sega (1989) Microsoft (1998)	The market went from boom to bust to boom. The bust occurred when home computers seemed likely to make video games obsolete. Kids lost interest when games lacked challenge. Price competition ruled. Nintendo rekindled interest with better games and restored market order with managed competition. Microsoft entered with its Xbox when they perceived gaming to be a possible component of its wired world.

- ■ The first mover's product or service strikes a positive chord but is flawed.

- ■ The first mover lacks a key complement, such as channel access, that a fast follower possesses.

- ■ The first mover's costs outweigh the benefits of its first-mover position. (Fast followers, for example, can often enter markets more cheaply because they don't face the initial costs incurred by the first mover.)

Status of Complementary Assets

Exhibit 6.10 First-Mover Dependencies

	Freely available or unimportant	Tightly held and important
Weak protection from imitation	It is difficult for anyone to make money: Industry incumbents may simply give new product or service away as part of its larger bundle of offerings	Value-creation opportunities favor the holder of complementary assets, who will probably pursue a fast-follower strategy
Strong protection from imitation	First mover can do well depending on the execution of its strategy	Value will go either to first mover or to party with the most bargaining power

Bases of First Mover Advantages

FIRST MOVERS AND COMPLEMENTARY ASSETS

An additional framework for assessing whether a firm should pursue a first-mover or fast-follower strategy incorporates the factor of *complementary assets*. Exhibit 6.10, for example, provides a framework that explains why a number of notable first movers fared poorly despite apparently advantageous positions one would expect them to extract by virtue of being a first mover.[23] What's the moral of the lessons collected in Exhibit 6.10? Basically, they remind us that any firm contemplating a first-mover strategy should consider the inimitability of its new product, the switching costs holding together current customer relationships, and the strength of its complementary assets. It should, for example, consider its distribution channels as important complementary assets. Industry key success factors are also complementary assets, as is access to capital.

Let's say, for instance, that a firm makes a critical breakthrough in cancer therapy. Before putting any product on the market, it will need to conduct a decade's worth of animal and clinical trials, and if it doesn't have hundreds of millions of dollars in the bank, it won't be able to pay for such extensive preliminary testing. New PC-software applications often depend on Microsoft because its operating system and bundled software constitute a whole set of complements—a product, a channel, and a potential competitor. As you can see from the illustrations in Exhibit 6.9, in the context of the framework summarized in Exhibit 6.10, first-movers tend to succeed if their initial advantages are unique and defensible *and* if they're in a position to exploit the complementary assets needed to bring a new product to market.

Defensive Strategies for Incumbents Caught Off-Guard

Incumbents, such as Anheuser Busch, deserve special attention because they are increasingly viewed as Goliaths in the many David-and-Goliath competitive interactions unfolding around the world. In the mid-1990s, the front pages of the business press were littered with stories decrying the demise of the brick-and-mortar business and the rise of e-commerce and the dot-com. Inasmuch as most firms currently occupied real estate rather than cyberspace, the trend—or at least warnings about its repercussions—threatened most of them with extinction. Some, of course, did disappear, but most did not. As a matter of fact, the Internet phenomenon—and especially the breakneck speed with which it became a regular feature of the cultural landscape—underscored a number of strategies that incumbents can adopt to respond to rapid changes in the environment of an industry. As usual, the success of these strategies depends on a given firm's strengths and weaknesses. They are, however, particularly attractive to incumbent firms because they depend on—and can even reinforce—a firm's basic strengths. Each seeks a resource-based competitive advantage—that is, a position in which the exploitation of a resource makes that resource stronger and more resilient. Hopefully, the firm is organized per the VRINE framework to realize value from the stronger and more resilient resource.

Competitor-response strategies can be thought about in a number of different ways. Incumbent firms can respond to sources of industry dynamism through any of the following strategies: (1) containment, (2) neutralization, (3) shaping, (4) absorption, or (5) annulment. These responses typically vary in terms of the ease with which the external threat can be controlled and the corresponding level of action taken in response. We'll discuss and provide examples of each strategy in the following sections.

CONTAINMENT

The containment strategy works well when the firm has identified the threat at an early stage. (You may detect facets of this strategy in the bundling or process-innovation strategies that we described in the context of industry evolution in Chapter 5.) Although firms sometimes select one of these strategies, they typically resort to a combination that aligns well with their particular resources and capabilities. American Airlines, for instance, can compete with Southwest not only by increasing the benefits of its frequent flier program but by using its bargaining power to secure more exclusive airport gates (thus effectively raising Southwest's distribution costs at airports where it used to share gates with American).

Similarly, a large consumer products company can release a copy-cat product that both leverages the new market created by a competitor and can be sold through its own existing channels. Consider, for example, the fact that retailers in industries from clothing to groceries typically charge *slotting fees*—fees that suppliers pay for access to retailers' shelf space. Because of this practice, any new product may bump an existing product from retail shelves, and if the one that gets bumped is a new entrant's only product, the containment strategy will have been highly effective.

NEUTRALIZATION

If containment does not work, then leaders will try to neutralize the threat. Incumbents who pursue a neutralization strategy aggressively often succeed in short-circuiting the moves of innovators or new entrants even *before* they make them—or at least in forcing them to seek out the incumbent as a partner or acquirer. Microsoft, for example, is so aggressive at adding free software features to its popular Windows platform that new software firms routinely include partnership with Microsoft as part of their entry strategies.

A more common neutralization tactic, however, is the threat or use of legal action. (Because such action is often taken in concert with partners, we'll revisit it as an aspect of cooperative strategy in Chapter 8.) Recall from our opening case that one reason for Napster's initial downfall was legal action taken by the recording industry. In fact, the Recording Industry Association of America (RIAA) launched such a fierce legal attack on Napster that it forced even smaller Napster-like firms to stay out of the fray.[24] The German media giant Bertelsmann AG later acquired the Napster name when it realized that the Internet upstart was trying to engage in a legitimate music-sharing business. (When Bertelsmann couldn't turn a profit in the music-sharing business, Roxio was later able to acquire Napster and its assets for only $5 million.) Meanwhile, the RIAA also attempted to neutralize the Napster model by setting up an industrywide sharing standard, but this initiative collapsed when the major record labels squabbled about intellectual property rights, technology, and pricing.

SHAPING

Sometimes, of course, it's simply not possible to contain or neutralize the growth of a new product, often due to antitrust laws. Moreover, in some cases, the new product may be attractive to the incumbent even if the incumbent can't gain full control of it. Today, for example, a state of peaceful coexistence prevails between the American Medical Association (AMA) and chiropractic medicine. For decades, however, the AMA characterized chiropractors as quacks. Eventually, the AMA used regulators and educators as part of a strategy to *shape* the evolution of chiropractic practice until chiropractics transformed itself into a complement to conventional healthcare, as defined by the AMA.

Large firms can also use funding to pursue shaping strategies. Intel, for example, maintains its Intel Capital unit as one of the world's largest corporate venture programs for investing in the technology segment. The concept is fairly simple: Each investment is aimed at helping businesses that, if successful, will need Intel products to grow. In many ways, then, Intel is not only creating future markets for its own products but discouraging demand for competing products and technology and co-opting potential future competitors at the same time.

ABSORPTION

The purpose of this strategy is to minimize the risks entailed by being either a first mover or an imitator. Sometimes, the approach is direct: The incumbent identifies and acquires the new entrant or establishes an alliance. In the late 1980s, for instance, Microsoft identified money-management software as a potentially attractive, high-growth market. It therefore entered into an agreement to acquire Intuit, the market leader, which offers such products as Quicken, QuickBooks, and TurboTax. However, antitrust action forced Microsoft to abandon the purchase, and it resorted to a containment strategy—namely, by developing its own product, Microsoft Money (although Intuit's Quicken still has an 80-percent market share). If it's difficult to acquire the new entrant, the incumbent may also try to leverage a buyout by taking control over industry suppliers or distribution channels.

ANNULMENT

Incumbents can annul the threat of new entrants by improving their own products. In many ways, for example, Kodak has so successfully improved the quality of film-based prints that they're superior to many digital-based alternatives. The annulment strategy, however, is less about quashing the competition than about making it irrelevant. Indeed, to excel at an annulment strategy a firm must often assume the role of first mover—a position that entails considerable risk. Kodak forestalled the advance of digital photography, but Kodak executives knew that in order to stay in the photo business, the company eventually had to shift to digital.[25] For this reason, firms usually resort to annulment only when the competition is otherwise unstoppable.

IBM provides another excellent example of a firm that annulled a competitive threat by sidestepping it.[26] In the early 1990s, IBM was faced with a flagging core business in PCs and minicomputers. Its first strategic shift catapulted IBM into second place behind Microsoft as a PC- and networking-software powerhouse. Its next move entrenched the company in the IT and Internet consulting markets, where it emerged as the largest firm among such competitors as Accenture. Next, IBM took on such companies as EDS to become the market leader in outsourcing IT and service solutions. Throughout this transition process, IBM leveraged its resources, capabilities, and dynamic capabilities in services and software. In many ways, IBM, though ostensibly on the defensive, was also wielding the tools of offensive strategy, effectively combining improvisation and experimentation with deft staging and pacing. As a result of this complex strategy, IBM not only emerged as a leader in information technology but, at the same time, avoided the commoditization pressures that affected PC firms such as HP-Compaq. Most recently, it has completely exited its core PC manufacturing business by spinning off this part of its operations to China-based Lenovo.

THE PITFALLS OF THE RETALIATORY MINDSET

A word of warning about the five strategies covered in this section. Although they are certainly viable strategies for dynamic markets, many of the strategies are nonetheless purely defensive. If you rely on them exclusively, you'll soon stumble over an important pitfall of purely defensive strategizing: *Any firm that invests in resources and capabilities that support retaliation to the exclusion of innovation and change may only be prolonging its inevitable demise.*

Here's a good example. Ralston Purina was long considered one of the most efficient and competitively aggressive pet-food companies in the world. Every time a competitor made a move or a new entrant set foot in the market, Ralston responded with a twofold defensive strategy: undermining prices in the competitor's stronghold markets while simultaneously attacking its weaker markets. Although its defensive posture secured Ralston's market leadership for over 20 years, it also ensured that the company lagged behind the industry in terms of innovation. In 2003, Ralston sold out to Nestlé, whose constant attention to innovative products had positioned it to take over Ralston's slot as industry leader.

Taking an Option on Revolutionary Strategies   Instead of retaliation, incumbent firms may strategically decide that waiting for uncertainty to clear is the best course of action. Rather than be an early mover in a new strategy, the firm might decide to make a small investment that will allow it to have an option on making a bolder move later. This type of investment is generally referred to as a **real option**. The idea behind real op-

For more than 20 years, Ralston Purina fiercely—and successfully—defended its position as top dog in the pet-food industry. Unfortunately, the company put so much energy into its defensive strategy that it had little left for innovation. Ralston sold out to Nestlé in 2003.

tions is to preserve flexibility so that the firm has an ability to be well-positioned in the future when the competitive environment shifts. A perfectly positioned firm can become ill-positioned as the industry evolves, as new competitors emerge, and as technology makes current core competencies obsolete. By making small investments that preserve the option of taking a new course of action in the future, a firm can maintain its advantage. As an example, Intel invests heavily in internal R&D; however, it determined that it was unlikely to be the source of most innovations that could change how processing technology is used. Consequently, Intel made a conscious decision to invest in startups. By being a partial owner of the startups, Intel would have inside information on many new technologies being developed elsewhere. Intel has no obligation to increase its investment in these operations or to buy the products or internalize these innovations. However, by making these small investments, it has the option of doing so in the future.

So, what are real options? Quite simply, a real option is *the opportunity (though by no means the obligation) to take action that will either maximize the upside or limit the downside of a capital investment.* Ironically, of course, the greater the uncertainty and flexibility in the project, the greater the potential value of having options in managing it. Increasingly, managers in industries characterized by large capital investments and high degrees of uncertainty and flexibility (such as oil and gas, mining, pharmaceuticals, and biotechnology) are beginning to think in terms of real options. These companies typically have plenty of the market and R&D data needed to make confident assumptions about uncertain outcomes. They also have the sort of engineering-oriented corporate culture that isn't averse to complex mathematical tools.

Although real-options analysis is not a cure-all for strategic uncertainty, the technique is getting much more attention not only in the fields of finance and strategic management but among other companies and industries as well. In addition to those industries cited earlier, the automotive, aerospace, consumer goods, industrial products, and high tech industries are also interested in real-options analysis. Intel, for example, now trains finance employees in real-options valuation and has used the technique to analyze a number of capital projects. As a starting point, we suggest that you introduce yourself to real options by considering the following five categories:[27]

- **Waiting-to-invest options.** The value of waiting to build a factory until better market information comes along may exceed the value of immediate expansion.

- **Growth options.** An entry investment may create opportunities to pursue valuable follow-up projects.

- **Flexibility options.** Serving markets on two continents by building two plants instead of one gives a firm the option of switching production from one plant to the other as conditions dictate.

- **Exit (or abandonment) options.** The option to walk away from a project in response to new information increases its value.

- **Learning options.** An initial investment may generate further information about a market opportunity and may help to determine whether the firm should add more capacity.

real-options Process of maximizing the upside or limiting the downside of an investment opportunity by uncovering and quantifying the options and discussion points embedded within it.

Formulating and Implementing Dynamic Strategies

In this final section we focus on the ways in which dynamic strategies should be reflected in your application of both the strategy diamond and the strategy implementation models. (Because we devote Chapter 11 to a more detailed discussion of implementation levers and organizational structure, our remarks in this section will provide just a basic introduction.)

The arenas and staging, in conjunction with the implementation levers, will be key decision areas as you move forward to put your strategy into place.

FOCUSING ON ARENAS AND STAGING

Let's look first at our model of strategy formulation, which is critical because it establishes a set of simple rules for describing the business and showing how it creates value. Of course, all five elements of strategy are important and must be managed in concert, but the *arenas* and *staging* diamonds are especially important. In addition to recognizing the need for dynamic capabilities, focusing on these facets of strategy is what differentiates a dynamic strategy from a strategy developed for more stable contexts.

 Arenas

The Role of Arenas   Arenas designate your choice of customers to be served and the products to be provided.◆ In each section of this chapter on dynamic strategy—sections dealing with industry and product evolution, technological discontinuity, and turbulence—we've tried to emphasize that the strategist is always making important and reasoned choices about the firm's mix of customers, noncustomers, products, and services. The remaining four diamonds of strategy—vehicles, differentiators, staging, and economic logic, will tell the strategist whether the mix of arenas is consistent with what we called a *coherent* strategy in Chapter 2.

Moreover, the role of arenas in the firm's strategy will vary according to the factor of the dynamic environment being considered. In the context of *industry evolution,* for example, arenas must fit with a firm's resources, capabilities, and dynamic capabilities. With regard to *technological discontinuities,* the role of arenas, though overlapping with its role in low-end disruption strategies, was broadened to include noncustomers, particularly when the strategy is designed to create new markets. *Globalization,* introduced in Chapter 4, adds yet another dimension to the role of arenas: If a firm is going global, managers need to apply what they have learned about competing in one geographic arena to the task of competing in others. Finally, in navigating *turbulent and hypercompetitive markets,* managers need to think of arenas as laboratories—sites in which to conduct experiments or launch probes into the possible future of the firm and its strategy.

 Staging & Pacing

The Role of Staging   Competing in turbulent environments requires finesse in addressing the staging element of the strategy diamond.◆ In many ways, strategies in this context require the regular deployment and testing of options—options with new growth initiatives, new businesses, and new ways of doing business. From the prior section you now have a sense of how you would evaluate these options, financially. In this section, we review the findings of recent research on how firms manage the staging of strategy in order to succeed in turbulent or hypercompetitive environments. Research on strategy in this particularly dynamic context is typically anchored in so-called *systems, chaos,* or *complexity theories.* They're peppered with such biological terms as *self-organizing systems* and *co-adaptation,* and they're concerned with the same phenomenon—adaptation to a changing external environment in which change may be rapid and its direction uncertain.[28] By and large, they all share a basic premise: Firms need some degree of ability to thrive in chaotic environments in order to survive. In one study of several firms competing on the edge of chaos, researchers encountered the following three levels of activity, summarized by the curves in Exhibit 6.11:[29]

■ Activities designed to test today's competitive strategy (defending today's business)

■ Activities designed to lead to tomorrow's competitive strategy (drive growth in emerging businesses)

■ Activities designed to influence the pacing and timing of change (seeding options for future new businesses and growth initiatives)

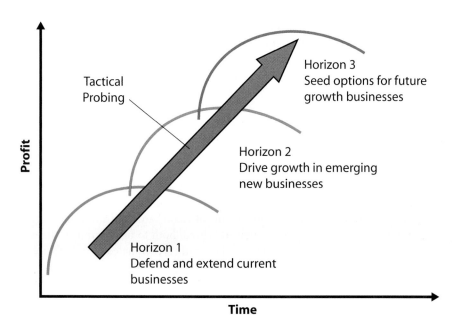

Exhibit 6.11 Creating Options for Future Competitive Advantage

The lower left-hand curve depicted in Exhibit 6.11 is the defense of existing businesses. The middle and upper right-hand curves represent activities focused on the future—the conditions toward which the change-oriented activities at the foundation of the strategy are aimed. At the same time, however, future products will embody indelible links to the past. In this model of business strategy, the bridge between past activities and future conditions is built on a substructure of experimentation and learning. For instance, S. C. Johnson found that one of its innovative home pesticide products in Europe could not pass U.S. regulatory hurdles, preventing its introduction in that country. However, through experimentation with its fragrances division, a key technology in the product was thought to be valuable and gave rise to the introduction of Glade PlugIn air fresheners in 1993. S. C. Johnson effectively joined knowledge embedded in previously disconnected and geographically removed operating units (pesticides and fragrances divisions) to create an entirely new product category in the home air-freshener industry.

Successful new-business conditions are a reflection of those strategies that have been most successful. Ineffective strategies are jettisoned or marginalized as customers migrate toward firms with strategies that best meet their needs. Thus, managers use their understanding of the competitive environment to guide their selection and reconfiguration of portions of yesterday's business practices. Dell, for example, developed its direct-sales model for the consumer and small-business PC market, and when it entered the large-business computer-server market, it adapted its direct-sales model by providing on-site customer service. The model, however, had evolved: In this sector, while maintaining a very modest level of on-site staff for its largest corporate clients, most of Dell's consumer service is provided by a Web-based platform. With virtually a single stroke, Dell had changed the industry business model in a way that favored and further strengthened the model that had long been its fundamental source of competitive advantage. In other words, Dell's dynamic move forward into the server market was anchored in its past strengths in the PC market, and it has had a profound effect on the strategies of other firms as they've attempted to adapt to signals from the environment.

Tactical Probing A striking feature of this model of dynamic strategy is the close relationship between tactical moves and strategy evolution. A clear strategy enables the firm to excel in a given business, but it also gives rise to experimentation that leads to options on future businesses—horizons 2 and 3 in Exhibit 6.11. Often, we don't think of the operating decisions that we call tactics as *strategic* activities because, in and of themselves, they're fairly inconsequential in affecting cost or competitive impact. In dynamic markets, however, many tactical moves can be used as low-cost "probes" for experimentation—testing the current strategy and suggesting future changes.

Tactics, in other words, can be both tools for competing today and experiments in new ways of competing tomorrow. Consider the case of discount broker Charles Schwab. When the company found itself being squeezed on one side by deep-discount Internet startups such as E*Trade and discount initiatives by full-service brokers such as Merrill Lynch on the other, it experimented with new ways of reinforcing customer relationships and identifying new markets. In particular, Schwab developed futures-trading programs, simplified its mutual-fund offerings, and launched Internet-based products and services. Some of these probes, of course, went nowhere (Schwab aborted a line of credit cards and a foray into on-line mortgages). But those that did succeed enabled Schwab both to further differentiate itself from bare-bones discounters and to gain ground in markets dominated by full-service brokers.

Setting Pace and Rhythm Finally, as managers move from one horizon to another they must concern themselves with the speed and pace of change. You're already familiar with this aspect of strategy because you're familiar with the staging diamond of the five-elements strategy model. Many managers, however, fail to appreciate fully the role played by time and timing in formulating and executing strategy. Consider, for example, the various approaches to staging and pacing described in Exhibit 6.12.[30] Obviously, attention to pacing and staging can prompt a company to think more seriously about the need for constant experimentation and probing. The concluding example of 3M may partially explain why that firm is consistently able to generate new and innovative products.

Exhibit 6.12 Staging and Pacing in the Real World

British Airways	"Five years is the maximum that you can go without refreshing the brand. . . We did it [relaunched Club Europe Service] because we wanted to stay ahead so that we could continue to win customers."
Emerson Electric	"In each of the last three years we've introduced more than 100 major new products, which is about 70 percent above our pace of the early 1990s. We plan to maintain this rate and, overall, have targeted increasing new products to [equal] 35 percent of total sales."
Intel	The inventor of Moore's Law stated that the power of the computer chip would double every 18 months. IBM builds a new manufacturing facility every nine months. "We build factories two years in advance of needing them, before we have the products to run in them, and before we know the industry is going to grow."
Gillette	Forty percent of Gillette's sales every five years must come from entirely new products (prior to its acquisition by P&G). Gillette raises prices at a pace set to match price increases in a basket of market goods (which includes items such as a newspaper, a candy bar, and a can of soda). Gillette prices are never raised faster than the price of the market basket.
3M	Thirty percent of sales must come from products that are fewer than four years old.

The Role of Implementation Levers   In terms of strategy implementation, the previous discussion provides you with some perspective on the type of strategy that needs to be implemented. In applying any implementation framework, the elements of the model must be balanced—in this case, a dynamic strategy should be reflected in organizational structures, systems, and processes that accommodate the strategic needs of firms in turbulent and hypercompetitive environments. One element of strategy formulation—staging— can also serve to bridge formulation and implementation because the staging component can specify how certain levers will be employed along the way.

Finally, both the strategic leadership of senior management and the culture of the organization that they foster should reflect a commitment to reasoned risk taking, learning, and responding to change. Indeed, it's hard to promote core values that support the strategy implementation in dynamic contexts if top management doesn't practice and champion them. That's just one reason why we studied strategic leadership in such detail in Chapter 2.

Summary of Challenges

1. *Distinguish the ways in which firms' strategies are related to dynamic contexts.* Dynamism can have dramatic effects on the quality of a firm's strategy and it can undermine competitive advantage—sometimes with blinding speed, but more typically over some extended period of time. Indeed, as noted in the opening vignette, although it may seem that the music industry has changed overnight, many of the seeds for that dramatic change were sown and nourished over an extended period of time. Technological discontinuities can alter the basis of competition and the requisite resources and capabilities for competitive advantage. The speed of change in an industry itself is a significant factor; it can either complement or compound the effects of industry evolution, technological discontinuities, and globalization.

2. *Identify, compare, and contrast the various routes to revolutionary strategies.* Revolutionary strategies are ones that do not take the existing rules of competition in the industry for granted but rather attempt to create value by approaching competition by violating some of these taken-for-granted rules. Reconceiving products and services, either by creating a new value curve or by separate function and form, can result in new offerings with high value-added for customers. Firms can also reconfigure the value chain, either by developing a new value chain or by compressing the existing value chain. Value can be created by redefining the arenas, either through focusing on the total possible market, rather than current customers served, or by spearheading industry convergence. Opportunities to increase margins are also found in rescaling the industry, either by consolidating the industry in search of greater economies of scale, or by downscaling the industry in search of profitable niche markets. Finally, revolutionary strategies can be found in reconsidering the competitive mindset, both by focusing on complementors and by shifting the competitive focus away from head-to-head competition and searching for areas where the competition has not yet ventured.

3. *Evaluate the advantages and disadvantages of choosing a first-mover strategy.* First movers are firms that initiate a strategic action before rivals, such as the introduction of a new product or service or a new process that provides a traditional product or service of dramatically higher quality or at a lower price, or both. Second movers are relatively early movers (because they are still not last-movers), but delayed enough to learn from first movers. Effective second movers are sometimes referred to as *fast followers.* They are distinguished from late movers, whose tardiness penalizes them when the market grows. First movers do not always have an advantage because there are significant risks associated with being the first to introduce new products, services, and business models.

4. *Recognize when an incumbent is caught off-guard by a revolutionary strategy and identify defensive tactics to reduce the effects of this competition.* As hard as they try, incumbents are not always successful in being the firm to revolutionize an industry and are caught off-guard by other incumbents or new entrants. In such cases, firms can resort to defensive tactics such as containment, neutralization, shaping, absorption, or annulment. They can also attempt to avoid surprise by taking out options on new businesses and technologies early in their life cycle (such as through investments in startups) that will give them the opportunity to acquire the new business at a later time on favorable terms should it prove to be a revolutionary idea.

5. *Explain the difficulties and solutions to implementing revolutionary strategies.* Vision is critical in that it serves as a set of simple rules that describe the business and how it creates value. Although all five elements of strategy are important and must be managed in concert, the arenas and staging diamonds are perhaps most important in dynamic markets. And, like the five elements of strategy, a balance among the implementation levers is critical.

These levers must accommodate environmental turbulence and hypercompetitive environments. The strategic flexibility demanded of these environments requires that organization structure and systems can be easily decoupled and recombined as circumstances change. Rigid bureaucracy is generally incompatible with turbulent environments. Strategic leadership must further support the firm's ability to identify the need for and undertake strategic change.

Review Questions

1. What are four sets of challenges to sustained competitive advantage outlined in this chapter?

2. What is the relationship between first and second movers?

3. What is industry commoditization? What are two strategies a firm may undertake to combat industry commoditization?

4. What is a new-market-creation strategy?

5. What is a low-end disruption strategy?

6. What are the three levels of activity that underlie strategies for turbulent and hypercompetitive markets?

7. What is the role of timing and pacing in revolutionary strategies?

8. What five defensive strategies might industry incumbents pursue in dynamic markets?

9. How might you apply real-options analysis, financially and conceptually, in the context of revolutionary strategies for turbulent and hypercompetitive markets?

10. What are the implications of dynamic strategies for strategy formulation and implementation?

Experiential Activities

Group Exercises

1. If you were the CEO of Napster (which started out as Roxio in the opening vignette), what material from this chapter would be most relevant to you? How would this material help you to formulate a strategy? What might key components of that strategy be? Now put yourself in Microsoft's shoes; would you see either Sonic Solutions or Napster as a threat? If so, what strategy would you formulate in response?

2. Review the list of first- and second-mover firms in Exhibit 6.9. What specific resources and capabilities do you think successful first movers must possess? What specific resources and capabilities do you think successful second movers and fast followers must possess? Do you think that a firm could be both a first mover and fast follower if it wanted to be?

Ethical Debates

1. Some firms manage disruptive strategy threats by investing in the firms that bring them to market, so that if the threat turns out to be wildly successful it can still benefit from it financially. Is this a purely business decision or are there ethical concerns as well?

2. You learned how incumbents can be blindsided by disruptive strategies. Litigation appears to be a prominent tool that incumbents can use to at least slow new entrants' growth. What might be some of your ethical concerns when using litigation to manage competition? Do you think that a firm's size will affect its ability to use this tactic? Does this matter?

How Would YOU DO THAT?

1. Pick an industry and use the box entitled "How Would *You* Do That? 6.1" as a template to map its value curve. What are the key success factors that define industry participation? Does there appear to be more than one strategic group in this industry operating with different value curves? Can you come up with a new value curve that would change the industry?

2. Identify a firm that you believe is pursuing a revolutionary strategy. How do its actions map onto the four-actions framework?

Go on to see How Would You Do That at www.prenhall.com/ carpenter&sanders

Endnotes

1. N. Wingfield and E. Smith, "With the Web Shaking Up Music, a Free-for-All in Online Songs," *Wall Street Journal,* November 19, 2003, A1; N. Wingfield and E. Smith, "Microsoft Plans to Sell Music over the Web," *Wall Street Journal,* November 17, 2003, A1; www.roxio.com (accessed June 28, 2005). "Napster Lives Again as Legal Distributor of Music on the Web," *The Wall Street Journal,* 25 February 2003, A10; N. Wingfield, "Roxio Agrees to Acquire Napster Assets," *The Wall Street Journal,* November 18, 2002, B4.

"Napster Achieves Number One Market Share in On Demand Music Subscriptions With Over 830,000 Subscribers and Will Exceed Fourth Quarter Guidance," *PR Newswire,* April 3, 2007; "Napster Subscriptions in Decline," *PC Magazine Online,* August 3, 2006; Emmanuel Legrand, "Napster: the Final Shutdown," *Music & Media, September* 14, 2002 p1(2); Gavin O'Malley, "Subscription Survivor?" *Advertising Age,* September 4, 2006 p6; "Market Commentary on Napster Inc." *M2 Presswire,* April 3, 2007.

2. Adapted from K. G. Smith, W. J. Ferrier, and C. M. Grimm, "King of the Hill: Dethroning the Industry Leader," *Academy of Management Executive* 15:2 (2001), 59–70.

3. D. C. Hambrick and J. W. Fredrickson, "Are You Sure You Have a Strategy?" *Academy of Management Executive* 15:4 (2001), 48–59.

4. M. Chen, "Competitor Analysis and Interfirm Rivalry: Toward a Theoretical Integration," *Academy of Management Review* 21 (1996), 100–134; M. Chen and D. C. Hambrick, "Speed, Stealth, and Selective Attack: How Small Firms Differ from Large Firms in Competitive Behavior," *Academy of Management Journal* 38 (1995), 453–482.

5. A. M. Brandenburger and B. J. Nalebuff, *Co-Opetition* (New York: Currency Doubleday, 1996).

6. K. G. Smith, W. J. Ferrier, and C. M. Grimm, "King of the Hill: Dethroning the Industry Leader," *Academy of Management Executive* 15:2 (2001), 59–70.

7. K. Rangan and G. Bowman, "Beating the Commodity Magnet," *Industrial Marketing Management* 21 (1992), 215–224; P. Kotler, "Managing Products through Their Product Life Cycle," in *Marketing Management: Planning, Implementation, and Control,* 7th ed. (Upper Saddle River, NJ: Prentice Hall, 1991); P. Kotler, "Product Life-Cycle Marketing Strategies," in *Marketing Management,* 11th ed. (Upper Saddle River, NJ: Prentice Hall, 2003), 328–339.

8. P. Anderson and M. L. Tushman, "Technological Discontinuities and Dominant Designs: A Cyclical Model of Technological Change," *Administrative Science Quarterly* 35 (1990), 604–633.

9. G. A. Moore, "Darwin and the Demon: Innovating within Established Enterprises" *Harvard Business Review* 82:7/8 (2004), 86–92.

10. S. Brown and K. Eisenhardt, *Competing on the Edge* (Boston: Harvard Business School Press, 1998).

11. These examples are drawn from an extensive and detailed list provided by C. Christensen and M. Raynor, *The Innovator's Solution* (Boston: Harvard Business School Press, 2003).

12. Adapted from W. C. Kim and R. Mauborgne, "Blue Ocean Strategy," *California Management Review* 47:3 (2005), 105–121.

13. W. C. Kim and R. Mauborgne, "Value Innovation: The Strategic Logic of High Growth," *Harvard Business Review* 75:1 (1997), 102–113; Kim and Mauborgne, "Charting Your Company's Future," *Harvard Business Review* 80:6 (2002), 76–82.

14. W. C. Kim and R. Mauborgne, "Blue Ocean Strategy," *California Management Review* 47:3 (2005), 105–121; Wine Institute, "Strong Sales Growth in 2004 for California Wine as Shipments Reached New High," April 5, 2005 (accessed July 12, 2005), www.wineinstitute.org; www.elitewine.com/site/index.php?lang=en&cat=news&art=159 (accessed July 12, 2005).

15. Adapted from W. C. Kim and R. Mauborgne, "Blue Ocean Strategy," *California Management Review* 47:3 (2005), 105–121.

16. The concept of the value net is common among game theorists, but was popularized by A. Brandenburger & B. Nalebuff in *Coopetition: A revolutionary mindset that combines competition and cooperation* (New York: Currency Doubleday, 1997).

17. M. E. Porter, *Competitive Strategy* (New York: Free Press, 1979), 232–233.

18. For a particularly rich discussion of these differences, see S. Schnaars, *Managing Imitation Strategies* (New York: Free Press, 1994), 12–14.

19. G. Tellis, S. Stremersch, and E. Yin, "The International Takeoff of New Products: Economics, Culture, and Country Innovativeness," *Marketing Science* 22:2 (2003), 161–187.

20. A. Goolsbee and J. Chevalier, "Price Competition Online: Amazon versus Barnes and Noble," *Quantitative Marketing and Economics* 1:2 (June, 2003), 203–222.

21. Adapted from S. Schnaars, *Managing Imitation Strategies* (New York Free Press, 1994), 37–43.

22. Schnaars, *Managing Imitation Strategies,* 37–43; J. Covin, D. Slevin, and M. Heeley, "Pioneers and Followers: Competitive Tactics, Environment, and Growth," *Journal of Business Venturing* 15:2 (1999), 175–210.

23. This framework is adapted from A. Afuah, *Innovation Management: Strategies, Implementation, and Profits,* 2nd ed. (New York: Oxford University Press, 2003). An earlier version appears in Schnaars, *Managing Imitation Strategies,* 12–14.

24. www.riaa.org (accessed July 28, 2005).

25. www.kodak.com (accessed July 15, 2005).

26. R. D'Aveni, "The Empire Strikes Back: Counterrevolutionary Strategies for Industry Leaders," *Harvard Business Review* 80:11 (November 2002), 5–12.

27. M. Amram and N. Kulatilaka, *Real Options: Managing Strategic Investment in an Uncertain World* (New York: Oxford University Press, 1998); E. Teach, "Will Real Options Take Root? Why Companies Have Been Slow to Adopt the Valuation Technique," *CFO Magazine,* July 1, 2003, 73.

28. See, for example, S. Kauffman, *At Home in the Universe: The Search for the Laws of Self-Organization and Complexity* (New York: Oxford University Press, 1995); M. Gell-Mann, *The Quark and the Jaguar* (New York: W. H. Freeman, 1994); J. Casti, *Complexification: Explaining a Paradoxical World through the Science of Surprise* (New York: HarperCollins, 1994); R. Lewin, *Complexity: Life at the Edge of Chaos* (New York: Macmillan, 1992).

29. Examples drawn from S. Brown and K. Eisenhardt, *Competing on the Edge: Strategy as Structured Chaos* (Boston: Harvard Business School Press, 1998).

30. Brown and Eisenhardt, *Competing on the Edge.*

7 Developing Corporate Strategy

In This Chapter We Challenge You To >>>

1. Define *corporate strategy*.

2. Understand the roles of economies of scope and revenue-enhancement synergy in corporate strategy.

3. Identify the different types of diversification.

4. Explain how companies can successfully enter attractive industries when those industries have the greatest barriers to entry.

5. Describe the relationship between corporate strategy and competitive advantage.

6. Explain the differences between corporate strategy in stable and dynamic contexts.

Diversification
at GE, 3M, *and*
MITY Enterprises

General Electric   General Electric (GE) was established in 1892 as a merger between two manufacturers of electrical equipment, Thomson-Houston Electric Co. and Edison General Electric Co. (of which Thomas Edison was one of the directors).[1] GE's early products included such Edison inventions as lightbulbs, elevators, motors, and toasters. In 1896, GE was among the 12 original companies to be included in the newly created Dow Jones Industrial Average stock index, and it's the only one that's still on the list.

By 1980, GE was earning $25 billion in revenues from such diverse businesses as plastics, consumer electronics, nuclear reactors, and jet engines. By 2007, its revenues were an astounding $163 billion and its businesses spanned consumer and commercial finance, health care, industrial, infrastructure, and news and entertainment. GE CEO Jeffrey Immelt described the range of GE: "We're not a monolithic company," Immelt said. "We have a $17 billion healthcare business that competes in a $4 trillion industry that's growing 8 percent a year. I can grow that business 8 percent. I've got a consumer-finance business in a $40 trillion global market growing 10 percent a year." How did GE evolve from an electronics company to an enormous conglomeration of many businesses? Over the years, GE developed some of the businesses through its own research and development (R&D) efforts. However, many of its current operations are the result of acquisitions. Indeed, GE is one of the most frequent acquirers of other businesses in the world. Between January 2000 and December 2004, GE acquired more than 250 different companies and spent more than $78 billion to do so. Despite its diversity of operations, GE stays competitive by following a vision that its CEO John F. (Jack) Welch formulated in 1981. Welch announced that GE would participate only in high-performing businesses in which it could be the number-one or number-two competitor. This gave GE a vision for growth as well as disciplined criteria for adding or divesting business lines. GE divested itself of many of its businesses, including air conditioning, housewares, and semiconductors, but it remains one of the most diversified companies in the U.S., if not the world. Today, the company's products and services include aircraft engines, locomotives and other transportation equipment, appliances (kitchen and laundry equipment), lighting, electric distribution and electric control equipment, generators and turbines, nuclear reactors, medical imaging equipment, commercial insurance, consumer finance, and network television (NBC).

Describing his strategy for the future, Immelt said in 2007, "We continue to execute on our strategy to invest in leadership businesses. Our focus remains on building faster growth, higher margin businesses. Since the beginning of the year, we have announced $15 billion of acquisitions in fast growth platforms in oil and gas, healthcare, and aviation. We continue to exit slower growth and more volatile businesses, and we are currently reviewing the potential disposition of our plastics business." The company's success has earned it the respect of the business community. In 2007, GE was named the top company on *Fortune* magazine's "America's Most Admired Companies" list, making 2007 the seventh year of the last ten in which GE was voted number one.

3M Minnesota Mining and Manufacturing (3M)—perhaps best known for its Post-it Notes and Scotch tape products—was originally founded in 1902 to sell corundum (an extremely hard mineral that is used as an abrasive) to grinding-wheel manufacturers. Within a couple of years, the fledgling company was specializing in sandpaper, but it wasn't until the 1920s, when it began focusing on technological innovation, that 3M hit its stride. Two products—Scotch-brand masking tape (introduced in 1925) and Scotch-brand cellophane tape (1930)—became so successful that they virtually guaranteed the company a long and prosperous future. Today, 3M has six operating units—industrial and transportation; display and graphics; health care; safety, security, and protection; electro and communications products; and consumer and office products. With nearly $23 billion in annual revenues, the company makes thousands of products, ranging from asthma inhalers to Scotchgard™ fabric coatings.

Coupled with enormous R&D spending (over $1 billion per year), 3M's policy of allowing scientists to dedicate 10 percent of their working time to experimentation has yielded a number of highly profitable innovations. Of course, not all divisions and innovations have been equally successful, and the company has spun off some divisions, including low-profit imaging and data storage ventures. 3M closed its audiotape and videotape businesses and got out of billboard advertising.

3M has entered most of its businesses through internal innovation, but it recently increased its pace of acquisitions. Between January 2000 and December 2004, 3M completed only 10 acquisitions and spent only a little more than $500 million on these deals in total. But in 2006 alone, the company completed 19 acquisitions and spent $900 million on them. The acquisitions ranged from a German firm that makes personalized passports to a Brazilian company that provides earplugs, eyewear, and hand cream. Despite the recent acquisitions, CEO George Buckley sees growth through external acquisitions as secondary to growth through internal invention. "We'll build first where 3M is strong, defend and expand market presence, and build size and scale," Buckley said. "We will also grow through continuous invention and reinvention in our core businesses—the marketplace manifestations of 3M imagination and 3M innovation." Beyond growing the core business, Buckley will look for acquisitions that expand 3M into adjacent markets. "Acquisitions will help us enter adjacent markets and build business in new spaces more quickly," Buckley said. 3M's healthy mix of businesses cushions the company from disruptions in any single market. "The unique nature of 3M's business model lends power unseen elsewhere," Buckley said. "At 3M, we have some real magic."

MITY Enterprises In contrast to corporate giants GE and 3M, MITY Enterprises is a small $55 million company founded just 20 years ago. MITY's first product was a lightweight, durable folding-leg table. Since then, the company has diversified into other product lines, including chairs and other low-cost furniture. The company looks for acquisitions, but for a company MITY's size, acquisition targets are not easy to find. Instead, MITY focuses on internal growth through innovation. "We believe that new product development will continue to propel our growth," said MITY CEO Bradley Nielson. "With that in mind, we are working on new chair lines, staging, dance floors, new healthcare chairs, and additional fencing and accessories."

Not all new product introductions work out. As Nielson said in 2006, "When we entered the year, we were just coming off a failed next-generation table experiment that was diluting our earnings base. However, rather than spending time licking our wounds, we quickly shifted gears and began executing a new plan." The new plan included taking the failed technology from the failed table experiment and applying it to a new area: fences. Like MITY's furniture, the fence panels are durable. "The panels are impact resistant, won't bow or sag in the sun, need no sanding, painting, or other kinds of maintenance, [and] are faster and easier to install than concrete or stone," Nielson said. The new product line is doing well, and MITY will continue developing innovative products. "Our growth is not dependent on making an acquisition," Nielson said. "We can do just fine going without."

As can be seen from these brief descriptions, many firms operate in more than one business. Some firms, like GE, participate in an incredible number of seemingly unrelated business operations. Others, like 3M, have grown into many businesses. Still others, like MITY Enterprises, are smaller companies, but they, too, seem to grow to a point where they venture out of their original businesses to experiment in other product lines. In this chapter, we will introduce you to the basic concepts necessary to understand and manage corporate strategy, including the diversification of firms. <<<

Corporate Strategy

Why would a firm that makes lightbulbs also make elevators? If you're in the table business, does it make sense to be in the chair business, too? If your core business activities result in innovative new products, should you retain ownership of these products and the units responsible for them, or does it make more sense to sell them? Questions such as these are fundamental to corporate strategy.

As we pointed out in Chapter 1 and have emphasized throughout this book, *corporate strategy* must address issues related to decisions about entering or exiting an industry. Specifically, effective corporate strategies must answer three interrelated questions:

- In which business *arenas* should our company compete?

- How can we, as a corporate parent, add value to our various lines of business?

- How will diversification or our entry into a new industry help us compete in our other businesses?

synergy   Condition under which the combined benefits of activities in two or more arenas are greater than the simple sum of those benefits.

At the same time, however, corporate strategy also deals with issues affecting the overall management of a multibusiness enterprise, such as top-level efforts to orchestrate synergies across business units. **Synergy** occurs when the combined benefits of a firm's activities in two or more arenas are more than the simple sum of those benefits alone. After all, corporate-level strategy must maintain strategic coherence across business units and facilitate cooperation (or competition) among units in order to create value for shareholders. Thus, although fundamentally related to each other through the common goal of achieving competitive advantage, business strategy and corporate strategy have different objectives.

Most large and publicly traded firms are amalgamations of business units operating in multiple product, service, and geographic markets (often globally); they are rarely single-business operations. Obviously, companies approach corporate strategy in different ways, and as you can see from Exhibit 7.1, corporate portfolios can be built in a number of different ways. Although MITY Enterprises has diversified into new products, they're all related to the institutional furniture market niche. At the other end of the spectrum, GE not only makes everything from lightbulbs to locomotives, but offers financial services for virtually any business or consumer need. In between is 3M. This company's business units, though highly diversified, reflect common core competencies—the unique resources and knowledge that a company's management must consider when developing strategy—in innovation and adhesive technology.[2]

diversification   Degree to which a firm conducts business in more than one arena.

Recall that we introduced the important fact that most firms are multiproduct organizations in our earlier discussions of industry analysis, value chains, and market segmentation. That's why we're now going to discuss in some detail the ways in which managers can create (and squander) value through **diversification**. In this chapter, we'll focus on six key aspects of corporate strategy as it affects diversification decisions:

1. We'll review our understanding of corporate strategy and define *diversification,* and show how both concepts have changed over time.

2. We'll identify the potential sources of economic gain that make diversification attractive.

3. We'll describe alternative forms of diversification.

4. We'll present a rationale, or logic, for guiding corporate decisions about adding businesses.

5. We'll revisit the relationship between corporate strategy and competitive advantage.

6. We'll amplify our discussion of the roles of corporate strategy in dynamic contexts.

Economic Logic

We will build our discussion around many of the elements of the strategy diamond. This framework is useful because it allows you to choose those elements of strategy formulation and implementation that are essential to developing a firm's corporate strategy under specific conditions. ◆ As was made apparent in the chapter's opening vignette, a firm's corporate strategy usually evolves over time. All three of our firms in the vignette have entered and/or exited business arenas. They have used the various major vehicles of strategy to facilitate these changes. The economic logic of diversification often incorporates such levers to achieve synergy and transfer

Exhibit 7.1 Diversification Profiles

GE Product Scope

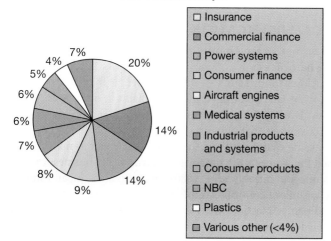

- □ Insurance
- □ Commercial finance
- □ Power systems
- □ Consumer finance
- □ Aircraft engines
- □ Medical systems
- □ Industrial products and systems
- □ Consumer products
- □ NBC
- □ Plastics
- □ Various other (<4%)

GE Geographic Scope

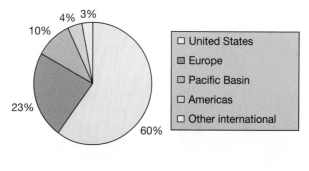

- □ United States
- □ Europe
- □ Pacific Basin
- □ Americas
- □ Other international

3M Product Scope

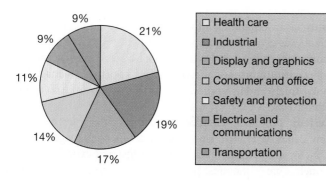

- □ Health care
- □ Industrial
- □ Display and graphics
- □ Consumer and office
- □ Safety and protection
- □ Electrical and communications
- □ Transportation

3M Geographic Scope

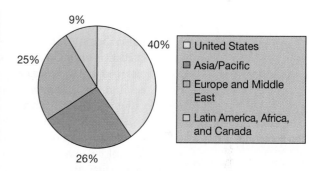

- □ United States
- □ Asia/Pacific
- □ Europe and Middle East
- □ Latin America, Africa, and Canada

MITY Enterprises Product Scope

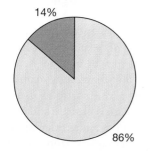

- □ Multipurpose room furniture
- □ Healthcare seating

MITY Enterprises Geographic Scope

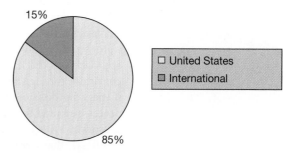

- □ United States
- □ International

knowledge between business units. The timing and pacing of such moves must be orchestrated in ways that do not negate the possible benefits of diversification.

THE EVOLUTION OF DIVERSIFICATION IN THE UNITED STATES

vertical integration
Diversification into upstream and/or downstream industries.

In the United States, the first form of organizational diversification was probably **vertical integration**. In order to secure needed resources, large firms often moved "upstream" in the industry value chain—that is, closer to the source of the raw materials they needed.[3] Early on, for example, General Motors began operating its own steel plants in order to supply its auto-frame and body factories. During the early phases of industrialization, many large firms also began investing in businesses that, though related to their operations, were not part of their original industry value chains. DuPont, for instance, started out making gunpowder and eventually applied the scientific discoveries generated by that business to enter new businesses, such as dynamite and nitroglycerin (1880), guncotton (1892), and smokeless powder (1894). Ultimately, DuPont controlled most of the U.S. explosives market. The company then diversified into paints, plastics, and dyes until antitrust action forced it to divest some of its explosive powder business.

In the late nineteenth century, the booming U.S. economy fostered a period of rapid consolidation. The Sherman Act of 1890 introduced U.S. federal antitrust law and led to the eventual breakup of many large monopolistic companies. In 1891, for instance, the courts ordered Standard Oil to split into six separate companies. Similar rulings broke up other companies deemed to be anticompetitive.

By the 1960s, many large firms began expanding into areas unrelated to their core businesses, because this type of growth was generally exempt from antitrust restrictions. Unrelated diversification became a corporate strategy of choice, and soon a breed of corporations emerged that was characterized by curious mixes of operations. ITT's portfolio managed to accommodate telephones, donuts, hotels, and insurance. For a brief history of the diversification of ITT over time, see Exhibit 7.2.

conglomerate Corporation consisting of many companies in different businesses or industries.

Although it addressed certain problems entailed by antitrust constraints, the **conglomerate** model raised new issues of its own. How could a company manage a portfolio of far-flung enterprises? The need to address such questions fostered experiments in new management tools and models. One of the most popular of these tools was **portfolio planning**. Without knowing it, you are probably already familiar with the conglomerate version of portfolio planning (see Exhibit 7.3).

portfolio planning Practice of mapping diversified businesses or products based on their relative strengths and market attractiveness.

Portfolio planning was initially intended to help managers evaluate the diversified firm and achieve a balanced portfolio of large, stable businesses and high growth ones, such that resources could be channeled to fuel growth. Its basic purpose was to guide resource allocation among businesses, help make choices that achieve a balanced portfolio (in terms of growth, cash generation, cash needs, and so on), set performance hurdles and reward structure, and set business unit strategy. A key assumption of the portfolio planning approach was that firms were capital constrained—while this may or may not be a real constraint for a given firm, it is a pretty strong assumption that may unduly constrain managerial decision making. Regardless, the starting point in the portfolio planning process required the firm to analyze businesses in terms of their market share and growth prospects. With one variation of this tool, for instance, a company identified all of its businesses that were "dogs"—those businesses in which it didn't have a strong competitive position, typically based on low relative market share, and that were located in bad industries (i.e., mature or low-growth industries). Such businesses were then earmarked to be sold. Businesses that had very strong competitive positions but were in slow-growth industries were referred to as "cash cows." Portfolio planning dictated that cash cows should be maintained because the cash flow could be channeled into promising high-growth businesses ("stars").

Exhibit 7.2   A Brief History and Genealogy of a Conglomerate

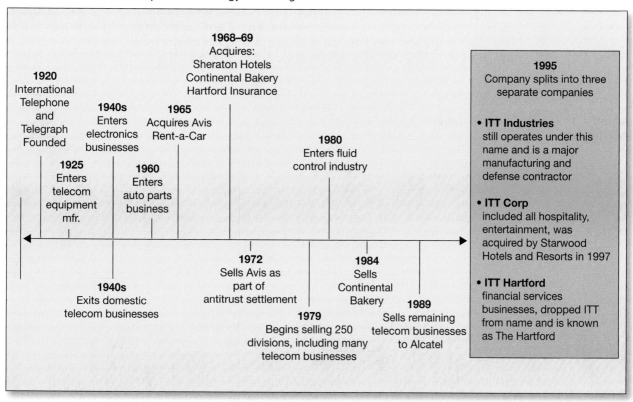

1920
International Telephone and Telegraph Founded

1925
Enters telecom equipment mfr.

1940s
Enters electronics businesses

1940s
Exits domestic telecom businesses

1960
Enters auto parts business

1965
Acquires Avis Rent-a-Car

1968–69
Acquires:
Sheraton Hotels
Continental Bakery
Hartford Insurance

1972
Sells Avis as part of antitrust settlement

1979
Begins selling 250 divisions, including many telecom businesses

1980
Enters fluid control industry

1984
Sells Continental Bakery

1989
Sells remaining telecom businesses to Alcatel

1995
Company splits into three separate companies

- **ITT Industries**
still operates under this name and is a major manufacturing and defense contractor

- **ITT Corp**
included all hospitality, entertainment, was acquired by Starwood Hotels and Resorts in 1997

- **ITT Hartford**
financial services businesses, dropped ITT from name and is known as The Hartford

Business Unit Competitve Position or Market Share

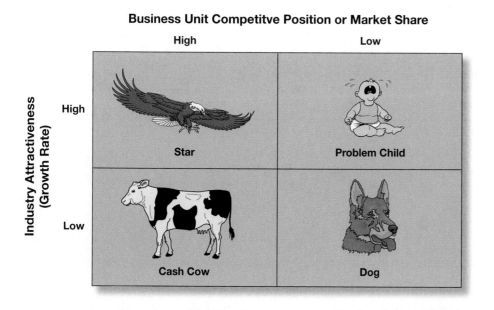

Industry Attractiveness (Growth Rate)

High — Low

High — Star / Problem Child

Low — Cash Cow / Dog

Exhibit 7.3   A Portfolio Planning Lens on Diversification

Exhibit 7.4 shows the portfolio models for MITY, along with one for a highly diversified financial services company in 2007. In simple matrices, like that for MITY, you can use the size of the circle to represent the market share of that business in a particular industry. More elaborate versions of the matrix involve plotting out the size and profitability of each business. For instance, with the diversified financial services firm in Exhibit 7.4, the size of the

Exhibit 7.4 Portfolio Planning at Two Firms

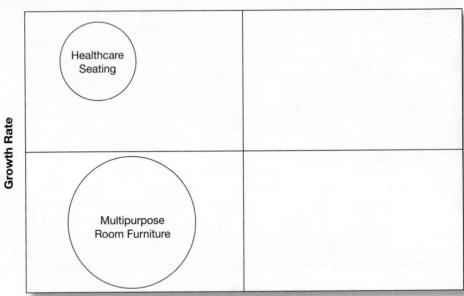

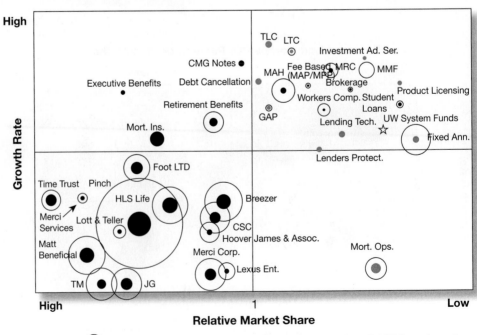

inner circle tells you the relative amount of revenue that business generates for the firm, while the color inside indicates whether or not it is profitable.

Several aspects of the more simplistic aspects of the portfolio planning approach have been debunked. The most basic reason is that it provides no fundamental competitive logic for which businesses should be entered and which should be maintained. Moreover, the sources of synergies among businesses—beyond the generation and usage of cash—are not recognized. Nor is there any accounting for the VRINE-based resources and capabilities that allow a firm to be successful in one business, but perhaps not another. Overly simplistic tools like this lead to questionable diversification moves such as a telecommunication company entering the hotel industry simply because the growth opportunities are attractive. Sears, for instance, used the model early in its history to diversify into growth industries like credit cards (Discovery), stock brokerage (Dean Witter), real estate brokerage (Coldwell-Banker), and insurance (Allstate). While Sears looked at these moves as logical, and aimed to develop a one-stop shopping strategy around what it perceived to be a mature retail business (Sears Department stores), these moves also led it to stop investing in the core retail business. Unfortunately for Sears, upstart Wal-Mart viewed retailing as a growth industry, and changed the rules of competition so dramatically in retailing that it almost put Sears out of business, and did lead to the demise of many retailers such as Kmart and others. Ironically, Wal-Mart is pursuing a similar one-stop shopping strategy (it has added groceries and is trying to enter the consumer banking industry), but Wal-Mart is still aggressively investing in its core retail business and making sure that it builds strong synergies among its portfolio of owned and partner businesses.

Despite the problems with the portfolio planning model, as demonstrated by Sears application of it, modified versions of the portfolio planning tool have been developed to help managers analyze the performance of single-industry and diversified companies as well as help them isolate performance problems. For instance, by plotting out businesses, managers can visually critique why and where there are or should be synergies between different business units, and identify those that might no longer fit the larger economic logic of the firm's corporate strategy. Similarly, managers can integrate what they know about product or industry life cycles with the portfolio visualization tool. As you can see in Exhibit 7.5, again using the example from the same diversified financial services firm portrayed in Exhibit 7.4,

Exhibit 7.5 A Portfolio Model that Accounts for the Life Cycle of Products

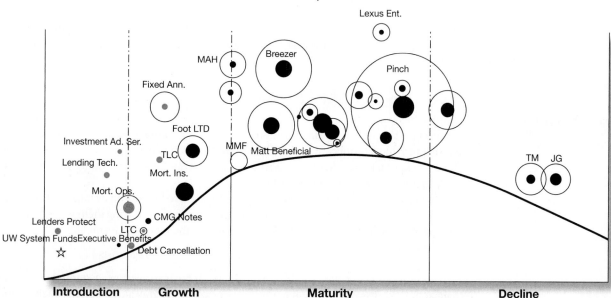

most of the firm's business activity is in relatively mature markets. This visual accounting of the businesses helped to motivate managers to invest more heavily in new product and service development. Beyond this modification, the portfolio management tool still helps managers communicate and align business unit managers' incentives and growth objectives. At a very basic level, particularly in firms with many business units, it provides a useful way to communicate and evaluate business unit strategies, and then relate them to corporate goals and objectives in changing environments. Since strategy is ultimately about making tradeoffs—what will the firm do and what won't it do—the portfolio approach clearly and visibly shows managers what the firm is doing, and what tradeoffs they are and are not making. We will introduce you to other portfolio models—ones that plot out industry characteristics or look at the intersection of industry characteristics and VRINE characteristics—that further incorporate aspects of dynamic strategy later in the chapter. You will have the opportunity to work with these portfolio-based tools in How Would *You* Do That? 7.1 and 7.2.

Shareholder dissatisfaction, especially on the part of institutional investors, coupled with the threat of hostile takeover opportunities, put pressure on conglomerates to reorganize in more manageable forms. Unwieldy portfolios of unrelated business units began to give way to more focused portfolios of related operations.[4] This move toward a more focused corporation can be seen in the more recent years of ITT, as illustrated in Exhibit 7.2.

Business history is littered with stories of failed growth and diversification strategies. The lesson taught by such cases is pretty clear: In and of itself, diversification not only doesn't necessarily create shareholder value but may in fact dissipate it. However, as we'll see later in the chapter, the logic behind *certain types* of diversification remains compelling. Indeed, substantial empirical evidence indicates that some forms of diversification can create significant shareholder wealth. Which types or forms of diversification are these? In the next part of the chapter, we'll identify and discuss the conditions necessary for value creation and the tools that can be used to increase its likelihood.

Economic Logic of Diversification: Synergy

Expanding the firm's scope—whether the addition of new vertical, horizontal, complementary, or geographic arenas—doesn't necessarily create value for shareholders. Strategists need to understand the sources of potential value creation from diversification, and they need to know how to determine whether a firm can leverage those sources. That's why we're going to turn to two concepts that are critical in evaluating opportunities for diversification and value creation: *economies of scope* and *revenue-enhancement*. Collectively, these are often referred to as *synergy*. However, they are two different economic logics for the possible profits from diversification. ◆

 Economic Logic

ECONOMY-OF-SCOPE SYNERGIES

economy of scope Condition under which lower total average costs result from sharing resources to produce more than one product or service.

We introduced the concept of **economy of scope** in Chapter 5, where we simply associated it with a firm's success in sharing a resource among two or more of its products. In this chapter, we'll provide a more complete definition and explain why economies of scope are one of the two key factors in determining whether a corporate strategy is adding value through the diversification of its business portfolio.

As you learned in Chapter 5, economies of scope are reductions in average costs that result from producing two or more products jointly instead of producing them separately. The concept of economies of scope can be represented by the following formula:

$$\text{Average costs } (X, Y) < \text{Average costs } (X) + \text{Average costs } (Y)$$

Economies of scope are possible when the company can leverage a resource or value chain activity across more than one product, service, or geographic arena. Although we focus on productive resources for the sake of presentation, you should recognize that economies of scope are possible in all value-chain activities, not simply production. For instance, comarketing of two products within one company may be less costly than marketing them separately in two companies (it may also help increase revenue-enhancement synergies, but we'll discuss that point later). For instance, it may have been less costly to market and distribute Sobe drinks within PepsiCo than it was to market it as a stand-alone product before PepsiCo purchased Sobe.

Sources of Economy-of-Scope Synergies

What tactics result in economies of scope? Economy-of-scope savings generally result when a firm uses common resources across business units. Or to put it another way: Whenever a common resource can be used across more than one business unit, the company has the *potential* to generate economies of scope. If, for instance, the cost of material that's common to two or more products is lower when purchased in greater quantity, then jointly producing two products may increase purchase volume and, therefore, cut costs. The ability to join the procurement function in this case and buy materials jointly creates an economy of scope.

Likewise, a manufacturing facility that achieves minimum efficient scale for one product may have excess capacity that it can put to use in producing other products. In this case, the total cost for both products will be lower because the cost of the common facility can be spread across two businesses. Sometimes the common resource is located farther down the firm's value chain. For instance, if a firm distributes products through a system with access to a large customer base, it may be able to add products to that system more cheaply than competitors launching similar new products that may need to create dedicated distribution networks from scratch. Coke and Pepsi enjoy such economies of scope in the markets for soft drinks, noncarbonated beverages, and bottled water.

REVENUE-ENHANCEMENT SYNERGIES

Another manifestation of synergy is revenue enhancement. **Revenue-enhancement synergy** exists when total sales are greater if two products are sold and distributed within one company than when they are owned by separate companies. Put another way, while economies of scope relate to cutting costs, revenue-enhancement synergies relate to growing revenues. In short, it's the difference between synergies that allow you to make more money by saving on expenses and those that allow you to grow the business! This can be represented by the following formula:

$$\text{Total revenues } (X, Y) > \text{Total revenues } (X) + \text{Total revenues } (Y)$$

Simply put, if two business units X and Y are able to generate more revenue because they're collectively owned by a single corporate parent than if they are in separate companies, the strategy of common ownership is synergistic.

> **revenue-enhancement synergy** When total sales are greater if two products are sold and distributed within one company than when they are owned by separate companies.

Sources of Revenue-Enhancement Synergies

Revenue-enhancement synergy may result from a variety of tactics, such as bundling products that were previously sold separately, sharing complementary knowledge in the interest of new-product innovation, or increasing shared distribution opportunities.

Consider how Disney leverages its various resources to create revenue-enhancement synergies. The result of its web of collaborative activities is a consistent stream of new revenue sources that demonstrate a direct line between creativity in product design and financial acumen.[5] At the same time, Disney's collaborative context doesn't specify the forms that synergies must take; it merely reflects the principle that they should be profitable for all of the units involved. Two movies, for example, *The Little Mermaid* and *The Lion King,* became television shows. Another, *Toy Story,* was rolled out as a video game. Both *The Lion King* and another movie, *Beauty and the Beast,* became smash-hit musicals. The managers of Disney

Tokyo share best practices with managers at Disney World in Orlando and Euro Disney outside Paris. Big Red Boat, a cruise line that specializes in Caribbean vacations, and Disney World, which offers vacation packages in Orlando on Florida's east coast, collaborate to build traffic in both venues. Characters from one animated series make cameos in others, and all shows are circulated through Disney's lineup of cable- and network-television channels. The voices of both live-action and animated characters circulate through Radio Disney.

Revenue-enhancement synergies generally arise from bundling and joint-selling opportunities. In recent years, for example, firms in the financial services industry have been actively acquiring or merging with firms in adjacent sectors in order to bundle products for current customers in different sectors.

A more specific example is found in the opening vignette. Founded in Orem, Utah, in 1987, MITY Enterprises originally made folding tables targeted at such institutional users as schools and churches. A decade later, when the company found itself with excess capacity in its Orem plant, managers began thinking about growth options. Because MITY's technology could be used to manufacture chairs and other types of furniture as well as tables, the company decided to expand into complementary products. MITY thus achieved synergy in two ways:

- Because expansion didn't require a new plant, the cost of the existing facility was spread across the various operations needed for different products.

- Because its manufacturing and distribution operations were geared toward multiple products, MITY's customers were more likely to buy more than one of its products, thus generating incremental sales that the firm could not otherwise have gained.

Similarly, firms in various sectors of the financial services industry have been actively acquiring and merging with firms in adjacent sectors in order to be able to bundle related products and cross-sell to existing customers.

ECONOMIC BENEFITS OF DIVERSIFICATION

Because mutual gains may be derived from either cost savings or revenue-enhancement synergies, a corporation that maintains ownership over multiple business units may have an advantage over competing businesses that are owned and managed separately. A company achieves this so-called "parenting advantage" when the joint cash flows of two or more collectively owned business units exceed the sum of the cash flows that they would generate independently.

When their collective market value exceeds the independent market values of a portfolio of business units, the financial markets will typically recognize the existence of a parenting advantage. Of course, the market doesn't compare business units by assigning both collective and independent value. Investors, however, can make reasonable estimates of a business unit's potential independent value. How? By using the market multiples (e.g., price earnings ratios or other similar multiples) of independent competitors in the industry within which its business units compete to compare the parent corporation's market value with the combined hypothetical values of its business units.

How and When to Seek Synergy   Two processes can generate synergy: sharing resources and transferring capabilities. We've discussed resource sharing extensively in our discussion of economies of scope. Transferring capabilities is actually a special case of resource sharing that can create both cost savings and revenue enhancement. Yum! Brands, for instance, can transfer knowledge about site location, franchise development, and internationalization from one restaurant brand to another. Black & Decker can share knowledge about small electric motors across its power tool and kitchen appliance units. Honda transfers knowledge gained about high-performance engines from its Formula 1 racing activities not only to its automobile division, but also to units that produce motorcycles and lawncare and recreational equipment.

LIMITS OF DIVERSIFICATION BENEFITS

Remember, however, that neither economies of scope nor revenue enhancement materialize simply because firms expand into new lines of business. In other words, it's not *necessarily* cheaper to produce two products jointly in a single firm than separately in distinct firms. Indeed, in many cases, diversification creates **diseconomies of scope**—average cost increases resulting from the joint output of two or more products within a single firm.

The critical question is *when economies of scope are likely to materialize.* Often, firms that can't demonstrate that diversification has generated economies of scope or revenue-enhancement synergies are forced to divest themselves of some units. During the 1990s, AT&T attempted to reap synergies across such businesses as long-distance telephone services, wireless cell phone service, and cable TV. However, it was never able to generate the cross-selling and synergistic outcomes it projected. Thus, in 2002 the company made the decision to split the company apart; some divisions were split off as separate companies, others were sold to competitors. The restructuring at AT&T reflects a failed diversification strategy; the sale of the surviving long-distance company to SBC Communications further testifies that AT&T's forays into new industries did not create the value and shareholder enthusiasm its leaders had hoped for. Ironically, SBC Communications changed their name to AT&T after acquiring the company. But, names can be deceiving; it is the shareholders and managers of SBC Communications that now own and manage the assets of the original AT&T long distance company. Of course, such divestitures are not always the result of failed diversification. Sometimes, a firm is quite successful but because of a change in strategy decides to divest itself of some successful businesses.

As the AT&T example illustrates, it often turns out that the collective value of a firm's portfolio is less than the total hypothetical value of the same businesses operated independently. In this case, the strategy of common ownership dissipates potential shareholder value. When investors—and corporate raiders, in particular—suspect the prospect of a significant diversification discount (i.e., the profits to be gained from buying the parent firm and selling off its portfolio piecemeal), a firm becomes a prime candidate for takeover and forced restructuring. Many investors have made huge profits by gaining control of an overly diversified company and selling various parts to firms in related areas—firms that are often willing to pay premium prices for operations related to their own.

Two things increase a firm's level of diversification: the number of separate businesses it operates and the degree of relatedness of those businesses. Relatedness is typically assessed by how similar the underlying industries are. The most diversified firms are those that own lots of businesses in very disparate industries; this is known as **unrelated diversification**. Firms that own many businesses clustered in a few industries are pursuing what is known as **related diversification**. Both forms of diversification can create management problems.

The harmful side effects of too much diversification include increased transaction and bureaucratic costs and burgeoning complexity. As firms become larger and multidivisional, corporate office functions tend to grow rapidly. If not held in check, these bureaucratic costs may exceed the benefits of diversification. Likewise, diverse firms may fall victim to doing too much internally and underutilize outside suppliers. Often the transaction costs of sourcing externally are sufficiently lower than the costs of organizing this activity internally. Finally, diversification increases firm complexity. For instance, the organization of a firm with ten businesses that span five industries is inherently more complex than a firm of the same size that operates only in one or a few industries. Complex firms are more difficult to manage than simple, focused firms. Research shows, for example, that diversified firms pay significantly higher compensation to attract and retain top management personnel than

diseconomies of scope Condition under which the joint output of two or more products within a single firm results in increased average costs.

unrelated diversification Form of diversification in which the business units that a firm operates are highly dissimilar.

related diversification Form of diversification in which the business units operated by a firm are highly related.

more focused firms of similar size.[6] Why? Because there are fewer top executives who are capable of managing complex firms. Bureaucratic costs, transaction costs, and complexity can all impede management's designs to create synergies.

If diversified firms are more difficult to manage—that is, if it's demonstrably harder to realize the benefits of diversification—then it stands to reason that there are real limits to those benefits. Indeed, research indicates that there's a point at which both the benefits of diversification and firm performance begin to decline. Exhibit 7.6 illustrates the relationship between diversification and two measures of firm performance—*return on assets* (ROA) and *total shareholder returns* (TSR).

In analyzing the data for the S&P 500 and S&P midcap firms over an eight-year period, we find that the relationship between diversification and performance takes the form of an inverted U (∩). At the median level of diversification, performance is much higher than at low levels of diversification (25th percentile) or high levels of diversification (75th percentile). These findings tell us that, on average, although diversification seems to benefit shareholders up to a point, it begins to dissipate value at high levels of diversification. Moderate values are typically achieved by firms which, like 3M, are active in several businesses that are somewhat related to each other.

When examining the relationship between diversification and performance reviewed in Exhibit 7.6, it is important to understand that there are exceptions to these averages. Some highly diversified firms perform quite well. For instance, GE is very diversified and over the long-term has performed very well, much better than most firms diversified at that level (and even single business firms). High levels of diversification, such as the conglomerate firm, can be very effective strategies in countries with developing capital markets. When capital markets are not as efficient as they are in developed countries, diversified firms can internally generate lower costs of capital than they can obtain in capital markets. Consequently, it can be efficient for firms to diversify and own more businesses than would be efficient in countries such as the United States, the United Kingdom, or Germany.

RESOURCE RELATEDNESS AND STRATEGIC SIMILARITY

To create economies of scope and revenue-enhancement synergies, a firm's resources should match its business activities. For this reason, whether they're thinking about en-

Exhibit 7.6
Diversification and
Performance in S&P 500
and S&P Midcap Firms

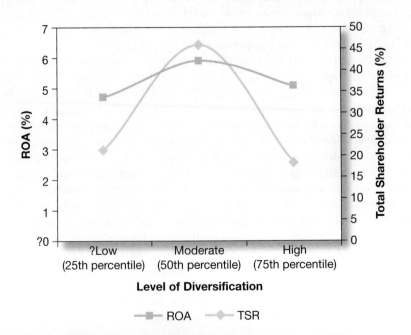

tering a new business arena or evaluating the suitability of a firm's portfolio for a proposed diversification move, strategists must assess the extent to which a firm's resources and capabilities match the needs of potential subsidiaries. One way to assess this match is in terms of how related the businesses are. When unrelated diversification is taken to the extreme—when there are many businesses and they are largely unrelated—firms are referred to as *conglomerates*. When there's a good match between the resource needs of parent and subsidiary—when diversification is related—it's more likely to create value. It's not critical, however, that both parent and subsidiary possess the *same* set of resources and capabilities. Indeed, in seeking to diversify, many firms are trying to acquire and bundle complementary resources and capabilities. The key issue is whether the match or fit between resources will help the parties compete more effectively.

Strategic Similarity   Parent firms and their subsidiaries need to assess their fit on more than just the resources it takes to compete. In determining fit, we want to know if the strategies required to compete in the various businesses of the firm are similar. A firm's strategy affects the way in which managers view the firm's competitive activities and make critical resource allocation decisions. In general, it is easier to manage a firm that does not require dissimilar strategies across business units. For instance, the jobs of the top executives at 3M and GE are significantly more complex than at MITY Enterprises—and this would be the case even if MITY were as large as these other firms.

If the strategies of its businesses are similar, a firm's managers can respond more quickly and effectively to strategic issues. Conversely, when strategies differ significantly, managers will generally be slower and less decisive. Decision-making delays can be hazardous, especially in high-speed industries such as cell phones and computer peripherals; perhaps more important, dissimilarity in dominant logic increases the likelihood that when managers finally do make decisions they'll make bad ones.

Not surprisingly, the strategic characteristics of businesses in a diversified portfolio may vary widely. Two businesses, for instance, may depend on very different technologies, industry competitive structures, and customer-buying routines. Strategic dissimilarity, therefore, can make it much more difficult to manage the portfolio. The more similar the contexts across which its businesses compete, the easier it is to manage a firm's portfolio and to create value through economies of scope and revenue-enhancement synergy.

The maximum opportunities to exploit potential economies of scope and revenue enhancement synergies lie at the intersection of two dimensions: (1) the fit among parent–subsidiary resources and (2) the fit of parent–subsidiary strategies. Conversely, the least promising opportunity for creating synergies occurs when there's a misfit on both of these same dimensions. When there's a misfit, managers need to make organizational adjustments. Later in this chapter, we'll present two models that can help determine these adjustments.

ULTERIOR MOTIVES FOR DIVERSIFICATION

In addition to reducing costs and increasing revenue-enhancement opportunities, managers may have self-serving motives for diversification—motives that aren't necessarily in shareholders' best interests. Among these, we'll mention three: *risk reduction, empire building*, and *compensation*.

At first glance, risk reduction would seem to be a natural reason for diversifying. In fact, it's probably the reason cited most often by students who haven't yet been formally introduced to the pros and cons of corporate diversification. Why isn't the strategy of reducing risk by diversifying generally in shareholders' best interests? Because it's much cheaper for the shareholders themselves to diversify in other ways. They can, for example, diversify equity risk by building a diversified stock portfolio—a strategy that, compared to the cost of diversifying a corporate portfolio, is fairly inexpensive.

When executives embark on growth and diversification because they desire to manage a larger company, they are said to be engaging in empire building. Rarely will empire building result in shareholder value or higher margins. However, empire building almost always results in greater notoriety and prestige for top executives. Although some executives may pursue empire building simply because of hubris, there are opportunistic reasons why they would do so as well. This simple reason is that executives of larger companies are paid more than executives of smaller companies. The main determinant of how much CEOs are paid is company size. Therefore, growing and diversifying the company generally results in executives being paid more.

Types of Diversification

A firm that wants to expand the scope of its operations has several options. In this section, we'll show how a company can expand its arenas, the three dimensions of *vertical*, *horizontal*, and *geographic*.

VERTICAL SCOPE

vertical scope The extent to which a firm is vertically integrated.

Sometimes a firm expands its **vertical scope** out of economic necessity. Perhaps it must protect its supply of a critical input, or perhaps firms in the industry that supply certain inputs are reluctant to invest sufficiently to satisfy the unique or heavy needs of a single buyer. Beyond such reasons as these—which are defensive—firms expand vertically to take advantage of growth opportunities. Vertical expansion in scope is often a logical growth option because a company is familiar with the arena that it's entering.

In some cases, a firm can create value by moving into suppliers' or buyers' value chains if it can bundle complementary products. If, for instance, you were to buy a new home, you'd go through a series of steps in making your purchase decision. Now, most homebuilders concentrate on a fairly narrow aspect of the homebuilding value chain. Some, however, have found it profitable to expand vertically into the home financing business by

Homebuilders like Pulte and D.R. Horton have found a way to create value by moving down the home-buyer's value chain. Both companies now offer mortgage services, a complementor to the home building industry, making it easier for customers to buy their homes. Pulte and D.R. Horton benefit as well because they earn the revenues associated with mortgage financing.

offering mortgage brokerage services. Pulte Homes Inc., one of the largest homebuilders in the United States, set up a wholly-owned subsidiary, Pulte Mortgage LLC, to help buyers get financing for new homes. This service not only simplifies the home buying process for many of Pulte's customers, but it also allows Pulte to reap profits in the home financing industry. Automakers and dealers have expanded into financing for similar reasons.

The Pitfalls of Increased Vertical Scope Although a firm's business segments lie adjacent along an industry's value chain, the structural features of the industries of these business segments (e.g., the industry five forces and complementors) may be fundamentally different. Thus, even though an adjacent segment is profitable, it doesn't follow that it's a good area for a firm to enter. Perhaps, for example, the firm doesn't have the resources needed to compete against established firms. Similarly, incumbents may enjoy significant cost advantages in performing the activities of their segment. Finally, the unwritten rules of competition in a segment, as well as the nature of strategic interactions, may be fundamentally different from those in a firm's base industry. A company should conduct thorough internal, industry, and competitor analyses before moving vertically into an adjacent segment of its industry value chain.

HORIZONTAL SCOPE

A firm increases its **horizontal scope** in one of two ways:

- By moving from an industry market segment into another, related segment; or

- By moving from one industry into another (unlike vertical-scope expansion, the movement here is into other industries not in the firm's existing value chain of activities).

> **horizontal scope** Extent to which firm participates in related market segments or industries outside its existing value-chain activities.

The degree to which horizontal expansion is desirable depends on the degree to which the new industry is related to a firm's home industry. Industries can be related in a number of different ways. They may, for example, rely on similar types of human capital, engage in similar value-chain activities, or share customers with similar needs. Obviously, the more such factors that are present, the greater the degree of relatedness. When, for example, Coke and Pepsi expanded into the bottled water business, they were able to take advantage of the skill sets that they'd already developed in bottling and distribution. Moreover, because bottled water and soft drinks are substitutes for one another, both appeal to customers with similar demands.

However, when Pepsi expanded into snack foods, it was clearly moving into a business with a lesser degree of relatedness. Although the distribution channels for both businesses are similar (both sell products through grocery stores, convenience stores, delis, and so forth), the technology for producing their products are fundamentally different. In addition, although the two industries sell complementary products—they're often sold at the same time to the same customers—they aren't substitutes.

Cost Savings and Revenue Enhancement Opportunities Why is increased horizontal scope attractive? Primarily because it offers opportunities in two areas:

- The firm can reduce costs by exploiting possible economies of scope.

- The firm can increase revenues through synergies.

Because segments in closely related industries often use similar assets and resources, a firm can frequently achieve cost savings by sharing them among businesses in different segments. The fast food industry, for instance, has many segments—burgers, fried chicken, tacos, pizza, and so on. YUM! Brands Inc., which operates KFC, Pizza Hut, Taco Bell, A&W Restaurants, and Long John Silvers, has embarked on what the company calls a "multibrand" store strategy. Rather than house all of its fast food restaurants in separate outlets, YUM! achieves economies of scope across its portfolio by bundling two outlets in a single facility. The strategy works, in part, because customer purchase decisions in horizontally related industries are often made simultaneously: In other words, two people walking into a bundled fast food outlet may desire different things to eat, but both want fast food, and both are going to eat at the same time. In addition, some of these combinations allow two food services that cater to purchases with different peak hours to share physical resources that would otherwise be largely unused during off-peak hours.

Profit Pools

profit pool   Analytical tool that enables managers to calculate profits at various points along an industry value chain.

One tool managers can use to evaluate adjacent market opportunities (whether vertical, horizontal, or complementary) is the **profit pool**. Beginning with a modified version of the firm and industry value chain, the profit pool can help you incorporate key complementary businesses near the point at which a firm is directly involved in customer transactions. The profit pool helps identify the size of value-chain segments (according to total sales) and the attractiveness of each segment (according to segment-by-segment profitability). Exhibit 7.7 illustrates the application of this tool to the auto industry in Europe and the global music industry.[7] Specifically, notice that sales volume for a segment is indicated visually by its width, while its profitability is shown by its height. As a map of the industry value chain, it reveals the breadth and depth of its alternative profit pools—each of the points along an industry's value chain at which total profits can be calculated.[8] The Western European profit pool is estimated to be approximately $62 billion, based on $885 billion in total revenues. In contrast, Exhibit 7.7 shows the United States' music industry profit pool to be about $10 billion, based on total industry revenues of $46 billion.

Some profit pools, of course, will be deeper (i.e., more profitable) than others. Moreover, depth may vary within a given value-chain segment. In the manufacturing segment of the PC industry, for instance, Dell enjoys much higher profit margins than Gateway. Segment profitability may also vary widely by product and customer group. Note that profit pools aren't stagnant; like industries in general, they change over time. Finally, and perhaps most importantly, the profit pool reminds us that *profit* concentration in an industry rarely occurs in the same place as *revenue* concentration.

Thinking in terms of profit pools also highlights a basic managerial mistake that's often made when developing corporate strategy. Firms often pursue strategies that focus on growth and market share on the assumption that profits automatically follow growth and size. *Profitable* growth, however, requires a clear understanding of an industry's profit pool. A profit-pool map, for example, will reveal the segments in which money is actually being made in an industry. More importantly, it may show where profits *could* be made. Consider, for instance, the U.S. consumer truck-rental business, in which U-Haul, Ryder, Hertz-Penske, and Budget are fierce competitors.[9] U-Haul, though the first entrant and largest player, faced significant disadvantages in the 1990s. Because its fleet was older, its maintenance expenses were considerably higher than those of competitors with newer fleets. U-Haul also charged lower prices than competitors. Lower revenues, coupled with higher expenses, generally result in lower margins. Indeed, U-Haul was barely breaking even on truck rentals. At the same time, however, U-Haul actually outperformed all of its competitors. Why? U-Haul beat its competitors because it went beyond its core business of truck rentals. It seized opportunities in complementary businesses that were relatively untapped, such as moving and storage accessories. By selling boxes, trailers, temporary storage space, tape, and other packing materials that truck renters needed, U-Haul squeezed out 10-percent operating margins in an industry in which the average was less than 3 percent. In How Would *You* Do That? 7.1, we walk you through the steps necessary to calculate the profit pool for a given industry.

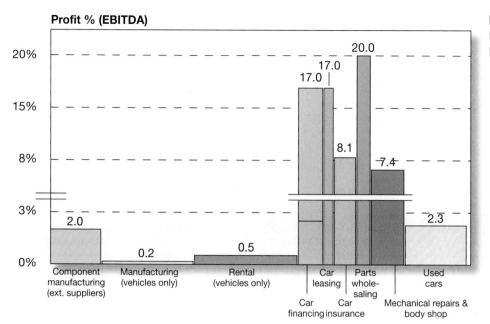

Exhibit 7.7a The European Auto Industry's Profit Pool

Exhibit 7.7b Global Music Industry's Profit Pool

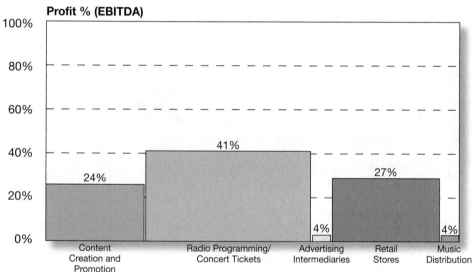

GEOGRAPHIC SCOPE

A firm typically increases **geographic scope** by moving into new geographic arenas without altering its business model. In its early growth period, for instance, a company may simply move into new locations in the same country. More often, however, increased geographic scope has come to mean *internationalization*—entering new markets in other parts of the world.

For a domestic firm whose operations are confined to its home country, the whole globe consists of potential arenas for expansion. Remember, however, that just as different industries can exhibit different degrees of relatedness, so, too, can different geographic markets, even those within the same industry. We can assess relatedness among different national

geographic scope Breadth and diversity of geographic arenas in which a firm operates.

Six Steps to a Profit Pool

The profit pool tool is an easy tool to understand. It also gives you a ready means for thinking about the boundaries of your focal industry where profits come from in a particular industry (or arena, in strategy diamond terms). Your profit pool analysis essentially follows six steps:

1. Define the profit pool in terms of its boundaries and the value-chain activities that are relevant to profit creation now and in the future. Think about the coffee industry, for example. For coffee, what are the key value chain inputs? You could go back as far as the farmers who grow the coffee beans, and even to specific coffee growing geographic arenas or arenas related to the variety or quality of coffee bean. Assuming that coffee growers are one end of the spectrum in this first step, you then want to identify the other end of the spectrum. So for coffee, does your interest in the industry stop at the coffee wholesalers (who sell bulk coffee to institutional and retail buyers), or do you move to institutional and retail buyers like Sysco Foods or Unilever, respectively, or all the way to consumer coffee purveyors like Costa Coffee or Starbucks, which sell ready-to-drink coffee products? Since you are already getting a good sense of what we mean by value chain activities in a given pool, you can see how those activities might vary by how narrowly or

broadly you define the beginning and end-points of the value chain. With this start and end-points in hand, now try to identify some of the intermediate value chain activities. Sticking with coffee, coffee-bean selection and roasting are important value chain activities in the larger coffee profit pool value chain since they determine the ultimate character of the final product.

2. Estimate the size of the profit pool. The size of the profit pool is the cumulative profits of all profit-pool activities for a given arena. One easy starting pointing in this step is to get figures on the total revenues and profits for all players in a given arena—this analysis has you starting at the top of the food chain since you want to know total revenues and profits for the finished product (though with coffee, recall that you could have been interested in wholesale product, product at the institutional or retail level, or the ultimate business to consumer level like a Starbucks coffee shop). In general, it is a good idea to think more broadly than narrowly about the scope of an industries value chain because, as in the case of coffee, if you stopped at wholesaling you would be missing pretty big pieces like institutional and retail sales, and ultimately the arena occupied by players like Starbucks (wouldn't you like to have been the

person who imagined that the coffee profit pool could become what Starbucks has achieved? 0). Taking Starbucks, or the business-to-consumer coffee arena as your profit pool, then in this step you would want to estimate the total sales and profitability of all players in this pool. While these data are hard to come by, market research companies like Mintel (often available through your library) can help you estimate market size and profitability, though typically on a country or regional basis. Investment bank reports, securities exchange filings, and data bases like Compustat will provide profitability and other data at a business unit level.

3. Estimate how profits are distributed among value chain activities. This is not as daunting of a task as it seems, when you remind yourself that every industry's cost-of-goods sold is the reflection of a downstream industry's total revenues and a determinant of that downstream industry's profitability. So where Step 2 has you aggregate revenues and profits for your focal profit pool, Step 3 has you disaggregate revenues and profits among the key value chain activities supporting the target profit pool. Keep in mind that this analysis is at an industry level so, in the case of the ready-to-drink coffee-consumer business, you would still want to

include coffee wholesalers, retailers, and roasters in your analysis (i.e., estimating their industry sales and profitability) even though you know that Starbucks has gone around them, roasts its own coffee, and works directly with coffee growers. Just like a good five-forces + complements industry analysis, your objective in profit pool analysis is to understand profit opportunities in an industry, now and in the future.

4. This is your reality-check step. Stand back and look at the value chain sales and profits across each of the activities and see how they reconcile with those of the focal profit pool. Try to reconcile inconsistencies by collecting additional data or doing further probing of the existing qualitative or quantitative data. Step 5 may give you some insights into why you are having difficulty reconciling the data in each value chain activity with the total revenue and profitability data you have compiled for the profit pool of interest.

5. Graph the profit pool. This fifth step is one reason why profit pool analysis is so powerful—because of the visual imagery it creates for you to explain industry profitability and the distribution and tradeoffs between sales and profitability across segments. The vertical axis on your profit pool grid, just as you see in the examples in Exhibit 7.7, should be industry profitability and the horizontal axis should be total industry revenues. You can play around with these, using percentages instead of absolute values, though the visual impression should be pretty similar across the two variants. The examples in 7.7 show percentages on the vertical access and actual dollars on the horizontal access. Just like a food chain, work from left to right where the first segment you plot on the left hand side is the first segment in the industry profit pool. So with coffee,

this would be the coffee bean growing industry (or different geographic, quality, or other (like organic, free-trade, etc.) segments of the coffee bean growing industry if they are relevant to your objectives. The height of each segment will reflect the segment's profitability, while the width will represent its sales. In the coffee profit pool, given that grocery stores are high volume but low profit businesses, you could imagine that segment of the profit pool to be very low (low profitability relative to other segments in the profit pool) but very wide in terms of sales volume.

6. You have probably learned a lot about the determinants of industry and firm profitability through the first five steps of your profit pool analysis. Though, the sixth and final step is the most interesting and creative. In this step you have the opportunity to do at least two things. First, you can step back and look at the value chain that comprises the profit pool and imagine the business potential were you to integrate some of these activities within a firm, or eliminate them altogether. You learned a bit about such strategies in Chapter 6 (revolutionary strategies), and step 5 of the profit pool tool is a great opportunity to do this. We've already given you the example of Starbucks, and how it bypassed the retail and wholesale channel, integrated roasting to provide distinctive coffee (ironically, they instruct their roasters to burn the beans more than other roasters!). IKEA would be an example of a firm that eliminated the value chain activity of furniture assembly, and actually outsourced it to you and me as consumers. Most recently, the T-shirt design house, ThreadFree, has eliminated fashion designers from its value chain cost structure. Through its web-site, thousands of customers submit T-shirt designs, its web-community picks one as the winner, and as a result 100% of the

new T-shirt design is sold out as quickly as it is produced (the design winner receives a $2000 design award).

Second, in this final step you can strive to identify *complements* and adjacent value chain arenas (sometimes called *adjacencies*) where additional value could be tapped or increased demand created. A traditional example of this is where General Motors has its own financial services arm (which is very profitable), and many car and recreational vehicle companies have found that they can sell more products when they also can provide on-the-spot financing. This is an example of a complementary business that has been integrated into the General Motor's corporate strategy. The European auto industry profit pool, shown in Exhibit 7.7a, shows this incorporation of financial services like insurance and financing into the industry profit pool. Complements like the iPod and SNOCAP (musician to consumer direct sales), are examples of complements that could be added to the music industry example in Exhibit 7.7b.

An adjacent business is somewhat different. The example of U-Haul presented earlier in the chapter is a great example of how U-Haul has exploited adjacencies. It makes much more profit on packaging material than it does on the rental of trucks. The use of adjacencies is not a new phenomenon. For instance, not long after Xerox introduced the photocopier (and actually created that industry), it found that it had a captive audience for copier paper sales, and had greater sales volume and profits on the sale of copy paper than on copiers! You have surely heard the saying that razor companies give away the handles to make money on the replacement razor blades.

markets by examining a number of factors, including laws, customs, cultures, consumer preferences, distances from home markets, common borders, language, socioeconomic development, and many others.

Economies of Scale and Scope Geographic expansion can be motivated by economies of scale or economies of scope. R&D, for example, represents a significant, relatively fixed cost for firms in many industries, and when they move into new regions of a country or global arenas, they often find that they can spread their R&D costs over a larger market. For instance, the marginal cost for a pharmaceutical firm to enter a new geographic market is lower compared to the R&D and clinical trial costs involved in bringing a new drug into the U.S. market. Once the costs of development and entry are covered, entering new geographic markets not only brings in new revenues, but because fixed costs have been spread over the new, larger market, the average cost for all the firm's customers goes down. It should come as no surprise, then, that industries with relatively high R&D expenditures, such as pharmaceuticals and high-tech products, are among the most globalized.

Strategy and the Local Environment Sometimes, firms expanding into new geographic markets find that they must adapt certain components of their strategies to accommodate local environments. In this country, for instance, Dell is famous for the business model that allows it to skip middlemen and go directly to suppliers and customers. In its early years, Dell experimented with a retail distribution strategy but quickly retrenched. As it has expanded into some international markets such as India and China, however, Dell has found that it must, even temporarily, delay the implementation of its direct model, at least for the consumer and small business markets, although it worked well for government and large business buyers. Why? Basically because it needs local intermediaries to help develop both a base of business and acceptable levels of awareness among those particular buyers. Once the market has been penetrated to a sufficient degree, the direct model is implemented and used to reach consumers and small businesses.

Although Dell provides a nice example of adaptation, most global firms tend to approach the subject of corporate strategy from the perspective of their domestic market—such an ap-

Dell has traditionally sold its computers straight to consumers without going through intervening middlemen or retail stores. In Asia, however, this strategy works only with institutional buyers, such as governments, schools, and businesses. As a result, Dell had to change its distribution strategy there.

proach can be problematic. Microsoft is a case in point here. The respective regulatory authorities of the U.S. and the countries of the EU employ very different traditions and models of competition, which in turn means that strategies must vary across these important markets. Had you not been aware of these differences, you might think that Microsoft implemented an ideal resource-based corporate strategy in its diversification into Europe. It bundled its Windows operating system with the Explorer browser and other software to increase customers' perceptions of value and, therefore, willingness to pay. It also used its extensive experience with PC software and operating systems and applications to better penetrate the market for software and operating systems in the server market, where customers are primarily businesses. Finally, Microsoft also tried to lock out competitors by including its Media Player as a standard feature in both its server and home PC operating systems.

The EU took exception to this strategy.[10] The European Commission recently signaled it would keep up the pressure on Microsoft, saying the company's "illegal behavior is still ongoing." It also warned that it remains concerned about Microsoft's "general business model," saying that it "deters innovation and reduces consumer choice in any technologies which Microsoft could conceivably take an interest in and tie with Windows in the future." In addition to a fine of over $600 million, the EU gave Microsoft 90 days to release versions of its Windows operating systems for home PCs and servers without the Windows Media Player and begin providing rivals access to the details of the code underlying its proprietary server systems. This is not the first time such differences in regulatory environments have been ignored or underestimated by global firms. Just a few years earlier, the European Commission's ruling dealt a fatal blow to the all-but-done merger between Honeywell and GE.[11]

Strategies for Entering Attractive New Businesses

So, what new businesses should a firm enter if it is contemplating diversification? We've already mentioned that the business should require the same or related resources and that it should have strategic similarity. But, there are literally thousands of possible businesses that a firm might enter, how else might managers narrow down the search? Certainly, some businesses will be more attractive than others. Recall that Chapter 4 taught you how to analyze the attractiveness of an industry. Among other things, attractive industries tend to benefit from higher levels of profitability. So, a manager might target a high-profit business that requires related resources and that is strategically similar to the firm's core business. However, Chapter 4 should have also taught you that there are reasons that industries have higher average profits; one critical reason is that it likely has strong entry barriers. Consequently, the most attractive markets are generally the hardest to enter. There are three ways to solve this paradox. First, entry barriers can be circumvented by acquiring a company already in the industry. Chapter 10 will address mergers and acquisitions as a vehicle for entering a new market. Second, a firm can enter in a manner that incumbents don't initially take notice of your entry. Third, entry should exploit something that the new entrant can do with a cost advantage over incumbents and other new entrants. We outline three methods for accomplishing this that are based on concepts you have already learned earlier.[12] These methods are not mutually exclusive strategies; they are often used in combination to formulate robust entry moves into attractive industries.

FOCUS ON A NICHE

Recall that in Chapter 5 you learned the concept of generic strategic positions. These were low cost leadership, differentiation, focus cost leadership, and focus differentiation. Entering an attractive industry is difficult to do if making a direct assault on incumbents' strongholds.

One way to enter and not attract lots of attention and retaliatory behavior is to focus the entry on a niche in the market. One type of niche to look for is a segment of the market whose needs are currently underserved. Consider the soft drink market. Coca-Cola and PepsiCo enjoy gross margins of more than 60 percent and return on assets of over 17 percent.[13] Many firms have attempted to enter the industry, but few have succeeded in establishing competitive positions. A successful niche entry to consider is the case of Red Bull. Rather than enter into the heart of the market, Red Bull entered the niche market of energy drinks.

Red Bull markets its nonalcoholic and functional energy drink in more than 100 countries. The nonalcoholic drink contains the amino acid taurine, B-complex vitamins, caffeine, and carbohydrates. Austrian Dietrich Mateschitz discovered the drink while doing business in Thailand. He formed a joint venture with the Thai businessman and adapted the drink for Austrian tastes.

Red Bull entered the United States in 1997 with little fanfare but city by city introduced the product and targeted the young adult market. The drink's popularity grew quickly and eventually captured more than 70 percent of the U.S. market for energy drinks, and rapid growth industry in and of itself. Of course, even though this was a niche market, that kind of growth captured the attention of Coca-Cola and PepsiCo, and many other firms and entrepreneurs. Red Bull's market share has slipped into the 40s, but the market has grown significantly as well, so Red Bull's sales continue to climb.

USING A REVOLUTIONARY STRATEGY

Entering an attractive industry is risky because it will get the attention of incumbents. In our first example, we suggested that entering by targeting a niche would provide some protection because incumbents often ignore niche markets. Likewise, entering with a revolutionary strategy will afford some protection because such a strategy breaks with the convention of the incumbents. Because it is so different from the status quo, incumbents generally are predisposed to think such a strategy is inferior, unwise, or risky. It is only after such a strategy proves successful that incumbents will rally to try to protect their ground. By then, it is often too late.

As you learned in Chapter 6, there are several ways a strategy can be revolutionary. For illustrative purposes, we use reconfiguring the value chain as an example, but successful new-business entry could be accomplished with any revolutionary strategy. One of those strategies was to reconfigure the value chain. Recall the example of Skype. How did Skype enter the telecom services industry with established and well-financed incumbents? It used a completely new value chain. Rather than rely on the existing telecom infrastructure, Skype used Voice-over-Internet-Protocol (VOIP) that allowed their customers to utilize their PCs to place calls, thereby bypassing the entire value chain of incumbents and giving them a totally different (and lower) cost structure. The service was targeted to price sensitive customers, so initially it was able to avoid direct retaliation from incumbents.

The film company Pixar, part of the Walt Disney Company since its acquisition in 2006, provides another example of diversification. You will see value-chain reconfiguration here, but facets of other revolutionary strategies as well. In 1986, Steve Jobs purchased the computer graphics division of Lucasfilm, Ltd. for $10 million and established an independent company named Pixar. With the new animation technologies that it developed and controlled, Pixar began to experiment with film shorts and commercials. The technology allowed Pixar to cast lifelike animal characters without the cost of their care and feeding. While you may not be familiar with Pixar as a technology company, you may have heard about Toy Story—the breakthrough film launched as a joint Disney/Pixar production in 1995. At that time, Toy Story provided the most dramatic glimpse of the promise of this new animation technology for global media market. Pixar is an example of a technology company diversifying into commercial (i.e., advertising) and then consumer animation (i.e., short and long animated feature films). As a result of this value-chain configuration, the core technology of many animated films was drastically changed, to the point that Disney abandoned its traditional animation approach in 2005.

LEVERAGE EXISTING RESOURCES

Successful new entrants use resources they already control, and possibly supplement these with a partner's resources, to leapfrog entry barriers. Consider Wal-Mart's entry into the soft drink business in the early 1990s. What resources Wal-Mart could bring to the table were shelf space and a top-flight distribution network. However, it did not have any capability in formulating soft drinks or bottling them. So, it partnered with Cott Corporation from Canada to develop Sam's Choice. By leveraging its resources with those of Cott, Wal-Mart has been able to capture approximately 5 percent of the soft drink market since its entry into softdrinks.

Recall the opening vignette from Chapter 1 about Under Armour. Under Armour initially entered the performance apparel market and established a loyal customer base. Its reputation for manufacturing high-quality performance apparel, combined with its brand image, were combined to help it enter the football cleat market. Under Armour leveraged these resources and product design to such an extent that they were able to capture 20 percent of the football cleat market share overall, and an amazing 40 percent of the market for cleats priced over $70! But Under Armour didn't enter the football cleat market as an end-game strategy. They view it as a stepping stone to allow entry into the broader athletic footwear market in future years. They used the resources they had to develop an entry strategy for cleats, but they plan to accumulate the resources (e.g., experience, expertise, distribution channels) in this niche area of footware to allow easier entry into the broader market later.

COMBINATION STRATEGIES

You have probably noticed in the examples of the three entry strategies reviewed above that several of the examples actually have elements of two or more of the strategies. For instance, Skype combined its reconfigured value chain with a niche strategy; they specifically targeted price-sensitive customers who would tolerate inferior quality. Wal-Mart's entry into soft drinks was a combination of leveraging their existing resources (e.g., shelf space and distribution network) with a reconfigured value chain; they did not distribute through typical retailers, they make no attempt to secure fountain drink contracts, and they do not stock vending machines except at their own properties.

The key to entering an attractive business is to do so in an indirect way; an entry strategy that does not directly assault the incumbents and immediately threaten their profitability. Pursuing niche markets initially is often ignored by incumbents because they represent customers that the incumbents were previously serving. Reconfiguring the value chain and leveraging existing resources help protect firms entering attractive markets. A reconfigured value chain gives the entrant a cost advantage and leveraging existing resources gives the entrant something to build off of that incumbents and other possible new entrants are likely to lack.

Competitive Advantage and Corporate Strategy

At the business level, competitive advantage reflects the relative position of a firm compared to positions of industry rivals. At the corporate level, it reflects management's success in creating more value from the firm's business units than those units could create as standalone enterprises or subsidiaries. Our goal is to identify the conditions under which the strategy of owning a corporate portfolio of businesses creates value for shareholders.

You are already familiar with the element of arenas in business strategy. Sometimes a firm chooses a corporate strategy of competing in only one arena. However, the corporate strategy of many firms involves operating in more than one arena. Corporate strategy becomes more complicated if the competitive or operational characteristics of those arenas differ in some way, whether subtly or substantially. Ultimately, it is the combination of arenas, resources (i.e., VRINE), and implementation that determines whether the corporate strategy leads to competitive advantage.

ARENAS

 Arenas

Theoretically, a firm can compete in any combination of discrete business arenas. In practice, of course, firms rarely enter arenas randomly but rather select those that are logically connected to the arenas in which they already participate. ◆ The key to logical connection is *relatedness*. Businesses can be related along several different dimensions, including similarity in markets, use of identical resources, and reliance on comparable dominant logic.

Resources provide the basis for corporate competitive advantage. The nature of corporate resources varies along a continuum, and whether the resources are specialized or general dictates the limits of a firm's scope, the manner of organizational control and coordination, and the effectiveness of corporate headquarters. Although most firms maintain some degree of relatedness among the various businesses in which they participate, some combinations require greater relatedness than others. Finally, it's not always easy to determine the dimensions along which corporate businesses are related.

Some conglomerates are actually portfolios of strategic business units within which several related businesses are combined for management purposes. GE, for instance, participates in such far-flung enterprises as jet engines, elevators, light bulbs, appliances, and financial services. Each of these businesses, however, is located in a business unit with conceptually similar units.

RESOURCES

As we saw in Chapter 3, resources and capabilities are tangible or intangible, and their usefulness in creating a competitive advantage depends on five factors: (1) how valuable they are, (2) whether they're rare in the industry, (3) whether they're costly to imitate, (4) the availability of substitutes, and (5) whether the firm has complementary capabilities to exploit them. At this point, we need to remember that these factors apply to the usefulness of resources in creating competitive advantage at the *business* level. At the corporate level in the VRINE framework (e.g., valuable, rare, inimitable, nonsubstitutable, exploitable), they must be supplemented by an additional factor: namely, how *specialized* or *general* a firm's resources are.

specialized resources
Resource with a narrow range of applicability.

Specialized Resources
Specialized resources have a narrow range of applicability. Knowledge about fiber-optics, for example, is fairly specialized, whereas managerial know-how and skill are more general in nature. Granted, fiber-optics has many uses in multiple contexts (such as telecommunications, electronics, routing and switching equipment), but its utility is more limited than that of a general resource such as general managerial skill.

general resources Resource that can be exploited across a wide range of activities.

General Resources
General resources can be exploited across a wide range of activities. For instance, expertise in efficient manufacturing and mass-marketing techniques can be exploited in any number of contexts. In fact, many companies have created significant shareholder value by leveraging these general resources across different businesses engaged in a variety of industries. General resources aren't confined to narrow applications, and the extent of resource specialization affects both a firm's scope and its organizational structure.

IMPLEMENTATION

As explained in Chapters 1 and 2 and will reaffirm in 11, *implementation levers* include organizational structure, systems and processes, and people and rewards. Strategic leaders use these levers to implement strategies. The success with which diversified firms are managed in accord with key organizational features has a significant effect on the level of value that can be created through their portfolios. Implementation levers that are critical for corporate strategy vary from firm to firm, but some of the more important levers to achieve successful diversification include knowledge-transfer mechanisms, coordination mechanisms, rewards, and corporate oversight.

Knowledge transfer enables a diversified firm to apply superior performance results observed in one organizational business unit to other units that are not performing as well. In practice, knowledge transfer is difficult because it may not be entirely clear what is causing the superior performance in the high-performing unit. Three mechanisms facilitate knowledge transfer. First, just the knowledge that superior results are being achieved in another business unit can be used to reset performance expectations for future performance in other units. In this case, no real knowledge of actual practices is transferred, but the superior performance is used to create stretch goals that motivate learning in other units. Second, underperforming units can study the operational practices of high-performing business units to determine the source of superior performance. Finally, knowledge transfer is perhaps best facilitated when members of lower-performing business units simply seek advice from the higher-performing units. It is often the case that high-performing business units have explicit routines and practices that can be detailed by key employees in those units.[14]

Coordination mechanisms are the management systems and processes that facilitate intrafirm activity. Coordination depends on a variety of structural mechanisms, including reporting relationships, informal meetings and exchanges, and detailed policies and procedures for such activities as intrafirm transfer pricing. Greater relatedness of businesses within a firm requires more intense coordination across business units. Why? Because resources in highly related diversified firms are often shared across business units. Illustratively, more cross-business coordination is needed at 3M than at GE. For instance, adhesive technology is used in multiple divisions in 3M, and this knowledge sharing requires coordination. Alternatively, knowledge transfer or resource sharing (other than cash) does not occur between GE's jet engine and consumer finance divisions. Consequently, 3M can generate more revenue-enhancement synergy between related units than GE can generate between unrelated businesses, but to reap these possible benefits requires that energy and resources be devoted to coordination efforts.

Successful diversification may require adjustments in how managers are compensated and rewarded. Generally speaking, a firm with a broad (highly diversified) portfolio should reward managers differently than a focused or related diversified firm.[15] Why? In a firm with a broad scope, division-level managers do not share resources and cooperate to implement their strategies. Consequently, it is more effective to reward managers for the performance of their divisions than to reward (and punish) them for the performance of divisions that they have no control of or influence over. Conversely, in a related diversified firm, managers of different divisions are generally required to share resources and cooperate to implement their strategies. As a result, it is more effective to reward managers for the firm's collective performance than to focus all rewards on division-level performance. For instance, when division-level profits drive bonuses, managers have little incentive to help other divisions.

When corporate-level management grows unwieldy, it can be a drag on corporate earnings. What factors should determine the size and organization of corporate-level management? Basically, two factors govern this decision: the firm's resources and the scope of its involvement in disparate arenas. When a firm's portfolio contains numerous unrelated units that aren't significantly interdependent, it doesn't need heavy corporate-level oversight;

there's not much that corporate-level management can do to add value on a day-to-day basis (a good example is investor Warren Buffet's Berkshire Hathaway Inc.). By contrast, when a firm's portfolio consists of highly interdependent businesses, more corporate-level control is needed to facilitate the sharing of resources and to oversee interbusiness transactions (e.g., S. C. Johnson, whose businesses include insect control, home cleaning, and plastic products).

Now that we've identified the ingredients of a good corporate strategy, we need to remind ourselves that it's the alignment of these ingredients in support of a firm's mission and vision that makes it possible for its managers to implement the firm's corporate strategy and create competitive advantage at the corporate level. Indeed, the configuration of these elements will determine whether a firm achieves corporate-level competitive advantage.

Corporate Strategy in Stable and Dynamic Contexts

By this point, you probably have a strong suspicion that corporate strategy is developed according to the relative dynamism of the context in which an organization operates. You are, of course, correct, and in this section we'll see how corporate strategy is designed to take dynamic context into account. Moreover, because alliances and acquisitions are vehicles for both business and corporate strategy, we'll elaborate on this theme in subsequent chapters as well. We'll see, for example, that, depending on whether a firm's context is stable or dynamic, different strategy vehicles are likely to play different roles. In particular, alliances and acquisitions have different implications for the allocation of a firm's resources and capabilities. We'll show that because certain issues arise in both stable and dynamic contexts, differences are often matters of emphasis. At the same time, however, we'll stress the point that even if the *content* of strategy is similar in both stable and dynamic contexts, the dynamism of the context will still have an effect on its *implementation*.

CORPORATE STRATEGY IN STABLE CONTEXTS

Many of the traditional notions of the relationship between diversification and corporate strategy are based on analyses of companies operating in relatively stable contexts. As we've seen, historically a firm may have diversified into a high-growth industry because growth prospects in its current industry were unattractive. That's why Kansas City Southern (KCS), a railroad, got into financial services in the late 1960s and soon owned almost 90 percent of the Janus Group of mutual funds. But recall, too, our observation that this form of unrelated diversification often fails. Indeed, due to an obvious lack of synergy between the rail industry and mutual funds—plus an increasing level of management conflict between its railroad and mutual-fund divisions—KCS divested Janus in 1999 (a move widely approved by the market).[16]

Stable Arenas and Formal Structures   As we've seen, creating synergies among its businesses is an important part of a corporation's strategy. Synergies can come from shared know-how, coordination of business-unit strategies, shared tangible resources, vertical integration, and pooled negotiating power.[17] In relatively stable environments, such synergies are typically conceived as functions of static business-unit arenas and the formal structural links among them. Corporate-strategy objectives focus primarily on synergies as means of achieving economies of scope and scale. In fact, corporate strategy explicitly defines the form and extent of the coordination and collaboration among business units. Thus, the managers of individual units are often compensated according to a combination of division- and corporate-level performance. Generally speaking, the overarching objective of corporate strategy in a stable environment is ensuring that the firm operates as a tightly interwoven whole.

The best example of such strategy in action is probably the related diversified firm. Masco Corporation, a multibillion-dollar manufacturer and distributor of plumbing fixtures and other home building and home repair supplies, is just such a firm. Starting with Delta Faucets in the early 1960s, Masco built a diversified portfolio of manufacturing businesses by acquiring well-run firms in a variety of industries. Today, Masco is one of the leading makers of home improvement and home building products and a powerhouse in the do-it-yourself industry dominated by such retail chains as Home Depot and Travis Perkins. We've summarized the breadth of Masco's holdings in Exhibit 7.8. Operating a tightly knit set of businesses is an effective corporate strategy for Masco. Why? Primarily because each business alone is unattractive, and by combining them under one corporate roof, Masco gives them greater selling and merchandising power in dealing with aggressive customers such as Home Depot. In addition, because its businesses are sufficiently related, Masco can leverage manufacturing, design, marketing, distribution, and merchandizing expertise across them.

CORPORATE STRATEGY IN DYNAMIC CONTEXTS

Masco's strategy would be problematic for firms competing in more dynamic contexts. Adaptec Inc., for instance, was once an integrated maker of both computer hardware and software. The strategy was logical because the firm could extract synergies from operations in such complementary businesses. Adaptec soon discovered, however, that rapid changes in technologies and advances by competitors were weakening its ability to maneuver well in both areas. In 1999, therefore, Adaptec spun off its software side as Roxio through an IPO.

Even a seemingly focused business like Palm, which makes PDAs, can find it difficult to perform well in both hardware (Palm Pilot PDAs) and software (the Palm operating system), accordingly, Palm actually split into two separate companies. Ironically, as late as 2000, 3Com, then a supplier of computer, communications, and compatibility (network-interfacing) products, spun off Palm as a separate business for similar reasons.[18] In turn, Palm used the proceeds from its own IPO to strengthen its position in the market for handheld devices and operating systems. 3Com now concentrates on its core networking business, along with research and development in emerging technologies.

Diversification in Dynamic Contexts
Despite the examples of Adaptec and 3Com, both of which have used divestitures to increase corporate focus, diversification can be a viable strategy in dynamic contexts. Bear in mind, however, that firms seeking to diversify in dynamic contexts usually need strong resources and capabilities in the areas of learning, knowledge transfer, and rapid responsiveness. If corporate ownership hinders nimbleness and response time in a dynamic environment, it's more likely to be an encumbrance than an advantage. It's hard enough to manage competitively in dynamic contexts without having to struggle under excess layers of corporate hierarchy.

Coevolution
The ebbs and flows of firms' corporate strategies in dynamic contexts are best described as a web of shifting linkages among evolving businesses—a process that some researchers call **coevolution**.[19] Borrowed from biology, the term *coevolution* describes successive changes among two or more ecologically interdependent species that adapt not only to their environment but also to each other. Business units coevolve when senior managers do not target specific synergies across business units but rather allow business-unit managers to determine which linkages do and don't work. As business-unit managers search for fresh opportunities for synergies and abandon deteriorating linkages, internal relationships tend to shift. As in the organic world, coevolution can result in competitive interdependence, with one unit eventually absorbing another or rendering it unnecessary. Coevolution means that cross-business synergies are usually temporary, and managers must learn to deal with the fundamental tension that results from the agility afforded by fewer linkages and the efficiency afforded by more. Finally, research suggests that in successful coevolving companies, managers, rather than trying to control, or even predict, cross-business-unit synergies, simply let them emerge in the "natural" course of corporate operations.[20]

coevolution Process by which diversification causes two or more interdependent businesses to adapt not only to their environment, but to each other.

Exhibit 7.8 Masco: A Holding Company at a Glance

United States	International
Cabinet and Related Products	
d-Scan Inc.	AlmaKüchen, Germany
Diversified Cabinet Distributors	Alvic, Spain
KraftMaid	Aran Group, Italy
Merillat	Berglen Group, UK
Mill's Pride	Grumal, Spain
Texwood Industries	Moores Group Ltd., UK
Zenith	Tvilum-Scanbirk, Denmark
	Xey, Spain
Plumbing Products	
Aqua Glass	A & J Gummers, UK
Brass Craft	Breuer, Germany
Brasstech	Bristan Ltd., UK
Delta Faucet	Damixa, Denmark
H&H Tube	Glass Indromassaggio SpA, Italy
Mirolin	Hansgrohe AG, Germany
Peerless Faucet	Heritage, UK
Plumb Shop	Hüppe, Germany
Watkins Manufacturing	NewTeam Limited, UK
	Rubinetterie Mariani, Italy
	S.T.S.R., Italy
Decorative Architectural Products	
Behr	Avocet, UK
Franklin Brass (Bath Unlimited)	SKS Group, Germany
GAMCO (Bath Unlimited)	
Ginger	
Liberty Hardware	
Masterchem	
Melard (Bath Unlimited)	
Vapor Technologies	
Specialty Products	
Arrow Fastener	Alfred Reinecke, Germany
Cobra	Brugman, Holland
Computerized Security Systems (CSS)	Cambrian Windows Ltd., UK
Faucet Queens	Duraflex Ltd., UK
Gamco/Morgantown Products	Gebhardt, Germany
MediaLab	Griffin Windows, UK
Milgard Manufacturing	Jung Pumpen, Germany
PowerShot Tool Company	Missel, Germany
	Premier Manufacturing Ltd., UK
	Superia Radiatoren, Belgium
	Vasco, Belgium

Ironically, of course, coevolution means that units owned by the same corporation are potentially both collaborators and competitors. This paradoxical relationship is perhaps easiest to detect when a firm operates both traditional and e-business units. It's less obvious when it arises because new technologies have emerged to threaten established processes, but the costs of allowing a competitor—even one with which you share a corporate umbrella—to gain a technological advantage are often steep. In dynamic contexts, corporate strategy usually takes the form of temporary networks among businesses, and if strategic alliances are added into the mix, the network may include companies that the corporation doesn't own as well as those it does.

Divestitures and corporate spinoffs can be effective strategic vehicles for dealing with the sort of disruptive innovations that we discussed in Chapters 4 and 6, and they also figure frequently in stories of corporate coevolution.[21] Because disruptive technologies compete with established technologies, it may not be enough to simply reorganize them as new units under the same corporate umbrella. The resulting problems from retaining ownership of the disruptive part of the business range from the creation of messy internal politics to simply starving the new business of resources so that it eventually fails. We've summarized the key differences between corporate strategies in stable and dynamic contexts in Exhibit 7.9. The box entitled "How Would *You* Do That? 7.2," demonstrates how you might evaluate dynamic corporate strategy at Disney.

 Vehicles

Stable Contexts	Dynamic Contexts
Top management team emphasizes collaboration among the businesses and the form of that collaboration.	Top management team emphasizes the creation of a collaborative context that is rich in terms of content and linkages.
Collaboration is solidified through stable structural arrangement among wholly-owned businesses.	Collaboration is fluid, with networks being created, changed, and disassembled between combinations of owned and alliance businesses.
Key objectives are the pursuit of economies of scale and scope.	Key objectives are growth, maneuverability, and economies of scope.
The business units' roles are to execute their given strategies.	The business units' roles are to execute their strategies and seek new collaborative opportunities.
Business units' incentives combine business with corporate-level rewards to promote cooperation.	Business units' incentives emphasize business-level rewards to promote aggressive execution and collaborative-search objectives.
Balanced-scorecard objectives emphasize performance against budget and in comparison to within-firm peer unit.	Balanced-scorecard objectives gauge performance relative to competitors in terms of growth, market share, and profitability.

Exhibit 7.9 Comparison of Corporate Strategies in Stable and Dynamic Contexts

Evaluating Diversification at Disney

To evaluate Disney's corporate strategy, we can use an adapted portfolio analysis. You learned about the problems with the traditional use of portfolio analysis, but it is still widely used in the modified form we present in this example. Disney's vision is to be the industry leader in providing creative entertainment experiences. The arenas in which Disney participates are focused on family entertainment and include media networks (41 percent), theme parks and resorts (28 percent), studio entertainment (24 percent), and consumer products (7 percent). A few of the fundamental resources that Disney shares across these arenas are the Disney name and legacy, the library of films and Disney's cast of animated and real-life characters, capabilities in the creation and management of world-class entertainment, and service-management expertise (this is obviously an abbreviated list of resources and capabilities).

Implementation is the glue holding these arenas and resources together. Although the company appears to be diversified into related arenas, each business is treated as a profit center, and managers are compensated according to business-unit performance. To overcome the lack of cross-division cooperation that this might motivate, Disney has historically relied on special "synergy management" positions. Imagine the powerful scope economies that are created when Disney launches a hit character and then leverages the

fictional personality through every channel, from toy licensing to Disney Radio. Just as important, however, is the skill with which Disney pulls the right implementation levers to make this synergistic dynamo work.

We want to evaluate how well Disney is doing with its corporate strategy. To do so, we will use a portfolio analysis tool that incorporates VRINE and other key strategy concepts that you have already learned about. We want to map Disney's business units along four dimensions: the size of the divisions, the VRINE characteristics of the division, the industry's five forces score, and the profitability of the divisions relative to competitors in these businesses. This 4-D exercise will allow us to visualize how well Disney is performing, given the industry contexts of each business and the resources and capabilities possessed by the divisions.

In Exhibit 7.10, we have tabulated the data for Disney's divisions using the tools you have learned earlier. For the five forces analysis, we rank each industry in which Disney participates using the tool that you learned in "How Would *You* Do That? 4.1" in Chapter 4.

For the VRINE analysis, we gave each division a score of 1 to 5, depending on whether its resources satisfy the VRINE requirements (e.g., 1 point given if the resources are valuable; 2 points if they are valuable and rare; 3 points if they are valuable, rare, and difficult to imitate; 4 points if they are valuable, rare, difficult to

imitate, and non-substitutable; and 5 points if they meet the first four requirements and the firm is able to exploit the resources. We also report the size of each division, the business unit profit margin, the weighted average profit margin for other firms in those industries, and the industry adjusted performance for each of Disney's business units (e.g., business unit profit margin minus the weighted average industry profit margin).

We can use this data to create a bubble chart in an Excel worksheet, which will make the data easier to interpret and present to managers. Bubble charts can plot three values. We use the VRINE scores for the X axis (i.e., the horizontal axis), the five forces score for the Y axis (i.e., the vertical axis), and the business unit size for the size of the bubble. After the chart is plotted, we then add the profit margin for each division using the text box feature. Exhibit 7.11 illustrates what we have found.

What do we learn from this type of portfolio analysis? Quite simply, it allows us to see whether Disney is creating synergy across its business units. Recall that synergy either results in economies of scope (which should lead to lower costs than competitors) or revenue enhancement, which should give us greater revenue relative to costs compared to competitors. Thus, if we've truly created synergy we should perform better than average. Portfolio analysis also helps us analyze the performance of the portfolio as a whole. For instance, we can see how business

Exhibit 7.10   Comparison Portfolio Data for Disney

	Business Unit VRINE Score	Strength of Five Force Score	Business Unit Size ($ millions)	Business Unit Profit Margin	Industry Weighted Average Profit Margin	Industry Adjusted Business Unit Profit Margin
Parks and Resorts	5	3	9023	13%	19%	−5.88%
Media Networks	2	2	13207	21%	10%	10.81%
Studio Entertainment	2	4	7587	?	10%	−7.28%
Consumer Products	3	2	2215	23%	30%	−6.75%

units perform relative to each other, which helps managers determine where they need to focus their attention.

So, how is Disney doing? Not too well, actually. Only Media Networks is performing above industry averages. The industry was scored as rather favorable (i.e., a low score for the level of the five forces). However, this will help all firms perform well in the industry, not just Disney. Perhaps Media Networks is best exploiting the synergies of all the divisions, allowing it to perform better than its competitors. The other divisions are all under-performing their competitors.

We need to emphasize that we are using industry-adjusted performance to evaluate the portfolio. Why? A firm (or business unit) might perform at what appears to be a healthy clip. For instance, the consumer product division of Disney achieves 23 percent profit margins, which are among the highest in the company. However, Disney's competitors in consumer products average more than 30 percent. So, actually, it would be a mistake to conclude that Disney is doing well in that division.

Exhibit 7.11   Disney Portfolio

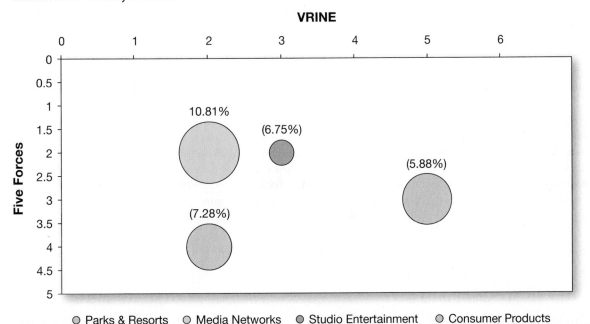

○ Parks & Resorts   ○ Media Networks   ○ Studio Entertainment   ○ Consumer Products

Summary of Challenges

1. *Define* corporate strategy. Corporate strategy encompasses issues related to decisions about entering and exiting businesses. A fundamental part of corporate strategy is the decision about what business *arenas* to enter and exit. However, corporate strategy also encompasses the overall management of the multibusiness enterprise, such as corporate headquarters' efforts to orchestrate the cross-business-unit synergies. Corporate strategy deals with the logic for owning more than one business within a firm.

2. *Understand the roles of economies of scope and revenue-enhancement synergy in corporate strategy.* Expanding the scope of the firm, whether vertically, horizontally, or geographically, does not necessarily create value. Value is created by either lowering costs or increasing revenues through diversification. This can take place when economies of scope result from diversification, such as when two businesses are able to share the same resources. Revenue-enhancement synergies can also create value. For synergies to be present because of joint ownership, the combined revenues of two distinct businesses must be greater when owned jointly than when operated independently. These economic gains are more likely when there is resource similarity between businesses and when the dominant logics necessary to manage the businesses are similar.

3. *Identify the different types of diversification.* Firms have several options when expanding the scope of their operations beyond the original business definition. In this chapter, we discussed the concept of diversification along three trajectories of new business arenas: vertical, horizontal, and geographic (global). Vertical scope is ownership of business activities along the firm's vertical value chain. Horizontal scope, typically called diversification, is increased by owning businesses in different industry segments or different industries entirely. Geographic scope entails moving into new geographic areas, typically new countries.

4. *Explain how companies can be successfully enter industries when those industries have the greatest barriers to entry.* In the evolution of firms over time, most decide to expand into new businesses. The industries that attract the most attempts for new entry are industries that are more profitable on average than others. However, entry barriers make it difficult for firms to enter these industries, as evidenced by the fact that most new entrants to such industries earn profits far below the average of the industry, and even below what entrants to unattractive industries earn. To successfully enter an attractive industry a firm needs to orchestrate an indirect assault, not attack the incumbents in their strongholds, such as by entering in a niche segment of the industry. In addition, successful entrants leverage their existing resources and enter with a fundamentally different value chain than incumbents.

5. *Describe the relationship between corporate strategy and competitive advantage.* Competitive advantage at the corporate level is a function of the fit among arenas, resources, and organizational systems, structures, and processes. When these are connected in a coherent fashion, the corporation is more likely to achieve its long-term objectives. When resources are specialized, the firm will likely find greater value creation opportunities in a narrow scope of business arenas. Conversely, general resources can be applied across a greater spectrum of businesses. Firms with a broad scope of business activities have different demands for organization structure, systems, and processes than firms that are narrowly focused on a specific set of business arenas.

6. *Explain the differences between corporate strategy in stable and dynamic contexts.* In relatively stable environments, synergies are typically achieved through static definitions of the business-unit arenas and formal structural links among them. Corporate strategy objectives are aimed primarily at using synergies to achieve economies of scope and scale and, in fact, the strategy explicitly defines the form and extent of business units' coordination and collaboration. Firms in dynamic contexts must usually have strong resources and capabilities in the areas of learning, knowledge transfer, and rapid responsiveness for diversification to yield benefits. Otherwise, the nimbleness and responsiveness required of business units in dynamic contexts is dampened as a consequence of corporate ownerships being more of an encumbrance than an advantage. In dynamic environments, allowing managers of business units to pursue a pattern of synergistic relationships that mimics biological coevolution is generally more advantageous than corporate-forced synergistic relationships.

Review Questions

1. How does corporate strategy differ from business strategy?

2. How has the practice of corporate strategy evolved over time?

3. What is a conglomerate?

4. How can managers decide whether they should diversify into a new business?

5. What are the types of diversification and how is value created by each type?

6. What is the difference between economies of scope and synergies?

7. What is the relationship between diversification and firm performance?

8. What factors tend to limit the attractiveness of diversification?

9. How does a dynamic industry context affect the possible benefits of diversification?

Experiential Activities

Group Exercises

1. Choose two firms that are well-known to your group members—perhaps firms that you've done case analyses on in the past. For each of these firms, identify their vertical, horizontal, and geographic scope. Having done that, evaluate the resources that are necessary for each business arena for the firms. How similar are the resource requirements? Identify the dominant logic in each of their main lines of business (if you picked a very diversified firm, just choose the largest two or three business segments). How similar are they across the business divisions?

2. Try to apply the profit pool tool to another industry. Where would you turn for data to do this? How "friendly" is that data for the purposes of using this tool? If you are having trouble being precise, make informed estimates for what you are missing. You will likely find some profit pools that are deeper than others. Why are there big differences between segments? Which firms in the value chain are best able to enter these attractive segments?

Ethical Debates

1. Textbook publishers face growing competition on numerous fronts, including new models of textbook delivery. One such model provides students with online textbook content for "free," on the condition that students provide personal information about themselves to vendors like credit card, student loan, and cell phone companies. For any publisher that is considering diversification into this new media space, what might be some of the ethical issues?

2. You can imagine that firms in the alcohol, tobacco, or firearms businesses may feel a need to diversify into less scrutinized or regulated businesses. How might ethical issues related to these core businesses affect their ability to enter, or costs of entry, into new businesses? How might these ethical issues affect their ability to exit, or costs of exiting, their traditional businesses?

How Would
YOU DO THAT?

1. The box entitled "How Would *You* Do That? 7.1" helps you see how a profit pool model is developed for a particular industry or geographic or product arena. You are given Starbucks and ready-to-drink coffee market as an example, but never shown a profit pool diagram for that industry. Using the resources you have available, try to map out the basic segment characteristics of this arena for the United States. Start with the narrow definition of the coffee business provided in the box. Finally, try to identify the complements or adjacencies that a company like Starbucks could exploit. Do you see new growth opportunities for Starbucks using all the steps of the profit pool tool?

2. "How Would *You* Do That? 7.2" applies a portfolio evaluation tool to Disney. Internally, Disney executives view one of their dynamic capabilities as that of being the best at creating world-class entertainment within financial constraints. What are your thoughts on this view? As you think about Disney and what you view as its resources and capabilities, and the insights you gain from evaluating Disney's portfolio of businesses, what arenas should it consider for future diversification or divestiture moves?

Go on to see How Would You Do That at www.prenhall.com/ carpenter&sanders

Endnotes

1. Corporate descriptions were compiled based on corporate histories on corporate Web sites (www.ge.com, www.3m.com, www.mityinc.com); business descriptions were compiled based on information available at www.hoovers.com (accessed July 15, 2005 and May 5, 2007); G. Colvin, "Q & A: On the Hot Seat," *Fortune*, November 27, 2006; "GE Reports Strong Fourth-Quarter and Full-Year Results for 2006," *Business Wire*, January 19, 2007; A. Fisher, "America's Most Admired Companies," *Fortune*, March 19, 2007, pp. 88–94; *MITY Enterprises Annual Report*, 2006; M. Moylan, "Whither 3M?" *Minnesota Public Radio*, February 28, 2007; "Economic Management," http://solutions.3m.com/wps/portal/3M/en_ US/global/sustainability/s/governance-systems/management-systems/ economic-management/ (accessed on May 4, 2007).

2. See especially C. K. Prahalad and G. Hamel, "The Core Competence of the Corporation," *Harvard Business Review* May–June (1990), 79–91; K. P. Coyne, S. Hall, J. D. Clifford, and P. Gorman, "Do You Really Have a Core Competency," *McKinsey Quarterly* 1 (1997), 40–54.

3. A. Chandler, *Strategy and Structure: Chapters in the History of the American Industrial Enterprise* (Boston: MIT Press, 1962).

4. G. F. Davis and S. K. Stout, "Organization Theory and the Market for Corporate Control: A Dynamic Analysis of Characteristics of Large Takeover Targets: 1980–1990," *Administrative Science Quarterly* 37 (1992), 605–633; G. F. Davis, K. A. Diekman, and C. H. Tinsley, "The Decline and Fall of the Conglomerate Firm in the 1980s: A Study in the Deinstitutionalization of an Organization Form," *American Sociological Review* 59 (1994), 547–570.

5. S. Wetlaufer, "Common Sense and Conflict: An Interview with Disney's Michael Eisner," *Harvard Business Review* 78:1 (2000), 44–48. See also K. Eisenhardt and C. Galunic, "Coevolving: At Last a Way to Make Synergies Work," *Harvard Business Review* (2000), 91–101.

6. A. D. Henderson and J. W. Fredrickson, "Information Processing Demands as a Determinant of CEO Compensation," *Academy of Management Journal* 39 (1996), 575–590; W. G. Sanders and M. A. Carpenter, "Internationalization and Firm Governance: The Roles of CEO Compensation,

Top-Team Composition, and Board Structure," *Academy of Management Journal* 41 (1998), 158–178.

7. The concept of profit pools has been around for decades but this particular tool is adapted from O. Gadiesh and J. L. Gilbert, "Profit Pools: A Fresh Look at Strategy." *Harvard Business Review* 76:3 (1998), 139–147.

8. O. Gadiesh and J. L. Gilbert, "Profit Pools: A Fresh Look at Strategy," *Harvard Business Review* 76:3 (1998), 139–148.

9. For more details on this example and other examples, see Gadiesh and Gilbert, "Profit Pools."

10. J. Kanter, D. Clark, and J. R. Wilke, "EU Imposes Sanctions on Microsoft— Fine, Disclosure Penalties Aim to Undercut Dominance; Continued Pressure Signaled," *Wall Street Journal*, March 25, 2004, A2; M. Wingfield, "DOJ Calls EC's Record Fine of Microsoft 'Unfortunate,'" *Dow Jones Newswires*, March 25, 2004; B. Mitchener and J. Kanter, "Monti's Initiatives on Commerce Leave an Enduring Mark," *Wall Street Journal*, March 25, 2004, A2.

11. Y. Akbar, "Grabbing Victory from the Jaws of Defeat: Can the GE-Honeywell Merger Force International Competition Policy Cooperation?" *World Competition* 25:4 (2002), 26–31.

12. The ideas in this section draw heavily from the work of Bryce and Dyer. D. J. Bryce and J. H. Dyer, 2007. Strategies to Crack Well-Guarded Markets. *Harvard Business Review* 85(5): 84–92.

13. Based on the companies' 10K filings for 2006. The averages over the past decade are consistent with these figures.

14. G. Szulanski, R. Cappetta, and R. J. Jensen, "When and How Trustworthiness Matters: Knowledge Transfer and the Moderating Effect of Causal Ambiguity," *Organization Science* 15 (2004), 600–613.

15. C. W. L. Hill, M. A. Hitt, and R. E. Hoskisson, "Cooperative versus Competitive Structures in Related and Unrelated Diversified Firms," *Organization Science* 3 (1992), 501–521.

16. A. Stone, "Can Kansas City Southern Keep Its Janus Spin-Off on Track?" *Business Week*, August 31, 1999, 27.

17. M. Goold and A. Campbell, "Desperately Seeking Synergy," *Harvard Business Review* 76:5 (1998), 131–143.

18. L. Bransten and S. Thurm, "For Palm Computers, an IPO and Flashy Rival," *Wall Street Journal*, September 14, 1999, B1.

19. Eisenhardt and Galunic, "Coevolving"; S. Brown and K. Eisenhardt, *Competing on the Edge* (Boston: Harvard Business School Press, 1998).

20. Eisenhardt and Galunic, "Coevolving"; Brown and Eisenhardt, *Competing on the Edge.*

21. C. Christensen, *The Innovator's Dilemma* (New York: Harper Collins, 1997).

8 Looking at International Strategies

In This Chapter We Challenge You To >>>

1. Define *international strategy* and identify its implications for the strategy diamond.

2. Understand why a firm would want to expand internationally and explain the relationship between international strategy and competitive advantage.

3. Use the CAGE framework to identify desirable international arenas.

4. Describe different vehicles for international expansion.

5. Apply different international strategy configurations.

6. Outline the international strategy implications of the static and dynamic perspectives.

Dell *goes* *to* China

"*T*oday there are one billion people on-line worldwide, and many of the world's second billion users are right here in China," said Michael Dell, chairman and chief executive of Dell Inc. "We intend to earn their confidence and their business." Mr. Dell was speaking in Shanghai in 2007. His company was the world's second-biggest PC maker and the third largest in China. The company had come a long way since 1999, when Mr. Dell first put plans for the company's expansion into China in motion.

In 1999, Dell had a negligible presence in many regions of the world, most notably China, where it ranked a distant seventh in PC sales. This lagging position bothered Dell executives because computer industry analysts were predicting that by 2002, China would become the world's second-largest PC market.

Consequently, in 1999 Dell set the ambitious goal of achieving 10 percent of its global PC sales from China by 2002, which would amount to nearly 50 percent of PC sales for the entire Asian region.

"Faster sales growth in China could really give Dell a boost because of how big the market is and how much potential it has," said William Bao Bean, an analyst with Deutsche Securities in Hong Kong. According to Dell, only about seven in 100 people own PCs in China. About 25 million PCs were sold in China in 2006. What's more, China's economy grew 10.7 percent in 2006, the fastest rate in more than a decade. Increasing wealth is making electronic goods like computers more affordable to a larger section of the population. "Smaller cities and towns are really where the growth is in China because incomes are rising and people are shopping for their first computers," Bean added.

Dell's overall approach in China is to stay flexible. Its direct-selling model works well with commercial buyers. But to reach first-time computer consumers, the company is opening physical stores—called "experience stores"—in Nanjing, Chongqing, and Tianjin. The reason, as Bryan Ma, a research director at International Data Corp., explained, is that "Consumers are accustomed to buying things with cash, touching and feeling a product in a store and getting instant gratification, rather than calling into a call center or placing an order on-line and waiting a few days for the machine to arrive." Dell China says that its purpose for opening the stores is to have Chinese consumers able to get in touch with Dell's products and enjoy the unique advantages of these products. On August 4, 2006, Dell opened its first product experience store in China in Chongqing. Opening an experience store may be a surprising move for the king of direct-sell, but Michael Dell understands the importance of flexibility: "The thing I've been saying internally is the direct model is not a religion. It's a great strategy, [and it] works well; there are things we can do with it. But that's not the only thing we can do as a company."

Michael Dell is optimistic about Dell's future in China: "We have a lot of opportunity" in the consumer market, he says, "You'll see a lot more products" like the ones he unveiled in March 2007.

For many companies, China is attractive simply due to its size, but it is also a competitive environment fraught with many hazards—and it can turn potential profits into a cash-flow black hole. Sourcing components and products from China has proven successful for many global firms, although some companies such as Mattel have faced serious quality and safety problems. The Chinese consumer market appears to be an entirely different matter. By 1999, for example, Motorola and Kodak had already sunk many millions of dollars into China hoping for large domestic market share and commensurate profits but instead were reeling from enormous and continuing losses. Dell's management was not ignorant of these warning signals but viewed the situation as "if we're not in what will soon be the second-biggest PC market in the world, then how can Dell possibly be a global player?"

The Dell-in-China situation showcases all five elements of the strategy diamond. It also shows how a firm must engage these elements flexibly and entrepreneurially to do business in markets different from their home markets. That is, internationalizing firms face challenges as to how to be global yet local at the same time and to what extent they should be global or local. China is a relatively new geographic arena for Dell. Within this country arena, Dell is targeting certain market segments, or subarenas; it is also using different channels as part of its market segmentation strategy.

In terms of vehicles, and regardless of global location, Dell typically goes it alone in assembly and distribution, entering into alliances only for its inputs and raw materials. A key facet of Dell's competitive advantage is distribution via its Dell Direct model—an on-line PC assembly and sales-on-demand powerhouse. In China, however, Dell initially formed alliances with independent distributors for the consumer market, a channel it had learned to exploit in its earlier entry into India. This was a risky move for Dell but also one that showed that management recognized that it had to be flexible and act in a locally sensitive fashion in approaching new geographic markets. Dell initially planned to use Chinese distributors, as it had in India, and then migrate sales over a five-year period to the typical kiosk sales model it employs in other parts of the world, further allowing it to leverage its Dell Direct model. Dell was able to draw immediately on the model for the large multinational-firm market, with which it already had established customer relationships. It could also use the Dell Direct model for the government-users market. As in all of its other markets, Dell's intended strategy was based on a performance-for-value logic and its Dell Direct service model to maintain its solid relationships with corporate and government clients in China.

In terms of staging, Dell flipped its distribution model on its head. This is a third example of how the company flexibly adapted its historic strategic approach to enter into China. In the United States, Dell built its Dell Direct model through the direct-to-consumer market; it entered the corporate-customer market only after it had established a strong, profitable foothold with consumers. In China, however, the Dell Direct market was more commercially viable with corporate customers, who have both the cash and access to infrastructure to make the Dell Direct model work effectively. Although Dell initially worked through distributors in China for the consumer market, its staging plan was to migrate these consumers eventually to its Dell Direct model.

Finally, Dell's economic logic is one of both scale and scope economies. It can leverage its size to gain the best terms and prices for the best technologies for the products it sells. It can use this cost advantage to compete in China and at the same time further enhance the Dell Direct model's footprint on the global computer market. So far, it appears that Dell's global strategy, and its flexible approach to entering countries like China, is paying off. Michael Dell said the company's overall business in China was strong, growing, and profitable. Dell's revenue in China increased 26 percent in 2006. Dell's revenue share in China is about 20 percent, which is double its 10-percent share of product shipments, because the company also sells services and other products beyond PCs there.

Nonetheless, Dell is facing strong competition. On December 9, 2004, IBM announced the sale of its entire PC division to Lenovo, a Chinese multinational firm. This left Dell, Hewlett-Packard, and Lenovo as the world's top three PC makers. At the time, industry analysts were placing their bets on wildly efficient Dell to broaden its lead, both globally and in China, by the middle of 2007. Dell seemed invincible using the low-cost model. Now, however, other companies have figured out how to make and sell PCs as cheaply as Dell. Exhibit 8.1 shows the respective market positions of the top five desktop, notebook, and PC makers, with HP leading the pack.

To respond to the fierce competition in China, Dell will have to cut its costs. Just a few weeks after CEO Michael Dell's heralded trip to the Middle Kingdom, local Chinese media report that Dell China has formulated a plan to reduce staff at the end of April 2007. According to the plan, Dell China will reduce up to 13 percent of the staff in each of its departments. The reports say that it is urgent for Dell to reduce its staff because its operational expenditures increased remarkably over ten consecutive quarters, but its revenue per employee dropped to the lowest level in seven years. <<<

Exhibit 8.1   Global PC Industry Market Share Comparables

Company	Global Market Share	Annual Sales Growth
HP	17.4%	23.9%
Dell	13.9%	−8.7%
Lenovo	7.1%	9.3%
Acer	6.8%	33.1%
Toshiba	3.8%	24.5%
Rest of Market	51.0%	3.8%
Total Market	100.0%	7.4%

International Strategy

international strategy
Process by which a firm approaches its cross-border activities and those of competitors and plans to approach them in the future.

What is *international strategy?* When should managers consider such a strategy? A firm's **international strategy** is how it approaches the cross-border business activities of its own firm and competitors and how it contemplates doing so in the future. In the narrowest sense, a firm's managers need only think about international strategy when they conduct some aspect of their business across national borders. Some international activities are designed to augment a firm's business strategy, such as sourcing key factors of production to cheaper labor markets (i.e., attempts to become more competitive within a core business). Other international activities represent key elements of the firm's corporate strategy (i.e., entering new businesses or new markets). Whether expanding internationally to reinforce a particular business's strategy or as part of a corporate strategy, international expansion is a form of diversification because the firm has chosen to operate in a different market.

Throughout this text, you have been exposed to many organizations, including those focused on one primary geographic region and others that are very global in their operating scope. For some organizations, a global mindset pervades managerial thinking and is explicit in the firm's vision, mission, goals, objectives, and strategy. With other firms, international strategy may be very new. Regardless of the case, a firm must carefully prepare for an international strategy through the analysis of all the dimensions of the strategy diamond.

The preventative cure for domestic-strategy myopia, and surefire pathway to a global mindset, is a broad awareness of the international landscape. Exhibit 8.2 highlights some of the top global trends that executives consider relevant to the competitive fortunes of their businesses.[1]

These trends suggest new market opportunities, such as the growth of consumer demand in emerging markets. They also suggest new concerns and constraints, particularly those related to natural resources and the environment. We encourage you to learn about these broader trends, different countries, and national cultures and internalize a cosmopolitan view of international strategy. In the broadest sense, a firm needs to consider its international strategy when any single or potential competitor is not domestic or otherwise conducts business across borders. Increasingly, it is this latter context that makes it imperative that almost all firms think about the international dimensions of their business, even if they have no international operations whatsoever. Thus, international strategy essentially reflects

Exhibit 8.2 Global Trends to Watch

Trend	Examples
Shifting of economic activity between countries and regions	Growth in demand for energy and basic materials (such as steel and copper) is moving from developed countries to developing ones, predominantly in Asia. Demand for oil in China and India, for example, will nearly double from 2003 to 2020, to 15.4 million barrels a day. Asia's oil consumption will approach that of the United States—the world's largest consumer—by the end of that period.
Shifting of economic activity within countries and regions	The story is not simply the march to Asia. Shifts within regions are as significant as those occurring across regions. For example, by 2015 the Hispanic population in the United States will have spending power equivalent to that of 60 percent of all Chinese consumers.
Growing number of consumers in emerging economies	Economic growth in the developing world will usher nearly a billion new consumers into the global marketplace over the next decade, as household incomes reach the level (around $5,000) associated with discretionary spending. Although these consumers will have less spending power than do their counterparts in the developed world, they will have similar demands as well as access to global brands. Many industries, therefore, face polarized markets where premium and no-frills offerings are squeezing middle-of-the-road offerings.
Increasing availability of knowledge and the ability to exploit it	Knowledge is increasingly available and, at the same time, increasingly specialized. The most obvious manifestation of this trend is the rise of search engines (such as Google) and online marketplaces (such as eBay and Amazon) that make an almost infinite amount of information available instantaneously.
Increasing global labor and talent markets	Ongoing shifts in labor and talent will be far more profound than the widely observed migration of jobs to low-wage countries. The shift to knowledge-intensive industries highlights the importance and scarcity of well-trained talent. The increasing integration of global labor markets, however, is opening up vast new talent sources. The 33 million university-educated young professionals in developing countries is more than double the number in developed ones. For many companies and governments, global labor and talent strategies will become as important as global sourcing and manufacturing strategies. For instance, in India there are about 245,000 Indians answering phones from all over the world about credit card and cell phone offers, along with bill collection. This type of skill shift is repeated across areas from data-input to programming to copyediting.
Resource and environmental strains	As economic growth accelerates—particulary in emerging markets—demand for natural resources is growing at unprecedented rates. Oil demand is projected to grow by 50 percent in the next two decades, and without large new discoveries or radical innovations supply is unlikely to keep up. Similar surges in demand across a broad range of commodities are being seen as well. In China, for example, demand for copper, steel, and aluminum has nearly tripled in the past decade. Evidence is emerging that one of our scarcest natural resources—the atmosphere—will require dramatic shifts in human behavior to keep it from being depleted further.

the choices a firm's executives make with respect to sourcing and selling its goods in foreign markets, and dealing with foreign competitors who enter their markets.

It probably comes as no surprise to you that all of the world's largest corporations are global as well. A simple review of the top-20 firms among *Fortune*'s Global 500 provides you with a snapshot of these global behemoths each year, in terms of who is largest and who has the best global reputation. As you can see in Exhibit 8.3, some of these large firms, seen at the beginning of 2007, had revenues greater than many countries' GDP!

And, with the exceptions of Wal-Mart and GE, the mix of top firms is clearly clustered among the oil and gas, automotive, banking, and insurance industries.[2] Even among this special group, you can see that firms vary significantly in terms of their international presence. What may be surprising, however, is the increasing presence of arguably tiny firms that are global very early in their lives, such as Logitech (which started in Switzerland and California and was global from inception) and Skype (which started in Sweden and went global in a year, and was recently acquired by EBay).

As you work through this chapter, you will see how international strategy must be reflected in all facets of the strategy diamond. Exhibit 8.4 summarizes some of the key strategic questions that firms must answer about the strategy diamond, such as Dell did in the opening vignette, as they expand into international markets.

Exhibit 8.3 Top 20 Global Companies Based on Revenue

Rank	Company	Country/HQ	Industry	Revenues ($ millions)	Profits ($ millions)	% Foreign Sales
1	Exxon Mobil	USA	Oil and Gas	339,938.0	36,130.0	69.14%
2	Wal-Mart Stores	USA	Retail	315,654.0	11,231.0	22.35%
3	Royal Dutch Shell	UK/Netherlands	Oil and Gas	306,731.0	25,311.0	57.25%*
4	BP	UK	Oil and Gas	267,600.0	22,341.0	70.17%
5	General Motors	USA	Automotive	192,604.0	−10,567.0	37.77%
6	Chevron	USA	Oil and Gas	189,481.0	14,099.0	55.19%
7	DaimlerChrysler	Germany	Automotive	186,106.3	3,536.3	14.64%
8	Toyota Motor	Japan	Automotive	185,805.0	12,119.6	63.23%
9	Ford Motor	USA	Automotive	177,210.0	2,024.0	49.32%
10	ConocoPhillips	USA	Oil and Gas	166,683.0	13,529.0	30.37%
11	General Electric	USA	Diversified	157,153.0	16,353.0	45.45%
12	Total	France	Oil and Gas	152,360.7	15,250.0	76.01%
13	ING Group	Netherlands	Banking	138,235.3	8,958.9	77.12%
14	Citigroup	USA	Banking	131,045.0	24,589.0	32.38%
15	AXA	France	Insurance	129,839.2	5,186.5	17.00%
16	Allianz	Germany	Insurance	121,406.0	5,442.4	70.72%
17	Volkswagen	Germany	Automotive	118,376.6	1,391.7	72.80%*
18	Fortis	Belgium	Banking	112,351.4	4,896.3	15.94%
19	Crédit Agricole	France	Banking	110,764.6	7,434.3	43.0%
20	American Intl. Group	USA	Insurance	108,905.0	10,477.0	48.77%

*Royal Dutch Shell and Volkswagen report domestic sales as sales in Europe.

Exhibit 8.4 The Five Elements in International Strategy

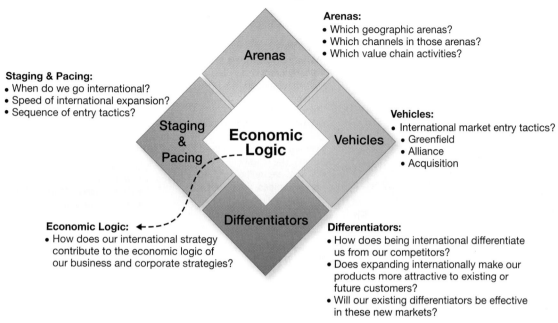

Arenas:
- Which geographic arenas?
- Which channels in those arenas?
- Which value chain activities?

Staging & Pacing:
- When do we go international?
- Speed of international expansion?
- Sequence of entry tactics?

Vehicles:
- International market entry tactics?
- Greenfield
- Alliance
- Acquisition

Economic Logic:
- How does our international strategy contribute to the economic logic of our business and corporate strategies?

Differentiators:
- How does being international differentiate us from our competitors?
- Does expanding internationally make our products more attractive to existing or future customers?
- Will our existing differentiators be effective in these new markets?

International Strategy and Competitive Advantage

Why, where, and how? Using the strategy diamond and another simple framework we refer to as the 1-2-3 Model, these are the three basic questions that international strategy must answer. While there is obviously a lot of analysis that must go into answering them, these three basic questions—summarized in Exhibit 8.5—will put you in a good position to determine the scale and scope of your international strategy.

Too often, executives make international strategy choices based on what competitors are doing, instead of starting with answers to fundamental strategy diamond questions like: (1) *Why* should we expand into another geographic arena (is the economic logic compelling and do our differentiators apply)?; (2) If so, *where*—which new geographic arena?; and (3) If this arena, then *how*—what vehicles will we use, and how should entry be staged and paced? Notice, for instance, that Dell identified the need to be a global player based on its growth objectives, customer needs, and opportunities to garner new customers. These needs fit with the economic logic of Dell's strategy. They also leveraged Dell's differentiators—relationships with customers and Dell's quality image. Dell then identified China as an important stepping stone—or stage—in its global growth aspirations. Finally, it chose an entry strategy—starting with an alliance with Indian distributors—for staging its efforts to do well in the new China market.

Given the complexities and risks of managing business activities across borders, it is imperative to understand why any firm would take on the often significant costs of doing so in terms of time, dollars, and managerial attention. One reason is simply necessity. Increasingly, many experts in the field of strategic management view global expansion as necessary for just about every medium and large corporation. This opinion is based on a few basic observations: (1) that capital markets and employees favor fast-growing firms, and many domestic markets in developed countries are becoming saturated; (2) that efficiencies in all value-chain activities are linked across borders, and the linkages and pressures for efficiency continue to escalate; (3) new market opportunities are present in developing economies; (4) that knowledge is not uniformly distributed around the world, and new ideas increasingly

Exhibit 8.5 Your 1-2-3 Model of Internationalization

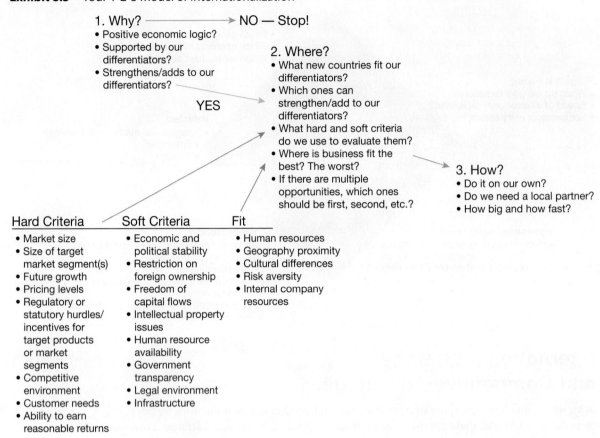

1. Why? ———————→ NO — Stop!
• Positive economic logic?
• Supported by our differentiators?
• Strengthens/adds to our differentiators?

YES

2. Where?
• What new countries fit our differentiators?
• Which ones can strengthen/add to our differentiators?
• What hard and soft criteria do we use to evaluate them?
• Where is business fit the best? The worst?
• If there are multiple opportunities, which ones should be first, second, etc.?

3. How?
• Do it on our own?
• Do we need a local partner?
• How big and how fast?

Hard Criteria	Soft Criteria	Fit
• Market size • Size of target market segment(s) • Future growth • Pricing levels • Regulatory or statutory hurdles/incentives for target products or market segments • Competitive environment • Customer needs • Ability to earn reasonable returns	• Economic and political stability • Restriction on foreign ownership • Freedom of capital flows • Intellectual property issues • Human resource availability • Government transparency • Legal environment • Infrastructure	• Human resources • Geography proximity • Cultural differences • Risk aversity • Internal company resources

are coming from emerging economies; (5) that customers themselves are becoming global at both the organizational level in terms of the growth and proliferation of multinationals and at the individual level in terms of consumer preferences; and (6) that competitors are globalizing, even if your organization is not.[3]

THE PROS AND CONS OF INTERNATIONAL EXPANSION

International expansion is no panacea for corporate-growth needs, and it is inherently hazardous even when it promises revenue opportunities. For instance, at the beginning of the 1990s, PepsiCo established an ambitious goal to triple its international sales from $1.5 billion to $5 billion within just five years. PepsiCo aggressively pursued this growth, yet it failed to keep pace with the growth of international markets and actually lost ground to Coca-Cola. While Coke was reaping the benefits of the growth of soft drinks in international markets, Pepsi's international market share actually shrank.[4] Pepsi's experience demonstrates that simply participating in international markets does not equate to having a competitive advantage to exploit international opportunities. Indeed, if you consult *Fortune*'s list of the largest global firms, you will typically find Wal-Mart at the top of that list. Yet, Wal-Mart's foreign operations do very poorly in comparison to its domestic business. Global expansion can just as easily contribute to profitability as it can detract from it. The key is to align international expansion with the firm's strategy in a way to exploit and further develop firm resources and capabilities.[5] Ultimately, the benefits must outweigh the costs, and more often than not, questions about a firm's nondomestic profitability take years to answer. The opening vignette on Dell demonstrates the ups and downs associated with international strategy and the necessary alignment of the elements of strategy and the firm's resources and capabilities. In addition to the possible benefits of international expansion, a firm incurs a number of costs when diversifying its business operations around the globe.[6] The costs of geographic diversification include the liabilities of newness and foreignness, and governance and coordination costs.

Liabilities of Newness and Foreignness

Liability of newness can be thought of as a disadvantage (cost disadvantage or other disadvantages) associated with being a new player in the market. For instance, a firm suffering from a liability of newness does not initially gain benefits from the learning curve. Likewise, *liability of foreignness* is the disadvantage a firm faces by not being a local player. This disadvantage may be cultural, in that the firm's managers do not understand local market conditions. It may also be political, such as when the firm does not understand local laws or have relationships in place to manage the local regulatory environment.

Firm managers contend with many challenges when establishing operations in a new country, including the logistics of purchasing and installing facilities, staffing, and establishing internal management systems and external business networks. Costs associated with establishing a new business can put a new foreign division in a disadvantageous position relative to local or more established foreign competitors. These types of disadvantages tend to dissipate with time as the division gains local experience, which in turn diminish the negative influence of liability of newness and foreignness.

Costs Associated with Governance and Coordination

Although the disadvantages of newness and foreignness typically decline over time, governance and coordination costs are disadvantages that tend to increase as international diversification increases. Some of the issues that increase governance and coordination costs include information distortion as it is transferred and translated across divisions and countries. Coordination difficulties and possible misalignment between headquarters and divisional managers in international firms increases as international diversification increases, much as in highly diversified domestic firms. Because every country has a relatively unique business environment, the more country environments a firm must deal with, the greater the difficulty and cost of coordinating operations across these diverse environments.

Offsetting Costs and Benefits

As shown in Exhibit 8.6, the costs associated with internationalization can offset the possible benefits of operating in multiple markets.[7] A firm's level of internationalization, shown on the horizontal axis, refers to the degree to which it has tapped foreign markets, particularly for product or service sales. The potential economic benefits of internationalization are modest at first, and then become quite significant before the marginal benefits level off. These potential increases in revenue must of course be balanced with the costs of internationalization. Costs are significant in early efforts to internationalize. After a presence is established, economies of scale and scope kick in, and the incremental costs of further expansion are minimal. However, bureaucratic and management costs can spike at extreme levels of internationalization. This increase in costs is similar to the notion of diseconomies of scale and scope introduced in earlier chapters. Consequently, research suggests that performance gains from internationalization come not at the early stages but at moderate to high levels; however, at very high levels of internationalization, firms tend to suffer performance declines.[8] The key for managers is to find a way to exploit the possible advantages of economies of scale and scope, location, and learning without having them offset by the excessive costs of internationalization. The tradeoff between costs and benefits of internationalization results in an S-curve relationship between internationalization and firm performance.

Exhibit 8.6 Costs and Benefits of Internationalization

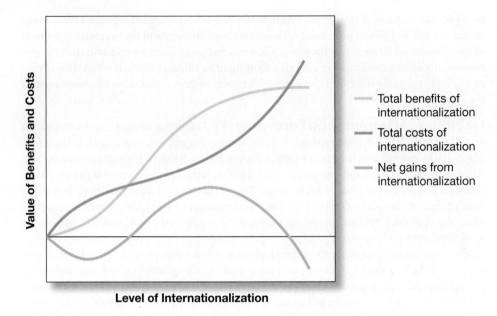

KEY FACTORS IN INTERNATIONAL EXPANSION

International strategy, particularly in the form of international expansion, can contribute to a firm's competitive advantage in a number of interrelated ways. The four most important aspects are *economies of scale and scope, location, multipoint competition,* and *learning.* While most of these aspects are directly related to the economic logic of a firm's strategy, they also can contribute to the differentiators. Firms must understand the specific benefits in one or more of these areas if they are to proceed with international expansion plans.

 **Global Economies of Scale and Scope**   Referring back to the strategy diamond, international strategy affects a firm's economic logic through its implications for economies of scale and scope. ◆ Larger firms are not necessarily more efficient or more profitable, but in some industries, such as pharmaceuticals and aircraft manufacturing, the enormous costs of new-product development require that the firm be able to generate commensurate sales, and this increasingly requires firms to have a global presence.

For instance, R&D costs are skyrocketing in many industries. This requires that firms in those industries seek a larger revenue base, typically outside of their home countries. This relationship is demonstrated by strategy research showing that the performance benefits from R&D increase with a firm's degree of internationalization: Firms generate more profits out of their R&D investments if they are also highly global.[9] One reason for this is that there is a minimum threshold of R&D investment necessary to launch a new product. When the firm can amortize those costs across many markets, it can in effect lower its average cost per sale. It is interesting to note that, when graphed, the relationship between performance, R&D investment, and internationalization further demonstrates the S-curve relationship between internationalization and firm performance discussed earlier in this chapter. Such economies of scale can also be realized for intangibles, such as a firm's brand, much as Nestlé, McDonald's, and Coca-Cola leverage their brands in practically every country in the world.

Scale and Operating Efficiency The larger scale that accompanies global expansion only creates competitive advantage if the firm translates scale into operating efficiency. As you learned in Chapter 5, cost savings are not axiomatic with larger scale. Larger scale must be managed to avoid diseconomies of scale. As with economies of scale in general, the potential scale economies from global expansion include spreading fixed costs over a larger sales and asset base and increasing purchasing power.[10] Attempts to gain scale advantages must be focused on resources and activities that are scale sensitive, and it means that these resources and activities must be concentrated in just a few locations.[11] However, if these resources and activities are concentrated in a few locations, they can become isolated from key markets, which may lead to delayed responses to market changes. For instance, until Dell established a regional office and manufacturing facility in Brazil (Eldorado do Sul), its sales and service record in Brazil suffered.

Economies of Global Scope A specialized form of scope economies is available to firms as they expand globally. Recall that scope economies were defined as the ability to lower average costs by sharing a resource across different products. Numerous scope economies are available to firms that expand globally. For example, Nestlé, McDonald's, and Coca-Cola profit from scope economies to the extent that the different country markets share the benefits of brand equity that these firms have built up over time. The opening vignette on Dell, too, provides several examples of scope as well as scale economies across different geographic and customer markets, starting with its ability to take advantage of its brand; its capability to leverage its Dell Direct sales model and related Internet sales and support technologies; its experience and relationships with distributors in India and then China; and its different geographic units' ability to pool their purchasing power for key components, such as CPUs, from powerful suppliers like Intel.

Consider how a supplier to McDonald's could exploit economies of global scope, which in turn provide it with economies of scale in production and other related value-chain activities. McDonald's needs the same ketchup products in Europe as it does in South America. A vendor with sufficient global scope to satisfy McDonald's worldwide demand for ketchup would be an attractive sourcing alternative to McDonald's compared with sourcing this supply from numerous local suppliers.[12] In this case, global scope gives a supplier an opportunity to generate revenue that it would be unable to generate in the absence of global scope. Of course, McDonalds' global scope also gives it access to more suppliers from around the globe, including local suppliers in many markets. Local suppliers may also have some advantages over global players in terms of being able to provide more immediate service and greater knowledge of local business practices. Thus, firms like McDonald's are in the enviable position of being able to source the lowest cost inputs and use lower local prices and service levels to force global suppliers to keep prices down and service levels high.

Attempts to gain economies of scope also face numerous hazards as well. Although economies of scope are possible as resources are shared across markets, strategy must still be executed at the national level.[13] In cases such as China, the United States, and Europe, where the "nation" is actually composed of distinctly different subgeographic markets (cantons in Switzerland, countries in other parts of Europe, states in the United States, and provinces in China), successful execution at the local level is further complicated. This can easily lead to tension between the need to identify and satisfy the local client contact and the aim of lowering costs by sharing resources and having actions coordinated across markets.

Location National and regional geographic location has an impact on competitive advantage as well, because of its implications for input costs, competitors, demand conditions, and complements. A basic five-forces industry analysis can be used to determine the importance of a given location. The analysis of industry structure should include such features as barriers to entry, new entrants, substitutes, and existing competitors, both domestic and international. Related and supporting industries that are forward and backward in the value chain, as well as true complements, also need to be identified.

With such an analysis in hand, the value chain and five-forces analysis can be geographically segmented to consider how and why rivalry may play out differently in different geographic arenas. ◆ In terms of customers, for instance, an analysis of consumption trends among the top 25 countries in the global soft drink industry shows that India and China

Arenas

Huge international chains, such as McDonald's, are able to achieve economies of scope, thereby lowering the costs of inputs they purchase both globally and in local markets.

exhibit fairly steady growth. A firm's managers can thus assess the desirability of investing in one market versus another, the competitive consequences of such an investment, and the value-chain activities needed to locate in each region. For instance, India and China may be prime locations to launch new growth initiatives for large players like Coca-Cola and Pepsi. Such an analysis should show how the firm's strategy has connected the dots, so to speak, in terms of linking resources, capabilities, and locations—and in this case, the choice of a new geographic arena should be consistent with the other facets of the firm's strategy, as seen in the strategy diamond.

Arbitrage Opportunities Beyond the five-forces and value-chain assessment, location differences also present an opportunity for arbitrage. Arbitrage represents the age-old practice of buying something in one market and selling it another market where it garners a higher price. Historically, the value added in such arbitrage was simply tracking down a desirable commodity, such as spice, tea, or silk, from a faraway land, and transporting it to a market that would pay a premium for it. Companies can improve performance and potentially build competitive advantage by optimizing the location of their value-chain activities. Significant cost differences for different types of value-chain activities exist around the globe. A firm that can optimize the intercountry cost differences better than its rivals will have a cost advantage. The caveat here is that arbitrage opportunities may be fleeting in that once they are identified, competitors who lack entry barriers can quickly realize them as well. Therefore, a firm that relies on arbitrage as a core part of its competitive strategy must possess greater capabilities in continually identifying new arbitrage opportunities as well as in increasing entry barriers for competitors trying to follow it.

Multipoint Competition Firms can develop competitive advantages through multipoint competition. **Multipoint competition** refers to the situation when a firm competes against another firm in multiple product markets or multiple geographic markets (or both). For instance, Proctor and Gamble and Unilever not only compete head to head in personal care products around the globe, they also compete in the soaps and detergents markets. When the firm competes in multiple international markets, as a special kind of multipoint

multipoint competition
When a firm competes against another firm in multiple product markets or multiple geographic markets (or both).

tactic, the stronghold assault becomes available. *Stronghold assault* refers to the competitive actions a firm takes in another firm's key markets, particularly when the attacking firm has little presence in that market. In the case of international strategy, stronghold assault refers to attacks on the geographic markets that are most important to a competitor's profitability and cash flow. A classic example of international stronghold assault is provided by the actions of French tire manufacturer Michelin and the U.S. tire company Goodyear in the 1970s.[14] Early on, both firms had negligible market presence in each other's respective domestic markets (Europe and the United States). Michelin became aware of Goodyear's intent to expand its presence in Europe, so it started selling its tires in the United States at or below its actual cost. Although these sales were a miniscule part of Michelin's overall sales, Michelin's sales tactic forced Goodyear to drop its prices in the United States, and hence lower the profitability of its largest market.

Such multipoint competitive tactics often initially benefit customers at the expense of competitors until a new market equilibrium is reached. Moreover, Michelin's low-price ploy earned it a larger share of the U.S. market, such that the lost profits in the United States began to take a toll on Michelin's overall profitability. In addition, nothing prevented Goodyear from doing the same thing in Michelin's home markets, further eroding both firms' profitability. Eventually, both firms ended up in the international courts charging each other with "dumping"—selling goods below cost in a foreign country.

Even today, stronghold assault is a motivation for global investment, but as the Michelin case highlights, it must be used with care and is typically not sustainable. Therefore, firms that employ this tactic should also have strategies in the staging component that take into account when and how the firm will shift from price competition to more sustainable bases of competition. For this reason, stronghold assault is used not only to underprice a competitor's products in its home market but also to simply eliminate the competitor's home market monopoly. Just as with the cola wars, the Michelin–Goodyear war left the industry landscape forever changed, and both firms had to adjust their strategies to survive in the new industry structure that resulted.

Learning and Knowledge Sharing   Learning is very important to the success of a firm's international strategy for a variety of reasons. At the very least, a firm with operations that cross borders must learn how to cope with different institutional, legal, and cultural environments. For the most successful firms, international expansion is used as a vehicle for innovation, improving existing products in existing markets, or coming up with new ideas for new markets. It is one thing to use such tools as the five-forces, value-chain, and other frameworks to identify profit or arbitrage opportunities, for instance, but it is quite another thing to exploit them successfully and profitably. For instance, Michelin initially shipped products to the United States and didn't care whether it made money on them because it viewed any losses as insignificant. But eventually that tactic caused the U.S. market to grow in importance as part of the French tire maker's overall global sales, and it had to reckon with making this part of its business profitable or admit defeat and abandon the U.S. market—one of the auto industry's largest and most profitable markets.

Similarly, Dell first used Indian then Chinese distributors in serving the consumer segment in China, but this is a much less profitable vehicle and differentiator than its core distribution and sales engine—the Dell Direct model. Dell's goal was to migrate from its Chinese distributors and eventually learn enough about the Chinese marketplace to use its direct-sales vehicle, which can be accessed through kiosks placed in busy foot-traffic locations. Like the product-diversified firm, the geographic-diversified firm must somehow learn how to ensure that the benefits of being international outweigh the added costs of the infrastructure necessary to support its nondomestic operations.

Learning and local adaptation appear to be particularly difficult for U.S. firms, even when they are very big firms that already have an international presence. For instance, with nearly a half-billion dollars in annual sales, Lincoln Electric completed its largest acquisition ever in 1991—the $70-million purchase of Germany's Messer Gresheim, a manufacturer of welding equipment, which was Lincoln's core business.[15] Although Lincoln maintained the bulk of its business in the United States, it had over 40 years of marketing and manufacturing experience in Canada, Australia, and France. Moreover, the company was in the process of aggressively ramping up manufacturing and sales operations in Japan, Venezuela, Brazil, the Netherlands, Norway, and the United Kingdom. With the acquisition of Gresheim, as with the other newly established international operations, Lincoln's management simply assumed that it could transplant its manufacturing approach, aggressive compensation and incentive systems (Lincoln pays employees only for what they produce), and culture—the three key success factors in the U.S. business—to the newly obtained German and other foreign operations. Within a year, the European operations were in disarray; losses were mounting in Japan and Latin America; and Lincoln reported a quarterly consolidated loss of $12 million—the first quarterly consolidated loss in the company's 97-year history.

Although Lincoln eventually recovered from the brink of disaster and ruin, it only did so after top management recognized and took steps to remedy the harsh reality that it had insufficient international experience, a dearth of experience in and knowledge about running a globally dispersed organization, and no understanding of how to manage foreign operations and foreign cultures. Part of its salvation involved scaling back many of the foreign operations it had acquired, giving the firm breathing room to develop its international operating and managerial capabilities. As a consequence of its learning from its failures abroad, Lincoln is now a global success story, as summarized in excerpts from its 2006 annual report shown in Exhibit 8.7.

Learning, Knowledge, Transfer, and Innovation   Beyond the rather obvious aspects of learning shown in the Lincoln Electric case, a firm that has operations in different coun-

Exhibit 8.7   Global Strategy at Lincoln Electric

To Our Shareholders: During 2006, the continued strong worldwide demand for our products, combined with the effective execution of our global strategy, contributed to another year of excellent performance for Lincoln Electric. By maintaining our focus on the five key components for excellence—people development, customer service, operational efficiency, global expansion, and innovative products—we have been able to take advantage of many opportunities in rapidly growing markets around the world.

We are expanding our footprint, strengthening our global leadership position in the welding industry and taking advantage of significant growth opportunities. Our performance has been strong everywhere we operate—in North America, Europe, Asia, the Middle East and Latin America—and we have gained market share in each of these regions.

From a global perspective, we are strengthening our position in emerging markets while continuing to serve existing markets. In Asia, specifically China, which stands to be the largest market for welding products for the foreseeable future, we are significantly increasing our manufacturing capacity for flux cored wire. We also are constructing a new facility in India to begin production of consumables in 2007, and we have recently expanded capacity at our Indonesia consumables plant.

Economic development is advancing rapidly on a global scale, evidenced by huge investments in infrastructure, transportation, manufacturing, energy production and transmission, and construction. All of these require substantial welding, and Lincoln Electric is **POWERING UP** in key markets and locations around the world to meet this growing demand.

Source: Lincoln Electric Annual Report

tries has the opportunity to increase innovation and transfer knowledge from one geographic market to another. For example, SC Johnson's European operations learned about a product that involved the combination of household pesticides and a simple plug-in device. In Europe, this product was sold in stores to consumers who needed a cheap and efficient deterrent for mosquitoes and other annoying insects. SC Johnson demonstrated its ability to learn from its European operation by transferring the technology to its fragrance division in the United States, thus giving rise to a whole new category of air fresheners called Glade PlugIns.[16]

A second facet of this form of learning is to locate a firm or a particular aspect of its operations in a part of the world where competition is the fiercest. So, for example, a European automaker might locate a product facility in Japan. Ironically, although one goal of such a move is actually to compete on Japan's own turf against incumbents Toyota and Honda, the learning objective is to try to emulate and learn from Japan's auto manufacturers' leading-edge production practices and transfer that advanced knowledge to the European company's plants in other parts of the world. Similarly, because France and Italy are leaders in the high-fashion industry, companies such as DuPont and W. L. Gore & Associates, which aim to compete with leading-edge fabrics such as Lycra and Gore-Tex, place high value on those countries as production and marketing locations because of the learning opportunities about future customer preferences (e.g., touch, feel, color, etc.). In this view, the strategically most important markets will be those that feature not only intrinsic market attractiveness but an opportunity to learn and innovate in ways that can improve the organization's operations, products, and services around the globe.[17]

Sharing Knowledge Across Business Units Finally, large multinationals can exploit opportunities for inter-business-unit collaboration, which results in valuable knowledge sharing.[18] Sharing knowledge across business units has several tangible benefits. First, it enables firms to transfer best practices across national and business-unit boundaries. Because these best practices are proprietary—and probably tailored to the idiosyncrasies of the firm— they are more likely to result in competitive advantage than borrowing best practices from other firms. Why? Because all competitors have access to that information as well.

An example of this type of knowledge sharing is illustrated by a case study of British Petroleum (BP). A U.S. business unit that operates service stations was looking for novel ways to reduce costs in BP convenience stores. A manager borrowed ideas from colleagues in the Netherlands and the United Kingdom about how to reduce working-capital requirements. Copying these practices and implementing them in the United States resulted in a 20-percent reduction in working capital.

Sharing knowledge across business units can also uncover revenue-enhancement opportunities. The country manager of GlaxoSmithKline in the Philippines found a new drug therapy for tuberculosis in the company's R&D lab in India. Although this therapy was not widely known within the company because it represented a very small slice of the multinational firm's business, it represented a huge market opportunity in the Philippines and other developing countries, where tuberculosis is more widespread than it is in Europe and the United States.

Using CAGE to Choose Foreign Countries

Now that you have answered the *why* question of international strategy, you must move on to answer the *where* question. But the world is a big place, so where do you start? Some markets are growing so quickly that their sheer size merits consideration. Exhibit 8.8 presents the top ten countries in terms of population, in addition to information on GDP, and GDP growth.[19]

The European Union and the United States have the most global Fortune 500 firms, 172 and 114 respectively, as of the start of 2007. And, as you might expect, Brazil, Russia,

Exhibit 8.8   Comparative Country Information of the Top 10 Markets by Population

Country	Est. Population 2007	Labor Force	Internet Users	GDP (in $ millions)	Average GDP Real Growth Rate (%)
China	1,321,851,888	798,000,000	123,000,000	10,000,000	10.50
India	1,129,866,154	509,300,000	60,000,000	4,042,000	8.50
European Union	460,827,146	222,700,000	247,000,000	12,820,000	2.80
United States	301,139,947	151,400,000	205,327,000	12,980,000	3.40
Indonesia	234,693,997	108,200,000	16,000,000	935,000	5.40
Brazil	190,010,647	96,340,000	25,900,000	1,616,000	2.80
Pakistan	164,741,924	48,290,000	10,500,000	427,300	6.50
Bangladesh	150,448,339	68,000,000	300,000	330,800	6.10
Russia	141,377,752	73,880,000	23,700,000	1,723,000	6.60
Nigeria	135,031,164	48,990,000	5,000,000	188,500	5.30

India, and China (you will often see them referred to collectively as BRIC) figure greatly into the landscape of developing economies where there is great opportunity married with great risk. Moreover, these four particular markets are giving rise to a new breed of savvy global competitor. They are shaking up entire industries, from farm equipment and refrigerators to aircraft and telecom services, and changing the rules of global competition (see Exhibit 8.9 for one view of how they are shaking things up in strategy and competition).[20]

The CAGE Framework   Generally, the greater the distance covered and the greater the value differences between the disconnected markets, the greater the profit potential that arises from arbitrage. However, greater distance also tends to be accompanied by greater entry costs and risks.

Although most people tend to think of distance in geographic terms, in the area of international strategy distance can also be viewed in terms of culture, administrative heritage, and economics. As summarized in Exhibit 8.10, this broader **CAGE framework**—Culture, Administrative, Geographic, and Economic—provides you with another way of thinking about location and the opportunities and concomitant risks associated with global arbitrage.[21] CAGE-related risks would be most relevant in industries in which language or cultural identity are important factors, the government views the products as staples or as essential to national security, or income or input costs are key determinants of product demand or cost. You learned about these broader cultural and socioeconomic factors through your use of the PESTEL framework in Chapter 4. CAGE asks you to look at countries and regions, try to assess the degree to which they are different or similar along many of the PESTEL dimensions, and then try to estimate the implications of such differences for a firm that wishes to move into a new geographic market.

Application of the CAGE framework requires managers to identify attractive locations based on raw material costs, access to markets or consumers, or other key decision criteria. For instance, a firm may be most interested in markets with high consumer buying power, so it uses per capita income as the first sorting cue. This would result in some type of ranking. For example, one researcher examined the fast food industry and found that based on per capita income, countries such as Germany and Japan would be the most attractive markets for the expansion of a North American-based fast food company. However, when the analysis was adjusted for distance using the CAGE framework, the revised results showed that Mexico ranked as the second-most-attractive market for international expansion, far ahead of Germany and Japan.[22]

CAGE framework   Tool that considers the dimensions of culture, administration, geography, and economics to assess the distance created by global expansion.

Exhibit 8.9 The Emerging Market Boom

In the world of global strategy and competition, new contenders are hailing from seemingly unlikely places, developing nations such as Brazil, Russia, India, China, and even Egypt and South Africa. They are shaking up entire industries, from farm equipment and refrigerators to aircraft and telecom services, and changing the rules of global competition. These changes are consistent with those presaged by the trends you learned about in Exhibit 8.2.

Emerging markets

Developed markets

Grey—Other

Unlike Japanese and Korean conglomerates, which benefited from protection and big profits at home before they took on the world, these emerging economy upstarts are mostly companies that have prevailed in brutally competitive domestic markets, where local companies have to duke it out with homegrown rivals and Western multinationals every day. As a result, these emerging champions must make profits at price levels unheard of in the United States or Europe. Indian generic drugmakers, for example, often charge customers in their home market as little as 1% to 2% of what people pay in the United States. Cellular outfits in North Africa, Brazil, and India offer phone service for pennies per minute. Yet these companies often thrive in such tough environments. Egyptian cellular operator Orascom boasts margins of 49%; Mahindra's pretax profit rose 81% in 2006.

Some already are marquee names. Lenovo Group, the Chinese computer maker, made waves in 2005 by buying IBM's $11 billion PC business. Indian software outfits Infosys, Tata Consultancy Services, and Wipro have revolutionized the $650 billion technology services industry. Johannesburg brewer SABMiller PLC is challenging Anheuser-Busch Cos.' leadership right in the United States.

These companies are just the first wave. The biggest international cellular provider? Soon it may be Mexico's América Móvil, which boasts more than 100 million Latin American subscribers and led BusinessWeeks's 2006 rankings of the world's top information technology companies. Never heard of Hong Kong's Techtronic Industries Ltd.? If you buy power tools at Home Depot Inc., where its products now fill the aisles, you probably know some of the brands it manufactures: Ryobi, Milwaukee, and RIDGID. Brazil's Embraer has surged past Canada's Bombardier as the world's No. 3 aircraft maker and is winning midsize-jet orders that otherwise

(continued)

Exhibit 8.9   Continued

would have gone to larger planes by Airbus and Boeing. Western telecom equipment leaders have long looked down on China's Huawei Technologies Co. as a mere copier of their designs. But in 2006, Huawei snared $8 billion in new orders, including contracts from British Telecommunications PLC for its $19 billion program to transform Britain's telecom network.

Many more companies are using their bases in the developing world as springboards to build global empires, such as Mexican cement giant Cemex, Indian drugmaker Ranbaxy, and Russia's Lukoil, which has hundreds of gas stations in New Jersey and Pennsylvania. Boston Consulting Group (BCG) recently published a report describing the amount of progress as "surprising," in view of the progress made by emerging-market companies in the last few years. BCG identified 100 emerging multinationals that appear positioned to radically transform industries and markets around the world. The 100 had combined $715 billion in revenue in 2005, $145 billion in operating profits, and a half-trillion dollars in assets. They have grown at a 24 percent annual clip in the past four years.

What makes these upstarts global contenders? Their key advantages are access to some of the world's most dynamic growth markets and immense pools of low-cost resources, be they production workers, engineers, land, petroleum, or iron ore. But these aspiring giants are about much more than low cost. The best of the pack are proving as innovative and expertly run as any in the business, astutely absorbing global consumer trends and technologies and getting new products to market faster than their rivals. Techtronic, for example, was the first to sell heavy-duty cordless tools powered by lightweight lithium ion batteries. Jetmaker Embraer's sleek EMB 190, which seats up to 118, has taken smaller commercial aircraft to a new level with the fuselage design that offers the legroom and overhead luggage space of much larger planes. Globalization and the Internet allow these emerging market firms to tap the same managerial talent, information, and capital as companies in more developed countries. In most industries, strategy and competition have clearly become a global game.

Any international expansion strategy would still need to be backed up by the specific resources and capabilities possessed by the firm, regardless of how rosy the CAGE analysis paints the picture. Think of international expansion as a movement along a continuum from known markets to less-known markets; a firm can move to more CAGE-proximate neighbors before venturing into markets that are portrayed as very different from a CAGE-framework perspective. Let's look at each dimension of CAGE.

Cultural Distance   Culture happens to be the first facet of CAGE, in terms of the acronym, but it also can be the most practically perplexing facet for managers. Culture is sometimes referred to as the software of the mind, in that it has a sometimes invisible but indelible influence on people's values and behaviors. *Cultural distance,* then, has to do with the possible differences existing in relation to the way individuals from different countries observe certain values and behaviors.

A number of researchers have identified significant cultural differences among countries. Among these, for instance, Geert Hofstede drew together distinct cultural differences he observed around the following dimensions: power distance (the extent to which individuals accept the existence of inequalities between subordinates and superiors within a hierarchical structure); uncertainty avoidance (individuals' willingness to coexist with uncertainty about the future); individualism (how the individuals in a society value individualistic behaviors as opposed to collective ones); predominant values (regarding quantity or quality of life, that is, whether more importance is given to material aspects or a stronger emphasis is laid on interpersonal relationships); and long-term or short-term orientation (the focus on future rewards or the concern about the maintenance of the stability related to the past and the present).[23] A cross-section of these cultural dimensions for a sampling of developed and developing countries around the world are presented in Exhibit 8.11.

Exhibit 8.10 The CAGE Framework

Cultural Distance	Administrative Distance	Geographic Distance	Economic Distance
Attributes Creating Distance			
Different languages Different ethnicities: lack of connective ethnic or social networks Different religions Different social norms	Absence of colonial ties Absence of shared monetary or political association Political hostility Government policies Institutional weakness	Physical remoteness Lack of a common border Lack of sea or river access Size of country Weak transportation or communication links Differences in climates	Differences in consumer incomes Differences in costs and quality of: • natural resources • financial resources • human resources • infrastructure • intermediate inputs • information or knowledge
Industries or Products Affected by Distance			
Products have high linguistic content (TV) Products affect cultural or national identity of consumers (foods) Product features vary in terms of size (cars), standards (electrical appliances), or packaging Products carry country-specific quality associations (wines)	Government involvement is high in industries that are: • producers of staple goods (electricity) • producers of other "entitlements" (drugs) • large employers (farming) • large suppliers to government (mass transportation) • national champions (aerospace) • vital to national security (telecom) • exploiters of natural resources (oil, mining) • subject to high sunk costs (infrastructure)	Products have a low value-of-weight or bulk ratio (cement) Products are fragile or perishable (glass, fruit) Communications and connectivity are important (financial services) Local supervision and operational requirements are high (many services)	Nature of demand varies with income level (cars) Economies of standardization or scale are important (mobile phones) Labour and other factor cost differences are salient (garments) Distribution or business systems are different (insurance) Companies need to be responsive and agile (home appliances)

From Exhibit 8.11 you can see, for instance, that the United States has one of the lowest scores for uncertainty avoidance (i.e., a culture with a high tolerance for uncertainty), and one of the highest scores for individualism (i.e., a highly individualistic culture). These differences may influence the success of a strategic initiative due to the way a new product is perceived by consumers, or the effect they have on how a firm traditionally manages its operations. You have already been introduced to the global trials and successes of Lincoln Electric, for example. One of its key strategic weapons was the use of highly individualistic pay practices, which resonate well with its U.S. employee stakeholders. However, as you can see from Exhibit 8.11, the German culture is not as individualistic, and this offers a partial explanation for the initial failure of this management tool in Germany.

Administrative Distance *Administrative distance* reflects the historical and present political and legal associations between trading partners; for example, colonial ties between trading partners, or participation in common trading blocs. This facet of CAGE asks you to examine whether there are historical or current political factors that might favor or impede a business relationship between a company and a new country market. NAFTA, for instance, decreased the administrative distance between firms in Mexico, Canada, and the United

Exhibit 8.11 Cultural Differences Among Countries

Country	Power Distance	Individualism	Masculinity	Uncertainty Avoidance	Long-term Orientation
Arab World	80	38	52	68	na
Brazil	69	38	49	76	65
China	80	20	66	30	118
Germany	35	67	66	65	31
India	77	48	56	40	61
Japan	54	46	95	92	80
Philippines	94	32	64	44	19
South Korea	60	18	39	85	75
Sweden	31	71	5	29	33
United Kingdom	35	89	66	35	25
United States	40	91	62	46	29

*Hofstede estimated these values for the region comprised of Egypt, Iraq, Kuwait, Lebanon, Libya, Saudi Arabia, and United Arab Emirates. Long-term orientation was not included in his estimates.

States. Similarly, historical political hostilities between the United States and Cuba make it virtually impossible (and illegal) for most U.S. firms to do business there.

As you can imagine, trade practices between countries can be significantly affected by laws and regulations enacted at the national or international level. Because they affect fundamental business practices, they often affect the competitive position of firms as well. Some of the key legal considerations for U.S. firms include the following:

■ **Free Trade Agreements.** Since presidential Trade Promotion Authority (TPA) was restored in 2002, the United States has embarked on an unprecedented effort to open foreign markets to U.S. exports by expanding its network of free trade agreements (FTAs). In 2003 and 2004, negotiations for FTAs with Chile, Singapore, Australia, and Morocco were concluded and subsequently approved by Congress. The latter two came into force in 2005; the FTAs with Chile and Singapore are already generating impressive results. U.S. exports to Chile, for example, increased by 28 percent in the first year of the agreement's implementation.

■ **Import Laws.** Under longstanding U.S. law, harm to U.S. companies caused by dumped products can be offset by antidumping duties if U.S. government investigating agencies—the Commerce Department and the International Trade Commission—are satisfied that certain criteria are met. Similarly, these two agencies can impose countervailing duties on subsidized imports to offset harm caused to U.S. industries by those imports. And numerous other laws are designed to restrict imports on grounds ranging from public health and safety to national security to protection of intellectual property. Such laws are still on the books, even though the recently established World Trade Organization has as a mandate continuing efforts to reduce such practices worldwide.

■ **Foreign Corrupt Practices Act (FCPA).** This U.S. federal law, amended to include OECD antibribery conventions, requires firms to have adequate accounting controls in place, but is most commonly known for its antibribery provisions. The antibribery provisions of the FCPA make it unlawful for a U.S. person, and certain foreign issuers of securities, to make a payment to a foreign official for the purpose of obtaining or retaining business for or with, or directing business to, any person. Since 1998, they also apply to foreign firms and persons who take any action in furtherance of such a corrupt payment while in the United States. The definition of foreign official is broad. For example, an owner of a bank who is also the brother of the minister of finance would qualify as a foreign official according to the U.S. government. There is no materiality to this act, which makes it illegal to offer even a penny as a bribe. The government focuses on the intent of the bribery more than the amount of it.

■ **Intellectual Property Protection.** Patents and trademarks are territorial and must be filed in each country where protection is sought. A U.S. patent or trademark does not afford protection in another country. However, the Patent Cooperation Treaty (PCT) streamlines the process of filing patents in multiple countries. By filing one patent application with the U.S. Patent and Trademark Office (USPTO), U.S. applicants can concurrently seek protection in up to 127 countries. Notable exceptions to this process include China. Indeed, if a firm enters the China market with a product but does not register its mark at China's Trademark Office, one of the firm's competitors, distributors, or partners may be able to register the trademark before them and bar them from manufacturing or selling the products with their mark in China. Despite international attention to the importance of intellectual property rights, their protection remains problematic in many developing countries. At the www.stopfakes.gov website, maintained by the U.S. Department of Commerce, there are intellectual property protection toolkits for Brazil, China, Korea, Malaysia, Mexico, Peru, Russia, and Taiwan—countries identified as among the most problematic.

Geographic Distance How far apart are trading partners in physical terms: the size of the country, differences in climates, and nature of transportation and information networks? You can think of *geographic distance* as absolute, in terms of the miles or kilometers that separate a firm from another market or supplier. Technology, however, has shrunk distance in terms of transportation time, and now with digital products and services, almost entirely eliminated geographic distance as a constraint of trade between some markets.

One of the most dramatic changes in trade was facilitated by the shipping container, which in many cases moves seamlessly between one country, shipping channels, and another country. The most recent example, of course, where distance has been reduced is with the case of the Internet. W.W. Grainger, for example, a leader in the U.S. maintenance, repair, and overhaul (MRO) industry, found that the Internet provided it a ready sales vehicle into European markets. Prior to the Internet it could not justify an investment in a far-flung European brick-and-mortar presence. With the Internet, its storefront in Europe became virtual.

Economic Distance Finally, *economic distance* captures fundamental differences relating to income, the distribution of wealth, and the relative purchasing power of segments of a geographic market. This has been one of the biggest barriers, for instance, in the way of firms' success selling products in emerging markets. In global terms, this is the four billion people who live on less than $2 per day. The phrase "bottom of the pyramid" is used in particular by people developing new models of doing business that deliberately target that market, typically using new technology. An example of a product that is designed with the needs of the very poor in mind is that of a shampoo that works best with cold water. Such a product is marketed by Hindustan Lever (part of the Unilever family of firms).

How would you calculate economic difference? You should have ready access to information on per capita income and relative purchasing power across countries. In the following "How Would *You* Do That? 8.1," you can see a sample per country per capita income difference for a cross-section of countries. This data will give you a sense of the income that individuals or companies may have to spend on a new product or service. At the same time, you should gain an understanding of the pricing for comparable products or services. This is why economic distance also includes the economics of supply for comparable or

Putting CAGE to Work at Virgin Mobile

The starting point for your CAGE analysis is something called a country attractiveness portfolio (CAP). A CAP is created using data on a country or region's per capita income, along with data on some aspect of the market's desirability, such as market penetration or per capita spending on a focal product or service. With this information, you would have two reference points that you plot on a grid, for each country. For instance, if you were Virgin Mobile, a U.K.-based cell phone company with an interest in entering a new geographic arena outside of its home European Union market, you would want to collect information on the percentage of the population that uses cell phones in other countries, along with country per capita income. By looking at the CIA's 2006 World Factbook, which is summarized in Exhibit 8.12, you found

the following information (you also happened to collect information on each country's population, since that will give you an idea of the percentage of people who have cell phones, or the current market penetration for cell phones in each country).

Since you were smart enough to rank order the data by cell phones, you can see that China has the biggest actual market. In some markets you see that the number of cell phones in use actually exceeds the labor force, which means that kids and retired people must be using them as well. Your next step is to plot out some of this data on a grid, so you have a better visual image of the possible market arenas. This is where the population data come in. You simply plot each country's location on the grid using number of cell phones on the X axis, and per capita income on the

Y axis—then use the bubble size to give you a rough impression of the relative opportunity presented by each market, in terms of the actual population. We picked population because it maps well to the idea of the potential cell phone market, but you could use other aggregated indicators like gross domestic product, number of factories, and so on. The best dimension is one that can give you an idea of the country's market size for the particular product or service you are analyzing. Exhibit 8.13 shows you your CAP, using population as an indicator of market size.

Had you not been reading this chapter, you would have concluded that you were done with your analysis. Based solely on the information in Exhibit 8.13, what country would you have chosen for Virgin's expansion move? And sadly, this is why so many

Exhibit 8.12 Market Characteristics

Rank	Country	Cell Phones	Per Capita Income	Population
1	China	334,824,000	$7,600	1,321,851,888
2	European Union	314,644,700	$29,400	460,827,146
3	United States	194,479,364	$43,500	301,139,947
4	Japan	91,473,900	$33,100	127,433,494
5	Russia	74,420,000	$12,100	141,377,752
6	India	69,193,321	$3,700	1,129,866,154
7	Brazil	65,605,000	$8,600	190,010,647
8	Mexico	38,451,100	$10,600	108,700,891
9	South Korea	36,586,100	$24,200	49,044,790

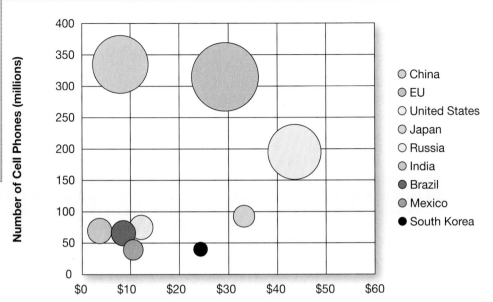

Exhibit 8.13 Country Attractiveness Portfolio

- ○ China
- ◔ EU
- ○ United States
- ◔ Japan
- ○ Russia
- ◔ India
- ● Brazil
- ◔ Mexico
- ● South Korea

CAP's are fundamentally flawed. The information in Exhibit 8.13 does give you an idea of the relative attractiveness of each country market, and you can see their relative size related to per capita income, and so on. For a company like Virgin, they would probably like to enter a new country market where income is high, and the market is very big. They do fine in Europe, and as you can see from Exhibit 8.12 (and 8.13), that market is both big and relatively rich. However, these exhibits do not tell you how well Virgin is prepared to enter those markets—you only know that they are big, but will they be big (as in a homerun) for Virgin? The third and final step is to adjust the size of the bubbles upward or downward for CAGE-based differences along the dimensions of culture, administration, geography, and economics. This will tell you how attractive each country is, *after adjusting for the critical CAGE differences*. For instance, this would probably lead you to discount all the markets, other than the U.S. market, and you might adjust the U.S. market upward. A CAGE-adjusted CAP is shown in Exhibit 8.14.

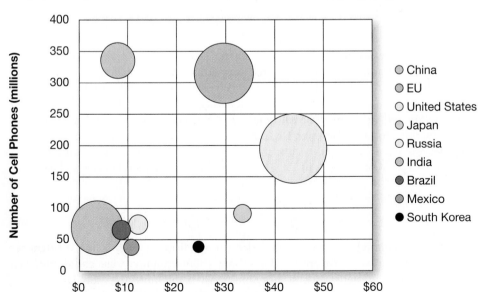

Exhibit 8.14 CAGE-Adjusted CAP for Virgin Mobile

- ○ China
- ◔ EU
- ○ United States
- ◔ Japan
- ○ Russia
- ◔ India
- ● Brazil
- ◔ Mexico
- ● South Korea

substitute products in a market. For instance, processed cheese (like Velveeta) tends to cost less than fresh cheese in U.S. supermarkets, and low relative price is a key selling point for processed cheese. A recent U.S. entrant to the Brazilian cheese market assumed this same price relationship. After setting up their factory, however, they found that fresh cheese was very good *and* cheap in Brazilian supermarkets. The company wrongly assumed they would have a price advantage, when in fact the economics of cheese production in Brazil typically made processed cheese a higher-priced, and relatively less attractive, product.

Based on the CAGE-adjusted CAP you calculated for Virgin, for instance, you would probably recommend that Virgin Mobile should think about entering the U.S. market. Beyond this work, a full analysis could consider how a company's own characteristics operate to increase or reduce distance from foreign arenas. Companies with a large cadre of cosmopolitan managers, for instance, will be less affected by cultural differences than companies whose managers are all from the home country. Other company characteristics can help or hurt as well. In Virgin's case, consideration of company-specific features make the United States even more attractive. For instance, Virgin's parent company, Virgin Atlantic Airways, has a pretty sexy image in the United States, particularly in the demographic that would be the ideal target market for Virgin Mobile. Despite starting well behind companies like Orange or Vodafone in the United Kingdom, Virgin has become the fastest-growing cell phone provider in that country, with more than 700,000 customers added in its first 15 months of operation.

So what have we learned by using CAGE in the context of Dell and Virgin Mobile, and international expansion more generally? You should now see that the CAGE framework can be used to address the questions of where to expand internationally (which arena) and how to expand (by which vehicle). It can also help you map out the staging and pacing of your strategic international expansion moves so as to maximize the strategy's anchoring in the firm's VRINE-based resources and capabilities. You can see the CAGE-based logic at work in recent moves by Indian and Chinese competitors, for instance. Chinese technology-based companies like Lenovo are offering their products (laptops in Lenovo's case), but outsourcing the service side to English-speaking Indian firms. In contrast, a number of Indian companies have bought third- and fourth-tier U.S. or European manufacturers, and used their proximity to China to outsource production to China. Finally, a firm with an already large, but diverse, global presence can use CAGE to reevaluate which countries to stay in, and which ones to exit.

The opening vignette about Dell further demonstrates the usefulness of the CAGE framework. As you saw in the case of Dell, the vehicles it used to enter China were just as important in its China strategy as the choice of geographic arena it entered. For Dell's corporate clients in China, a CAGE framework would reveal relatively little distance on all four dimensions, even geographic, given the fact that many PC components are sourced from China. However, for the consumer segment, the distance is rather great, particularly on the dimensions of culture, administration, and economics. One outcome here could have been Dell's avoidance of the consumer market altogether. However, Dell opted to choose an alliance with distributors whose knowledge base and capabilities enabled it to better bridge the CAGE-framework distances until it was in a position to engage its Dell Direct model with consumers (staging and pacing).

Entry Vehicles into Foreign Countries

The strategy diamond says that a critical element of a firm's strategy is how it enters new markets. Now that you have answered questions about economic logic and desired geographic arena, your international strategy must answer the "how" question. How will you enter that new market? With international strategy, these new markets just happen to be in different countries, with different laws, infrastructure, cultures, and consumer preferences. The various entry mechanisms are referred to as *vehicles of strategy*. Consequently, a critical

Exhibit 8.15   Choice of Entry Vehicles

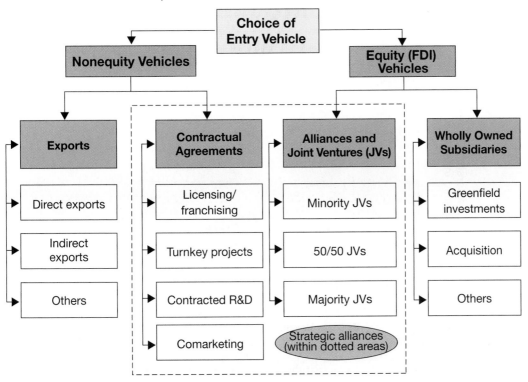

element of international expansion is determining which vehicles to use to enter new global markets. The first choice that managers must make is whether they will enter a foreign country with a vehicle that requires the firm to put some, or even considerable, capital at risk. As shown in Exhibit 8.15, firms can choose among a variety of nonequity and equity vehicles for entering a foreign country.[24] ◆ Exhibit 8.16 provides you with examples of the vehicles chosen by different firms around the world.[25]

The second choice that managers must make is the type of the vehicle. Typically, each type of vehicle offers differing levels of ownership control and local presence. Although firms can expand internationally in a number of different ways, we present them to you under three overarching foreign-country entry vehicles: *exporting, contractual agreements* and *alliances,* and *foreign direct investment (FDI),* either through the acquisition of a company or simply starting one from scratch. At the end of this section, we will briefly discuss the use of importing as a foreign-country entry vehicle; it is somewhat of a stealth form of internationalization.

Foreign-country entry has been viewed historically as a staged process. Like the industry life cycle, the internationalization life cycle starts with a firm importing some of its raw materials or finished product for resale at home, followed perhaps by exporting products or raw materials abroad, and lastly ending in some type of partial or full ownership of plant, equipment, or other more extensive physical presence in a foreign country. These stages could be accomplished using vehicles ranging from simple contracts for purchases or sales on a transaction basis, through alliances, and perhaps even via mergers or wholesale acquisitions. Lincoln Electric, which was discussed in the previous section, offers an example of international growth through acquisition.

Over time, research has suggested that although some firms do follow such stages, they are better viewed as being more descriptive than predictive. Specifically, some firms follow the stages, starting with importing through foreign direct investment, whereas others jump right to the direct investment stage as their first internationalization effort.[26]

Exhibit 8.16 Vehicles for Entering Foreign Markets

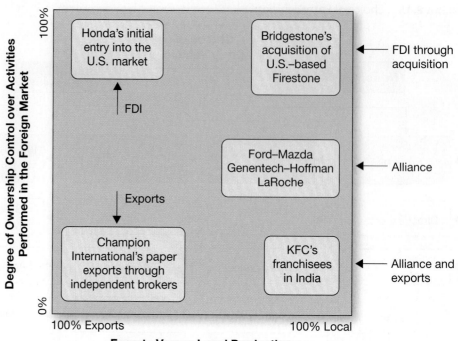

It is also helpful to note that the different entry vehicles have differing degrees of risk and control. For instance, a company that is only exporting its products abroad is typically risking its payment for the product, and perhaps its reputation if the product is not serviced well in the foreign locale. This also shows how little control the exporter has over the downstream activities once it has shipped the product. Although the exporter may have some legal or distribution agreement with local firms, this is very little control compared

South African Breweries, the maker of Castle Lager, successfully entered one of the largest beer markets in the world—the United States—by acquiring Miller Brewing Company in 2002. The combined corporation is known as SABMiller.

to ownership of local factories or distribution, or partial ownership through some form of alliance. In this section, we will walk you through these alternative entry vehicles.

EXPORTING

Exporting is exactly the opposite of importing; it can take the form of selling production or service inputs or actual products and services abroad. With the advent of the Internet and electronic banking, the physical entry barriers to becoming an exporter are lower than ever before. Although the importer is ultimately responsible for the issues relating to customs, packaging, and other trade requirements, the exporting firm will generally only be successful to the extent that it can deliver a product or service that meets customers' needs.

exporting Foreign-country entry vehicle in which a firm uses an intermediary to perform most foreign marketing functions.

Costs of Exporting Exporting is a popular internationalization vehicle with small firms because the costs of entering new markets are relatively minimal with this vehicle. Exporters generally use local representatives or distributors to sell their products in new international markets. The main costs associated with exporting are transportation and meeting the packaging and ingredient requirements of the target country. Consequently, exporting is most common to international markets that are relatively close to the domestic market or to markets in which competitors and substitutes for the firm's products are not readily available. A large percentage of the born-global firms discussed later in the chapter used exporting as a vehicle to go global quickly.[27]

Contractual Agreements **Contractual agreements** are an entry vehicle where a firm typically relies on another to manage their market presence. The contract itself can take a variety of forms, from a verbal agreement to an extensive legal document, but often relates to one of the following four types of agreements.

contractual agreement An exchange of promises or agreement between parties that is often enforceable by the law.

Licensing and Franchising Exporting can take the form of shipping a product overseas and leaving marketing and distribution up to a foreign customer. It can also take the form of licensing or franchising, turnkey projects, R&D contracts, and comarketing. Due to some of the characteristics of these latter vehicles, as shown in Exhibit 8.15, such contractual arrangements are often considered a form of strategic alliance. Licensing and franchising provide a case in point. When a firm licenses its products or technologies in another country, it transfers the risk of actually implementing market entry to another firm, which pays the licensor a fee for the right to use its name in the local country. Franchising in a foreign country works similarly to franchising in a domestic market. A firm receives a sign-up fee and ongoing franchise royalties in exchange for teaching the franchisee how to open and operate the franchisor's business in the local market.

The risk, of course, to the licensor or franchisor is that the licensee or franchisee will violate the terms of the agreement, either to the detriment of the product or service itself, by refusing to pay agreed-upon fees or royalties or simply selling a copy of the product or service under another name (that is essentially stealing the intellectual property entirely). The primary risks to the franchisee or licensee are that the product or service will not perform as promised or that the licensor or franchisor will do something that diminishes the market attractiveness of the product or service.

Turnkey Projects, R&D Contracts, and Comarketing The latter three forms—turnkey projects, R&D contracts, and comarketing—are specialized contractual agreements whereby a firm agrees to build a factory, conduct a specific R&D project, or comarket or cobrand a product such that the contracting firm has used it as a foreign-market entry vehicle. For example, the Norwegian firm Kvaerner A/S contracts to build paper mills and deep-sea oil rigs for Brazilian paper and petroleum companies; the German firm Bayer AG contracts a large R&D project to the U.S. firm Millennium pharmaceuticals with the work undertaken in both firms' respective countries; McDonald's in Japan packages its kids meals with characters that are familiar to Japanese children based on characters like Pokémon or Hello Kitty that are popular at the time.

ALLIANCES

Alliances are another common foreign-market entry vehicle. Because we devote an entire chapter to alliances later in the text, here we simply explain why alliances are so commonly used for international expansion. Often, alliances are chosen because of government regulations. For example, only recently did the Chinese government allow non-Chinese ownership of companies in China. As a result, firms could only enter China through various partnerships. Alliances may also be used as an international-strategy vehicle due to management's lack of familiarity with the local culture or institutions or because the complexity of operating internationally requires the firm to focus on the activities it does best and to outsource the rest. Some combination of these three factors—regulations, market familiarity, or operational complexity—typically explain why alliances are so often used by firms competing internationally. For instance, Virgin Mobile partnered with Sprint when it initially entered the U.S. market in 2002.

FOREIGN DIRECT INVESTMENT

foreign direct investment (FDI) Foreign-country entry vehicle by which a firm commits to the direct ownership of a foreign subsidiary or division.

greenfield investment Form of FDI in which a firm starts a new foreign business from the ground up.

Foreign direct investment (FDI), as the term implies, is an international entry strategy whereby a firm makes a financial investment in a foreign market to facilitate the startup of a new venture. FDI tends to be the most expensive international entry tactic because it requires the greatest commitment of a firm's time and resources. FDI can be implemented in several ways, such as through acquisitions or through a so-called greenfield alliance—the startup of a foreign entity from scratch. This latter form of FDI is called **greenfield investment**. In the previous section, we reviewed how alliances can be a vehicle to foreign market entry. As you will learn in Chapter 9, alliances do not require any equity investment. However, many alliances do involve equity investment, and when they do in the context of foreign market entry, it is a special case of greenfield investment. For instance, DaimlerChrysler and BMW each invested $250 million to start a new engine factory in Curitiba, Brazil.

Acquisitions and Equity Alliances

Because greenfield investment usually involves the greatest risk, expense, and time, many firms pursue FDI through acquisitions or alliances (you will learn more about these particular strategy vehicles in Chapters 9 and 10). Acquisitions provide the firm with rapid entry because the firm purchases existing businesses that are already staffed and successfully operating. For instance, when the battery maker Rayovac entered Brazil in 2005, it did so by purchasing Microlite, the dominant battery maker in Brazil. Similarly, South African Breweries purchased Miller Brewing in 2002 to gain an instant presence and production capacity in one of the largest beer markets in the world, the United States.

After its horrendous experiences with rapid international expansion, Lincoln Electric amended its corporate policy on FDI: It now engages only in FDI through alliances with local players in order to maximize the knowledge needed about local market conditions, both in terms of production and market demand. Sometimes alliances are dictated by the necessity to have a certain proportion of local content in a product, such as a car or motorcycle, in order to sell the product into a nonlocal market. Brazil and China are two examples of countries that have stringent local-content laws. Minimum efficient scale is another explanation for the use of alliances as an FDI foreign-entry tactic.

For example, the DaimlerChrysler and BMW alliance mentioned earlier was necessary because neither company could justify the volume of production needed by the new plant to justify it economically. Therefore, the two firms joined forces to form Tritec, a state-of-the-art automotive engine factory that supplies parts for BMW's Mini Cooper assembly plant in the United Kingdom and DaimlerChrysler's PT Cruiser assembly plants in Mexico, the United States, and South Africa.[28]

IMPORTING AND INTERNATIONAL STRATEGY

In many ways, **importing** is a stealth form of internationalization because firms will often claim they have no international operations and yet directly or indirectly base their production or services on inputs obtained from outside their home country. Firms that engage in importing must be knowledgeable about customs requirements and informed about compliance with customs regulations, entry of goods, invoices, classification and value, determination and assessment of duty, special requirements, fraud, marketing, trade finance and insurance, and foreign trade zones. Importing can take many forms, from the sourcing of components, machinery, and raw materials to the purchase of finished goods for domestic resale to outsourcing production or services to nondomestic providers.

> **importing** Internationalization strategy by which a firm brings a good, service, or capital into the home country from abroad.

Outsourcing and Offshoring

This latter activity, international outsourcing, has taken on the most visible role in business and corporate strategy in recent years. International outsourcing is not a new phenomenon. For instance, Nike has been designing shoes and other apparel for decades and manufacturing them abroad. Similarly, Pacific Cycle does not make a single Schwinn or Mongoose bicycle in the United States but instead imports them from Taiwanese and Chinese manufacturers. It just seems that international outsourcing is new because of the increasingly rapid pace with which businesses are sourcing services, components, and raw materials from developing countries such as China, Brazil, and India.

Information technologies (IT), such as telecommunications and the widespread diffusion of the Internet, have provided the impetus for the international outsourcing of services as well as factors of production. Such *business process outsourcing (BPO)* is the delegation of one or more IT-intensive business processes to an external nondomestic provider which, in turn, owns, administers, and manages the selected process based on defined and measurable performance criteria. Sometimes this is referred to as **offshoring** because the business processes (including production/manufacturing) are outsourced to a lower-cost location, usually overseas. Offshoring refers to taking advantage of lower-cost labor in another country. Although outsourced processes are handed off to third-party vendors, offshored processes may be handed off to third-party vendors or remain in-house. This definition of offshoring includes organizations that build dedicated captive centers of their own in remote, lower-cost locations. The many U.S. and Canadian firms that have established *maquiladoras* (assembly plants) in Mexico are examples of offshoring without outsourcing.

> **offshoring** Moving a value chain activity or set of activities to another country, typically where key costs are lower.

Firms in such service- and IT-intensive industries as insurance, banking, pharmaceuticals, telecommunications, automobiles, and airlines seem to be the early adopters of BPO. Of the industries just mentioned, insurance and banking are able to generate savings purely because of the large proportion of processes they can outsource, such as claim processing, loan processing, and client servicing through call centers. Among those countries housing BPO operations, India appears to be experiencing the most dramatic growth for services that require English-language skills and education. BPO operations have been growing 70 percent a year and are now a $1.6 billion industry, employing approximately 100,000 people. In India alone, BPO has to grow only 27 percent annually until 2008 to deliver $17 billion in revenues and employ a million people.[29]

More generally, foreign outsourcing and offshoring locations tend to be defined by how automated a production process or service can be made, the relative labor costs, and the transportation costs involved. When transportation costs and automation are both high, then the knowledge-worker component of the location calculation becomes less important. You can see how you might employ the CAGE framework to evaluate potential outsourcing locations. However, in some cases firms invest in both plant and equipment and the training and development of the local workforce. Brazil is but one case in point, with examples from BMW, Daimler-Benz, Ford, and Cargill. Each of these multinational organizations is making significant investments in the educational infrastructure of this enormous emerging economy.[30]

International Strategy Configurations

How a firm becomes involved in international markets—which appears to be increasingly important, if not obligatory, for many if not all firms—differs from how it configures the interactions between headquarters and country operations. It is important to note that international-strategy configuration is as much about strategy formulation as it is about implementation, because management is making choices about which value-chain components to centralize, where to centralize those operations geographically, and the degree to which those decentralized and centralized value-chain activities will be managed and coordinated. Remember, too, that strategy helps a firm manage important tradeoffs that differentiate it and its products from competitors.

RESOLVING THE TENSION BETWEEN LOCAL PREFERENCES AND GLOBAL STANDARDS

In this section, we discuss the underlying tensions created between a firm's attempts to be responsive to the local needs of diverse sets of customers and yet remain globally efficient. Meeting the ideal tradeoff between customizing for local needs and achieving cost efficiencies requires further tradeoffs with respect to the firm's value chain regarding which activities will be standardized and which will be locally tailored. These are the central tradeoffs a firm must wrestle with in designing and managing its international strategy.

Globalizing firms must reconcile the natural tension that exists between local preferences and global standards. The domination of local preferences over the search for global efficiencies, left unchecked, often leads to what strategy researchers describe as *market fragmentation*.[31] In addition, local adaptation of products and services is significantly more expensive than relying on global standards. Consequently, attempting to achieve high levels of local responsiveness will almost always lead to higher cost structure.[32] A product that is uniform across markets is highly efficient to produce because the firm can simply design a factory of the most efficient size in a location that most efficiently balances the costs of inputs with the transportation costs of getting outputs to the desired markets. If this product has the same brand around the world, then marketing and promotion efforts are similarly focused on that single brand. However, even products like Coca-Cola, which appear to be ubiquitous, have different flavorings, packaging, and promotion constraints in each market. Some of these constraints are a function of local regulatory pressures; others reflect underlying differences in consumers' tastes. Just as important, other constraints are a function of the competitive norms that have prevailed in the industry, either globally or locally. The variations of international strategy configurations that we cover in this section—making tradeoffs between local responsiveness and global efficiency—are summarized in Exhibit 8.17.[33]

We will also speak briefly about born-global firms in this section because more and more organizations appear to have operations that span national borders early in their existence. As you will see, born-global firms employ an amalgam of exporting and FDI, but do so much more rapidly than firms have in the past. In the strategy diamond, exporting and FDI are considered vehicles, and the timing and sequencing of the usage are viewed in the context of staging. Each of these vehicles provides a firm and its management with experience and knowledge about cross-border business practices.

Exhibit 8.17   International Strategy Configurations and Local/Global Tradeoffs

	Relatively Few Opportunities to Gain Global Efficiencies	**Many Opportunities to Gain Global Efficiencies**
Relatively High Local Responsiveness	**Multinational Vision** Build flexibility to respond to national differences through strong, resourceful, entrepreneurial, and somewhat independent national or regional operations. Requires decentralized and relatively self-sufficient units. **Example:** MTV initially adopted an international configuration (using only American programming in foreign markets) but then changed its strategy to a multinational one. It now tailors its Western European programming to each market, offering eight channels, each in a different language.	**Transnational Vision** Develop global efficiency, flexibility, and worldwide learning. Requires dispersed, interdependent, and specialized capabilities simultaneously. **Example:** Nestlé has taken steps to move in this direction, starting first with what might be described as a multinational configuration. Today, Nestlé aims to evolve from a decentralized, profit-center configuration to one that operates as a single, global company. Firms like Nestlé have taken lessons from leading consulting firms such as McKinsey and Company, which are globally dispersed but have a hard-driving, one-firm culture at their core.
Relatively Low Local Responsiveness	**International Vision** Exploit parent-company knowledge and capabilities through worldwide diffusion, local marketing, and adaptation. The most valuable resources and capabilities are centralized; others, such as local marketing and distribution, are decentralized. **Example:** When Wal-Mart initially set up its operations in Brazil, it used its U.S. stores as a model for international expansion.	**Global Vision** Build cost advantages through centralized, global-scale operations. Requires centralized and globally scaled resources and capabilities. **Example:** Companies such as Merck and Hewlett-Packard give particular subsidiaries a worldwide mandate to leverage and disseminate their unique capabilities and specialized knowledge worldwide.

Emphasize Local Responsiveness   Each of the configurations identified in Exhibit 8.17 presents tradeoffs between global efficiency and local responsiveness. Recognize that in reality, most firms' international strategy configurations vary slightly or significantly from those shown in Exhibit 8.17. By definition, strategy must be internally consistent and externally oriented. However, management must make judgments as to what an external orientation means in terms of how the strategy takes competitive pressures and consumer preferences into account. At the same time, management must also make judgments about the firm's internal resources and capabilities to support a particular international-strategy configuration. This explains why firms with seemingly very different international-strategy configurations can coexist in the same industry.

When Lincoln Electric first embarked on becoming a global firm, it had relatively independent operations in many markets around the world. It used its strongest national

cross-subsidizing Practice by which a firm uses profits from one aspect of a product, service, or region to support other aspects of competitive activity.

positions to **cross-subsidize** market-share battles or growth initiatives in other countries. Such an approach is essentially a portfolio of geographically removed business units that have devoted most of their resources and capabilities to maximizing local responsiveness and uniqueness. Firms which, like Lincoln Electric, employ this configuration have the objective to develop a global presence but may or may not use the same brand names in each market or consolidate their buying power or distribution capabilities.

Emphasize Global Efficiencies with Some Local Advantages

Another configuration centralizes some resources, such as global brand and distribution capabilities, in order to achieve costs savings; but decentralizes others, such as marketing, in order to achieve some level of localization. This strategy is common among firms that have created something in their home market that they wish to replicate in foreign markets, allowing them the economies of scale and scope necessary to create and exploit innovations on a worldwide basis. Heavy R&D companies such as Intel and Pfizer fit this mold: Even though the products that they produce are relatively standardized around the world, local marketing and distribution channels differ.

Emphasize Global Efficiencies

This configuration focuses only on global efficiency. A tradeoff is made between local responsiveness and the lower costs associated with global efficiency. With this configuration, production and sourcing decisions are designed to achieve the greatest economies of scale. Firms following this configuration potentially sacrifice the higher prices that follow customization, but they are counting on the likelihood that their products or services will meet enough needs to be demanded without finely tuned customization. Firms in commodity industries such as steel and copper, such as BHP-Billeton, fall into this category. Because end customers make purchase decisions based on price alone, the firm is organized to realize the lowest possible production costs.

Seek to Exploit Local Advantages and Global Efficiencies

The final international-strategy configuration that we discuss is one that attempts to capitalize on both local responsiveness and global efficiency. When successfully implemented, this approach enables firms to achieve global economies of scale, cross-subsidization across markets, and the ability to engage in retaliatory and responsive competition across markets. This configuration is available to companies with high degrees of internationalization. However, as with any other strategic tradeoff, it is extremely difficult to find the balance between cost efficiencies and the ability to customize to local tastes and standards. McDonald's is often used as an example of a firm that fits this configuration because it uses its purchasing power to get the best prices on the global commodities it uses for inputs, yet tries to tailor its menu offerings to fit local tastes and cultural preferences.

BORN-GLOBAL FIRMS

One reason that global strategy—and the four international strategy configurations—will become an increasingly important topic is the fact that more and more firms, even very small ones, have operations that bridge national borders very soon after their founding. Perhaps appropriate for the Internet age, this new breed of firms that emerged in the 1990s is being dubbed "born global" because their operations often span the globe early in their existence. A common characteristic of such firms is that their offerings complement the products or capabilities of other global players, take advantage of global IT infrastructure, or otherwise tap into a demand for a product or service that at its core is somewhat uniform across national geographic markets. Although many firms may fall into this category by virtue of their products, the operations and customers of born-global firms do actually span the globe. Born-global firms position themselves globally, exploiting a combination of exporting and FDI.

Logitech, the computer-mouse and peripherals company, is perhaps one of the best early examples of a successful born-global firm.[34] It was founded by two Italians and a Swiss, with operations and R&D initially split between California and Switzerland. Logitech's primary focus was on the PC mouse, and it rapidly expanded production to Ireland and Taiwan. With its stylish and ergonomic products, Logitech had captured 30 percent of the global mouse business by 1989, garnering the startup a healthy $140 million in revenues. Today, Logitech is an industry leader in the design and manufacture of computer-peripheral devices. It has manufacturing facilities in Asia and offices in major cities in North America, Europe, and Asia Pacific and employs more than 6,000 people worldwide.[35]

How to Succeed as a Global Startup   Successful global startups must complete two phases. In the first phase, managers ask, "Should my firm be a global startup?" If they can answer "yes" to all or most of the follow-up questions entailed by phase 1, then they need to be sure that they can quickly build the resources and capabilities identified in phase 2. Research has shown that those firms unable to connect the dots in phase 2 were forced to cease operations after short, albeit sometimes lively, adventures.[36]

During phase 1—*and before moving on to phase 2*—managers should consider questions that will help them determine whether the firm should be a global startup:

- Does the firm need human resources from other countries in order to succeed?

- Does the firm need financial capital from other countries in order to succeed?

- If the firm goes global, will target customers prefer its services over those of competitors?

- Can the firm put an international system in place more quickly than domestic competitors?

- Does the firm need global scale and scope to justify the financial and human capital investment in the venture?

- Will a purely domestic focus now make it harder for the firm to go global in the future?

If the answer to all or most of these questions is "yes," managers can commit to moving the firm into phase 2 and put together the tools they will need to move the firm into the global market:

- Strong management team with international experience

- Broad and deep international network among suppliers, customers, and complements

- Preemptive marketing or technology that will provide first-mover advantage with customers and lock out competitors from key suppliers and complements

- Strong intangible assets (Logitech has style, hipness, and mindshare via their brand)

- Ability to keep customers locked in by linking new products and services to the core business, while constantly innovating the core product or service

- Close worldwide coordination and communication among business units, suppliers, complements, and customers

So why do we introduce the concept of global startups at this point in the text? One reason is because of their increasing prevalence, which is driven, in part, by globalizing consumer preferences, mobile consumers, large global firms, and the pervasiveness of the Internet and its effects. The second reason, which should become clear after reading the next section, is that dynamic contexts typically give rise to the need for firms to strive for a global presence and to understand global markets early in their evolution.

International Strategy in Stable and Dynamic Contexts

Staging & Pacing

A recent McKinsey study suggests that the creativity that some companies have found in emerging economies, and that have resulted in inexpensive but high-quality products, will now compel incumbents to go down the same road.[37] This assertion gets at the heart—the question of urgency and timing—of how international strategy is approached in relatively stable versus dynamic contexts. ◆ Moreover, it also suggests that industries that might have been considered relatively stable will increasingly take on dynamic characteristics as a result of global competition. In many ways, what you have learned so far about business and corporate strategies in dynamic contexts is equally applicable in purely domestic and already globalizing organizations. The key difference, however—a difference that we hope is apparent after reading this chapter—is that cross-border business adds another level of complexity to both strategy formulation and execution and, that unfortunately, such complexity may be unavoidable for firms in dynamic contexts.

GLOBAL CONTEXT AND INDUSTRY LIFE CYCLE

Recall from earlier chapters that we differentiated between external- and internal-based views of strategy. The internal view emphasizes resources, capabilities, and activities as the source of competitive advantage; whereas the external view draws attention to how firms need to adapt or modify their competitive positions and strategies to the external environment to position themselves in a manner conducive to superior returns. These views have implications for the dynamic nature of international strategic action, as well. Taking the external perspective, for instance, typically draws managerial attention to the dynamic nature of the industry life cycle and how that drives decisions to internationalize. Specifically, as an industry matures, the international implications of industry structure—and therefore strategic choices and firm behavior—should change in fundamental ways.[38]

First-Mover Advantage   In the introductory stage of an industry's life cycle, the external perspective would expect firms to engage in few exports, largely because the market for the industry's products is still highly uncertain and there are few accepted quality, service, or technological standards. As you will see, the length of this stage may vary significantly by country. Firms should begin to export during the growth stage of industry life cycle because new firms enter the market and compete for existing customers. Early movers in the domestic market then have an opportunity to be early movers in foreign markets as well and to continue growth even as domestic competition heats up. As the industry matures, exports gain even more steam in the face of domestic market saturation, and firms start producing products abroad to satisfy foreign demand and to search for global efficiencies. Industry shakeout and consolidation also tend to follow industry maturity, and consolidation through acquisitions leads to a few large global companies.

Staging and Geographic Markets   Similarly, when discussing international strategy from an external perspective, the fact that geographic markets differ in many legal, cultural, and institutional ways—differences which, in turn, are likely to have implications for product demand—must also be taken into account. Indeed, demand characteristics of geographic markets have been shown to evolve at different rates. For example, the time from new-product introduction to the growth stage (sometimes called market takeoff) in Portugal may occur after a longer period of time than the same transition in Denmark. Indeed, although the average period of time between a new-product or new-service introduction and market takeoff is 6 years, a new product takes only about 4 years to take off in Denmark, Norway, and Sweden, compared to 9 years in Greece and Portugal (the United States averages 5.3 years).[39]

Role of Arenas in Global Strategies   Identification of arenas ensures that the most critical national markets are identified and brought into the plan. Similarly, even with thoughtful treatment of staging and arenas, structures, systems, and processes must be in complete alignment with the firm's vision and global intent. A firm that strives to execute the most complex global strategy—the transnational strategy—must have enormous investments in its ability to coordinate and integrate activities around the globe, complemented by customer characteristics that enable such a global strategy to create true value.

Resources and Global Strategy   The resource-based perspective has important implications for international strategy in dynamic contexts as well. It is here, too, that the questions of staging and geographic arenas from the strategy diamond model are critically important to effective international strategies. From the resource-based perspective, staging is important because the firm's global resources and capabilities do not materialize overnight. Lincoln Electric's experience is a case in point here. Lincoln's pace of international expansion exceeded its organizational capabilities to integrate foreign acquisitions, let alone manage them once they were integrated. Lincoln also attempted to internationalize almost exclusively through acquisitions. However, research on foreign expansion reveals that the firms most successful at internationalizing combine greenfield investments with acquisitions and alliances.[40] Simply expanding through greenfield investment can lead to inertia and lack of learning. Acquisitions help broaden a firm's knowledge base. However, exclusive reliance on acquisitions is not only costly but makes knowledge transfer and learning more difficult. Firms that balance greenfield investments and acquisitions seem to transfer more knowledge and create more value than firms that rely on either process exclusively.

Capabilities and Global Strategy   One of the fundamental ideas of having a dynamic view of strategy is to continuously build and renew firm capabilities. Many born-global firms fall into this dynamic-context category nearly from inception. By continuously evolving its stock of resources and capabilities, a firm maximizes its chances of adapting to changing environmental conditions. Thus, when a firm decides to enter a particular new foreign market, it must also embark on developing the resources necessary to make that market-entry decision a success. At the same time, what it learns in those new geographic markets should be evaluated for application or adaptation to existing market positions.

In addition, as a firm internationalizes and becomes more dependent on a particular foreign location, the need for high-level capabilities to perform the local activities increases commensurately.[41] For instance, as Ikea expands around the globe, its ability to understand local furniture markets increases. However, these needs are greatest in markets where it faces the most exposure; Ikea's early missteps in the United States have been attributed to lack of market intelligence.[42] This leads us to our closing section on global strategy in dynamic contexts.

DEVELOPING A MINDSET FOR GLOBAL DYNAMIC COMPETITIVENESS

Given the emphasis on the importance of leadership skills throughout this text, it should come as no surprise that what may make or break the effectiveness of a firm's international strategy is the internationally related capabilities and global mindset of the firm's executives, particularly in dynamic markets. Moreover, such capabilities and mindset may enable one firm to change a once relatively stable competitive context into a dynamic and vibrant one.

Global Perspective   The global mindset has two distinct but related dimensions. The first dimension is something that strategy researchers simply refer to as global perspective.[43] Executives with a global perspective require a combination of specific knowledge and skills. In terms of knowledge, executives with a global mindset have an appreciation for the fact that countries and their peoples differ culturally, socioeconomically, and sociopolitically; view those differences as potential opportunities as opposed to threats; and can link such differences to necessary adaptations in business operations. In addition, they also recognize that the management processes guiding those business operations must also be adapted to cultural, socioeconomic, and sociopolitical differences.

As opposed to conventional and routine cross-country transfers, companies are exposing managers to problem-solving situations in different business environments. An interesting example in this context is Dell Computer. Traditionally, Dell's practice has been to use local managers to run its outfits in different parts of the world. For important functions, Dell uses teams of specialists who move around the world providing expertise in specific areas. One such team which picked up design expertise while setting up Dell's manufacturing facilities in Texas, has been spending time in countries such as Ireland, Malaysia, China, and Brazil to set up plants there. In each of these countries, the team spends typically six months to one year.

Learning on a Worldwide Scale   In many ways, the second dimension of a global mindset requires the first dimension as a foundation. The second dimension is the capacity to learn from participation in one geographic market and transfer that knowledge to other operations elsewhere in the world. This means that the firm not only has globally savvy executives, but that these executives form an effective network of communication throughout the organization on a worldwide scale. You can tell that a firm and its managers possess this second dimension when the firm is routinely able to take knowledge gained in one market and apply it elsewhere, as was demonstrated in the case of SC Johnson's transfer of a plug-in household insect repellent product from Europe to the development of a new category of air-freshener products in the United States—Glade PlugIns.

Ironically, many global firms, and even more so with less global ones, are not very effective at retaining their managers once they return from an international assignment. These managers are either *expatriates*—someone from the home country who has moved abroad temporarily—or, increasingly, *inpatriates*—a manager recruited from the "local" market for their local business savvy. This apparent disconnect between a need for globally-seasoned executives and their retention by the firms that need them most can be explained by two factors. First, when the managers accept an international work assignment they often lose contact with the elements of the organization where strategy is formulated, such as corporate headquarters. In the case of inpatriates, they may never have had an opportunity to establish a strong network and power base at headquarters. Second, the expatriates' or inpatriates' firms do not have a repatriation plan in place to take advantage of their expertise. Because they have been-out-of-sight-and-out-of-mind, there is no ready way to plug them into the top management team.

Obviously, the development of a global mindset is more easily said than done. Our hope is that, given the fact that there are very few industries or markets untouched by global competition (just look around your classroom, for instance, and you will likely see at least one person from another country), you will take it upon yourself to start investing in your own global mindset.

Summary of Challenges

1. *Define* **international strategy** *and identify its implications for the strategy diamond.*   A firm's international strategy is how it approaches the cross-border business activities of its own firm and competitors and how it contemplates doing so in the future. International strategy essentially reflects the choices a firm's executives make with respect to sourcing and selling its goods in foreign markets. A firm's international activities affect both its business strategy and its corporate strategy. Each component of the strategy diamond may be affected by international activities.

2. *Understand why a firm would want to expand internationally and explain the relationship between international strategy and* *competitive advantage.* Firms often expand internationally to fuel growth; however, international expansion does not guarantee profitable growth and should be pursued to help a firm build or exploit a competitive advantage. International expansion can exploit four principle drivers of competitive advantage: economies of scale and scope, location, multipoint competition, and learning. However, these benefits can be offset by the costs of international expansion, such as the liabilities of newness and foreignness, and governance and coordination costs.

3. *Use the CAGE framework to identify international arenas.* CAGE stands for *c*ultural distance, *a*dministrative distance, *g*eographic distance, and *e*conomic distance and is a tool to help you better understand the firm-specific implication of a country attractiveness portfolio (CAP). You learned how to identify a portfolio of geographic markets and rank them on their relative attractiveness. The first step involved gathering data on personal income and market performance for a particular segment or industry. The second step involved creating a CAP by plotting the data on a grid to observe relative differences in attractiveness across countries. The third step asked you to make judgments about relevant CAGE dimensions and apply them to your CAP.

4. *Describe different vehicles for international expansion.* Foreign-country entry vehicles include exporting, alliances, and foreign direct investment (FDI). Exporters generally use local representatives or distributors to sell their products in new international markets. Two specialized forms of exporting are licensing and franchising. Alliances involve partnering with another firm to enter a foreign market or undertake an aspect of the value chain in that market. FDI can facilitate entry into a new foreign market and can be accomplished by greenfield investment or acquisition.

Although importing is not technically a form of international expansion, it does provide firms with knowledge, experience, and relationships on which future international expansion choices and activities can be based.

5. *Apply different international strategy configurations.* The different forms that international strategies may take are driven by tradeoffs in attempts to customize for local needs and to pursue global cost efficiencies. The first configuration seeks to achieve high levels of local responsiveness while downplaying the search for global efficiencies. The second configuration seeks relatively few global efficiencies and markets relatively standard products across different markets. The third configuration seeks to exploit global economies and efficiencies and accepts less local customer responsiveness (i.e., more standardized products). The fourth configuration attempts to simultaneously achieve global efficiencies and a high degree of local product specialization.

6. *Outline the international strategy implications of the stable and dynamic perspectives.* Cross-border business adds another level of complexity to both strategy formulation and execution, and unfortunately such complexity may be unavoidable for firms in dynamic contexts. As products mature, firms' international strategies evolve, often moving from little global involvement during the introductory phase to high degrees of internationalization in mature markets. Resources need to be renewed more rapidly in dynamic markets. Thus, when a firm enters a new foreign market, it must also embark on developing the resources necessary to make that market-entry decision a success. In addition, what is learned in new markets can be leveraged for application in existing markets. Obviously, these objectives can be best achieved when managers with an international mindset are in place.

Review Questions

1. What is meant by *international strategy*?

2. Which aspects of the strategy diamond are related to international strategy?

3. What are the four most important ways a firm's international strategy can be related to its competitive advantage?

4. What three foreign-country entry vehicles are emphasized in this chapter?

5. What is typically the most cost- and time-intensive entry vehicle?

6. What are characteristics of firms that fit the four international strategy configurations discussed in this chapter?

7. On what two dimensions do the four international strategy configurations differ?

8. What does the external perspective tell you about international strategy in dynamic contexts?

9. What does the resource-and-capabilities-based perspective tell you about international strategy in dynamic contexts?

10. What role do managers play in effective international strategies, particularly in dynamic contexts?

Experiential Activities

Group Exercises

1. Why have firms typically followed an international strategy path that started with importing or exporting, followed by alliances, and then FDI? What risks do born-global firms face in trying to do all of these at once? What resources and capabilities must they possess to do all of these effectively?

2. Are all Internet firms global by definition? What opportunities and barriers does the Internet present to firm internationalization?

Ethical Debates

1. You have successfully grown your local pasta company and while traveling in other countries you found that you might be able to produce and sell your product profitably there as well. In exploring these opportunities further, you were surprised to find that one of these countries has much stricter ingredients labeling and contents laws, while the other country much looser ones (in comparison to those of your home country, which you considered to be pretty strict to begin with). All three opportunities look to be profitable, regardless of the differences in regulations. Which regulations do you abide by in each country? The strictest ones, or the respective country standards, even if they are different?

2. As you learned in the section exploring CAGE, the Foreign Corrupt Practices Act is a U.S. federal law that makes it illegal for a citizen or corporation of the United States or a person or corporation acting within the United States to influence, bribe, or seek an advantage from a public official of another country. You, as an employee of a U.S. firm, are bidding for a contract in a foreign country where you understand that bribery is a common practice. Does the U.S. law put your firm at a competitive disadvantage? What should you do?

How Would YOU DO THAT?

1. Refer to the box entitled "How Would *You* Do That? 8.1." Pick another industry that is of interest to you. What did you identify as your indicator of potential market size? What market performance indicator did you use (for instance, in the example we used current cell phone usage)? How different were your CAP and CAGE-adjusted CAPs?

Go on to see How Would You Do That at www.prenhall.com/ carpenter&sanders

Endnotes

1. "Acting on Global Trends: A McKinsey Global Survey," *The McKinsey Quarterly*, 7, May 2007, www.McKinsey.com.

2. Information provided on companies' respective websites. General information on the global Fortune 500 can be found at www.Fortune.com.

3. The imperatives are summarized in A. Gupta and V. Govindarajan, "Managing Global Expansion: A Conceptual Framework," *Business Horizons* 43:2 (2000), 45–54.

4. R. Tomkins, "Battered PepsiCo Licks Its Wounds," *The Financial Times*, May 30, 1997, 26.

5. A. K. Gupta and V. Govindarajan, "Converting Global Presence into Global Competitive Advantage," *Academy of Management Executive* 15 (2001), 45–56.

6. J. W. Lu and P. W. Beamish, "International Diversification and Firm Performance: The S-Curve Hypothesis," *Academy of Management Journal* 47 (2004), 598–609.

7. J. W. Lu and P. W. Beamish, "International Diversification and Firm Performance: The S-Curve Hypothesis," *Academy of Management Journal* 47 (2004), 598–609.

8. Lu and Beamish, "International Diversification and Firm Performance."

9. Lu and Beamish, "International Diversification and Firm Performance."

10. A. D. Chandler, *Scale and Scope: The Dynamics of Industrial Capitalism* (Cambridge, MA: Harvard University Press, 1990).

11. Gupta and Govindarajan, "Converting Global Presence into Global Competitive Advantage."

12. Gupta and Govindarajan, "Converting Global Presence into Global Competitive Advantage."

13. Gupta and Govindarajan, "Converting Global Presence into Global Competitive Advantage."

14. K. Ito and E. L. Rose, "Foreign Direct Investment Location Strategies in the Tire Industry," *Journal of International Business Studies* 33:3 (2002), 593–602.

15. This anecdote is based on an interview with Lincoln Electric's chairman emeritus in D. Hastings, "Lincoln Electric's Harsh Lessons from International Expansion," *Harvard Business Review* 77:3 (1999), 163–174.

16. Based on information from a personal interview with Sam Johnson.

17. Adapted from A. Gupta and V. Govindarajan, "Managing Global Expansion: A Conceptual Framework," *Business Horizons* 43:2 (2000), 45–54.

18. The points in this paragraph draw heavily on the work of M. T. Hansen and N. Nohria, "See How to Build a Collaborative Advantage," *Sloan Management Review* Fall (2004), 22–30.

19. CIA World Factbook, www.cia.gov.

20. Based on surveys reported in *Business Week* and Grant Thornton LLP. See *2007 Grant Thornton International Business Report* at www.gti.org, and "Emerging Giants Multinationals from China, India, Brazil, Russia, and even Egypt are coming on strong. They're hungry—and want your customers. They're changing the global game," *BusinessWeek*, July 31, 2006, Cover Story.

21. P. Ghemawat, "The Forgotten Strategy," *Harvard Business Review* 81:11 (2003), 76–84. Recreated from www.business-standard.com/general/pdf/113004_01.pdf.

22. P. Ghemawat, "Distance Still Matters," *Harvard Business Review* 79:8 (2001), 1–11.

23. G. Hofstede, *Culture's Consequences. International Differences in Work-Related Values* (Newbury Park, CA: Sage Publications, 1980); G. Hofstede, *Culture's and Organizations. Software of the Mind* (London: McGraw-Hill, 1991).

24. Adapted from Y. Pan and D. Tse, "The Hierarchical Model of Market Entry Modes," *Journal of International Business Studies* 31 (2000), 535–554.

25. Examples drawn from A. Gupta and V. Govindarajan, "Managing Global Expansion: A Conceptual Framework," *Business Horizons*, March/April 2002, 45–54.

26. J. Johanson and J. Vahlne, "The Internationalization Process of the Firm," *Journal of International Business Studies* 8 (1977), 23–32; F. Weidershiem-Paul, H. Olson, and L. Welch, "Pre-Export Activity: The First Step in Internationalization," *Journal of International Business Studies* 9 (1978), 47–58; A. Millington and B. Bayliss, "The Process of Internationalization: UK Companies in the EC," *Management International Review* 30 (1990), 151–161; B. Oviatt and P. McDougall, "Toward a Theory of International New Ventures," *Journal of International Business Studies* 25 (1994), 45–64.

27. O. Moen, "The Born Globals: A New Generation of Small European Exporters," *International Marketing Review* 19 (2002), 156–175.

28. www.tritecmotors.com.br

29. Gupta and Govindarajan, "Managing Global Expansion."

30. www.fordfound.org, www.tritecmotors.com.br, and www.cargill.com.br.

31. G. Hamel and C. K. Prahalad, "Do You Really Have a Global Strategy?" *Harvard Business Review* 63:4 (1985), 139–148.

32. Gupta and Govindarajan, "Converting Global Presence into Global Competitive Advantage."

33. Adapted from C. Bartlett, S. Ghoshal, and J. Birkenshaw, *Transnational Management* (New York: Irwin, 2004). Note that Bartlett and Ghoshal distinguish among international, multinational, global, and transnational strategies. We have found these distinctions are difficult for students to apply and have chosen to use the underlying dimensions of local responsiveness and global efficiency as the tradeoffs that international strategy emphasizes.

34. B. Oviatt and P. McDougall, "Global Start-Ups: Entrepreneurs on a Worldwide Stage," *Academy of Management Executive* 9:2 (1995), 30–44.

35. www.logitech.com.

36. Summarized from Oviatt and McDougall, "Global Start-Ups."

37. J. S. Brown and J. Hagel, "Innovation Blowback: Disruptive Management Practices from Asia," *McKinsey Quarterly* January (2005).

38. M. Porter, *Competitive Advantage* (New York: Free Press, 1998).

39. G. Tellis, S. Stremersch, and E. Yin. "The International Takeoff of New Products: Economics, Culture and Country Innovativeness," *Marketing Science* 22:2 (2003), 161–187.

40. F. Vermeulen and H. Barkema, "Learning Through Acquisitions," *Academy of Management Journal* 44 (2001), 457–476; M. A. Hitt, M. T. Dacin, E. Levitas, and J. Arregle, "Partner Selection in Emerging and Developed Market Contexts: Resource-Based and Organizational Learning Perspectives," *Academy of Management Journal* 43 (2000), 449–467.

41. Gupta and Govindarajan, "Converting Global Presence into Global Competitive Advantage."

42. "Furnishing the World," *The Economist*, November 19, 1994, 79–80.

43. B. Kedia and A. Mukherji, "Global Managers: Developing a Mindset for Global Competitiveness," *Journal of World Business* 34:3 (1999), 230–251.

9 Understanding Alliances and Cooperative Strategies

In This Chapter We Challenge You To >>>

1. Explain why strategic alliances are important strategy vehicles.

2. Identify the motivations behind alliances and show how they've changed over time.

3. Compare and contrast the various forms and structures of strategic alliances.

4. Explain alliances as both business- and corporate-level strategy vehicles.

5. Understand the characteristics of alliances in stable and dynamic competitive contexts.

6. Summarize the criteria for successful alliances.

An Alliance *that* Fits Like *a* Glove[1]

*P*rocter & Gamble's Mr. Clean brand, launched in 1958 with a muscle-man sailor as the mascot, had become a 98-pound weakling in the liquid cleaner segment by the 1990s. Jeffrey Weedman, P&G Vice President of External Business Development, saw the problem. "Mr. Clean is a singleproduct line and we aren't focusing enough on it," he told Nancy Bailey of Nancy Bailey & Associates. "Nancy, why don't you take the Mr. Clean brand and see what you can do with it." Bailey & Associates specializes in brand extension licensing, and Bailey went right to work finding an alliance partner who could help revitalize the Mr. Clean brand. Bailey found Jordan Glatt, President of Magla, a $30 million unbranded manufacturer of household gloves. Magla excelled at making high-quality products, but gloves are a commodity product, which, if undifferentiated and unbranded, can't command a premium price. Mr. Clean, on the other hand, was a well-known brand looking to expand beyond its core liquid-cleaner line. An alliance between the two companies could help both. In just 60 days, P&G and Magla signed an agreement to market a line of Magla household gloves under the Mr. Clean name. Glatt was "excited about the prospects of producing upscale household gloves under the Mr. Clean brand name and developing creative packaging and promotions to further distinguish our products," he said. Magla would use the Mr. Clean trademark and pay P&G royalties, but Magla would remain separate from P&G and would sell directly to the big retailers. The deal brought a strategic line extension for Mr. Clean while expanding the customer base and distribution channels for Magla. Describing the agreement, Glatt said, "A partnership with P&G provides Magla with a great niche-marketing opportunity. Mr. Clean has widespread name recognition." Similarly, Scott Lazarczyk, Brand Manager of Mr. Clean, explained the benefit to P&G: "This licensing agreement is a great example of how we're leveraging the Mr. Clean brand across product categories that add to our current offerings."

In an age of speed, alliances make sense. If done right, they can help a company grow faster, introduce new products faster, or expand into new areas less expensively. As Glatt said, "An added benefit from working with P&G is that we could hook in to their national FSCIs [free-standing coupon inserts] that appear in newspapers, which make the P&G and Magla products look like a seamless Mr. Clean product line. A company our size could never afford this type of investment." What's more, the alliance helped Magla expand overseas. Mr. Clean is known overseas as Mr. Proper in mainland Europe, Don Limpio in Spain (*limpiar* is the Spanish verb for "to clean") and Mastro Lindo ("Master Clean") in Italy. Glatt said, "The Mr. Clean brand provides us with a wonderful opportunity to enter the European market with a leading brand with high awareness and an exceptional reputation."

Pursuing an alliance is an important strategic consideration for growth. Indeed, Glatt initially came up with the idea of using alliances long before the Mr. Clean opportunity presented itself. In the 1990s, Glatt was debating with his top managers about whether to launch a line of work gloves. Magla already made gloves for household chores, so adding a line of work gloves made strategic sense. But Glatt and his team realized that pursuing such an expansion strategy would be risky because Glatt knew that Magla had neither the brand name nor the retail connections to enter the home improvement market. Glatt worried that a big player like Stanley Works (a company known for its hardware and tools) could easily get into the market. Glatt decided to circumvent the potential problems of expansion and potential competition through an alliance with Stanley. He signed a licensing deal for Magla to make and sell work gloves under the Stanley name. In 2005, Glatt continued with his alliance strategy, this time entering into an agreement with the American Red Cross to market a complete line of branded medical gloves. The partnership was the first of its kind for the American Red Cross, with a portion of the proceeds from the sale of each retail package going directly to benefit the organization's relief efforts. The alliance strategy has paid off for Glatt—by 2006, his company's revenues had more than tripled to $100 million. Said Glatt: "Partnerships have turned us into a new company."

For its part, giant P&G is likewise benefiting from its alliances. P&G expanded the Mr. Clean brand even further through alliances with other companies. Its alliance with automotive and chemical supplier Old World Industries yielded a Mr. Clean Premium Windshield Wash. Even better, P&G's strategic alliance with Old World covers other P&G brands beyond Mr. Clean. For example, Old World is producing a specialty automotive version of P&G's Febreze air fresheners and Swiffer dusters that bring these two brands out of the home and into the car. For the Febreze auto line, Old World tailored Febreze into a lightly scented formula made specifically to eliminate odors in car interiors.

Successful alliances have led P&G's Jeff Weedman to coin "Weedman's Corollary": The second deal takes one-half of the time of the first deal. The third deal takes one-third of the time, and so on. And that law appears to have worked well for P&G, Magla, and Stanley. The subsequent deals are not only faster, but they also tend to be more profitable. Weedman's corollary means that P&G looks for ways to extend its alliances with good partners. P&G benefits from sustained collaborations and discovers new value creation opportunities that it previously did not know about. Small businesses can bring the giant company ideas it needs. As Jeff Weedman says, "This isn't a revolutionary idea. It's just smart business." <<<

Strategic Alliances

Why do firms enter alliances? Are most alliances successful? Was the agreement between P&G and Magla typical? How long do typical alliances last? Are alliances really a form of courting prior to the acquisition of one party by another? Or, does one party use the alliance to gain knowledge at the expense of the other party? By the end of this chapter, you should be able to answer these and many other questions about the formation, implementation, and termination of strategic alliances. Like most relationships, alliances have a beginning and an end. As you work through the chapter, you'll see that the opening vignette on P&G and Magla features many of the characteristics of strategic alliances. Alliances often enable participants to share in investments and rewards while reducing the risk and uncertainty that each firm would otherwise face on its own. In addition, shared activities enable each organization to focus its resources on what it does best. Finally, alliances foster economies of scale and scope—both within the partner firms and between partners and the alliance vehicle—that companies wouldn't otherwise be able to achieve, at least not in the same cost-effective manner.

Studies have shown that companies that participate most actively in alliances outperform the least-active firms by 5 to 7 percent.[2] And most alliances average seven years in duration before they are dissolved, or one of the parties to the alliance buys out the other. Some might argue that this 5 to 7 percent performance premium results from the fact that better-run firms are also simply better at initiating and managing alliances. In the early 1990s, for instance, BMW and DaimlerChrysler determined jointly that the minimum efficient economic scale of a small automobile engine facility would be a plant capable of producing 400,000 engines annually. Separately, however, each firm had internal demand for only 200,000 engines per year. The solution? An alliance through which they shared the cost of building a new plant large enough to turn out 400,000 engines. BMW uses the motors in its line of Mini Coopers, and DaimlerChrysler uses them in both its Neon and PT Cruiser lines.

Remember, however, that alliances are not strategies in and of themselves. Rather, as you will recall from the strategy diamond, which represents the five elements of the strategy diamond, an alliance is simply one *vehicle* for realizing a strategy. ◆ In addition, an effective alliance must be consistent with the economic logic of the strategy. The firm must also have the managerial capabilities to create economic value through cooperative arrangements, not simply the actions that are internal to the firm. In this chapter, we'll review the critical features that firms must master if they're going to use alliances effectively and in a manner that's consistent with the economic logic underpinning their overall strategies.

Exhibit 9.1 The Value Chain

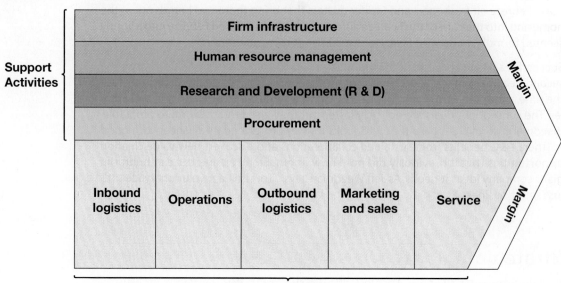

Support
Activities

Primary Activities

---

strategic alliance Relationship in which two or more firms combine resources and capabilities in order to enhance the competitive advantage of all parties.

A **strategic alliance** is a partnership in which two or more firms combine resources and capabilities with the goal of creating mutual competitive advantage. An alliance may involve sharing resources related to only one key activity in the partners' value chain, such as R&D. Recall the value chain you studied in Chapter 3 (see Exhibit 9.1 for a generic reproduction of the value chain model).

As shown in Exhibit 9.2, however, an alliance may involve coordination across many value chain activities. For example, the partners may work together to develop new products via shared R&D and also cooperate on the production and marketing of the new products. Indeed, the number and combinations of linkages is practically endless.

Note, too, that an alliance may be strategic to one firm and only tactical or operational to the other. This distinction is typically a function of the relative size of the alliance partners, and the truly unique character of the alliance function. Wal-Mart, for example, has long sought to reduce the number of its suppliers through a variety of so-called *sole-sourcing* and *just-in-time supply agreements*. Both types of agreements mean that a buyer has chosen only one or a few suppliers for its raw materials, and with the just-in-time arrangement, it expects that the supplier will provide the buyer with those materials at the exact point in time that they are needed in the production or sales cycle. In terms of investment in distribution infrastructure, sales volume, and concentration of sales to one buyer, such agreements may be strategic for the supplier but not necessarily to Wal-Mart, which is rarely dependent on any one supplier. In 1994, for instance, when Rubbermaid sought to raise its prices to Wal-Mart, its single largest customer, the giant retailer responded by dropping Rubbermaid products from every one of its stores.[3] Only after Rubbermaid was acquired by Newell in 1999 was it restored to Wal-Mart's good graces.

GROWTH OF ALLIANCES

Given its attractive features—as well as increasing competitive intensity in most industries—it shouldn't be surprising that the use of alliances as a strategy vehicle has grown dramatically in the last few decades. As a percentage of revenues, alliances ballooned from 2 to nearly 16 percent between 1980 through 1995. In particular, as of 2007, it is believed that large multinational corporations will have over 20 percent of their total assets tied up in al-

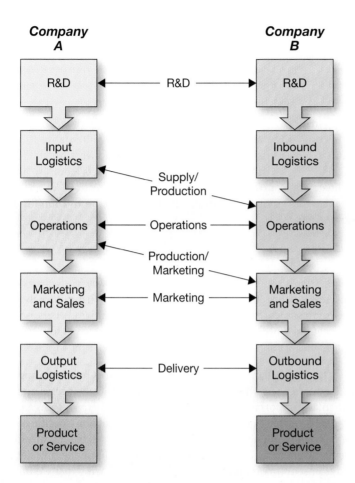

Company A

Company B

R&D ←——— R&D ———→ R&D

Input Logistics / Inbound Logistics

Supply/ Production

Operations ←——— Operations ———→ Operations

Production/ Marketing

Marketing and Sales ←——— Marketing ———→ Marketing and Sales

Output Logistics ←——— Delivery ———→ Outbound Logistics

Product or Service

Product or Service

Exhibit 9.2 Possible Points of Value Chain Coordination in an Alliance

liances.[4] If outsourcing arrangements were factored into this calculation, then the percentage of assets related to alliances would surely be much higher.

FAILURE RATES

Note, however, that despite their apparent popular use, the failure rate for alliances is about 50 percent (and nearly 70 percent in some cases). An alliance can be deemed a failure when one or more of the partners did not achieve its objectives and, in more dismal cases, when one partner benefited but the other partner was left worse off competitively. Clearly, alliances can be high-risk as well as high-return vehicles for realizing a firm's strategy.[5]

Interestingly, however, such a high failure rate doesn't surprise economists and many other experts. Why? Most economic theories assume that, left to their own devices, individual entities will behave in their own *self-interest.* The success of an alliance, of course, depends on the willingness of partners to subordinate their own interests to those of the alliance, but even when partners start out by suspending self-interest, circumstances can change dramatically over time, compromising even the best of intentions.

In the remaining sections of this chapter, we'll examine the various forms that alliances can take, and we'll show how the objectives underlying them have evolved over time. We'll discuss alliances as strategy vehicles and explain the risks to which they're prone. We'll also focus on the ways in which both the objectives and structures of alliances vary in stable versus dynamic contexts. Finally, because so many alliance failures are due to faulty implementation, we'll conclude by discussing four specific ways to improve the probability of alliance success.

Why Alliances?

Not surprisingly, firms participating in effective alliances can improve their competitive position and gain competitive advantage. Remember that one alternative to an alliance is a purchase contract. However, there are significant limits as to what can and cannot be contracted, particularly in dynamic contexts. Put bluntly, contracts alone are not always sufficient to coordinate and control partners' behaviors. In this section, we review how the use of alliances is related to competitive advantage and how the motivation for using alliances has evolved over time.

ALLIANCES AND COMPETITIVE ADVANTAGE

Alliances can help firms achieve their objectives in several ways. Alliances not only spread the risk of business ventures by sharing that risk with other firms; they also give firms access to knowledge, resources, and capabilities that the firm might otherwise lack. Alliances achieve these potential building blocks of competitive advantage in four ways: *joint investment, knowledge sharing, complementary resources*, and *effective management*.[6]

Joint Investment   Alliances can help to increase returns by motivating firms to make investments that they'd be unwilling to make outside a formal alliance relationship. This advantage is particularly important in light of the fact that productivity gains are possible when activities linked in the value chain are supported with transaction-specific investments.

In many situations, a supplier won't make an investment pertaining specifically to an exchange with one buyer. Why? Because the investment would tie the supplier too closely to one buyer and expose it to too much risk, the greatest risk being that the buyer reneges on its commitment to buy the supplier's products or services or grinds the supplier down on price due to its dependence on the single buyer.[7] For instance, if you invested $10 million in a piece of equipment that made products that could be sold only by Wal-Mart, you would be very dependent on Wal-Mart because of the asset specificity of such an investment. A buyer, therefore, often integrates backward vertically in the value chain, making the necessary investment to internalize the supply. The supplier's hesitancy, however, can be overcome if the buyer is willing to enter a formal arrangement that reduces the supplier's risk. Both supplier and buyer can benefit not only from gains in efficiency but also from savings in the bureaucratic costs entailed by vertical integration.

Knowledge Sharing   One common reason of entering into alliances is to learn from partners. Learning, however, requires partners to cooperate in transferring knowledge. Although partners may not be equally capable of absorbing knowledge, two factors can help to facilitate the transfer of knowledge: (1) mutual trust and familiarity between partners; and (2) consistent information-sharing routines, such as that obtained through higher-level executive contact, integrated information systems, and employee swapping and cross-company career paths. As an example of the latter, the farming-equipment manufacturer John Deere regularly exchanges key employees with alliance partner Hitachi in certain product segments.

Complementary Resources   In Chapter 3, we saw that a firm's resources and capabilities are the primary sources of competitive advantage. When partners combine resources and capabilities, they may be able to create a stock of resources that's unavailable to other competitors in the industry. If that stock combines complementary resources and capabilities, then the alliance may be able to generate a shared advantage. Finally, if the combination of resources and capabilities is valuable and rare, the alliance may be able to generate greater profits than the sum of the partners' individual profits. Thus, when Nestlé and Coke combined resources to offer canned tea and coffee products, the alliance offered a vehicle that was more attractive than going it alone due to complementarities between the parties.[8]

Effective Management   One way to judge the appropriateness and effectiveness of an alliance is through comparing its costs with the alternatives of an arm's-length transaction or formal internal integration (providing the activity internally or buying a company that can provide the activity). The second way to judge whether an alliance is effective is if it helps build a competitive advantage. This evaluation process is referred to as a *buy or make* decision, with alliances lying somewhere in between the two extremes—this is sometimes called make, buy, or ally.

Look at the principle from the following perspective: A potential problem in any alliance is that one partner may take advantage of another. To minimize this risk, many alliances call for formal protection mechanisms, such as equity investments (which should align incentives) or formal contracts (which should outline expected behavior and remedies for violations). Although such mechanisms are costly, they may still be cheaper than formal integration of activities within one firm. However, some experts argue that the true cost savings of alliances comes to those firms that can rely on less formal managerial control over their partners' behavior and instead depend on self-enforcement and informal agreements. Informal arrangements, of course, require a great deal of trust, which is likely to develop only after multiple dealings between partners.[9] We'll address the subjects of learning and trust more fully in the concluding section of this chapter.

Recall from the VRINE framework that resources and capabilities are the basis of competitive advantage only when they satisfy certain criteria: They must be valuable, rare, difficult to imitate, and supported by organizational arrangements. If an alliance (or network of alliances) is a vehicle that helps the firm's strategy satisfy these criteria, it has probably developed a collaborative advantage that helps one or more of the member firms achieve a competitive advantage over rivals outside the alliance.

ALLIANCE MOTIVATION OVER TIME

Although the overarching motivation behind alliances—the pursuit of competitive advantage—hasn't changed, the ways in which alliances contribute to such advantage have. This is one reason why it is so critical for you to understand strategic management from a dynamic perspective. In the late 1980s, in an effort to better understand why alliances were becoming increasingly common, the consulting firm Booz-Allen began studying the alliance practices of 1,000 firms. Among other things, the study revealed dramatic changes in the motivations that impelled firms to enter alliances over the course of several decades.[10] Note, these drivers represent *cumulative* needs.

As shown in Exhibit 9.3, alliances formed during the 1970s emphasized product and service performance.[11] The alliance strategy of Corning Glass Works (now called Corning) exemplifies this focus. Its alliance with Dow (Dow-Corning) allowed Corning to leverage its advanced glass-making capabilities in new products and new markets, and creating scale and scope economies, both at home and abroad. In the 1980s, firms tended to stress the building and reinforcing of market position. Microsoft and Intel, for example, joined to informally establish the Wintel alliance. Microsoft's Windows family of operating systems functioned best on PCs with Intel's chips, and as long as Microsoft kept increasing processing-speed requirements, Intel could count on consistent product demand. In some ways, P&G's alliance with Magla is a position alliance, since P&G can leverage Magla's strengths in gloves with its own brands to enter new markets or reinforce existing market positions.

Exhibit 9.3 Cumulative Motivation of Alliances Over Time

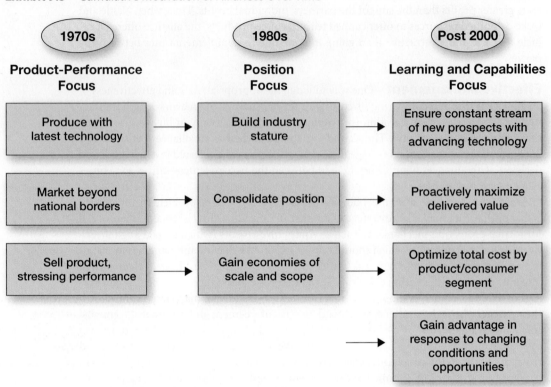

More recently, corporations have begun to emphasize more complex benefits, such as organizational learning and the development and accumulation of valuable resources and capabilities. In this vein, we can look at the case of the bicycle distributor Pacific Cycle. Recall that Pacific is sort of the Nike of bikes—it designs and distributes its bikes, but outsources production entirely to overseas factories in China. While Pacific does have its own design team in the United States, it relies heavily on its suppliers for new product ideas. In fact, these suppliers have the capability of rapidly building prototypes of new bikes that Pacific can then quickly test market in its major venues. As a reward for such innovativeness, Pacific will often grant the production contract for the new bike to the factory that invented it. Thus, Pacific and its suppliers have a shared gain in any successful products that are brought to market.

Form and Structure of Alliances

Note that we've been using the term *strategic alliances* as a catchall term. In reality, cooperative arrangements can take a number of forms. Exhibit 9.4 summarizes the vast continuum of forms that cooperative arrangements, including strategic alliances, may take. As you can see, the two primary dimensions on which alliances can be categorized are the nature of the *time commitment* (e.g., timeframe and resources) and respective *investment commitment* of the alliance and inputs into the alliance (ranging from cash to people to technology).

Whether or not a particular alliance is deemed as strategic will depend on the degree to which one or both parties' survival or competitive advantage depends on the alliance. For instance, a contract to supply coffee to a company's offices might be important, but there is no shared equity involved (no cross investment), and the relationship can probably be easily replaced by another provider. However, a contractual relationship between an enterprise software provider like SAP and its client, while perhaps not strategic for SAP, is mission critical for SAP's customer because such software is likely to be the lifeblood of their operations.

Exhibit 9.4 Degrees of Alliance Intensity

	No Linkages Beyond Transaction	Information Sharing	Asset, Resource, and Capability Sharing	Cross-Equity (partners take ownership in one party or each other)	Shared Equity
Long-term				*Keiretsu* in Japan or *chaebols* in South Korea	Caltrex, which was jointly owned by Chevron and Texaco prior to their merger
	Outsourcing	Many technology standards consortia	Examples include technology collaborations such as the PowerPC chip between Motorola, IBM, and Apple	Anheuser-Busch's cross-ownership with Kirin in Japan and Modelo in Mexico	Standalone joint ventures such as Dow-Corning
	Purchase agreements that are renewable annually or every several years	Agreements to distribute products or services	Cross-licensing such as that between Disney and Pixar or R&D partnerships as between Millennium Pharmaceuticals and some of its smaller partners		
Transactional	Simple purchase order for commodities, sometimes called a spot transaction	Short-term agreements on functions such as advertising or manufacturing to achieve efficiencies—for example, contract brewing of Miller Beer by Anheuser-Busch			
		Nonequity Alliances		**Equity Alliances**	

Level of Commitment

Time Commitment   **Financial Commitment** ⟶

JOINT VENTURES AND OTHER EQUITY ALLIANCES

The form of an alliance depends on such factors as legal structure and the number and objectives of participants. In a **joint venture**, for instance, two companies make equity investments in the creation of a third, which exists as an independent legal entity. This is the case with Dow-Corning, which, as the name suggests, is a joint venture between Dow and Corning; if mapped to Exhibit 9.3, it would fall under the shared-equity category. Many joint ventures are 50/50 splits in ownership and control, but they need not be equal partnerships. As you can probably imagine, each partner typically wants 51% ownership, so that they have technical control over the alliance. In reality, partners usually identify the specific aspects of the alliance that they are most interested in, so the respective ownership question becomes less of a stumbling block.

It isn't necessary, however, for an alliance to create a separate legal entity or share equal ownership. In many cases, **equity alliances** involve unequal partners. This may be the case when one partner owns a greater percentage of the alliance's equity than another partner; when a separate legal entity is not established, and one partner instead takes partial ownership of the other partner; or when contracts are used to govern the sharing and respective rights regarding contributed assets, resources, or capabilities. Millennium Pharmaceuticals, for example, prefers arrangements in which larger partners take a percentage ownership not only in Millennium itself, but also a minority-percentage interest in any alliance with a separate legal structure. (It also manages several strategic alliances with traditional 50/50 splits.[12])

joint venture Alliance in which two firms make equity investments in a third legal entity.

equity alliance Alliance in which one or more partners assumes a greater ownership interest in either the alliance or another partner.

Dow Corning Corporation, the silicone-products maker, is a joint venture between Dow and Corning, as its name suggests. In joint ventures, partners often invest on an equal basis and split corporate ownership and control down the middle.

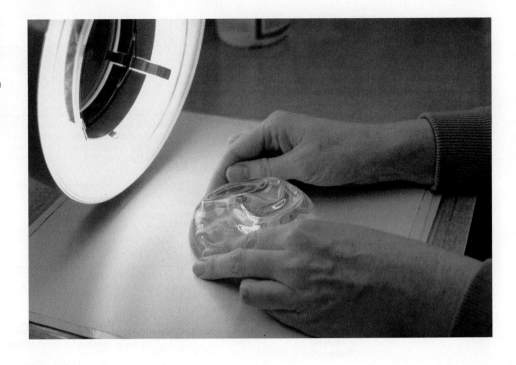

NONEQUITY ALLIANCES

The most common form of strategic alliance involves neither equity interest nor separate organizations. Arrangements such as *sole-sourcing, just-in-time supply agreements, licensing, cobranding,* and *franchising* often fall under the heading of *nonequity alliances.* The coffee company example provided earlier fits this category.

nonequity alliance Alliance that involves neither the assumption of equity interest nor the creation of separate organizations.

Nonequity alliances are typically contracts that call for one firm to supply, produce, market, or distribute another's goods or services over an extended period of time, but without substantial ownership investments in the alliance. Starbucks, for instance, has extended the presence of its brand into a number of customer-contact locations through alliances with such companies as Barnes & Noble (bookstore cafés), United Airlines (in-flight coffee service), Dreyer's (coffee ice cream), Pepsi (Frappuccino ready-to-drink coffee), and Kraft (ground and whole coffee beans distributed through grocery stores). The various strategic roles that these nonequity alliances play for Starbucks are shown in Exhibit 9.5.[13]

MULTIPARTY ALLIANCES

consortia Association of several companies and/or governments for some definite strategic purpose.

Thus far, we've described alliances involving two partners. Other types of alliances, such as **consortia**, usually involve many participants, perhaps even governments. The primary contribution to these cooperative arrangements is information, though there may be some cost sharing as well. Perhaps the most complex multifirm alliances are those in the technology arena. SEMATECH, for example, is a consortium of semiconductor manufacturers established in the mid-1980s to prop up the U.S. semiconductor industry, which at the time was considered to be of strategic importance to national defense. To some extent, SEMATECH's cooperative structure was modeled after joint projects by which Japanese semiconductor producers were responsible for advancing their collective technological competencies in the late 1970s.[14] The consortium has since evolved to include both U.S. and non–U.S. firms, and a related venture called SEMI/SEMATECH (or SEMI) is an alliance of suppliers to the semiconductor industry.[15]

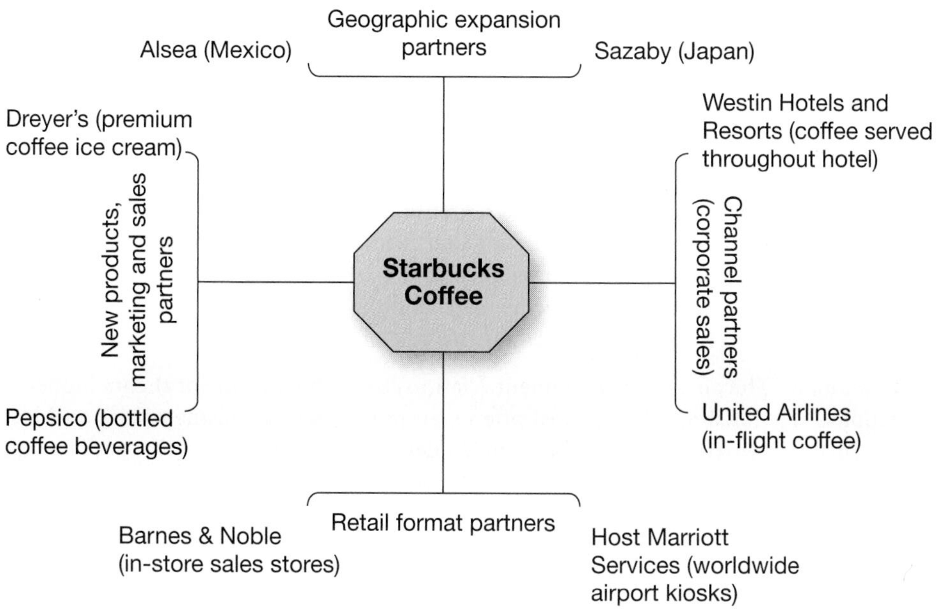

Exhibit 9.5 Starbuck's Universe of Alliances

Alliances as Strategy Vehicles

You probably are beginning to realize this, but almost any organization is a potential alliance partner, and deciding with whom to partner is a matter of a firm's business and corporate strategies. The challenge is to, first, determine if you are going to use alliances as a strategy vehicle and then, second, begin to identify potential partners.

ALLIANCES AND BUSINESS STRATEGY

Let's start by considering factors related to business strategy—strategy that determines how a firm competes in a chosen industry. A quick review of the five-forces model and related complementors of industry structure that we introduced in Chapter 4 reinforces the number and variety of a firm's potential partners. Who might these allies be?

■ **Rivals.** Are there opportunities to partner with rivals? Although there are certainly legal prohibitions against cooperative arrangements among competitors that harm consumers, rivals will often engage in strategic alliances. The various airline alliances, such as One World and Star, are a case in point. Sometimes a company may partner with a competitor to manage surplus production demand or to help it manage excess capacity. Beer companies collaborate in production and distribution for instance—if a truck can deliver two breweries' products to the same market then both companies benefit from the cost sharing. Similarly, breweries often contract with competitors to brew their beer when their demand outstrips capacity. This has been one of the secrets of success for Sam Adams. Sam Adams creates the beer recipes but then has the beer produced by Anheuser-Busch, Miller Beer, and others.

■ **New entrants.** Industry incumbents can ally with new entrants to diversify or to co-opt a future potential rival. Wal-Mart's alliance with the Mexican retailer Cifra is a good example of this. If you know a new competitor has an interest in your market, one firm can take the initiative to work together with the other, usually with the end-game strategy of merging the two entities.

■ **Suppliers.** Increasingly, firms are developing alliances with key suppliers. These can take on the form of sole-sourcing and just-in-time arrangements or include more complex forms, such as Tritec, in which the supplier is formed by two rivals. This alliance approach can take several forms. For instance, SC Johnson sells many of its products in Wal-Mart. However, since SC Johnson is so good at merchandising its products, Wal-Mart has designated SC Johnson as the category manager for several lines of products. What this means is that SC Johnson is responsible for stocking its own goods on Wal-Mart's shelves, but also for coordinating and merchandising all the other producers' products in, say, the category of household cleansers. As a result, SC Johnson is in a much stronger position, and can improve its merchandising skills, and Wal-Mart benefits by having the best in the business managing this part of its in-store merchandising.

■ **Customers.** The customer-incumbent relationship is the flip side of the incumbent-supplier relationship. This is most often seen in business-to-business relationships. For instance, when Copeland Corporation developed a new line of air conditioning units, it partnered with its customers to provide that part, while the end-user like Trane or Rheem manufactured the rest of the air conditioning unit. This situation is very analogous to the Intel inside story. Intel makes the chips, but its alliances with Apple and Dell and others ensures that they are the leading edge processor in those machines.

■ **Substitutes.** These products and services pose a threat to the incumbent. Through an alliance, this threat can actually be exploited. For instance, soy milk is a clear substitute for dairy milk. Instead of actively competing against the growing market for soy milk, Dean Foods established a joint venture with, and then acquired, industry leader Silk. You can see how you can employ this same logic with any substitute. If there is an opportunity to collaborate, and offer consumers broader choices, then perhaps both parties will gain through the alliance.

■ **Complementors.** Recall that complements are those products or services that, when bundled together, create greater value than when acquired separately. An alliance between an industry incumbent and a complement can lock out competitors. As a case in point, most major fast-food chains provide Coke or Pepsi products, not both. We elaborate further on this aspect of managing alliance strategy below.

The Value Net Model and Co-opetition

One way to think about all of the players identified in the industry structure model in a manner that highlight possible alliance possibilities is to rearrange the players into the **value net model**. You were introduced to this model in Chapter 6, and it is reproduced for you here in Exhibit 9.6.[16] Notice that in this model we place the firm of interest in the center and link it to all possible exchange partners. In allowing them to identify opportunities for cooperative relationships among all possible exchange partners and even competitors, the value net model helps managers find alternatives to conventional win-lose business scenarios.

How might a firm establish a cooperative relationship with a competitor? Consider a firm like Motorola, which may in some business situations be a competitor to Intel, such as in the sale of microprocessors. In other situations, it may be in a partnership with Intel, such as in the development of a new technology. Still in other situations, Motorola might be a customer of Intel, sourcing key components for a particular product.

Co-opetition The term **co-opetition** refers to a situation in which firms are both competitors and cooperative partners. The purpose of co-opetition is to find ways of increasing the total value created by parties in the value net, not just determining how to compete for

value net model Map of a firm's existing and potential exchange relationships.

co-opetition Situation in which firms are simultaneously competitors in one market and collaborators in another.

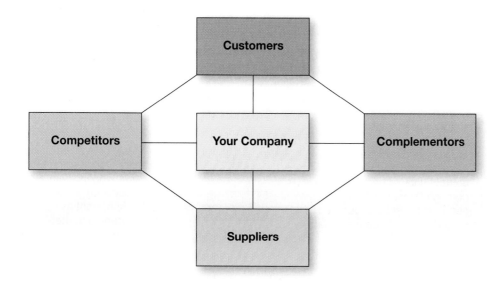

Exhibit 9.6 The Value Net

industry profits. The value net helps managers find potential partners; in other words, it helps them to identify those parties that are possible complementors rather than just competitors. In the following two sections we illustrate how the value net can be applied to various types of alliances.

Alliances can figure into most aspects of business strategy, but they generally provide a means of managing competitive pressures, uncertainty, or both. Business-strategy alliances tend to fall into two major categories: *vertical alliances* or *horizontal alliances.*

Vertical Alliances   A **vertical alliance** is formed when a firm partners with one or more of its suppliers or customers (typically, the latter only occurs in business-to-business relationships). This is exactly the type of alliance we referred to in the section about supplier and customer alliances earlier. The purpose of a vertical alliance is to leverage partners' resources and capabilities in order to meet two goals: (1) to create more value for the end customer and (2) to lower total production costs along the value chain. In a sense, the vertical alliance is an alternative for vertical integration, the *corporate* strategy whereby a firm takes ownership of downstream supply or upstream distribution or other marketing functions.

Jeffrey H. Dyer, a prominent strategy professor who specializes in the study of strategic alliances, has found that vertical alliances can create lean value chains by reducing total supply-chain costs in four areas: transaction, quality, product-development, and logistics costs:[17]

■ *Transaction costs* are often lower among alliance partners than among firms in third-party arm's-length transactions.

■ Because quality is often improved, *quality-related costs*—those associated with defects, returns, and warranty work—go down.

■ When partners share knowledge and human capital and focus their efforts on improving product design and quality, vertical alliances can control *product-development costs.*

■ Reduced warehousing and transportation costs not only reduce inbound *logistics costs* but result in lower inventory costs as well.

vertical alliance Alliance involving a focal firm and a supplier or customer.

Exhibit 9.7 An Example of Co-opetition

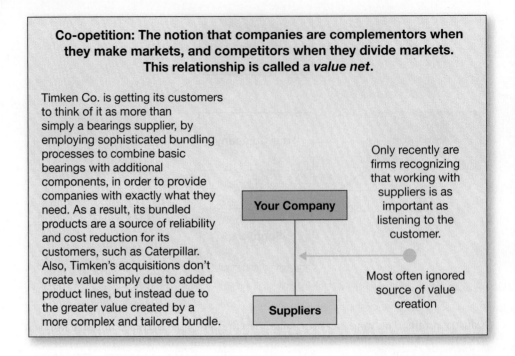

Co-opetition: The notion that companies are complementors when they make markets, and competitors when they divide markets. This relationship is called a *value net*.

Timken Co. is getting its customers to think of it as more than simply a bearings supplier, by employing sophisticated bundling processes to combine basic bearings with additional components, in order to provide companies with exactly what they need. As a result, its bundled products are a source of reliability and cost reduction for its customers, such as Caterpillar. Also, Timken's acquisitions don't create value simply due to added product lines, but instead due to the greater value created by a more complex and tailored bundle.

Your Company

Suppliers

Only recently are firms recognizing that working with suppliers is as important as listening to the customer.

Most often ignored source of value creation

Vertical alliances also improve value to the customer by making it possible for alliance partners to increase speed to market, improve quality, introduce newer technologies and features, and respond more quickly to market changes. Exhibit 9.7 shows how Timken applies the net value to vertical integration alliances by bundling its product offerings.

horizontal alliance Alliance involving a focal firm and another firm in the same industry.

Horizontal Alliances

Horizontal alliances are partnerships between firms in the same industry. These types of alliances enable competitors, or potential competitors, to gain a presence in multiple segments of an industry. As a component of a firm's value net, a horizontal alliance, which gives a company access to multiple segments of an industry, can create value in a number of ways. First, it can reduce risk. For instance, when two oil exploration firms enter into a joint venture, they spread the risk entailed by the costs of drilling. Likewise, Kraft's alliance with Starbucks gives it a super-premium coffee brand that it can distribute through the grocery channel to complement not only its Maxwell House and Yuban brands in the same channel but also its Gevalia brand in the direct-marketing and business-to-business channels. Mondavi's various alliances with top wine producers in Chile, Italy, Argentina, and France give it access to a broader range of high-quality wines than it could support if it had to rely solely on its own resources.

Horizontal alliances can also help partners achieve greater efficiency. Thus, when McDonald's and Disney cooperate in promotions, each leverages its advertising expenditures. In addition, although Disney benefits from McDonald's promotion of Disney characters and programming, McDonald's benefits from the popular appeal of Disney characters, which appear as toys in products aimed at kids.

Finally, horizontal alliances foster learning in the development and innovation of new products. SEMATECH and the Automotive and Composites Consortium (launched by GM, Ford, and Chrysler) are good examples of learning alliances. In the case of SEMATECH, for instance, all U.S.–based semiconductor manufacturers pooled their knowledge to improve the production process and were collectively able to turn the competitive tide against the rising dominance of Japanese firms. The Apple–Sony partnership that developed the PowerBook is a good example of firms using horizontal alliances to access complementary skills. Finally, horizontal alliances can help firms overcome political obstacles. In China, for example, the Otis Elevator–Tianjin joint venture enabled Otis to enter an attractive and growing market that at the time was inaccessible without a local partner.

Let's return for a moment to the concept of co-opetition, which is based on the principle that firms must often cooperate and compete simultaneously. Because horizontal alliances make allies of competitors, it's crucial that all parties understand the conditions that favor success in such ventures. First, they're potentially beneficial when partners' strategic goals converge and competitive goals diverge. When, for instance, Philips and DuPont collaborated to make compact discs (CDs), neither firm was invading the other's markets for other products. In addition, horizontal alliances are more likely to succeed when the partners are chasing industry leaders, as when Asian semiconductor-chip makers collaborated in making memory chips in an effort to cut into Intel's market share. Finally, in successful horizontal alliances, all partners acknowledge the fact that, though each must be willing to share knowledge, each can and must protect proprietary skills. For example, the Fuji Photo–Xerox alliance, established in 1962, allows the two makers of copiers and printers to collaborate in the Japanese and Pacific Rim markets. In return for access to these markets, Fuji is entitled to a 75-percent share in the joint profits. Fuji agreed to the arrangement because it believed that it could protect its film business in these markets; Xerox, meanwhile, believed that the venture would not endanger its copier business elsewhere in the world.

CORPORATE AND INTERNATIONAL STRATEGIC ALLIANCES

Although alliances are typical business strategy vehicles, they can also be vehicles for corporate and international strategy. In the first case, the alliance facilitates product or service diversification within an existing market, while in the second case the alliance facilitates entry and competition in another geographic market. ◆

 Arenas

Alliances and Corporate Strategy   As we saw in Chapter 7, corporate strategy is largely concerned with two activities:

- Determining the right mix of businesses in the corporate portfolio

- Ensuring that this mix creates shareholder value

Let's consider each of these activities in terms of decisions about alliances. As for portfolio mix, alliances are vehicles for exploring and implementing diversification options. Through its office-copier business, for instance, a company like Xerox may have developed a set of technologies that may provide access into the intensely competitive desktop-copier and computer-printer businesses. In an alliance with a strong partner like Fuji Photo of Japan, it can share the risk and development costs related to an uncertain diversification move. Similarly, through its alliance with Magla, P&G diversified into household gloves and Magla diversified into branded consumer products.

Corporations can also use alliances to create value across a portfolio of individual businesses. At first glance, for example, you might think of venture capitalists (VCs) and their various investments as independent entities. They do, however, represent strategic alliances. How so? Whereas the VC provides capital and managerial expertise, the entrepreneurial firm provides an opportunity for new products. From a corporate-strategy perspective, the VC firm can create more value for its investments by identifying key individuals in one firm who could help create value for its other units. The VC firm Softbank, for example, leverages its investments in broadband-application and broadband-provider companies by circulating its best and brightest managers and technologists among its wholly owned companies as well as those in which it has investments.[18] Likewise, a diversified firm can also broker relationships among its portfolio businesses.

Alliances and International Strategy   Finally, as shown in the example of the international partnership between Dell Computer and the Asian distributors in the opening vignette in Chapter 8, a firm's international strategy should issue from its business- and corporate-strategy objectives. Many of the alliances that we've described in this chapter are international in nature: either they involve partners from different countries or the alliance itself is headquartered in a country different from those of the partners. Cross-border alliances differ from domestic alliances in that governments, public policies, and national cultures often play significant roles. Also important, of course, are differences in workplace regulations and socioeconomic conditions.

In some cases, a firm can only do business in another country through an alliance. For instance, a U.S. firm that wishes to do business in Saudi Arabia can only do so if it has a partner with a local firm. In fact, the partner has to be a member of the Saudi Royal family. Many Chinese companies are buying U.S. and European high-technology firms, and then partnering with Indian companies for the customer service component. Similarly, Indian firms are buying large manufacturing firms in Latin America, the United States, and Europe, and then through alliances outsourcing production to more efficient facilities in China.

Not surprisingly, in international contexts, decisions about internal and external vehicles through which to execute a firm's strategy are much more complex than in domestic contexts. Multinational corporations, for instance, may be better than alliances in facilitating the flow of knowledge across borders. Analysis of patent citations by semiconductor companies suggests that multinationals are better than both alliances and market forces in fostering cross-border knowledge transfer, primarily because they can use multiple mechanisms for transferring knowledge and are more flexible in moving, integrating, and developing technical knowledge.[19]

ALLIANCE NETWORKS

Related to the study of the strategic functions of alliances is the concept that alliances are taking on characteristics of networks. Network theory has two implications for organizational practice. First, as alliances become a larger component of a firm's strategy, the strategy discussion will shift from particular alliances as a vehicle to networks of alliances as a vehicle. In this sense, the firm is operating as a hub, or node, in a complex array of owned, partially owned, and nonowned businesses. Looking back at the value net portrayed in Exhibit 9.6, you can imagine how multiple alliances among complementors, competitors, suppliers, and customers might easily come to resemble a web of complex network relationships.

Second, as networks themselves take on the characteristics of organizations, competition among networks should arise both within and across industries. Exhibit 9.8 lists several alliance networks formed in the past, some of which have been dissolved or restructured as the nature of the partners' relationships or the competitive environment has evolved. The clearest current example of network competition can probably be found in the airline industry, where three alliances—Star, One World, and Sky Team—are battling for air passengers.[20]

Perhaps more dramatic still are the alliance networks that are battling over emerging technological standards. As you can see in Exhibit 9.9, Sun, HP, IBM, and MIPS, are all plac-

Business or Industry	Selective Rival Constellations
Hardware and Software for Interactive TV	► Motorola, Scientific Atlanta, Kaleida ► Time Warner, Silicon Graphics ► Intel, Microsoft, General Instruments ► H.P., TV Answer
Video CDs	► Sony and Philips ► Toshiba, Time Warner, Matsushita, others
Global Telecommunications	► AT&T Worldpartners (includes 12 partners) ► British Telecom and MCI ► Sprint, Deutsche Telekom, France Telecom
Automobiles and Trucks	► G.M., Toyota, Isuzu, Suzuki, Volvo ► Ford, Mazda, Kia, Nissan, Fiat, VW ► Chrysler, Mitsubishi, Daimler-Benz
Biotechnology Research	► Genentech network ► Centocor network
Pharmaceutical Marketing	► Merck and Medco (merger) ► SmithKline and DPS (merger) ► Eli Lilly and PCS (merger) ► Pfizer and Value Health ► Pfizer, Rhône-Poulenc, Caremark, others
Global Airline Services	► Delta, Swissair, Singapore Airlines, SAS ► KLM and Northwest ► British Airways and USAir
Global Comercial Real Estate Services	► Colliers International (44 companies) ► International Commercial (23 companies) ► Oncore International (36 companies) ► New America Network (150 companies) ► Cushman & Wakefield (52 alliances) ► CB Commercial (70 affiliates) ► Grubb & Ellis (six affiliates)

Exhibit 9.8   Different Alliance Networks

ing bets on certain technological standards, and they have a vast array of partners helping them to battle their respective parts of the fray.[21]

Importantly, the fortunes of the many small firms in the network are dependent upon the success of the larger group. Just as beta and VHS battled it out, with VHS being the eventual winner, so too will this battle have its winners and losers. What is clear, however, is that the loser is typically not a single firm, but instead many of the smaller players aligned with the network core. If one of these battles is lost, it means less to SUN, HP, IBM, or MIPS, but it can make or break the fortunes of a much smaller firm.

Finally, there is another variation of alliance networks where a focal firm sets itself out as the hub of an enormous wheel of alliance relationships. The most dramatic example of the new organization form is P&G, and it has dubbed this aspect of its strategy as "Connect +

Exhibit 9.9 Alliance Networks of Sun, HP, IBM, and MIPS

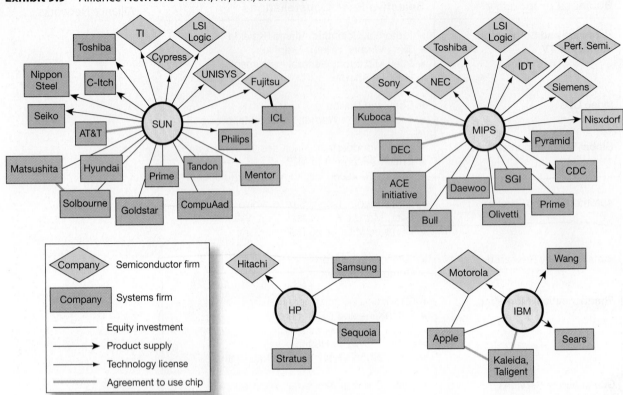

Develop," instead of the traditional notion of research and development. Exhibit 9.10 summarizes P&G's view, and in particular, how it comes from the CEO himself.

P&G even maintains a Connect + Develop (C+D) website that invites new potential partners. While P&G is no slacker when it comes to investment in new products—2006 R&D spending amounted to about $2 billion across 150 science areas—by the company's own calculations, its C&D activities with just its top 15 suppliers provides it access to more than 10,000 new products, and an estimated combined R&D staff of 50,000! P&G's goal is to have over 50 percent of its new products originated through the C&D process by 2010.

RISKS ARISING FROM ALLIANCES

As we mentioned in the introduction to this chapter, one of the potential benefits of an alliance is the reduction of risk or uncertainty borne by any one party. With that said, however, we must point out that cooperative ventures can be risky. There are six potential alliance risks:

- **Poor Contract Development** This problem is relatively self-explanatory. Typically, the hardest part of drawing up good alliance contracts is negotiating rights, particularly those pertaining to termination prior to the intended maturity date.

- **Misrepresentation of Resources and Capabilities** This issue arises when a partner *misrepresents*, intentionally or unintentionally, the quality or quantity of a resource or capability—say, a crucial technology or the availability of staff with particular skill sets—that its partners deem critical to the success of the venture.

Exhibit 9.10   Welcome to P&G's Connect + Develop Website

Connecting with the world's most inspired minds. Developing products that improve consumers' lives.

We've collaborated with outside partners for generations—but the importance of these alliances to P&G has never been greater.

Our vision is simple. We want P&G to be known as the company that collaborates—inside and out—better than any other company in the world.

I want us to be the absolute best at spotting, developing and leveraging relationships with best-in-class partners in every part of our business. In fact, I want P&G to be a magnet for the best-in-class. The company you most want to work with because you know a partnership with P&G will be more rewarding than any other option available to you.

A. G. Lafley

Chairman of the Board,

President and Chief Executive

The Procter & Gamble Company

Source: The Procter & Gamble Company http://pg.t2h.yet2.com/t2h/page/homepage

■ **Misappropriation of Resources and Capabilities** *Misappropriation* occurs when one partner takes something of value, whether to the partner itself, to the alliance, or to both. Sometimes misappropriation is so endemic that would-be partners garner reputations for misappropriation. China, for example, has a notoriously poor reputation when it comes to protecting intellectual and trademark property rights.

■ **Failure to Make Complementary Resources Available** Related to the risk of misappropriation is the risk that a partner may fail to make available a promised complementary resource, such as a valuable technology or the people with the skills needed to implement or design new products or processes.

■ **Being Held Hostage Through Specific Investments** Sometimes, even when such resources are made available, the firm that needs them may become so dependent on the alliance that it's virtually held hostage. Resources can range from a proprietary technology that the partnership controls or simply a production capability controlled by one of the partners. Trek Bicycles, for example, outsources much of its production to an Asian manufacturer called Giant. The alliance allows Trek to focus on the design, marketing, and distribution of high-quality bikes. In turn, Giant enjoys economies of scale in production. Giant, however, is also a competitor of Trek and, given Trek's dependence on Giant's production capabilities, Giant could conceivably raise its prices to Trek in order to gain price advantage over Trek in the latter's primary markets. Or consider the arrangement by which Rayovac (Spectrum) licenses its core battery technology from Matsushita, on whom it was dependent for a key technology.

■ **Misunderstanding a Partner's Strategic Intent** The Trek and Rayovac examples provide a jumping off point for exploring another alliance risk. Both Trek and Rayovac are not only dependent on their partners for a critical resource, but they're much smaller than their partners and much weaker financially. It would be relatively easy for Giant to exploit and weaken Trek—perhaps eventually buy it out for relatively little investment. Likewise, Matsushita could raise licensing fees for its battery technology or even suspend Rayovac's access to it altogether. In addition, although Matsushita sells consumer electronics products (under the Panasonic label), its share of the U.S. battery market is quite small. Conceivably, one way of increasing it would be to weaken Rayovac, undermining its U.S. competitor to the point at which it would become an easy acquisition target. In each case, then, it's crucial for the vulnerable partner to have a strong sense of whether its larger partner is interested in a co-opetition strategy or a winner-take-all strategy.

Alliances in Stable and Dynamic Contexts

Another factor in determining whether an alliance is a suitable strategic vehicle is the level of stability or dynamism of a firm's competitive context. Relative dynamism of an industry context may affect an alliance decision in two ways:

■ From a practical standpoint, relatively stable environments are much more forgiving of mistakes, such as poor choices in partners or alliance structures.

■ Because they make maintenance and management easier, stable environments allow firms to participate in more alliances. Likewise, although wasted time, effort, and resources are undesirable in any situation, relatively stable contexts provide firms with the luxury of learning from their mistakes and regrouping.

Consider, for example, an alliance between Nestlé and Mars that allows Nestlé to put Mars-brand M&Ms in its ice creams. The success or failure of this alliance is not going to make or break either company. As we'll soon see, however, in dynamic contexts, competitive stakes are typically much higher, and any distraction of a firm's resources or managerial time and attention can have serious consequences. Particularly when dynamism is coupled with technological intensity. If, for instance, Millennium Pharmaceuticals chooses an unsuitable partner, it will lose time and money, and it also risks the possibility that while it's busy trying to manage the alliance, a competitor will make some advance in product or technology that gives it a significant advantage. Such risks place tremendous pressure on firms not only to choose the

Nestlé and Mars share an alliance whereby Nestlé is allowed to put Mars' M&Ms in its ice creams. Because the companies compete in a relatively stable competitive environment, however, the success or failure of the alliance isn't likely to make or break either firm.

right partners (and the right number of partners), but to structure alliances so that they contribute to the development and enhanced value of its resources and capabilities.

RELATIVE STABILITY AND ALLIANCE MOTIVATION

Relative environmental stability of a firm's external context also affects the objectives that partners set for an alliance. In many ways, relative stability has played a role in the evolution of alliance motivation that we discussed previously. In relatively stable environments, for example, partners are typically seeking access to production technologies or markets. Their objective is essentially to consolidate market positions and generate economies of scope and scale.[22] These objectives also motivate firms in dynamic contexts, but under such conditions, firms are also motivated to use alliances as means of identifying new market threats and opportunities and of providing dynamic capabilities with which to respond to changes (and perhaps even to drive changes) in the competitive landscape.

RELATIVE STABILITY AND THE COEVOLUTION MODEL OF CORPORATE STRATEGY

Focusing on relative stability will also help us to better understand the coevolution model of corporate strategy that we outlined in Chapter 7. Recall that *coevolution* means orchestrating a web of shifting linkages among evolving businesses. In making alliances, a firm opts to develop vertical, horizontal, or complementary linkages with other firms instead of seeking them solely among wholly owned businesses. The use of alliances in such a web enables a firm to develop its specific dynamic capabilities in concert with the best resources and capabilities available. Just as important, alliances sustain a specific focused strategy. Periodically, for instance, certain alliances can be abandoned and others added. Thus, if a firm is pursuing, say, a growth strategy, the coevolution approach suggests that it drop alliances developed around commoditized products and add those with partners who are active on the technology frontier or in other forward-looking strategies for enhancing competitive advantage.[23]

What Makes an Alliance Successful?

Given the prevalence of alliances as a critical and valuable strategy vehicle, it is imperative for managers to understand the ingredients that make them successful, as well as the factors that can derail them. Professor Ben Gomes-Casseres, one of the world's leading experts in alliances, identifies ten features that separate successful alliances from unsuccessful ones. These are summarized in Exhibit 9.11.[24]

But how do you put these features into place? Strategy research has considered the ten features identified in Exhibit 9.11, and distilled out of them five particular areas where organizations can increase the probability of alliance success. As you will see in the final section of this chapter, some of these areas are related to relationships between the partners, while others relate to the experience and supporting structures put into place in a focal firm. These five areas are:

- Understanding the determinants of trust

- Being able to manage knowledge and learning

- Understanding alliance evolution

- Knowing how to measure alliance performance

- Creating a dedicated alliance function

The first four apply readily to firms of all sizes, both domestic and international. The last usually pertains to larger firms and those that otherwise use alliances as a key vehicle for strategy execution. Understanding what's involved in all five areas puts managers in a better position to design alliances that will contribute to a firm's competitive advantage.

Exhibit 9.11   Features of Successful Alliances

1. The alliance has a clear strategic purpose—alliances are never an end in or of themselves, they provide tools to achieve a business strategy

2. Good partner fit—a partner with compatible goals and complementary capabilities

3. Specialized partner roles—allocate tasks and responsibilities in the alliances in a way that enables each party to do what they do best

4. Create incentives for cooperation—working together never happens automatically, particularly when partners were former rivals

5. Minimize conflicts between partners—the scope of alliance and of partners' roles should avoid pitting one against the other in the market

6. Share information—continual communication develops trust and keeps joint projects on target

7. Exchange personnel—regardless of the form of the alliance, personal contact and site visits are essential for maintaining communication and trust

8. Operate with long time-horizons—mutual forbearance in solving short-run conflicts is enhanced by the expectation of long-term gains

9. Develop multiple joint projects—successful cooperation on one project can help partners weather the storm in less successful joint projects

10. Be flexible—alliances are open-ended and dynamic relationships that need to evolve in pace with their environment and in pursuit of new opportunities

UNDERSTANDING THE DETERMINANTS OF TRUST

It may be stating the obvious to say that alliances perform better when partners trust each other. Research suggests that a network of trustworthy partners can itself be a competitive advantage, as can be a reputation for trustworthiness.[25] Unfortunately, because not all partners are equally trustworthy, parties in alliances often must rely on a variety of mechanisms to safeguard their interests. Formal mechanisms, such as long-term contracts, stock ownership, and collateral bonds, can signal credible long-term commitments to alliance partners. They do not, however, ensure information sharing, which is critical to alliance success. Partners foster interorganizational trust by using understandable and predictable processes. Informal mechanisms, such as firm reputation and personal trust among managers and officers, are also keys to creating long-term value.

Mutual trust generates several benefits. It results in conditions that increase the value of the alliance and, therefore, the probability that it will contribute to competitive advantage.[26] As you might expect, trust leads to a greater willingness to make investments in assets customized to the alliance. When such partnership-specific investments raise the potential for hold-up, they're also more likely to yield the economies of scope and scale that make such partnerships pay off economically. The investment in Tritec by BMW and DaimlerChrysler is a good example, because both firms invested considerable time and dollars in the plant and it is delivering some of the most dependable and efficiently produced four-cylinder car engines in the industry.

Besides increasing learning by encouraging investment in mechanisms that promote greater information sharing, trust reduces the costs of monitoring and maintaining an alliance. Savings can result from such simple gestures as foregoing new legal agreements for small changes in the arrangement or from such critical decisions as an agreement to rely on a simple management structure rather than a more complicated structure requiring a board of directors.

Relational Quality   Because trust is so important to alliance performance, firms need to focus on the areas that affect it most. One approach to identifying these areas is called **relational quality**, which identifies four key elements in establishing and maintaining interorganizational trust.[27] You'll probably find one or more of these elements to be intuitively obvious, but research suggests that organizations don't do a good or consistent job of paying attention to them.

> **relational quality**   Principle identifying four key elements (initial conditions, negotiation process, reciprocal experiences, outside behavior) in establishing and maintaining interorganizational trust.

Initial Conditions   The first element refers to the mutual attitudes of the parties before negotiations begin. Attitudes may be based on prior experiences or on reputation. Sometimes they reflect a larger set of political and economic circumstances. As we noted earlier, for example, China's reputation for condoning property-rights abuses would probably make a prospective partner wary of allying with a Chinese firm.

The Negotiation Process   Prior experience with the process can influence the attitudes that any party brings to the negotiating table. Initial conditions provide a foundation for the development and upgrading of resources and capabilities, but the social interactions that characterize the negotiations process will determine whether any promise in the negotiations is eventually realized. Your own relationships provide a relevant example here. When you meet someone, for instance, you may feel positive about that person due to his or her behaviors or prior reputation. However, your interaction with that person after the initial meeting will determine whether a friendship and otherwise productive relationship develops.

Reciprocal Experiences Once some level of interorganizational trust is established, stock and flow reflect the partners' reciprocal experiences. Do they, for instance, share information openly, disclose potential problems, or behave in other ways that add to the stock of existing interorganizational trust?

Outside Behavior Trust is also a function of the reputation the organization develops as a consequence of its interactions with other organizations outside of the alliance. When Wal-Mart dropped Rubbermaid as a supplier, other suppliers undoubtedly became concerned about the degree to which the retailer could be trusted as a partner.

MANAGING KNOWLEDGE AND LEARNING

For many firms, learning from alliance partners is one of the primary objectives of entering an alliance. In addition to reflecting trust, the ability of a partner to learn increases the collective benefits derived by every partner in the alliance. However, wanting to learn, though obviously important, isn't enough to make learning take place.[28] Learning is enhanced if a firm develops specific processes for managing knowledge exchange. Some explicit activities enable firms to learn from alliances.

Learning and Supplier Support at Toyota Toyota is one of the most successful firms at managing learning through alliance networks and provides a helpful example of knowledge management best practices. Research by Jeffrey H. Dyer highlights Toyota's success in managing its alliances so that knowledge and productivity gains accrue to all alliance members.[29] In studying Toyota's U.S. alliance networks, Dyer found that Toyota's U.S. suppliers were able to achieve efficiency gains in manufacturing that suppliers for GM and Ford couldn't match. In fact, Toyota's suppliers outperformed the other automakers' suppliers despite the disadvantage of being newer and at an earlier stage of the learning curve. Performance *improvements* far outpaced those of other suppliers, and *absolute* performance rapidly surpassed that of suppliers to American firms. Dyer suggests that these efficiency gains resulted from concentrated efforts to ensure that learning flowed both ways and that suppliers learned from each other, not just from Toyota. The strategy depends on the carmaker's Toyota Supplier Support Center (TSSC), which has twenty consultants working with U.S. suppliers.

Let's look at the process a little more closely. Toyota divides its suppliers into groups of six to twelve, with direct competitors assigned to separate groups. To keep interactions fresh, group composition changes every three years. Each group meets with Toyota consultants to decide on a theme for the year, such as styling, demographic fit, supplier relations, and so on. Representatives from each group visit each supplier's plant over a four-month period, examining operations and offering suggestions for improvement. Finally, Toyota hosts an annual meeting at which each group reports on the results of the year's learning activities.

The results have been impressive—an average improvement of 124 percent in labor productivity and inventory reductions of 75 percent. The lesson is quite clear: Alliances result in significant productivity gains when learning is facilitated by coordinated efforts to exchange knowledge and disseminate best practices within the network. Note, too, that such a high level of learning is made possible by an overarching commitment to mutual trust.

UNDERSTANDING ALLIANCE EVOLUTION

At the outset of this chapter, we asked whether you thought the outcome of Magla's alliance with P&G was a common one. You may not be surprised to learn that what starts out as an alliance may eventually become an acquisition.[30] In fact, one study found that nearly 80 percent of equity joint ventures end in the sale of one partner to another.[31] The researchers suggested that managers who don't look out for this twist in the road may run head-on into an unplanned divestiture or acquisition. Although some alliances are actually structured to terminate in the eventual transfer of ownership, most are not, and unplanned sales may erode shareholder value.

Of course, a sale that's well managed and planned in advance can be to a firm's advantage. The same study indicated that alliances can advance a firm's long-term strategy by providing companies with a low-cost, low-risk means of previewing possible acquisitions.

At the same time, it should come as no surprise that relationships between partners may change over time. Indeed, if one partner is aggressively pursuing a coevolution strategy that involves alliances, these changes should be monitored closely and included in the ongoing strategy of both the alliance and its partners. The box entitled Exhibit 9.12 provides a good example of well-managed coevolution through the Fuji-Xerox alliance.[32]

MEASURING ALLIANCE PERFORMANCE

Ironically, one reason for the high failure rate of alliances is the fact that few firms have effective systems for monitoring alliance performance.[33] In the short term, a lack of monitoring systems means that managers who are responsible for the alliance must rely more on intuition than on good information. The long-term consequences are even more serious: When problems do surface, it's much more expensive to fix them. Moreover, performance may have declined so drastically that one or more of the partners starts looking for ways to exit the alliance—an event that often starts a downward spiral toward more performance problems and eventual termination.

Although it may, therefore, seem eminently logical for firms to put monitoring systems in place, there are at least three barriers to getting it done:

■ Partner firms often have different information and reporting systems. DaimlerChrysler and BMW, for instance, have quite different quality, production, and financial reporting systems. The systems at their alliance firm, Tritec, differ from those of both partners. The two carmakers have recently decided that, despite the expense in time and money, Tritec will "translate" its performance data into information that can be accessed through both DaimlerChrysler's and BMW's systems.

■ Even when firms go to great lengths to gauge performance, the inputs that the alliance receives from its corporate parents can be difficult to track and account for. For example, say a manager from DaimlerChrysler joins a Tritec team and that team develops a novel new manufacturing approach. Very often it is difficult to determine whether it was the specific team member or the larger team that came up with the new idea.

■ Similarly, it's also difficult to put a precise value on alliance outputs. What price or value, for example, would you attach to the alliance-based knowledge that a partner uses to improve operations in other parts of the organization?

DEDICATED ALLIANCE FUNCTION

Recent research indicates that cooperative strategies are more likely to succeed when a firm has a dedicated alliance function.[34] A dedicated alliance function may simply be one manager who is responsible for setting up, tracking, and dissolving the firm's alliances; however, typically this function is managed by a group of individuals working together as a team. In many ways, such a function is a structural solution to the need to manage trust, learning, evolution, and performance in a systematic fashion. Although some firms can't afford this added management function, the benefits make it worth looking for a way to fill this role. A

Exhibit 9.12
Coevolution in the
Fuji-Xerox Alliance

Some of the best examples of coevolution reinforce the important roles played by time and investments. Take the case of Fuji-Xerox, which provides some insight into the resources and capabilities acquired through alliances. This alliance between Fuji Photo and Xerox also provided fertile ground for the successful turnaround of Xerox itself by Anne Mulcahy, which you read about in the opening vignette to Chapter 2.

The Fuji-Xerox alliance had been in place for several years, but it was not until early 1970 that it began to bear fruit as a source of competitive capabilities and knowledge for both the alliance and the partners. Xerox was in dire financial straits at the time, having positioned its products against then high-powered rivals such as Eastman Kodak and IBM but being undermined at the same time by low-cost Japanese manufacturers. The first transition was the transfer of Fuji Photo's manufacturing plants in 1970 to the Fuji-Xerox alliance and the resulting development of low-cost manufacturing capabilities by the venture. Following the development of these capabilities, from 1976 to 1978, Xerox initiated R&D and technology-reimbursement agreements between itself and Fuji-Xerox. This transfer agreement fostered the design and fabrication of copy machines for distribution in Europe and the United States.

Over the next decade, Fuji-Xerox continued to upgrade its resources and capabilities in low-end copiers and printers, and Xerox aggressively absorbed these advantages as they grew in importance in the global marketplace. For instance, following an agreement to allow Fuji-Xerox control over its own R&D, Fuji-Xerox began to internalize Japanese total-quality-control manufacturing processes. Xerox, in turn, adopted these processes, and at the same time used the Fuji-Xerox alliance as a platform to expand its own products' presence in Japan.

Ironically, the success and rapid growth for the Fuji-Xerox alliance was a function of the autonomy granted to it by its parents. By 1991, those parents established a new alliance, Xerox International Partners, to market the Fuji-Xerox printer mechanism outside of Japan to companies such as Hewlett-Packard, which were largely captive to the industry leader, Canon. At the same time, this same mechanism satisfied the majority of Xerox and Rank Xerox (another alliance) low-end copier sales. Although the alliances were largely autonomous, top executives at Xerox and Fuji-Xerox were careful to hold top-executive "summits" twice a year, exchange key personnel, and fund joint research programs to avoid redundant and wasteful R&D efforts.

It was on this platform of global success that Anne Mulcahy made a case for the acquisition of the color-printer division of Tektronix by Xerox in 2000. These color-printer capabilities were shared, not surprisingly, with Fuji-Xerox, which flourishes to this day, with Xerox owning 25 percent and Fuji Photo owning 75 percent. As for Xerox? Well, you know much of the rest of that story from the vignette in Chapter 2.

firm might, for example, assign a chief alliance officer, whose responsibilities are outlined in Exhibit 9.13.[35]

The first two roles in the components of a dedicated-alliance-function process are often the most critical. Regardless of the levels of trust, learning, and capabilities that an alliance boasts, it won't be productive under either of the two following situations:

- When there isn't a strong business case for the alliance as a vehicle

- When assessment fails and there simply isn't a good fit between partners

Exhibit 9.13   A Dedicated Alliance Function

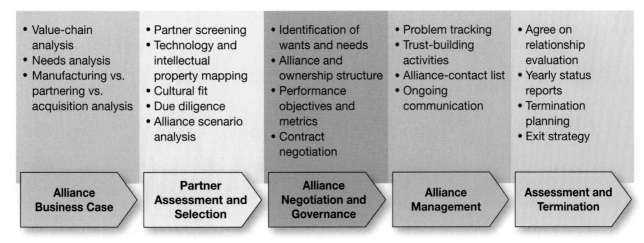

Alliance Business Case	Partner Assessment and Selection	Alliance Negotiation and Governance	Alliance Management	Assessment and Termination
• Value-chain analysis • Needs analysis • Manufacturing vs. partnering vs. acquisition analysis	• Partner screening • Technology and intellectual property mapping • Cultural fit • Due diligence • Alliance scenario analysis	• Identification of wants and needs • Alliance and ownership structure • Performance objectives and metrics • Contract negotiation	• Problem tracking • Trust-building activities • Alliance-contact list • Ongoing communication	• Agree on relationship evaluation • Yearly status reports • Termination planning • Exit strategy

Good intentions alone do not make alliances work. Nothing can replace a good strategy that spells out the role of alliances in a firm's strategy and partner fit.

WHEN DO PARTNERS FIT?

The issue of fit isn't easy to resolve, and to do so, firms must be able to answer yes to the following questions:

■ *Strategic fit:* Are the partners' objectives compatible? For how long?

■ *Resource and financial fit:* Are the partners willing and able to contribute the resources and competencies?

■ *Cultural fit:* Can the partners understand each other? Do they share the same business logic and commitment?

■ *Structure, systems, and processes fit:* Can the decision-making and control mechanisms be aligned?

■ *Additional fit criteria:* What other key questions should be on the table, such as timing, other alliances, alliance alternatives, environmental context, and competitive pressures?

Because we're interested in alliances as a strategy vehicle, the first question pertains to *strategic fit.* Researchers at the consulting firm of McKinsey and Company have identified lack of strategic fit as a common starting point for those alliances that eventually failed.[36] In many ways, the opening vignette on Magla provides an example of an alliance where strategic fit was good because Magla needed better access to the mass-market channels and capital than it could attain on its own. Sometimes, alliances between weaker and stronger firms even lead the weaker firm to a position of strength, in which case the alliance is usually dissolved, or in other cases in which the stronger partner acquires the weaker one. Partnerships among complementary equals tend to be the strongest and longest lasting. In some cases, competitive tensions and industry conditions may lead one partner to acquire the other, usually after about seven years. In other cases, the partners remain strong and independent. Some alliances, such as Fuji-Xerox, exemplify true co-evolution and are most likely to survive for much longer than seven years. In the case of Fuji-Xerox, the alliance has lasted several decades and has spawned additional complementary alliances.

Assessing Alliance Fit at Millennium Pharmaceuticals

Evaluating alliance opportunities is not simple, but you do have the advantage of a framework that helps you start the process. The first step is to develop a grid, shown in Exhibit 9.14 that lays out how well the potential partner fits with your firm.

Note that you should always include alternative potential partners, since you may be more likely to enter a bad deal when you have nothing to compare it to. This may sound silly, but many CEOs say that some of the most important alliance or acquisition decisions they have made, are the decisions not to do them! In this example, Millennium Pharmaceuticals was faced with a huge alliance opportunity with German firm Lundberg—it involved lots of cash and a savvy global partner with a great deal of experience. Why, then, would Millennium turn such a deal down? Using the following alliance-fit framework, and setting up Abbott Labs as the comparison alliance, Millennium decided that it was best to pass on the Lundberg alliance (though it turns out that the Abbott alliance was in the works):

- *Strategic fit?* In general, the strategic fit was good. However, Millennium had recently put together a very similar large alliance with Monsanto, and it was not clear how another deal would move Millennium's strategy forward.
- *Resource fit?* Other than money, the Lundberg did not bring much to the table in terms of new resources and capabilities. In fact, Millennium would be putting most of its unique capabilities to work, which in turn could stretch its technical and research staff with no benefit other than additional cash in the bank. At the time, Millennium was strong financially.
- *Cultural fit?* The potential partner was a large, private agribusiness firm, whereas Millennium was a relatively small, public biotech firm. In initial meetings, there was some indication with the potential partner that top management was keen on an alliance but that lower-level managers were out of the loop. Cultural misfit often arises when line managers are not involved in the alliance-building process from the very start.
- *Structural fit?* This, too, was a big question mark. Millennium's management had the impression that the partner would not grant it the autonomy or flexibility that it desired in its alliances. Thus, the structure appeared too rigid from Millennium's perspective.
- *Other questions?* Because Millennium was still contemplating other options and partnerships, it was not as if this was the only opportunity in the market. Finally, the top-management team determined that it was not excited about the alliance beyond the fact that the partner had a great reputation and brought lots of cash to the relationship.

So, you are probably asking what happened to Millennium after it passed up such a lucrative deal. Shortly thereafter, Millennium and Abbott formed a five-year alliance primarily for collaborative research and development in the area of metabolic diseases. The companies agreed to share equally the cost of developing, manufacturing, and marketing products on a worldwide basis. The arrangement with Abbott also includes an equity investment by Abbott in Millennium, amounting in total to $250 million over several years, and a technology exchange and development agreement. Moreover, Millennium and Aventis expanded their existing joint development pipeline to include an aggregate of eleven additional discovery projects that were previously pursued outside the joint collaboration by Millennium or Aventis. These new assets included chemokine receptors, kinases, and integrins, which are important as potential drug-development target classes in inflammatory disease research. As a result of this expansion, that alliance yielded approximately fifty jointly funded discovery projects. Soon, Millennium had created more than twenty alliances with leading pharmaceutical and biotechnology companies—close to $2 billion of committed funding. You can learn more about why Millennium sees such a network of alliances as a central vehicle in its strategy—to eventually become a full-fledged pharmaceutical firm—through its R&D page at www.millennium.com.

Exhibit 9.14 Comparing Alliance Opportunities

	Partner A—Lundberg	Partner B—Abbott Labs
Strategic Fit?	Good, but no new learning opportunities	Good and ample learning and growth opportunities
Resource Fit?	Cash resources, but cash is generic	Cash and technology resources, and technology is unique
Cultural Fit?	Likely to be poor	Good
Structural Fit?	Unknown	Good
Other Key Questions? • Capital market demands—who drives strategy here? • Timing—are capital markets hot or cold? • Timing—do we need another deal like this? • Timing—how plentiful and attractive are other alliance options? • Does "no" here mean no more options? • Again, other criteria? • What other key questions should be on the table?	Management was not excited about the deal	Management was excited about the deal—high level of motivation

The second question concerns *resource and financial fit.* This question deals with either the availability of a resource or the willingness and ability of a partner to make that resource available. Questions of *cultural fit* typically relate to the cultural characteristics of the organizations themselves. In the early years of SEMATECH, for instance, Intel's participation was problematic because Intel's highly competitive culture clashed with the cooperative culture being fostered by the consortium.[37] Though *structural fit* can be a simple matter of making financial reporting systems compatible, conflicts may arise over arrangements of authority and decision making.

Finally, in determining fit, a company should take situation-specific factors into consideration. Is the firm, for example, already involved in too many alliances? Is the timing right? Do competitive conditions currently favor alliances as a strategy vehicle? The box entitled "How Would *You* Do That? 9.1" shows what happened when Millennium Pharmaceuticals applied a checklist for assessing partner fit in determining whether to enter into an alliance with a potential partner. The answer, as you can see, was no.

Dyer's research shows that it's difficult to develop the rich alliance capabilities that will satisfy a checklist like Millennium's. At the same time, however, Dyer notes that firms that succeed in developing the requisite capabilities may be better competitors as a result. Not only may such capabilities contribute to near-term performance and competitive position, but they may also enhance the reputation of a company as a preferred partner. Wal-Mart, for example, though known as a very aggressive competitor, has established a solid reputation in Latin America as a dependable partner. As noted earlier, Wal-Mart is now leveraging these alliance skills and the reputation built through local partnerships to fuel its growth in China and Japan.

Summary of Challenges

1. *Explain why strategic alliances are important strategy vehicles.* Alliances enable participants to share in investments and rewards, while reducing the risk and uncertainty that each firm must bear on its own. Such sharing also enables firms to focus their efforts on what they do best, while benefiting from the similarly focused efforts of their partner firms. In economic terms, alliances may lead to higher firm performance by enabling firms to realize economies of scope and scale that would otherwise not be realized if they had to operate on their own.

2. *Describe the motivations behind alliances and show how they've changed over time.* Although firms seek economies of scope and scale from alliances, their ultimate objective is that the alliance contributes to their competitive advantage. The VRINE framework can be applied to alliances. If the alliance creates something of value, has benefits that are both rare and difficult to imitate (including less costly imitation by a simple market purchase agreement or wholly owned business), and the partners are able to extract value from the alliance (i.e., the resources and capabilities in the alliance are supported by features of the organization), then a firm can reap competitive advantages. Over time, the basis for alliance advantage has shifted from simple efficiencies and economies of scope and scale to a vehicle for organizational learning and innovation.

3. *Identify the various forms and structures of strategic alliances.* Alliances can take many forms. A joint venture is the most complex form because it results in the establishment of a third, independent entity. Joint ventures, in which partners contribute cash and other resources to the partnership, fall into the broader category of equity alliances. Nonequity alliances are the most common form of alliance. These typically take the form of contracts to supply, produce, market, or distribute a firm's goods or services. Sole-sourcing, just-in-time supply agreements, licensing, and cobranding are examples of nonequity alliances. Equity and nonequity alliances may involve many participants. Such alliances are sometimes called *industry associations, cooperatives,* or *consortia.*

4. *Compare and contrast alliances as business- and corporate-level strategy vehicles.* The five-forces model and value net are good tools for both identifying potential partners and reaffirming that just about any firm related to the business can be considered a potential partner. Business strategy alliances fall into two categories: vertical and horizontal. Vertical alliances link a focal firm to downstream raw materials and other critical inputs; upstream they link that same firm to marketing, arenas, and other channels of distribution. Horizontal alliances enable firms in one segment of the industry to partner with firms in other segments. Strategic alliances are also a useful vehicle for a firm's corporate and international strategies. Cross-border alliances differ from domestic-only alliances in that government, public policies, and national culture often play a more visible role. Alliances can also take on the characteristic of a network when clusters of companies compete against each other for customers or new technology standards. Finally, cutting across all these alliances are six risks that contribute to their failure or lackluster performance. These risks range from poor contract development to the misinterpretation of a partner's strategic intent.

5. *Understand the characteristics of alliances in stable and dynamic competitive contexts.* Just as strategies may vary according to context, so, too, should the expectations and design features of alliances as a strategy vehicle. Stable contexts afford firms the luxury of managing many alliances. Although the choice of alliance partners is always important, any one alliance failure is unlikely to break the company. However, in dynamic contexts the stakes are much higher. Such heightened stakes can take the simple form of greater dollar investments in new technological platforms but typically are manifest in a rapidly evolving environment where being in the wrong partnership today could mean the ultimate demise of the firm later. The use and design of alliances in dynamic contexts fits well with the coevolution model introduced in Chapter 7. That is, alliances are included in the firm's orchestration of a web of shifting linkages among evolving businesses.

6. *Summarize the criteria for successful alliances.* Five interrelated criteria for effective alliance implementation were emphasized in this chapter. First, firms must understand the determinants and benefits of trust. Alliances that are based on trust benefit from lower transaction costs, greater economies of scope and scale, and greater learning and knowledge management. Second, firms must be good at managing knowledge and knowledge flows. This means that they should establish learning objectives for each alliance and mechanisms for realizing them. The third criterion is the need to understand alliance evolution. Alliances may follow different pathways depending on their initial conditions and partner relations, and an understanding of both the role of initial conditions and the potential pathways will inform the establishment of an alliance and its management once it is in place. Linking the alliance to a performance management system is the fourth criterion. Such tracking will help to ensure both near-term benefits and the avoidance of problems that may fester for lack of attention. Finally, firms should consider the establishment of some systematic and coherent structural response to the unique and complex management challenges that alliances give rise to. This structure can take the form of an individual with the title of chief alliance officer or, where appropriate and financially feasible, the establishment of a dedicated alliance function.

Review Questions

1. What is a strategic alliance?

2. Do most strategic alliances succeed?

3. What forms can strategic alliances take?

4. What is the difference between an equity and a nonequity strategic alliance?

5. Provide an example of a nonequity strategic alliance.

6. Why do firms enter into alliances?

7. What are the three forms of strategic alliance that support business strategy?

8. What do the value net and industry structure models tell you about potential alliance partners?

9. How do alliances serve as a vehicle for corporate strategy?

10. What risks do alliances pose to partner firms?

11. How do alliances differ in stable and dynamic contexts?

12. What are the five critical criteria for successful alliances (hint: don't confuse these with the ten observations made about alliances in Exhibit 9.11)?

Experiential Activities

Group Exercises

1. Increasingly, firms such as P&G, Corning (www.corning.com) and Millennium Pharmaceuticals (www.millennium.com) claim to have a core competency and competitive advantage based on their ability to manage alliances. Develop statements that both defend and critique this proposition. Identify risks that firms run when their strategy is essentially a network of alliances.

2. Identify a firm and document its alliance activity over the past five to ten years (visit the Web site of a public firm, particularly the "history" page). Examine the list of officers at the company (these are always detailed in the annual report and often on the firm's Web site). Do they appear to have a dedicated alliance function? What kinds of changes would they have to make if they were to follow the recommendations on implementation levers necessary to achieve an effective dedicated alliance function? What would be the costs and benefits of such a change?

Ethical Debates

1. One of the biggest barriers for firms entering into alliances with foreign partners, and even domestic ones, are issues of trust. Does a well-crafted legal agreement prevent breaches of ethics by either party to the agreement?

2. You have seen many reports in the press about Adidas or Nike and how the working conditions of the foreign partners and suppliers are sometimes abysmal. Is this just a cost of doing business through foreign alliances or can firms do something to manage these situations?

How Would YOU DO THAT?

1. The box entitled "How Would *You* Do That? 9.1" shows how Millennium Pharmaceuticals evaluated a potential alliance partner. Apply the Millennium fit framework to the alliances of another firm you are familiar with. Do these appear to be good alliances? Do any of the alliances suggest that your focal firm is on a pathway to acquire its partner or be acquired by it?

Go on to see How Would You Do That at www.prenhall.com/carpenter&sanders

Endnotes

1. "Growth: Hand In Glove," *Business Week*, Fall 2006, (accessed August 15, 2007), at http://www.businessweek.com/magazine/content/06_38/b4001838.htm; D. G. Thomson, *Blueprint to a Billion: 7 Essentials to Achieve Exponential Growth* (New York: Wiley, 2005); "Mr. Clean Expands Licensing Program Internationally," *PR Newswire*, January 10, 2002; "Magla Plans to Sell Household Gloves Under Procter & Gamble Mr. Clean Brand Name," *Business Wire*, January 16, 2000; *Magla Company Story* (accessed on April 25, 2007) at http://www.magla.com/geninfo/Type.cfm?Type=About&Level=General&Width=1878; "Magla Signs Licensing Agreement to Sell Disposable Exam Gloves Under the American Red Cross Brand Name," Press Release, February 23, 2006, accessed June 21, 2007; "Inspirational Consumers," *Brand Strategy*, July 12, 2005, p. 24; "Driving with Mr. Clean." *Grocery Headquarters*, January 2006, p. 96; "P&G Keeps Expanding Its Far-flung Empire," *Household & Personal Products Industry*, January 2007, p. 100; H. Chesbrough and K. Schwartz, "Innovating Business Models with Co-Development Partnerships," *Research-Technology Management*, January–February 2007, p. 55(5).

2. J. Harbison and P. Pekar, *Smart Alliances: A Practical Guide to Repeatable Success* (San Francisco: Jossey-Bass, 1998).

3. C. Wolf, "Rubbermaid Struggles to Put Lid on Problems: Company's Earnings Tumble after Price Increase Backfires," *Cincinnati Enquirer*, April 8, 1996, D1.

4. J. Cook, T. Halevy, and B. Hastie, "Alliances in Consumer Packaged Goods," *McKinsey on Finance*, Autumn 2003, 16–20.

5. J. Bleeke and D. Ernst, *Collaborating to Compete* (New York: John Wiley & Sons, 1993); D. Ernst and T. Halevy, "When to Think Alliance," *McKinsey Quarterly* 4 (2000), 46–55.

6. J. H. Dyer and H. Singh, "The Relational View: Cooperative Strategies and Sources of Interorganizational Competitive Advantage," *Academy of Management Review* 23 (1998), 660–679.

7. O. E. Williamson, *The Economic Institutions of Capitalism* (New York: Free Press, 1985).

8. G. Hamel and C. K. Prahalad, *Competing for the Future* (Boston: Harvard Business School Press, 1994).

9. J. B. Barney and M. H. Hansen, "Trustworthiness as a Source of Competitive Advantage," *Strategic Management Journal* 15 (1995), 175–190; Dyer and Singh, "The Relational View."

10. Harbison and Pekar, *Smart Alliances.*

11. Adapted from J. Harbison and P. Pekar, *Smart Alliances: A Practical Guide to Repeatable Success* (San Francisco: Jossey-Bass, 1998).

12. www.mlnm.com/media/strategy/index.asp (accessed July 15, 2005).

13. Adapted from J. D. Bamford, B. Gomes-Casseres, and M. S. Robinson, *Mastering Alliance Strategy: A Comprehensive Guide to Design, Management, and Organization* (San Francisco: John Wiley & Sons, 2003), p. 22.

14. For detailed discussions of the Japanese projects, see K. Flamm, *Mismanaged Trade? Strategic Policy and the Semiconductor Industry* (Washington, D.C.: Brookings Institution, 1996), 39–126; J. Sigurdson, *Industry and State Partnership in Japan: The Very Large Scale Integrated Circuits (VLSI) Project* (Lund, Sweden: Research Policy Institute, 1986). For a dissenting assessment, see M. Fransman, *The Market and Beyond: Cooperation and Competition in Information Technology Development in the Japanese System* (Cambridge: Cambridge University Press, 1992).

15. Semiconductor Equipment and Materials International, About Us (accessed June 6, 2005), at http://wps2a.semi.org/wps/portal/_pagr/103/_pa.103/259.

16. Adapted from A. Brandendburger and B. Nalebuff, *Co-Opetition* (New York: Doubleday, 1996).

17. J. H. Dyer, *Collaborative Advantage: Winning through Extended Enterprise Supplier Networks* (New York: Oxford University Press, 2000).

18. www.softbank.co.jp (accessed August 12, 2005).

19. P. Almeida, J. Song, and R. M. Grant, "Are Firms Superior to Alliances and Markets? An Empirical Test of Cross-Border Knowledge Building," *Organization Science* 14 (2002), 157–171.

20. Adapted from B. Gomes-Casseres, "Competing in Constellations: The Case of Fuji-Xerox," *Strategy and Business* First Quarter (1997), 4–16; www.fujixerox.co.jp/eng/company/history (accessed July 15, 2005) and the Xerox Fact Book (2005–2006), at www.xerox.com (accessed November 8, 2005).

21. Adapted from B. Gomes-Casseres, "Alliance Strategies of Small Firms," *Small Business Economics* 9 (1997), 33–44.

22. Harbison and Pekar, *Smart Alliances;* E. Bailey and W. Shan, "Sustainable Competitive Advantage Through Alliances," in E. Bowman and B. Kogut, eds., *Redesigning the Firm* (New York: Oxford University Press, 1995).

23. S. Brown and K. Eisenhardt, *Competing on the Edge* (Boston: Harvard Business School Press, 1997).

24. Adapted from B. Gomes-Casseres, "Critical Eye," www.criticaleye.net, June–August, 2004. See http://www.alliancestrategy.com/, for more alliance resources.

25. Barney and Hansen, "Trustworthiness as a Source of Competitive Advantage."

26. Dyer, *Collaborative Advantage.*

27. A. Arino, J. de la Torre, P. S. Ring, "Relational Quality: Managing Trust in Corporate Alliances," *California Management Review* 44:1 (2001), 109–134.

28. G. Probst, "Practical Knowledge Management: A Model That Works," *Prism* (Arthur D. Little Consultants), Second Quarter (1998), 17–29.

29. Information in this section is drawn from J. H. Dyer, *Collaborative Advantage.*

30. J. Bleeke and D. Ernst, *Collaborating to Compete* (New York: Wiley, 1993).

31. Bleeke and Ernst, *Collaborating to Compete.*

32. Adapted from B. Gomes-Casseres, "Competing in Constellations: The Case of Fuji-Xerox," *Strategy and Business* First Quarter (1997), 4–16; www.fujixerox.co.jp/eng/company/history (accessed July 15, 2005) and the Xerox Fact Book (2005–2006), at www.xerox.com (accessed November 8, 2005).

33. J. H. Dyer, P. Kale, and H. Singh, "How to Make Strategic Alliances Work," *Sloan Management Review* 42 (2001), 121–136. According to the authors, 51 percent of the alliances surveyed had no performance monitoring systems, and only 11 percent believed that they had good systems in place.

34. Dyer, Kale, and Singh, "How to Make Strategic Alliances Work."

35. Adapted from J. H. Dyer, P. Kale, and H. Singh, "How to Make Strategic Alliances Work," *Sloan Management Review* 42:4 (2001), 121–136.

36. J. Bleeke and D. Ernst, "Is Your Strategic Alliance Really a Sale?" *Harvard Business Review* 73:1 (1995), 97–102.

37. L. D. Browning, J. M. Beyer, and J. C. Shetler, "Building Cooperation in a Competitive Industry: SEMATECH," *Academy of Management Journal* 38:1 (1995), 113–151.

10 Studying Mergers and Acquisitions

In This Chapter We Challenge You To >>>

1. Explain the motivations behind acquisitions and show how they've changed over time.

2. Explain why mergers and acquisitions are important to strategy.

3. Identify the various types of acquisitions.

4. Understand how the pricing of acquisitions affects the realization of synergies.

5. Outline the alternative ways to integrate acquisitions and explain the implementation process.

6. Discuss the characteristics of acquisitions in different industry contexts.

eBay + Paypal + Skype
How to Acquire Customers

*S*trategy is important at every firm, but Meg Whitman, CEO of eBay, says that on the Internet "the landscape changes quarterly," which elevates strategy to a mission-critical task.[1] eBay, as most people know, is an Internet-based auction and marketplace site on which some 233 million registered customers buy and sell tens of thousands of products ranging from Beanie Babies to used cars. The company generates revenues through advertising and by charging listing and selling fees. For the 2007 year, eBay expected revenues between $7.2 billion and $7.45 billion.

eBay has grown fast, and acquisitions are part of Whitman's toolkit. Some acquisitions, like the purchase of Butterfields (a 140-year-old auctioneer of high-end merchandise) didn't work well and Butterfields was sold off three years later. Others, like eBay's purchase of PayPal in 2002, were greeted skeptically but have paid off. Whitman said she thought the PayPal acquisition was "one of the all-time great acquisitions, even though at the time people about had a heart attack that we paid $1.5 billion for PayPal. I mean, I got creamed in the press. 'The woman is crazy. I cannot believe she paid $1.5 billion dollars for this, you know, stupid little company.'"

Indeed, PayPal didn't come cheap. The sale entailed a 100-percent stock transaction, and the price—about $1.5 billion—represented a 20-percent premium over PayPal's stock value prior to the announced acquisition. Thus, eBay paid a premium of about $250 million, and on the day that the sale was announced the market discounted eBay's stock price by 7 percent. After successfully negotiating and closing this transaction, Whitman was left with the reality of trying to make it work. She either had to identify significant cost savings or find new revenue-enhancement opportunities (i.e., synergies) in order to recoup the capital that was necessary to snag PayPal. Whitman's approach was to look for synergies. "The magic is, what opportunities do various combinations of our two assets open up?" As Whitman sees it, "eBay and PayPal was one of the most remarkable combinations because they made each business stronger on their own, and then created a whole new opportunity called merchant services." Most payment companies faced the problem that they couldn't get enough buyers to use the payment system and therefore couldn't get merchants to accept the payment form. But eBay provided PayPal with ready-made droves of customers. "PayPal became the *de facto* payment standard on the biggest locus of small business in the world, and as a result was able to extend off that market place," Whitman said. At the end of March 2007, PayPal had 143 million total accounts. Those accounts helped drive record TPV (total payment volume) of $11.36 billion the first three months of 2007 alone.

Let's take a closer look at the synergies between PayPal and eBay: PayPal's network builds on the existing financial infrastructure of bank accounts and credit cards to create a global payment system. Its revenue comes from the float in the personal accounts and fees charged for Premier and Business Accounts. Float can mean many things in finance, but in this case it refers to the fact that eBay has buyers' money, via PayPal, for a period of time and can invest those monies for profit between the time it receives the money and the time it pays it out to sellers. eBay management viewed PayPal's strategy as complementary to its own. Both business models, shown in Exhibit 10.1, for example, relied on transaction-based revenue sources. Neither required inventory or warehousing of merchandise, and neither maintained any sales force to speak of. Finally, both strategies called for high operating leverage and low capital requirements.

Just because there are synergies between two companies, however, doesn't mean that executing the acquisition plan is easy. For example, when eBay first bought PayPal, eBay executives debated whether to rename the company something like "eBay Payments" rather than PayPal. "In fact," Whitman admitted, "for a while on the website, it was called 'eBay Payments.' We were a little confused." Ultimately, however, the team decided that if PayPal was to grow as a system used by merchants beyond the eBay space, it had to retain its own brand identity. "We decided that eBay stands for e-commerce, it stands for connecting buyers and sellers. PayPal stands for payments," Whitman said. Had eBay called it eBay Payments, Whitman continued, "I don't think we'd have a merchant services business, because I'm not sure Dell.com would necessarily want eBay Payments as a payment module."

One of Whitman's latest acquisitions was of the Internet phone service startup Skype, which eBay bought in 2005 for as much as $4.1 billion (depending on how Skype performs). Whitman made the acquisition for several reasons: "We loved the Skype viral effect of how it had grown its user base—it looked a lot like eBay. You know, in the earliest

eBay Business Model

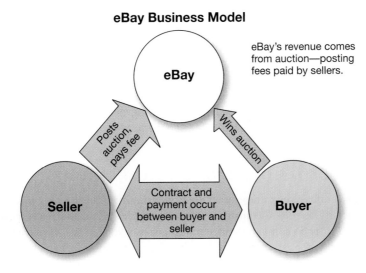

eBay's revenue comes from auction—posting fees paid by sellers.

Exhibit 10.1   eBay and PayPal Business Models

PayPal Business Model

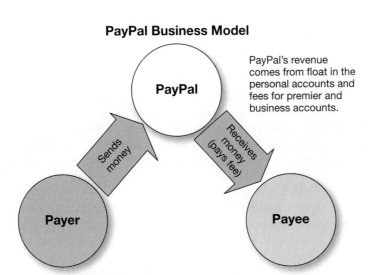

PayPal's revenue comes from float in the personal accounts and fees for premier and business accounts.

days, [it had] even more rapid adoption. So it was very clear to me that something quite unique was going on at Skype—it was pioneering a whole new technology, but building a thriving ecosystem of users, developers, hardware manufacturers, and chipset manufacturers."

Most of all, however, Skype added to synergies with Paypal and eBay. "In the case of eBay, [there is] communication synergy. And with PayPal, this whole notion of PayPal being the wallet on Skype, and every new Skype user getting a PayPal account and vice versa," Whitman said. "That's why we were so excited when we saw Skype—there's something here that will unlock the Skype business, and will enable each business to grow on its own," Whitman said. Skype had grown to 196 million registered users at the end of March 2007, representing a 107 percent increase from the 95 million users at the end of March 2006.

In short, Whitman's strategy boils down to three critical synergies among eBay's properties: that eBay buyers and sellers will talk using Skype (generating ad revenue for eBay);

that Skype callers will use PayPal to pay for their calls (the ones that aren't free, that is); and that Skype will encourage PayPal's expanding cross-border remittance business. This economic logic of eBay's strategy is summarized by Whitman: "We want to build the synergies between these businesses," Whitman said at a shareholder conference in 2006, "so that one plus one plus one equals a lot more than three." The jury is still out on the actual synergies and other benefits to be gained by eBay through the high-profile Skype acquisition, but as you will see later in the chapter, it appears that the PayPal leg of the trio is paying off handsomely in eBay's strategy. <<<

Motives for Mergers and Acquisitions

Why do firms acquire companies rather than entering new businesses on their own or through alliances? Was eBay's acquisition of PayPal a typical acquisition? Are most acquisitions successful? Why do companies often pay huge costs, such as the 20-percent premium that eBay paid for PayPal, to acquire another firm? By the end of this chapter, you should be able to answer these and other questions about mergers and acquisitions (M&As). Indeed, as you work through the chapter, you'll see that our opening vignette on eBay and PayPal introduces many of the features common to acquisitions.

DIFFERENCES BETWEEN ACQUISITIONS AND MERGERS

Although it is regular practice to use the terms *mergers* and *acquisitions* together, and sometimes interchangeably, they aren't the same thing. The differences can be subtle, and depending on who's using the terms and in what country, each term tends to have different meanings. Disputes over differences in legal definitions can end up in court. For instance, Chrysler investor Kirk Kerkorian sued DaimlerChrysler in 2001 for billions based on the argument that the marriage of Daimler with Chrysler in 1997 was actually an acquisition by Daimler and not a merger. What was Kerkorian's interest in the transaction being labeled an acquisition? An acquisition would result in much more money being paid to Chrysler shareholders, including Kerkorian.[2]

acquisition Strategy by which one firm acquires another through stock purchase or exchange.	Technically, the term **acquisition** means that a transfer of ownership has taken place—that one firm has bought another. A **merger** is the consolidation or combination of one firm with another.[3] When the term *merger* is used, it often refers to a class of mergers known as *mergers of equals*. These mergers are typically between firms of relatively equal size and influence that fuse together to form one new larger firm. Although there are many technical, legal, and detailed differences between mergers and acquisitions, for our purposes in understanding how they serve as vehicles of strategy, they are more similar than dissimilar. Consequently, we will focus on how firms use M&As to pursue their objectives.
merger Consolidation or combination of two or more firms.	

We will emphasize the motives for M&As and the strategic implications of those motives. The motives behind M&As fall into three basic categories: *managerial self-interest, hubris,* and *synergy.* In this section, we'll review these three types of motives and assess the effects of M&As undertaken in pursuit of each of them. Because the first two motives usually don't reflect shareholders' best interests, the rest of the chapter will focus on M&As undertaken in pursuit of synergy.

MANAGERIAL SELF-INTEREST

managerialism Tendency of managers to make decisions based on personal self-interest rather than the best interests of shareholders.

Sometimes senior managers make decisions based on personal self-interest rather than the best interests of shareholders. We call this behavior **managerialism**. Conceivably, managers can make acquisitions—and even willingly overpay in M&As—in order to maximize their own interests at the expense of shareholder wealth. Executive compensation, for instance, tends to be linked to firm size. Managers might, therefore, enhance their paychecks by making acquisitions that accomplish nothing more than enlarging the firm.[4] As you have learned, getting bigger, in and of itself, does not create shareholder wealth.

Likewise, because year-end bonuses (and job security) are often tied to the firm's earnings, some managers might pursue diversification through M&A in order to stabilize annual earnings. Managers could, therefore, make acquisitions in order to boost earnings by diversifying the firm's revenue stream.[5] Certainly, organic growth could achieve the same goal but not as quickly. In any case, diversification of a firm's revenue stream creates little value for shareholders. Why? Because, as we've seen, they can diversify their personal securities portfolios much more cheaply.

HUBRIS

In the mid-1980s, economist Richard Roll proposed what he called the *hubris hypothesis* to explain, at least in part, why acquisition premiums are so large and yet acquisitions remain so common.[6]

As we've already pointed out, when a publicly traded firm is acquired by another firm, the purchase price almost always exceeds the target firm's market value. The average premium—the amount received by the target firm's shareholders in excess of the value of their stock—was between 30 and 45 percent during the 15-year period between 1989 and 2004. Why would anyone pay such a generous premium? After all, the target firm's market value prior to the acquisition bid was the market's best estimate of the present value of target firm's future cash flows.

According to Roll, managers not only make mistaken valuations but often have unwarranted confidence both in their valuations and in their ability to create value. This attitude, says Roll, reflects **hubris**—a Greek term denoting excessive pride, overconfidence, or arrogance. Hubristic managers may overestimate their own abilities to implement potential synergies.

A final word: Although we're going to focus on synergy as a motivation for acquisitions, you shouldn't ignore the other two motivations—managerialism and managerial hubris—when you're evaluating M&As. When managerialism and hubris are kept in check, acquiring firms are more likely to realize synergies and positive performance benefits.

hubris Exaggerated self-confidence that can result in managers' overestimating the value of a potential acquisition, having unrealistic assumptions about the ability to create synergies, and a willingness to pay too much for a transaction.

SYNERGY

When M&As are undertaken in pursuit of synergy, managers are guided by the belief that the value of two firms combined can be greater than the sum value of the two firms independently. This category includes all forms of M&As that are motivated by value creation. Synergy may derive from a number of sources, including reduced threats from suppliers, increased market power, potential cost savings, superior financial strength, economies of scope and scale, and the sharing and leveraging of capabilities.

Reducing Threats   As was noted in Chapter 7, sometimes a supplier cannot or will not make an investment that's specific to an exchange with one buyer. Why might this situation arise? Perhaps the investment would tie the company too closely to one buyer, expose it to too much risk, or overtax its financial means. In such cases firms may need to integrate vertically, backward into the supply chain.[7] The quickest way to do this is through an acquisition. Some of Cisco Systems' acquisitions of network switch technology companies are examples of this type of backward integration.

Increasing Market Power and Access   If a company improves its competitive position by means of a merger or acquisition, it may be possible to derive potential market power from the deal. Firms have market power when they can influence prices, and price competition is reduced significantly when rivalry is reduced. In the banking industry, for example, some mergers—especially those involving two moderate-sized banks—seem to have been motivated by a desire to improve market power. Thus, when First Union purchased Wachovia, the combined company vaulted into the number-four slot among U.S. banks. When Daimler merged with Chrysler in an effort to exploit potential synergies, its share in the global automotive market increased significantly. And the merger was designed to improve market access for both companies in geographic arenas where they were weak but their merger partner was strong. Another example of improved access is provided by PepsiCo. In 1992, for example, when PepsiCo still owned Pizza Hut, Taco Bell, and Kentucky Fried Chicken, it purchased Carts of Colorado (CC), a small food cart (e.g., kiosk) manufacturer, for $7 million, seeing it as the ideal means of installing new restaurants quickly and cheaply. Not only did the purchase give PepsiCo access to new cart technology, but it also provided it with an inexpensive means for quickly establishing fast food outlets in high-traffic locations. One of PepsiCo's first successful cart locations was in the Moscow metro system.

Realizing Cost Savings   Cost savings are the most common synergy and the easiest to estimate. Financial markets tend to understand and accept cost savings as a rationale and are more likely to reward savings-motivated M&As with higher stock prices than other forms of synergy. Revenue-enhancement opportunities, such as increasing total sales through cross-selling and enhanced distribution, also represent a significant upside in many M&As. It's more difficult, however, to calculate and implement revenue enhancement synergies (sometimes called *soft synergies*) than cost-saving synergies.

Increasing Financial Strength   Other synergies can be created by various forms of financial engineering. An acquisition, for instance, can lower the financing costs of the target firm when the two firms' respective credit ratings are markedly different and significant debt is involved. Such would be the case if a company with AAA-rated debt were to buy a B-rated company. Various tax benefits also provide unique financial synergies. If, for example, the target company has operating loss carry-forwards (i.e., financial losses that the IRS allows firms to apply to future years' earnings) that can't be fully utilized, the acquiring company can use them to reduce the tax bill of the combined firm.

Sharing and Leveraging Capabilities   Transferring best practices and core competencies can create value. This form of synergy is important in the resource-based view of competitive advantage. According to this view, one reason for acquiring another firm would be to absorb and assimilate the target's resource, knowledge, and capabilities—all of which, as we saw in Chapter 3, may be primary sources of competitive advantage. When firms combine resources and capabilities through M&As, they may be able to create a bundle of resources that is unavailable to competitors. If the combined resources and capabilities are complementary, the competitive advantage may be long-term. If the combination is valuable and rare, the acquiring firm may be able to generate profits greater than the sum of the two firms' individual profits. Bear in mind, however, that transferring resources, knowledge, or capabilities can create long-term competitive advantage only if the cost of the acquisition doesn't exceed the cost to other firms of accumulating comparable resource stocks.

Mergers, Acquisitions, and Strategy

Three points need to be kept in mind when considering acquisitions as a part of a firm's corporate strategy. First, as with other elements of strategy, managers need to be clear about the economic logic: How does the acquisition help the firm earn profits? Second, managers need to consider alternatives to the acquisition, such as developing the new business internally rather than buying it. Third, acquisitions are fraught with hazards that can end up ruining the projected returns, and managers need to know what these hazards are and how to navigate around them.

THE VEHICLE AND ITS ECONOMIC LOGIC

Acquisitions enable firms to enter new businesses quickly, reduce the time and risks entailed by the process of starting new businesses internally, and rapidly reach minimum efficient scale. Research shows, however, that M&As come with significant risks and uncertainties of their own. Although some acquisitions succeed, such as eBay's acquisition of PayPal, others fail to produce anticipated synergies, resulting in small losses, and some fail miserably, resulting in huge losses. eBay, for instance, was forced to sell Butterfields at a significant loss in terms of both dollars and managerial time and attention. In this chapter, we'll discuss some of the keys to making acquisitions serve as an effective vehicle for growth and, at the same time, avoiding common potential pitfalls.

What we said of alliances in Chapter 9 also holds true for mergers and acquisitions: They are not strategies in and of themselves; rather, as we're reminded in the strategy diamond shown in Exhibit 10.2, M&As simply represent one element of a strategy. Specifically, they are *vehicles* for realizing a strategy—that is, for entering or exiting a business.[8]

However, acquisitions have significant implications for other elements of strategy. Acquisitions take firms into new arenas. Acquisitions that result in diversification are used in the staging of corporate strategies. And finally, acquisitions have implications for the financial success of strategies—for the realization of the anticipated economic logic of the strategy.

Perhaps because they enable companies to accelerate their strategies, acquisitions are quite popular. The number of acquisitions over the past few decades suggests that they constitute a fundamental element of many firms' strategies. Exhibit 10.3 shows that M&A is not a new strategy vehicle, but its usage has grown dramatically in recent years.[9] The graph of aggregate M&A activity clearly displays a wave-like behavior with several notable peaks. The most intense quarter of M&A activity in Exhibit 10.3 is 1899:1, while the least intense quarter occurred during the Great Depression (1932:1). However, current M&A activity, as you will see in later exhibits, dwarfs these early peaks in both dollar volume and number of deals.

Research suggests that firms average about one acquisition per year, but of course, there's tremendous variance in firms' propensity for using acquisitions as a growth vehicle.[10] Not

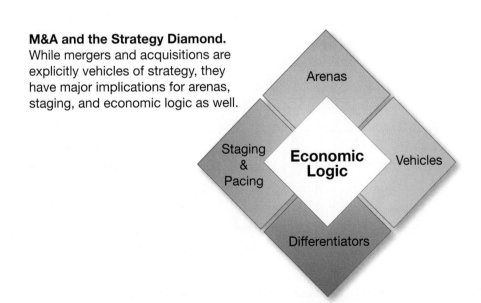

M&A and the Strategy Diamond.
While mergers and acquisitions are explicitly vehicles of strategy, they have major implications for arenas, staging, and economic logic as well.

Arenas

Staging & Pacing

Economic Logic

Vehicles

Differentiators

Exhibit 10.2 The Place of Acquisitions in the Strategy Diamond

Exhibit 10.3 Long-term View of M&A Activity (Relative Frequency of Deals)

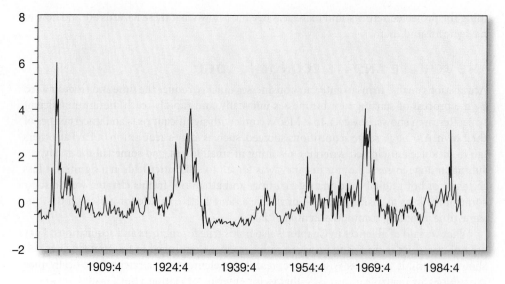

surprisingly, the financial success of any given acquisition depends on a number of factors and has a significant effect on the overall economic logic of a firm's strategy. As you can see in Exhibit 10.4, which summarizes acquisition activity involving U.S. firms between 1995 and 2006, the value of acquisitions involving U.S. firms demonstrates that acquisitions represent a major economic activity.[11]

Also, as shown in Exhibit 10.5, the frequency of cross-border M&A is on the rise.[12] Across all deals, over 40 percent of transactions were valued in excess of $1 billion; about 30 percent were in the $100 million to $500 billion range.

As you can also see from Exhibit 10.5, recent acquisition activity peaked near the turn of the century. That wave coincided with the tremendous bull market when firms used their inflated stock prices as currency to purchase other firms.

Exhibit 10.4 Recent M&A Activity

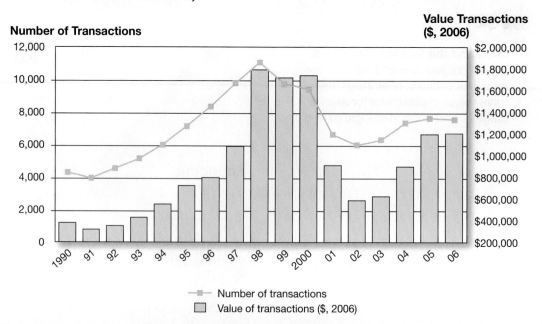

Exhibit 10.5   Global M&A Activity

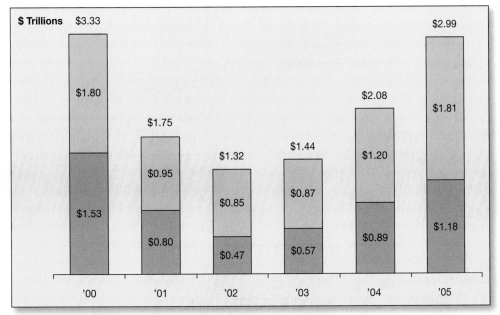

Despite—and because of—their economic consequences, M&As get a lot of bad press and receive criticism from scholars and consultants as well. We can attribute this criticism—at least in part—to the high visibility of many spectacular acquisition mistakes. Notable acquisition "mistakes" include AT&T's acquisition of NCR, Quaker's acquisition of the drink-maker Snapple, and AOL's acquisition of Time Warner. As is the case of so many acquisitions, the managers who made these deals seemed to be unable to make them work.

Quaker, for instance, purchased Snapple thinking that it could create profitable synergies between Snapple and its own Gatorade.[13] Apparently, however, Quaker failed to do its preacquisition homework, particularly when it came to the differences in the distribution networks of the two products. There were troublesome delays in implementing key aspects of the acquisition, and Snapple's market position in relation to newer brands was seriously eroded. The pressure from analysts and shareholders grew so intense that just two years after acquiring Snapple, Quaker pulled the plug on the acquisition and sold it for $300 million—a hefty $1.5 billion less than it paid for it. After just three years of repositioning Snapple, the new owner, Triarc, sold the brand for $1.45 billion to Cadbury Schweppes PLC, where it's now successfully positioned in a portfolio of brands run by a company with the capabilities necessary to build the Snapple brand. Snapple's financial-market roller coaster ride, which is illustrated in Exhibit 10.6, provides a good lesson in the combination of risks and opportunities that often accompany acquisitions as a strategy vehicle.

And while you might think that firms would learn from others' M&A mistakes, Daimler's recent sale of Chrysler for $7.4 billion, after having paid $36 billion for it in 1998, is striking evidence that hubris is alive and well in the world of M&A.

From what we've seen so far, it's clear that **divestiture**—the selling off of a business and the flip side of acquisition—is also a key strategic vehicle. eBay, AT&T, and Quaker all exited businesses by selling business units to competitors. In this chapter, we focus primarily on acquisitions as vehicles for entering or expanding businesses, but remember that closely related types of transactions enable firms to exit businesses as well.

When deciding to enter a new business, companies have alternative vehicles from which to choose, including *internal development*, *alliances*, and *acquisition*. Here, we'll explain why the

divestiture   Strategy whereby a company sells off a business or division.

Exhibit 10.6 Ups and Downs at Snapple

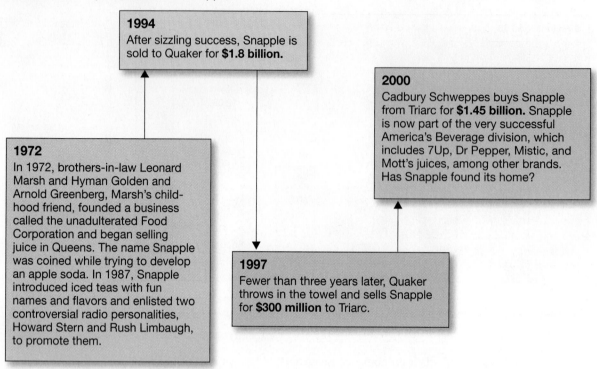

1994
After sizzling success, Snapple is sold to Quaker for **$1.8 billion.**

1972
In 1972, brothers-in-law Leonard Marsh and Hyman Golden and Arnold Greenberg, Marsh's childhood friend, founded a business called the unadulterated Food Corporation and began selling juice in Queens. The name Snapple was coined while trying to develop an apple soda. In 1987, Snapple introduced iced teas with fun names and flavors and enlisted two controversial radio personalities, Howard Stern and Rush Limbaugh, to promote them.

1997
Fewer than three years later, Quaker throws in the towel and sells Snapple for **$300 million** to Triarc.

2000
Cadbury Schweppes buys Snapple from Triarc for **$1.45 billion.** Snapple is now part of the very successful America's Beverage division, which includes 7Up, Dr Pepper, Mistic, and Mott's juices, among other brands. Has Snapple found its home?

tradeoffs between internal development and acquisition—make or buy decisions—are important considerations when deciding whether to enter a new business through acquisition.

BENEFITS OF ACQUISITION OVER INTERNAL DEVELOPMENT

One of the primary advantages of acquisition over internal development is *speed*. Although an acquisition quickly establishes a foothold in a new business, internal development can take years. A corollary benefit is critical mass. An acquisition ensures that a firm enters a new business with sufficient size and viable competitive strength. The acquiring firm, for example, can be assured of entering at minimum efficient scale for cost purposes. As another advantage, acquisitions can provide access to complementary assets and resources. In developing a new business, a firm invests its existing stock of resources and capabilities, and although it may develop new resources and capabilities in the process, there's always the chance that it may simply expend existing resources. With an acquisition, new resources and capabilities can be integrated with those of the buyer, who may actually improve its competitive position in other businesses as well. Finally, entry by acquisition may foster a less competitive environment. By acquiring an existing firm in a new business, the buyer eliminates a competitor that would otherwise remain in the market.

DRAWBACKS OF ACQUISITION OVER INTERNAL DEVELOPMENT

Conversely, firms may find it preferable for several reasons to enter new businesses by means of internal development. First, acquisitions can be more expensive than internal development. Buyers often pay steep premiums for existing companies. In many cases, these premiums outweigh any potential benefits of the acquisition, and in some cases, they make it economically more viable either to enter through internal development or to avoid entry altogether. In short, firms may decide against entering new businesses because they aren't likely to generate sufficient return on capital to justify the premium cost. In addition, the acquiring firm will often inherit several unnecessary adjunct businesses. As an acquirer, you must either be willing to run these unwanted businesses or go through the administrative hassle of spinning them off.

Second, although acquisitions represent a major one-time commitment of resources, internal development entails incremental investment over time. The internal development process, therefore, allows for many points at which the project can be assessed and reevaluated before further investment is made. If, for example, economic circumstances change, a firm can pull the plug. Acquisitions, on the other hand, are typically all-or-nothing propositions.

Finally, organizational conflict may emerge as a potential problem; the eruption of *cultural clashes* can impede the integration of two firms. The process of integration requires significant effort, and firms may encounter setbacks or even failure. Because integration is such a major factor in making M&As work, we'll discuss it in greater detail later in the chapter.

As you can see, many potential roadblocks can make it difficult for firms to realize economic gains from acquisitions. And the greater the cost in capital and time required for integration, the more synergies managers will have to squeeze out of the deal.

Types of Mergers and Acquisitions

There are many types of M&As, and each has a particular purpose—a specific rationale for creating synergies. In this section, we'll survey the different forms of M&As and link the economic logic of each form to firm strategy.[14] Because the logic behind each form varies, so, too, do the criteria for their success.

TYPES OF ACQUISITIONS

Acquisitions can figure into most aspects of business strategy, but they're generally regarded as a means of managing competitive pressures, uncertainty, or both. Thus, business-strategy acquisitions, like business-strategy alliances, tend to be fundamentally related to the firm's core business through *vertical, horizontal,* or *complementary relationships.*

A vertical acquisition has three purposes:

- To secure a reliable supply

- To leverage the resources and capabilities of upstream activities in order to create more value for the end customer

- To reduce total production costs across the value chain

Coca-Cola and Pepsi each have engaged in several vertical acquisitions over the years as they have purchased independent bottling operations. These acquisitions are downstream vertical acquisitions. Recall from the opening vignette in Chapter 4 that Coke and Pepsi sell most of their core product (concentrate) to bottlers who then mix the concentrate with other ingredients, bottle the product, and distribute it to retail outlets. Coke and Pepsi were able to reduce some threats that were beginning to emerge from large bottlers, as well as infuse more efficiency into these downstream activities, by consolidating bottling operations into more efficient regional operations.

In contrast, horizontal acquisitions help expand the company's product offerings. The Cadbury Schweppes purchase of Snapple was a horizontal acquisition that helped expand the buyer's beverage portfolio, particularly in the growing juice and tea segment.

A complementary acquisition involves a complementary business—one that increases the sale of another product. The electronics retailer Best Buy's recent acquisition of the

Best Buy's 2002 acquisition of the Geek Squad, a computer-support service, was a product-market extension.

Geek Squad, a computer-support service, is a complementary acquisition: When computer-service capability is bundled with retail computer sales, each business potentially increases sales of the other's product.

A Complete Classification   Because this simple breakdown of acquisitions into vertical, horizontal, and complementary relationships is a little oversimplified, let's take a look at the typology proposed by Harvard professor Joseph Bower, illustrated in Exhibit 10.7. It will give us a better understanding of the strategic logic behind five more commonly employed forms of acquisition.[15]

Though developed through a study of extremely large acquisitions (over $500 million), this schema provides a useful way of thinking generally about M&As.

Product and Market Extension   In a *product-extension acquisition*, the acquiring company expands its product line by purchasing another company. Basically, the buyer has decided that it can reap higher rewards by buying a company with an existing product than by developing a competitive product internally. In a *market-extension acquisition*, one company buys another that offers essentially the same products as the buyer but has a platform in a geographic market in which the buyer has no presence.

The journey of Snapple that we described earlier in this chapter is an interesting example of two different companies using the same acquired firm for the purpose of product extension. Conceivably, Quaker Oats could have developed its own line of fruit juices, lemonades, and teas. At the time, however, Quaker management believed that an internally developed line would lag too far behind those of incumbent firms in the market segment. Likewise, Cadbury Schweppes certainly has the capability to develop new drinks internally but chose to cultivate expertise in extending product offerings through the acquisition of established brands.

geographic roll-up   Strategy whereby a firm acquires many other firms in the same industry segment but in different geographic arenas in an attempt to create significant scale and scope advantages.

Geographic Roll-Ups   A **geographic roll-up** occurs when a firm acquires several firms that are in the same *industry* segment but in many different *geographic* arenas. It's not the same strategy as market extension. With a roll-up, the acquiring company is trying to change the nature of industry competition in a fundamental way; it seeks to become a large

Exhibit 10.7 Bower's Classification of Acquisitions

	Product/Market Extension	Roll-up M&A	M&A as R&D	Overcapacity M&A	Industry Convergence
Example	Pepsi's acquisition of Gatorade	Service Corporation International's more than 100 acquisitions of funeral homes	Intel's dozens of acquisitions of small high-tech companies	DaimlerChrysler merger	AOL's acquisition of TimeWarner
Objectives	Synergy of similar but expanded product lines or geographic markets	Efficiency of larger operations (e.g., economies of scale, superior management)	Short cut innovation by buying it from small companies	Eliminating capacity, gaining market share, and increasing efficiency	Anticipation of new industry emerging; culling resources from firms in multiple industries whose boundaries are eroding
Percent of All M&A Deals	36%	9%	1%	37%	4%

regional, national, or international player in what's probably been a fragmented industry. The purpose of a roll-up is to achieve economies of scale and scope. Prior to its merger with First Chicago, for example, Banc One had grown from a small U.S. regional bank to a large national bank by buying smaller local and regional banks around the country. (The merged company is called Bank One.) In a roll-up, the acquiring company usually retains the resources and management of acquired companies but imposes its processes on them.

Entrepreneur Bradley Jacobs made a fortune deploying the roll-up strategy to build two extremely successful companies in two different industries. In the waste-management business, Jacobs used United Waste Systems as a roll-up company to buy small trash-hauling firms in a fragmented industry. He later sold the company to USA Waste Services (now Waste Management) and used the proceeds to launch another startup—one that would use the same roll-up strategy to consolidate the equipment rental industry. He launched United Rentals by purchasing six heavy-equipment leasing firms and then proceeded to buy equipment rental companies all across the country. Through a series of more than sixty acquisitions in seven years, it has become the largest equipment rental company in the United States.

What's the rationale behind a roll-up strategy? Basically it's that a large regional or national player can achieve economies of scale that smaller local firms can't. Centralized management, for example, may improve overall operational effectiveness through large volume supply discounts. In addition, a national firm may have the resources to win customer accounts that smaller local firms don't have. United Rentals, for instance, may be able to win equipment rental contracts with large customers who want a single national provider for all of their heavy equipment needs.

M&As as R&D Some firms use acquisitions in lieu of or in addition to internal R&D. Usually, the acquiring firm buys another company in order to gain ownership of its technology. The strategy is common in industries in which technology advances rapidly and in which no single company can do all the innovating that it needs to continue competing effectively.

Exhibit 10.8   M&A
as R&D

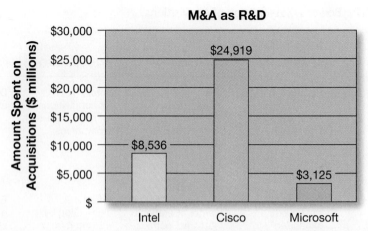

In the telecommunications equipment and computer industries, this strategy has been used to good effect by such firms as Cisco, Microsoft, and Intel. Exhibit 10.8 indicates how important acquisitions are to these companies as R&D vehicles.

First of all, bear in mind that the average U.S. company engages in approximately one acquisition per year. In the five-year period between 1999 and 2003, each of these three companies averaged more than ten acquisitions per year. All three companies allocate money for internal R&D, but each also spends considerable sums to acquire new technologies by buying startups that have made promising innovations. The strategy, of course, represents a tradeoff.

To get a better idea of what this tradeoff entails, consider the acquisition expenses of Intel and AMD. Both firms devote significant capital to traditional internal R&D projects. However, Intel made dozens of acquisitions during the past several years, whereas AMD made only three. This suggests that these two firms in the same industry have very different approaches to R&D. Intel apparently uses acquisitions as an opportunity to acquire potential future innovations from small startup companies with promising technologies.

Overcapacity M&As   The purpose of an *overcapacity acquisition* is to reduce the number of competitors in a mature industry in which capacity exceeds decreasing demand. In essence, parties to an overcapacity acquisition are trying to consolidate the industry. Such is the case, for instance, when two companies in the same industry merge (or one acquires another) in order to rationalize the industry and reduce overcapacity. Overcapacity mergers are often explained as attempts to create economies of scale, but in many cases both companies are already large enough to be operating at a minimum efficient scale. Improved efficiencies come from reducing redundant operations and trimming the size of combined units. This was the rationale behind Daimler's acquisition of Chrysler (Daimler's recent sale of Chrysler for a significant loss is evidence of the difficulty implementing large acquisitions). The banking industry, in which firms are jockeying for market position and trying to create greater economies of scale, has experienced extensive overcapacity-M&A volume in the past decade.

Industry Convergence M&As   When two industries start to overlap and become highly complementary, they begin to *converge*. When this happens, we see an increase in the level of M&As involving firms in the converging industries. In the media and entertainment industries, for example, Time Inc. had an extensive print media business and some cable operations. Warner Brothers Inc. had a bigger presence in cable operations and a huge library of movies. In 1990, the two companies combined through Time's acquisition of Warner to form Time Warner (which acquired Turner Broadcasting in 1996 and which was later acquired by AOL in 2001) in order to consolidate media content and distribution. In response to the AOL–Time Warner combination, Viacom, whose core business was cable TV production and distribution, bought Paramount, a movie and TV producer (1993); Blockbuster, a chain of video outlets (1994); and the TV network CBS (2000). In 1996, Disney, already a media conglomerate, bought ABC, including cable broadcaster ESPN (1996). The entertainment industry's landscape continues to shift as firms try to find the right mix of businesses to compete effectively in converging industries.

The logic behind M&As in converging industries holds that such calculated investments will put firms in a better competitive position if and when industry boundaries erode. One can also view acquisitions in this environment as attempts by companies to acquire resources that, although less valuable in the present competitive environment, will be critical in projected new industry contexts.

Investor/Holding Company M&As Although we won't discuss this category in much detail, investor holding company M&A represents a significant portion of total acquisition activity. In investor/holding company transactions, independent investors or holding companies purchase existing firms. Such might be the case when an investment fund engages in a leveraged buyout of a company. Rather than merge the purchased company with other firms in its portfolio, the buyer tries to bring some management, operating, and financial discipline to the company, intending to sell it later at a profit. In other cases, investors purchase companies for long-term ownership and management.

International Acquisitions

Bower's classification doesn't provide a specific category for international M&As, but in Exhibit 10.5 you learned that they are fairly prevalent. Our analysis of data compiled by Thomson Financial Services reveals that since 1990, cross-border M&As have accounted for an increasing percentage of all M&A activity. However, the issues confronting firms during international acquisitions are significant and you may need to examine the issues of differing cultures, laws, and competitors very closely before executing an international acquisition. An international acquisition can be of any of the types reviewed (e.g., R&D, product/market extension, roll-up, convergence, overcapacity, holding company). Obviously, the use of acquisitions as a strategy vehicle by any firm wanting to enter a new international arena should flow from its business- and corporate-strategy objectives, but firms must be aware that the international context introduces significant complexity into M&A transactions.

Pricing and Premiums

In this section, we'll review some of the basic financial issues relating to potential M&A success. These issues include pricing, premiums, and the benefits of establishing a walk-away price.

PRICING

What is the right price to pay for an acquisition? You might imagine such an assignment from a future boss (or a finance professor on an exam!); however, in the real world there really is no single correct price for an acquisition or merger. Why? Simply because the value of a target depends on how well it fits with the acquiring company. A potential acquisition will have a different value for different buyers. The ultimate purchase price will depend on a number of specific factors, including the target's current market value, its intrinsic value, and the value to be gained from any potential synergies between the target and buyer. Intrinsic value and the value of potential synergies cannot be known with certainty; these values are estimated by managers of the acquiring firm, investment bankers, and outside analysts. The firm contemplating an acquisition can consider a number of factors when determining its offer price for another firm.

Market and Intrinsic Value Of course, one of the first (and easiest) things to consider when evaluating a possible acquisition is the target's current market value. As the term suggests, **market value** is the current market capitalization of a firm, which is typically

market value Current market capitalization of a firm.

intrinsic value   Present value of a company's future cash flows from existing assets and businesses.

calculated by multiplying the number of shares outstanding by the firm's stock price. This value is theoretically the market's estimates of the current value of the firm's future cash flows. A firm's **intrinsic value**, however, is the present value of a company's future cash flows from existing assets and businesses for a particular owner or buyer. It can be higher or lower than a company's market value, with the difference reflecting a number of factors. Markets make important adjustments in the valuation of a firm, evaluating future growth opportunities that will result in products and generate additional cash flows, assessing discounts for bad management or excessive diversification, or awarding premiums to firms that are likely to become the targets of bidding wars themselves.

purchase price   Final price actually paid to the target firm's shareholders of an acquired company.

The **purchase price** is the value actually paid to the target firm's shareholders. Like market price, it may be either higher or lower than intrinsic value, but it's almost always greater than current market value. The only exception to this rule involves target firms that are in dire financial condition (e.g., Daimler recently had to pay a buyer to take Chrysler off its hands).

Why would a potential acquirer offer to pay more than a firm's market price in an acquisition? Recall that synergy is the economic value created by being able to reduce costs or increase revenues by operating in two or more businesses instead of a single business. Synergy is essentially another way of saying that two or more combined entities create economies of scope and scale. If a buyer perceives that an acquisition will offer synergy potential, it may rationally pay more than the current market value for another firm. When synergies exist, they have the effect of increasing the intrinsic value of a target firm for that buyer.

Because synergy is a function of the *strategic fit* of the acquiring and the target firms, each bidding firm may value the target differently. In addition, the market may react differently in evaluating different bidding firms. When, for instance, Vodafone and Bell Atlantic both made bids for AirTouch, Bell Atlantic's stock price dropped while Vodafone's price went up—even though Vodafone entered the bidding with a higher offer. Why? The market believed that Vodafone and AirTouch could achieve greater synergies than Bell Atlantic and AirTouch.

PREMIUMS

acquisition premium   Difference between current market value of a target firm and purchase price paid to induce its shareholders to turn its control over to new owners.

The difference between current market value and the final purchase price is called the **acquisition premium**. A premium is what induces shareholders of the target to sell their shares to new owners. Our analysis of the acquisitions tracked by Thompson Financial Services finds that in the United States, average acquisition premiums have ranged between 30 and 45 percent during each of the past fifteen years. For instance, a firm with a market value of $100 million would normally sell for a purchase price of between $130 and $145 million.

Paying premiums for acquisitions, however, presents a basic problem for managers of would-be acquirers. When the managers of an acquiring firm agree to pay a premium for a target firm, they must expect that they will be able to generate better returns by combining the firms than the firms would achieve independently. In other words, to justify paying a premium of 30 to 45 percent, managers will need to generate more net income from the combined companies than the market assumed would be realized before the announcement of the acquisition. Where is this increase in return supposed to come from? Apparently it is from the synergies achieved by the combined firms. Synergies, however, are not guaranteed and there are several managerial traps that can make synergies difficult to achieve. Some of the managerial problems will be discussed in more detail later in the chapter. First, let's consider the practical implication of premiums.

The Synergy Trap   In a study of acquisition premiums, Mark Sirower of the Boston Consulting Group (BCG) discussed what he called the "synergy trap."[16] He argued that premiums present two problems for managers:

1. Premiums increase the level of returns that must be extracted from the combined businesses.

2. Because of the time value of money, the longer it takes to implement performance improvements, the lower the likelihood that the acquisition will be successful. Consequently, any delays in implementing and extracting synergies increase the ante on required performance improvements.

Not surprisingly, paying too much for an acquisition can not only jeopardize the success of an acquisition, but it can also cause irreparable damage to the acquiring firm. Regularly in his letters to shareholders, investment guru Warren Buffett has reminded shareholders of Berkshire Hathaway that paying too much for a company can lead to disastrous effects. The box entitled "How Would *You* Do That? 10.1" goes into more depth on the issue of premiums and their effects on acquisition success and helps you gain confidence in calculating the required performance improvements associated with a particular acquisition premium. **Required performance improvements** are the annual increases in cash flow that are necessary to justify the level of premium paid. Calculating required performance improvements utilizes simple principles from discounted cash flow analysis that you've learned in your finance classes. The tools we provide you with in "How Would *You* Do That? 10.1" make the calculations even easier.

> **required performance improvements** The increases in combined cash flow of the acquiror and target that are necessary to justify the acquisition premium.

Reaching a Walk-away Price Given what you now know about the synergy trap (and perhaps about Warren Buffett's shrewdness as a strategic investor), it shouldn't surprise you to learn that in 2000, when Coke CEO Douglas Daft tried to buy Quaker Oats in order to add Gatorade to the company's product line, board member Buffett opposed the idea. Buffett argued that the bidding by Coke and Pepsi had driven the premium too high and Coke should walk away from the negotiations. (The board sided with Buffett and withdrew from the bidding.) Similarly, in 2004, cable operator Comcast made a tender offer for Disney of 0.78 share of Comcast Class A stock for each Disney share. The stock market wasn't overly thrilled with the proposed deal and Comcast's share price dropped while Disney's increased. Comcast was forced to withdraw the offer, however, because the value of its stock subsequently dropped too far: There came a point at which Comcast would have to pay out too many shares to reach the offered value. In effect, that point was Comcast's "walk-away price."

Escalation of Commitment and the Winner's Curse Establishing a walk-away price is relatively easy; sticking to it is not. One reason for this is that executives escalate the commitment to their initiative as they proceed through a transaction. This—coupled with excessive fear of failure—means that bidders are sometimes seduced into making questionable decisions. Bidders who allow their prices to get carried away (or allow themselves to get carried away with their bidding) often suffer from the so-called **winner's curse**. Although the bidders win the "prize," they're saddled with the consequences of having paid too much.

> **winner's curse** Situation in which a winning M&A bidder must live with the consequences of paying too much for the target.

The Acquisition Process

So far we've focused mostly on the technical side of M&As: what they are and how they're used as strategy vehicles, along with the roles of pricing and premiums. The success of M&As as a strategy vehicle, however, depends on much more than the choice of a good target and paying the right price. The process by which M&As are completed and targeted firms are integrated into acquiring firms can have a significant bearing on success or failure. Indeed, some experts say that the acquisition process is the single largest factor.[17]

The Impact of Premiums on Required Synergies

Assume that you worked for eBay prior to its acquisition of PayPal. You have learned from your division manager that PayPal will be folded into your division after the acquisition. Your boss, in a moment of pause from the hysteria surrounding the deal, has suddenly realized that she will be held responsible for integrating the acquisition and generating the synergies that Meg Whitman has been touting in discussions with Wall Street analysts. She turns to you and asks you to calculate just how much synergy she will have to deliver to make the deal a success. How would you translate the premium paid in this acquisition into actionable division budgets for the coming years?

This is not an entirely hypothetical question. Every time an acquisition is completed, it affects how division managers operate. Indeed, it often affects the targets that the CEO imposes upon them in terms of revenue targets and expense containment. To illustrate how this happens, let's go back to eBay's acquisition of PayPal. The opening vignette noted that eBay paid a premium of $250 million (a 20-percent premium over PayPal's market value prior to the acquisition).

Let's start with our objective: We need to know the synergy required to make the deal a success. Let's call this *required performance improvement*, or RPI for short. Understanding how to calculate RPI is a useful managerial tool here. The RPI to justify a premium paid can be calculated with various degrees of sophistication, including the use of discounted uneven cash flows and probability statistics. But that level of sophistication isn't necessary to get in the ballpark.

We have simplified the various formulas and created a simple table of factors in Exhibit 10.9 that will help you understand the concept. The three factors that you'll need to know are (1) the premium expected to be paid, (2) the number of years before you expect synergies to be implemented (on the vertical axis) and (3) the cost of capital of the firm (on the vertical axis). Together, these are the factors that can be used to determine the annual synergies required to make the acquisition a success. The synergy trap calculation also assumes synergies are captured over a 10-year period, so if synergies start in year 1, that amount would need to be captured in each of the remaining 9 years as well. If they start in year 9, then they would need to be captured in 9 and 10, and so on.

Locate the intersection of the years assumed to make the synergies materialize and the cost of capital. Then multiply that factor by the premium paid to determine just how much synergy must be generated *each year* over the 10-year synergy period, depending upon when the synergies start, through the combination of annual cost savings and new revenue improvements. If we assume that synergies will materialize immediately after the acquisition, then the amount of synergy that must be achieved is determined by simply multiplying the cost of capital by the premium. However, as you can see, as the years increase before synergies are implemented, or as the cost of capital increases, the amount of synergy that must be generated increases very quickly (the amount of synergy required is reflected in the yellow area of the exhibit).

In the case of eBay's acquisition of PayPal, the premium was approximately $250,000,000. So if the company thought that it would take two years to implement the synergies and it knew that their cost of capital was 15 percent, then the operational synergies required could be estimated by multiplying the premium by the factor as follows: $250,000,000 × 0.198 = $49,500,000. What does this number represent? It is the amount of additional net income that is needed *each* of the eight remaining years in a 10-year period. The acquisition of PayPal over and above the existing net income of both companies combined. eBay would have to find almost an additional $50 million in synergies just to pay for the premium.

Recall that synergies can take the form of increased revenues or reduced

Years Until Synergies Are Implemented	Cost of Capital		
	10%	15%	20%
0	0.100	0.150	0.200
1	0.110	0.173	0.240
2	0.121	0.198	0.288
3	0.133	0.228	0.346
4	0.146	0.262	0.415
5	0.161	0.302	0.498

Exhibit 10.9 Synergies Required to Justify a $10 Million Premium

costs for the combined firm, or both an increase in revenues and reduction of costs. Synergies can also be found in specific parts of the business such that one unit can grow faster or have a better cost position than it had previously. Ultimately, if it is considered a successful acquisition, the acquisition must leave the acquired and the acquiror better off than had the acquisition not been consummated.

While it is too early to tell how the Skype acquisition will turn out, and it is less obvious where the synergies from that deal might come from, we can at least provide a post-mortem on the PayPal deal. Here are the facts:

- eBay launches BillPoint in 1999 for online payments (though took a year to launch, and when finally up and running, PayPal had registered its millionth user)

- By mid-2001, eBay is losing $10–15 million yearly on BillPoint

- eBay buys PayPal in July 2002 for $1.5 billion, and eBay's cost of capital at the time was 15 percent

- eBay integrated PayPal in *one year*, with 74 percent of all eBay transactions by 2004, and 9 percent of U.S. e-commerce (5 percent globally)

- Experts point to the availability of PayPal as partial explanation for the exponential growth of eBay's total revenues, beyond those garnered by PayPal. While it is hard to point to the PayPal acquisition as the single source of eBay's growth, all indicators suggest that PayPal is a great example of a complement obtained through acquisition!

In summary, the synergy trap tool will help you evaluate what must be done with an acquisition if it takes place and considering some basic financial assumptions. Ironically, CEOs will comment that the best acquisitions are sometimes the ones they did not make, and the synergy trap tool lets the managers who must eventually integrate and make good on the purchase wrestle with whether or not the numbers made sense. Recall from our opening vignette that the business press considered the PayPal acquisition to be more hubristic than synergistic, but that in the end the deal proved a home run for eBay. You can bet though, as is the case in most acquisitions, that had the strategy not worked, many a critic would have said "I told you so!"

STAGES OF THE ACQUISITION PROCESS

Exhibit 10.10 summarizes the four major stages in an acquisition: *idea generation, justification* (including due diligence and negotiation), *integration*, and *results*. As the exhibit suggests, the M&A process really begins with the strategy because management has identified and prepared for M&A as a strategy vehicle, understands what strategic differentiators the firm will gain, bolster, or develop as a result of M&A, and has accounted for all the acquisition process stages in the staging and pacing facet of its strategy.

Problems at any of the first three stages can sow the seeds of failure.[18] This model identifies two types of problems: *decision-making problems* and *implementation* or *integration problems*. Decision-making problems can arise during the idea-generation, justification, and integration stages, whereas implementation problems occur during the integration stage. However, these integration problems could have their roots in an earlier stage of the process.

Idea Integration starts with the strategy itself, since the strategy will have foreseen M&A as a critical vehicle for success. But once M&A is part of the strategy, then the *idea* is the impetus for the acquisition. Some firms have well-articulated strategies that state the conditions under which acquisitions will be the vehicle of choice for implementing strategic plans. Recall, for instance, the case of United Rentals' roll-up strategy: Acquisitions were a key vehicle in the firm's strategy. Conversely, Quaker Oats' purchase of Snapple was an opportunistic (and ill-considered) move. Whereas some firms have well-defined strategies, in terms of the role of M&A as strategy vehicles, others don't. Firms that do have clear concepts about the role of M&A in their strategy, and have the requisite M&A capabilities, can be more opportunistic in the use of acquisitions.[19]

Justification, Due Diligence, and Negotiation The major analytical stage of an acquisition includes the processes that a firm goes through to develop the internal and external logic for the acquisition. Researchers Philippe Haspeslagh and David Jemison contend that several critical decisions must be made at this stage: strategic assessment, devel-

Exhibit 10.10
Acquisition Process
Stages

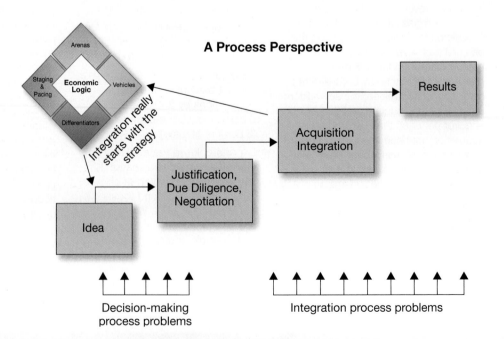

oping a widely shared view, a degree of specificity, organizational conditions, implementation timing, and a walk-away price.

- *Strategic assessment* is the process of determining how an acquisition will contribute to overall strategy and competitive position. It should do more than analyze the target: It should address the issue of how the acquisition will affect the acquiring firm's pursuit of its core objectives. Managers should also make sure that their assessment isn't too static: It should consider the firm's future needs as its industry evolves.

- Because many people will be involved in implementing an acquisition and integrating the target firm into the parent, it's important that the purpose and strategic logic of the acquisition be widely understood by members of the organization. The following is a list of eight questions that managers should ask at this stage of an acquisition:[20]

  1. What is the strategic logic behind this acquisition? Does it correspond with the firm's strategy? Why this company?

  2. Is the target industry attractive? What are the key segments? What is the prognosis about industry evolution?

  3. If this is an international acquisition, what are the key differences between this country and our experience? Do these differences have performance implications?

  4. Does an analysis of the target company (products and services, market position, customers, suppliers, distribution channels, costs, etc.) suggest that it is healthy and viable in the long term?

  5. How well does this company fit with ours? What are the expected benefits, and what might impinge on the realization of those benefits?

  6. How will the acquisition be integrated? Who will lead this process? How will we be organized?

  7. Have alternative *scenarios* been considered? What is the outcome given reasonable, optimistic, baseline, and pessimistic assumptions?

  8. Is the valuation reasonable? Is this acquisition priced at a premium or distress—priced? What do alternative valuation methods conclude (accounting-based, market-based, NPV, option)?

- Managers should be as specific as possible in identifying the possible benefits and problems of an acquisition throughout the organization. This step is important for two reasons:

  1. If operational managers aren't aware of the potential sources of synergies identified by upper management and the acquisition team, they'll have a hard time determining what's expected of them. Moreover, if they understand that synergies are needed but have little idea about how to gain them, the task is just as daunting. Let's go back to Quaker Oats' purchase of Snapple. Perhaps some acquisition managers understood Snapple's operations but no one seemed to understand fully the differences between the two industries' distribution systems. Operating-level managers were thus left to discover and deal with them through trial and error. A good deal of time and effort was wasted in trying to implement the acquisition in ways that simply were not in sync with Quaker Oats' business model.

  2. Although identifying possible problems is also important, some acquisition teams tend to understate them, usually because they're afraid of causing key decision makers to shy away from the deal.[21] All in all, it's much better for all parties to know what

the potential roadblocks are; they can be dealt with more effectively if the acquisition team provides some suggested solutions.

Understand the Conditions Required for Creating Synergies Managers must understand the organizational factors on which key synergies hinge and the organizational conditions necessary to implement desired synergies. Synergies in a cross-border acquisition, for example, may depend on the transfer of a functional skill from one company to another. If so, executives at the acquiring firm must identify the managers and key employees who are critical to the transfer. Even when the numbers look good, more and more firms are scuttling acquisitions because of a lack of organizational fit—which can undermine possible synergies. Cisco Systems is one of the most successful high-technology acquirers; their screening criteria and means of achieving these criteria are summarized in Exhibit 10.11. Cisco regularly uses acquisitions to supplement internal R&D. However, Cisco discovered that the ability to realize synergies was to manage the entire process actively, from screening possible acquisitions to diligently managing the integration process.

Control the Timing of Implementation and Integration Timing is critical in most acquisitions. It's important because of the time value of money. In addition, stock markets can be volatile, which is important when a firm is paying for an acquisition with its own stock. Moreover, timing is critical because acquisitions cause major disruptions in both the target and acquiring firms. Many organizational problems arise from disruption in the lives of affected employees who may be impacted by the acquisition; such problems can be lessened if implementation and integration are achieved quickly. As you learned from the synergy trap tool, the more quickly that synergies can be realized through implementation and integration measures, the greater the premium a firm can afford to pay for the acquisition.

Establish a Walk-away Price Finally, managers should settle on the maximum price that they're willing to pay for the target firm. As we've already seen, it's wise to set a walk-away price early in the process, before rival bidders succumb to *escalation of commitment* and overestimate the value that they believe will be derived from the acquisition. Potential synergies are often uncertain and ambiguous, and they'll vary from one prospective buyer to

Exhibit 10.11
Organizational-Fit
Acquisitions Screening
by Cisco Systems

Screening Criteria	Means of Achieving Criteria
Offer both short- and long-term win-wins for Cisco and acquired company	• Have complementary technology that fills a need in Cisco's core product space • Have a technology that can be delivered through Cisco's existing distribution channels • Have a technology and products that can be supported by Cisco's support organization • Is able to leverage Cisco's existing infrastructure and resource base to increase its overall value
Share a common vision and chemistry with Cisco	• Have a similar understanding and vision of the market • Have a similar culture • Have a similar risk-taking style
Be located (preferably) in Silicon Valley or near one of Cisco's remote sites	• Have a company headquarters and most manufacturing facilities close to one of Cisco's main sites

the next. Problems arise when managers mistake a rival's higher bid as a signal that they've overlooked some attractive feature of the deal; in responding with a more competitive offer, they're often overpaying.

Integration   Many acquisitions fail during the integration stage. The best means of integrating an acquisition varies from case to case, and failure to identify it can cancel any potential synergies that may have been derived from the deal. Determining the best process for implementing and integrating an acquisition means understanding potential interactions between the target and the acquiring firm. Because this stage is so important, we'll devote the next section to presenting a model for dealing with integration problems.

Integrating and Implementing an Acquisition

When one company acquires another it has several options for how the acquired company will be integrated into the firm. At one extreme, the acquired company may be granted near-complete autonomy. Warren Buffett's Berkshire Hathaway often treats its acquired companies this way. Alternatively, the acquiring company may attempt to fully integrate the acquired firm into its operations so that the two firms are melded into one.

How should managers decide whether an acquisition should be treated in a rather hands-off approach or be tightly integrated? Two concepts should be considered in making this decision—the strategic interdependence of the businesses and the need for organizational autonomy of the acquired business.

STRATEGIC INTERDEPENDENCE

Let's go back to one of the basic principles identified in this chapter: The primary purpose of M&As is to create synergies—value that can be created by combining two firms that isn't available to them as standalone firms. To what extent should the target firm and acquiring firm remain strategically interdependent? It depends on the types of resource sharing and skill transfers anticipated by the two firms. When the logic of the acquisition requires that they share tangible and intangible resources, the success of the deal usually requires a relatively high level of interdependence. Likewise, when the logic of the deal calls for transferring people with different functional skills in order to share knowledge, it entails more interdependence between the two organizational units than if it called simply for a transfer of general management skills. Alternatively, when the resources being transferred are primarily financial (say, borrowing power or excess cash), very little interdependence is required. Thus the first factor that determines how integration should be handled is the level of strategic interdependence between the acquiring firm and the acquired firm.

NEED FOR AUTONOMY

The second factor that should be considered is the target's need for autonomy. The value of some acquisitions lies largely in the retention of key people and transfers of capabilities. Key people, however, often leave once their firm has been acquired—especially when the acquisition disrupts their operating procedures and their autonomy in conducting them. Just how much autonomy should be granted an acquired firm? There's no single answer, of course, but the following is a good rule of thumb: The appropriate amount of autonomy depends on whether it is necessary to create value. Granted, even this response is a little too simple. Perhaps, for example, autonomy is necessary only in certain facets of the acquired firm's operations, whereas others can be easily assimilated.

When Swiss giant Nestlé set out to purchase British candy maker Rowntree York (makers of such candies as Kit Kat and Rolo) in order to extend its reach in chocolates and confectionary markets, it found that it could not, in accord with its usual policy, fully integrate its latest acquisition. Rather, to get the deal approved by Rowntree, Nestlé had to allow Rowntree executives to remain in the United Kingdom and run the strategic office in charge of all confectionary businesses. Thus, in this case, autonomy was needed simply to get the managers of the target firm to support the acquisition and agree to the buyout. Cisco, the network company, has used acquisitions extensively as part of its strategy. Generally, they try to integrate the target as soon after the closing as possible. For instance, they attempt to have the target's products in its sales peoples' catalogues the moment the acquisition closes. In order to achieve this, they need the target firms to adopt all of Cisco's systems and be fully integrated. However, periodically, Cisco acquires a target that resists some aspect of Cisco integration. They claim that to be innovative, they need some organizational autonomy, and that their engineers want to work for a small and dynamic company, not a big, "bureaucratic" Cisco. Consequently, in a few cases, Cisco has deviated from their normal integration policy in order to complete a transaction that they deem is of strategic imperative.

THE IMPLEMENTATION PROCESS

No matter what approach managers take—fostering interdependence, autonomy, or some combination of these—they will be well served by reminding themselves that acquisition integration is a *process* and not an *event*. By analogy, think of acquisition integration as a comma in a sentence, not a period. To this end we can learn some lessons from so-called **serial acquirers**—companies that engage in frequent acquisitions—that will be useful in understanding how the process can be handled smoothly and effectively.

It's a Continual Process, Not an Event
The best serial acquirers start the integration process during initial screening interviews and negotiations, well before closing the deal. M&A is already designed into the arenas, differentiators, vehicles, staging and pacing, and economic facets of their strategy (notice these comprise *all* five facets of the strategy diamond). During this process, called **due diligence**, executives and lower-level managers at both companies begin to plan for the postdeal structure of the combined firm. Although some pretransaction discussions can be awkward, they're essential in identifying both potential obstacles and additional opportunities. Once the deal is closed, specific decisions must be executed and prearranged organizational structures implemented. The lesson, in short, is that it's better to make tough decisions early rather than delaying them. Firms such as GE Capital and Cisco, which have successfully integrated many acquisitions (and some not so successfully), have found that initiating and pursuing a comprehensive integration and communications process is the lynchpin for success.

Integration Management Is a Full-time Job
Many firms make the mistake of assuming that people at all levels in both organizations will work together to make the acquisition as seamless as possible. Unfortunately, so many organizational issues are involved in integrating an acquired company that line managers often can't oversee operations *and* manage the integration process. Many successful acquirers, therefore, appoint an *integration manager*. Ideally, this person will be someone from the due-diligence team who understands both companies. Having met many line managers in both organizations, the integration manager spearheads integration efforts, guiding newly acquired managers through the maze of the new organizational hierarchy.

At GE Capital, for instance, integration managers introduce both executives and employees of the acquired firm to the business requirements and organizational standards of the new parent company. They also deal with a number of seemingly mundane issues that have been found to hamper integration efforts, such as communicating information about benefits and human resources policies. They educate new employees about such idiosyn-

serial acquirers Company that engages in frequent acquisitions.

due diligence Initial pre-closing screening, analysis, and negotiations for an acquisition.

cratic features of the firm as culture, business customs, and even acronyms. Finally, in order to prevent unnecessary overload and redundant activities, they channel information requests from the parent company to both new managers and those who are veterans of the original organization.

GE Capital has found that individuals with strong personal and technical skills make the best integration managers and typically draws candidates from one of two pools. First, the company recruits "high-potential individuals"—people with strong functional-area management credentials and leadership potential. These people function best as integration managers when the integration is highly structured and relatively uncomplicated. For more complex integrations, GE Capital relies on seasoned veterans who know the company well. Experience has shown that these individuals can be drawn from every functional area.

Key Decisions Should Be Made Swiftly As we've already seen, speed is of the essence in the acquisition process simply because of the cost and the time value of money. Certain organizational factors also dictate swift integration. For one, employees—both those of the target firm and those of the acquiring firm—are naturally concerned about the impact of the acquisition on their jobs. As much as executives and managers would like everyone to feel like a team player with a secure place in the organizational lineup, when they're worried about their jobs, people succumb to distractions. Successful acquirers have found that it's best not to prolong the suspense: Decisions about management structure, key roles, reporting relationships, layoffs, restructuring, cost-cutting, and other career-affecting aspects of the acquisition should be announced as soon as possible—even within days of the acquisition announcement. Telling employees that everything will be "business as usual" is almost never being honest and will probably hamper the integration process. In addition, swift implementation of the integration process allows the firm to get on with its primary task—creating value. Because sluggish integration makes it more difficult to focus on this task, it weakens the value-creation process.

Integration Should Address Technical and Cultural Issues When integrating acquisitions, most managers tend to focus on technical issues. At Cisco, for example, a key technical issue is the rapid integration of the target's products into the Cisco system so that sales representatives can begin selling the new product line. Successful integration means identifying and addressing such issues as early as possible.

Issues related to corporate culture should also be addressed immediately. Some of these issues are as simple as meeting and greeting new employees. The cultures of any two firms are bound to be different, and the faster managers and employees can meld the two organizations, the more smoothly the integration will proceed. Even when two organizations seem to have a lot in common, profound cultural differences may exist that could threaten successful integration. When, for instance, Franklin Quest merged with Covey, many observers expected cultural integration to be smooth. After all, the two makers of time-management products were highly complementary, and because both firms were located in Utah, they had similar employee bases. In addition, the two CEOs were well acquainted with one another. Surprisingly, however, the two cultures were highly dissimilar. For instance, Franklin Quest was built on a culture of efficiency, whereas Covey eschewed efficiency for effectiveness. Everything from products to company vision statements were tied to these critical underlying philosophies. During the acquisition process, executives dismissed these differences as semantics, but discovered during the integration phase that these were rather incongruent philosophies. In addition, more functional things, such as incompatible accounting systems, also impeded quick integration. Successful acquirers identify cultural clashes early; in fact, they may walk away from deals when the potential clashes are too severe.

Acquisitions in Different Industry Contexts

Not surprisingly, M&A activity varies across industries. It is determined largely by the development phase in which a given industry finds itself and by the extent of industry dynamism. In addition, competitive conditions will determine whether acquisition is a suitable strategy vehicle for a firm in a given industry and what the most viable type of acquisition may be. In this section, we'll discuss the role of M&As and industry context in terms of the industry life cycle and the level of industry-wide turbulence.

M&AS AND INDUSTRY LIFE CYCLE

Recall the model of industry life cycle and industry dynamics that we presented in Chapter 4. In this section, we'll use this model to illustrate how different types of acquisitions play different roles in each stage.

Introduction   During the introduction stage, acquisitions tend to involve the purchase of startup firms by well-established firms in related but more mature industry segments. Many partial acquisitions may occur, with established companies making equity investments in startups but not acquiring them outright. Thus, at this stage M&As tend to be R&D and product- and market-extension acquisitions.

Growth   During this phase, we see several types of acquisitions. Established companies from one industry segment may start entering other segments with greater frequency, looking mostly for proven and growing targets. Although some M&A activity may be for R&D, most of it is likely to be for the purpose of acquiring products that are proven and gaining customer acceptance. The geographic roll-up also becomes more common, especially at the end of the growth stage and through the maturity stage. In high-velocity industries, industry-convergence acquisitions appear and continue into the maturity stage.

Maturity   At this point, we begin to see overcapacity acquisitions. Why? During the growth stage, the industry witnessed the entry of new firms and aggressive expansion, with numerous competitors jockeying for competitive position. Capacity built during this period often exceeds the long-term needs of the segment, and as demand starts to flatten, companies see consolidation as a way to rationalize the industry. Overcapacity M&A activity continues throughout the decline stage of the cycle.

M&AS IN DYNAMIC CONTEXTS

Dynamic contexts are often home to firms that engage in acquisitions at a frantic pace. What is it about dynamic contexts that makes acquisitions such popular strategy vehicles? In Chapter 4, we discussed factors that can alter an industry landscape, particularly discontinuities and globalization. These factors tend to accelerate acquisitions. Note that within these two broad categories, many factors can affect the attractiveness of acquisitions as strategy vehicles. We'll focus on *technological change, demographic change, geopolitical change, trade liberalization,* and *deregulation.*[22]

Technological Change   In high-velocity industries, technological change and innovation can transpire at lightning speed, and some firms respond with aggressive acquisition campaigns. Both Cisco and Microsoft, for example, use acquisitions to ensure that innovation and technological change among competitors don't contribute to the erosion of their strong competitive positions.

Demographic Change   Demographic changes, such as the aging of the population and mass emigration, may alter customer profiles significantly. Spanish-language speakers, for instance, are an increasingly important market segment for U.S. media companies: Thus, when the Tribune Company merged with Times-Mirror in 2000, it acquired *Hoy,* the leading Spanish-language daily in New York and one of the fastest-growing publications of its kind. The Tribune Company has recently launched editions of *Hoy* in Chicago and Los Angeles.

Geopolitical Change   Such events as the fall of the Iron Curtain, the emergence of the European Union, the opening of China, and conflict in the Middle East all have significant effects on the operations of global companies. In some cases, changes enhance opportunities for acquiring established companies in new locations. In others, they foster divestiture. For example, IBM was able to divest its personal computer division to the Chinese firm Lenova in 2005 largely because of the rapid growth and commercialization of the domestic Chinese marketplace, which was fostered by the loosening of some government interventions.

Trade Liberalization   Trade liberalization also opens new opportunities for doing business. In the wake of the European Union and the North American Free Trade Agreement (NAFTA), for example, cross-border acquisition activity increased in industries conducting business in those regions. Wal-Mart's acquisition of the successful Mexican retailing giant, Cifra, is a case in point. Geographic proximity and NAFTA make it cost-effective for Wal-Mart to stock its shelves in the United States with goods assembled in Mexico as well as provide otherwise more expensive U.S.–made goods to Mexican consumers through Cifra's outlets. Wal-Mart gained improved economies of scope and scale as a result of NAFTA.

Deregulation   Finally, deregulation has had a major impact on the volume of M&A activity in a number of industries. Prior to deregulation, for instance, the wave of M&As that swept the banking industry would not have been possible. Regulation and deregulation have also affected acquisitions and divestitures in the telecommunications industry. AT&T, for example, was allowed to exist as a virtual monopoly until 1984, when antitrust action forced its breakup. The seven so-called Baby Bells divided up local service, leaving the parent company, AT&T, with long-distance and telecom equipment businesses. Following subsequent deregulation, M&A activity has put the industry in a state of almost constant change.

M&AS AND COEVOLUTION

As with alliances, the use of acquisitions in dynamic contexts fits into the coevolution model of corporate strategy. Recall our definition of coevolution as the orchestration of a web of shifting linkages among evolving businesses. In the case of acquisitions, acquisitions can enable a firm to absorb the capabilities of their targets in order to develop specific dynamic capabilities in concert with the best resources and capabilities available on the market. Just as important, acquisitions (at least well-conceived ones) support a specific, focused strategy. Consequently, in keeping with this strategy, certain businesses are periodically pared off through divestitures and others added through acquisitions. If, for instance, the firm is pursuing a growth strategy, the coevolution perspective would suggest that it divest slow-growth businesses and products and acquire firms that are operating on the technology frontier or that offer some other basis for future competitive advantage.[23]

Summary of Challenges

1. *Explain the motivations behind acquisitions and show how they've changed over time.* The three basic motivations for acquisitions are synergy, manager self-interest, and hubris. Synergy is the primary motivation for acquisitions, and it can be generated in many different ways. Synergies can come from cost savings, revenue enhancements, improved competitive position, financial engineering, and the transfer of resources, best practices, and core competencies between targets and acquiring firms. Manager self-interest can motivate some acquisitions because many managers find it attractive to lead larger organizations, size and diversification can help smooth earnings, and compensation is higher for managers of large firms. This motive is known as *managerialism*. Hubris is exaggerated self-confidence, and it can result in managers overestimating the value of a potential acquisition, having unrealistic assumptions about the ability of an acquisition to create synergies, and being too willing to pay too much for a transaction. Thus, hubris results in more acquisitions than would be the case if it were kept in check.

2. *Explain why mergers and acquisitions are important to strategy.* Acquisitions enable firms to enter new businesses quickly. One of the key benefits of an acquisition over internal development of a new business is that the time and risks associated with business startup are reduced significantly. For instance, if the acquisition is of a firm of sufficient size, minimum efficient scale is achieved immediately. In addition, proven products are already in distribution. Acquisitions can also put firms in a position to achieve significant synergies—they can create value when the two firms combined are more valuable than when owned separately.

3. *Identify the various types of acquisitions.* Several types of acquisitions are possible, and each has a specific purpose. A product- or market-extension acquisition has the aim of expanding the products offered or markets served. A geographic roll-up is a series of acquisitions of firms in the same industry segment but in different geographic segments. A R&D acquisition is the purchase of another company for the purpose of acquiring its technology. An overcapacity, or consolidation, acquisition is the combination of two large firms in a mature industry that has excess capacity for slowing demand. An industry-convergence acquisition occurs when the boundaries between two industries start to fade and firms need to participate increasingly in both industries to be competitive; firms often use acquisitions to enter the converging industry. Finally, a significant portion of acquisitions are transactions by investors or holding companies (not an existing operating company) that are purchasing a company as an investment.

4. *Understand how the pricing of acquisitions affects the realization of synergies.* The pricing of an acquisition is critical to its success. The price of an acquisition normally exceeds its current market value by a significant premium. And although there is no one correct price for an acquisition target, managers of each potential acquiring firm can estimate the potential synergies between their company and the target. The price a firm is willing to pay for a target should be based on these synergies. Using Sirower's formula for acquisition premiums, managers can calculate the maximum premium they should be willing to pay. Likewise, if the price that is needed to make the acquisition is known first (such as in bidding situations), managers can easily estimate the required performance improvements that would be necessary. The greater the premium paid, the more synergies that must be extracted from the deal to make it economical. Likewise, the greater the premium, the more important it is to realize the synergies quickly.

5. *Outline the alternative ways to integrate an acquisition and explain the implementation process.* How an acquisition is integrated should be a function of the target firm's need for autonomy and the strategic interdependence between the target and the acquired company. Successful implementation requires recognition that acquisition integration is a continual process, that dedicated managers are required to oversee the process, that the process is enhanced by swift decisions, and that it focuses on both technical and cultural issues.

6. *Discuss the characteristics of acquisitions in different industry contexts.* Different types of acquisitions are seen with greater frequency at different stages of the industry life cycle. During the introduction stage, acquisitions tend to be by firms in related segments acquiring technology (R&D acquisitions) or products of startups (product extensions). During the growth phase of the industry life cycle, several types of acquisitions are common. Some R&D acquisitions of a now-proven technology by later-moving established companies from related industry segments still take place. But given that in the growth phase, products have achieved more accepted status, many more product-extension acquisitions are seen. The geographic roll-up tends to appear at the waning stages of the growth phase. In high-velocity industries, industry-convergence acquisitions also start to appear. During the maturity stage, overcapacity acquisitions start to emerge, and roll-ups and product-extension acquisitions continue. Overcapacity acquisitions continue throughout industry decline. Industry turbulence, such as technological change, demographic change, geopolitical change, trade liberalization, and deregulation are all forms of industry shock that tend to increase acquisition activity because they change the competitive landscape.

Review Questions

1. What is an acquisition?

2. Why would firms use acquisitions rather than create a new business internally?

3. What are the possible motives for acquisitions?

4. What are the ways in which synergies can be created in acquisitions?

5. How easy or difficult is it to achieve the alternative types of synergies?

6. What are the various types of acquisitions?

7. How do market-extension acquisitions and geographic roll-ups differ?

8. Give examples of product extension, overcapacity, and R&D acquisitions.

9. What is an acquisition premium?

10. How can you calculate the synergies that must be extracted from an acquisition with a given premium?

11. How do acquisitions tend to be used in different stages of the industry life cycle?

Experiential Activities

Group Exercises

1. Pick a firm of interest to your group. Identify potential acquisition candidates. Explain why these companies would make sense as an acquisition target. Evaluate and describe possible implementation barriers to this acquisition.

2. Pick a firm of interest and peruse its annual reports over a 5- to 10-year period. Assess the information presented on M&As in the annual reports. Do you see any explicit mention of the link between strategy formulation and implementation with respect to the acquisition mentioned in the annual reports? (As a starting place, see the chairman's letter to the shareholders.) What are the before-and-after scenarios that you find regarding the M&As?

Ethical Debates

1. During the due diligence phase of a pharmaceutical company's acquisition, you discover that an executive of the po-tential target may have funneled payments to government regulators overseeing the company's drug approval process. The case in question only represents a minor drug in the target's portfolio of therapies. What should you do?

2. While negotiating a possible buyout with the management of a firm, the CEO of the target starts to play hardball. He continues to add contingencies to the deal. In addition, he has recently raised the issue of a golden parachute for himself if he can convince the largest shareholder to agree to the deal. The CFO of the target pulls you aside and indicates that he can persuade the largest shareholder to sell and that he can do it for much less than the CEO is asking for in his golden parachute. What should you do?

How Would YOU DO THAT?

1. Identify a company that has recently announced an acquisition. Study the terms of the deal and identify to the extent possible the market value of the target, its intrinsic value, and the acquisition price. What was the acquisition premium? Using the synergy trap formula presented in the box entitled "How Would *You* Do That? 10.1," determine the performance improvements required to justify this acquisition premium. Calculate the required performance improvements with dif-ferent assumptions as to how long it will take to implement them in, say, one, three, and five years. What is the difference in these required performance improvements if the acquisition premium is 50 percent lower than what was paid? What if it is 50 percent higher?

Go on to see How Would You Do That at www.prenhall.com/ carpenter&sanders

Endnotes

1. N. Wingfield and J. Sapsford, "eBay to Buy PayPal for $1.4 Billion," *Wall Street Journal*, July 9, 2002, A6; N. Wingfield, "eBay Completes PayPal Deal, Gaining Web-Payments Heft," *Wall Street Journal*, October 4, 2002, B8; N. Wingfield, "eBay's Profit More Than Triples as Transaction Revenue Surges," *Wall Street Journal*, October 18, 2002, B4; Adam Lashinsky, "Building eBay 2.0," *Fortune*, October 5, 2006; "Interview Transcript: Meg Whitman, eBay," *Financial Times*, June 18, 2006; "Analysis: eBay's Growth To Come From Community" *InformationWeek*, June 19, 2006; "eBay Inc. Announces Financial Results for First Quarter 2007," *M2 Presswire*, April 19, 2007; "eBay Quarterly Net Beats Expectations, Raises Outlook," *eWeek*, April 18, 2007.

2. "Kerkorian Files Briefs in Lawsuit Alleging Deception by Daimler," *Wall Street Journal*, June 19, 2001, A4.

3. See R. F. Bruner, *Applied Mergers and Acquisitions* (Hoboken, NJ: John Wiley & Sons, 2004).

4. P. Wright, M. Kroll, and D. Elenkov, "Acquisition Returns, Increase in Firm Size, and Chief Executive Officer Compensation: The Moderating Role of Monitoring," *Academy of Management Journal* 45 (2002), 599–608.

5. Y. Amihud and B. Lev, "Risk Reduction as a Managerial Motive for Conglomerate Acquisitions," *The Bell Journal of Economics* 12 (1983), 605–617.

6. R. Roll, "The Hubris Hypothesis of Corporate Takeovers," *Journal of Business* 59 (1986), 197–216.

7. O. E. Williamson, *The Economic Institutions of Capitalism* (New York: Free Press, 1985).

8. Adapted from Hambrick and Fredrickson, "Are You Sure You Have a Strategy?" *Academy of Management Executive* 15:4 (2001), 48–59.

9. Data drawn from U.S. Department of Commerce sources.

10. P. Haunschild, "How Much Is That Company Worth?: Interorganizational Relationships, Uncertainty, and Acquisition Premiums," *Adminis-trative Science Quarterly* 39 (1994), 391–411; W. G. Sanders, "Behavioral Responses of CEOs to Stock Ownership and Stock Option Pay," *Academy of Management Journal* 44 (2001), 477–492.

11. Data compiled from SDC Platinum, a product of Thompson Financial.

12. Data compiled from SDC Platinum, a product of Thompson Financial.

13. R. F. Bruner, *Deals from Hell: M&A Deals That Rise Above the Ashes* (New York: Wiley, 2005).

14. Figure is adapted. This typology was developed by J. T. Bower, "Not All M&As Are Alike—and That Matters," *Harvard Business Review* 79:3 (2001), 92–101.

15. Bower, "Not All M&As Are Alike."

16. M. L. Sirower, *The Synergy Trap: How Companies Lose at the Acquisition Game* (New York: Free Press, 1997).

17. Haspeslagh and Jemison, *Managing Acquisitions*; D. B. Jemison and S. B. Sitkin, "Corporate Acquisitions: A Process Perspective," *Academy of Management Review* 11:1 (1986), 145–163.

18. Brunner, *Applied Mergers and Acquisitions*; Haspeslagh and Jemison, *Managing Acquisitions*.

19. Haspeslagh and Jemison, *Managing Acquisitions*, 42.

20. Haspeslagh and Jemison, *Managing Acquisitions*.

21. Haspeslagh and Jemison, *Managing Acquisitions*.

22. Brunner, *Applied Mergers and Acquisitions*, 88.

23. S. L. Brown and K. M. Eisenhardt, *Competing on the Edge: Strategy as Structured Chaos* (Boston: Harvard Business School Press, 1998).

11 Organizational Structure, Systems, and Processes

In This Chapter We Challenge You To >>>

1. Outline the interdependence between strategy formulation and implementation.

2. Demonstrate how to use organizational structure as a strategy implementation lever.

3. Illustrate the use of systems and processes as strategy implementation levers.

4. Identify the roles of people and rewards as implementation levers.

5. Explain the dual roles that strategic leadership plays in strategy implementation.

6. Describe how global and dynamic contexts affect the use of implementation levers.

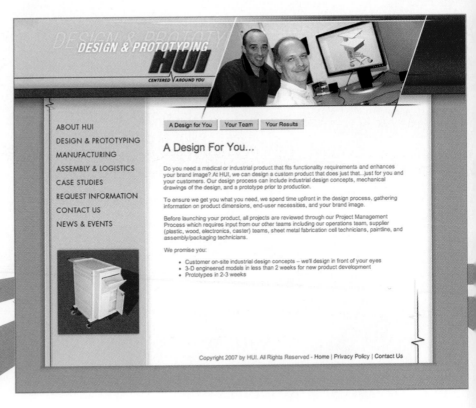

The "Leaning" of HUI

Success *as a* Journey, *not a* Destinations

The notion of "Lean" manufacturing (commonly referred to simply as *Lean*) is typically associated with the enduring success stories of Toyota Motors of Japan or Danaher Corp. in the

United States. Lean is a generic process management philosophy derived mostly from the Toyota Production System (TPS) but also from other sources. It is renowned for its focus on reduction of the original Toyota 'seven wastes' in order to improve overall customer value (you will learn more about lean throughout the chapter). However, when the CEO of a small metal fabricator—HUI—successfully rebuilds his business based on Lean principles, it points out the far-reaching strategic implications of the Lean revolution well beyond the context of global, large-scale manufacturers.

HUI (previously known as Household Utilities, Inc.) has been in the Kiel, Wisconsin area since 1933, and was originally founded as a metal fabrication business by Albert Deibele Sr., a German immigrant to the Kiel area. Metal fabrication involves the stamping, bending, coating, and finishing of sheet metal and other raw material to form product parts to trays and rolling carts used in hospitals. You should also know that metal fabrication is a cutthroat business—the barriers to entry are trivial, amounting to $800,000 and three people, and any single firm faces 100–300 competitors that are just a speed-dial number away. In 1996, Kurt Bell, who had been Operations Manager at HUI, accepted the position of President/CEO and purchased a majority ownership position in 2002. Prior to joining HUI, Kurt had been a CPA with one of the large global consulting and accounting firms. Under Kurt's guidance, HUI has grown and prospered, both in revenue growth and, more importantly, in employee development. Today, the company is 135-people strong, and garners a profitable $20 million in annual revenues. HUI has reinvented itself from a traditional family business, with limited sharing of information and authority, to an open-book managed company with defined roles and responsibilities and authority spread throughout the company.

This reinvention required HUI to create alignment between its revamped strategy and key pieces like marketing, organizational structure, employee evaluation methodology and pay systems, decision-making processes, performance metrics, and group dynamics. Lean principles provided the catalyst for bringing the pieces together.

In the CEO's Message, posted on the firm's website, Kurt Bell tells of HUI's Lean story like this:[1]

> HUI embarked on the Lean journey in September of 1998. At that time it was done for all the normal reasons: decrease lead-times, reduce costs, better satisfy our customers and improve profitability.

> Although those are good reasons to start with they are not what we've discovered to be the compelling factors that keep us going. Those have proven to be quite a bit loftier and more comprehensive.

> HUI aspires to be "The Company of Choice in all that we do today and tomorrow." Pretty inspirational and we may never get there but the journey is proving to be worthwhile and very rewarding.

> What is the role of Lean in all this? Lean is being utilized company-wide and does many things for HUI, our customers, and our suppliers. Above all, Lean increases our speed and adulthood.

> In today's world there are two types of companies, the quick and the dead. In order to play, HUI has to produce the right part at the right time, at the right price, the right way. All of this must be done quicker than the customer expects and quicker than last time. This is the world we live in.

> Lean increases our speed. It allows us to reduce the roadblocks and speed bumps that get in the way of our ability to quickly add value. This is accomplished with set-up reduction, standardized work, adhering to a process, visual systems, cross-trained teammates and quality at the source. The list goes on and on. These tools and principles are being used company-wide at HUI, from the front door to the back door. By doing these things well we will constantly increase our ability to deliver value quicker.

> Lean increases our degree of adulthood. As an adult you should be able to know what is expected, know what to do, know when to do it, know how you are doing, and know what to do to improve performance, all without being told. In other words, Lean helps to create an environment where people can be adults at work. Many of the same tools that deliver measurable waste reductions also put people in a position to act as adults. A good visual

system increases the likelihood that people can decide for themselves what needs to be done and how things are going. Being on a well functioning, self-directed work team leads to greater accountability, responsibility and personal growth.

So why we started is pretty normal, why we keep going is NOT NORMAL to most companies. For us at HUI, it's a way of life. Each day we strive to be faster and more adult like than yesterday.

This is not an easy journey, but the road to greatness rarely is.

Kurt Bell, CEO

The move to Lean by HUI also meant that it would embrace cellular manufacturing. This involves significant organizational changes, but also has big benefits. With cellular manufacturing, you make one product at a time immediately—the opposite of the mass-batch method, where products are processed and set aside for assembly. Exhibit 11.1 shows the way that the traditional manufacturing line is converted to a U-shaped work cell.

An obvious reward is that errors are detected quickly because a welded product, for instance, won't sit around for days waiting for the next step. If the welding isn't right, production is stopped immediately and the error is fixed, which enhances productivity and creates less waste. More benefits include scheduling flexibility, reduced lead-time and decreased inventory. Finally, in the best cases—as is the case at HUI—these cells are self-managing, so that there is no need for a supervisor to oversee the traditional line. Members of the cell coordinate activities collectively, instead of following the direction of the line manager. A full layer of management, and the time and cost associated with it, is thus eliminated.

The Lean revolution at HUI, however, did not stop with manufacturing. Bell restructured his back office to a cellular structure as well, and created cells comprised of sales, customer service, engineering, purchasing, and accounting staff, organized by customer. The restructuring process started with viewing the back office as a factory, and asking questions like: What will my customers (external and internal) pay me to do? What are our products? And, what are the flows required to produce those products? For instance, "products" were identified such as project quotes, engineering designs, and shop-floor routing instructions. Like manufacturing at HUI, this U-shaped customer-business-development cell is self-directed. Moreover, it is responsible for its own sales.

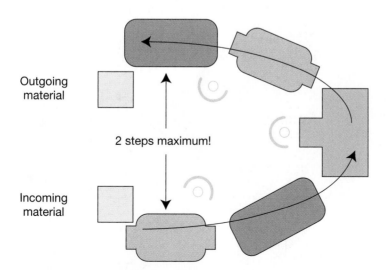

Exhibit 11.1 The U-Shaped Work Cell in Lean

Outgoing material

2 steps maximum!

Incoming material

For Lean to work well, experts say that the organization's culture must change in significant ways—and Bell saw that this type of change had to start with him—particularly the need to shift operating control from "management" to the employees. From a command-and-control culture, which is typically associated with efficiency, HUI moved to a culture of customer and process ownership by employees, with a team-based structure, and a broader orientation toward learning and individual growth. Where employees had deep knowledge of specialized areas in the old model, the Lean model asked them to cross-train each other, and complement depth with breadth so that they could better coordinate activities to benefit the customer and lower costs. This deep cultural change took a decade to build, resulted in the departure of many employees who could not adapt to the aggressively cooperative and performance-demanding climate, but also created a more enduring source of competitive advantage for HUI. This advantage can be seen in the firm's agility, creativity, product quality, and production efficiency. Ironically, CEO Bell sees Lean as a table stake in future battles for market share, though it is clear that the culture that enables it is not easily duplicated. **<<<**

Interdependence of Strategy Formulation and Implementation

By now, you should have a very good idea of what makes a good strategy: Good strategies enable an organization to achieve its objectives. You've also learned how to describe and evaluate business and corporate strategy formulation according to the strategy diamond. You know that *strategy formulation* is *deciding what to do* and that *strategy implementation* is the process of *executing what you've planned to do*.[2] You understand that neither formulation nor implementation can succeed without the other, and you're aware that the most successful firms often adjust strategies and execution according to feedback from the implementation process itself. That's why the processes of formulation and implementation are iterative and interdependent, with the objective being a consistent and coherent set of strategy elements and implementation levers. As Exhibit 11.2 reminds us, the overarching model of strategy hinges on the integral relationship among *formulation* (the process of aligning the five elements of the strategy diamond), *implementation levers*, and *strategic leadership*.

Exhibit 11.2 Formulation and Implementation

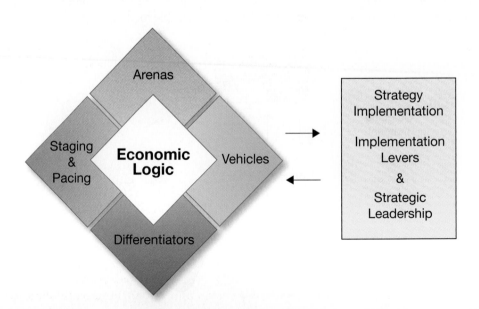

In this chapter, we'll focus on issues concerning strategy implementation—specifically, such implementation levers as organization structure, systems, and processes, and the aspects of strategic leadership that facilitate successful implementation.

When a firm is experiencing difficulties, it's always good to ask three questions:

■ Is the strategy flawed?

■ Is the implementation of the strategy flawed?

■ Are both the strategy and implementation flawed?

It shouldn't come as any surprise that, more often than not, implementation problems are the source of performance problems.[3] Obviously, no strategy can be effective if it's implemented poorly. By the same token, although we tend to attribute success to effective strategies, some of the most stellar performers achieve competitive advantage because of *how* they execute their strategies.

A MODEL COMPANY

The opening vignette on HUI describes a company whose strategy implementation integrates all of the key elements of the overarching implementation model outlined in Exhibit 11.2 (and indeed, it hits on all the points of the more detailed implementation framework we will review later in the chapter):

■ HUI's implementation levers function in unison to support a focused strategy of growth through innovative new products.

■ The lack of formal titles, hierarchy, and bureaucracy reflect a flat organizational structure that facilitates both the flow of information and quick decision making (though this presents a challenge to coordination and rapid change at an organizational level).

■ Systems are in place to identify new-product opportunities, to ensure that they have product champions, and to reward employees for their contributions to both product lines and the company's overall profitability.

■ Because the selection and retention of people, in terms of both necessary skills and personal fit with the organization, are a critical factor in HUI's success, these functions are rigorously managed. Attention to human resources also reinforces a deep culture that values leading-edge innovation, and top management reiterates the importance of the firm's "core values."

By the end of this chapter, you should be able to identify the implementation levers and strategic leadership functions that drive successful strategies. You should be able to identify levers that are in need of repair and propose a plan for using certain levers to implement a strategy more effectively.

THE KNOWING-DOING GAP

Let's go back to a couple of admonitions that we cited in Chapter 1:

■ "A strategy . . . is only as good as its execution."[4]

■ "The important decisions, the decisions that really matter, are strategic. . . . [But] more important and more difficult is to make effective the course of action decided upon."[5]

These principles apply to our focus in this chapter as well: By and large, firms find it much more difficult to implement good ideas than to generate new ideas and knowledge. A recent study, for instance, found that 46 percent of large companies surveyed regarded themselves as good or excellent at generating new knowledge; only 14 percent of the same

knowing-doing gap
Phenomenon whereby firms tend to be better at generating new knowledge than at creating new products based on that knowledge.

firms reported having launched new products based on the application of new knowledge.[6] This difference between what firms *know* and what they *do* has been dubbed the **knowing-doing gap**.[7] Let's look a little more closely at this phenomenon.

What Causes the Knowing-Doing Gap?

One explanation of the knowing-doing gap is the fact that the strategy formulation process itself isn't shared with those stakeholders, including lower-level managers, who will be integral in rolling out the strategy. Other observers argue that, even if all the right stakeholders are included in the strategy formulation process, management often fails either to determine whether the proper implementation levers are in place or to take appropriate strategic leadership actions.

Obstacles, External and Internal Some experts believe that strategy implementation failures result from management's inability to assess potential implementation obstacles. Some obstacles reside in the external environment. Prior to its merger with Hewlett-Packard, for example, Compaq's attempts to mimic Dell's direct-sales model met with stiff resistance from its existing retail base, including such outlets as CompUSA and Best Buy. Of course, obstacles also exist inside the firm—a fact that we've already touched on by emphasizing the importance of assessing existing resources, implementation levers, and management action plans. In diversified firms, the parent company itself may be an internal obstacle, particularly if one business unit is proposing a strategy that puts it in direct competition with another.

The Impact of Culture One of the most critical, and yet most overlooked, internal implementation factor is a firm's *culture*. Exhibit 11.3 sums up Lou Gerstner's view of culture as he came on board to revive a dying IBM.[8]

culture Core organizational values widely held and shared by an organization's members.

Ironically, Gerstner's challenge was not to change the IBM culture, but instead to harness and direct the aspects of that culture that had previously made IBM great. Culture sometimes presents management with a persistent challenge: It's both difficult and time-consuming to change, and it can be a source of competitive advantage.[9] **Culture** consists of the core organizational values that are widely held and shared by organizational members (including employees, managers, and owners). Recent studies have found evidence confirming the theory that firms with strong shared values are better at implementing strategies and achieving higher levels of performance than firms with weaker values. Across industries, for example, firms with strong cultures generally achieve higher average levels of return on investment, net income growth, and change in share price.[10] In addition, firms

Exhibit 11.3 Lou Gerstner's View on the Role of Culture

"Along the way, something happened—something that quite frankly surprised me. I fell in love with IBM. I came to see, in my decade at IBM, that culture isn't just one aspect of the game—it is the game. We changed almost every process in this company, but none of those changes would have gotten done if we didn't convince the IBM team that a whole new set of values and behaviors had to emerge. And interestingly many of them were a return to IBM's true values, not the grotesque misalignment of those values that had emerged during the bad years. Once IBM was reminded of its core culture, it helped rally the company, bind it together in ways that had been absent for years."

with strong cultures seem to be less variable in their performance outcomes.[11] Finally, these positive effects of shared values on performance appear to be even stronger in highly competitive markets.[12] Why? Perhaps because effective strategy implementation is even more important in highly competitive industries, where there's less room for error. The opening example on HUI shows how important the shared culture was to the successful implementation of Lean processes.

Sometimes, company culture reflects the values of the CEO and other top managers, whereas at others, leaders steward and protect existing values. Shared values are typically few in number, deeply embedded in the organization, give meaning and identity to the firm's members, and state the purpose of the firm's work. The shared values of HUI may be one of the reasons why it thrives despite having a structure that seems too chaotic for a firm of its size. HUI's values can be summed up as fairness, freedom, commitment, and consultation. Associates, for instance, are expected to treat one another fairly. They're given the freedom to grow in knowledge, skill, and scope of responsibility. Finally, although everyone is empowered to make decisions, any management decision that may affect the firm's image or performance must be run past other associates.

In short, a firm's strategy must be consistent with its shared values if it's to be implemented successfully. Thus, it's crucial that strategists understand what's really important to members of the organization. First, of course, they need to ask whether employees have any shared values. If the answer is no, top management may have to spend some time developing and communicating a core set of values, starting with the vision and mission statements, and getting organizational members to buy into them.

Mismatches Not surprisingly, mismatches between strategy and implementation levers or between strategy and strategic leadership actions are easy to recognize in hindsight. Of course, they're much more difficult to catch in real time. Executives who are responsible for formulating strategy are often prone to making overly optimistic projections and downplaying the obstacles to execution. Consider, for instance, the number of hardware and software firms that have attempted to become IT solution providers by adding a consulting arm to their existing business. Most have failed, usually because they lacked the organization to execute the strategy.[13] SAP provides a good example of this.

As a provider of ERP software, SAP grew quickly at first because of demand for its unique product. In its zeal for growth, however, the firm neglected to focus on structure, employee retention, and balance between rewards for sales and rewards for profitability. SAP eventually recovered (as you will see in Exhibit 11.4), but only after a new CEO dramatically revamped the firm's infrastructure, cost controls, and human resource policies.[14]

As the SAP example in Exhibit 11.4 shows, implementation levers tend to be interrelated, which means that a change in one will probably require a change in all or some of the others.[15]

We'll deal with further examples of these interrelationships in the following sections, but at this point we suggest that you use the following statement to guide you in your study of the material in this chapter:

> [T]he strategist will not be able to nail down every action step when the strategy is first crafted, nor should this even be attempted. However, he or she must have the ability to look ahead at the major implementation obstacles and ask, "Is this strategy workable? Can I make it happen?"[16]

By the end of this chapter, you'll be able not only to answer questions such as these, but also offer recommendations for employing implementation levers and taking strategic leadership actions. These two facets of strategy implementation—levers and leadership—are summarized in Exhibit 11.5.[17]

Exhibit 11.4 Picking Up the Pieces at SAP

The enterprise software company SAP dodged a bullet, but just barely. It did so not by overhauling its strategy but rather by dramatically changing its leadership and implementation approach. We will focus on SAP America, one of the largest subsidiaries of the German firm SAP, because it characterizes much of what took place globally in this firm. From 1992 through most of 1996, SAP America's revenues grew at an astounding triple-digit annual rate, from $49 million to an annualized $818 million. The number of employees over that same period grew from 284 to 1,621. This rapid growth was spurred by two things. First, SAP had what many multinationals perceived to be the best ERP product on the market. The product was highly profitable due to its relatively standardized design and high market demand. Second, SAP was a fairly decentralized organization, with functional emphasis primarily in sales and on an incentive system that rewarded sales and sales growth. Career paths were unclear and focused on regions, but because the compensation was so lucrative, employees could earn huge salaries based on sales and then jump ship to a firm where their career and mobility might be more clearly laid out. As a result, SAP America was built for speed (though not efficiency), and its rocket-like sales growth reflected the levers and leadership that were in place.

Coming into late 1995, however, the rocket seemed to be running out of fuel. The combination of growing competition from the likes of Oracle and Siebel systems, market saturation, and a lack of organizational account-ability that was a by-product of the growth focus was beginning to undermine SAP's profitability, customer service, and reputation. SAP Germany's kick in the pants to SAP America started with the promotion of then-CFO Kevin McKay to the position of CEO (and the departure of the old CEO, Paul Wahl, to competitor Siebel Systems). McKay moved quickly to increase cultural sensitivity to costs and cost management, implement an administrative structure to bolster the organization's overall professionalism, and formalize human resource policies. This latter step took the form of hiring an HR director (no one had held that role at SAP America before, despite all of the hiring that had gone on) who put a formal HR system in place. These decisions were comple-mented by increased R&D funding to explore the Internet applications of SAP software, a platform that the software giant had ignored up to that point. At the same time, McKay subtly shifted SAP's strategy from one of pure growth through new accounts to account "farming"—an increased focus on garnering a greater share of each existing customer's IS business needs, coupled with the modification of the firm's reward system to reward such behaviors.

While these changes caused many people to leave SAP, this loss was more than offset by the hiring of new executives and workers who bought into the new organizational arrangements and SAP's vision. By 2000, the firm had successfully launched a Web-based version of its software, called MySAP, and regained its position of industry leadership.

Exhibit 11.5 Key Facets of Strategy Implementation

Implementation Levers

- Organizational structure
- Systems and processes
- People and rewards

Intended Strategy

Realized Strategy

Strategic Leadership

- Lever and resource allocation decisions
- Support among stakeholders

Implementation Levers

We have been using the term *implementation lever* without providing a precise definition. Before we explore the concept in detail, therefore, it may be useful to make clear that **implementation levers** are mechanisms that a strategic leader has at his or her disposal to help execute a strategy. Although anything that enables an executive to get leverage to execute change can be considered an implementation lever, we categorize the major levers as *structure, systems and processes,* and *people and rewards.* In this section, we will go into some depth on each of these.

implementation levers
Mechanisms used by strategic leaders to help execute a firm's strategy.

STRUCTURE

Because structure is the implementation lever that usually gets the most attention in an organization, we'll start with it. Alfred Chandler's classic research on the interdependence of strategy and structure based on studies of General Motors, DuPont, and Sears raised the topic to prominence in the 1960s.[18] Today, practically every issue of the *Wall Street Journal* announces that some firm is busy "restructuring" or reporting decreased earnings due to "restructuring charges." Most firms develop *organizational charts,* which are static representations of their structure. But what is *structure* itself? We'll define **organizational structure** as the relatively stable arrangement and division of responsibilities, tasks, and people within an organization. Organizations are composed of people who are assigned to certain divisions and who perform certain delegated and specialized tasks. The *structure* of an *organization,* therefore, is the framework that management has devised to divide tasks, deploy resources, and coordinate departments.[19] Structure provides a way for information to flow efficiently from the people and departments who generate it to those who need it. Structure also spells out *decision rights*—policies that tell individuals who's responsible for generating particular information and who's authorized to act on it.

organizational structure
Relatively stable arrangement of responsibilities, tasks, and people within an organization.

Control and Coordination Briefly, structure includes a firm's authority hierarchy, its organizational units and divisions, and its mechanisms for coordinating internal activities. Organizational structure performs two essential functions:

- It ensures control.

- It coordinates information, decisions, and the activities of employees at all levels.

As both functions become more complex, firms generally modify their structure accordingly. Structure should be consistent with the firm's strategy. The more diversified the firm, the more the structure that will have to be designed to accommodate coordination. After all, if a firm is participating in related businesses, it is probably trying to exploit synergies—a task that, as we saw in our chapters on corporate and international strategy, often requires sharing information and resources across product or geographic divisions. Conversely, the more focused the firm is on a single business (or even on each of multiple unrelated businesses), the more its structure should be designed to emphasize control. As we'll see, the popular means of organizing firm structure include the *functional, multidivisional, matrix,* and *network* forms.[20]

Traditionally, both scholars and managers have thought of structure as being determined by a firm's strategy,[21] and in most cases, this assumption is valid. We'll soon see, however, that structure can result in new or modified strategies. In fact, the way in which tasks are delegated and resources deployed can produce rather dramatic changes in a firm's strategy.

With respect to structure, a key question is whether the firm's current structure facilitates the implementation of its strategy and provides the information it needs to revise its existing strategy. At all times, a firm's structure should seek a balance between the control needed to achieve efficiency and unity of direction and the delegation of authority required to make timely decisions in a competitive environment. Let's examine two cases in which new structure resulted directly in changes in strategy.

How Structure Influences Strategy (I)　After developing an innovative process for economically producing industrial gas onsite at customers' factories, the French firm Air Liquide (translated as *liquid air*) began locating personnel at client sites. This restructuring gave employees at customer sites more decision-making autonomy. Before long, on-site employees discovered a host of new services that Air Liquide could offer its clients, such as handling hazardous materials, troubleshooting quality-control systems, and managing inventory. The result, of course, was a wealth of new business opportunities—most of which offered higher margins than the company's core gas production and distribution business. Such services now account for 25 percent of Air Liquide's revenues, as opposed to just 7 percent before the restructuring.[22]

How Structure Influences Strategy (II)　Part of this next story was presented in the opening vignette to Chapter 3. In the early 1980s, Intel derived more than 90 percent of its revenue from the manufacture of memory chips. A feature of its organizational structure is credited with being the key to its transformation into a maker of PC microprocessors in a span of less than two years. Although they appear similar, the capabilities underlying effective competition in memory versus microprocessors differ. Originally, Intel's structure permitted production managers to make production decisions based on a set of established rules. Among other things, these rules stipulated that managers allocate production capacity based on margins per square inch of silicon wafer. In response to this requirement, production managers started shifting manufacturing capacity from memory chips to microprocessors (previously just a small side business), because the margins were much greater. Interestingly, this shift wasn't dictated or orchestrated by senior management. In fact, Intel's senior management didn't ratify the decision to become a microprocessor manufacturer until well after microprocessors had come to account for about 90 percent of companywide output.[23]

FORMS OF ORGANIZATIONAL STRUCTURE

In this section, we'll review four basic forms of organizational structure: *functional, multidivisional, matrix,* and *network.* We also briefly describe partnerships and franchises. Consider these structures to be "pure" forms. In reality, they're just basic models on which many variations have been played. Later in the chapter, we'll show how they've been modified to accommodate global and dynamic contexts.

functional structure Form of organization revolving around specific value-chain functions.

Functional Structure　A **functional structure** organizes activities according to the specific functions that a company performs. As shown in Exhibit 11.6, common units include finance, sales and marketing, production, and R&D. From a practical standpoint, any of the functions in a firm's value chain can be organized as a unit in a functional structure.

　　Functional structures tend to work best in smaller firms and those with few products or services. Platypus Technologies, for instance, is a small nanotechnology firm with thirty em-

Exhibit 11.6　Functional Structure

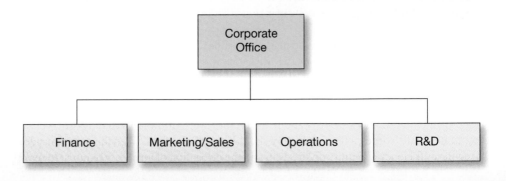

ployees,[24] most of whom are R&D scientists working in the lab. Obviously, however, Platypus also has small departments dedicated to finance, marketing, and human resources.

Functional organization helps managers of smaller firms improve efficiency and quality by fostering professionalism in the performance of specialized tasks. Bear in mind, however, that as firms grow and become more complex (perhaps by venturing into multiple lines), a functional firm can become downright dysfunctional. Often, problems arise if each functional unit begins to focus too narrowly on its own goals and operations, thus losing sight not only of other functional activities but also of customer needs and corporate objectives. This phenomenon has given rise to the term *functional silos.*

The functional organizational model may also exacerbate problems in multiproduct, multimarket firms. Expansion, whether into product or geographic markets, can become problematic if the strategy that's appropriate in one market doesn't work very well in another. The types of products, for example, that enjoy dominant domestic share may not meet the needs of foreign consumers. Similarly, a firm involved in two different product markets may find that the same competitive methods don't work equally well in both or that different markets call for different sales channels. When a functional structure is used in contexts characterized by varying market demands and sales characteristics, functionally structured organizations may be sluggish in responding to changing customer demands and in accessing potential new customers.

Multidivisional Structure   One solution to the problems of managing activities in multiple markets is the **multidivisional structure**, illustrated in Exhibit 11.7 for the Walt Disney Company. Divisions can be organized around geographic markets, products, or groups of related businesses, with division heads being responsible for the strategy of a coherent group of businesses or markets. Such strategic specialization means that strategic decisions are more likely to be appropriate and timely. It also enables firms to design compensation systems that reward performance at the business-unit, versus functional, level.

One of the first companies to adopt a multidivisional structure, GM is mostly organized according to product divisions (GM Trucks, Chevrolet, Buick, Cadillac, Saturn, and so forth). Each division maintains a finance function, a marketing function, and so on. Multidivisional structure makes it possible to implement division-specific incentives and performance accountability standards, and because each division has ready access to key resources, multidivisional structure also fosters speedier reactions to opportunities and challenges.

multidivisional structure
Form of organization in which divisions are organized around product or geographic markets and are often self-sufficient in terms of functional expertise.

Exhibit 11.7   Multidivisional Structure at Disney

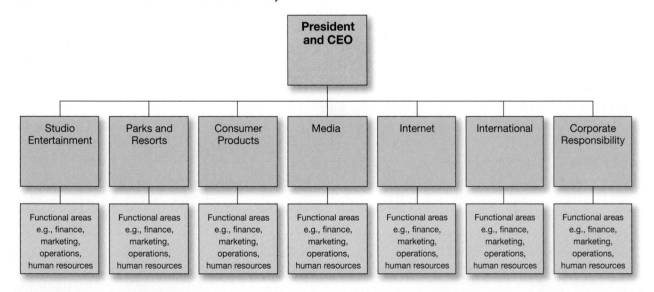

Multidivisional structure is also effective in coordinating diverse economic activities. Headquarters, for example, plans, coordinates, and evaluates all operating divisions, allocating the personnel, facilities, funds, and other resources needed to execute divisional strategies. Divisional managers, meanwhile, are in charge of most of the functions revolving around major product lines and, as such, are typically responsible for divisional financial performance.

For instance, Emageon, a 225-employee provider of advanced visualization tools to hospitals and other medical organizations, has two divisions.[25] One offers electronic hardware, and its sales force works with executives who are responsible for IT decisions at target customers. The second division specializes in software for X-rays and CAT scans, and because physicians usually make the software purchase recommendations, Emageon's software sales force focuses on them. Together, the two divisions provide a complete solution for firms in Emageon's target industry, and as it so happens, each can cross-sell the other's products.

Of course, multidivisional structure is not without drawbacks. It can, for instance, foster undesirable competition between divisions. Emageon doesn't have this problem, but it's not hard to see how GM's higher-end Buicks bump up against its lower-priced Cadillacs.

In addition, when each division is functionally self-contained, there may be costly duplications of staff functions that could be handled more efficiently under some other form of organization. Finally, coordination across divisions can be difficult if cooperation is in the best interests of one division but not those of another.

Matrix Structure   The matrix structure, which is represented in Exhibit 11.8, is a hybrid between the functional and multidivisional structures.

Exhibit 11.8   Matrix Structure

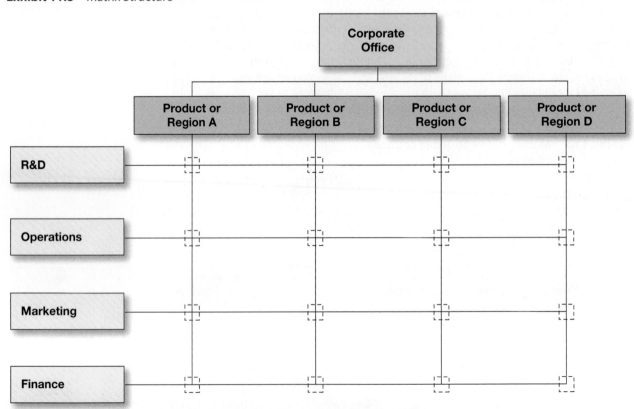

E. Prewitt, "GM's Matrix Reloads," CIO, September 1, 2003. http://www.cio.com/archive/090103/hs_reload.html

A **matrix structure** is designed to take advantage of the benefits of both basic forms—namely, functional specialization and divisional autonomy. As you can see in Exhibit 11.8, two reporting channels exist simultaneously. In our hypothetical company, for instance, there are functional divisions for finance and marketing, but personnel from both divisions are assigned to specific product or geographic divisions. A finance specialist, therefore, reports simultaneously to a finance executive and an executive in one or another of the product or geographic divisions.

matrix structure Form of organization in which specialists from functional departments are assigned to work for one or more product or geographic units.

The Swiss–Swedish technology giant Asea Brown Boveri (ABB) furnishes perhaps the most dramatic example of the matrix structure in action. In the early 1990s, the firm was composed of more than 900 matrix units. Any structure that sets up so many loci of authority is going to have problems with conflicts over authority and accountability. At ABB, however, managers in one matrix unit rarely exercise direct authority over their counterparts in other units. (Dealings between units, therefore, often depend on managers' skills in the arts of negotiation and persuasion.) Moreover, the matrix provides flexibility by making it possible to organize teams around specific projects, products, or markets.

The utility of a matrix structure increases when the pressures facing a firm are unpredictable and require both high degrees of control and extensive coordination of resources. Many firms find it difficult to implement the matrix structure because it calls for high levels of resource sharing across divisions; in fact, it's generally feasible only when strong culture and shared values support cross-division collaboration. As it turns out, even though ABB enjoyed a strong culture, the company eventually realized that coordinating 900 matrix units was far too complex. Massive restructuring began in early 2000, and today, though ABB is still operating under a matrix structure, it has reduced the number of its operating units by about half.

One word of caution here to those firms that may view a matrix structure as a panacea to organizational problems: While the matrix is great for collaboration, particularly when it is focused around customer needs, it also requires a very different managerial skill set. For instance, in the functional and multidivisional structures, each employee typically reports to one or several bosses. In a matrix, the reporting structure is much more of an adhocracy, and managers with the best power bases and negotiating skills get their agendas accomplished. In general, this means that a shift to a matrix structure, while perhaps desirable, also requires attention to the negotiation and communication skill-sets of the managers tasked with making the matrix work. This is another example of how implementation levers—in this case structure, people, and skills—need to be orchestrated in concert.

Network Structure

A more recent development in organization design, the **network structure** consists of small, semi-autonomous, and potentially temporary groups that are brought together for specific purposes—a team, for example, that's been assembled to work on a new product idea. A network structure also includes external linkages with such groups as suppliers and customers. Sometimes these external linkages take the form of strategic alliances, which you learned about in Chapter 9. Authority is based on the control of resources, knowledge, and expertise, rather than on hierarchical rank, and because it's highly flexible, a firm can reconfigure staff and resources rapidly enough to exploit rich but fleeting bubbles of opportunity. Drawbacks include the potential for confusion and ambiguity.

network structure Form of organization in which small, semiautonomous, and potentially temporary groups are brought together for specific purposes.

Gore Industries provides a good example of the network structure in action. You probably know about Gore through its popular GORE-TEX fabrics. Although difficult to diagram here, imagine what an organizational structure would look like for Gore, with its approximately 7,400 associates working in more than forty-five plants and sales locations worldwide. Sales and customer service sites are located in Argentina, Australia, Austria, Brazil, China, Finland, France, Germany, Greece, Hong Kong, India, Italy, Japan, Korea, Malaysia, the Netherlands, New Zealand, Poland, Russia, Scotland, Singapore, Spain, Sweden, Taiwan, and the United States. Manufacturing operations are clustered in the United States, Germany, Scotland, Japan, and China. Gore separates its products into ten categories:

aerospace, automotive, chemical processing, computers/telecommunications/ electronics, energy, environment, industrial/manufacturing, medical/healthcare, military, and textiles. As with the typical network organization, Gore employees work in small teams and are encouraged to participate in direct one-on-one communication with other Gore associates, customers, and suppliers. So, Gore employees do not report through the normal hierarchical structure, but through shifting project teams.

The Real Network You have likely heard the saying that it's not *what* you know, but *who* you know, that matters. Increasingly, organizations are recognizing that it is the informal networks, and not the formal reporting relationships in the organization chart, that matter most. These informal networks operate beyond the boundaries of the formal structure and actually help the firm evolve in positive ways that the fixed organizational structure might otherwise prevent. Research on social networks has shown that the most productive firms are those that identify "brokers"—individuals who are successful and effective at linking otherwise unconnected parts of the organization. They also identify and promote "central connectors"—individuals whom others frequently consult for information, decision-making help, or expertise. Regardless of the actual formal structure, firms that foster these fluid and living network relationships are more likely to see achievement of desired results.[26]

Partnerships and Franchises

Before leaving this section, we should mention two additional forms of organization structure—the professional partnership and the franchise system. Although both are as much forms of legal ownership as they are organizational structures, they offer a few unique structural characteristics that can impact persistent organizational problems. In addition, because both are common fixtures on the business landscape, it's important that you understand their role in the national economy.

Professional Partnerships In several industries, the professional partnership is the structural form of choice. In a professional partnership, the company is organized as a group of partners who own shares or units in the company. Generally, the partners vote on a managing partner who will act as a supervisor, but this person serves at their pleasure. Consequently, a senior partner has significant authority and prestige but perhaps not nearly the power that a CEO of a large firm has over subordinates. Partnerships are pyramid-shaped structures, with each partner having a number of associates (of various levels). Industries in which the partnership form is common include legal offices, accounting firms, consulting firms, advertising agencies, and real estate companies. Until recently, investment banking firms were structured as partnerships, but most have converted to publicly held corporations. The management structure of investment banking firms has remained relatively the same, but the change to a corporate form has enabled firms to increase their capitalization.

Franchise Structure The franchise system not only transfers ownership of local facilities to a franchisee, it likewise shifts all local management responsibility to the franchisee. One purpose of using a franchise model is that it enables a firm to grow rapidly because much of the capital costs are picked up by the franchisees. However, the franchise model fundamentally changes the organizational structure of the firm. A franchisee assumes all management responsibility for individual business locations. For the right to the franchisor's business model and brand name, the franchisee pays a royalty percentage and other fees to the franchisor.

SYSTEMS AND PROCESSES

When asked to think about the systems and processes needed to manage an organization, people usually mention information systems (IS). In reality, an IS is just one type of vital system. Systems and processes make it possible to manage budgeting, quality control, planning, distribution, and resource allocation in complex contemporary organizations. However, two particular systems are taking root in many firms and it is important that you are at least familiar with them. These are the balanced scorecard and Lean process improvement. You learned a little about Lean through the opening vignette on HUI, and before talking more about it, we will give you a primer on the balance scorecard.

In Chapter 2, we pointed out that ambitious vision and mission statements don't automatically translate into higher levels of financial performance.[27] Conversely, of course, a myopic focus on financial accounting results, such as return on equity or return on sales, may cause managers to lose sight of long-term strategic initiatives and divert their attention from other key stakeholders.[28] For this reason, many firms are developing performance-measurement and management systems that enable them to balance the need to report short-term financial returns with the need to pursue longer-term (and often intangible) objectives. Various approaches can be used to gauge the success with which implementation levers are aligned with strategic objectives; the most common term for these performance management systems is the *balanced scorecard.*

The Balanced Scorecard   For the firms that utilize this practice best, the **balanced scorecard** has evolved into what might just as well be called a *strategy scorecard.* It's a strategic management support system devised to help managers measure vision and strategy against business- and operating-unit-level performance along several critical dimensions.[29] It provides balance because it requires managers to reconcile priorities across functions, over time, and across initiatives. It is important to note that the balanced scorecard and strategy map are not strategies in and of themselves. Instead, they serve to (1) translate the strategy into operational terms, (2) align the organization with the strategy, (3) make strategy everyone's job, (4) make strategy a continual process, and (5) mobilize change through executive leadership. The cascading nature of vision through the balanced scorecard and strategy map is summarized in Exhibit 11.9.[30]

> **balanced scorecard**
> Strategic management support system for measuring vision and strategy against business- and operating-unit-level performance.

What this diagram should make clear, is that the balanced scorecard and strategy map are the means for achieving the strategy—particularly the staging and pacing components of the strategy diamond—too often firms go through the expensive exercise of formulating a strategy, and then leaving it in a three-ring binder on a shelf. The scorecard and mapping process pushes the company to act on what it said it was going to do in terms of strategy. It provides a coherent mechanism for managing tradeoffs, since the scorecard is driven by the staging and pacing of the strategy itself.

Beyond these larger issues, the balanced scorecard approach teaches three fundamental lessons:

1. Translate strategy into tangible and intangible performance metrics (recall the summary of financial and nonfinancial performance measures summarized in Exhibit 2.10 of Chapter 2).

2. Use a *strategy map* to align metrics with strategy.

3. Make strategy a continuous and dynamic process.[31]

Let's look a little more closely at each of these principles.

Relying on a Range of Metrics   Managers should pay attention to a variety of performance metrics, not just to short-term financial performance indicators. Granted, financial performance is the easiest metric to apply, but other indicators are just as critical in diagnosing and maintaining the long-term health of an organization. The balanced scorecard prevents managers from relying solely on short-term financial or other outcome measures and forces them to focus instead on those measures, both tangible and intangible, that are relevant to the elements of value being delivered to key stakeholders.

Exhibit 11.9 Cascading Nature of the Balanced Scorecard

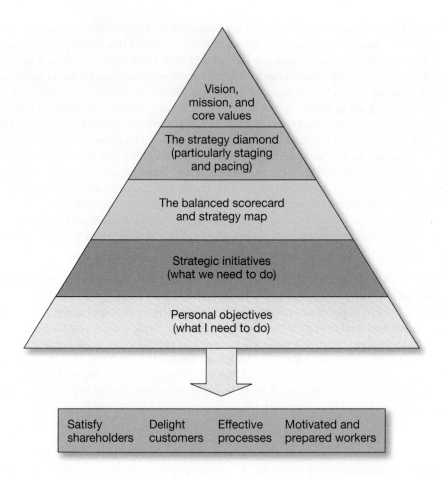

Leading proponents of this approach advise managers to consider four perspectives on performance: *financial, external, internal business process,* and *learning and growth:*

1. The *financial perspective* involves strategy for growth, profitability, and risk when viewed from the shareholder's or owner's perspective.

2. The *external relations perspective* pertains to strategy for creating value and differentiation from the perspective of the customer.

3. The *internal business process perspective* reflects strategic priorities among processes according to their contributions to customer and shareholder satisfaction.

4. The *learning and growth perspective* focuses on the organization's priorities for fostering change, innovation, and growth.

Exhibit 11.10 illustrates the links among these four perspectives and a firm's vision and strategy. It can also serve as a worksheet for identifying a performance metric, its target level, and the specific initiatives aimed at achieving the target.

Recall that the overarching strategic management process introduced in Chapter 1 flows from vision to goals and objectives and then to the strategy diamond, which sets out how those goals and objectives are to be achieved. You can think of the balanced scorecard as an elaborate summary of the goals and objectives in the strategic management process. Essentially, management must distill tangible and intangible strategic objectives for each area down into specific measures that will be used to gauge those

Exhibit 11.10   The Balanced Scorecard System

External			
Objectives	Measures	Targets	Initiatives

"To achieve our vision, how should we appear to our customers?"

Financial			
Objectives	Measures	Targets	Initiatives

"To succeed financially, how should we appear to our shareholders?"

Vision and Strategy

Internal Business Process			
Objectives	Measures	Targets	Initiatives

"To satisfy our shareholders and customers, what business processes must we excel at?"

Learning and Growth			
Objectives	Measures	Targets	Initiatives

"To achieve our vision, how will we sustain our ability to change and improve?"

objectives. Are our goals growth goals, profitability goals, market share goals, or some combination of these? The balanced scorecard communicates these perspectives clearly and coherently; since strategy tells managers what they should do and what they should not do, this visual aspect of the balanced scorecard becomes very powerful. Targets are then set for those measures and initiatives that are launched to reach the desired targets. Ideally, these measures will have leading, pacing, and lagging characteristics such that management can tell if they are moving forward, how well and quickly they are doing so, and when initiatives are drawing to a successful conclusion. For instance, GE uses a very simple leading indicator to determine if business is growing or slowing: sales people ask their customer if they would refer them to another prospective client. GE has found this to be a very reliable indicator of future business. The beauty of the balanced scorecard process is, with this type of knowledge, GE can direct resources to the types of actions that lead to more customer referrals. Previously, it was investing in many different marketing approaches with no idea as to which marketing approach generated the greatest yields.

Developing a Strategy Map   Exhibit 11.10 shows how managers can begin the strategy-mapping process.[32] This is not an easy process, and requires that managers talk through their interests, share information about their functions and businesses, and reconcile their priorities. Through this process, the most important objectives are identified, measures are assigned to those objectives (again, leading, lagging, and pacing indicators), and then specific targets are designed. ◆

The purpose of the targets is to help the firm understand if the staging and pacing of the strategy is on track. Specific initiatives are then designed to achieve the desired targets, and so on. The benefit of this visual tool is that managers now understand what other initiatives

Staging & Pacing

are being invested in across the business. In some cases this prevents duplication of effort, and in other cases lets parts of the firm pool their resources to realize greater or quicker gains.

The next, and most critical, step of the process is to develop a *strategy map* wherein managers link all performance metrics to the firm's strategy. Many managers begin mapping systems and processes by diagramming activities across the four perspectives that we've already developed: (1) financial, (2) external relations, (3) internal business processes, and (4) learning and growth. An example of this cause-and-effect approach to strategy mapping is shown in Exhibit 11.11.[33]

The strategy map states objectives—in terms of business processes, cycle time, productivity, and other important internal processes—to guide key activities. It is important to note that the bubbles you see in the chart are not generic, but instead are agreed upon by the management team as those most relevant to the respective perspectives. When mapping learning-and-growth objectives, managers should indicate what must be done—in terms of people and product and process development—if learning-and-growth processes are to be developed and sustained.

The two remaining perspectives shown in Exhibit 11.11—customer and financial—state objectives that reflect the desired outcomes. How, for instance, does the firm want customers, partners, and other external stakeholders to perceive it? How will planned activities ultimately translate into financial results and economic value? The arrows that connect the various boxes and bubbles are important, in that they should demonstrate expected cause and effect relationships. Just as importantly, if a bubble or box does not have an arrow coming from or to it, then it either means that activity is not important or that there is nothing in place to achieve it.

As the box entitled "How Would *You* Do That? 11.1" demonstrates, a balanced scorecard can smooth the process of strategy implementation—for all of the reasons described so far. Linking objectives in this way helps managers articulate causality between objectives—a key factor in linking strategy to relevant performance measures.[34]

Making Strategy a Continuous and Dynamic Process   To ensure that a strategy remains continuous and dynamic, managers must succeed at two tasks:

1. Disseminating the key features of a strategy and stipulating responsibilities for executing it throughout the organization

2. Linking the strategy with the financial budget

In one important sense, the balanced scorecard can serve as a tool for communicating vision, mission, and strategy throughout an organization—a theme which we'll return to later in the chapter when we discuss the roles of strategic leadership in strategy implementation. Employees who've participated in developing and revising a balanced scorecard should have a fairly in-depth understanding of a firm's strategy and of the ways in which underlying maps come together to support it. During the process, they should also develop a good sense of whether the organization's culture will support the strategy. Finally, beyond simple communication, the dissemination process can foster broader support for the strategy among stakeholders, improve understanding of how the balanced scorecard works to ensure that the strategy is effectively implemented, and furnish a mechanism for receiving feedback.

To be sure, in the form of operational budgets, the process of financial budgeting not only provides a feedback tool, but also helps to determine resource allocation. However, operational budgets impose a form of outcome control that, by its very nature, tends to constrain managers and hamper investment in new capabilities and products.

In contrast, a *strategic* budget focuses on identifying and acquiring new customers, new capabilities, new operations, and new products. The balanced scorecard is important in de-

Exhibit 11.11   The Strategy Map Basis for the Balanced Scorecard

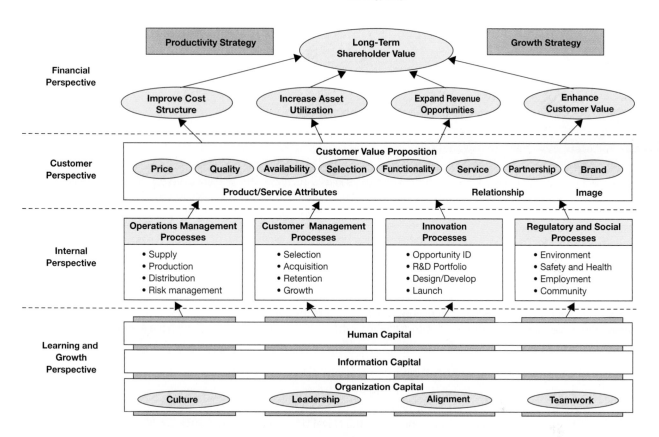

termining the mix and amount of spending in the strategic budget. The relationship between strategic priorities and the scorecard is further reinforced when compensation is tied to financial and nonfinancial measures. Microsoft, for instance, now ties the compensation of its top 600 officers to customer satisfaction scores, a critical nonfinancial performance measure in the company's balanced scorecard.[35]

What Is Lean?   Beyond the balanced scorecard, another profound process change in manufacturing and service operations is the adoption of lean practices. As you learned in the opening vignette on HUI, Lean is a generic process management philosophy derived mostly from the Toyota Production System (TPS) but also from other sources. It is renowned for its focus on reduction of the original Toyota 'seven wastes' in order to improve overall customer value. Lean is often linked with Six Sigma because of that methodology's emphasis on reduction of process variation (or its converse, smoothness). Toyota's steady growth from a small player to the most valuable and the biggest car company in the world has focused attention upon how it has achieved this, making "Lean" a hot topic in management science in the first decade of the twenty-first century. The opening vignette on HUI, and its success through its adoption of lean initiatives, should tell you that Lean would likely be a necessary part of any future leader's vocabulary.

For many, Lean is the set of TPS "tools" that assist in the identification and then steady elimination of waste (*muda*), quality improvement, and production time and cost reductions. While the use of Japanese terms may appear distracting at first, you will quickly find

Developing a Balanced Scorecard for the NUWC

Exhibit 11.12 shows the first steps in the mapping process at the U.S. Naval Undersea Warfare Center (NUWC), the Navy's full-spectrum research, testing, and engineering center for submarines, autonomous underwater systems, and weapons systems associated with undersea warfare.[36]

As a result of the strategic-mapping process, which involved communication among managers in all parts and levels of the organization in addition to external stakeholders, three organizational themes emerged—innovation, affordability, and putting the customer first. In turn, these themes led to the development of a system of performance metrics that is aligned with the clearly articulated strategic direction of NUWC. (This example, by the way, shows that the concept of the balanced scorecard can be applied to both nonprofit and for-profit organizations.)

The next step (for NUWC or any other organization) is to develop objectives, measures, targets, and initiatives for each of the key perspectives. These perspectives should then be used to develop the overarching strategy map. If there are inconsistencies between pieces in the map, then the relevant stakeholders

Exhibit 11.12   Balanced Scorecard Development at the Naval Undersea Warfare Center (NUWC)

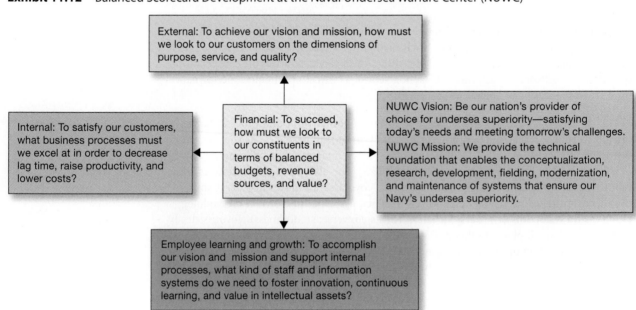

can use this information as an opportunity to refine the implementation of the strategy, including revision of the objectives, measures, targets, and initiatives. Because the perspectives and their underlying objectives are related to strategic priorities, the system goes well beyond a mere listing of things to do or key performance indicators. By means of the mapping process, all metrics are related to strategic objectives.

The next step in the process for NUWC would be to create the strategy map. For this scenario, a simple strategy map like the one shown in Exhibit 11.13 will do.

You can see that we have further simplified the form to let you identify the relationships among financial, external, internal, and learning perspectives, alongside the measures, targets, and initiatives you would align with those perspectives. When you are done with the mapping process, you can imagine that you will have a good idea what it will take to implement the strategy you have outlined with your strategy diamond, as well as what activities are not mission-critical. Given what you know in general about NUWC or perhaps what you can glean from the web, take a stab at filling out this map for NUWC.

Exhibit 11.13   Strategy Map Worksheet

Overarching Themes	Measurement	Target	Initiative
Financial Quality Balance Revenue			
External			
Internal			
Learning			

Exhibit 11.14　Elimination of Waste as the Soul of Lean

Muda 無駄 is a Japanese term for activity that is wasteful and doesn't add value. It is also a key concept in the Toyota Production System and is one of the three types of waste (Muda, Mura, Muri) that it identifies. Waste reduction is an effective way to increase profitability. Following are the seven deadly wastes, along with their definitions:

1. Defects Quality defects prevent the customer from accepting the product produced. The effort to create these defects is wasted. New waste management processes must be added in an effort to reclaim some value for the otherwise scrap product.

2. Overproduction Overproduction is the production or acquisition of items before they are actually required. It is the most dangerous waste of the company, because it hides the production problems. Overproduction must be stored, managed, and protected.

3. Transportation Each time a product is moved it stands the risk of being damaged, lost, delayed, etc. as well as being a cost for no added value. Transportation does not make any transformation to the product that the consumer is willing to pay for.

4. Waiting Refers to both the time spent by the workers waiting for resources to arrive, the queue for their products to empty as well as the capital sunk in goods and services that are not yet delivered to the customer. It is often the case that there are processes to manage this waiting.

5. Inventory Inventory—be it in the form of raw materials, work-in-progress (WIP), or finished goods—represent a capital outlay that has not yet produced an income either by the producer or for the consumer. Waste occurs when any of these three items are not actively processed to add value.

6. Motion As compared to transportation, motion refers to the producer or worker or equipment. This has significance to damage, wear, or safety. It also includes the fixed assets and expenses incurred in the production process.

7. Overprocessing Using a more expensive or otherwise valuable resource than is needed for the task or adding features that are unneeded by the customer. There is a particular problem with this item with regard to people. People may need to perform tasks that they are overqualified for so as to maintain their competency. This training cost can be used to offset the waste associated with overprocessing.

that it is the common vocabulary surrounding Lean thinking. You have a brief introduction to these seven wastes in Exhibit 11.14. To solve the problem of waste, Lean has several "tools" at its disposal. These include continuous process improvement (*kaizen*), the "5 Whys," and mistake-proofing (*poka-yoke*).

There is a second approach to Lean promoted by Toyota in which the focus is upon implementing the "flow" or smoothness of work (*mura*) through the system and not upon "waste reduction" per se. Techniques to improve flow include production leveling, "pull" production (by means of *kanban*), and the Heijunka box. The implementation of smooth flow exposes quality problems that always existed and thus waste reduction naturally happens as a consequence. The advantage of this approach is that it naturally takes a system-wide perspective, whereas a "waste" focus assumes this perspective.

Lean was originally developed and applied in a manufacturing context, but is now seen as relevant to service firms, and all value chain aspects of the firm. Sales, human resources, and customer service, for instance, all can provide a context for the application of Lean principles. As you began to see in the introductory vignette on HUI, key Lean principles are:

- Perfect first-time quality through quest for zero defects, revealing and solving problems at their ultimate source, achieving higher quality and productivity simultaneously, teamwork, and worker empowerment

- Waste minimization by removing all non-value-added activities, making the most efficient use of scarce resources (capital, people, space), just-in-time inventory, and eliminating any safety nets

- Continuous improvement (reducing costs, improving quality, increasing productivity) through dynamic process of change, simultaneous and integrated product/process development, rapid cycle time and time-to-market, and openness and information sharing

- Flexibility in producing different mixes or greater diversity of products quickly, without sacrificing efficiency at lower volumes of production, through rapid set-up and manufacturing at small lot sizes

- Long-term relationships between suppliers and primary producers (assemblers, system integrators) through collaborative risk-sharing, cost-sharing, and information-sharing arrangements

PEOPLE AND REWARDS

This next subset of implementation levers draws attention to the importance of people and the rewards that can be used to align their energies and actions with the organization's objectives. We'll treat people and rewards together because inappropriate incentives and controls can frustrate the efforts of even the best people. Let's go back to our earlier example of the impact of inadequate compensation policies on SAP's strategy. One problem was that the company's compensation system rewarded people for generating new sales regardless of whether SAP product packages were priced to yield a profit for the firm. In terms of sales, the firm grew quickly, but SAP eventually realized that, over time, many of its customer relationships were costing it more money than it was making.

People   Employees are sometimes called a firm's *human capital* in order to distinguish them from fixed assets and financial capital. Individually, people are a critical component in strategy formulation and implementation. Collectively, people comprise the firm's culture, and such culture contributes strongly to a firm's dynamic capabilities and competitive advantage. Barclay's Global Investors (BGI) provides a good case in point of how a firm's culture of action orientation and self-reliance can and must be aggressively nurtured and protected:

> One of the things we discovered was that there are certain basic things—values, vision, the culture of the firm—that are not up for discussion. You can discuss it in the sense of explaining it and understanding it, but it's not something that is going to be changed. It's important for people to understand that. When you become part of BGI, this is what you are signing up for. And quite frankly, we've still got a small hard-core group of our managing directors that still are questioning it. So we are at the point of saying to them, "Well, maybe it's best that you go someplace else, because these things aren't up for discussion."[37]

As we've indicated on several occasions, a strategy will succeed only if a firm has the right people with the right experience and competencies. As the BGI example demonstrates, this also includes people who share and steward the corporate culture. Thus, recruitment, selection, and training with an eye to competencies and values are critical to strategy implementation. In a recent study, management researcher Jim Collins examined eleven firms that went from good to excellent performance and sustained it over a 15-year period. He then compared these firms with peer companies that had similar prestudy performance but never reached the level of great performance. In all eleven cases of good-to-great companies, making sure they had the right people working was a major priority for CEOs early in their tenures. Collins reports that many executives believe the people lever to be the most crucial to the successful implementation of strategy. Successful CEOs, according to Collins, "attended to people first [and] strategy second. They got the right people on the bus, moved the wrong people off, ushered the right people to the right seats—and then they figured out where to drive it."[38] In BGI's case, for example, management's clarity on the requisite values and principles each employee should hold enabled managers to identify quickly those individuals who fit the desired BGI culture.

So how do people influence firm performance? In many organizations, of course, the skills of their people make it possible for them to do what they do best.[39] That's why the VRINE framework regards such expertise as an important part of a firm's bundle of strategic capabilities. Some consultants and scholars think that these bundles of skills, all the way down to the level of those possessed by teams and even specific individuals, are the key factor in a firm's long-term viability and its ability to innovate new products.[40] People decisions are critical to performance because decisions about which and how many people to employ hinge on the desire either to improve efficiency or generate new revenues.[41]

Because human resources are generally a firm's largest operating cost, many managers focus on reducing this cost.[42] Moreover, the stock market tends to react positively to downsizing.[42] Ironically, however, research shows that although downsizing results in a short-term stock-price improvement, it's often followed by productivity declines that can take several years to correct.[43] These results are consistent with research showing that when a firm's HR policies focus on enhancing its human capital, there are positive effects on several dimensions of operational performance (such as employee productivity, machine efficiency, and the alignment of product and service capabilities with customers' needs).[44]

The continued success of highly profitable growth companies results largely from skill in recruiting people who fit the organization, adhere to its values, and work toward common goals. Both JetBlue and Southwest Airlines, for example, expend considerable effort making sure that new hires will fit the firm.

Regardless of the specifics of the strategy, at the end of the day, success depends on hiring the right people and developing and training them in ways that support a firm's strategy. Competitive advantage, therefore, is inextricably bound up in a firm's human capital.[45] Unfortunately, many firms don't seem to appreciate fully the role of people in developing and sustaining a competitive advantage. One study found that only 50 percent of managers in firms today believe that human capital matters; only about half of those actually launch human-resource initiatives, and only about half of those stick to those initiatives.[46] Not surprisingly, the remaining one-eighth includes such world-class companies as Southwest Airlines, General Electric, and Microsoft. According to the authors of another recent study, few leaders seem to understand that their "most important asset walks out the door every night."[47]

The importance of having the right people is accentuated in human-capital-intensive industries. If, for instance, a key resource in a firm's industry is access to oilfields, it doesn't have the same concern about human resources as a firm whose key resource is access to scientific knowledge. Oil fields can't quit and jump to a competitor, demand higher wages, reject authority, lose motivation, or become dissatisfied with management and coworkers.[48] Consequently, firms in human-capital-intensive industries must develop strategies to reduce the risk of losing the human capital. Besides fostering job satisfaction, companies can develop firm-specific knowledge that's less transferable to other firms. Profit-sharing initiatives encourage valuable people to stay with an employer because they have a stake in any value that they help to create. Adjusting organization

Many companies focus on staffing cuts because employees represent their largest expense. Although stock markets often react positively to such moves, firms that downsize often experience long-term performance declines.

structure to eliminate authoritative and mechanistic processes and to accommodate more egalitarian and participative models reduces turnover.[49]

Rewards   Although rewards are technically the function of a system, we discuss them in this section because of their obvious relationship to people. An old management adage is *you get what you measure.* In reality, however, this proposition may need to be altered slightly: In the real workplace, it seems that what gets done is that which is rewarded.[50] Some experts grant that although organizational culture may be difficult to change, **reward systems**, which determine the compensation and promotion of an organization's employees, express and reinforce the values and expectations embedded in its culture.[51] Thus, any strategist who wants to get things done must think and act flexibly with regard to compensation and align rewards not only with strategy, but also with other implementation levers.

> **reward system**   Bases on which employees are compensated and promoted.

The Components of the Reward System   Reward systems have two components:

1. Performance evaluation and feedback

2. Compensation, which can consist of salary, bonuses, stock, stock options, promotions, and even such perquisites as cars and coveted office spaces

Single-business firms usually have one reward system, although the compensation component will probably vary by functional area. Salespeople, for instance, will have incentives based on sales growth, particularly profitable sales growth; whereas employees in production and procurement will have incentives based on quality, cost control, and customer service. Again, rewards are designed to encourage achievement of the organization's strategic objectives, and neither rewards nor penalties apply to performance that's unrelated to those objectives.

Rewards as a Form of Control   Like structure, systems, and processes, rewards also serve as a form of control. Rewards necessarily require that performance and behavior targets be stipulated, but their control function can take one of two forms: outcome controls or behavioral controls.

Outcome Controls   **Outcome controls** monitor and reward individuals and groups based on whether a measurable goal has been achieved. Such controls are generally preferable when just one or two performance measures (say, return on investment or return on assets) are good gauges of a business's health. Outcome controls are effective when there's little external interference between managerial decision-making and business performance. It also helps if little or no coordination with other business units is required, because each unit's people will be seeking to maximize their performance on the targeted measure. Because of this, outcome controls often provide a disincentive for cross-unit collaboration.

> **outcome controls**   Practice of tying rewards to narrowly defined financial criteria.

Behavioral Controls   **Behavioral controls** involve the direct evaluation of managerial decision-making, not of the results of managerial decisions. Behavioral controls tie rewards to a broader range of criteria, such as those identified in the balanced scorecard. Behavioral controls and commensurate rewards are typically more appropriate when many external and internal factors can affect the relationship between a manager's decisions and organizational performance. They're also appropriate when managers must coordinate resources and capabilities across different business units.

> **behavioral controls**   Practice of tying rewards to criteria other than simply financial performance, such as those broadly identified in the balanced scorecard.

Compensation in the Diversified Firm   Although diversified firms may rely on a single reward system for all business units, reward systems usually vary in order to reflect both overall corporate strategy and the competitive environment and strategy of each business unit. A diversified company like GE, which owns several unrelated businesses, achieves the best results by linking the pay of division managers to the performance of the units that they manage. On the business-unit level, therefore, outcome-based controls and reward systems are aligned with both corporate strategy and organization structure.

However, in a diversified firm that expects divisions to share resources and otherwise cross-subsidize each other, the same sort of compensation would provide *disincentives* for resource sharing. Division managers who are paid solely on the basis of business-unit performance, for instance, might reasonably conclude that it's not in their best interest to subsidize other divisions because doing so may jeopardize their own units' performance and, therefore, their pay.

Conversely, a diversified firm that's trying to generate synergies across business units can increase the likelihood of desired outcomes by linking unit managers' rewards to actual decisions and other balanced-scorecard criteria rather than to individual unit performance.[52] To encourage managers to recognize their own stakes in organizational prospects, rewards often include stock-based incentives or bonuses based on firmwide performance.

To further illustrate how reward systems can affect strategy implementation, let's consider the ways in which incentive systems can impact the realization of postmerger synergies. Many mergers are driven by the belief that two companies can generate net new revenue if they're combined in one firm. But what if compensation systems don't reward employees for sharing knowledge and resources? Obviously, synergies probably won't materialize. Mergers between commercial and investment banks, for instance, are often hampered by incongruent incentive systems.[53] Key employees of commercial banks are typically rewarded for managing relationships, whereas investment bankers are rewarded for doing deals. Paying bankers to do deals is generally at odds with the need for commercial banks to minimize risk and retain customers. Alternatively, investment bankers generally earn bigger bonuses on larger and higher-risk deals.

Contingency Framework for Analyzing Pay People are an essential element in strategy execution, but the employment relationship with them can vary by context, which is typically a function of firm strategy. Some organizations view their relationships with employees as passive and transactional, while others view them as enduring or family-like. On a second dimension, the employees themselves may have a weak or highly committed relationship with their employer. Taken together, these factors have been shown to play out in different compensation profiles, as summarized in Exhibit 11.15.[54]

These characterizations are intended to give you an idea of how compensation can take on different flavors, depending on the employer-employee relationships. Obviously, there will be many exceptions to the examples in this typology but it at least gives you a way to

Exhibit 11.15 Employer/Employee Relationship Matrix

	Low	High
High Employer transactional relationship	High Pay—Low Commitment • Hired Guns—Investment Bankers	High Pay—High Commitment • Cultlike—Google
Low	Low Pay—Low Commitment • Workers as Commodity • Employers of Migrant Laborers	Low Pay—High Commitment • Family—Starbucks

Employee Relations

Exhibit 11.16   Pay Philosophies at Medtronic and AES

Stated Pay Objectives at Medtronic and AES	
Medtronic	**AES**
• Support objectives and increased complexity of business • Minimize increases in fixed costs • Emphasize performance through variable pay and stock • Competitiveness aligned with financial performance: 50th percentile performance paid at 50th percentile of market, 75th percentile performance paid at 75th percentile of market	• Our guiding principles are to act with integrity, treat people fairly, have fun, and be involved in projects that provide social benefits. This means that we will: • Help AES attract self-motivated, dependable people who want to keep learning new things • Hire people who really like the place and believe in the AES system • Pay what others are paid both inside and outside AES, but hire people who are willing to take less to join AES • Use teams of employees and managers to manage the compensation system • Make all employees stockholders

think about the employee-employer relationships, as it relates to compensation. The best way to see how these objectives play out is to look at examples of statements of pay practices by such firms as Medtronic, a medical device manufacturer, and AES, a global energy company, shown in Exhibit 11.16. [55]

Rewarding A, While Hoping for B   We can't conclude this discussion of rewards without reminding you of the classic article by Steven Kerr titled "On the folly of rewarding A, while hoping for B."[56] This section is more of a reminder than a toolkit item for you, but we hope that you take it to heart. The essential message is that organizations often have a strategy to achieve certain objectives, but then set out a reward system and incentivize behaviors that work at odds to that strategy. The balanced scorecard, by the way, is one tool that can help firms avoid these all-too-common problems. Some of the common management follies are summarized in Exhibit 11.17.[57]

Exhibit 11.17   Common Management Follies with Regard to Reward Systems

We Hope For . . .	But We Reward For . . .
Long-term growth; environmental responsibility	Quarterly earnings
Teamwork	Individual effort
Setting challenging "stretch" objectives	Achieving goals; "making the numbers"
Downsizing; rightsizing; delayering; restructuring	Adding staff; adding budget; adding Hay points
Commitment to total quality	Shipping on schedule, even with defects
Candor; surfacing bad news early	Reporting good news, whether it's true or not; agreeing with the boss, whether or not (s)he's right

Strategic Leadership and Strategy Implementation

Strategic leadership plays two critical roles in successful strategy implementation. We're going to highlight them here so that you can incorporate them into your assessment of a strategy's feasibility and include them in your implementation plans. Specifically, strategic leadership is responsible for:

- Making substantive implementation lever and resource-allocation decisions
- Communicating the strategy to key stakeholders

Let's take a closer look at both of these roles.

DECISIONS ABOUT LEVERS

We hope that it is obvious to you that the choices about which levers to employ and when to employ them do not appear out of thin air as a result of executive action (and sometimes inaction or neglect). The examples you have seen in this chapter, and in other parts of the text, have emphasized the importance of aligning strategy with the appropriate implementation levers. For instance, the executives at HUI are very careful to preserve the organization's deep culture of innovation and the unique levers that reinforce this culture and, ultimately, the firm's strategy and competitive advantage. New ventures by HUI are also launched with all of these key supporting implementation levers in place.

Like strategy-formulation decisions, decisions about levers involve important tradeoffs regarding what the firm will and will not do. Misalignment between the levers and the strategy can arise because management has made poor choices about which levers to employ, is employing too simple or too complex a repertoire of levers for the given situation, or the organization or its competitive environment has changed such that the levers need to be changed but have not been. For example, a firm that is small, experiencing the growth stage of its respective arena, and facing little direct competition may be well served by a functional structure, relatively little bureaucracy, and an incentive system that emphasizes growth and innovation. However, as the firm grows, its operations typically become more complex, including diversification into new product and geographic markets. Similarly, it is likely that it will face growing competition and cost pressures. Top management should probably be in the process of changing the implementation levers to favor some form of multibusiness or matrix structure and a compensation system that rewards financial accountability and not just growth. Absent such important management choices about which levers to employ, the firm may lose its once-strong competitive foothold.

DECISIONS ABOUT RESOURCE ALLOCATION

A good strategy guides managers in making decisions about the allocation of resources. Again, a good strategy tells managers what the firm should and shouldn't be doing, and thus helps them decide on important tradeoffs—an extremely important function because an organization that tries to be all things to all people by investing equally in every value-chain activity is doomed to mediocrity at best. Top managers must allocate resources in ways that are consistent with the firm's strategy and make the tradeoffs that this entails. Unfortunately, internal interests—whether political, self-serving, or misguided—can sabotage effective resource allocation decisions and undermine even well-crafted strategies.

Both the misallocation of resources and the failure to make hard investment choices often result from a firm basing its resource allocation on that of its competitors. As a result, not only does the firm become less distinctive from a competitive standpoint, but many of the key players in an industry start to look like clones of one another.

Let's look at the ways in which different carriers in the airline industry manage—and don't manage—certain tradeoffs.[58] Exhibit 11.18 summarizes the key areas in which commercial airlines make strategic resource allocation decisions (if you look back at the example of [yellow tail] wine in Chapter 6, you will see a similar picture of the importance of resource allocation tradeoff choices in the wine industry).[59]

As you can see, in the airline industry, the key resource allocation choices are numerous and range from price for tickets to frequent departure times. Recall that these lines are not meant to depict trends but rather the different patterns of resource allocation choices made by the respective parties. What's striking is the fact that most major airlines seem to be mimicking each other's resource allocation decisions. Two exceptions are Southwest and JetBlue, which, as you can tell from their resource allocation decisions, are following decidedly different strategies. Some have even suggested that for Southwest, with its extensive network of short routes and frequent departures, the greatest competition actually comes from customers' automobiles! JetBlue's management committed itself to allocation decisions that would support the airline's overarching strategy, even when tempted with less expensive options. As a low-cost airline, for instance, JetBlue decided that it needed a modern fleet of new, fuel-efficient aircraft. Used aircraft would have been significantly cheaper (but only in the short run), and management could have rationalized the savings of precious startup capital. Such a shortcut, however, would have been inconsistent with the specific low-cost economic logic of the firm's strategy.

The point to be made here—and which we've made throughout this book—is that competitive advantage goes to those firms who develop unique advantages. Most of the time, such firms develop unique advantages because they make independent resource allocation decisions instead of mimicking those of everybody else in the industry. Remember, too, that resources and capabilities—especially those that are likely to distinguish a firm from its competitors—are usually scarce. Scarcity takes many forms; a firm, for example, may have a team of brilliant researchers who can only work on so many projects for so many hours in a week. Managers, therefore, must revisit their strategy diamond and make at least two

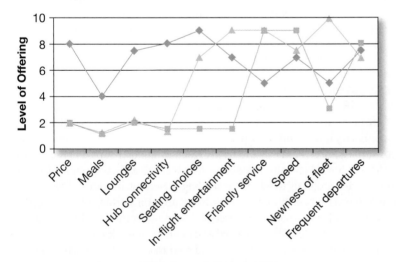

Exhibit 11.18 Resource Allocation Decisions in the Airline Industry

difficult decisions when allocating the firm's resources and capabilities: (1) what to direct at each arena and (2) what to direct to each differentiator.

One additional point bears mention here. You are already aware, from earlier chapters, of how well Intel reoriented its resource allocation to favor a much more profitable and successful computer chip—one that essentially wrote the winning ticket for Intel. What you might not know is that it took another year for Intel to figure out that it was still spending over a billion dollars of R&D investment on the discontinued product! This is a poignant reminder that if strategy is about what you do and don't do, you still need the systems and processes in place to stop doing the things you should not be doing.

COMMUNICATING WITH KEY STAKEHOLDERS ABOUT STRATEGY

From the outset, we've emphasized the interdependence of strategy formulation and implementation. In many ways, because suppliers, customers, and an organization's own managers will ultimately contribute to the strategy's success or failure, the process of communicating with stakeholders about strategy begins in the strategy formulation process itself. It is, therefore, a strategic leadership function.

In performing this strategic leadership role, managers must evaluate both the need and the necessary tactics for persuasively communicating a strategy in four different directions: *upward*, *downward*, *across*, and *outward*.[60]

Communicating Upward   Increasingly, firms rely on bottom-up innovation processes that encourage and empower middle-level and division managers to take ownership of strategy formulation and propose new strategies. Such is particularly the case at highly diversified firms, but even fairly focused firms such as HUI endorse bottom-up processes. Communicating upward means that someone or some group has championed the strategy internally and has succeeded in convincing top management of its merits and feasibility.

Communicating Downward   Communicating downward means enlisting the support of the people who'll be needed to implement the strategy. Too often, managers undertake this task only after a strategy has been set in stone, thereby running the risk of undermining both the strategy and any culture of trust and cooperation that may have existed previously. Starting on the communication process early is the best way to identify and surmount obstacles, and it usually ensures that a management team is working with a common purpose and intensity that will be important when it's time to implement the strategy.

Communicating Across and Outward   The need to communicate across and outward reflects the fact that implementation of a strategy will probably require cooperation from other units of the firm (*across*) and from key external stakeholders, such as material and capital providers, complementors, and customers (*outward*). Internally, for example, the strategy may call for raw materials or services to be provided by another subsidiary; perhaps it depends on sales leads from other units. Recall, for instance, our earlier example of Emageon. Emageon couldn't get hospitals to adopt the leading-edge visualization software that was produced and sold by one subsidiary until its hardware division started cross-selling the software as well. This internal coordination required a champion from the software side to convince managers on the hardware side of the need and benefits of working together.

External constituencies play a comparable role, and a strategy must similarly be communicated to them. Managers can use stakeholder analysis to identify these key players and determine whether suppliers, customers, complementors, and relevant regulatory agencies support the firm's strategy. In the early 1990s, for instance, when IBM first launched its ThinkPad, the product was an unexpected hit with customers. The launch,

IBM's ThinkPad, launched in the early 1990s, was an unexpected hit. However, IBM couldn't produce ThinkPads fast enough to keep up with demand, so potential sales suffered.

however, was so successful that IBM's key component suppliers couldn't keep up with IBM's demand, thus costing the company sales on what should have been an even more profitable rollout.

The Three Cs of Strategy Communication   Just as communicating the strategy to stakeholders is a key factor in successful strategy implementation, so, too, is having the right people in place to communicate it. As one researcher puts it, "The strategy champion must have three Cs—contacts, cultural understanding, and credibility."[61]

Contacts   Contacts are key because implementing a strategy—particularly one that's dynamic and innovative—often entails some back-channel maneuvering. 3M's PostIt notes, for instance, made it to market only because an enterprising manager convinced internal people to supply clerical and other support staff with experimental versions of the product as a means of demonstrating that there was actually a market.

Cultural Understanding   Cultural understanding refers to the fact that the people communicating the strategy need to have a rich familiarity with the organization's culture, policies, and procedures. In an earlier example on BGI, you saw how culture provides a screen for recruitment, retention, and promotion. It may also provide strategy communicators with insights into internal and external network dependencies that may not be obvious but that nonetheless will be essential to the effort to sell across and outward.

Credibility   Needless to say, it helps if strategy communicators are respected by management, peers, and staff, all of whom expect them to present ideas with a good chance of success. Credibility is based on perceptions of trustworthiness, reliability, and integrity. Yet studies indicate that many employees just don't believe or trust their organizational leaders. According to Bruce Katcher, president of Discovery Surveys, a Massachusetts–based firm specializing in employee opinion and customer satisfaction surveys and focus groups, just 53 percent "of employees believe the information they receive from senior management."[62] He bases the figure on a review of the company's database of 30,000 respondents from forty-four international companies. Closing the credibility gap can be helped by developing regular—at least annual—processes to gauge real employee perceptions about their managers' level of leadership as well as other issues, including morale, obstacles to higher performance, pet peeves, or key irritants. Managers must then pay attention to the findings and demonstrate real commitment to act on them. When actions speak louder than words, employees will have more reason to trust those above them.

Implementation Levers in Global Firms and Dynamic Contexts

As we've observed throughout this text, firms are increasingly facing challenges that are both global and dynamic in nature. In this section, we'll show how implementation levers can be adapted to these particularly important contingencies. We'll also link strategy implementation explicitly to strategy formulation through the staging component of the strategy diamond model.

IMPLEMENTATION SOLUTIONS FOR GLOBAL FIRMS

As you learned in Chapter 8, two critical needs confront firms in implementing global strategies: the need for *efficiency* and the need for *local responsiveness*.[63] In this section, we want to stress their role in terms of implementation levers and their function in executing globalization strategies. Paralleling the strategy research on global strategy, research has found that firms deeply involved in international business adopt one of four structural forms in the effort to manage the tension between the need for efficiency and the need for local responsiveness.[64] As we'll see, most of these forms place more emphasis on one or the other of these two competing forces and build on the general understanding of structure you have amassed thus far from this chapter. These four structural solutions accommodate the four international strategy configurations discussed in Chapter 8.

Emphasize Local Responsiveness
This structural solution resembles a decentralized federation. Assets and resources are decentralized, and foreign offices are given the authority to respond to local needs when they differ from those of the home market. Control and coordination are managed primarily through the interactions of home-office corporate executives and overseas executives, who are usually home-country managers who've been dispatched to run foreign offices.

From the perspective of top management, the corporation is a portfolio of relatively independent businesses located around the globe. SAP, for example, adhered to this model for much of the 1990s, until it determined that it fostered costly duplications of effort across markets and inadequate coordination among units across borders. Indeed, because SAP's customers were global firms with better coordination and integration than SAP itself, many of them managed to get SAP to compete against itself for new system sales. Nestlé, for instance, would get bids from SAP U.S. and SAP U.K. without informing either party that they were actually bidding against one another.

Emphasize Global Efficiencies with Some Local Advantages
The structure supporting this tradeoff reveals an organization that is a coordinated group of federations over which more administrative control is exerted by home-country headquarters. For reasons of both efficiency and strategy, firms like SAP typically evolve into this structure. SAP itself, for example, adopted it at the end of the 1990s when it realized that its customers were taking advantage of its Balkans-like structure.

Under this model, although resources, assets, and responsibilities are delegated to foreign offices, additional control—usually in the form of more formal management systems, such as centralized planning and budgeting—is exercised centrally. This control facilitates global account management, so that the quality and price of services provided to global clients can be made uniform. As a rule, top management regards overseas operations as appendages to the domestic firm. Local units, therefore, are highly dependent on home-office coordination of resource allocation, knowledge sharing, and decision approval.

Emphasize Global Efficiencies   Ideally, firms adopting this configuration have a structure that is based on the centralization of assets, resources, and responsibilities. Foreign offices are used to access customers, but demand is filled by centralized production. This form of organization was pioneered by firms such as Ford, which exported standardized products around the globe, and was popular among Japanese companies undertaking globalization in the 1970s and 1980s. The global configuration affords much less autonomy to foreign offices or subsidiaries than the two preceding models. Operational control is tight and most decisions centralized. Top management views foreign operations as pipelines for distributing products to a global, but homogeneous, marketplace.

Seek to Exploit Local Advantages and Global Efficiencies   Each of the three preceding organizational models responds in a different strategic fashion to the challenge of balancing the two fundamental demands of managing across borders. The global efficiencies configuration, for example, is clearly designed to achieve maximum efficiencies, largely through scale economies derived from centralized production. Because decisions and resources are controlled locally, the first form is well-suited to respond to local needs. The second model attempts to meet local needs while retaining central control. This fourth configuration is designed to accommodate both demands.

This configuration was designed to achieve not only efficiency and local responsiveness but innovation, as well. Its structural characteristics enable firms—at least those that are able to manage it—to achieve multidimensional strategic objectives. The key functions in this multidimensional strategy are *dispersion, specialization,* and *interdependence.* Resources and capabilities are dispersed to local units, and a networked control system is designed to achieve both coordination and cooperation. Because geographically dispersed organizational units are strategically interdependent, large flows of products, resources, and personnel, as well as value-chain activities, are channeled through the structure. To some extent, McDonald's, which features both standard and locally tailored menu items at outlets around the globe, depends on this structure. The structure fits with McDonald's transnational strategy and affords the global food company greater flexibility in adapting to local tastes while enabling it at the same time to exploit the global economies of scale that it enjoys by virtue of its size and geographic breadth.

People and Rewards Solutions in Global Firms   As firms expand globally, they face the critical issue of how to find and reward managers. On the one hand, using local managers can enhance a firm's understanding of local markets. On the other hand, using home-country managers strengthens the relationship between the foreign subsidiary and the parent company.

Naturally, operating subsidiaries in culturally distant locations gives rise to a great deal of uncertainty. Research suggests that a company's policy for finding and rewarding foreign managerial staff can have a significant bearing on its performance. For instance, multinationals that use overseas management positions as a training ground for future executives of the parent significantly outperform those that allow senior managers to ascend to the top ranks without spending time in overseas posts.[65]

The performance of foreign subsidiaries may be affected when parent-country nationals, or expatriates, are sent to manage them. When multinationals have subsidiaries in culturally distant locations (as opposed to those that are just geographically distant), costs and risks increase because of a so-called *information asymmetry* problem: Onsite overseas information may not be readily available to the parent company.[66] When a multinational relies more on parent-country nationals than local managers, the information asymmetry problem gradually diminishes: As subsidiaries gain experience in conducting transactions with home-country nationals, there's less need for deploying expatriates. Indeed, research shows that when a multinational firm staffs a culturally distant foreign subsidiary with parent-country managers, it improves subsidiary performance, largely because it's easier to exercise cultural control and enhances the transfer of firm-specific resources from the parent to the subsidiary.[67]

Apparently, however, this positive effect decreases over time because host-country nationals not only acquire knowledge and skills from expatriate managers, but also adopt the shared values of the parent company. Not surprisingly, given the high cost of managing an expatriate workforce (not to mention the high expatriate failure rate), reliance on expatriates is declining.

IMPLEMENTATION LEVERS IN DYNAMIC CONTEXTS

We observed early in this text that, because competitive pressures are compounded in dynamic, "high-velocity" industries, companies' strategies necessarily grow more complex. Moreover, the difficulties in *implementing* strategies in such industries are an order of magnitude more challenging than those of implementing strategies in relatively stable industries. As we've also seen, the task is becoming even more complex and difficult because dynamic markets are increasingly becoming global markets as well. Consider, for instance, the threat to a firm in a global industry that needs to develop or adopt a radically new technology in order to survive industry evolution. In Chapter 4 we described a special problem known as the innovator's dilemma—a situation where new entrants innovate in low-end, unattractive segments of the market that leaders tend to overlook because margins are apparently lower there, only to have those new entrants migrate into the more profitable segments with lower cost structures and increasingly popular products.[68] Firms have developed several structural adaptations to deal with the problems of implementing strategies in dynamic contexts, and in this section, we'll examine two of the most effective adaptations: the *ambidextrous organization* and the use of *patching* among diversified firms.

The Ambidextrous Organization
Even a firm that's successful at executing a strategy can face a problem as its industry becomes well-established: In particular, it's difficult to retain market leadership when a new disruptive technology (product or process) is pioneered and introduced by another firm. The incumbent also faces a disadvantage because it invests in order to sustain an advantage, not (like the new entrant) to destroy one.

Incremental Change Versus Radical Innovation: Revisiting the Innovator's Dilemma
This is the essence of the innovator's dilemma, and despite leaders who are perfectly capable of recognizing the problem, it often persists because of structural deficiencies among many organizations. When, for example, one division of a leading incumbent tries to pioneer its own version of disruptive technology, the rest of the organization may resist. Why? Perhaps because the status quo is perceived to be in the best interests of managers and employees. Or perhaps submerged but strong facets of the organizational culture favor the continued influence of large, established divisions.

Granted, many firms are skilled at introducing refinements into their current product lines. Usually such organizations don't resist moderate innovation because it's perceived as a means of sustaining or improving current competitive positions. At the same time, however, the same firms may face monumental obstacles when they try to introduce *radical* changes or offer products that require disruptive technologies. In that case, of course, they're faced with a paradoxical problem: To flourish in the long run, they must exploit existing advantages and explore innovations that will probably alter the industry significantly in the future. In other words, if a firm wants to sustain long-term competitiveness in a dynamic context (and most, of course, do), it must learn to integrate both incremental changes and radical innovations.

The **ambidextrous structure** is one response to this problem.[69] In fact, the idea evolved from studies of how firms dealt with the problem of simultaneously integrating two types of innovations:

- *Incremental innovations* are those that make small improvements in existing products and operations and that are aimed at existing customers.

- *Discontinuous innovations* are those that make radical advances that may alter the basis of competition in an industry and that are aimed at new customers.[70]

Four Structures for Handling Innovation   Researchers identified four basic forms of organization among the companies studied:

- A functional form in which innovation efforts are completely integrated into an existing organization structure.

- A cross-functional or matrix-style form in which groups of people from established organizational divisions are formed to work outside the functional hierarchy.

- A form in which teams or units, though nominally independent and working outside the established hierarchy, are limited in their independence and relatively unsupported by the organizational hierarchy.

- An "ambidextrous" form in which project teams focusing on radical improvements are organized as structurally independent units and encouraged to develop their own structures, systems, and processes. As you can see in Exhibit 11.19, these semiautonomous units may be integrated into the organizational hierarchy only at the senior-management level.[71]

Researchers found that the ambidextrous structure was quite effective in facilitating the integration of radical innovations; 93 percent of radical innovations were launched by firms characterized as ambidextrous. Firms that pursued radical innovation through autonomous units bound to the organizational hierarchy only through senior management had very high success rates for launching new products or operations. Conversely, firms trying to achieve radical innovation within the existing corporate hierarchy found that their efforts were often stymied. Finally, the ambidextrous form also fostered innovations that were initiated under some other organizational form and only later moved into an ambidextrous structure.

Among other things, these findings reveal just how difficult it is for firms to compete in dynamic industry environments that require not only constant incremental innovations, but periodic radical innovations as well. Ambidexterity allows for the simultaneous maintenance of the status quo (incremental business improvements made through conventional organizational units) and proactive preparation for future industry-wide alterations (radical innovation made through units that are unencumbered by existing organizational practices and allowed to implement strategies consistent with the requirements of competitive conditions).

Diversified Firms in Dynamic Markets: Patching   A multidivisional firm

operating in diverse product markets can create new synergies by actively managing the structure of its corporate portfolio through a process known as *patching*. **Patching** is the process of regularly remapping businesses in accordance with changing market conditions

ambidextrous structure
Organizational structure for dynamic contexts in which project teams are organized as structurally independent units and encouraged to develop their own structures, systems, and processes.

patching   Process of remapping businesses in accordance with changing market conditions and restitches them into new internal business structures.

Exhibit 11.19   The Ambidextrous Organization

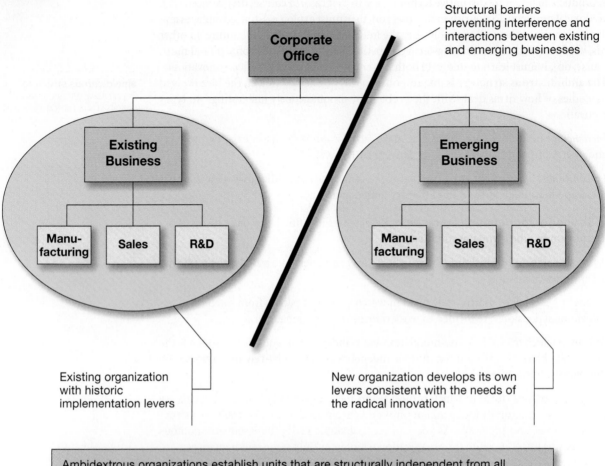

Ambidextrous organizations establish units that are structurally independent from all other units. The emerging business units are to develop their own structures, processes, systems, cultures, strategies, etc. They are only integrated into the mother organization at the level of senior management.

and restitching them into new internal business structures.[72] It can mean combining, splitting, or transferring units or exiting businesses or adding new ones. Patching is particularly effective in dynamic markets because it enables managers to exploit the best business opportunities while bypassing less promising ones. However, as you can imagine, patching is very complex to manage and requires a culture and workforce that is action-oriented and flexible, such as the one described at BGI.

Here's an example of patching at work. Originally, Hewlett-Packard's laser-printing business was a small startup operation with only modest growth expectations. Shortly after launch, however, sales climbed to ten times the expected level (100,000 units per month instead of the forecasted 10,000). As new applications for related technologies, such as the ink-jet printer, emerged, management stripped them away from the laser-printer business and patched them onto other business units. This technique of patching units not only allowed managers in the laser-printer unit to focus on their core growth business but ensconced the ink-jet business in a unit where it could get the support it needed to get off the ground, develop into a growth business, and become a major source of cash flow. In this case, patching required the transfer not only of a business but of related resources and personnel as well.

With patching, therefore, structure is intentionally altered so that managers can better maintain focus on core and growth businesses while seeding and protecting new opportunities. Because it requires managers to view organizational structure as flexible and contingent, they tend not to fret about getting a new structure exactly right. In addition, although patching is a proactive tool, it usually involves relatively small and incremental changes. Change, however, is ongoing, as managers constantly search for new combinations. To make patching work, firms need to adjust internal systems so that when a business is detached from one division and restitched elsewhere, companywide systems don't require extensive modification. Compensation systems, for instance, need to be fairly consistent across organizational borders.

Finally, we should note some key differences between patching and the ambidextrous organizational structure. Patching is a tool that helps diversified firms operate in multiple product or geographic markets. It doesn't involve radical technologies, but rather leverages either existing businesses or new but related businesses. It works when systems are consistent across the organization. In contrast, the ambidextrous organization is designed to enable radically new businesses to develop unencumbered by existing structures and processes.

LINKING STRATEGY IMPLEMENTATION TO STAGING

Before wrapping up this chapter, we'd like to underscore the relationship between implementation levers and a specific facet of strategy formulation. Recall that the staging element of the strategy diamond refers to the timing and pacing of strategic moves. ◆ Staging decisions typically depend on available resources—resources that include structures, systems and processes, and people and rewards. From the opening vignette on HUI, you gained some insight into how the firm coupled a unique resource base—its knowledge and intellectual property relating to Teflon—with the implementation levers necessary to launch new and highly innovative ventures. Thus, management of the implementation process should anticipate the staging objectives of the strategy.

Staging
&
Pacing

More generally, it would be a rare case in which a change in strategy did not have implications for implementation. Consider, for instance, a firm that's considering expansion into foreign markets. It can achieve this strategic goal through a variety of vehicles, including exporting, alliances or acquisitions, and the establishment of foreign offices from which to conduct value-chain activities. If international staging is an explicit component of the firm's strategy, then managers must start modifying other implementation levers. In other words, they must determine whether the firm has the appropriate structure, systems, human capital, expertise, and culture to support its evolution into a global competitor. If, for example, the vehicle of choice calls for alliances or acquisitions, then the related skills and capabilities must be acquired as well. If the vehicle is exporting, the firm will need to acquire people who understand customer demands and distribution channels in foreign markets.

Summary of Challenges

1. *Outline the interdependence between strategy formulation and implementation.* Strategy formulation and implementation are interrelated. The introductory section of the chapter showed you the various ways in which formulation and implementation are interrelated and provided you with an overarching model for thinking about how to translate an abstract strategy into concrete action. You also learned that the relationship between formulation and implementation is not necessarily a linear one. In some cases, the iterative evolution of strategy is advantageous and desirable. The section closed with a discussion of why implementation efforts can and often do fail. Organizational culture can be one barrier to (or facilitator of) effective strategy execution and strategic change.

2. *Demonstrate how to use organizational structure as a strategy implementation lever.* Organizational structure exists to perform two essential functions within the organization: ensuring control and coordinating the efforts of managers and employees. As control and coordination become more difficult, firms generally modify their structure to improve control and coordination. Popular forms of organizing firm structure include the functional, divisional, matrix, and network forms. The structure chosen should be consistent with the firm's strategy. For instance, the more diversified the firm, the more the structure will need to accommodate coordination. The more focused the firm is in a single business, or in several unrelated businesses, the more the structure should emphasize control.

3. *Illustrate the use of systems and processes as strategy implementation levers.* Formal processes and procedures used by a firm should support the execution of strategy. Information systems are the most common systems, but all systems should be considered for their alignment with strategy (and other implementation levers). For instance, management control, performance and rewards, budgeting, quality, planning, distribution, client management, and resource allocation are all managed by systems. Systems can affect what people pay attention to and what information they have access to.

4. *Identify the roles of people and rewards as implementation levers.* For a strategy to succeed, a firm needs the right people with the right experiences and competencies. As a result, recruitment, selection, and training are critical to strategy implementation. Because human resources, or staffing issues, are often large sources of operating costs, too much focus may be placed on reducing the staffing costs. Investments in human resource systems have positive effects on multiple dimensions of firm performance. The importance of people is even more important in high-human-capital industries. Rewards are an important implementation lever. They reflect the degree to which a firm employs outcome versus behavioral controls. Rewards are composed of both performance evaluation and feedback and incentives, such as compensation and promotion. Ultimately, rewards enable the firm to get the right people to do the right things for the firm, such that it can achieve its goals and objectives.

5. *Explain the dual roles that strategic leadership plays in strategy implementation.* This section showed you that strategy implementation is much more than simply putting the right levers into place. The levers are important, but they must also be complemented by strategic leadership actions. The two actions we emphasized were decisions about resource allocation and levers and communicating the strategy to stakeholders. The resources and capabilities that differentiate a firm from its competitors are by definition scarce. Strategic leadership shows its mettle by making difficult tradeoffs in terms of the levers chosen and when and where not to deploy scarce resources. Communicating the strategy to stakeholders requires that managers promote and get strategic buy-in from top management, lower-level workers, other key organizational units; and external stakeholders, such as suppliers, customers, and complementors.

6. *Describe how global and dynamic contexts affect the use of implementation levers.* As a firm becomes more global, it faces contradictory needs for efficiency and local responsiveness. Depending on the primacy of these two demands, four configurations are possible. The most complex configuration aims to simultaneously achieve global efficiency and maximum local responsiveness. As in global contexts, coordination and control are made more difficult in dynamic contexts. In addition, being able to protect potentially radical innovations can be accommodated through the ambidextrous structure. Diversified firms in high-velocity environments can increase the likelihood of synergies by using patching techniques, which essentially assumes that the organizational structure is flexible and allows for the constant reconfiguration of business units. This enables managers to remain focused on high-volume businesses by placing high-potential-growth businesses in units that can better exploit these opportunities. This section closed by showing you how to link formulation and implementation through the staging component of the strategy diamond.

Review Questions

1. What is strategy implementation?

2. How are formulation and implementation related?

3. What are the basic forms of organizational structure? When is each appropriate?

4. What are some common systems and processes that are relevant to strategy implementation?

5. How are people relevant to strategy formulation and implementation?

6. How can rewards affect strategy?

7. What are the roles of strategic leadership in successful strategy implementation?

8. How does globalization affect organization structure?

9. What are organizational solutions to the problems caused by dynamic environments?

10. What component of the strategy diamond maps most closely to issues related to strategy implementation?

Experiential Activities

Group Exercises

1. Apply the concepts of strategy formulation and implementation to your college experience. What was your objective in going to college? When did your strategy for achieving this objective emerge? Has it ever changed? How would you adapt the implementation levers and strategic leadership roles to evaluate how well you have implemented your strategy? What is your overall personal evaluation?

2. Refer to the opening case on HUI. Assume that, for reasons of estate planning, the owners decided to take the company public through an IPO. What would be the effect on the firm's strategy and implementation practices if this were to happen? What, if anything, would need to change?

Ethical Debates

1. As part of a corporate restructuring, your analysis helps you conclude that you have rather extensive redundancy in corporate finance and accounting positions. Management concludes that through consolidation, cross training, and other shifts in responsibility, you could do the same work with 30 percent fewer staff. How do you downsize these jobs in the next twelve months without damaging morale of the surviving employees and while trying to treat the terminated employees in a fair manner?

2. Your company acquires another company in China. When you start to transform the organizational structure to that commonly used by your company at home and in other countries, you encounter significant resistance from local management. They claim that this new structure will never work in China. What do you do?

How Would YOU DO THAT?

1. In the box entitled "How Would *You* Do That? 11.1," you learned how SAP America responded to performance problems primarily through changes in strategy implementation. Find one or two firms that were once high flyers but that have recently fallen on hard times. Are these hard times primarily a function of a flawed strategy, flawed strategy implementation, or both? Using SAP as an example, what changes would you suggest in terms of implementation?

2. The example of the NUWC in the box entitled "How Would *You* Do That? 11.1" demonstrated the strategy mapping process and how to develop a balanced scorecard. Review Exhibits 11.12 and 11.13 and generate suggestions for specific objectives, measures, targets, and initiatives that would complete NUWC's use of the scorecard. If you prefer using the scorecard with a for-profit firm then apply the framework from scratch to a firm of your choosing.

Go on to see How Would You Do That at http://www.prenhall.com/ carpenter&sanders

Endnotes

1. http://www.huimfg.com/aboutus_president.html

2. K. R. Andrews, *The Concept of Corporate Strategy* (Homewood, IL: Irwin, 1987); *The Strategy Execution Imperative: Leading Practices for Implementing Strategic Initiatives* (Corporate Executive Board, 2001); C. M. Christensen, "Making Strategy: Learning by Doing," *Harvard Business Review* 75:6 (1997), 141–156.

3. D. Hambrick and A. Cannella, "Strategy Implementation as Substance and Selling," *Academy of Management Executive* 3:4 (1989), 278–285.

4. M. Porter, "Know Your Place: How to Assess the Attractiveness of Your Industry and Your Company's Position in It," *Inc.*, September 1991, 90.

5. P. F. Drucker, *The Practice of Management* (New York: HarperCollins, 1954), 352–353.

6. R. Ruggles, "The State of the Notion: Knowledge Management in Practice," *California Management Review* 40 (1998), 82–83.

7. J. Pfeffer and R. I. Sutton, *The Knowing-Doing Gap* (Boston: Harvard Business School Press, 2000).

8. L. Gerstner, *Who Says Elephants Can't Dance?* (New York: HarperBusiness, 2002).

9. J. R. Kotter and J. L. Heskett, *Corporate Culture and Performance* (New York: Free Press, 1992); C. A. O'Reilly and J. A. Chatman, "Culture as Social Control: Corporations, Culture and Commitment," in B. M. Staw and L. L. Cummings, eds., *Research in Organizational Behavior* 18 (Greenwich, CT: JAI Press, 1996), 157–200; J. B. Sønrensen, "The Strength of Corporate Culture and the Reliability of Firm Performance," *Administrative Science Quarterly* 47 (2002), 70–91.

10. Kotter and Heskett, *Corporate Culture and Performance.*

11. Sønrensen, "The Strength of Corporate Culture and the Reliability of Firm Performance."

12. R. S. Burt, S. M. Gabbay, G. Holt, and P. Moran, "Contingent Organization as a Network Theory: The Culture Performance Contingency Function," *Acta Sociologica* 37 (1994), 345–370; Sønrensen, "The Strength of Corporate Culture and the Reliability of Firm Performance."

13. A. Slywotzky and D. Nadler, "The Strategy Is the Structure," *Harvard Business Review* 82:2 (2004), 16.

14. SAP Harvard Business School Case, SAP America 9-397-067, December 3, 1996.

15. SAP Annual General Shareholders' Meeting, Mannheim, Germany, May 3, 1997; SAP 1997–2003 Financial Reports (accessed on July 15, 2005),www.sap.com/company/investor/reports/pastfinancials/index.epx; Harvard Business School Case 9-397-067, SAP America, December 3, 1996; N. Boudette, "How a German Software Titan Missed the Internet Revolution," *Wall Street Journal*, January 18, 2000, A1.

16. Hambrick and Cannella, "Strategy Implementation as Substance and Selling," 278.

17. Hambrick and Cannella, "Strategy Implementation as Substance and Selling," 278.

18. A. Chandler, *Strategy and Structure* (Cambridge, MA: MIT Press, 1962).

19. R. L. Daft, *Management*, 6th ed. (New York: Southwestern, 2003).

20. L. G. Hrebiniak and W. Joyce, *Implementing Strategy* (New York: MacMillan, 1984).

21. Chandler, *Strategy and Structure.*

22. Slywotzky and Nadler, "The Strategy Is the Structure," 16.

23. R. A. Burgelman, "Fading Memories: A Process Theory of Strategic Business Exit in Dynamic Environments," *Administrative Science Quarterly* 39 (1994), 24–56.

24. www.platypustech.com (accessed July 15, 2005).

25. www.emageon.com (accessed July 15, 2005).

26. R. Cross, "The role of networks in organizational change," *McKinsey Quarterly*, Web Exclusive, April 2007; J. McGregor, "The office chart that really counts," *Business Week*, February 27, 2006, 48.

27. C. K. Bart and M. C. Baetz, "The Relationship Between Mission Statements and Firm Performance: An Exploratory Study," *Journal of Management Studies* 35:6 (1998), 823–853.

28. W. G. Sanders and M. A. Carpenter, "Strategic Satisficing? A Behavioral-Agency Perspective on Stock Repurchase Announcements," *Academy of Management Journal* 46 (2003), 160–178.

29. G. Reilly and R. Reilly, "Using a Measure Network to Understand and Deliver Value," *Journal of Cost Management* 14:6 (2000), 5–14; R. Kaplan and D. Norton, *The Strategy-Focused Organization* (Watertown, MA: Harvard Business School Press, 2001).

30. Adapted from R. Kaplan and D. Norton, *The Strategy-Focused Organization.*

31. "The Balanced Scorecard's Lessons for Managers," *Harvard Management Update*, October 2000, 4–5.

32. Adapted from R. Kaplan and D. Norton, *The Strategy-Focused Organization.*

33. Adapted from R. Kaplan and D. Norton, *The Strategy-Focused Organization.*

34. R. Simons, *Levers of Control: How Managers Use Innovative Control Systems* (Boston: Harvard Business School Press, 1995); M. J. Epstein and J. F. Manzoni, "The Balanced Scorecard & Tableau de Bord: A Global Perspective on Translating Strategy into Action," INSEAD Working Paper 97/63/ AC/SM (1997).

35. E. Schonfeld, "Baby Bills," *Business 2.0* 4:9 (2003), 76–84.

36. Adapted from G. Harrigan and R. Miller, "Managing Change Through an Aligned and Cascading Balanced Scorecard," *Perform* 2:2 (2003), 20–26.

37. Quote from BGI's head of human resources, Garret Bouton, in J. Pfeffer and R. I. Sutton, *The Knowing-Doing Gap*, 227.

38. J. Collins, "Level 5 Leadership," *Harvard Business Review* July–August (2001), 66–76.

39. J. Bradach, *Organizational Alignment: The 7-S Model* (Boston: Harvard Business School Publishing, 1996).

40. C. K. Prahalad and G. Hamel, "The Core Competence of the Corporation," *Harvard Business Review* 79:1 (1990), 1–14; R. Nelson and S. Winter, *An Evolutionary Theory of Economic Change* (Cambridge, MA: Harvard University Press, 1982); D. J. Teece, G. Pisano, and A. Shuen, "Dynamic Capabilities and Strategic Management," *Strategic Management Journal* 18 (1997), 509–534; K. M. Eisenhardt and J. A. Martin, "Dynamic Capabilities: What Are They?" *Strategic Management Journal* 21 (2000), 1105–1121.

41. B. Becker and B. Gerhart, "The Impact of Human Resource Management on Organizational Performance: Progress and Prospects," *Academy of Management Journal* 39 (1996), 779–802.

42. W. N. Davidson III, D. L. Worrell, and J. B. Fox, "Early Retirement Programs and Firm Performance," *Academy of Management Journal* 39 (1996), 970–985.

43. C. Chadwick, L. W. Hunter, and S. M. Walston, "The Effects of Downsizing Practices on Hospital Performance," *Strategic Management Journal* 25:5 (2004), 405–428.

44. M. A. Youndt, S. A. Snell, J. W. Dean Jr., and D. P. Lepak, "Human Resource Management, Manufacturing Strategy, and Firm Performance," *Academy of Management Journal* 39 (1996), 836–866.

45. See J. B. Barney and P. M. Wright, "On Becoming a Strategic Partner: The Role of Human Resources in Gaining Competitive Advantage," *Human Resource Management* 37 (1998), 31–46; J. Pfeffer, *Competitive Advantage Through People* (Boston: Harvard Business School Press, 1994).

46. J. Pfeffer, *The Human Equation* (Boston: Harvard Business School Press, 1998).

47. F. Luthans and C. M. Youssef, "Human, Social, and Now Positive Psychological Capital Management: Investing in People for Competitive Advantage," *Organization Dynamics* 33:2 (2004), 143–160.

48. R. W. Coff, "Human Assets and Management Dilemmas: Coping with Hazards on the Road to Resource-Based Theory," *Academy of Management Review* 22 (1997), 374–402.

49. See Coff, "Human Assets and Management Dilemmas."

50. B. Gerhart and S. Rynes, *Compensation* (Beverly Hills, CA: Sage Publications, 2003).

51. J. Kerr and J. Slocum, "Managing Corporate Culture Through Reward Systems," *Academy of Management Executive* 1:2 (1987), 99–108.

52. C. W. L. Hill, M. A. Hitt, and R. E. Hoskisson, "Cooperative Versus Competitive Structures in Related and Unrelated Diversified Firms," *Organization Science* 3 (1992), 501–521.

53. CIBC Corporate and Investment Banking (A). Harvard Business School Publishing, 1999.

54. For an extensive review see Milkovich & Newman, *Compensation*, 8th Edition (New York, McGraw-Hill, 2004).

55. For an extensive review see Milkovich & Newman, *Compensation*, 8th Edition.

56. S. Kerr, "On the Folly of **Rewarding for A** while Hoping for B." *Academy of Management Journal*, December 1975, 18(4), pp. 769–83.

57. S. Kerr, "On the Folly of **Rewarding for A** while Hoping for B."

58. Adapted from W. C. Kim and R. Mauborgne, "Charting Your Company's Future," *Harvard Business Review* 80:6 (2002), 76–82.

59. Adapted from W. C. Kim and R. Mauborgne, "Charting Your Company's Future," *Harvard Business Review* 80:6 (2002), 76–82.

60. Hambrick and Cannella, "Strategy Implementation as Substance and Selling," 278–285.

61. N. Wreden, "Executive Champions: The Vital Link Between Strategy Formulation and Implementation," *Harvard Management Update* 7:9 (2002), 3–5.

62. www.clemmer.net/excerpts/pf_credibility.html (accessed October 25, 2005).

63. The information in this section draws heavily upon the work of Christopher Bartlett and Sumantra Ghoshal, *Managing Across Borders: The Transnational Solution* (Boston: Harvard Business School Press, 1989).

64. Bartlett and Ghoshal, *Managing Across Borders.*

65. M. A. Carpenter, W. G. Sanders, and H. B. Gregersen, "Bundling Human Capital with Organizational Context: The Impact of International Assignment Experience on Multinational Firm Performance and CEO Pay," *Academy of Management Journal* 44 (2001), 493–511.

66. Y. Gong, "Subsidiary Staffing in Multinational Enterprises: Agency, Resources, and Performance," *Academy of Management Journal* 46 (2003), 728–739.

67. Gong, "Subsidiary Staffing in Multinational Enterprises."

68. C. Christensen, *The Innovator's Dilemma* (Boston: Harvard Business School Press, 1997).

69. C. A. O'Reilly and M. L. Tushman, "The Ambidextrous Organization," *Harvard Business Review* 82:4 May–June 2004), 74–81.

70. For details of this study, see O'Reilly and Tushman, "The Ambidextrous Organization."

71. Adapted from C. A. O'Reilly and M. L. Tushman, "The Ambidextrous Organization," *Harvard Business Review* 82:4 (2004), 74–81.

72. This section draws heavily on K. M. Eisenhardt and S. L. Brown, "Patching: Restitching Business Portfolios in Dynamic Markets," *Harvard Business Review* 77:3 (1999), 72–82.

12 Considering New Ventures *and* Corporate Renewal

In This Chapter We Challenge You To >>>

1. Define *new ventures, initial public offerings (IPOs),* and *corporate renewal* and explain how they are related to strategic management.

2. Understand entrepreneurship and the entrepreneurial process.

3. Describe the steps involved in new-venture creation and corporate new-venturing.

4. Map out the stages leading up to an initial public offering (IPO).

5. Understand the external and internal causes of organizational failure.

6. Outline an action plan for strategic change and corporate renewal.

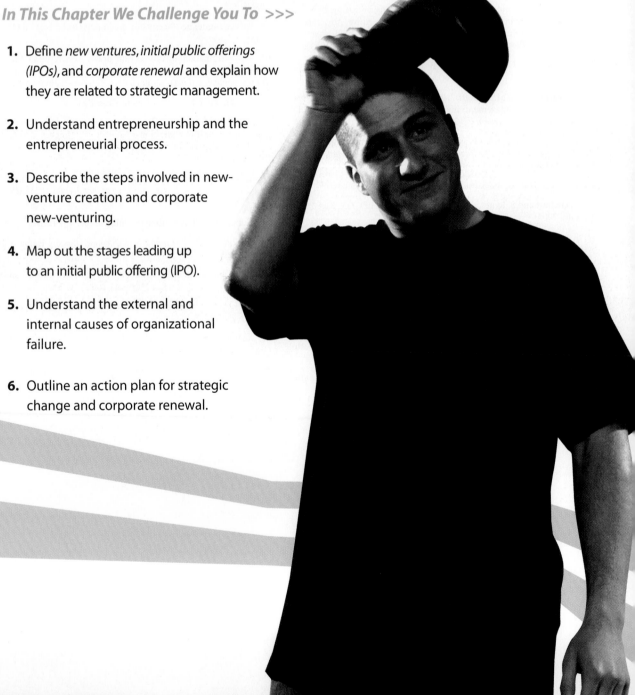

From Napster *to* Snocap: Shawn Fanning *as* Serial Entrepreneur

f you want to download new music today, you can buy it from a centralized site like iTunes, or Rhapsody, or you can get it directly from the artist's website or MySpace page. Snocap, however, is the company that is helping artists and copyright owners sell their music directly to their fans.

Snocap's founding team includes Shawn Fanning, the brain behind the original Napster. In 1999 Napster rocked the foundations of the music industry by making it easy to share music **"peer-to-peer,"** directly from one fan to another. With the advent of peer-to-peer music sharing services, music lovers no longer had to depend on radio stations or music stores, or even recording labels, to hear about new music. The only problem was that file sharing cut out any compensation for the artists who make the music.

peer-to-peer Where individual network members can engage in exchange with any other member of the network.

long-tail When the selling of individual products that each have low sales volume add up to huge revenues.

With Snocap, Fanning's goal was to keep the "many-to-many" or "granular" concept of Napster, but this time to extend it directly from artists to their audiences. The business model is based on the idea of the **"long tail"**—a concept coined by Chris Anderson, the Editor and Chief of Wired Magazine, that selling many individual products that each have low sales volume can add up to huge revenues. In essence, forget squeezing millions from a few megahits at the top of the charts. The future of entertainment is in the millions of niche markets at the shallow end of the bitstream. Anderson argued that products that are in low demand or have low sales volume can collectively make up a market share that rivals or exceeds the relatively few current bestsellers and blockbusters, if the store or distribution channel is large enough. Anderson cites earlier research that described the relationship between Amazon sales and Amazon sales ranking and found that a large proportion of Amazon.com's book sales come from obscure books that are not available in brick-and-mortar stores. The long tail is a potential market and, as the examples illustrate, the distribution and sales channel opportunities created by the Internet often enable businesses to tap into that market successfully. On the artists' side, a band may make only pocket change for the sale of each song, but when the music is available to millions of listeners, that change can add up quickly. And if a company like Snocap is the middleman on the transactions, then that could add up to lots of profits. The basic economics of the long tail are summarized in Exhibit 12.1.[1]

While Shawn Fanning is truly a creative genius—he invented Napster when he was 19—he also knew that he needed the best in the business when it came to directing a highly dynamic business in a fluid industry. Rusty Reuff was the perfect guy for the job, and joined Snocap as CEO in 2005. He had spent seven years in the videogame industry, as Executive VP of Human Resources at Electronic Arts. Reuff joined Snocap at a difficult time. Everyone

Exhibit 12.1 The Economics of the Long Tail

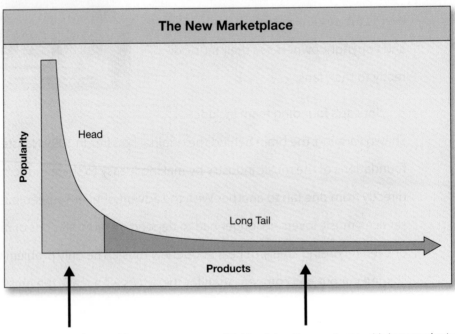

Traditional products with big, homogenous markets

Highly niche-like products with low products for single product sales, low volumes for single product sales, but huge collective volumes for similar products

knew the old business models for selling music were disintegrating, but there were, and still are, many new ventures claiming to have the best model to replace it. Artists and labels were not jumping on SNOCAP's bandwagon as fast as they had hoped.

After careful examination of the external environment, Reuff and his team noted the similarities between peer-to-peer music sharing and the new **social networking** sites like FaceBook, Friendster, and MySpace. In 2006 they announced the creation of a partnership to offer digital music through MySpace pages.

> **social network** The collection of ties between people and the strength of those ties.

Snocap's differentiators are based on two elements: rights protection and commerce. The first involves software that digitally fingerprints the songs to protect the copyright, and tracks the sales so copyright owners can be paid monthly. Artists (or content owners) can choose which songs they want to sell, and set the price themselves. To help with the commerce side, Snocap provides a ready-made "storefront," that can be added to a MySpace page or any webpage. Songs can also be sold through a list of "Snocap powered retailers" to expand distribution.

Snocap is betting that both music lovers and creators will see the potential of the Internet for sharing and supporting their music. There are about three million songs available for download through iTunes. But estimates are that there are ten times as many available in the marketplace as a whole. And music is only the beginning: one day Snocap hopes to bring the same tools to writers, videographers, and any creative artist who can sell their work on the Internet.

Perhaps the complete irony of this story is that whereas Fanning created Napster, a bootleg software engine that could virtually doom the entire music business as we know it, Snocap's business model is built around the total protection of artists' rights to the music they create. Snocap hopes that by targeting the long tail of the music industry it can carve out a competitive advantage. <<<

From New-Venture Creation to Corporate Renewal

Why are we going to discuss entrepreneurship and turnaround management (otherwise known as *corporate renewal*) in the same chapter? Throughout this text, we've described companies of various ages, sizes, and competitive positions. In this chapter, we want to focus on three particularly important phases or stages that can punctuate the life cycle of a firm:

■ The birth of new ventures

■ The transition from new venture to a more established firm, either as a public company via an initial public offering (IPO) or the incorporation of more professional management

■ The rescue of established but struggling ventures

Not surprisingly, strategic management is critical to firms in all three of these phases. At first glance, it may seem that these three stages are far removed from one another, but by the end of this chapter, we will show that the entrepreneurial process is an important common thread that runs through all of them. Managers of startups, for example, must learn firsthand what it takes to develop and grow a business, whereas managers of distressed firms must recover the entrepreneurial orientation from which the firm originally emerged. This approach will demonstrate why what you've learned about strategy is equally applicable to both small and large firms as well as new and old ones.

If we've underscored any one concept in this book, it's that *strategies provide solutions to problems.* It just so happens that today new ventures face problems whose solutions involve not only the identification of new opportunities but the development of organizational resources and capabilities to operate profitably in that domain. The IPO, meanwhile, enables a firm not only to capitalize (literally as well as figuratively) on its initial success but to gain access to the financial resources needed to fuel future growth. Some firms do not need to resort to an IPO to support their growth, but they do at least make a transition from a visionary leadership style to one that increasingly incorporates aspects of professional management practices. While SNOCAP is not a public firm yet, if they succeed, an IPO would be one of the logical steps in their development path. In established firms, such entrepreneurial behavior faces the same growth management problems as those faced by startup firms. (An established firm, of course, must also deal with problems arising from its history and prior activities.) Finally, the five elements of a strategy are critical to any firm—established or new—that is engaged in entrepreneurial activity. Indeed, all of the tools of strategic management can be applied to problems arising from both new-venture creation and corporate renewal.

NEW-VENTURE CREATION VERSUS CORPORATE RENEWAL

Note that in emphasizing new ventures, IPOs, and turnarounds, we're presenting a slightly simplified view of the organizational life cycle. **New-venture creation** refers to entrepreneurship and the creation of a new business from scratch, whereas **corporate renewal** refers to successful strategic change. **Initial public offerings** (**IPOs**) and/or the institutionalization of professional management often occur in the relatively early stages of a firm's life cycle. All firms start somewhere, and some firms go public. In addition, nearly all firms experience distress at some point, and corporate renewal prevents established firms—and sometimes even new and newly public ones as well—from vanishing from the face of the competitive landscape. As we already noted, because all three involve the creation of something new, all three stages in the organizational life cycle can engage in the entrepreneurial process. Indeed, a firm's success gives it a lot of options: It may remain independent, seek savvy private investors with deep pockets (as did SNOCAP), go public, or merge with an established firm seeking to enhance its future prospects.

In the sections that follow, you'll get a better idea of what entrepreneurship is and how the entrepreneurial process works. You'll also see how the same process may either lead to an IPO and professional management or provide an impetus for corporate renewal. By the end of the chapter, you'll understand the range of strategic ventures from startup to turnaround and see how strategic management is relevant to new enterprises. You'll also be able to identify the warning signs of organizational trouble and outline a resource-based turnaround plan for a struggling organization.

new-venture creation
Entrepreneurship and the creation of a new business from scratch.

corporate renewal   Outcome of successful strategic change in the context of an established business.

initial public offering (IPO)
First sale of a company's stock to the public market.

Entrepreneurship and the Entrepreneurial Process

Because of stories like the one in our opening vignette, you probably think of lone, self-reliant individuals like Shawn Fanning when you think about entrepreneurship and the creation of new ventures. Research shows, however, that no matter how important one individual is to an organization, its ultimate success depends as much on the entrepreneurial team as on the lead entrepreneur.[2] Dell, for instance, would have gone bankrupt in the early 1990s had it not recruited talented executives from IBM and Apple.

WHAT IS ENTREPRENEURSHIP?

Beyond the common misconception of entrepreneurship as an individual enterprise, people tend to associate it with a variety of images, from garage inventors to rogue executives who leave established employers to form their own companies. Such images have some validity, and throughout this chapter, you'll encounter certain behaviors that tend to characterize successful entrepreneurs. With this fact in mind, let's define **entrepreneurship** as the consequence of actions based on the identification and exploration of opportunity in the absence of obviously available resources. The **entrepreneurial process**, then, is the set of activities leading up to and driving the entrepreneurial venture.

Successful entrepreneurs, whether those who start new firms or who work within companies, are often those who challenge orthodoxy. *Orthodoxies* are the deeply held and broadly shared beliefs about what drives success within "the industry." Orthodoxies are not necessarily incorrect conceptualizations of the current market. Indeed, orthodoxies achieve their status because they do represent the status quo. However, orthodoxies also create blind spots to the recognition of new opportunities. Most industries have orthodoxies along several dimensions:

- Who the customer or end user is

- The type of interface and interaction with the customer or end user

- How benefit is defined and value is delivered

- How product/service functionality is defined

- What form the product/service should take

- How processes are structured and managed

- The "ideal" cost and pricing structure

Consider the examples reviewed in Exhibit 12.2 of a few notable business ideas and the orthodoxies they had to surmount to see the light of day.[3] Consider how the fortunes of some companies may have been different had they been able to overcome the orthodoxy internally and capitalize on the ideas and opportunities these innovations represent.

entrepreneurship Recognition of opportunities and the use of resources and capabilities to implement innovative ideas for new ventures.

entrepreneurial process Integration of opportunity recognition, key resources and capabilities, and an entrepreneur and entrepreneurial team to create a new venture.

- "This 'telephone' has too many shortcomings to be seriously considered as a means of communication. The device is inherently of no value to us."
—Western Union internal memo, 1876
- "The wireless music box has no imaginable commercial value. Who would pay for a message sent to nobody in particular?"—David Sarnhoff's associates in response to his urgings for investment in the radio in the 1920s
- "There is no reason anyone would want a computer in their home."—Ken Olson, President, Chairman and Founder of Digital Equipment Corp., 1977
- "The concept is interesting and well-formed, but in order to earn better than a 'C,' the idea must be feasible."—A Yale University management professor in response to Fred Smith's paper proposing reliable overnight delivery service. Smith went on to found Federal Express Corp.
- "A cookie store is a bad idea. Besides, the market research reports say America likes crispy cookies, not soft and chewy cookies like you make."
—Response to Debbi Fields' idea of starting Mrs. Fields' Cookies
- "There will never be a market in selling stock over the Internet."
—David Komansky, Merrill Lynch Chairman & CEO, 1999

Exhibit 12.2
Orthodoxies That Have Created Entrepreneurial Blind Spots

THE ENTREPRENEURIAL PROCESS

In this section, we'll elaborate on the entrepreneurial process, which, as you can see in Exhibit 12.3, integrates and coordinates three elements:

1. Opportunity

2. Key resources and capabilities

3. The entrepreneur and the entrepreneurial team

Because it emphasizes a need for balance and symmetry among its elements, this process model fits well with most of the theories that we've discussed throughout this book. It's also consistent with emerging research that considers entrepreneurship a function in most firms, regardless of their age or size.[4] For that reason alone, you'll see strong affinities with the resource- and dynamic-capabilities-based perspectives that we've described throughout the book.

The Starting Point: Opportunity

SNOCAP is an example of an entrepreneurial starting point. Fanning identified a need to (1) protect the property rights of individual musicians and (2) connect individual musicians with individual consumers. Perhaps the biggest difference between strategy in existing firms and new ventures is the starting point. Most researchers agree that the starting point for new ventures is opportunity, whereas the strategy for existing firms typically begins with an assessment of the firm's underlying resources and capabilities.[5] You might be surprised to learn that you already possess some of the tools that may help you unearth a valuable business opportunity. Recall our discussion of revolutionary strategies in Chapter 6: All the revolutionary strategies provide a solid basis for identifying market opportunities. For instance, new market-creation strategies are designed to eliminate, reduce, create, or raise some previously assumed dimension of product/market supply and demand. For instance, new market-disruption strategies are an entrepreneur's dream because they're designed to enable a firm that's created a new market to grow into a dominant player in a new but

Exhibit 12.3 The Entrepreneurial Process

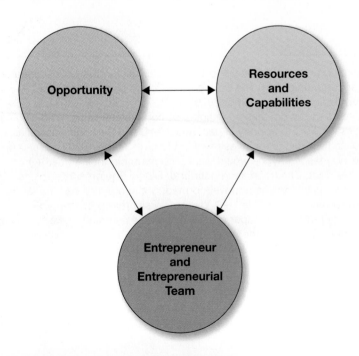

potentially huge industry. Google is a good example of this. Just a scant six years before it went public in 2004, a firm that now has more than $10 billion in revenue was bringing in less than $100,000 in a virtually nonexistent industry.[6] Low-end-disruption strategies involve identifying a business that will let a firm shift customers from a high-cost-to-serve to a low-cost-to-serve business model.

Like Fanning at SNOCAP, an entrepreneur identifies an opportunity and then seeks to cobble together the resources and capabilities to exploit it. Opportunities also can be identified by individuals who have close contact with scientific breakthroughs. In fact, scientific, technological, or process discoveries often inspire people to seek market opportunities. This is one reason why universities are increasing investments to support research faculty in the protection of intellectual property and identification of commercial opportunities. Universities like Stanford and the University of Wisconsin-Madison, for instance, maintain Offices of Corporate Relations that, among other services, assists individual researchers in the creation of new ventures. After all, faculty and staff members who create an early stage technology are often in the best position to develop it. Not only do they possess unsurpassed technical knowledge about their discoveries, they're often in a position to appreciate the promise that they hold.

Resources, Capabilities, and the Entrepreneurial Team

So far, we've focused on the element of opportunity in the entrepreneurial process. Our context, however—the intersection of technology and entrepreneurship—already suggests ways in which other elements—namely, resources and capabilities and people (the entrepreneur and entrepreneurial team)—are involved in the process. We discussed resources and capabilities in Chapter 3, and the VRINE framework that we presented there is as relevant in an entrepreneurial setting as it is in that of an established firm. Within the entrepreneurial firm, however, there's likely to be significant overlap between the people element and the resource-and-capabilities element. Why? Sometimes, the new opportunity is based in a technology whose benefits are recognizable only when it's complemented by the specific technical knowledge and experience of the people who created it. Similarly, if

Six years before going public in 2004, Google, founded by Sergey Brin and Larry Page, was bringing in less than $100,000 a year. Today Google Inc.'s annual revenues exceed $4 billion.

the opportunity is revealed by a "good idea," the entrepreneur and entrepreneurial team must often rely on their own personal resources, experience, and persuasiveness to acquire the needed resources and capabilities, including financial capital. In the case of SNOCAP, the firm has propriety technology to protect the property rights of the musicians, connect musicians with customers, and process and track payments for music purchased. In SNOCAP's lingo, "uploading and registering your music with SNOCAP enables you to sell tracks through your own SNOCAP MyStore and multiple retailers—all from one interface. It's non-exclusive and you keep all the rights to your music. Set licensing terms in the SNOCAP Digital Registry so SNOCAP-powered online retailers can sell your music. You determine the price, format, and digital rights (DRM) restrictions."

Although there is no litmus test for determining the characteristics of successful entrepreneurs and the people who make the best members of an entrepreneurial team, it's clear that without them, a new venture will never get off the ground. Sometimes, as we've already

Exhibit 12.4 The Google Management Team and Their Management Philosophy

"We run Google as a triumvirate. Sergey and I have worked closely together for the last eight years, five at Google. Eric, our CEO, joined Google three years ago. The three of us run the company collaboratively with Sergey and me as Presidents. The structure is unconventional, but we have worked successfully in this way.

To facilitate timely decisions, Eric, Sergey, and I meet daily to update each other on the business and to focus our collaborative thinking on the most important and immediate issues. Decisions are often made by one of us, with the other being briefed later. This works because we have tremendous trust and respect for each other and we generally think alike. Because of our intense, long-term working relationship, we can often predict differences of opinion among the three of us. We know that when we disagree, the correct decision is far from obvious. For important decisions, we discuss the issue with a larger team appropriate to the task. Differences are resolved through discussion and analysis and by reaching consensus. Eric, Sergey, and I run the company without any significant internal conflict, but with healthy debate. As different topics come up, we often delegate decision-making responsibility to one of us.

We hired Eric as a more experienced complement to Sergey and me to help us run the business. Eric was CTO of Sun Microsystems. He was also CEO of Novell and has a Ph.D. in computer science, a very unusual and important combination for Google given our scientific and technical culture. This partnership among the three of us has worked very well and we expect it to continue. The shared judgments and extra energy available from all three of us has significantly benefited Google.

Eric has the legal responsibilities of the CEO and focuses on management of our vice presidents and the sales organization. Sergey focuses on engineering and business deals. I focus on engineering and product management. All three of us devote considerable time to overall management of the company and other fluctuating needs. We also have a distinguished board of directors to oversee the management of Google. We have a talented executive staff that manages day-to-day operations in areas such as finance, sales, engineering, human resources, public relations, legal and product management. We are extremely fortunate to have talented management that has grown the company to where it is today—they operate the company and deserve the credit."
—Larry Page

seen, key people are among the intangible resources and capabilities that distinguish the potential new venture as an opportunity rather than just another good idea. For instance, Shawn Fanning is the creative genius behind SNOCAP, and Rusty Reuff is the innovative leader who connects the dots between the leading edge SNOCAP technology and the creative types who not only buy and sell through SNOCAP, but also work there. As a practical matter, it's the entrepreneur who drives the entrepreneurial process and ensures that all three elements—opportunity, resources and capabilities, and people—are in place and balanced. Because individuals have limits, team members are often selected because they bring skills that complement those of the lead entrepreneur and will ensure that the firm has the necessary human capital to achieve the objectives that it has set. This is why the positive chemistry between Fanning and Reuff is so important.

While the interplay among key team members is not always obvious, the letter to shareholders issued by Google in its 2004 IPO provides a rare and intriguing glimpse into this incredibly important context. Recall that Google was founded by Larry Page and Sergey Brin, and they soon brought in Dr. Eric Schmidt to serve as Chairman of the Board and CEO. Exhibit 12.4 summarizes their special, if not unique, relationship.

New-Venture Creation and Corporate New-Venturing

Entrepreneurship, which is the outcome of the entrepreneurial process, is embodied in the launch of a new venture. As we've already explained, the first step in new-venture creation is identifying an opportunity. Unfortunately, there's no rule of thumb for deciding on the next step. All we can say is that, typically, entrepreneurs begin a process of experimentation involving the confluence of several activities over time.

NEW-VENTURE SCENARIOS

Exhibit 12.5 summarizes these activities. As you can imagine, the traditional view of new-venture creation calls for the entrepreneur to exploit an opportunity by drawing up a business plan, obtaining external financing, and then launching the new product.[7]

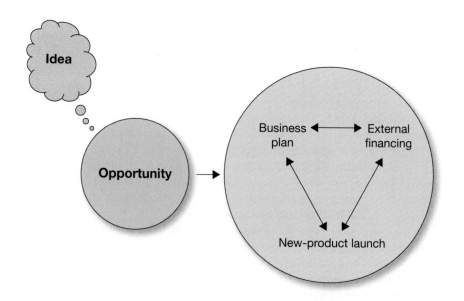

Exhibit 12.5 Activities in New-Venture Creation

A more realistic view allows for an alternative sequence of events that begins when the entrepreneur uses his or her own resources to launch a product and then seeks financing to stay in the game. The business plan often comes after the launch because its purpose is to obtain financing or to generate market interest (in the form of additional financing or purchase of the business) by explaining the venture's history and prospects.

Financing the New Venture   Commercializing a new venture requires capital for startup needs. The financing activity of the new venture can take many forms, with sources ranging from credit cards to venture capitalists to banks. You might expect most successful ventures to have access to adequate capital, but you'd be surprised. In fact, many successful entrepreneurs (and their investors) suspect that too much money, too early, produces more damage than good.[8] How, you're probably asking yourself, can excess cash possibly be a problem? Remember, first of all, that financing rarely comes without strings attached. Thus, entrepreneurs who depend on significant cash flow from loans or investor capital often find their flexibility considerably reduced. Second, ample funding can obscure potential problems until their consequences become irreversible. Finally, deep financial pockets shelter the new firm from the need to innovate in all aspects of its business. For instance, if you look at SNOCAP's website you will notice that they have venture capital financing from Ron Conway. Ron, besides being one of SNOCAP's founders, is a seasoned angel investor whose company, Angel Investors LLC, was an early investor in Napster. SNOCAP is also supported by Morgenthaler Ventures, WaldenVC, and Court Square Ventures. Nevertheless, without adequate startup financing, a new venture has difficulty getting off the ground.

bootstrapping   Process of finding creative ways to support a startup business financially until it turns profitable.

Bootstrapping means exploiting a new business opportunity with limited funds. Many new ventures are bootstrapped: A study of about 100 of *Inc.* magazine's list of the 500 fastest-growing small companies in the United States found median startup capital to be around $22,000 in real terms.[9] Ironically, the fastest-growing firms typically require the most money because they have to support increases in inventories, accounts receivable, staffing, and production and service facilities.

The Business Plan   Once the new product has been launched and startup financing secured, many entrepreneurs draw up a formal business plan that brings all the elements of the new venture together for a specific purpose: namely, to assure key stakeholders that the firm has a well-considered strategy and managerial acumen. Even if such a plan isn't necessary for communicating with external stakeholders, preparing one is still a good idea. At the very least, it will help the entrepreneur to reexamine the five elements of strategy and look for ways of bringing them together to create a viable and profitable firm.

In addition, a business plan provides the entrepreneur with a vehicle for sharing goals and objectives—and plans for implementing them—with members of the entrepreneurial team. Focusing on the staging component of the five elements of strategy, for example, is a good way to set milestones and time lines and otherwise manage the scale and pace of a new company's growth. Finally, when it does come time to seek external funding to support the firm's growth, the plan provides a coherent basis for engaging professionals who can not only help the entrepreneur obtain financing, but also offer advice on strengthening customer relationships and finding strategic suppliers.

Familiarity with the five elements of the strategy diamond, implementation levers, and frameworks for analyzing external organizational context is helpful with drawing up a business plan. Although there are variations in form, the content of most plans covers the same topics. A multitude of examples—as well as software packages for creating a detailed and professional-looking document—are available on the Web.[10] Exhibit 12.6 provides a sum-

Exhibit 12.6   Table of Contents of a Typical Business Plan

1. **Executive summary.** One to three pages highlighting all key points in a way that captures the interest of the reader. Stress the business concept here, notthe numbers. It is the unique value proposition and business model that reallymatter.

2. **Company description.** Provide a brief description of the company's business,organization, structure and strategy. Provide a summary of how thecompany's patents or licenses to patents are connected with the developmentand introduction of products.

3. **Products and services.** Include a layman's overview of how the company's technology and patents relate to its products and services. Describe the products or services the company will sell, including a discussion of why people will want them, what problems they solve, and how much customers are likely to pay for them (i.e., the willingness to pay criteria).

4. **Market analysis.** Identify the need for the product, the extent of that need,who the customers will be, and why they will buy your product. This sectionshould also include a discussion of competitors or potential competitors andwhy the product will have a competitive advantage over their offerings.Include considerations of barriers to entry in this market.

5. **Proprietary position.** If the new venture's market position will rely on patentsor licenses to patents, discuss how these patents will contribute to thecompany's competitive position and whether other patents (competitors orotherwise) might limit the company's ability to market its products. If similarproducts do not already exist, discuss the alternative means by whichcustomers are likely to meet the needs the product addresses.

6. **Marketing and sales plan.** Show how the company plans to attract and maintain customers. Discuss product pricing, promotion, and positioning strategy.

7. **Management team.** Describe the management team with special emphasis onits track record at accomplishing tasks similar to those it will face in makingthe company successful. Investors place major emphasis on the managementteam, viewing it as the critical ingredient in catalyzing the growth of thecompany and responding to the unexpected.

8. **Operations plan.** Describe how the day-to-day operations of the company willbe organized and carried out to produce the products and services describedabove.

9. **Finances.** Identify the capital that will be required to build the business and how it will be used. Include projections of revenues and expenses that show investors how they will get their money back and what return they can expecton their investment.

mary of what is normally contained in a comprehensive business plan. It is important to keep in mind that the process of systematically thinking through the nine steps in the exhibit is probably more important than the business plan document itself.

Finally, a word of warning. All too often, would-be entrepreneurs tend to equate a good business plan with the probability of success in running a business. Needless to say, however, a well-crafted plan does not ensure a successful business. At this point in the process, the probability of success depends more heavily on the strength of the three elements that were present at the start of the process—a good opportunity (including the right timing), the right entrepreneurial team, and the necessary resources and capabilities. A business plan is no more a substitute for strategy and strong execution than a clear vision and mission or even such strategic vehicles as alliances and acquisitions. That's why consultants often suggest that entrepreneurs think of the business plan not only as a helpful and necessary starting point but as a continuous work in progress.[11]

CORPORATE NEW-VENTURING

The previous section discussed new-venturing as a process engaged in by entrepreneurs. However, many successful innovations and new ventures are sponsored by existing organizations. What you have learned about entrepreneurial new-venturing applies equally well to the process of **corporate new-venturing**—the creation of new businesses by established firms. In addition, your knowledge of co-opetition and coevolution should give you a pretty good idea of some of the challenges and opportunities encountered during the process of corporate new-venturing. However, the resources and capabilities of established firms and the corporate environment in which they do business differ. These factors often kill corporate new ventures before they get off the ground (or at least keep performance below levels that firms might have achieved through other investments or even by simply buying a portfolio of market stocks).[12] The stellar innovation track records of firms such as Merck, 3M, Motorola, Rubbermaid, Johnson & Johnson, Corning, General Electric, Raychem, Hewlett-Packard, Wal-Mart, and many others demonstrate that bigness is not in itself antithetical to new-venturing. At the same time, however, these are but a few of the thousands of large firms around the world.[13] Understanding the obstacles to entrepreneurship in large, established firms will put you on firmer ground when it comes time to translate what you know about entrepreneurship into the process of corporate new-venturing. Corporate new-venturing can take on one or a combination of two forms: establishing a new business or creating a new-ventures division.

corporate new-venturing
New-venture creation by established firms.

Establishing a New Business

A firm may seek to develop a new business around some valuable process or technological breakthrough. Typically, an executive or group of executives will champion the innovation, and the process will proceed when the business concept has been tentatively validated and many of the major uncertainties resolved or reduced.[14] Attention then shifts from opportunity validation to the process of bringing the new business to life. Efforts are directed at assembling resources and capabilities, meeting production and sales goals, and solidifying organization. Interestingly, researchers note that creating a business climate supportive of entrepreneurial activity is the most difficult task faced by a large company trying to integrate an innovative new business.[15]

As a general rule, new-venture activities are less predictable and are, therefore, riskier than those in which a firm traditionally engages. In particular, such activities face three obstacles:

1. Although false starts and failures can sometimes be important learning mechanisms, most large firms naturally try to mitigate them by improving efficiency.

2. Moreover, new ventures often meet resistance because they challenge long-established assumptions, work practices, and employee skills. After all, by definition *new* means *different*.

3. Ironically—and most importantly—large organizations often lavish *too many resources*, including cash, on new ventures. How can this practice be a problem? To be successful at corporate new-venturing, large firms must learn to be simultaneously patient and tolerant of risk on the one hand, and stingy on the other. The need for stinginess comes from the observation by strategy researchers that corporate new ventures tend to thrive when their managers must face new markets on the same realistic terms that startups typically do outside the corporate bureaucracy.

New-Venture Division

The second form of corporate new-venturing, in which the firm sets up an internal new-venture division, is actually a structural solution to these obstacles. In many ways, this division acts like a venture capitalist or business incubator, working to provide expertise and resources and impart structure to the process of developing the new opportunity.

In this case, too, the opportunity may revolve around some proprietary process, product, or technological breakthrough. This approach is designed to achieve one of two possible objectives:

1. The creation and retention of a new business that will fuel growth and perhaps foster corporate renewal

2. The creation of a high-growth new venture that the firm can sell off through an IPO at a significant profit

The advantage of the structural approach is that it provides a system for investing in a team that's assigned specifically to new-venture creation. If the system is managed properly, new-venture divisions can function like the best venture-capital operations—that is, they can be cost conscious while still encouraging risk taking, experimentation, and novel, market-oriented solutions. A new-venture division—for that matter, new-venturing in any form—is a form of diversification, with the firm betting that it has the resources and capabilities to do something new.

The structural approach first became popular in the late 1960s, when 25 percent of the *Fortune* 500 maintained internal venture divisions.[16] The next wave came in the late 1970s and early 1980s, when large players such as Gillette, IBM, Levi Strauss, and Xerox launched internal new-venture groups.[17] Next came the Internet boom, when many firms set up divisions to run e-commerce operations that mirrored their traditional brick-and-mortar operations.

The success of new-venture divisions can be measured in several ways. Using an internal rate of return metric, many of these divisions perform quite well. However, the performances of these divisions are generally not up to the levels of those achieved by private equity venture capital firms.[18] Why? Although a firm may have proprietary access to a valuable technology, it probably doesn't possess the necessary venture-capitalist managerial skills and experience. In addition, when it's in the hands of a new-venture division, the new business is isolated from the rest of the organization. This separation is often necessary to protect the new venture, as you saw with the discussion of the ambidextrous organizational structure in Chapter 11. However, if the loose linkages with the parent company, which are necessary to secure resources and transfer information, are severe or dysfunctional, then the parent firm is insulated from the new business and thus less likely to learn from its successes and failures. In addition, the new venture risks being starved for resources and capabilities possessed by the parent firm.

Is corporate new-venturing, then, doomed to failure? Of course not. Firms must, however, be careful to balance the requirements of entrepreneurial ventures—such as a supportive entrepreneurial climate—with the benefits of sustained linkage to the parent firm. The natural tension and potential dysfunction created by the need for separateness yet connectedness must be carefully managed. Entrepreneurship Professor David Garvin of Harvard Business School recently reviewed the history of corporate new-venturing. He suggested that corporate new ventures are more likely to succeed when they:[19]

- Are developed and validated in firms with supportive, entrepreneurial climates

- Have senior executive sponsorship

- Are based on related, rather than radically different, products and services

- Appeal to an emerging subset or current set of customers

- Employ market-experienced personnel

- Test concepts and business models directly with potential users

- Experiment, probe, and prototype repeatedly during early development

- Balance demands for early profitability with realistic time lines

- Introduce required systems and processes in time, but not earlier than the new venture's evolution required

- Combine disciplined oversight and stinginess with entrepreneurial autonomy

Professor Garvin's guidelines for successful corporate venturing suggest that there are other inherent tensions in the decision-making process as well. Many of the guidelines in this list call for incorporating a resource-based approach into the new-venturing process. Even when a firm succeeds in creating a climate that's supportive of entrepreneurship, the evolving characteristics of the new venture may result in a unit that's more distinctive from—than complementary to—the core businesses. In that case, it might be wise for the parent firm to allow the new business to function independently—physically and legally. In part, the increase in new-venture public offerings can be attributed to the willingness of firms to take this advice. With this fact in mind, we turn in the next section to a discussion of initial public offerings (IPOs).

Initial Public Offerings and Managerial Professionalism

As firms grow, they face the need to transition to a more complex organizational form. Sometimes this form is dictated by the need for access to additional capital and professional management or managerial professionalism alone. Increasingly, experts are starting to view the IPO as a pivotal point in a firm's transition from small and entrepreneurial to large and established.[20] An IPO takes place when a firm offers ownership shares through a public stock market.[20] In 2000, for instance, Krispy Kreme was a highly successful private company that decided to facilitate expansion by issuing an IPO. Typically, investment bankers (underwriters) and stockbrokers value the firm and place the stock with investors. Of course, a number of different transition vehicles are possible—alliances, mergers, sales, outright failure (the most common exit route). Given their recent visibility and rise to virtual holy-grail status among entrepreneurs, it's important to understand the workings of IPOs in greater detail.

HOW DOES AN IPO WORK?

How does an organization orchestrate an IPO? Once it's decided to make a securities offering, the company establishes a market value in the private sector. This value is estimated by an investment-banking institution, which will also sell the firm's shares to public investors. During this process, the company files an **S-1 statement**, which states its value proposition and financial prospects, with the Securities and Exchange Commission (SEC) and various state securities commissions. It is a good idea for you to track down the S-1 of recently IPO'd firms like TomoTherapy just to see the impressive amount of information that is provided about the firm, its strategy, competition, operating risks, and financial prospects. It also provides detailed information about the backgrounds of the management team and board of directors, as well as the schedule of their compensation. The front page of one of these statements is shown in Exhibit 12.7. Finally, the company and its brokerage firm "time" the offering to get maximum value from the sale of its stock.

One thing that companies are required to discuss at length is the challenges they face that could adversely affect shareholders. Google, for example, discloses in its S-1 prospectus that "We face significant competition from Microsoft and Yahoo."

Usually, the *prospectus* describes the perceived business opportunity, outlines the firm's strategy for exploiting it, and details its current products and activities, generally in the con-

S-1 statement Legal document outlining a firm's financial position in preparation for an initial public stock offering.

As filed with the Securities and Exchange Commission on February 12, 2007

Registration No. 333

SECURITIES AND EXCHANGE COMMISSION
Washington, D.C. 20549

Form S-1
REGISTRATION STATEMENT
UNDER
THE SECURITIES ACT OF 1933

TomoTherapy Incorporated
(Exact Name of Registrant as Specified in its Charter)

Wisconsin	3845	39-1914727
(State or Other Jurisdiction of Incorporation or Organization)	*(Primary Standard Industrial Classification Code Number)*	*(I.R.S. Employer Identification Number)*

1240 Deming Way
Madison, Wisconsin 53717
(608) 824-2800
(Address, including zip code, and telephone number, including area code, of registrar's principal executive offices)

Stephen C. Hathaway
Chief Financial Officer and Treasurer
1240 Deming Way
Madison, Wisconsin 53717
(608) 824-2800
(Name, address, including zip code and telephone number, including area code, of agent for service)

Copies to:

Gregory J. Lynch, Esq.	Shawn Guse, Esq.	Colin J. Diamond, Esq.
Geoffrey R. Morgan, Esq.	Vice President, General Counsel and	White & Case LLP
Michael Best & Friedrich LLP	Secretary	1155 Avenue of the Americas
100 East Wisconsin Avenue	TomoTherapy Incorporated	New York, NY 10036
Suite 3300	1240 Deming Way	Telephone: (212) 819-8200
Milwaukee, Wisconsin 53202	Madison, Wisconsin 53717	Facsimile: (212) 354-8113
Telephone: (414) 225-2752	Telephone: (608) 824-2800	
Facsimile: (414) 277-0656	Facsimile: (608) 824-2996	

Approximate date of commencement of proposed sale to the public: As soon as practicable after the effective date of this registration statement.

Exhibit 12.7 Opening Page of TomoTherapy's S-1 Statement

text of the company's overall expansion strategy. The firm must clearly define its vision and describe its mission, business initiatives, and objectives. As we observed earlier in this chapter, the business plan should also spell out the firm's approach to the five elements of strategy and the implementation levers necessary for executing its strategy, and it should do so in a way that's clear and compelling for potential investors. Because investors will want to know what goals the firm has set for itself, treatment of staging is especially important.

COST OF AN IPO

When preparing a securities offering, consider the old saying that you need money to make money. While exact figures will vary by transaction level and complexity, the IPO process could easily require $400,000 in professional fees alone. Investment bankers exact a heavy toll for shepherding a firm through an IPO. A normal 6.5-percent commission would skim $1,625,000 off the top of a $25-million offering! As an illustration, Exhibit 12.8 breaks out the underlying IPO costs for a $25-million offering.[21] Some of the line items, such as the "road show," are discussed further in the next section.

Financial and Legal Requirements   The firm will have to pass certain financial tests. An independent U.S. Securities Exchange Commission (SEC)-approved CPA (Certified Public Accounting) firm, for example, must audit the firm's financial statements for the previous three years. If the firm hasn't been audited over that period, the process may take months. If the company has been around for more than five years, it will have to include financial information from previous years in the (S-1) registration and prospectus statement.[22]

An SEC-approved CPA will require that all legal work be done and be done properly. If the firm doesn't pass the CPA's audit tests, it won't be issued an *unqualified opinion* on its financial statements. Instead, it will receive a *qualified opinion*—a statement of the auditor's

Exhibit 12.8   Minimum Costs of Going Public to Raise $25 Million

Source: P. Downing, 1998. IPO launch fraught with perils. The Ottawa Citizen, High Tech Report, October 12, 1998.

Pre-IPO costs over two years,		
1. Upgrading accounting and MIS	$150,000	
2. New personnel and board members	150,000	
3. Management/administrative time	100,000	
Minimum Pre-IPO Costs		**$400,000**

IPO-Process costs 90 days,		
6.5% underwriter commission		
$25 million IPO		$1,625,000
IPO professional fees		
1. Legal fees	$ 150,000	
2. Preliminary/final prospectus printing	100,000	
3. Translation	30,000	
4. Investors relations	40,000	
5. Accounting	50,000	
6. Road show and preparations	50,000	
7. Initial stock exchange listing fee	10,000	
Minimum IPO professional fees		430,000
Minimum IPO-Process Costs		**$2,055,000**

Post-IPO costs every year thereafter,		
1. Investor relations and Web site	100,000	
2. Directors' fees, travel costs, etc.	100,000	
3. Directors' liability insurance	50,000	
4. Corporate image, public relations	50,000	
5. Annual stock exchange fee	5,000	
6. Management/administration costs	100,000	
Minimum Annual Post IPO-Costs		**$405,000**

Total Minimum Cost of a $25 million IPO		$2,860,000

opinion that the audit reflects certain limitations, such as financial irregularities, lack of controls, and so forth. That's not good: In the securities world, an unqualified opinion is sometimes called the "blue screen of death," and it's particularly grave for the IPO.

The "Road Show"   Once the firm has met the financial and legal requirements, it enters the pre-IPO period and launches a **road show**, which is a series of presentations in which members of the top-management team, particularly the CEO, promote the company to interested investors and analysts. Depending on the quality of the road show, the firm may even get commitments from investors to buy shares of its stock. However, bear in mind that there are restrictions on the people to whom managers can talk and what they can talk about, and what's more, these rules change frequently. Obviously, top executives need to know the rules before they hit the road.

As pressure for financial transparency increases, the SEC may eventually require companies to open road-show presentations, which are now restricted to analysts and institutional investors, to individual investors, not only to expand the audience for promotional activities but to level the playing field in terms of access to information. The SEC hasn't yet worked out the logistics, but one way to give individuals access to road shows would be to broadcast them on the Internet. Road-show meetings with stock analysts, which must be open to the public, are often broadcast over the Internet.

Once the road show is over, the firm's brokers will want to time the offering so that shares become available under the most favorable market conditions.[23] For example, a high-tech company wouldn't want its stock brought to market during a sell-off in technology stocks. The firm's brokers may prefer things to be uneventful so that the IPO can make news. They might try to time the firm's offering to coincide with other attractive IPOs, taking advantage of a window during which investors feel eager to get in the game.

AN IPO OR A MORE FORMAL ORGANIZATION?

Given the complexities and costs of an IPO, it is no surprise that not all growing firms go public. Recall that an IPO is part of the growth path of a firm because it provides access to additional capital as well as the opportunity and motivation to put more professional management in place. Professional management may take the form of executives experienced with running larger firms, rapidly growing firms, or those that require management of significant organizational change. The need to shift from purely entrepreneurial management to more formal or professional management was initially discovered by Professor Daryl Wyckoff in his study of the trucking industry.[24] Wyckoff coined the term the *Bermuda Triangle of Management* to describe the region where firms are faced with the need to cross over from entrepreneurial to formal management. The Bermuda Triangle is an infamous area in the Atlantic Ocean where legend has it that ships and planes enter but never escape; Wyckoff argued that firms face a similar scenario and that those trucking firms that never completed the shift from informal to formal, professional management is apt to fail and disappear from the scene.

Part of the explanation for the Bermuda Triangle effect is economic. Wyckoff found that the operating ratio (expenses as a percentage of revenues) in the trucking industry varied by firm size; large and small companies were generally more profitable than midsized companies (those ostensibly stuck in or trying to get through the Bermuda Triangle). Part of the effect was managerial. Wyckoff noted that small firms were informally managed and large firms were professionally managed.

What does formal, professional management entail? Based on his work with the trucking industry, Wyckoff concluded that formal management includes delegation of authority; detailed and frequent measurement systems; formalized, performance-based reward systems; formal ground rules, procedures, and resource-allocation systems; and separation of ownership and management. Although Wyckoff's work dates from the 1970s, more recent

road show Series of presentations in which top management promotes an IPO to interested investors and analysts.

examples are easy to find. Recall the saga of SAP in the late 1990s, which struggled as it grew but ultimately succeeded by successfully transitioning from an informal to a formal management system.

Why Do Organizations Fail?

The new-venture process, whether undertaken by a new firm or within an existing firm, represents the beginning of a new organization. However, successful new ventures do not ensure long-term prosperity. Firms often must make major changes in order to survive, and the Bermuda Triangle phenomenon aptly demonstrates this. Before considering how firms can change to return to prosperity, it may be useful to review the broader set of explanations as to why organizations fail. Knowing the causes of failure will help us better understand what is needed to guide a firm through a strategic change to correct problems and avoid complete failure.[25]

Both public and private firms may experience distress at any point in their life cycle, and research indicates that a set of common factors underlies business failure. To be fair, it's usually much easier to determine the cause of organizational failure after the failure rather than before, but understanding and learning from the mistakes of other management teams is the responsibility of everyone charged with leading a business.

In the United States, publicly traded firms are required to disclose known risks that could lead to business failure. These risks are disclosed in the firm's annual 10-K filings and in S-1 filings when the firm first goes public. For instance, Google lists a number of risks that could affect the viability of its business. Some of these risks are summarized in Exhibit 12.9.

As you can see from reviewing the risks that have been identified by the managers (or more likely the investment bankers and attorneys) of Google, most of the risks identified as sources of potential business failure fall into two broad categories: *external* and *internal*. In the next section, we look at both categories in some detail.

EXTERNAL CAUSES OF ORGANIZATIONAL FAILURE

You will recall that there are two major contexts facing firms that determine the success of their strategies: in Chapter 3 you were introduced to the internal context of strategy and in Chapter 4 you learned about the external context. Just as these factors affect the success of strategies, it should not be surprising that causes of failure can also be categorized similarly. External causes of organizational failure reflect trends and events that strike at the core of a company's business. Some of these changes, such as population trends in peacetime, occur slowly and predictably. Others, such as natural disasters and wars, occur suddenly and with a severity that may change the shape of much more than the business world. Failure to foresee the possibility of such events and to consider their implications is an invitation to trouble. Remarkably enough, a recent study of fifty-one failed organizations found that not one of the failures was the result of unforeseeable events.[26] In each case, managers observed, discussed, and then disregarded the relevant change in the external environment.

External change may take one of four forms: *economic, competitive, social,* and *technological.*

Economic Change Managers are often heard to say that "the trend is your friend." A boom can cover many sins, and good economic times often mask organizational problems. A bust, however, can turn many small glitches into big problems. A list of economic problems includes (but is certainly not limited to) slackening overall demand, currency devaluation, international monetary crises, interest-rate hikes, and credit squeezes. Common sense would suggest that when economic activity levels off or declines, the number of failures will increase and vice versa. As a matter of fact, that's exactly how it works out.

Exhibit 12.9 Some of Google's Risk Listed in S-1

RISK FACTORS

An investment in Google involves significant risks. You should read these risk factors carefully before deciding whether to invest in our company. The following is a description of what we consider our key challenges and risks.

Risks Related to Our Business and Industry

We face significant competition from Microsoft and Yahoo.

We face competition from other Internet companies, including web search providers, Internet advertising companies and destination web sites that may also bundle their services with Internet access.

We face competition from traditional media companies, and we may not be included in the advertising budgets of large advertisers, which could harm our operating results.

We expect our growth rates to decline and anticipate downward pressure on our operating margin in the future.

Our operating results may fluctuate.

If we do not continue to innovate and provide products and services that are useful to users, we may not remain competitive, and our revenues and operating results could suffer.

We generate our revenue almost entirely from advertising, and the reduction in spending by or loss of advertisers could seriously harm our business.

We rely on our Google Network members for a significant portion of our net revenues, and otherwise benefit from our association with them, and the loss of these members could adversely affect our business.

Our business and operations are experiencing rapid growth. If we fail to manage our growth, our business and operating results could be harmed.

If we fail to maintain an effective system of internal controls, we may not be able to accurately report our financial results or prevent fraud. As a result, current and potential stockholders could lose confidence in our financial reporting, which would harm our business and the trading price of our stock.

Our business depends on a strong brand, and if we are not able to maintain and enhance our brand, our business and operating results would be harmed.

Proprietary document formats may limit the effectiveness of our search technology by excluding the content of documents in such formats.

New technologies could block our ads, which would harm our business.

Our corporate culture has contributed to our success, and if we cannot maintain this culture as we grow, our business may be harmed.

Our intellectual property rights are valuable, and any inability to protect them could reduce the value of our products, services and brand.

(continued)

Exhibit 12.9 Continued

We are, and may in the future be, subject to intellectual property rights claims, which are costly to defend, could require us to pay damages and could limit our ability to use certain technologies in the future.

Expansion into international markets is important to our long-term success, and our inexperience in the operation of our business outside the U.S. increases the risk that our international expansion efforts will not be successful.

We compete internationally with local information providers and with U.S. competitors who are currently more successful than we are in various markets.

Our business may be adversely affected by malicious third-party applications that interfere with the Google experience.

If we fail to detect click-through fraud, we could lose the confidence of our advertisers, thereby causing our business to suffer.

We are susceptible to index spammers who could harm the integrity of our web search results.

Our ability to offer our products and services may be affected by a variety of U.S. and foreign laws.

If we were to lose the services of Eric, Larry, Sergey or our senior management team, we may not be able to execute our business strategy.

The initial option grants to many of our senior management and key employees are fully vested. Therefore, these employees may not have sufficient financial incentive to stay with us.

If we are unable to retain or motivate key personnel or hire qualified personnel, we may not be able to grow effectively.

Our CEO and our two founders run the business and affairs of the company collectively, which may harm their ability to manage effectively.

We have a short operating history and a relatively new business model in an emerging and rapidly evolving market. This makes it difficult to evaluate our future prospects and may increase the risk of your investment.

At the same time, however, although economic change does indeed contribute to decline and failure, we should keep its role in proper perspective. According to one study, only 9 percent of all failures are caused chiefly by economic factors. The same study also found that during any economic cycle, good performers outperformed laggards by astonishing rates: While good performers' earnings per share grew at 33 percent annually, those of poor performers declined by 23 percent.[27] Can we draw any conclusions from these findings? One conclusion is perhaps that good management can offset poor economic conditions.

Competitive Change   Because so many events can drastically change the competitive landscape—the emergence of low-cost foreign competitors, the entry of new companies in an industry, the merger of two competitors—most companies operate in a world of constantly shifting competition. Thirty-five percent of all business failures are related to competitive change (i.e., the emergence of competition plus loss of market).[28] Usually, competitive change takes the form of price competition, as competitors lower prices in order to introduce products into new markets (a trend that's particularly common during economic downturns). In response, incumbents often try to keep factories at near-capacity production despite decreased demand.

A more sudden and less predictable type of competition comes from foreign countries or the appearance of a new technology. Foreign competition has been a fact of life for many years now, and in the United States, it's had a particularly devastating impact on clothing (shoes and textiles), consumer electronics, and steel. Failures in these industries highlight the importance of monitoring the external competitive environment.

Social Change

Because it generally takes a fairly long time for a society to accommodate significant changes, social change is usually less abrupt and less obvious than other forms of external change. The first signs of changes in people's attitudes toward work, such as the balance of men and women professionals and an aging workforce, have been evident for decades, but many companies still don't fully understand how the shift affects them.

Although such trends are hard to quantify, companies must realize that failure to recognize and respond to social changes can be extremely costly. Numerous companies have lost touch with markets or customers because they failed to observe or react to such social trends as changes in lifestyles, in the composition of given populations, or in attitudes toward such issues as pollution and personal health. Krispy Kreme, for example, the acclaimed purveyor of fried donuts, blamed a slowdown in business on the changing dietary habits of carbohydrate-conscious consumers. Apparently taken by surprise, the company issued its first profit warning since going public, thereby adding fuel to investor worries about its growth prospects.[29] Companies can even lose touch with their own employees, and the consequences may range from declining productivity to work stoppages.

Again, however, we should repeat that changes such as these tend to occur slowly, over long periods of time, and in one recent survey, CEOs agreed that in most industries reasonably astute management should be able to keep up with them.[30]

Technological Change

It's not overstating the case to say that global markets are what they are today because today's technologies make it possible to move information, products, and people quite easily. Technological change is a result of advances in information transportation technology.

Information Technology The absolute amount of knowledge in the world has been growing at an increasing rate. Between 1965 and 1980, for example, the number of scientific articles published per day rose from 3,000 to 8,000, and because knowledge feeds on itself, this pattern isn't likely to change. In any case, even if the rate of increase were to diminish, the existing knowledge base would still be so large that the absolute increase in units of knowledge per unit of time would remain large throughout at least the first half of the next century.

Just as important, the growing number of advanced communications technologies will greatly increase the availability of all knowledge that is produced. Combined with the rate at which new knowledge is being generated, technology has also increased the *availability* of information substantially.

Transportation Technology Transportation technology has increased the number of markets to which a business has access and the speed with which they can be accessed. Moreover, we now know a lot more about markets to which we've long had access, and not surprisingly, the effects of changes in information and transportation technology are closely related. The decline in U.S. manufacturing employment, for example, is a direct consequence of automation (information technology) and importation (manufacturing and transportation technologies).

The increasing availability and complexity of information make the task of focusing on relevant information more daunting than ever. This fact is especially important. As we said at the beginning of this section, organizational failure is rarely a consequence of unforeseen events. Rather, it very often results from management's failure to make the best use of relevant information.

INTERNAL CAUSES OF ORGANIZATIONAL FAILURE

It's nearly impossible to say exactly what percentage of business failures result from internal causes, but most experts agree that internal causes of failure are more common than external ones. Failure is generally the result of a bad strategy, poor executive judgment, or financial mismanagement.

Strategy Failure   By now it should be clear that a good strategy is preferable to a poor one and that expert implementation will always outperform poor implementation. Also, recall that a quality strategy exploits opportunities in the marketplace. It also enables the firm to fit with the current competitive environment and adapt to changes so that it will be well-positioned when the competitive environment changes. When a firm's strategy is poorly adapted to the current environment or a change in the environment results in a major misalignment, quick decline may result.

Management Failure   Why does poor management lead to failure? A recent study addressed the common assumption that failures are due to inept or incompetent CEOs or senior executives. After interviewing executives from over fifty failed firms, the researcher concluded that people who become CEOs of large corporations are almost always remarkably intelligent.[31] That's not surprising: They reach the top because they are regarded as the most capable, and are repeatedly chosen for positions over their fellow managers. So, how do smart managers lead organizations to failure? Some of these concepts were reviewed in Chapter 2, but we revisit a few of them here.

Dictatorial management styles, for instance, can be problematic. In a dictatorship, leaders ignore input from others, who soon stop offering it. Dictatorial managers tend to be-

Economic changes, such as rising crude oil and gasoline prices, can certainly contribute to business failures, but research shows they aren't the main cause. If anything, downturns "magnify" a company's shortcomings and put managers and their strategies to the test.

come either averse to change or unable to implement it effectively because they lack information they need.

A related problem is *lack of managerial depth*, which is often a by-product of dictatorial leadership. It arises when a strong leader refuses to be surrounded by equally strong people. When this problem sets in, it tends to compound itself. Lack of managerial depth has been cited as a contributing factor to the failure of several organizations. CEO Roger Smith of GM was notorious for getting rid of fellow executives who regularly disagreed with him, either firing them or exiling them to relatively desolate corners of the organization. As a result, the organization lost touch with a changing marketplace and saw its market share decline precipitously.

Another effect of flawed leadership is the tendency of top management to become unbalanced. A management team is unbalanced when experience in one product or functional area dominates the team, the board of directors, or both. Let's say, for example, that the CEO and the board of directors are executives with financial backgrounds. Once they reach a financial decision, it's not likely to be questioned, even by other top managers with financial experience.

Finally, although individual dishonesty and fraud are not as common as we might be led to believe by such cases as Enron, WorldCom, and Tyco, they can and do cause severe damage to organizations. They're especially dangerous when they involve systemic failures in a company's accounting and auditing functions. WorldCom, for example, admitted that in order to meet Wall Street expectations, it had inflated its profits by $3.8 billion between January 2001 and March 2002. Only *systemic* financial failure could lead to such a mammoth collapse.

A weak finance function can have a devastating impact on an organization, in part because it's ultimately a reflection of larger management problems. It may present itself in the form of an unbalanced executive team with little financial knowledge or experience or as a more general organizational defect that fosters inadequate financial controls, a weak auditing function, or both. One of the greatest dangers of a weak financial function—*creative accounting*—emerges during economic downturns. Fudging earnings or sales is a great temptation during a downturn, but it's a less attractive option in a firm with a strong financial function.

Warning Signals of Organizational Decline   At this point, you undoubtedly realize that organizations are complex and that a lot can go wrong with them. You may also be wondering if there are any early warning signals that would prompt someone to start questioning a firm's strategy or its execution, or simply the reliability or competency of its leaders. You can rely on certain indicators that reflect a variety of factors. The tools presented in Chapter 4—PESTEL, industry structure, and value-chain analysis tools—can be good *qualitative* indicators. Regular evaluation of the quality of a firm's strategy is another qualitative indicator. A strategy that does not fit with current external environmental conditions or the near-term environment will lead to organizational decline.

Not surprisingly, financial indicators are a common signal of the potential for decline. For instance, unexpected declines in earnings or revenues are always a red flag. So are declining customer satisfaction scores. WorldCom's rapid demise was foreshadowed by several quarters of record-breaking numbers of customer complaints about service quality. Sometimes incipient problems can be discovered by assessing financial ratios (profitability, operating, liquidity, and debt ratios are a good start) in terms of historical or industry data. In addition to the signals provided by operating leverage and sustainable growth rate, discussed later in the chapter, you can also use a combination of ratios to predict financial problems. Several of these tools are showcased in the box entitled "How Would *You* Do That? 12.1."

Are Ford's Numbers Fizzy or Flat?

Here we will use the 2005 and 2006 annual results from Ford Motor Company to walk you through a handful of financial analysis tools that you can use quickly to get a sense of a firm's financial strength. The breadth of Ford's activities once spanned the traditional Ford, Lincoln, and Mercury brands, plus import brands like Aston Martin, Jaguar, Volvo, Land Rover, and an equity interest in Mazda. Recently however, Ford sold off Aston Martin, and many auto industry experts speculate that Jaguar, Volvo, and Land Rover are on the auction block as well (and may have another home by the time you read this). This provides a good example given the recent press about their financial troubles, and we can use quantitative tools to see if there is substance behind the rumors. These tools are most often used to gauge the financial health and prospects of large firms, but they can be used to assess any new venture. These types of analyses can be used to determine whether the economic logic underlying the firm's strategy is actually paying off and to suggest implementation levers that may need to be pulled in case problems are discovered or predicted.

Z-SCORE MODEL

Let's start with the Z-Score model, the brainchild of Edward I. Altman, who is considered to be the dean of insolvency predictors. Altman was the first person to develop a highly accurate prediction model. A recent test of Altman's Z-Score found that it was 95-percent accurate in classifying companies. Altman's model takes the following form:

$$Z = 1.2A + 1.4B + 3.3C + 0.6D + .99E$$

where

A = Working capital/total assets
B = Retained earnings/total assets
C = Earnings before interest and taxes/total assets
D = Market value of equity/book value of total debt
E = Sales/total assets

If Z is less than 1.8, then the firm is classified as "high likelihood of failure."

Although the model was developed to analyze manufacturing companies, it can also be applied to nonmanufacturing organizations by modifying the formula. The formula is modified by omitting the fifth component (E). The adjusted formula seems to provide equally valid predictive results. Applying the model to Ford's 2006 annual report, the numbers summarized in Exhibit 12.10, you would find:

$$Z = 1.2(.0038) + 1.4(-.0001) + 3.3(-.0250) + .6(.09147) + .99(.5517) = .52$$

Because Z is less than 1.8, it suggests that Ford is at great risk of failure.

SUSTAINABLE GROWTH

Another useful model for evaluating a firm's financial health is the sustainable growth rate. The value obtained from this analysis is the rate of growth the company can sustain with its current capital structure. Inasmuch as many firms get into trouble because they simply "grow broke," the sustainable growth rate is a useful tool.

To calculate the sustainable growth rate for a company, you need to know how profitable the company is as determined by its return on equity (ROE). You also need to know what percentage of a company's earnings per share is paid out in dividends, which is called the dividend-payout ratio. From there, multiply the company's ROE by its plowback ratio, which is equal to 1 minus the dividend-payout ratio.

Sustainable-growth rate = ROE × (1 − dividend-payout ratio)

Let's go through another example using Ford. Ford's ROE is a negative number (since they lost money in 2006) percent and yet dividends are still paid out of its earnings. Based on the formula, Ford has no sustainable growth, unless it finances that growth through new debt or equity. In fact, given its losses, it is using debt to finance dividend payments! So you should expect the next big step in any Ford turnaround to be the discontinuation of dividend payments (which Ford announced at the end of 2006). Now that we know Ford's sustainable-growth rate is basically zero (given current profitability or lack thereof), we should be concerned if the company promises that it can sustain a

Exhibit 12.10 Key Numbers at Ford Motor Company

	2005 (in U.S. millions)	2006 (in U.S. millions)
Working Capital (Current Assets—Current Liabilities)	$(5,072)	$1090
Total Assets	275,936	290,217
Retained Earnings	13,064	(17)
Earnings Before Interest and Taxes	8,276	(7,263)
Market Value of Equity	15,000	14,500
Total Liabilities	153,777	158,575
Revenues	176,896	160,123
Net Cash Flow	20,387	9,609
Liquidation Value We use current Assets minus all debt because that gives a value that might reasonably be achieved if the company had to be sold	(107,296)	(101,250)
Gross Profit Margin	18%	7%
Net Profit Margin	1%	(8%)
Return on Equity	10.7%	(na) Ford had negative equity of ($3,465) and an operating loss of ($12,613)
Dividend Payout Rate	.52	(na) lost $6.72 per share and paid out $.25 per share dividend

growth rate of well above that from now until eternity. From 2005 to 2006, Ford's sales actually declined by $16 billion. If you had calculated Ford's sustainable growth rate in 2005, you would have come up with 5.13 percent. This means that Ford was continually growing faster than the growth it can support using the existing debt and equity. To maintain this or a higher growth rate, Ford would have to become more profitable (which would boost its ROE), pay out fewer dividends as a percentage of earnings (which would reduce the dividend-payout ratio, but that is already at zero), or obtain more money through borrowing or the equity markets (as it did with the additional equity acquired in 2003).

OPERATING LEVERAGE

Finally, operating leverage can give you an idea how sensitive a firm's profits are to small increases or decreases in revenues. If scenario planning shows that many able competitors are liable to jump into the fray or that the firm's revenues will likely go down in the future for other reasons, this metric can be used to determine if fixed costs need to be cut immediately, before profitability suffers.

Operating leverage can be calculated simply by dividing *gross margin* (sometimes called *gross profit*) by *net profit margin*. The beauty of this indicator is that it shows very quickly the extent to which a percentage-profit decrease will be reflected in a percentage decrease in profitability. In

2005, for instance, Ford had a gross margin of 18 percent and a net profit margin of 1 percent. If you do the math, you'll find that Ford had an operating leverage of 18. What does this number mean? It means that a 1-percent decrease in revenues would result in an 18-percent decrease in profits (unless some element of the firm's fixed-cost structure was dramatically reduced). From this exercise, you should conclude that Ford is reasonably unhealthy, at least in financial terms. However, given that most of its competitors, such as GM and Toyota, are huge, many financial changes would need to be made for it to regain its historical financial strength.

Strategic Change and Organizational Renewal

Not surprisingly, strategic management—particularly in dynamic contexts—is a process for dealing with strategic change and organizational renewal. As was discussed in Chapter 11, implementing a change in strategy involves transforming the firm from its current state to a different one through the use of implementation levers and strategic leadership. In many ways, therefore, you already have a good foundation for understanding the processes of change and renewal in certain situations—namely, in firms that aren't yet facing crises.

A key premise is that all business environments are in a state of change. To remain successful, firms must take one of two actions: stay aligned with changes in their environments by responding quickly or actively anticipate changes in customer demographics, future technologies, and potential new products/services, and thereby recreate their industries.

Strategic change can be defined as significant changes in resource-allocation choices or business activities that align the firm's strategy with its vision. Strategic change could also encompass changes that are undertaken to inform the firm what its new vision should be. Strategic change is difficult. Consider the problem of orthodoxies reviewed earlier in the chapter. When a firm explicitly or tacitly adheres to orthodoxies to the point that it creates rigidities in the way management thinks about the firm and its environment or rigidities in internal practices, the difficulty of strategic change is compounded. The most traditional types of change processes involve some combination of cost reduction, asset reduction or redeployment, or restructuring.

strategic change Significant changes in resource allocation choices in the business and implementation activities that align the firm's strategy with its vision, or in its vision.

Cost Reduction This tactic is as straightforward as it sounds. Sometimes this requires short-term reduction in staffing, or the elimination of expenses that don't clearly affect the quality or attractiveness of a product or service. One common consulting trick to control costs is to take stock of all the inputs that a firm uses, identify those that are high volume inputs but purchased in a decentralized fashion, then centralize the purchase of these key inputs to gain lower costs through larger average orders.

Asset Reduction or Redeployment This tactic typically asks managers to identify assets that may be undervalued on the books (like real estate) and then sold to realize their true market value. Another variation is to use a piece of equipment on higher margin products, instead of wasting its productive capacity on lower margin products. For instance, a brewery can make much more money on craft beers than low-priced beers, but both essentially use the same fixed assets for the beers production. A common consulting trick here is to look at the portfolio of a firm's products and services and identify those that seem to command the highest margins, and then focus productive and sales resources on those products. This may sound silly, but firms often have a large inventory of product or service offerings, even though only a few of these offerings account for the lion's share of profitability.

Restructuring Whereas cost and asset restructuring are typically narrowly defined tactics, restructuring is typically defined by a major change in the composition of a firm's assets combined with a major change in its business or corporate strategy. It usually involves selling off (or liquidating) businesses in multidivisional firms, either voluntarily through spin-offs or involuntarily through hostile takeovers. Restructuring also can occur once a leveraged buyout (LBO) of a firm has been completed. Thus, you should view restructuring as more than the simple divestiture of a single business unit, or reduction of assets or costs.

THE CHANGE PROCESS

Although change is rarely a linear process, it can be helpful to think of the elements of change in such a fashion in order to appreciate the magnitude of the effort. Using the principles you've already learned about the strategic management process, let's consider all that must happen in order to implement a strategic change successfully. The best place to start is with a broader understanding of the steps that lead to positive organizational transformation. Exhibit 12.11 provides you with this broader picture of what it takes to get change going.[32] This model was pioneered by John Kotter of the Harvard Business School, a professor long recognized as the guru of organizational transformation.

Exhibit 12.11 Essential Transformation Steps

Eight Steps to Transforming Your Organization

1
Establishing a Sense of Urgency
Examining market and competitive realities
Identifying and discussing crises, potential crises, or major opportunities

2
Forming a Powerful Guiding Coalition
Assembling a group with enough power to lead the change effort
Encouraging the group to work together as a team

3
Creating a Vision
Creating a vision to help direct the change effort
Developing strategies for achieving that vision

4
Communicating the Vision
Using every vehicle possible to communicate the new vision
    and strategies
Teaching new behaviors by the example of the guiding coalition

5
Empowering Others to Act on the Vision
Getting rid of obstacles to change
Changing systems or structures that seriously undermine the vision
Encouraging risk taking and nontraditional ideas, activities, and actions

6
Planning for and Creating Short-Term Wins
Planning for visible performance improvements
Creating those improvements
Recognizing and rewarding employees involved in the improvements

7
Consolidating Improvements and Producing Still More Change
Using increased credibility to change systems, structures, and
    policies that don't fit the vision
Hiring, promoting, and developing employees who can implement
    the vision
Reinvigorating the process with new projects, themes, and change agents

8
Institutionalizing New Approaches
Articulating the connections between the new behaviors and
    corporate success
Developing the means to ensure leadership development and succession

The first step, establishing a sense of urgency, is sometimes referred to as the "burning platform." A "burning platform" is a term used to describe an extremely urgent or compelling business situation in order to convey, in the strongest terms, the need for change. Using this process, you can get people's attention and build awareness of the need for change very quickly. The second part, a guiding coalition, is in essence a group of missionaries who believe in the need for change, are in positions of power where they can see that it is effected, work well as a team, and are good communicators of the vision. Often, some members of the coalition have been with the firm for a long time, so have deep respect from their colleagues in addition to good knowledge of the company's deep culture. The vision component you already know well. It is the first part of the strategy framework that you were introduced to in Exhibit 1.3 from Chapter 1. Without a clear and compelling vision, the change effort has no direction. We have already mentioned the fact that the guiding coalition needs to be comprised of good communicators, and this fourth transformation step means that they act on those abilities—there probably cannot be too much communication when so much is at stake in big transformation efforts.

Staging & Pacing

While the guiding coalition is critical, they cannot accomplish transformation alone. Through their communication and empowerment of others, the transformation movement can take on a life of its own. This is why it is designated separately as a fifth step. Planning for and creating short-term wins is the essential sixth step. These successes need to be celebrated and shared so the firm sees that it is making progress with the transformation. An example of an early win was SAP's signing of Exxon as a client for its enterprise resource package software. This win signified that the SAP strategy was paying off, and suggested that better things were sure to come. Step 6 maps well to the staging facet of your strategy diamond. ◆ This is the point where the guiding coalition, and those that they have empowered, take stock of their successes and begin to map out the next staging and pacing of the transformation effort. Recall that strategy is about tradeoffs and choices, and through the consolidation process you are able to make choices about what should no longer be done, and what activities need added attention or additional direction. Finally, the accumulation of the activities undertaken to accomplish or work through steps 1 through 7, will have likely changed the culture in such a profound way that the transformational change is institutionalized. The term *institutionalization* is widely used in social theory to denote the process of making something (for example a concept, a social role, particular values and norms, or modes of behavior) become embedded within an organization as an established custom or norm within that system. In essence, what may have been considered novel, difficult, or even revolutionary at the beginning of the change process now becomes almost taken for granted, and new hires to the organization will often assume that the firm always operated that way.

Whereas Exhibit 12.11 gives you the larger agenda, Exhibit 12.12 lays out the nuts and bolts necessary for the change to be achieved, along with the possible repercussions if any particular nut or bolt is neglected.

Specifically, it illustrates this process and the possible outcomes if any of the elements of the change effort are missing. Consultants love this tool for this very reason—it is prescriptive, predictive, and diagnostic. The model should also reinforce your understanding of the interdependence of strategy formulation and implementation. There are some necessary and obvious areas of overlap between the two frameworks. For instance, a clear vision and the ability to communicate it clearly are identified as desirable and essential in both frameworks. Beyond this specific point of overlap, Exhibit 12.12 actually guides you in prescribing interventions that would lead to positive strategic change.[33] The upper path in the model, where all the conditions are present—from vision to an execution plan—suggests that strategic change is most likely to be effective (assuming the correct implementation of the components). However, when any individual component is weak or missing, then you can see that negative consequences are likely to occur. Let's talk through each of the scenarios, working with the boxes from left to right.

Exhibit 12.12 The Levers of Organizational Transformation

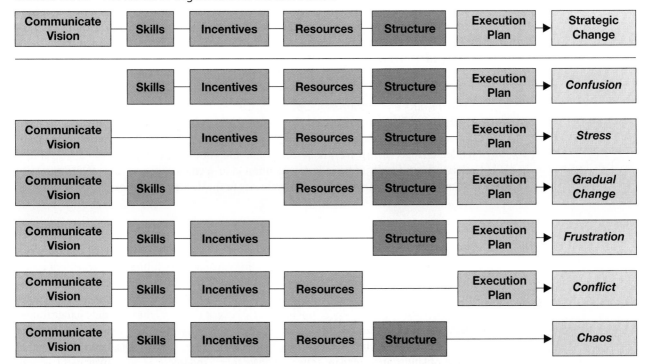

Vision First, in order to change, the firm must have a new vision of the desired end state. This was pretty clear in the framework discussed in Exhibit 12.11, just as it is here. This new vision must be communicated to those who will effect the change. As we have noted numerous times, because a vision is not a strategy, the new vision will require an executive plan—a strategy—that will serve as a map of the strategic-change process.

Skills Executing strategy is a task of all managers, indeed all employees, not just the work of those who dream up new strategies. Consequently, the change effort requires skills embodied in the people of the organization.

Incentives However, what tasks people spend their time on is heavily influenced by incentives. To get people to change their behaviors, as is often needed when an organization is trying to change its strategy, the firm will have to provide incentives.

Resources Next, it is critical to recognize that talented people with proper incentives will find it much easier to work toward the new vision if the organization allocates the resources necessary to accommodate the desired changes. These resources can be evaluated using the VRINE framework to gain a richer understanding of the unique opportunities or challenges faced by a particular change effort.

Structure An effective strategy, and in this case a strategic change, often requires modification, or at least clarification, of organizational structure. Finally, a plan that connects the dots in the change process must be put into place and widely communicated.

When all of these pieces of the change process are in place, a firm is likely to manage successfully the shift from one strategy to another—and the outcome is likely to be successful strategic change. Yet if any single step is missing, it undermines the entire change effort. Note that each missing step has different potential consequences for the change effort. Consider a few possible outcomes should we remove any one of the steps of strategic change.

First, if there is no guiding vision, organization members are likely to be extremely confused about why all these efforts are to be undertaken. If the organization does not have the right people who possess the skills necessary to carry out the efforts, extreme levels of stress will probably result among those who are left to shoulder the burden they are ill-equipped to carry.

Should the wrong incentives be in place, the organization is likely to change much slower than it could, or worse, actually pursue an unintended pathway because that is what is actually rewarded. If resources are not allocated, extreme levels of frustration are likely to emerge because managers and employees feel that they have been given a difficult goal without any institutional support. If the organizational structure does not accommodate the intended change, then there will be confusion and conflict over reporting and cooperative relationships. Finally, if there is no execution plan, a chaotic state is likely to emerge, with various managers pursuing different pathways to the desired end state.

TURNAROUND MANAGEMENT

The strategic-change process as just described is difficult work. However, all change is not created equal. Sometimes, there comes a point when a firm's future prospects seem hopeless, and this section is about strategy from that point forward. When an organization is going downhill fast, what can be done to turn it around? When the word *turnaround* comes into play, managers typically do not have the luxury of time, and the strategic-change framework presented in the previous section, though relevant, is also time-consuming. Ford and GM are examples of historically strong firms facing current dire straits. Remembering that causes of failure are rooted in strategy, management, and financial mismanagement, we will now walk through five stages of the turnaround-management process summarized in Exhibit 12.13.[34]

We identify five distinct stages, but before we proceed, here are five caveats that you should bear in mind in thinking about these stages:

1. Because every turnaround is unique, each stage is not necessarily distinguishable in every turnaround.

2. The number of stages involved in each turnaround stage will depend on the seriousness of the financial crisis facing a given company: The more dire the trouble, the more stages the turnaround process is likely to involve.

3. The importance of each stage will vary from case to case. Sometimes, for instance, analysis will be more important than action, whereas the opposite will be true in other cases.

4. A company can find itself involved in more than one stage at a time. Stages can overlap, and some tasks may affect more than one stage.

5. The length of time required to address each stage is not only fluid but can vary greatly. The major factors in determining the amount of time entailed by each stage include the size of the company and the severity of its financial straits. Addressing every stage in the process may take 12 to 36 months.

The following stage-by-stage description of the turnaround process can be used as a template for designing a change-management program for a company in financial trouble. Exhibit 12.14 shows you how all these pieces work together in the successful turnaround of ISH, a German cable company.[35]

Stage 1: Changing Management Changing management means one of two things: either changing the way management approaches organizational problems or changing the personnel at the top of the organization, which is more often the case. Most

Exhibit 12.13   Stages in the Turnaround Process

Stages	Management Change	Evaluation	Emergency	Stabilization	Return-to-Normal
Objectives and Action Items	1. Select new top-management team. 2. Weed out impediments.	1. Can it survive? 2. Identify strategy.	1. Survival. 2. Positive cash flow through cost reduction, asset reduction and restructuring.	1. Enhance profitability. 2. Restructure business to increase ROI.	1. Seek profitable growth. 2. Build competitive strengths.
	3. Select a turnaround manager.	3. Develop plan. 4. Determine nature of turnaround.	3. Raise cash. 4. Take charge. 5. Get control of cash.		

CEOs and other officers will not relinquish power easily. Often egos make it difficult for them to admit that a downturn is really happening or that they're incapable of pulling the company out of its nosedive. The first step, therefore, is setting up a top-management team to lead the turnaround effort. In some cases, the board of directors may recruit turnaround specialists; bankers and corporate attorneys are also usually involved. As outsiders, turnaround specialists come aboard unfettered by obligations to the incumbent management team or the firm's current strategy. During this stage, the turnaround team will weed out and replace any top officials who may impede the turnaround effort. In general, it is believed that the benefits of the leadership capabilities that outsiders bring far outweigh their lack of organizational or industry experience.[36]

Stage 2: Analyzing the Situation   Before making any major changes, turnaround leaders must determine the chances of the firm's survival, identify appropriate strategies for turning it around, and develop a preliminary action plan. The first days, therefore, are devoted to fact finding and diagnosing the scope and severity of the problems at hand.

In the meantime, the team must deal with various stakeholder groups. The first group often consists of angry creditors who may have been kept in the dark about the company's financial status. Employees are confused and nervous. Customers, vendors, and suppliers are wary about the firm's future. It's essential that the turnaround team be open and frank with all of these groups.

Once the major problems have been identified, the team develops a strategic plan with specific goals and detailed functional actions. To keep the process moving and to make sure that priorities are adhered to, goals should be sequenced to correspond directly with the staging facet of the strategy diamond. Then the team must sell its plan to the key members of the organization, including the board of directors, the management team, and employees. Presenting the plan to key external parties—bankers, major creditors, and vendors—goes a long way toward regaining their confidence and financial support.

Exhibit 12.14 A Successful Turnaround at ISH

How exactly would you implement the turnaround steps shown in Exhibit 12.13? Here we illustrate the turnaround process for ISH GmbH, one of Europe's largest and most successful cable companies. Formerly part of Deutsche Telekom, in April 2002 this supplier of cable services to approximately four million homes in the German state of North Rhine Westphalia (NRW) was in a state of total business failure—bleeding cash, losing money, and in default on nearly €2.7 billion (€ is the symbol for euros) in debt. This is the story of ISH's resurrection from the organizational graveyard.

Stage 1: Changing Management

In April 2002, ISH's management brought in the strategy-consulting and turnaround firm AlixPartners to help it analyze its books and cash flow. AlixPartners is a professional turnaround firm recently credited with profit improvement at beleaguered Kmart. Nearly 120 days later, ISH shareholders appointed Jim Bonsall to fill the role of CEO. Bonsall is a principal with AlixPartners and has 25 years of experience working with European and multinational public and private companies.

Stage 2: Situation Analysis

Ironically, when AlixPartners was brought in, ISH management was completely unaware of the depth of the firm's problems. Although this may sound surprising, a management team may lose track of the need for change when its members are too heavily invested in the status quo. Initial analyses revealed that, although the firm had recorded current liabilities of €7 million, the actual number was €500 million! Management was also unaware that ISH was in default on many of its secured-debt facilities. These amounted to nearly €2.5 billion; thus, its total liabilities were approximately €3 billion.

Stage 3: Emergency Action

The complexities of Germany's insolvency code nearly always result in the total liquidation of a firm's assets. Once difficulties are discovered, a troubled firm has 21 days to resolve relationships with creditors prior to being declared insolvent. To take advantage of this three-week window of opportunity, AlixPartners worked quickly to gain 120 days of additional short-term bank financing and assigned teams of AlixPartners professionals to ISH's 17 largest vendors. Teams met weekly, and the objective was to educate bankers and vendors on the balance sheet and operating strengths of ISH while preventing a premature declaration of insolvency. By the end of the 120-day period, not only had insolvency been avoided, but the firm had reached agreement among the major creditors on an operating plan for going forward.

Stage 4: Restructuring ISH

Shareholders officially appointed Bonsall as CEO of ISH in late 2002. However, restructuring had actually started in the emergency-action stage in April of that year. Bonsall's early agenda for his tenure as CEO included establishing core organizational values, improving the company's image, solving problems using a team approach, and achieving profitability and industry leadership. He sought to do this by institutionalizing a balanced-scorecard system and tying a reward system to it that supported his objective of transforming the firm into a customer- and data-driven organization. Bonsall achieved these objectives the hard way: by achieving results and restoring trust and confidence in the company's goals. One of the biggest early restructuring tasks was to reorient ISH away from the Internet and back to its cable-television business. The company had put the vast majority of its time, money, and effort on building up its Internet subscriber base and had only 5,000 Internet subscribers to show for these efforts (versus its core, but neglected, resource of 4 million cable subscribers).

Stage 5: Normalcy and ISH's Return to Industry Leadership

Bonsall's management team agreed that the best way to grow the cable business would be to offer more selection and technical innovation through a digital-program offering in the key cities of Cologne, Düsseldorf, Bochum, and Neuss. All this would have to be achieved in the first year following the restructuring, starting in December 2003. ISH overcame numerous institutional and technical complications to achieve the digitalization objectives.

Signs that the ISH turnaround was succeeding was the fact that by January 2004, cable outages had become a thing of the past and customer satisfaction was increasing. ISH saw itself as a company that provided its four million customers with entertainment. Soon, the company would launch a showcase with up to 50 additional channels and Near Video on Demand. Bonsall expected a standard offering for the whole of Germany to be marketed jointly by all cable regions. ISH continued to offer high-speed Internet—with download speeds of 2 MB and upload speeds of 512 KB, leaving the competition behind in the residential customer segment.

Stage 3: Implementing an Emergency Action Plan

When the firm's condition is critical, the team's plan is usually both drastic and simple. Emergency surgery is performed to stop the bleeding and improve the organization's chances of pulling through. At this time, as employees are laid off or entire departments eliminated, emotions tend to run high. Such cuts should be made thoughtfully and objectively, but swiftly.

The turnaround team must also turn its attention to cash, which is the lifeblood of the business. It must establish a positive operating cash flow as quickly as possible, and it must make sure that there's enough cash to implement its turnaround strategies. Unprofitable divisions or units are often unloaded, sometimes after some quick, corrective surgery. As we mentioned in our opening comments on strategic change, the fundamental leverage points are cost reduction, asset reduction, and restructuring.

Stage 4: Stabilization

Once the bleeding has stopped, losing divisions sold off, and administrative costs cut, the turnaround team directs its efforts toward making current operations effective and efficient. Increasing profits and return on assets and equity usually means restructuring. In many ways, this stage is the most difficult: Cutting losses is one thing, but achieving an acceptable return on investment is another. In the new, leaner company, some facilities may be closed; the company may even withdraw from certain markets or target its products toward different markets.

Finally, as the company restructures for competitive effectiveness, the right mix of people becomes quite important. Reward and compensation systems, another implementation lever, are changed to reinforce the turnaround effort and to get people thinking "profits" and "return on investment." Everyone who still has a job must remember that survival, not tradition, is the number-one priority in reshaping the business.

Stage 5: Returning to Normal

In the final stage of the turnaround process, the company slowly returns to profitability. At earlier stages, the turnaround team focused on correcting problems. Now, however, it focuses on institutionalizing an emphasis on profitability, return on equity, and enhancing economic value. At this point, for example, the company may initiate new marketing programs to broaden its business base and increase market penetration. Financially, the firm shifts its emphasis from generating cash flow to maintaining a strong balance sheet, finding long-term financing, and setting up strategic accounting and control systems. Return to normalcy also entails a psychological shift: Rebuilding momentum and morale is almost as important as restoring ROI. Corporate culture must be renewed and reshaped, and negative attitudes must be transformed into positive attitudes.

Summary of Challenges

1. *Define new ventures, initial public offerings (IPOs), and corporate renewal and explain how they are related to strategic management.* New-venture creation is the creation of a new business from scratch. Young entrepreneurial firms often use initial public offerings (IPOs) to access the world's stock markets for capital. Corporate renewal is the outcome of actions and processes that return a failing or potentially failing firm to firm financial footing and resumption of profitable growth. All three activities require good strategies and solid execution.

2. *Understand entrepreneurship and the entrepreneurial process.* Entrepreneurship is the consequence of actions taken based on the perception and exploration of opportunity in the absence of obviously available resources. The entrepreneurial process leads to entrepreneurship and consists of the coordination of opportunity, key resources and capabilities, and the entrepreneur and entrepreneurial team.

3. *Describe the steps involved in new-venture creation and corporate new-venturing.* Entrepreneurial firms and established large firms follow the same steps in the new-venture creation process. The biggest difference between entrepreneurial new-venturing and corporate new-venturing is that the new venture in the latter context must overcome the fact that most large organizations are driven by the need to protect and optimize the use of existing resources and capabilities and discourage entrepreneurship and the pursuit of opportunity. New-venture creation starts with the identification of an opportunity. Opportunities can be distinguished from ideas in that they pass tests relating to market demand, market structure and size, and potential profitability. The remaining steps in new-venture creation are the drafting of a business plan, obtaining financing, and launching the new product or service. The order of these final three steps will vary significantly.

4. *Map out the stages leading up to an IPO.* Once a firm has validated a good opportunity and has some amount of prior success, its owners may seek to access capital through an IPO. First, the firm undergoes the legal and accounting preparation for a securities offering. Second, the firm contracts with an investment banker to establish a value for the firm and eventually sell its shares. During this process, the firm files a registration document called an S-1 statement with the appropriate legal authorities. Finally, the firm and its investment bankers time the offering to coincide with a market that will likely provide the highest initial bids for the company's stock. An IPO typically provides access to capital and motivation to install more formal and professional management processes. If the firm does not have the capital needs, it may bypass the IPO and install professional management directly.

5. *Understand the external and internal causes of organizational failure.* The four main sources of external change that may lead to organizational failure are economic change, competitive change, social change, and technological change. Although there are many possible internal causes of organizational failure, most can be traced back to either management problems or an ineffective finance function. However, an ineffective finance function is essentially a reflection of larger management problems.

6. *Outline a plan of action for strategic change and corporate renewal.* Successful strategic-change efforts require communicating a new vision, defining an executive plan, having the right people and skills, getting incentives right, allocating needed resources, and altering the organizational structure if necessary. However, if the firm's financial condition has deteriorated to the point of near failure, a turnaround plan is necessary. The first stage of a turnaround plan is a change of management. It may also mean that the existing team must be replaced with executives who are able to assess the situation quickly and develop a plan to remedy the firm's woes. During the second stage, the management team determines the business' chances of survival, identifies appropriate strategies, and develops a preliminary action plan. The third stage is not required in all firms. The third stage is the implementation of an emergency-action plan when an assessment in the previous stage has determined that the firm is in critical condition. Oftentimes, assets are sold and parts of the business shuttered to avoid further crisis. The fourth stage is the actual restructuring of the business to align the organizational structure with the five elements of the strategy diamond. If all has gone as planned, the firm enters the fifth stage, during which it returns to normalcy and profitable growth.

Review Questions

1. What is entrepreneurship?

2. What is the entrepreneurial process?

3. How is the entrepreneurial process related to strategy?

4. What steps are involved in new-venture creation?

5. What is a business plan?

6. How do entrepreneurial new-venture creation and corporate new-venture creation differ?

7. What must organizations do to prepare for an IPO?

8. What are some of the external causes of organizational failure?

9. What are some of the internal causes of organizational failure?

10. What are the stages of a turnaround plan?

11. How do you know that a turnaround has been successful?

Experiential Activities

Group Exercises

1. Entrepreneurship starts with an idea. Without being critical or judgmental, brainstorm a set of 10 ideas that could lead to the startup of a new business. Screen your ideas and select those that would enjoy the greatest market demand, the most attractive market structure and size, and the best profit margins. Which of these screens caused most of the ideas to be discarded? What additional information would you need to seek out to answer all the screening questions?

2. This second exercise relates to turnaround and change management. Identify a company that is in dire financial straits. What are the financial symptoms of this distress? Do you think the cause of this distress is a bad strategy, bad implementation, or both? Again, using the brainstorming skills you applied with activity 1, flesh out a new product and strategy proposal that might put the firm on better financial and strategic footing.

Ethical Debates

1. You are the cofounder and president of a new venture, manufacturing products for the recreational market. Five months after launching the business, one of your key suppliers informs you it can no longer supply you with a critical raw material since you are not a large-quantity user. Without the raw material the business cannot continue. There is a 50/50 chance that your new product may take off, which would let you provide the supplier with a demand estimate that could lead the supplier to think you are a larger prospect, and therefore worth investing in as a large-quantity purchaser. What do you do?

2. Your small manufacturing company is in serious financial difficulty. A large order of your products is ready to be delivered to a key customer, when you discover that the product is simply not right. It will not meet all performance specifications, will cause problems for your customer, and will require rework in the field; but this, you know, will not become evident until after the customer has received and paid for the order. If you do not ship the order and receive the payment as expected, your business may be forced into bankruptcy. And if you delay the shipment or inform the customer of these problems, you may lose the order and also go bankrupt. What do you do?

How Would
YOU DO THAT?

1. The box entitled "How Would *You* Do That? 12.1" introduced a number of financial tools for predicting a firm's financial troubles. Pick a public company that has recently announced financial woes and run these analyses on its financial results for the past three years. Do any of the indicators seem to detect looming problems? What might be the limits of these financial tools?

2. Exhibit 12.14 presented the successful turnaround of ISH GmbH. Identify another company in the business press that

you believe to be in the turnaround process. Based on Exhibit 12.13, which stages has it entered and what have managers chosen to do in those stages? What stages remain? What do you think are the key challenges facing management in returning this firm to normalcy?

Go on to see How Would You Do That at www.prenhall.com/ carpenter&sanders

Endnotes

1. Adapted from C. Anderson, *The Long Tail* (London: Hyperion, 2006).

2. W. Bygrave and J. Timmons, *Venture Capital at the Crossroads* (Boston: Harvard Business School Press, 1992).

3. Adapted from G. Hamel and C. K. Prahalad, *Competing for the Future* (Boston: Harvard Business School Press, 1994).

4. For a comprehensive discussion, see J. Timmons, *New Venture Creation* (New York: Irwin-McGraw-Hill, 1999).

5. J. Eckhardt and S. Shane, "Opportunities and Entrepreneurship," *Journal of Management* 29:3 (2003), 333–349; J. Eckhardt and S. Shane, "The Individual-Opportunity Nexus: A New Perspective on Entrepreneurship," in Z. Acs and D. Audretsch, eds., *The Handbook of Entrepreneurship Research* (Boston: Kluwer, 2003), 161–191.

6. From Google, S-1 statement, 2004.

7. Adapted from J. Timmons, *New Venture Creation* (New York: Irwin-McGraw-Hill, 1999).

8. Timmons, *New Venture Creation*; A. Bhide, "Bootstrap Finance," *Harvard Business Review* 70:6 (1992), 109–117.

9. Bhide, "Bootstrap Finance."

10. Among other sites, try www.bplans.com, www.sba.gov/starting/businessplan.html, www.morebusiness.com, and www.businessplans.org.

11. Timmons, *New Venture Creation*.

12. H. Chesbrough, "Designing Corporate Ventures in the Shadow of Private Venture Capital," *California Management Review* 42:3 (2000), 31–49.

13. Z. Block and I. MacMillan, *Corporate Venturing* (Boston: Harvard Business School Press, 1995).

14. D. Day, "Raising Radicals: Different Processes for Championing Innovative Corporate Ventures," *Organization Science* 9 (1994), 148–172.

15. D. Garvin, *A Note on Corporate Venturing and New Business Creation* (Boston: Harvard Business School, 1997).

16. N. Fast, *The Rise and Fall of Corporate New Venture Divisions* (Ann Arbor: UMI, 1978).

17. R. Gee, "Finding and Commercializing New Business," *Research-Technology Management* 37:1 (1994), 49–56.

18. Chesbrough, "Designing Corporate Ventures."

19. D. A. Garvin, "What Every CEO Should Know About Creating New Businesses," *Harvard Business Review* 82:7–8 (July–August 2004).

20. M. Pagano, F. Panetta, and L. Zingales, "Why Do Companies Go Public? An Empirical Analysis," *Journal of Finance* 53:1 (1998), 27–64.

21. Adapted from P. Downing, "IPO Launch Fraught with Perils," *The Ottawa Citizen*, High-Tech Report, October 12, 1998.

22. Because the regulations on IPOs are constantly changing, you may find it interesting to consult the source of these changes at www.sec.gov/index.htm.

23. R. Rajan and H. Servaes, "Analyst Following of Initial Public Offerings," *Journal of Finance* 52:2 (1997), 507–529; J. Ritter and I. Welch, "A Review of IPO Activity, Pricing, and Allocation," *Journal of Finance* 57:4 (2002), 1795–1828.

24. D. Wyckoff, *Organizational Formality and Performance in the Motor Carrier Industry* (Lexington, MA: Lexington Books, 1973).

25. Much of this material is drawn from M. A. Carpenter, *A Primer on Turnarounds* (Chicago: Association of Certified Turnaround Professionals, 2004).

26. S. Finkelstein, *Why Smart Executives Fail* (New York: Portfolio Press, 2003).

27. D. B. Bibeault, *Corporate Turnaround: How Managers Turn Losers Into Winners!* (New York: Beard Books, 2001).

28. Bibeault, *Corporate Turnaround*.

29. C. Terhune, "Krispy Kreme Issues Profit Warning—After 1st Forecast Reduction Since IPO, Stock Falls 29%; Low-Carb Fervor Is Blamed," *Wall Street Journal*, May 10, 2004, A8.

30. Finkelstein, *Why Smart Executives Fail.*

31. Finkelstein, *Why Smart Executives Fail.*

32. Adapted from J. Kotter, "Why transformation efforts fail," *Harvard Business Review.* March–April, 1995: 59–67.

33. Adapted from A. Marcus, *Management Strategy* (New York: McGraw-Hill, 2004).

34. Thomas D. Hays, III, CTP, Certified Turnaround Professional, Nachman Hays Brownstein, Chicago, IL.

35. This turnaround summary was compiled from information available from www.turnaround.org, www.ish.com, www.alixpartners.com, and a summary of the turnaround in J. Bonsall, "Inside a German Turnaround," *Turnaround Management* Spring (2004). For information on Kmart, see K. Dybis, "Kmart Rings Up $200 Million Profit: Stock Soars as Embattled Retailer Reports Upswing for Nov., Dec., Its First Since 2000," *The Detroit News,* January 6, 2004, A1. Tecumseh Announces Performance Improvement Program, www.alixpartners.com/EN/pr_tecumseh.html, accessed December 16, 2005.

36. P. Tourtellot, "Turnarounds: How Outsiders Find the Inside Track," *Turnaround Management,* Spring (2004).

13 Corporate Governance *in the* Twenty-First Century

In This Chapter We Challenge You To >>>

1. Describe what *corporate governance* means and understand its basic principles and practices.

2. Explain how corporate governance relates to competitive advantage.

3. Identify the roles of owners and different types of ownership profiles in corporate governance.

4. Show how boards of directors are structured and explain the roles they play in corporate governance.

5. Analyze and design executive incentives as a corporate governance device.

6. Illustrate how the market for corporate control is related to corporate governance.

7. Compare and contrast corporate governance practices around the world.

Corporate Governance *in* Action *at* Hewlett-Packard

$\mathcal{B}$ill Hewlett and David Packard started Hewlett-Packard (HP) in Palo Alto, California in 1938. Packard was the business operations partner and Hewlett was known as the one with the big ideas. The first product ended up being an audio oscillator. An audio oscillator is an instrument that generates one pure tone or frequency at a time. Through the years, HP oscillators were used to design, produce, and maintain telephones, stereos, radios, and other audio equipment. According to HP's corporate history, Bill and Dave made the first of these oscillators in the garage behind Dave's house and baked the paint on the panels in Lucile Packard's oven. Lucile claimed the roast beef never tasted right after Bill and Dave started using the oven as HP's first paint-baking facility.

Test and measurement devices were HP's first products. Its first product was an audio oscillator—a device used to test sound equipment—introduced in 1938. In later years, HP continued as a leader in this category, making instruments for measurement, medical technology and chemical analysis.

From those modest beginnings, the company went on to become the largest manufacturer of electronic instruments in the world. Along the way, HP became known for its prowess in innovation.

The company is credited with making the world's first handheld scientific calculator, one of the first PCs, the first desktop mainframe, and the LaserJet printer. Its initial PCs were known for their rugged build, tailored for factory operations. HP's early PCs were targeted for industrial uses, such as in factory operations. Consequently, they were ruggedly built but not suited as well for personal or office use and did not enjoy strong sales.

In 1999, HP recruited its first outsider as CEO, Carly Fiorina, a flashy telecommunications executive. HP and Ms. Fiorina bet their future on the controversial and strongly contested 2002 takeover of Compaq Computer Corp. Ironically, the contest wasn't with Compaq shareholders, but with HP's. The families of Hewlett and Packard were dead set against the deal. However, shareholders finally approved the deal, valued at $19 billion.

The Compaq merger was so large and complex that it took several years to integrate. Debate over the wisdom of the merger continued in its wake and continued to hound Fiorina in the years following the closing of the deal. HP management claimed that operating synergies amounted to about $3 billion and that they were realized within about 2 years of the closing. HP's market share in the PC business did increase and recently they passed Dell as the number-one manufacturer of PCs in the world. However, HP's stock price continued to languish. And Fiorina's leadership was now being questioned in the boardroom.

Ms. Fiorina's relationship with the board became strained in 2004. Stakeholders were questioning the acquisition of Compaq, the stock price was languishing, and board politics became problematic. Fiorina became very upset when confidential board discussions were leaked to the press. She confronted the board, which collectively supported her in maintaining that all conversations as a board were confidential. Fiorina was concerned that details of strategic plans were being fed to the press by one or more board members. She used legal counsel to interview each board member in an attempt to identify the leak.

Before the issue could be settled, the board asked Ms. Fiorina to step down. In public statements, the board and succeeding management indicated that the reason for Fiorina's dismissal had to do with personal leadership style and not strategy. The questions and problems were execution and not formulation. In the summer before her dismissal, Fiorina herself dismissed several top executives. Some suggested that this was a last-ditch scapegoating effort in an attempt to solidify her leadership.

Fiorina's dismissal left two holes at HP, the job of the CEO and that of the Chairman of the Board. The board quickly asked Patricia Dunn to step in as Chairman and appointed one of Fiorina's top executives, Mark Hurd, as CEO. In Hurd's early interviews with the press, he maintained that he would not be changing the strategy, just trying to fix the execution.

Ironically, Dunn took up two important issues. First, she thought the board needed some new heavy weight directors. Second, she carried on with Fiorina's quest to get to the bottom of the board leaks. She personally interviewed all directors and felt she had a mandate to plug the leaks.

In looking for new directors, Dunn proposed to the board that they recruit established CEOs from large U.S. firms. Because she felt that the business of HP was so complex, she maintained that they needed directors who had experience with large, diverse firms. She ran into resistance with some directors, particularly Tom Perkins, the famous Silicon Valley venture capitalist. He maintained that HP needed directors from high-tech companies who had experience in "fast cycle" industries. He claimed that some of the CEOs Dunn was recruiting had never dealt with products that change every year and that this experience was crucial to proper governance of HP.

On the issue of board leaks, rather than relying just on in-house counsel, Ms. Dunn authorized a more daring strategy: outside private investigators were hired to track down the truth. As a result of this investigation, the term "pretexting" is now part of the business vocabulary. Investigators felt sure that some directors were lying. So, they approached phone companies pretending to be a director seeking copies of their billing records (i.e., approaching a company under the pretext of being someone else).

Examination of these records revealed that long-time director George Keyworth had placed phone calls to the reporter at CNet.com who printed the detailed information about the HP board's contemplations. The *Wall Street Journal* estimates that HP private investigators spent more than $350,000 to finger Mr. Keyworth.

The HP scandal didn't end there; in fact, it was just getting warmed up. When Dunn convened the board and confronted Mr. Keyworth without prior notice, Tom Perkins, abruptly quit. He argued that the methods used to entrap Keyworth were unethical. In addition, he maintained that the information that was leaked was inconsequential. After his departure, Perkins was furious because in HP's filings with the SEC about his departure, they did not disclose his reasons for leaving. So, Perkins took matters into his own hands and contacted the SEC and the press on his own.

In the ensuing months, HP was regularly on the front page of the *Wall Street Journal* and the *New York Times* as they and other media outlets competed in a race to uncover what really happened at HP. Dunn and HP maintained that their methods were legal and ethical. When they were pressed on the practice of pretexting, they maintained that they were not in control of the methods used by the investigators. Later examination of internal emails revealed that Dunn and other executives were aware of the methods being used and had acquiesced because the issue of leaks was of so much importance.

The Hewlett-Packard board scandal resulted in hearings before congress and charges in California courts against the company and specific officers and directors. Eventually, HP agreed to pay a $14.5 million settlement and adopt corporate reforms to clean up its "pretexting" scandal. HP also fired Ms. Dunn and agreed to pay $650,000 in civil penalties and $350,000 to cover the cost of the attorney general's investigation. The 12-page injunction also requires the tech company to adopt a series of corporate governance reforms. HP will bolster its code of conduct; appoint a new, independent director to serve as the compliance watchdog for the board of directors; and expand the oversight of the company's privacy officer. In addition, HP's ethics and compliance officer will report to the board's audit committee as well as Chairman and CEO Mark Hurd. "We are pleased to settle this matter with the attorney general and are committed to ensuring that HP regains its standing as a global leader in corporate ethics and responsibility," Hurd said in a written statement. <<<

What Is Corporate Governance?

This chapter brings the strategy dialogue full circle. As the opening vignette illustrates, shareholders, employees, and other stakeholders run the risk that managers will engage in practices detrimental to the value, health, and vitality of the firm. As you learned in Chapters 1 and 2, the CEO and members of the top management team set and guide the vision for the firm and its stakeholders and are responsible for formulating and implementing the strategy that realizes that vision. Carly Fiorina was a rising corporate star when she was hired at HP in 1999. She was hired as HP's new CEO to help formulate a strategy that would restore HP to a dominant position. Six years later she was dismissed, as performance problems led to lack of confidence in her leadership.

Once shareholders invest in a firm, they have relatively little direct control over what happens within the firm. This separation of the ownership of the capital necessary to fund a business enterprise from the day-to-day operational management of business affairs is the crux of what is known as the **agency problem**. From shareholders' perspectives, the solution to the agency problem is to find ways to ensure that corporate resources and profits are not squandered, that executives will not make choices that benefit themselves at shareholders' expense, and that shareholders will receive a positive return on their investment.[1] The means and mechanisms used to ensure that managers act in accordance with investors' best interests are the topics of this chapter.

It should also be noted that whether a company resides in a country with a strong orientation toward shareholders' rights, such as the United States or the United Kingdom, or is located in a country with relatively weak shareholders' rights and stronger protection for other stakeholders, such as Germany or France, all companies have a corporate governance system. The differences across these national contexts are discussed later in the chapter.

Corporate governance is the system by which organizations, particularly business corporations, are directed and controlled by their owners. However, all organizations—public,

agency problem Separation of its ownership from managerial control of a firm.

corporate governance The system by which owners of firms direct and control the affairs of the firm.

private, and nonprofit—have some form of governance in place. Corporate governance addresses the distribution of rights and responsibilities among different participants in the organization, such as the board, managers, shareholders, and other stakeholders, and spells out the rules and procedures for making decisions on corporate affairs. By doing this, governance also provides the structure through which the company's objectives are set and the means of attaining those objectives and monitoring performance.[2] A broader stakeholder view of governance is that the firm, as a function of its governance, has the responsibility to benefit other stakeholders beyond shareholders. This is sometimes called the "triple bottom line" in the corporate world, because a firm's strategy and related investments have financial performance objectives and social and environmental objectives as well. In this chapter, we introduce you to the language and principles of corporate governance.

Corporate Governance and Competitive Advantage

Before considering specific governance mechanisms that can protect shareholders, consider the following overarching question: *What effect does corporate governance have on firm survival, performance, and competitive advantage?* Although the answer to this question is actually very complex and the governance mechanisms themselves required by regulators and peer pressure are very costly to implement and maintain, strong evidence suggests that shareholders favor good governance and that it can help firms outperform those with poor governance.

EVIDENCE THAT GOVERNANCE WORKS

Germany provides a case in point with respect to an important governance mechanism—stock-based incentive plans. Prior to 1998, German law did not permit firms to issue U.K.- and U.S.-styled stock-option pay to executives. A few firms found creative ways around this legal roadblock and implemented pay schemes that mimicked stock options. This led the German legislature to reconsider the prohibition. By 1998, the law had been rewritten to allow limited forms of stock-based compensation. Once the legal obstacle was removed, about half of Germany's largest firms quickly adopted stock-based incentive plans. Early adopters of such plans were rewarded by the stock market with higher share prices; however, these incentives also seemed to lead to new strategies in these firms; many started to restructure by divesting non-core business operations.[3]

Similar effects for governance mechanisms have been illustrated among Italian firms. In Italy, large investors have traditionally shied away from small and midsize companies because of concerns about liquidity and poor standards of corporate governance. To alleviate these concerns and help attract capital to this important economic segment, the Italian stock exchange, the Mercato Italiano di Borsa, started a new exchange called STAR. It was designed to be a separate market for small and midsize companies that follow strict governance prescriptions. Some of these prescriptions include provisions that the board must include a minimum number of independent directors and use performance-based compensation to reward both management and members of the board. Comparing the results of this index of well-governed firms with the general index of other small and midsized firms that do not adhere to these governance profiles illustrates

Small- and midsized Italian firms typically have been poorly governed. To encourage investment in these companies, the Italian Stock Exchange, called the Mercato Italiano di Borsa, started a new exchange for them called STAR. Companies listed on STAR adhere to strict corporate governance rules. As a group, these companies consistently outperform those listed on the Borsa.

the potential value of good governance. Even taking into consideration the possibility that better-managed firms are more likely to join the new STAR exchange, the companies on the STAR exchange have consistently outperformed their counterparts on the Borsa; during 2004, STAR firms achieved 24.5-percent greater returns than their counterparts.[4]

Consider the effect of governance mechanisms on the survival and market capitalization of Internet-based companies launched in the United States. These companies were risky for investors because they used new business models and lacked objective operating data that investors could analyze. This created significant uncertainty in the valuation of these new firms. Because of the lack of traditional indicators of quality that would enable analysts to value the firms objectively, the markets seemed to turn to secondary information sources as indicators of the underlying quality of these risky firms. Market valuations of these firms have been tightly linked to the firms' corporate governance characteristics (e.g., executive and director stock-based incentives, institutional and large-block stock ownership, board structure, and venture capital participation). Indeed, these governance factors were much stronger predictors of firm valuation and survival than things such as firm sales and profits.[5] The market seems to put more faith in risky new firms with good governance characteristics than in their counterparts with loose oversight by rewarding firms perceived to have good governance with significantly higher valuations.

Finally, consider the recent cases of corporate fraud and malfeasance in the United States. Corporate scandals have shaken the foundations of American business. In a short period, investors watched billions of dollars of wealth evaporate and dozens of individual managers and employees suddenly found themselves on the street or, worse, incarcerated. As it turns out, firms that engaged in the most egregious scandals exhibited several warning signs, as evidenced in the nature of how the corporate governance was structured. Sometimes effective governance may not prevent executive fraud, but it enables the firm to recover from its consequences. In summary, corporate governance has a strong bearing on the ability of firms to create a competitive advantage and exploit that advantage for the benefit of shareholders.

The Case of Krispy Kreme   Some of these warning signals, as shown in the case of Krispy Kreme in Exhibit 13.1, were actually detected by organizations such as Governance Metrics International (GMI), which rates the quality of a firm's governance practices.[6]

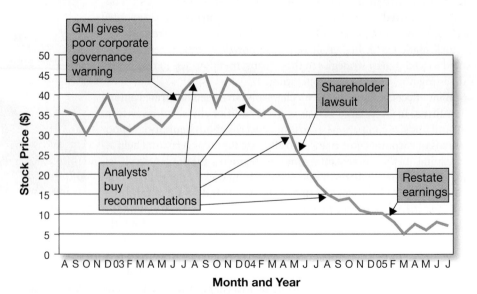

Exhibit 13.1   Early Warning Signals of Problems with Krispy Kreme from GMI

Could careful attention to corporate governance issues have saved Krispy Kreme investors lots of money? In other words, is corporate governance some kind of expensive window dressing, or does it actually impact the bottom line? Analysis of Krispy Kreme's stock price performance, analysts' recommendations, and the warnings of a GMI suggest that good governance has a positive impact on firm performance.

On January 4, 2005, Krispy Kreme Doughnuts Inc. announced that it was filing a financial restatement; its stock had fallen 73 percent over the previous 12 months. How did Krispy Kreme lose so much of its value in such a short period of time? GMI, which had begun evaluating firms in 2002, first rated Krispy Kreme in June 2003, and compared to all other U.S. companies, Krispy Kreme scored a below-average 4.0 for its corporate governance practices. (On the GMI 10-point scale, an average company earns about 6 points.) Among other things, GMI cited a relatively large number of nonindependent directors and related-party transactions and a lack of disclosure about ethical codes of conduct. In short, GMI concluded that the company did not have a strong overall governance record. Seven months later, in January 2004, GMI rerated the company, and its score had dropped to 2.5. At this stage, none of Krispy Kreme's financial woes had been discovered or announced, but the declining GMI scores clearly pointed to risk. Five months later, in May 2004, a shareholder suit was initiated, and in July, an SEC investigation was announced.

However, over this same period, several Wall Street firms were recommending the stock. On August 22, 2003, one had an outperform rating on the stock (even though it was a downgrade from a top pick), and as of January 2005, Krispy Kreme still had an outperform rating. On December 17, 2003, another Wall Street firm initiated coverage with a buy recommendation, as did another on March 30, 2004. Another initiated coverage on September 13, 2004, with a hold recommendation, and yet another issued a strong buy on September 28, 2004.

GMI is the first to admit that governance should not be the only screen in stock selection, but with this kind of downward move in ratings, one would think that financial analysts would have tempered their enthusiasm. Some analysts now believe that corporate governance attributes can have a strong influence on the quality of earnings. Further evidence of this belief is the recent action of Morningstar, one of the most respected investment advisory firms, to grade firms on an *A*-through-*F* scale based on the degree to which companies align their corporate governance practices with shareholders' interests.[7]

CORPORATE GOVERNANCE AND STRATEGY

Corporate governance is related to strategy formulation and implementation in several ways. The most visible roles are in establishing controls and incentives. Boards should ensure that the firm's vision and mission are reflected in its strategy, monitor the way that strategy is executed, and ensure that the top executives reap appropriate career and financial consequences in cases of failure or success.

The risk that managers will deviate from an organization's stated purpose and its guiding documents increases when managers are not the owners of the firm.[8] For instance, when the founders of a company raise capital through an IPO, they generally exchange a significant portion of the firm's stock for the financial capital needed to fund the operations and growth of the firm. After going public, the founders of an IPO firm dilute their ownership, often become minority owners of the firm, and instantly accept accountability for their actions to independent outside shareholders. Likewise, executives of older or large publicly held firms are generally owners of very small percentages of the firm.[9] For instance, research shows that the median level of executive ownership is 0.06 percent of outstanding shares.[10]

How do shareholders hold executives accountable for their actions and ensure that the firm is operated in a manner consistent with the firm's mission? What recourse do shareholders have if they find executives formulating strategies that lack coherence or fail to create value or, worse, engaging in unethical or illegal practices? A number of corporate governance mechanisms help shareholders avoid losing control of the corporation to unscrupulous or incompetent management.

THE MAJOR PARTIES IN CORPORATE GOVERNANCE

agent   Party, such as a manager, who acts on behalf of another party.

An agency relationship exists when one party, the **agent**, acts on behalf of another party, the **principal**. In corporations like Hewlett-Packard, shareholders are viewed as principals, and key executives like Fiorina are viewed as agents.[11] Generally, a few assumptions can be made about principals and agents that highlight the potential problems in an agency relationship.

principal   Party, such as a shareholder, who hires an agent to act on his or her behalf.

First, let's consider the interests of agents and principals in a corporation. What is it that each party wants from the relationship? Most theoretical treatments of the agency relationship in a modern corporation assume that both shareholders and executives are self-interested decision makers. This does not mean that they have no interest in the well-being of the other party; it simply means that they will generally make decisions that are in their own best interests. When the interests of shareholders and executives are virtually identical—when their goals are in alignment—then the agency problem is small. In this situation, executives will do what shareholders want them to do because it serves their own interests as well as those of the firm's shareholders.

However, in most situations, the interests of principals and agents do not naturally overlap completely; some things that would be in shareholders' best interests may be detrimental to those of executives and vice versa. For example, high executive salaries logically reduce corporate profits, which may be reflected in lower relative earnings per share if the higher pay has not led to higher firm performance in the first place. Similarly, executives may choose to diversify the firm to smooth earnings and reduce their own employment (or unemployment) risk without actually improving the competitive position of the firm. Thus, the key for shareholders is either to find a way to align the interests of executives with their own or to closely monitor and control what executives do so that shareholders' interests are protected.

CODES OF GOVERNANCE

codes of governance   Ideal governance standards formulated by regulatory, market, and government institutions.

Many markets and investor groups around the globe have formulated **codes of governance**— ideal governance standards to which firms should adhere. Some of these are followed voluntarily; others are formalized by law. Codes of governance are aimed at four main issues: shareholder equality—upholding all shareholder rights; accountability by the board and management; disclosure and transparency through accurate and timely financial and nonfinancial reporting; and independence (audits and oversight; directors).

The Cadbury Code   Following a series of corporate scandals in the United Kingdom and the United States, Sir Adrian Cadbury, former chairman of Cadbury Schweppes, raised the public's awareness and stimulated debate on corporate governance. His most celebrated achievement is the Cadbury Code of Best Practice, his namesake and a code of prescribed practices that has served as a model for reform around the world.

What is the Cadbury Code's history? In 1991, the Cadbury Commission was established in the United Kingdom to help raise corporate governance standards and increase the level of confidence in financial reporting and auditing by clarifying the respective responsibilities and obligations of relevant entities. In 1992, the Cadbury Committee issued a report with suggestions for corporate governance reform among U.K. companies. The report made nineteen recommendations for better firm governance. Since that time, similar codes have been crafted in many countries around the world, including Brazil, the Netherlands, Oman, the Philippines, Russia, Switzerland, Canada, France, Germany, Italy, and the United States. In all, more than fifty countries have adopted their own codes (see Exhibit 13.2 for examples of several of these codes). The burden placed on firms by these codes varies across the globe. However, all of these new codes significantly increased the stringency of recommended governance standards within their respective countries.

Some codes impose a comply-or-explain burden on firms. For instance, the U.S. Securities and Exchange Commission (SEC) now requires companies to disclose whether they have financial experts on their audit committees and, if not, to explain why. As indicated in Exhibit 13.2, although all of the codes do not impose the same requirements, their aims and recommendations overlap considerably.

The Sarbanes-Oxley Act Perhaps the most far-reaching governance reforms in the United States—at least from the standpoint that they are legal requirements—are seen in the Sarbanes-Oxley Act of 2002. What was the motivation for these new requirements? Just a few U.S. household names: Adelphia, Enron, Arthur Andersen, WorldCom, and Tyco. When corporate names like these synonymous with scandal and greed, public confidence in stock as a secure investment wavers. The Sarbanes-Oxley Act was signed into law on July 30, 2002, in response to these corporate scandals. Now, all companies are required to file periodic reports with the SEC. Noncompliance comes with significant penalties. The essential components of Sarbanes-Oxley deal with accounting oversight,

Exhibit 13.2 Examples of Codes of Governance

Country	What Is the Recommendation on Director Independence?	Can the Same Executive Be Both CEO and Chairperson?	Is Auditor Rotation Required?	Is Disclosure Required If the Company Does Not Comply with the Recommendations?
Brazil CVM Code (2002)	As many as possible	Split recommended	Not addressed	No
Russia CG Code (2002)	At least one-quarter	Split required by law	Not addressed	No
Singapore CG Committee (2001)	At least one-third	Split recommended	Not addressed	Yes
United Kingdom Cadbury Code[1] (1992)	Majority	Split recommended	Periodic rotation of lead auditor	Yes
United States Conference Board and CalPers (2003)[2]	Substantial majority	Separation is one of three acceptable alternatives	Recommended[3]	No

[1]In 2003, a Combined Code made further additions to the code, but these basic principles remain.
[2]Just one of several codes in existence in the United States.
[3]The Sarbanes-Oxley Act requires that the lead audit partner be rotated every 5 years changing audit firms either after 10 years of continual relationship or if former audit partner is employed by the company.

auditor independence, disclosure, analysts' conflicts of interests, accountability for fraud, and attorney's responsibilities.[12]

Public Company Accounting Oversight Board

Sarbanes-Oxley resulted in the creation of the Public Company Accounting Oversight Board to oversee the audits of public companies. This board sets standards and rules for audit reports. All accounting firms that audit public companies must register with the oversight board. This board also inspects, investigates, and enforces compliance by these registered firms. A few of the new governance compliance rules that resulted from Sarbanes-Oxley include:

- Auditors must list the nonaudit services they are unable to perform during an audit.
- Audit-firm employees who leave an accounting firm must wait 1 year to become an executive for a former client.
- Transactions and relationships that are off the balance sheet but that may affect financial status must now be disclosed.
- Personal loans from a corporation to its executives are now largely prohibited.
- Research analysts for securities firms must now file conflict-of-interest disclosures. For instance, analysts must report whether they hold any securities in a company or have received corporate compensation.
- Brokers and dealers must disclose if the public company is a client.
- Altering, destroying, concealing, or falsifying records or documents with the intent to influence a federal investigation or bankruptcy case is subject to fines and up to 20 years of imprisonment.

Securities laws like Sarbanes-Oxley are complicated and confusing. For these reasons, there are a number of government initiatives underway to simplify these overwhelming and highly costly regulations. Regardless, failing to follow the Act's new restrictions and procedures can result in severe penalties.

Whether legal or voluntary, all governance guidelines appear to have four agency control mechanisms in common. These relate to (1) ownership concentration and power, (2) boards of directors, (3) incentive compensation, and (4) the market for corporate control. Each of these mechanisms, reviewed in the following sections, can work to decrease the likelihood that managers will act in ways detrimental to shareholders.

Ownership and the Roles of Owners

The ownership of for-profit firms can be subdivided into different ownership types, such as public and private firms (although the definition of public versus private varies from the U.S. definition in different parts of the world). A private firm is one in which the owner(s) has not listed shares of the firm on a public exchange; shares are typically owned largely by the founding families or by an investment group, such as a leveraged-buyout firm or venture capitalist. A public firm has sold shares to the general investing public, but how those publicly traded shares are dispersed or concentrated varies significantly and leads to another way to categorize public firms.

Dispersion of Ownership

Some firms have a few select owners who control significant stakes in the firm. Consequently, these parties have so much voting power that they can have significant influence and control over the firm's strategy and governance. Sometimes they use that influence to determine who stays in power as CEO or chair of the board. An example of an owner-controlled firm is Nike; founder Philip Knight resigned as CEO, but he still owns

92 percent of the firm's class A stock and remains chair of the board of directors. Other firms have highly dispersed ownership, and managers also own small percentages of the firm's stock.

The dispersion of stock ownership affects the type and magnitude of agency problems that investors face. However, the presence of a powerful owner does not remove all forms of agency problems. One specific type of problem arises when a single powerful owner uses that power to extract private benefits from the company at the expense of other, less powerful owners. The fraud case against Adelphia alleges just such behavior. Members of the Rigas family were convicted of using their ownership power and board control to enable them to use corporate assets as collateral for personal and family loans, ultimately squandering the company's fortunes.[13]

Even when ownership is dispersed and no shareholder's ownership approaches a majority interest, some shareholders are in a position to influence corporate policies. In the United States, the SEC considers an ownership position of 5 percent sufficient to wield significant influence. Owners who control 5 percent or more of a firm's shares are referred to as *blockholders,* and this level of ownership or control must be publicly disclosed. Blockholders are considered powerful because voting blocks that large can sway boards of directors on important votes.

Exhibit 13.3 demonstrates a few different ownership profiles. The nature of executive/shareholder relationships varies across the firms in the exhibit. At Coca-Cola for instance, managers are very cognizant that over 13 percent of the company's stock is controlled by two individuals: Warren Buffet and James Williams. Both of these investors are members of the board of directors as a result of their sizeable investments. Contrast that profile with that of Dell, where the only major individual investor is founder Michael Dell.

Institutional Owners   FedEx has another type of powerful owner to deal with. Vanguard, Barclays, and Capital Research and Management Company each owned more than 5 percent of the company in 2004. Investors such as Vanguard are known as **institutional investors**; the money they control is capital invested in mutual funds and pension funds controlled by the company. Sometimes these institutional investors own large blocks of

institutional investors
Pension or mutual fund that manages large sums of money for third-party investors.

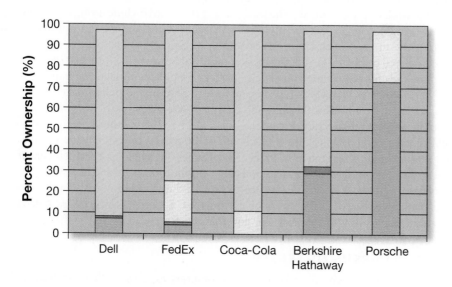

Exhibit 13.3   Ownership Structure Comparison

Other shareholders (mutual funds, individuals, etc.)
Blockholders (any ownership position >5%)
Management team
Founder and family

individual companies. Most institutional investors are relatively passive investors: They essentially vote with their feet by purchasing or selling a stock based on their outlook for the firm's performance, and therefore the potential performance of the firm's stock. But they can also become quite active should the need arise, and some institutional investors, such as CalPers (the California Public Employees' Retirement System) and SWIB (State of Wisconsin Investment Board), are by their charter activist investors.[14]

Different types of institutional investors seem to have preferences for firms with different strategies. For instance, recent research has found that the managers of public pension funds prefer to invest in firms that follow strategies that attempt to exploit internal innovation, whereas investments made by managers of professional investment funds revealed preferences for firms that attempt to acquire innovations externally through acquisitions.[15] For sure, managers of these two types of institutional funds do not limit their investments to these types of firms, but their portfolios demonstrate nonrandom preferences.

Perhaps the most important lesson in this observation for managers of firms is the idea that owners do not have a unified voice. Economic theories make assumptions about shareholders and their preferences, but in reality different types of shareholders have different preferences. For instance, examine the types of owners that control Porsche, the German sports car manufacturer. It is unlikely that the family who owns most of Porsche would vote the same way on many corporate issues that independent mutual-fund managers would because the issues that are important to each are not always the same. Indeed, as you examine the marketing material for different mutual funds, you will notice that many of them have different objectives. The implication for managers is that they must understand who owns the company and what their interests are.

The Board of Directors

One of the chief monitoring devices available to shareholders is the board of directors. All publicly held companies are required to have a **board of directors**. A board of directors—a group of individuals who formally represents the firm's shareholders—is charged with overseeing the work of top executives. The legal roles of the board include hiring and firing top executives, monitoring management, ensuring that shareholders' interests are protected, establishing executive compensation, and reviewing and approving the firm's strategy. Informal roles played by boards include acting as conduits of information from external sources, providing leads for acquisition and alliance partner candidates, influencing important external parties such as industry regulators and foreign government policy makers, and providing advice and counsel for the CEO and other top executives.

> **board of directors**   Group of individuals that formally represents the firm's shareholders and oversees the work of top executives.

Although corporate laws vary around the globe, which results in some differences in board practices, the general responsibility of the board of directors is to ensure that executives are acting in shareholders' best interests. In the United States, shareholders elect members of the board of directors. In the wake of numerous high-profile financial scandals in recent years, boards have been under increasing pressure to exercise their monitoring responsibility with greater vigilance.[16] Part of this pressure comes from the U.S. Congress, which has created laws that require public firms to put particular governance reforms into place.[17]

INSIDERS VERSUS OUTSIDERS

A board of directors is typically composed of several very experienced individuals. Most of these individuals are generally not officers of the company but, rather, are employed by other companies. Executives of the firm who also serve on the board are often referred to as *insiders;* those on the board who are not employed by the firm otherwise are known as *outsiders.* Outsiders can typically be more independent in fulfilling their board responsibilities, but being an outsider does not necessarily make a director independent. For instance, the independent judgement of a director who has another business relationship with the company may be compromised.

Most institutional investors and watchdog groups prefer a large majority of independent directors. This helps to avoid conflicts of interests in carrying out fundamental responsibilities. As a result, there is a strong movement to increase the percentage of board members who are independent outsiders. However, insiders, although not independent, have access to more critical knowledge of the business and its environment and have the potential to add critical insight to board deliberations.[18]

Boards in the United States are typically comprised of a majority of outside directors, along with one or more senior executives of the firm. Although there is the presumption that outside directors make for a more vigilant board, this is not always the case. First, outside directors may not be independent; they may have business dealings with the firm or friendship ties to the CEO. Similarly, by virtue of their position, CEOs have considerable control over outside directors, which may make it difficult for them to be truly independent. These relationships can affect how they monitor and advise management. Although watchdog groups seem to clamor for more independent outsiders on boards, research reveals that in some circumstances, increasing the number of insiders (i.e., executives) on the board can increase the board's effectiveness. For instance, when the firm operates in highly technical areas, insiders can provide better information than can many independent outsiders.[19]

What to Do About the CEO Chair   In approximately 70 percent of U.S. public firms, the CEO also serves as the chair of the board of directors. Debate continues as to the wisdom of an "independent chair" structure in American corporate culture. As evidenced by the prevalence of dual CEO/chairs in the United States, corporations are generally resistant to the idea of separating the two positions. Although separating the roles of CEO and board chair is more common in European corporations[20] (and is one of the Cadbury guidelines in the United Kingdom), it remains the exception in the United States. However, the two roles are actually quite distinct, and there is a movement to separate the two jobs. In other countries, norms and laws lead to other configurations. In Germany, because such duality is prohibited, the CEO and the board chair are always different people. When the roles are split, it is critical that the board chair not take operational roles, just as the CEO shouldn't attempt to run the board.

The logic for combining the posts includes the need for specialized information that an outsider could not have, and a lack of qualified candidates. The logic for splitting is the need for monitoring: One cannot effectively serve as referee and player at the same time. Many critics of U.S. corporate governance practices believe, however, that true board independence may ultimately—within the next decade—require a serious reexamination of this historic combination of powers.[21] Consequently, pressure is increasing to separate these two positions so that the board can more effectively monitor top executives. Some large U.S. companies that have recently transitioned from a combined chair/CEO to a split model include Boeing, Walt Disney, and Oracle.

THE BOARD'S ACTIVITIES AND THE COMPANY'S STRATEGY

Boards generally are organized into several committees, with key board responsibilities being assigned to different committees. For instance, all companies listed on the New York Stock Exchange (NYSE) must have an audit committee, which is responsible for selecting the independent auditor and reviewing the reports provided by that outside auditor. Because independent audits of books and records is critical to effective monitoring, the NYSE requires that the audit committee be composed only of outsiders; insiders may not be responsible for ensuring the independence of the audit. In addition, boards have compensation committees that are charged with setting the level of executive compensation.

Exhibit 13.4 Board Roles and Actions

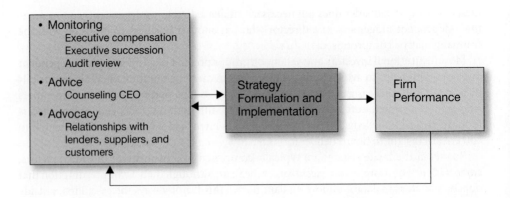

The relationship between the board and firm strategy and performance is illustrated in Exhibit 13.4. Let's review each of these mechanisms and discuss how managers can utilize the board to further the purposes of the firm.

Monitoring   One of the key roles of the board of directors is to monitor the performance of top executives and potentially replace management when necessary. **Monitoring** is the process of the board acting in its legal and fiduciary responsibility to oversee executives' behaviors and performance and to take action when necessary to replace management. The opening vignette on HP provides an example of this role. Some of the most important decisions made by the board are hiring and firing the CEO and other senior executives. Effective boards make sure that they have an executive succession plan that keeps the firm prepared in the event that a new CEO is needed. Some forms of succession, such as retirement, are easier to plan for than others. Orderly succession seems to have better results than sudden termination and turning to a new outsider to fix the firm's problems. A recent study of CEO successions in U.S. companies illustrates this point (see Exhibit 13.5).[22] Indeed the left-hand graph shows that firm's generally performed more poorly two years after an incumbent CEO was dismissed, while the right-hand graph demonstrates that firms with an orderly CEO succession process improved their stock-market and accounting-based performance.

Firing is a drastic monitoring device that should be used judiciously. More routine monitoring mechanisms include meeting regularly as a board, hiring competent external auditors, and diligently reviewing financial and operating results. Evidence suggests that when a CEO is fired for firm-performance reasons, it is more likely that the board will recruit an

monitoring   Functioning of the board in exercising its legal and fiduciary responsibility to oversee executives' behavior and performance and to take action when it's necessary to replace management.

Exhibit 13.5 CEO Firing

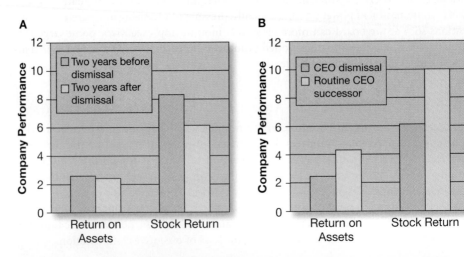

outsider as a replacement. Although outsiders do bring a fresh perspective, research shows that they are more likely than not to deploy strategies that lead their firms to underperform, not outperform, their competition. Indeed, the best-performing firms, following the forced replacement of the CEO, appear to be those run by executives who already have experience at the company they are leading.[23] Perhaps the best case-in-point here is the placement of Jack Welch, a GE manager, into the CEO role. Welch dramatically changed the firm's strategy and created the diversified powerhouse we know today.

Advising Managers Although increasing emphasis is being placed on the monitoring roles of boards, recent research has shown that just as much, if not more, value is to be had by tapping into the expertise and contacts of the board and using board members as confidants and information sources. On the other hand, many critics of corporate governance argue that CEOs who have social ties and friendships with board members could put shareholders at risk because these relationships may make the board less likely to monitor the CEO effectively.

Research indicates that social ties typically fail to reduce the level of board-monitoring activity and that, in fact, such social ties improve the ability of the CEO to tap board members for advice and counsel on strategic issues. This suggests that social ties between CEOs and board members may increase board involvement rather than decrease it.[24] The same research found that CEOs were more willing to turn to board members for advice when they had social ties to these members—when they considered the relationship to be friendship-based, not solely monitoring-based. This suggests that when CEOs perceive they have a loyal board, they will involve the board more in strategic decision-making.

Finally, the research also demonstrated that firms in which CEOs collaborate with board members on strategic issues outside of board meetings perform significantly better than firms that limit CEO/board interactions to purely monitoring roles. The trend is to encourage board members to be more actively involved, as opposed to passively involved (i.e., simply a rubber stamp on the executive team's recommendations). For instance, General Electric now requires that its board members spend time at its various facilities around the world in addition to the regular boardroom meetings.

Because more advice and counsel interactions between board members and executives leads to improved firm performance, managers and board members alike are interested in how these interactions can be exploited for shareholders' benefit. How can the board be structured to maximize the positive strategic counsel that can take place between the board and the CEO? Simply adding more directors to the board is not an effective method for increasing these interactions; increasing the number of board members who can provide CEOs with appropriate strategic knowledge does increase board–CEO involvement.[25] Research shows that positive CEO–board interactions are maximized when the selection of outside board members matches the competitive environment facing the firm. When firms are in relatively stable competitive environments, the advice and monitoring of board members is enhanced when outside board members are drawn from other firms that are strategically related to the firm. In these stable environments, the knowledge and experience that board members gain in their own firm translates well to the firm they monitor.

However, when the firm is located in a very unstable competitive environment, board involvement is most effective when outside board members are drawn from strategically dissimilar firms. This is probably due to the fact that in unstable environments, boards need to tap into multiple experiential backgrounds to help make sense of the firm's competitive environment. Given the increasingly active role that directors play in strategy and the greater demands of the job, it should come as no surprise that the complexion of the boardroom is changing. Boards today are typically larger and more diverse, and members are more highly paid, than in years past.[26]

Using the Board as a Lever of Power and Influence Finally, boards also provide access to external resources, and it is not uncommon for a director to sit on multiple boards (a characteristic called a *board interlock*). These resources can range from access to capital, to new knowledge, to the ability to influence other external stakeholders, such as investors, banks, and regulators. CEOs often sit on the boards of other firms as well, though, given their time constraints, they often sit on only one or two others at the most. When asked why they would invest the required time and effort in another firm's success, they often respond that it is the learning component that drives their choice. They report that they learn from the CEO and executives of the other firm and benefit from the knowledge and contacts possessed by their peer directors.[27]

Beyond the straightforward fact that a board position may provide access to resources and be a lever of power or influence over other important stakeholders, some believe that such influence and power can get out of hand. One aspect of this perspective is CEOcentric from the standpoint that CEOs may be tempted to seek out other CEOs to sit on their boards if those potential board members are highly paid at their home firms. Landing highly paid CEOs as directors will probably lead to a board that will be supportive of paying high wages for CEOs. For instance, critics of corporate excess, such as the Conference Board or Institutional Shareholders Services, point to research showing that the CEOs of the boards of companies on which Home Depot's former CEO Bob Nardelli sat were overpaid relative to their peers and that Nardelli himself was overpaid.[28]

As you learned in the opening paragraph of this section, it is not unusual for directors to sit on multiple boards or for companies to be interconnected via their directors. For instance, PepsiCo director Robert E. Allen also sits on the board of Bristol-Myers Squibb. Ironically, Coca-Cola director James D. Robinson III, also sits on the board of Bristol-Myers Squibb, leaving you to wonder how the Cola Wars play out in the Bristol-Myers' boardroom. Debate continues as to whether such board interlocks help firms perform better by virtue of their access to better information or simply allow corporations to collude at the expense of the public at large. Although there is no evidence that consumers are generally harmed by such interrelationships at the board level, strategy research has shown that directors themselves may be more effective as monitors if they are linked to certain firms given the competitive standing and environmental turbulence facing the focal firms.[29] It has also been shown that common board ties can influence many other important factors, ranging from the choice of CEO to a firm's strategy in the face of failing performance.[30]

Executive Compensation

One of the fundamental conditions that leads to a potential agency problem in publicly held companies is the separation of firm ownership from company management. When professional managers, rather than the owners themselves, run the operations of a firm, situations can arise in which there may be conflicts of interest—where what is best for shareholders is not necessarily what is best for management. For instance, consider a situation in which the company could receive an attractive buyout proposal from a competitor. Shareholders might be interested in pursuing this buyout if the premium they are being offered for their shares is attractive. However, management may not be as interested in the buyout if their employment is threatened. Incentives are sometimes used to alleviate this potential conflict. Of course, it is also true that sometimes incentives can unwittingly exacerbate conflicts of interest. This is why it is important to understand how incentives work, including how people tend to respond to different types of incentives.

One possible solution to these potential conflicts of interest is to structure incentive arrangements so that managers are rewarded for doing what is in shareholders' best interests. **Incentive alignment** can be used to solve the agency problem. For instance, to avoid managers' hesitancy to examine acquisition-buyout options, boards can include "golden parachute" provisions in managers' compensation packages, which offer significant bonuses when loss of employment is a consequence of an acquisition with an acceptable premium.

In practice, it is impossible to structure executive compensation to completely overcome all possible conflicts of interest. A number of mechanisms are frequently used to increase the incentive alignment between shareholders and executives. We review some of these common mechanisms in this section, but we also point out how each mechanism has its limitations.

incentive alignment Use of incentives to align managerial self-interest with shareholders'.

EXECUTIVE OWNERSHIP

Perhaps the most direct way to align incentives is to require that executives own stock in the firm. The theory here is rather obvious: If you are an owner of the company you should behave more like an owner and less like a hired hand. In recent years, many firms have established ownership guidelines for senior executives. Consider the case of Dendrite International, which is discussed in Exhibit 13.6.[31] However, the ownership requirement may backfire. Executives cannot diversify their risk exposure as well as large shareholders.

Exhibit 13.6 Establishing Executive-Ownership Requirements at Dendrite International

As an illustration of a recent adopter of an executive stock-ownership plan, consider Dendrite. Dendrite (DRTE), a leading supplier of specialized software to the global pharmaceutical industry that was founded in Australia in 1986 and is now headquartered in the United States, implemented a formal stock-ownership plan for its twenty senior-most executives and all of its nonemployee directors. The new program mandates ownership of Dendrite stock, ranging from 15,000 to 100,000 shares, depending on the executive's position.

The ownership requirements set by Dendrite are based on owned common stock, not stock options. Ownership of the predetermined number of shares must be achieved within 5 years, with an initial number attained in three years. Restrictions have been placed on the receipt of additional equity-based compensation and sale of Dendrite shares until ownership commitments are attained. The executive participants may obtain shares through purchase on the open market, receiving incentive compensation in shares or exercising options and holding shares.

In addition to instituting share-ownership requirements, Dendrite also made changes to its executive compensation program. Executives may now elect to receive incentive compensation in stock instead of cash. If the executive elects to receive stock, these shares are restricted from sale for 1 year, and the executive will receive a number of options equal to the number of restricted shares. Replacement options will be granted for shares used to exercise vested options.

By the start of 2005, Dendrite's executive stock ownership plan was fully in place. In addition, all of Dendrite's directors—executive and independent—owned at least some Dendrite stock, further aligning the board, top manager, and shareholder interests. While Dendrite is in a highly competitive and dynamic industry, it is notable that since beginning the implementation of the executive stock ownership plan in 2000, the firm has managed to garner shareholders a strong return. For instance, as of the end of 2005 shareholders had earned a 3-year average return of 28 percent, versus the S&P 1500 return of 12 percent. Standard and Poor also ranked the firm among the top tier of its peers, in terms of overall performance and outlook.

Is an executive stock ownership plan an easy pathway to competitive advantage? Probably not, but at least it is an important lever in a firm's corporate governance repertoire to provide executives and directors an incentive to see that the right strategy is being executed well.

Shareholders can spread their risks across many firms, but an individual executive who is required to invest heavily in the company is likely to have a very unbalanced investment portfolio.

In addition, executives risk their human capital—that is, their reputation and future job opportunities—through the employment relationship. For U.S. firms in particular, the Sarbanes-Oxley governance reforms now require that the CEO and CFO certify that the firm's financial statements are accurate, and they can be jailed if the statements are proven to be fraudulent or misrepresentative of the facts. This increases the pressures of top executives' jobs, one indication of which is the fact that CFO turnover has increased by about 23 percent over the last three years.[32] Consequently, executives suffer heavy exposure to firm-specific risk. This type of risk exposure could lead some executives to become very risk averse. Consequently, boards need to be very careful in structuring executive compensation so that they understand just what types of behaviors they are encouraging through the economic incentives they provide.

Stock-Ownership Policies   As mentioned earlier, many firms have established executive stock ownership policies. How prevalent are these programs, how are they put into place, and what do they require of executives? Based on research by F. W. Cook, a large executive compensation consulting firm, the prevalence of executive and director stock ownership guidelines has increased and is expected to continue to increase over the next several years because of the perception that it is one of the best forms of governance (see Exhibit 13.7).[33]

Ownership guidelines are generally grouped into two types: traditional and retention programs. Traditional stock ownership guidelines establish ownership levels through a multiple-of-salary approach. Retention programs express ownership as a percentage of the gains resulting from the exercise of stock options and other equity-based incentives, such as restricted stock. These two types of stock ownership are sometimes used together. For example, some firms may require that executives retain their shares (or some percentage of their shares) acquired through stock options until they own five times their salary in company stock.

Stock ownership requirements vary among firms that have such plans. For instance, among firms that have multiple-of-salary plans, the median value of stock ownership required is about $5 million, but it ranges from a mere $100,000 to over $20 million. The median multiple is five times the executive's salary; the highest requirement is at Mellon Financial Corporation, where the CEO is required to have twenty-five times the executive's salary.

Implementing a stock ownership plan requires time. Most CEOs do not have sufficient liquid assets to immediately buy the needed shares when a plan is implemented. Consequently, firms often allow CEOs several years to acquire the required shares (most companies allow 5 years). Alternatively, if companies use the retention method, no time requirement is necessary because they are only concerned with what is retained from granted options.

Exhibit 13.7   Comparison Executive Stock Ownership

	Largest 250 Companies with Stock Ownership Guidelines		
	Number of Companies	**Percent of Companies**	**Percent Increase from 2001 to 2004**
Executives	142	57	58
Directors	123	49	127

As noted in Exhibit 13.6, firms are increasingly requiring that their members of the board also own stock. The level of required ownership is much lower than for CEOs. The median level of required ownership among firms that have such requirements is either five times their annual director retainer or 5,000 shares. These levels equate to approximately $200,000.

INCENTIVE COMPENSATION

Firms use various forms of incentive compensation to reward executives and align the interests of their top-management team with those of shareholders. The two most common incentives are annual bonus plans and stock options. In recent years, firms have been increasing their reliance on newer forms of pay, such as restricted stock grants and long-term accounting-based incentive plans. Exhibit 13.8 illustrates how different firms in the food industry emphasize various incentive mechanisms when paying their CEOs.

Bonus Plans   Perhaps the oldest form of incentive pay is the bonus plan. The idea behind bonus plans is that the board can subjectively evaluate executives' performance on multiple dimensions and allocate a year-end cash award as appropriate. In theory, bonus plans should be linked to firm performance indicators. The bonus-plan incentive has two principle drawbacks. First, when bonuses are tied to accounting indicators of performance, executives may be motivated to make accounting decisions that maximize their possible bonus payout. For instance, research has found that firms are more likely to increase income deferrals when senior executives have reached the maximum payout under terms of their bonus plan.[34] Second, linking pay to annual firm performance can have the unintended consequence of short-term bias and inattention to long-term strategic needs. For instance, some research shows that bonus plans can lead to the underfunding of R&D initiatives.[35] To get around this problem, many firms are now tying bonus payouts to long-term performance, rather than annual performance. (These are often called Long-term Incentive Plans, or LTIPS, because incentives are based on firm performance over a period longer than one

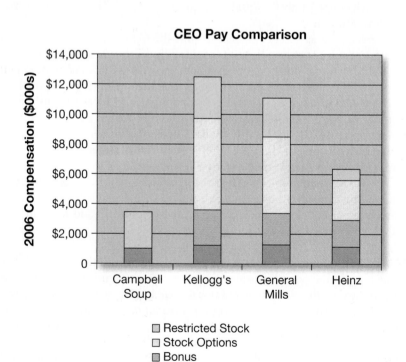

Exhibit 13.8   Comparison of Incentive Pay Usage in the Food Industry

year, but excludes other long-term incentives like restricted stock, stock options or stock appreciation rights plans.) Options and restricted stock are discussed in the next section.

However, bonuses do have some appealing characteristics. For instance, the board can tie them to multiple desired outcomes, including both financial performance and other important outcomes such as customer satisfaction and quality. In addition, the board can more easily revoke or withhold bonuses than it can other long-term incentives that it loses control of once they are granted. The effectiveness of annual bonus programs really comes down to how well the board links them to the achievement of desired objectives.

Stock Options One of the most popular incentive devices of the past 20 years has been the executive stock option plan. The idea behind stock options is to simulate stock ownership for executives who do not or cannot buy lots of stock.

stock options Incentive device giving an employee the right to buy a share of company stock at a later date for a predetermined price.

When a company grants a stock option, the executive's cash pay does not increase in the year the option is granted. Rather, a **stock option** gives an employee the right to buy a share of company stock at a later date for a predetermined price. Usually, stock option plans impose a vesting period, generally 3 years. After that period of time, the executive can redeem the option. If the company's stock price has increased, then the executive can buy the stock at a discount, sometimes a very significant discount. In addition, many companies do not require the executive to actually buy the stock, they sometimes allow them to receive the difference between the stock price and the option price as compensation at that future date. The rationale for the use of stock options is that they motivate executives to act like owners and take reasonable risks that will result in the company's stock price increasing. Advocates of stock options like their supposed win–win attributes: If executives do not create shareholder value in the form of higher stock prices, the options will be worthless.

Like most incentive plans, options do have their downside. Although used to simulate stock ownership, in reality they do not always achieve this objective. This is because options do not make executives bear any financial risk like stock ownership does. When executives own stock, they win if the stock price increases and they lose actual wealth if the stock price declines. With stock options, only the upside potential is conveyed. The only cost to executives is an opportunity cost.

Decision makers, such as executives, behave quite differently when they have something to lose. Indeed, upside potential and downside risks seem to motivate different behaviors. Research shows that stock options may increase excessive risk taking beyond the level of risk desired by shareholders.[36] For instance, executives with large proportions of their pay package derived from stock options tend to pursue aggressive acquisition and divestiture strategies; buying and selling divisions frequently is a key part of their corporate strategy. For instance, GE has historically used stock options heavily, and it may be no coincidence that it is one of the most prolific acquirers of other companies in the world. Likewise, in the opening vignette, Carly Fiorina was quick to use acquisitions to solve her company's revenue problems rather than exercising patience with internal development programs. Conversely, firms run by executives with high levels of stock ownership are much less likely to pursue acquisitions and divestitures and focus more on internally developed strategies.[37]

Restricted Stock Restricted stock is a rather recent compensation initiative that is designed to help avoid the potential problems associated with annual bonus plans and stock options. To tie executives' financial rewards to shareholder value while avoiding the lack of downside risk associated with stock options (recall that executive's make money through options when the stock price goes up, but since they don't actually own any stock, they do not lose money if the stock price falls), companies can grant actual stock shares to executives. These shares are generally referred to as a *restricted stock grant* because the grants have restrictions built in to ensure that managers do not sell the stock to convert it to cash (and thus lose the incentive power of stock ownership). The restrictions usually entail vesting over a period of 3 to 5 years and prohibitions on the sale of the stock for some extended period of time. The popularity of restricted stock has grown significantly in the past several years because of the wave of bad press associated with stock option abuses. With restricted stock grants, the executive has upside incentive associated with the stock, but they are also exposed to the downside risk. When the stock price drops, the value of the executives restricted stock declines as well. And because restricted stock has real value when granted (i.e., the value of the stock) and not only potential value like stock options, some boards think they are better at truly aligning the incentives of managers with those of shareholders.

Unions, shareholder watchdog groups, and other interested stakeholders often criticize the level of pay that CEOs are able to make, claiming that their rewards are excessive and that they sometimes achieve these high levels of pay without achieving stellar performance. How do some CEOs achieve high levels of pay without high levels of performance? Usually because they were given lots of stock options. Executives can make a great deal of money from options because any increase in the firm's stock price results in money for the CEO even if the firm's stock price gains are far outpaced by competitors. Exhibit 13.9 illustrates that star compensation can attract attention because it is so grandiose. You can see from the exhibit the average level of CEO pay among large U.S. companies and the two highest-paid executives in the United States as well as the two highest-paid female CEOs in the world. It is no wonder that CEO pay createsheadlines every year in the business press. CEO pay is very high relative to that of almost everyone else. (except perhaps movie stars and star athletes!).

The Well-Designed Incentive Plan   Notwithstanding recent abuses, if firms are careful about how they use incentives, monetary rewards are powerful tools that can be used to increase the likelihood that executives act in shareholders' interests. Proper use of incentives tied to long-term performance metrics (as opposed to the current stock price) increases the likelihood that executives will make necessary capital investments.[38] For instance, facing intense competition, cutbacks in military spending, and years of

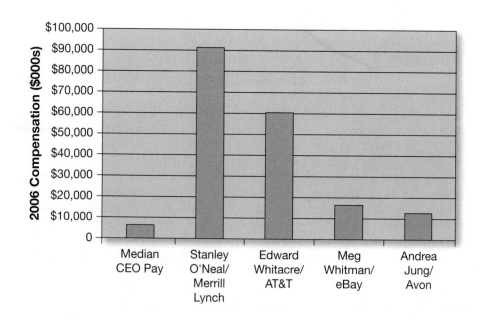

Exhibit 13.9   Variation Among CEOs' Pay

underperformance, in 1991 the board of directors of General Dynamics hired a new management team and charged it with formulating a strategy to create shareholder wealth. The company established strong links between shareholder wealth and managerial compensation through a combination of bonuses, options, and restricted stock. This pay-for-performance plan is largely credited with providing the incentive to devise a strategy that was politically unpopular but economically successful. The new management team downsized, restructured, and exited some of its businesses by selling divisions to competitors but in the process, it created gains for shareholders of approximately $4.5 billion. Scholars documenting this case suggest that such a dramatic and successful strategy would have been unlikely without these financial incentives.[39] The key to using incentives is to find the appropriate performance metrics (i.e., those identified in the balanced scorecard) and to link executive pay to these outcomes.

Options can be a part of a well-designed incentive package, but evidence suggests that option pay should be used in moderation and balanced with other types of incentives, such as annual bonus plans and stock ownership. In addition, research suggests that too much focus has been placed on keeping the CEO's pay level in line with market forces and not enough focus has been placed on the incentives of other key executives. For instance, the best-performing firms tend to compensate their second-level managers (i.e., CFO, COO, etc.) at levels more closely related to the pay of the CEO rather than have a star system where the CEO's pay significantly outpaces that of other top managers. This is probably due to the fact that strategic management is inherently a team function, and huge gaps in pay between the CEO and other officers creates an unhealthy social context in which to operate as an effective team.[40]

Firms that have large gaps in pay across top managerial ranks suffer negative effects. For instance, firms with large pay gaps seem to undermine their ability to develop managerial talent because manager turnover increases significantly when pay gaps are large.[41] Thus, to maximize performance, firms need to adjust both absolute and relative pay levels to achieve the proper fit with their strategic context.

The box entitled "How Would *You* Do That? 13.1" examines some of the factors that firms should consider when structuring CEO compensation. When establishing CEO pay and aligning it with a firm's intended strategy, recognize that boards of directors are often criticized but rarely praised for how they structure CEO incentives.

The Market for Corporate Control

The final corporate governance mechanism we review is not a mechanism that the board puts in place to protect shareholders, but rather is a reflection of national and global institutions and their effect on the relative ease or difficulty of an individual or company simply taking full or partial control of another company. The **market for corporate control** is the idea that every public company is theoretically for sale. To explain this concept, let's take the phrase in its parts. The "market" is the sum of all the possible buyers of corporate stock and the individual shareholders of the company (who might be "sellers" in this market). The term "control" refers to what can be bought and sold in this market. Control of what? Control of corporations. Don't confuse this market with the stock market where you can go buy lots of shares. The stock market is merely the mechanism that the market for corporate control uses to allow one party to take control away from another. Several types of battles for the control of large corporations can take place. For instance, the problems HP faced during the Carly Fiorina's period were tied to her strategy to acquire Compaq. The acquisition and integration of Compaq's assets and product lines into HP was the outcome of an active market for corporate control.

market for corporate control Control over public corporations is traded, and this theoretically puts some pressure on managers to perform, otherwise their corporation can be taken over.

Doing Some Repairs at Home Depot

Hiring (and firing) and compensating the CEO are some of the chief responsibilities of the board of directors. After all, the CEO is expected to foster the formulation of a leading-edge strategy and champion it. Ultimately, the CEO is held accountable for the strategy's successful execution. When Home Depot and Bob Nardelli parted ways in 2006 because of poor performance, the board decided that the best candidate was Frank Blake, a senior executive of the firm. By deciding to hire an insider, the Home Depot board in some ways simplified their job because they would not have to offer a big carrot to recruit an executive from another firm to come to Home Depot. When a board goes outside the firm to hire a CEO, they usually pay a premium because they need to lure an executive from another position. But, deciding what, and how, to pay the CEO is still a major challenge for the board. The

board's objective is to offer a compensation package that will result in incentives consistent with Home Depot's objectives—incentives that will motivate the CEO to formulate a strategy that achieved its vision and mission. When the Home Depot board had identified Blake as the new CEO, they stated that the firm's objectives were to improve its strategy and tie CEO pay more closely to firm performance.

In setting Blake's pay, three of the key considerations are: (1) Blake's prior compensation as an executive vice president of the company, (2) Nardelli's compensation as the former CEO, and (3) the compensation of the CEO of Home Depot's chief rival, Lowe's. These data are provided in Exhibit 13.10.

With Home Depot's objectives in mind, the board initially offered Mr. Blake a contract that included a mixture of incentives, including bonus payments, restricted stock, and stock

options. Surprisingly, Mr. Blake rejected the pay package because it was *too* generous and because he was opposed to restricted stock grants. His argument was that restricted stock didn't offer enough incentive because if the stock price declined he would still have some value in the shares make money. He ended up settling on the following package:[48]

Annual salary: $975,000

Annual bonus: A target 100 percent of salary, with the possibility of double salary if performance is high enough

Long-term bonus: A target of $2,500,000, contingent on performance over the next 3 years

Restricted stock awards: None

Stock options: A present value of $2,500,000, but contingent on increasing stock price

Exhibit 13.10 Pay Comparison Between CEOs at Home Depot and Lowe's

	Salary	Bonus	Restricted Stock	Stock Options
Blake's Pay as EVP	$685,000	$825,000	$2,900,000	$0
Nardelli's Pay as former CEO	$2,200,000	$7,000,000	$14,000,000	$0
CEO Pay at Lowe's	$850,000	$2,600,000	$4,000,000	$0

Corporate control literally refers to who controls the corporation. Thus, corporate control is achieved by having sufficient power and votes to choose the CEO and members of the board of directors of a company and to control all major decisions made by a company.[42] One of the principle ways of gaining corporate control is through mergers and acquisitions. Corporate raiders, competitors, and leveraged-buyout firms are investors who buy underperforming firms, restructure them, and then sell them for a profit. Because misbehavior or underperformance may lead to shareholders replacing the board and the CEO or other firms or investors attempting to buy out a firm and replace its management, the market for corporate control helps to keep managers in line.

The Trend Toward Takeovers and Buyouts   In the United States, the market for corporate control was spurred by hostile takeover activity and leveraged buyouts in the 1980s. Corporate raiders discovered great financial opportunities in seizing control of someone else's business, often at bargain prices. With millions of dollars at stake, these raiders aroused massive public attention and, depending on one's point of view, were either the villains or the saviors of American business.[43] The hostile takeover threat is alive and well today. Beginning in 2003 and eventually culminating in a successful acquisition in 2005, Oracle engaged in an 18-month battle to gain control of PeopleSoft.

Overall, researchers have concluded that corporate takeovers generate positive gains, that the target firm's shareholders benefit, and that the bidding firm's shareholders do not lose out. However, the success of a hostile takeover depends on the takeover premium paid. This work ties in well with the notion of resources and competitive advantage because the market for corporate control can be viewed as an arena in which managerial teams compete for the rights to manage corporate resources.[44]

Although the market for corporate control may indeed be the last line in the sand, in terms of corporate governance, it should also be evident that it is one of the most costly and emotion-wrenched governance remedies beyond the replacement of the CEO by a firm's board. When a firm is the target of a raider or a fight for control of a board, it is a potential signal that the firm's board and its management has been ineffective or, at the very least, that the board and management see no way to combat the competition without merging with or being acquired by another entity. In Chapter 10 on mergers and acquisitions, you learned that many of the gains associated with acquisitions go to the seller, not the buyer. Therefore, although the market for corporate control may serve to discipline management, it is a very costly and time-consuming remedy to implement, and its benefits to the buyer will always be of concern. Moreover, as you will learn in the following section, the market for corporate control can only be an effective governance mechanism to the extent that the capital markets and governance mechanisms in place in a country allow hostile acquisitions to occur in the first place.

The Faces of Corporate Governance Around the World

Although conflicts between managers and owners occur around the globe, the specific nature of the problems and the norms for guarding against them vary markedly. Governance problems are not unique to the United States, for instance, the Netherlands' Ahold Group (grocery stores), Italy's Parmalat (dairy and food products), France's Vivendi (entertainment), and the French-Belgian firm Elf (petroleum) are all very recent examples of scandal-ridden non-U.S. multinationals.

Most of these firms' problems can be traced to faulty governance and, in the end, fraudulent accounting and executive excess much like that which eventually brought down Enron, MCI, and Tyco. Some of these differences are illustrated by recent cross-national comparisons of corporate governance practices, which differ considerably around the globe. For instance, ownership is heavily dispersed in the United States but is much more concentrated in Canada, Germany, Japan, and China. In the last three countries, national and state governments also often own major stakes of public companies. In countries where ownership is highly concentrated, owners typically have a corresponding high level of influence over corporate affairs. Finally, board composition differs greatly from country to country: Owners and workers typically sit on the board in France, Germany, Japan, and China, whereas outsiders and managers occupy those seats in U.K., U.S., and Canadian companies.[45]

DIFFERING NATIONAL GOVERNANCE PRACTICES

As implied by these differences in governance practices across the globe, the effects of particular governance mechanisms are somewhat dependent on the national context in question. For instance, a recent comparison of the relationship between ownership structure and R&D investment revealed that in the United States, the owner-manager relationship tends to be more adversarial, whereas in Japan it is more cooperative. Managers and shareholders in Japan are often members of the same *keiretsu,* which is a set of companies with interlocking business relationships and shareholdings. This often creates ties between potential adversaries.

On the basis of these differences, ownership concentration in the United States serves as a control mechanism and affects how resources are allocated in the firm; in Japan, because the relationship is not adversarial and monitoring in nature, it does not tend to have an effect on investment behaviors.[46] This difference is dramatized by U.S. investor T. Boone Pickens' hostile-takeover attempt of Japanese firm Koito Manufacturing in 1989. At the time, Pickens' firm Mesa Petroleum owned a 20-percent stake in Koito, which in the United States would guarantee him a position on the board and a large say in corporate matters. In Japan, Pickens was snubbed by the Japanese directors because of his hostile approach. As a result, he was unable to negotiate a board seat, ultimately foiling his takeover attempt. Although it appears that the governance environment is changing in Japan, as evidenced by the more recent successful hostile takeover of Yushiro Chemicals by American-led Steel Partners in 2004, these changes are taking effect very slowly.[47]

French and German firms have different types of owners than those found in the United Kingdom and the United States. In France, nonfinancial corporations and state governments are the largest shareholders, particularly with regard to some of the country's largest employers. The same holds true for Germany, but banks are also major owners there. It is not unusual for German banks to own both debt and equity in the same corporation. In addition to the direct voting power that banks have due to their ownership position, banks also control a significant number of proxy voting positions from depositors who use the bank as a trustee for ownership purposes.

THE CASE OF GERMANY

Boards of directors are structured very differently across countries. For instance, Germany has a two-board system (sometimes called a *two-tiered board*): the management board and the supervisory board. The management board is responsible for managing the enterprise. Its members are jointly accountable for the firm's management. The chair of the management board coordinates its work. The supervisory board appoints, supervises, and advises the members of the management board and is directly involved in decisions of fundamental importance to the enterprise. The chair of the supervisory board coordinates its work. The supervisory board is similar to the board of directors of U.S. firms, with two major exceptions. First, one-half of the board's seats are allocated to representatives of shareholders and one-half to representatives of labor. To break potential tie votes, the board chair (who is always a representative of owners) is given two votes. Second, executives are not permitted to serve on the supervisory board.

Contrast the situation in Germany with U.S. firms, where about 75 percent of the board's seats are occupied by outsiders and 25 percent by insiders. Much more often than not, the chair of the board in a U.S. firm is also the CEO of the firm. Also note that members of the board in U.S. firms are elected by shareholders; no seats are allocated to any other stakeholder by right. That would seem to give shareholders considerable power. However, potential board members nominated by people other than the current board are rarely elected to the board in the United States. Consequently, CEOs have considerable power over the board in many U.S. companies. Conversely, in France and Germany it is relatively easy for owners to nominate and elect members of the board. The board-election processes in Canada and the United Kingdom resemble those in the United States more so than in the continental European countries.

THE CASE OF CHINA

China is perhaps the newest market to face corporate governance issues. With its flagship stock exchanges set up in Shanghai and Shenzhen, the China securities market started in 1990. At that time, only 10 companies were listed on the stock exchanges. After 17 years of exponential growth, the Chinese securities market has reached a considerable size, and Chinese as well as non-Chinese individuals and firms are allowed to own stock. At the end of 2005, well over 1,000 firms were listed on Chinese exchanges, with shares owned by Chinese citizens (these types of shares being referred to as A-class shares). The number of companies listed in the local market with shares owned by foreign investors (B-class shares) was 108; among them, 26 companies issued B shares only, while the rest issued both A and B shares. Forty-six companies have overseas listings (H-class shares).[49]

Given China's history of operating as a closed economy, it is probably not surprising that the majority of companies listed on the Chinese exchanges started off as state-owned enterprises. This heritage is also evident in the ownership structure of public firms, where the percentage of state ownership remains relatively high across all industries. As a result, in virtually all cases, Chinese public firms are controlled by state-owned or state-controlled shareholders. The remaining trading shares are typically owned by a combination of individual and institutional investors.[50] Such government control of public corporations is most often seen in countries where, historically, the government owned the largest companies and gradually privatized them. In Brazil, for instance, the government still has veto power over the operations of Embraer and Petrobras, two of the world's largest airplane and oil companies, respectively. French and Russian residual ownership of many large organizations reflects this heritage, as well.

Summary of Challenges

1. *Describe what* **corporate governance** *means.* Corporate governance is the means and mechanisms used to ensure that managers act in accordance with investors' best interests. It encompasses the system by which organizations are directed and controlled by their owners. Corporate governance is related to strategy formulation and implementation in several ways. Corporate governance ensures that the firm's vision and mission are reflected in its strategy and the way that strategy is executed. Governance mechanisms include monitoring and incentive devices, such as pay and promotion, that can bring managements' actions in line with shareholders' interests.

2. *Explain how corporate governance relates to competitive advantage.* Evidence suggests that shareholders favor good governance and that it can help firms outperform those with poor governance characteristics. To the extent that governance helps firms maximize returns and minimize agency problems, firms with good governance may have a competitive advantage over those lacking appropriate oversight and incentives. Young firms with good governance outperform their counterparts with loose oversight and poor incentives. Corporate scandals, such as those at Enron, Tyco, and WorldCom, are more likely to affect firms with inappropriate incentives and lax boards.

3. *Identify the roles of owners and different types of ownership profiles in corporate governance.* A public firm is one that has sold shares to the general investing public. How those publicly traded shares are dispersed and traded in the stock market varies significantly. Some firms have a few select owners who control significant stakes in the firm. Consequently, these parties have so much voting power that they can have significant influence and control over the firm's strategy and governance. Generally, the presence of strong owners minimizes agency problems. However, the presence of a powerful owner does not remove all agency problems. One specific type of problem arises when a single powerful owner uses that power to extract private benefits from the company at the expense of other, less powerful owners.

4. *Show how boards of directors are structured and explain the roles they play in corporate governance.* One of the chief monitoring devices available to shareholders is the board of directors. The general responsibility of the board of directors is to ensure that executives act in shareholders' best interests. All publicly held companies are required to have a board of directors. The legal roles of the board include hiring and firing top executives, monitoring management, ensuring that shareholders' interests are pro-

tected, establishing executive compensation, and reviewing and approving the firm's strategy. There is the presumption that independent outsiders make for a more vigilant board; however, insiders on the board can improve governance when the firm operates in highly technical areas and technical expertise is needed on the board to help board members better understand the firms' environment and internal resources. The three key roles played by boards include (1) monitoring the activities of senior executives, thereby protecting shareholders' interests; (2) providing advice to managers; and (3) using their power, influence, and networks in the business community and political circles to aid the company.

5. *Analyze and design executive incentives as a corporate governance device.* Incentives can be used to lessen potential conflicts of interests between executives and shareholders. Compensation can be structured so that managers are rewarded for doing what is in shareholders' best interests. Stock ownership is the strongest way to link shareholders' and executives' incentives. Bonus pay is a subjective incentive that can link pay to performance. Its potential drawbacks are short-term bias and that it provides executives with incentives to manipulate earnings. Stock options have been the most heavily used incentive. Although they provide upside financial benefits, such as stock ownership, they do not convey a downside financial risk beyond opportunity cost. Recently, restricted stock grants and long-term incentive plans have become popular because they seem to overcome the limitations of bonuses and options.

6. *Illustrate how the market for corporate control is related to corporate governance.* The threat that a firm may become the target of a battle for corporate control and takeover is an external governance mechanism that helps to limit the consequences of bad management. When management performs poorly, the firm may become the target of a hostile takeover, either by disgruntled investors who want to replace the management and the board or by opportunistic investors looking to buy a company on the cheap and reap profits through dramatic restructuring. In either case, the existing management team will typically be terminated. Thus, this mechanism is a draconian backstop to the other internal mechanisms.

7. *Compare and contrast corporate governance practices around the world.* Governance practices differ around the globe in accordance with local laws and societal norms. Governance in the United States and the United Kingdom is shareholder-centric; in other countries, other stakeholders have much greater formal standing. For instance, in Germany labor has the right to appoint one-half of the board members. Ownership structure in Europe and Asia differs dramatically from the ownership of U.S. companies, and these differences have profound consequences for strategy formulation and implementation. Large corporate and government ownership blocks are common in Europe and Asia, whereas in the United States the majority of stock ownership is through pension plans and mutual funds. These funds tend to own relatively small percentages of any given company.

Review Questions

1. Explain what is meant by corporate governance.

2. Who are the principals and agents in the modern corporation? How do their interests differ?

3. How does governance affect firm performance and competitive advantage?

4. How can large, powerful owners reduce the agency problem? How can they exacerbate the problem?

5. When are inside directors beneficial to the functioning of the board of directors?

6. What are the three primary roles played by boards? How do boards carry out these roles?

7. What is the difference between stock options and restricted stock? What are the advantages and disadvantages of each?

8. What is the market for corporate control? What role does it play in solving or exacerbating the agency problem?

9. What are some primary differences and similarities in governance practices between the United States and other countries?

Experiential Activities

Group Exercises

1. Prior to class, visit the Web site www.theyrule.net. This site provides a convenient way to map out the interlocking boards of directors of U.S. firms. Develop or pick from the various interlock arrangements, print out your example, and bring it to class for discussion. What are the implications of the interlocks you identified for strategy formulation and implementation? What is provocative about your network structure? How might it affect the formulation and implementation of strategy?

2. Identify a company that is currently subject to an attempted hostile takeover (the *Wall Street Journal* or various online sources can help you do this quickly). What are the dynamics that are involved in this potential takeover? Who are the key stakeholders in this battle? Who do you see benefiting and losing if this takeover is successful? Does it appear that this hostile takeover would create value?

Ethical Debates

1. In a business dinner at which a few board members and top executives are attending, you overhear directors mentioning that the CEO's office has been bugged because they think he is negotiating behind their backs for a sale of the company. What do you do with this information?

2. You work in the HR department of a large international high-tech company. During the annual process of preparing for the closing of year-end books, your manager comes to you and tells you to pull out the documents for executive stock option grants and change the grant date from April 1st to July 13th. Why would he do this? What should be done?

How Would YOU DO THAT?

1. Refer back to the box entitled Exhibit 13.6 which discussed the establishment of executive stock ownership requirements at Dendrite International. Many business press outlets, such as *Business Week* and *Fortune,* publish articles that are critical of the corporate governance practices, particularly executive compensation, of one firm or another. Using these outlets, identify a recent example of a company that has been criticized for its governance practices and determine whether executive or director stock ownership was a factor in this criticism. What action plan for remedying this situation would you propose?

2. Identify a firm that is looking for a new CEO (or pick one whose CEO you think should be replaced!). Using the box entitled "How Would *You* Do That? 13.1" as a model, imagine that a firm is turning toward a compensation model that requires the CEO to own stock. What, specifically, do you think the compensation package should look like? How different will your company be from the competition in terms of the compensation package offered to the new CEO? (Hint: Pull up competitors' 10-K statements on the Internet.) What are the implications of these differences?

Go on to see How Would You Do That at www.prenhall.com/ carpenter&sanders

Endnotes

1. A. Shleifer and R. W. Vishny, "A Survey of Corporate Governance," *The Journal of Finance* 52:2 (1997), 737–783.

2. E. F. Fama and M. C. Jensen, "Separation of Ownership and Control," *Journal of Law and Economics* 26 (1983), 301–325; A. Shleifer and R. W. Vishny, "A Survey of Corporate Governance," *The Journal of Finance* 52:2 (1997), 737–783.

3. A. Tuschke and W. G. Sanders, "Antecedents and Consequences of Corporate Governance Reform: The Case of Germany," *Strategic Management Journal* 24 (2003), 631–649.

4. Exchange News: Statements from Angelo Tantazzi, Chairman of Borsa Italiana and Massimo Capuano, CEO of Borsa Italiana, www.exchange-handbook.co.uk/news_story.cfm?id=50739 (accessed November 29, 2005); T. C. Hoschka, "A Market for the Well Governed," *The McKinsey Quarterly* 3 (2002), 26–27.

5. W. G. Sanders and S. Boivie, "Sorting Things Out: Valuation of New Firms in Uncertain Markets," *Strategic Management Journal* 25 (2004), 167–186.

6. This exhibit summarizes a press release from Governance Metrics International (GMI), a New York City organization that provides governance ratings on public companies around the world. Source: M. Maremont and R. Brooks, "Fresh Woes Batter Krispy Kreme; Doughnut Firm to Restate Results, Delay SEC Filing; Shares Take a 15% Tumble," *Wall Street Journal* (Eastern edition), January 5, 2005, A3.

7. For more information, see www.gmiratings.com and www.morningstar.com (accessed July 15, 2005).

8. E. F. Fama and M. C. Jensen, "Separation of Ownership and Control," *Journal of Law and Economics* 26 (1983), 301–325; M. C. Jensen and W. H. Meckling, "Theory of the Firm: Managerial Behavior, Agency Costs and Ownership Structure," *Journal of Financial Economics* 3 (1976), 305–360; Shleifer and Vishny, "A Survey of Corporate Governance"; J. P. Walsh and J. K. Seward, "On the Efficiency of Internal and External Corporate Control Mechanisms," *Academy of Management Review* 15 (1990), 421–458.

9. A. A. Berle, Jr. and G. C. Means, *The Modern Corporation and Private Property* (New York: McMillan, 1932).

10. E. Ofek and D. Yermack, "Taking Stock: Equity-Based Compensation and the Evolution of Managerial Ownership," *Journal of Finance* 55:3 (2000), 1367–1384.

11. P. Milgrom and J. Roberts, *Economics, Organization, and Management* (Upper Saddle River, NJ: Prentice Hall, 1992).

12. www.sec.gov (accessed July 15, 2005).

13. "Prosecutors Say Rigases Owe $2.5 Billion," *New York Times,* December 15, 2004, C2. Jack Hitt, "American Kabuki: The Ritual of Scandal." *New York Times,* July 18, 2004, 1.

14. www.calpers.org and www.swib.state.wi.us (accessed July 15, 2005).

15. R. E. Hoskisson, M. A. Hitt, R. A. Johnson, and W. Grossman, "Conflicting Voices: The Effects of Institutional Ownership Heterogeneity and Internal Governance on Corporate Strategies," *Academy of Management Journal* 45 (2002), 697–716.

16. M. Peers, J. Carreyrou, and B. Orwall, "Vivendi CEO Loses Key Board Support, Endangering His Job," *Wall Street Journal,* (2002) July 1: A1; L. Panetta, "It's Not Just What You Do, It's the Way You Do It," *Directors & Boards* 27 (2003), 17–21.

17. www.aicpa.org/info/sarbanes_oxley_summary.htm (accessed November 29, 2005).

18. B. Baysinger and R. E. Hoskisson, "The Composition of Boards of Directors and Strategic Control: Effects on Corporate Strategy," *Academy of Management Review* 15 (1990), 72–87.

19. Baysinger and Hoskisson, "The Composition of Boards of Directors and Strategic Control."

20. J. Dahya, A. Lonie, D. Power, "The Case for Separating the Roles of Chairman and CEO: An Analysis of Stock Market and Accounting Data," *Corporate Governance* 4 (1996), 71, 76. This study examined the impact of separating or combining the roles of CEO and chair in the United Kingdom. The authors found that a "significant positive market reaction . . . followed the separation of the responsibilities of chairman and CEO." Also, companies that announced a separation subsequently performed better than their counterparts based on several accounting measures. Conversely, companies that announced combination of the positions resulted in "the largest negative market response the day after the announcement."

21. "The function of the chairman is to run board meetings and oversee the process of hiring, firing, evaluating, and compensating the CEO . . . Without the direction of an independent leader, it is much more difficult for the board to perform its critical function," M. C. Jensen, "Presidential Address: The Modern Revolution, Exit and the Failure of Internal Control Systems," *Journal of Finance* 48 (1993), 831, 866; "Wearing both hats is like grading your own paper," A. Hansen, deputy director of the Council of Institutional Investors, as quoted in "A Walk on the Corporate Side," *Trustee* 49:10 (1996), 9, 10. See also, C. E. Bagley and Richard H. Koppes, "Leader of the Pack: A Proposal for Disclosure of Board Leadership Structure," *San Diego Law Review* 34:1 (1997), 149, 157–158.

22. Adapted from M. Wiersema, "Holes at the Top: Why CEO Firings Backfire," *Harvard Business Review* 80:12 (2002), 70–77.

23. C. Lucier, R. Schuyt, and J. Handa, "The Perils of Good Governance," *Strategy+Business* 35 (2004), 1–17.

24. J. D. Westphal, "Collaboration in the Boardroom: Behavioral and Performance Consequences of CEO–Board Social Ties," *Academy of Management Journal* 42 (1999), 7–24.

25. M. A. Carpenter and J. D. Westphal, "The Strategic Context of External Network Ties: Examining the Impact of Director Appointments on Board Involvement in Strategic Decision Making," *Academy of Management Journal* 44 (2001), 639–651.

26. G. Strauss, "Board Pay Gets Fatter as Job Gets Hairier," *USA TODAY,* March 7, 2005, B1; T. Johnson-Elie, "Boards Slowly Opening up to Women, Minorities—Time Is Right, Seasoned Executive Jackson Says," *Milwaukee Journal Sentinel,* June 1, 2005, 1.

27. B. Lechem, *Chairman of the Board* (London: Wiley, 2002).

28. www.thecorporatelibrary.com and www.issproxy.com (accessed July 15, 2005).

29. M. A. Carpenter and J. D. Westphal, "The Strategic Context of External Network Ties."

30. M. McDonald and J. D. Westphal, "Getting by with the Advice of Their Friends: CEOs' Advice Networks and Firms' Strategic Responses to Poor Performance," *Administrative Science Quarterly* 48 (2003), 1–32; J. D. Westphal and J. W. Fredrickson, "Who Directs Strategic Change? Director Experience, the Selection of New CEOs, and Change in Corporate Strategy," *Strategic Management Journal* 22 (2001), 1113–1138; J. D. Westphal, M. D. Seidel, and K. S. Stewart, "Second-Order Imitation: Uncovering Latent Effects of Board Network Ties," *Administrative Science Quarterly* 46 (2001), 717–747.

31. "Dendrite International Board Mandates New Executive Share Ownership Policy; Program Reflects Positive Expectations," *BusinessWire,* February 8, 2000; Standard and Poor's Quantitative Stock Report; DRTE (Dendrite International), December 17, 2005.

32. E. White, "Call It Sarbanes-Oxley Burnout: Finance-Chief Turnover Is Rising," *Wall Street Journal,* April 5, 2005, A1.

33. Adapted from Fredrick W. Cook & Co., Inc., "Stock Ownership Policies: Prevalence and Design of Executive and Director Ownership Policies Among the Top 250 Companies," www.fwcook.com/surveys.html (accessed November 29, 2005), September 2004.

34. P. M. Healy and J. M. Wahlen, "A Review of the Earnings Management Literature and Its Implications for Standard Setting," *Accounting Horizons* 13 (1999), 365–383.

35. R. E. Hoskisson, M. A. Hitt, and C. W. L. Hill, "Managerial Incentives and Investment in R&D in Large Multiproduct Firms," *Organization Science* 4 (1993), 325–341.

36. W. G. Sanders, "Behavioral Responses of CEOs to Stock Ownership and Stock Option Pay," *Academy of Management Journal* 44 (2001), 477–492; W. G. Sanders, "Incentive Alignment, CEO Pay Level, and Firm Performance: A Case of 'Heads I Win, Tails You Lose'?" *Human Resource Management* 40 (2001), 159–170.

37. W. G. Sanders, "Behavioral Responses of CEOs to Stock Ownership and Stock Option Pay," *Academy of Management Journal* 44 (2001), 477–492.

38. D. F. Larcker, "The Association Between Performance Plan Adoption and Corporate Capital Investment," *Journal of Accounting and Economics* 5 (1983), 3–30.

39. J. Dial and K. J. Murphy, "Incentives, Downsizing, and Value Creation at General Dynamics," *Journal of Financial Economics* 37 (1995), 261–314.

40. M. A. Carpenter and W. G. Sanders, "Top Management Team Compensation: The Missing Link Between CEO Pay and Firm Performance," *Strategic Management Journal* 23 (2002), 367–374.

41. M. Bloom and J. G. Michel, "The Relationships Among Organizational Context, Pay Dispersion, and Managerial Turnover," *Academy of Management Journal* 45 (2002), 33–42.

42. Berle and Means, *The Modern Corporation and Private Property.*

43. R. Slater, *The Titans of Takeover* (New York: Beard Books, 1999).

44. M. C. Jensen and R. S. Ruback, "The Market for Corporate Control: The Scientific Evidence," *Journal of Financial Economics* 11 (1983), 5–50.

45. E. R. Gedajlovic and D. M. Shapiro, "Management and Ownership Effects: Evidence from Five Countries," *Strategic Management Journal* 19 (1998), 533–553; R. Tricker, *Pocket Director* (London: The Economist Books, 1999).

46. P. M. Lee and H. M. O'Neill, "Ownership Structures and R&D Investments of U.S. and Japanese Firms: Agency and Stewardship Perspectives," *Academy of Management Journal* 46 (2003), 212–225.

47. B. Bremner and M. der Hovanesian, "So 'Takeover' Does Translate: Foreigners Are After Japanese Companies—With Better Governance as One Result," *BusinessWeek,* February 9, 2004, 51.

48. *Home Depot proxy statement filing (form DEF 14A), April 20, 2007.*

49. www.oecd.org (accessed July 15, 2005).

50. www.oecd.org (accessed July 15, 2005).

Pulling It
All Together

Preparing for
Case Discussions

The case method is one of the most effective means of management education. It is widely used in schools of business throughout the world, and this use is predicated upon the belief that tackling real business problems is the best way to develop practitioners. Real problems are messy, complex, and very interesting.

Unlike other pedagogical techniques, many of which make you the recipient of large amounts of information but do not require its use, the case method requires you to be an active participant in the closest thing to the real situation. It is a way of gaining experience without spending a lot of time. It is also a way to learn a great deal about how certain industries and businesses operate, and how managers manage in them. There are few programmable, textbook solutions to the kinds of problems faced by real general managers and other leaders. When a problem becomes programmable, the leader gives it to someone else to solve on a repeated basis using the guidelines he or she has set down. Thus the case situations that you will face will require the use of analytical tools and the application of your personal judgment.

Sources of Cases

Most of the cases in this course are about real companies. You will recognize many of the names of the companies, although some of them may be new to you. These cases were developed in several different ways. In some instances, a company came to a business-school professor and requested that a case be written on that company. In other situations, a professor sought out a company because he or she knew that the company was in an interesting or difficult situation. Often, the company agreed to allow a case to be written. Sometimes, cases were written solely from public sources. In these instances, there may be less "inside" information about the company incorporated in the case, but generally there is still enough rich information to motivate a rigorous analysis and discussion of the situation at hand.

In rare instances a true company was disguised because the case content is rich for learning but the company desires anonymity or is a private firm.

Overview of Case Preparation

There is only one secret to good case-based learning, and that is good preparation on the part of the participants. Because this course has been designed to "build" as it progresses, class attendance is also very important. But, what you learn from case discussion will be a function of how well you prepare.

When you prepare for class, we recommend that you plan on reading the case at least three times. The first reading should be a quick run-through of the text in the case. It should give you a feeling for what the case is about, who the major players are, and the types of data that are contained in the case. For example, you will want to differentiate between facts and opinions that may be expressed. In every industry, there is a certain amount of "conventional wisdom" that may or may not reflect the truth.

On your second reading you should read in more depth. Many people like to underline or otherwise mark up their cases to pick out important points that they know will be needed later. Your major effort on a second reading should be to understand the business and the situation'. You should ask yourself questions like: (1) Why has this company survived? (2) How does this business work? (3) What are the basic economics of this business? It is important that you clearly spell out the five elements of the strategy diamond here. During this reading, you should also carefully examine the exhibits in the case. It is generally true that the case writer has put the exhibit there for a purpose. It contains some information that will be useful to you in analyzing the situation. Ask yourself what that information is when you study each exhibit. You often will find that you will need to apply some analytical technique (e.g., ratio analysis or growth rate analysis) to the exhibit in order to benefit from the information in the raw data. More often than not, data from more than one exhibit will need to be combined to develop innovative and meaningful insights about the case.

By the time you read the case the third time, you should already have a good idea of the fundamentals of the case. Now you will be searching to understand the specific situation. Your objective will be to get at the root causes of problems and gather data from the case that will enable you to make specific action recommendations. Before the third reading, you may want to review the assignment questions in the course description. It is during and after the third reading that you should be able to outline your answers to the assignment questions. Just as important, you should be able to determine whether these are the most relevant and important questions facing the organization and its management.

Class Discussions

Often an instructor will ask a few class members several leadoff questions. If you have prepared the case, and are capable of answering the assignment question, you should have no difficulty with these leadoff questions. An effective leadoff assignment can do a great deal to enhance a class discussion. It sets a tone that enables the class to probe more deeply into the issues of the case. Although instructors may differ in their preferences, it is often desirable to take a particular stand, even take on the role of devil's advocate, regarding case questions. One benefit of the case method is that it offers a better context in which to experience missteps and miscalculations than does your first job assignment. In this regard, cases give you an opportunity to exercise reasoned risk taking and make specific recommendations under conditions of uncertainty, just as real leaders would. If you are asked to make recommendations, they will be more compelling if they are specific, grounded in analysis of case data and information, and demonstrate a solution that the firm may be uniquely able to exploit.

The instructor's role in the class discussion is to help, through intensive questioning, to develop your ideas. This use of the Socratic method has proved to be an effective way to develop thinking capability in individuals. The instructor's primary role is to manage the class process and to ensure that the class achieves an understanding of the case situation. There is no single correct solution to any of these problems. There are, however, a lot of wrong solutions. Therefore, you will try to come up with a solution that will enable you to deal effectively with the problems presented in the case.

The Use of Extra- or Post-Case Data

Unless otherwise instructed, you are encouraged to deal with the case as it is presented. You should put yourself in the position of the general manager involved in the situation and look at the situation through his or her eyes. Part of the unique job of being a general manager is that many of the problems they face are dilemmas. There is no way to come out a winner on all counts. Although additional data might be interesting or useful, being a "Monday morning quarterback" is not an effective way to learn about strategic management. Therefore, you are strongly discouraged from acquiring or using extra- or post-case data.

Some case method purists argue that a class should never be told what actually happened in a situation! Each person should leave the classroom situation with his or her plan for solving the problem, and none should be falsely legitimized. The outcome of a situation may not reflect what is, or is not, a good solution. You must remember that because a company did something different from your recommendations and was successful or unsuccessful, this is not an indication of the value of your approach. It is, however, interesting and occasionally useful to know what actually occurred. Therefore, your professor may decide to tell you what happened to a company since the time of the case, but you should draw your own conclusions from that.

Case Preparation Details

We just reviewed our logic for case preparation. In this section, we outline in a worksheet format the type of analysis that you might complete before coming to class. Note that in this worksheet, we do not segment the three readings reviewed above. During your three readings you should simply fill in the relevant information, and at the conclusion of your third pass you should have collected enough information, analyzed the material, and come to a personal view as to what should be done.

Case Title:

Case Assignment Questions:

Who are the main players (name and position)?

_____

_____

_____

What business(es) and industry or industries is the company in?

_____

_____

What are the issues and problems facing the company? (Sort them by *importance* and *urgency.*)

_____

_____

_____

Why did this problem emerge? (Identify causal chain.)

_____

_____

_____

Are the apparent problems the real problems or only symptoms of the real problems?

_____

_____

_____

What are the characteristics of the environment in which the company operates?

_____

_____

_____

What are the characteristics of the industry that the company is in and how is the industry changing over time?

_____

_____

_____

What is the firm's strategy, in terms of the five strategy elements, for competing in this context?

_____

_____

_____

What are possible solutions to the identified problems?

_____

_____

_____

Are there any possible problems with your suggested recommendations? What contingencies need to be accommodated?

_____

_____

_____

Try to model the problem and solution by drawing a diagram. Identify the problem, what is causing it, what is making the problem worse (or potentially hiding the problem), and what can be done to mitigate or eliminate it. Use the strategy models to help you think through the steps that must be taken to intervene and solve this problem.

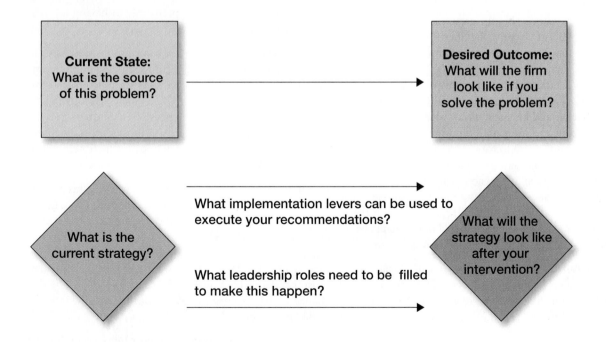

Case 1

Robin Hood

It was in the spring of the second year of his insurrection against the High Sheriff of Nottingham that Robin Hood took a walk in Sherwood forest. As he walked he pondered the progress of the campaign, the disposition of his forces, the Sheriff's recent moves, and the options that confronted him.

The revolt against the Sheriff had begun as a personal crusade, it erupted out of Robin's conflict with the Sheriff and his administration. However, alone Robin Hood could do little. He therefore sought allies, men with grievances and a deep sense of justice. Later he welcomed all who came, asking few questions, and only demanding a willingness to serve. Strength, he believed, lay in numbers.

He spent the first year forging the group into a disciplined band, united in enmity against the Sheriff, and willing to live outside the law. The band's organization was simple. Robin ruled supreme, making all important decisions. He delegated specific tasks to his lieutenants. Will Scarlett was in charge of intelligence and scouting. His main job was to shadow the Sheriff and his men, always alert to their next move. He also collected information on the travel plans of rich merchants and tax collectors. Little John kept discipline among the men, and saw to it that their archery was at the high peak that their profession demanded. Scarlock took care of the finances, converting loot to cash, paying shares of the take, and finding suitable hiding places for the surplus. Finally, Much the Miller's son had the difficult task of provisioning the ever-increasing band of Merrymen.

The increasing size of the band was a source of satisfaction for Robin, but also a source of concern. The fame of his Merrymen was spreading, and new recruits poured in from every corner of England. As the band grew larger, their small bivouac became a major encampment. Between raids the men milled about, talking and playing games. Vigilance was in decline, and discipline was becoming harder to enforce. "Why?" Robin reflected, "I don't know half the men I run into these days."

The growing band was also beginning to exceed the food capacity of the forest. Game was becoming scarce, and supplies had to be obtained from outlying villages. The cost of buying food was beginning to drain the band's financial reserves at the very moment when revenues were in decline. Travelers, especially those with the most to lose, were now giving the forest a wide berth. This was costly and inconvenient to them, but it was preferable to having all their goods confiscated.

Robin believed that the time had come for the Merrymen to change their policy of outright confiscation of goods to one of a fixed transit tax. His lieutenants strongly resisted this idea. They were proud of the Merrymen's famous motto: "Rob the rich and give to the poor." "The farmers and the townspeople," they argued, "are our most important allies." "How can we tax them, and still hope for their help in our fight against the Sheriff?"

Robin wondered how long the Merrymen could keep to the ways and methods of their early days. The Sheriff was growing stronger and better organized. He now had the money and the men, and was beginning to harass the band, probing for its weaknesses. The tide of events was beginning to turn against the Merrymen. Robin felt that the campaign must be decisively concluded before the Sheriff had a chance to deliver a mortal blow. "But how," he wondered, "could this be done?"

Robin had often entertained the possibility of killing the Sheriff, but the chances for this seemed increasingly remote. Besides, killing the Sheriff might satisfy his personal thirst for revenge, but it would not improve the situation. Robin

Prepared by Joseph Lampel, New York University. Copyright Joseph Lampel © 1985 revised 1991.

had hoped that the perpetual state of unrest, and the Sheriff's failure to collect taxes, would lead to his removal from office. Instead, the Sheriff used his political connections to obtain reinforcement. He had powerful friends at court, and was well regarded by the regent, Prince John.

Prince John was vicious and volatile. He was consumed by his unpopularity among the people, who wanted the imprisoned King Richard back. He also lived in constant fear of the barons, who had first given him the regency, but were now beginning to dispute his claim to the throne. Several of these barons had set out to collect the ransom that would

release Richard the Lionheart from his jail in Austria. Robin was invited to join the conspiracy in return for future amnesty. It was a dangerous proposition. Provincial banditry was one thing, court intrigue another. Prince John's spies were everywhere. If the plan failed the pursuit would be relentless, and retribution swift.

The sound of the supper horn startled Robin from his thoughts. There was the smell of roasting venison in the air. Nothing was resolved or settled. Robin headed for camp promising himself that he would give these problems his utmost attention after tomorrow's raid.

Case 2

Three Dimensional Printing

UVA-ENT-0006

On December 8, 1989, the MIT Technology Licensing Office (TLO) filed for a U.S. patent on the Three Dimensional Printing Process (3DP), invented by a team of four MIT researchers: Emmanuel Sachs, John Haggerty, Michael Cima, and Paul Williams. As the U.S. patent explains, 3DP is

> a process for making a component by depositing a first layer of a fluent porous material, such as a powder, in a confined region and then depositing a binder material to selected regions of the layer of powder material to produce a layer of bonded powder material at the selected regions. Such steps are repeated a selected number of times to produce successive layers of selected regions of bonded powder material so as to form the desired component. The unbonded powder material is then removed. In some cases the component may be further processed as, for example, by heating it to further strengthen the bonding thereof.[1]

[1]Abstract for "Three-dimensional Printing Techniques," US Patent number 5,204,055 <http://164.195.100.11/netacgi/nph-Parser?Sectl=PTOl&Sect2=HITOFF&d=PALL&p=1&u=/netahtml/srchnum.htm&r=1&f=G&1=50&s1='5,204,055'.WKU.&OS=PN/5,204,055&RS=PN/5,204,055> (Accessed on July 10, 2000).

True to MIT form, the four inventors of 3DP were primarily motivated by academic research, not in starting a company to exploit the technology. The TLO was in the business of attracting licensees in an effort to promote MIT inventions. Over the next nine years, the 3DP process was presented in conference presentations, academic publications, a website, and TLO mailings. Several trade and popular publications including *Fortune*, the *Financial Times*, and the *Economist* have written stories about it. Eight teams of entrepreneurs have investigated the possibility of forming new companies to exploit the technology. Why did eight entrepreneurs discover opportunities to exploit the 3DP process? What business opportunities did these entrepreneurs discover in the 3DP process and how did they discover them?

Soligen

Yehoramo Uziel, vice president of engineering at 3D Systems, a rapid prototyping firm where he worked from 1989–1992, was first introduced to the 3DP process in 1990. Uziel had a strong background in the manufacture of capital equipment. He had previously founded a manufacturer of capital equipment for printed circuit board inspection, and had extensive experience on the machine development side of rapid prototyping at 3D Systems. In fact, he was a key participant in the design and manufacture of rapid prototyping machines that employed stereolithography, a technique for using a laser to solidify liquid resin into solid plastic and forming, in successive layers, a three dimensional "print" of a part.

While at 3D Systems, Uziel had developed rapid prototyping machines based on stereolithography for Ford Motor Company, General Motors, and Chrysler. In fact, General Motors was the first customer for 3D System's machine. Uziel was part of the team that helped proliferate stereolithography initially as a way to visualize design of three-dimensional objects and subsequently for making masters that were duplicated in short runs by using "soft tooling." (Soft tooling uses RTV silicone to rapidly make molds for the injection of resin plastic.) Using these techniques to make the prototype for the 1994 1/2 Ford Explorer, Ford was able to reduce costs by 45 percent and development time by 40 percent.

Working with these companies made Uziel aware of the problems of prototyping "real" or functional parts. Anticipating that computer graphics would soon replace "physical visualization," Uziel's team explored the use of rapid prototyping to make functional metal parts. The team developed the use of rapid prototyping patterns for "lost plastic," a modification of investment casting that used a stereolithographic plastic prototype as a replacement for the traditional expandable wax pattern in the production of metal parts through investment casting. He knew that the automobile industry, for example, faced the problem of producing metal parts through investment casting because investment casting has never been suitable for mass production of automotive parts. Uziel reasoned that, since product launching required production tools, auto firms spent twice the time on design tooling for new cars as they did on production tooling. By enabling the testing of a functional part prior to the design of the tool, Uziel increased the probability of making an accurate tool the first time, thus saving time and costs in tooling.

Uziel recalls when he first heard about the 3DP process:

> I was at 3D Systems where Ely Sachs presented at a couple of conferences. I heard through the grapevine that someone else was planning to commercialize this new technology. 3D Systems was not interested in exploring new rapid prototyping methods. However, as a VP of engineering you are obliged to look around and know who your potential competitors are. So I went to MIT to take a look at the technology. I quickly became very interested in Ely's machine because I realized that the 3DP process was the only technology that would eliminate patternmaking and allow ceramic casing models directly from a CAD file. Since my interest in rapid prototyping was not so much for making visualization models or non-functional prototypes, I realized that three-dimensional printing would be the only process to cast complex metal parts with integral cores, such as cylinder heads.

> It had became apparent to me that metal casting was one of the industries that no one had tried to revolutionize. All of the developments in metal casting were in metallurgy, with a little bit in putting robots to replace some physical work. Metal casting is relying on a paradigm that in order to make a part, you first have to make a tool. Thus a CAD design of a part has to be modified by a casting expert into a tool even if the end user wishes to produce a mingle casting. Any attempt to expedite metal casting prototypes was in making a prototype. In recent years, the developments in metal casting focused on metallurgy, with a little bit on putting robots to replace physical work.

> I saw a great opportunity in the 3DP process to create a paradigm shift by making the ceramic casting molds with all the integral cores as net shaped cavities of the CAD file of the part and move from a CAD file into a castable ceramic mold and thus a functional part. I thought that if you can make a machine to give you even a small quantity of functional metal parts, you can enable the delay of the making of the tool until after you are done making design changes on the cast part. This allows you to get production tooling right the first time. I wrote up that concept in 1984 and that's what I was looking for. I joined 3D Systems as vice president of Engineering because I wanted to use stereolithography to make patterns for casting. So I was looking to create a revolution in the metal casting industry way before I had ever even heard about Ely Sachs and Mike Cima.

> I was trying to push changes in how we used stereolithography at 3D Systems because I knew that non-functional parts will not make it for more than five to ten years. In the future there will be no need for prototypes or mock-ups because everything will be done in cyberspace. So the benefit of an engineer holding a plastic prototype of an engine component is not there. While a plastic prototype might make a person able to see the component better, one day you'll be able to supplant most of the trial and error in engineering design with computer simulation. Moreover, rapid prototyping uses exotic fabrication processes that will never become production methods. For example, there is no way that anyone will be able to drive a laser as fast as needed to create something that will compete with the injection mold piece. So rapid prototyping can never yield functional parts. Even if you solidify a liquid which is exactly nylon, this is not the same properties of nylon which is injection molding. . . . [B]uilding parts from CAD can only work if you do something intermediary like make an expendable mold.

One of the biggest obstacles to accelerating manufacturing is the fabrication of parts. Metal parts are made by creating ceramic molds; and existing rapid prototyping technology does not allow for ceramic casting. MIT's 3DP process allows a person to combine colloidal silica, the liquid component of a ceramic shelf, with powder elements that you would normally mix together in a dip wax. By combining the liquids and powders directly, ceramic shell molds can be created, reducing the need for costly tooling.

Uziel explains,

> The main roadblock in foundries using rapid prototyping more intensely is the incompatibility of rapid prototyping to casting technology . . . Plastic patterns are not durable enough and have long-term dimensional instability. (They may warp or distort as time goes by and internal stresses are relieved.) For investment casting, plastic patterns do not dissolve easily and may crack the shells, and wax patterns made by laser sintering (joining wax powder particles into a wax object using a laser beam) cannot incorporate cores as they are limited to simple geometries. They also do not have the required accuracy and surface finish.[2]

Uziel decided that the 3DP process was a great opportunity and approached Ely Sachs to license it. He traveled to Boston to meet with Ely Sachs, Mike Cima, and John Preston, who was the head of the TLO at the time. With his colleague Adam Cohen he made a presentation to MIT in August of 1991, which explained his opportunity:

> Soligen recognizes a genuine problem in the investment casting industry: We feel that with increased pressure to accelerate product development and achieve just-in-time manufacturing, the long lead times needed for investment castings are a serious liability. We recognize that a major barrier to shortening this lead time is the requirement for complex and expensive tooling, which even prototypes require. All rapid prototyping companies feel their technologies are capable for eliminating the need for tooling. But our evaluation of these technologies has convinced us that Three Dimensional Printing (3DP) has the greatest chance for success and goes much further than any competing approach. Because it bypasses not only tooling for wax and cores but several other steps as well, 3DP can offer tangible benefits which will ultimately revolutionize investment casting.

Uziel told MIT that he wanted to license the 3DP process for metal casting only. He did not want to be responsible for other applications. Uziel believed that the 3DP process would change the foundry industry by allowing him to au-

tomatically create ceramic casting molds with integral cores for the general casting market directly from a computer aided design file. Uziel estimated the applicable portion of the casting market to be at least $20 billion. By implementing the 3DP process for the parts applicable, he estimated that the program for developing the foundry industry would be $1 billion per year and would achieve 25 percent annual growth in the first ten years. He projected that a company could use the technology to generate sales revenues of $40 to $60 million and throw off an operating profit of $8.5 million in five years. To do this he needed to raise a $5 million initial investment.

The presentation was successful, and MIT granted Soligen the rights to the 3DP process for metal casting. Uziel explains:

> What we licensed from MIT was a concept. Anything beyond that we had to go and develop. When we looked at MIT's technology, we saw a prototype to prove the feasibility of printing a binder onto powder. It was not the machine that Soligen would ultimately build. MIT's prototype apparatus had a single jet printing machine, and the printer jet was something that MIT made from a syringe. While it worked okay on a single jet, there was no way to make a commercial machine with a single jet. To develop DSPC (Direct Shell Production Casting), one actually had to use a different and substantially faster printing technology. So we ended up developing all of the hardware and software. The only thing that we used is the concept of printing liquid on to sequential layers of powder.

Soligen was founded in 1992 in Uziel's garage to build a machine that would postpone the design and creativity of casting tooling until after the design is proven, thus eliminating the need to prototype tooling. Soligen's Direct Shell Production Casting (DSPC) was based on the 3DP process and allowed Soligen to make a ceramic mold directly from a CAD model, using a powder and binder, without the need for wax forms or tooling. This technology allowed Soligen to develop cast metal parts with a much shorter lead time and at a lower investment cost than with existing technology, allowing customers to speed product introduction.

3D Orthopedics

Stephen Campbell first learned about the 3DP process from Michael Cima. At the time, Campbell was treating patients and running an advanced education program at the Harvard School of Dental Medicine. He had previously attended dental school at the University of Virginia and then did a specialty training program in prosthodontics at Harvard,

---

[2]Yehoramo Uziel, "Functional Prototyping—Has The Future Arrived?" *Foundry,* March 3, 1993.

with advanced materials training at MIT. His specialty was prosthodontics: the replacement of body parts with artificial substitutes. At the time, Harvard Dental School had a formalized program with the ceramic processing research lab at MIT. Campbell had two students at the ceramics processing lab and had gotten to know a few of the faculty members by writing grants or supervising students.

Campbell described his first encounter with the 3DP process:

> I was working on a program at Brigham and Women's Hospital to reconstruct images from MRIs and CAT scans for the head and neck region, to construct 3-D models of maxillofacial bones. While these models were crude and hand-constructed, the technological alternatives at the time were not very good. There were a few startup companies involved in laser lithography. This allowed three dimensional forming of some polymer-based materials. This was very limiting because if you are going to make replacement body parts, you have to be able to use many materials not just a narrow scope. One thing that the 3DP process did was to allow you to use the whole world of materials. I was aware of the new imaging technologies that were developing, as well as the materials, and the idea of providing these replacement bones just clicked. I saw that my little world of dental restorations was opening up to CAD/CAM. When the 3DP process came along, the whole idea of a service to provide replacement parts just clicked.

At the time Campbell was exploring this entrepreneurial opportunity, there were no ways to make artificial bone for weight bearing indications; doctors had to graft a patient's own bone, use cadaver bones, or grind bones or artificial substitutes in surgery. Medical professionals were aware of the shortcomings of these techniques. In many cases, surgeons were literally handgrinding a large block of material during surgery to insert it. The inserts did not fit well and controlling and restoring normal form and contours was difficult, if not impossible.

However, the use of the 3DP process to make artificial bone was far from obvious. One needed to have knowledge of the materials that make up the compositions and an understanding of the biology of the human system to know how the 3DP process could be used to create artificial bone. Moreover, one had to know the microstructural aspects of bone and artificial bone replacements, as well as the emerging field of 3D imaging. However, Campbell knew from the outset that there was a market for using the 3DP process to replace bones and teeth, because the creation of replacement parts was one of his areas of exper-

tise. As a dental specialist, he was aware of what services were being provided to surgeons and what services were not. Campbell proposed using the 3DP process to provide custom-fitted orthopedic devices for the medical and dental market as a service for individual patients, physicians, and hospitals. The 3DP process would allow Campbell to make artificial bone out of materials that were hard enough for weightbearing indications, eliminating the need for other alternatives. The potential to form custom shapes that accurately fit bony defects was a huge step forward for surgeons and patients. In addition, being able to control the microstructure and macrostructure of the formed parts during manufacturing was critical. No other process allowed such flexibility from start to finish. The 3DP process allowed for three dimentional forming of a biologically compatible replacement bone which could be printed out of any material and implanted. One could provide an anatomically accurate form that fit the defect, restoring the area to normal contours and avoiding aesthetic and functional problems.

Campbell's idea was that doctors would digitally submit patient information scanned from an MRI. This 3-D digital information would be downloaded to a central site where the piece would be designed and manufactured out of ceramics using the 3DP process. The ceramic piece would then be formed and returned to the physician in sterile form for implantation during the surgical phase.

Campbell brought his opportunity to Medical Science Partners, a Boston-area venture capital firm affiliated with Harvard University. Since Johnson and Johnson had funded the 3DP research at MIT, the company held an option to exploit the technology for medical applications. Therefore, Medical Science Partners began discussions with Johnson and Johnson to jointly finance the opportunity. In April of 1993, Medical Science Partners decided not to pursue the development of Campbell's plan.

Therics

At the end of 1992, Jean-Pierre Nagle, an analyst for the Committee on Science and Technology at Johnson and Johnson (J&J) Development Corporation, received a call from an engineer at Johnson and Johnson Orthopedics. The engineer had seen the 3DP process and was calling about J&J's option for medical use of it. MIT had already licensed the 3DP process to Soligen. The J&J engineer had participated in industry consortium meetings at the 3DP lab in which he had discussed using the 3DP process to speed the fabrication of ceramic molds for casting artificial hips and knees. Nagle called his colleague, Brad Vale, and the two of them went to MIT to discuss the technology with Ely Sachs and Mike Cima. Nagle and Vale visited MIT several times, believing that there was a possibility of brokering a deal to help J&J's operating companies make use of the technology. However, the message came back from several J&J operating companies that the technology was too new; they would rather wait until it was closer to the production stage before they did something with it.

In February 1993, Vale asked Walter Flamenbaum, an entrepreneur he had worked with in the past, to attend a brainstorming meeting about J&J's option. Flamenbaum had 25 years of experience as an academic, entrepreneur, and pharmaceutical industry executive, as well as serving as consultant for a number of pharmaceutical, biotechnology, and medical product firms that developed a diverse variety of therapeutic agents and medical devices. He had initiated, directed, and completed hundreds of clinical research and product development projects involving pharmaceutical and biotechnology agents and medical devices. He had served as group vice president of TSI-Clinical Research Group, which provided comprehensive services for the development of pharmaceutical drugs and biotechnology products. Flamenbaum spent eight years as the founder, president, and CEO of Health and Sciences Research, Inc., a contract research organization providing the medical device and pharmaceutical industries with clinical trials required by the FDA for new drug and device development. He had been responsible for all phases of clinical and regulatory development from Phase I to Phase III clinical research, all elements from Investigational New Drug (IND) to New Drug Application (NDA) submissions, as well as 510(k) (a submission to the FDA to market a medical device) and Investigational Device Exemption/Pre-Marketing Approval (IDE/PMA) submissions.

Flamenbaum had 25 years of experience in clinical pharmacology. He had served on the editorial board of the *Journal of Clinical Pharmacology* and was certified by the American Board of Clinical Pharmacology in clinical pharmacology. He was also an expert on hypertension, having served on the editorial board of the *American Journal of Hypertension*, as chief of the Division of Nephrology and Hypertension at Beth Israel Medical Center and as a professor of Clinical Medicine at Mount Sinai School of Medicine. He authored and co-authored articles, abstracts, and books on clinical pharmacology, clinical and experimental hypertension, and cardiovascular disease.

Vale gave Flamenbaum some background reading, which included a few relevant papers by the inventors of the 3DP process, and a copy of a report by two consultants who had previously done medical device development and who had been hired to investigate J&J's option. Flamenbaum recounts his meeting with the group:

> We sat around a room and talked about the process and how it could be used. The consultants had engineering backgrounds so they talked a lot about the process from an electro-mechanical point of view. They were looking at this after Soligen. So they were looking from the view of casting hips and knees using the Soligen process.

> I took a different approach. My background is in clinical pharmacology and the holy grail for me has been chronopharmacology, based on the fact that a lot of my clinical pharmacology experience is in the area of hypertension. There was a lot of evidence indicating that we were not appropriately treating high blood pressure because we weren't appropriately taking into consideration the variations in blood pressure during the course of the day, despite the fact that we have effective blood pressure lowering agents. Even when we give people drugs, there continues to be arterial sclerotic cardiovascular disease resulting in myocardial infarction because we don't hit a morning rapid change in the rate of rise in blood pressure. If you can control the amount and time of drug release to changes in blood pressure over a person's daily cycle, you can solve problems with hypertension drugs.

> If you are a clinical pharmacologist with an interest in chronopharmacology, you look at something that you can control with microarchitecture and materials. I had this "chronopharmacological logic," and intuitively looked at the technology and thought we could use it to compartmentalize the release of drugs and use it to do chronopharmacological delivery of drugs. If you know this, seeing three dimensional printing as a way to make time release drugs is quite reasonable, intuitive reasoning. Drugs are typically fabricated through a process by which a powder and liquid are fed together to create a "wet mass." This mass is typically dried and then formed into tablets. This process makes it difficult to achieve optimized control over time and amount and sequence of drug release. While pseudo-pulsative release can be created by manipulating coatings or mixing populations of beads with different release characteristics, these procedures do not effectively control release, are limited to certain materials, and are costly. The 3DP process allows the precise positioning and protection of microgram doses of highly potent drugs in the epicenter of a dosage form. By allowing the accurate placement of reservoirs, walls, and channels in micro-structures,

the 3DP process makes possible optimized control over time and amount and sequence of drug release.

I had enough commercial experience in the pharmaceutical industry that I know what the markets are. I know about drug delivery systems and thought about the percentage of that market that were for drugs that would benefit from chronopharmacologic drug delivery. I knew that there were some huge markets like hypertension and angina that you could clearly capture. So I waxed prolific on this point because my sole interest in this technology was for chronopharmacology.

Flamenbaum and the other consultants then went their separate ways. Flamenbaum decided to resign from his position as the president and CEO of Health and Sciences Research, Inc. When the announcement came out in March, Vale called Flamenbaum: "Okay, you asked for this," Vale said. "J&J is looking for someone to run this thing and see if we have established proof of principle and value in this option we have at MIT on the 3DP process. I want you to help us to investigate the medical applications of the 3DP process."

When Flarnenbaum joined the effort that April, MIT's process was far from medically acceptable and was not based on good manufacturing principles. The lab did not operate at the level of cleanliness required for the development of pharmaceutics, and the engineers were using all sorts of parts, many of them scavenged from various places. The products were not protected from the outside environment. Moreover, all of the 3DP lab's work used only one ceramic powder and one fluid, and medical applications require multiple fluids and multiple powders, specifically polymers. Drugs require more than a single solution as well as things like polymers and polyesters. Also, MIT had a bubble jet printer. A bubble jet printer works by heating a liquid to make a bubble and spitting it out the other end. The Food and Drug Administration (FDA) would not likely be convinced that the liquid that went in was the same as the liquid that came out. In addition, if the liquid was heat labile, there would be problems.

To make drug delivery systems for ethical drugs, one has to build a machine that makes very accurate, very precise pills out of hundreds of drugs, powders, and binders in a sterile environment that meets with FDA approval. One problem with the fabrication of drug products and components at the time was that the same design and fabrication were not used in downstream manufacturing. This created discontinuities in regulatory approval and process validation. Since faulty drugs posed a significant human health risk, the process by which they were made was heavily regulated. Each step in the manufacturing process had to be validated, and its effect on the final product assessed, and each piece of equipment had to be individually validated as well.

In September of 1993, Flamenbaum told Vale that the MIT team had established proof of principle. He believed that the technology could be transferred from MIT and used for broad development in the fabrication of medical products.

At the time, the researchers were not looking at commercial scale manufacturing. However, Flamenbaum and some of the pharmaceutical scientists he recruited pointed out that because of the small volume of pills involved, they could easily scale up to commercial production and not just do prototyping. Since the 3DP process was a fully integrated process for the manufacture of products, not requiring intervening tooling or molding steps, it integrated product development from initial design through final manufacturing. Therefore, it allowed direct scalability of pre-production prototypes to full quantities using the same process. This meant that the prototypes and the full production were made with the same FDA general manufacturing principles and validated processes thus eliminating the need to go through validation of different batch sizes, proving that a larger volume process produced exactly the same drug. By eliminating this step, the 3DP process facilitated approval for new drugs from regulatory agencies.

So far Vale had funded Flamenbaum's operations without co-investors. This was not consistent with J & J's usual practice of investing in new companies, and it raised a lot of questions from his management. Around that time, the Pharmaceutical Research Institute had become interested in a research project that would prove that sequential dosing could be done for a specific collection of female hormones. Vale explains:

> Pharmaceutical Research Institute was standing there with a checkbook in hand saying let's try this specific concept of sequential drug delivery. To make an investment in a start up with no co-investors is a high-risk decision. It raises a lot of questions from management and even the venture community. So keeping this alive even for one year with Johnson and Johnson Development Corporation as the sole investor would have been a bit precarious. So in a very simple minded way, our attention and our interest got aligned with somebody who had a specific problem to solve. That problem happened to support the drug delivery opportunity in the 3DP process. So we went with that.

Therics was founded with $900,000 from New York State's Science and Technology Fund, J&J, and several private investors. A second round of financing raised another $3 million. The money was used for technology transfer, to pay for more research and development at MIT, and to start the engineering process. The founders believed that the worldwide market for Therics's drug delivery system was worth $9 billion. The company projected five-year revenues of $2 million and a net loss of $7.5 million on those revenues.

Conferences, Inc.

Michael Padnos learned about the 3DP process for the first time in 1992 from John Preston, the director of the TLO. Padnos was a University of Chicago-trained lawyer who ran a company called Conferences, Inc., which provided translation and conference services to firms interested in doing business in other countries. He was also in the art business and had served as the chairman of the Cambridge Art Association. He collected art, primarily sculpture, and lived in a house full of folk art, primarily sculptures of human heads.

In the late 1980s Padnos organized a conference for the TLO on doing business in France. He brought over a group of French high-technology companies and arranged for them to meet their U.S. counterparts. The conference was a big success, and in 1991, when Russia was opening up, John Preston suggested that Padnos organize a similar conference for MIT with Russian companies. Padnos organized the conference and found it fascinating. He explains, "People were literally grabbing me on the street and asking me to help them start companies with these incredibly interesting inventions." The conferences he organized for MIT got Padnos hooked on the "whole technology creativity angle of life." He called Preston:

> I said, "I see that you have all these interesting things. Why don't I do something?" John said, "Whatever you want. Talk to my people. Talk to whomever you want." I explained to John's people that I am a lawyer and not a technology guy. I said that I would be interested in a consumer product. I talked to various people in the office and eventually learned about the 3DP process. I said, "That sounds interesting. What do you think it is good for?" They said, "Well, it's very good if you have an individual tool or something and it's outdated. For example, if you need a new gizmo for a 1913 Ford, you can show it the piece and it will manufacture a new one without having to go through the whole manufacturing process." So that sounded interesting, but I wasn't interested in that kind of stuff. I was interested in the consumer market.

> I knew that people go to malls. What do they do? They buy clothes. What else do they do? They buy photographs of themselves and their families. So I decided, why not start a business in which a person could three dimensionalize these pictures, like a bronzed head. Like an emperor of Rome, and everybody could have a statue of themselves or whatever he wanted. People would come in and we would make sculptures of them.

So Mike proposed using the 3DP process to establish a chain of stores to make three dimensional heads and busts of people from photographs. Mike describes his investigation of that opportunity:

> I looked into the idea and concluded that the technology could do what I thought it could do. In fact, several people had tried it. I found this company in California who had done it and I talked to them. They had manufactured the things, but when they tried to sell them, the public said that they looked like emperors' busts and it made them think they were dead. I said, "Well, how about if you made them smaller or bigger so it didn't look like a life-sized head?" They said, "we've tried all that and nobody was interested." The person I talked to seemed quite intelligent and competent and I didn't have any reason to think that I was a lot cleverer than he was and that's the end of that.

Specific Surface Corporation

Mark Parrish first heard about the 3DP process from an engineer at Albany International Corporation in early 1993. Parrish was an expert in ceramics who held a B.S. in ceramic engineering from SUNY College of Ceramics at Alfred University, and an S.M. and Ph.D. in ceramics from MIT. He worked as a development ceramic engineer throughout his schooling and had eight years of experience as the founder of CPS, a manufacturer of high-performance electronic ceramics. He founded and managed Ceranova, a research and development company in advanced materials, focusing on ceramics, including porous ceramics. On one project, Ceranova had subcontracted with Albany International Corporation (AIC) to help develop an extruded ceramic product. That project took Parrish to Albany frequently to meet with Albany Internationals engineers. At one of these meetings in early 1993, one of the engineers started discussing a process that had been demonstrated at MIT, which involved Mike Cima, a professor of material science. Parrish knew Cima—he had served as a consultant for Cerinova—and so he asked him about the project, which turned out to be the 3DP process. Parrish recounts his investigation of the 3DP process:

> Mike [Cima] had set up a small three-dimensional printing operation in his lab. His job was to make a very high density ceramic. The mechanical engineering department had designed the rapid prototype process to make casting shells. Mike was brought in to make the ceramic. To make a mold that you pour liquid metal into, and then break away once it solidifies, you need a very porous ceramic, with very good dimensional tolerances and uniform porosity. I asked Mike, "Is anybody using this to make filters?" He said, "No, why don't you do it?"
>
> So I started looking at the idea. I went to the TLO and made arrangements with them to get an option. They required me to write a business plan and find investors as a condition for the option. I was having a heck of a time doing that. I couldn't find any information about ceramic filters in industry. Coors uses ceramics to filter their cold filtered beer, but that wasn't a big industry.
>
> At lunch one day, I was telling an engineer at Albany International this story, including about all of my frustration. He happened to have invited Andy Jeffrey, his best buddy at work with him, along to the lunch.

Andrew Jeffrey was a chemical engineer who was working in product development at AIC, where he worked with flexible fabric filters. His position included finding new market opportunities for industrial filtration using fabric filter media. Jeffrey had spent a lot of time working on rigid filter structures. He owned four patents on filter elements, including one for "High-efficiency, self-supporting filter element made from fibers" and one for "Method of making a rigidized fiber filter element." These patents involved the creation of filter elements at high temperatures and in cylindrical form. He also had several publications on filtration, including "Rigidified Fiber Filter Elements" in the *Proceedings of the Powder and Bulk Solids Show*, 1994, and "Ceramic Filter Elements with Tailored Macro- and Microstructure," in *Filtration and Separation*. He was a member of the American Filtration Society and the Air and Waste Management Association.

Jeffrey had previously been employed by two major institutional manufacturers of fabric filtration media for industrial processes, and had been responsible for divisions within major corporations targeting filter elements using ceramics. At Birkmyre Pty, he had advised on the development of polymer coatings as a technology for filtration and had defined quality control procedures for manufacturing filter media. He had also worked on an air/gas stream filtration project for coal-fired plants in Australia for the supplier to the two largest coal-fired power-generation plants in that country. At AIC, he developed and commercialized microporous foam coated fabrics for large-scale gas-cleaning filters for coal-burning power stations. This work led to several publications in the area of gas filtration, including a 1993 article, "Rigidified Fiber Filter Elements for Industrial Gas Filtration" in the *Proceedings of the Sixth World Filtration Congress*.

Jeffrey explains his introduction to Parrish and the problem:

> We're eating pizza and discussing this problem and I told Mark that I had just been to a conference on filters in Europe that covered rigid filters. I was looking at rapid prototyping technology to see if you could use it to filter liquids in paper making. Filter making is very labor-intensive and it takes a lot of steps. I was working on a way to reduce the number of steps from raw materials to finished products and rapid prototyping allows you to do that. Also, I was working on a flexible fiber filter. It became clear to me that efficiency of the filter could be improved if we had a rigid structure. So I spent a lot of time working on rigid structures. The 3DP process combined the rapid prototyping and the rigid structures. I thought that it would solve problems in the power generation industry.
>
> My take on the industry was that there were two things that were happening. One, people didn't want to cool down gasses to filter them, everyone wanted to filter hot at the source. Two, people want more compact filters. Filters had grown very large and costly just by virtue of their size. And people said, "Can we get the filter smaller?" To do that, you have to get more surface area in the same volume or the same surface area in a smaller volume of filter. A trend was emerging that I could see clearly with the rise of cartridge filter people getting into the industrial area. The same thing had started to happen in hot gas filtration and that's where I saw the real benefit of the process was being able to get a lot of surface into a smaller filter. I told Mark to contact these guys at ABB and Westinghouse working on high temperature gas filtration, who are having some problems.

When Parrish called ABB and Westinghouse, the engineers told him that they were very interested in ceramic filters and asked what he could do with them to solve their problems.

Parrish offered Jeffrey the opportunity to join him in pursuing this market. Jeffrey read Parrish's initial plan. He decided that if the 3DP process could do what he and Parrish thought it could, it would be a great way to make a filter. The two men decided to pursue the opportunity. They estimated the market for industrial filter elements was $800 million per year. With a $1.75 million investment, they believed that they could generate sales of $31.5 million in their fifth year, and earnings before interest and taxes of $13 million in that year. In January of 1995, after a year of writing business plans and finding people that said that they would be interested in purchasing the filters, Parrish and Jeffrey found investors and started their company.

At the time Parrish and Jeffrey licensed the technology, MIT had a machine that did not bear much resemblance to the one that they used, except that it operated on the same principle. Ely Sachs' machine could not be used for manufacturing; it put out something only every two days. The binder that MIT was using was not compatible with chemical binder systems used to make ceramic filters. Also, filters must be of very high quality. They have to have high building integrity, no holes, and must hold together in a very hot environment. The MIT process was not concerned with any of those things. In addition, the MIT researchers were not focusing on the creation of a finished product; they were focusing instead on the creation of molds and prototypes that were intermediate steps. Moreover, they were emphasizing accuracy and precision, which were not the areas of emphasis for Parrish and Jeffrey's needs.

Parrish and Jeffrey's company, Specific Surface Corporation (SSC), manufactured a final product: ceramic filters for the power generation market directly from computer drawings, without tooling, dies, or molds. The 3DP process allowed SSC to manufacture filters with geometries and performance not possible with alternative processes. This enabled them to provide customers with filters that more efficiently removed particulates from dirty hot flue gas streams, and thereby provided customers with greater power generation efficiency. Parrish and Jeffrey had decided that it was better to develop the market by using an existing machine and so made their filters using a modified Soligen machine.

Z Corp

Marina Hatsopoulos and her husband, Walter Bornhorst, learned about the 3DP process from Jack Turner, a licensing officer at the TLO.

Bornhorst was a former executive who had spent 25 years working at Thermo Electron. George Hatsopoulos, the founder of Thermo Electron, had been Bornhorst's thesis adviser in mechanical engineering at MIT. Bornhorst started working with George Hatsopoulos as a consultant for the newly formed company when he was teaching at MIT. Over the years at Thermo Electron, Bornhorst had oc-

cupied many different positions. Most recently he had served as senior vice president and sector manager of the Industrial Products and Service Sector. He served as a member of the five-person operating committee which made all of the major decisions at Thermo Electron. A couple of years before, Bornhorst had decided to leave Thermo Electron, and was currently rehabilitating houses with his son.

Marina Hatsopoulos, George's daughter, had attended Brown University, where she obtained a bachelor's degree in mathematics in 1987. From there she worked for three years at Chase Manhattan Bank as a corporate finance associate and then joined Thermo Electron in 1990 to get some industrial experience. Marina Hatsopoulos left Thermo Electron in 1992 to get a master's degree in mechanical engineering at MIT, where she worked with Professor Woody Flowers, an industrial design expert.

When Marina Hatsopoulos graduated from MIT, she decided that she wanted to start a business. While looking for a business, she did some consulting and helped Bornhorst with his rehab business. Bornhorst explains:

> We did everything ourselves. We did the architectural work and then we'd buy the buildings, gut them, turn them into luxury apartments and rent them or sell them as condominiums.

Marina Hatsopoulos worked with Bornhorst on four major real estate rehabilitations, in which she participated in the architectural layout and interior and exterior design. She explains:

> We've done renovations of buildings and in all those cases there are certain views that get really tricky to visualize from a two-dimensional diagram. Architects are designing very much in three dimensions and so for them, three-dimensional models are useful. Even more importantly, architects are interacting with lay people who want to build a golf course or a house or whatever and cannot read a CAD drawing at all.

Meanwhile, Marina began to search for a business that she could buy. After a year of searching, she had become frustrated at the lack of product differentiation among the companies she saw. So she decided to call her old professor, Woody Flowers, to ask him if he had any ideas. He suggested that she talk to the TLO at MIT. She describes her meeting with Jack Turner at the TLO:

> I went to the TLO with my set of criteria. I have a mechanical engineering background, so I wanted something electro-mechanical, a physical product as opposed to a service. I did not want software. I wanted something that could be developed and com-

mercialized in a few years. When I looked at the MIT technologies, there were basically two that fit the criteria. The other one was Sensable Technologies.

Turner sent Hatsopoulos to see Jim Brecht and Tim Anderson in the 3DP Lab. Brecht was a Ph.D. student in the 3DP lab. He held a B.S. in materials science and engineering from MIT and had worked with plastics, ceramics and other materials in previous employment and research. He solely held the patent for a binder composition that could be used in the 3DP process and had developed CAD debugging and rasterization programs at the 3DP laboratory.

Tim Anderson was a technician in the lab who had previously served as a database programming consultant for Staples, Inc., and Carnbrex Group, conducted software testing for EDC, Inc., and was the first maker of PC clones in central Minnesota. He had a B.S. in computer science and electrical engineering from St. Cloud State University.

Brecht and Anderson had become good friends while working together in the 3DP lab. Both of them loved the 3D printers, but felt that the focus on accuracy and making durable parts was detracting from the entertaining aspect of simply being able to build models. They preferred figuring out how to slice software and watching the layers crop up on the screen. They were interested in the 3DP process largely so that they could make something that their friends would think was cool.

Their joint interest in the 3DP process led Brecht and Anderson to use cannibalized computers and printers scavenged from junk piles around MIT to build their own 3DP machine. Their first machine—the "Kitty Machine"—used Elmer's glue to draw patterns on kitty litter. Unfortunately, the "Kitty Machine" could only produce things that looked like puddles of dried vomit. Eventually, they began using starches and built a machine that combined a Macintosh computer with old ink jet printer parts. When they figured out a way to make rocker arms and heads with their machine, they showed the machine to Ely Sachs. Brecht explains:

> Ely was just getting over his shock when we told him we were going to start a company with the technology in our garage to make models. Specific Surface, Therics, and Soligen were all started by then, but none of them had expressed any interest in appearance models. All the companies in the rapid prototyping industry thought that it was saturated. Ely and Jack said, "no, you have to start a rapid prototyping company— a real company. You have to get financing and you have to know how to manage a small company." We knew that there was no way that we could do that alone. So Jack started sending around people who

might be interested. None of the people clicked. The concept was very early-stage. It was a proof of principle prototype and it made pretty poor models.

Then Turner sent Marina Hatsopoulos to the lab. Brecht and Anderson set up their machine and printed a rocker arm in about 20 minutes. She described the visit:

> Once I saw the rocker arm, it was clear that it would have to be for appearance models, not for functional parts. The parts were very fragile and they were made out of nontoxic material. The machine was very small. You could easily envision it being located in an office environment. I could envision getting rid of the duct tape and the rubber band and beefing up certain parts of the machine. The value of the 3DP process to rapid prototyping inherently made sense to me because I've done design on a computer screen and I know how difficult it is to visualize a three-dimensional model.

Marina Hatsopoulos called Bornhorst on her cellular phone and told him to come over to look at the machine. Since he could not come that night, Marina and Bornhorst came back a few days later. Bornhorst describes the visit:

> The device that they showed me was a proof of principle device which really did prove the principle. That sort of shocked me. I would never in a million years have expected it to work. But they were demonstrating that it did. Once I saw that it worked, the rest was easy. It would not be hard to make it a useful device. Jim Brecht and Tim Anderson had proved the hard part. It wasn't going to take a rocket scientist to go from there to a salable machine.

> Now other people might have looked at it and said, "Wow, this is a long way from a machine." When you went to the lab, you saw this duct tape, rubber bands, and chewing gum. And these guys are a little bit different. So if you had a suit on, you'd feel pretty uncomfortable just being there. Also, most people who looked at it were coming to it with a pretty specific need that was not quick and dirty printing. Most of them wanted extreme accuracy and looked at three-dimensional printing from that point of view. We saw what they were trying to do as a quick and dirty way, almost a sloppy way to do what MIT was trying to do.

> Maybe I saw something because I have done some design myself and have watched other people do design. I immediately recognized how valuable it would be to have an object in front of me when I'm trying to sort out a three-dimensional problem. It was natural to me because I have struggled with trying to visualize three dimensional things.

Once Marina and Bornhorst decided that the technology looked interesting, Marina started to do market research. She went onto the internet and did searches. She obtained magazines, journals, and annual reports that described the industry. She read books about the industry. In none of the material that she obtained was there anybody who paid any attention to the earlier stage of the design cycle. Marina realized that there was a definite pull in the marketplace that nobody was addressing: the need for early-stage design models that would be easy to make, cheap, nontoxic, office-compatible, and fast. Marina figured that a company could generate a $2-million EBIT in five years on sales of $10 million if it filled this niche.

In December 1994, Marina Hatsopoulos, Walter Bornhorst, Jim Brecht, and Tim Anderson founded Z Corp. intending to manufacture a fast, inexpensive, office-compatible machine to tap the $100-million market for three-dimensional concept models for engineering and architectural design. Design engineers and architects used concept models to review design changes early in the design process and to present ideas to others who could not read CAD designs, but who were involved in the design process. The Z Corp. machine made rapid prototypes 20 times faster than existing rapid prototyping processes and made them out of less expensive materials, reducing the cost of prototyping, accelerating the process, and allowing for more design alterations. Z Corp used an off-the-shelf ink-jet head to deposit a water-based binder on an inexpensive starch. This made their machine less than half the price of the high-end unit of their major competitor, 3D Systems, whose machines ranged from $100,000 to $490,000 and required the use of resins costing $70 per gallon. The Z Corp. machine, at $59,000, was slightly less expensive than 3D System's low-end system, which sold for $65,000.

The Z Corp. machine was sold in conjunction with a software program that ran under Windows 95 and allowed the user to import an STL file. The machine incorporated a proprietary software interface with the customer's CAD machine, which checked for faulty CAD designs. This solved the problem of working with rapid prototyping service bureaus, because designers sometimes sent files that had faults and could not be made in three dimensions without the computer file being modified. While existing high-end systems had been sold in large part to service bureaus, which built parts as an outsourced service to designers, Z Corp.'s system was placed right next to the designer in his or her office. The biggest advantage of using the 3DP process for concept models was speed, which would be lost if a service bureau had to wait to get a file from a customer, give them a quote, do the backlog, print it out, and send it out.

3D Partners

Andrew Kelly was a second-year master's student in mechanical engineering at MIT in 1996, when one of the other people working in the 3DP lab came up with the idea of using the 3DP process to a create a service bureau to provide architectural models.[3] Kelly describes the identification of the opportunity:

> My friend in the lab was an architect who had worked in an architectural firm for a year and a half making study models. He also had a general design background, mechanical engineering, and civil engineering experience. It so happens that 3DP sponsors receive mosque trinkets, which are, in essence, the same as an architectural study model. So if you know about the problems of making concept models, then it stands to reason that there is money to be made by applying the 3DP process to making architectural models.

> The architectural model-making industry still uses exacto knives, mylar and foam. These are fairly primitive manufacturing tools. We figured that you could revolutionize the industry by taking advantage of advances in computer tools like Alias and CAD/CAM. With CAD and the 3DP process, there is the potential to spin out models in a couple of minutes rather than a couple of hours. Also, training a person to run the machine is easier than training a person in the traditional architectural model-making craft.

> Our business would receive CAD drawings electronically and then send back finished architectural models faster and at a lower cost than existing alternatives. We saw the opportunity in providing study models but, as novices, we didn't know how to make machines. To make machines, you would need to be familiar with material systems, infiltration kinetics, surface chemistry, fluid delivery systems, and machine design. You would need to know some of these areas in grand detail. These were not things I knew at the time. To effectively make machines to build concept models, one would need a Ph.D. with expertise like Jim Brecht.

Kelly explained that the team dropped the business opportunity when they discovered that the architectural model-

---

[3]The individual who developed the concept of 3D Partners still works in the 3DP lab. Andrew Kelly was unwilling to identify this individual because it could "compromise that person's security in the lab."

making industry nationwide was only worth $10 million. After brainstorming ways to adapt the technology to other markets, the team developed an idea for an electronic white board that retrofit a dumb white board.

3D Imaging

Lau Christianson was a Sloan MBA student who had worked in pharmo-economics and health care consulting. Like many Sloan students, Christianson was interested in entering the 50K business plan competition. In early 1997, he ran into a high school friend, Todd Jackson, who was doing a Ph.D. at MIT. Since Jackson was also interested in entering the 50K competition, the two started talking and began to try to figure out a way to make Jackson's dissertation become the basis for a company.

Jackson's research focused on designing the CAD interface program that would take an image as constructed on a computer and allow a new generation of 3D printers to place differing materials next to each other. While the existing 3D printer used a single material to create a shape, Jackson was working on the equivalent of color printing with multiple colors or materials. In particular, his dissertation examined how to represent smoothly varying compositions within the computer by assigning different materials or colors to the computer commands. Jackson explains:

> I knew that the 3DP process could solve this problem and that stereolithography could not. In stereolithography, you are working with one material—one vat of goo. The layer the laser hits turns solid. If you hit it again, there are some materials which could change color so you could have red and white, but that's it. Now for the 3DP process, it's completely analogous to an inkjet printer except that you are squirting a binder into a powder. So, in theory, you could vary the powder and binder and change the composition gradually. And if you really stick to the analogy of inkjet printing, the simplest way of changing composition is to just add food coloring or dye to the binder material. This will blend colors in a three-dimensional model in the same way that you can blend colors in your inkjet printer to make shaded images.

To develop a business concept to make use of Jackson's dissertation, Jackson and Christianson started thinking about how the 3DP process was already being used. They tried to capitalize on the next-generation ability to use different material in the same printing job. Jackson's process was very memory intensive and this suggested making something that would take advantage of this complexity. Information from medical file data was one example. Christianson explains:

> We tried to think of things that were three dimensional that could possibly benefit from using this technology. We knew that CAT scan and MRI data tried to get a three-dimensional image of whatever part of the human anatomy was being scanned. However, the only way that a physician could really access that was through a series of two dimensional pictures that ultimately required the physician or surgeon to abstract from these pictures laid out in front of him or her and try to imagine what it's going to be like once the surgery actually begins. Our idea was to reassemble these two-dimensional images into an actual three-dimensional object so that a surgeon could explore what they were really going to find once the surgery began without having to deal with that secondary abstraction.

> One of the problems of stereolithography is that while you could model hardtissue objects, it is not very good making things that require multiple materials. Surgeons need three-dimensional models that deal with multiple materials and colors. This will provide better surgical planning and reduce failure rates in surgery. If the models are in one material or color, there is not much advantage over the abstraction of looking at MRI and CAT scan data.

Christianson and Jackson proposed using three-dimensional printing to provide a modeling service for surgeons. At that time, surgeons had to abstract from two-dimensional CAT scans and MRI images when planning for surgery. The 3DP process would create multicolor, three-dimensional models of the human brain for surgical planning that would reduce error and malpractice exposure. Their company would provide a service based on complex computer software that would make direct use of Jackson's Ph.D. dissertation research on the processing of composition information into machine instructions. They would provide a service: overnight delivery of models of the human head for surgery, rather than machines. Their company would own the printers and programs to translate the MRI and CAT scan data. It would get data from the hospitals, print out the models, and ship them back. Since these entrepreneurs did not have any experience in the manufacturing of the machines themselves, they planned to outsource their manufacture.

Case 3

Southwest Airlines

UVA-OM-0743

It was March 1992, and Herb Kelleher, Southwest Airline's chief executive officer, was laughingly describing the way in which he was about to settle a dispute with Stevens Aviation over the right to use the ad slogan "Just Plain Smart," which Stevens maintained it had developed first. Kurt Herwald, chairman of Stevens Aviation, and Kelleher had decided they would settle things the "old-fashioned way" in a best-of-three arm-wrestling match in the Dallas Sportatorium.

This unusual method of negotiation was entirely in keeping with Herb Kelleher's "disarming" style, which, for some observers, was the principal reason for Southwest's 19 straight profitable years. Many in the industry, however, pointed to a variety of other factors that ensured the Dallas-based airline would continue to maintain its top record of achievement. The bottom line for Southwest Airlines was that it provided high value for low cost and consistently delivered what it promised.

DARDEN

This case was prepared by Charlotte Thompson under the supervision of Professor Elliott N. Weiss. It was written as a basis for class discussion rather than to illustrate effective or ineffective handling of an administrative situation. Copyright © 1993 by the University of Virginia Darden School Foundation, Charlottesville, VA. All rights reserved. *To order copies, send an e-mail to sales@dardenpublishing.com. No part of this publication may be reproduced, stored in a retrieval system, used in a spreadsheet, or transmitted in any form or by any means—electronic, mechanical, photocopying, recording, or otherwise—without the permission of the Darden School Foundation.*

History

Southwest Airlines was founded in 1967 by Rollin King, a former investment counselor who had been operating a small air-taxi service in Texas. The impetus behind King's organization of Southwest Airlines was his perception of a growing unmet need for improved intercity air service within Texas.

In the late 1960s, Houston, Dallas, San Antonio, and Fort Worth were among the fastest growing cities in the United States. Although each had its own airport, a huge new airport, the Dallas/Fort Worth Regional Airport, was then under construction that would serve both Dallas and Fort Worth. These four cities were primarily served by two Texas-based carriers, Braniff International Airways and Texas International Airlines (TI). For the most part, service to these cities by Braniff and TI consisted of "legs" of interstate flights; in other words, a Braniff flight might stop at Dallas on its way from New York to San Antonio.

In his talks with consumers prior to embarking on the Southwest venture, King was struck by the amount of dissatisfaction with the current service and discovered that the market was bigger than many realized. Together with his lawyer Herb Kelleher, King was able to raise enough capital to incorporate the airline. On February 20, 1968, Kelleher obtained the Certificate of Public Convenience and Necessity from the Texas Aeronautics Commission, which granted Southwest Airlines the right to provide intrastate air service between Dallas/Fort Worth, Houston, and San Antonio. Southwest's competitors reacted immediately by asking the Texas courts to enjoin issuance of the certificate, maintaining that service was already provided on the proposed routes and that the market was not large enough to support another carrier. The ensuing litigation kept the company's lawyers occupied for several years.

In 1970, King brought Lamar Muse aboard as president, director, and treasurer. An independent financial consultant and former president of Universal Airlines, Muse had become attracted to Southwest after reading about its legal battles and realizing that the market for this kind of carrier was growing: "There was so much interline traffic that most of the seats were occupied by those people. While Braniff had hourly service, there really weren't many seats available for local passengers." Muse also commented that both Braniff and TI, in part because their local service was merely a leg of interstate flights, were rarely on time, and people thus tended to fly only when they absolutely had to.

On June 18, 1971, amid a heavy advertising campaign to promote the new airline and restraining orders issued by judges after complaints by its competitors, Southwest launched six round-trip flights between Dallas's Love Field and San Antonio and 12 round-trip flights between Dallas and Houston. The takeoff proved to be less than auspicious. In its first eleven months of operation, Southwest lost $3.7 million. Some days saw the airline carrying a total of only 150 passengers on its 18 round-trip flights. Nevertheless, Muse persevered with his ideas by offering unbelievable prices, gimmicks, and creative advertising.

In Texas, 1972 became the year of the fare war. To compete with Southwest, competitors slashed fares and began offering more in terms of service, e.g., free beer, hot and cold towels, one-dollar drinks on routes Southwest flew, and more frequent service. When Braniff decided to offer a half-price fare, Muse countered with a give-away: free bottles of premium liquor to passengers who paid full fare; passengers who did not want the liquor would pay half fare. Because corporations were used to paying full fare, business travelers became the happy recipients of premium liquor. During the promotion, Southwest became not only the largest distributor in Texas of Chivas, Crown Royal, and Smirnoff, but also the winner in the fare war. After 1972, Southwest consistently made a profit (see Exhibit 1).

Herb Kelleher

In March 1977, Lamar Muse resigned as president and chief executive officer of Southwest Airlines, and Herb Kelleher was named to replace him. Kelleher, a student of philosophy and literature who later graduated at the top of his law-school class at New York University, was wedded to the Southwest cause from the very

Exhibit 1	Southwest Airlines

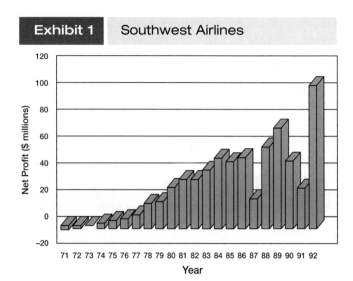

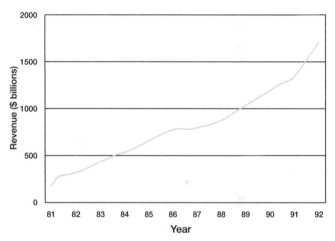

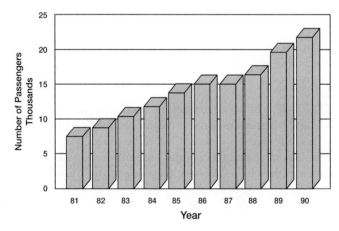

beginning. Kelleher did not merely believe in Southwest's mission; in some ways, the initial legal battles with Southwest's competitors enraged him to the point where he knew he had to win. Kelleher likened Southwest's struggles with its competitors to the trench warfare of World War II, and he was determined that Southwest would eventually be able to engage the enemy on its terms, not theirs.

Early on, Kelleher established a reputation for doing the unusual. At company functions he would appear as Elvis Presley or Roy Orbison and perform "Jailhouse Rock" or "Pretty Woman." One Halloween night he showed up at Southwest's hangar in drag, as Corporal Klinger from *M*A*S*H*, to thank mechanics for working overtime. Although Kelleher's behavior was somewhat unconventional for a chief executive officer, his efforts paid off. His colleagues credited much of Southwest's "magic" to him. "Herb has a nice, light perspective on life," stated Jim Wimberly, head of Southwest's ground operations. "We both like Wild Turkey, and we smoke a little too much."

Known for his extreme tenacity and limitless energy, Kelleher slept only four hours a night, read two or three books a week, and chain-smoked. Gary Barron, Southwest's chief operations officer, called Kelleher "the smartest, quickest lawyer—not to mention the best judge of people" he had ever seen.[1] Kelleher was widely credited with much of the airline's success for promoting and maintaining both a culture that favored people and a coherent business strategy that was consistently successful yet deceptively simple. "People always want high-quality service at a lower price, provided by people who enjoy what they do," he maintained.[2] The results of Kelleher's efforts: Southwest's overall costs were the lowest of any major carrier, yet its workers were among the best paid.

Operations

START-UP Initial operations for Southwest Airlines began under extreme pressure and tight deadlines. Additional capital for start-up expenses had to be raised, personnel had to be hired and trained, and a multitude of marketing problems had to be resolved. Most important, Muse and King had to make key decisions on the number and type of aircraft to be used. Many weeks of high-pressure negotiations with representatives of several airplane manufacturers resulted in the purchase of three Boeing 737-200 aircraft. This decision proved to be a crucial one for South-

west, not only because the airline would continue to use the same type of aircraft for many years, but also because the planes required fewer crew members than the aircraft used by Southwest's competitors.

SCHEDULING Initial decisions regarding scheduling were constrained by the fact that Southwest only had three airplanes. After studying flight times and on-the-ground (turnaround) times, Muse and King concluded that they could offer flights at 75-minute intervals using two planes between Dallas and Houston (the most important route) and at 150-minute intervals (2.5 hours) between Dallas and San Antonio using one plane, which amounted to 12 round-trips per day between Dallas and Houston and 6 round-trips per day between Dallas and San Antonio. Because of low weekend demand, Muse and King decided to fly less frequently on Saturdays and Sundays.

In spite of all their well-laid plans, however, scheduling proved to be a problem. In the first two weeks, the airline reported an average of 13.1 passengers per flight on the Dallas-Houston route and 12.9 passengers on the Dallas-San Antonio route. Because of the lack of planes, management concluded that Southwest was unable to compete effectively and thus set about improving its schedule frequencies. The delivery of the fourth plane in late September helped immensely; but perhaps more important than the arrival of the fourth plane was the company's ability to deliver a turnaround time of ten minutes. Proving its ability to turn a constraint into a competitive advantage, Southwest was able to initiate hourly service between Dallas and Houston and flights every two hours between Dallas and San Antonio by orchestrating maintenance and servicing to the point that no plane stayed on the ground more than ten minutes. This development proved to be a real innovation in the industry; the company became known for its "quick turns."

STRATEGY AND SERVICE From the beginning, Southwest management's idea was to offer no-frills, low-cost flights to and from secondary airports, and the airline clung tenaciously to this initial strategy. Management's focus was the "short-haul, point-to point" strategy, which advocated short flights (average flight time of 55 minutes) to uncrowded airports for quick turnarounds. This adherence to a short-haul strategy enabled Southwest to distinguish itself from its competitors, many of whom failed. Several airlines started out in the short-haul business, only to become tempted by the more glamorous routes. "Suddenly they were competing with big people who knew what they were doing," stated Gary Barron. "They got their brains beat out. Southwest will take Lubbock to Little Rock any old time." As

[1] *Inc.*, January 1992, p. 67.
[2] *Inc.*, January 1992, p. 66.

Salomon Brothers analyst Julius Maldutis pointed out, "They stay out of the major vegetable patches with big elephants."[3]

Most of Southwest's competitors used a "hub-and-spoke" system in which big planes fly to major airports (hubs) and then link up with smaller airports (spokes). Southwest developed no recognizable hub, preferring instead to maintain a "spiderweb" system in which one strand at a time is spun.[4] Kelleher's reason for implementing this strategy was that a hub-and-spoke network tied up too many valuable assets at too few pressure points, whereas a spiderweb system would allow maximum flexibility to disperse assets and reduce stress in the system.

Southwest's "no-frills" policy included no baggage transfers, no meals, no assigned seats, and reusable boarding cards. When a passenger decided to fly Southwest, he or she would show up at the airport at the designated time, get a ticket at the counter printed out by a machine (at the time, the competition was issuing handwritten tickets), take a reusable boarding card, and board the plane to sit wherever he or she preferred. On board, the passenger could enjoy a drink or two and some peanuts, but nothing more. The reason behind the no-frills policy was that there were other things to offer customers that gave better value: frequent, reliable, on-time flights and very low prices. For Southwest,

[3] *Financial World,* May 28, 1991, p. 19.
[4] *Inc.,* January 1992, p. 66.

quality was not a filet mignon dinner with a fine wine, it was on-time flights and no lost baggage.

Southwest's management also made a decision not to subscribe to expensive computerized reservation systems that would link them with travel agencies, opting instead to market the airline through other means. Although initially the airline hired a small sales force that promoted Southwest among travel agents and corporate accounts (companies whose personnel flew Southwest on a regular basis), Southwest used travel agents relatively infrequently because of the small margins it made on ticket sales.

One way the airline was able to keep its costs down was through contracting for such things as major maintenance, data processing, and legal services. Southwest also contracted for about two-thirds of its monthly jet-fuel supply and purchased the rest on the spot market.

Southwest's policy with regard to costs and service paid off: its average number of flights per plane per day was 10.5, whereas the industry average was 4.5; its planes were in the air 11 hours a day (industry average, 8 hours a day), which was an especially significant statistic in that its flights were the shortest of any airline. Given that short flights made for higher fuel costs and a greater number of landing fees than did long flights, Southwest could be especially proud of its cost of 6.5 cents per available seat-mile, the lowest in the industry. Southwest's secret was that it made extremely good use of its most expensive asset: its planes (see Exhibit 2).

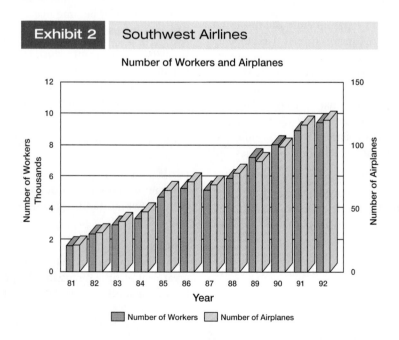

Exhibit 2　**Southwest Airlines**

Number of Workers and Airplanes

New Markets

Part of Southwest's strategy was to investigate potential markets carefully. As flamboyant as Kelleher often portrayed himself, he admitted to being a very cautious businessman. In 1991, 34 cities formally requested that Southwest operate from their airports. Southwest chose only one, Sacramento, and it did so only after USAir left. As Gary Barron put it, "We search out markets that are overpriced and underserved."[5] Small cities and small airports meant that Southwest could get its planes in and out quickly.

Once Southwest decided to enter a market, however, it did so with full force. The airline offered so many flights that customers merely had to show up at the airport and take the next cheap flight out. This part of the strategy not only enabled the airline to spread its fixed costs over many seats, but also served a marketing function in that Southwest could really "make a statement" in a new airport.

After years of patient watchfulness and careful consideration, Southwest decided to enter the California market. In 1983, it began offering flights on the San Diego–San Francisco route but did not expand service until 1989. The California intrastate market was ideal for Southwest: it combined short-haul, high-frequency routes with good weather and a populace appreciative of Southwest's "unconventional behavior." The airline employed a relatively simple strategy of offering service in the mainly suburban areas outside Los Angeles and San Francisco at prices as low as $19 and no higher than $64 for a one-way flight.

Not surprisingly, Southwest's expansion into California led to a series of fare wars as the major airlines tried to keep Southwest from stealing customers. The intensely competitive market in California saw some losers: USAir and American were forced out of the California intrastate market almost entirely. As airline analyst Harold Shenton noted, "Most of the big airlines are trying to protect long-haul revenue, so they're not dependent on local traffic and they're weakening in the markets outside Los Angeles and San Francisco."[6]

Southwest undercut its California competitors and emerged victorious in the fare battles. The airline continued to use such tactics as offering free tickets in a "Fly One Way,

Get One Way Free" campaign and a $59 unrestricted one-way fare for all intrastate California flights as part of the airline's "California State Fare" promotion. Southwest's California campaign was so successful that Southwest saved its California fliers more than $40 million in 1991.

Marketing

POSITIONING Southwest decided from the beginning that it would differentiate itself from its competitors by creating a "fun" image. In contrast to Texas International, which was perceived as dull, and Braniff, which was seen as conservative, Southwest's personality and theme were focused on the concept of "love"; flight attendants wore brightly colored hot pants, and inflight drinks and peanuts were known as "Love Potions" and "Love Bites."

As Southwest began working with the Bloom Agency, a large regional advertising agency, to create its public image, it concurrently came up with a model for the type of person it wanted to hire: the "entire personality description model," which was used as a guide in the recruiting process. Adjectives such as "young and vital," "exciting," and "dynamic" were sprinkled throughout the personality-model statement.

Herb Kelleher's fun-loving personality served to reinforce Southwest's lively image among its employees and encouraged them to pass it on to passengers. Employees took to donning holiday costumes such as rabbit garb for Easter, and every holiday became an excuse for inflight parties with balloons and cake.

In 1986, the airline introduced the concept of "Fun Fares," which ranged in price from $19 to $85 for a one-way ticket. A new summer uniform for flight attendants was used to promote the fares: surfer shorts, knit shirts, and tennis shoes.

Under an agreement signed with Sea World of Texas in 1988, Southwest launched "Shamu One," its flying killer whale in the form of a 737-300 airplane. The painted plane became so popular throughout Texas that Southwest painted two more to resemble Sea World's most popular attraction.

PRICING Pricing decisions were a particularly important part of Southwest's overall strategy. Muse and King spent a great deal of time discussing the pricing issue with executives of Pacific Southwest Airlines, which had revolutionized

[5] *Inc.*, January 1992, p. 68.
[6] UPI, June 2, 1991, p. 70.

commuter air travel in California through a combined strategy of low fares and aggressive promotion. At the time, Braniff and TI fares from Dallas to Houston were $27 and from Dallas to San Antonio, $28. Muse and King looked carefully at preoperating expenditures, operating costs, and market potential and finally decided on an initial fare of $20 for both routes. To operate at a breakeven capacity, Southwest would require an average of 39 passengers per trip, a number the two executives considered reasonable given that the airline would have an initial price advantage over its competition. Before the breakeven figure of 39 passengers per flight could be reached, however, they expected an initial period of deficit operations, a development they were willing to accept to get the airline off the ground. Clearly, the marketing campaign would be crucial to their future decisions on pricing.

Southwest was only five months old when Muse decided to try something revolutionary in the airline industry. Because the crew had been flying an empty plane from Houston to Dallas at the end of each week for weekend servicing, Muse came up with the idea of offering a fare of $10 for this last flight of the week. Within a period of two weeks, the plane was flying from Houston to Dallas with a full passenger load.

The success of the two-tier pricing system did not escape Muse, who soon decided to cut fares on the last flight of *each day* in all directions, which meant that any passenger flying Southwest after 7:00 p.m. on any day of the week would need a mere $10 to climb aboard. A few months later he was able to raise both prices (regular and "night"), but he continued the two-tier pricing system because of its ability to attract passengers.

Pricing was a key part of Southwest's strategy, and the company was leery of fare increases. From 1972 to 1978, Southwest did not have a single fare increase. "We base our pricing on profit rather than market share," contended Southwest Vice President for Finance Gary C. Kelly.[7]

Southwest's rock-bottom prices won both admiration and scorn from competitors, many of whom immediately dropped their prices when Southwest entered their markets. Many were also resentful: one American Airlines executive commented, "Value isn't quality; it's getting what you pay for."[8] Some competitors accused Southwest of "airline-

seat dumping," although the airline made money on its routes from day one.

PROMOTION   Southwest defined its target market not as the passengers flying with other airlines, but as the people who were using other modes of transportation. As Southwest's director of sales and marketing stated, "We're not competing with other carriers. We want to pull people out of backyards and automobiles, and get them off the bus."

Southwest's promotions were aimed primarily at regular business commuters, who constituted 89 percent of Southwest's traffic. Accordingly, the airline used a heavy advertising campaign and a small sales force targeted specifically at the business traveler. Initially, the airline was striving for name recognition, but its marketing efforts quickly expanded to create an image via mass communications. With a first-year advertising budget of $700,000, this strategy was implemented in a number of ways, including teaser ads announcing incredibly low fares and a follow-up phone number, and the Sweetheart Club, in which secretaries received one "sweetheart stamp" for each Southwest reservation they made for their bosses. For every 15 stamps, the secretary would receive one free ride on Southwest.

BUILDING A REPUTATION   Although at first many observers believed Southwest's "fun" image and no-frills flights would be the last choice for business travelers and cause the airline to take an immediate nose dive into bankruptcy, the skeptics soon stopped laughing. Initially unprofitable, Southwest ended 1973 in the black and celebrated its millionth passenger early in 1974. As the airline continued to expand its routes to cities such as Corpus Christi, Austin, El Paso, Oklahoma City, New Orleans, and Albuquerque, its management continued to maintain its reputation as the feisty underdog that was consistently able to offer low prices and superior, reliable service. (See Exhibit 3 for a comparison of 1991 revenues, profits, and passenger-miles for the major U.S. airlines.)

In 1988, the U.S. Department of Transportation rated Southwest as having the best on-time performance, the lowest number of lost-baggage complaints, and the lowest number of customer complaints among all domestic airlines (see Exhibit 4). Southwest was particularly proud that it was the first airline to "win" all three categories since the department began tracking airline performance. Southwest then proceeded to win the "Triple Crown" the following four years.

---

[7] *AW*, March 5, 1990, p. 36.
[8] *Time*, March 2, 1992, p. 15.

Exhibit 3	Southwest Airlines

Airline Revenues, Profits, and Passenger-Miles for 1991

Airline	Revenue ($ millions)	Profit ($ millions)	Passenger-Miles (billions)
Alaska Air Group	1,116	10.3	5.4
America West	1,420	−222.0	3.0
American	12,993	−240.0	82.3
Continental	5,551	−305.7	41.4
Delta[1]	9,171	−324.4	62.1
Northwest	7,534	−3.1	53.2
Southwest	1,324	26.9	11.3
Trans World	3,688	34.6	28.0
UAL	11,748	−331.9	82.3
US Air Group	6,533	−305.3	34.1

[1]Fiscal year ended June 30, 1991.

Source: "Unfriendly Skies," *Fortune*, November 2, 1992, p. 92.

Exhibit 4	Southwest Airlines

Performance of Major U.S. Air Carriers for 1992

Airline	On-Time Performance[1] (rank)	Baggage Problems[2] (rank)	Consumer Complaints[3] (rank)
Alaska Air Group	84.6 (4)	6.04 (7)	0.48 (2)
America West	88.9 (2)	4.42 (2)	1.50 (9)
American	82.1 (6)	4.73 (3)	1.40 (8)
Continental	79.0 (10)	6.13 (10)	1.17 (7)
Delta	79.1 (9)	5.71 (6)	0.58 (3)
Northwest	86.1 (3)	5.49 (5)	0.74 (4)
Southwest	92.1 (1)	3.72 (1)	0.24 (1)
Trans World	82.1 (5)	6.06 (8)	2.82 (10)
UAL	81.3 (7)	5.30 (4)	1.05 (6)
US Air Group	79.6 (8)	6.10 (9)	0.85 (5)
Average	**82.3**	**5.36**	**1.03**

[1]Percentage of flights operating within 15 minutes of their scheduled times.
[2]Reported baggage problems per 1,000 passengers.
[3]Complaints per 100,000 passengers.

Source: U.S. Department of Transportation's *Air Travel Consumer Reports*.

Personnel

The company's philosophy toward recruitment and its employees remained consistent throughout its history: Southwest looked for people who were energetic and who wanted to work hard and have fun at the same time. Kelleher maintained that the most important step was choosing the right people, because "if the employees aren't satisfied, they won't provide the product we need."[9]

This philosophy proved effective. Although Southwest's work force was over 90 percent unionized, the employees owned 11 percent of the company. The average employee age was 34 years, one of the industry's lowest, yet the annual average employee pay ($42,000) was among the industry's highest. Although the airline industry was notorious for contentious labor-management relations, Southwest's employees enjoyed sunny relations with management. One reason for the smooth sailing was that employees had a stake in the company's success. Another reason was that Southwest managed to make employees feel as if they were part of an extended family, even if it was a $1.2 billion family.

Southwest management did not try to hide the fact that the main reason for the airline's success was the commitment of its employees. The quick turnaround time was a perfect example. As Gary Barron stated,

> Our employees bust their butts out there. Ground crews of six (12 is the industry average) perform 40 or 50 tasks during the 15 minutes that the plane is on the ground. [Jim] Wimberly [head of ground operations] likens those 15 minutes to a ballet, in which everything must be perfectly executed, and if it isn't, the employees have to be flexible enough to adjust. Because of employee commitment, Southwest has consistently kept to its 15-minute "turn" (planes of major airlines spend usually an hour at the gate) and is consequently on time.

Another example of employee loyalty was the automatic ticket machines at Southwest counters that took credit cards and dispensed tickets in just 20 seconds. These efficient machines were built by Southwest employees in their off-hours. Stated Andy Donelson, station manager at Dallas's Love Field, "The machine was thought up by a bunch of guys in a bar one night in Denver."[10]

Annual turnover was 7 percent, the industry's lowest. In 1990, 62,000 people applied for jobs at Southwest. Only 1,400 were hired.

Corporate Culture

Southwest's culture was perhaps best experienced by strolling down the hallway of the company's Dallas headquarters, where 20 years of Southwest Airlines history could be witnessed through mannequins attired in the various uniforms of Southwest personnel and hundreds of photos of employees. Each year the company hosted a banquet at which outstanding employees were recognized, much in the manner of the Emmy Awards. Kelleher could be seen at these functions mingling with employees from all levels of the company, calling them by name, laughing uproariously with them, and hugging, and kissing them.

Even customers were brought into the family circle. Each month Southwest invited its frequent fliers to company headquarters to interview prospective employees, the logic being that the company wanted to hire people who matched customers in personality. The 5,000 letters a month Southwest received from its customers were all answered by the staff; Kelleher himself usually read around 200 letters a week.

Kelleher's role in the formation of Southwest's familial culture was crucial. Jim Wimberly stated that Kelleher had "a knack of really being with you, even if you're one person in a crowd of 1,000."[11] Kelleher firmly believed that employees who were committed to a mission would be more productive than uncommitted employees, and he spent a lot of his time fostering this attitude: "Southwest has its customers, the passengers; and I have my customers, the airline's employees. If the passengers aren't satisfied, they won't fly with us. If the employees aren't satisfied, they won't provide the product we need."

Once a quarter, Kelleher would join his employees to load baggage, serve drinks at 30,000 feet, or hand out boarding passes. Every Friday he wore brightly colored shirts and shorts, regardless of the business to be conducted that day.

Kelleher seemed to have found a formula that worked. During 1990, rising fuel costs caused Southwest to suffer a fourth-quarter loss of $4,581,000. Employees voluntarily created a "Fuel from the Heart" program in which they incurred payroll deductions to purchase fuel for the airplanes. Kelleher was so moved that he dedicated his opening letter to them in the company's 1990 annual report.

As bright as Southwest's history had been, there had also been a few dark clouds. Perhaps the darkest cloud was Southwest's purchase of Muse Air in June 1985. Kelleher

---

[9]*AW*, March 5, 1990, p. 36.

[10]*Inc.*, January 1992, p. 70.

[11]*Inc.*, January 1992, p. 67.

changed the airline's name to TranStar and it operated profitably for two years, until the larger Continental Airlines began an "impossible fare war" by moving into Houston's Hobby Airport. TranStar, with only 18 operating planes, proved to be no match for Continental with its fleet of 618 planes and considerable financial resources. In 1987, Kelleher was forced to liquidate TranStar's assets and report a loss in the first quarter of that year.

Although many observers were quick to praise the airline, some analysts were not as enthusiastic about Southwest's future. The industry itself has always been a risky one, and the prospects of endless competition, unpredictable fuel prices, and fickle customers gave financial analysts reason to advise caution when investing in Southwest. The TranStar case was a good example of how quickly success could turn sour in such a high-risk industry, and how even bright, savvy managers could make disastrous mistakes. Analysts also pointed out that large airlines had the deep pockets necessary to subsidize some of the more important routes if they deemed them important, whereas Southwest did not have much of a cushion.

Conclusion

The Southwest success story served as a model for others in the airline business, but none were able to match the airline's stellar record. Southwest's strategy of high value and low cost had worked for 20 years; what would the future hold? Kelleher's goal for the airline was simple: increase the number of seats by 15 percent each year and keep costs down. He feared the complacency suffered by many airlines when things appear to be going well. "Our job is to never lose focus on keeping our costs low and to never suffer an excess of hubris so we take on too much debt," he commented. "When you think you've got it all figured out, then you're probably already heading downhill."[12]

[12] *Inc.*, January 1992, p. 72.

Case 4

Pleasant Valley Elementary School: Celebrating Success One Student at a Time

UVA-OB-0882

We have to create the instructional strategies that will work with every child. We have a team at Pleasant Valley that works together with individual students, because every child is so different. Children have different personalities, different backgrounds, and different life experiences. We look at their performance—academically, socially, emotionally—and we develop a plan to help each child succeed in whatever way possible.

—**Pleasant Valley Elementary Principal Paula Frazier**

At the start of the 2005–06 school year, Pleasant Valley was the top-performing elementary school in the Rockingham County Public School District. Principals from around the county visited Pleasant Valley to discuss teaching strategies and curriculum models, and the superintendent asked the school's third-grade teaching team to present its successful methods to elementary teachers across the district.

There had not always been so much to celebrate at Pleasant Valley, though. Seven years earlier, it had been one of the lowest-performing schools in the district, and a new principal had been hired to lead the school in a fresh direction.

DARDEN

This case was written by Pleasant Valley Elementary School Principal Paula Frazier and Michael J. Salmonowicz, PhD candidate, under the supervision of Gerry Yemen, Darden School senior case writer. Copyright © 2006 by the University of Virginia Darden School Foundation, Charlottesville, VA. All rights reserved. *To order copies, send an e-mail to sales@dardenpublishing.com. No part of this publication may be reproduced, stored in a retrieval system, used in a spreadsheet, or transmitted in any form or by any means—electronic, mechanical, photocopying, recording, or otherwise—without the permission of the Darden School Foundation.*

How had the school turned around? And how had it managed to achieve distinction year after year?

PLEASANT VALLEY ELEMENTARY SCHOOL

Pleasant Valley Elementary was located in Harrisonburg, Virginia. Opened in 1963, it was one of 13 elementary schools in Rockingham County. It served more than 300 students in grades prekindergarten through five, including large numbers of students classified as English as a Second Language (ESL) (30%), special education (14%), Title I (29%), and low-income (63%). The instructional staff included two administrators (one principal, one administrative intern), 18 full-time classroom teachers, and 27 instructional assistants. The faculty was stable, consisting primarily of veteran teachers who had taught in the community for many years.

School Accountability

Educational accountability was formally introduced across Virginia in 1995 with a sweeping revision of the Standards of Learning (SOL). Those standards were implemented to guide teachers through their curricula in core subject areas and were the basis for the state's annual standardized tests. Each spring, all third- and fifth-grade students were tested in reading/language arts, math, science, and history/social science. The SOLs quickly became the criteria by which school effectiveness and individual student achievement in the commonwealth were measured and monitored.

Pleasant Valley struggled during the early years of SOL testing, regularly achieving scores below those of the county and commonwealth. In the 2001–02 school year, however, the school made dramatic gains in nearly all tested areas (Exhibits 1 and 2). By 2005, its students' test scores were highest among its peers in four of the six state accreditation categories, and third-highest in a fifth category (Exhibit 3).

Exhibit 1	Pleasant Valley Elementary School: Celebrating Success One Student at a Time

Percentage of Students Receiving Passing Scores on SOL Tests, 1998–2005

Third Grade

Year	Reading/ Language Arts			Mathematics			History/ Social Science			Science		
	PV	RC	VA	PV	RC	VA	PV	RC	VA	PV	RC	VA
1997–1998	50	57	53	75	68	63	70	56	49	80	90	63
1998–1999	62	62	61	60	72	68	59	68	62	73	71	68
1999–2000	60	66	61	79	80	71	65	77	65	80	79	73
2000–01	63	75	65	77	88	77	74	87	72	74	83	74
2001–02	78	78	72	97	91	80	89	90	76	93	91	78
2002–03	79	77	72	90	85	83	100	88	82	91	87	82
2003–04	81	75	71	100	93	87	100	93	87	98	91	86
2004–05	93	80	77	98	93	88	100	94	89	100	93	89

PV = Pleasant Valley Elementary School
RC = Rockingham County
VA = Commonwealth of Virginia

Exhibit 2	Pleasant Valley Elementary School: Celebrating Success One Student at a Time

Percentage of Students Receiving Passing Scores on SOL Tests, 1998–2005

Fifth Grade

Year	Reading/ Language Arts			Mathematics			History/ Social Science			Science		
	PV	RC	VA	PV	RC	VA	PV	RC	VA	PV	RC	VA
1997–1998	71	66	68	43	49	47	30	33	33	68	62	59
1998–1999	69	73	69	73	56	51	38	49	46	67	72	67
1999–2000	70	76	68	67	72	63	53	60	51	67	75	64
2000–01	69	78	73	83	77	67	90	77	63	73	83	75
2001–02	95	85	78	90	84	74	85	79	72	83	86	76
2002–03	96	90	83	92	85	74	91	84	79	88	88	80
2003–04	91	87	85	95	89	78	85	88	87	98	93	84
2004–05	95	90	85	95	86	81	86	86	85	84	86	81

PV = Pleasant Valley Elementary School
RC = Rockingham County
VA = Commonwealth of Virginia

Exhibit 3	Pleasant Valley Elementary School: Celebrating Success One Student at a Time

Rockingham County Elementary School Test Scores as Calculated for 2005–06 State Accreditation

Date	3/5 English	3/5 Math	3 History	3/5 History	3 Science	3/5 Science
Elkton	88	83	94	98	91	83
Fulks Run	87	90	96	100	95	96
John C. Myers	92	94	95	93	91	91
John W. Wayland	89	90	99	95	99	91
Lacey Spring	90	93	95	91	96	92
Linville-Edom	88	89	100	93	97	88
McGaheysville	89	91	93	89	92	93
Mountain View	86	87	93	95	91	87
Ottobine	90	90	96	93	96	97
Peak View	95	97	100	98	100	93
Plains	90	94	97	87	94	88
Pleasant Valley	98	98	100	93	100	93
South River	87	91	92	95	92	87

Paula Frazier

Frazier, 52, had been principal of Pleasant Valley since the fall of 1998. Prior to this principalship, she spent 15 years as a classroom teacher in grades one through five and seven years as an assistant principal in two different middle schools. Frazier took pride in having lived and worked in the community all her life.

Turning Around

The enormous challenge of turning around Pleasant Valley was evident to Frazier from the very beginning. She recalled:

> I received the job a week before school began. When I walked into this school for the first time, it was in disarray. Furniture was everywhere; I couldn't see the hallways because they were filled with desks and chairs. The building reeked of urine. I thought, "Oh, my goodness. What have I gotten myself into?"

There were other problems beyond the physical plant. No schoolwide system existed for recordkeeping or accountability, which left teachers unable to accurately communicate students' academic performance. Instruction still included topics that were not SOL content areas, and classes frequently took field trips that had little or no correlation with the curriculum. Grade levels were not housed in the same hallways, making it difficult for "teaming" to occur. Under the previous administration, a contingent of teachers had been empowered to make their own decisions and had tried to conceal the results of their shortcomings in their classrooms.

After working with the janitorial staff to clean up the school, Frazier's first order of business was to assess each grade level, classroom, and student. She developed achievement inventories for teachers to determine students' reading, spelling, writing, and math levels at the beginning and end of each semester. Following classroom visits, she asked teachers specific questions about individual students she had observed, such as how a student was currently doing with a certain-level book and where the teacher projected the student to be by the end of the year. Armed with data, Frazier began charting test results to show where improvement was occurring and where it was still needed in individual classrooms and at each grade level.

Frazier's other major goal was to build trust with and inspire teamwork among the faculty. Her initial step in that endeavor was to make herself accessible to the staff. In addition to informally visiting classrooms throughout the day, she had an open-door policy so teachers would feel comfortable coming to her with questions or problems. To encourage a greater sense of ownership in the school, Frazier invited each teacher to become involved with at least two committees. She moved some teachers into different classrooms so they were grouped by grade level and could more easily collaborate and team-teach. Though Frazier asked teachers to be more accountable than they had been in the past, she also gave them increased freedom:

> I think it's important to allow teachers a sense of professional leeway in decision-making. This is their school. They know our vision and mission. If their decisions promote success with children and it's a win-win situation for our students, parents, and school, then they have my blessing to go for it. All I ask is that they keep me informed. My ultimate goal is to be the leader of leaders, not the leader of followers.

Some faculty members had difficulty adjusting to Frazier's high expectations and emphasis on using data. Realizing that this was probably the first time teachers had been asked to talk about academics on this level, she committed to spend one year working intensely with struggling teachers. Those who were unable to reach her expectations after that period of time were encouraged to find another school where they might find more success. Other faculty members, especially those who were not accountable under the previous administration, resisted Frazier's changes; she worked with the district office to have them transferred as soon as possible.

At the end of the 2001–02 school year, Frazier's fourth at Pleasant Valley, test scores showed that the school had indeed turned around. Another challenge remained, however, proving that the school was more than just a one-year wonder.

Sustaining and Celebrating Success

Frazier knew by fall 2002 that her school had in place a formula for success. Her focus therefore moved from effecting major change to improving what was already being done. Using the achievement data they regularly collected, teachers identified students in need of remediation in reading and math. Those students attended a newly created after-school tutoring program from 3 P.M. to 5 P.M., two days per week. Improvements were made in the regular school day as well. When score trends showed that third-grade students regularly scored well below fifth graders in reading/language arts, Frazier blocked every morning for reading and math in the third-grade classrooms; during that time, students would not be interrupted by physical education, art, music, or other specialty classes. She assigned her master teacher to the 15 lowest readers, and supported the group with Title I and ESL teachers so the student-to-teacher ratio was never more than 5:1. At the end of the day, the master teacher creatively retaught concepts to students who had not grasped them earlier.

State testing was another area targeted for improvement. To increase students' confidence, teachers equipped them with testing strategies such as underlining important words; scanning the questions before reading a passage; properly bubbling in answer sheets; and using process of elimination to derive correct answers. ESL students were taught how to get beyond names and places they could not pronounce. Rather than get frustrated because they were stumbling over the name "Mr. Alexander," for example, they knew to simply call him "Mr. A" and stay focused on the main idea of the paragraph. To ensure students knew their material well, students in testing grades attended review sessions at the end of each day in the four core areas. Then, when test results came in, the faculty undertook what Frazier called the science of teaching:

> We analyze our test results each year, question by question. How well we did on this question? What can we do next year in our annual school plan? We look at the lowest five questions in each of the core subjects in the SOL tests, and that becomes part of our annual school plan. And then we come up with activities, ways to assess each of those questions and topics. I consider it the science of teaching—breaking components down, and determining where we are and where we need to go.

Though test scores were a high priority, they were not the sole emphasis at Pleasant Valley. Frazier explained that her evaluation of the school went well beyond state test results:

> I look at teacher morale and student morale. Each day, I look at student attendance and teacher attendance. I look at ways in which we recognize students, whether it be through assemblies, in the classroom, or in the way teachers talk to students. I call it the "Language of Learning." How do we respond to students when they don't get a concept? That is so important, and I think there is a right way to do it. Let's say John, coming into fifth grade, had a hard time picking up his pencil and writing a sentence. When he gets to the point of picking up his pencil and writing a few sentences, how do we talk to him about that? He needs more than "Great job!" Praise has to be immediate, sincere, and specific. What are those ways in which we can motivate him? I look very carefully at the dialogue that we have with students.

The excellent work of both teachers and students did not escape Frazier. She believed that taking time to celebrate their accomplishments was not only appropriate, but also essential to the school's continued success. Since SOL results generally came back over the summer, when teachers were on vacation, Frazier made sure to congratulate them (along with the entire staff) at the start of in-service days in the fall. Celebrations ranged from cake, party hats, and party horns at the school to enjoying hors d'oeuvres at a local restaurant. Students were likewise acknowledged. Those who showed improvement in their work on the SOL test in math received a ride in her dune buggy on the last day of school; third-grade classes that met their quarterly benchmark goals were rewarded with pizza parties; Frazier autographed softballs and gave them to all the students who received perfect attendance; and fifth graders who studied homework packets with their parents were treated to lunch with their principal on the cafeteria stage, complete with linen tablecloths, candlelight, homemade delicacies, and Kenny G. music in the background. Frazier also recognized the daily victories achieved by individual students:

> A fifth-grade teacher had informed me of the lack of progress of a particular student struggling with two-digit multiplication. The teacher had implemented numerous instructional strategies with little success, until the "light" finally came on for this student. The teacher shared the news so that I could be a part of celebrating her success. I quickly found the student in the hall and brought her to my office to be our "Math Queen for the Day." She wore a fuchsia-colored crown and was extremely proud as she entered the hallway to her classroom.

Though Pleasant Valley appeared to be a well-oiled machine, Paula Frazier emphasized that the school's record of success did not come easily:

> I've never been at the very bottom of school performance, and I know it must be tough to be at that place. But it's tough to be at the top as well because you have that expectation every year to maintain your performance. We have met that expectation in the past, though, and I'm confident that we will again this year. School improvement is a continuous journey and each year we begin the journey anew.

Case 5

Prince Edward Island Preserve Co.

9A91G005

In August 1991, Bruce MacNaughton, president of Prince Edward Island Preserve Co. Ltd. (P.E.I. Preserves), was contemplating future expansion. Two cities were of particular interest: Toronto and Tokyo. At issue was whether consumers in either or both markets should be pursued, and if so, how. The choices available for achieving further growth included mail order, distributors, and company controlled stores.

Background

Prince Edward Island Preserve Co. was a manufacturing company located in New Glasgow, P.E.I. which produced and marketed specialty food products. The company founder and majority shareholder, Bruce MacNaughton, had realized that an opportunity existed to present P.E.I. strawberries as a world-class food product and to introduce the finished product to an "up-scale" specialty market. With

IVEY

Richard Ivey School of Business
The University of Western Ontario

Professor Paul W. Beamish prepared this case solely to provide material for class discussion. The author does not intend to illustrate either effective or ineffective handling of a managerial situation. The author may have disguised certain names and other identifying information to protect confidentiality.

total sales in the coming year expected to exceed $1 million for the first time, MacNaughton had made good on the opportunity he had perceived years earlier. It had not been easy, however.

MacNaughton arrived in P.E.I. from Moncton, New Brunswick in 1978. Without a job, he slept on the beach for much of that first summer. Over the next few years he worked in commission sales, waited tables in restaurants, and then moved to Toronto. There he studied to become a chef at George Brown Community College. After working in the restaurant trade for several years, he found a job with "Preserves by Amelia" in Toronto. After six months, he returned to P.E.I. where he opened a restaurant. The restaurant was not successful and MacNaughton lost the $25,000 stake he had accumulated. With nothing left but 100 kilograms of strawberries, Bruce decided to make these into preserves in order to have gifts for Christmas 1984. Early the following year, P.E.I. Preserves was founded.

The products produced by the company were priced and packaged for the gift/gourmet and specialty food markets. The primary purchasers of these products were conscious of quality and were seeking a product which they considered tasteful and natural. P.E.I. Preserves felt their product met this standard of quality at a price that made it attractive to all segments of the marketplace.

Over the next few years as the business grew, improvements were made to the building in New Glasgow. The sense of style which was characteristic of the company was evident from the beginning in its attractive layout and design.

In 1989 the company diversified and opened "The Perfect Cup," a small restaurant in P.E.I.'s capital city of Charlottetown. This restaurant continued the theme of quality, specializing in wholesome, home-made food featuring the products manufactured by the company. The success of this

Table 1

Operation	Year Opened				
	1985	1989	1990	1991	Projected 1992
New Glasgow—Manufacturing and Retail	X	X	X	X	X
Charlottetown—Restaurant (Perfect Cup)		X	X	X	X
New Glasgow—Restaurant (Tea Room)			X	X	X
Charlottetown—Retail (CP Hotel)				X	X
Toronto or Tokyo?					X

operation led to the opening in 1990 of a small tea room at the New Glasgow location. Both of these locations showcased the products manufactured by the P.E.I. Preserve Co.

In August 1991, the company opened a small (22 square metre) retail branch in the CP Prince Edward Hotel. Mac-Naughton hoped this locale would expand visibility in the local and national marketplace, and serve as an off-season sales office. P.E.I. Preserves had been given very favourable lease arrangements (well below the normal $275 per month for space this size) and the location would require minimal financial investment. As Table 1 suggests, the company had experienced steady growth in its scope of operations.

Marketplace

Prince Edward Island was Canada's smallest province, both in size and population. Located in the Gulf of St. Lawrence, it was separated from Nova Scotia and New Brunswick by the Northumberland Strait. The major employer in P.E.I. was the various levels of government. Many people in P.E.I. worked seasonally, in either farming (especially potato), fishing, or tourism. During the peak tourist months of July and August, the island population would swell dramatically from its base of 125,000. P.E.I.'s half million annual visitors came "home" to enjoy the long sandy beaches, picturesque scenery, lobster dinners, arguably the best tasting strawberries in the world, and slower pace of life. P.E.I. was best known in Canada and elsewhere for the books, movies and (current) television series about Lucy Maud Montgomery's turn-of-the-century literary creation, Anne of Green Gables.

P.E.I. Preserves felt they were competing in a worldwide market. Their visitors were from all over the world and in 1991 they expected the numbers to exceed 100,000 in the New Glasgow location alone. New Glasgow (population 200) was located in a rural setting equidistant (15 kilometres) from

Charlottetown and P.E.I.'s best-known North Shore beaches. In their mailings they planned to continue to promote Prince Edward Island as "Canada's Garden Province" and the "little jewel it was in everyone's heart!" They had benefitted, and would continue to benefit, from that image.

Marketing

PRODUCTS The company had developed numerous products since its inception. These included many original varieties of preserves as well as honey, vinegar, mustard, and tea (repackaged). (Exhibit 1 contains a 1990 price list, ordering instructions, and a product picture used for mail order purposes.) The company had also added to the appeal of these products by offering gift packs composed of different products and packaging. With over 80 items, it felt that it had achieved a diverse product line and efforts in developing new product lines were expected to decrease in the future. Approximately three-quarters of total retail sales (including wholesale and mail order) came from the products the company made itself. Of these, three quarters were jam preserves.

With the success of P.E.I. Preserves, imitation was inevitable. In recent years, several other small firms in P.E.I. had begun to retail specialty preserves. Another company which produced preserves in Ontario emphasized the Green Gables tie-in on its labels.

PRICE P.E.I. Preserves were not competing with "low-end" products, and felt their price reinforced their customers' perception of quality. The 11 types of jam preserves retailed for $5.89 for a 250-millilitre jar, significantly more than any grocery store product. However, grocery stores did not offer jam products made with such a high fruit content and with champagne, liqueur or whisky.

In mid-1991, the company introduced a 10 per cent increase in price (to $5.89) and, to date, had not received any negative

Exhibit 1	P.E.I. Preserves Mail Order Catalogue

Prince Edward Island Preserve Co.

Mail Order

Canada

Prince Edward Island Preserve Co.
RR# 2 Hunter River
Prince Edward Island
Canada
C0A 1N0
Tel. (902) 964-2524
Fax. (902) 566-5565

PRODUCTS

Preserves
1. Strawberry & Grand Marnier 250ml 5.69
2. Raspberry & Champagne 250ml 5.69
3. Wild Blueberry & Raspberry in Champagne 250ml 5.69
4. Strawberry, Orange & Rhubarb 250ml 5.69
5. Raspberry & Peach 250ml 5.69
6. Blueberry, Lemon & Fresh Mint 250ml 5.69
7. Black Currant 250ml 5.69
8. Gooseberry & Red Currant 250ml 5.69
9. Sour Cherry Marmalade 250ml 5.69
10. Orange Marmalade with Chivas Regal 250ml 5.69
11. Lemon & Ginger Marmalade with Amaretto 250ml 5.69
12. Strawberry & Grand Marnier 125ml 3.60
13. Raspberry & Champagne 125ml 3.60
14. Wild Blueberry & Raspberry in Champagne 125ml 3.60
15. Raspberry & Peach 125ml 3.60
16. Black Currant 125ml 3.60
17. Orange Marmalade with Chivas Regal 125ml 3.60

Honeys
18. Summer Honey with Grand Marnier 250ml 5.95
19. Summer Honey with Amaretto 250ml 5.95
20. Summer Honey with Grand Marnier 125ml 3.50
21. Summer Honey with Amaretto 125ml 3.50

Mustards
22. Hot & Spicy Mustard 250ml 3.95
23. Champagne & Dill Mustard 250ml 3.95
24. Honey & Thyme Mustard 250ml 3.95
25. Hot & Spicy Mustard 125ml 2.75
26. Champagne & Dill Mustard 125ml 2.75
27. Honey & Thyme Mustard 125ml 2.75

Vinegars
28. Raspberry Vinegar 350ml 5.95
29. Black Currant Vinegar 350ml 5.95
30. Peach Vinegar 350ml 5.95
31. Raspberry Vinegar 150ml 3.50
32. Black Currant Vinegar 150ml 3.50
33. Peach Vinegar 150ml 3.50

Specials
34A. Catharines Hors d'oeuvre & Pasta Sauce . 250 ml 6.49
35. Catharines Hot Antipasto............................250 ml 5.69
36. Catharines Antipasto..................................250 ml 5.69

Spices *(recipes included)*
37A. Bloody Mary, Bloody Caesar Mix 3.95
38A. Apple Spices - for pies, butters, chutneys................3.95
39A. Mulling Spices - for wine, cider, or ale...................4.95
40A. Hot Chocolate - rich & tasty, just add hot water....4.95

Tea - *No tea is fresher than ours*
41. a) Monks Blend   b) Strawberry   c) Raspberry
41. d) Earl Grey   e) English Breakfast   f) Blackcurrant
42. Sachets..50 g   2.95
43. Tea by the Pound, all blends ....1 lb   14.95
   order tea by # and letter, i.e. 43c is 1 lb. of raspberry tea.

Maple Products
44A. Pure Maple Syrup .... 100 ml   3.95
45A. Pure Maple Syrup .... 250 ml   5.95
46A. Pure Maple Syrup .... 500 ml   10.95
47A. Maple Syrup with Light Rum .... 250 ml   5.95
48A. Maple Butter, excellent on pancakes, toast or baking
   ....250 ml   5.95

Coffees - *We think this is the best coffee available*
First Colony - ground coffee, available 8 oz. and 2 oz.
49A. Columbian Supremo ....8 oz.   6.49
50A. Irish Cream   50B. Swiss Chocolate Almond
                            8 oz.   6.49
50C. Chocolate Raspberry Truffle.................8 oz.   6.49
51A. Special House Blend.............................2 oz.   2.25
52. All flavours available in 2 oz. packs
   (order coffee by # and letter, i.e. 52C is a 2 oz Chocolate
   Raspberry Truffle)

Teapots - If you've had tea with us, these are the ones!
56. Executive Tea set Black with Sterling Silver   49.95
57.   Sky Blue with Sterling Silver   49.95
58. [1-2 cup teapot 1 cup & saucer]   Fern Green with Gold Inlay   49.95
59.   Rust with Gold Inlay   49.95
60. Romance Tea set Black with Sterling Silver   59.95
61.   Sky Blue with Sterling Silver   59.95
62. [1-2 cup teapot 2 cups & saucers]   Fern Green with Gold Inlay   59.95
63.   Rust with Gold Inlay 59.95
64. Gift Packages - We pack all for long journeys!
A. P.E.I.Summer House 24.99
B. Taster's Choice Duo ....2: 125 ml Preserves Crated 8.25
C. Taster's Choice Trio .2: 125 ml Preserves,1: 125 Honey Crated 11.95
D. Crated vinegars ....2: 150ml Fruit Vinegars Crated 7.49
E. Crated Preserves (2 jars) ....250 ml size 12.49
F. Crated Preserves (3 jars) ....250 ml size 17.95
G. Tea-for-Two ....1: 125 ml Preserves, Tea, 1: 125 ml Honey 11.95
75. 8" Brass Planter - filled with Swiss Chocolate, Hot
   Chocolate, Chocolate Coffee and more
   Chocolate 23.99
76. 6" Brass Planter - 1-125 ml Preserve, 1-125 ml
   Honey with Liqueur, Honey Dipper and
   Chocolate 16.50
77. 4" Brass Planter - 125 ml Honey with Liqueur and
   Honey Dipper 10.95
78. Wicker House - 2-250 ml Preserves with Liqueur,
   1-250 ml Honey with Liqueur, 100 ml Maple Syrup,
   Irish Cream Coffee, Strawberry Tea 39.95
79. 14" Wicker Hamper - 1-125 ml Preserve, 1-125 ml
   Honey with Liqueur, 1 Raspberry Tea, 1 Irish
   Cream Coffee, Honey Dipper 32.95
80. Hunter Green S M L XL Sweatshirt 29.95
   87% Cotton, 13% Poly, Preshrunk
81. Deep Lavender S M L XL Sweatshirt 29.95
   87% Cotton, 13% Poly, Preshrunk

---

reaction from customers. The food products were not subject to the seven per cent National Goods and Services Tax or P.E.I.'s 10 per cent Provincial Sales Tax, an advantage over other gift products which the company would be stressing.

PROMOTION Product promotion had been focused in two areas—personal contact with the consumer and catalogue distribution. Visitors to the New Glasgow location (approximately 80,000 in 1990) were enthusiastic upon meeting Bruce, "resplendent in the family kilt," reciting history and generally providing live entertainment. Bruce and the other staff members realized the value of this "Island Touch" and strove to ensure that all visitors to New Glasgow left with both a positive feeling and purchased products.

Visitors were also encouraged to visit the New Glasgow location through a cooperative scheme whereby other spe-

cialty retailers provided a coupon for a free cup of coffee or tea at P.E.I. Preserves. In 1991, roughly 2,000 of these coupons were redeemed.

Approximately 5,000 people received their mail order catalogue annually. They had experienced an order rate of 7.5 per cent with the average order being $66. They hoped to devote more time and effort to their mail order business in an effort to extend their marketing and production period. For 1991 to 1992, the order rate was expected to increase by as much as 15 per cent because the catalogue was to be mailed two weeks earlier than in the previous year. The catalogues cost $1 each to print and mail.

In addition to mail order, the company operated with an ad hoc group of wholesale distributors. These wholesalers were divided between Nova Scotia, Ontario, and other loca-

Exhibit 1	P.E.I. Preserves Mail Order Catalogue—Continued

Shipping cost per Address

Value of Order	*Shipping Cost
$ 0. - $30.	5.00
$31. - $40.	6.00
$41. - $55.	7.00
$56. - $65.	8.00
$66. - $75.	9.00
$76. - $100.	10.00
$101. & over	5% of order

All packages are packed well for shipping. We use double strength corrugated boxes and finish the packages with a heavy brown paper wrap.

*Please note that if the postage cost is less than the amount charged to you, we then will charge you the least amount. That is why we prefer if you paid by credit card. Thank you, Bruce.

Gift Wrapping $3.50 per package

Using the appropriate gift wrap for the season, we'll give your package that little extra. We can supply a small card with your salutation, or if you send us your card with your order, we will include it.

Gift Packaging
Friends, we have many packaging ideas, too many for our catalogue. If you wish us to do up a basket in a certain price range, or any special order for that matter just give us a call, fax or mail in your request. We are here for you!

Method of Payment

☐MasterCard ☐Visa

CREDIT CARD NUMBER

Cardholder Name
Please Print

We require a signature

mo./ yr.
Expiry Date

---

① **SOLD TO:** ☐Mr. ☐Mrs. ☐Ms.

Name _____ Please Print

Address _____

City _____ Prov _____ PostalCode _____
May we have your phone number in case of a question about your order?

Home ( ) _____ Work ( ) _____

Send to me at the above address.
Ship to arrive: ☐ Now ☐ Christmas ☐ Other_____

Prod.#	Quantity	Price Each	Gift Wrap	Total Price
			3.50☐	
			3.50☐	
			3.50☐	
			3.50☐	
			3.50☐	
			3.50☐	
			3.50☐	
			3.50☐	
		Shipping		
		Total Cost		

② **Send to:** ☐Mr. ☐Mrs. ☐Ms. ☐Firm

Name _____ Please Print

Address _____

City _____ Prov. _____ Postal _____
Greetings from:
Ship to arrive: ☐Now ☐Christmas ☐Other_____

Prod.#	Quantity	Price Each	Gift Wrap	Total Price
			3.50☐	
			3.50☐	
			3.50☐	
			3.50☐	
			3.50☐	
			3.50☐	
			3.50☐	
			3.50☐	
		Shipping		
		Total Cost		

Dear Shopper,
If you have visited our store recently, and wish to purchase an item which is not on this list, please feel free to do so.
On a separate sheet of paper, write a description of the item to the best of your ability, and we will do our best to satisfy your request.

sincerely,

Bruce MacNaughton

For *FAST* delivery call:
(9:00 am to 5:00 pm A.S.T.)
(902) 964-2524
Fax (902) 566-5565

*Prices subject to change without notice.

---

tions. For orders as small as $150, buyers could purchase from the wholesalers' price list. Wholesale prices were on average 60 per cent of the retail/mail order price. Total wholesale trade for the coming year was projected at $150,000, but had been higher in the past.

Danamar Imports was a Toronto-based specialty food store supplier which had previously provided P.E.I. Preserves to hundreds of specialty food stores in Ontario. Danamar had annually ordered $80,000 worth of P.E.I. Preserves at 30 per cent below the wholesale price. This arrangement was amicably discontinued in 1990 by MacNaughton due to uncertainty about whether he was profiting from this contract. P.E.I. Preserves had a list of the specialty stores which Danamar had previously supplied, and was planning to contact them directly in late 1991.

Over the past few years, the company had received numerous enquiries for quotations on large-scale shipments. Mitsubishi had asked for a price on a container load of preserves. Airlines and hotels were interested in obtaining preserves in 28 or 30 gram single-service bottles. One hotel chain, for example, had expressed interest in purchasing three million bottles if the cost could be kept under $0.40 per unit. (Bruce had not proceeded due to the need to purchase $65,000 worth of bottling equipment, and uncertainty about his production costs.) This same hotel chain had more recently been assessing the ecological implications of the packaging waste which would be created with the use of so many small bottles. They were now weighing the hygiene implications of serving jam out of multicustomer use larger containers in their restaurants. They

Exhibit 1	P.E.I. Preserves Mail Order Catalogue—Continued

had asked MacNaughton to quote on $300,000 worth of jam in two-litre bottles.

Financial

The company had enjoyed a remarkable rate of growth since its inception. Sales volumes had increased in each of the six years of operations, from an initial level of $30,000 to 1990's total of $785,000. These sales were made up of $478,000 from retail sales (including mail order) of what they manufactured and/or distributed, and $307,000 from the restaurants (the Tea Room in New Glasgow, and Perfect Cup Restaurant in Charlottetown). Exhibits 2 and 3 provide Income Statements from these operations, while Exhibit 4 contains a consolidated balance sheet.

This growth, although indicative of the success of the product, has also created its share of problems. Typical of many small businesses which experience such rapid growth, the company had not secured financing suitable to its needs. This, coupled with the seasonal nature of the manufacturing operation, had caused numerous periods of severe cash shortages. From Bruce's perspective, the company's banker (Bank of Nova Scotia) had not been as supportive as it might have been. (The bank manager in Charlottetown had last visited the facility three years ago.) Bruce felt the solution to the problem of cash shortages was the issuance of preferred shares. "An infusion of 'long term' working capital, at a relatively low rate of interest, will provide a stable financial base for the future," he said.

Exhibit 2	P.E.I. Preserve Co. Ltd. (Manufacturing and Retail) Statement of Earnings and Retained Earnings Year Ended January 31, 1991 (Unaudited)

	1991	1990
Sales	$478,406	$425,588
Cost of sales	217,550	186,890
Gross margin	260,856	238,698
Expenses		
Advertising and promotional items	20,632	6,324
Automobile	7,832	3,540
Doubtful accounts	1,261	—
Depreciation and amortization	11,589	12,818
Dues and fees	1,246	2,025
Electricity	7,937	4,951
Heat	4,096	4,433
Insurance	2,426	1,780
Interest and bank charges	5,667	17,482
Interest on long-term debt	23,562	9,219
Management salary	29,515	32,600
Office and supplies	12,176	10,412
Professional fees	19,672	10,816
Property tax	879	621
Rent	—	975
Repairs and maintenance	6,876	9,168
Salaries and wages	70,132	96,386
Telephone and facsimile	5,284	5,549
Trade shows	18,588	12,946
	249,370	242,045
Earnings (loss) from manufacturing operation	11,486	(3,347)
Management fees	—	7,250
Loss from restaurant operations— Schedule 2	3,368	—
Earnings before income taxes	8,118	3,903
Income taxes	181	1,273
Net earnings	7,937	2,630
Retained earnings, beginning of year	9,290	6,660
Retained earnings, end of year	$ 17,227	$ 9,290

At this time, MacNaughton was attempting to provide a sound financial base for the continued operation of the company. He had decided to offer a preferred share issue in the amount of $100,000. These shares would bear interest at the rate of eight per cent cumulative and would be non-voting, non-participating. He anticipated that the sale of

Exhibit 3	P.E.I. Preserve Co. Ltd. Schedule of Restaurant Operations (Charlottetown and New Glasgow) Year Ended January 31, 1991 (Unaudited)

	SCHEDULE 2 1991
Sales	$306,427
Cost of Sales	
Purchases and freight	122,719
Inventory, end of year	11,864
	110,855
Salaries and wages for food preparation	42,883
	153,738
Gross Margin	152,689
Expenses	
Advertising	2,927
Depreciation	6,219
Electricity	4,897
Equipment lease	857
Insurance	389
Interest and bank charges	1,584
Interest on long-term debt	2,190
Office and supplies	2,864
Propane	2,717
Rent	22,431
Repairs and maintenance	3,930
Salaries and wages for service	90,590
Supplies	12,765
Telephone	1,697
	156,057
Loss from Restaurant Operations	$ 3,368

these shares would be complete by December 31, 1991. In the interim he required a line of credit in the amount of $100,000 which he requested to be guaranteed by the Prince Edward Island Development Agency.

Projected Sales for the Year Ended January 31, 1992 were:

New Glasgow Restaurant	$ 110,000
Charlottetown Restaurant	265,000
Retail (New Glasgow)	360,000
Wholesale (New Glasgow)	150,000
Mail Order (New Glasgow)	50,000
Retail (Charlottetown)	75,000
Total	$1,010,000

Exhibit 4	P.E.I. Preserve Co. Ltd. Balance Sheet as at January 31, 1991 (Unaudited)	
	1991	**1990**
Current Assets		
Cash	$ 5,942	$ 592
Accounts Receivable		
Trade	12,573	6,511
Investment tax credit	1,645	2,856
Other	13,349	35,816
Inventory	96,062	85,974
Prepaid expenses	2,664	6,990
	132,235	138,739
Grant Receivable	2,800	1,374
Property, Plant and Equipment	280,809	162,143
Recipes and Trade Name, at Cost	10,000	10,000
	$425,844	$312,256
Current Liabilities		
Bank indebtedness	$ 2,031	$ 9,483
Operating and other loans	54,478	79,000
Accounts Payable and accrued liabilities	64,143	32,113
Current portion of long-term debt	23,657	14,704
	144,309	135,300
Long-term Debt	97,825	99,679
Deferred Government Assistance	54,810	—
Payable to Shareholder, non-interest bearing, no set terms of repayment	43,373	49,687
	340,317	284,666
Shareholders' Equity		
Share capital	55,000	5,000
Contributed surplus	13,300	13,300
Retained earnings	17,227	9,290
	85,527	27,590
	$425,844	$312,256

Operations

Preserve production took place on site, in an area visible through glass windows from the retail floor. Many visitors, in fact, would videotape operations during their visit to the New Glasgow store, or would watch the process while tasting the broad selection of sample products freely available.

Production took place on a batch basis. Ample production capacity existed for the $30,000 main kettle used to cook the preserves. Preserves were made five months a year, on a single shift, five day per week basis. Even then, the main kettle was in use only 50 per cent of the time.

Only top quality fruit was purchased. As much as possible, P.E.I. raw materials were used. For a short period the fruit could be frozen until time for processing.

The production process was labour intensive. Bruce was considering the feasibility of moving to an incentive-based salary system to increase productivity and control costs. Because a decorative cloth fringe was tied over the lid of each bottle, bottling could not be completely automated. A detailed production cost analysis had recently been completed. While there were some minor differences due to ingredients, the variable costs averaged $1.25 per 250-millilitre bottle. This was made up of ingredients ($0.56), labour ($0.28) and packaging ($0.20 per bottle, $0.11 per lid, $0.03 per label and $0.07 per fabric and ribbon).

Restaurant operations were the source of many of Bruce's headaches. The New Glasgow Restaurant had evolved over time from offering "dessert and coffee/tea" to its present status where it was also open for meals all day.

MANAGEMENT During the peak summer period, P.E.I. Preserves employed 45 people among the restaurants, manufacturing area and retail locations. Of these, five were managerial positions (see Exhibit 5). The company was considered a good place to work, with high morale and limited turnover. Nonetheless, most employees (including some management) were with the company on a seasonal basis. This was a concern to MacNaughton who felt that if he could provide year round employment, he would be able to attract and keep the best quality staff.

Carol Rombough was an effective assistant general manager and bookkeeper. Maureen Dickieson handled production with little input required from Bruce. Kathy MacPherson was in the process of providing, for the first time, accurate cost information. Natalie Leblanc was managing the new retail outlet in Charlottetown, and assisting on some of the more proactive marketing initiatives Bruce was considering.

Bruce felt that the company had survived on the basis of word-of-mouth. Few follow-up calls on mail order had ever been done. Bruce did not enjoy participating in trade shows—even though he received regular solicitations for them from across North America. In 1992, he planned to participate in four *retail* shows, all of them in or close to P.E.I. Bruce hoped to be able eventually to hire a sales/marketing manager, but could not yet afford $30,000 for the necessary salary.

The key manager continued to be MacNaughton. He described himself as "a fair person to deal with, but shrewd when it comes to purchasing. However, I like to spend

Exhibit 5	Key Executives

President and General Manager—Bruce MacNaughton, Age 35

Experience:	Seventeen years of "front line" involvement with the public in various capacities;
	Seven years of managing and promoting Prince Edward Island Preserve Co. Ltd;
	Past director of the Canadian Specialty Food Association.

Responsibilities:	To develop and oversee the short-, mid-, and long-term goals of the company;
	To develop and maintain quality products for the marketplace;
	To oversee the management of personnel;
	To develop and maintain customer relations at both the wholesale and retail level;
	To develop and maintain harmonious relations with government and the banking community.

Assistant General Manager—Carol Rombough, Age 44

Experience:	Twenty years as owner/operator of a manufacturing business;
	Product marketing at both the wholesale and retail level;
	Personnel management;
	Bookkeeping in a manufacturing environment;
	Three years with the Prince Edward Island Preserve Co. Ltd.

Responsibilities:	All bookkeeping functions (i.e. Accounts Receivable, Accounts Payable, Payroll);
	Staff management—scheduling and hiring;
	Customer relations.

Production Manager—Maureen Dickieson, Age 29

Experience:	Seven years of production experience in the dairy industry;
	Three years with the Prince Edward Island Preserve Co. Ltd.

Responsibilities:	Oversee and participate in all production;
	Planning and scheduling production;
	Requisition of supplies.

Consultant—Kathy MacPherson, Certified General Accountant, Age 37

Experience:	Eight years as a small business owner/manager;
	Eight years in financial planning and management.

Responsibilities:	To implement an improved system of product costing;
	To assist in the development of internal controls;
	To compile monthly internal financial statements;
	To provide assistance and/or advice as required by management.

Store Manager—Natalie Leblanc, Age 33

Experience:	Fifteen years in retail.

Responsibilities:	To manage the retail store in the CP Hotel;
	Assist with mail order business;
	Marketing duties as assigned.

enough money to ensure that what we do—we do right." Financial and managerial constraints meant that Bruce felt stretched ("I haven't had a vacation in years") and unable to pursue all of the ideas he had for developing the business.

The Japanese Consumer

MacNaughton's interest in the possibility of reaching the Tokyo consumer had been formed from two factors: the large number of Japanese visitors to P.E.I. Preserves, and the fact that the largest export shipment the company had ever made had been to Japan. MacNaughton had never visited Japan, although he had been encouraged by Canadian federal government trade representatives to participate in food and gift shows in Japan. He was debating whether he should visit Japan during the coming year. Most of the information he had on Japan had been collected for him by a friend.

Japan was Canada's second most important source of foreign tourists. In 1990, there were 474,000 Japanese visitors to Canada, a figure which was expected to rise to one million by 1995. Most Japanese visitors entered through the Vancouver or Toronto airports. Within Canada, the most popular destination was the Rocky Mountains (in Banff, Alberta numerous stores catered specifically to Japanese consumers). Nearly 15,000 Japanese visited P.E.I. each year. Excluding airfare, these visitors to Canada spent an estimated $314 million, the highest per-capita amount from any country.

The Japanese fascination with Prince Edward Island could be traced to the popularity of Anne of Green Gables. The Japanese translation of this and other books in the same series had been available for many years.However, the adoption of the book as required reading in the Japanese school system since the 1950s had resulted in widespread awareness and affection for "Anne with red hair" *and* P.E.I.

The high level of spending by Japanese tourists was due to a multitude of factors: the amount of disposable income available to them, one of the world's highest per person duty-free allowances ([¥]200,000), and gift-giving traditions in the country. Gift giving and entertainment expenses at the corporate level are enormous in Japan. In 1990, corporate entertainment expenses were almost ¥5 trillion, more than triple the U.S. level of ¥1.4 trillion. Corporate gift giving, while focused at both year end (seibo) and the summer (chugen), in fact, occurred throughout the year.

Gift giving at the personal level was also widespread. The amount spent would vary depending on one's relationship with the recipient; however, one of the most common price points used by Japanese retailers for gift giving was offering choices for under ¥2,000.

THE JAPANESE JAM MARKET Japanese annual consumption of jam was approximately 80,000 tons. Imports made up six to nine per cent of consumption, with higher-grade products (¥470 or more per kilo wholesale CIF) making up a third of this total. Several dozen firms imported jam, and utilized a mix of distribution channels (see Exhibit 6). Prices varied, in part, according to the type of channel structure used. Exhibit 7 provides a common structure. Import duties for jams were high—averaging about 28 per cent. Despite such a high tariff barrier, some firms had been successful in exporting to Japan. Excerpts from a report on how to access Japan's jam market successfully are contained in Exhibit 8.

Canadian World

In spring 1990, P.E.I. Preserves received its biggest ever export order; $50,000 worth of product was ordered (FOB New Glasgow) for ultimate shipment to Ashibetsu, on the northern Japanese island of Hokkaido. These products were to be offered for sale at Canadian World, a new theme park scheduled to open in July 1990.

In 1981, Japan's first theme park was built outside Tokyo. Called Tokyo Disneyland, in 1989 it had an annual revenue of $815 million, 14.7 million visitors, and profits of $119 million. Not surprisingly, this success has spawned a theme park industry in Japan. Over the past decade, 20 parks with wide-ranging themes have opened. Another 16 were expected to open in 1991–1992.

The idea to construct a theme park about Canada was conceived by a Japanese advertising agency hired by the Ashibetsu city council to stop the city's declining economy. The city's population had decreased from 75,000 in 1958 to 26,000 in 1984 due principally to mine closures.

With capital investment of ¥750 million, construction started in mid 1989 on 48 of the 156 available hectares. The finished site included six restaurants, 18 souvenir stores, 16 exhibit event halls, an outdoor stage with 12,000 seats, and 20 hectares planted in herbs and lavender.

The theme of Canadian World was less a mosaic of Canada than it was a park devoted to the world of Anne of Green Gables. The entrance to the Canadian World was a replica of Kensingston Station in P.E.I. The north gateway was Brightriver Station, where Anne first met with Matthew. There was a full-scale copy of the Green Gables house,

Exhibit 6	Jam Distribution Channel in Japan

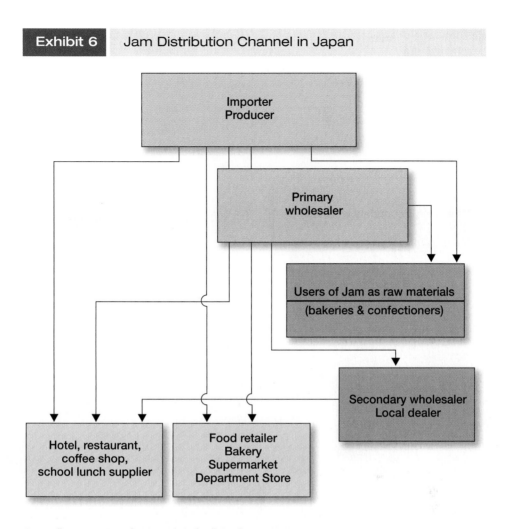

Source: "Access to Japan's Import Market," *Tradescope,* June 1989.

Orwell School where you could actually learn English like Anne did, and so forth. Canadian World employed 55 full-time and 330 part-time staff. This included a high school girl from P.E.I. who played Anne—complete with (dyed) red hair—dressed in Victorian period costume.

In late August 1991, Canadian World still had a lot of P.E.I. Preserves' products for sale. Lower than expected sales could be traced to a variety of problems. First, overall attendance at Canadian World had been 205,000 in the first year, significantly lower than the expected 300,000. Second, the product was priced higher than many competitive offerings. For reasons unknown to Canadian World staff, the product sold for 10 per cent more than expected (¥1,200 versus ¥1,086).

Wholesale price in P.E.I.	$3.50
Freight ($4.20/kilo, P.E.I. to Hokkaido)	0.80
Duty (28% of wholesale price + freight)	1.20
Landed cost in Japan	5.50
Importer's Margin (15%)	0.83
Price to Primary Wholesaler	6.33
Wholesaler Margin (10%)	0.63
Price to Retailer	6.96
Canadian World mark up (30%)	2.09
Expected retail price	$9.05
Exchange (Cdn$1.00 = 120 yen)	¥1,086

Exhibit 7	Example of Price Markups in Japan

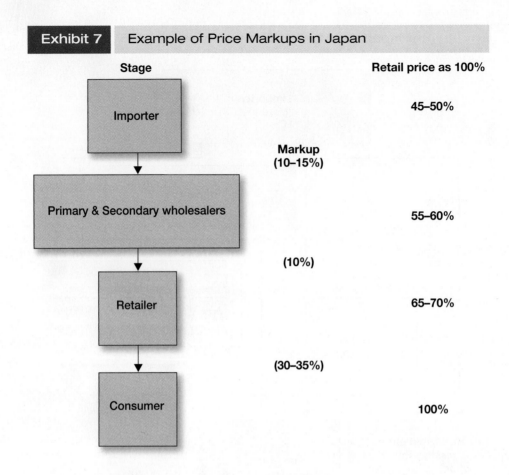

Stage   **Retail price as 100%**

Importer   45–50%

                                         **Markup
                                         (10–15%)**

Primary & Secondary wholesalers   55–60%

                                             (10%)

Retailer   65–70%

                                           (30–35%)

Consumer   100%

Source: "Access to Japan's Import Market," *Tradescope,* June 1989.

Third, the product mix chosen by the Japanese buyers appeared to be inappropriate. While it was difficult to locate any of the company's remaining strawberry preserves in the various Canadian World outlets which carried it, other products had not moved at all. Canadian World personnel did not have a tracking system for product-by-product sales. Fourth, the company's gift packs were not always appropriately sized or priced. One suggestion had been to package the preserves in cardboard gift boxes of three large (250-millilitre) or five small (125-millilitre) bottles for eventual sale for under ¥2,000.

An increasing portion of all of the gifts being sold at Canadian World were, in fact, being made in Japan. Japanese sourcing was common due to the high Japanese duties on imports, the transportation costs from Canada, and the unfamiliarity of Canadian companies with Japanese consumer preferences.

The Tokyo Market

With 10 million residents, Tokyo was the largest city in Japan and one of the most crowded cities anywhere. Thirty million people lived within 50 kilometres of Tokyo's Imperial Palace. As the economic centre of the nation, Tokyo also had the most expensive land in the world—US$150,000 per square metre in the city centre. Retail space in one of Tokyo's major shopping districts would cost $75 to $160 per square metre or $1,600 to $3,400 per month for a shop equivalent in size to that in the CP Prince Edward Hotel. Prices in the Ginza were even higher. In addition to basic rent, all locations required a deposit (guarantee money which would be repaid when the tenant gave up the lease) of at least $25,000. Half of the locations available in a recent survey also charged administrative/maintenance fees (five to 12 per cent of rent), while in about one-third of the

Exhibit 8	The Japanese Jam Market

To expand sales of imported jam or to enter the Japanese market for the first time, it is necessary to develop products after precise study of the market's needs. Importers who are making efforts to tailor their products to the Japanese market have been successfully expanding their sales by 10 per cent each year. Based on the analysis of successful cases of imported jam, the following factors may be considered very important.

Diversification of consumer preferences: Strawberry jam occupies about 50 per cent of the total demand for jam and its share is continuing to rise. Simultaneously, more and more varieties of jam are being introduced.

Low sugar content: European exporters have successfully exported low sugar jam that meets the needs of the Japanese market. Jam with a sugar content of less than 65 per cent occupies a share of 65 to 70 per cent of the market on a volume basis.

Smaller containers: Foreign manufacturers who stick to packaging products in large-sized containers (650 grams, 440 grams, 250 grams), even though their products are designed for household use, have been failing to expand their sales. On the other hand, foreign manufacturers who have developed products in smaller containers (14 grams, 30 grams, 42 grams) specifically for the Japanese market have achieved successful results.

Fashionable items: Contents and quantity are not the only important aspects of jam. The shape and material quality of the containers and their caps, label design and product name can also influence sales. It is also important that the label not be damaged in any way.

Development of gift items: Sets of various types of imported jams are popular as gift items. For example, there are sets of 10 kinds of jam in 40-gram mini-jars (retail price ¥2,000) sold as gift sets.

Selection of distribution channel: Since general trading companies, specialty importers and jam manufacturers each have their own established distribution channels, the selection of the most appropriate channel is of the utmost importance.

Source: "Access to Japan's Import Market," *Tradescope,* June 1989.

locations a "reward" (gift) was paid by tenants to the owner at the time the contract was signed. For a small site it might amount to $10,000 to $15,000.

The Toronto Market

With three million people, Toronto was Canada's largest city and economic centre. It contained the country's busiest airport (15 million people used it each year) and was a popular destination for tourists. Each year, roughly 20 million people visited Toronto for business or vacation.

MacNaughton's interest in Toronto was due to its size, the local awareness of P.E.I., and the high perceived potential volume of sales. The company did not have a sales agent in Toronto.

The Toronto market was well served by mass market and specialty jam producers at all price points. Numerous domestic and imported products were available. Prices started as low as $1.00 (or less) for a 250-millilitre bottle of high sugar/low fruit product. Prices increased to $2.00 to $2.50 for higher fruit, natural brands and increased again to $3.00 to $3.50 for many of the popular branded imports. The highest priced products, such as P.E.I. Preserves, were characterized by even higher fruit content, highest quality ingredients, and a broader selection of product offerings. The specialty domestic producers were from various provinces and tended to have limited distribution areas.

The specialty imports were frequently from France or England. The Canadian tariff on imports was 15 per cent for most countries. From the United States, it was 10.5 per cent and declining.

The cost of retail space in Toronto varied according to location but was slightly lower than that in Tokyo. The cost of renting 22 square metres would be $100 per square metre per month (plus common area charges and taxes of $15 per square metre per month) in a major suburban shopping mall, and somewhat higher in the downtown core. Retail staff salaries were similar in Toronto and Tokyo, both of which were higher than those paid in P.E.I.

FUTURE DIRECTIONS MacNaughton was the first to acknowledge that, while the business had been "built on gut and emotion, rather than analysis," this was insufficient for the future. The challenge was to determine the direction and timing of the desired change.

Case 6

ESRI: Changing World

© Jyoti Bachani
University of Redlands
Jyoti_Bachani@Redlands.edu
909 748 0545
909 748 8763

In August of 2005, Jack Dangermond, the founder and CEO of Environmental Systems Research Institute, Inc. (ESRI), the company that had been at the forefront of geographic information systems (GIS) for forty years, spoke at the ESRI user conference in San Diego, CA, and said:

> " 'The Web is the new platform for GIS' and it is becoming 'geographically enabled.' It will 'change the way we do things and the way we talk about them . . . GIS on the Web, provides many additional possibilities for sharing, integrating, and leveraging the full stack of geographic knowledge,' allowing users to 'share maps and data, models, analyses.' This, he argued, will create 'a whole new way of thinking about GIS at all scales.' Meanwhile, the enabling technology is 'evolving nicely:' faster machines, increased bandwidth, larger storage, Web servers providing real-time information, and a new generation of geographic software. 'I believe this will improve our ability to share dynamically in this real-time environment.' He calls it the 'geo-web.' "

Jack Dangermond and his wife Laura had dedicated their lives to creating and spreading the GIS technology, through ESRI, since they founded it in 1969. For almost four decades they had pursued the mission, "to make a difference in the world by using computers and technology to collect, organize, analyze and communicate geographical information". In 1973, ESRI had created the first commercial State-wide GIS system for the State of Maryland. Later, they also created and supported the online portal www.GIS.com, to disseminate information about the geographic information systems. According to ESRI's website, they have the largest GIS software installed base in the world with more than a million users in more than 100,000 organizations representing government, NGOs, academia, utilities, healthcare, transportations, telecommunications, homeland security, retail and agriculture. According to industry analyst Daratech, in 2001, ESRI was the number one GIS software provider with estimated software revenues of $427 million and 34.6% of total worldwide GIS software market.

Since 1995, with the commercial adoption of the Internet, several new technology companies started to offer consumers computer based geographic information simply at the click of a mouse button. Initially, it was the ability to simply look up electronic maps online with any PC connected to the Internet. Mapquest, Yahoo Maps, and other similar services. Overtime, additional functionality was added to these maps, for example, one could get directions from one location to another. Other businesses started adding these electronic maps to their web-sites in order to give their customers a way to locate their business and get directions to it. By the end of 2006, many additional interactive features were available on these electronic maps. For example, getting real time traffic information along the route of the directions, locating a hotel or other nearby businesses and tourist attractions. Related technologies appeared in mobile devices like cell-phones and automobiles. Cars could be equipped with devices that linked to the satellite Global Positioning System that could provide driving directions and local information as one drove through an area, and cell-phones could be tracked to their exact locations.

Jack's vision of a geographically enabled world had come true, even though it was happening with technologies and companies that were unrelated to ESRI or even GIS. Will this visionary pioneer of geographic information systems be a pioneer in this geographically enabled world that they have championed for four decades? How, if at all, should

ESRI respond to these technologies and companies that were redefining the market?

GIS Technology and Industry

GIS is computer software that links geographic information (where things are) with descriptive information (what things are like). GIS produces electronic maps that have layers of information representing different themes, or features, of the map. For example, the plotted map may contain information about roads in an area, or cables buried underground, or lakes or cities, in the same area. The stack of information about the same geographic area can be visualized and analyzed by being turned off or on, and 'mashed-up' on the same map with a GIS system. There are three underlying technologies that work together within any GIS system: a database, a visualization system and a spatial analysis system. The spatial analysis system is the engine that brings together the data and visualized information and allows for spatial analysis to be conducted complete with data manipulation, 3D and network visualizations, and other ways of analysis that use data and its geographic component together. For example, a company may have addresses of their customers in an Oracle database, which can be displayed on Yahoo Maps or similar visualization package. Such visual representation adds information to the data since one can see the geographic distribution or density or other patterns in the customer address database by having it visually displayed. Further spatial analysis can be conducted to highlight some features, say, customers with homes on an acre or more of land, by some other parameter. A GIS system can add a component of data, the lot size, from the county land-records, for the customer addresses, and overlay that on the previously visualized map of customer addresses and highlight the ones that have lot sizes of acre or more of land.

GIS software was originally designed for mainframe computers that were owned and operated by the large organizations, like the government departments or utility companies that collected and maintained their own data. Over the years, it has evolved to have multiple incarnations: a desktop personal computer version, server platform based GIS, GIS as a service delivered over the Internet, and a mobile GIS version. GIS was a tool for making better business decisions that were expected to provide substantial sustainable competitive advantage. The traditional customers for GIS software were larger organizations, the government departments that maintained land records, Oil and Gas companies that analyzed geological information and made location decisions about oil and gas exploration, Telecom companies that analyzed information to route their service personnel most effectively, or kept updated data on exact locations of their buried cables, or found the best locations for transmitters of cell phone calls, large retail businesses, from banks to coffee shops, who used GIS in combination with demographic databases, to make decisions about their branch locations, delivery truck routings, and their product and service mix. A GIS system required substantial investment in expensive computers, custom-made software to address their special business needs and ongoing maintenance and support with data updates. Thus, only larger organizations with businesses big enough to recover adequate returns on this investment could use GIS.

In 2006, the six leading companies in the Geo-Spatial industry were[1]: The Autodesk, Inc., Bentley Systems, Inc., Environmental Systems Research Institute (ESRI), GE Energy, Intergraph Corporation, and NAVTEQ Corporation. Since 2000, several new players have entered the market. Oracle, SAP, Microsoft Maps, Google Earth, and others, have become aware of the value of adding a spatial dimension to their product offerings. Some of these companies acquired smaller firms and start-ups that had the spatial visualization technologies. Their technologies were developed in the Internet enabled world and focused on ease of use. They served up visualization with limited interactive or analytic ability. Only in the mid-2000s, these technologies advanced enough to add real-time data on to the visuals. Their primary consumer was anyone with a personal computer connected to the Internet, since they delivered their maps online, mostly for free for the individual user, and at a subscription based rate for the other businesses. Google Earth had by far the furthest reach amongst the consumers as it continued to add new features and aggressively pushed towards its goal of cataloging the world's information and knowledge.

History and Leadership

ESRI was started in 1969 as Environmental Systems Research Institute, a land use consulting company, by the husband and wife team of Jack and Laura Dangermond. They had worked together at the Harvard Design Lab, designing systems that allowed geographic information to be visualized on computers. In 1973, when ESRI was selected to provide the first commercially developed State-wide GIS for the State of Maryland, entitled the Maryland Automated Geographic Information System, they decided to incorporate it as a company.

---

[1]www.Daratech.com.

The early mission of ESRI focused on the principles of organizing and analyzing geographic information. In 2007, according to the ESRI website, its mission is, "The company's focus remains on producing excellent software and delivering exceptional service to users. Our reputation is built on contributing our technical knowledge, our special people, and valuable experience to the collection, analysis, and communication of geographic information."[2]

The Dangermonds focused on creating and disseminating the GIS technology while being financially responsible. They carefully managed project work to ensure growth without the need for venture capital or taking the company public. ESRI remained a privately held company, owned by Jack and Laura, who remained actively involved with its operations. This private ownership structure was important as it allowed them to stay focused on their mission of changing the world by spreading the GIS technology. They were not driven by external pressures from venture capitalists or Wall street to focus on pure financial gain, and could continuously reinvest in furthering the technology. In the year 2004, ESRI had revenues of more than $560 million with an average annual growth rate of more than 20%. ESRI had enjoyed steady growth of 10–15% per year for almost four decades. The conservative financial management also created a debt free company.

During the 1980s ESRI devoted its resources to developing and applying a core set of application tools for GIS systems. The commercial success of the technology was used to reinvest in the technology, thus setting off a virtuous cycle of continuing growth and success. The major milestones in ESRI's history are shown in the timeline in appendix 1. ESRI continued to pursue steady business along with its mission of bringing geospatial technology to the world, and emerged as an organization of global stature.

ESRI was headquartered in Redlands, a small town of 60,000 people located an hour east of Los Angeles in the USA. The main office was a sprawling campus of 22 buildings, some old, others new, all in close proximity, amongst beautifully landscaped grounds. Ponds with fish, turtles, fountains, and large rocks placed to enhance the Japanese garden-like ambiance of the grounds with several outdoor seating areas, offered ESRI employees and visitors a serene place to sit under the trees and work or take their lunch breaks. The campus landscaping was planned by Jack, who grew up in Redlands, where his father used to own a plant nursery. ESRI had 11 US regional offices and 90 worldwide offices and affiliates. ESRI had a business partner program with more than 2,000 developers, consultants, resellers, and

data providers; and a network of more than 75 international distributors. As a privately held company, ESRI did not make its profits and financial statements public but the continuing growth and expansion of the firm were ample evidence of its commercial success. In 2005, it was an organization of 2,900 employees, known internationally for GIS software development, training, and services.

As the founder-leaders Jack and Laura Dangermond had a powerful influence on ESRI's mission and culture. Their involvement in the day-to-day affairs of the company was low-profile, but strong. They both had modest offices in one of the older low-rise buildings on the ESRI campus in Redlands. There was a complete absence of any bio or photos of these two pioneers and founder-leaders, either on the company's website or in its publicity materials. They were both in their 60s and commanded great respect within the company and amongst the professionals in the industry. Jack Dangermond was a pioneer in spatial analysis methods and one of the most influential people in GIS. See appendix 2 for Jack's professional bio and how others in the industry see him.

Organization

ESRI adopted a project based organization to support its focus on creating technology. The top management of ESRI consisted of a small team of managers reporting directly to Jack Dangermond. Most of them had been with ESRI for over a decade, and some for over two decades. There was a team approach to handling all responsibilities although they had assigned areas of responsibility as well. Being in offices in close proximity to each other encouraged team work and information sharing on a daily basis. The rest of the organization was made up of several teams handling specific aspects of the technology and business. The marketing and sales function are described below.

MARKETING In 2006, the director of marketing group said: "My marketing mission is to educate the world about the Geographic Information System (GIS) technology we create to help organizations make better, more informed decisions by adding the spatial component to their businesses."[3] The marketing department at ESRI had 180 marketing professionals, organized into seven broad teams, three strategic and four tactical, who marketed the 40 products and services ESRI offered, to 40 industries worldwide. The three strategic groups—Corporate Marketing, Industry Solutions, and Product Marketing—developed market-

---

[2]From www.Esri.com downloaded on May 22nd 2006.

[3]Reaching the world with your message. ASPATORE Books: Inside the Minds.

ing plans, strategies, campaigns, and promotional programs to build brand equity and effectively market ESRI products and services. The four tactical groups—Events Marketing, Marketing Communications, Marketing Operations, and Technical Marketing—executed the plans and programs developed by the three strategic groups. The tactical groups were responsible for managing ESRI events (seminars, trade shows, conferences), developing ESRI's presence on the Internet, generating exposure through the press and ESRI publications, implementing direct mail and e-mail campaigns, and developing product demonstrations and benchmarks.

"Half or more of what we do is building a relationship with our customers," the marketing director said. "It helps build a relationship, and then we can upsell them." That "half or more" encompasses a lot of efforts. "ESRI's marketing strategy relies on a number of customer touches every year. These include ArcNews, a quarterly general-interest print publication for geographic information users; ArcWatch, a technical newsletter for more sophisticated users of the global information systems; and a variety of permission-based e-mail alerts, including conference notices and advanced-use training sessions."[4] ESRI also surveyed its customers regularly and builds relationships with them by using the information from the surveys. Customers could get a book just for completing an online survey, and after they had filled the survey, ESRI had information to direct them to other users in their area or to conferences that may be of interest to them. One major annual event was the international GIS user conference hosted by ESRI and attended by about 15,000 users from around the world.

SALES Sales function resided primarily in the regional offices, and with the partner network of regional, national and global partner firms. Partnering was critical to the technology as database companies, applications developers, resellers and others were needed to make the GIS platform broadly useful and accessible. ESRI had about 1400 domestic partners, ranging from consultants (OEMs like Telecordia or Bell Labs who visualize and analyze their telecom networks using GIS, and then sell to Telecom companies) to resellers.

Some of the other functional teams were consulting, professional services, administrative services, corporate strategies and software development. Each of these had teams within their domains to handle business as needed.

[4]*In Getting to Know Them* by Richard H Levy, published March 1, 2005, © 2006 Prism Business Media Inc. downloaded from www.directmag.com/mag/marketing_getting_know/index.html (on 6/19/2006).

Products and Services

ESRI offered a range of GIS focused products and services, driven by customer need. The software ran on different hardware platforms, desktop, mobile devices, in-house main-frames, servers, and over the Internet. Most of these products and services allow several layers of data to be 'mashed-up' into a single multi-layered electronic visual map, in which the different layers of data could be switched on or off the display, depending on the needs of the various users of the system. The systems were designed to solve certain problems within their virtual worlds by focusing on certain information, e.g. oil wells, flooding, logistical planning, etc. Several of the original users from the 80s continued to use the ESRI product into the mid-2000s. ESRI remained committed to supporting the large established user base on whatever product and version they happened to be using, while also keeping pace with changing technologies and customer needs by modifying the products.

The original mainframe code based product was ArcInfo. It evolved in the era of mini-computers and Unix based workstations, and in the PC era, ArcView was introduced with Microsoft Windows interface. In the late 90s, in response to the Internet, ArcGIS was launched. Internet also offered the opportunity to integrate various products that used to be sold separately before, into a suite called ArcInfo. ArcInfo contained pieces of software that could also be purchased separately, like ArcView for visualization tools, and ArcEditor for editing and manipulating data that was to be subjected to geo-spatial analysis. In 1998, ArcData Online was launched for internet mapping. ESRI was continuously adding new features and functionality to the core GIS product in order to meet the customer needs. A new version of the flagship product was released roughly every eighteen months. ESRI organized an annual user conference, and in 2006, they released the ArcGIS 9.2 product at the conference. ArcGIS 9.2 essentially offered the ArcInfo product functionality delivered over the Internet from a server.

The pricing for the products and services varied depending on the customer, usage and other factors. Users could buy packaged software that they would own, bundled with support and service including training contracts. Users could also simply use ESRI software or services as a paid-service to solve specific problems. For example, a large retailer like Sears purchased and owned the ArcInfo product that it used for several in-house operational decisions, e.g. for routing delivery trucks most efficiently between the various distribution warehouses and the store locations. A smaller business, say a delivery service with a dozen trucks that services clients within a specified geographic area, could get the same benefit of planning its delivery routes without the big investment required for buying and maintaining an ArcInfo system. Such a firm could purchase the spatial analysis of its delivery routes as a service from ESRI. It had a choice to either use an ArcGIS Server based application for route-planning or use an online product like the Business Analyst, to access the technology to come up with the optimal solution to their routing problem.

ESRI products had customers at two different levels: the end-use customers who use the applications as described above and the developers who build applications for the ESRI products to solve specific problems for the end-users. The developers used Java and other tools to develop applications on the ESRI system for the final end-user customer. For example, a county land use office had a GIS system and GIS developers that created the applications on the GIS system for the city planners and citizens who actually use the final output. These developers created many unanticipated uses for the GIS products. This made product development

at ESRI more challenging as new versions had to anticipate the end-users needs as well as the unanticipated uses that the developer-users may create. ESRI emphasized the need to get close to the customer, and often hired product engineers from the user community. They provided a voice in product development by contributing the language and user-centric understanding of the business problems. See appendix 3 for a detailed list of ESRI products and services and their descriptions.

If ESRI continued with its strategies, should it expect to enjoy the same success in the future as it had until now? Or will success be redefined? After all, Google measures its success in terms of the number of eye-balls it attracts or the revenue from advertising, while ESRI has been a financially conservative company that has remained debt free for almost four decades as it continued to change the world with pioneering technology. Whether the new world of geographically enabled Internet will have room for all the companies in the industry or not remains to be seen.

Appendix 1: TimeLine: Major Milestones

ESRI Product Milestones

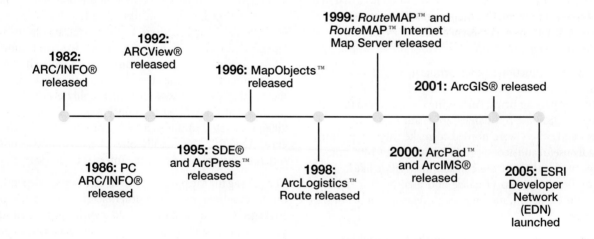

ESRI User Conferences

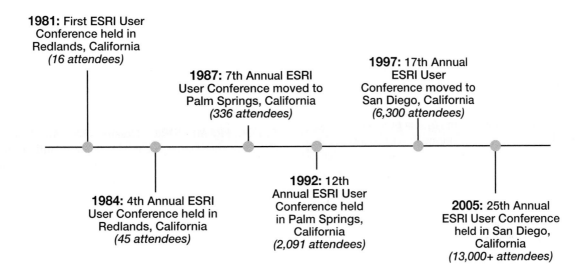

Appendix 2: Jack Dangermond's Bio

Jack grew up in Redlands, California when it was primarily an orange growing community. He graduated with a bachelor of science in environmental science from California State Polytechnic University in Pomona, California. He holds a Master of Science degree in urban planning from the Institute of Technology at the University of Minnesota and a Master of Science degree in landscape architecture from the Graduate School of Design, Harvard University, where he worked in the Laboratory for Computer Graphics and Spatial Design. Laura was also at Harvard and their partnership formed while at the Laboratory. Jack also holds honorary doctorates from The City University of London, University of Redlands, and Ferris State University. Over the last 30 years, Jack has delivered keynote addresses at numerous international conferences, published hundreds of papers on GIS, and given thousands of presentations on GIS around the world. He is the recipient of a number of awards, honorary degrees, lectureships, and medals including the 2000 LaGasse Medal for his notable contributions to the management of natural resources, public lands, or other lands in the public interest by the American Society of Landscape Architects, the Brock Gold Medal of the International Society for Photogrammetry and Remote Sensing, the Cullum Geographical Medal of the American Geographical Society, the EDUCAUSE Medal of EDUCAUSE, the Horwood Award of the Urban and Regional Information Systems Association, the Anderson Medal of the Association of American Geographers, and the John Wesley Powell Award of the U.S. Geological Survey. He is a member of many professional organizations and has served on advisory committees for U.S. agencies including the National Aeronautics and Space Administration's (NASA) Science and Technology Advisory Committee, the U.S. Environmental Protection Agency, the National Academy of Sciences, the National Science Foundation, and the National Center for Geographic Information and Analysis (NCGIA). In 2003, he met India's president, Dr. A.P.J. Abdul Kalam, and Thailand's prime minister, Pol. Lt. Col. Thaksin Shinawatra, to discuss the role of GIS technology. He also met with Dr. Jorge Batlle Ibanez, president of the Republic of Uruguay, to discuss various national GIS initiatives. In recent years, in addition to several key note speeches, he has also been a featured speaker at the U.S. Department of State's Open Forum entitled 'A Conversation on Geographic Information for Diplomacy, Development, and Homeland Security.'

WHAT OTHERS THINK OF JACK AND LAURA DANGER-MOND Matteo, the editor of www.gismonitor.com writes this about Jack and Laura Dangermond:

> "In a world dominated by ideology, faith, and narrow self-interest, in which we continue to devastate the environment and underfund education, I greatly appreciate Jack Dangermond's steady emphasis on rationality, scientific analysis, interdependency, collaboration, and social responsibility, and his strong support for environmental protection and education.
>
> Though the leader of a company that produces sophisticated technology, Dangermond never gets lost in the technical details. His focus is always on the big challenges, on big ideas (one of his favorite words is "interesting"), and on people. . . . Off-stage, too, Jack is personable and engaging. Despite the fact that ESRI now has more than 3,100 staff, he and his wife, Laura, are still intimately involved in every aspect of the company. When I was trying to figure out in which line to stand on Monday morning, to get my conference materials and then enter the huge room in which the plenary session was about to begin, Laura was on hand to give me directions. She also signs the company's checks and supervises the gardeners at the Redlands campus.
>
> Until a couple of years ago, when ESRI bought electric vehicles, every morning Jack loaned his Ford Taurus to the mailroom staff to deliver mail around campus. Recently, when a new sidewalk was being built, he supervised the pouring of the concrete. When I needed a book that was not currently on display in the ESRI Press area of the Exhibit Pavilion, a staffer told me that he would mail it to me, because "only Jack and Laura can authorize books to be checked out of inventory."[5]

[5]http://www.gismonitor.com/news/newsletter/archive/archives.php?issue=20060811&style=web&length=full#introduction (taken on Sept 20th 2006 at 4:16pm)

Appendix 3: ESRI Products and Services and Their Descriptions
PRODUCTS

ArcGIS is an integrated collection of GIS software products for building a complete GIS. ArcGIS enables users to deploy GIS functionality wherever it is needed in desktops, servers, or custom applications; over the Web; or in the field.

ARCGIS FRAMEWORK Desktop GIS—ArcGIS Desktop GIS software products are used to compile, author, analyze, map, and publish geographic information and knowledge. ArcGIS Desktop is a scalable suite of GIS products that starts with ArcReader and extends to ArcView, ArcEditor, and ArcInfo—the most powerful GIS product available today. Each product exposes progressively more GIS capabilities. An extensive collection of desktop extensions provides additional capabilities.

Server GIS—ArcGIS Server, ArcIMS, and ArcSDE are used to create and manage server-based GIS applications that share GIS functionality and data within organizations and many other users on the Internet. ArcGIS Server is a central application server that is used to build serverside GIS applications that run in enterprise and Web computing frameworks. ArcIMS is a scalable Internet Map Server for publishing maps, data, and metadata over the Web using standard Internet protocols. ArcSDE is an advanced spatial data server for accessing geographic information in relational database management systems.

Developer GIS—The ESRI Developer Network (EDN) is an annual subscription-based program that provides software developers with the resources needed to build a wide range of custom GIS solutions. EDN subscribers will receive the latest versions of ArcGIS Engine Developer Kit, ArcGIS Server, ArcIMS, ArcSDE, and ArcWeb Services, with a license that expires when their EDN subscription expires.

Mobile GIS—ArcPad coupled with a wireless mobile device that is location enabled is widely used for data collection and GIS information access in the field. ArcGIS Desktop and ArcGIS Engine running on laptop and Tablet PC computers are being used for field tasks that require GIS data collection, analysis, and decision making.

GIS Web Services—ArcWeb Services offer a cost-effective way to include mapping and location services in Web-enabled applications. Because data storage, maintenance, and updates are handled by ESRI, ArcWeb Services eliminate the overhead of purchasing and maintaining large datasets. An ArcWeb Services subscription provides you with instant access to imagery and aerial photos, real-time weather and traffic incidents, extensive demographic data, and much more. You can use ArcWeb Services in ArcGIS, or you can use them to build unique Web-based applications.

GEODATABASE TECHNOLOGY   All these software products utilize geodatabase technology—the core ArcGIS geographic information model and data management functions.

SERVICES

Consulting Services and Technology Solutions

ESRI Professional Services

Systems Integration Services

Developer Support Program

ESRI Enterprise Advantage Program: provides technical advisory and GIS strategy consulting

Business Information Solutions

Data Publishing Tools and Services

Web Services

ArcWeb Services

Business Analyst Web Services

Partner Solutions

Business Partners

Corporate Alliances

Corporate Hardware Partners

Case 7

ICMR Case Collection

BSTR/149

Li & Fung—The Global Value Chain Configurator

"In an age when the Internet is supposedly going to eliminate the middleman, here's a middleman, an old Asian trading company that has made itself indispensable."[1]

—An Article in Forbes.

"We deliver a new type of value added, truly global product that has never been seen before. We're pulling apart the value chain and optimising each step—and we're doing it globally."[2]

—Victor Fung, Chairman, Li & Fung, in June 2000.

Strengthening Its Fort

In January 2004, Li & Fung Limited (Li & Fung), a Hong Kong based global consumer goods trading giant, announced that Li & Fung Trading (Shanghai), its wholly-owned subsidiary, had been granted an export company license by the Ministry of Commerce of the People's Republic of China (China). After receiving the license, Li &

Fung Trading (Shanghai) became the first wholly owned foreign trading company to be offered direct export rights in China. The company was authorized to export China-sourced goods directly to customers worldwide and import raw materials for manufacturing in China. Li & Fung was until then dependent on its Chinese partners for exporting from China.

According to William Fung (William), managing director, Li & Fung, the license freed the group companies (See Exhibit 1 for Li & Fung's Major Subsidiaries & Associate Companies) from the many trading restrictions in China. It would enhance the company's competitiveness and increase its share in the global market. William said, "With the ability to directly export products from China to our customers worldwide, Li & Fung is now able to offer an even more complete supply chain service."[3]

ICFAI

This case was written by **A. Neela Radhika** under the direction of **Vivek Gupta,** ICFAI Center for Management Research (ICMR). It was compiled from published sources, and is intended to be used as a basis for class discussion rather than to illustrate either effective or ineffective handling of a management situation.

[1]"Stitches in Time," www.forbes.com, June 09, 1999.

[2]"Winning at a Global Game: Part Five of an Eleven Part Series," www.asiabusinesstoday.org, June 10, 2000.

[3]"First Hong Kong Trading Firm to Gain China Licence," www.hktrader.net, February 2004.

Exhibit 1	Li & Fung's Major Subsidiaries and Associated Companies

Held Directly	Place of Incorporation and Operation	Issued and Fully Paid Share Capital	Principal Activities
Li & Fung (B.V.I.) Limited	British Virgin Islands	US$ 400,010	Marketing services and investment holding
Basic & More Fashion Limited	Hong Kong	HK$ 1,000,000	Export trading
Black Cat Fireworks Limited	England	GBP 1,200,000	Wholesaling
Camberley Enterprises Limited	Hong Kong	HK$ 250,000	Apparel exporting
Civati Limited	Hong Kong	US$ 450,000	Export trading
Colby International Limited	Hong Kong	HK$ 1,500,000	Exporting of garments and sundry goods
Colby Tekstil ve Dis Ticaret Limited Sirketi	Turkey	TL50,000,000,000	Export trading
CS International Limited	Hong Kong	HK$ 1,000,000	Provision of export assistance service
Dodwell (Mauritius) Limited	Hong Kong	HK$ 500,000	Export trading
Golden Gate Fireworks Inc.	U.S.A.	US$ 600,000	Commission agent and investment holding
GSCM (HK) Limited	Hong Kong	HK$ 140,000	Export trading
Hillung Enterprises Limited	Hong Kong	HK$ 300,000	Export trading
International Sourcing Group, LLC	U.S.A.	US$ 300,000	Trading of apparel
Janco Overseas Limited	Hong Kong	HK$ 760,000	Buying agent
Kariya Industries Limited	Hong Kong	HK$ 1,000,000	Manufacturing and trading
LF Maclaine (Thailand) Limited	Thailand	Baht 4,000,000	Export trading
Li & Fung Agencia De Compras em Portugal, Limitada	Portugal	PTE 20,000,000	Export trading
Li & Fung (Exports) Limited	Hong Kong	HK$ 8,610,000	Export trading
Li & Fung (Fashion Accessories) Limited	Hong Kong	HK$ 600,000	Export trading
Li & Fung (India)	India	Rupees 64,000,200	Export trading
Li & Fung (Italia) S.r.l.	Italy	Lire 90,000,000	Export trading
Li & Fung (Korea) Limited	Korea	Won 200,000,000	Export trading
Li & Fung (Korea) Limited	Mauritius	Rupees 1,250,000	Export trading
Li & Fung Mumes sillik, Pazarlama Limited	Turkey	TL 25,000,000,000	Export trading
Li & Fung (Philippines) Inc.	The Philippines	Peso 500,000	Export trading
Li & Fung (Properties) Limited	Hong Kong	HK$ 1,000,000	Property investment
Li & Fung Taiwan Holdings Limited	Taiwan	NT$ 287,996,000	Investment holding
Li & Fung Taiwan Investments Limited	British Virgin Islands	US$ 4,912,180	Investment holding
Li & Fung (Taiwan) Limited	Taiwan	NT$ 63,000,000	Export trading
Li & Fung (Thailand) Limited	Thailand	Baht 6,000,000	Export trading
Li & Fung (Trading) Limited	Hong Kong	HK$ 10,000,200	Export trading and investment holding
Li & Fung Trading (Shanghai) Limited	The People's Republic of China	RMB 50,000,000	Export trading
Li & Fung (Zhanjiang) Limited	The People's Republic of China	US$ 1,999,055	Packaging
Livring Limited	Mauritius	Rs 250,000	Export trading

(continued)

Exhibit 1	Li & Fung's Major Subsidiaries and Associated Companies—Continued

Held Directly	Place of Incorporation and Operation	Issued and Fully Paid Share Capital	Principal Activities
Lloyd Textile Trading Limited	Hong Kong	HK$ 1,000,000	Export trading
Maclaine Limited	Hong Kong	HK$ 5,570,150	Export trading
Perfect Trading Inc.	Egypt	LE 2,480,000	Export trading
Shiu Fung Fireworks Company Limited	Hong Kong	HK$ 1,200,000	Export trading
The Millwork Trading Co., Ltd	U.S.A.	US$ 1,331,000	Distribution and wholesaling
Toy Island Manufacturing Company Limited	Hong Kong	HK$ 62,000,000	Design and marketing
Verity Enterprises Limited	Hong Kong	HK$ 2,000,000	Export trading
W S Trading Limited	Hong Kong	HK$ 1,000,000	Export trading

Source: Li & Fung Annual Report, 2003.

Notes:

1. Li & Fung (B.V.I.) Limited provides the subsidiaries with promotional and marketing services outside Hong Kong.

2. Subsidiaries not audited by PricewaterhouseCoopers, Hong Kong. The aggregate net assets of subsidiaries not audited by PricewaterhouseCoopers, Hong Kong amounted to approximately 5% of the Group's total net assets.

The above table lists out the principal subsidiaries of the Company as at 31 December 2003 which, in the opinion of the directors, principally affected the results for the year or form a substantial portion of the net assets of the Group. To give details of other subsidiaries would, in the opinion of the directors, result in particulars of excessive length.

After China joined the World Trade Organization (WTO) in 2001, it emerged as the world's largest exporter of textile and clothing. The country also consolidated its position as one of the world's largest and fastest growing manufacturing economies. According to the US International Textiles Association, export of textiles and clothing from China to the US doubled from US$ 6.5 bn in 2001 to US$ 11.6 bn in 2003. With export quotas among WTO members proposed to be eliminated from January 2005, China would be free of restrictions on quantity of exports to the US, enabling further growth.

In this light, analysts felt Li & Fung stood to benefit significantly from its new license as it was one of the world's leading textile export traders, and the largest to the US. The company was well-placed to leverage China's leadership position in textile manufacturing and exports, as that country was the company's largest manufacturing hub, from where it sourced over US$ 2 bn worth products annually. Li & Fung had 16 offices in China, which it planned to take to 36 by 2007. The downside was that in early 2004, Li & Fung faced many challenges like a slowdown in its overall revenues and net profit growth, over dependence on the US market, declining share of revenues from the European market and negligible growth in revenues from the rapidly growing Asian markets.

Background Note

The history of Li & Fung goes back to the early 1900s, making it the oldest trading company in Hong Kong. The company was founded in 1906 by Fung Pak-Liu (Pak-Liu) and Li To-ming (To-ming) in Guangzhou (South China) and was one of the first Chinese-owned export companies. Trade in China at that time was controlled by foreign commercial houses. Li & Fung began operations by exporting porcelain and silk, mainly to the US. It later expanded its product portfolio to include bamboo, jade, ivory, rattan ware, fireworks and handicrafts.

During the early 1900s, since US buyers did not know Chinese and Chinese sellers did not know English, traders who could speak both the languages became essential mediators between buyers and sellers. Li & Fung, being one among this lot, prospered, earning commissions as high as 15% on each export deal. Li & Fung was formally established in Hong Kong as a limited company in 1937.

World War II disrupted trading in the early 1940s, forcing Li & Fung to cease trading for some years. In 1943, Pak-Liu passed away. Shortly after the end of the war, To-ming, who had been a silent partner, retired and sold his stake to Pak-Liu's family. With this, the Fung family became sole owners of Li & Fung.

In 1949, Pak-Liu's son, Fung Hon-chu (Hon-chu), restarted trading operations in Hong Kong, which had come under British control. Hon-chu was instrumental in leading Li & Fung into the new era. The trading business picked up momentum in Hong Kong during the mid 1900s, driven by the influx of refugees, which transformed China into a manufacturing economy that exported labour intensive consumer products. Li & Fung began exporting consumer products such as garments, electronics, plastic flowers and toys and was soon Hong Kong's biggest exporter.

By the early 1970s, the trading business in Hong Kong began to struggle owing to stiff competition from other manufacturing economies in Asia such as Taiwan and Singapore. Trading margins also went down significantly to 3%, as buyers and sellers became comfortable dealing directly with each other, doing away with intermediaries.

Under these circumstances, Hon-chu called his sons—William and Victor Fung (Victor)—back home from the US. Victor was teaching at the Harvard Business School and William had just finished his MBA from the same business school. Despite their friends' warning that trading would die out in a decade, the two brothers returned to Hong Kong to join their family firm.

Victor and William worked hard to modernize and rebuild Li & Fung into a well-structured organization, professionally managed at all levels. In 1973, the company went public and was listed on the Hong Kong Stock Exchange. Li & Fung's initial public offering was oversubscribed 113 times—a record that stood for 14 years.

With the opening up of the Chinese economy in 1979, many manufacturers in Hong Kong relocated their factories to southern China, which was more cost effective thanks to low labour costs. The rapid industrialization of underdeveloped Asian countries widened the choice of supply sources. Li & Fung realized that there was a huge potential for the trading business. To benefit, the company established a regional network of sourcing offices in Asian countries such as Taiwan, Singapore and Korea in the 1980s. It emerged as a major regional trading company in Asia.

In 1989, with trading margins decreasing further, Victor and William realized the need for drastic changes to safeguard the company's business. As a result, in that year, Li & Fung was again made a private company, in one of the first management buyouts in Hong Kong. The company was then restructured into a diversified group with export trading and retail as its core businesses. In 1992, the firm's export trading business, Li & Fung (Trading) Pvt. Limited., was re-listed on the Hong Kong Stock Exchange.

As Li & Fung expanded its business, it understood that sourcing could no longer be restricted to a few countries but required a vast network of sourcing offices to sustain trading business. Thus, the company established sourcing offices across the world, mainly around its major markets, the US and Europe. Li & Fung also went in for acquisitions to strengthen its sourcing and distribution networks and expand its product lines and customer networks. It pursued an active information technology (IT) and Internet strategy to enhance efficiency and effectiveness of its internal and external communications.

By the turn of the 20th century, Li & Fung was a premier global trading company, with more than 95% of its revenues coming from North America and Europe. East Asia and the South Hemisphere accounted for the rest. In the fiscal year 2002, North America and Europe accounted for 76% and 19% of the group's total revenues, while East Asia and the South Hemisphere were placed at 3% and 2% respectively (See Table 1 for Li & Fung's revenues by geographic segments in percentage terms).

Table 1	Revenues by Geographic Segments (1999–2003)				
Geographic Regions	1999	2000	2001	2002	2003
North America	69%	70%	75%	76%	75%
Europe	27%	26%	21%	19%	19%
East Asia	1%	1%	1%	3%	3%
South Hemisphere	3%	3%	3%	2%	2%
Total (%)	100%	100%	100%	100%	100%
Total Revenues (in HK$ bn)	16.298	24.992	32.941	37.281	42.631

Source: Li & Fung Annual Report 2003.

Table 2	Li & Fung's Product Lines
Soft Goods	Hard Goods
Garments	Fashion Accessories
	Footwear
	Furnishing
	Gifts
	Handicrafts
	Home Products
	Promotional Merchandize
	Toys
	Stationery
	Sporting Goods
	Travel Goods

Source: www.lifung.com.

The group's major product segments were both soft and hard goods. While soft goods included garments, hard goods constituted product lines such as fashion accessories, footwear, gifts and furnishings (See Table 2 for Li & Fung's major product lines). Soft goods contributed to majority of the group's revenues. In 2002, this segment accounted for 68% of Li & Fung's total revenues, while hard goods generated the remaining 32% (See Table 3 for Li & Fung's revenues by product segments in percentage terms).

In 2002, export trading remained Li & Fung's major business, but it also actively operated in the retailing and distribution business through its privately held companies. The retailing business was confined to China and the Asian market, where it operated as a regional license holder for Toys 'R' Us, the biggest US toy products chain and was the franchisee for the Hong-Kong based Circle K convenience store chain. The distribution business too was confined to China and the Asian region. Li & Fung was also involved in other businesses such as venture capital, investment holding and property investment.

In the fiscal 2002, Li & Fung registered revenues of HK$ 37.3 bn, a 13% increase over HK$ 32.94 bn revenues in 2001. The company recorded a net profit of HK$ 1.08 bn in 2002, an increase of 38% over the figure of HK$ 782 mn in 2001. The company's largest customer in the US was Kohl's Department Store Chain, accounting for nearly 13% of Li & Fung's total revenues in 2002. Other major clients included Abercrombie & Fitch, Ann Taylor, Disney, American Eagle Outfitters, Guess, Laura Ashley Jeans, Levi Strauss & Company (Levis), Reebok, The Limited Inc. and Warner Bros.

By this time, Li & Fung had successfully positioned itself as a cutting edge sourcing company in the world, with a well-established sourcing network of 68 offices across 40 countries and over 4,500 employees. In 2002, Li & Fung was reportedly one of the best professionally run companies in Hong Kong. The company's commitment to excellence and high standards in corporate governance practices earned it many awards and recognitions. Li & Fung was named one of Hong Kong's best companies, by the *Euromoney* magazine, in the category "Asia's Best Company 2002." The same year, Li & Fung was named the "Best Managed Company 2002" and "Company most committed to Corporate Governance" by *Finance Asia* magazine (See figure 1 for the corporate governance structure of Li & Fung).

Analysts credited the growth and success of Li & Fung to the visionary leadership and managerial capabilities of Victor and William. Since the early 1970s, the duo had led Li & Fung through a series of transformations in line with changes in the external environment. The major factors that helped Li & Fung evolve into a major global export trading company were the focus on efficiently managing the supply chain of its clients, a unique customer-centric organizational structure, leveraging IT & the Internet and global expansion strategies.

Table 3	Revenues by Product Segments (1999–2003)				
	(In Percentage Terms)				
Product Segments	1999	2000	2001	2002	2003
Soft Goods	75%	78%	72%	68%	67%
Hard Goods	25%	22%	28%	32%	33%
Total (%)	100%	100%	100%	100%	100%
Total Revenues (in HK$ bn)	16.298	24.992	32.941	37.281	42.631

Source: Li & Fung Annual Report 2003.

| Figure I | Li & Fung's Corporate Governance Structure |

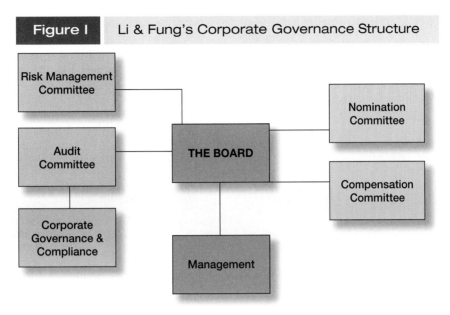

Source: Li & Fung Annual Report, 2003.

Managing the Global Supply Chain

Li & Fung's evolution into a supply chain manager took place in three stages, driven by significant changes in the global retailing industry, customer and retailer preferences and economic trends across Asia through the early 1970s.

In the first stage (during the 1970–78 period), Li & Fung acted as a regional sourcing agent. The company extended its geographic reach by establishing sourcing offices in Singapore, Korea and Taiwan. Li & Fung's knowledge and reach in the Asian region held value for customers. This was because many big buyers could manage their own sourcing if they needed to deal only in Hong-Kong. Dealing with the whole region was far more complex and buyers did not have the necessary resources. Commenting on the complexity of sourcing from the region, in an interview to *Harvard Business Review*, Victor said that as quotas governed world trade in the textiles industry, knowledge on which quotas had been used up in Hong Kong and which was the next best place to source textiles from, where quotas had not been exhausted, enabled Li & Fung to provide customers with a complete product package.

In the second stage (1979–82), Li & Fung evolved from a sourcing agent into a manager and deliverer of production programmes. When a customer came up with an idea of a product and gave specifications such as look, colour and quality, the company developed a detailed manufacturing programme for that product. In other words, the firm created an entire manufacturing programme for its customers for a particular fashion season. The programme involved all tasks from specifying the product mix to scheduling the manufacturing process and delivery time. Li & Fung worked with factories to plan and monitor the manufacturing process, to ensure quality and on-time delivery.

This strategy worked well for Li & Fung. Yet, the 1980s brought a new challenge. This led to its third stage of evolution (1983 to the present period). Other countries in Asia such as Korea, Taiwan and Thailand had by then emerged as labour-intensive manufacturing hubs, while Hong-Kong had become an expensive and non-competitive place to manufacture. The Chinese economy was being liberalized, and the company soon took the advantage by moving the labour intensive portion of production to southern China.

Dispersed Manufacturing

Li & Fung broke the value chain into parts which it called 'Dispersed Manufacturing.' Under this, the company performed all high end value-added activities such as design and quality control in Hong Kong and outsourced low end activities like manufacturing to the best possible locations across the world. For every order, the company aimed at customizing the supply chain to meet the client's specific requirements. For example, when Li & Fung got an order for transistor radios, it created little kits (plastic bags) filled with all the components necessary to build a radio and shipped the kits to China, where they were assembled. The assembled radios were then shipped back to Hong Kong, where they underwent final testing and inspection.

Similarly, to fulfil an order for baby dolls, Li & Fung designed them in Hong Kong, produced moulds for the dolls using sophisticated machinery, and then shipped the moulds to China; where plastic was injected into the moulds, the dolls were assembled, their fingers were painted

| Exhibit 2 | Exports and Imports of Services in Hong Kong (2000–02) | | | | | | | |

| Major service group | Year | Exports of services | | | Imports of services | | | Net exports of services |
		HK$ mn	Share (%)	Year-on-year % change	HK$ mn	Share (%)	Year-on-year % change	HK$ mn
Transportation	2000	99,513	33.0	11.5	48,628	25.4	23.9	50,885
	2001	93,675	30.4	−5.9	50,916	26.5	4.7	42,759
	2002	103,751	30.9	10.8	48,518	24.3	−4.7	55,233
Travel	2000	46,019	15.2	7.4	97,402	50.9	−4.4	−51,383
	2001	46,362	15.1	0.7	96,057	49.9	−1.4	−49,695
	2002	58,855	17.5	26.9	96,846	48.5	0.8	−37,991
Insurance services	2000	3,452	1.1	12.6	4,111	2.1	−17.4	−659
	2001	3,556	1.2	3.0	4,028	2.1	−2.0	−472
	2002	3,421	1.0	−3.8	4,618	2.3	14.6	−1,197
Financial services	2000	20,859	6.9	8.6	5,536	2.9	−3.4	15,323
	2001	21,823	7.1	4.6	5,242	2.7	−5.3	16,581
	2002	19,564	5.8	−10.4	4,876	2.4	−7.0	14,688
Merchanting and other trade-related services	2000	97,616	32.3	19.7	11,170	5.8	6.3	86,446
	2001	106,447	34,6	9.0	11,802	6.1	5.7	94,645
	2002	115,996	34.6	9.0	14,660	7.3	24.2	101,336
Other services	2000	34,355	11.4	15.8	24,695	12.9	13.7	9,660
	2001	35,794	11.6	4.2	24,408	12.7	−1.2	11,386
	2002	33,826	10.1	−5.5	30,158	15.1	23.6	101,336
All services	2000	301,813	100.0	13.7	191,543	100.0	4.1	110,270
	2001	307,657	100.0	1.9	192,453	100.0	0.5	115,204
	2002	335,412	100.0	9.0	199,676	100.0	3.8	135,736

Source: www.info.gov.hk.

Notes:

1. Figures for exports of travel services have incorporated the new data released by the Hong Kong Tourism Board in November 2003 on destination consumption expenditure of incoming visitors and travellers. For details, please refer to the feature article "Statistics on Inbound Tourism" in the December 2003 issues of the *Hong Kong Monthly Digest of Statistics*.

2. The sum of individual items and the corresponding total shown in the table may not tally because of rounding.

and their clothes were tailored. After the completion of such labour intensive work in China, the dolls were shipped back to Hong Kong for final testing, inspection, packaging, transportation and distribution. So, while the front and back ends of the value chain were taken care of in Hong Kong, the middle portion was performed in China.

Once Li & Fung understood the benefits of dispersed manufacturing and gained expertise in it, the company extended its network beyond southern China. It moved into the inner parts of China, where wages were even lower. Li & Fung also began searching for other labour intensive and potential sources of supply outside China and established a strong global network of suppliers by the late 1990s. Soon, the concept of 'dispersed manufacturing' spread to other industries in Hong Kong, which led to the transformation of Hong Kong from a manufacturing economy into a service economy. By 1997, 84% of Hong Kong's gross domestic product[4] came from services (See Exhibit 2 and Exhibit 3 for Hong Kong's Trade Statistics).

[4]GDP is used to measure the growth and health of an economy and is defined as the total market value of all final goods and services produced in a country in a given year, equal to total customer, investment, and government spending, plus the value of the total exports, minus the value of total imports.

| Exhibit 3 | Hong Kong's External Trade Performance |

			% Change	
	2003 (HK% Mn)	2004 JAN–MAY (HK$ Mn)	03/02	04/03 J–M
Overall				
Domestic Exports	121,687	44,668	−7	1
Re-exports	1,620,749	713,531	13	16
Imports	1,805,770	816,918	12	19
Total Trade	3,548,206	1,575,117	12	17
Balance	−63,334	−58,719	8	99
Total Exports—Major Markets				
All Markets	1,742,436	758,199	12	15
China	742,544	334,450	21	18
U.S.A.	324,215	122,950	−3	5
E.U.	231,033	98,469	12	13
Japan	94,003	41,241	12	13
Singapore	35,704	16,866	13	27
Taiwan	42,269	20,334	22	23
Rep. of Korea	35,526	18,054	17	29
Total Exports—Major Products				
All Products	1,742,436	758,199	12	15
Electronics #	732,653	332,023	20	23
Clothing	180,357	65,408	3	5
Electrical Products #	192,485	88,524	13	21
Textile Yarn & Fabrics	101,923	45,067	5	9
Toys & Games	75,008	22,538	1	−3
Footwear	44,755	17,874	−1	−3
Watches and Clocks	41,903	17,237	9	8
Travel Goods & Handbags	32,070	14,333	*	12
Plastic Articles	23,872	9,309	−8	−6
Food	15,404	5,597	−8	−7
Jewellery	22,231	9,794	17	21

(continued)

| Exhibit 3 | Hong Kong's External Trade Performance—Continued |

	2003 (HK% Mn)	2004 JAN–MAY (HK$ Mn)	% Change 03/02	% Change 04/03 J–M
Re-exports—with China				
Total Re-exports	1,620,749	713,531	13	16
To China	705,787	321,126	23	19
Of China Origin	967,104	418,816	12	16
Imports—End-use Categories				
Total Imports	1,805,770	816,918	12	19
Foodstuffs	53,439	22,747	−3	8
Consumer Goods	573,926	235,109	5	9
Raw Materials	654,452	319,439	17	27
Fuels	35,398	18,026	13	28
Capital Goods	481,081	218,494	12	18

\# Overlap with other products   *Insignificant

Source: http://stat.tdctrade.com.

Meanwhile, owing to maturing markets, intense competition and changing consumer trends, many companies in the Western countries were compelled to outsource not only their manufacturing, but the entire supply chain management (SCM), to reap time and cost benefits. Li & Fung, with its extensive sourcing depth and network, grew from a deliverer of production programmes into a potential manager of supply chains for companies looking for optimum SCM.

Li & Fung described SCM as 'tackling the soft $3' in the structure—that is, if the price of a consumer product when it leaves a factory in China was $1, it would end up on retail shelves at $4. The company felt there was very little companies could do to further reduce production costs, as they had already exhausted all possible ways. It would be easier to cut on costs that were spread across distribution channels—i.e. the $3 (difference between the product price on retail shelves and price when it left the factory).

Li & Fung took its dispersed manufacturing technique further, dissecting the entire value chain and optimising every step of the chain, from product design and development, raw material sourcing, production planning, conducting quality assurance and factory inspections, managing production and logistics of exporting, timely delivery and complying with import and export quota restrictions, imposed by the buyer and seller countries, respectively. The company became a much broader intermediary by connecting and co-ordinating many links in the supply chain.

It made its services more valuable by delivering a better product, which translated into better price and margins for customers (See Exhibit 4 for Li & Fung's Supply Chain).

Global Supplier Network

When Li & Fung got an order from a customer, it sifted through its global supplier network (See Exhibit 5 for Li & Fung's Global Sourcing Network) to find the right manufacturer for the specific product and the most attractive combination of cost and quality. The company broke up its supply chain to disperse different production processes to manufacturers in various countries, based on factors such as labour costs, quality, trade barriers, transportation costs and so on. The company coordinated all processes in the value chain, managing the logistics and arranging the shipment of the finished order to the client. Li & Fung also ensured that suppliers complied with rules and regulations pertaining to environmental standards, child labour etc. in the importing countries (See Exhibit 6 for Li & Fung's Code of Conduct for Suppliers).

For instance, when Li & Fung got an order from Levis, a leading retail clothes chain in the US, with garment designs for the next fashion season, the company took the basic product concepts and researched the market to find the right kind of raw materials such as yarn, dye and buttons. The company then assembled the raw materials to create a prototype, which was sent to Levis for inspection. Once the

Exhibit 4   Li & Fung's Supply Chain

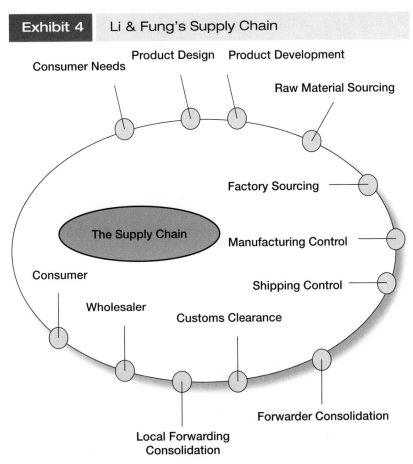

Source: Li & Fung Annual Report, 2003.

prototype was approved, Levis placed an order for the garments with Li & Fung, asking for delivery within six weeks.

Li & Fung immediately went to work—it distributed various tasks of the overall manufacturing process to different producers based on their capabilities and costs. It decided to purchase yarn from a Korean supplier but have it woven and dyed in Taiwan. The yarn was picked up from Korea and shipped to Taiwan. As the Japanese offered best quality zippers and buttons, which they got manufactured in China, Li & Fung approached the leading zipper manufacturer in Japan to order the right zippers from Chinese factories. Li & Fung decided to manufacture the final garments in Thailand, based on factors like quota availability and favourable labour conditions. It moved all the materials to Thailand. Since the order had to be fulfilled within six weeks, the order was divided across five factories in Thailand. Li & Fung ensured that within the scheduled date of delivery, the finished products, all looking as if they came from one factory, arrived at Levis retail stores.

Efficient SCM also addressed the problem of obsolete inventory, a major area of concern for fast-moving consumer goods (FMCG) companies, which were consumer-driven. FMCG companies preferred buying closer to the market as it shortened the buying cycle and gave them more time to get a better sense of the changing needs and preferences of consumers. Such quick changes led to shorter product cycles and the problem of obsolete inventories went up significantly. This was where Li & Fung's global SCM expertise was useful, as it aimed at buying the right things at the right place, at the right cost and quality.

The Scm Strategy

To ensure shorter product delivery cycles, Li & Fung managed the whole supply chain of its customers. To shrink the delivery cycle, the company reached upstream to organize production and ensured small production runs, which resulted in improved response time for retailers, enabling them to alter production in tandem with market trends. For

Exhibit 5	Li & Fung's Global Sourcing Network

EUROPE & THE MEDITERRANEAN	THE AMERICAS	NORTH ASIA
Amsterdam	Boston	Beijing
Bucharest	Guadalajara	Dalian
Cairo	Guatemala City	Dongguan
Denizli	Managua	Guangzhou
Florence	Mexico City	Hepu
Huddersfield	New York City	Hong Kong
Istanbul	San Francisco	Huizhu
Izmir	San Pedro Sula	Liuyang
London	Santo Domingo	Longhua
Oporto		Macau
Tunis	SOUTHEAST ASIA	Nanjing
Turin	Bangkok	Ningbo
	Hanoi	Qingdao
SOUTH ASIA	Ho Chi Minh City	Seoul
Amman	Jakarta	Shanghai
Bahrain	Makati	Shantou
Bangalore	Phnom Penh	Shenzhen
Chennai	Saipan	Taipei
Colombo	Shan Alam	Tokyo
Delhi	Singapore	Zhanjiang
Dhaka		Zhongshan
Karachi	SOUTH AFRICA	
Lahore	Durban	
Mumbai	Madagascar	
Sharjah	Mauritius	

Source: Li & Fung Annual Report, 2003.

Exhibit 6	Li & Fung's Code of Conduct for Suppliers

Li & Fung (Trading) Limited Code of Conduct ("Code of Conduct") outlines the basic requirements on working conditions that must be satisfied by all vendors ("Vendors") to principals of Li & Fung (Trading) Limited ("Li & Fung"). Li & Fung and its principals can supplement these requirements at any time.

Child Labour: Vendors shall not use child labour. A "Child" is defined as a person who is not older than the local age for completing compulsory education, but in no event is less than 15 years old. Vendors must verify the age of their workers and maintain copies of proof of age. Vendors must follow all applicable laws and regulations regarding working hours and conditions for minors.

Involuntary Labour: Vendor shall not use involuntary labour. "Involuntary Labour" is defined as work or service extracted from any person under threat or penalty for its non-performance, and for which the worker does not offer himself or herself voluntarily. It includes prison, bonded, indentured and forced labour.

Disciplinary Practices: Vendors shall not use corporal punishment, any form of physical or psychological coercion or intimidation against workers.

Non-discrimination: Vendors shall employ workers solely on the basis of their ability to do the job. They shall not discriminate on the basis of age, gender, racial characteristics, maternity or marital

Exhibit 6	Li & Fung's Code of Conduct for Suppliers—Continued

status, nationality or cultural, religious or personal beliefs in relation to hiring, wages, benefits, termination or retirement.

Health and Safety: Vendors shall maintain a clean, safe and healthy workplace in compliance with applicable laws and regulations. They shall ensure that workers have access to clean drinking water, sanitary washing facilities and adequate number of toilets, fire-extinguishers and fire exits. Workplaces should provide adequate lighting and ventilation. Vendors shall ensure that these standards are also met in any canteen and/or dormitory provided for workers.

Environmental Protection: Vendors shall comply with all applicable laws and regulations to protect the environment and maintain procedures for notifying the local authorities in the event of an environmental accident resulting from the vendors' operations.

Wages and Benefits: Vendors shall provide wages and benefits that comply with all applicable laws and regulations or match prevailing local manufacturing or industry rates, whichever is higher. Overtime pay shall be calculated at the legally required rate, regardless of whether workers are compensated hourly or by piece rate.

Working Hours: Vendors shall not require workers to work, including overtime, more than 60 hours per week or more than the maximum number of hours per week set by applicable laws and regulations, whichever is less. Vendors shall guarantee that workers receive at least one day off during each seven-day period.

Freedom of Association: Vendors shall respect the right of workers to associate, organize and bargain collectively in a legal and peaceful manner.

Familiarization and Display of this Code of Conduct: Vendors shall familiarize workers with this Code of Conduct and display it, translated in the local language, at each of their facilities in a place readily visible and accessible to workers.

Legal Requirements: Vendors shall comply with all legal requirements applicable to the conduct of their businesses, including those set out above.

Contractors and Suppliers: Vendors shall ensure that their contractors and suppliers adhere to this Code of Conduct.

Monitoring of Compliance: Vendors authorize Li & Fung and its principals to conduct scheduled and unscheduled inspections of vendors' facilities for ensuring compliance with the Code of Conduct. During these inspections, Li & Fung and its principals have the right to review all employee-related books and records maintained by vendors and to interview workers.

Corrective Action: When violations are found, Li & Fung and the vendor concerned will agree on a corrective action plan that eliminates the problem in a timely manner. If it is determined that a vendor is knowingly and/or repeatedly in violation of this Code of Conduct, Li & Fung and its principals shall take appropriate corrective action. This may include cancellation of orders and/or termination of business with that vendor.

Source: www.lifung.com.

instance, Li & Fung got to know that Levis would order 1 mn pieces of garments, but did not have specific details of style or colours. This would be disclosed only four weeks before delivery was due. Under these circumstances, Li & Fung, based on trust and its strong relationship with suppliers, reserved un-dyed yarn and locked up capacity at mills for weaving and dying. It told suppliers that they would receive an order for a specific size and colours, six days before delivery. Then the company intimidated factory owners, stating that it did not know product specifications yet, but it had organized the colours, fabric and trim for them and

they should deliver the order on a specific date, say two weeks from the raw materials arriving at their factories.

Having a vast network of suppliers enabled Li & Fung to configure activities as if they were modules in a process. For instance, a South Korean yarn provider might be appropriate for a product line, but an Indonesian supplier who used different raw materials and production technology might be a better choice for the needs and preferences of a specific customer. Li & Fung assembled the right modules for each job, customizing value chain solutions for its clients. Such flexible modules also meant that the company could quickly change its plans if there were unforeseen problems at the manufacturing site. The company could tap its worldwide network and send the order to another company to avoid delays in order fulfillment. For example, Li & Fung quickly shifted production from high-risk countries to lower-risk countries following the September 11, 2001 terrorist attacks in the US.

A major supplier management strategy of Li & Fung was to utilize anywhere from 30% to 70% of factory capacity of suppliers, ensuring that at such a capacity, the company would be one of their important customers. Most times, Li & Fung would be their largest customer. Li & Fung also ensured that it did not use up the entire capacity of any manufacturer, to give itself flexibility. It did not want manufacturers to be completely dependent on the company. This strategy also enabled the company to gain exposure to new suppliers.

To improve suppliers' performance, Li & Fung managers, based on their interactions with them, provided a detailed performance feedback to each supplier, mentioning strengths and weaknesses. Faltering suppliers were dropped from a project or from the company's network if they failed to improve. According to analysts, as Li & Fung offered many economic incentives to suppliers, they willingly customized their own operations to fit Li & Fung's supply chain strategy. The major benefits to suppliers were substantial and steady business from Li & Fung and the opportunity to improve their performance, as the company set detailed benchmarks across its entire process network and gave all partners valuable insights into their specific strengths and weaknesses. It also helped them address performance gaps.

To further strengthen its supplier network, Li & Fung constantly looked out for new suppliers. The company evaluated the experience and skills of each prospect to determine whether its operational standards could be met. By the early 2000s, Li & Fung had an extensive network of over 7,500 regular suppliers, each on an average having about 200 employees. Li & Fung described itself as a smokeless factory. Though it did not own any manufacturing concern, it was involved in various functions that qualified it as a manufacturer.

Customer-Centric Organizational Structure

Li & Fung had an organizational structure that masked its size. In line with the transformation of the company's business strategy during the 1980s, Li & Fung revamped its organizational structure to manage its global sourcing network better and meet customer needs. The company discarded its traditional structure of geographic division as it found inefficiencies in this. During this period, all large trading companies in the world with vast supplier networks were organized geographically with country units as profit centres. Such a structure made it tough for the companies to optimise the value chains for their customers, as the country units competed against each other for business. The lack of co-operation and co-ordination among country units also resulted in loss of customers, affecting a company's business.

To eliminate this, Li & Fung adopted a new customer-centric structure, where it organized itself into various small customer-centric divisions.[5] Under the new structure, an entire division focused on serving a big customer such as The Limited, Levis, Kohl's and Abercrombie & Fitch. A single division aimed at fulfilling the needs of a group of smaller customers, with similar needs. For example, the company's theme-store division served a group of customers like Warner Bros. stores chain and Rainforest Café. According to company sources, this new model assisted them in creating a customized value chain for each customer order.

As part of its customer-centric strategy, Li & Fung created small divisions dedicated to serving one customer, and a person managing the unit as if it was his/her own company. Li & Fung hired people who were entrepreneurial in nature and whose ultimate aim was to run their own business. Thus, each division was run by a lead entrepreneur, designated as division manager, who was responsible for understanding customers' needs and fulfilling them by mobilizing resources from the group's sourcing and process network. For instance, the Gymboree division, which served Gymboree, a leading US-based clothing store, was headquartered in a separate office within the Li & Fung building in Hong Kong. It had 40 plus employees focused on meeting Gymboree's needs. The division was further broken up into specialized teams in areas such as technical support, raw material purchase, quality assurance, merchandising and shipping. Apart from the employees at its head office, the division also had dedicated sourcing teams across the branch offices of Li & Fung in China, Indonesia and Philippines, the countries from where the division purchased in high volumes.

These divisions also promoted knowledge sharing during their interactions with customers, which benefited customers. Commenting on this, Frank Leong (Leong), CFO

---

[5] In 2002, Li & Fung had about 120 business divisions across 40 countries.

and Head of the Operation Support Group (OSG), Li & Fung, said, "Our people sit down to share with them the latest information from the production side—what sort of material is hot, what new colours are available, where a product can be produced."[6] Such discussions not only expanded the fashion retailers' knowledge, but also gave them scope for more creativity and financial liberty in designing garments for a season. If required, the divisions also offered trade financing services to customers, through Letters of Credit (L/C).[7]

To preserve the entrepreneurial spirit, Li & Fung kept each division relatively small, with average revenues ranging between HK$ 30 mn and HK$ 50 mn. The company allowed each division to act as an independent unit with its own customers and profit and loss accounts. Li & Fung gave considerable freedom to division managers to run their divisions, as it believed that autonomy would encourage a free spirit. To further ensure the commitment of division managers, Li & Fung tied up their compensation to their division's bottom line. To motivate them to achieve their division's targets, the company gave out substantial financial incentives. Reportedly, Li & Fung did not fix any ceilings on bonuses. The company followed the same policy of performance based compensation and incentives for other employees too.

Li & Fung provided the divisions with all necessary financial resources and administrative support, mainly through the OSG, which provided back-end support to the entire group operations. The OSG supplied all divisions with personal computers and network connections, at a charge per PC, which covered the entire network including order processing, production tracking and e-mail communication. These charges were paid from the division's revenues.

The OSG also acted as an in-house HR provider, as it supplied recruitment services by internally matching staff from across various divisions, to meet some specific requirements of clients, and training them. It also acted as the divisions' chief banker as all divisional revenues finally went to the OSG. According to company sources, the divisions could take loans from the OSG at an interest rate cheaper than the market rate.

The OSG's performance was measured against its profit and loss account as was the case of any other division in the group. According to Leong, such a performance measurement strategy ensured that the OSG provided advanced high quality services to its customers (other divisions) and at the same time optimised its costs.

The logic behind such an organizational structure was to allow each division to function like an independent company without worrying about back-end needs. Such a model provided the group with the flexibility of a small company, while having the strengths of a large, global company. As Leong said, "We're marrying the strength of being small and big together. Big companies tend to get bureaucratic, while small companies can do specialized products. Our small business units act extremely fast, but at the back-end, they get the level of service of a huge company"[8]

However, while Li & Fung believed in flexibility in some things, the company was highly conservative when it came to financial control and operating procedures. These were centralized and tightly managed. Li & Fung also maintained tight control over its working capital. All cash flows were centrally managed through headquarters in Hong Kong. For instance, L/Cs from all divisions came to headquarters for approval and were then reissued. The company also had a standardized and fully computerized order executing and tracking system used by all divisions.

Leveraging It and the Internet

To leverage the potential of IT, Li & Fung took many initiatives through the mid 1990s. It tied up its global network of offices with intranet[9] since 1995, to enable free information flow. In 1998, the company began creating dedicated extranet[10] sites for major customers. These sites enabled the company to interact with customers, track their orders, help in product development and perform many other tasks in a cost efficient manner. The extranet also enabled customers to track their orders and gain access to related information through Li & Fung's Electronic Trading System, known as XTS, which was linked to Li & Fung's global network of offices.

---

[6]"Asset Lite," www.cfoasia.com, April 2002.

[7]A document, consisting of specific instructions by the buyer of goods, that is issued by a bank to the seller who is authorized to draw a specified sum of money under certain conditions, i.e., the receipt by the bank of certain documents within a given time. A confirmed L/C is one issued by a foreign bank, which is validated or guaranteed by a Hong Kong bank for a Hong Kong exporter in the case of default by the foreign buyer or bank.

[8]"Asset Lite," www.cfoasia.com, April 2002.

[9]An intranet is a restricted-access network that works like the Internet. Usually owned and managed by a corporation, an intranet enables an organization to provide content and services to its employees across its various divisions, without allowing external people to view it.

[10]An extranet is an Internet site that is offered to a select group of people such as customers, suppliers and business partners, usually to provide or share non-public information.

The major benefits of a dedicated extranet site can be understood from the following example. In the late 1990s, Coca-Cola, the leading soft drinks company, and many of its independent bottlers worldwide largely relied on merchandize tied to sporting events to promote the company's core brand, 'Coca-Cola.' As Coca-Cola was mainly a beverage company, with no exposure to manufacturing, the company found managing the manufacturing activity (for its merchandise) expensive and outside its area of core expertise. The company also feared that its manufacturing process might be too slow to respond to sporting and entertainment events. As a result, in March 2001, the company turned to Li & Fung for managing its manufacturing activities. Li & Fung designed and built an extranet site, called Kodimsum.com ('KO' for Coke's stock symbol, and dimsum for a Hong Kong food delicacy), enabling Coca-Cola's executives and bottlers to place online orders. The extranet also allowed bottlers to check orders placed by other bottlers of the company, enabling them to place a similar order if they found that the product would be useful in their own markets.

With the emergence of the Internet as a major communication medium, industry observers felt it would make trading companies like Li & Fung redundant. Li & Fung opposed this view, stating that the key to its business was not hardware but information and its application to the management of client supply chains. The company believed that instead of being a threat, the Internet and e-commerce would offer more opportunities by helping it drive supply chain costs down and integrating management of supply chain via IT. Analysts too felt that this was true. They said that the real value of Li & Fung's business model lay not just in its ability to link suppliers and buyers, but in its power to influence suppliers and manufacturers, with whom the company had a strong relationship of trust.

Thus, Li & Fung used the Internet as a tool to make supply chains more transparent. When Li & Fung received an order from a customer, it used extranet sites and the Internet to fine-tune specifications. It then took instructions from customer and fed the information on to its intranet to find the right raw material suppliers and right factory or factories to assemble the product. The Web also aided customers in quickly assessing shifting consumer demands. Thus, as an order moved through different phases of production, customers could make last-minute changes through Li and Fung's website, which hosted real-time information on the entire production process.

This real-time tracking by customers was not possible until the mid-1990s, when Li & Fung began using phone and fax. For instance, when a customer ordered 50,000 khaki cargo pants, the company delivered the pants five months later,

leaving the customer with little chance of altering their orders in line with changing market trends. By the early 2000s, once the web-based communication system was established, customers could cancel their order until the time the material was woven, change the colour till the fabric was dyed and alter design or size, until the fabric was cut.

In March 2000, Li & Fung announced its Internet strategy to enter the e-commerce market, through its Business-to-Business (B2B) initiatives. Li & Fung aimed at creating economies of scale and scope for small and medium-sized enterprises by bundling their orders for the same products and then customizing the mass-produced product to meet the requirements of each customer.

Commenting on this, William said, "Li & Fung has done private-label manufacturing for a long time. We can only do this if the customers are very large and they have the scale, since you need intensive interaction when you do private-label work. To capture economies of scale, we need large customers, not small ones. . . . What the Internet does is allow us to reach the small and midsize guys we could never reach before. What do they want? What the big guys have— a private label, their own differentiated line, and at the same price as the big guys. . . . The Internet allows us to reach those people—without intensive interaction—and to aggregate their orders. We can allow you different style, limited customisation using American yarn, knitted in China, assembled in Bangladesh. And we can allow you to put in your own label, embroidery, colours, packages, boxes. We can reap the economics of mass production, but with enough customisation."[11]

As part of Li & Fung's Internet strategy, StudioDirect Inc. was formed in April 2000, as an e-commerce subsidiary of the company (57% controlling stake) with an investment of US$19 mn. StudioDirect's website, www.studiodirect.com, launched in March 2001, allowed placement of highly individualized orders from small and medium sized retailers, enabling them to choose from a wide variety of fabrics, colours and accessories such as cuffs, pockets, buttons and embroidery. According to Li & Fung sources, StudioDirect had customisation options that could satisfy 90% of the smaller retailers.

StudioDirect aggregated all orders placed on its website and put them on to Li & Fung's manufacturers, resulting in a series of private-label lines ready for delivery. To handle the logistics needed to deliver finished goods to retailers across the world, StudioDirect tied up with Danzas AEI Intercon-

[11]"A Different Kind of B2B Play in China?" www.businessweek.com, May 08, 2000.

tinental, a business division of the Danzas Group, which specialized in logistics services and had already worked with Li & Fung.

Reportedly, StudioDirect was capable of beginning production within six hours of receiving an order from a client over the Internet. For marketing its B2B initiative, the company chose the strategy of direct mailing. Through this, the company aimed at reaching about 1,000 small and medium sized retailers in the first year and expected to do business of $2 mn with each of them, in the next five years. The initiative was launched in the US in early 2001.

Analysts felt that Li & Fung, with its sound global sourcing network and strong financials (US$ 270 mn in cash reserves) was poised to establish itself as a strong player in the B2B market place. Commenting on what Li & Fung could provide small and medium size customers with, Barnett, a Goldman Sachs' analyst, said, "A large company that uses Li & Fung typically pays 4% to 12% of the value of the order [because of economies of scale]. It's about 30% for a small company. Those costs come down to 4% to 12% if clients use the studiodirect.com Internet site."[12]

In the early 2000s, Li & Fung maintained Internet-based communication with all its major customers worldwide. About 75% of them were large retailers in the US, who reaped significant benefits from the transparent SCM attained due to the use of IT and the Internet.[13] Laurence H. Alberts, managing partner, Mercer Management Consulting (Asia), said, "They (Li and Fung) are the leaders in Asia in providing this full solution of sourcing and supply-chain management. They've built up a very considerable barrier to anyone else trying to replicate it."[14]

Global Expansion

During the late 1990s, with the growing popularity of private label brands, shortening product life cycles and acute competition in the retailing industry, companies had to focus on their supply chain processes. As many companies did not have expertise in SCM and outsourcing was a cost-efficient alternative, the demand for companies that offered SCM services increased. Li & Fung, which already had an impressive sourcing network and SCM expertise, increased

efforts to position itself as a global consumer goods trading company. The company devised an acquisition strategy to strengthen its position in the global trading market. The strategy aimed at expanding the sourcing network, product lines and customer base.

In 1995, Li & Fung acquired Inchcape Buying Services (also known as Dodwell) from Inchcape Pacific, a leading British trading conglomerate. That company had an established network of offices in South Asia, the Mediterranean and Caribbean regions, where Li & Fung had little or no presence. The acquisition nearly doubled the size and geographic reach of Li & Fung and brought with it a vast European customer base that complemented Li & Fung's strength in North America. The acquisition also contributed significantly to the company's success in achieving its three year plan (1995–98) target of doubling its profits from HK$ 225 mn in 1995 to HK $455 mn in 1998.

As a part of its proximity strategy, which aimed at producing products closer to the customer market (North America and Europe), Li & Fung began establishing and expanding its sourcing networks in regions such as the Mediterranean, Eastern Europe, North Africa, South Africa and Central America in the late 1990s.

In December 1999, Li & Fung acquired Swire & Maclaine and Camberley Enterprises, the trading businesses of the Hong Kong-based group, Swire Pacific, for HK$ 450 mn. While Swire & Maclaine was a major provider of product sourcing and quality assurance services in Hong Kong, Camberley Enterprises made high-quality ladies sportswear, ready-to-wear garments and home accessories. These acquisitions offered Li & Fung design process expertise and helped it further strengthen its customer base in the US and Europe, by adding some major customers like Laura Ashley and Ann Taylor. As Swire & Maclaine had been a major competitor of Li & Fung in Hong Kong, its acquisition helped Li & Fung further consolidate its business in Hong Kong and strengthened its position as one of the world's leading sourcing and supply chain management companies.

In November 2000, Li & Fung announced the acquisition of Colby Group Holdings Limited; a Hong Kong based leading consumer goods trading company, for HK$ 2.2 bn to consolidate its global competitive position further and helped it emerge as the largest consumer goods export trading groups in Hong Kong. Commenting on the rationale behind the acquisition, William said, "Colby has strong brand recognition, especially among US department stores. Its seasoned staff and diversified sourcing capabilities will complement our existing business. With this acquisition,

---

[12]"Picking Asian Winners in the Internet Age," www.asiaweek.com, 2000.

[13]However, in countries such as China, Bangladesh, Philippines, Africa and Caribbean, where communication systems are still under developed, Li & Fung relied on personal visits, phones, faxes and couriers to communicate information and manage operations.

[14]"Middleman Become Master," www.chiefexecutive.net, October 2002.

we will be able to expand our customer base and further penetrate what is an important new market segment."[15] Even after the acquisition, Colby continued to operate under its own company name, as a subsidiary of Li & Fung.

In the early 2000s, Li & Fung focused its acquisition strategy on hard goods companies. In mid 2002, Li & Fung acquired Janco Overseas, a Hong Kong-based buying agent, specializing in hard goods, for HK$ 249.6 mn. According to company sources, the acquisition was expected to increase Li & Fung's turnover by HK $1.4 bn. Reportedly, Janco's strengths in the hard goods segment and focus on large food retailers, who were rapidly expanding their non-food offerings, was expected to strengthen Li & Fung's position in the hard goods segment. It was also expected to open up new customer segments and opportunities on account of expansion in its hard goods product portfolio.

In the fiscal year 2002, the hard goods segment accounted for 32% of Li & Fung's revenues compared to 28% in 2001. The segment registered a 29% increase in revenues and 70% in operating profits over 2001. Li & Fung sources said the acquisition of Janco was a major factor that contributed to such a significant growth in its hard goods business.

In August 2003, Li & Fung announced plans to purchase the remaining one-third stake in the group's New York based garment importer unit, International Sourcing Group (ISG), for US$ 5.22 mn, from ISG's chief executive, Alan Chartash, who owned that stake. The acquisition was expected to increase Li & Fung's profitability. Victor said, "By further leveraging the group's financial resources, management strength and entrepreneurial corporate culture, it is envisaged that a more comprehensive service will be provided to ISG's customers."[16]

During the early 2000s, Li & Fung focused on expanding its customer base in non-US markets to balance the group's overall revenue portfolio, which was highly skewed towards the US. It concentrated on the fast developing economies in Asia and the Southern Hemisphere, where more and more companies were outsourcing manufacturing and SCM on account of increasing globalization and resulting competitive pressures that were forcing companies to optimize resources.

Li & Fung identified Japan as a potential market, where the fashion retailing business was booming. In October 2003, Li & Fung entered into an alliance with Nichimen Corporation (Nichimen), a leading general trading firm in Japan, to offer higher value for Japanese retailers. This was possible due to the integration of Li & Fung's global sourcing network with Nichimen's customer servicing capabilities.

In December 2003, Li & Fung acquired the sourcing business of the Hong Kong-based Firstworld Garments Limited and the US-based International Porcelain Inc. for US$ 27 mn. These two companies would together operate under the name "International Sources." They were expected to strengthen Li & Fung's presence in the hard goods business and enable it to reach out to Mexico.

The Challenges

By the end of 2003, Li & Fung emerged as one of the few global consumer goods trading companies with geographical flexibility and depth of expertise required for success in the fiercely competitive business environment of the early 21st century. In the fiscal year ending December 31, 2003, the group's revenues amounted to HK$ 42.6 bn, a 14.3% rise over HK$ 37.3 bn in 2002. Net profits amounted to HK$ 1.22 bn in fiscal 2003, a 13.2% increase over the HK$ 1.08 bn in fiscal 2002. In December 2003, the share price of Li & Fung was quoting around HK$ 13 (See Exhibit 7 for Li & Fung's Five-Year Stock Price Chart).

However, according to company sources, revenues and profits were below expectations. The Iraq War,[17] the SARS epidemic,[18] and poor business performance in the holiday season of some major customers were cited as reasons. The drop in the group's non-trading income also had an unfavourable effect on overall financial results. Reportedly, the net loss from Li & Fung's venture capital business amounted to HK$ 8 mn in the fiscal 2003.

---

[17]The US government believed that Osama Bin Laden led terrorist organization, Al-Qaida, which was responsible for the September 11, 2001, terrorist attacks on the World Trade Centre in the US may obtain weapons of mass destruction (WMD) from Iraq. As Iraq was ruled by Saddam Hussein (Hussain), who was openly hostile to the US, the US officials considered it a severe threat to the country's security, and felt the need for pre-emptive war against Iraq to prevent further damage from occurring in the US. In March 2003, the US declared war against Iraq (the second war, the first being in January 1991), called 'Operation Iraqi Freedom,' aimed at freeing Iraq from the ruling Hussain government and gaining control over the WMD. The war ended in May 2003, following the capture of Tikrit, the birthplace of Hussain. Hussain was captured by the US army in December 2003.

[18]According to www.cdc.gov, Severe Acute Respiratory Syndrome (SARS) is a viral respiratory illness caused by a corona virus called the SARS associated corona virus (SARS - CoV). The first case of SARS was reported in Asia in February 2003. Within a few months, the illness spread to more than 24 countries throughout the world. The outbreak of SARS in the Asian region severely damaged its economic performance—the hardest-hit business was the region's tourism industry.

[15]"Li & Fung to Acquire Colby," www.irasia.com, November 09, 2000.

[16]Li & Fung to Buy Out Last Stake of US Unit, Hong Kong iMail (China), August 20, 2003.

Exhibit 7	Li & Fung's Five-Year Stock Price Chart (August 1999–July 2004)

Source: www.prophet.net.

That year, the soft goods segment accounted for 67% of Li & Fung's total revenues, while hard goods accounted for the remaining 33%. Geographically, North America continued to be the company's largest export market, accounting for 75% of its total revenues. It was followed by Europe (19%), East Asia (3%) and the South Hemisphere (3%). As part of achieving its three year plan (2001–04) goal of doubling profits by the fiscal 2004, Li & Fung announced that it would continue its aggressive acquisition drive, focused at non-US companies, and new product lines that could open up more revenue opportunities.

In August 2003, Li & Fung finalized a licensing agreement with Levis, under which the former would design, manufacture and market clothing under the latter's Levi Strauss Signature label. According to company sources, these products would be marketed in the US by late 2004. In early 2004, Li & Fung also signed similar licensing deals with Official Pillowtex LLC, a US-based company that owned the Royal Velvet linen brand. Commenting on these deals, William said, "Leveraging our strong position in the supply chain, we are building a higher-margin business model of licensing well-known brand names. This new business model will augment our core sourcing business and will be an important growth driver for the group in our next three-year plan for 2005–2007."[19]

By mid 2004, Li & Fung had an extensive network of over 65 offices in 40 countries worldwide, managed by a dedicated employee base of over 6,000. Reportedly, the company faced very little competition, which analysts attributed to its unique positioning as a supply chain manager for its clients and its focused acquisition strategy. William E. Connor & Associates (WEC&A), an American-owned, Hong-Kong-based trading company, was the closest competitor to Li & Fung in Hong Kong as textiles was WEC&A's major product line. But, as WEC&A focused on large department store customers, and Li & Fung concentrated on specialty store chains, analysts felt that competition between them was not intense (See Exhibit 8 for a note on Hong Kong's Export Trade Industry).

[19]"Hong Kong Li & Fung Posts 13% Net Profit Rise on Sales Growth," www.prophet.net, March 24, 2004.

| Exhibit 8 | A Note on Hong Kong's Export Trade Industry |

The Export Trade Industry:

Hong Kong has always been one of the world's major export trade centres. Until the 1970s, Hong Kong was a manufacturing economy, supplying the world with textiles, handbags, toys, plastic flowers, watches and footwear. Most of its exports were to the US and Europe. After the Chinese economy was liberalized in 1979 (initially only some coastal regions were opened up for foreign investors) many companies across all the major industrial segments and trading companies in Hong Kong moved the labour-intensive part of manufacturing to China.

The rapid industrialization of Asian countries from the 1980s resulted in expansion of production capabilities in the manufacturing sector and related supporting services especially in other low cost countries like Taiwan and Korea. This in turn led to trading companies expanding their sourcing reach beyond China to optimise sourcing costs for their clients. By the late 1990s, Hong-Kong emerged as a service economy with 84% of GDP derived from services. According to a survey by the Hong Kong Trade Development Council (TDC) in 1998, 64% of international buyers sourced China-made products through trading companies in Hong Kong. The country's strategic location, good physical infrastructure, expertise in international trade and well-established legal framework made trading reliable, simple and convenient. By the turn of the 20th century, Hong Kong became one of the world's largest export trade countries.

In 2001, Hong Kong earned HK$ 106 bn from exporting trade-related services, accounting for 32.7% of total services exports. In 2002, one in five employed persons in Hong Kong were engaged in the import-export trade. The sector produced a net output of HK$ 249 bn and accounted for 21% of Hong Kong's GDP. In 2002, there were more than 1,133 companies involved in the wholesale, retail and import and export trade businesses.

In the early 2000s, off shore export trading was increasing rapidly on account of many factors. The use of advanced technology, sophisticated production processes and on-site inspections by trading firms eliminated the need for further processing of products like final assembly, packaging and imposing quality control procedures. At the same time, the increased availability of cost-effective and reliable transport services contributed to the rise in off shore export trade. Some expected changes in the regional trade regimes including the China-ASEAN Free Trade Agreement and the Closer Economic Partnership Arrangement (CEPA) between Hong Kong and mainland China were expected to further boost the trading industry in Hong Kong.

In 2003, Hong Kong was the world's freest and 10th largest trading economy. It was a major trading centre with total merchandize trade amounting to US$ 457 bn, equivalent to 289% of GDP for that year. Major exports included clothing, electrical machinery, apparatus, textiles, jewellery, insurance services, financial services, transportation and travel services. In 2003, Hong Kong earned US$287.9 bn from exporting goods and services. Major export trading partners included mainland China (39.3%), US (21.3%), Japan (5.4%) and the UK (3.5%). With trading volumes of such magnitude, Hong Kong became a leading sourcing hub in the Asia-Pacific region in the early 21st century.

Export Trading Firms in Hong Kong:

Export trading firms in Hong Kong can be divided into three categories:

Left Hand-Right Hand Traders: Traditional trading firms that matched sellers and buyers but did not add significant value. These firms identified goods produced in Hong Kong or neighbouring countries and shipped them to their customers.

Traders with some value-added services: These firms, apart from sourcing raw material for their customers, offered some additional value such as providing trade finance and freight forwarding services.

Traders with sophisticated value-added services: These exporting firms went beyond traditional trading services. Additional services included product designing and development, manufacturing prototypes, offering supply chain management services, undertaking distribution and delivery of finished goods.

Exhibit 8	A Note on Hong Kong's Export Trade Industry—Continued

Hong Kong's export trading firms source garments, toys, electronic items and other manufactured goods. The sourcing activities are of three types:

- Sourcing goods produced in Hong Kong.

- Sourcing goods from the Asian region for re-export from Hong Kong.

- Sourcing goods from one country for direct shipping to another country, without touching Hong Kong. This is called offshore trade.

Trading firms in Hong Kong usually specialize in one product. In most cases, they offer shipping services to customers and manage their own warehousing facilities. Such facilities enable exporters of durable goods to offer better customer service, as a certain quantity of stock is always readily available for shipment. For goods like textiles, trading firms use temporary storage, with emphasis placed on prompt dispatch for shipping.

Most export trading firms in Hong Kong are closely involved in manufacturing activities, though indirectly, as actual production is usually sub-contracted. Short production cycles, a preference for smaller quantities of more product lines and keeping tight deadlines ensured that companies met customer needs. They provided supplier factories with advanced production techniques and know-how and helped solve production bottlenecks.

Profile of William E. Conner & Associates (Li & Fung's Major Competitor)

William E. Conner & Associates (WEC&A) was founded in 1949 in Tokyo and moved to Hong Kong in 1985. It is one of the major export trade companies in Hong-Kong in the early 21st century and the closest competitor to the market leader, Li & Fung, in the consumer goods trading market. WEC&A optimised the supply chain for its clients by managing every aspect of sourcing, right from product design & development to distribution and delivery of the finished product. The company's products included apparel, fabrics, fashion accessories, footwear, decorative accessories, textiles, house ware, furniture, lighting, office products, stationery and fashion-related products.

In the early 2000s, WEC&A had a global network of 35 offices in 20 countries. With an employee base of over 1,400, the company fulfilled the requirements of over 70 customers, which included leading department stores, specialty stores, catalogue companies, e-commerce retailers and importers, mainly in North America, Australia, Europe, Latin America and Japan. In 2002, WEC&A's net worth amounted to US$ 850 mn.

Source: www.tdc.trade.com & www.weconnor.com.

While Li & Fung's business model might seem error free and its future bright, analysts were quick to point out that every business had its negative side and Li & Fung also had made miscalculations. They said the company's much hyped B2B initiative "StudioDirect," had failed to get the expected response, forcing Li & Fung to restructure its operations. In 2002, Li & Fung converted StudioDirect from a full-service e-commerce company into a private label golf-wear specialist, offering services to customers through the Internet. The company also reduced its stake in StudioDirect from 57% to 15%. Li & Fung attributed this restructuring to changes in market conditions in the US, which were not conducive to the growth of StudioDirect's business. It stated that it was still committed to e-commerce and its aim was to reach smaller and mid-sized retailers. However, even by

early 2004, StudioDirect had failed to make major progress on this front.

The continuous fall in the annual growth of revenues and profitability through the early 2000s was also perceived as an area of concern by many analysts (See Exhibit 9 for Li & Fung's Seven Year Financial Summary). While Li & Fung registered a high growth in revenues and profit after taxation of 53.35% and 49% respectively, for the fiscal year ending December 31, 2000, the growth in revenues and profit after taxation came down to 14.35% and 12.06% respectively by the fiscal 2003. Analysts felt that the sharp decline in the share of overall revenues derived from European markets, during the early 2000s, was not a good sign for the company. They felt the company had failed to come up

Exhibit 9 Li & Fung—Consolidated Statements of Income (1997–2003)

Year Ending December 31	2003 HK$'000	2002 HK$'000	2001 HK$'000	2000 HK$'000	1999 HK$'000	1998 HK$'000	1997 HK$'000
Continuing operations	42,630,510	37,281,360	32,941,392	24,992,227	16,297,501	14,312,618	13,345,722
Discontinued operations	—	—	87,183	791	—	—	—
Total Turnover	**42,630,510**	**37,281,360**	**33,028,575**	**24,993,018**	**16,297,501**	**14,312,618**	**13,345,772**
Counting operations	1,285,952	1,134,605	904,520	830,223	592,885	469,501	361,289
Discontinued operations	—	—	(237,955)	(39,375)	—	—	—
Gross Profit	**1,285,952**	**1,134,605**	**666,565**	**790,848**	**592,885**	**469,501**	**361,289**
Interest income	38,373	49,581	112,837	140,330	43,830	56,093	37,772
Interest expenses	(9,813)	(8,987)	(12,464)	(20,585)	(32,243)	(61,346)	(6,270)
Share of profit less losses of associated companies	2,015	393	1,443	13,677	9,389	6,850	6,666
Profit before taxation	1,316,527	1,175,592	768,381	924,270	613,861	471,098	399,457
Taxation	(105,513)	(94,896)	(55,637)	(64,178)	(36,638)	(16,425)	(25,326)
Profit after taxation	1,211,014	1,080,696	712,744	860,092	577,223	454,673	374,131
Minority interests	12,104	(228)	69,567	10,296	(2,585)	495	974
Continuing operations	1,223,118	1,080468	951,307	893,118	574,638	455,168	375,105
Discontinued operations	—	—	(168,996)	(22,730)	—	—	—
Net Profit	**1,223,118**	**1,080,468**	**782,311**	**870,388**	**574,638**	**455,168**	**375,105**

Source: Li & Fung Annual Report, 2003.

with effective strategies to increase revenue share from the European market, which, next to the US, had immense potential for fashion goods, especially garments, Li & Fung's major business. They criticized Li & Fung for failing to build on the opportunities provided by its acquisition of Inchcape Buying Services, which had a strong presence in Europe.

Analysts also felt that Li & Fung's high dependence on large retailers, especially in the US and Europe, might prove a threat for the company in the long run, given the uncertainties in the retailing industry. They pointed out that a major consolidation in the North American retailing industry, Li & Fung's largest export market, might severely affect the company's business. For instance, if a retailing giant such as Wal-Mart, which rarely outsourced its manufacturing activities, acquired other major American retailers, or put them out of business, it could lead to an 8% to 10% cut in margins for Li & Fung. Such consolidation might also result in only a few large retailing giants surviving (with other companies either having been acquired or forced to quit) in the market, which might also have se-

vere implications on Li & Fung's revenues. This was because the company mainly derived its revenues from a large base of companies in US, with revenues of over US$ 100 mn.

Analysts further added that Li & Fung's hopes of benefiting from increased manufacturing activity in China to strengthen its competitive position in the US, after the removal of the quota system in January 2005, might fail. They were of the view that according to WTO rules, the US and Europe were entitled to impose 'anti-surge' quotas until the end of 2008, in case they felt any threat to domestic industry from exports. Anti-surge quotas restricted annual growth of imports from a country to 7.5% per product category. Analysts also said that it was very likely that the anti-surge quotas would come into existence in 2005.

Despite these challenges, industry observers felt that with Li & Fung focusing on expanding its customer base outside the US, especially in Asia, in the years to come the company could reduce its dependence on the US, its largest market. Meanwhile, Li & Fung had already achieved considerable success in lessening its dependence on soft goods over the years, reducing some risks in its business.

Media reports expressed optimism for Li & Fung's future. They wrote that the company, powered by its depth of sourcing knowledge and positioning as an efficient manager of global supply chains, was well poised for growth, in the light of increasing globalisation. An *Economist* article had quoted in 2001, "Li & Fung appears to have as bright a future as globalisation itself."[20]

Assignment Questions

The following questions can be given as an assignment to the students/executives. Each student/executive is supposed to write the answers individually and submit the same to the moderator/concerned faculty for evaluation.

1. Li & Fung owes much of its ongoing success to its expertise in global value chain configuration. Define the concept of value chain and critically discuss the importance of value chain management for global companies. How did Li & Fung use the value chain configuration in its globalization process?

2. According to John Mathews, a Professor of Management in Macquarie Graduate School of Management, Sydney; and the author of "*Dragon Multinational: A New Model for Global Growth*," Li & Fung is one of the first truly global companies. Describe the various stages in the globalization process. Examine the role played by alliances and acquisitions in a company's globalization strategy, with specific reference to Li & Fung.

3. William Fung believes that Li & Fung is an information and knowledge-based business. Discuss the importance of knowledge management for global companies. Describe the knowledge management initiatives typically taken by global companies and examine the implementation process of a knowledge management system at a company. Study Li & Fung's organizational structure and examine how such a structure enables efficient and effective knowledge management at the company.

4. According to William Fung, it has always been a policy at Li & Fung to embrace information technology (IT) in all aspects of the company's business to provide more value added services to its customers worldwide. Critically comment on the importance of IT for global companies. How did Li & Fung use IT to enhance its global competitiveness?

[20]"Li & Fung: Optimising Supply Chain for Other Companies," The Economist, May 31, 2001.

Suggested Additional Readings and References

1. **Li & Fung Reports Profit Growth on Track,** www.irasia.com, August 15, 1997.
2. **Li & Fung Reports Continued Profit Growth,** www.irasia.com, August 26, 1998.
3. Joan Magretta, Victor Fung, **Fast, Global, and Entrepreneurial: Supply Chain Management, Hong Kong Style: An Interview with Victor Fung,** Harvard Business Review, September/October 1998.
4. **Li & Fung Maintains Strong Track Record,** www.irasia.com, March 29, 1998.
5. **The Ever-Spending Tentacles of Hong Kong,** http://fox.rollins.edu, June 18, 1998.
6. **Cash-Rich Li & Fung Keeps $ 500 mn for New Acquisitions,** Hong Kong Standard (China), May 19, 1999.
7. **Did You Know You Were Buying Li & Fung?** www.forbes.com, June 09, 1999.
8. Tanzer Andrew, **Stitches in Time,** www.forbes.com, June 09, 1999.
9. **Improved Margins Boost Li & Fung Interim by 23pc,** Hong Kong Standard (China), August 19, 1999.
10. Ng Ada, **Li & Fung's Group Managing Director William Fung Kwok-lun,** Hong Kong Standard (China), December 30, 1999.
11. **The Old and the New: Li & Fung Looks Like an e-Commerce Winner,** www.asiaweek.com, 2000.
12. **E-Companies to Watch,** www.asia.com, 2000.
13. **Li & Fung Maintains Strong Growth,** www.irasia.com, March 27, 2000.
14. **A Different Kind of B2B Play in China?** www.businessweek.com, May 08, 2000.
15. **Winning at a Global Game: Part Five of an Eleven Part Series,** www.asiabusinesstoday.org, June 10, 2000.
16. **Li & Fung Powering Ahead at the Half,** www.irasia.com, August 17, 2000.
17. **Fung Brothers Increase their Shareholding of Li & Fung Limited,** www.irasia.com, September 06, 2000.
18. **E-engineering the Business Models in Asia,** www.weforum.org, September 12, 2000.
19. Wong Eunice, **Li & Fung to Source for Disney,** Hong Kong iMail (China), September 19, 2000.
20. **Taking Control from Start to Finish,** www.tdctrade.com, October 2000.
21. **Li & Fung Sets to Buy M&S Sweater Supplier for $ 566 m,** Hong Kong iMail (China), October 17, 2000.
22. **Li & Fung to Acquire Colby,** www.irasia.com, November 09, 2000.

23. **Li & Fung Acquires Colby Group for HK$ 2.2 bn,** http://asia.internet.com, November 11, 2000.

24. Tam Jonathan, **Acquisition Drive Lifts Profit 51pc to $ 870 mn,** March 27, 2001.

25. **Li & Fung Sustains Strong Growth on Track to Achieve Three-Year Plan,** March 26, 2001.

26. **Streetwalker,** www.forbes.com, May 03, 2001.

27. **Li & Fung: Optimising Supply Chain for Other Companies,** Economist, May 21, 2001.

28. **Li & Fung: Link in the Global Chain,** Economist, June 02, 2001.

29. **Furiously Fast Fashions,** The Industry Standard, June 11, 2001.

30. **StudioDirect: In Search of a Sourcer's Apprentice,** www.glscs.com, July 2001.

31. **Colby Allows Li & Fung to Boost Profits 15pc,** Hong Kong iMail (China), August 21, 2001.

32. **Caught in the Middle,** www.asiaweek.com, October 12, 2001.

33. **Li & Fung Allies with Nichimen for Market Expansion in Japan,** www.lifung.com, October 31, 2001.

34. **Cut Loose from Old Business Processes,** www.optimizemag.com, December 2001, Issue 2.

35. **Hong Kong's Oldest Trading Company, Remains at the Global Cutting Edge,** www.tdctrade.com, 2001.

36. Wong Foster, **Slump Takes Toll on Trading Giant,** Hong Kong iMail (China), March 22, 2002.

37. **Asset Lite,** www.cfoasia.com, April 2002.

38. **Li & Fung Partners with Microsoft to Further Enhance the Connectivity of the Trading Firm's Global Supply Chain System,** www.lifung.com, July 08, 2002.

39. **Li & Fung Defies Downturn,** Hong Kong iMail (China), August 16, 2002.

40. **Loosening up: The Bottom Line Benefit,** http://news.com.com, August 17, 2002.

41. **Loosening up: How Process Networks Unlock the Power of Specialization,** www.euractiv.com, September 18, 2002.

42. **Hooking up Suppliers,** www.idg.com.sg, September 2002.

43. **Middleman Becomes Master,** www.chiefexecutive.net, October 2002.

44. **Leveraged Growth: Expanding Sales without Sacrificing Profits,** Harvard Business Review, October 2002.

45. **Apparel Globalization: The Big Picture,** www.apparelmag.com, January 01, 2003.

46. **Analysts Agree on 32.6pc Earnings Rise at Li & Fung,** Hong Kong iMail (China), March 20, 2003.

47. **War-Wary Li & Fung Sees Profit Rise 38pc,** Hong Kong iMail (China), March 25, 2003.

48. **The Private Label Supply Chain,** Apparel Magazine, June 2003.

49. **Lucky Li & Fung in Levi Strauss Deal,** www.thestandard.com, August 15, 2003.

50. **Li & Fung to Buy Out Last Stake of US Unit,** Hong Kong iMail (China), August 20, 2003.

51. **Hong Kong Shares Close Higher,** Xinhua (China), September 23, 2003.

52. **Levi's Pillowtex Deals Worth Billions to Li & Fung,** www.thestandard.com, January 09, 2004.

53. **Easy Access for HK, Macao Traders,** www2.chinadaily.com.cn, January 09, 2004.

54. **First Hong Kong Trading Firm to Gain Chinese License,** www.hktrader.net, February 2004.

55. **Import and Export Trade,** www.tdctrade.com, April 16, 2004.

56. **Executive Speeches: China and the Supply Chain, by Dr. Victor K. Fung,** http://pressroom.ups.com, April 29, 2004.

57. **Li & Fung Signs New Licensing Agreement with Levi Strauss & Co,** www.lifung.com, June 24, 2004.

58. **Made by HK – Local Companies Move up the Value Chain,** www.hktrader.net, June 30, 2004.

59. **HK Textile Firms See Gains from Quota Scrapping,** http://finance.lycos.com, July 05, 2004.

60. **China Gets Set to Cloth America when Quota End,** http://news.ft.com, July 20, 2004.

61. **Li & Fung Annual Reports 1997, 1998, 1999, 2000, 2001, 2002 and 2003.**

62. www.lifung.com.

63. http://cgfair.com

64. http://cf.heritage.org.

Case 8

Update: The Music Industry in 2006

9-707-531

February 27, 2007

John R. Wells
Elizabeth A. Raabe

Introduction

The global recorded music industry was undergoing a major transition in 2006. Sales had been declining for a decade and consumers were buying music in new formats and through different channels. CD sales still accounted for 86% of U.S. recorded music sales in 2005, but sales revenues had decreased 20% since 2000. (See Exhibit 1.) On the other hand, digital music purchases—such as single track and album downloads, subscriptions, mobile phone ringtones, and music videos—were growing significantly. Only 1.5% of U.S. recorded music sales in 2004, digital had reached 4% in 2005, and looked to exceed 7% in 2006. The International Federation of the Phonographic Industry (IFPI) antici-

HARVARD BUSINESS SCHOOL

Professor John R. Wells and Research Associate Elizabeth A. Raabe prepared this case. This case was developed from published sources. HBS cases are developed solely as the basis for class discussion. Cases are not intended to serve as endorsements, sources of primary data, or illustrations of effective or ineffective management.

pated that digital sales would account for more than 25% of worldwide industry revenues by 2010.[1] Meanwhile, big box retailers such as Wal-Mart and Best Buy were becoming increasingly important purveyors of recorded music. These shifts were causing the specialty retail base to shrink. Tower Records, formerly one of the leading music retailers in the United States, filed for bankruptcy in 2006 claiming in court papers, "The brick-and-mortar specialty music retail industry has suffered substantial deterioration recently."[2]

Many considered digital the future of the music business but the format posed both opportunities and challenges. While it had revitalized the singles market, for instance, digital had also facilitated rampant piracy. The industry estimated it lost $4.5 billion in revenues from piracy in 2005, and that nearly 20 billion audio files were downloaded illegally.[a] One research source estimated that 26% of the decrease of CDs units in 2005 in the U.S. was replaced by music obtained through illegal file-sharing.[3] The music industry was retaliating, launching lawsuits against illegitimate peer-to-peer operators such as Kazaa and large groups of people, such as college students, caught downloading illegally. Whether this would be enough to stop the trend was a matter of much debate.

Meanwhile, the industry was continuing to consolidate. In 2004, Sony Music and BMG, the third- and fifth-largest record firms at the time, merged to form Sony BMG. Surprisingly, in 2006 the European Union's Court of First Instance annulled the merger—which the European Commission had approved two years earlier—after a group of

---

[a] Approximately 37% of all CDs purchased worldwide in 2005 were pirate copies, according to the IFPI.

569

Exhibit 1	U.S. Manufacturers' Unit Shipments (in millions) and Dollar Value (In Millions, Net After Returns), 1995–2005

	1995	1996	1997	1998	1999	2000	2001	2002	2003	2004	2005
PHYSICAL											
CD (unit shipments)	723	779	753	847	939	943	882	803	746	767	705
(dollar value)	9,377	9,935	9,915	11,416	12,816	13,215	12,909	12,044	11,233	11,447	10,520
CD Single	22	43	67	56	56	34	17	5	8	3	3
	111	184	273	213	222	143	79	20	36	15	11
Cassette	273	225	173	159	124	76	45	31	17	5	3
	2,304	1,905	1,523	1,420	1,062	626	363	210	108	24	13
Cassette Single	71	60	42	26	14	1	-2	-1	N/A	N/A	N/A
	236	189	134	94	48	5	-5	-2	N/A	N/A	N/A
LP/EP	2	3	3	3	3	2	2	2	2	1	1
	25	37	33	34	32	28	27	21	22	19	14
Vinyl Single	10	10	8	5	5	5	6	4	4	4	2
	47	48	36	26	28	26	31	25	22	20	13
Music Video	13	17	19	27	20	18	18	15	20	33	34
	220	236	324	508	377	282	329	288	400	607	602
DVD Audio	—	—	—	—	—	0	0	0	0	0	1
	—	—	—	—	—	0	6	9	8	7	11
SACD	—	—	—	—	—	—	—	—	1	1	1
	—	—	—	—	—	—	—	—	26	17	10
DVD Video	—	—	—	1	3	3	8	11	18	29	28
	—	—	—	12	66	80	191	236	370	561	540
Total Units	1,113	1,137	1,063	1,124	1,161	1,079	969	860	798	814	749
Total Value	12,320	12,,534	12,237	13,711	14,585	14,324	13,741	12,614	11,854	12,155	11,195
DIGITAL											
Download Single	—	—	—	—	—	—	—	—	—	139	367
	—	—	—	—	—	—	—	—	—	138	363
Download Album	—	—	—	—	—	—	—	—	—	5	14
	—	—	—	—	—	—	—	—	—	46	136
Kiosk	—	—	—	—	—	—	—	—	—	—	1
	—	—	—	—	—	—	—	—	—	—	1
Music Video	—	—	—	—	—	—	—	—	—	—	2
	—	—	—	—	—	—	—	—	—	—	4
Total Units										144	383
Total Value										183	504
Mobile	—	—	—	—	—	—	—	—	—	—	170
	—	—	—	—	—	—	—	—	—	—	422
Subscription	—	—	—	—	—	—	—	—	—	—	1
	—	—	—	—	—	—	—	—	—	—	149
TOTAL DIGITAL & PHYSICAL											
Total Units	1,113	1,137	1,063	1,124	1,161	1,079	969	860	798	958	1,302
Total Value	12,320	12,534	12,237	13,711	14,585	14,324	13,741	12,614	11,854	12,338	12,270
Real GDP Index	100	106	112	118	125	133	137	142	148	158	168

Source: Recording Industry Association of America (RIAA), 2005 Year-End Statistics, http://www.riaa.com, accessed January 2007.

independent music labels complained about the merger's effect on competition. While Sony and BMG were defending the merger in court, EMI Group plc wondered if its desired takeover of Warner Music Group—which it had been pursuing since 2000—would ever happen.[4] If it did, how much business would the new entity have in the rapidly changing environment? All wondered how the industry would evolve.

The Majors

By 2006, approximately 72% of the global market for recorded music rested in the hands of the four "majors": EMI Group plc, Sony BMG Music Entertainment, Universal Music Group, and Warner Music Group.[5] (See Exhibit 2.)

UNIVERSAL MUSIC GROUP

With a 26% global share of the recorded music market, Universal Music Group (UMG) was the leading music major, having attained that position in 1998 by acquiring PolyGram, the world's largest record firm at the time. UMG generated $6.2 billion in revenues in 2006, $599 million of which was from digital channels.[6] UMG was a subsidiary of French telecommunications conglomerate Vivendi, which generated $24.3 billion in revenues and $2.6 billion in net income in 2006.[7]

UMG's recorded music division signed artists, recorded their music, and sold CDs and digital downloads; the company also had a music publishing division that actively sold the rights to use its catalog of music for advertisements, live performances, films, computer games, karaoke, etc. UMG had a 13% share of the music publishing business, and was number three in the world. It planned to grow the

division and had purchased BMG's music publishing unit in December 2006.

The company had recently outsourced its manufacturing by selling its CD and DVD production unit to Glenayre Technologies. Glenayre manufactured the majority of UMG's CDs and DVDs in North America and Europe.[8]

SONY BMG MUSIC ENTERTAINMENT

In 2004, Bertelsmann A.G. and Sony Corporation of America established the 50-50 joint venture Sony BMG Music Entertainment (Sony BMG), becoming the second largest major in the industry. Whether the merger would be allowed to stand was still uncertain in 2006. With a combined market share of 20%, Credit Suisse analysts noted the scale benefits that would accrue to the new entity. Furthermore, Sony BMG had a strong artist roster, producing 20 of the top 50 albums in 2004. The analysts also reported, "Cost reductions as a result of the merger are supporting better-than-expected profit growth."[9]

However, Sony BMG faced challenges. Its management team was equally composed of executives from Sony and Bertelsmann, and there was dissention among the members regarding the direction of the firm. In addition, the company faced a hailstorm of negative publicity and lawsuits when an attempt to combat piracy backfired. Some of Sony BMG's CDs had been loaded with hidden antipiracy software which installed itself on computers to monitor consumers' behavior and prevent them from illegally copying the disks. The software acted like spyware and posed security problems, and when individuals tried to remove it, it damaged their CD-ROM drives. The situation went from bad to worse when a patch that Sony issued to combat the problem created greater security breaches than the original software.[10] In late 2006,

Exhibit 2	Financial Statistics for Recording Industry Majors (In $ Millions), 2005/2006			
	EMI	Sony BMG	Warner Music	Universal Music
Year End	3/31/2006	3/31/2006	9/30/2006	12/31/2005
Total Sales	3,618	4,283	3,516	6,091
EBITDA	402	556	518	946
Operating Income	358	336	283	598

Source: Compiled from Hoover's, Inc., http://www.hoovers.com; William B. Drewry, Global Music Industry: "Just the Two of Us," Credit Suisse, June 19, 2006, pp. 48, 51, via Thomson Research/Investext; and Warner Music Group, 2006 Annual Report (New York: Warner, 2007).

the firm settled with nearly all U.S. states to pay $5.75 million to resolve the situation; it also placed claims forms on its website, offering to reimburse consumers' computer repair expenses associated with the removal of the software.[11]

EMI GROUP PLC

By 2006, EMI Group plc was the world's third largest record company with revenues of $3.6 billion annually.[12] The firm was composed of two divisions. *EMI Music* produced artists' recordings in various formats (e.g., CD and digital) and sold them into the retail trade. It accounted for 80% of the company's total revenues and had a 13.1% share of the global market in 2005, up from 12.9% in 2004. *EMI Music Publishing*, the largest music publisher in terms of revenues, handled the rights to over one million songs and had a 20% share of the music publishing market.[13]

EMI produced the world's best selling albums in 2003 and 2005, Norah Jones's *Come Away With Me* and Coldplay's *X&Y*. However, its share of the top 50 trailed the other majors. The company's biggest challenge, according to Hoover's, was "to build a more robust stable of artists and generate more hit album releases."[14] It had replaced the head of its Virgin Records label with the former chief of Atlantic Records to help accomplish this aim.

Digital sales represented 5.4% of EMI's 2005 revenues—a 139% increase over the previous year—and it was striving to sell more of its music through digital channels. The firm noted in its 2006 annual report: "We currently have relationships with almost 400 digital partners for products and services ranging from a la carte audio and video downloads to ringtones, ring tunes, subscription and legalized peer to peer services."[15]

In mid-2006, Warner rejected EMI's takeover offer of $4.2 billion. Warner subsequently made a counter-offer for EMI for $4.6 million but it also was rebuffed. Like the other majors, EMI had outsourced its manufacturing by 2006.

WARNER MUSIC GROUP

U.S. media conglomerate Time Warner sold Warner Music Group (WMG) in 2004; the firm went public the following year. WMG boasted 29 of the 100 U.S. best-selling albums of all time, including the number one album, *The Eagles: Their Greatest Hits 1971–1975*.[16] By 2006, WMG had a 12% market share of the recorded music business and a 16% market share of the music publishing business.[17]

Like the other music majors, WMG was increasingly focused on effectively selling its wares through digital channels. Sales of digital music products (e.g., ringtones, music videos, downloaded single tracks and albums) accounted for approximately 10% of the firm's total revenues in 2006, up from 4% in 2005. WMG added bonus tracks, music videos, and "behind the scenes" footage to its digital albums and sold these premium-priced album bundles on websites such as Apple's iTunes. The firm had formed partnerships with leading mobile companies in China, Korea, and Russia to take advantage of opportunities presented by the growing mobile music arena.[b] It had also established deals with websites YouTube and Google to share advertising sales related to the streaming of its music videos.[18]

Credit Suisse analysts noted the firm's strengths included its strong artist roster (e.g., Enya, Madonna, and the Red Hot Chili Peppers)[c], management acumen (Chairman and CEO Edgar Bronfman had been an executive at Vivendi Universal), and its cost-cutting program—the firm had decreased its cost base by $250 million since it split with Time Warner.[19] The company had outsourced its manufacturing and distribution in 2003 to Canadian firm Cinram, which continued to produce and distribute WMG's products.[20]

Music Retail Channels

BRICK-AND-MORTAR ESTABLISHMENTS

Music specialty retailers were facing intense competition from big-box retailers such as Wal-Mart and online stores such as Apple's iTunes. (See Exhibit 3.) Tower Records had succumbed and filed for bankruptcy, and other players such as Virgin Megastores and HMV also faced financial woes in the face of decreasing sales. According to market research firm NPD, Wal-Mart was the top retailer of music in the U.S in 2005, in terms of units sold. (See Exhibit 4.) Big-box retailers' strategies included stocking only the top titles—Wal-Mart stocked 5,000 CDs; Tower carried 60,000—and actually taking a loss or accepting a very small margin on CDs to drive store traffic.[d] Music sales at Wal-Mart ac-

---

[b]Credit Suisse analysts estimated that online purchases (e.g., downloads and subscriptions) accounted for 51% of global digital sales and mobile purchases the remainder.

[c]The analysts noted, however, that the firm had decreased its artist roster by 30% since 2004.

[d]Wal-Mart also sold songs online for 88 cents each. It recently began offering custom CDs on its website as well, charging $4.62 for the first three songs and 88 cents for each additional song (up to 20 songs total). Customers chose the CD's name and cover design and could have the product mailed to their homes or they could pick them up in the store in one hour. Wal-Mart, "Create a Customer CD," http://www.walmart.com/catalog/catalog.gsp?cat=197184, accessed February 2007.

Exhibit 3	Music Sales by Type of Outlet in the United States (% of Total Dollar Sales)									
	1996	1997	1998	1999	2000	2001	2002	2003	2004	2005
Record store	49.9	51.8	50.8	44.5	42.4	42.5	36.8	33.2	32.5	39.4
Other store	31.5	31.9	34.4	38.3	40.8	42.4	50.7	52.8	53.8	32.0
Total stores	81.4	83.7	85.2	82.8	83.2	84.9	87.5	86.0	86.3	71.4
Tape/record club	14.3	11.6	9.0	7.9	7.6	6.1	4.0	4.1	4.4	8.5
Mail order	2.9	2.7	2.9	2.5	2.4	3.0	2.0	1.5	1.7	2.4
Internet	N/A	0.3	1.1	2.4	3.2	2.9	3.4	5.0	5.9	8.2
Digital Download	N/A	N/A	N/A	N/A	N/A	N/A	N/A	N/A	N/A	6.0
Concert	N/A	N/A	N/A	N/A	N/A	N/A	N/A	N/A	1.6	2.7

Source: Recording Industry Association of America (RIAA), 2005 Consumer Profile, http://www.riaa.com/news/marketingdata/purchasing.asp, accessed January 2007.

Note: Totals many not add up to 100% due to 'don't know/no answer' responses.

Exhibit 4	Top 10 Music Retailers in the U.S., Q3 2005
Rank	Retailer
1.	Wal-Mart (1)
2.	Best Buy (2)
3.	Target (3)
4.	Amazon.com (4)
5.	FYE (10)
6.	Circuit City (Tied for 5)
7.	Apple/iTunes (14)
8.	Tower Records (Tied for 7)
9.	Sam Good (Tied for 5)
10.	Borders (9)

Source: The NPD Group, Inc., "iTunes Music Store Cracks Top 10 List of Leading Music Retailers in Q3 2005," November 21, 2005, http://www.npd.com/press/releases/press_051121a.html, accessed February 2007.

Note: NPD used an equivalency of 12 songs per album to establish a comparison between singles and physical CDs. The number in parentheses indicates each retailer's ranking in the third quarter of 2004.

counted for approximately 20% of major-label music sales.[e] *Rolling Stone* estimated that half of all major-label music was sold through Wal-Mart, Target, and Best Buy.[21]

ELECTRONIC RETAILERS

A number of Internet retailers were established in the late 1990s that offered music products digitally; in the intervening years, many failed. By 2006, nearly 500 legal online music sites offered four million songs to consumers in 40 countries.[22] A handful dominated the market in the U.S.

APPLE'S iTUNES MUSIC STORE   Apple launched the iTunes Music Store in 2003 as a complement to its portable digital music player, the iPod, which it had debuted in late 2001. In the subsequent years, Apple introduced new models of the iPod that were smaller and less expensive (e.g., the Mini, the Shuffle, and the Nano). In 2006, Apple had a 75% share of the U.S. portable audio player market, and analysts estimated that 18% of U.S. inhabitants and 1% of people globally owned an iPod.[23]

iTunes sold individual recorded music tracks for 99 cents as well as complete albums in digital format.[f] Apple, which licensed rights from the four major record firms to distribute their music, used a digital rights management (DRM) system to "envelop[e] each song purchased from the iTunes store in special and secret software so that it cannot be played on unauthorized devices."[24] iTunes customers could play their purchased music on up to five computers and on an unlimited number of iPods. iPod owners could transfer songs from their own CDs, which were generally unprotected and DRM-free, onto their iPods.[25]

The iTunes Music Store was the undisputed leader of legally downloaded music products. BusinessWeek Online reported,

---

[e]Music sales accounted for only 2% of Wal-Mart's total sales.

[f]iTunes added music videos, movies, television shows, audio books, and iPod games to its line-up of offerings.

"The iTunes Music Store . . . revolutionized how music was sold. If you doubt that statement, go visit your local Tower records store—if it's still open."[26] While it faced a host of competitors, iTunes commanded 88% of online music sales.[27] By the end of 2006, it was available in 22 countries and had sold 1.5 billion songs.[28]

Piper Jaffray analysts reported that Apple sold 390 million downloads during the first nine months in 2005 and 695 million songs during the same period in 2006.[29] A report by Forrester Research indicated that 3% of online households made an iTunes purchase in 2006 and that Apple sold approximately 20 iTunes songs for each iPod it sold.[30]

eMUSIC.COM eMusic.com was established in 1998 and was the first website to offer a general music subscription service which allowed customers to download an unlimited number of music files for $9.99 per month. After several years of operation, it started losing customers to newer services such as Apple's iTunes store. Hence, in 2004 it refashioned itself as a purveyor of independent music.[31] By 2006 eMusic had a 10% share of the online music market. On its website, it claimed to be the "world's largest retailer of independent music and the world's second-largest digital music retailer overall, offering more than 2 million tracks from more than 13,000 independent labels."[32] The site had modified its subscription service. Customers could download up to 30 songs for $9.99 per month, 50 songs for $14.99 per month, or 75 songs for $19.99 per month.

eMusic also noted on its website that it was "the only major digital service to deliver music in the universally [i.e., unprotected] MP3 format," allowing users to "burn as many CDs as [they] like and copy downloads to an unlimited number of computers and portable MP3 players, including the iPod." That is, none of the songs in its catalogue was protected by DRM.[33]

The company was seeking to expand its customer base by targeting those who mostly purchased physical CDs. At Borders stores, it offered a "prepackaged digital music in a box" which contained an informational booklet and a code for purchasers to use to download music on their computers.[34]

NAPSTER In 2003, music software firm Roxio purchased subscription-based service pressplay and merged it with the Napster brand, which it had also acquired in 2003.[8] Head-quartered in Los Angeles with offices in Frankfurt, London, and Tokyo, Napster licensed three million songs from major and independent record labels and offered users several different options for legally accessing music from its site. Its digital lineup included an advertisement-supported free service whereby users could listen to songs on a limited basis on the Web[h]; a subscription service that gave individuals access to music and music-related content without advertisements; Napster To Go, which allowed a subscriber to transfer songs to a portable music player (excluding an iPod) for $14.95 per month; and Napster Mobile, which proffered ringtones.[35]

Napster's aim was to move the four million users of its free service to subscription accounts, of which it had approximately 518,000.[36]

RHAPSODY Digital media firm Real Networks, Inc., acquired Rhapsody when it bought Listen.com, another subscription service which charged users a monthly fee, in 2003. By 2006, Rhapsody offered three membership subscription plans. It entered into a three-way partnership with number-two MP3 player manufacturer SanDisk and electronics retailer Best Buy. The former produced the Sansa e200R Rhapsody MP3 player, which was developed especially for Rhapsody, and Best Buy was promoting the device along with the Best Buy Digital Music Store, which was powered by Rhapsody.[37]

YAHOO! MUSIC UNLIMITED A Yahoo! executive in charge of the website's music division explained, "You've got to figure out a way to get that large base of consumers who right now think music should be free. . . . And you've got to figure out a way to monetize them."[38] In an attempt to do so, Yahoo! launched its Yahoo! Music Unlimited service for just $4.99 per month in 2005. The service allowed users to listen to unlimited amounts of music and, for an additional monthly fee, transfer files to portable music players (not including iPods); when the users stopped paying, the music would no longer play. In 2006, the basic service was available for $8.99 per month or $71.88 per year.[39]

The firm was also striving to integrate its music service with a number of cell phones and personal digital assistants.

ZUNE MARKETPLACE In November 2006, Microsoft launched its own portable digital music device—the 30-gigabyte Zune—for $249. Surprisingly, Microsoft did not make Zune compatible with its PlaysForSure software, which was used by most other digital music players (but not the iPod).

---

[8]In 1999, Northwestern freshman Shawn Fanning created the Napster website, which offered free software that allowed peer-to-peer music file sharing. It became hugely popular with millions of music-loving fans but was the target of several lawsuits by record companies since no royalties were paid on the copyrighted music shared via the site. Napster eventually filed for bankruptcy in mid-2002.

[h]Users could only listen to a song three times per month, and they could not copy them.

Inevitably, industry observers compared the device to the iPod, criticizing Zune for its heavier weight and shorter battery life but praising its for its larger screen, built-in FM radio, and Zune-to-Zune Wi-Fi communication feature which allowed users to share audio files with other users. (However, the shared files could only be played up to three times and expired after three days.)[40]

To complement Zune, Microsoft created the online Zune Marketplace where customers could purchase single tracks for 99 cents or a subscription plan (the Zune Pass) allowing them unlimited downloads for $14.99 per month.

The Digital Music Market and the Piracy Problem

In its *Digital Music Report 2007*, the International Federation of the Phonographic Industry (IFPI) reported that global digital music revenues doubled in 2006 to $2 billion. (See Exhibit 5.) In particular, the growth was driven by the popularity of single tracks available online; portable music players (e.g., iPods and music phones); and mobile formats such as ringtones, mastertones, ringback tones[i], and full

[i]Mastertones were ringtones that featured a song's original recording, and ringback tones were songs a caller heard while waiting for his or her call to be answered.

song mobile downloads. Record firms and Internet retailers were using a variety of business models, including advertising-supported services and subscription-based offerings, to meet customer demand and generate revenue. Record companies were also establishing deals with popular social network sites such as MySpace and YouTube to sell singles, albums, and music videos. Some independent artists had used these sites to digitally launch new albums.[41]

However, IFPI's chairman and CEO, John Kennedy, explained, "Digital music has not yet achieved its holy grail: growth has not offset the fall in CD sales. The recording industry's single greatest challenge is the widespread unauthorized availability of its product for free. Digital piracy and the devaluation of music content is a real threat to the emerging digital music business."[42]

In *The Recording Industry 2006 Piracy Report*, the IFPI detailed the music industry's efforts to contain piracy. Curtailing rampant CD piracy was an ongoing effort between the IFPI and law enforcement agencies around the globe.

Also, the industry was taking legal action against unauthorized online music distributors throughout the world. Many in the music industry were heartened by its triumph over leading peer-to-peer operator Kazaa, which the Australian Federal Court found guilty of copyright infringement. Kazaa paid $115 million to various record companies and agreed to disseminate music legally. The IFPI believed

Exhibit 5	Global Digital Music Market (in millions)		
	2005	2006	Change
Broadband lines	209	280	34%
Song catalogue online	2	4	100%
Single tracks downloaded	420	795	89%
Subscription service users	2.8	3.5	25%
Mobile subscriptions	1,817	2,017	11%
3G mobile subscriptions	90	137	52%
Portable player sales	84	120	43%

Source: IFPI, Digital Music Report 2007, p. 4, http://www.ifpi.org, accessed January 2007.

Note: Broadband lines = number of households with high-speed Internet connection

Song catalogue online = number of songs available for purchase online

Single tracks downloaded = number of individual songs purchased in digital format via the Internet

Subscription service users = number of individuals with a subscription plan to an online retailer such as eMusic

Mobile subscriptions = number of music subscriptions for cell phones

3G mobile subscriptions = number of music subscriptions for mobile phones with the advanced third generation mobile technology, which allowed users to quickly download singles and videos

Portable player sales = number of portable digital music devices (e.g., iPods) sold worldwide

that legal victories like those against Kazaa were making a palpable difference in the digital music business: "Victory over Kazaa in the courts was a major development in the evolution of a healthy legitimate market. The legitimate sector cannot compete on price with illegal sites that pay no royalties or copyright fees and so legal action is needed to clear a path for growth for such music services."[43]

Digital piracy was a formidable problem, however, and new forms such as mobile piracy were appearing. One industry observer noted, "The pirate market—if we considered that a market—would command better than 90% of the online marketplace."[44] The IFPI was calling for governments and ISPs (Internet service providers) to take bigger roles in the fight against piracy.

Some in the industry—including Apple's Steve Jobs[45]— argued that the majors should sell their music online in the unprotected MP3 format, i.e., without DRM. Their reasoning? Millions of songs were available on CDs already without copyright protection, DRM had not made a significant difference in the fight against piracy, and the available music would create greater interoperability among portable music devices and online music vendors, giving consumers greater flexibility. Some noted that the move would actually decrease Apple's power in the digital music arena.

While many executives in the industry were resistant to the proposal, some were testing it. For example, in late 2006 EMI's Blue Note Records label sold a single from jazz-pop singer Norah Jones's latest CD in MP3 format via Yahoo! Sony BMG and Warner Music Group had also made select singles available in MP3 format earlier in the year.[46]

Whether the majors would embrace the strategy and release more singles and even entire albums online in MP3 format remained to be seen. However, music firms, artists, retailers and the fans watched the direction the recorded music industry was headed with great interest.

Endnotes

1. IFPI, *Digital Music Report 2007*, http://www.ifpi.org, p. 3, accessed January 2007.
2. As quoted in "Tower Records Will Auction Its Assets," *The New York Times*, August 22, 2006, http://www.nytimes.com, accessed January 2007.
3. IFPI, *The Recording Industry 2006 Piracy Report*, http://www.ifpi.org, accessed January 2007.
4. "Review of the Year: Merger Glitches," *Music Week*, December 23, 2006, via ProQuest, ABI/Inform, http://www.proquest.com, accessed January 2007.
5. William B. Drewry et al., Global Music Industry: "Just the Two of Us," Credit Suisse, June 19, 2006, via Thomson Research/Investext, accessed February 2007.
6. Vivendi, "Vivendi Full Year 2006 Revenues Reach €20 Billion," January 31, 2007, http://www.vivendi.com/ir/download/pdf/CA%202006%20anglais.pdf, accessed February 2007.
7. Vivendi, Corporate—Group Profile, http://www.vivendi.com/corp/en/group/profile.php, accessed February 2007.
8. Hoover's, Inc., http://www.hoovers.com, accessed February 2007.
9. William B. Drewry et al.
10. Morgan O'Rourke, "The Great Anti-Piracy Debacle," *Risk Management* 53 (January 2006): 48.
11. Chris Walsh, "Sony BMG Settles," *Billboard*, January 6, 2007, p. 8.
12. Hoover's, Inc.
13. EMI Group plc, 2006 Annual Report (London: EMI, 2006).
14. Hoover's, Inc.
15. EMI Group plc, 2006 Annual Report.
16. Warner Music Group, 2006 Annual Report (New York: Warner, 2007), p. 1.
17. William B. Drewry et al.
18. Warner Music Group, 2006 Annual Report, pp. 2, 52.
19. William B. Drewry et al., p. 53.
20. Warner Music Group, 2006 Annual Report, p. 2.
21. Warren Cohen, "Wal-Mart Wants $10 CDs," *Rolling Stone*, October 12, 2004, http://www.rollingstone.com/news/story/6558540/walmart_wants_10_cds, accessed January 2007.
22. IFPI, *Digital Music Report 2007*, p. 4.
23. C. Eugene Munster and Michael J. Olsen, Apple Computer, Inc., Piper Jaffray, August 2006, p. 1, via Thomson Research/Investext, accessed January 2007.
24. Steve Jobs, "Thoughts on Music," Apple—Hot News, February 6, 2007, http://www.apple.com/hotnews/thoughtsonmusic/, accessed February 2007.
25. Ibid.
26. Arik Hesseldahl, "The Apple iPod Turns Five," BusinessWeek.com, October 23, 2006, http://www.businessweek.com/technology/content/oct2006/tc20061021_515771.htm?campaign_id=rss_tech, accessed February 2007.
27. Jefferson Graham, "Closed Systems Leave Song Buyers Out in the Cold," USA Today.com, October 16, 2006, http://www.usatoday.com/tech/products/2006-10-15-music-war_x.htm, accessed February 2007.

28. Carl Bialik, "A Research Report on iTunes Sales Becomes Shot Heard 'Round the Net," *The Wall Street Journal*, December 20, 2006.

29. Gene Munster and Michael J. Olson, Apple Computer, Inc., Piper Jaffray, December 13, 2006, p. 1, via Thomson Research/Investext, accessed February 2007.

30. Josh Bernoff and Remy Fiorentino, "Few iPod Owners Are Big iTunes Buyers," Forrester, December 6, 2006, http://www.forrester.com/Research/Document/Excerpt/0,7211,40858,00.html.

31. Hoovers, Inc.

32. eMusic.com, http://www.emusic.com/about/index.html?fref=700736, accessed February 2007.

33. Ibid.

34. Ethan Smith, "Can Anybody Catch iTunes?" *The Wall Street Journal*, November 27, 2006, via ProQuest, ABI/Inform, accessed February 2007.

35. Napster, http://www.napster.com, accessed February 2007.

36. Ethan Smith, "Can Anybody Catch iTunes?"

37. Ibid.

38. Quoted in Ethan Smith, "Can Anybody Catch iTunes?"

39. Yahoo! Yahoo! Music Unlimited, http://music.yahoo.com/ymu/default.asp?, accessed February 2007.

40. Carmen Fleetwood, "Microsoft's Zune Falls Off Sales Pace for Media Players," *The Wall Street Journal*, November 28, 2006, via ProQuest, ABI/Inform, accessed February 2007.

41. IFPI, *Digital Music Report 2007*, pp. 3, 4, 10, 12, http://www.ifpi.org, accessed January 2007.

42. Ibid., p. 4.

43. IFPI, *The Recording Industry 2006 Piracy Report*, p. 7.

44. Ethan Smith and Nick Wingfield, "In a Turnabout, Record Industry Releases MP3s," *The Wall Street Journal*, December 6, 2006, via ProQuest, ABI/Inform, http://www.proquest.com, accessed February 2007.

45. See Steve Jobs, "Thoughts on Music," Apple—Hot News, February 6, 2007, http://www.apple.com/hotnews/thoughtsonmusic/, accessed February 2007.

46. Ethan Smith and Nick Wingfield.

Case 9

Razorfish

1042-2587

Daniel P. Forbes
Carla Pavone

Two childhood friends, Jeff Dachis and Craig Kanarick, founded Razorfish in early 1995 as a specialized consulting firm offering sophisticated web technology and design services. Geographically, the firm began in a small, cramped office in an artistic neighborhood of downtown Manhattan in New York City, only a short walk from Wall Street. But in a figurative sense, the distance between the company's origins as a boutique start-up and its future as a global, publicly traded company could be measured in light years. In a span of just a few years, Dachis and Kanarick came to know the full measure of that distance, as they led Razorfish through the best and worst of what the Internet business had to offer.

During its first 5 years, Razorfish grew from two employees to over 1,300, from one location in New York to 15 locations in nine countries, and from zero to $268 million in annual revenues. In the second half of 2000, however, growth screeched

ET&P Founded at the dawn of the Internet industry in 1995, Razorfish's pioneering technology, marketing, human resource, and acquisition strategies enabled it to become a paragon of global success in just 5 years. In 2000 and 2001, it appeared that this success would be short-lived. Increased competition, declining demand, and an economic recession all combined to threaten Razorfish's future. This case chronicles the rise of Razorfish and the Internet industry, as well as the challenges presented by a changing industry and economic context. In the spring of 2001, Razorfish management faced options that appeared as either high-risk or highly distasteful.

Please send correspondence to: Daniel P. Forbes, tel.: 612-625-2989; fax: 612–626-1316; e-mail: dforbes@csom.umn.edu at the Carlson School of Management, University of Minnesota, 321 19th Avenue S.— Room 3-365 Minneapolis, MN 55455.

to a halt. The company was hit with a class-action shareholder lawsuit and booked a net loss of over $148 million.

By April 2001, Razorfish management faced wrenching decisions. Business had not improved in the first quarter. Cash flow was negative, even after painful fourth quarter 2000 layoffs. Management estimated that, at the current "burn rate," there was sufficient cash to carry the company for 5–10 months. By the release of first-quarter earnings on May 15, the continuing deterioration of Razorfish would become public information. Investors would be expecting an explanation and an action plan. In April 2001, chief executive officer (CEO) Jeff Dachis, chief operating officer (COO) Jean-Philippe Maheu, and their worldwide management team met to decide what to do. Each of their options was either high-risk or highly distasteful:

- They could retain their employees and offices around the world, while modestly cutting expenses and making a concerted push for new funding and new revenue.
- They could drastically shrink Razorfish by laying off additional employees and shedding unprofitable offices (to the degree allowed by law in various countries).
- They could attempt to sell Razorfish to a larger corporation.
- They could shut down the business completely (again within international legal constraints) and return the remaining cash, net of closing and severance costs, to investors.

Founding: A New Company in a New Industry

Jeff Dachis and Craig Kanarick grew up together in suburban Minneapolis and moved to the East Coast after high school. Although they fell out of touch for a while, both had interests at the intersection of art and technology. Dachis earned a master's degree in performing arts administration from New York University and had worked in arts management and in several media-related businesses. Kanarick, meanwhile, received a master's from the Massachusetts Institute of Technology Media Lab, a major center for the research and study of emerging technologies, and began work as a freelance consultant, becoming a recognized leader in the emerging technologies of digital media, or "new media." When the two met again in Manhattan in late 1994, they envisioned ways to commercialize the technologies with which Kanarick worked.

At the time that Dachis and Kanarick reconnected, a vibrant entrepreneurial community was developing in New York. While the growth of the Internet spawned clusters of start-ups in many large cities throughout the 1990s, the New York City "Silicon Alley" community was larger and better developed than most. Concentrated in lower Manhattan but extending throughout the New York City metropolitan area, Silicon Alley was already home to over 4,000 new media businesses generating nearly $4 billion in revenues (Coopers & Lybrand, 1996). In contrast with the more technically oriented communities that existed in some regions, Silicon Alley had a distinctly "content-oriented" character that drew upon the area's traditional strengths in publishing, media, advertising, and other cultural industries. Content of some sort played a role in many of the prominent firms that have emerged from Silicon Alley, such as advertising brokers Doubleclick and 24/7 Media, online communities theglobe and iVillage, and portal sites StarMedia and Juno.

In this context, Razorfish set out to provide "digital solutions" by integrating technology, strategy, and design. As Dachis later explained, Razorfish was not a dot-com, meaning that they did not generate revenue through a website. Instead, as he put it, Razorfish "sold shovels during the Gold Rush" by creating websites and development tools for both traditional organizations and the new dot-coms (J. Dachis, personal communication, August 2, 2004).

Dachis and Kanarick incorporated their new company in early 1995, choosing the name Razorfish at random from the dictionary. The company's first assignments were not lucrative but were highly visible. For example, they designed Time Warner's Pathfinder site for $20,000. This assignment came after Kanarick had conducted a speaking engagement at a Time Warner conference. Through capable, creative project execution combined with vigorous self-promotion, Razorfish began to pick up a steady stream of engagements as more large companies began to

focus on the Internet. Some of these early, high-profile projects included design development for Microsoft and America Online.

Early Razorfish: A High-Profile Boutique

Razorfish's early clients ranged from cultural institutions to small high-tech companies to Fortune 500 firms, many of which feared that they might miss the opportunities presented by the Internet. Sample engagements included a user interface incorporating wireless application protocol technology for Nokia, an open collaborative business environment delivering SAP AG's personalized enterprise resource planning software solutions, and a multiple digital channel strategy for NatWest Bank (Razorfish, 1999).

As a 1995 *New York Times* article put it,

> To fill the need, small studios are popping up around the country, like Avalanche Design and year-old Razorfish in New York . . . [The founders of Razorfish] offer what they call dynamic digital design, with navigational tools and the latest hot software. "We understand the technology," said Mr. Dachis, whose company designed Websites for Bankers Trust and Sony's Handycam division. "We eat and breathe it. With technology changing every six weeks I'm not sure the big companies or the ad agencies can compete at that pace" (Rifkin, 1995).

Despite its cutting-edge technology, Razorfish depended on a relatively traditional consulting business model. Razorfish attracted a workforce of highly educated, creative, and technically knowledgeable employees who utilized a common set of proprietary tools and processes. These employees would be shifted among engagements as projects were completed and new projects were initiated. Customers were typically billed for each project on a time-and-materials basis. However, unlike traditional strategy or technology consulting firms, whose engagements would often last for months or years, the projects of Razorfish and other new media firms typically lasted for only several weeks or months. Thus, while it might have been relatively easy for Razorfish to attract initial, small-scale projects, it was also necessary for them continually to refill the pipeline with additional projects from either new or existing customers.

To achieve this growth, Razorfish engaged in an unorthodox branding effort to differentiate itself from other Silicon Alley new media start-ups. As Jean-Philippe Maheu (who joined Razorfish in 1996 and became COO in 2000) later recalled,

"A company decides a branding strategy in various ways. [It might] decide that the work speaks for itself, that it will do the branding for you. That was not the decision [Razorfish] made at the time" (J.P. Maheu & B. Lord, personal communication, February 25, 2004). Instead, Razorfish drew wide attention by throwing high-profile parties, issuing blizzards of press releases, and publishing a series of white papers about the Internet. The Razorfish branding effort highlighted the firm's cutting-edge technological and artistic sensibilities along with an impression of marketing savvy. Dachis regularly invited journalists to visit the firm's offices, and the firm sought high-profile ways to apply its technology. In July 1997, e.g., Razorfish sponsored a web-based real-time illustrated diary of Spencer Tunick's "Naked States" project to photograph nudes in public settings in each of the 50 states.

Although aggressive public relations campaigns are often viewed as a substitute for substance, this was not the case for Razorfish. The company's strong branding efforts were also backed by technological prowess and a comprehensive methodology that reassured corporate clients. The company offered an integrated package of services including strategic consulting, information architecture and end-user interface design, and customized software development.

To deliver on its technological and marketing promise, Razorfish needed to attract top talent. Razorfish cultivated a strong cultural identity that appealed to young workers who were eager to learn and who possessed cutting-edge technology and design skills. This identity revolved around a sense of "hipness" that was intended to convey certain characteristics, such as creativity, intellectual curiosity, social informality, the possession of cutting-edge technological expertise, and confidence. Projecting these cultural characteristics helped Razorfish compete in an industry that relied heavily on intangible assets both by defining and reinforcing the firm's reputation and by strengthening its bonds with its employees, whose knowledge and skill were integral to the company's competitiveness.

For most of the firm's history, its workforce exhibited deep loyalty and a willingness to work hard, sometimes for less pay than they might have been offered elsewhere. As Dachis later recalled, "It was a religion. It was a unique, unified way of doing business" (J. Dachis, personal communication, August 2, 2004). As far as employees were concerned, Razorfish was "as good as it gets in corporate America" (Ross, 2003). As a result, turnover at Razorfish was minimal even in an industry where job-hopping among organizations was common. Dachis was quoted in an industry newspaper

article that "Razorfish has essentially no turnover whatsoever. You ask the recruiters where the resumes are coming from. It's not here. Even our first, second, and third employees are still here" (Goldberg, 1998).

Razorfish's pursuit of hipness was reinforced by both founders' strong interests in the arts. One manifestation of these interests was the Razorfish Subnetwork, or RSUB. RSUB was a series of artists' websites, which showed the artistic potential of interactive technology. RSUB eventually became Razorfish Studios, with offices in New York and Los Angeles. Razorfish Studios' offerings included online art and interactive multimedia galleries, online magazines, and communities, book and music publishing, and television and film production. While Razorfish Studios was spun off formally in 1997, it continued to serve as a source of "cultural gravity" for the firm. It remained located in the same offices as Razorfish and provided a creative outlet for many Razorfish employees involved in experimental projects related to the development of video, music, and art.

Private Investment and Firm Growth

In the fourth quarter of 1996, Omnicom announced the creation of a corporate venture capital unit (soon called Communicade) with $10 million in initial capital. Omnicom was a global, multibillion-dollar conglomerate of advertising agencies, public relations firms, and marketing services companies. The purpose of Communicade was to invest in "digital and interactive media." Communicade invested in multiple Silicon Alley companies, several of which competed directly with each other and with initial interactive work within Omnicom. In 1996, Omnicom invested in Razorfish with $3.5 million in cash, a line of credit for working capital, and a second line of credit to enable Razorfish to acquire new media companies.

Communicade's line of credit helped finance Razorfish's initial acquisitions. In early 1998, the company acquired Avalanche Systems of New York and CHBi of London for $1.3 million and $2.0 million, respectively. Three smaller acquisitions followed, adding companies in San Francisco, London, and Los Angeles to the Razorfish fold. Table 1 shows Razorfish's 1995–1998 financial results.

In January 1999, in conjunction with its plans to go public later that year, Razorfish used an acquisition to more than double its size and extend its reach in Europe. The company acquired Spray Network, a Swedish firm with which

Table 1 Razorfish in the Early Years

Income Statement (Million $)	1995	1996	1997	1998
Revenues	31.0	1.22	3.62	13.84
Direct salaries and costs	0.11	0.90	1.91	7.77
Gross profit	0.21	0.32	1.71	6.11
Sales and marketing expenses	0.02	0.13	0.18	0.44
General and administrative expenses	0.14	0.50	0.88	2.90
Amortization of goodwill	—	—	—	0.11
Noncash compensation	—	—	0.08	1.94
Income (loss) from operations	0.05	(0.31)	0.58	0.70
Interest expense	—	—	0.02	0.24
Income (loss) before taxes	0.05	(0.31)	0.56	0.45
Provision (benefit) for taxes	0.01	(0.57)	0.27	0.46
Net income (loss)	0.04	(0.25)	0.29	0

Balance sheet information (million $)	1995	1996	1997	1998
Cash and cash equivalents	—	0.06	1.18	0.60
Total assets	0.01	0.59	4.27	12.09
Total long-term debt	0.02	0.06	0.08	3.21
Total debt	0.02	0.06	0.08	5.54
Shareholders' equity	0.04	0.28	0.66	2.73

Source: Prospectus filed in April 1999.

Razorfish had been partnering since October 1997. Spray had 1998 revenues of about $15.4 million and offices in Stockholm, Oslo, Helsinki, and Hamburg. The deal involved payment of $54.1 million in Razorfish's privately traded stock to Spray's shareholders, an amount representing 50% of Razorfish's own common stock after the acquisition. Several of Spray's European investors joined the Razorfish board, reflecting the major role that they had gained in the ownership and governance of Razorfish through the transaction.

The initial acquisitions were primarily to expand the firm's geographic scope. Accordingly, the aquired firms offered Razorfish access to additional interactive talent and a broader range of clientele in both the United States and Europe. The acquisitions also gave the firm access to talented workers from around the world, a critical consideration because Razorfish preferred to have its work done by full-time employees rather than by freelance workers. Although Razorfish's core business stayed consistent, the acquisitions profoundly changed the size of the company. Razorfish was transformed from a small group of employees based in a single Manhattan loft office to a medium-sized, geographically dispersed, and genuinely multinational firm.

Rather than operate as a network of independent, locally managed firms, the company chose to convert its various acquisitions to a single corporate identity. In other words, all the acquisitions were rebranded; they adopted the name, the global image, the culture, and the technology development processes of Razorfish. As Dachis later recalled, "It wasn't you were being acquired by us, you were joining us. That was always my spiel. That was always my handshake at the end of the deal . . . welcome to the family" (J. Dachis, personal communication, August 2, 2004). By and large, the effort was successful. Jonathan Nelson, the CEO of rival consulting firm Organic Online, conceded, "They've done a better job of integrating their acquisitions than a lot of their competitors. Razorfish isn't perceived as a roll-up [acquisitions purely for financial reasons]. They have an integrity of brand that's really impressive" (Goldberg, 1998).

Industry Growth and Convergence

The new media industry (which was sometimes called by different names, such as the "Internet industry" or the "interactive industry") was on fast-forward in 1999. The Center for Research on Electronic Commerce at the University of Texas at Austin estimated that the worldwide "Internet economy" had revenues of $301 billion in 1998 and predicted that it would grow at a double-digit rate in subsequent years (Barua, Pinnell, Shutter, & Whinston, 1999).

Many types of organizations vied for this exploding source of business. Accordingly, Razorfish identified four major categories of competitors. They included traditional strategy consulting firms (e.g., Boston Consulting Group), recently formed Internet services firms (e.g., Agency.com), old-line technology consulting firms and integrators (e.g., Accenture), as well as the in-house information technology (IT) or marketing departments of current or prospective clients.

The scope of services offered by firms in this industry varied with their strategies. Some of the technology specialists were content to stay specialized. For example, Jonathan Nelson, CEO of Organic Online, said, "We're not here to tell GE how to run its business. We're here to develop a channel for GE, if it wants it" (Brown, 1999). Other firms sought a more diversified approach. The top-tier strategy consulting firms aggressively sought to develop Internet-focused practices. Table 2 shows the income statements of typical competitors.

To some degree, these efforts reflected a desire to attract and retain high-level talent and an acknowledgement that Internet-related activity appealed strongly to such people. David Pecaut of Booz-Allen and Hamilton's e-commerce practice explained in April 1999, "We've got to be relevant to today's MBAs" (Brown, 1999). But the move toward Internet-related markets also reflected the perception of genuine economic opportunity. International Business Machine (IBM)'s earnings report for the first quarter of 2000, e.g., registered flat demand for its standard services unit but a 70% revenue growth in its e-business consulting services (Farmer, 2000a).

Table 2 Historical Income Statements of Selected Competitors

Accenture	Year Ended August 31 (Million $)				
	1996	1997	1998	1999	2000
Revenues	5,710	7,447	9,640	11,079	11,540
Cost of services	3,446	4,642	6,125	6,986	7,274
Sales, general, and admininistrative costs	1,191	1,430	1,732	2,061	2,180
Operating income	1,073	1,375	1,783	2,032	2,086
Net income	937	1,242	1,685	2,023	2,464

Agency.com	Year Ended December 31 (Thousand $)				
	1996	1997	1998	1999	2000
Revenues	6,095	12,975	26,452	87,786	202,090
Cost of services	2,217	6,200	15,930	45,458	98,953
Sales, general, and administrative costs	955	4,343	11,540	38,501	97,114
Operating income	2,923	2,432	(1,018)	3,827	6,023
Net income	1,502	1,182	(2,481)	(12,879)	(14,686)

Organic Online	Year Ended December 31 (Thousand $)				
	1996	1997	1998	1999	2000
Revenues	4,294	6,780	27,734	77,800	128,614
Cost of services	1,889	4,285	16,801	46,254	72,682
Sales, general, and administrative costs	2,104	5,473	12,068	40,513	90,167
Operating income	301	(2,978)	(1,135)	(8,967)	(34,235)
Net income	237	(1,785)	(2,766)	(38,875)	(86,293)

Firms in the industry were also divided by differences in the pace with which they worked. One analyst explained, "Unlike the McKinseys, e-consultants don't expect to work on a single project for years and years. On the Internet, you get your play up first—some kind of play, any kind of play—and then you 'iterate,' constantly updating and improving in a mad effort to stay competitive. Speed is the name of the game" (Brown, 1999). In this regard, the ability of smaller firms to move quickly served the smaller consultancies well. Their relative nimbleness enabled them to adopt some of the newer technologies sooner than their larger, older counterparts, and some customers valued the greater depth of experience they possessed in the short-lived but quickly moving Internet area (Farmer, 2000b).

Many large corporations, afraid of being left behind by a new technology, invested in and/or acquired interactive start-ups. For instance, after much criticism for avoiding channel conflict with its brokers by not joining the Internet brokerage movement, Merrill Lynch finally acquired online firm D.E. Shaw. Other start-ups felt the need to build mass in order to compete effectively against the traditional technology behemoths and to provide the broad range of services demanded by Fortune 500 clients. Examples of roll-ups were MarchFirst and Agency.com, each of which acquired numerous small Internet agencies in the mid to late 1990s.

Public Investment and Expanding Scope

In April 1999, Razorfish sold 3 million shares of its stock in an initial public offering (IPO) at $16 per share, netting

about $44 million. Like many Internet stocks at that time, Razorfish stock debuted favorably: In the 4 months following the IPO, the company's stock price fluctuated between $24:50 and $58 per share, roughly 1.5 to 3.5 times its initial offering price.

Razorfish's prospectus stated that it would use the proceeds to increase employee retention and recruitment through the expansion of the company's human resources department, to hire additional technology personnel, to develop its sales and marketing department, to expand into international markets, and to perform internal systems upgrades. For example, Razorfish formed a unit devoted to mobile and wireless devices and their applications, including mobile phones, watches, and handheld personal digital assistants. It also continued to expand geographically, with new offices in Milan, Frankfurt, and Silicon Valley. Table 3 shows the geographic spread of Razorfish offices and revenues.

Razorfish's strong stock market valuation gave it the means to execute an even more ambitious acquisition strategy. While some acquisitions continued to be in the new media arena, others were meant to broaden its capabilities beyond those associated with the company's original focus on Internet strategy and web design. These broader capabilities would enable Razorfish to take on bigger and longer client engagements. For instance, the company's July 1999 acquisition of Fuel, a Los Angeles-based company with operations in broadcast design and television commercial production, added to the firm's broadband capabilities and was intended to position the company to exploit the anticipated convergence of personal computer and television technologies.

Table 3	Business Segment Breakdown			
Year	U.S. Locations	Non-U.S. Locations	U.S. Revenue (Million $)	Non-U.S. Revenue (Million $)
1995	New York	None	22.3	0
1996	New York	None	32.4	0
1997	New York	None	42.1	16.0
1998	New York, Los Angeles, San Francisco	London	62.1	21.8
1999	New York, Los Angeles, San Francisco, Boston	London, Stockholm, Oslo, Helsinki, Hamburg, Amsterdam, Mannheim	109.7	60.5
2000	New York, Los Angeles, San Francisco, Boston, San Jose	London, Stockholm, Oslo, Helsinki, Hamburg, Amsterdam, Munich, Frankfurt, Tokyo, Milan	180.1	88.2

Sources: 10-Ks from 1999, 2000, and 2001.

Note: Includes consolidated revenues from acquisitions.

Table 4	Acquisitions			
Date	Company	Description	Location	Price ($)
January 1998	Avalanche	New media company with capabilities in creative design	New York	1,294,000
May 1998	CHBi	New media company	London	2,028,000
June 1998	Plastic	New media company with technical expertise	San Francisco	686,000
July 1998	Media	New media entertainment consultant to film and record companies	Los Angeles	256,000
October 1998	Sunbather	New media company with expertise in interactive and digital television	London	289,653
January 1999	Spray	Interactive media development and consultancy	Stockholm	9,881,034 shares
June 1999	Electrokinetics		New York	847,000
September 1999	Fuel and Tonga	Graphic design and branding for television, TV commercial production	Los Angeles	1,312,000 shares + 750,000
November 1999	i-Cube	Electronic business and transformation services for complex IT environments	Boston	36,069,224 shares plus assumption to purchase 12,103,000 options
December 1999	Lee Hunt	Strategic marketing and creative production for the entertainment industry	New York	1,250,000 shares
December 1999	TSDesign	Internet strategy and product design firm	New York	180,000 shares
January 2000	QB International	IT/strategic consulting	Stockholm	407,000 shares + 3,100,000
May 2000	Limage	Visual communications agency	Rotterdam	141,000 shares
August 2000	Medialab	E-business solutions provider	Munich	446,000 shares + 1,400,000

Sources: 2001 10-K, 2000 10-K, April 1999 initial public offering prospectus.
IT, information technology.

The largest acquisition was the Cambridge, Massachusetts-based systems developer and integrator i-Cube, which Razorfish bought in August 1999 for $677 million in stock. At the time, i-Cube had trailing 12-month revenues of nearly $54 million and trailing 12-month earnings of $6.6 million. The i-Cube acquisition added expertise in the development of the "back-end" operations of corporate websites. It also added management expertise. The i-Cube chief financial officer (CFO), Larry Begley, became CFO of Razorfish, while i-Cube founder and CEO Michael Pehl became COO of Razorfish. Table 4 shows Razorfish's acquisitions.

2000: A Roller Coaster Year

The year 2000 started out well for Razorfish. Although the stock market had declined somewhat since its peak the previous spring, Razorfish's market capitalization still stood at about $4 billion, and revenues continued to rise. Like other

early outside investors in Razorfish, Omnicom's Communicade unit cashed out much of its stake, generating a $65 million gain on its initial investment. See Table 5 for major shareholders at the time of the Razorfish IPO and in 2000.

The company planned to raise additional capital, potentially several hundred million dollars, to fund even more growth via a secondary stock offering in the second quarter. Then, worrying signs began to appear. Although Razorfish had won praise for its ability to manage acquisitions in previous years, there were signs that the integration of i-Cube and other recent acquisitions was faring less well. In February, CFO Larry Begley and most of the i-Cube senior management team left the company and cashed out their Razorfish stock. They left behind founder Michael Pehl, who had been promoted to Razorfish president, who then left Razorfish in August (Olsen & Farmer, 2000). In addition, there were reports of a "mass exodus" of employees from Fuel in the months following its acquisition. Some re-

Table 5	Ownership by Major Shareholders	
Owner	At IPO (%)	Year End 2000 (%)
Communicade/Omnicom	33.0	12.1
Spray Ventures AB	32.8	6.4
Jeffrey A. Dachis	9.5	6.1
Craig M. Kanarick	9.5	5.0

Source: Company prospectus, filed April 1999; 10-K, filed April 2001.
IPO, initial public offering.

ports indicated that those who were leaving cited a clash of corporate cultures as the reason for their departures (Saunderson, 2001). The company's problems were not entirely internal. In April 2000, the National Association of Securities Dealers Automated Quotations fell 25.3%, and new IPO offerings ground to a halt. The stock market's dramatic reassessment of its valuations of Internet-related stocks had several important business implications. The pool of talented technology-oriented employees, many of whom were drawn to new ventures like Razorfish in part by the potential of their stock-option packages, grew cautious and restive about their affiliations with such firms. Venture capitalists, who had looked to the public markets as an exit strategy, refused to invest further in Internet start-ups. Corporate marketing and IT managers also began to scrutinize their Internet-related investments more carefully. Even if there had been no management turnover among its acquisitions, it would have been difficult for Razorfish to raise additional equity capital. In this environment, Razorfish decided not to pursue the secondary stock offering.

In general, by the middle of 2000, the market seemed to move away from demanding consulting services related to the Internet and other new technologies, and had returned to a demand for more conventional IT services. Razorfish and other consultancies, for whom cash-rich Internet start-ups and large, blue-chip companies had composed a major portion of their customer base, found themselves faced with clients who refused to extend additional engagements and in some cases were unable to pay for past services (Farmer, 2000b). More established firms like IBM and Accenture were perceived to be better suited to such projects than the newer, envelope-pushing firms like Razorfish (Farmer, 2000b).

In this tighter environment, Internet consulting became a buyers' market. Customers aggressively negotiated lower hourly fees and firmer project deadlines. In addition, many customers challenged the traditional technology consulting business model. Traditionally, customers had borne the risk of project-cost overruns by paying consultants on a time-and-materials basis. Accurate estimation was especially an issue for Internet projects, because they involved relatively untested technologies and methodologies. With the glut of technology consultants, customers could increasingly insist on fixed-price engagements, thus forcing their vendors to bear the risk of cost and time overruns. This combination of lower demand, lower rates, and increased risk put pressure on margins throughout the Internet services business.

Fixed-price contracts were a matter of intense debate within Razorfish. On the one hand, they were easier to sell and helped bolster the firm's top line. On the other hand, fixed-price contracts reduced profitability because Razorfish's cost structure compounded the margin issue. Back when there had been a shortage of web design and development talent, Razorfish's intense culture and strong brand identity had attracted top people and high-status customers to the firm, but also resulted in high fixed costs. An element of that identity was that employees—not external freelancers or outsourcing firms or internal contractors—executed Razorfish projects. As Dachis explained, "We don't outsource. We have too many smart people inside" (J. Dachis, personal communication, August 2, 2004). Another manifestation of the Razorfish identity was its high-priced real estate. Razorfish offices were more than places to work. In their prime locations in major cities around the world, Razorfish offices were architecturally interesting gathering places for employees and customers alike. Long-term office leases and an implied no-layoffs social contract reduced Razorfish's flexibility in adjusting its cost structure to an industry downturn.

Despite the third-quarter dip in IT revenues and Internet stock valuations, many industry observers believed that this would be a temporary breather and the industry growth would resume. Headlines in industry trade journals proclaimed, "Companies Throwing More $$$ Into E-Biz" (Shah, 2000) and "Believe It or Not, IT Spending Will Increase and It Will Be Permanent" (Gomolski, 2000). While small dot-coms began to fail, management at large Internet services firms felt that they could ride out a short dip. In many respects, Razorfish was in better shape than its smaller competitors, with blue-chip customers, a strong balance sheet, and third-quarter revenues slightly higher than its record second-quarter revenues. As Dachis later recalled, "The third quarter was our best quarter . . . You could smell what's going on around you, but it doesn't seem to be affecting you . . . We heard there was a slow down, but we're not feeling it" (J. Dachis, personal communication, August 2, 2004). However, third-quarter expenses increased faster than revenue, resulting in the first quarterly net loss in 4 years.

Fueled by the publicity and personal wealth they had generated by taking the company public, Kanarick and Dachis continued to pursue their personal interests in ways that seemed to seamlessly blend Razorfish's hip culture, its artistic creativity, and its penchant for attracting attention. In late 2000, they invested in a nightclub managed by a Razorfish employee and her husband. The Slipper Room was located on Manhattan's cutting-edge Lower East Side. Dark, smoky, and loud, the club billed itself as a "restaurant, lounge, and Victorian stage." It featured an ongoing series of theme parties, campy burlesque shows, high-priced martinis, and gourmet appetizer selections from around the world. The milieu appealed to the same set of arts—and technology-minded young adults who worked at Razorfish. "The whole place is tacky," Kanarick explained, "but it's gorgeous, like Ivana [Trump]'s house meets Bugsy Siegel circa 1929" (Grigoriadis, 2001).

Cutbacks and Losses

After the third quarter 2000 plateau, revenues plummeted in the fourth quarter. The company continued to lose money. Under intense pressure from Wall Street analysts, it was clear that Razorfish had to reduce its costs. Despite earlier no-layoff promises, Dachis reluctantly laid off 200 employees (about as many people as had been added earlier that year) in October. The cuts were a severe blow to the morale of a firm that had prided itself on the integrity of its culture and the loyalty of its staff.

With revenues continuing to decline during the fourth quarter, disgruntled shareholders filed a class-action lawsuit against the company, claiming it had misled investors by lying about the magnitude of the integration difficulties encountered by the i-Cube acquisition. Many technology-oriented firms with battered stock prices, including March-First and Cisco, also faced shareholder lawsuits. Ultimately, the Razorfish lawsuit would be dismissed, but at the time, it placed additional pressure on a management team already under increasing scrutiny from disappointed Wall Street analysts (Gilliard, 2001).

Razorfish COO Jean-Philippe Maheu and Executive Vice President for Sales Bob Lord developed a series of more dramatic budget-cutting scenarios designed to match company costs to lower revenues. However, Dachis refused to consider additional layoffs, saying that he was concerned they would destroy the company. Furthermore, like many technology executives, he continued to believe that the downturn would be short-lived. Maheu and Lord did not press their point because they, too, did not believe that the situation was urgent (J.-P. Maheu & B. Lord, personal communication, February 25, 2004). In December, with Razorfish stock at an all-time low, Dachis and Kanarick held a revival-style meeting for all New York-based employees. "We're a company, not a stock," Dachis reminded them, "and we're playing to win the revolution not the stock market. This company is a company of true believers." Kanarick added, "We're not going to feed the beast of revenue simply for the public markets . . . I'm willing to wait out two quarters [of losses]" (Ross, 2003).

By December 31, the company's stock—which had traded for as much as $100 per share in January—had sunk below $2 per share. Razorfish posted a pretax loss of $165 million in the fourth quarter (including a write-down of good will from acquisitions of $126 million) and a pretax loss of $149 million for the full year of 2000. Although the company still had $51 million in cash, something had to change or Razorfish would be out of business within months. Table 6 shows Razorfish's financial and headcount information (adjusted for acquisitions) for 1995–2000.

Difficult Options in an Uncertain Environment

The first quarter of 2001 was a time of great uncertainty in the U.S. economy in general, and in IT in particular. Despite a recent slowdown in growth, economists were moderately optimistic that the U.S. economy would have a "soft landing," as opposed to a full-blown recession (Fox, 2001). This cautious optimism was reflected among IT industry observers. For instance, the trade newspaper *Information Week* reported on an IT U.S. executive survey in which respondents predicted slower growth (but not decline) in IT spending, with an increased emphasis on wireless technology and e-commerce, both of which were areas of strength for Razorfish (McGee, 2001). *Interactive Week* predicted, "Tech's Soft Landing in Rough Economy: 2001 Will Prove Better Than Expected for IT Community" (Duvall & Cleary, 2001).

Still, Razorfish struggled across the globe for enough profitable business to support its cost structure. By the end of

Table 6 Razorfish Historical Financial and Headcount Information, 1995–2000[†]

Income statement (millions U.S.$)	1995	1996	1997	1998	1999	2000
Revenues	22.3	32.4	56.2	83.9	170.2	267.9
Project personnel costs	10.5	16.0	27.5	44.2	81.0	147.9
Gross profit	11.8	16.4	28.7	39.7	89.1	119.9
Sales and marketing expenses	1.2	2.1	4.0	6.3	12.6	22.5
General and administrative expenses	6.8	11.5	16.3	22.5	48.5	109.7
Amortization of intangibles	0	0	0	.1	3.5	8.9
Nonrecurring items[‡]	0	(0.1)	0	1.9	21.0[‡]	124.9[‡]
Income from operations	3.9	2.9	8.2	8.1	(0.2)	(149.5)
Other income			0.1	.8	3.7	3.5
Income before taxes	3.9	2.9	8.3	8.9	3.5	(146.0)
Provision for taxes	1.5	1.1	3.3	4.8	18.1	2.9
Net income (loss)	2.4	1.8	5.0	4.1	(14.5)	(148.9)
Shares outstanding (millions)	49.2	49.2	46.2	50.1	83.1	93.7
Net per share (in dollars)	0.05	0.04	0.11	0.08	(0.17)	(1.59)

Balance sheet information (millions U.S.$)	1995	1996	1997	1998	1999	2000
Cash and cash equivalents	3.8	5.5	13.0	36.6	98.8	51.5
Total assets[§]	12.2	16.9	35.4	75.8	251.6	205.0
Long-term obligations	0.6	0.7	2.7	6.8	1.8	1.0
Stockholders' equity	2.5	4.9	10.7	45.8	198.4	169.2

Employees (at period end)	1995	1996	1997	1998	1999	2000
Full-time employees	NA	26	40	414	1,355	1,900

[†] 1995–1998 results are restated to include financials of acquisitions made in 1998, 1999, and 2000.

[‡] In 1999, merger-related costs aggregating $24.6 million were charged to operations. The costs included professional services fees, integration-related activities, and miscellaneous other costs.

[§] In the fourth quarter of 2000, Razorfish recalculated the present value of expected cash flows of certain business units to determine the fair value of those assets. Accordingly, the company recorded noncash impairment charges and wrote down goodwill by $126.0 million from the acquisitions of Spray, CHBi, Tag Media, and Fuel.

Sources: Company 10-Ks, filed April 1999, April 2000, and April 2001; initial public offering prospectus filed April 1999; quarterly report for first quarter 2001.

the first quarter, it was clear that no major revenue rebound was in the offing. In fact, revenues had continued to decline, and the company burned through another $20 million of cash. See Table 7 for quarterly income statements, balance sheet information, and the company stock price in 2000 and the first quarter of 2001.

As a public U.S. company, Razorfish had to announce its first-quarter results within 45 days of the end of the quarter. Investors, analysts, and board members would be looking for

an action plan for how Razorfish would return to profitability. In mid-April, top management met with the 15 general managers of Razorfish offices from around the world. In this meeting, the leaders of Razorfish needed to come to terms with the company's finances and decide how to improve its prospects. See Table 8 for profiles of top managers.

The company's choices were either high-risk or highly distasteful. They ranged from forging ahead with the current strategy to shuttering the company. Contradictory company

| Table 7 | Quarterly Income Statements, Balance Sheet Information, and Stock Prices (January 2000–March 2001) |

Income Statement	2000 (Millions $)				2001 (Millions $)
	Q1	Q2	Q3	Q4	Q1
Revenues	64.1	76.6	77.1	50.1	42.7
Project personnel costs	<u>29.8</u>	<u>36.4</u>	<u>41.7</u>	<u>40.0</u>	28.9
Gross profit	34.3	40.2	35.4	10.1	13.8
Sales and marketing	4.1	4.9	6.2	7.3	4.7
General and administrative	20.4	23.7	22.9	2.3	20.5
Amortization of intangibles	2.0	2.1	2.3	2.5	0.9
Nonrecurring items[†]	<u>0</u>	<u>0.7</u>	<u>5.6</u>	<u>143.7</u>	<u>12.8</u>
Income from operations	7.8	8.8	(1.6)	(164.5)	(25.1)

Balance sheet information	2000 (Millions $)				2001 (Millions $)
	Q1	Q2	Q3	Q4	Q1
Cash and cash equivalents	89.6	89.6	84.1	51.5	30.3
Total assets[‡]	367.1	374.4	385.6	205.0	176.0
Long-term obligations	0.7	1.4	2.0	1.0	0.7
Stockholders' equity	321.2	324.4	327.5	169.2	141.8

Stock price	2000 ($ per Share)				2001 ($ per Share)
	Q1	Q2	Q3	Q4	Q1
High	56.93	30.12	23.31	10.75	3.00
Low	26.75	12.62	8.03	1.00	0.38

[†] Line includes provision for doubtful accounts, restructuring costs, and impairment loss.
[‡] Q4 2000 includes $126 million write-down of goodwill from acquisitions of Spray, CHBi, Tag Media, and Fuel.
Sources: 2000 10-K; March 31, 2000 10-Q; June 30, 2000 quarterly report (10-Q); September 30, 2000 10-Q; and 2001 10-K; March 2001 10-Q.Q1, first quarter; Q2, second quarter; Q3, third quarter; Q4, fourth quarter.

and industry information made it impossible to predict the future, even for the short term. For instance, while Razorfish revenues had weakened further, industry publications continued to be optimistic (a typical March 2001 headline proclaimed, "Despite Spending Slowdown, It's Full E-Speed Ahead") (Gantz, 2001). In this context, there was no obvious best choice among the alternatives:

- **Attempt to ride out the storm with modest cutbacks, aggressive marketing, and (if necessary) additional funding.** This was the option Dachis had initially advocated back in December 2000. His hope had been to retain talent, culture, and morale until the industry turned around. A few months later, the firm still had great talent, proprietary methods, a core of loyal customers, and, even though the equity markets were weak, the balance sheet was strong enough to obtain debt. Although additional cutbacks would clearly be needed, most of his general managers still preferred a modest approach. They wanted to keep Razorfish poised to take advantage of any rebound in demand by retaining its global reach (and keeping their own offices open).

- **Drastically downsize Razorfish to its most profitable operations.** Dachis, Lord, and Maheu had come to prefer some variant of this option, although they differed on the specifics. Lord and Maheu had analyzed the customer base and their sources of reliable revenue, both within the United States and in other parts of the world. They advocated shrinking the firm to serve core cus-

Table 8 Senior Management of Razorfish (January 2001)

Name	Position	Age	Year Joined	Experience	Educational Background
Jeffrey Dachis	Cofounder and Chief Executive Officer	33		Positions with various media-related companies	MA, New York University; BA, State University of New York
Craig Kanarick	Cofounder and Chief Strategic Officer	33		Independent consultant and designer	MS, Massachusetts Institute of Technology; BS, University of Pennsylvania
Jean-Philippe Maheu	COO	37	1997	Consultant, Gunn Partners and A.T. Kearney	MBA, Northwestern University; diploma, Curie University, Paris
John Robert	Chief Financial Officer	33	2001	Partner, PricewaterhouseCoopers; certified public accountant	BA, Boston College
Ed Godin	EVP, Human Resources		2001	Vice President for Human Resources, Prism, Inc.	BA, Holy Cross
Michael Simon	EVP, Business Affairs and General Counsel	36	1996	Senior Director of Legal Affairs, Polygram Records; Founder and President, Simon Ventures, an artist management firm acquired by Razorfish Studios in 1999	JD, Columbia University; BA, Amherst
Clayton Hubner	EVP, Infrastructure		2000	Chief Information Officer, Applied Power, Inc., a $1.9 billion manufacturer; professor of operations and information technology, College of William and Mary	PhD, operations management, Michigan; MBA, BS, Brigham Young University
Hyo Yeon	EVP, Strategic Development	36	1998	Strategy, client service, and business development positions at firms which later became Sapient and MarchFirst; management consultant, Andersen Consulting; positions with various design firms	MBA, Northwestern University; diploma, School of the Art Institute of Chicago; BA, Stanford University
Bob Lord	EVP, North America	38	2000	Vice President for Alliances and Business Development, Pretzel Logic Software; COO, Prism Rehab Systems	MBA, Harvard University; BS, Syracuse University
Michael Moore	EVP, Europe	34	1999	Management consultant, Monitor Company and Andersen Consulting	MBA, Nyenrode; BS, Manchester Institute of Science and Technology

Source: Company website as of July 2001 and 10-K, filed April 2001.
MA, master of arts; MBA, master of business administration; BA, bachelor of arts, BS, bachelor of science; JD, doctor of jurisprudence; COO, chief operating officer; EVP, executive vice president.

tomers and shedding Razorfish's European operations (J.P. Maheu & B. Lord, personal communication, February 25, 2004). Dachis went even further. As he later recalled, "Choice number one would be to cut off all the subsidiaries . . . fire 13 out of 15 offices, keeping San Francisco and New York open" (J. Dachis, personal communication, August 2, 2004). However, many members of the management team were against drastic cutbacks. They especially expressed concern about European labor laws, many of which restrict layoffs and business closings.

■ **Attempt to be acquired.** Despite its recent troubles, Razorfish still had something to offer to traditional technology consulting firms. With over 1,300 talented employees around the world, it had developed sophisticated web development processes and expertise at integrating web development with consumer and business-to-business marketing. It had a core of what Lord called "anchor clients" such as Ford, Cisco, and Genentech (J.P. Maheu & B. Lord, personal communication, February 25, 2004). These employees, capabilities, and client relationships could be attractive to more established marketing/advertising firms or to technology firms. Maheu had raised this idea back in 2000 with Dachis, who had immediately rejected it. From Dachis' perspective, this was the worst option of all. As he later recalled, "That's something morally I just couldn't do . . . That's throwing in the towel . . . It was a means of winding down that I didn't comprehend as palatable" (J. Dachis, personal communication, August 2, 2004). Also, at this point, the window may have closed for an acquisition at a valuation that management would consider reasonable. With a first quarter 2001 price range of $0.38 to $3.00 (which translated into a market valuation range of about $36 million to $282 million), it could be argued that Razorfish's stock was as drastically undervalued as it had been overvalued in the first quarter of 2000, when the price range was $27.75 to $56.93 (a market valuation range of $2.3 billion to $4.7 billion).

■ **Close up shop and distribute the assets to shareholders.** The firm still had about $30 million in cash, $33 million in receivables, and virtually no debt. This option conflicted drastically with the passion that Razorfish's managers still felt for the company and its potential. However, compared with the prospect of a sale, this kind of corporate *hara-kiri* might actually have been more palatable to the hard-core believers in what Dachis had described as the "religion" of Razorfish.

For an organization that had been in growth mode only 6 months earlier and now appeared to be in free fall, Razorfish management faced a wrenching decision. Neither acquisition nor closure came under serious consideration. However, there was a great deal of debate about the first two options. The meeting ended without consensus. Shortly after the meeting, Dachis and Kanarick notified the board of directors that they would resign from Razorfish. Dachis received a $750,000 severance payment, while Kanarick received a $450,000 (Razorfish, 2001). As far as Dachis was concerned, "It was the last day of Silicon Alley . . . When Craig [Kanarick] and I stopped going to work on May fifth, there wasn't really a Silicon Alley anymore" (J. Dachis, personal communication, August 2, 2004).

But, like many Silicon Alley businesses, Razorfish was still there, and something still needed to be done. First-quarter results would be announced on May 15, 2001, and the available options had not changed. Jean-Philippe Maheu was named CEO, and Bob Lord was named COO. Both men brought strengths to the leadership of Razorfish. Maheu had a credible profile for the manager of a large multinational firm: He was a French-born management consultant

with an MBA from Northwestern University and work experience at established consulting firms on both sides of the Atlantic. But he was also in tune with Razorfish: He was young (37) and had proven himself, having joined the company in 1996 and helping build its North American operations. Lord, who was 38 and had earned an MBA from Harvard Business School, came with external high-tech business development experience when he joined Razorfish in 2000. Now it was up to Maheu and Lord to determine the next steps for Razorfish.

References

Barua, A., Pinnell, J., Shutter, J., & Whinston, A. (1999). *Measuring the Internet economy: An exploratory study.* Austin, TX: Center for Research on Electronic Commerce at the University of Texas, Austin.

Brown, E. (1999). The e-consultants. *Fortune,* April, 12.

Coopers & Lybrand (1996). *New York new media industry survey.* New York: Coopers & Lybrand.

Duvall, M. & Cleary, M. (2001). Tech's soft landing in rough economy. *Interactive Week,* January 8.

Farmer, M. (2000a). Net consultancies look to rebuild after sobering year. *CNETNews.com,* December 20.

Farmer, M. (2000b). Services firms run circles around tech giants. *CNETNews.com,* April 26.

Fox, J. (2001). The slowdown: How much will it hurt? *Fortune,* January 8.

Gantz, J. (2001). Despite spending slowdown, it's full e-speed ahead. *Computerworld,* March 19.

Gilliard, S. (2001). How to read a 10-Q: Razorfish. *NetSlaves,* April 23.

Goldberg, M. (1998). Razorfish's secret recipe. *Silicon Alley Reporter, 16.*

Gomolski, B. (2000). Believe it or not, IT spending will increase and it will be permanent. *InfoWorld,* October 23.

Grigoriadis, V. (2001). Silicon Alley 10003. *New York Magazine,* May 31.

McGee, M.K. (2001). Outlook for 2001. *InformationWeek,* January 8.

Olsen, S. & Farmer, M. (2000). Razorfish shares slide after president resigns. *CNETNews.com,* April 25.

Razorfish. (1999). Document 10-K filed with the U.S. Securities and Exchange Commission.

Razorfish. (2001). 10-Q for first quarter.

Rifkin, G. (1995). Increasingly, top designers are drawn to web. *The New York Times*, November 27.

Ross, A. (2003). *No collar: The humane workplace and its hidden costs.* New York: Basic Books.

Saunderson, L. (2001). Marquis launches Milk Bar. *Boards*, March 1.

Shah, J. B. (2000). Companies throwing more $$$ into e-biz. *Electronic Buyers' News*, September 11.

Daniel P. Forbes is an assistant professor at the University of Minnesota, Carlson School of Management.

Carla Pavone is a doctoral candidate at the University of Minnesota, Carlson School of Management.

We are grateful to many people for giving us constructive feedback on this case, including former Razorfish employees Tom Byun and Elisa Vargas; our former students, especially Sean Sciara, Sarah Youngerman, and Jason Harrison; and our academic colleagues, including Theresa Lant, Phil Bromiley, Suresh Kotha, *Entrepreneurship Theory and Practice* editor Bill Sandberg, and the anonymous case reviewers. We also extend a special thanks to Jeff Dachis, Jean-Philippe Maheu, and Bob Lord for sharing their recollections about Razorfish.

Case 10

Embraer: Shaking Up the Aircraft Manufacturing Market

UVA-S-0135

While traveling to an investor conference in Montreal, Canada, on Embraer's Legacy business jet, Mauricio Botelho, CEO of Embraer, reflected on his company's dramatic ascent to its position as the world's leading regional aircraft manufacturer. Since becoming a private company, Embraer had successfully introduced seven commercial aircraft models to the market, including its latest, the 118-seat EMBRAER 195. As the jet began its runway approach just a few miles from the headquarters of rival company Bombardier, Botelho pondered the potential competitive response to his company's recent attacks on the commercial aircraft market.

The U.S. Airline Industry

With the passing of the Airline Deregulation Act of 1978 by the U.S. Congress, government control of routes and fare pricing were eliminated, resulting in growth, increased competition, and emergence of three new business models: major, regional, and low-cost carriers.

MAJOR CARRIERS The distinguishing feature in the business model of a major carrier (or a "major") was the hub-and-spoke system. This system was based on central hubs to which feeder flights were directed. Passengers from the feeder flights transferred to numerous other flights provided at the hub to their final destinations.[1]

The enormous capital required to expand geographically was a substantial barrier to entry for new airlines. As low-cost and regional carriers primarily competed on price and local market convenience, the rationale for the majors' costly model lay largely on the improved customer loyalty generated by the convenience and reach of these airlines.

To further enhance breadth of service and increase the number of customers while limiting capital outlays, most majors turned to code-sharing and global alliances with other major and regional airlines. The major global alliances included Star Alliance, Sky Team, and One World.

REGIONAL CARRIERS Regional airlines (or "regionals") operated short- and medium-haul scheduled airline service connecting smaller communities with larger cities and with the hubs of the major airlines. Although most were independently owned, several of the largest regional carriers were actually subsidiaries of the major airlines, including Atlantic Southwest, Comair (Delta), and AMR Eagle (American Airlines).

Many regionals benefited from arrangements with the majors, including code-sharing arrangements, scheduling

[1]"Air Transportation," *Encyclopedia of Global Industries*, online edition, Thomson Gale, 2005. Reproduced in Business and Company Resource Center (Michigan: Gale Group, 2005) http://galenet.galegroup.com/servlet/BCRC.

assistance to ensure flight connections in majors' hubs, and the branding of a major airline.

With low-cost structure and improved service levels, regionals as a whole became the most profitable segment in the air carrier business. Regionals continued to replace turboprops on low-density routes and developed new routes that extended airline networks, enabling those carriers to serve unserved or underserved markets more cost-efficiently. Regionals were able to do that because newer, smaller jets were significantly faster than existing fleets of turboprop planes, had greater range, and burned less fuel (a major per-flight fixed cost). The regionals were the fastest-growing segment of commercial aviation and continued to serve a valuable segment of travelers unaddressed by low-cost and major carriers.

LOW-COST CARRIERS Low-cost carriers (LCCs) offered airfares at a lower price than major and regional carriers. The largest LCCs included JetBlue, AirTran, Southwest Airlines, and America West, as well as new upstarts Song and Ted, which were owned by Delta and United, respectively.

Many of the LLCs started off as regionals, offering short-haul service connecting business and leisure travelers between high-volume destinations. By operating out of underutilized airports in those markets, the LLCs were able to keep a low profile. The largest LCCs were already operating nonstop transcontinental flights.

Contrary to the major airlines' hub-and-spoke system, LCCs generally operated a point-to-point route system. This feature was credited in the air carrier industry with providing higher levels in the quality of passenger service in terms of on-time departures and arrivals, limited lost luggage, etc. In order to effectively utilize the point-to-point system, LCCs offered service to the same general destinations as majors and regionals but used satellite airports, which were typically less congested than hub airports and charged lower fees.

LCCs limited its fleet of planes to one or two midsize, more fuel-efficient models, thus reducing training and maintenance costs. Moreover, by avoiding congested airports, LCCs were able to achieve faster turnaround times. The net effect was that planes were kept in the air longer, increasing the asset utilization. Additionally, LCCs tended to have lower labor costs because of the nonunion work force.

U.S. Market Conditions

The airline industry experienced uninterrupted growth in revenues throughout the 1990s. A weakening global econ-

omy, however, coupled with the September 11, 2001, terrorist attacks, had drastically reduced airline traffic by the end of 2001. As a result, the industry posted unprecedented losses of $7.7 billion for the year, as revenues dropped 13.5% from a record high of $93.6 billion in 2000. The slowdown continued into 2002 and 2003 as major airlines, faced with reduced sales, continued to reduce capacity and trim ranks. United Airlines, the second-largest airline in the world, filed for bankruptcy at the end of 2002.[2] The U.S. domestic available seat miles (ASM)[3] evolution (Exhibit 1) demonstrates the shift in capacity from majors to regionals and LCCs.

LCCs, whose cost structures were already tailored to the current fare environment, had not been affected as greatly as the majors. In fact, they continually reported profits even in the difficult post-September 11 environment.[4]

Market Conditions in Europe

In Europe, major airlines were faced with many of the same competitive issues as majors in the United States. Successful low-fare carriers exerted downward pressure on fares, and fall-off in passenger demand made it more difficult to maintain presence in existing markets, much less expand to new ones. Regional operators had softened the blow of the downturn. With their lower cost structures and greater flexibility, they had proven less vulnerable to outside market forces and capable of growth under adverse conditions.

The milestones in the airline industry for both the United States and Europe are presented in Exhibits 2 and 3.

It is important to highlight that these trends in the global airline industry were a key driver of the recent developments in the commercial aircraft industry.

The Commercial Aircraft Industry

OVERVIEW Since most modern aircraft were incredibly complex (the Boeing 747, for example, had six million parts), a worldwide network of approximately 400 subcontractors was required to supply major structures and subassemblies, such as wings and fuselages, to manufacturers of

---

[2]"Air Transportation," Encyclopedia of Global Industries, Gale Research International Ltd., Pub ID: GE66 (1 December 2002).

[3]Available seat miles (ASM) measure available passenger capacity.

[4]"Airline Industry: A Business in Transition," Optimizing Air Travel Mini-Conference Presentation, Boston, Massachussets, 24 March 2004.

Exhibit 1	Embraer: Shaking Up the Aircraft Manufacturing Market

Shifting Capacity among Business Models

U.S. Domestic ASM Evolution (Index 100)[1]

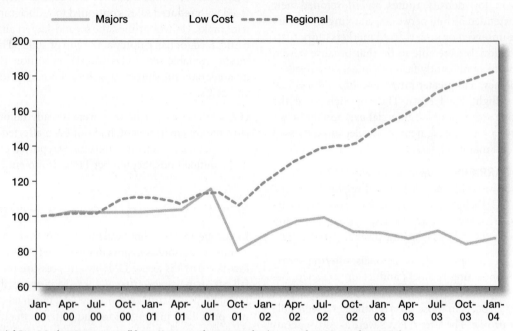

[1]"Commercial Jets Market Assessment," http://www.embraer.com.br (accessed 10 November 2006).

Exhibit 2	Embraer: Shaking Up the Aircraft Manufacturing Market

Milestones in the Airline Industry—United States[1]

Hub-and-Spoke
- U.S. Congress passes the Airline Deregulation Act of 1978, initiating a period of intense competition and paving the way for a new operational model, the hub-and-spoke system.
- Deregulation makes room for low-fare, point-to-point service expansion.
- By 1984, code-sharing alliances between major carriers and regional operators begin to be formed.
- Majors begin to rely more on low-cost regionals. Number of short-haul turboprop routes increase.

Market Outsourcing
- Regional jets are introduced in 1992.
- In 2002, U.S. orders for regional jets near 400. Turboprop orders collapse.
- Regional jet networks grow dramatically as majors shift routes to the lower-cost aircrafts and deploy them to expand into new markets.
- Regional jets become crucial part of airline strategy to remain profitable in pre-September 11 downturn.

Regional Jets
- Terrorist attacks in the United States on September 11, 2001, deliver crippling blow to airline industry.
- FAA enacts its Operational Evolution Plan.
- Airlines respond to plunging demand by cutting frequencies and trimming networks. Regional jets' ability to operate profitably with low load factors offset losses from airlines operating with overcapacity.
- Regional jets used to complement or replace narrow-body aircraft on unprofitable short-haul routes.

[1]"2004–2023 Embraer Market Outlook."

Exhibit 3	Embraer: Shaking Up the Aircraft Manufacturing Market

Milestones in the Airline Industry—Europe[1]

Liberalization in Europe

- European airlines evolved a hub-and-spoke system independently, primarily operating from each nation's capital city.
- Europe takes a four-step approach to liberalization. The first phase is implemented in 1988.
- Airlines begin to be restructured and privatized.
- High labor costs in a competitive, deregulated environment force airlines to take drastic measures.

Market Expansion

- Regional jets are introduced in 1992.
- European airlines successfully deploy regional jets in the current established air transport system.
- Regional jets replace many turboprops, but turboprops with 40-plus seats remain in service.
- Low-fare carriers such as Ryanair and EasyJet see dramatic growth in RPK from 1995 to 2001.

Regional Jets

- The regional airline market in Europe averages 12% growth during the period from 1995 to 2002.
- Terrorist attacks in the United States on September 11, 2001, deliver crippling blow to airline industry.
- As in the United States, the regional jets' ability to adapt to different demand environments helps sustain allied majors through crisis.

[1]"2004–2023 Embraer Market Outlook."

finished aircraft. Those subcontractors, in turn, were supplied by up to 4,000 firms that manufactured components or raw materials. Parts that differentiated a product, or those strongly identified with a company, were usually produced in-house given their strategic and competitive importance.

A strong customer base and careful order-book management were needed to recoup the cost of developing new commercial or business jets. Standards for safety, quality, and value were crucial. Because of the capital-intensive nature of the industry, manufacturers needed to sell hundreds of units globally in order to break even on the design and manufacture of new aircraft.

The 1990s were years of consolidation in the aircraft industry. In 1997, two of the industry's largest producers, Boeing Company and McDonnell Douglas Corporation, merged. Other well-known companies, such as Piper Aircraft Corporation and Fairchild Aircraft in the United States, as well as Fokker N. V. of the Netherlands, filed for bankruptcy during that period.

The market for commercial aircraft was typically divided into two product categories: narrow-body and wide-body aircraft. Narrow-body aircraft were single-aisle, short-range aircraft (up to 6,000 km or roughly 3,700 miles) that typically carried up to 200 passengers. Leading aircraft in that category were the Boeing 737, the Boeing 757, and the Airbus A-320. Wide-body aircraft were double-aisle, medium- to long-range aircraft (up to 14,000 km or

roughly 8,700 miles) that could carry from 200 to 450 passengers. Leading aircraft in that category were the Boeing 747, the Boeing 777, and the Airbus A-300. Boeing and Airbus were the industry leaders in these segments.

REGIONAL JETS The regional jets segment, which was included within the narrow-body category, was traditionally composed of aircraft that carried between 20 and 70 passengers. Bombardier and Embraer were the market leaders in this segment, which had consistently expanded since 1992, when Bombardier introduced the first regional jet as a replacement for turboprop planes.

Even before regional jets became widely available, growth among regional airlines was consistently robust. Between 1971 and 1993, regional carriers outgrew the majors virtually every year. The expansion could be traced to two contributing factors. First, in the years leading up to 1978, many cities previously unserved had been introduced to air service, mainly on turboprop aircraft. Second, regional carriers in the years after the Deregulation Act of 1978 began to fill gaps in the ever-expanding hub-and-spoke networks of the majors.

By 1989, the majors changed its airline operation to increase the number of passengers flowing into the networks by adding capacity on its feeder routes, offering more destinations, and increasing frequency. It was a strategy that played against the strengths of regional turboprops, whose shorter range made them ineffective in reaching new markets.

The net effect was a surge in regional jet adoption and deployment, largely because of the replacement of turboprops on low-density routes and the development of new routes that extended airline networks. As the regional jets segment expanded, the capability of the jets themselves expanded to comprise roomy and cost-effective modern aircraft that flew up to 4,000 km (3,700 miles), enough to operate within most continents.

Based on expected growth of LCCs and regional carriers, as well as the aging of aircraft currently in use, the market for regional planes appeared to be poised for significant growth. Embraer had projected deliveries of 30- to 120-seat planes to total nearly 8,500 units over the next 20 years, representing a US$175 billion business. The United States was expected to generate 56% of this demand, while 19% of demand would come from Europe (Exhibit 4).

EMBRAER In 2004, Embraer was the fourth-largest commercial airplane manufacturer in the world in terms of volume, behind Boeing, Airbus, and Bombardier. Airbus and Boeing led the market with deliveries of 320 and 285 commercial airplanes, respectively. In the regional market, Bombardier and Embraer demonstrated a close rivalry by achieving 158 and 148 deliveries, respectively (see Exhibit 5 for Embraer market share evolution).

Exhibit 4	**Embraer: Shaking Up the Aircraft Manufacturing Market**

Market Outlook

Delivery Forecast by Segment and Region[1]

30- to 120-seat Commercial Jet Category, World Deliveries by Seat Segment

Segment	2004–13	2014–23	2004–23
30–60	1,150	1,450	2,600
61–90	1,300	1,600	2,900
91–120	1,250	1,700	2,950
Total	**3,700**	**4,750**	**8,450**

Deliveries by Region, 30- to 120-seat Segment

Regions	2004–13	2014–23	2004–23
North America	2,245	2,495	4,740
Latin America	255	370	625
Europe	636	944	1,580
Africa & Middle East	154	236	390
China	240	395	635
Asia Pacific	170	310	480
Total	**3,700**	**4,750**	**8,450**

Deliveries by Region and Segment

Regions	30- to 60-seat Segment			61- to 90-seat Segment			91- to 120-seat Segment		
	2004–13	2014–23	2004–23	2004–13	2014–23	2004–23	2004–13	2014–23	2004–23
North America	840	1,030	1,870	715	650	1,365	690	815	1,505
Latin America	25	70	95	90	130	220	140	170	310
Europe	85	152	237	263	424	687	288	368	656
Africa & Middle East	80	38	118	52	106	158	22	92	114
China	100	100	200	90	160	250	50	135	185
Asia Pacific	20	60	80	90	130	220	60	120	180
Total	**1,150**	**1,450**	**2,600**	**1,300**	**1,600**	**2,900**	**1,250**	**1,700**	**2,950**

[1]"2004–2023 Embraer Market Outlook."

Exhibit 5	Embraer: Shaking Up the Aircraft Manufacturing Market

Embraer Market Share Evolution

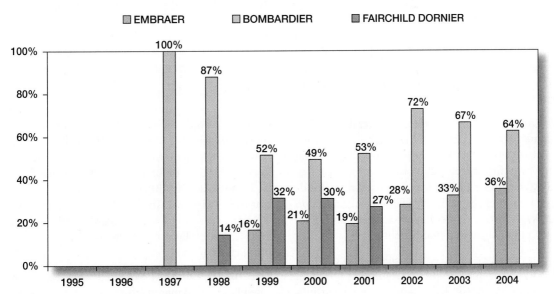

Data source: http://www.embraer.com.br (accessed 10 November 2006).

Data source: http://www.embraer.com.br (accessed 10 November 2006).

(continued)

Exhibit 5	Embraer: Shaking Up the Aircraft Manufacturing Market—Continued

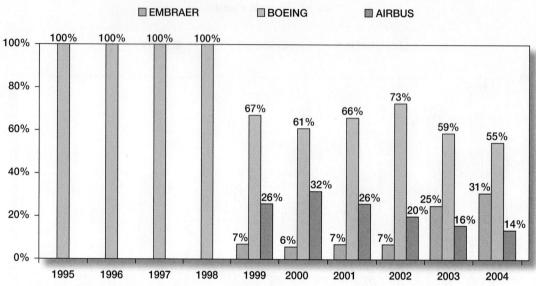

91- to 120-seat Planes

Data source: http://www.embraer.com.br (accessed 10 November 2006).

Embraer, founded in 1969, was the product of an aeronautical technology center (CTA) that had been established in 1945 by Brazil's Ministry of Aeronautics. Together with Embraer, the CTA also generated one of the world's leading aeronautical engineering schools, the Aeronautical Technological Institute (ITA). Most of Embraer's aeronautical engineers had been hired out of ITA.

Moreover, Embraer's first great commercial success was the Bandeirante, a 15-seat plane with a design based on an eight-seat prototype assembled inside the CTA. Overall, 500 Bandeirantes were sold over a 10-year period. The first 80 were sold to the Brazilian military, as an indirect government support to the new enterprise.

From 1972 to 1983, Embraer introduced several small turboprop planes. Embraer's first international success, introduced in 1983, was the EMB 120 Brasilia, a 30-seat pressurized twin turboprop. In 2006, the Brasilia was still in production, with more than 350 planes operating worldwide. Embraer's jet era began in 1985 with the introduction of the AMX, a military jet developed in partnership with Aermacchi, an Italian aircraft manufacturer.

Embraer was privatized in December 1994 as part of President Fernando Henrique Cardoso's privatization program. Cia. Bozano, Simonsen (CBS), the leader of the consortium that took Embraer private, was a conglomerate with diversified investments in financial services, agriculture, real state, and industrial products (see Exhibit 6 for Embraer's ownership structure).

In 1995, Embraer entered the commercial jet market with the introduction of its ERJ family. The ERJ 145 (introduced in 1995), ERJ 135 (introduced in 1998) and ERJ 140 (introduced in 2000) had seating capacity of 50, 37, and 44 seats, respectively. Those planes were developed in accordance with Embraer's strategy of entering the 30- to 50-seat market to compete against Bombardier's Q-Series turboprop planes as well as its CRJ family of regional jets.

In 1999, while still celebrating the successful introduction of the ERJ family, Embraer began developing a new aircraft family that would serve the 70- to 120-seat market. In February 2002, the 70- to 78-seat EMBRAER 170 completed its first flight, taking off from São José dos Campos. In the following two years, Embraer completed the maiden flights of its 78- to 86-seat EMBRAER 175 as well as the 98- to 106-seat EMBRAER 190. To complete the family, in December 2004, the 108- to 118-seat EMBRAER 195 accomplished its first successful flight (see Exhibit 7 for a list of Embraer's products as of 2006).

THE 70- TO 120-SEAT MARKET Several reasons motivated Embraer to manufacture 70- to 120-seat planes. First, Embraer identified a gap between capacity and demand for

| Exhibit 6 | Embraer: Shaking Up the Aircraft Manufacturing Market |

Embraer Capital Structure

Common Shares (242,544,448 Shares)—33% of Shares

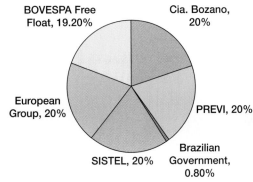

The European group includes: Thales (5.67%), Dassault (5.67%), Snecma (2.99%), and EADS (5.67%).

Preferred Shares (476,720,786 Shares)—66% of Shares

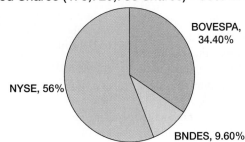

Total (719,265,234 Shares)

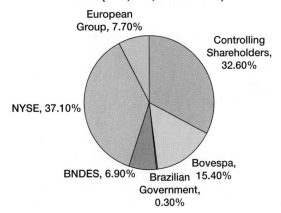

Data source: http://www.embraer.com.br (accessed 10 November 2006).

Exhibit 7	Embraer: Shaking Up the Aircraft Manufacturing Market

Embraer's 2006 Product Mix

Commercial Aviation	Military Aviation	Corporate Aviation
EMB 120	Super Tucano	Legacy
ERJ 135	AMX	
ERJ 140	EMB 145 AEW&C	
ERJ 145	EMB 145 RS/AGS	
Embraer 170	P 99	
Embraer 175	Legacy	
Embraer 190		
Embraer 195		

Data source: http://www.embraer.com.br (accessed 10 November 2006).

this range of planes. The absence of a true 70- to 120-seat jet family had forced airlines to deploy planes that were either too large or too small to operate efficiently in the intermediate-demand market. In 2002, 61% of flights in the United States departed the airport with loads appropriate for 70- to 110-seat aircraft.

Several trends in the airline industry also contributed to Embraer's interest in this segment. First, the continued growth of LCCs had created a shift in aircraft demand toward smaller, more efficient planes. In addition, the downturn in the airline industry that began with September 11, 2001, along with the resulting price wars, had highlighted the fact that the majors required a high-load factor to compete effectively against the LCCs. Furthermore, the increased volatility of passenger demand created a greater need for flexibility among airlines. As a result, the majors were becoming increasingly receptive to the notion of using smaller planes for short- to intermediate-range flights. As well, the financial problems experienced by the majors during this period had prompted its U.S.-based unions to relax clauses that limited the scope of its regional airlines to 50-seat jets. As a result, several airlines were beginning to expand regional operations to include planes with more than 70 seats.

Another key reason was related to aging fleets. More than one-third of the planes serving the 61- to 120-seat market were more than 20 years old. Those planes amounted to approximately 690 units, which would be gradually replaced within the next five to 10 years (see Exhibit 8 for details).

Embraer already delivered nine EMBRAER 170s to customers, including US Airways, which had broken in its new 170s with flights from Pittsburgh, Pennsylvania to Albany, New York on April 4, 2004. JetBlue Airways had 100 EMBRAER 190s on firm order—at a total cost of $3 billion—having chosen that model over the 107-seat Airbus A318. The total number of firm orders for the 170/190 family, as of December 2004, was 343.

BOMBARDIER Founded in 1942 by Armand Bombardier as a snowmobile manufacturer, Bombardier has been publicly listed on the Toronto Stock Exchange since 1969, yet has remained under the majority control of the Bombardier family throughout the company's history. In the 1970s, Bombardier began to diversify into other transportation industries through acquisitions of various train, plane, bus, and boat manufacturers. Notable aerospace acquisitions included the purchases of Canadian aircraft manufacturer Canadair in 1986, business jet manufacturer Learjet Corporation in 1990, and de Havilland, manufacturer of the Dash-8 turboprop, in 1992.

In 1992, Bombardier entered the regional jet market with the launch of its 50-seat CRJ100/200. After Embraer's entry into that market in 1995, Bombardier began to face a significant erosion of its competitive position. Financial problems compounded the challenges posed by Embraer; they prevented Bombardier from launching major development projects outside of the CRJ family of jets. Instead, Bombardier raced to beat Embraer to the emerging 70- to 90-seat regional jet market by announcing in 1997 its plans to introduce the 64- to 75-seat CRJ700/705, a stretched version

Exhibit 8	Embraer: Shaking Up the Aircraft Manufacturing Market

The 70– to 110-Seat Capacity Gap

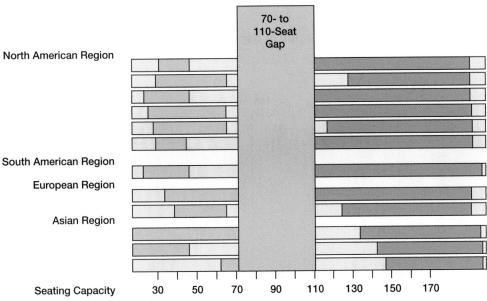

Data source: http://www.embraer.com.br (accessed 10 November 2006).

How Overcapacity or Undercapacity Hurts the Bottom Line

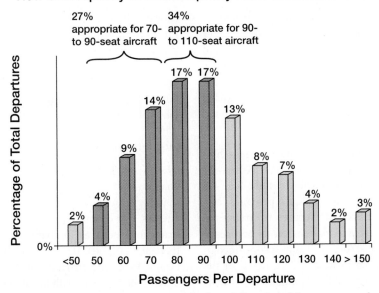

Note: More than half of all U.S. domestic airlines operating narrow-body mainline aircraft have passenger loads better suited for 70- to 110-seat aircraft.

(continued)

Exhibit 8	Embraer: Shaking Up the Aircraft Manufacturing Market—Continued

Seating Gap

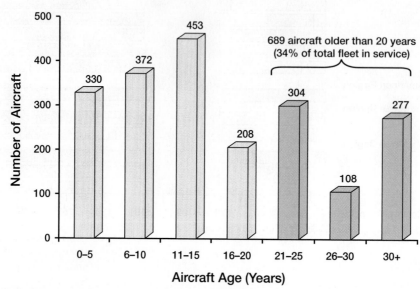

Aircraft in Service (as of 2002)

Note: More than one-third of the world's jet fleet serving the 51- to 120-seat segment is more than 20 years old and should be retired in the coming years.

Data source: http://www.embraer.com.br (accessed 10 November 2006).

of the CRJ100/200. The CRJ700/705, first delivered in 2001, was followed by the 86- to 90-seat CRJ900, another stretched CRJ100/200, which was announced in 1999 and in service by 2003. In 2000, Bombardier's plans to develop a new generation jet that could have beaten Embraer to the 100-plus-seat market were abandoned owing to financial constraints, and Bombardier was forced to continue relying on its existing platform.

After several years of escalating financial and business challenges, in 2003, Bombardier appointed former CN Railway CEO Paul Tellier as the company's president and CEO. Tellier quickly implemented a recapitalization program, featuring an equity issue and asset divestitures, to strengthen Bombardier's balance sheet and refocus on its aerospace and railcar businesses. The aerospace business continued to struggle, however, with 2005 production estimates for the 50-seat CRJ200 reduced from 98 to 54, as the market continued to migrate toward larger regional planes. Furthermore, the financial strength of airlines still interested in 50-seat jets, such as US Airways and Delta Airlines, continued to decline. In November 2004, Standard & Poor's and

Moody's Investor Service downgraded Bombardier's credit rating to junk status. One month later, after less than two years on the job, Tellier was removed from his position as president and CEO of Bombardier. Replacing Tellier was Laurent Beaudoin, a member of Bombardier's founding family, chairman of Bombardier since 1979, and previously CEO of the company from 1979–1999. Beaudoin had reportedly pushed Tellier aside after disagreeing with his long-term vision for Bombardier.

The CSeries: The entrepreneurial Beaudoin was believed to be an enthusiastic supporter of the CSeries development project that began feasibility studies at Bombardier in 2004. The CSeries, a new family of three jets ranging from 110 to 135 seats, would serve as Bombardier's entry vehicle into the commercial jet market. Bombardier's board of directors was expected to decide in early 2005 whether to proceed with development efforts, with the objective of launching the project in spring of 2006 and delivering the first jet in 2010. The Canadian government, attracted to the opportunity to replace the thousands of jobs that had been lost because of the scaled-back production of Bombardier's CRJ200, had reportedly agreed to finance one-third of the expected $2 billion of capital costs associated with the prototype development. In exchange, Bombardier would commit to locating the CSeries manufacturing and development facilities in Canada.

The CSeries jets were expected to compete directly with Embraer's EMBRAER 190, Airbus's A318, and Boeing's 737–600. Bombardier claimed the CSeries would be the only jet specifically designed for the 110- to 135-seat market, as Embraer's 190 was an upward stretch from the 170, and Airbus's and Boeing's jets were downsized versions of their larger narrow-body jets. As a result, Bombardier claimed the CSeries would outperform each competing jet with respect to weight, size, or range. Bombardier expected the CSeries to achieve unmatched operating efficiency, reducing costs to 15% to 20% below the cost of operating competing planes.

Bombardier's recent hiring of former Boeing executive Gary Scott, who had previously worked on Boeing's development of the 737, to direct the CSeries program sparked conjecture in the Canadian press of a Bombardier plan to create a joint venture with Boeing. Bombardier called the reports "pure speculation," but Boeing Commercial Airplanes President Alan Mulally confirmed that his company had served as a "consultant" to Bombardier. A relationship with Boeing could add significant value to the CSeries, particularly if it allowed Bombardier to create cockpit commonality with Boeing's 737.

BOEING Boeing was the world's second-largest manufacturer of large commercial jets behind Airbus, as well as the world's largest aerospace company, focusing on military aircraft, satellites, missile defense, human space flight, and launch systems and services. Since 2001, Boeing's commercial airplane sales had plummeted from 60% to 40% of Boeing sales. Boeing responded to that downturn by cutting costs, curtailing product development, and placing more emphasis on its military and space operations. In 2005, Boeing's commercial development efforts were primarily focused on the 787 Dreamliner, a super-efficient, long-range (9,500 km to 11,000 km, or 7,000 to 8,000 miles), 200- to 250-seat aircraft that was expected to be in service by 2008.

The smallest Boeing airplane in full-scale production as of 2005 was the 162- to 189-seat 737. Boeing announced in January 2005 that the 106- to 114-seat 717, which was inherited in Boeing's 1997 acquisition of McDonnell Douglas, would be taken out of production as soon as its existing orders were filled. Boeing cited insufficient demand as the reason for the decision, adding that the 717's market niche was simply too small for Boeing to continue serving. The 717 was considered by market analysts to be too big and heavy to operate efficiently relative to smaller regional jets such as Bombardier's CRJ900 and Embraer's EMBRAER 190. Furthermore, the 717 was an orphan product, with no cockpit or engine commonality with other Boeing jets, and had not received a great deal of marketing and development support from Boeing during its six years of production.

AIRBUS S.A.S. The world's largest commercial aircraft maker, Airbus, was 80% owned by the European Aeronautic Defense and Space Company (EADS), with U.K.-based BAE Systems controlling the remaining 20%. Airbus was founded in 1970 to address several European governments' wishes to have a European competitor in the aerospace industry. In 2005, Airbus was the manufacturer of the world's largest, lowest-cost, and longest-range aircraft. The company had recently been focused on the super-jumbo market, with the development of the 550-seat A380. In December 2004, however, Airbus announced plans to develop a midsized plane, the A350, to compete directly against Boeing's 787, seating 245 to 285 passengers.

Airbus's product line comprised four families: the single-aisle A320 family, the wide-body A300/310 family, the long-range A330/340 family, and the new super-jumbo A380 family. Airbus's smallest airplane, the 318, was a 107- to 132-seat short-haul jet launched in 1999 to compete with Boeing's 717. The A318 benefited from a high degree of commonality with the entire A320 family in terms of airframes, on-board systems, cockpits, and handling characteristics, which meant that the entire family could be flown by the same pilots and maintained by the same engineers. Still, as a downsized version of the 150-seat A320, detractors considered the A318 to be larger and heavier than is desirable for jets in the 100-seat market.

Competitive History (1989–2005)

1989	Embraer began development of the ERJ 145.
1992	Bombardier entered the regional jet market with the 50-seat CRJ100/200, developed from the CL-601 Challenger business jet.
1993	Airbus launched development of the 120-seat A319.
1996	Embraer began delivering the ERJ 145.
1997	Embraer launched the 37-seat ERJ 135. Bombardier announced plans to develop the 64- to 75-seat CRJ700/705.
1998	Embraer began delivering the ERJ 135.
1999	Bombardier began development of the 86- to 90-seat CRJ900. Embraer launched development of the 44-seat ERJ 140 and launched its EMBRAER 170/190 family beginning with the development of the 70-seat EMBRAER 170.

Airbus launched development of the 107- to 132-seat A318.

After two years of discussion about government subsidies, Canada challenged the Brazilian subsidy program PROEX before the WTO. The WTO decided that the Brazilian PROEX was a prohibitive export program that had to be withdrawn. The value of the PROEX subsidy to Embraer was worth $1.4 billion. Following that, Canada chose to retaliate by imposing tariffs on the Brazilian exports including a temporary ban on Brazilian beef.

2000	Bombardier abandoned plans for development of a new 100-seat jet, the BRJ-X.
2001	Bombardier's CRJ700/705 began service.
2003	Bombardier's CRJ900 began service.
	Embraer's EMBRAER 170 began service.
2004	Bombardier announced that it is studying the feasibility of a new jet family, the CSeries, which would serve the 110- to 135-seat market.
	Embraer began delivery of the EMBRAER 175 and EMBRAER 190.
2005	Boeing announced plans to stop production of the 717 because of insufficient market demand.

The Decision

As he made final preparations for his upcoming investor presentation, Mauricio Botelho was concerned that Embraer still did not know what to expect from Bombardier, Boeing, and Airbus. How would they respond to Embraer's successful launch of its recent family of jets? Would Bombardier really follow through with its launch of the CSeries? Would Airbus and Boeing perceive the latest attacks by Embraer and Bombardier as attacks on their own families of jets? Most importantly, given Botelho's expectations of rivals' future competitive moves, what should Embraer do next to protect its position and influence its competitors' actions?

Case 11

Wal-Mart in the 21st Century: A Global Perspective

UVA-S-0100

The world's largest retailer still thinks of itself as a small-town outfit. That might be its greatest strength.[1]

By 2002, ten years after its folksy founder Sam Walton died, Wal-Mart was the largest company in the world, having surpassed even ExxonMobil and General Electric. By January 31, 2002, its reported sales were $218 billion; worldwide, there were 1,647 Wal-Mart stores, 1,066 Supercenters, 500 Sam's Clubs, 1,170 international stores, and 1.3 million "associates." Wal-Mart had opened 107 stores in foreign countries that year and reported experimenting internationally with new operational elements, including jewelry, one-hour photos, optical labs, and online home-delivery programs. Domestically, Wal-Mart was trying out products not normally associated with the retailer, such as used cars.[2] While the 1990s had been a decade of global expansion for the retail giant, its 2001 international business, $35.5 billion, represented less than 20 percent of its $218 billion business. Still, Wal-Mart International as a stand-alone business would have ranked 42nd on the Fortune 500, ahead of such stalwart retailers as J.C. Penney and Costco.[3] The going had not been easy; Wal-Mart International did not show a profit until 1997, six years after starting global expansion. At the end of January 2002, the breakdown of stores in the international community was as follows:

Argentina: 11 Brazil: 22 Canada: 207
China: 22 Germany: 95 Great Britain: 258
Mexico: 593 Puerto Rico: 19 South Korea: 14

At that point, there were 45,000 suppliers for the international division, and it was estimated that 100 million people shopped in Wal-Mart stores throughout the world on a weekly basis.[4] In Wal-Mart's 2002 Annual Report, in a section titled "What's in Store for Our Global Community," the company reported a 10.5 percent growth in international sales to $35.5 billion and a 31 percent operating income increase over 2001. To enhance cross-cultural retail skills, Wal-Mart reported the 2001 launch of "an International Leadership Development Program (ILDP) to ensure that an

DARDEN

This case was prepared by Research Assistant Jenny Mead under the supervision of Elizabeth Olmstead Teisberg, associate professor of Business Administration and R. Edward Freeman, Elis and Signe Olsson Professor of Business Administration and Director of the Olsson Center, at the Darden School, University of Virginia.

[1]"Wal Around the World," *Economist* (December 6, 2001): 49.

[2]In the summer of 2002, Wal-Mart set up a partnership with Asbury Automotive Group, Inc., and set up four used-car dealerships, called Price 1 Auto Sales, in Houston. Aside from "no-haggle" pricing, Price 1 offered the following customer perks: "a 5-day money-back guarantee (no questions asked), a 3,300-mile warranty, and, most remarkable of all, 12 months of roadside assistance, a feature unheard of in the used-car business." Bill Breen, "What's Selling in America," *Fast Company* 66 (January 1, 2003).

[3]"Global Reach Gets Broader Every Day," *Chain Store Age* 78 (August 1, 2002): 66.

[4]"Behind the Scenes at Wal-Mart International," *Australian Hardware Journal* (May 8, 2002).

ample pool of operations teams and store managers are pre-pared to support our growth in the years to come."[5] (See Exhibit 1 for International Operations Datasheet.)

[5]Wal-Mart 2002 Annual Report, pp. 8–9.

By 2002, Wal-Mart had three distinct types of stores:

- *Discount stores* that usually were around 90,000–100,000 square feet in size.
- *Sam's Clubs* or warehouse/membership clubs, that "used high-volume, low-cost merchandising, minimized handling costs, leveraged their buying power, and passed the

Exhibit 1	Wal-Mart in the 21st Century: A Global Perspective

International Operations Datasheet

INTERNATIONAL DATA SHEET	September 2002
Wal-Mart International	1,227 total units
	Mexico (593)
	Puerto Rico (19)
	Canada (207)
	Argentina (11)
	Brazil (22)
	China (22)
	Korea (14)
	Germany (95)
	United Kingdom (258)
History	Entered Mexico in November 1991.
	Entered Puerto Rico in August 1992.
	Entered Canada in November 1994.*
	Entered Argentina in November 1995.
	Entered Brazil in November 1995.
	Entered China in August 1996.
	Entered Germany in January 1998.*
	Entered Korea in July 1998.*
	Entered United Kingdom in July 1999.*
	*Entered these countries through acquisitions.
Company Trade Territory	Wal-Mart Stores, Inc. serves more than 100 million customers weekly in 50 states, Mexico, Puerto Rico, Canada, Argentina, Brazil, China, Korea, Germany and United Kingdom.
Total Associates	Internationally—more than 300,000
	Total Company Associates—more than 1.3 million worldwide
Total Company Sales	FYE 1/31/02: $217.7 billion—13.8 percent increase over the previous year.
Total International Sales	FYE 1/31/02: $35.4 billion—10.5 percent increase over the previous year. Operating profit was $1.4 billion, an increase of 31.1 percent compared to the previous fiscal year.
	For the second quarter ending 10/31/02: $9.9 billion—14.4 percent increase over the same period last year. Operating profit was $447 million for the quarter, an increase of 42.4% over the same period last year.

Source: Wal-Mart 2002 Annual Report

savings on to members, with gross margins of 9%–10%."[6] These clubs were primarily cash-and-carry, catered to businesses, and charged a membership fee, which made up approximately two-thirds of the operating profits. By the early 1990s, Sam's Club had far outstripped and was twice as big as Price Club, its original model.[7]

■ *Supercenters* averaging 120,000 to 130,000 square feet, combined regular retail items (clothes, appliances, etc.) with food products and limited its packages and brands to keep down costs. Supercenters also offered other services like photo developing, hair salons, and optical shops. These stores were generally so large that employees often wore rollerblades to get around.

■ *Neighborhood markets*, which were smaller than the other formats and designed for urban centers where space was limited. These approximately 45,000 square-foot venues were "Wal-Mart's answer to consumer needs in between weekly trips to a Supercenter" and were "no-frills food, drug, and limited merchandise supermarkets built on real estate locations generally pursued by grocery stores and convenience stores."[8]

Despite the strong international presence in the early 21st century, Wal-Mart President and CEO Lee Scott[9] claimed no "firm blueprint or time line"[10] in international expansion. To an audience of international retailers and suppliers, Scott said:

> We're more opportunistic than strategic.... There are differences between markets, and we've never been confused about that fact ... We'd never take a U.S. store and put it in Argentina and expect customers to flock there. But although we understand there are differences, we're not always as good at understanding what those differences are."[11]

Nonetheless, Scott claimed that, internationally as well as domestically, the Wal-Mart key values—every-day low prices and the focus on the customer—remained and would never be abandoned. (See Exhibit 2 for Wal-Mart's 11-Year Financial Summary and Exhibit 3 for Stock History.)

Why Go Global?

In the early 1990s, Wal-Mart was a hugely successful domestic retail chain that, as the brainchild of the legendary homespun Sam Walton and with roots in Bentonville, Arkansas, was distinctly American. The retailer had a 20-year average return on equity of 33 percent and compound average sales growth of 35 percent. At the end of 1993, Wal-Mart had a market value of $57.5 billion, with per square-foot sales of $300, compared to the $210 industry average.[12] Did the retail giant need to expand into global markets? Would it be successful internationally? Would its trademark attributes—deeply discounted prices, associates instead of salespeople, greeters at every Wal-Mart front door, bulk buying that limited the brand variety—translate well into other cultures? That remained to be seen, but Wal-Mart started its global expansion with next-door neighbors Canada and Mexico, followed soon thereafter with Brazil and Argentina, and then into Western Europe, the United Kingdom, and Asia. By 2002, Wal-Mart was a presence on other continents, but global expansion had not been without its difficulties. The company was unable to penetrate France, largely because of the powerful French retail chain Carrefour and had abandoned efforts to establish a presence in Indonesia and Hong Kong.

In the 1990s, the United States comprised only 4 percent of the world population; Wal-Mart management, like other U.S. companies, was determined to tap into the other 96 percent. Wal-Mart foresaw opportunities to serve customers in other countries, using its management and IT skills, purchasing scale, and corporate mentality of keeping costs low.[13] But transferring capabilities and culture internationally was a challenging proposition. What is folksy in Arkansas or even suburban California might prove off-putting in another country. Also, the best business location in foreign urban centers (China for example) was in the heart of the large cities. How would Wal-Mart, which was accustomed to large and sprawling retail stores with ample parking lots in America, adjust to the space constraints dictated by the crowded, space-precious international cities?

---

[6]"Wal-Mart Stores, Inc.," Harvard Business School Case (9-794-024); Rev. 1996, Harvard Business School Publishing, p. 11.

[7]Price Club was sold to Costco Wholesale Corp. in 1993. The Price Club spin off, PriceSmart Inc., competed with Costco. PriceSmart's 2002 revenues were $647 million, its profits $3.8 million. Costco's 2002 revenues were $38.7 billion. In January 2003, Costco had 401 warehouses (295 in the United States, 60 in Canada, 15 in the United Kingdom, five in Korea, three in Taiwan, three in Japan, and 20 in Mexico).

[8]"Wal-Mart in 2002," Harvard Business School Case (9-702-466), Harvard Business School Publishing, 2002.

[9]Scott, who had joined Wal-Mart in 1979, became president and CEO in 2000. He had spent most of his professional career in the Wal-Mart ranks and had known Sam Walton very well.

[10]David Orgel, "Wal-Mart Lacks Firm Strategy for International Expansion" *Supermarket News* (June 24, 2002): I.

[11]Ibid.

[12]"Wal-Mart Stores, Inc.," 1.

[13]David Yoffie, "Wal-Mart 1997; Wal-Mart Ventures into Mexico; Wal-Mart in East Asia," Harvard Business School Teaching Note (5-798-110), 1998.

Exhibit 2	Wal-Mart in the 21st Century: A Global Perspective

Financial Summary

(Dollar amounts in millions except per share data)	2002	2001	2000
Net sales	$ 217,799	$ 191,329	$ 165,013
Net sales increase	14%	16%	20%
Domestic comparative store sales increase	6%	5%	8%
Other income-net	2,013	1,966	1,796
Cost of sales	171,562	150,255	129,664
Operating, selling and general and administrative expenses	36,173	31,550	27,040
Interest costs:			
Debt	1,052	1,095	756
Capital leases	274	279	266
Provision for income taxes	3,897	3,692	3,338
Minority interest and equity in unconsolidated subsidiaries	(183)	(129)	(170)
Cumulative effect of accounting change, net of tax	—	—	(198)
Net income	6,671	6,295	5,377
Per share of common stock:			
Basic net income	1.49	1.41	1.21
Diluted net income	1.49	1.40	1.20
Dividends	0.28	0.24	0.20

Financial Position

Current assets	$ 28,246	$ 26,555	$ 24,356
Inventories at replacement cost	22,749	21,644	20,171
Less LIFO reserve	135	202	378
Inventories at LIFO cost	22,614	21,442	19,793
Net property, plant and equipment and capital leases	45,750	40,934	35,969
Total assets	83,451	78,130	70,349
Current liabilities	27,282	28,949	25,803
Long-term debt	15,687	12,501	13,672
Long-term obligations under capital leases	3,045	3,154	3,002
Shareholders' equity	35,102	31,343	25,834

Financial Ratios

Current ratio	1.0	0.9	0.9
Inventories/working capital	23.5	(9.0)	(13.7)
Return on assets*	8.5%	8.7%	9.5%***
Return on shareholders' equity**	20.1%	22.0%	22.9%

Other Year-End Data

Number of U.S. Wal-Mart stores	1,647	1,736	1,801
Number of U.S. Supercenters	1,066	888	721
Number of U.S. SAM'S CLUBS	500	475	463
Number of U.S. Neighborhood Markets	31	19	7
International units	1,170	1,071	1,004
Number of Associates	1,383,000	1,244,000	1,140,000
Number of Shareholders of record (as of March 31)	324,000	317,000	307,000

*Net income before minority interest, equity in unconsolidated subsidiaries and cumulative effect of accounting change/average assets

**Net income/average shareholders' equity

***Calculated giving effect to the amount by which a lawsuit settlement exceeded established reserves. If this settlement were not considered, the return would have been 9.8%.

Exhibit 2	Wal-Mart in the 21st Century: A Global Perspective—Continued						
1999	1998	1997	1996	1995	1994	1993	1992
$ 137.634	$ 117.958	$ 104,859	$ 93,627	$ 82,494	$ 67,344	$ 55,484	$ 43,887
17%	12%	12%	13%	22%	21%	26%	35%
9%	6%	5%	4%	7%	6%	11%	10%
1,574	1,341	1,319	1,146	914	645	497	404
108,725	93,438	83,510	74,505	65,586	53,444	44,175	34,786
22,363	19,358	16,946	15,021	12,858	10,333	8,321	6,684
529	555	629	692	520	331	143	113
268	229	216	196	186	186	180	153
2,740	2,115	1,794	1,606	1,581	1,358	1,171	945
(153)	(78)	(27)	(13)	4	(4)	4	(4)
—	—	—	—	—	—	—	—
4,430	3,526	3,056	2,740	2,681	2,333	1,995	1,609
0.99	0.78	0.67	0.60	0.59	0.51	0.44	0.35
0.99	0.78	0.67	0.60	0.59	0.51	0.44	0.35
0.16	0.14	0.11	0.10	0.09	0.07	0.05	0.04
$ 21,132	$ 19,352	$ 17,993	$ 17,331	$ 15,338	$ 12,114	$ 10,198	$ 8,575
17,549	16,845	16,193	16,300	14,415	11,483	9,780	7,857
473	348	296	311	351	469	512	473
17,076	16,497	15,897	15,989	14,064	11,014	9,268	7,384
25,973	23,606	20,324	18,894	15,874	13,176	9,793	6,434
49,996	45,384	39,604	37,541	32,819	26,441	20,565	15,443
16,762	14,460	10,957	11,454	9,973	7,406	6,754	5,004
6,908	7,191	7,709	8,508	7,871	6,156	3,073	1,722
2,699	2,483	2,307	2,092	1,838	1,804	1,772	1,556
21,112	18,503	17,143	14,756	12,726	10,753	8,759	6,990
1.3	1.3	1.6	1.5	1.5	1.6	1.5	1.7
3.9	3.4	2.3	2.7	2.6	2.3	2.7	2.1
9.6%	8.5%	7.9%	7.8%	9.0%	9.9%	11.1%	12.0%
22.4%	19.8%	19.2%	19.9%	22.8%	23.9%	25.3%	26.0%
1,869	1,921	1,960	1,995	1,985	1,950	1,848	1,714
564	441	344	239	147	72	34	10
451	443	436	433	426	417	256	208
4	—	—	—	—	—	—	—
715	601	314	276	226	24	10	—
910,000	825,000	728,000	675,000	622,000	528,000	434,000	371,000
261,000	246,000	257,000	244,000	259,000	258,000	181,000	150,000

Years prior to 1998 have not been restated for the effects of the change in accounting method for SAM'S CLUB membership revenue recognition as the effects of this change would not have a material impact on this summary. Therefore, pro forma information as if the accounting change had been in effect for all years presented has not been provided. The acquisition of the ASDA Group PLC and the Company's related debt issuance had a significant impact on the fiscal 2000 amounts in this summary. See Note 7 to the Consolidated Financial Statements.

Source: Wal-Mart 2002 Annual Report

Exhibit 3	Wal-Mart in the 21st Century: A Global Perspective

Wal-Mart Stock Performance: 1993–2002

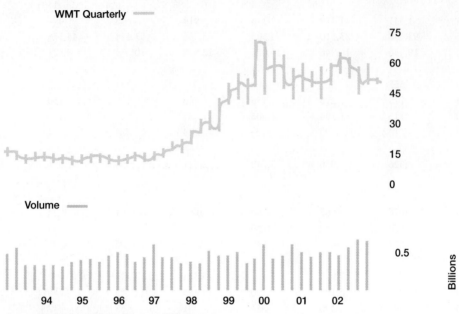

Source: Wal-Mart Website, Investor Relations:
http://investor.walmartstores.com/ireye/ir_site.zhtml?ticker=wmt&script=300&layout=-6

International Expansion

In taking its operations global, Wal-Mart hoped to use domestically developed knowledge bases and processes for "efficient store management, the effective use of technology vis-á-vis suppliers, merchandising skills, logistics,"[14] and a tremendous and highly sophisticated computer system. It also hoped to continue benefiting from its influence with large and powerful suppliers like Proctor & Gamble, Kellogg, and Coke, among others. Also, whatever it learned in international operations, Wal-Mart might then apply to its domestic operations. Although Sam Walton reportedly "thought 'damn computer' was one word,"[15] he gave the nod to developing the technology early and comprehensively in the mid-1970s. And develop Wal-Mart did; its computer system, housed in Bentonville, in 2002 reportedly held three times more data than the computers of the

United States Internal Revenue Service[16] and was second only to the technology system of the Pentagon.[17]

Wal-Mart's plan of global expansion involved moving ahead country by country to learn from its experiences in each market. It chose to start with the markets of Mexico, Latin America, and Asia, rather than Europe, where well-entrenched retailers presented enormous competition. To prepare and integrate foreign management and personnel for the Wal-Mart experience, the retailer took a number of steps. It sent a transition team to each country to define the company's practices and train the staff. Many of the foreign employees were sent to the Walton Institute where they learned about Sam Walton's best practices and Three

[14]Vijay Govindarajan and Anil K. Gupta, "Taking Wal-Mart Global: Lessons from Retailing's Giant," *Strategy & Business* 17 (1999): 16.

[15]Eryn Brown, "America's Most Admired Companies," *Fortune* 139 (March 1, 1999).

[16]Richard Ernsberger, Jr., Stefan Theil, Bianca Toness, Alexandra A. Seno, William Underhill, and Amy L. Webb, "Wal-Mart World; Can the Arkansas Giant Export Its Price-Cutting Culture Around the World?," *Newsweek International* (May 20, 2002): 50.

[17]The Pentagon, located just outside Washington, D.C., is the headquarters of the United States Department of Defense and the nerve center for military and defense command and control. In the early 21st century, approximately 23,000 military and civilian employees and about 3,000 non-defense support personnel were based at the Pentagon.

Basic Beliefs (respect for the individual, service to our customers, and to strive for excellence), the 10-Foot Rule (employees must greet every customer who comes within ten feet of them), and the Sundown Rule (any employee or customer request must be addressed before sundown). Many employees were brought to the United States to experience the original Wal-Mart culture and operations firsthand.

To establish a foreign presence, Wal-Mart relied on three basic approaches.[18] The first was to acquire an entrenched, dominant player, as it did in Germany by acquiring the Wertkauf hypermarket chain. Second was acquiring a weaker player, as the company did in Canada when it bought the suffering Woolco chain. The third method was to build its own stores and go head-to-head with existing competition, as it did with the powerful Carrefour in Brazil.

MEXICO   To prepare for its journey into global expansion, Wal-Mart began in Mexico where customers had been crossing the border for years to shop at U.S. stores. In 1991, largely because of the opening of trade between the United States and Mexico, Wal-Mart formed a $20 million joint venture with the Mexican Cifra, S.A. de C.V. to open Club Aurrera stores based on the popular U.S. Sam's Club. Wal-Mart thus got the benefit of Cifra's operational expertise in this market. In 1992, Wal-Mart's role in the joint venture expanded tremendously, when Wal-Mart and Cipra joined forces to develop new stores; the American company also had the option to partner 50-50 in future Cipra ventures. Then, in 1993, Wal-Mart applied for and received permission to establish a foreign trade zone in Buckeye, Arizona, where the company built a 1.5 million square-foot distribution center on 145 acres.[19] When Wal-Mart finally acquired Cifra in 1997, it formed Walmart de Mexico or Walmex. By the 21st century, Walmex operated 62 Supercenters, 46 Sam's Clubs, and an assortment of supermarkets, department stores, and restaurants with names like Bodega, Suburbia, Superama, and VIPS. Wal-Mart in general was well-received in Mexico, in part because many Mexicans having shopped at the stores across the border in the United States were familiar with the giant retailer. However, there were occasional gaffes in this foreign country, like when Wal-Mart caused consternation by violating a code that required products to be labeled in Spanish.

PUERTO RICO   Wal-Mart first entered Puerto Rico in 1992, shortly after expanding into Mexico. K-Mart already had a presence there, having opened its first store in 1964, and over the years other big retailers such as Home Depot and J.C. Penney appeared. Wal-Mart and these other retailers benefited not only from the tourist industry in Puerto Rico but also from a strong upper- and middle-class component of the population and from the very nature of shopping in this U.S. territory. "Unlike shopping trends in the United States, where busy consumers view a trip to the local shopping center as one more errand on a long 'to do' list, a typical Puerto Rican shopping trip becomes a family outing, the visit itself is a source of entertainment," according to the vice-president of one New York-based real estate management firm with a large presence in Puerto Rico.[20]

Nonetheless, Puerto Rico (a self-governing commonwealth associated with the United States and subject to its laws) produced its own challenges for Wal-Mart. In December 2002, Puerto Rico Justice Secretary Anabelle Rodriquez sued in a Puerto Rican court to stop Wal-Mart from buying Supermercados Amigo, a local supermarket (with 37 stores, employing 4,500 people). Although the $22.5 million deal had been approved by the U.S. Federal Trade Commission earlier that year, Rodriquez claimed that it would violate Puerto Rico's anti-monopoly laws and would hurt Puerto Rican businesses. U.S. District Judge Juan Perez Gimenez in San Juan disagreed and in late December 2002 ordered Rodriquez to stop interfering with the deal. Puerto Rico's Department of Justice then asked for a hearing in the U.S. Court of Appeals for the First Circuit (in Boston). As of early 2003, no hearing had been set, and the case was still unresolved.

CANADA   Wal-Mart entered Canada in 1993, when it bought 120 Canadian Woolworth's/Woolco stores. Canadian customers were familiar with the Wal-Mart culture and offerings because many had crossed into the United States to shop. By 2002, Wal-Mart was the dominant retailer in Canada, "with 40 percent of the Canadian department store/mass merchandiser market and 5 percent of total retail sales. On a store-by-store basis, Wal-Mart's 196 Canadian stores were more profitable than U.S. operations."[21]

---

[18]Govindarajan, 22, 24, 25.

[19]"Foreign-trade zones are designated sites licensed by the Foreign-Trade Zones (FTZ) Board (the Secretary of Commerce is Chairman) at which special Customs procedures may be used. FTZ procedures allow domestic activity involving foreign items to take place as if it were outside U.S. Customs territory, thus offsetting Customs advantages available to overseas producers who export in competition with products made here. Subzones are special-purpose zones, usually at manufacturing plants." From Foreign Trade Zones Board website: http://ia.ita.doc.gov/ftzpage.

[20]"'Grande Opportunidads' in South America," *Chain Store Age* (May 2000): 116.

[21]"Wal-Mart in 2002," Harvard Business School Case, p. 3.

There were, however, gaffes and tactical errors. It distributed English-only flyers in the province of Quebec where, by law, both the English and French languages must be used. Also, the company's written request that managers work extra hours without pay generated bad publicity for the newly installed retailer.

BRAZIL Wal-Mart entered Brazil in 1994. As it had done in Mexico, Wal-Mart chose to partner with a Brazilian retailer, Lojas Americana, to make its entry. However, this time Wal-Mart had a controlling stake (60-40) in the joint venture. Initially, Wal-Mart found mixed results in Brazil. While its Osasco store was the company's top-grossing store in 1996, other stores scattered throughout Brazil did not fare as well. Part of the problem was fierce competition from Carrefour, already deeply entrenched in the country and offering a number of inventive promotions to fend off the American retailer. Carrefour also benefited by stocking a smaller selection of items than Wal-Mart, thus keeping down its overhead. Wal-Mart found it hard to streamline the Brazilian supply chain, a factor that made it so successful elsewhere. Not helping matters were Brazil's overwhelming traffic and congestion, particularly in the larger cities, that made it difficult for suppliers' trucks to get to the stores to unload. Wal-Mart did not own its own distribution system in Brazil, so it was dependent on distributors to get goods to the store in a timely fashion, which—as Wal-Mart discovered—was no easy task between the traffic, distributor theft and the sheer volume of suppliers (for example, deliveries at Wal-Mart stores in the United States averaged seven daily while in Brazil there could be 300 daily).[22] In 2001, Wal-Mart opened only two stores in Brazil. Because it was experimenting with stores with smaller formats (akin to the domestic neighborhood markets), which were often more suitable for foreign cities with an existing culture of smaller, neighborhood shops, these two Brazilian shops were the small format *Todo Dia.*

There were other bumps along the Wal-Mart Brazilian highway. At the beginning of 1999, the Brazilian Central Bank devalued the country's currency, the *real* and then stopped pegging it to the U.S. dollar; the *real's* value plunged, touching off a sharp recession. This was Wal-Mart's first foray into a Portuguese-speaking country, so the retailer had few employees who could speak the language. Local suppliers had difficulty with the easily handled and quality control packaging that the company required, forcing Wal-Mart to rely on imported goods. Angered by Wal-Mart's demands, some local distributors refused to stock its

shelves. Wal-Mart's stock-handling equipment didn't work with the standardized local pallet designs, and its computerized bookkeeping system did not fit the Brazilian system. Some stocked items were complete failures: cordless tools, which Brazilians do not use, and leaf blowers, useless in big, concrete cities like Sao Paulo. Wal-Mart also refused to take postdated checks, which were customary in Brazil. The Sam's Clubs were less than successful because the concepts of a membership fee and bulk buying were foreign to customers. Cultural differences were often pronounced. In 1997, a reporter took note of the differences. "Tanks of live trout are out; sushi is in. American footballs have been replaced by soccer balls. The fixings for *feijoada*, a medley of beef and pork in black-bean stew, are now displayed on the deli counter. American-style jeans priced at $19.99 have been dropped in favor of $9.99 knockoffs."[23]

In November 2002, Brazil was plagued by high inflation; wholesale inflation had risen to 21 percent, and the *real* had lost 37 percent of its value in the preceding year. Also, adding to the dismal financial situation was the country's concern about the future government of President-elect Luiz Inacio da Silva, Brazil's first leftist president in 40 years.

ARGENTINA Having gained experience in the Latin American retail business, Wal-Mart entered Argentina through a wholly owned subsidiary. On the day that Wal-Mart opened its first Argentinean store in November 1995, the company posted a one-day sales record of $1 million. Wal-Mart's entry into Argentina (as well as Brazil) touched off price wars, with France's Carrefour and Holland's Makro, also in Latin America, struggling to keep up by turning to increased volume-based buying and focusing on "customer service, inventory management, and product mix."[24] Despite the rivals' efforts, Argentinean customers flocked to the newly opened Wal-Marts. Nonetheless, Wal-Mart struggled from the start when taking on the formidable Carrefour, which had been in Argentina since 1982.

Wal-Mart maintained its *modus operandi* in Argentina, refusing to accept suppliers' price-setting demands and selling some items at a loss to maintain its competitive stance. The company angered Argentinean beverage behemoth Quilmes, for example, by selling the popular Quilmes beer for 50 cents a can, six cents below wholesale; as a result, Quilmes stopped selling their beverages to the retailer.[25] In stocking their Latin America shelves, Wal-Mart en-

[22]Jonathan Friedland and Louise Lee, "Foreign Aisles: The Wal-Mart Way Sometimes Gets Lost in Translation Overseas," *Wall Street Journal,* October 8, 1997, p. A-1.

[23]Ibid.

[24]Louisa Shepard and Ian Katz, "Wal-Mart Undercuts the Price-Cutters: The U.S. Giant Is Squeezing Rivals in Argentina and Brazil," *Business Week* (February 26, 1996): 19.

[25]Ibid.

countered cultural differences and often erred in picking products:

> The meat counters featured American cuts like T-bone steaks, not the rib strips and tail rumps that Argentines prefer. Cosmetic counters were filled with bright-colored rouge and lipstick, though Argentine women tend to like a softer, more natural look. And jewelry displays gave prominent placement to emeralds, sapphires, and diamonds, while most women here prefer wearing gold and silver.[26]

In addition, the first Wal-Mart stores in Argentina carried 110-volt tools and appliances when the Argentine standard was 220 volts.

Several years after opening its doors in Argentina, Wal-Mart was still struggling. Despite its partnerships with large, entrenched chain stores, in 1997 the retailer "remain[ed] too all-American for its market. The 'Everyday Low Prices' policy on hundreds of goods that works so well domestically has not fared as well in Argentina, where customers care less about vast selection than creatively priced and promoted specials."[27] In December 2001, the country defaulted on its debts to the private sector in the biggest ($140 million) default in history. That triggered an economic crash as well as a banking system and government crash. Argentina remained problematic for Wal-Mart in 2002, in large part because of the country's chaotic financial and political situation. By late 2002, the country was on its fourth president in a year, after Fernando de la Rua was ousted. John Menzer,[28] Wal-Mart International president and CEO, said that Wal-Mart operations in the country had "been in a 'hold' strategy for about the last two years while we're waiting to see where the economy shakes out. Argentina is currently the most difficult market we're in, and we don't know when that will change."

CHINA Wal-Mart International stepped into China in 1996, with its first Supercenter and Sam's Club in Shenzhen, a mainland city of 3.8 million residents located on the opposite shore of Hong Kong and one of the eight special economic zones that China had set up to attract foreign investments. The Shenzhen store was a first for the retailer, a multi-level store housed in a four-tower, 30-story residential complex; the Sam's Club was located across the city in a

newly built 123,000 square-foot building. Wal-Mart added another Supercenter in 1997; two more in 1998; one in 1999; five in 2000; and 22 total by the close of 2002.

Wal-Mart quickly began catering to customers' tastes, which included traditional Chinese food items such as dim sum, barbecued pigeons, turtle blood, live frogs, fried rice-flour buns, pickled lettuce, chicken feet, and pork sausages in the food sections. In this manner, Wal-Mart was replicating the *xiaomaibu*[29] neighborhood markets and shops of China. Customer response was positive with food accounting for 50 percent of sales in the Chinese stores. Wal-Mart also catered to the Chinese concept that "fresh" meant "live," with tanks containing live fish, snakes, and frogs. Of all the Asian countries where Wal-Mart had a presence, China was by far the poorest. Many Chinese customers toted their purchases by bike, rather than car, and made repeated visits to the same store: "it can take five times as many Chinese customers to achieve the same volume as a U.S. store."[30] Thus, there was far more congestion in the foot traffic patterns in these stores. To adapt to the Chinese purchasing customs, Wal-Mart also fashioned smaller shopping bags. As in other countries, Wal-Mart's greatest Chinese competitors were Carrefour and Metro.

Chinese associates in general seemed to be happy with the Wal-Mart culture; managers often staged Ping-Pong tournaments for the employees, and the Shenzhen store introduced its own song: "My heart is filled with pride . . . I long to tell you how deep my love for Wal-Mart is . . . ,"[31] which was the Chinese equivalent of the "Give me a W! Give me an A!" cheer that American associates chanted each morning. Wal-Mart also sent its Chinese store managers to the Walton Institute to learn the company's best practices.

In the fall of 2002, Wal-Mart entered a joint venture with CITIC Group (China International Trust and Investment Corporation) to open stores in eastern China, starting in Shanghai. CITIC was a well-established, prominent conglomerate of 38 subsidiaries, which had been in existence since 1979. Wal-Mart needed this prominent edge, because it was competing with the powerful Carrefour, which had a far bigger presence in China as well as in Europe. Nonetheless, an editorial in *DSN Retailing Today* compared the strengths and weaknesses of Wal-Mart and Carrefour in market share, formats, Asian presence, global sourcing and pricing, among others and gave Wal-Mart the edge in this rivalry. "The battle for dominance in China will redefine the meaning of

[26]Clifford Krauss, "French Give Wal-Mart a Sales Lesson: U.S. Retailer Finds Argentina Adventure to Be a Bit Unsettling," *San Diego Union-Tribune*, January 16, 2000, p. 1–2.

[27]Matt Adams and Susan Dentzer, "How the Big Guys Do It," *Working Woman* (December 10, 1997): 48.

[28]Menzer was president of Ben Franklin Stores before joining Wal-Mart as CFO. In 2000, Menzer left that position to become president and CEO of Wal-Mart International.

[29]In Chinese, 小卖部, means "convenience store."

[30]"Asian Aspirations," *Chain Store Age* (June 2001): 67.

[31]Bill Saporito, "Can Wal-Mart Get Any Bigger?," *Time* (January 2003): 38–43.

global retailing. In turn, it will define the future for these two retailers, as well as also for hundreds of other companies that recognize the multitude of opportunities that retailing in China will offer over the next decade and beyond."[32]

Indeed, China, with 1.3 billion people in 2001 (in contrast, the United States population was 270 million), was the one country where Wal-Mart, according to Menzer, could "replicate the scale of our U.S. operations." He predicted that 2002's 22 Chinese stores could potentially become 3000 by the year 2028.[33] In 2002, Chinese retail sales in general were $492.6 billion and were expected to hit $579.5 billion by 2008. Analysts also predicted that of this $579.5 billion, 2008 could see Wal-Mart's share at $35.7 billion or approximately 5 percent of the market.[34] In 2002, Wal-Mart did an estimated $12 billion in sales in China.

GERMANY Many observers were surprised when Wal-Mart chose Germany rather than the traditional and easier point-of-entry, Great Britain, to enter markets across the Atlantic Ocean. Wal-Mart forayed into Germany, considered Western Europe's largest and most price-sensitive market, in 1998 with the acquisition for $880 million of the 21-store chain Wertkauf Hypermarts. The following year, the U.S. retailer bought 74 Interspar stores. The Interspar stores were not as profitable as the Wertkauf chain, however. Germany presented a number of challenges: competition from Germany's biggest retailer, Metro A.G., the stiff German regulatory atmosphere, the powerful trade unions, and a different shopping culture. Indeed, early on, Wal-Mart lost some top management talent, faced contentious vendor relations, and in trying to centralize distribution (Germany still used an inefficient vendor drop system), constantly had an overstock problem.

Wal-Mart's entry into Germany caused an enormous furor. German retailers had already endured a six-year slump in profits, and the presence of a new rival touched off price competition as the German stores attempted to fend off the Arkansas retailer. German regulations of what retailers charged were so stiff that "price wars" were essentially nonexistent. By law, retailers could not sell below cost and could only offer sales for two specified weeks in February and two in August. Regulators paid keen attention. Wal-Mart, of course, avoided the sale prohibition by pointing out its classic "everyday low prices." By German law, Wal-Mart could not stay open 24 hours and could not open on Sunday.

Wal-Mart had to make concessions to the German culture. For example, Germans did not like the ubiquitous greeters or employees who welcomed customers at the door. "Germans are skeptical. Customers said that they didn't want to be paying the salary of that guy at the door," said a Deutsche Bank Research analyst in 1999.[35] Germans also found the associates, attempting to be helpful, merely intrusive. Particularly distasteful to the Germans was Sam Walton's 10-Foot Rule.

Wal-Mart was not able to catch up to Metro AG in sales, which in 2001 operated 246 Real hypermarkets, 500 Extra supermarkets, 81 cash-and-carry Metro outlets, and 220 consumer-electronic stores, either under the Media Market or Saturn moniker. Nonetheless, in an attempt to increase sales, Wal-Mart in 2001 renovated a number of its German holdings, even bringing in workers from the United States to help make over its supercenter in Bad Soderheim, near Frankfurt. Part of the renovations included widening the aisles, painting in brighter colors, and installing sophisticated computer systems.

Some analysts remained sanguine about Wal-Mart's German prospects. A veteran retail forecaster, commenting in 2000 about the retailer's struggles in Germany, said: "You don't capture markets with high gross margins, but once you've sent your rivals packing, then the gross margins are going to grow mightily." Nonetheless, in 2001, Wal-Mart scuttled plans to add another 50 German stores by the year 2003.

In 2002, Wal-Mart Germany was still having difficulty and closed two stores for the first time in its international division. The clash of shopping cultures was a factor, and buying everything under one roof seemed an anathema to the Germans. Also, they were more environmentally conscious, preferring Spartan stores where they could bag their own purchases with containers brought from home rather than waste plastic. There was stiff competition from the Aldi chain, a no-frills, even austere, "bring-your-own-bag" German discounter. Sam's Clubs, where bringing your own bag or box was *de rigueur*, were not allowed in Germany because of the country's planning restrictions. Wal-Mart often butted heads with Germany's powerful trade unions; in July 2002, the retail workers' union held a two-day strike, ultimately unsuccessful, at several of the stores in an effort to get Wal-Mart to join the country's regional wage bargaining system.

KOREA It took four years of deliberation, study and planning before, in 1998, Wal-Mart International entered South Korea, then the world's 11th largest economy and, with a population of 47 million, one of the world's densest. In a $179 million deal, Wal-Mart acquired four stores and six

[32]Tony Lisanti, "Wal-Mart Has Edge in China Battle," *DSN Retailing Today* (October 28, 2002): 13.

[33]Ernsberger, Jr., et al., 50.

[34]"A Great Wall Worth Hurdling," *Discount Store News* Special Issue (October 1999): 91 & 167.

[35]Heidi Dawley, "Watch Out: Here Comes Wal-Mart," *Business Week* (June 28, 1999): 48.

sites from Makro, the Korean club store retailer. Makro owner H.S. Chang retained a minority interest in the business. There were several reasons for Wal-Mart's caution, including the ongoing tension between North and South Korea and the retail giant's initial inability to use its trade name (by late 1999, Wal-Mart was able to do so). Three of the stores were in the Seoul area, in Inchon, Ilsan, and Pundang; the fourth was in the centrally located city of Taejon. When a fifth store opened in 1999 in Kangnam, space constraints required it to be built on two subterranean floors of a ten-level shopping center. By December 2002, Wal-Mart's Korean operations included 15 stores and over 3,000 associates. Recognizing the tight family structure in the Korean culture, the newest Supercenter had, among its merchandise and convenience facilities (such as beauty parlors), an indoor playground, nursery facility, and family bathroom for customers with infants.

The Wal-Mart stores were popular in South Korea and analysts predicted that by 2007, there would be fifty to sixty more stores in the country.

UNITED KINGDOM   In June 1999, Wal-Mart acquired, in a $10.7 billion deal, 229 stores of Asda Group PLC, the United Kingdom's third largest supermarket chain. Immediately, shares of competing chains—Britain's supermarkets Tesco PLC and J. Sainsbury—plummeted, in anticipation of Wal-Mart's arrival. Asda kept its store logo instead of assuming Wal-Mart's. Its format, which included conventional supermarkets, superstores, and hypermarkets, was similar to Wal-Mart's. Like the Bentonville company, Asda emphasized low prices, customer service, and motivation of its "colleagues" (associates to Wal-Mart) "by involving them in the business, recognizing their contributions and value, sharing with them key operating information, and positioning them, collectively, as the people most responsible for ensuring that the customer comes first."[36] Asda's top management team was skilled and motivated and led by Alan Leighton who, years earlier, had adopted the Wal-Mart "operating system, philosophy and culture" to keep the near-bankrupt Asda alive. Both sets of management (many of the Asda executives stayed) worked well together, trading skills and technologies, and, by 2002, Wal-Mart was thriving in Great Britain.

JAPAN   Wal-Mart had tested the waters in Japan in 1992 when it linked up with retailer Ito-Yokado. The results were dismal, as Japanese consumers—with a reputation for fastidiousness in product quality—rejected what they considered the inferior quality of Wal-Mart products. In March 2002, Wal-Mart once again approached Japan, the world's second-largest retail market, by structuring a unique deal that gave the chain an opportunity to acquire a majority interest in Seiyu Ltd., a Japanese chain of 400 stores. This deal was "seen as an inexpensive, low-risk way for Wal-Mart to enter a market with long-term potential, but that is currently suffering economic weakness and price deflation."[37] With an initial investment of $46 million giving it a 6 percent ownership interest, Wal-Mart joined forces with a diversified retailer whose Japanese stores, ranging from 10,000 to 80,000 square feet, combined general merchandise with supermarket grocery items. The following December, Wal-Mart raised its stake in Seiyu by exercising an option to purchase shares that brought its ownership to 34 percent. With that move, Wal-Mart was poised to go head-to-head with Japan's largest retailers, Ito-Yokado and Aeon Corp. Other international retailers—France's Carrefour, the United Kingdom's Tesco, and Germany's Metro—had also already established a presence in Japan. "The price of future share purchases will rise 5% per year, meaning Wal-Mart will invest about $2 billion in Seiyu if it decides to buy up the full 66.7% stake."[38]

The possible hurdles that Wal-Mart faced in 2002, just as they had in the 1990s, extended beyond the attitudes and concerns of the Japanese consumer. Japanese retailers were notoriously aggressive in fighting competitors; many of them eschewed the Wal-Mart tradition of bypassing wholesalers because of old relationships. Japan had gone through a major financial slump in the 1990s and in addition had a complex distribution system, making direct purchases from producers difficult. Several other international concerns—the United Kingdom's healthcare chain store Boots, the French cosmetics group Sephora, and even France's Carrefour—had encountered a myriad of problems in the Japanese market. "The challenge facing Wal-Mart and other new entrants is finding a way to meet the fastidious Japanese consumers' expectations for service and quality while maintaining their streamlined cost structure, despite high labor costs and a multi-layered distribution system."[39]

RUSSIA   In April 2002, Wal-Mart representatives, led by strategic planning director Jeffrey Gruner, visited Moscow in its first business exploratory trip. Along with the global companies Pepsi, MacDonald's, and Procter and Gamble, Gruner and his associates met with the management of Russia's Perekrestok trading house, as well as with Western

[36]"Asda: Key Acquisition in Wal-Mart's Global Expansion," *MMR* 18 (October 15, 2001): 17.

[37]Mike Troy, "Wal-Mart Invests in Japan, Buys 6% Share of Seiyu," *DSN Retailing Today* (March 25, 2002): 1.

[38]Charles Smith, "Wal-Mart Stocks Up On Seiyu," *Daily Deal*, The Deal LLC, December 13, 2002.

[39]Bayan Rahman, "Retailers Set Sights on Japan," *Financial Times*, December 13, 2002, p. 30.

suppliers. Traveling incognito, the representatives visited the department stores Ramstore and Seventh Continent. But it was no secret that Wal-Mart was interested in the Eastern European market. "Gruner frequently spoke about the interest of his company in the Russian retail market. . . . According to Gruner, by 2008 Wal-Mart plans to increase turnover of operations outside of the U.S. from $22.7 billion to $142.5 billion."[40] Russia and Eastern European countries were predicted to be the next global destination for the retailing giant.

Wal-Mart International: What's Next?

By bringing its everyday low prices to different countries, Wal-Mart had often created turmoil and fear in the local retailers, but one result was lower, more competitive prices in the various countries. Wal-Mart was "credited with holding down inflation in Mexico, with improving Britain's cost of living and with helping to revolutionize the distribution system in China."[41]

John Menzer described performance results in Canada, the United Kingdom, and Mexico as "stellar." While the outlook for stores in Puerto Rico, Korea, China, and Brazil were not as rosy, Menzer said they were "trending upwards." Still

problematic at the end of 2002 were stores in Germany and Argentina.[42] The close of 2002 found Wal-Mart with even grander expansion plans. Domestically, it announced plans to open 45–55 new stores, 200 new Supercenters, 20–25 new Neighborhood Markets, and 40 to 45 new Sam's Clubs. Some of these stores would be relocations or expansions of existing stores. On the international front, Wal-Mart announced plans to open 120–130 new stores in existing markets.[43] The retailer also had plans to build a global hub in Derby, England, for its exclusive apparel line, George, which it planned to manufacture and distribute to domestic and international stores. Wal-Mart was also investigating the use of Radio Frequency Identification (RFID), a state-of-the-art microchip process that had the potential to streamline and enhance inventory tracking, receiving, stocking, and scanning.

As Wal-Mart CEO Lee Scott said in early 2003, "Simply put, our long-term strategy is to be where we're not."[44]

In the 2003 *Financial Times*/PricewaterhouseCoopers annual survey of "The World's Most Respected Companies" and "Most Respected Business Leaders," Wal-Mart was ranked 8th and CEO Lee Scott ranked 11th.[45]

---

[40]"Delegation of Wal-Mart Visited Moscow," *Russian Business Monitor*, December 16, 2002.

[41]Ernsberger, Jr., et al., 50.

[42]Don Longo, "Sam's Goes Back to Business, George Goes Global," *Retail Merchandiser* 42 (November 1, 2002): 8.

[43]"Wal-Mart Tells Expansion Plans," *Arkansas Business* 19 (October 7, 2002): 10.

[44]Saporito, 38–43.

[45]*Financial Times*, Special Report Section, January 20, 2003, p. 2.

Case 12

Home Depot's Strategy Under Bob Nardelli

BSTR141

"What I'm known for is transferring best practices. That's particularly important in this economic environment, when you have to maximize revenues through existing assets."

—Bob Nardelli, CEO of Home Depot, in 2001[1]

First Manhattan Store

In September 2004, The Home Depot Inc. (Home Depot), the biggest home improvement retailer in the world, opened a new store in New York's up-market Manhattan region. The store, spread over 105,000 square feet, employed over 300 'associates'[2] and featured a range of home improvement products, specially geared to the needs of Manhattan's residents.

ICFAI This case was written by **Shirisha Regani,** under the direction of **Sanjib Dutta,** ICFAI Center for Management Research (ICMR). It was compiled from published sources, and is intended to be used as a basis for class discussion rather than to illustrate either effective or ineffective handling of a management situation.

For enquiries regarding bulk purchases and reprint permissions, please call 91-40-23430462/63 or write to ICFAI Center for Management Research, 49, Nagarjuna Hills, Panjagutta, Hyderabad 500082, India or email icmr@icfai.org. Copies of this case can also be purchased online from the ICMR website, www.icmrindia.org.

Based on the findings of extensive consumer research, Home Depot incorporated a number of features in the new store that would appeal to an urban customer base. For instance, the store had a door attendant to hail cabs, and a help desk to offer information and schedule appointments with in-house designers. The products in the store were also more upscale than in the company's traditional stores, which stocked mainly cheap and functional items. "We've got nails. We've got electrical sockets. But we've also got $7,000 rugs," said Tom Taylor, the company's Eastern Division president, on the products on offer at the new store.[3]

The company also planned to offer special "how-to" clinics on themes like "how to create a garden on a fire escape," "how to make 500 square feet seem like 5000," etc. "Our new Manhattan location is a retail marvel and proof positive that The Home Depot continues to break the mold in how we approach new formats, new markets and new customers," said Bob Nardelli (Nardelli), the company's CEO.[4] The company also planned to open a second store in Manhattan by the end of 2004.

Over the years, Home Depot had grown chiefly by opening stores in new locations. However, the Manhattan store was a departure from the norm in that it was the first store to be opened in a large metropolitan area as against the company's earlier strategy of concentrating on suburban areas and small towns. Analysts said that the reason for the changed approach was a saturation of markets in suburban localities, which was

---

[1] Patricia Sellers, "Exit the Builder, Enter the Repairman," *Fortune,* 2001.

[2] Home Depot called its employees 'associates.'

[3] Elizabeth Lazarowitz, "Home Depot Goes Urban, Opens First Manhattan Store," news.yahoo.com, September 9, 2004.

[4] ir.homedepot.com.

limiting Home Depot's growth and revenue. By targeting metropolitan locations, Home Depot aimed to offset the saturation setting in its traditional suburban outlets. Nardelli said that if the format worked in Manhattan, it would give the company access to other large metropolitan areas.

Background Note

Home Depot traces its roots to 1978, when Bernie Marcus (Marcus) and Arthur Blank (Blank) developed the concept of large, warehouse-like stores, which stocked large varieties of home-related products, and sold them at the lowest possible prices. The stores targeted mainly "do-it-yourselfers,"[5] and adopted a "no-frills" approach to selling [merchandise]. On June 22, 1979, the first three Home Depot stores were opened in Atlanta. By the end of 1979, Home Depot had 200 associates, and had crossed $7 million dollars in sales.

In 1981, Home Depot made a public issue, raising over $4 million. Most of the money was ploughed into opening new stores. In 1984, Home Depot's shares were listed on the New York Stock Exchange. In the early 1980s, Home Depot grew very rapidly, and by 1985, the company had 50 stores and $700 million in revenues. In 1986, the stores' sales touched the $1 billion mark.

In 1991, Home Depot established its first Expo Design Center in San Diego. The Expo Design Centers carried higher-end products compared to Home Depot and sold complete solutions to household needs, such as modular kitchens, assembled bathrooms, etc. In the same year, the company's sales crossed five billion dollars. In the mid 1990s, Home Depot collaborated with the Discovery Channel and Lynette Jennings (a popular television personality and authority on home decorating and design in the U.S.) on a home improvement program, called *HouseSmart,* which was televised daily. By 1996, there were over 500 Home Depot outlets. Most of the outlets were in suburban areas and near small towns.

In 1997, Marcus stepped down and Blank became the CEO of Home Depot. In the same year, the company entered into a joint agreement with S.A.C.I. Falabella, the top departmental store in Chile and Peru, to open home improvement stores in Chile. By 1998, the company had entered South America, opening stores first in Chile and later in Puerto Rico. In 1998, Home Depot initiated its Tool Rental program, which allowed customers to rent tools for their home improvement projects. Another important event that year was the introduction of a computerized job application process, which made the recruitment process simpler and more efficient. In 1999, the company announced its environment-friendly wood policy, through which it vowed to stop selling goods that were made from wood cut in ancient and ecologically important forests. In his announcement of the policy, Blank affirmed that Home Depot would eliminate wood products from endangered sources like the rain forests, and some types of wood like cedar, redwood and lauan, giving preference instead to certified wood.

In 2000, Nardelli became the CEO of the company. The company opened stores in Canada and Argentina and expanded its international operations. However, the Argentinean and Chilean operations were not successful and the company withdrew from South America in 2001. In 2002, Marcus retired and Nardelli was appointed chairman in his place. The company expanded into Mexico, mainly through the acquisition of Mexican home improvement chains like Total Home, and Del Norte. It also opened sourcing offices in China to enable the purchase of cheap products from China and other labor-intensive Asian countries.

In 2003, Home Depot had sales of $64.8 billion and $4.3 billion in earnings (Refer [to] Exhibit 1 for annual financials of Home Depot). By the end of 2003, it had 1635 stores and

Exhibit 1	Home Depot—Annual Financials (2002–04)		
Income Statement (All Amounts in Millions of USD Except Share Data)	**January 04**	**January 03**	**January 02**
Revenue	64,816.0	58,247.0	53,553.0
Cost of Goods Sold	43,160.0	39,236.0	36,642.0
Gross Profit	21,656.0	19,011.0	16,911.0
Gross Profit Margin	33.4%	32.6%	31.6%
SG&A Expense	13,734.0	12,278.0	11,215.0
Depreciation & Amortization	1,076.0	903.0	764.0
Operating Income	6,846.0	5,830.0	4,932.0
Operating Margin	10.6%	10.0%	9.2%
Nonoperating Income	59.0	79.0	53.0
Nonoperating Expenses	62.0	37.0	28.0
Income Before Taxes	6,843.0	5,872.0	4,957.0
Income Taxes	2,539.0	2,208.0	1,913.0
Net Income After Taxes	4,304.0	3,664.0	3,044.0
Continuing Operations	4,304.0	3,664.0	3,044.0
Discontinued Operations	0.0	0.0	0.0
Total Operations	4,304.0	3,664.0	3,044.0
Total Net Income	4,304.0	3,664.0	3,044.0
Net Profit Margin	6.6%	6.3%	5.7%

Source: www.hoovers.com.

---

[5]Customers who preferred to purchase products and do their home improvements themselves instead of contracting them out.

Exhibit 2	Home Depot's Product Categories

- Building and Remodeling
- Home Décor and Organizing
- Outdoor Living
- Tools and Hardware

Source: www.homedepot.com.

employed over 300,000 associates. The stores stocked over 40,000 products related to home building, improvement and repair. (Refer [to] Exhibit 2.) In addition to Home Depot stores, the company also operated several specialized subsidiaries (Refer [to] Exhibit 3 for a profile of Home Depot's subsidiaries). In 2004, Home Depot was the largest home improvement store in the world, and the second largest retailer in the U.S. (behind Wal-Mart) and the third largest retailer globally.

CHANGES UNDER NARDELLI When Nardelli became the CEO of Home Depot in late 2000, there was widespread interest in industrial circles. Home Depot had thus far been managed only by its founders (Marcus until 1997 and then Blank till 2000). Marcus had an iconic status at Home Depot, and analysts often compared his position in the company to that of Wal-Mart's Sam Walton.

Although Blank's personality was distinct from that of Marcus, there were no significant changes in the company's operations or its culture under him. "If you like the package of the last 19 years, you can count on more of the same," Blank said when he succeeded Marcus.[6] Analysts expected that when Blank retired, the board would choose someone from within the company to succeed him, even though there was no heir apparent in the company. Nardelli's appointment came as a surprise to many analysts and company insiders because he was a complete outsider, and one with no retail experience.

Nardelli had a detail-oriented style of management. He had worked at General Electric (GE) for 27 years, and was one of the three contenders to succeed Jack Welch in 2000. Like many of the top executives at GE, Nardelli had a deep belief in "processes" and believed that better processes led to better products, and consequently, better profits. Many analysts felt that Nardelli, with his experience [with] GE and its focus on processes and systems, was the right person for Home Depot at that juncture, when it was passing through a difficult phase.

[6]Nicole Harris, "Home Depot: Beyond Do It Yourselfers," *BusinessWeek*, June 30, 1997.

Exhibit 3	Home Depot's Specialized Ventures

Expo Design Centers

Expo Design Centers were showrooms, which put customers in complete and finished settings. For instance, a completely set-up kitchen or bathroom was displayed and customers were allowed to make modifications in the setting. They featured more lifestyle and designer products than general Home Depot Stores, which emphasized functionality. Most of the products at Expo Centers had to be special ordered and they stocked very few items in the stores.

The Home Depot Supply

The Home Depot Supply was part of Home Depot's growth strategy to expand into emerging markets and professional customer channels. The division served professional customers' needs by offering products and services that complemented Home Depot's core retail business. Home Depot Supply served the diverse needs of business-to-business customers, with a national focus on production homebuilders, facility maintenance professionals, construction contractors and government customers.

The Home Depot Landscape Supply

Home Depot Landscape Supply was a store selling a complete range of landscape products and services, including delivery, tool rental, etc. The stores stocked products like saplings, shrubs, indoor plants and gardening tools, and catered to professional landscapers as well as amateur gardeners.

The Home Depot Floor Store

This was a specialized division selling flooring materials and accessories like rugs and carpets, targeting professional flooring contractors as well as do-it-yourself customers. The company even provided installation to customers. These stores also stocked minimum [merchandise] and most of the sales were through special order.

Georgia Lighting

Georgia Lighting sold an extensive collection of fine decorative and antique lighting, accent furniture, antiques, and a complete line of unique accessories. This division boasted the largest lighting showroom in the U.S.

Adapted from www.homedepot.com.

The rapid growth in Home Depot in its first two decades came largely from its setting up of new stores. In the late 1990s, the company's growth rate began to slow. The company said that the lower rate of growth was a reflection of the slowing economy (which resulted in a slump in home building), expensive labor and falling lumber prices (which resulted in a lower level of total sales). However, analysts believed that the main reason for the slowdown was market saturation.

In the first quarter of 2001, Home Depot's profits rose only 16 percent, which was considerably lower than the company's five-year annual average of 25 percent. Soon after the announcement of the first quarter 2001 results, David Buchsbaum (Buchsbaum), an analyst at Wachovia Securities, said, "They're certainly at or near their store-saturation point. From now on, they have to garner growth through more efficient operation of the existing store base."[7] Analysts agreed that major changes were imperative in Home Depot's culture and strategic direction to put the company on a high growth trajectory again, and many of them were confident that Nardelli was well qualified to bring about these changes. Over the early 2000s, Nardelli made several changes in Home Depot's operations and business strategy, which helped the company streamline its activities and grow in a balanced manner.

RATIONALIZING STORE OPENINGS   One of the biggest threats for retail businesses is unplanned and excessive growth, which can result in stores being set up too close to each other, eventually cannibalizing each other's customer base. Traditionally, Home Depot increased its number of stores by 20 percent every year. While this rate of expansion worked well in the initial years, by the late 1990s analysts felt that the number of stores was growing too fast. By the late 1990s, the company had set up more stores than it could conveniently manage, while failing to invest in the systems that would help in their management. "Same store" or "comparable store" sales[8] had been declining since the mid-1990s, and while new stores were successful in increasing their revenues, the older stores were not performing well. In 2000, comparable store sales increased only four percent, as compared to around ten percent in the 1990s. "Store growth will need to slow at some point. Investors are starting to see that we're very close to the saturation point," said Buchsbaum.[9]

Nardelli decided to stop the proliferation of stores and to ensure that expansion was balanced. The first thing that Nardelli did on being appointed CEO was to lower the target for store openings in 2001 by nine percent. Home Depot eventually opened 204 stores in 2001, which was the same number as in 2000. Nardelli reasoned that growth should come from internal changes in existing stores, rather than new store openings, so that the overall performance of the company would be positive and strong. The company also began to choose locations for new stores more carefully to ensure that they were not set up too close to other Home Depots.

IMPROVING THE SUPPLY CHAIN   Until 2000, Home Depot did not have any formal system for inventory management or purchasing. While many of its competitors were switching to automated inventory management systems, Home Depot was still logging in each shipment manually. In the stores, employees spent more time restocking shelves and taking inventory counts than in assisting customers. One survey conducted in the late 1990s revealed that Home Depot's sales associates spent 70 percent of their time restocking and 30 percent helping customers.

Soon after Nardelli became CEO, he introduced a new service program for all the stores, which required employees to restock at night and spend maximum time with customers during service hours. He also mandated that the new program be adopted in all the stores by the end of 2001. A survey conducted after the new program was adopted showed that the time associates spent with customers and the time they took to restock shelves had been reversed. This improved the service at the stores considerably and Nardelli estimated that the change would bring in additional revenues of $2.8 billion in 2001.

To cut down on excess inventories, Nardelli decided to adopt a leaner approach. Storekeepers were trained to take a scientific approach to ordering new stocks and avoid excessive inventory. He also told managers to increase "inventory velocity," or the speed at which products flowed through the store. This would ensure that stores did not purchase more goods than they needed, keeping inventory costs as low as possible.

Purchasing at Home Depot was also ridden with inefficiencies. Home Depot had nine operating regions, and purchasing was fully decentralized in all the regions. Individual buyers from the nine regions dealt separately with suppliers for their regional purchases. This created a number of inefficiencies in the overall system.

To correct this situation, Nardelli centralized Home Depot's purchasing function, locating it at Atlanta. He believed that centralization would eliminate inefficiencies, as well as increase negotiating power with sellers. The number of suppliers was also cut down to facilitate standardization. The company estimated that centralization of purchasing and standardization of suppliers increased the company's gross margins by one percentage point—a major achievement in the retailing industry.

---

[7]Sam Jaffe, "New Tricks in Home Depot's Toolbox?" *BusinessWeek*, June 5, 2001.

[8]A retail industry metric used to measure the growth from stores that have been open a year or more.

[9]Sam Jaffe, "What's Hammering Home Depot?" *BusinessWeek*, October 18, 2000.

BETTING ON IT Home Depot was a laggard in the adoption of Information Technology (IT). Most of the systems—inventory, purchasing, recruitment, performance appraisal—were not up to date. In fact, when Nardelli joined the firm, there wasn't even a system for the different stores to be connected through e-mail. This increased the cost of coordination between stores.

Nardelli moved to apply IT constructively throughout the company. Systems like inventory, appraisal, etc., were taken up for automation. "There's an enormous amount of room to improve margins just by advancing its information technology," said Robert Morse, manager of the Wall Street Fund.[10]

In the early 2000s, Home Depot began introducing self-checkout kiosks at some of its stores. This reduced the time spent by customers on their check-outs and cut the queues at cashiers. In 2004, the company started deploying a massive software program that would automate quotes, scheduling and order tracking. Nardelli said that the company was spending 12 times more on IT in 2004 than in 2000. By 2004, the company had self-checkout [facilities] at more than 800 of its stores, and it was estimated that 32 percent of the customers used them.

IN-STORE IMPROVEMENTS Home Depot stores had always been laid out like warehouses, with a large number of products displayed [on] huge shelves from the ceiling to the floor. The idea was to create a warehouse-like atmosphere where people could purchase all that they needed for home improvement at discount prices. However, surveys in the early 2000s revealed that this layout had lost its appeal for most people. Improvements in the retailing industry in the early 2000s led shoppers to favor stores that were bright, clean and open and contributed to the enjoyment of the shopping experience.

In the early 2000s, Home Depot began making changes to its store layouts on these lines. For instance, lighting displays were moved to the front in many stores, so as to make them brighter and more inviting. The stores also did away with floor to ceiling displays and began displaying many of the products at eye level for customers to look at easily. "You'll see a lot more of our sets come down. It makes for a better shopping experience," said Carol Tomé, the company's CFO.[11] This also made the stores more customer-friendly as products were easier to access. In-store innovations also helped improve customer service. For instance, instead of stacking up paint cans on shelves, most

Home Depots set up color solution centers, where customers could consult with experts in the field to choose colors or order special colors for their homes. Better store displays helped Home Depot keep up with competitor Lowe's Companies Inc. (Lowe['s]), a company that had a good reputation for its customer-friendly store layout.

EMPHASIZING THE SERVICE ANGLE Nardelli also shifted the focus in Home Depot from its traditional customer base of "do-it-yourselfers" to people who preferred a full basket of services. Nardelli reasoned that, while some people liked to purchase products and do their home improvements themselves, a far greater number of them preferred to hire someone to do it for them. He believed that Home Depot could increase its margins considerably by offering installation and other services to people who purchased merchandise from the stores.

Prior to 2000, Home Depot offered installation services in some of its stores, but the service was not standardized or uniform across stores. Besides, it was restricted to the surrounding locality and even within those areas, not all the customers were aware that such services were available.

The company moved to increase awareness about these services in the early 2000s, by putting up toll-free installation numbers on all the company's signboards and advertisements. It also set up service desks in front of all its stores, where customers could register for home consultations regarding their home improvement projects. Customers could also register over the Internet.

Home Depot entered into tie-ups with contractors, who did the installations on behalf of the company. Before selection, a contractor had to go through a comprehensive screening process, which included a detailed criminal and immigration background check. The contractors were also required to wear an identity card issued by Home Depot. In early 2004, the company had tie-ups with over 6000 contractors all over the U.S. It also acquired a few small installation companies to expand the business. In 2003, Home Depot spent $248 million on the acquisition of several small installation companies, including Installed Products USA, which installed roofing and fences, and RMA Home Services, which provided siding and window installation.

Nardelli believed that many customers would find it more convenient to get their installations done by someone from Home Depot, rather than appointing a contractor themselves. It would also endear Home Depot to contractors, who took up 30 percent of the company's sales. After tying up with Home Depot, many contractors increased their purchases and stocks of Home Depot [merchandise] to use in installations that did not originate at Home Depot.

---

[10]Sam Jaffe, "New Tricks in Home Depot's Toolbox?" *BusinessWeek*, June 5, 2001

[11]Dean Foust, "Home Depot's Remodeling Project," *BusinessWeek*, January 9, 2004.

In 2004, the installation unit was the fastest-growing unit of the company, expanding at 40 percent per year. The company had 25 national installation programs, covering roofing, siding, fencing, windows, decking and sheds. The company ensured that high standards were maintained in the installation business through its careful screening of the contractors with whom it tied up. In addition to this, customers were required to call in and rate the installation job before the contractors were paid. The company said that most of the callers rated the jobs eight or higher on a scale of ten.

Home Depot also began targeting professionals like plumbers, carpenters and builders, who, according to the company's research, spent three times more than amateur customers. The company set up Home Depot Pro in 2001 to cater specifically to professionals. The Pro stores were laid out differently from the regular Home Depot outlets and were staffed by experienced store assistants. Products were also sold in larger packs or in bulk. Some of the regular Home Depot stores also introduced hours catering specially to professionals, and many of them took up the Pro initiative program, where there was a special desk to serve professionals. Targeting professionals pitted Home Depot against smaller companies that specialized in specific areas of home-building supply, but analysts felt that Home Depot's huge size gave it a competitive advantage in the home improvement market.

EXPLORING NEW MARKETS   In the early 2000s, as the market in the U.S. was getting saturated and competition from other stores was increasing, Home Depot began exploring options overseas. In the late 1990s, the company had made a foray into Chile and Argentina. However, the ventures were not very successful and it had to withdraw from the markets.

But [the] next time around, Home Depot was more successful and by 2004, it had stores in Canada, Mexico, Puerto Rico and the District of Columbia. Analysts also believed that, given its good cash position (around $5.2 billion in cash reserves in 2003) and strong balance sheet, the company was likely to try for some acquisitions in Europe. They said that Home Depot had the potential to become a strong player in Europe.

Home Depot was also looking at China as a market with great potential. In 2002, the company opened offices in Shanghai and Shenzhen to obtain customer data as a preliminary to setting up shop in the country. "We have studied China for some time. It's got a great capability in terms of a growing economy," said Bill Patterson, who was appointed to the newly created position of Home Depot president of Asia.[12]

In addition to overseas expansion, the company also began to focus on setting up more stores in urban areas in the U.S. during the 2000s. The urban stores were smaller than regular Home Depot stores and carried products that city people were interested in. The company opened its first urban format store in Brooklyn, New York, in 2001. The company maintained that the store was getting a mixed response, and it was clear that the higher overhead costs in urban areas would not justify the setting up of too many urban stores.

The Challenges

It was not easy for Nardelli to initiate changes at Home Depot. While most people acknowledged that significant changes in Home Depot's strategy of the 1990s were required, Nardelli faced a large amount of criticism from various quarters for the changes he made at Home Depot.

Firstly, critics said that Nardelli was moving too fast and that the changes that he was making were too drastic. Analysts said that this rate of transformation could upset old timers at Home Depot, who would not take revolutionary changes kindly. "There's the fear that Home Depot is changing too much, too fast," said UBS Warburg analyst Aram Rubinson.[13] But Nardelli pointed out that speed was required to bring in positive results faster. He also said that speed in adapting to new conditions was a very critical factor for success in the retail business. "The rate of internal change must be greater than the rate of external change, or we will fall behind," said Nardelli.[14]

Secondly, Nardelli's application of GE's numbers-oriented management did not go down well with executives at Home Depot. Soon after Nardelli joined, many top executives at Home Depot resigned or threatened to resign, as they were not able to accept the sudden change in orientation at the company. "It was time to infuse some different thinking in the company, but his 'do it my way' style undercut the sense of ownership employees had," said one longtime human-resources manager who left Home Depot for a job at another Atlanta company, taking along several employees. "It was revolution, not evolution," he added.[15]

Thirdly, analysts feared that some of Nardelli's revolutionary policies could alienate customers. For instance, Nardelli's elimination of the "cash return" policy of the company was widely criticized. Home Depot's original cash return policy

[12]"Home Depot Preparing to Expand to China," *The Boston Herald*, June 7, 2004.

[13]Patricia Sellers, Julie Schlosser "Its His Home Depot Now," *Fortune*, September 20, 2004.

[14]Patricia Sellers, "Something to Prove," *Fortune*, June 24, 2002.

[15]Carol Hymowitz, "How One Savvy Executive Led a Winning Revolution," *Career Journal*, March 17, 2004.

allowed customers to return any product they bought at Home Depot, to any store, without any time limitations and even without proof of purchase, to claim [a] full refund. In the 2000s, Nardelli and Tome conducted a study to see the efficacy of this policy and realized that it was highly abused. Consequently, Nardelli abolished it and introduced a new policy, which allowed customers to return goods only with a proof of purchase and within 90 days of purchase. It was estimated that the new policy would save Home Depot $10 million annually, but some analysts still felt that it would harm the company's goodwill with customers.

Home Depot vs. Lowe['s] in the Early 2000s

In the early 2000s, Lowe['s] became a major competitor to Home Depot. Lowe['s], which was initially set up as a regional operator in North Carolina, was the top home improvement retailer in the U.S. in the 1980s, but was overtaken by Home Depot's rapid expansion in the 1990s. Lowe['s] changed its strategy in the 1990s, opening more stores in metropolitan areas, and consequently, grew rapidly in the 1990s and early 2000s.

By 2004, Lowe['s] had over 950 stores in the U.S. (the company's store expansion rate was around 14 percent in the 2000s, while Home Depot had lowered its expansion rate to around 10 percent). It was the second largest home improvement retailer in the U.S. at this time. Lowe['s] planned to open 140 more stores in 2004. Some company insiders and shareholders blamed Nardelli for Lowe's closing in on Home Depot. They said that Lowe['s] had a good chance of overtaking Home Depot, considering that Nardelli had slowed Home Depot's store expansion rate. Lowe['s] was also performing better than Home Depot on the financial front and the company's stock had tripled in the first three years of the 2000s, as against Home Depot's, which fell by 12 percent. Lowe's profits also rose by nearly 40 percent in 2003, while Home Depot's profits were increasing at about 18 percent.

Lowe's entry into city markets led analysts to fear that it would overtake Home Depot in these areas. "Lowe's has the opportunity to grab market share. It's a tight, tough business, but there's definitely room for them," said Mike Porter, an analyst at Morningstar.[16]

Some analysts also said that Lowe['s] had a competitive advantage over Home Depot in that its stores were generally perceived to be better laid out and more appealing, espe-

cially to women. Lowe['s] had made a conscious decision to make stores more appealing to women as its research indicated that women made a majority of the purchasing decisions. Executive Vice-President for Merchandising Dale C. Pond said, "Eighty percent of (home) projects are initiated by females."[17] Therefore, Lowe['s] made its stores brighter, cleaner and more spacious, to attract women as well as other non-professional shoppers, who hesitated to buy things in "lumber shops." Sandy Cooper, a homemaker and loyal customer of Lowe['s] said about Lowe['s], "I have to sing their praises, because they were very nice. At Home Depot, you can't find anybody to help—and if you do, they just point."[18]

Home Depot had a practice of employing more part-time staff to operate the stores. Analysts said that part-time staff did not take much interest in closing sales because they did not have a sense of responsibility. On the other hand, Lowe's store assistants, most of whom were permanent employees, were found to be more friendly and helpful. (In 2004, 60 percent of Home Depot's staff was permanent compared to Lowe's 80 percent.) Analysts said that, because store assistants were the main points of contact for the customer with the store, they played an important role in determining the image that customers formed of a store.

The Share Price Paradox

While analysts were speculating about whether Lowe['s] would be able to overtake Home Depot to become the biggest retailer in its segment, Home Depot's executives, especially Nardelli, were trying to analyze the reasons for the fall in the company's share price. The stock, which traded at around $70 in late 1999 and early 2000, fell to an all-time low of around $22 in early 2003 and was trading at around $38 in 2004 (Refer [to] Exhibit 4 for stock price movements). Executives were worried that the market was not responding to the company's growth. Nardelli was reported to have said, "I can understand not getting rewarded, but I don't understand getting punished."[19] It was also said that shareholders blamed Nardelli for the poor performance of the stock, considering that the stock fell by around 50 percent from 2000. "I think there are people on Wall Street who are questioning his ability to make the change and run a retail organization," said Erik Becker, an analyst at Waddell & Reed Financial, an investment fund.[20]

[16]Amy Tsao, "How Home Depot and Lowe Measure Up," *BusinessWeek*, December 5, 2001.

[17]Aixa M. Pascual, "Lowe is Sprucing up Its House," *BusinessWeek*, June 3, 2002.

[18]Aixa M. Pascual, "Lowe is Sprucing up Its House," *BusinessWeek*, June 3, 2002.

[19]Patricia Sellers, "Something to Prove," *Fortune*, June 24, 2002.

[20]Dean Foust, "The GE Way Isn't Working at Home Depot," *BusinessWeek*, January 17, 2003.

Exhibit 4	Stock Price Movement

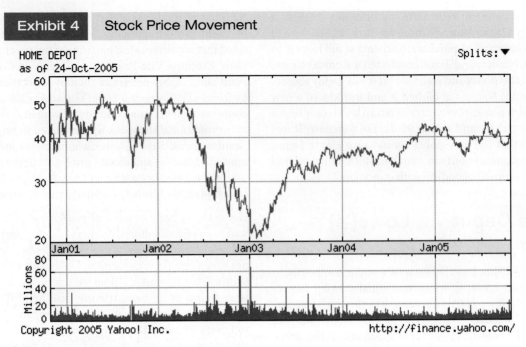

HOME DEPOT
as of 24-Oct-2005   Splits:▼

Copyright 2005 Yahoo! Inc.   http://finance.yahoo.com/

Source: finance.yahoo.com.

What was even more perplexing was that the price failed to rise despite the improving financial performance of Home Depot. In the first quarter of 2004, same store sales rose 7.7 percent, which was the highest rate of growth experienced in the last five years.

Some analysts explained that although Home Depot had made some changes for the better since 2000, the company was by no means stable in the market. Competition had increased not only from Lowe['s], but also from other smaller companies, which sold home improvement items over the [Internet], at prices much lower than Home Depot's. Of these companies, some were suppliers to Home Depot.

Although Nardelli made some positive changes to Home Depot's operations and strategy, analysts said that most of the steps he took were more relevant to manufacturing than to retail. They said that Nardelli had moved too fast, considering that he had no experience in retail. One example of this was his new inventory management system, which made stores run on leaner inventory. Store managers said that leaner inventory often led to under-stocking of high demand goods, which created a shortfall and led to customer complaints.

However, Nardelli's supporters said that his numbers-oriented and scientific style of management managed to streamline the somewhat haphazard growth path that Home Depot followed until 2000. "They had been in start-up mode for 22 years," said Nardelli soon after becoming CEO.[21] His supporters believed that Nardelli was the right person to shift Home Depot from its startup mode to that of a mature industry leader.

Additional Readings & References

1. Patricia Sellers, **Can Home Depot Fix Its Sagging Stock?** *Fortune,* March 4, 1996.
2. Nicole Harris, **Home Depot: Beyond Do It Yourselfers,** *BusinessWeek,* June 30, 1997.
3. Jennifer Bresnahan, **Home Depot's Ron Griffin on How IS Benefits from Corporate Values,** *CIO Magazine,* May 1, 1998.
4. Roy Johnson, **Home Depot Renovates,** *Fortune,* November 23, 1998.
5. Lawrence Armour, **Home Depot: Now It Can Be Told,** *Fortune,* May 1, 1999.
6. Katrina Brooker, **E-Rivals Seem to Have Home Depot Awfully Nervous,** *Fortune,* August 16, 1999.
7. Cora Daniels, **To Hire a Lumber Expert, Click Here,** *Fortune,* April 3, 2000.
8. Nicholas Stein, **Winning the War to Keep Top Talent,** *Fortune,* May 29, 2000.

[21]Carol Hymowitz, "How One Savvy Executive Led a Winning Revolution," *Career Journal,* March 17, 2004.

9. Sam Jaffe, **What's Hammering Home Depot?** *BusinessWeek,* October 18, 2000.

10. **Co-Founder Trades Depot's Orange Apron for Family and Community,** www.findarticles.com, March 5, 2001.

11. Patricia Sellers, **Exit the Builder, Enter the Repairman,** *Fortune,* March 19, 2001.

12. Sam Jaffe, **New Tricks in Home Depot's Toolbox?** *BusinessWeek,* June 5, 2001.

13. Patricia Sellers, **Home Depot's Home Defense,** *Fortune,* October 15, 2001.

14. Aixa M. Pascual, **Tidying Up At Home Depot,** *BusinessWeek,* November 26, 2001.

15. Amy Tsao, **How Home Depot and Lowe Measure Up,** *BusinessWeek,* December 5, 2001.

16. Anthony Williams, **What? Now We Have to Make a Profit *and* Be Ethical?** *Business 2.0,* February 1, 2002.

17. Axia M. Pascual, **Lowe Is Sprucing up Its House,** *BusinessWeek,* June 3, 2002.

18. Amy Tsao, **Reading Home Depot's Fuzzy Blueprint,** *BusinessWeek,* June 4, 2002.

19. Patricia Sellers, **Something to Prove,** *Fortune,* June 24, 2002.

20. Dean Foust, **Home Depot's "Big Disappointment": Sales,** *BusinessWeek,* January 17, 2003.

21. Dean Foust, **The GE Way Isn't Working at Home Depot,** *BusinessWeek,* January 17, 2003.

22. Janice Revell, **Can Home Depot Get Its Groove Back?** *Fortune,* February 3, 2003.

23. Matthew Maier, **How to Revive Home Depot,** *Business 2.0,* May 1, 2003.

24. Dean Foust, **Home Depot Still Hasn't Nailed Lowe's,** *BusinessWeek,* November 20, 2003.

25. Dean Foust, **Home Depot's Remodeling Project,** *BusinessWeek,* January 9, 2004.

26. Carol Hymowitz, **How One Savvy Executive Led a Winning Revolution,** *Career Journal,* March 17, 2004.

27. Janice Revell, **More Room for Improvement?** *Fortune,* March 22, 2004.

28. **Home Depot Preparing to Expand to China,** *The Boston Herald,* June 7, 2004.

29. Jyothi Thottam, **Bob the Builder,** *Time,* June 21, 2004.

30. Rebecca Zicarelli, **Home Depot's Hardware Warriors,** *Fast Company,* September 2004.

31. Chana R. Schoenberger, **House Call,** *Forbes,* September 6, 2004.

32. Elizabeth Lazarowitz, **Home Depot Goes Urban, Opens First Manhattan Store,** news.yahoo.com, September 9, 2004.

33. Patricia Sellers, Julie Schlosser, **Its His Home Depot Now,** *Fortune,* September 20, 2004.

34. Kelvin Taylor, **The Windfall of Hurricanes,** www.fool.com, September 20, 2004.

35. Julie Schlosser, **He'll Take Manhattan,** *Fortune,* September 20, 2004.

36. Karen Jacobs, **Home Depot, Lowe's Sees Strong Post-Hurricane Demand,** about.reuters.com.

37. www.rabble.ca.

38. www.sprawl-busters.com.

39. www.youareworthmore.org.

40. www.hoovers.com.

41. ir.homedepot.com.

42. www.homedepot.com.

Case 13

Ryanair—The "Southwest" of European Airlines

BSTR059

> *"Everyone always says, 'What's your secret?' It's very simple. We're like Wal-Mart in the U.S.— we pile it high and sell it cheap."*
>
> **–Michael` O'Leary, CEO of Ryanair**[1]

> *"Ryanair is the best imitation of Southwest Airlines that I have seen."*
>
> **–Herbert D. Kelleher, founder of Southwest Airlines**[2]

> *"He (O'Leary) is almost certainly one of the most successful leaders in the industry, with a unique business model, discipline and an extraordinary level of confidence."*
>
> **–Sir Michael Bishop, chairman, BMI British Midland**[3]

> *"Ryanair has the financial and operational capacity to maintain its position as the dominant player in the low fares, no frills market, and indeed become one of Europe's largest airlines."*
>
> **–Stephen Furlong, airline analyst, Davy Stockbrokers**[4]

Ryanair Challenges easyJet

In the summer of 2003, Michael O'Leary (O'Leary), the CEO of Ryanair, one of the oldest and most successful low-

ICFAI This case was written by **Shirisha Regani,** under the direction of **Sanjib Dutta,** ICFAI Center for Management Research (ICMR). It is intended to be used as a basis for class discussion rather than to illustrate either effective or ineffective handling of a management situation.

The case was compiled from published sources. © 2003, ICFAI Center for Management Research. All rights reserved. No part of this publication may be reproduced, stored in a retrieval system, used in a spreadsheet, or transmitted in any form or by any means—electronic or mechanical—without permission.

To order copies, call 0091-40-2343-0462/63 or write to ICFAI Center for Management Research, Plot # 49, Nagarjuna Hills, Hyderabad 500 082, India or email icmr@icfai.org. [Web site] www.icmrindia.org.

cost airlines of Europe, outfitted himself in combat gear and led a small army of Ryanair's employees to Luton airport, the base of rival easyJet.[5] An old World War II battle tank was also roped in to complete the effect. This was Ryanair's way of "attacking" the fares of easyJet, which, it claimed, were very high for a low-cost airline. O'Leary said he wanted to "liberate" the public from the high fares of easyJet. Through this unconventional publicity stunt, O'Leary was able to get his message across successfully and create positive media attention for his airline.

Ryanair was one of the first independent airlines in Ireland. Until Ryanair was set up in 1985, the Irish air services were

---

[1]Kerry Capell, Carlos Tromben, William Echikson, Wendy Zellner, "Renegade Ryanair," *Business Week,* May 14, 2001.

[2]Kerry Capell, Carlos Tromben, William Echikson, Wendy Zellner, "Renegade Ryanair," *Business Week,* May 14, 2001.

[3]"The Life of Ryan," www.easyprotest2.com.

[4]www.ryanair.com.

[5]easyJet is a low-cost airline based in London. It was set up [by] Stelios Haji-Ioannou, a Greek shipping magnate.

almost exclusively under the control of Aer Lingus, the national carrier. Some other airlines, notably Avair, had been set up in Ireland before Ryanair, but most of them collapsed due to their inability to compete with the more powerful national carrier. The setting up of Ryanair was an important landmark in Irish airline history. Ryanair went through a few turbulent years of operation, but soon it managed to refocus itself successfully as a low-cost no-frills carrier, capturing a large share of the market for air services between England and Ireland. By the late 1990s, it was the largest low-cost airline in Europe. However, it was overtaken by easyJet when the latter took over Go, the low-cost subsidiary of British Airways (BA), to gain a larger market and a bigger combined fleet. (Refer [to] Exhibit 1 for note[s] on low-cost airlines in Europe.)

Exhibit 1	Low-Cost Airlines in Europe

In the mid-1990s, after the European Union deregulated air travel, a number of upstart airlines came up, providing no-frills travel around Europe. easyJet, Ryanair, Buzz,[13] bmibaby[14] and Go[15] were some of the airlines fighting for airspace. Low-cost airlines had a large market in Europe because the number of people traveling between the different countries increased after the formation of the European Union. Train travel was slow and expensive. Therefore, people looked to airlines to meet their travel needs. Low-cost airlines identified the business opportunity and offered tickets which were about half the price of a train ticket. They thrived on volumes rather than profit margins. So successful were the low-cost airlines that some of the national carriers also set up low-cost subsidiaries. (Go was set up by British Airways, Buzz by Dutch carrier KLM, and bmibaby by British Midlands Airlines.)

The low-cost airline industry was characterized by high competition. The standard of service of all these airlines was almost the same and they competed within the same markets. This made rivalry intense. In the early 2000s, the low-cost airline industry began getting consolidated, with Go being taken over by easyJet and Ryanair taking over Buzz.

easyJet and Ryanair became the biggest low-cost airlines in Europe. Ryanair had the advantage of age and experience, as it had been set up ten years before easyJet. But easyJet, with its fleet of new planes and practice of flying to airports in the main cities (unlike Ryanair) overtook Ryanair to the top position in 2002.

[13] The low-cost subsidiary of Dutch carrier KLM.
[14] The low-cost subsidiary of British Midland [A]irlines.
[15] Go was the low-cost subsidiary of British Airways.

Source: Compiled from various sources.

Background Note

Ryanair started operations in July 1985, flying between Waterford in the southeast of Ireland and London's Gatwick airport. Three brothers, Catlan, Declan and Shane Ryan, were the founding shareholders of Ryanair, which was set up to offer low-cost, no-frills services between Ireland and London. The airline began operations with a fifteen-seater turbo prop commuter plane which was leased to the company by Guinness Peat Aviation (GPA),[6] of which their father, Tony Ryan, was the chairman.

Ryanair got an early break when, shortly after its formation, the UK and Irish governments signed a new air services agreement that deregulated air traffic between the two countries. In anticipation of the increased air traffic between the two countries, the Irish government decided to license a second Irish operator on the route from Dublin to London. Ryanair happened to be the only airline to apply for the license. It was granted the license to operate on the Dublin (Ireland)–Luton (London) route. By the end of the first year, Ryanair had carried 5,000 passengers and had a staff of 57.

To meet increased operational requirements, Ryanair purchased two more planes (24-year-old 50-seaters) from Dan Air. The airline quickly realized that it could capitalize on the market by offering cheap fares, and set its initial fare at IR£95 (1 Ireland pound was equal to approximately 1.44 U.S. dollars) for a return ticket. The price was 20 percent lower than the cheapest fare of its competitors. Gradually, the airline replaced its old aircraft with newer aircraft purchased from TAROM, a Romanian air transport company.

By the end of 1986, services to London were firmly established. However, further expansion had been blocked because the requisite licenses could not be obtained. To overcome this, Ryanair acquired an 85 percent stake in London European Airways (LEA, a Luton-based airline). LEA had been flying scheduled flights to Amsterdam and Brussels from London, but the flights had been suspended in early 1987. By May 1987, Ryanair had resumed services to both the cities. However, load factors were low on both the routes (around 45 percent), and the Amsterdam route had to be dropped later that year. The Brussels route also had problems and had to be more closely integrated with the parent company which was called Ryanair Europe. However, several difficulties cropped up and the scheduled routes had to be abandoned. The company repositioned itself as a charter tour operator flying to various destinations in the Mediterranean and Europe.

[6] GPA was set up in 1975 as an aircraft leasing company. Tony Ryan was a founder member of GPA.

In the summer of 1987, Ryanair started its first charter operation to over 65 locations around Europe. By the end of that year, the airline had carried over 400,000 passengers. 1988 started well, with Ryanair getting more licenses on new routes from Dublin, Knock, Cork and Shannon. However, attempts to develop new routes from Dublin to Manchester and Glasgow came up against entrenched competition from Aer Lingus, which slashed prices and increased capacity.

In the face of this competition, Ryanair's losses on the Manchester route rose alarmingly to IR£700,000. In April that year, Eugene O'Neil, who became Chief Executive within a year of the airline's formation, was removed from his post. The company released a statement citing differences with the management. Declan Ryan was named acting chief executive and both the Glasgow and Manchester routes were axed. Shortly afterwards, P.J. McGoldrick (McGoldrick) was brought in from a similar position at Heavylift Cargo Airlines (a UK-based cargo company), to take over as chief executive.

On October 20, 1988, Ryanair carried its 1,000,000th passenger, Jane O'Keefe, on the flight to Dublin from London. She was presented with a golden voucher entitling her and a nominated friend free travel for life on any Ryanair route. By the end of 1988, Ryanair's total fleet had increased to six aircraft. Losses, however, were continuing to mount, reaching IR£6 million in 1988.

In September 1989, the Irish government announced a "two airline policy," which would be valid for three years (till October 1992). The new policy was directed at benefiting both the Irish carriers, Aer Lingus and Ryanair, and eliminating the cut-throat competition between them that was harming both. The new policy ruled that the airlines would not compete on any international route and allotted them separate routes. (Aer Lingus would fly from Dublin to Paris and Manchester and Ryanair, from Dublin to Liverpool and Munich.)

Ryanair continued to expand and carried 100,000 passengers on the Dublin–London route in 1990. Some new routes were also added. However, the Gulf War (1990–1991) caused a general downturn in the market, and at the AGM held in November 1990, the management announced losses of IR£4.5 million for 1989. The situation in 1990 looked even worse. The airline had to cut down some routes, retrench staff and shift its base from central Dublin, to Dublin airport. In 1990, the losses amounted to IR£7 million. Realizing that its position was becoming increasingly weak, Ryanair refocused its activities on providing low-cost, no-frills services. It also moved its base in London from Luton airport to Stansted. Services to regional airports were also reorganized.

In late 1991, senior management changes were announced, with McGoldrick relinquishing his position as chief executive. Patrick Murphy (Murphy), who had earlier worked for Aer Lingus, was brought in to replace him. A few weeks later, Conor Hayes was appointed chief executive and Murphy became non-executive chairman. In financial year 1991, Ryanair made its first profit of IR£300,000 since it was started in 1986. In 1992, a new livery was introduced for the planes in the fleet, with the Ryanair logo and the Irish harp painted on them in a white and blue scheme. In 1992, the airline made a profit of IR£0.8 million. In 1993, O'Leary, who had joined as chief operating officer in 1991, took over as CEO.

In 1994, Ryanair took delivery of its first Boeing 737–204. By 1995, when Ryanair completed 10 years in service, it had become the biggest passenger carrier on the London–Dublin route and the largest Irish carrier on every route it operated. The airline carried a total of 2.25 million passengers in 1995. In 1997, the European Union deregulated the airline business and a number of low-cost airlines (notably easyJet) offering no-frills services were set up. The deregulation of the market enabled Ryanair to open new routes to continental Europe. The same year, the airline also came out with an IPO on NASDAQ and the Dublin Stock Exchange for $500 million. With the money raised from the IPO, it ordered 45 new Boeing planes.

In 2000, the airline opened Ryanair.com, an online booking site. Within three months, the site was taking over 50,000 bookings a week. By the next year, over 75 percent of the bookings were made over the internet. In 2002, Ryanair made Frankfurt-Hahn (Germany) its second continental European base, after Brussels-Charleroi (Belgium). The airline also entered into a partnership with Boeing for the purchase of about 150 new aircraft over the next eight years (till 2008). By the end of 2002, the internet accounted for almost 95 percent of the tickets booked with Ryanair. By the end of 2002, the airline's fleet had 44 aircraft.

In early 2003, the airline took over Buzz, the low-cost subsidiary of Dutch carrier KLM, for £15 million. Until then Ryanair had not gone in for acquisitions, but O'Leary said that this offer was too good to pass over. Ryanair later shut down the operations of Buzz as it undertook a massive restructuring program to make the ailing airline more profitable.

In the financial year ended March 31st, 2003, Ryanair had carried 15.74 million passengers and earned revenues of £842.5m. (Refer [to] Exhibit 2.) O'Leary declared that he would double the numbers of passengers to 30 million in 5 years.

Exhibit 2	Summary Table of Results (Irish Gaap)—in Euro		
Year ended	March 31st, 2002	March 31st, 2003	% Increase
Passengers	11.09m	15.74m	(+)42%
Revenue	€621.1m	€842.5m	(+)35%
Profit After Tax	€150.4m	€239.4m	(+)59%
Basic EP (euro cents)	20.64	31.71	(+)54%

Source: www.ryanair.com.

The Recipe for Low Fares

Ryanair followed a strategy of cost focus. The airline served a class of flyers who looked for functional and efficient service rather than luxury. It did not aim to satisfy all segments of the market. The airline's operational policies supported its strategy of cost focus. The operational model of the airline included the following components:

SIMPLE FLEET   Ryanair flew a fleet compris[ed] entirely of Boeing 737s. This focus on standardization was a key feature in keeping the costs of the airline low, thus allowing it to offer low fares. Flying a standard fleet had the advantage of simplifying the maintenance function of the planes. The airline did not have to stock spares for different types of planes. As spares and other aircraft parts could be purchased in bulk, it resulted in economies of scale. It also reduced training requirements for the pilots and the cabin crew, as they had to only learn to operate a single type of plane. This ensured interchange ability of crews, spares and furnishings between planes which made operations easier.

SECONDARY AIRPORTS   Ryanair used secondary airports. This was one of the important elements in keeping costs low. Using airports located outside city centers (many of them were former military airfields) saved time and money for the airline, as secondary airports had relatively lower landing charges. Besides, due to lower traffic, there were no delays, allowing the planes to turn around (turnaround is the time required for a plane after landing, to be ready for its next flight) in a very short time. In exchange for bringing in passengers to airports which normally witnessed little or no traffic, Ryanair negotiated 15- [to] 20-year deals on landing fees and other agreements to the advantage of the airline. In these airports, Ryanair negotiated airport fees of as little as $1.50 per passenger (much lower than the average rate of $15 to $22 per passenger charged by Europe's major hubs).

FASTER TURNAROUNDS   The turnaround time for Ryanair planes was approximately 25 minutes (the major carriers took about an hour). Most low-cost airlines based on the Southwest model (Refer [to] Exhibit 3) emphasized faster turnaround times to allow a plane to fly more times a day rather than spending time on the ground. This increased the efficiency of the asset. By taking about half the time of the larger airlines like British Airways (BA) or Lufthansa, Ryanair's planes made an average of nine trips per day as [opposed to] the average six of larger airlines. This made Ryanair's planes more productive than the planes of the major carriers.

HIGHER PRODUCTIVITY   Ryanair used fewer employees per plane than other airlines. This increased the productivity per employee for the airline and also helped keep the wage bill low. Consequently, Ryanair's revenue per employee was approximately 40 percent higher than that of other airlines. The simple service model also allowed Ryanair to have only two flight attendants per flight, compared to the five attendants that major carriers required.

Ryanair sweated its assets. The airline flew its planes for an average 11 hours per day as [opposed to] the 7 hours of BA. The pilots at Ryanair also clocked in 900 hours a year, which was 50 percent more than the pilots at BA. The airline did not keep many planes on standby to meet unforeseen contingencies. All the assets were put to work, unlike BA which usually kept about ten planes at any given time on standby.

ONLINE SALES   After Ryanair.com was launched in 2000, a large number of tickets began to be booked online. By early 2003, almost 95 percent of the bookings were done through the internet. This allowed the airline to make the booking process cheaper as transaction costs came down considerably. The benefits of lower costs were passed on to customers in the form of lower prices. Although some bookings were done over the telephone and some through agents, the internet brought in the major part of business. So, the airline decided to slash the commissions of agents from 7.5 percent to 5 percent. Analysts estimated that bookings over the internet saved the airline about $6 million a year on an average.

NO FREEBIES   Like other discount airlines, Ryanair did not serve food or drinks on its flights. Snacks, however, could be purchased on the airline. Unlike Southwest, which served drinks and light snacks, Ryanair even charged for water on the flights (a bottle of water cost about $3). Analysts said that Ryanair transformed a cost into a revenue opportunity, as it not only eliminated all expenses on food (which formed a major portion of the expenditure per passenger), but also made additional revenues through the sale of food and

Exhibit 3	Southwest Airlines

Southwest Airlines (Southwest) was started in 1967 by Rollin King, John Parker and Herb Kelleher. King, an entrepreneur from San Antonio, Texas, owned a small commuter air service. Parker was his banker, while Kelleher was the legal advisor to King's air service. The airline aimed to provide the best service with the lowest fares for short-haul, frequent-flying and point-to-point "non-interlining"[16] travelers. Over 30 years of operation, Southwest became one of the most successful airlines in the U.S. In fact, it was the only airline that was able to stay profitable even after the September 11th terrorist attacks on the [U.S.] in 2001.

The success of Southwest spawned a number of other airlines which tried to imitate Southwest's model of providing low-cost and high quality services. Some of the components of the Southwest operational model are given below.

1. **Low fares:** Southwest offered one of the simplest and most inexpensive fare structures in the U.S. The low fares were made possible by adopting a number of techniques which brought down the operating expenses of the airline. The airline also had a frequent flyer program which gave a free round trip to a customer who purchased eight round trips on a particular route.

2. **Customer focus:** Southwest geared its operations to the needs of its customers. It therefore developed a flight schedule with frequent departures to meet the customers' need for flexibility. Airports were also conveniently located near city centers to make flying more convenient.

3. **Standard fleet:** To simplify operations, Southwest used only one type of aircraft—the Boeing 737, in an all coach configuration. This simplified the maintenance function and resulted in economies of scale due to bulk purchase of spares and other parts.

4. **Secondary airports:** Southwest flew into less congested, secondary airports. This helped negotiate better landing terms and also save time. This also allowed it to turn around the planes faster.

5. **Turnarounds:** Southwest had one of the fastest turnaround records of all airlines. It turned around planes in about 15 minutes, which was a quarter of the time taken by major airlines. This allowed better utilization of the fleet.

6. **Point-to-point flights:** Southwest flew point-to-point, short haul flights, which made operations simple and inexpensive, and allowed the airline to save time. It could also operate with fewer staff than airlines which adopted a hub-and-spoke system.

7. **No food:** Southwest pioneered the concept of not serving food on short haul flights. Instead of meals, the airline served drinks and light snacks. On the shortest flights, even these were eliminated. This helped the airline save a considerable amount of money and consequently keep fares low.

[16] Southwest did not arrange connections with other airlines; passengers transported their own luggage to recheck themselves onto connecting airlines.

Source: Compiled from various sources.

drinks. According to a published report of the airline, Ryanair saved $50,000 a year, simply by not serving ice on its flights.

None of the services provided by the airline were free either. Baggage check-in cost the passenger according to the amount of baggage carried. It meant that users paid for what they needed and didn't pay for anything they didn't need. Since Ryanair charged for all the optional parts of a flight, it was able to fix the basic ticket price very low.

VOLUMES What was distinctive about Ryanair was its focus on filling its planes to capacity. If tickets did not get sold at a high price, it tried to sell them by lowering prices. It realized that it was more profitable for it to fly its planes full at lowered ticket prices rather than half-empty at its standard rates, as the per unit cost of flying a person came down. Besides, since Ryanair charged for all additional services like food and baggage, it stood to profit even if the ticket was sold at a huge discount.

SIMPLIFIED OPERATIONS The airline did not assign seat numbers; this simplified the ticketing and administration processes. It helped the airline save time as it ensured that passengers came to the airport on time to be able to sit together or get seats of their choice on the plane. The decision to fly short and medium haul point-to-point[7] flights also enabled the airline to work with a smaller number of personnel than it would have required if it adopted the more complicated hub-and-spoke system.[8] Transfer of baggage and people from one plane to another is generally considered a vulnerable area for airlines. Flying point-to-point avoided the need for any kind of transfer, thus keeping operations simple and inexpensive. Ryanair had very low operating costs. The $50 average cost of a Ryanair ticket could be broken down into approximately $35 operating costs and $15 profit. Thirty-five dollars as operating cost per passenger was low by any standards.

PARTNERING Ryanair entered into partnerships and agreements with car rental companies and hotels so that it could earn commissions by selling these products to passengers. These commissions bridged the gap between the airline's cost and profit, which allowed it to sell its tickets for very low prices. Ryanair viewed each passenger as an opportunity to make money in more ways than just transporting them somewhere by plane. By charging them for additional services and earning commissions through them, the airline could constantly drop ticket prices. Ryanair.com also hooked up with hotel chains, car-rental companies, life insurers, and mobile-phone companies to expand the website's range of offerings.

Ryanair's Publicity

Ryanair had a publicity program, which though sometimes unconventional, nearly always achieved its aim. The "attack" on easyJet was one of the typical publicity exercises of Ryanair. The CEO of an airline blatantly waging war against another airline was a topic guaranteed to generate publicity, and Ryanair leveraged the publicity by bringing it to the notice of the public that easyJet's fares were much higher than those of Ryanair.

One ad released by the airline featured the Pope whispering into a nun's ear. Many people felt the ad had gone too far and was in bad taste. The Vatican even sent out a press release accusing the airline of insulting the Pope. The release attracted so much attention that it got reported in newspa-

pers as far away as India, and generated a great deal of free publicity. "I thought I died and went to heaven," said O'Leary.[9] Added David Bonderman, the chairman of Ryanair, "It's hard to think of another CEO of a company with a $4 billion market cap who would run those ads. They accomplished everything he set out to and more."[10]

Ryanair also often released ads comparing its prices to competitors' prices. In 2001, it was involved in a controversy with BA for claiming through an ad that BA's fares were five times higher than those of Ryanair. BA complained to the Advertising Standards Authority that Ryanair was exaggerating the situation and that the fares were, in fact only about three times higher. The advertising standards authority asked Ryanair to withdraw the ads and behave more responsibly in the future.

Ryanair's Competitive Position

Being the oldest low-cost carrier in Europe, Ryanair had some advantages over its competitors. For one thing, it had the advantage of experience, and secondly, its brand enjoyed good recognition. However, after the deregulation of air travel in Europe in the late 1990s, a number of startup airlines came up in the low-cost market. Notable among the competitors was easyJet, the discount airline set up in 1995 by Greek shipping magnate Stelios Haji-Iaonnou. easyJet was based in London's Luton airport and competed on some of the same routes as Ryanair. In 2002, with the takeover of Go, easyJet beat Ryanair to the top position as the biggest low-cost airline in Europe. O'Leary declared that Ryanair would soon bounce back to reclaim its number one position.

Although Ryanair and easyJet both operated in the low-cost segment and had similar operational models, there were some inherent differences between the two airlines. Firstly, Ryanair made a major portion of its profits by flying to secondary airports which were a long distance away from the main cities. For instance, the destination advertised as Frankfurt actually flew to Hahn, 60 miles away from the main city. A trip to Paris meant a flight to Beauvais, 43 miles north of the city, where the terminal looked like a bus depot and the baggage handlers were local firemen. The claimed flight to Copenhagen in Denmark actually landed in Malmo in Sweden. Flying secondary airports gave Ryanair a cost advantage, but put passengers to a lot of trouble as

---

[7]In the point-to-point system the [plane] has a simple flight route and flies from the origin to destination.

[8]A hub-and-spoke system uses a strategically located airport (the hub) as a passenger exchange point for flights to and from outlying towns and cities (the spokes).

[9]Kerry Capell, Carlos Tromben, William Echikson, Wendy Zellner, "Renegade Ryanair," *BusinessWeek*, May 14, 2001.

[10]Kerry Capell, Carlos Tromben, William Echikson, Wendy Zellner, "Renegade Ryanair," *BusinessWeek*, May 14, 200[1].

they had to seek other forms of conveyance from the place of landing to their final destination. This resulted in a lot of delay as well as additional expenses for the passengers.

Analysts said that, while leisure travelers may not really mind having to put up with additional travel, business travelers would not appreciate the inconvenience. This might put them off Ryanair. In contrast, easyJet flew to main destination airports around Europe, which made it the favorite of business travelers or people who were pressed for time.

Not flying to main destination airports did not affect the market for Ryanair too much, because, unlike easyJet which sought to serve leisure as well as business markets, Ryanair only targeted leisure travelers. Additionally, analysts said that flying to main destination airports could affect easyJet adversely, because the major carriers which also flew there had begun to defend their positions against low-cost airlines aggressively. The increased aggressiveness of major carriers, who had more resources than low-cost airlines as well as more governmental support, could lead to the withdrawal of easyJet from those airports. Thus, there appeared some doubt as to whether easyJet would be able to withstand the intense competition from flag carriers.

Secondly, Ryanair flew older planes than easyJet. Where easyJet emphasized passenger safety by buying and flying new planes, Ryanair had some planes in its fleet which were over 20 years old. The average age of the easyJet fleet was three years, while the average age of Ryanair's fleet was about 15 years. The founder of easyJet, Stelios Haji-Ioannou, publicly expressed doubts about Ryanair's use of 20-year-old aircraft on some of its routes, pointing out that though they flattered profits in the short term, they put the future of the airline at risk in the event of an accident. In response, O'Leary said that easyJet was only trying to harm its rival's reputation. He pointed out that Ryanair had an unblemished safety record in the eighteen years that it had been in operation. Nevertheless it was clear that a single airline accident (even in another airline) could make passengers think twice about an airline with an older fleet. Realizing this, Ryanair had already begun phasing out its older aircraft as it purchased new ones.

In terms of price, however, Ryanair had a distinct advantage over easyJet. easyJet's fares were almost 60–70 percent higher than those of Ryanair. Ryanair's lowest fare, on flights between Glasgow's Prestwick and London's Stansted was $71, round-trip, while easyJet's round-trip flight between Glasgow International and London's Luton was $123. Ryanair's average fares in 2002 were 30% cheaper than easyJet, and its unit costs were 80% less. Ryanair also had [a] better punctuality record than easyJet, taking off and landing on time more often than its rival (Refer [to] Exhibit 4 for punctuality statistics of early 2003).

Exhibit 4	Punctuality Statistics		
Week Ended (2003)		Ryanair	easyJet	Ryanair Position
1	06-Jan	81%	72%	1
2	12-Jan	84%	76%	1
3	19-Jan	93%	86%	1
4	26-Jan	97%	88%	1
5	02-Feb	81%	64%	1
6	09-Feb	90%	63%	1
7	16-Feb	89%	73%	1
8	23-Feb	86%	72%	1
9	02-Mar	91%	79%	1
10	09-Mar	88%	81%	1
11	16-Mar	94%	86%	1
12	23-Mar	86%	82%	1
13	30-Mar	93%	78%	1
14	6-Apr	92%	68%	1
15	13-Apr	95%	79%	1
16	20-Apr	93%	78%	1
17	27-Apr	97%	81%	1
18	05-May	91%	75%	1
19	11-May	94%	81%	1
20	18-May	92%	70%	1
21	25-May	91%	NA	1
22	01-Jun	90%	63%	1
23	8-Jun	90%	62%	1
24	15-Jun	95%	77%	1
25	22-Jun	94%	74%	1
26	29-Jun	92%	72%	1

Source: www.ryanair.com.

To steal customers from easyJet, Ryanair announced that it would lower fares 5% a year for the foreseeable future. O'Leary believed that he could launch a new price war and still stay highly profitable, mainly because of the profitable agreements he had with the airports. Ryanair also got a huge discount from plane manufacturer Boeing for the purchase of new planes. Boeing offered Ryanair this discount in order to be able to beat competitor Airbus in the European market. Ireland, where Ryanair was based, was also eligible for U.S. aircraft subsidies as it did not manufacture aircraft domestically. This helped the airline substantially in terms of price. In 1998, the airline ordered 25 737–800 planes for about $30 million each ($15 million below the list price) from Boeing, when it was engaged in a price war with Airbus Industrie.

In addition to this, easyJet's break-even load factor (the percentage of total available seats to be sold each month to break even) was 71 percent compared to Ryanair's 53 percent. This meant that easyJet needed more passengers than

Ryanair to break even. The profits of easyJet were correspondingly lower. Ryanair's 27% operating margin (ratio of operating income to sales revenue) was also higher than British Airways 3.8%, easyJet's 8.7%, and the 8.6% of Southwest Airlines. Ryanair had a built-up cash pile of $1 billion and its $5 billion market capitalization exceeded that of BA, Lufthansa,[11] and Air France.

O'Leary believed that his biggest advantage was that Ryanair did not compete head-on with Europe's biggest carriers. It targeted the discount market which the majors shunned in favor of the business-class traveler. "These [low-cost] companies are opening up new segments of the market without really taking clients from the regular carriers," said Air France CEO Jean-Cyril Spinetta.[12] [Forty-eight percent] of Ryanair's passengers were budget-conscious leisure travelers who did not care about luxury and only wanted the lowest possible fares.

No other low-cost airline managed to replicate Ryanair's results. According to analysts, its "cost per available seat mile," (the yardstick used by the airline industry to measure costs) was 30% lower than the average for Europe's major airlines, and its productivity—as measured by the number of passengers per employee—was 40% higher. As a result, Ryanair could break even when its planes were just over half-full.

With the acquisition of Go, easyJet may have become the bigger low-cost airline (with 19 million passengers in 2002 to Ryanair's 16 million), but Ryanair was in a better financial position, with net incomes higher than those of easyJet, from lower revenues. (Refer [to] Exhibit 5.) easyJet had reported losses for the first quarter of 2003, due to the acquisition costs of Go for which it paid a phenomenal £374 million; however, Ryanair had made a profit, in spite of the acquisition of Buzz.

Analysts wondered how Ryanair would fare if there was new competition in the European airline market. O'Leary, however, felt that there was unlikely to be any major new competition. "There are huge barriers to entry now, and none of the new airlines are going to be able to find a price point below Ryanair or easyJet," he said. He said that Ryanair was poised to become the counterpart of Southwest Airlines in Europe, while easyJet was imitating the strategy of JetBlue, which flew to major airports and did not cut costs quite as drastically as Southwest. "Air transport is just a glorified bus operation. You get on, you want to get there quickly, with the least amount of delays, and cheaply," said O'Leary. He believed that those who could provide the fastest and cheapest means of transport were likely to survive in the long run.

---

[11]The national airline of Germany.

[12]Kerry Capell, Carlos Tromben, William Echikson, Wendy Zellner, "Renegade Ryanair," *BusinessWeek*, May 14, 2001.

Exhibit 5	Ryanair vs. easyJet			
	Ryanair		easyJet	
	March 2002	March 2001	Sept 2002	Sept 2001
Revenue (in dollars)	543.4m	427.2m	861.5m	525.7m
Total Net Income (in dollars)	130.9m	91.6m	76.5m	55.8m

Adapted from www.hoovers.com.

Questions for Discussion

1. Ryanair is one of the oldest low-cost airlines in Europe. Discuss the growth of Ryanair and comment on its present position in the European low-cost market vis-à-vis rivals.

2. Ryanair offered the lowest airfares across various routes in Europe. The airline was able to do this because of the operational advantages it enjoyed. Discuss the components of Ryan air's operational model and how they supported the low fares offered by the airline. Also discuss the role of publicity in helping create brand awareness.

3. Examine the competitive advantages Ryanair had over rival easyJet. According to you, which of the two airlines has a higher long-run sustainability? Discuss this in the light of the operational advantages of the two airlines.

Additional Readings & References

1. Kerry Capell, Carlos Tromben, William Echikson, Wendy Zellner, **"Renegade Ryanair,"** *BusinessWeek*, May 14, 2001.

2. **"How Ryanair Keeps the Cost Down,"** *BusinessWeek*, May 14, 2001.

3. **"Ryanair Brothers Make £33.4m from Shares Sell-Off,"** *The Irish Examiner*, July 06, 2001.

4. O'Connell, Patricia, **"Full-Service Airlines Are 'Basket Cases,'"** *BusinessWeek*, September 12, 2002.

5. Day, Julia, **"Ryanair Sells 1m Seats for Less Than a Tenner,"** *The Guardian Review*, September 24, 2001.

6. Tomlinson, Richard, **"Europe's Businessman of the Year,"** *Fortune*, December 9, 2001.

7. **"The Pluck of the Irish,"** *The Economist*, January 24, 2002.

8. Peachey, Paul, **"Ryanair 'Misled' Public over Flight Destinations,"** *The Independent*, March 13, 2002.

9. Eoghan, Nolan, **"Good Product, Bad Brand,"** *Marketing Magazine*, July 3, 2002.

10. Capell, Kerry, **"Ryanair Rising,"** *BusinessWeek*, June 2, 2003.

11. Capell, Kerry, **"Suddenly, Life Is Hard for easyJet,"** *BusinessWeek,* June 2, 2003.

12. Wachman, Richard, **"Can Ryanair Soar Higher?"** *The Observer,* June 8, 2003.

13. Smith, V. Kenneth, **"easyJet Leads Low Fare Airline Battle in Europe,"** www.webtravelnews.com, September 27, 1999.

14. **"Business Profile: High Flier Who Built a Fortune on Low Fares,"** www.telegraph.co.uk.

15. Lee, James, **"Ryanair: The First Ten Years,"** www.iol.ie.

16. www.thetravelinsider.info.

17. www.easyprotest.com.

18. www.theolivehouse.it.

19. www.bbc.co.uk.

20. www.legal500.com.

21. www.msnbc.com.

22. www.hoovers.com.

23. www.ryanair.com.

Case 14

Airbus—From Challenger to Leader

BSTR/046

"In prior years we found customers somewhat cautious about supporting Airbus. This year it has become acceptable and, frankly, even stylish to laud Airbus and to chastise Boeing."

–Excerpt from Bear Stearns Analyst Report as reported in *Fortune* in August 1999

"We are not here to buy market share."

–Noel Forgeard, Chairman, Airbus Industrie, in August 1999

Boeing's Nightmare

In October 2002, *The Seattle Times,* a local newspaper published from Seattle, USA, where Boeing is headquartered, carried a headline story, *Boeing Is Slipping to No. 2.* According to the newspaper report, Boeing's sole competitor, Airbus Industrie (Airbus) had bagged an order from easyJet[1] for 120 A-319 jets. easyJet was one of Boeing's most loyal customers (Refer [to] Exhibit 1 for a profile of Boeing).

ICFAI

This case was written by **K. Subhadra,** under the direction of **Sanjib Dutta,** ICFAI Center for Management Research (ICMR). It is intended to be used as a basis for class discussion rather than to illustrate either effective or ineffective handling of a management situation.

The case was compiled from published sources.

To order copies, call 0091-40-2343-0462/63 or write to ICFAI Center for Management Research, Plot # 49, Nagarjuna Hills, Hyderabad 500 082, India or email icmr@icfai.org. Website: www.icmrindia.org.

[1]Europe's biggest low-cost airliner.

Analysts felt that after easyJet's shift away from Boeing, other low-cost airlines would follow suit in opting for Airbus. Airbus seemed all set to take market leadership in the low cost segment from Boeing for the first time. From the mid-1990s onwards, Airbus had steadily increased its market share. By the late 1990s, Boeing and Airbus had an equal share in the market.

Rival Boeing accused Airbus of resorting to heavy price cutting in order to beat off the competition. It also accused Airbus of producing aircraft for which it had not received orders and creating a glut in the market. But Airbus rejected the allegations, saying that it was in the market to make money and not to buy market share. Some analysts were of the opinion that Airbus was able to increase its market share because of the financial support it received from its consortium partners. However, others attributed Airbus' success to its fuel-efficient jets, which were economical to run.

The Takeoff

The history of Airbus dates back to the late 1960s, when Britain, France and West Germany launched the Airbus Project. Airbus was a desperate attempt by the European governments to end the monopoly of American manufacturers in the aerospace industry. At that time, American manufacturers dominated the global aerospace industry and European aircraft manufacturers were unable to compete with American players.

635

Exhibit 1	Profile of Boeing

The leading airplane manufacturer in the U.S., Boeing Airplane Company (Boeing), was formed in 1916 by William Boeing (W. Boeing) and George Westervelt (Westervelt). At the time, it was called the Pacific Aero Products Company. The company's name was changed to Boeing in 1917. Boeing began by manufacturing [aircraft] for the U.S. military during the First World War. In 1922, Edgar Scott became the company's president and during his tenure the navy awarded Boeing a contract to build a primary trainer (a plane for test flights). In 1927, the Model 40A mail plane won the U.S. Post Office contract to deliver mail between San Francisco and Chicago. The Boeing Air Transport (BAT) [company] was formed to run the new airmail services. BAT also trained pilots, set up airfields and provided maintenance staff for the new service.

However, Boeing realized that to grow, it needed to design and go in for mass production and sell its own aircraft. After the Second World War, the company shifted its focus from the defense industry to commercial jets. In 1952, Boeing launched its first commercial jet, the Boeing 707, a short-range jet. In 1960, William M. Allen (Allen) became the company's CEO. The same year, Boeing began manufacturing its first jumbo jet—the Boeing 747. During Allen's tenure, Boeing launched one of its most successful jets, the 737. In 1962, Boeing manufactured the Air Force One for the American president's use. In late 1969, Boeing entered the spacecraft manufacturing business by contributing to the Apollo program.

In the early 1970s, Boeing faced a host of problems due to the recession in the aviation industry. When Airbus Industrie was formed in 1970, Boeing's market share (70% in the early 1970s) began to decline. In the mid-1970s, Boeing launched long-range planes (the 757 and the 767). By the mid-1980s, Boeing expanded its presence in the consumer electronics business through joint ventures, mergers and subcontracting. In March 1984, Boeing took over the De Havilliard Aircraft [company] of Canada to enter the commuter planes market. In the early 1990s, Boeing completed the manufacture of the 727 and the 737. By October 1994, the company launched the new 737 series, the 737-800.

In the mid-1990s, Boeing's revenues plunged and it had to retrench around 9,300 employees due to the economic slowdown. The company faced a 10-week strike in the fourth quarter of 1995. In late 1996, Boeing and McDonnell Douglas announced plans to merge. In 1997, Boeing had approximately 70% of the world market for passenger aircraft. By the end of 1997, Boeing was severely affected by the Asian economic crisis[2] that put in doubt over one-third of the $1.1 trillion projected commercial aircraft sales for the next 20 years. The company's internal problems such as excessive bureaucracy, redundant manufacturing processes and an outdated information technology setup further aggravated the situation. Boeing lost 17% of its market value as a result of the Asian crisis.

In 2002, Boeing was a $54 billion company operating in 145 countries with around 112,000 employees worldwide. The company was divided into six major units: Air Traffic Management, Boeing Capital Corporation, Commercial Airplanes, Space and Communications, Military Aircraft and Missile Systems, and Connexion by Boeing. The commercial aircraft division contributed around 60% of the total revenues. Boeing's manufacturing plants were located at Renton, Everett (Washington), Wichita (Kansas) and Long Beach (California).

Source: ICFAI Center for Management Research.

[2]The Asian financial crisis started in early July 1997, when international currency speculators as well as many Thai nationals started selling Thailand's currency, the Baht, to buy U.S. dollars, causing a flight of capital out of the country. As a result, capital became scarce and interest rates on borrowed money rose sharply, leading to the Baht losing about 20% of its value. Then the Thailand stock and real markets collapsed, pushing the country into its worst recession, as production decreased, unemployment rose sharply and businesses went bankrupt. The crisis spread quickly to other countries in the southeast Asian region like Indonesia, South Korea and Japan, significantly damaging the region's economy.

The big three of Europe—Britain, France and West Germany—came together to salvage European pride and industry. Due to differences with the other partners, Britain quit the project in July 1967, and in 1970 the Airbus Project was reorganized and named Airbus Industrie, a Franco-German company under French law.

In 1971, Spain joined the consortium with [a] 4.2% stake through state-owned Construcciones Aeronautics S.A (CASA). Initially, Airbus had its headquarters in Paris; in 1974, the headquarters were shifted to Toulouse (France). Each partner in the consortium was assigned specific production and assembly tasks, and the consortium was responsible for coordinating designing, development, financing and production activities of the partners.

Airbus' first product was the A-300-B—a widebody twin-jet plane with a capacity of 226 passengers. The next product was the A-300-B2, a 250-seater. By 1975, Airbus was able to garner 10% of market share, and received first time contracts from Eastern Airlines[3] and Thai Airways.[4] By the end of 1975, Airbus had orders for 55 aircraft. By 1978, Airbus' orders had increased to 133, and it had a 26% market share by value. It also launched [the] A-310 with a 218-passenger capacity in the two-class configuration. The A-310 had a two-man cockpit with a six-cathode ray tube display, replacing dials—the first of its kind in the aviation industry. In 1979, British Aerospace Systems (BAE Systems) entered the consortium with a 20% stake, and in the same year, Airbus announced that it would launch a single-aisle aircraft with a seating capacity of 130–170; the aircraft was later called the A-320.

In the early 1980s, Airbus experienced difficulties in financing the A-320 project, since all the Airbus partner governments had not approved the program. While the French government had approved the project, both British and German partner governments wanted more time to measure the market potential for the plane. Another problem was that the consortium had not yet made money on products already in the market.

By 1985–86, Boeing's market share had decreased to 46%, with Airbus having increased its share to 25%. With Airbus' increasing market share, Boeing began to accuse Airbus of using unfair trade practices by getting heavy subsidies from its European governing partners. The U.S. government too started [pressuring] the EU to reduce subsidies to Airbus. The then President of the United States, Ronald Reagan,

cited Airbus as a classic example of violation of international trade agreements.

In the late 1980s, [the] U.S. government filed a complaint against Airbus at The General Agreement on Trade and Tariffs (GATT). It complained of unfair competition against two U.S. airline manufacturers, McDonnell Douglas and Boeing, by Airbus. Airbus, it said, had the financial support of four European governments, who provided cheap loans to the consortium with no repayment conditions. Airbus responded by denying that it received heavy subsidies from the governments concerned. The governments of the four European states also stated that U.S. aircraft manufacturers received indirect government subsidies through the U.S. defense department. After protracted discussions, in 1992 a bilateral deal was signed between the European governments on one side and the U.S. government on the other, that limited the financial help that could be given to Airbus to develop any new model, to 33% of its total development costs. The agreement also stipulated that the aid would have to be repaid with interest within 17 years.

In the mid-90s, the main problem for Airbus was to raise finance for its major projects, such as the development of a new super jet. Airbus wanted to bring in more partners; however, no new partner was willing to invest money because of the uncertain financial health of the consortium. Under French law, Airbus was not obliged to publish its annual accounts or reveal cost and revenue details. With no financial data on the consortium, no new partner was forthcoming. Another negative feature of Airbus was its slow decision-making process—every partner (representing [each] different country) tried to safeguard its own interests rather than [make] decisions that would benefit [the] consortium as a whole.

Airbus came under strong pressure to corporatize itself. Despite its success in attracting orders and increasing its market share, many were skeptical about its ability to compete with Boeing with its existing structure.

Airbus announced its decision to restructure itself on the lines of an integrated company. However, the managing partners could not reach agreement on the nature of the restructuring. Around the same time, Boeing announced its decision to take over U.S. aircraft manufacturer McDonnell Douglas. *BusinessWeek* summarized the challenges that Airbus faced: "With 35% of the world jet market, Airbus has so far proved a spirited challenger to Boeing. But to face up the new behemoth, Airbus must change itself from an unwieldy, four-partner consortium into one for-profit company. It must develop planes with more than 400 seats to compete with Boeing's 747 series and develop a next-generation

---

[3]Eastern Airlines was one of the largest airlines in [the] U.S., which operated on eastern coast routes. It was liquidated in 1991 due to heavy losses.

[4]Thai Airways is an airline company, operating from Thailand.

superjumbo that can carry up to 700 passengers. And it must overhaul its inefficient manufacturing, which is geared more toward making sure each partner gets its share of jobs than it is toward making money."[5]

Reports said that though British Aerospace and Daimler-Chrysler Aerospace AG (DASA) were in agreement over the plan for revamping Airbus' organizational structure, the French partner—Aerospatiale—was opposed to it. The French company did not want to pool manufacturing assets, fearing that rationalization of production might lead to massive layoffs. This was politically unacceptable to France, a country with an already high unemployment rate.

In early 1998, the Airbus partners re-started discussions on revamping the organizational structure of the consortium. In the same year Noel Forgeard (Forgeard)[6] was appointed as CEO of Airbus. However, there were serious differences between the consortium partners over the valuation of the assets to be pooled in the new corporate structure. The fact that accounting standards differed from country to country was also a hindrance in the valuation of assets.

In 1999, the stumbling blocks to restructuring were finally cleared, when Aerospatiale was merged with Marta Hautes Technologies, and DASA (Germany) [took] over the Spanish partner CASA. Aerospatiale Marta and DASA together formed the European Aeronautic Defense and Space Company (EADS). By 2001, Airbus was incorporated into an integrated company, with EADS and BAE owning stakes of 80% and 20% respectively. In 2002, Airbus employed around 45,000 employees, with manufacturing plants spread all over Europe (Refer [to] Table 1). In 2002, it reported a turnover of 24.3 billion[7] (Refer [to] Table 2).

Note on Aerospace Industry

The history of the aerospace industry dates back to 1917, when the U.S. government built an aeronautics research center in Langley, Virginia. In the subsequent years, there was close private and public sector collaboration in the industry. The U.S. government's investment in the aerospace industry was substantial, before and during the Second World War. After the Second World War, U.S. manufacturers had distinct technological and financial advantages over their European competitors. Prior to the Second World War, Britain had been the leader in the aerospace industry.

5"Angst at Airbus," *BusinessWeek*, December 23, 1996.

6Former CEO of French missile and satellites maker Matra Hautes Technologies.

7On June 6, 2003, 1 Euro = $1.18.

Table 1 | Plants of Airbus

Parts Manufactured	Location
Cabin Interior	Buxtehude, Laupheim (Germany)
Fuselage (forward & aft)	Hamburg, Nordenham, Bremen, Varel (Germany)
Fuselage (cockpit & centre)	Meaulte, Saint Nazaire, Nantes (France)
Wing	Broughton, Filton (England)
Pylon, Nacelle	Toulouse (France)
Empennage—horizontal tail plane	Puerto Real (France), Getafe & Illescas (Spain)
Empennage—vertical tail plane	Stade (Germany)
FINAL ASSEMBLY LINES	
A-320 Family	Hamburg (Germany) & Toulouse (France)
A-300/A-310 & A-330/A-340	Toulouse (France)
A-380	Hamburg (Germany) & Toulouse (France)

Source: www.airbus.com.

Table 2 | Turnover of Airbus

Year	Turnover (in Billions)
1997	$11.6
1998	$13.3
1999	$16.7
2000	$17.2
2001	€20.5
2002	€24.3

Source: www.airbus.com.

However, it failed to retain its leadership position due to the lack of a proper corporate and regulatory climate.

The industry continued to be a high priority area for governments after the Second World War. Western governments invested in the industry to an increasing extent after the war. While military aviation received federal funding in the U.S., in Europe, governments provided funds for civil aviation.

The aerospace industry can be broadly divided into three categories: defense contracts, space programs, and commercial aircraft. The aerospace industry is one of the most capital-intensive industries in the world. It is characterized by high labor and research [and] development costs. R&D, apart from developing new commercial aircraft designs, provides technological inputs for the defense and space programs.

Investment in the aerospace industry involves a high degree of risk. The investment risk can be gauged from Airbus' investment in its A-380 aircraft; the investment required was equivalent to the company's net worth. The cost structure of the aerospace industry is also very high. It is estimated that the cost of development of a new aircraft model from designing to launching, is around $4 billion. The cost structure in developing a new aircraft can be broken up as follows:

Development	40%
Tooling	20%
Work-in-progress and overhead expenses	40%

Product development of an aircraft begins with a "paper airplane"—a three-dimensional model, estimating the performance and the operating costs of the aircraft. The manufacturers generally [use] these models to demonstrate new technology and most importantly to assess the response of potential buyers. Generally, before initiating production of new aircraft, companies hold discussions with key airline companies about adaptations and options that need to be incorporated into the prototype. Often, these airlines [become] launch customers, placing initial orders that [guarantee] the minimum volume, while sending signals to potential buyers that the aircraft is worth considering.

One of the important characteristics of the global aerospace industry was the high entry barrier of heavy capital investment required. Another characteristic was the high level of involvement of governments in the industry. Prior to the Second World War, [the] British ruled the aerospace industry. But after the war, the Americans began to dominate the global aerospace industry. Many European aircraft manufacturers became bankrupt, being unable to compete with the American aircraft companies. The main players in the aerospace industry were [the] Boeing, McDonnell, Douglas and Lockheed companies, all [from] the U.S. Over the years, there was strong consolidation in the aerospace industry through mergers and acquisitions. One of the first moves towards consolidation was made in the 1960s, when McDonnell and Douglas merged, forming a new company—McDonnell Douglas. In the late 1960s, in order to challenge American dominance in the industry, the big three of [. . .] Europe joined together, forming the consortium Airbus Industrie. From this point, American and European companies competed for dominance in the global aerospace industry.

Table 3	Global Aerospace Industry—Market Shares (in %)	
Year	Boeing	Airbus
1995	69.7	13
1996	64	32
1997	60	35
1998	50	50
1999	45	55
2000	45	55
2001	47	53
2002	43	57

Source: Compiled from various articles.

In the early 1980s, the American company Lockheed announced that it was stopping production of commercial aircraft to concentrate on the military and space segments. The commercial aircraft market was now divided between the three dominant players—Boeing, McDonnell Douglas and Airbus Industrie. There was further consolidation in the industry when, in the late 1990s, the two American majors, Boeing and McDonnell Douglas, announced their merger. The merger resulted in a situation of duopoly in the commercial aircraft market with only two players—Boeing and Airbus Industrie (Refer [to] Table 3 for market share).

In the late 1990s and early 2000s, the worldwide economic recession compounded by terrorist attacks in the USA resulted in turbulent times for the industry. The September 11, 2001 attacks on the U.S. had a devastating [effect] on [airline] companies all over the world, with a decline in the world air passenger traffic. Many airline companies went broke and filed for bankruptcy. The U.S. government stepped in and announced a bailout package for the U.S. airline industry. The slump in airline services had a very negative impact on aircraft manufacturers, with most airline companies canceling orders for new aircraft.

Flight to Success

In 1970, when Airbus Industrie was set up, the commercial aircraft market was totally dominated by U.S. aircraft manufacturers led by Boeing. Boeing dominated the world market with its 747 jumbo jet family of aircraft. Although Airbus had great difficulty in breaking into the market initially, over the years, it managed to attract more and more customers. Though some attributed Airbus' success to the subsidies it received from European governments, others felt that Airbus succeeded because of its production efficiency and innovative product development.

INNOVATIVE PRODUCT DEVELOPMENT In the 1970s, the aerospace industry was in a transition. The regulatory set-up in the American market restricted price wars among existing carriers and the entry of new carriers. However, existing airlines were allowed to fly any number of flights on [a] route, resulting in an increasing number of flights on the popular routes. Airlines found that the use of Boeing aircraft (Boeing 727s) was expensive for frequent flying. There was a demand for wide-body aircraft with twin engines and twin aisles, and with passenger capacities of 250 passengers.

However, Boeing was not interested in manufacturing such aircraft. Though both McDonnell Douglas and Lockheed came out with the wide-body planes, their aircrafts had three engines and a range of 3,500 miles. Airbus was able to identify the niche left by the U.S. aircraft manufacturers, and decided to launch a wide-body aircraft with twin engines and with a range of 2,100 miles. Thus Airbus launched its first product—[the] A-300—in 1974, a wide-body aircraft with twin engines and twin aisles, which reduced flying costs for the airliners. However, the A-300 model was not as popular as expected and for around 18 months there were no orders for [it].

The first breakthrough for Airbus came in 1978, with Eastern Airlines[8] placing an order for 23 A-300s, and soon Airbus started receiving more orders for the A-300. In the same year, Airbus decided to develop a new model—[the] A-310—an extension of the A-300, with a budget of $1 billion. Till the late 1980s, Airbus had only two aircraft models on the market—[the] A-300 and [the] A-310. Soon it realized that it needed to increase its product range in order to compete with Boeing in all product categories. During the 1990s, Airbus focused on introducing new aircraft. It launched 4 product families with nine airplane models during the 1990s; in the same period Boeing launched only two product families—717[9] and 777—and revamped its old models in other product lines. Commenting on the Airbus products, Ned Laird, managing director of Air Cargo Management Group, said, "Airbus airplanes are newer in design, and in most cases they are cheaper to own than Boeing

Exhibit 2	Product Range of Airbus & Boeing	
Category	Airbus	Boeing
Single Aisle Family Model	A-319	757
	A-320	757–200
	A-321	767
	A-318	757–300
		717
Wide Bodied Aircraft Model	A-300–600R	767–200ER
	A-330–200	767–300ER
	A-340–200	767–400ER
	A-330–300	
	A-340–200	
	A-340–300	
	A-340–500	
	A-340–600	
Super Jet Jumbo	A-380	747–400

Source: www.airbus.com & www.Boeing.com.

alternatives."[10] In 1989, Airbus launched the A-321 with increased seating capacity (185 passengers), and in 1992, [the] A-319—a 124-seater—was launched. In 1993, Airbus launched the A-319 with a seating capacity of 124 passengers (Refer [to] Exhibit 2 for [the] Airbus product range).

Airbus was able to emerge as a serious threat to Boeing chiefly because of the success of the A-320 family of aircraft, which included [the] A-318, A-319, A-320 and A-321. Instead of imitating Boeing's products, Airbus came out with product innovations to differentiate itself from Boeing. For instance, Airbus offered similar cockpits across every model, unlike Boeing, which designed the cockpit differently for every plane. The identical cockpit design was an instant hit with airline companies. Similar cockpits meant that airline companies could use the same crew across Airbus aircraft, right from the 107-seat A-318 to the 380-seat A-340. Said Tim Bennett and Alex Hunter, analysts at Morgan Stanley, "Airbus has taken the technological lead by offering a common cockpit configuration. We believe this is helping to consolidate Airbus' position with airlines operating a mixture of short-haul and long-haul aircraft."[11]

Airbus also differentiated itself from Boeing in its aircraft design. For instance, the A-320 was designed with [a] 7½-[inch] wider fuselage than Boeing's 737 (designed during

---

[8]Eastern Airlines was one of the largest airlines in [the] U.S., which operated on eastern coast routes. It was liquidated in 1991 due to heavy losses.

[9]Some analysts pointed out that Boeing inherited [the] 717 aircraft family from McDonnell Douglas, which was acquired by it in 1997, so they pointed out that effectively, Boeing came out with only one new product—[the] 777—during the 1990s.

[10]"Upstart Airbus Threatens to Leave Giant Boeing in Its Jet Stream," *The Seattle Times,* May 13, 2002.

[11]"Upstart Airbus Threatens to Leave Giant Boeing in Its Jet Stream," *The Seattle Times,* May 13, 2002.

the 1960s), giving the airlines extra space to add more seats in a six-across configuration. Richard Aboulafia, director [of] aviation [at] Teal Group, said, "That inch makes a difference, because North American rear ends aren't getting any smaller."[12]

The wider choice of aircrafts encouraged airlines to switch to Airbus in order to spread their maintenance costs. Commenting on the economies of using Airbus aircraft, Frederic Brace, vice president [of] finance [at] United Airlines, said, "Once you get an Airbus in your fleet, you tend to want more of them. They make a good plane that is very economical to operate."[13]

Over the years Airbus has come out with aircraft in line with the market demand, and [has incorporated] technological innovations, unlike Boeing's aircraft, which were extensions of its 747 technology. Boeing had failed to introduce new technology in its commercial jets after its Super Jumbo 747.

Airbus' A-320, launched in 1984, had new technology, resulting in better operating efficiencies and performance. The A-320 was the first commercial jet with 'fly-by-wire'[14] controls and side sticks, and was designed to meet the requirements of short-distance routes. In 1986, Airbus launched the medium capacity A-330/-340 for long-distance routes. While Airbus was coming out with new models, Boeing was offering its existing 747 and 737 product lines only.

Unlike Airbus, Boeing did not use computers for designing its aircraft. Its designing activities were done manually, consuming a huge number of engineering hours, while Airbus used computer software to design its aircraft. The use of computer-aided design reduced the number of engineering hours spent on designing, and also helped Airbus bring out better designs.

PRODUCTION EFFICIENCY In 1995, Boeing started offering huge discounts of about 25% on its aircraft in a bid to draw customers back from Airbus. However, though it succeeded in getting more orders than Airbus that year, it was unable to stick to its delivery schedule. Two of its production plants were shut down due to shortage[s] of parts and [workers]. As a result of the delays, many clients can-

celled their orders with Boeing and returned to Airbus, raising Airbus' market share over that of Boeing.

The main problem for Boeing, as many analysts saw it, was that its production processes dated back to [the] Second World War period, after which the company had never comprehensively revamped its production processes. It followed traditional aircraft manufacturing methods. In Boeing factories, planes were docked in stalls on either side of the factory floor. Each plane was surrounded by ramps and workers found the parts and installed them, and during the night, partly-finished planes were moved into the stall using cranes, for the next stage of assembly.

Compared to Boeing's cumbersome production practices that were decades old, Airbus had very sophisticated production practices. Airbus adopted the line-manufacturing method, which made the process of assembling aircraft easier. Boeing employed 216 workers per aircraft, while Airbus employed only 143 workers. This amounted to a 51% productivity difference between the two companies. Boeing's 119,000 workers manufactured 550 jets, while Airbus manufactured 230 jets with [the] help of 33,000 employees per year.

Airbus also benefited from the transnational element of its organizational structure. It could exploit the expertise of its four partners to the full, resulting in low designing and manufacturing costs. This enabled Airbus to price its aircraft lower than Boeing. The company had manufacturing units (all over Europe) which made cockpits, fuselages and wings.

Airbus also had much fewer HR problems than Boeing. During the mid-1990s, when its orders were up, Boeing hired 38,000 people and trained them. However due to production problems, it was forced to reduce its workforce and lay off around 26,000 employees in late 1998. By the late 1990s, workforce salaries and overhead expenses [at] Boeing were around 30% of total overhead costs—very high for any company. In addition, Boeing had difficulties with its employee unions. Boeing unions went on strike over 4 times between 1998 and 2002, resulting in serious production problems for the company.

Airbus, on the other hand, managed its workforce well. Although Airbus was regularly criticized on the grounds that it was set up to provide jobs for Europeans, Airbus had a lean workforce. Due to Europe's strict lay-off rules, Airbus had, right from the start, relied on contract workers. It could increase or decrease the workers hired on contract on the basis of its order-book position. Further, its sophisticated manufacturing practices enabled it to work with fewer people.

---

[12]"Blue Skies for Airbus," *Fortune,* August 2, 1999.

[13]"Blue Skies for Airbus," *Fortune,* August 2, 1999.

[14]Fly-by-wire is a means of aircraft control that uses electronic circuits to send inputs from the pilot to the motors that move the various flight controls on the aircraft. There are no direct hydraulic or mechanical linkages between the pilot and the flight controls. Digital fly-by-wire uses an electronic flight control system coupled with a digital computer to replace conventional mechanical flight controls.

The Gamble

In order to increase its market share, Airbus decided to enter the super jet category (400 seater). In 1998 it announced that it would be developing a super jumbo jet with a planned initial investment of $10 billion. If it took off, Airbus's A-3XX (later called A-380) would end the monopoly of Boeing's 747 in the over-400-seats category. According to company sources, the A-380 would be a double-decker plane with a seating capacity of 555 passengers (137 more than the Boeing 747). The super jumbo would be priced at $213 million and was expected to fly by 2004 (later the launch date was postponed to 2006). The main challenge for Airbus was to raise the funds required to manufacture [the] A-380. Finally, Airbus was able to split the total costs of development of the project as follows: around 40% would be funded by its suppliers such as Saab (Sweden), 30% would be in the form of government loans [brought] in by partners, and the remaining 30% would be the consortium's own funds.

Boeing questioned Airbus' wisdom in putting funds into the development of a super jumbo. While both Airbus and Boeing were [in agreement about] the expectation that air traffic would increase 5% annually over the next 20 years, they differed in their expectation regarding the type of aircraft the market would absorb. Airbus felt that airlines would opt to buy larger aircraft to accommodate growing consumer demand, whereas Boeing felt that airlines would be buying smaller aircraft such as [the] 777, as there would be increased demand for point-to-point services rather than long-haul flights requiring bigger planes. Said Allan Mullay, head [of the] commercial airplane division [at] Boeing, "We think the lineup we have is what airlines want, and there is no economic justification for a bigger airplane."[15]

Airbus disagreed, saying that with increasing restrictions in airports regarding noise and pollution, airlines would opt for big planes, as they would require few takeoffs and landings. Said Philippe Jarry, head [of] Airbus market development, "Boeing acts as if there are no constraints on airports, runways, or the environment. I'm really surprised that the leading American manufacturer is so concerned about the bottom line that it says, 'Flying is more fun in our smaller planes. You should buy more of them.'"[16]

The Airbus super jet project received further encouragement when airline companies also showed interest in the aircraft. Companies such as Federal Express were reportedly interested in the super jumbo as freight shipments were predicted to grow fast—in fact, faster than passenger volumes. Commenting on their interest in [the] A-380, Don Barber, senior vice president of FedEx air operations, said, "The A-3XX may be an option to increase our capacity per trip."[17]

Airbus consulted more than 60 airports worldwide to ascertain whether or not its super jumbo jet would take off and land easily. To reduce the weight of the aircraft, a crucial element in take-off and landing, Airbus developed a new material called *Glare*.[18] During the design of the aircraft, the Airbus staff had to give careful consideration to seating arrangements and arrangements for evacuating 555 people from the aircraft in case of an emergency. Initially, passenger seating [was] on a single deck or in side-by-side fuselages; however, later on designers hit upon double-deck seating arrangements as it would be easier to get passengers off the plane quickly. Another advantage was that double-deck planes would not require more space on runways. In order to avoid the problem of claustrophobia among passengers, Airbus announced that it would create an ambience of leisure on the plane. [The] A-380 would have a staircase connecting both decks, and also exercise rooms, and sleeping rooms with bunk beds. It enlisted 1,200 frequent fliers from eight cities across the world to assess and provide suggestions for its mock cabins.

In response to fears that operational costs of the super jet would be high, Airbus sources said that the use of new technology meant that the A-380 would be 15% cheaper to operate than the Boeing 747. Airbus also said that the 656-seater A-380 would [. . .] reduce operating costs by around 25%. Boeing officials, however, calculated that cost savings through the super jet would amount to half the level claimed by Airbus.

As Airbus went ahead with its super jet plan, Boeing too started considering the manufacture of similar large planes. Although reports came out on Boeing's plans to design a 550-seat aircraft with a wide single deck and three aisles, company officials denied any firm designs. Later the project was dropped due to lack of orders.

Meanwhile, the response to Airbus' super jumbo jet was good. In 2000, the super jet project received a boost with Britain's Virgin Atlantic airline (owned by Richard Branson), and Qantas—Australia's major airliner—placing orders for the A-380 aircraft. Geoff Dixon, CEO [at] Qantas, said, "The aircraft will also enable us to further enhance our

---

[15]"Blue Skies for Airbus," *Fortune*, August 2, 1999.

[16]"Blue Skies for Airbus," *Fortune*, August 2, 1999.

[17]"Blue Skies for Airbus," *Fortune*, August 2, 1999.

[18]Glare was made of aluminum alloy and glass-fiber tape, which reduced the weight of the aircraft.

onboard customer product consistent with our recognized tradition as a pioneer in the development of long-haul air travel."[19]

A major concern that arose for Airbus was Boeing's decision to extend its 747 family. In March 2001, Boeing announced that it would be extending the family of 747s with its 747-X planes that would be on par with Airbus A-380s[20] and would carry around 522 passengers. It was also reported that Boeing's costs for [the] 747-X would be around a quarter of the A-380's budget. However, by the end of 2001, Boeing abandoned its plans to go for [the] 747-X due to weak market projections for the large super jet. It announced that it would launch a 'Sonic Cruiser' that would travel at 98% of the speed of sound. However, this project too failed to arouse any interest among airline companies due to the turbulent conditions in the industry.

After the September 11th (2001) attacks, the airline industry was down and out because of the sharp [fall] in air travel. The worldwide economic slowdown also affected the industry very badly. Both Airbus and Boeing announced declines in their revenues due to recession. However, in October 2002, Airbus had 276 orders, while Boeing had just 186 orders. Analysts felt the lower operational costs of Airbus aircraft might have brought about this situation. However, as far as the A-380 project was concerned, Airbus would need around 100 orders to break even, but it actually had only 50 orders by the end of 2002.

While Airbus was gearing up to consolidate its position through its A-380, Boeing also started re-focusing on operational efficiencies in order to regain market leadership. In June 2003, Boeing announced the launch of a new plane—[the] 7E7, with a seating capacity of 200–250 passengers. Boeing sources said that with the help of new technology and operational processes it would be able to assemble the plane in only 3 days. With Boeing seemingly set to face up to the challenge from Airbus, it remains to be seen how long Airbus will be able to sustain its leadership position.

Questions for Discussion

1. When Airbus was set up, it failed to attract customers and did not get any orders over a period of 18 months. Discuss the problems faced by Airbus initially, and analyze the strategies adopted by the company to overcome them.

2. By the early 2000s, Airbus had acquired market leadership in the aerospace industry. Discuss the nature of the competition between Airbus and Boeing. What differentiating strategies did Airbus adopt in order to survive and succeed over the past few decades? How far do you think the advantages are sustainable in the long run? Justify.

3. Analyze the changes in the structure of the aerospace industry over the years and evaluate [their] effect on competition in the industry.

Additional Readings & References

1. Healy, Tim, **Competition: Battle for Asia,** www.asiaweek.com, March 29, 1996.
2. **Can Airbus Partners Unite?** *BusinessWeek,* July 22, 1996.
3. Edmondson, Gail & Browder, Seanna, **Angst at Airbus,** *BusinessWeek,* December 23, 1996.
4. Edmondson, Gail & Browder, Seanna, **A Wake Up Call for Airbus,** *BusinessWeek,* December 30, 1996.
5. **Peace in Our Time,** *The Economist,* July 24, 1997.
6. Guyon, Janet, **The Sole Competitor,** *Fortune,* January 12, 1998.
7. Henkoff, Ronald, **Boeing's Big Problem,** *Fortune,* January 12, 1998.
8. Edmondson, Gail, **Up, Up, and Away at Last for Airbus?** *BusinessWeek,* February 9, 1998.
9. **Airbus Highflier Grounded,** *BusinessWeek,* February 2, 1998.
10. **Hubris at Airbus, Boeing Rebuilds,** *The Economist,* November 26, 1998.
11. **Boeing Admits It "Let Clients Down,"** www.news.bbc.co.uk, September 8, 1998.
12. **Fearful Boeing,** *The Economist,* February 25, 1999.
13. Taylor, III Alex, **Blue Skies for Airbus,** *Fortune,* August 2, 1999.
14. Edmondson, Gail, **Overhauling Airbus,** *BusinessWeek,* August 2, 1999.
15. Burgner, Norbert, **The Airbus Story,** www.flugrevue.com, February 2000.
16. **Airbus Gets a Boost,** *The Economist,* April 6, 2000.
17. **Rivals in the Air,** www.news.bbc.co.uk, June 23, 2000.
18. **Airbus Steals Boeing Ground,** www.news.bbc.co.uk, November 30, 2000.
19. Useem, Jerry, **Boeing vs Boeing,** *Fortune,* October 2, 2000.
20. **Airbus Draws First Blood,** www.news.bbc.co.uk, June 18, 2001.
21. Matlack, Carol & Holmes, Stanley, **Trouble Ahead for Airbus?** *BusinessWeek,* October 1, 2001.

---

[19]"Airbus Steals Boeing Ground," www.news.bbc.co.uk, November 30, 2002.

[20][The] A3XX was renamed [the] A380 in early 2001.

22. **Bettering Boeing,** *The Economist,* July 18, 2002.

23. Holmes, Stanley, **Showdown at 30,000 Feet,** *BusinessWeek,* July 22, 2002.

24. **Airbus Just May Win This Dogfight,** *BusinessWeek,* August 5, 2002.

25. **Bashing Boeing,** *The Economist,* October 17, 2002.

26. Matlack, Carol & Holmes, Stanley, **Look Out, Boeing,** *BusinessWeek,* October 28, 2002.

27. **Boeing vs Airbus,** *The Economist,* April 17, 2003.

28. **Boeing Can Assemble 7E7 in 72 Hours,** *The Economic Times,* June 6, 2003.

29. www.flugrevue.com.

30. www.airwise.com.

31. www.aviationnow.com.

32. www.seattletimes.com.

33. www.news.bbc.co.uk.

34. www.airbus.com.

35. www.speednews.com.

36. www.boeing.com.

Case 15

Hornby Plc: Building Communities

307-147-1

It was a cold January morning. In 2001 Frank Martin rubbed his hands, watched his breath vapourise in front of him, and stared pensively at the seagulls circling over the office of Hornby Plc in Margate, a small seaside town on the southeast coast of England. It was his first day on the job as the company's new CEO, and he was about to enter the building. Once, many years ago, Margate had been a bustling seaside resort where thousands of workers and upper-class Londoners spend their holidays in search of fine beaches, fresh air, quality restaurants, luxurious hotels, and a wide choice of entertainment options that ranged from donkey rides on the beach to glamorous nightclubs and theatres and the country's oldest wooden roller coaster. But much had changed since the Victorian and Georgian days of abundance; the piers had crumbled, the esplanadas were all but empty, and the seafront hotels looked tatty and deserted.

Hornby, the renowned manufacturer of model trains and race tracks, had followed a fate similar to that of the town of Margate. Once it had been the city's largest employer, providing for thousands of jobs in its factory, its products were adored and owned by a vast proportion of English schoolboys, and its brand recognition was such that its racecar brand "Scalextric" had even become synonymous with the product in English vocabulary. But with increasing competition from the Far East and new toys such as game computers quickly gaining popularity among children it had fallen on hard times. Most recently, four years of patchy performance had seen sales plummet 35% and the institutional shareholders, who had run out of patience with the company's management, had unsuccessfully attempted to sell the company. In a desperate attempt to cut costs, Peter Newey, Hornby's then CEO, had slashed headcount and moved all manufacturing from Margate to China. But it was too late for him: On January 3, 2001, Frank Martin replaced Peter Newey as Hornby's CEO.

Frank Martin, who had been working for Airfix, a rival company in the hobby sector, and who at the time had unsuccessfully tried to acquire Hornby, was convinced that Hornby's trains and racecars had great potential. He was confident that peter Newey's cost-cutting initiatives would help the company's bottom line but, when he opened the door to the office for the first time to meet his employees, he also felt anxious. He feared they might not share his optimism. After all, they had been faced with many years of decline. How was he going to restore his employees' confidence and trust, and convince them that there was a future for them, and Hornby Plc.? And, equally challenging, how was he going to convince retailers to help him increase sales, and how was he going to convince investors to put up the money necessary for the expansion? And, last but not least, how was he going to recoup the product's former popularity among customers? He knew the product had potential, but he also realised there was still a long and arduous way to go.

Historical Background

In 1907, Frank Hornby founded Meccano Ltd, a company that manufactured educational toys to help teach construction and mechanics to children. The product comprised metal pieces punched with holes which children could screw and bolt together into elaborate models of vehicles,

LONDON BUSINESS SCHOOL

Freek Vermeulen, Associate Professor of Strategic & International Management, and *Rahul Mathur*, MBA2005, prepared this case.

buildings and bridges. The models were an instant success and the company rapidly expanded its range of products and accessories to include freight trucks, passenger carriages and battery powered train engines. By the mid 1920s, Meccano Ltd was the biggest toy manufacturer in Britain.

Business prospered until the late 1950s when Meccano started to come under pressure from its rival Triang Railways, which was owned by Lines Brothers. Model railway manufacturers were experiencing a severe recession in the early 1960s and this eventually led to Triang Railways acquiring a part of Meccano Ltd in 1964 to form Triang Hornby. Following the acquisition, manufacturing was consolidated at Triang's purpose-built factory in Margate, Kent, UK.

Lines Brothers, the parent company of Triang Railways and the largest UK toy manufacturer in the 1960s, also acquired another company called Minimodels Limited in 1958. Minimodels had recently introduced a new range of metal bodied model cars of the sports and racing variety. The cars, named Scalextric, were powered by an electric motor and ran on a rubber based track system. The popularity of these model racing cars quickly grew to such an extent that a Scalextric World Championship event was staged in London in 1964, to be repeated in alternate years into the 1970s. While Scalextric cars were initially manufactured in Triang factories in France, Australia and New Zealand, the recession of the 1960s forced the company to relocate manufacturing to Margate.

The Triang Group was disbanded and sold in 1971 and the model railway system which had until 1972 been known as Triang Hornby was renamed Hornby Railways in January. Even though the name changed production continued at the Margate factory.

In 1981 the demand for traditional toys such as model trains and cars was hit hard by the growing popularity of electronic toys and home computer systems such as Atari. The resulting business pressures saw Hornby undergo a management buyout that brought both product lines (Hornby trains and Scalextric racing cars) together under Wiltminster Limited, a consortium of financial institutions and management. Wiltminster later changed its name to Hornby Group Plc in 1986. In the years following the MBO, the company went through some turnover in its senior management. Keith Ness, who had previously worked for a toy company named Pedigree Dolls, took over as Hornby's new Managing Director in 1983.

Product Diversification

Until 1983, Hornby had very much been a hobby company mainly focussing on making model trains and racing cars. However, the launch of electronic games in 1981 almost halved the company's turnover forcing management to rethink its strategy. Simon Kohler, Marketing Manager for Hornby recalls,

> "The market for Hornby, Scalextric and traditional toys disappeared overnight. We had a turnover in the late 70s/early 80s of £26 million; that was a lot of money, and it fell virtually in one year to about £8 million. We went from employing about 2000 people down to the hundreds very quickly."

In a bid to stabilise the business, Hornby's new management decided to diversify the company's product line into new toys. Investment was channelled away from trains and cars into producing soft toys, pre-school toys and dolls. In 1983, Keith Ness oversaw the launch of a new product named Flower Fairies, a range of collectable dolls. The idea was to broaden the appeal of Hornby's products to include girls as well as boys. Other popular Hornby toys of this era were Pound Puppies (soft toys), Thomas the Tank Engine and Boo Boos Care (a baby doll).

The diversification strategy worked well: Hornby was consistently profitable in the latter half of the 1980s with turnover eventually rising to £40 million by 1990. In December 1986, the company decided to reduce its debt and went public at an earnings multiple of 11.

While the late eighties did bring some prosperity to the business, Hornby's strategy to diversify its product line came at a cost. For the past several years, management had chosen to focus the company's limited resources on toys and had deliberately refrained from investing in its core products. By the early nineties, Hornby was coming out with just one new Scaletrix model per year and a new locomotive only every 3–4 years. The lack of investment and innovation in what many still regarded the company's core business worried many of the firm's long-serving employees. Chris Harwood, Field Sales Manager explains,

> "I always believed that our foray into the toy market was exploratory. The established businesses of Hornby trains and Scalextric cars were used to subsidize the toy product line. Now, toys are a very fashion-oriented market. Even if you put an awful lot of money into bringing out a new product and manage to brand it properly, the thing might die in less than a year's time, which is clearly insufficient to recover your costs. And if you carry on like that, you eventually disappear."

The recession of the early nineties started to make things difficult for Hornby Competitors in the traditional hobby market for trains and racing cars started snatching market share away from the company and sales declined. Even so, management continued pouring money into developing new toys in the hope of finding a winner. In 1992, a decision was taken to go up against Mattel, the American toy company which, along with Hasbro, continues to dominate the global toy market today. Hornby invested a significant sum of money to develop and launch a doll named Cassy, with the intent of snatching some market share from Mattel's popular Barbie doll. Unfortunately for Hornby, the plan backfired and Cassy's sales never took off. Hornby's shareholders were outraged and demanded that the company's senior management be replaced immediately.

A New Strategy

The company's strategy to focus on toys came to an abrupt end when Peter Newey replaced Keith Ness as Hornby's Chief Executive in 1995. Newey came from Lazard, the British investment bank. Mike Walters, Hornby's Product Development Director describes Newey's management style,

> "If he were a consultant who came into the company, spent two years here telling you what to do to put your company right and then moved on, he would have been a fantastic guy. [But] if you consider Peter as a man manager, he was perhaps not the easiest person to get on with. And you know, perhaps some very, very clever people are not always the easiest people to deal with; I think we did suffer a little bit from his [lack of] interpersonal skills."

Peter believed that the way forward for Hornby was to focus on its core products that people identified with. Traditionally, Hornby had been a hobby company; people did not identify with its toys in the same way that they did with its model trains and Scalextric cars. Peter's strategy was three-pronged:

Firstly, he sold off the toys business and realigned the company's budget, product development efforts, personnel allocation and marketing and sales focus to just focus on model railways and Scalextric cars. The company now invested money into building new tools and machinery for producing improved models of trains and cars.

Secondly, he started moving Hornby's manufacturing from Margate to two Chinese factories close to Hong Kong. This significantly reduced the company's manufacturing costs and freed up management's time allowing them to focus on commercial issues, such as obtaining licenses for new cars Scalextric planned to manufacture, instead of manufacturing issues. Peter further realised that product quality could be significantly improved if the cost savings were invested back into the product rather than passed along to customers. Hence, he decided not to lower prices even after the move to China. Instead, twice as many hours were now dedicated to each model which improved the quality substantially. Frank Martin explains,

> "The gains resulted from reduced labour cost. For example, if you are building a locomotive model in the UK, the tendency would be to create a number of sub-assemblies, put the sub-assemblies together and then test the finished item. In China each sub-assembly is individually tested so for example, to put wheels onto the axle, the wheels are first pressed onto the axle and then that axle is tested; they have a slope that they roll the wheels down and if they go outside of a certain channel, then they fix it until it stays within the channel, so then when you finally assemble the locomotive everything is perfectly set. This improvement is purely due to the number of man hours that are put into manufacturing the product."

The improvement in product quality had an important ramification: Parents buy train sets for their children and build a large proportion of the layouts themselves. This rekindles their enthusiasm for model trains in adulthood. The move to China already allowed a lot more detail to be built into the model trains, making them look more authentic. Consequently Hornby products suddenly took on a new appeal to a growing segment of the market, namely enthusiasts and collectors.

The first product that was launched under the new strategy was a model of the Eurostar Channel Tunnel train in 1996. The UK railway industry had just been privatised and the Channel Tunnel was opened to rail traffic. Consequently, the distinctive traditional livery of British Railways along with its locomotives and carriages was replaced by more modern services such as Virgin Railways and Midland Mainline Hornby's new product aimed to immortalise this lost tradition for hobbyists.

Unfortunately, the gains from the improved quality of Hornby's products were slow to materialise and sales continued to drop. In 2000, recorded sales had dropped to £21.5 million with pre-tax profits of £1.2 million. Shareholder pressure resulted in the company being put up for sale. A number of parties expressed an interest in buying in the business, however none of the valuations met the expectations of Hornby's Board. In late 2000, Peter Newey was asked to leave with a golden handshake of £385,682.

A New Beginning with Frank Martin

Hornby's failed sale earlier in the year had caught the attention of Frank Martin who worked for Airfix, a rival company in the hobby sector. Frank had a marketing background. In the past, he had held senior management positions at various companies in the consumer goods sector, such as Humbrol, Denby Potteries and Hasbro. While at Airfix, Frank was attracted by the ongoing changes at Hornby and felt that there was a real opportunity to put the companies together. He tried to convince Airfix's owners to bid for Hornby when the company was put up for sale in early 2000. Although due to other commitments, ultimately no bid was made, Frank was able to build a relationship with Hornby's Board in the process. The Board subsequently approached Frank later that year and offered him the role of Chief Executive at Hornby. Frank accepted the offer and took over as Hornby's CEO on January 3, 2001.

Frank strongly believed that the way forward was to build confidence in all the stakeholders of the company, both internally among the employees as well as externally among distributors, shareholders and most importantly, the customers. At the time that Frank took over, adult collectors were starting to show a renewed interest in Hornby trains. For example, a new engine manufactured in China, called the Merchant Navy Class was launched in 2001. It notched up sales of 25000 units in its very first year, a significant number considering Hornby's total annual sales were around 70000 units. Frank wanted to leverage this new customer segment of adult collectors and hobbyists to rebuild the company's image. He recalls,

> "Hornby is a well-known brand and loved by the British public. It has been around for over a 100 years and many of us have memories of it from our youth. So the press were very keen to run positive stories on Hornby. And I said [to the press] that we need to tell people that if you're in your 40s or 50s, looking for a hobby and have got more money, more time and more space than you ever thought you would have, look at Hornby because it is different to the way you remember it."

Rebuilding Sales in the UK

Throughout the nineties, Hornby had steadily been losing ground in the UK, the very market that had traditionally been its mainstay. The decline manifested itself as a drop in the number of retail outlets across the country. For example, the number of outlets in Manchester had dropped from 12 twenty years ago, to only 2 independent retailers in the late nineties. Peter Newey, who was CEO in the late nineties, felt that the answer lay in getting Hornby's products out in front of customers and making them visual. He came up with the

concept of "concessions." His original idea was to put Hornby and Scalextric products on the shelves of the toy departments in large stores without actually selling the stock to the retailer upfront. The retailer just had to commit to making shelf space available, essentially allowing Hornby to set up a "shop within a shop." All stock would still be owned by Hornby while the retailer benefited from any sales that actually look place.

The "concessions" strategy had mixed results. Sales did improve, but most of the sales taking place around Christmas. Moreover, the cost of maintaining a dedicated Hornby employee in each concession was high as a proportion of sales. Consequently, departmental stores started offering resistance to carrying Hornby products. In response, Frank and Hornby's marketing team decided to supplement Newey's original idea of retailing through departmental stores by focussing on the "concessions" scheme on specialty stores and upscale toy shops located on high streets. The concept has since then proven very successful. In 2004, sales climbed back to £39 million and pre-tax profits rose to £6.5 million.

Building Trust among Employees and Customers

Given the intense competition in the toy and hobby market, Frank believed that the only way to continue building market share both in the UK and overseas was by constantly investing in new product ideas and designs early, thus keeping Hornby's product line one step ahead of the competition. He actively involved Hornby's senior management in coming up with new product ideas and formulating the company's strategy on an ongoing basis. Every morning, Frank would hold an informal meeting with senior management to discuss new ideas, check on outstanding issues, review sales figures and revise targets if necessary. These morning meetings were typically attended by sales and marketing managers, product development directors and production schedulers. The agenda was very flexible and often included a demonstration of products and catalogues still under development to get everyone's opinion or how these could be further improved. The atmosphere in the morning meetings was relaxed and constructive criticism was freely exchanged.

One of the ideas that came out of these meetings was the Hornby Collectors' Club. It brought Hornby and its customers closer together. Already, improved product quality arising out of the move to China was starting to attract a different customer segment. Information gathered through registration cards put inside train sets revealed that Hornby's customer base had started to grow beyond the three to sixteen year age group. In fact, customers with an average age of fifty five were starting to become a significant chunk of Hornby's business. Through the Collectors' Club, Hornby sought to attract more of these customers by offering them: (1) bi-monthly magazines targeting enthusiasts, (2) club competitions in every issue, (3) a free fully functional Hornby model, (4) an opportunity to come aboard the "Hornby Roadshow vehicle" in the member's residential locality to see the company's latest products. In addition to running the Collectors' Club, Frank encouraged Hornby employees to interact extensively with customers and other players in the hobby sector by actively participating in international toy fairs as well as local hobby shows. This gave product designers and the marketing folks a sense of the sort of products customers wanted and also helped them keep abreast of market trends.

Frank's efforts to get employees more involved in defining the strategy and direction of the firm had a positive effect on their morale. Mike Walters, Product Development Director, explains this shift in the attitude of employees.

> "The difference between the company today and the company in the early 90s is that now when people who work here go into a store and pick up a Scalextric car or a Hornby train, they say to their friend or partner, "I was involved in marketing that!" And when they pick it up, they are proud of it. In development, you have to be proud of the product you're putting into the market place. Over the past few years, we have set ourselves the goal of producing the best model railway and best slot car product system in the world within commonsensical commercial boundaries. And that's what we've striven to do over the last couple of years.

Peter Newey's vision of the company was very different from Frank's. Given a choice, Peter would have liked to run Hornby as a virtual company with production in China and all of the development somewhere else.

Frank on the other hand is a very pleasant person to work for: He is approachable and open to new ideas. For example, had I ever gone to Frank and said, "Frank, I think we are spending an awful lot of money in artwork and I feel it is time that we opened our own in-house design facility," Frank's response would have been, "Yes, commercially it makes sense to do that. Let us bring the right people on board, let's start slowly and if it improves the bottom line, let's do it." One the other hand, Peter's answer to the same request would have been, "No, I want to get fixed overheads down to the lowest possible denominator."

Building Trust with the City[1]

Given the company's performance until Frank took over, it was no surprise that three of Hornby's major shareholders who collectively owned over 30% of the equity wanted to sell their stakes and get out. These shareholders were institutional investors who were just not interested in holding what they saw as a small, poorly capitalised company belonging to "the old economy." Thus, part of Frank's mandate was to either improve the share price or return cash to shareholders. Upon Frank's suggestion, Hornby repurchased 13% of its outstanding shares, thereby sending a positive signal to the market and immediately putting a floor under the share price. This also allowed the institutions to sell their holdings in the company easily and get out.

To further build the credibility of the company in the eyes of the market, Frank made presentations to potential institutional investors who were considering investing in Hornby as well as to key journalists. As Hornby's shareholder base grew, the company started getting into analyst presentations during the earnings announcement season.

Growing Sales Overseas

In the past Hornby had mainly focussed on the UK market. Exports constituted a mere 14% of the total sales even as late as 1998. However, the crisis of the late nineties forced the company to seriously rethink its international strategy. Frits Passet was appointed as International Director in 1998 and given the mandate to extend the Hornby community overseas. At the time Hornby did not have products which were specifically targeted towards a particular international market. For example, models of cars such as Jaguar and Vauxhall did not have the same appeal in Germany as they did in the UK with the result that sales of these models overseas had been disappointing. Even Hornby trains had limited success internationally given that only people familiar with British culture were able to relate to them. Predictably, international sales of model trains mainly came from commonwealth nations such as Australia and Canada. Frits recognised that the real potential for international growth lay in Scalextric cars since they were not as steeped in British culture as Hornby's model trains were. Geographically, Western Europe and the US seemed the most promising.

When Frits joined Hornby, most of Hornby's existing distributors internationally were carrying only a single product and were reluctant to take on new products. To overcome this

---

[1]"The City" is London's financial district.

barrier, Frits told the distributors that they had the right of first refusal on the other product categories, however should they choose not to take these on, Hornby would enter into exclusive distribution agreements with competing distributors in the same region. The threat of being locked out of other product lines and seeing these go to local competitors forced most distributors to open up to Hornby. In return, Frits offered complete transparency in terms and prices to all of Hornby's distributors. However, only one distributor was maintained in every region to pre-empt price wars.

To strengthen relationships with distributors, Frits started inviting them to annual international conferences. Hornby would fly in all its key distributors from different parts of the world for a get-together hosted in different locations every year. These events gave distributors an opportunity to network with each other and with Hornby personnel. The company used the forum to unveil its product lines for the coming year and also solicit input from attendees on product designs. A "Distributor of the Year" award was announced for the year gone by. The award generated much enthusiasm and healthy competition among the distributor community. Occasionally, Frits accompanied distributors to their major clients to build rapport with clients and better assess their needs. These meetings gave him an opportunity to negotiate prices and contract details directly with clients and also get a sense of the competition in the region.

Hornby worked closely with its distributors in organizing local toy fairs around the world in locations such as New York, Hong Kong, London and Nuremberg. Sometimes distributors also organized events on their own. For example, one of Hornby's distributors in Trinidad who has been with the company for forty years regularly organizes local Scalextric competitions for both children and adults.

Frits Passet explains his attitude towards toy fairs,

> "I try and create a family atmosphere at our stand in toy fairs; I encourage my distributors to use our stand as theirs. For example, when I see any of them with their customers, I invite them all over to our stand for lunch. The expense of a few dozen extra sandwiches is insignificant compared to the loyalty and sense of belonging that this fosters in our distributors. They feel proud to be representatives of Hornby."

The Road Ahead

By 2004, Hornby had increased its profit as well as its shareholder return by a factor 5, in comparison to the year 2000. Its brands were again firmly established, employees were

optimistic, and the 2002 PLC "Company of the Year Award" as well as the 2003 "Best Investor Communication Award"[2] indicated the City's confidence in the company. However, Frank Martin realized that soon investors would start asking him how he planned to maintain such a high level of growth. He pondered what his answer might be, and turned his eye abroad.

In March 2004, Hornby acquired one of its Spanish distributors named Electrotren S.A. for 7.9 million Euros. Electrotren, based near Madrid, was the brand leader in model railways in Spain. It had also been the exclusive distributor of Scalextric cars in the country. Prior to the acquisition, Hornby and Electrotren had had a three year long history of collaborative efforts towards designing and marketing model trains and cars in the Spanish market. This effort resulted in a trebling of Scalextric sales in Spain since the inception of the partnership in June 2001.

Similarly, in December 2004, Hornby acquired the principle assets of Lima, one of the best known model railway companies in Europe. Lima went into liquidation in 2003 when excessive overhead costs associated with its European manufacturing operations resulted in poor cash flow. Frank, and the Hornby Board, saw an opportunity to reinvigorate Lima's brands by reducing production costs mainly through outsourcing production to China and concentrating on improving sales and distribution channels to ensure a recovery in sales in Lima's key European markets. The acquisition brought with it more than 10,000 moulds for engines and rolling stock which were dispatched to China to be used as the basis for forthcoming ranges.

In addition to the Lima brand, which sold mainly in Italy, the acquired company owned Rivarossi, a pan-European brand also widely recognized in the USA; Jouef, the brand leader in France, Arnold, which specialized in the smaller N-guage railways, and Pocher, which made high-end die-cast collectable kits. This portfolio of brands, models and distributions relations provide a huge potential for aggressive, international growth.

---

[2]The annual PLC Awards event was founded in 1987 to reward excellence in the smaller quoted company sector and is sponsored by PricewaterhouseCoopers, the London Stock Exchange and the Financial Times.

Exhibit 1	Total Shareholder Return

Total Shareholder Return 1/4/1999 to 31/3/2004

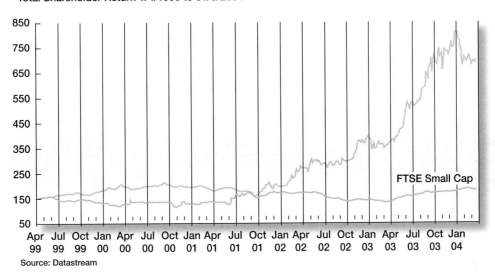

Source: Datastream

Exhibit 2a	Segmental Information of Model Products

BY ORIGIN	Turnover		Profit before tax		Net assets	
	2004	2003	2004	2003	2004	2003
	£'000	£'000	£'000	£'000	£'000	£'000
						As restated
United Kingdom	36,028	30,680	6,399	5,347	15,762	14,951
United States of America	2,942	3,462	70	64	254	235
Spain	–	–	–	–	1,313	–
Group	38,970	34,142	6,469	5,411	17,329	15,186

TURNOVER BY DESTINATION		2004	2003
		£'000	£'000
United Kingdom		30,961	26,473
Rest of World		8,009	7,669
Group		38,970	34,142

Exhibit 2b	Segmental Information of Model Products

BY ORIGIN	Turnover		Profit before tax		Net assets	
	2002	2001	2002	2001	2002	2001
	£'000	£'000	£'000	£'000	£'000	£'000
United Kingdom	25,746	22,224	3,839	1,352	12,950	11,714
United States of America	2,743	2,380	(117)	143	212	289
Group	28,489	24,604	3,722	1,495	13,162	12,003

TURNOVER BY DESTINATION		2002	2001
		£'000	£'000
United Kingdom		22,439	19,159
Rest of World		6,050	5,445
Group		28,489	24,604

Exhibit 3	Summary of Key Financial Information

	2004 £'000	2003 £'000	2002 £'000	2001 £'000	2000 £'000
Turnover	38,970	34,142	28,489	24,604	21,477
Profit after interest before exceptional items	6,469	5,411	3,722	2,292	1,402
Exceptional items				(797)	(195)
Profit on ordinary activities before taxation	6,469	5,411	3,722	1,495	1,207
Taxation	(1,974)	(1,519)	(1,329)	(520)	(398)
Profit on ordinary activities after taxation	4,495	3,892	2,393	975	809
Assets employed:					
Fixed assets	8,453	3,600	3,661	3,739	4,518
Net current assets	9,506	12,094	10,145	9,122	9,932
Creditors due after more than one year	(103)	(22)	(16)	(96)	(148)
Provisions for liabilities and charges	(527)	(486)	(628)	(762)	(806)
Net assets	17,329	15,186*	13,162*	12,003	13,496
Total capital employed	17,329	15,186*	13,162*	12,003	13,496
Earnings per share					
– basic	61.0p	53.3p	33.0p	11.7p	9.7p
– diluted	58.2p	52.0p	32.6p	11.7p	9.7p
Dividend per share (net)	30.0p	25.0p	17.0p	12.0p	7.0p
Net assets per share (net)	234.4p	206.8p	181.4p	165.4p	161.5p

Case 16

Oracle Corporation: Transformation to an e-business

Larry Ellison, Founder and CEO of Oracle Corporation, had made a big bet on his vision of the future of computer industry in the Internet era. In May 2000, Oracle had introduced Oracle 11i, a product that integrated a broad suite of Internet-based e-business applications and aimed to be a single product that would fully integrate the software needs of any company. Oracle 11i had software modules for Customer Relationship Management (CRM), Employee Resource Planning (ERP), Supply Chain Management (SCM), online requisitions, Internet exchanges, financial management and human resources. It was meant to eliminate the need for customers to be purchasing several different software components from several different vendors.

This was a new direction for both the computer industry as well as Oracle. Internet had only been around commercially for less than five years. Most established computer companies still sold packaged software to handle some critical area of enterprise management, be it CRM, ERP or SCM. Customers bought these packages and customized them to suit their individual needs by hiring consultants. Larry Ellison had declared that the Internet would change this forever. He said,

> "It's like if you want to buy a car, would you get an engine from BMW, a chassis from Jaguar, windshield wipers from Ford? No, of course not. Right now with the software that's out there, you need a glue gun—or hire all these consultants to put it together. They call it best-of-breed. I call it a mess."

Ellison vision of the future of the computer industry was that the Internet would transform it into a utility industry, rather like electricity or water. Computers, data and applications would reside in a centralized location and customers all over the world would be able to use these over the Internet, with only a personal computer and a browser. The customers would no longer be tying up their resources heavily in IT investments, but would instead just pay for what they used. Successful computer companies would be providing the hardware, software and maintenance as a service over the Internet. According to him,

> "You don't need a nuclear power plant in every backyard to use electricity, so why do you need to buy, run and maintain computers when all you really care about is the service."

Ellison had bet on transforming Oracle from a database company to an e-business that would offer applications as a service over the Internet, including hosting the database, applications for front and back office operations as well as development tools for writing specialized programs to meet the unique needs of customers everywhere. In 2000, Oracle was the world's second largest software company with a market capitalization of $184 billion and annual sales of US $ 10.1 billion. Oracle software could run on PCs, workstations, minicomputers, mainframes and massively parallel computers as well as personal digital assistants and set-top devices. Oracle had 42,000 employees of which 21,000 were in the US. Oracle sold relational databases, tools and application products and related consulting, education and support services in over 145 countries around the world. (See Exhibit 1 for product and service offerings). It had customers in various industries including manufacturing, financial, automotive, aerospace, aviation and defense, consumer, energy, pharmaceutical, utilities, shipping and telecommunications. "Oracle had over $3 billion in operating profits, which are growing at 40% a year."[1]

Will Ellison's vision of the computer industry turn out to be right? Will he be able to transform Oracle, the largest database vendor successfully selling packaged software, into an Application Services Provider (ASP)?

Exhibit 1

(From Oracle Corp report on Competitive Assessment—August 2000, p9)

Oracle Products Can Be Segmented into Three Primary Product Families:

Server Technologies

Application Development

Business Intelligence Tools & Business Applications

Business Operations

Products			Services
Server	Tools	Applications	Support
			Consulting
Oracle 8	Designer	Financials	Education
Oracle 8i	Developer	SCM	
Oracle Lite	Jdeveloper	Manufacturing	
Oracle8 Enterprise edition	Reports	Projects	
Oracle 8i Lite	Discoverer	HR	
Web Application Server	Express	Front Office Applications	
Express Server		Web Self Service Applications	
Oracle Open Gateway		Data Warehousing	

Larry Ellison: Founder and CEO

Lawrence (Larry) Joseph Ellison was adopted by his aunt, Lillian Ellison, and her Russian Jewish immigrant husband Louise Ellison, who adopted the name Ellison after Ellis Island. Louise was a quiet accountant and Lillian worked as a bookkeeper. Larry Ellison was raised on the affluent North Side of Chicago and graduated from South Shore High School in 1962. He enrolled at the University of Illinois in Champaign Urbana, only to drop out after his sophomore year. Ellison later enrolled at the University of Chicago, only to drop out again, but not before he had discovered computing, which was a way to make some money at student jobs. Friends remember him as being very intelligent, good at thinking on his feet and intensely competitive. He could talk about anything and read a lot but did not bother much about exams.

Ellison moved to California in the summer of 1966 and took up various programming jobs, working during nights and weekends just so he could spend the days at Yosemite. Some of the companies he worked for are Wellsco Data Systems, Fireman's Insurance Co, Amdahl, Ampex and Precision Instruments. Into his thirties, he was still drifting from one job to another, while enjoying other interests, with little evidence to hint at such a successful future.

ORACLE'S ORIGINS   In June of 1977, Ellison invited two former colleagues, Bob Miner and Ed Oates, to start a company that would provide contract-programming services to his then employer Precision Instruments (PI). They called it Software Development Laboratories (SDL), and made Ellison the CEO, Miner the president and Oates the vice president.

After the initial contract with (PI) ended, they decided to develop a product-platform that could be sold over and over again. Oates discovered the idea for a product; it was to build a relational database that would be a better alternative to the hierarchical and the network databases—since the structure of data storage would not limit the speed with which one could query the data and convert it into information. He read about a group of IBM engineers at San Jose developing System R and Structured Query Language (SQL), and he decided to join the race. SDL's name was changed to Relational Software Inc (RSI).

Ellison sold the early version of the database to the Central Intelligence Agency (CIA). The second customer was the Office of Navy Intelligence. RSI changed its name to Oracle and re-located to a prestigious address at Sand Hill Road in Menlo Park. Oracle's two customers operated several computers with different operating systems; forcing Oracle to find a way to make its product 'portable', i.e. adapt it so that it could run on a range of computers from different manufacturers. By version 3, Oracle had re-written their product entirely in C, a language for which compilers were available for many machines. This created a remarkable first, a 'promiscuous' software that ran on many different machines irrespective of hardware.

By making the Oracle database portable, Ellison and his team were able to shift the balance of power in the computing industry from hardware manufacturers towards software. The choice of hardware went from being a key strategic decision to a mere commodity detail. With the winning combination of a relational database that could run on different computers, Oracle quickly became the favored database provider for large companies and government agencies. It became one of the star companies of Silicon Valley by selling its innovative packaged software, database and applications, to large global companies with multiple computer systems.

Oracle doubled in size every year until 1990 and retained a technically innovative spirit. See Exhibit 2 for key events in Oracle's history. Oracle went public on March 15, 1986 at $15 a share, closing the day at $20.75, giving it a market value of $270 million.[1] See Exhibit 3 for recent performance numbers. It re-located to a brand new sprawling office complex, called the Oracle campus, with gleaming new glass towers around a lagoon at Redwood Shores in the heart of Silicon Valley.

[1]Fortune Nov 13, 2000
[2]The Oracle Edge by Stewart Read

Exhibit 2

Oracle History—Some Milestones

1979	Offers the first commercial SQL relational database management system (RDBMS)
1983	Offers a database written entirely in C for portability
1986	First client-server database
1992	Offers a full applications implementation methodology (AIM)
1995	First 64-bit relational database management system (RDBMS)
1996	Announces an open standards based, web-enabled architecture Breaks the 30,000 tpc-c barrier
1997	First Web database. Moves client/server applications to the Web
1998	Launches Business Online, the first hosting service for enterprise applications designed to be run over the Web Offers full Web deployment of all applications Offers the first set of application modelling tools that generate 100 percent of the application Breaks the 100,000 tpc-c barrier First database with Java support
1999	First to offer a full featured internet database Launches complete e-business initiative Launches first industry exchange, AutoXchange, with Ford First to integrate Java and XML into an application development tool
2000	Launches e-business network Launches Oracle Mobile, wireless applications service provider Launches Oracle technology Network Xchange, first online developers skills exchange Industry's first Developer Service Provider (DSP) First to offer complete and simple software for information management, including the Oracle9i database, Oracle 9i Application Server and Oracle 9i Developer Suite

Exhibit 3

Chart 1

Years	Revenue Trend (in Millions of Dollars)
1988	282
1989	570
1990	916
1991	1027
1992	1179
1993	1503
1994	2001
1995	2967
1996	4226
1997	5684
1998	7100
1999	8800
2000	10100

Source Oracle annual report 2000

License Revenue by Product		Revenue by Line of Business		Revenue by Geography	
Database Platform	77%	Services	58%	Americas	58%
Applications	23%	License	42%	EMEA	29%
				Asia Pacific	13%

Revenue by Geographic Regions (in Thousands)

	2000	1999	% (in 2000) p91
American Operations	5,913.4	5,053.2	58.4%
Europe Middle East Africa	2,983.1	2,855.2	29.4%
Asia-Pacific Operations	1,233.5	918.8	12.2%
Total	10,130.1	8,827.2	

Oracle: The Organization

Oracle had adopted an aggressive 'can-do' style in both technology and sales from the very beginning. Ellison's competitive nature had driven the organization towards systematically targeting and eliminating competitors, with tools like extra bonuses for winning customer-sales away from competition and comparative advertising campaigns. Oracle had systematically hired people who were entrepreneurial and thrived in the rapidly changing environment. Oracle's rapid growth was further accelerated by Oracle's customers, a majority of whom were Fortune 100 global firms, who expected to be served globally.

Oracle was organized as a more or less independent business in each country, under a country manager responsible for selling the database and applications as packaged products developed in Silicon Valley. The country managers were entrepreneurial in developing their markets and systems to best meet their local needs. They had their own marketing, finance, planning and technology staff, with freedom to determine their own strategies in order to meet the aggressive revenue growth targets set by the corporate head office. His technical staff set-up and maintained the country's IT infrastructure and serviced their local clients. The marketing campaigns in each country were designed and developed independently to best suit the needs of their particular market.

THE COMPETITION It was hard to find organizations that were Oracle's true peers. Microsoft and IBM were the other major players in the industry but their products and services were rather different. The core Oracle database competed with IBM's SQL database and a few others. In specific products and services, Oracle faced intense competition from a number of different companies. In applications, in the ERP market, Oracle competed against Peoplesoft, SAP, J.D. Edwards, Baan and others; in the CRM market it competed with Siebel Systems, Clarify, Peoplesoft/Vantive, Broadvision, Epiphany, Kana, eGain, Baan and others, and in the SCM market, it competed with i2 technologies, Manugistics, Vitria and so on. In Procurement and Online Exchange applications businesses, its competition came from Commerceone and Ariba. Always the aggressive competitor, Ellison had a very public competition with Microsoft's Bill Gates, who was the richest man in America, making Ellison only the second richest.

See Exhibit 4 for market-shares of Oracle and its competition in different products.

The competing firms concentrated in separate areas of applications because these systems were highly complex. According to *eCompany* magazine "building global real-time systems to tie together corporate data was very hard to do with the network architecture of the day, way back in 1997. Applications had to reside on both desktop machines and servers. Such systems became hideously complex and glacially slow as they were expanded."[2] By focusing on one specific business application, be it CRM or ERP, or whatever else, these companies claimed to be providing the 'best-of-breed' products. Every company, including Oracle, maintained a small army of consultants who 'integrated' these applications into the customer's enterprise, so that it was able to communicate and operate with the enterprise's existing software. In fact, the largest cost to customers of any new software was not the actual cost of licensing the software, but the cost of integrating that software into the enterprise. Integration costs could run to be five to ten times the cost of actual licenses. By being the largest database vendor and offering a variety of applications as well as consulting services, Oracle continued to enjoy market success.

THE INTERNET: ORACLE'S EARLY RESPONSE TO IT

Internet started as an infrastructure initiative by the Department of Defense in the USA in 1960s. In 1986, the initial version of Internet was created with five supercomputers linked by the National Science Foundation to allow scientific researchers from around the country to connect with each other. But until 1991, it remained a limited tool for the military and academic researchers. Between 1991 and 1994, with enabling technologies like HTML and browsers being invented and cheaper PCs becoming rapidly available, the modern Internet was fast emerging as a network of distributed interconnected computers.

Oracle's early foray into the world of Internet computing was due to an initiative taken by one of its many programmers. Mark Jarvis, Senior Vice President of Global Marketing started his career at Oracle in 1987 as a programmer with the European Development Team. He had a degree in computer science from Leeds University and had worked for Philips in Netherlands before joining Oracle. Being a network guy, he traveled frequently to the head office and eventually moved to Redwood Shores. He recalls his experience at Oracle:

> "In late 1994—Internet came along. It was mostly a university thing at the time but once browsing came along and the web spread outside the University, I became really interested in it. I thought that connecting a web browser to Oracle databases would be a cool thing to do. I set up a development team to do it. We showed the results of our efforts to the head of development. He promptly asked me to show it to Larry (Ellison). I was reluctant at first because being a developer I felt more comfortable in the back-office, but then I

Exhibit 4	

Database Market Share

Oracle	42%
IBM DB2	20.40%
Microsoft SQL Server	7.80%
Other	29.40%

ERP Market Share 1998 (market sales in 1999 $20.3 billion, CAGR 37%)

Players	Marketshare
Sap	31%
Oracle	10%
Peoplesoft	9%
J.D.Edwards	7%
Baan	6%
Others	37%

CRM Market share 1999 (market size in 1999 was $3.7 billion with CAGR 49%)

Siebel Systems	19%
Oracle	10%
Clarify	6%
Peoplesoft/Vantive	5%
Bann	4%
Others	56%

[2]eCompany Nov 2000 p 172

went along. As I presented, I noticed that Larry sat up and really listened. He understood the technology and asked questions that required me to drill down into the details of technology."

Oracle country organizations, being entrepreneurial and independent, were adopting the Internet at a pace suitable for their local markets. Country managers in most of the developed countries had set up their own web-sites with information about their products, services and organizations. They also harnessed the new technology for their organization by setting up their e-mail, administrative and employee systems on Inter and Intranets. Each of these websites and systems was custom designed to meet their country's needs. By mid-1990s, Oracle was using the Internet as a tool for internal organization as well as external customer sales and services and public interface. Mike Rocha, Senior Vice President in charge of Oracle's IT—infrastructure, operations and worldwide support, explained what it was like.

"Oracle.com, at its peak, had sixty different country developed and maintained web-sites, many of them with a different logo for Oracle and almost all of them with a different design. Each one was meant to be best suited for its country, so the Portugal organization, had designed it's website in Portuguese for its customers. There were 97 e-mail servers, each running a different version of the program."

In 1995, Ray Lane, Senior Vice President in charge of Globalization, organized a globalization convention where 400 Oracle managers from all over the world came together, and were rallied to globalize. The motivation, at the time, was to better serve Oracle's global customers, like GE, Ford, etc. more consistently. The assumption at the time was that to be global, Oracle had to have a local country-specific staff, and the challenge was to organize them to be consistent. The Internet only made the need for consistency more urgent.

Forever in the search of the next golden goose, Ellison re-engaged in running the business after having spent time away trying to buy an Italian fighter jet and racing his sailboat. His objective was to understand the implications of this new Internet technology and how it would be making waves in the industry. According to him,

"I tried to create an Oracle web-store. Just trying to create an on-line product catalogue made me realize how complex and fragmented the organization had become. Despite having the same products worldwide, the Oracle organization had packaged, bundled and priced them differently for each market, creating an explosion in the offerings. It was alarming to see what Oracle's global customers were seeing."

According to *eCompany* magazine:

"He (Ellison) didn't understand at the time, he admits, because he had never used his applications. "The earliest revelation was that I've never even seen the applications, because the applications don't provide any information," he says. The purchasing system, for example, couldn't identify who the best suppliers were by price, quality, and other metrics. That information was scattered among 70 different computer systems and 70 databases in 70 different countries. Ditto for human-resources and sales data."

With all the clever IT infrastructure, Oracle systems could still not answer simple questions like exactly how many employees Oracle had. Someone would literally have to go out and touch 60 databases, and make sure the numbers were consistent before consolidating the answer for the company. The country based proliferation of the systems had created some problems. One was duplication of effort as each country re-invented the wheel with everything from technical systems to marketing mailers being designed and developed independently. This duplication may have provided country specific local targeting initially but with the coming of Internet, and the customers being able to access web-sites globally, this had become a problem of lack of consistency. Each country manager believed that the needs of his organization were unique and special and deserved custom-made solutions. Only the Oracle head-office was in a position to see and care about customers on a global basis. The Brazilian customers, because of the common language, were accessing information about Oracle from a website designed for the Portuguese market only. Another problem was one of support and maintenance of software. Oracle released new software approximately every eighteen months. With different customized software kits in each country, every upgrade became a time and resource intensive effort. According to Rocha,

"Oracle was still growing rapidly and we could not hire fast enough. Support was swamped and was handling over 3000 calls per month, with different versions of the software running in different countries with different customized kits."

Even when software applications that incorporated standardized business processes, like Enterprise Resource Planning (ERP), became available, it was near impossible to implement these in a centralized manner. Vance Kearny, Senior Vice President of Human Resources for Oracle in Europe Middle East and Africa (EMEA) tells of the challenges he faced.

"In mid 1990s, I had been trying to implement the Oracle ERP system within the 32 countries under me. I had only managed to get four countries live on it in that time. Experience at implementation had made us really good, which meant that we could plan, install, customize and get the system up and running in a country in as little as three months. At this rate of three months for each country and 30 countries, it would have taken us over six years before we got to some of the smaller countries, like Luxembourg. In the meantime, we would also have to deal with the new releases and updates of the software. Due to different customization in each country, these upgrades were going to be just as challenging as the initial installation."

Ellison realized some of the implications of the Internet technology that went beyond the ad-hoc responses to it that he saw within the Oracle organization. Firstly, Internet could enable software applications to be deployed centrally while allowing distributed computing. Secondly, designing an integrated suite of internet-enabled applications could potentially eliminate the need for expensive customized interfaces to link the front and back office applications. Deploying software over the Internet could also minimize the need for manual intervention to consolidate data into meaningful information. Internet virtually eliminated the country boundaries of the business as every customer could see the product and services offered in every other country as well as compare prices and discounts offered. He also realized that the upgrade and support problems faced by the large Oracle organization due to the rapid proliferation and customization of IT infrastructure were also common to their customer's organizations. The CEO of every large corporation was facing the same issues as Ellison in not being able to get meaningful information or productivity gains despite increasingly huge investments in their firm's IT infrastructure.

The New Vision: Oracle e-business

Ellison decided to take on the challenge of creating the first ever Internet enabled integrated suite of applications for business. He declared,

"If we're going to do applications, let's do it. Let's really do it. We're the big guys. We have the size and the brainpower to do this. No other software company does. Oracle will build a suite of Internet-based enterprise applications software. These enterprise applications would work perfectly with Oracle databases. The resulting combination would be irresistible to corporate IT guys looking to make their lives simpler."

This vision to create a hugely complex new technology based product required a massive shift in how Oracle used its human, capital and technology resources. It was unlike creating a new version of existing products, which Oracle was used to doing every eighteen months. This e-business vision required a radical transformation of Oracle, its technology, its organization and business. Technical developers would have to re-create several existing applications with added functionality of being seamlessly integrated with other applications, and being deployable over the Internet.

Ellison's vision was also to not sell this new product outright to Oracle's customers but to merely sell them the service of computing. The product would be hosted by Oracle and deployed at the various customer-sites over the Internet. The customers would use the applications they needed and just pay for what they used. Oracle would go from being in the business of selling packaged software products to being an Applications Services Provider (ASP).

An Oracle white paper called 'War on Complexity' spelled out this new approach, as follows:

"[A] Standardized, repeatable, quantifiable approach to enterprise software deployments, Oracle envisions a New World Order for its e-business customers, based on internet business practices (IBPs) that define new rules of engagement:
- Centralize critical business information and make it accessible via a standard web browser.
- Deploy globally rather than locally.
- Implement complete Internet business flows rather than dated business rules.
- Use standardized, certified configurations rather than modifying packaged applications.
- Invest in integrated software suites designed and engineered to work together.
- Focus on your core competency: shift complexity out of your IT organization by deploying online services."

Ellison was so convinced and committed to the change to e-business that not only did he stop all client server development, but he also pushed for Oracle to start using its own product in a centralized manner. Under this initiative, called 'Eat your own dogfood', Oracle was to be its own beta test site so that the benefits from standardization and globalization of business processes could be realized and thus powerfully demonstrated. In April 1999, Ellison told his board that Oracle would chop expenses by $500 million dollars in one year. After he saw some early results, he upped the ante to $1 billion, equal to about 10% of Oracle's revenue. The head office at Redwood Shores would become the centralized location for computers, data and applications, which the field offices would access using a browser. This initiative required a transformation in Oracle's organization and business processes.

Historically successful Oracle with independent regional and field operations was to be transformed to a globally consistent Oracle with standardized business processes and technology deployed from a centralized location. It required standardization of business practices across different countries and field offices, while for software, it translated into development priorities that required reusing and integrating pieces to create a suite that could be deployed over the Internet from a centralized location.

ORGANIZATIONAL CHANGES The sheer scope of changes required to make e-business vision a reality demanded commitment from the highest levels of Oracle leadership. It was very important that Ellison was personally driving this transformation. Jeff Henley, Senior Vice President and Chief Financial Officer, said:

> "Ellison was fanatical about e-business—and you needed a fanatic driving it from the top—to get people to cooperate."

The focus of globalization shifted from being multi-local with representatives in every country to being centralized with the same standardized technology driven processes implemented in every country. Ellison started talking about the new strategy during meetings, including the budget meetings in the spring. He wrote a letter to management outlining this strategy. He centralized marketing, human resources and other support functions, leaving the country mangers to focus on sales alone. Ellison changed the technical development priorities, supporting the early Internet initiatives and later stopping all local and client-server development initiatives. When the new Internet enabling projects competed for development resources with existing products, Ellison finally pulled the plug on all client-server development. This sent a clear message to the entire organization that the future of the company was riding on this bet.

Ellison changed management responsibilities and incentives to ensure that the organization got behind this transformation. Ellison then changed the reward structure of country managers to be based on margins instead of sales. The centralized data-processing services were offered for free while any local country IT infrastructure had to be maintained from the local revenues, negatively impacting the margins. The choice to accept the centralization became a lot easier than trying to keep the local infrastructure. Ellison consistently set tough standards and drove the target margins up. Everyone knew that it was his (Ellison's) way or the highway. With one global website for Oracle, the pricing

and discount packages that were originally set by each country also had to be standardized. Ellison changed the pricing strategy. Oracle products were offered for sale on the website for the same published price worldwide. The discount schemes were standardized too. These changes could not have been made by anyone with a smaller mandate than a CEO, and the results indicated success.

> "Between 1998 and 2000, Oracle's annualized operating margins improved by 14 percent, up from 21 percent to 35 percent, with savings of over a billion dollars in the first year alone. Even as Oracle revenue grew almost 15% over last fiscal year, its head count actually fell 5.6% from 43,800 to 41,320."[1] These savings came as technology changes led to changes in the business practices. In June 2000, Oracle reported that profits for the fiscal year ending May 31 had jumped a stunning 61 percent, to $2.1 billion, far outpacing its 15 percent revenue growth. Its operating expenses were, indeed, nearly $1 billion below where they had been if they had grown at the same rate as sales."[3]

Risks and Challenges

The ambition behind integrated applications suites can be understood if we consider what these really did: "They take whole segments of a company's operations and streamline them—sifting through all the sales, financial, and customer data that a company might have and then distributing them to managers and employees in all sorts of usable packages. And now, thanks to the Internet, a company can tie suppliers and customers into this movable data feast as well."[1] Even if Oracle has the brainpower for such an engineering feat, is the rest of the world ready for it? Adopting it would require companies to throw away not one or two but a number of customized applications that may even have been tailor-made to suit their needs, and accept a standardized package. Company inertia is likely to keep them from pursuing such a radical move. And even if they manage to overcome the inertial forces, will a standardized product that treats a trucking business the same as a pizza chain and a bank as similar to a manufacturing company, fulfill their expectations?

Andy Grove of Intel, a friend of Ellison's, had expressed his doubts: "So often, when you see companies try to move from one area of dominance to another, they fail. I have my doubts about this one." And he is not the only one. Analyst Upin of Robertson Stephens was scared by Ellison's aggressive strategy. He says "Oracle hasn't been a leader in this

[3]eCompany Nov 2000 p 171

business and all of a sudden they are talking about $1.3 billion in applications revenue for fiscal 2001."[1] "Even after the stock's incredible run over the past two years, lots of Wall Streeters have a traumatic history with Oracle. "The feeling is that this is a stock you can ride, but if you don't watch it, at some point Ellison will burn you," says one trader. Witness the big air pocket in the fall of 1997 when the company began to move to Web-based applications. Sales dropped, the Street got scared and the stock caved 40%."[1] Others feel that even if the strategy succeeded, there were no gains to be had in the stock market because Oracle's current valuation already reflected the factored in value of this strategy.

Oracle's founder and CEO Larry Ellison, according to *Fortune* magazine, "is the only technology company CEO who has launched a business in the era of mainframes and taken it to client/server and then to the internet."[1] Oracle's ambition is implied in the tag lines of its ubiquitous advertisements; "Oracle software powers the internet," and "Oracle.com, Big business. Small business. All business."

Case 17

McDonald's and the McCafé Coffee Initiative

9B04M008

Ralph Sgro, on his usual morning tour of the Burlington-area McDonald's restaurants, stopped at a traffic light and counted the number of cars ordering through the Tim Hortons drive-through. The number of cars in his competitor's drive-through had been continually increasing over the last few years. Sgro was concerned that, although McDonald's breakfast sales were increasing, the breakfast market share had declined. As well, the snack business segment of McDonald's sales had not kept pace with industry growth. Sgro attributed the loss of market share predominantly to the growth of strong coffee competitors (including Tim Hortons) and McDonald's poor reputation for coffee. In response, Sgro introduced the McCafé concept to Canada, in May 2001, at restaurants in Burlington, Ontario.

McCafé was a full-service coffee bar located either as an extension of a McDonald's front counter or as a stand-alone restaurant. It had also been introduced in Australia,

New Zealand, Brazil and many European countries. While McCafé was well received in Burlington, Sgro wondered if the McCafé concept would help McDonald's regain dominance in breakfast and snack-time sales and rebuild McDonald's competitive advantage.

The Canadian Foodservice Industry

The Canadian foodservice industry, which includes those businesses that transport, cook and serve prepared foods, grossed $32.7 billion and accounted for 4.3 per cent of Canada's gross domestic product (GDP).[1] Restaurant sales dominated this industry, accounting for 66 per cent of the foodservice industry, and of all the meals services, quick service (commonly known as fast food) accounted for about 60 per cent (see Exhibits 1 and 2). In 2001, Canadians spent $0.41 of every designated food dollar on meals prepared outside the home.[2]

Commercial restaurant growth had been attributed largely to an increase in franchising activity.[3] In the last 10 years, independently owned restaurants decreased by nearly 10 per cent. In the quick service industry, restaurants such as McDonald's, Wendy's and Burger King competed with similar product lines, prices, speed of service and convenience. Industry players often fought for high traffic locations—it was not unusual to see a busy corner with two or three fast food restaurants clustered together.

IVEY
Richard Ivey School of Business
The University of Western Ontario

Lindsay Sgro prepared this case under the supervision of Professor Tima Bansal solely to provide material for class discussion. The authors do not intend to illustrate either effective or ineffective handling of a managerial situation. The authors may have disguised certain names and other identifying information to protect confidentiality.

[1]Kostuch Information Services, *Canada Multi-Unit Report of 125 Foodservice Operators,* International Foodservice Manufacturers Association, Edition Canada, 1997.

[2]Kimberley Noble, "Fast Food Whole in One," *Maclean's,* August 20, 2001.

[3]Kostuch Information Services, *Canada Multi-Unit Report of 125 Foodservice Operators,* International Foodservice Manufacturers Association, Edition Canada, 1997.

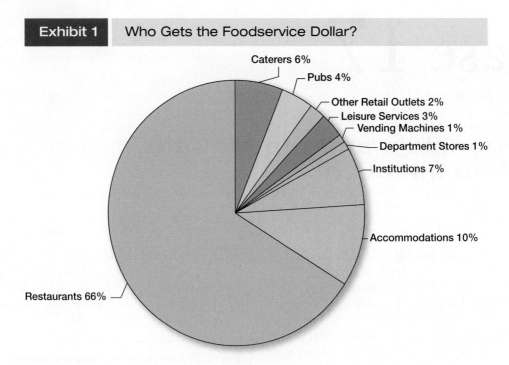

| Exhibit 1 | Who Gets the Foodservice Dollar? |

Source: Canadian Restaurant and Foodservices Association (CRFA) and Statistics Canada.

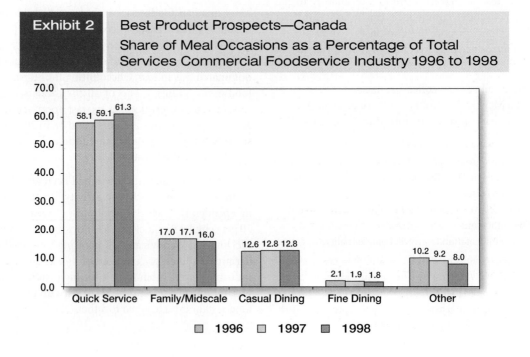

| Exhibit 2 | Best Product Prospects—Canada |

Share of Meal Occasions as a Percentage of Total Services Commercial Foodservice Industry 1996 to 1998

Mergers, acquisitions and alliances were commonplace in this industry. In 1995, Wendy's International acquired Tim Hortons (TDL Group Ltd.) for $542 million. After acquiring some smaller American coffee chains, the Second Cup sold 37 per cent of their shares to Cara Foods (the owner of Harvey's and Swiss Chalet). The Second Cup entered into a distribution contract with The Great Canadian Bagel. In spite of this consolidation of the industry and the co-operative agreements, McDonald's continued to be the Canadian quick-service industry market share leader, second only to the Four Seasons Hotels and Resorts.

Quick-service consumers were both time and value conscious. They demanded low prices, good quality, safe food and fast service. Although Canadian consumption decisions were impacted by brand image and marketing, value and convenience were high on the priority list. While each competitor attempted to provide a unique offering, it was difficult to build customer loyalty, given the large number of restaurant choices.

The Retail Coffee Industry in Canada

Tim Hortons, McDonald's, Second Cup, Country Style, Coffee Time, Starbucks, as well as many independent coffee retailers, drove the coffee industry. Tim Hortons had the largest share of coffee consumption in Canada at 33 per cent. In Ontario, Tim Hortons lead with a 41.4 per cent market share, followed by independent coffee chains at 22.1 per cent, McDonald's at 7.1 per cent, Second Cup at 4.4 per cent and Starbucks at one per cent. While many competitors focused on brewed coffee, specialty teas and specialty coffees, many were expanding their product lines to offer sandwiches, soups and other gourmet treats. Canadian consumers appeared to receive this product line extension well, as reflected by the 39 per cent increase in Tim Hortons lunch sales in 2000.

Each coffee competitor had a different value proposition. Reliability, quality and service all positively impacted the retailer's brand image. Further, some coffee houses catered to the coffee connoisseur, while others were simply convenient locations to consume good quality coffee. Producing consistent quality and taste in specialty coffee, however, required skill and training. Service was slower for specialty coffee retailers because the specialty coffee production process took approximately three to four minutes, compared to simply pouring a cup of brewed coffee. Specialty coffee customers seemed to accept long queues, long service times, varying quality and high prices.

Although coffee competitors distributed their products primarily through their individual retail outlets, many experimented with unique distribution strategies. For example, the drive-through had traditionally served brewed coffee, but many specialty coffee retailers had started to also offer drive-through service. Also, distribution alliances had formed in the coffee industry. Starbucks had joined with Chapters, and Second Cup with the Home Depot. Tim Hortons had partnered with Wendy's in 1995. Together, they

opened Wendy's/Tim Hortons food court–styled restaurants where a customer could order both Wendy's and Tim Hortons products at the same location.

The Canadian retail coffee industry had experienced explosive growth over the last five years. Annual retail coffee consumption had increased by 15 per cent to more than 16 million cups of coffee purchased every week in Canada. Although most Canadians still consumed their coffee in traditional sit-down retail coffee outlets, 29 per cent of the industry's coffee consumed was purchased from drive-throughs. Drive-through coffee consumption had grown almost fourfold since 1995.

Canadians, who consumed on average two or more cups of coffee per day, expected a different experience at different times of the day. Their morning consumption was driven by a "get up and go" ritual that required a convenient, dependable coffee source. In the afternoon, consumers wanted a coffee break—a "pick me up" or reward for their hard work. At night, coffee consumption was often a way to finish the evening meal. While specialty coffee growth had been significant, brewed coffee continued to be the dominant purchase throughout the day.

McDonald's Corporation

Ray Kroc, the founder of the McDonald's system, opened the first McDonald's Restaurant in Des Plaines, Illinois, in 1955. Although McDonald's was originally a hamburger restaurant, McDonald's now offered a diverse menu and quick service in 121 countries worldwide. While each country offered a slightly different dining experience to cater to the local culture, food preparation and marketing were standardized across the globe—from Tokyo to Toronto, the Big Mac was the same. According to Tom Peters, the three most recognized brands in the world were McDonald's golden arches, Coca-Cola and Disney.[4] In fact, these three brands often jointly marketed their products, further securing the primacy of their brands.

In the 1980s McDonald's experienced rapid growth, partly attributable to the successful "Big Mac Attack" ad promotion. By 2000, the McDonald's brand represented value and fast service. Through product innovation, McDonald's attracted many customer segments including families, teens and adults. After partnering with Disney, McDonald's Happy Meals revolutionized children's dining. With Ronald McDonald as the spokesperson, no other competitor was able to match the brand equity associated with the McDonald's Happy Meal. Furthermore, the introduction of

[4]www.worklifechoices.org/brandyou.htm, referenced January 12, 2001.

the "combo meal" made McDonald's another favorite at both lunch and dinner for a variety of adult customers. In 2000, McDonald's in the United States and Canada initiated the "Value Campaign." This promotion slashed the prices of McDonald's small and large sandwiches, to bring "value" to the customer. McDonald's also built its reputation through community activities. Ronald McDonald Children's Charities (RMCC), for example, was established to help fund children's charitable causes.

McDonald's Corporation was a publicly held company based in Chicago, Illinois. The head office established standard marketing, operations and quality practices, but the international subsidiaries could make independent decisions that addressed the needs of their particular customers. International subsidiaries were accountable to the head office for profitability and had to regularly remit their financial statements and strategic positions to the international headquarters.

McDonald's Corporation adopted a growth by acquisition strategy. To leverage the strong McDonald's brand, it acquired Aroma Café, Boston Market, Chipotle Mexican Grill, Donatos Pizza and Pret A Manger. In 2000, McDonald's Corporation was the quick service industry leader with sales of $14.7 billion and the industry's highest profit margin of 12.4 per cent.

Competition

The discussion below identifies the primary competitors to McDonald's.

WENDY'S Wendy's International, Inc. opened its first restaurant in 1969 and operated, developed and franchised a system of distinctive quick-service restaurants. Wendy's was known for its founder, Dave Thomas, and its unique menu blend of burgers, fries and healthy alternatives. Wendy's flagship products included the introduction of the salad in 1979, the baked potato in 1983 and the Super Value Menu in 1989. Furthermore, the introduction of the late night drive-through window allowed Wendy's customers to "eat great, even late." As of December 31, 2000, there were 5,792 Wendy's restaurants in the United States, Canada and 25 other countries and territories. Of these restaurants, 1,153 were operated by the company and 4,639 by the company's franchisees. The merger with the Canadian coffee and doughnuts icon, Tim Hortons, provided Wendy's the opportunity to expand into the coffee business in the United States, even though Tim Hortons continued to operate as a separate entity. Although Tim Hortons was best known for its coffee and doughnuts, the introduction of deli-style sandwiches, bagels and Tim's Own soups and chili made it a major player

in lunch sales. As of December 31, 2000, there were 1,980 Tim Hortons restaurants in Canada and the United States, of which 95 per cent were owned by franchisees.

In 2001, Wendy's International, Inc. enjoyed significant financial success. Its revenues increased by seven per cent as a result of strong domestic and international sales and its net income increased nine per cent largely attributed to improved operating performance at the Tim Hortons restaurants. More recently, Wendy's International focused much of its expansion through "combo units" of Wendy's and Tim Hortons in a food court–style [restaurant].

BURGER KING Burger King's reputation was associated with inexpensive food served quickly, in an attractive, clean environment. Founded in 1954, in Miami, Florida, there were more than 11,370 Burger King restaurants in 58 countries and international territories worldwide by 2002. The restaurants were owned and operated by independent franchisees. Burger King was best known for its flagship flame-broiled Whopper, its "Have It Your Way" motto (that enabled customers to design their own hamburgers) and its drive-through and take-out services (that accounted for 50 per cent and 15 per cent, respectively, of their sales). In fiscal year 2002, Burger King, part of Diageo (an international food and drinks corporation), had system-wide sales of $11.4 billion.

KFC, PIZZA HUT AND TACO BELL Tricon Global Restaurants, through its three brands, KFC, Pizza Hut and Taco Bell, developed, operated, franchised and licensed a worldwide system of restaurants which prepared, packaged and sold a menu of competitively priced food items. The Tricon organization operated more than 30,400 units in more than 100 countries and territories, and was the global leader in the chicken, pizza and Mexican restaurant categories. Tricon was also the leader in multi-branded quick-service restaurants with more than 1,100 locations worldwide. Multi-branding had proven to be a growth vehicle for Tricon in the United States, as consumers appeared to enjoy the variety of two or three dining options at the same location. In 2001, in spite of a three per cent drop in revenues as a result of foreign currency exchange issues and refranchising, net income rose 15 per cent due to restrained corporate and project spending.

McDonald's Canada

McDonald's Canada had approximately 1,200 locations throughout the country with 70 per cent owned and operated by franchisees. McDonald's Canada developed its own strategy, marketing plan and product line, although it was often similar to that of McDonald's USA. Canada based its success on the "three-legged stool": the company, the suppliers and the franchisees. Each leg brought stability to the partnership. Supplier "partners" included Coca-Cola, Disney, Nestlé, Cuddy Foods, Mother Parkers, and Cossette Communications-Marketing.

McDonald's entered the Canadian breakfast industry in April 1976, and for many years, dominated the industry with its flagship Egg McMuffin sandwich and other hand-held product features. Tim Hortons was essentially ignored by McDonald's and was allowed free reign to develop its brand, based on the slogan of "Always Fresh" coffee and doughnuts. Even though the McDonald's breakfast business had grown, Sgro believed that McDonald's Canada did not allocate the necessary operational expertise and marketing drive to develop its coffee equity or breakfast business.

Corporate/Franchisee Relationship

Franchisees played important roles in the McDonald's system because of their customer contact and their entrepreneurial spirit. Although some franchisees were employees of McDonald's who were promoted through the corporate ladder, most franchisees applied from outside of the system because they saw the tremendous business opportunity. Franchisees were screened and selected for their entrepreneurial drive and prior business success. Franchisees were expected to act as owner-operators, not strictly as investors. They were required to be active in the day-to-day operations of their franchise and assume the responsibility of building the McDonald's system within the community. Franchisees paid a monthly rent and service fee to McDonald's Canada, based on a percentage of top-line sales. In addition, franchisees were required to meet the corporate standards of quality, service and cleanliness. They were obliged to contribute to the marketing fund and take an active involvement in all marketing initiatives. It was the franchisees' responsibility to represent the company well in their community, and to grow the business to the best of their ability. In return, franchisees leveraged McDonald's brand equity and received considerable support for every facet of their business. McDonald's Canada offered support in training, human resources, operations, marketing, construction, purchasing and product development. Through involvement in most of the functional areas of the business, the franchisees played active roles in the strategic direction of McDonald's Canada. Finally, McDonald's corporation and the franchisee shared in the cost of each restaurant. McDonald's owned the land (or the head lease) and the building, while the franchisee owned the equipment and décor package. A strong corporate/franchisee relationship was the cornerstone of the McDonald's philosophy.

Operations and Training

In Canada, all operations and training requirements were set and standardized by McDonald's Canada and were followed precisely in the restaurants. Each store was equipped with an operations and training manual that dictated everything from cooking times and temperatures, to drive-through service standards and appearance standards. All products were prepared on the spot, offering "Made for You" service. Using clamshell grills, timed fryers and high-tech holding cabinets, McDonald's restaurants could produce quality products quickly. In recent years, drive-through service had been a priority throughout Canada, with numerous management initiatives focused both on the speed and accuracy of service. The overarching goal was to ensure that customers received the same food and service in Vancouver, B.C., as they did in Tokyo, Japan.

All salaried managers received standardized business training from the McDonald's Institute of Hamburgerology, which was based in Chicago and had affiliate campuses in Vancouver, Montreal and Toronto. McDonald's functioned as a meritocracy. Managers were evaluated through annual performance and compensation reviews based on standardized goals set by McDonald's Canada, goals set by the market franchisee and their ability to attain objectives that they set themselves to enhance personal development. Managers were offered competitive salaries and there existed considerable opportunity for advancement. They received regular feedback through Management Visitation Reports that graded the overall efficiency of their shift. They also received a performance review every six months and a formal wage review once a year.

Outside of the management team, McDonald's restaurants were staffed by part-time employees. These part-time workers were often teenagers looking to build their work experience or adults looking for a flexible job. Management tried to create an environment built on mutual respect, hard work and fun. Managers often organized monthly crew social outings, treat days and crew operational competitions. In addition, McDonald's offered all employees flexible scheduling, regular wage reviews, free uniforms and benefits. All McDonald's crew members were also given a McGold Card that allowed employees McDonald's food at half price, as well as a variety of discounts at local and national retail restaurants. To support their business, all McDonald's crew received an orientation class, at least three training shifts, and were evaluated bi-monthly through a Station Observation Checklist that dictated precisely how to operate their particular station. Crew received a wage review every six months, which evaluated their Station Observation Checklist grades, as well as their versatility, initiative and leadership ability.

Burlington Operations

Ralph Sgro, the owner-operator of the Burlington market, had more than 30 years of McDonald's experience. He began his career in 1973 as a front line manager in London, Ontario, and advanced through the system to become the senior field service manager of Eastern Canada in 1985. Within the corporate system, Sgro worked in a variety of operational areas, product development and menu management. In 1988, Sgro and his wife purchased the four-store market in Burlington, Ontario. In 2002, the Burlington market was home to seven restaurants. Although Sgro focused on Burlington, he continued to be involved with strategic planning for McDonald's Canada as the Ontario representative on the Partnering Committee. Sgro was recognized throughout the McDonald's for his operational involvement and commitment to the McDonald's system.

McCafé

On a recent vacation to Italy, the Sgros encountered McCafé, a full-service coffee bar located inside a downtown Rome McDonald's. McCafé offered espressos, cappuccinos and lattes, as well as cookies and pastries, complete with a marble countertop. Sgro believed that this European concept could be successful in Canada and could address the issue of Tim Hortons' increasing market share. Looking into the McCafé concept, Sgro discovered that there were more than 300 McCafés in 19 countries worldwide, including the United States.

After discussing the McCafé opportunity with his friend, the McDonald's Canada chief operating officer (COO), Bill Johnson, Sgro was given the go-ahead to introduce it to Canada. The implementation team, led by Sgro, comprised entrepreneurial and experienced corporate employees with diverse backgrounds in operations, marketing and menu management, as well as representatives from Cossette Advertising. The McCafé operational prototype was scheduled to open as an extension of the front counter at the Millcroft location in Burlington, Ontario.

In Canada, McCafé was positioned for working adults who enjoy coffee. McCafé was among the few restaurants that offered specialty coffee conveniently, quickly and relatively inexpensively. Its products included a full selection of specialty coffees and teas, 100 per cent Arabica-brewed coffee, baked goods and tins of the McCafé blend. All products could be purchased at both the front counter and through the drive-through. The McCafé design had a mahogany wood backdrop, stainless steel appliances and dark green accents. The baked goods were presented in a rounded, refrigerated, glass display case. The overall McCafé package was modern, sophisticated.

McCafé Burlington

On May 26, 2001, McCafé Burlington opened its doors. The McCafé prototype restaurant was designed as an addition to the front counter at the Millcroft location in Burlington, Ontario. The purpose of this location was purely operational— an opportunity to work out the operational kinks before taking McCafé public.

Compared to the space requirements of other McDonald's equipment, McCafé equipment was relatively small, inexpensive and easy to fit into an existing counter. McCafé construction took less than four days, and did not significantly disrupt the McDonald's operations during construction. As with other McDonald's operations, McCafés were also standardized. Specialty coffee machinery poured lattes, cappuccinos and espressos at the push of a button, in 22 seconds. The McCafé equipment did not require the expertise of well trained baristas. The brewed coffee was prepackaged to ensure every pot of coffee had the same strength. Other than the cookies and muffins, none of the baked goods was prepared on site. The cakes were delivered in bulk packaging and cut as needed.

Local billboards and newspapers were used to advertise the new Burlington McCafé and in-store samples and promotions allowed customers to sample the new products. Comment cards were distributed to collect customer feedback on the new venture.

The Future of McCafé in Canada

Sgro and his team were excited about McCafé. The initial customer response was positive; the quantity of coffee sold in the first six months of operation increased over 30 per cent from the previous year. Moreover, McCafé had fit seamlessly into McDonald's operations. However, there was still much to learn about the product lines that were successful and those that were not. Further, the competition had not responded yet to McCafé. While breakfast sales had improved with McCafé, it was not clear whether the increase in sales would be sustained. While Sgro was optimistic about the future of McCafé, he was unsure if McCafé was the white knight needed to stem the loss of McDonald's market share in breakfast sales over the long term.

Case 18

House of Tata, 1995: The Next Generation (A)

9-798-037
Rev: August 30, 2006

Tarun Khanna
Krishna Palepu
Danielle Melito Wu

Ratan Tata has his own vision for the group and there is never any doubt that he will hold it together.[1]

The House of Tata, India's oldest and largest group of companies, was also one of the country's most respected business organizations. The Tata Group enterprises, worth a market value of Rs. 290 billion in FY96, included 84 separately traded companies spanning 25 sectors of the economy, with 270,000 employees and FY95 sales of Rs. 220 billion.[2] Ratan Tata, chairman since 1991 of the group holding company, Tata Sons, had already launched

HARVARD BUSINESS SCHOOL

Professors Tarun Khanna and Krishna Palepu and Research Associate Danielle Melito Wu prepared this case. HBS cases are developed solely as the basis for class discussion. Cases are not intended to serve as endorsements, sources of primary data, or illustrations of effective or ineffective management.

[1]N. Radhakrishnan, "Let Us Go Anywhere, I Do Not Care Where . . ." *Business India*, December 6–19, 1993.

[2]1996 average exchange rate: Rs. 35.4 : $1. 1995 average exchange rate: Rs. 32.4 : $1. (Rs. = rupee.)

several strategic initiatives that were changing the very character of the group.

In early 1995, Ratan proposed a fee scheme whereby, for the first time, Tata companies would have to pay for the use of the Tata brand name. This proposition met healthy questioning and debate from several Tata company heads. In addition, Ratan was taking steps to increase the degree of group ownership in the individual companies, to revitalize its management development programs through Tata Adminstrative Services, and to move into uncharted territories in new industries. Finally, in late 1995, Ratan contemplated selling a 20% private equity stake in Tata Industries Limited (TIL), a holding company wholly owned by Tata Sons, to a Hong Kong conglomerate.

At a time when conventional wisdom argued against the continued existence of diversified business groups, Ratan's bold decisions seemed especially puzzling to many of his colleagues and admirers. At the March 31 close of FY96, Ratan, the various Tata companies, the media, and the Indian business world at large all waited to see how his plans would unfold in the new year.

The Indian Economy

Following a balance of payments crisis in 1991, the incoming Indian National Congress (Indira) introduced drastic reforms to liberalize the old central planning economy. Far-ranging policies began the process of decreasing government control and moving India towards an increasingly market-based economy. Within just a few years, there was a change away from the license regime and the old, protected mindset that had permeated the nation.[3] Product expansion and new market entry became easier as centralized planning ceased. The number of industries in which only public sector (state and central government) firms were allowed to operate decreased from seventeen to six. This opened fast growing industries such as electronics and motor vehicles to the private sector. The government also divested minority shares of its state-owned enterprises (in some cases up to 25%), most notably in the steel, oil refining, air transport, and mining industries. See Exhibit 1 for market indicators.

A new sealed bid system helped combat a culture of bribery in industries that still required licenses, but corrupt officials could still extract "speed money" to help businesses avoid project delays. Greedy officials could also change the bidding requirements after the bidding had been completed, thereby leaving bidders scrambling to secure favor. Officials had also been known to accept payment from the losing bidders to declare all former bids insufficient and to start the bidding process again.

The reforms had a positive effect on the growth of domestic capital markets. New banking regulations aimed at aiding priority sectors and small firms, but had the effect of restricting lending to the largest 20 groups. These regulations were easily enforced, as the public sector held 87% of the nation's total deposits and received over half of all bank loans.[4] As a result, global depository receipts (GDRs) and private equity investment became popular methods of fundraising among large business groups.[5]

As a way of bringing capital, technology, and modern management practices into the country, the government encouraged foreign investment by reducing red tape and easing the restrictions on ownership stakes for foreigners in 34 high priority industries. For example, foreigners could now own up to 40% of a domestic airline. In priority sectors, such as power, foreigners were permitted to invest up to 100%. As a result of these reforms, foreign direct investment increased from $230 million in 1991 to $8.8 billion in 1995.

However, as foreign investment increased, so did anti-foreign sentiment. With a new takeover code which no longer protected companies from hostile takeovers, the arrival of cash-rich foreign firms appeared as a threat to some incumbent managers. Only investors with at least 26% ownership of a company had the legal right to block takeover resolutions.

BUSINESS GROUPS

Diversified business groups dominated the Indian private sector. The modern groups grew out of the 19th century British "managing agency" system, under which a central agency controlled several companies across a range of industries, with limited liability to the agency. After the government abolished the managing agency system in 1970, diverse family-controlled companies formed identifiable business groups. Group companies were often linked through a maze of cross-holdings and interlocking directorates, and often emphasized a common identity. To venture into a new area of activity the group typically put up some fraction of the capital for the new area, with the remainder provided by state-run financial institutions.

The promoter's own capital often came through other group companies who purchased part of the equity in the new venture.[6] During the 1970s the strict government regulations stifled competition and thereby basically guaranteed success in any line of business. But since liberalization, many Indian promoters had been quietly increasing company holdings in order to deal with the threat of takeovers.

Despite the ongoing debate over whether business groups were a dying breed, they continued to be an important component of the post-liberalized economy. The largest and most successful modern business groups tended to be run by politically savvy entrepreneurs. One study examined the "industrial embassies" that many large groups maintained in New Delhi to interact with the regulators.[7] Other observers claimed that powerful groups sometimes secured licenses solely to preempt others from a particular activity, that they often exceeded their licensed production levels, and that they engaged in "financial preemption" in an environment of capital scarcity.

The House of Tata

Jamsetji Tata planted the roots of the Tata Group by establishing a single textile mill in 1874. Throughout his expansive career, he never lost sight of his goal to encourage India's industrial and intellectual development. The House

---

[3]Prior to reform, businesses were required to obtain licenses in order to enter and exit new markets, and create or expand product lines.

[4]In 1994 and 1995, applications were approved for the launching of 18 new private sector banks.

[5]GDRs allow companies in Europe, Asia, the United States, and Latin America to offer shares in world markets. Local investors can buy shares on their own home exchange and receive dividends in their home currency.

[6]In the Indian business context, a promoter was a person (or an entity) who started a business, by investing personal or corporate funds and/or soliciting funds from other investors.

[7]Dennis G. Encarnation, *Dislodging Multinationals: India's Strategy in Comparative Perspective,* Cornell University Press, 1989.

Exhibit 1	The Indian Economy in 1995 as Compared to the Economy of the UK and US in 1995

Indicators and Ratings Index	India	UK	US
Local currency : $1[a] (1995 ave.)	Rs. 32.4	£0.63	
Population[a] (m)	937	59	
GDP[a] ($bn)	335	1,111	
GDP % real growth[a]	7.0%	2.4%	2.0%
Financial, business & other services as % of GDP[b]	11.1%	22.2%	35.6%[c]
Capital Market			
Bank assets as % of GDP[d]	49%	103%	78%
No. of listed domestic companies[e]	5,000[f]	2,078	7,671
No. of companies followed by at least one analyst[g]	153	n/a	n/a
No. of equity analyst firms[g]	17	59	396
Price index (Dec. 29; 1/31/91=100)[h]	184.3	179.7	186.7
Market Value (Dec. 29; $bn)[h]	85	1,321	5,367
Volume of shares traded (Dec. 29; m of shares)[h]	161,239	10,594	9,375
Value of volume (Dec. 29; $m)[h]	829	57,070	409,962
Ratings Index[e]			
(Ratings are on a scale of 1 to 10. Higher scores indicate higher likelihood of scenario.)			
Ability of foreign investors to control domestic companies	6.57	9.38	8.46
Local capital markets accessible to domestic & foreign companies	5.66	8.72	8.22
Stock markets reflect real value of companies	4.32	6.35	6.91
Availability of venture capital	4.58	7.64	8.31
Information & Infrastructure			
Urban population[e] (1993)	26%	89%	76%
No. of business student as % of population[i]	0.1%	0.4%	0.9%
Radios per 1,000 population[i]	81	1,429	2,122
Phone lines in use per 1,000 population[e]	11	494	599
TVs per 1,000 (1994)[i]	40	439	817
Newspaper circulation per 1,000 population[e] (1992)	31	383	236
Ratings Index[e]			
Adequacy of roads	2.15	5.49	8.34
Adequacy of telecommunications infrastructure	4.00	8.26	9.09
Overall efficiency of distribution systems	5.14	7.54	8.78
Political Risk Factors			
Ratings Index[j]			
Efficiency of judicial system	8.00	10.00	10.00
Rule of law	4.17	8.57	10.00
Corruption	4.58	9.10	8.63
Risk of expropriation	7.75	9.71	9.98
Risk of contract repudiation by government	6.11	9.63	9.00

[a]As reported in *Economic Intelligence Unit (EIU) Country Reports*, various countries, 4th quarter, 1996. India data is based on EIU estimates. [b]As reported in *EIU Country Profiles*, various countries, 1996–1997. [c]1993 data. [d]Bank assets from "Bank Survey, Domestic Credit," *International Financial Statistics*, IMF, July 1997. [e]*World Competitiveness Yearbook*, 1996. [f]Author's estimate. Companies are traded on multiple stock exchanges for which data is often unavailable. Estimates vary widely. [g]*Nelson's Directory of Investment Research*, volume II, 1995 (India). Phone interview with Nelson's (US and UK). [h]Datastream International, 1997. Indian data from CRISIL 500 Equity Index, Bombay, India. [i]*UNESCO Statistical Yearbook*, 1996. [j]*Law and Finance*, by Raphael La Porta, Florencio Lopez-de-Silanes, Andrei Shleifer, and Robert W. Vishny, working paper #5661, The National Bureau of Economic Research, Inc., July 1996, Table 7. The ratings are an average of the months of April and October from the *International Country Risk's* monthly index between 1982 and 1995. The "Efficiency of judicial system" rating is a 1980–1983 average of raw numbers provided by the Business International Corporation.

of Tata built world-class capacity in steel and hydroelectric power, and developed modern manufacturing methods, technical education, and research capabilities. Jamsetji founded the J.N. Tata Endowment Trust in 1892 to provide loan scholarships for Indian nationals with outstanding academic records to pursue higher studies abroad. The later Tatas lived up to their patriarch's legacy, and by the mid 20th century, 85% of the Tata family's original share in Tata Sons was transferred to two charitable trusts, the Sir Dorabji Tata Trust and the Sir Ratan Tata Trust.

Tata Sons, the initial investor in many Tata companies, eventually became the group holding company. As such, it administered current business activities as well as financed new projects. J.R.D. Tata, the son of Jamsetji Tata's cousin, was elected chairman of Tata Sons in 1938. At that time, the group held just 13 companies. J.R.D. hand-picked many of the Tata company chairmen, including Darbari Seth (Tata Chemicals) and Ajit Kerkar (Indian Hotels). J.R.D. presided over the Tata companies during the nationalization of many of India's businesses, including Tata Airlines (nationalized in 1953), later to become India's two national airlines, Air India and Air India International; and Tata's insurance arm, New India Assurance Company Limited (nationalized in 1971).

The Tata companies became legally independent after the dismantling of the managing agency system in 1970. Nevertheless, the force of J.R.D.'s personality, along with a network of inter-corporate shareholdings and weekly cross-company directors' meetings, helped maintain a sense of unity. J.R.D. encouraged his hand-picked chairmen to expand and operate their companies autonomously within the Tata philosophy of professionalism and ethical business practices. As a result, the chairmen of the larger Tata companies grew accustomed to ruling their empires without interference from the Tatas for decades. Ajit Kerkar reminisced, "He [J.R.D.] was the kind of chairman any professional manager should have. He laid down the policies but never interfered with the day-to-day working. Even those areas where he and the board did not agree with me . . . he never imposed his own will on anything. That was his greatness."[8] Although these company commanders all traded on the Tata name—one of the most respected brand names in India—they cherished their independence, and vehemently protected their own domains.

J.R.D. fostered this entrepreneurial spirit and believed that it was the main ingredient in the outstanding success of the Tata companies. Among the more notable were the two flagship companies, Tata Engineering and Locomotive Company (Telco) and Tata Iron and Steel Company (Tisco); Tata Power (one of the three Tata Electric Companies); Associated Cement Company (ACC); Tata Chemicals; Tata Tea; and Indian Hotels. These seven companies together accounted for nearly 80% of the Tata Group's sales in FY95. Exhibit 2 diagrams the intercompany relationships and investment flows. Exhibits 3, 4a b, and 5 provide an overview of the publicly listed Tata companies and a comparison of the major Tata companies with corresponding industry averages.

RATAN TATA

Ratan Tata, the son of one of J.R.D.'s cousins, was an open, trusting man who had never worn his wealth with comfort and as a result developed into a shy, soft-spoken individual. He was an unfailingly ethical man who believed that "the end never justifies the means." After studying engineering at Cornell University, Ratan embarked upon a career in architecture in the United States. He was called back to India in 1962 to work for the House of Tata. He rotated through various Tata companies, attended the Harvard Business School's Advanced Management Program in 1975, and was elected chairman of Tata Industries Limited (TIL) in 1981. Ratan then attempted to turn TIL from a small holding company, with 1981 profits of Rs. 35,000, into a group strategy think tank.

Ratan's 1983 "Tata Strategic Plan" proposed placing TIL as the group's vehicle for growth in high-technology businesses in four areas (advanced electronics, biotechnology, advanced materials, and alternative energy), and simultaneously phasing out "sunset" businesses like textiles and cooking oils. Its other goals included defining the group companies in terms of eight business areas, increasing Tata ownership in group companies, and exploring joint ventures with the government. TIL generally maintained a 10% to 20% stake in the few new ventures that they promoted in the 1980s, including a highly successful entry into several high technology areas and a joint venture in contract drilling for oil and gas.

Ratan's friendship with India's Prime Minister Rajiv Gandhi (PM from 1984 to 1989) sparked a warm relationship between the Tata companies and the government. During Prime Minister Gandhi's tenure, new projects that had been awaiting approval for years were finally granted the necessary licenses. However, the implementation of the "Tata Strategic Plan" was held back by the Tata culture of independence—the various Tata company chairmen, who collectively held TIL's entire share capital, were unwilling to fully support Ratan's plans.

In 1988 the aging J.R.D. promised succession of the Tata Sons chair to Russi Mody, a good friend and long-time

[8]N. Radhakrishnan, "Let Us Go Anywhere, I Do Not Care Where . . . ," *Business India,* December 6–19, 1993, p. 67.

Exhibit 2	Tata Group Company Relationships

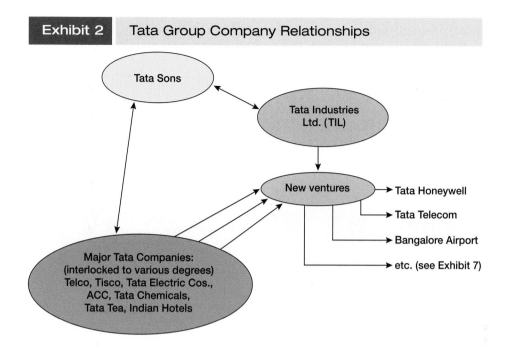

Arrows indicate investment flows.

Exhibit 3	Activity between Tata Group Companies by Publicly Listed Tata Company, FY94 (Year-End Mar 31; Rs. Million; 1994 Ave.: Rs. 30.5 : $1)

Company	Loans from grp. cos.	Receivables from grp. cos.	Investment in grp. cos.	Net Worth
Agricultural Products				
Asian Coffee	0	0	0	150.7
Consolidated Coffee	0	3.2	4.3	245.4
Tata Tea	0	119.8	1,016.50	2,588.80
Base Metals				
India Steel Rolling Mills	0	0	0	−125.2
ACC-Nihon Castings	18	0	0	82.5
Tata-Yodogawa	0	0	3.3	181.7
Ipitata Sponge Iron	71.1	44	0	220.8
Tata Metaliks	0	0	0	263.6
Tata Metals & Strips	0	0	15	352.5
Tinplate Co. of India	0	0	0	1,037.3
Special Steels	0	0	7.0	1,437.2
Tata Iron & Steel (Tisco)	0	140.7	1,920.60	25,247.4
Non-Metallic Mineral Products				
Ipitata Refractories	6.2	0	0	−04.6
Premium Granites	10.0	0	0	36.9
Tata Refractories	0	1.7	17.6	447.8
Associated Cement (ACC)[a]	0	52.3	186.8	4,099.90
Chemicals				
Tata Pigments	0.1	0	0	15.4
Industrial Perfumes	0	0	0	74.0
Lakme Exports	0	1.3	42.1	167.6
Vashisti Detergents	0	0	0	183.9
Merind	0	0	0	214.7
Lakme	0	0	18.4	299.6
Goodlass Nerolac Paints	0	10.3	11.4	465.3
Tata Oil Mills	0	12.2	29.1	652.2

(continued)

Exhibit 3	Activity between Tata Group Companies by Publicly Listed Tata Company, FY94 (Year-End Mar 31; Rs. Million; 1994 Ave.: Rs. 30.5 : $1)—Continued

Company	Loans from grp. cos.	Receivables from grp. cos.	Investment in grp. cos.	Net worth
Tata Chemicals	0	72.8	996.4	8249.3
Construction & Allied Activities				
Tata Constructions & Proj.	0	0	0	−120.0
Babcock & Wilcox of India	0	0	0	−03.3
Tata Korf Engg. Services	0	0	0	07.1
Stewarts & Lloyds of India	0	0	0	7.7
Tata Projects	0	0	1.4	123.8
Tata Industries[b]	0	0	728.9	504.3
Electrical & Non-Electrical Machinery				
Voltas Transformers	48.0	0	0	36.1
Voltas Switchgear	130.0	0	0	52.5
AP Industrial Components	0	0	0	21.8
FAL Industries	0	0	7.3	164.2
Associated Tire Machinery	0	0	0	25.3
TRF	0	0	13.2	95.2
Tata Timken	25.2	02.4	0	272.2
Electricity & Non-Conventional Energy				
Tata Hydro-Electric Power	0	37.7	158.4	2,602.5
Andhra Valley Power	0	56.6	154.4	3776.1
Tata Power	0	94.3	201.8	6,582.7
Electronics				
Tata Elxsi (India)	0	0	0	83.3
Tata Honeywell	0	0	0	158.6
Nat'l Radio & Electronic	0	0	2.6	322.2
Tata Telecom	0	0	74.4	433.7
Tata Unisys	0	0	6.0	457.0
Services				
Forbes Shipping Corp.	0	0	0	0.7
Tata Klockner Indl. Plants	0	0	0	4.0
Tata Services	0	0	8.0	9.4
Voltas Food & Beverages	0	02.5	0	10.1
Latham India	0	0	0	12.9
Bradma of India	0	1.0	3.0	14.2
Benares Hotels	0	0	0	36.2
Indian Resort Hotels	0	0	4.0	58.2
Investa	0	0	33.5	97.9
Eureka Forbes	0	7.5	20.5	101.1
Voltas International	6.1	1.8	24.8	118.6
Piem Hotels	0	13.6	74.6	241.4
Hitech Drilling Serv. India	0	0	0	416.1
Tata Exports	0	0	147.6	550.4
Investment Corp. of India	0	0	370.7	716.1
Tata Finance	0	0	56.1	886.7
Indian Hotels	0	20.0	303.1	1,856.1
Other				
Timex Watches (mfr.)	0	0	0	341.4
Titan Industries (mfr.)	0	0	143.3	1,286.2
Rallis India (diversified)	0	1	05.1	563.9
Voltas (diversified)	0	224.5	371.3	1,546.2
Tata Adv. Mat. (plastics)	0	0	0	11.7
Tata Press (pulp & paper)	0	25.9	20.0	295.5
Svadeshi Mills Co.	0	0	01.2	184.1
Forbes Gokak	0	38.3	228.5	1,344.3
Tata Eng. & Loc. (Telco)	0	113.6	1,363.3	8,361.2

Source: Center for Monitoring the Indian Economy (CIMM). Note: Major companies in boldface. [a]ACC is technically referred to as a Tata associate company. [b]Tata Industries is a separate company from TIL.

Exhibit 4a   Financials of Tata's Major Companies Compared to Industry Average, FY94 (Year-End Mar 31; Rs. Millions; 1994 Ave.: Rs. 30.5 : $1)

Rs. 30.5 : $1 (# of companies)	Telco Heavy Vehicles	Industry Average: Transport Equipment (118 cos.)	ACC Cement	Industry Average: Non-metal Minerals (154 cos.)	Tisco Finished Steel	Industry Average: Base Metals (319 cos.)	Tata Power[a] Electricity	Industry Average: Electricity (19 cos.)	Tata Chemicals Sodium Carbonate	Industry Average: Chemical (415 cos.)	Tata Tea	Industry Average: Agric. Product (55 cos.)	Indian Hotels & Restaurant	Industry Average: Services (508 cos.)
Sales	36,688	1,492	16,349	935	37,259	1,159	9,498	5,864	4,983	1,049	4,158	759	2,983	1,740
PBDIT[b]	4,057	13	1,592	147	5,940	29	2,240	2,175	3,655	167	1,159	128	981	525
Liabilities	33,686	1,531	14,224	1,127	73,191	2,116	16,304	30,606	23,296	1,269	5,173	888	3,606	5,234
Net worth	8,361	280	4,100	365	25,247	689	6,583	14,674	8,249	398	2,589	544	1,856	1,057
Borrowings	14,132	501	6,788	515	34,285	977	8,044	12,722	12,522	496	1,566	172	956	1,708
Current liabilities	11,192	750	3,336	246	13,658	450	1,678	3,210	2,525	375	1,019	172	794	964
Assets	33,686	1,531	14,224	1,127	73,191	2,116	16,304	30,606	23,296	1,269	5,173	888	3,606	5,234
Current assets	22,606	1,062	6,239	265	23,588	843	4,385	7,882	6,052	690	3,776	424	2,044	3,234
Sources of funds	1,057	287	2,425	187	12,817	338	4,001	4,097	6,727	259	516	95	573	599
Internal	1,288	63	635	52	2,444	71	1,115	1,436	2,286	57	402	48	515	168
External	−231	224	1,790	135	10,373	267	2,887	2,661	4,441	202	114	47	58	431
Uses of Funds	1,057	287	2,425	187	12,817	338	4,001	4,097	6,727	259	516	95	573	599
GFA[c]	2,390	87	2,575	97	9,772	229	2,133	3,253	7,459	98	116	40	162	247

Exhibit 4b Financials and Activity of Tata Companies Compared FY91 and FY95 (year-end Mar 31; Rs. millions; 1995 ave.: 32.5 : $1; 1991 ave.: 22.8 : $1)

	Telco		ACC		Tisco		Tata Power[a]		Tata Chemicals		Tata Tea		Indian Hotels	
	1991	1995	1991	1995	1991	1995	1991	1995	1991	1994	1991	1995	1991	1994
Loans f/ grp. cos.	0	0	0	0	0	0	0	0	0	0	0	0	0	0
Receivables f/ grp. cos.	27	724	8	64	106	60	0	54	83	73	138	120	34	20
Investment in grp. cos.	0	1,909	2	391	405	2,057	0	1,922	2	996	226	1,207	30	303
Sales	25,508	56,403	11,513	20,658	21,922	45,487	4,740	10,599	2,994	4,983	2,943	3,991	1,563	2,983
PBDIT[b]	3,704	7,527	2,058	2,810	4,861	7,909	791	3,082	1,316	3,655	1,061	1,085	367	981
Assets	16,975	41,396	6,984	16,960	33,854	77,845	6,510	21,539	10,417	23,296	3,593	5,467	2,325	3,606
Net worth	5,831	14,203	2,384	5,954	14,241	26,880	2,309	10,445	3,345	8,249	1,628	2,888	716	1,856
Internal fund sources	1,520	3,472	1,282	1,550	2,156	3,799	458	1,553	709	2,286	390	383	331	515
External fund sources	894	5,328	–418	1,567	3,391	3,194	666	4,204	2,395	4,441	529	–5	287	58
GFA[c]	10,065	3,860	5,933	2,184	27,029	5,230	5,779	1,634	4,999	7,459	1,404	205	1286	162

Source: Center for Monitoring the Indian Economy (CIMM). Note: Figures may not add up due to rounding. Note for Exhibit 4a: The companies being compared were not included in the industry average. Note for Exhibit 4b: 1995 CIMM data not available for Tata Chemicals and Indian Hotels. [a]Tata Power is the largest of Tata's two other companies in the electricity sector, Tata Hydro-Electric Power Supply Co. and Andhra Valley Power Supply Co. The three companies together hold a 17% market share of publicly listed power companies. [b]Profit before depreciation, interest, and taxes. [c]Gross fixed asset.

Exhibit 5 Stock Indices of Tata's Major Companies Compared to Industry Average, 12/29/95 (Rs. 35.2 : $1)

	CRISIL 500[a]	Telco	CRISIL 500: Travel & Transport	Tisco	CRISIL 500: Metals	Tata Power	CRISIL 500: Power
(# of companies)	(508 cos.)		(2 cos.)		(7 cos.)		(9 cos.)
Price Index 1/31/91 = 100	184.3	372.7	286.5	141.6	96.7	199.0	121.8
Return Index 1/31/91 = 100	n/a	397.0	n/a	151.4	n/a	218.8	n/a
Market value Rs. billions	2,750.6	83.3	2.3	66.4	29.2	12.5	58.2

	ACC	CRISIL 500: Cement Products	Tata Chemicals	CRISIL 500: Inorganic Chemicals	Tata Tea	CRISIL 500: Tea & Coffee	Indian Hotels	CRISIL 500: Hotels
(# of companies)		(14 cos.)		(7 cos.)		(9 cos.)		(8 cos.)
Price Index 1/31/91 = 100	274.1	265.1	337.9	370.6	224.9	179.7	1148.7	866.3
Return Index 1/31/91 = 100	288.0	n/a	371.33	n/a	239.5	n/a	1202.9	n/a
Market value Rs. billions	24.0	80.5	23.4	49.1	14.1	59.8	25.9	60.5

Source: Datastream International.

Note: The tables above compare each major Tata company to a corresponding portfolio of the CRISIL 500. Price index is a measure of capital gains. Return Index is a measure of capital gains and dividends.

[a]CRISIL 500 is a stock information database comprised of 508 actively traded Indian companies. The CRISIL 500 industry averages include data for Tata companies, with the exception of "travel and transport" (Telco) and "metals" (Tisco).

chairman of Tata Iron & Steel Company (Tisco). Like many of his contemporaries, Mody figured the shy and soft-spoken Ratan for a lightweight, not viewing him as a serious contender for the chair. A consequent error, and overconfidence on Mody's part, caused J.R.D. to rethink the succession plan. He started with bypassing Mody in favor of inviting Ratan to take over the Telco chair from 82-year-old Sumant Moolgaokar in December 1988. Mody was incensed.

J.R.D., then 88, nominated Ratan, then 54, to the Tata Sons chair on March 25, 1991. Ratan found himself as the head of a conglomeration of companies one Tata director described as "no longer existing as a group except in their culture and name. Legally, none of the companies has any reason to show allegiance to Tata Sons. It is only because of the financial institutions, who are the major shareholders, that Tata management is allowed in these companies."[9]

Russi Mody and Ratan had a major confrontation when Mody unilaterally decided to change the succession hierarchy in Tisco. Ratan objected, saying that such changes warranted a full-fledged board discussion. Mody disagreed, but after a series of meetings with J.R.D. and other Tata directors was held, Mody withdrew his new management succession plan. A few months later, Mody relinquished his position as managing director in favor of Dr. Irani. Mody remained as non-executive chairman but over the next several months the growing tension between Mody and Irani resulted in open conflict within the company. On April 19, 1993, then 75-year-old Mody was terminated from his position as Tisco chairman.

In the meantime, Ratan revived a much-ignored policy which set the mandatory retirement age for executive directors at 65 and non-executive directors at 75. Enforcement of this policy would make it difficult for the powerful but aging chairmen to remain within the Tata companies. After the episode with Mody, most old-guard chairmen relinquished their posts with little fuss in deference to the new order. Darbari Seth, 73, continued at Associated Cement as a non-executive director and was recognized as chairman emeritus at both Tata Chemicals and Tata Tea. At that time, the remaining powerful chairmen were Ajit Kerkar, 60, of Indian Hotels; N.A. Palkhivala, 72, of Associated Cement; H.N. Sethna, 70, of the Tata Electric Companies; and A.H. Tobaccowala, 68, of Voltas. See Exhibit 6 for the chairmen and boards of directors of major Tata companies.

Before Ratan could craft a group strategy, he would have to get Tata's two flagship companies, which together accounted for more than half of sales, back into shape. Telco's earnings had dropped 77% in FY93 and Tisco had suffered a 41% earnings loss the same year. Under Ratan's leadership, both Telco and Tisco managed to increase earnings in FY94 and by FY95, earnings for both companies had rebounded. By Ratan's account, "I made no effort to play a group role until Tisco and Telco were doing extremely well."[10]

Between the mid-1980s and mid-1990s, Ratan promoted—through TIL—a total of 20 solo and joint ventures, with combined sales of Rs. 7.5 billion in FY96 (see Exhibit 7). These sales were expected to increase tremendously. TIL maintained a 25% to 50% share in all solo ventures. In the case of joint ventures, TIL signed all joint venture contracts, while the Tata company involved usually commanded the controlling interest. Other Tata companies were encouraged to become co-promoters only in those ventures in which they had a strategic interest. Although TIL tended to exclude external investors from its promotion projects, the company had on occasion taken a few of their promoted companies public.

RATAN TATA'S STRATEGY, 1995

We have somehow to consider ourselves as one group. That's what we're trying to do in terms of corporate communications. We need to get the companies to operate synergetically [sic] with each other. After that, we will have to evolve a structure that has to be accepted, not mandated.[11]

THE TATA BRAND Ratan Tata was considering several steps that he hoped would give the group a stronger collective identity. The principal of these was for Tata Sons to take responsibility for promoting a unified Tata brand which could be used by all companies that subscribed to the Tata Brand Equity Scheme. Each subscribing company would derive the benefits of the centrally promoted Tata brand and of the Tata affiliation. Tata Sons would require an annual contribution related to each company's net income in order to meet the costs of the development, promotion, and protection of the unified Tata brand.

---

[9]India's financial institutions had strong ties with, and had historically always supported, the Tata family.

[10]Cesar Bacani and Shirish Nadkarni, "The Tata Emperor," *Asiaweek,* January 24, 1997, p. 41

[11]Ibid, quote from Ratan Tata.

Exhibit 6				Major Tata Companies: Chairmen (1985 and 1995) and Board of Directors (1995)

Company	Est.	Chairman, 1985	Chairman, 1995	Board of Directors, 1995
Tata Sons	1917	J.R.D. Tata	Ratan Tata	Directors: J.J. Bhabha, B.G. Deshmukh, Syamal Gupta, A.B. Kerkar, F.K. Kavarana, F.C. Kohli, Dr. F.A. Mehta, P.S. Mistry, N.A. Palkhivala, S.A. Sabavala, D.S. Seth, H.N. Sethna, J.K. Setna, N.A. Soonawala, J.E. Talaulicar, A.H. Tobaccowala, S.R. Vakil.
Tata Industries (TIL)	1945	Ratan Tata	Ratan Tata	Directors: K.M. Chinnappa, Sujit Gupta, Syamal Gupta, Dr. J.J. Irani, John MacKenzie, Dr. F.A. Mehta, S.A. Sabavala, A.B. Kerkar, F.K. Kavarana, F.C. Kohli, N.A. Palkhivala, D.S. Seth, N.A. Soonawala, J.E. Talaulicar, Mrs. S.N. Tata, S.R. Vakil.
Telco	1945	Sumant Moolgaonkar	Ratan Tata	Exec. Dir.: S.J. Ghandy. Exec. Dir.: V.M. Raval. Exec. Dir.: F.K. Kavarana.
				Directors: J.J. Irani, S. Jagannathan, A.P. Kurian, A.N. Mafatlal, S.A. Naik, N.A. Palkhivala, F. Plattner, J.K. Setna, N.A. Soonawala, S.R. Vakil, H. Werner.
Tisco	1907	Russi Mody	Ratan Tata	Managing Dir.: J.J. Irani. Exec. Dir.: K.C. Mehra. Exec. Dir.: I. Hussain. Exec. Dir.: R.K. Bhasin.
				Directors: G.P. Gupta, A. Hydari, P.K. Kaul, S. Krishna, K. Mahindra, S.M. Palia, N.A. Palkhivala, S.A. Sabavala, L.P. Singh, M. Sondhi, N.N. Wadia.
Tata Chemicals	1929	Darbari Seth	Ratan Tata	Chair Emeritus: D. Seth. Managing Dir.: M. Seth.
				Directors: G. Chidambar, D.M. Ghia, F.J. Heredia, N.J. Jhaveri, D.V. Kapur, R.C. Khanna, A.N. Lalbhai, K. Mahindra, H. Mangaldas, M. Ramaswamy, S. Shervani, N.A. Soonawala, N.N. Wadia.
Tata Tea	1962	Darbari Seth	Ratan Tata	Chair Emeritus: D. Seth. Dep. Chair: N.A. Soonawala. Managing Dir.: K. Kumar. Exec. Dir.: S.M. Kidwai. Exec. Dir.: M.H. Ashraff.
				Directors: A.S. Bam, B.V. Bhargava, D.B. Engineer, D.N. Ghosh, F.K. Kavarana Y.H. Malegam, M.M. Appaiya, U.M. Rao, Y.T. Shah.
Tata Power	1919	N.H. Tata	H.N. Sethna	Vice Chair: K.M. Gherda. Dep. Chair: Ratan Tata.
				Directors: N.M. Govardhan, M.S. Patwadhan, B.K. Shah, H.S. Vachha, S.R. Vakil, D.G. Mehra.
Indian Hotels	1902	Ajit Kerkar	Ajit Kerkar	
				Directors: J.J. Bhabha, N.B. Daruwala, A. Ghosh, S.K. Kandhari, L.A. Menezes, N.A. Palkhivala, Ms. C. Panjabi, J.M.R. Pillai, N.A. Soonawala, Ratan Tata, S.R. Vakil.
ACC	1936	Sumant Moolgaonkar	N.A. Palkhivala	Vice Chair: S. Ganguly. Dep. Chair: P.S. Mistry. Exec. Dir.: T.M.M. Nambiar. Exec. Dir.: R. Bhattacharya. Exec. Dir.: M.M. Rajoria.
				Directors: A. Ghosh, G. Goswami, P.J. Jagus, H. Mahindra, P.K. Mistry, K.P. Narasimhan, B. Ramakrishna, K.J. Reddy, D. Seth, N.A. Soonawala, S.R. Vakil.

Source: Center for Monitoring the Indian Economy (CIMM).

Exhibit 7	New Ventures Promoted by Tata Industries		
Year	Name	Sector/product	Alliance
1984	Tata Finance	Finance	
1984	Tata-Honeywell	IT	Honeywell
1984	Tata Keltron	Terminal instruments, phones	
1985	Hitech Drilling Services	Services	
1986	Tata Telecom	Communications	
1989	Tata Interactive Systems	IT	
1989	Tata Elexsi	IT	Silicon Graphics
1989	Tata Advanced Materials	Composites	
1990	Oriental Floratech	Agro	
1991	Tata Strategic Management Group	Services	
1991	Tata Information Systems	IT	IBM
1992	AT&T Switching Systems	Communications	AT&T
1993	Tata Petrodyne	Energy	
1993	Utkal Alumina International	Metals	Norsk Hydro, Indal
1993	Oriental Seritech	Agro	
1994	Information Technology Park	Industrial park	Singapore consortium, Karnataka state government
1995	Tata Autocomp Systems	Automotive Components	
1995	Tata Communications, Ltd.	Cellular telecom services	Bell Canada
1995	Tata Teleservices Ltd.	Fixed line telecom services	Bell Canada
future	Tata-Singapore Airlines	Airline	Singapore Airlines
future	Bangalore Airport Project	Airport / infrastructure	Singapore consortium, Raytheon

Source: Sanjoy Narayan, "Ratan Tata's New Gameplan," *BusinessWorld*, May 1–14, 1996, p. 58; and Tata Industries Limited.

Ratan proposed that each subscribing company pay a contribution (he adamantly avoided using the term "royalty"), based on its degree of association with the brand.[12] Contribution rates would range between 0.10% to 0.25% of a company's net income before taxes and non-operating income, and would be capped at a maximum of 5% of the profit before tax (i.e., profit after interest and depreciation). Participating companies would be required to subscribe to a code of conduct to ensure uniformly high quality and ethical business practices. Participating companies would be eligible for recognition of outstanding representation of Tata values with the J.R.D. Quality Value Award, modeled after the Malcolm Baldrige National Quality Award in the United States.

Many Tata companies had urged Tata Sons to adopt a strong, global Tata corporate campaign, and were pleased with Ratan Tata's plan. The managing director of Titan Industries Ltd., a Tata company, wrote, "[Tata] companies have, in recent years, been pressing Tata Sons to put their act together with some speed so that they can both take advantage of the opportunities and ward off the competitive threats which have suddenly and so dramatically emerged with the opening up of the Indian economy. The Tata name is a powerful force and hugely valuable commercial property."[13]

Tata Sons planned to use the fee money to build a national, and later international, group brand image by emphasizing a set of core values and ethics, largely through advertising. Tata Sons estimated that meaningful domestic brand pro-

[12]Fee schedule: right to use the Tata name in both company banner and products, 0.25%; right to use the Tata name in either the company banner or products, 0.15%; right to be perceived as a Tata company, 0.10%.

[13]Xerxes Desai, "Much Ado About Nothing," *Business India,* December 2–15, 1996.

motion alone would cost at least Rs. 300 million per annum. A central committee would be set up to facilitate decisions regarding brand promotion.

The boards of directors of the various Tata companies passed a resolution in the last half of FY95 approving this arrangement. However, the Scheme generated debate in the investing public and in the media. The implementation of the Scheme, slated to be retroactively effective April 1, 1995, was deferred to incorporate additional features based on evolving views. Some Tata shareholders resented Tata Sons' attempt to assert itself beyond the limits of an ordinary shareholder (even though the role of Tata Sons in the Scheme had nothing to do with its status as a shareholder of the major Tata companies). Some others doubted whether the brand subscription would offer an immediate benefit to their individual companies. Still others went so far as to claim that the Tata name had not necessarily been the reason for their companies' success. Many of the companies that did openly derive the benefit of the Tata name had enjoyed free access and, therefore, some of their shareholders opposed paying a subscription fee now. Ratan countered these arguments:

> The intention has been that it [brand] would create a single strong equity that will benefit all the companies. . . . If you are to fight a Mitsubishi or an X or Y in the free India of tomorrow, you better have one rather than 40 brands. You better have the ability to promote that brand in a meaningful manner. . . . Do we have a common thread that runs through the Tata Group? In the past, that thread was embodied in a personality, maybe J.R.D. Tata. But I think times are different now. You have to institutionalize certain things. You cannot be forever on personalities[*sic*]. There may be a Mr. Tata as a chairman, or there may not be a Mr. Tata as chairman of the group.[14]

Companies not using the Tata name or the Tata brand to market their products, such as Indian Hotels, Voltas, and Rallis, were also invited to subscribe to the Scheme.[15] Tata Sons' rationale was that such companies did make use of the Tata reputation when raising money in global and domestic markets, and often accessed managerial and financial support from the group. For example, Indian Hotels (IHC), better known as the Taj Group of Hotels (TGH), devoted four pages of its GDR offer prospectus to its ties with the House of Tata, although management claimed that they did not refer to themselves as a "group company" per se. At one stage, Ajit Kerkar publicly denied that IHC's name would be changed to reflect the Tata brand. One disgruntled IHC share-holder complained:

> Any payment made by the company for questionable returns substantially affects my income from IHC. . . . It will only tighten the grip of TSL [Tata Sons] over IHC at our expense. . . . By advertising that our hotels belong to the Tata Group, we will confuse prospective clients and undermine the significance of the TGH brand name which has been built up over 92 years.[16]

RESTRUCTURING   In 1993 Ratan began taking steps to convert the Tata Group into a tighter, leaner organization by selling the loss-making Tata Oil Mills Company Ltd. (Tomco) to Hindustan Lever Ltd., a subsidiary of the Anglo-Dutch group Unilever. Ratan also favored a merger of Tata's three electric companies, but by 1996 he had yet to coordinate such a transition:

> I think we were in many more areas than we should have been in and we were perhaps not concerned about our market position in each of those businesses. I think the needs today are that we define our businesses much more articulately and that we remain focused rather than diffused, and that we become more aggressive than we used to be, much more market driven, much more concerned about customer satisfaction.[17]

Yet independent-minded Tata companies continued to diversify with little coordination. Despite Tata Sons' concern about Tata companies entering into disparate joint ventures, Associated Cement Company continued to do so. ACC's managing director rationalized, "We are looking at these new areas of business because of the opportunities that exist."[18] In some cases, the lack of coordination was so great that several Tata companies competed with each other, both in domestic and export markets. For example, Tisco, Tata Chemicals, and ACC were each setting up huge cement plants, leading to the possibility of conflict.

INCREASING TATA SONS' INVESTMENT CAPABILITIES
Through Tata Sons, the Tatas held minority shares ranging from 0.01% to 15% in Tata companies. By comparison,

---

[14]"Brand Name to Survive Personalities: Ratan," *The Economic Times,* October 14, 1996.

[15]Unprofitable companies and joint venture companies in which the non-Tata joint venture partner company did not charge a brand fee would not be required to pay the subscription.

[16]"The Tatas: Trust Deserved or Belied?," *The Economic Times* (New Delhi), November 28, 1996.

[17]"The Problems of Being a Tata," *The Hindu,* November 24, 1996. Excerpt from Gita Piramal, *Business Maharajas,* Viking Penguin India.

[18]D. N. Mukerjea, "ACC's Quest for a Stable Future," *Business World,* May 29–June 11, 1996, p. 52.

Indian entrepreneur Pallonji Shapoorji Mistry, with 18.4%, owned more of Tata Sons than the entire Tata family together. In order to increase (and in some cases, maintain) its stake in various companies and fuel growth in its core divisions, Tata Sons determined that they would need to raise a total of Rs. 7 billion in FY95 and FY96, to realize a 1% stake increase in each of the major Tata companies. To raise the necessary funds, Tata Sons announced a Rs. 3 billion rights issue on September 25, 1995.[19] The shares were made available to Tata companies (at a premium) through a re-

nunciation of shares by various trusts.[20] The additional Rs. 4 billion would be raised through internal generation and debt. See Exhibit 8a, 8b for the new share ownership.

Group companies could legally purchase Tata Sons shares and vice versa, but collusion between companies to exchange shares would violate the law. The media queried Ratan's plan to increase Tata Sons' equity holdings, raising concerns that (among other issues) the selling price overvalued the Tata Sons' shares. From an analyst's point of view, the deal seemed to lack any benefit for the investing compa-

[19]A rights issue is the offering of common stock to existing shareholders who hold rights that entitle them to buy newly issued shares at a discount from the price at which shares will later be offered to the public. (Source: *Barron's Dictionary of Finance and Investment*, 1995.)

[20]A few years earlier, the government had adopted a regulation forbidding public charitable trusts to invest in the private corporate sector.

Exhibit 8a		Cross Ownership between Tata Sons and Major Group Companies, FY95 and FY96 (year-end Mar 31; Rs. millions; 1996 ave.: Rs. 35.4 : $1)				
Tata Sons		Major Group Companies	Sales	Value of Tata Sons' Shares Bought By Companies 1995-96	Tata Sons' Stake in Group Companies	
FY96		FY96	FY96	FY96	FY95	FY96
Book value	8,990	Tisco	53,720	688	2.35%	8.46%
Market value	19,900	Telco	77,910	688	1.78%	2.67%
Paid-up cap.	179	Tata Power	11,700	370	5.63%	6.35%
Reserves	6,236	Tata Chemicals	15,150	569	7.91%	8.18%
Net profit	1,240	Tata Tea	5,190	n/a	7.56%	8.58%
Indian Hotels	5,470			250	13.34%	13.34%
		ACC	n/a	n/a	n/a	n/a

Source: Adapted from Robin Abreu, "Controversial Defense," *India Today*, November 15, 1996, p. 105, and from information provided by Tata Industries Limited.

Exhibit 8b	Ownership Structure of Tata Sons (After Rights Issue), FY96

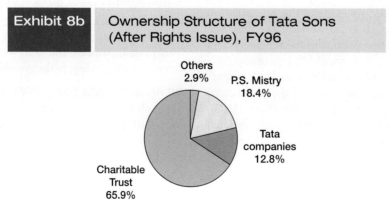

Source: Adapted from Robin Abreu, "Controversial Defence," *India Today*, November 15, 1996, p. 105, and from information provided by Tata Industries Limited.

nies. It was estimated that the interest cost on the Rs. 3 billion investment would be Rs. 450 million, whereas even a 100% dividend declaration by Tata Sons would yield only Rs. 30 million. Ratan argued that the shares would appreciate immensely if Tata Sons were to go public, and no shareholders had yet officially complained of the illiquid nature of the Tata Sons investment. But one foreign investor criticized the participation of Tata companies in the Tata Sons rights issue, "Industrial companies in India will need capital to invest to compete over the next decade. . . . This [diversion of capital] won't do the Tatas any good [long term]."[21]

TATA ADMINISTRATIVE SERVICES (TAS)   TAS, a department of Tata Services, Ltd., had been recruiting talented individuals for accelerated management careers within the Tata companies since the 1950s. Although TAS had been relatively successful—maintaining an average TAS officer retention rate of 67% over the ten-year period 1986–1995, compared to a 10% to 25% annual attrition rate experienced by many Indian organizations—the prestige had waned somewhat in recent years. Ratan planned to promote TAS as a "premium career" and elevate the program's status among up-and-coming business leaders through media exposure, including high profile TAS coverage in business publications. TAS also planned to develop an audio-visual presentation that would promote TAS and the Tata Group to prospective employees.

Ratan hoped to redefine and develop TAS as a group resource, enlarge the program, and increase the mobility of the TAS participants among group companies. New TAS recruits (mostly MBAs) would be encouraged to take advantage of the opportunity to work in a range of industries within the group by rotating among the Tata companies. Individual Tata companies that opted to participate in the TAS program would receive a newsletter advertising TAS officer openings as well as TAS officers looking for new positions.

During the first ten years of the new and improved program, TAS officers would gain exposure to three different industries through planned job rotation within the Tata companies. Special programs would foster leadership, teamwork, and group values for TAS officers in years 1, 5, and 10. During years 11 to 15, TAS program coordinators would take special pains to match TAS officers with appropriate senior job opportunities in Tata companies.

TAS was prepared to recruit 25 exceptional new officers in the coming year and planned to increase the annual number of recruits if necessary. TAS coordinators were aware that to become competitive TAS would have to be in the top 10th percentile of MBA compensation packages, while TAS' current MBA compensation package was below the 35th percentile. To rectify this, TAS calculated that they would need to offer an entry level compensation package of Rs. 20,000 per month in 1996 and Rs. 25,000 per month in 1997 (more than double the current rate). Exhibit 9 compares TAS' MBA compensation packages with those of other top companies in India.

TAIPANS AND MAHARAJAS[22]   Ignoring the concern of Indian industrialists over the entry of foreign firms into Indian industry, Ratan contemplated selling a 20% stake in TIL to the colossal Hong Kong-based Jardine Matheson

---

[21]Manjeet Kripalani, "Tut-Tutting over Tata's Way of Doing Business," *Business Week*, November 11, 1996.

[22]Taipan: a powerful business person, particularly a foreigner who does business in Hong Kong and China. Maharaja: a Hindu prince.

Exhibit 9	MBA Compensation Packages, 1994 (Rupees/mo.)			
Top Overall Companies		Gross Pay	Top Groups/Diversified Companies	Gross Pay
1	Boston Consulting Group	50,000	1 J.K. Organization	15,000
2	McKinsey & Company	41,667	2 RPG Enterprises	14,145
3	Morgan Stanley Indian Securities Ltd.	33,333	3 Reliance Industries Ltd.	14,006
4	Union Bank of Switzerland	30,000	4 Ballarpur Industries Ltd.	11,750
5	HCL Corporation	25,866	5 Tata Services Ltd. (TAS)	11,250
6	Citibank N.A.	24,333	6 UB Group	10,875
7	SBI Capital Markets Ltd.	23,374	7 Mafatlal Industries Ltd.	10,000
8	Pepsico India Holdings	23,000	8 Essar Group	8,333
9	Coopers & Lybrand, SRF Finance Ltd.	22,917	9 Walchandnagar Industries	7,000

Source: Tata Administrative Service Secretariat document.

group (worth Rs. 612 billion) for Rs. 1.26 billion. Jardine, a firm which already boasted significant influence throughout most of Asia, was anxious to get into India's newly liberalized market. The deal was expected to push TIL's share capital up from Rs. 476 million to Rs. 595 million. Ratan planned to use this capital influx for venture start-ups promoted through TIL. Although Jardine probably would not receive a dividend for five years, the Hong Kong company would have the same rights as the other Tata companies: to occupy a TIL board seat, to be involved in project planning, and to invest in new projects promoted by TIL.

Ratan anticipated that Jardine would contribute expertise in a wide range of business activities, such as retailing and distribution, real estate, hotels, engineering, construction, and financial services. Specifically, both Jardine and Tata had interests in exploring the potential synergy between their financial businesses (Tata Finance and Jardine Fleming) and in creating a major car distribution network. A Jardine associate described Ratan as "a careful planner and thinker, and his long-term decisions seem to be spot-on. But he's not good when consumer demand patterns change rapidly."[23] For example, sales of the Telco-assembled Mercedes Benz had been 50% off initial projections and Ratan admitted that the joint venture had not read the market accurately.

FORTHCOMING VENTURES

> If everyone is told not to go into unrelated businesses, how will the airlines, oil, and telecommunications industries develop? The government has said that they can't do it. So there's a social benefit to all this diversification.
>
> —N. A. Soonawala, Tata Sons Director

Indeed, Ratan had several projects in mind which necessitated the deep pockets and clout of a conglomerate like Jardine. For example, the Tata Group was considering joint ventures with AIG (insurance), a Singapore consortium (technology park in Bangalore), Singapore Airlines (airline), and Bell Canada (telecommunications). In addition,

many more technology companies would be introduced through TIL.

One of TIL's latest plans was a joint venture with Singapore Airlines (SIA) to create a domestic Indian airline. In February 1995 TIL submitted a bid to the Indian government within the framework of the current government guidelines. If the joint venture were approved, Singapore Airlines would hold a 40% stake, Tata companies would hold another 40%, and Indian institutional investors 20%. In comparison, India's two major airlines, Air India and Indian Airlines, each of which held an equity base of less than Rs. 1 billion, were government owned. One aviation analyst predicted that such a venture would change the entire nature of India's airline industry. "The airline business needs large amounts of capital. Only a venture with big players such as Tata and SIA could really get a handle on it. They can give Indian Airlines a run for its money."[24]

The project required the approval of the Foreign Investment Promotion Board (FIPB) of the Ministry of Industry, and the Ministry of Civil Aviation. It was expected that the FIPB would eventually approve TIL's joint venture with Singapore Airlines. However, the Ministry of Civil Aviation was strongly opposed to permitting foreign direct investment in the airline industry and planned to adopt a policy to prevent such an occurrence. The civil aviation minister reasoned, "Indian Airlines is the national carrier and we have to protect its interests. Otherwise the future of thousands of employees working for Indian Airlines will be at stake."[25]

Looking Ahead

The plans Ratan had implemented thus far—from the brand fee and share increase to continued diversification—had generated much criticism both inside the group and beyond. It was apparent that the character of the Tata companies had already changed, and Ratan now had to ask himself whether he had chosen the appropriate course for the future.

---

[23]Cesar Bacani and Shirish Nadkarni, "The Tata Emperor," *Asiaweek*, January 24, 1997, p. 43.

[24]Ibid.

[25]Mark Nicholson, "Indian Ministers Face Fierce Airline Battle," *Financial Times*, January 8, 1997.

Case 19

Apple's iPod System: iPod, iTunes and Fairplay[1]

9B06M080

In January 2007, Apple unveiled its latest innovative product, the iPhone, a mobile telephone and PDA with iPod capabilities. Apple Computer, Inc. (Apple) commanded 62 per cent of the portable digital music player market with its popular iPod, which was launched in 2001. Apple's online iTunes Music Store, accessed via its iTunes music jukebox software, had a 70 per cent share of paid-music downloads.

Despite Apple's success thus far—Apple's iPod and music sales combined accounted for a third of company sales in 2005 (see Exhibit 1)—observers could not help but wonder whether the iPod-iTunes combination would experience the same fate as Apple's personal computer business, especially so since Microsoft's new Zune MP3 player captured two per cent of the market within a month of its November 2006 launch.

IVEY

Richard Ivey School of Business
The University of Western Ontario

Ken Mark wrote this case under the supervision of Professor Rod White solely to provide material for class discussion. The authors do not intend to illustrate either effective or ineffective handling of a managerial situation. The authors may have disguised certain names and other identifying information to protect confidentiality.

Ivey Management Services prohibits any form of reproduction, storage or transmittal without its written permission. Reproduction of this material is not covered under authorization by any reproduction rights organization. To order copies or request permission to reproduce materials, contact Ivey Publishing, Ivey Management Services, c/o Richard Ivey School of Business, The University of Western Ontario, London, Ontario, Canada, N6A 3K7; phone (519) 661-3208; fax (519) 661-3882; e-mail cases@ivey.uwo.ca.

Copyright © 2006, Ivey Management Services
Version: (A) 2007-02-07

[1]This case has been written on the basis of published sources only. Consequently, the interpretation and perspectives presented in this case are not necessarily those of Apple Computer, Inc. or any of its employees.

When introduced in January 1985, Apple's Macintosh computers were better designed, easier to use and generally more advanced than its personal computer (PC) rivals. Even so Apple saw its share of the computer market fall from more than 30 per cent to less than five per cent in about a decade. Most experts attributed this outcome to Apple's insistence on a closed computer system, where it controlled (and limited) access to both the hardware and software, especially the operating system. In contrast, in the competing PC format, originally dubbed the IBM standard and later the WINTEL (Windows + Intel) standard, one player, Microsoft supplied the operating system to numerous hardware equipment manufacturers, including Dell, Hewlett-Packard and Lenovo, made PCs using components from a wide range of suppliers. Most independent applications software developers preferred to write for the dominant WINTEL platform.

Drawing a parallel between the Macintosh and iPod-iTunes, a *Fast Company* article noted:

> The battle over digital music is just another verse in Apple's sad song: this amazingly imaginative company keeps getting muscled out of the markets it creates. So what does Apple have to tell us about innovation?

The Launch of the Apple iPod and iTunes Software

On October 23, 2001, Apple released the Apple iPod, a music player with a five gigabyte hard drive, almost 21 times more capacity than the leading MP3 player. The iTunes "jukebox" digital media player software was bundled with each iPod. The iTunes software for use on Macs was launched earlier, in January 2001. The digital audio encoding format Apple chose for the iPod was Advanced Audio

685

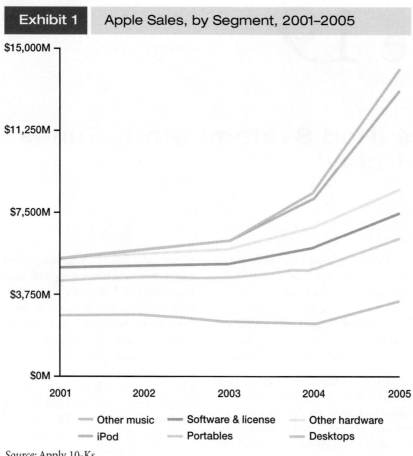

Exhibit 1 — Apple Sales, by Segment, 2001–2005

Source: Apply 10-Ks

Coding (AAC), an international standard declared by the Moving Pictures Experts Group (MPEG) in 1997.

Although iPods were originally available only for Macintosh users, a Windows-compatible iPod was released in July 2002, followed by a Windows version of iTunes, released during October 2003. Previously, Windows users needed third-party software, such as Yahoo!'s MusicMatch Jukebox (included with Windows iPods before the release of the iTunes Windows version) to manage their music.

FAIRPLAY: APPLE'S DIGITAL RIGHTS MANAGEMENT SYSTEM   Using FairPlay, Apple's digital rights management (DRM) system, iTunes was the only program that allowed legally acquired copyrighted media to be played on Apple iPods. DRM systems enabled digital content vendors to control how media was used on any electronic device with such measures installed. The iTunes software converted MP3 files or music files from compact discs (CDs) into AAC (and iTunes also wrapped the file in FairPlay) before the songs could be played on an iPod. This process

prevented protected media from being played on "unauthorized" computers, or traded illegally on peer-to-peer (P2P) networks. Music executives were very worried about the illegal copying of their product. FairPlay helped Steve Jobs, Apple's co-founder and chief executive officer (CEO), convince the music industry to support the iTunes Music Store.

THE LAUNCH OF ITUNES MUSIC STORE   With licensing agreements from the major music companies in hand, Apple launched the first substantial legal music download site in May 2003, approximately two years after the iPod and iTunes software had been introduced. At the download site, called "iTunes Music Store," users paid $0.99 per song. The user interface for iTunes Music Store was built into iTunes version 4.0, enabling customers to log on to the Apple website and buy music. The store began with 200,000 songs available to download. As was the case with iTunes software, the iTunes Music Store was initially only accessible to Mac users; a PC version became available in October 2003.

Apple's iPod-iTunes Developments Post-Launch (2001–2006)

Competitors of iPod, such as Sony, Creative Labs and Rio, tried to break Apple's hold on the market. Despite their efforts, the iPod, along with the iPod mini, the iPod nano and the iPod shuffle, controlled 70 per cent of the portable digital media player market. Sony had previously dominated the portable music player market with its Walkman personal stereo players but the company had made little impact with its digital music players, which could only play songs encoded in the company's own ATRAC3 format. In January 2006, Microsoft confirmed that it was considering plans to build its own portable music player to rival the iPod.

In the media player market, iTunes faced dozens of large competitors (such as Microsoft's Windows Media Player, Yahoo!'s MusicMatch Jukebox and RealNetworks' RealPlayer) and smaller entrants (such as Beep Media Player and Songbird). In the legal online music download market, there were more than 30 competitors, including Napster, Puretracks and Wal-Mart. Competitors distributing music from the large music companies encrypted music with DRM systems (most often Microsoft's PlayForSure DRM). Despite their efforts to unseat Apple, their total market share hovered around 30 per cent.

The updates of iTunes software were available for download free of charge from Apple's website. Regular updating allowed Apple to fix glitches in the software and to remove any vulnerabilities. When a computer programmer wrote a piece of software that cracked Apple's DRM system, Apple responded with a fix to iTunes within a week. When Apple discovered that unscrupulous hackers could gain access to iTunes on unsuspecting users' computers and download their songs, Apple fixed the problem, again within a week. In contrast, competitors such as Microsoft were known for their slow response to fixing software security problems.

Competitors had tried to force Apple to open up its closely linked iPod-iTunes-FairPlay system. When RealNetworks announced that its Harmony technology allowed music purchased from its online store to play on the iPod (via iTunes), Apple threatened to sue RealNetworks. In a subsequent iTunes software release, Apple broke Harmony's compatibility with iTunes. Recently, a piece of computer software called hymn (Hear Your Music aNywhere) was anonymously released, allowing users to remove FairPlay from songs purchased from the iTunes Music Store. Although hymn only functioned with iTunes versions 5.0.1

(released September 20, 2005) and older, a quick response by Apple was anticipated.

Apple's iPod, iTunes and Fairplay (as of January 2007)

For a chronology of the significant iPod and iTunes developments, see Exhibit 2.

IPOD IN 2007 In January 2007, Apple's iPod, in its fifth generation, was the world's best-selling digital media player. It had quickly evolved, however, to encompass a variety of extra features to complement its original purpose as a portable music player. The current version of the iPod had video playback capabilities, could play podcasts (audio and video files downloaded for free or purchased), had picture display capabilities and could be used as an organizer. The smaller iPod nano with flash memory, could be used as both a digital music player and, with Nike's Nike+ iPod Sport Kit," as a training device that captured workout data.

The iPod played songs from a variety of audio formats, including AAC, Apple Lossless, MP3, WAV and video file formats. However, iPods did not play music files encrypted with rival DRM technologies, such as Microsoft's PlayForSure or RealNetworks' Helix. Thus, DRM-protected music purchased from rival download sites did not play on the iPod. Although iTunes was the only official method for synchronizing with the iPod, there were other programs that allowed the iPod to be synchronized with other software players.

ITUNES IN 2007 The iTunes software allowed users to organize music as playlists, edit file information, record CDs and DVDs, copy files to the iPod, download increasingly popular podcasts, back up songs and encode music between a number of different audio formats (MP3, AIFF, WAV, MPEG-4, AAC and Apple Lossless) as well as purchase music and video content through the built-in iTunes Music Store. It could also play QuickTime files, including Audible.com audio books. Another popular format, podcasts were currently growing at 15 per cent per month. Most podcasts were free, but a few, such as *The Daily Show with Jon Stewart*, sold for a fee ($1.99 per episode).

The iTunes songs could be shared over a local network using software from Apple; songs could be streamed (but not copied by the recipients) to a maximum of five users every 24 hours. The iTunes software did not allow songs purchased from iTunes Music Store (which were encrypted with FairPlay) to be loaded directly onto any device other than an iPod. However, iTunes supported a number of popular portable music players from firms such as Creative

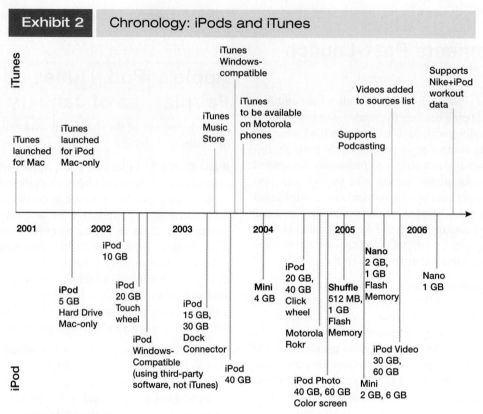

Exhibit 2	Chronology: iPods and iTunes

Source: Apple 10-Ks.

Labs, Rio Audio and Archos, allowing non-encrypted files, such as MP3 files, to be transferred to those players. For less popular portable music players, a number of third-party programs had been created to help iTunes users synchronize songs with any music player mounted as an external hard drive.

More than one billion songs had been downloaded since the iTunes Music Store first opened in May 2003. Downloads cost consumers $0.99 per song, of which $0.65 was remitted to record labels and $0.24 was spent on direct distribution costs, leaving at most $0.10 in operating margin for Apple. But according to Jobs, Apple continued to operate the iTunes Music Store at minimal profit "(b)ecause we're selling iPods." Each iPod, with some models costing into the hundreds of dollars, generated up to 35 per cent in net profit for the firm.

The iTunes software was being employed in other portable devices. Notably, the Motorola ROKR cellphone with iTunes onboard was introduced into North America in late 2005. It had a capacity of 100 songs and Cingular was the exclusive service provider.

FAIRPLAY IN 2007 Apple refused to license FairPlay to competitors. FairPlay allowed a protected track to be copied to any number of iPods (though not the other way around); played on up to five (originally three) authorized computers simultaneously and copied to a standard Audio CD any number of times. The resulting CD had no DRM and could be ripped, encoded and distributed like any other CD. However, as the CD audio bore the artifacts of compression, converting it back to a lossy format, such as an MP3 file, aggravated the sound artifacts of encoding; a particular playlist within iTunes containing a protected track could be copied to a CD only up to seven times before the playlist had to be changed

CLOSED OR OPEN? Apple's closed system strategy differed from the longstanding Microsoft strategy of licensing software to work on any device, an approach begun with PC operating systems and continued in the world of digital music. Microsoft licensed its digital-audio format (WMA) and PlaysForSure. WMA was compatible with more than 500 different types of digital players and WMA files worked on desktop software jukeboxes by MusicMatch, Roxio, Yahoo!, Real and many others. PlaysForSure was a certification given by Microsoft to portable devices and content services that had passed several hundred compatibility and performance requirements including DRM support used by Windows Media Player version 10.

In November 2006, Microsoft launched Zune, a new 30 GB portable music player. Selling for $249.99, Zune offered a Wi-Fi connection allowing users to share songs between Zune units wirelessly and with wireless networks. Zune supported several general audio formats, but did not allow users to purchase downloaded music from sites other than Microsoft's Zune Marketplace. The Zune Marketplace website offered subscribers access to over two million songs for $14.95 per month. In an interesting development MS had offered at least one major music house a small (undis-

closed) per cent of each Zune sold as a inducement for listing their songs on Zune Marketplace and as recognition for the "pirated" downloaded songs carried and played on many, if not most digital music players.

To access the Zune Marketplace, users had to download and install Zune Software onto their PCs. Microsoft allowed prospective subscribers to listen to songs for three days or three plays, whichever came first, after which the songs would expire unless a subscription was purchased. Zune was incompatible with PlaysForSure-certified content. In making Zune compatible only with Zune Marketplace and its own DRM, Microsoft seemed to be emulating Apple's "closed" approach. Apple had not yet responded to Microsoft's entry into the digital music business.

Case 20

Coca-Cola's Re-Entry and Growth Strategies in China

BSTR140

"Putting cold bottles on shelves is the best marketing we can do, we don't have to ask ourselves if our product will sell, only, how do we get it to the consumer?"

–E. Neville Isdell, Chairman and CEO, The Coca-Cola Company, in a trade publication in 1992[1]

"Any of you with experience operating in China know that to have a shot at success, you've really got to take the time to invest in the country. China is large and diverse and it's a long-term proposition. So you have to make the effort to patiently and diligently build your business over time. That's where our focus was decade after decade and our results today prove the wisdom of this approach."

–Patrick T. Siewert, President, East and South Asia Group, the Coca-Cola Company, at the 8th Annual International Conference on "The Future of Asia" in 2002[2]

Introduction

The Coca-Cola Company (Coke) re-entered China in 1979. Today it is recognized as one of China's most trusted brands according to Interbrand.[3] It was voted number 5 of the top 10 multinational companies doing business in Asia in the 2003 Review 200,[4] a survey conducted by *Far Eastern Economic Review* (*FEER*).[5] Since 1990 it has been making profits in China and according to AC Nielsen[6] it had a market share of over 50 percent [...] of the Chinese beverages market in 2002.

[1]"Coke's Big Gamble in Asia: Digging Deeper in China, India," by Leslie Chang in Kunyang, China and Chad Terhune and Bets Mckay in Atlanta, USA, August 11, 2004, *The Wall Street Journal.*

[2]Press center, www.coca-cola.com.

[3]Interbrand is a global brand consultancy firm founded in 1974. It attempts to identify, build and express the right idea for a brand, so that positive business results can be achieved.

[4]Review 200 is a survey designed to identify the companies that Asia's [businesspeople] regard as leaders in their class.

[5]*FEER* is one of Asia's leading business magazines, published every Thursday in Hong Kong. It is fully owned by Dow Jones & Company, the publishers of [the] *Wall Street Journal.* The magazine covers politics, business, economics, technology and social and cultural issues throughout Asia, with a particular emphasis on Southeast Asia and China.

[6]AC Nielsen, a market research company, was established in the United States of America by Arthur C. Nielsen Sr. in 1923. It gradually spread its operations [all over] the world. In 2001, AC Nielsen became part of VNU, a world leader in marketing information, media measurement and information, business media and directories.

How did Coke achieve this success in China? Coke's top managers and industry observers too believe that it is the company's winning approach of "Think local, act local" that has enabled it to capture markets outside of the United States. This is particularly true of the Asian markets where the diversity of cultures and income levels makes for a rather diverse consumer base. Coke encourages local managers to develop strategies that are best suited for their areas, and regional offices have the freedom to approve local initiatives.

From the very beginning, Coke's strategy for re-entry into the Chinese market has been based on localization of the entire Coca-Cola system. In order to achieve this, Coke had to work closely with Chinese state-owned enterprises and develop strong relationships with the Chinese government. Since China had just opened up to foreign investment at the time of its re-entry, Coke had to deal with its restrictive policies. It brought its technology and equipment to China and built bottling plants, which it then handed over to the Chinese government. Later it formed joint ventures with state-owned enterprises to set up more bottling plants. Coke formed joint ventures with local Chinese companies as well. Even though initially it had to import certain inputs for the production process, Coke eventually sourced them from Chinese companies. Coke developed its own infrastructure for distribution but gradually came to mainly rely upon state-owned distribution companies and local Chinese distribution companies. This strategy of localization of the Coca-Cola system in China proved to be a success and China grew to be its second largest market in Asia in 2003 (in terms of volume).

Background Note

In the early 1920s, Coke made its entry into China with bottles imported from its plant in the Philippines. In an effort to localize production, two bottling plants were opened in 1927. These plants were located in Shanghai and Tianjin, and in 1930 another was opened in Qingdao. Coke faced setbacks during [. . .] World War II when the Japanese occupied China and took over its plants. However, in 1946, after the war ended Coke opened a bottling plant in Guangzhou. The Shanghai plant had the distinction of being the most up-to-date and fastest bottling line in China, and in 1948 became the first overseas plant to make annual sales of more than 1 million cases. This was great progress for Coke, even though the customers in Shanghai were mostly expatriates.

When the People's Republic of China (PRC) was formed in 1949, all foreign companies were asked to cease operations and leave the country. Coke shut down operations in China and its bottling plants were nationalized by the government. State-owned companies were formed to produce beverages and some of these companies used the former Coke plants to produce soft drinks. In [the] case of the Shanghai plant, the equipment was shipped to Beijing to be re-installed in a factory there. For almost 30 years after the PRC was formed, foreign direct investment and direct production activity by a foreign company were not allowed. Only the state-owned foreign trade corporations were allowed to have contact with foreign businesses and to carry out exporting and importing of goods.

COKE'S RE-ENTRY IN CHINA In December 1978, Deng Xiaoping (Deng)[7] announced the "open door policy." This policy was part of Deng's larger plan for economic reforms in China. An open door policy meant that China would allow foreign trade and investment. December 1978 was an important time for Coke as well. Soon after China made its announcement, Coke initiated discussions with the Chinese government. Coke expressed its commitment to making long-term investments and to economic development in China.

In 1979, Coke began importing cans from California and bottles from Hong Kong to sell in China. Initially, these were sold only to foreigners through hotels and special stores called friendship stores where only foreigners could shop. Even though Coke made its re-entry into the Chinese market with imported products, its intention was to localize every aspect of the business from sourcing inputs and production to sales and distribution, eventually. Establishing the localized Coca-Cola system in China was a difficult and a long process. China had opened its doors to foreign companies but at the same time, had set in place policies to control and closely monitor the foreign investments. Most areas of business were heavily regulated and needed approvals from various government officials. Nevertheless, Coke was determined to establish itself in China.

Localisation Strategies

Long before Coke was given permission to sell its products to the Chinese people, it began developing production capabilities through various joint ventures with the Chinese government. In sharp contrast to its strategies in the past (in China and other countries as well), initially Coke did not own any bottling plants in China. It imported the concentrate and

---

[7]Deng Xiaoping was the Vice-Chairman of the Central Committee. The Central Committee is the highest authority within the Communist Party of China, the sole political party in the People's Republic of China. He was also the Vice-Premier of the State Council, which is the chief civilian administrative body of the country. The State Council is chaired by the Premier and consists of the heads of each governmental department and agency. There are about 50 members in the Council.

sold it to bottling plants. The bottling plants (that it sold the concentrate to) had been built by Coke and handed over to the Chinese government. The first of these plants was built in Beijing and was operational in 1981. According to an agreement between Coke and the state-owned China National Cereals, Oils, and Foodstuffs Import and Export Corporation (COFCO) in 1980, Coke agreed to build a plant and hand it over to the government in exchange for approval to expand distribution and sales in China. The second bottling plant was built in Guangzhou and was also handed over to the Chinese government in 1982. However, this time it was agreed that both plants would pay for the concentrate supplied to them. This agreement was approved by the Chinese government's Export Committee, of which President Jiang Zemin was also a member.

In 1983, Coke began constructing a bottling plant in the Xiamen SEZ,[8] and on completion in 1984 handed it over to the Ministry of Light Industry. This Ministry later became the State Light Industry Bureau. The year 1984 was a special year for Coke as many significant events took place that year. In 1984, the plant in the Xiamen SEZ, in addition to producing Coca-Cola also started producing Sprite and Fanta. Coke became the first company to air a foreign commercial on China's Central Television station (CCTV). Even though Coke's products were not sold to the Chinese at that time, it decided to advertise in order to develop brand recognition. Coke was allowed to air its commercials in exchange for underwriting CCTV's coverage of the Queen of England's trip to China. In 1984, Coke signed an agreement with the Ministry of Light Industry to establish its first joint venture in China, a bottling plant in the Zhuhai SEZ. Construction of this plant began in 1984 and it became operational in 1985.

In 1984, the Chinese government signed a letter of cooperation with Coke to set up cooperative bottling plants in China. The proposed locations for these plants were Shanghai, Tianjin and Qingdao. Also in 1984, Coke signed proposals to build a wholly owned concentrate plant in Shanghai, and to build a bottling plant as a joint venture close to the proposed concentrate plant. The agreement stated that Coke would be the sole owner of the concentrate plant and the Ministry of Light Industry and the Shanghai Investment and Trust Corporation (SITCO)[9] would own the bottling plant.

Finally, in 1985 the Chinese government gave Coke its approval to sell its products to the Chinese. However, construction work for both plants would not begin until 1986 when President Jiang Zemin gave his approval. Also in 1986, Coke sponsored and organized the first Asian Coca-Cola Cup football tournament in China. In 1988, construction of the Shanghai concentrate plant was completed and it began production. The opening of the concentrate plant marked the localization of the inputs of Coke's production process, as it began producing the concentrate locally using local inputs. The bottling plant in Tianjin was also completed in 1988 and produced local Chinese brands of soft drinks in addition to Coke's products. Production of local Chinese brands was another feature of Coke's localization strategy.

By 1993 Coke had set up a total of 14 bottling plants in China, and had obtained permission from the Ministry of Light Industry and the State Economic and Trade Commission to build 10 more plants. However, the approval to build bottling plants came with certain stipulations. The provinces in which the bottling plants were to be built were specified by the Chinese government, and in addition the plants had to be located in the capital cities of these provinces. Another stipulation was that Coke should, in addition to Coke's brands, produce local Chinese beverages at these new plants.

Since Coke already had 14 plants and had permission to open 10 more it decided to restructure its bottling operations to form bottling alliances. In 1993, it formed alliances with two Hong Kong–based multinational companies, Swire Pacific (Swire)[10] and Kerry Beverages Group (Kerry).[11] These two firms became its key partners in China. Coke signed an agreement with Swire to produce and distribute its products in southern China and certain interior provinces. Coke also acquired a 12.5 percent stake in Swire. By the year 2000, Coke and Swire [had become] partners in nine joint ventures in China. Also in 1993, Coke bought [a] 12.5 percent stake in Kerry Bottling Company, which is part of the Kerry Beverages Group.

---

[8]In order to promote economic growth and foreign direct investment, the Chinese government began setting up Special Economic Zones (SEZs) in 1980. China has established SEZs in Shenzhen, Zhuhai and Shantou in Guangdong Province and Xiamen in Fujian Province, and the entire province of Hainan. A SEZ is a geographical region that has economic laws that are different from the country's economic laws. A SEZ has special economic systems and policies [that] are designed to promote foreign investment and economic growth in that particular region. SEZs usually have special tax incentives for foreign investments and greater independence regarding international trade activities.

[9]SITCO was established in July 1981, with the Shanghai Municipal Government as the major shareholder. It is an investment and finance company with a presence in real estate, international trading, tendering and consulting. In January 1993, SITCO was renamed Shanghai International Trust & Investment Corporation (SITICO).

[10]Swire Pacific is a Hong Kong–based company [that] was established in the 1960s. It is also a partner in Coca-Cola's bottling operations in Taiwan and the United States.

[11]A privately owned Hong Kong–based group. Robert Kuok, a Malaysian Chinese, owns a major share in the company.

Kerry Bottling focused on bottling operations in northern and interior China, and partnered with Coke for ten joint ventures.

In 1995, Coke set up separate production lines for its own products and for the local Chinese brands produced at the Tianjin plant. The existing facility in Tianjin became the Tianjin Jin Mei Beverage Company, which produced the beverage base for all domestic brands and also provided training to professionals in the Chinese soft drink industry. In the same year, the Tianjin Coca-Cola Bottling Company was built in the Tianjin Economic and Technological Development Zone to produce Coke's brands.

When Coke realized that many Chinese consumers preferred non-carbonated beverages with Chinese [flavors], it decided to enter the domestic non-carbonated beverages market. In 1996, Coke launched the "Tian Yu Di"[12] a non-carbonated beverage brand [that] was the first domestic non-carbonated beverage brand to be produced by a multi-national company. Under this brand, the Tianjin Jin Mei Beverage Company produced fruit juices like mango and lychee (a popular Chinese dessert fruit), ready-to-drink teas in oolong and jasmine flavors, and bottled water. Also in 1996 Coke sponsored the Asian Games in China. In 1997, it also started producing carbonated beverages under the brand name "Xingmu."[13] Once again in an effort to cater to the tastes of the Chinese consumers, this line of domestic beverages came in fruit flavors such as green apple, watermelon, coconut, peach and orange. The flavors were a huge hit and soon the brand's sales had surpassed those of Tian Yu Di. Over the years Coke opened several bottling facilities and by 1999, it had 28 bottling plants and 2 concentrate plants; one for Coke's brands and one for the local brands.

LOCALIZING THE COCA-COLA SYSTEM The central part of the Coca-Cola system [is comprised] of the concentrate plants and bottling enterprises [that] produce the final product. But many inputs and services go into producing the final product and it also takes a good distribution network to get the product to the consumer. Therefore, the network of suppliers of inputs and services and the distribution network are extensions of the Coca-Cola system.

When Coke re-entered China, it formed local partnerships to open several bottling plants. These bottling plants were owned by bottling enterprises that operated as joint ventures (Refer to Exhibit 1). Typically the joint venture consisted of Coke, one of its key bottlers (either Swire or Kerry) and either a state-owned enterprise or a local Chinese company (based in the city where the joint venture was located), or both the state enterprise and the private local firm. In some cities the bottling enterprise ran more than one bottling plant. Coke also had independent bottling enterprises where its key bottlers were not involved. These bottlers operated under a franchise arrangement with Coke and were allowed to use its trademark. The local bottlers needed to invest in the land, building, machinery, trucks, crates and bottles.

Localization of the Coca-Cola system was not limited to the bottlers and production of the beverages. It extended to the inputs that went into making the final product and the distribution of the product.

The bottling enterprises depended upon local suppliers for various inputs and services and each of these enterprises handled its own procurement of inputs based upon its production schedule. Since bottlers order supplies according to their immediate requirements, they choose suppliers on the basis of how efficiently they can deliver supplies on demand. Bottlers only accepted inputs that met Coke's global standards. Initially, Coke could not find suppliers that met its standards so it had to import certain inputs. For example, in the early 1980s it had to import PET bottles. However, in 1986 Coke began procuring PET bottles from the Zhong Fu Industrial Group (Zhong Fu).[14] Zhong Fu began manufacturing PET bottles in 1986, after it received technical advice and training from Coke. Zhong Fu went on to become one of China's biggest suppliers of PET bottles to Coke, and also to other beverage companies.

Unlike the bottling enterprises, Coke had no share of ownership in the companies that supplied the inputs for production. The bottling enterprises developed good relationships with their local suppliers as they were usually among the suppliers' biggest customers. [Ninety-eight] percent of the final product consisted of local inputs such as water, sugar, CO_2, PET bottles, glass, paper, closures, crowns and other packaging material. The bottlers relied upon Chinese companies for bottling line machinery, trucks, and lifting machinery as well. Coke also engaged local firms for business services such as legal services, financial services, repair services, accounting services, advertising, design, travel, construction, etc. The services of local construction companies were hired when building new plants or for expansion of existing plants.

---

[12]The brand name "Tian Yu Di" translates as "Heaven and Earth" in English.

[13]The brand name "Xingmu" translates as "Smart" in English.

[14]The Zhong Fu Industrial Group was founded by Huang Le Fu, who started out with a small plastics company in 1971. Then in the 1980s he started manufacturing fiber material for the garment industry.

Exhibit 1	Coca-Cola China Ltd.'s List of Bottling Enterprises (as of March 2000)		
Name	City/Province	Key Shareholders	Key/Anchor Bottler
Beijing Coca-Cola Beverage Co. Ltd.	Beijing	Kerry Beverages National COFCO Beijing COFCO	Kerry
Swire Guangdong Coca-Cola Ltd.	Guangdong	Swire Coca-Cola HK Ltd. Guangdong Foodstuffs Imp & Export (Group) Corporation COFCO Industries Development Co.	Swire
Guangmei Foods Co. Ltd.	Guangdong (for Xingmu & Meijin)	BFC International (Asia) Ltd. Guangzhou Eagle Coin Enterprise Group Corporation	Swire
Swire Coca-Cola Beverages Xiamen Ltd.	Xiamen, Fujian	Swire Beverages Xiamen Luquan Industrial Co. Ltd.	Swire
Zhuhai Coca-Cola Beverage Co. Ltd.	Zhuhai, Guangdong	Macau Industrial Limitada Zhuhai Food & Beverage Co. Ltd.	Independent
Nanning Coca-Cola Beverage Co. Ltd.	Nanning, Guangxi	Kerry Bottlers (Nanning) Co. Ltd. Nanning Kangle Shareholding Co. Ltd.	Kerry
Dalian Coca-Cola Beverage Co. Ltd.	Dalian, Liaoning	Kerry Beverages Dalian Fruits Co.	Kerry
Shanghai Shen-Mei Beverage & Foods Co. Ltd.	Shanghai	Coca-Cola China Ltd. National COFCO Shanghai SITICO & Shanghai Food Industrial Investment	Independent
Nanjing BC Foods Co. Ltd.	Nanjing, Jiangsu	BCD National COFCO Nanjing Perfumery Factories	Swire
Hangzhou BC Foods Co. Ltd.	Hangzhou, Zhejiang	BC Development Co. Ltd. National COFCO Hangzhou Tea Factory	Swire
Tianjin Jin Mei Beverage Co. Ltd.	Tianjin, Hebei	Coca-Cola (Asia) Holdings Ltd. Tianjin Beverage Factory China National Food Industry Corporation China Light Industrial Corp for Foreign Economic & Technical Cooperation	Independent
Hainan Coca-Cola Beverage Co. Ltd.	Hainan	Coca-Cola China Ltd. National COFCO Hainan COFCO	Independent
Tianjin Coca-Cola Bottling Co. Ltd.	Tianjin, Hebei	Coca-Cola (Asia) Holdings Tianjin Beverages Factory China National Food Industry Corporation	Independent
Xian BC Hans Foods Co. Ltd.	Xian, Shaanxi	BCD Xian Hans Brewery	Swire
Wuhan Coca-Cola Beverage Co. Ltd.	Wuhan, Hubei	Kerry Beverage National COFCO Wuhan Second Beverage Factory	Kerry
Shenyang Coca-Cola Beverage Co. Ltd.	Shenyang, Liaoning	Kerry Beverages Ba Wangshi Beverage Beijing COFCO	Kerry
Harbin Coca-Cola Beverage Co. Ltd.	Harbin, Heilongjiang	Kerry Beverages Harbin Economic & Technology Area Industrial Development Co. Ltd. Beijing COFCO	Kerry

Source: www.moore.sc.edu.

Exhibit 1	Coca-Cola China Ltd.'s List of Bottling Enterprises (as of March 2000)—Continued		
Name	City/Province	Key Shareholders	Key/Anchor Bottler
Swire Coca-Cola Beverages Zhengzhou Ltd.	Zhengzhou, Henan	BCD, Beijing Beijing Zhong Yin Industrial & Trading Co. Zhengzhou General Food Products Factory	Swire
Qingdao Coca-Cola Beverage Co. Ltd.	Qingdao, Shandong	Kerry Beverages Qingdao Yiqing Industrial Corp.	Kerry
Swire Coca-Cola Beverages Hefei Ltd.	Hefei, Anhui	BCD CITIC Anhui Jiushi Group	Swire
Swire Beverages (Dongguan) Ltd.	Dongguan, Guangdong	Swire Coca-Cola HK Ltd. Dongguan Huaxin Industrial Co.	Swire
Taiyuan Coca-Cola Beverage Co. Ltd.	Taiyuan, Shanxi	Kerry Beverages National COFCO Xishan Coal & Electricity (Group) Co. Ltd.	Kerry
Chengdu Coca-Cola Beverage Co. Ltd.	Chengdu, Sichuan	Kerry Beverages Chengdu Hua Jin Group	Kerry
Kunming Coca-Cola Beverage Co. Ltd.	Kunming, Yunnan	Kerry Beverages COFCO Hong Kong Yuan Tong Investment Co. Ltd.	Kerry

Source: www.moore.sc.edu.

During the 1980s, demand for Coke's products far exceeded the supply. However, it had difficulty distributing its products beyond the major cities and towns due to lack of proper infrastructure such as roads and railways, at that time. In most other countries, Coke's main method of distribution is the 'direct store delivery.' It [runs] its own sales centers [and] trucks, and [employs] sales and delivery staff to sell and deliver soft drinks directly to retail outlets and restaurants. But this method of distribution [is] effective only in developed markets and economies. To overcome the challenges of covering a large geographical area and lack of good infrastructure, Coke had to develop a different kind of distribution network in China. Coke based its distribution network on where the demand was and where the consumers could actually buy a Coke product. Since a method that would work for one geographical area might not work for another, Coke had to customize its methods of distribution for each market. It used both wholesalers and the direct store delivery system to distribute products in China.

The Coke bottlers owned and operated direct store delivery systems, but it was not the primary method of distribution. This system accounted for only about 20 percent of its sales while wholesalers accounted for the rest. The bottlers had warehouses, sales centers, fleets of trucks, sales personnel and other staff to manage sales and delivery to retail customers as well as wholesale customers. Depending upon the size of the city and market as well as its proximity to a bottling plant, the bottler would have either a warehouse or a sales center or sometimes both. In a large city the bottler had a big warehouse from which it would transport products to its smaller warehouses in other locations and to retailers. In smaller cities the bottlers ran sales centers as well as warehouses. Salesmen from these sales centers visited customers every day to take orders; the turnaround time (the time between placement of an order by the customer and delivery of product) for an order was usually 24 hours. In some cities bottlers ran the sales center at the bottling plant itself instead of at a different location. However, the bottler-owned direct store delivery system was not enough to reach all retail outlets such as restaurants, small stores and vendors.

As mentioned earlier, in addition to selling directly to retail outlets, the bottlers also sold the products to the wholesalers who in turn distributed them to the retail outlets. Therefore, Coke was dependent on the local Chinese distributors to get its products to the final consumer. For various reasons this proved to be an effective method of distribution. Firstly, Coke did not need to invest a large amount of capital in the distribution network. Secondly, the local Chinese companies had more expertise in wholesaling in the area that they were located in, as they were more familiar with the area as well as the requirements of the retailers. Over the years Coke has developed strong relationships with different kinds of wholesalers in China. During the 1980s, most of Coke's distributors were state-owned enterprises as most of the wholesale sector was state-owned. Later in the 1990s, many state-owned distribution companies were privatized and individual private entrepreneurs were also encouraged to set up their own wholesale companies. So, more and more local Chinese private wholesale companies began to distribute Coke products.

MARKETING AND ADVERTISING STRATEGIES Back in 1927 when Coke first entered China, it faced the challenge of communicating with the Chinese. The company needed to transliterate "Coca-Cola" into Chinese characters if it wanted to reach the millions of Chinese consumers. However, finding the nearest phonetic equivalent to Coca-Cola proved to be a difficult task. Not only did the transliteration need to sound like Coca-Cola but it also needed to have an appropriate meaning. Some shopkeepers who made their own transliterations and put up signs, proved how disastrous it could be if the meaning of the characters is not considered. Some of them put up signs that had ridiculous meanings such as "female horse fastened with wax" and "bite the wax tadpole." The Chinese language is made up of thousands of characters and out of these only 200 would even remotely sound like Coca-Cola. Also, most of the characters have more than one meaning. After extensive research the company finalized K'o K'ou K'o Le^ (the aspirates designated by ^ are necessary to approximate the English sounds) in Mandarin, a dialect understood by most Chinese. K'o means to permit, be able, may, can; K'ou means mouth, hole, pass, harbor; and Le^ means joy, to rejoice, to laugh, to be happy. So, K'o K'ou K'o Le^ can be interpreted as "to permit [the] mouth to be able to rejoice" or "something palatable from which one derives pleasure."

Coke believed that it needed to use music, color, arts and sports that the Chinese could identify with in order to connect with them. It gave its local managers autonomy over advertising and promotions. During the 1996 Chinese New Year it aired a television commercial using a Chinese dragon, which is something all Chinese would recognize. In the commercial the dragon was decorated with red Coke cans from head to tail and danced in a parade. Towards the end of the commercial a voice said, "For many centuries, the color red has been the color for good luck and prosperity.

Who are we to argue with ancient wisdom?" In July 2001, when China announced that it would host the 2008 Olympics, Coke immediately introduced a commemorative gold Coke can in the market.

Recognizing the Chinese people's love for soccer, Coke designed some of its marketing and promotions around the FIFA World Cup. In January 2001, Coke became the official beverage and a main sponsor of the national Chinese soccer team. It also commissioned a special song sung by eight popular Chinese singers during a live telecast of the Chinese team's first match. The song became popularly known as the 'Team China Anthem.' From the time the Chinese team started playing the qualifying matches Coke aired different TV commercials and organized other promotions based on the World Cup. In August 2001, during the World Cup Asian Qualifying Matches, Coke launched "The Dream Never Dies," an advertisement that showed the Chinese soccer fans' enormous support for their national team. Then in October 2001, marking the occasion of the Chinese team qualifying for the finals, Coke introduced a commemorative can and video disc called "The Road to the World Cup."

Later, in early 2002, Coke organized a road show called "Hero Tours" so that soccer fans all over China could meet with the team. It also ran special customized local promotions such as special packaging, World Cup star cards, ticket give-aways, flag bearer selections, and "Finger Soccer"[15] tournaments for school kids. In May 2002, Coke aired another advertisement about the Chinese team and the soccer fans' support to the team. The advertisement, which was called "Home Ground Advantage," showed a Chinese boy giving the players a Coke bottle filled with soil to wish them "home ground advantage" in the World Cup.

Coke also used SMS to run promotions and increase interaction between the company and its consumers. This was an effective method to use in China because, according to Teleconomy, a London-based market research company, China had 176 million mobile phone users in 2002. In 2002, during the end of summer, Coke ran [an] SMS contest for 35 days. The contest, which was called Coke Cool Summer, was announced through a television advertisement. Who ever guessed the correct highest daily temperature in Beijing and sent the reply through SMS, won a year's supply of Coke or Siemens cell phones. According to Coke, it received

---

[15]"Finger Soccer" is a very popular game in Latin America and has been brought to China by Coca-Cola. The soccer match is [. . .] played using fingers instead of feet, with 2 members [on] each team. The game kit consists of a pair of miniature replica soccer boots [that] are slipped onto two fingers of one hand.

over 4 million messages during the contest. "We are thrilled with the results, which frankly exceeded expectations; consumers can look forward to Coke adding more fizz on this platform, which is now clearly a key part of our consumers' lifestyle," said Sumanta Dutta, Coca-Cola China's Brand director.[16] In early 2004, Coke introduced "Modern Tea Workshop," a new line of tea drinks. To promote this new line of tea drinks, it hired Hong Kong movie stars Tony Leung and Shu Qi. It also hired Taiwanese pop stars S.H.E. and Will Pan to promote Coca-Cola.

China, Coca-Cola's Second Largest Market in Asia

Coke has enjoyed great success in China and in the Asian markets on the whole. According to the 2003 annual report, Coke's Asian operating segments boosted its revenues when growth in its U.S. market was slowing down. In terms of volume, China was Coke's second largest market in Asia in 2003 (Refer to Exhibit 2) and Coke estimates that China will beat Japan to the top position in 2004. Encouraged by its success in big cities and towns, Coke wants to reach more customers in rural areas. "We'd grown well by reaching the top 100 cities, but how many people were we reaching? Rather than continuing to focus solely on those highly competitive urban areas, Coke must push aggressively into the rest of China and India," said Patrick Siewert, Coke's East and South Asia group president.[17] In early 2004, Coke announced plans to build two new bottling plants in China's western provinces to tap the market potential of China's rural areas. Kerry signed an agreement with Chongqing Economic and Technological Development Zone to build [an] $11 million bottling plant in Chongqing, Western China. COFCO Coca-Cola, a Coke bottling enterprise, announced plans to build a bottling plant in Lanzhou, the capital city of Gansu Province in Northwest China. COFCO Coca-Cola also announced plans to build two new plants in Guangdong province in Southern China. These plants will be built in Zhanjiang and Huizhou. The construction of the Zhanjiang plant began in mid-2004 and construction of the Huizhou plant began in September 2004.

| Exhibit 2 | Percentage-Wise Breakup of Total Unit Case Volume in Asia Operating Segment |

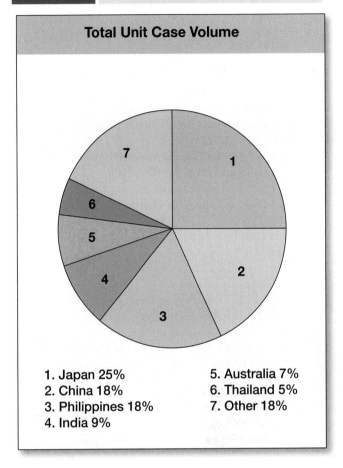

1. Japan 25%
2. China 18%
3. Philippines 18%
4. India 9%
5. Australia 7%
6. Thailand 5%
7. Other 18%

Source: 2003 Annual Report Summary, www.coca-cola.com.

[16]"Coke Judges China SMS Campaign a Success," by Brian Morrissey, October 30, 2002, www.boston.internet.com.

[17]"Coke's Big Gamble in Asia: Digging Deeper in China, India" by Leslie Chang in Kunyang, China, and Chad Terhune and Bets McKay in Atlanta, *The Wall Street Journal.* Gabriel Kahn in Hong Kong and Eric Bellman in Kithore, India, contributed to this article, August 11, 2004, www.mlive.com.

Additional Reading & References

1. **Two Reasons Why Coke Is It: China and Russia**, March 7, 1994, www.businessweek.com.
2. Mark L. Clifford in Hong Kong and Nicole Harris in Atlanta, with Dexter Roberts in Beidaihe and Manjeet Kripalani in Bombay, **Coke Pours into Asia,** October 28, 1996, www.businessweek.com.
3. Zeng Min, **Is China the Real Thing for Coca-Cola?** February 18, 2000, www.chinadaily.com.
4. Anil K. Joseph, **Coca Cola to Double its China Business in Five Years, Says Company Official,** August 15, 2000, www.financialexpress.com.

5. Drake Weisert, **Coca-Cola in China: Quenching the Thirst of a Billion,** July–August 2001, www.chinabusinessreview.com.

6. **Coca-Cola Eyes Western China,** September 2, 2002, www.peopledaily.com.cn.

7. Li Heng, **Coca-Cola Has over 50 Percent Market Share in China,** September 4, 2002, www.peopledaily.com.cn.

8. **Basketball Player Yao Ming Sues Coca-Cola,** May 26, 2003, www.china.org.cn.

9. **Coca-Cola Launches Its World Cup Marketing Initiative "It's Our Turn,"** March 25, 2002, www.coca-cola.com.

10. **Coca-Cola's First Chinese Majority-Owned Bottling Plant Set Up,** April 16, 2000, www.fpeng.peopledaily.com.cn.

11. **China Seen as Coca-Cola's Largest Market in 10 Years,** February 20, 2003, www.peopledaily.com.cn.

12. **Coca-Cola Tops Again,** 2001, www.bjreview.com.

13. **China Recognizes Coca-Cola for Its Social, Environmental Contributions,** January 19, 2003, www.peopledaily.com.cn.

14. Jane Tian, **Beverage Maker Thirsty: Coca-Cola Rosy About Potentials in China,** November 28, 2000, *Shanghai Star.*

15. Brian Morrissey, **Coke Judges China SMS Campaign a Success,** October 30, 2002, www.boston.internet.com.

16. **Coca-Cola Launches New 2008 Beijing Olympic Games Commemorative Cans,** August 4, 2003, www.coca-cola.com.

17. **First New Chinese Logo for Coca-Cola in 24 Years Marks Start of "Year of Coke" in China,** February 18, 2003, www.coca-cola.com.

18. **Cola War Rages on as Can Suppliers Cut Off Supplies,** Feb 11, 2002, *Asian Economic News,* www.findarticles.com.

19. **Investment of Coca-Cola in China Hit US$1.1b,** July 27, 2001, www.fpeng.peopledaily.com.

20. H. F. Allman, formerly Legal Counsel in China for The Coca-Cola Company, **Transliteration of Coca-Cola Trademark to Chinese Characters,** www.tafkac.org.

21. Ann Chen and Vijay Vishwanath, **Be the Top Pick in China,** January 16, 2004, www.business-times.asia1.com.

22. **Coca-Cola.com.cn Debuts in China,** July 26, 2000, www.chicagopride.com.

23. Geoffrey A. Fowler, Shanghai and Ramin Setoodeh, Hong Kong, **A Question of Taste,** August 12, 2004, www.feer.com.

24. **Is Diet Coke Drugged?** September 7, 2004, www.chinadaily.com.

25. Craig Simmons, **Marketing to the Masses,** September 4, 2003, www.feer.com.

Case 21

Neilson International in Mexico (A)

9A95G003

In January 1993, Howard Bateman, vice-president of International Operations for Neilson International, a division of William Neilson Limited, was assessing a recent proposal from Sabritas, a division of Pepsico Foods in Mexico, to launch Neilson's brands in the Mexican market. Neilson, a leading producer of high quality confectionery products, had grown to achieve a leadership position in the Canadian market and was currently producing Canada's top selling chocolate bar, "Crispy Crunch." In the world chocolate bar market, however, Neilson was dwarfed by major players such as M&M/Mars, Hershey/Lowney and Nestlé-Rowntree. Recognizing their position as a smaller player with fewer resources, in a stagnant domestic market, Neilson in 1990 formed its International Division to develop competitive strategies for their exporting efforts.

Recent attempts to expand into several foreign markets, including the United States, had taught them some valuable

IVEY Gayle Duncan and Shari Ann Wortel prepared this case under the supervision of Professors P. W. Beamish and C. B. Johnston solely to provide material for class discussion. The authors do not intend to illustrate either effective or ineffective handling of a managerial situation. The authors may have disguised certain names and other identifying information to protect confidentiality.

lessons. Although it was now evident that they had world class products to offer to global markets, their competitive performance was being constrained by limited resources. Pepsico's joint branding proposal would allow greater market penetration than Neilson could afford. But, at what cost?

Given the decision to pursue international opportunities more aggressively, Bateman's biggest challenge was to determine the distributor relationships Neilson should pursue in order to become a global competitor.

The Chocolate Confectionery Industry[1]

The "confectionery" industry consisted of the "sugar" segment, including all types of sugar confectionery [and] chewing gum, and the "chocolate" segment, which included chocolates and other cocoa based products. Most large chocolate operations were dedicated to two major products: boxed chocolates and bar chocolates, which represented nearly 50 per cent of the confectionery industry by volume.

Competition from imports was significant, with the majority of products coming from the United States (39 percent). European countries such as Switzerland, Germany, the United Kingdom and Belgium were also major sources of confectionery, especially for premium products such as boxed chocolates. (See Exhibit 1 for a profile of chocolate exporting countries.) In order to maintain production volumes and to relieve the burden of fixed costs on operations, Canadian manufacturers used excess capacity to produce goods for exporting. Although nearly all of these products were traditionally exported to the United States, in the early

[1]Some information in this section was derived from: J. C. Ellert, J. Peter Killing and Dana Hyde, "Nestlé-Rowntree (A)," in *Business Policy, A Canadian Casebook*, Joseph N. Fry et al. (Eds.), Prentice Hall Canada Inc., 1992, pp. 655–667.

Exhibit 1	World Chocolate Exports (Value as % of Total) [1987]–1990			
	1987	1988	1989	1990
Africa	x1.5	x1.0	x1.1	x0.7
Americas	8.1	9.1	9.2	x9.1
LAIC[1]	2.1	1.9	1.4	x1.4
CACM[2]	0.1	x0.1	x0.1	x0.1
Asia	2.5	3.2	3.4	2.9
Middle East	x0.5	x0.5	x0.7	x0.4
Europe	86.4	85.0	84.2	85.4
EEC (12)[3]	73.3	71.8	71.3	73.5
EFTA[4]	12.5	12.7	12.1	11.5
Oceania	x1.5	1.8	x2.1	x1.8

Figures denoted with an "x" are provisional or estimated.

Adapted from: The United Nations' "International Trade Statistics Yearbook," Vol. II, 1990.

[1]LAIC = Latin American Industrialists Association

[2]CACM = Central American Common Market

[3]EEC(12) = The twelve nations of the European Economic Community

[4]EFTA = European Free Trade Association

nineties, the world market had become increasingly more attractive.

Firms in the confectionery industry competed on the basis of brand name products, product quality and cost of production. Although Canadian producers had the advantage of being able to purchase sugar at the usually lower world price, savings were offset by the higher prices for dairy ingredients used in products manufactured for domestic consumption. Other commodity ingredients, often experiencing widely fluctuating prices, caused significant variations in manufacturing costs. Producers were reluctant to raise their prices due to the highly elastic demand for chocolate. Consequently, they sometimes reformatted or reformulated their products through size or ingredient changes to sustain margins. Three major product types were manufactured for domestic and export sales:

Blocks These products are molded blocks of chocolate that are sold by weight and manufactured in a variety of [flavors], with or without additional ingredients such as fruit or nuts. Block chocolate was sold primarily in grocery outlets or directly to confectionery manufacturers. (Examples: baking chocolate, Hershey's Chocolate Bar, Suchard's Toblerone.)

Boxed Chocolates These products included a variety of bite-sized sweets and were generally regarded as "gift" or "occasion" purchases. Sales in grocery outlets tended to be more seasonal than for other chocolate products, with 80 per cent sold at Christmas and Easter. Sales in other outlets remained steady year round. (Examples: Cadbury's Milk Tray, Rowntree's Black Magic and After Eights.)

Countlines These were chocolate covered products sold by count rather than by weight, and were generally referred to by consumers as "chocolate bars." The products varied widely in size, shape, weight and composition, and had a wider distribution than the other two product types. Most countlines were sold through non-grocery outlets such as convenience and drug stores. (Examples: Neilson's Crispy Crunch, Nestlé-Rowntree's Coffee Crisp, M&M/Mars' Snickers, and Hershey/Lowney's Oh Henry!)

Sweet chocolate was the basic semi-finished product used in the manufacture of block, countline, and boxed chocolate products. Average costs of sweet chocolate for a representative portfolio of all three product types could be broken down as follows:

Raw material	35%
Packaging	10
Production	20
Distribution	5
Marketing/sales	20
Trading profit	10
Total	100% (of manufacturer's selling price)

For countline products, raw material costs were proportionately lower because a smaller amount of cocoa was used.

In value terms, more chocolate was consumed than any other manufactured food product in the world. In the late eighties, the world's eight major markets (representing over 60 per cent of the total world chocolate market) consumed nearly three million [tons] with a retail value close to $20 billion. During the 1980s, countline was the fastest growing segment with close to 50 per cent of the world chocolate market by volume and an average annual rate of growth of seven per cent. An increasing trend towards indulgence in snack and "comfort" foods strongly suggested that future growth would remain strong.

Competitive Environment

In 1993, chocolate producers in the world included: M&M/Mars, Hershey Foods, Cadbury-Schweppes, Jacobs Suchard, Nestlé-Rowntree, United Biscuits, Ferrero, Nabisco and George Weston Ltd. (Neilson). Chocolate represented varying proportions of these manufacturers' total sales.

For the most part, it was difficult to sustain competitive advantages in manufacturing or product features due to a lack of proprietary technology. There was also limited potential for new product development since the basic ingredients in countline product manufacturing could only be blended in a limited variety of combinations. This forced an emphasis on competition through distribution and advertising.

Product promotion played a critical role in establishing brand name recognition. Demand was typified by high-impulse and discretionary purchasing [behavior]. Since consumers, generally, had a selection of at least three or four [favorite] brands from which to choose, the biggest challenge facing producers was to create the brand awareness necessary to break into these menus. In recognition of the wide selection of competing brands and the broad range of snack food substitutes available, expenditures for media and trade promotions were considerable. For example, Canadian chocolate bar makers spent more than $30 million for advertising in Canada, in 1992, mostly on television. This was often a barrier to entry for smaller producers.

Major Competitors

M&M/MARS As the world leader in chocolate confectionery M&M/Mars dominated the countline sector, particularly in North America and Europe, with such famous global brands as Snickers, M&Ms and Milky Way. However, in Canada, in 1992, M&M/Mars held fourth place with an 18.7 per cent market share of single bars. (Exhibits 2 and 3 compare Canadian market positions for major competitors.)

M&M/Mars' strategy was to produce high quality products which were simple to manufacture and which allowed for high volume and automated production processes. They supported their products with heavy advertising and aggressive sales, focusing marketing efforts on strengthening their global brands.

HERSHEY/LOWNEY Hershey's strength in North America was in the block chocolate category, in which it held the leading market position. Hershey also supplied export markets in Asia, Australia, Sweden, and Mexico from their chocolate production facilities in Pennsylvania. In Canada, in 1992, Hershey held third place in the countline segment with a 21.6 per cent share of the market.

Hershey's strategy was to reduce exposure to volatile cocoa prices by diversifying within the confectionery and snack businesses. By 1987, only 45 per cent of Hershey's sales

Exhibit 2	Single Bars Canadian Market Share: 1991–1992	
Manufacturer	1992	1991
Neilson	28.1%	29.4%
Nestlé/Rowntree	26.9%	26.2%
Hershey/Lowney	21.6%	21.9%
M&M/Mars	18.7%	19.0%
Others	4.7%	3.5%

Source: Nielson News, Issue #1, 1993.

Exhibit 3	Top Single Bars in Canada: 1991–1992		
Top Single Bars	Manufacturer	1992	1991
Crispy Crunch	Neilson	1	1
Coffee Crisp	Nestlé/Rowntree	2	3
Kit Kat	Nestlé/Rowntree	3	2
Mars Bar	M&M/Mars	4	4
Caramilk	Cadbury Schweppes	5	6
Oh Henry!	Hershey/Lowney	6	5
Smarties	Nestlé/Rowntree	7	7
Peanut Butter Cups	Hershey/Lowney	8	8
Mr. Big	Neilson	9	11
Aero	Hershey/Lowney	10	10
Snickers	M&M/Mars	11	9
Crunchie	Cadbury Schweppes	12	12

Source: Nielson News, Issue #1, 1993.

came from products with 70 per cent or more chocolate content. This was down from 80 per cent in 1963.

CADBURY SCHWEPPES Cadbury was a major world name in chocolate, with a portfolio of brands such as Dairy Milk, Creme Eggs and Crunchie. Although its main business was in the United Kingdom, it was also a strong competitor in major markets such as Australia and South Africa.

Cadbury Schweppes diversified its product line and expanded into new geographic markets throughout the 1980's. In 1987, Cadbury International sold the Canadian distribution rights for their chocolate products to William Neilson Ltd. Only in Canada were the Cadbury brands incorporated into the Neilson confectionery division under the name Neilson/Cadbury. In 1988, Cadbury sold its U.S. operations to Hershey.

NESTLÉ-ROWNTREE In 1991, chocolate and confectionery comprised 16 per cent of Nestlé's SFr 50.5 billion revenue, up sharply from only eight per cent in 1987. (In January 1993, 1SFr = $0.88 CAD = 0.69 U.S.) This was largely a result of their move into the countline sector through the acquisition in 1988 of Rowntree PLC, a leading British manufacturer with strong global brands such as Kit Kat, After Eights and Smarties. In 1990, they also added Baby Ruth and Butterfinger to their portfolio, both "Top 20" brands in the U.S. Considering these recent heavy investments to acquire global brands and expertise, it was clear that Nestlé-Rowntree intended to remain a significant player in growing global markets.

Neilson

COMPANY HISTORY William Neilson Ltd. was founded in 1893, when the Neilson family began selling milk and [homemade] ice cream to the Toronto market. By 1905 they had erected a house and factory at 277 Gladstone Ave., from which they shipped ice cream as far west as Winnipeg and as far east as Quebec City. Chocolate bar production was initiated to offset the decreased demand for ice cream during the colder winter months and as a way of retaining the skilled [labor] pool. By 1914, the company was producing one million pounds of ice cream and 500,000 pounds of chocolate per year.

William Neilson died in 1915, and the business was handed down to his son Morden, who had been involved since its inception. Between 1924 and 1934, the "Jersey Milk," "Crispy Crunch" and "Malted Milk" bars were introduced. Upon the death of Morden Neilson in 1947, the company was sold to George Weston Foods for $4.5 million.

By 1974, "Crispy Crunch" was the number one selling bar in Canada. In 1977, "Mr. Big" was introduced and became the number one teen bar by 1986. By 1991, the Neilson dairy operations had been moved to a separate location and the ice cream division had been sold to Ault Foods. The Gladstone location continued to be used to manufacture Neilson chocolate and confectionery.

Bateman explained that Neilson's efforts under the direction of the new president, Arthur Soler, had become more competitive in the domestic market over the past three years, through improved customer service and retail merchandising. Significant improvements had already been made in Administration and Operations. All of these initiatives had assisted in reversing decades of consumer share erosion. As a result, Neilson was now in a position to defend its share of the domestic market and to develop an international business that would enhance shareholder value. (Exhibit 4 outlines the Canadian [...] confectionery market.)

Exhibit 4	Canadian Confectionery Market—1993	
	Dollars (Millions)	%
Total Confectionery Category	$1,301.4	100.0
Gum	296.5	22.8
Boxed Chocolates	159.7	12.3
Cough Drops	77.0	5.9
Rolled Candy	61.3	4.7
Bagged Chocolates	30.3	2.3
Easter Eggs	22.0	1.7
Valentines	9.4	0.7
Lunch Pack	3.6	0.3
Countline Chocolate Bars	641.6	49.3
Total Chocolate Bar Market Growth	+ 8%	

Source: Neilson Marketing Department estimates.

NEILSON'S EXPORTING EFFORTS Initial export efforts prior to 1990 were contracted to a local export broker—Grenadier International. The original company objective was to determine "what could be done in foreign markets" using only working capital resources and avoiding capital investments in equipment or new markets.

Through careful selection of markets on the basis of distributor interest, Grenadier's export manager, Scott Begg, had begun the slow process of introducing Neilson brands into the Far East. The results were impressive. Orders were secured for containers of "Mr. Big" and "Crispy Crunch" countlines from local distributors in Korea, Taiwan, and Japan. "Canadian Classics" boxed chocolates were developed for the vast Japanese gift ("Omiyagi") market. Total 1993 sales to these markets were projected to be $1.6 million.

For each of these markets, Neilson retained the responsibility for packaging design and product formulation. While distributors offered suggestions as to how products could be improved to suit local tastes, they were not formally obliged to do so. To secure distribution in Taiwan, Neilson had agreed to launch the "Mr. Big" bar under the distributor's private brand name "Bang Bang," which was expected to generate a [favorable] impression with consumers. Although sales were strong, Bateman realized that since consumer loyalty was linked to brand names, the brand equity being generated for "Bang Bang" ultimately would belong to the distributor. This put the distributor in a powerful position from which they were able to place significant downward pressure on operating margins.

MARKET EVALUATION STUDY In response to these successful early exporting efforts Bateman began exploring the possible launch of Neilson brands into the United States (discussed later). With limited working capital and numerous export opportunities, it became obvious to the International Division that some kind of formal strategy was required to evaluate and to compare these new markets.

Accordingly, a set of weighted criteria was developed during the summer of 1992 to evaluate countries that were being considered by the International Division. (See Exhibit 5 for a profile of the world's major chocolate importers.) The study was intended to provide a standard means of evaluating potential markets. Resources could then be allocated among those markets that promised long-term incremental growth and those which were strictly opportunistic. While the revenues from opportunistic markets would contribute to the fixed costs of domestic production, the long-term efforts could be pursued for more strategic reasons. By the end of the summer, the study had been applied to thirteen international markets, including the United States. (See Exhibit 6 for a summary of this study.)

Meanwhile, Grenadier had added Hong Kong/China, Singapore and New Zealand to Neilson's portfolio of export markets, and Bateman had contracted a second local broker, CANCON Corp. Ltd, to initiate sales to the Middle East. By the end of 1992, the International Division comprised nine people who had achieved penetration of 11 countries for export sales (see Exhibit 7 for a description of these markets). As of January 1993, market shares in these countries [were] very small.

The U.S. Experience

In 1991, the American chocolate confectionery market was worth US$5.1 billion wholesale. Neilson had wanted to sneak into this vast market with the intention of quietly selling off excess capacity. However, as Bateman explained, the quiet U.S. launch became a Canadian celebration:

> Next thing we knew, there were bands in the streets, Neilson t-shirts and baseball caps, and newspaper articles and T.V. specials describing our big U.S. launch!

The publicity greatly increased the pressure to succeed. After careful consideration, Pro Set, a collectible trading card manufacturer and marketer, was selected as a distributor. This relationship developed into a joint venture by which the Neilson Import Division was later appointed distributor of the Pro Set cards in Canada. With an internal sales management team, full distribution and invoicing infrastructures and a 45-broker national sales network, Pro Set seemed ideally suited to diversify into confectionery products.

Unfortunately, Pro Set quickly proved to be an inadequate partner in this venture. Although they had access to the right outlets, the confectionery selling task differed significantly from card sales. Confectionery items demanded more sensitive product handling and a greater amount of sales effort by the Pro Set representatives, who were used to carrying a self-promoting line.

To compound these difficulties, Pro Set sales plummeted as the trading-card market became over-saturated. Trapped by intense cashflow problems and increasing fixed costs, Pro Set filed for Chapter 11 bankruptcy, leaving Neilson with huge inventory losses and a customer base that associated them with their defunct distributor. Although it was tempting to attribute the U.S. failure to inappropriate partner selection, the U.S. had also ranked poorly relative to other markets in the criteria study that had just been completed that summer. In addition to their distribution problems, Neilson was at a serious disadvantage due to intense competition from the major industry players in the form of advertising expenditures, trade promotions and brand proliferation. Faced with duties and a

Exhibit 5	World Chocolate Imports (Value as % of Total) [1987]–1990			
	1987	1988	1989	1990
Africa	x0.7	x0.7	x0.7	x0.7
Americas	x15.6	x15.0	x13.9	x13.2
LAIC[1]	0.2	0.4	1.1	x1.3
CACM[2]	x0.1	x0.1	x0.1	x0.1
Asia	11.7	x13.9	x15.6	x12.9
Middle East	x3.5	x3.3	x3.9	x2.8
Europe	70.8	68.9	67.7	71.4
EEC (12)[3]	61.1	59.5	57.7	59.3
EFTA[4]	9.3	9.0	8.9	8.4
Oceania	x1.3	x1.7	x2.1	x1.8

Figures denoted with an "x" are provisional or estimated.

Adapted from: The United Nations' "International Trade Statistics Yearbook," Vol. II, 1990.

[1]LAIC = Latin American Industrialists Association

[2]CACM = Central American Common Market

[3]EEC (12) = The twelve nations of the European Economic Community

[4]EFTA = European Free Trade Association

Exhibit 6 Summary of Criteria for Market Study (1992)

CRITERIA	Weight	Australia	China	Hong Kong	Indonesia	Japan	Korea	Malaysia	New [Zealand]	Singapore	Taiwan	Mexico	EEC	USA
* U.S. Countline	—	4	4	4	4	4	4	4	4	4	4	4	4	4
1 Candy Bar Economics	30	20	20	30	20	20	28	20	15	25	15	20	10	10
2 Target Market	22	12.5	14	13	15.5	19	15	10	7	9.5	12.5	21	22	22
3 Competitor Dynamics	20	12	15	8	7.5	11	13.5	10	12	14.5	12	11	20	6.5
4 Distribution Access	10	9	4	4	3.5	5	6	6.5	9	3.5	7.5	9.5	9	9
5 Industry Economics	9	2.5	3.5	6	5.5	2	5	2.5	7	4.5	3	3.5	3.5	4.5
6 Product Fit	8	7	6	6	6	3	7.5	7.5	7.5	8	4	8	5	8
7 Payback	5	4	4	1	2.5	4	5	2.5	4	2	2	5	2	1
8 Country Dynamics	5	5	1	4	3	5	3.5	4.5	4.5	5	4	3	2	4
TOTAL	109	72	67.5	72	63.5	69	83.5	63.5	66	72	60	81	73.5	65

COMPETITOR DYNAMICS	Score	Mexico
Financial Success of Other Exporters	0–8	5
Nature (Passivity) of Competition	0–6	2.5
Brand Image (vs. Price) Positioning	0–6	3.5
SCORE/20	/20	11

Due to Neilson/Cadbury's limited resources, it was not feasible to launch the first western-style brands into new markets. The basic minimum criteria for a given market, therefore, was the presence of major western industry players (i.e., Mars or Hershey). Countries were then measured on the basis of 8 criteria which were weighted by the International Group according to their perceived importance as determinants of a successful market entry. (See above table.) Each criterion was then subdivided into several elements as defined by the International Group, which allocated the total weighted score accordingly. (See table, right.)

This illustration depicts a single [criterion,] subdivided and scored for Mexico.

Source: Company Records.

Exhibit 7	Neilson Export Markets—1993	

Agent (Commission)	Country	Brands
Grenadier International	Taiwan	Bang Bang
	Japan	Mr. Big, Crispy Crunch, Canadian Classics
	Korea	Mr. Big, Crispy Crunch
	Hong Kong/China	Mr. Big, Crispy Crunch, Canadian Classics
	Singapore	Mr. Big, Crispy Crunch
CANCON Corp. Ltd.	Saudi Arabia	Mr. Big, Crispy Crunch, Malted Milk
	Bahrain	Mr. Big, Crispy Crunch, Malted Milk
	U.A.E.	Mr. Big, Crispy Crunch, Malted Milk
	Kuwait	Mr. Big, Crispy Crunch, Malted Milk
Neilson International	Mexico	Mr. Big, Crispy Crunch, Malted Milk
	U.S.A.	Mr. Big, Crispy Crunch, Malted Milk

Source: Company records.

higher cost of production, Neilson was unable to maintain price competitiveness.

The International Division was now faced with the task of internalizing distribution in the U.S., including sales management, broker contact, warehousing, shipping and collections. Neilson managed to reestablish a limited presence in the American market using several local brokers to target profitable niches. For example, they placed strong emphasis on vending-machine sales to increase product trial with minimal advertising. Since consumer purchasing patterns demanded product variety in vending machines, Neilson's presence in this segment was not considered threatening by major competitors.

In the autumn of 1992, as the International Division made the changes necessary to salvage past efforts in the U.S., several options for entering the Mexican confectionery market were also being considered.

Mexico

Neilson made the decision to enter the Mexican market late in 1992, prompted by its parent company's, Weston Foods Ltd., own investigations into possible market opportunities which would emerge as a result of the North American Free Trade Agreement (NAFTA). Mexico was an attractive market which scored very highly in the market evaluation study. Due to their [favorable] demographics (50 per cent of the population was within the target age group), Mexico offered huge potential for countline sales. The rapid adoption of American tastes resulted in an increasing demand for U.S. snack foods. With only a limited number of competitors, the untapped demand afforded a

window of opportunity for smaller players to enter the market.

Working through the Ontario Ministry of Agriculture and Food (OMAF), Neilson found two potential independent distributors:

Grupo Corvi A Mexican food manufacturer operated seven plants and had an extensive sales force reaching local wholesalers. They also had access to a convoluted infrastructure which indirectly supplied an estimated 100,000 street vendor stands or kiosks (known as "tiendas") representing nearly 70 per cent of the Mexican confectionery market. (This informal segment was usually overlooked by marketing research services and competitors alike.) Grupo Corvi currently had no American or European style countline products.

Grupo Hajj A Mexican distributor with some experience in confectionery, offered access to only a small number of retail stores. This limited network made Grupo Hajj relatively unattractive when compared to other distributors. Like Grupo Corvi, this local firm dealt exclusively in Mexican pesos, historically a volatile currency. (In January 1993, 1 peso = CDN$0.41.)

While considering these distributors, Neilson was approached by Sabritas, the snack food division of Pepsico Foods in Mexico, who felt that there was a strategic fit between their organizations. Although Sabritas had no previous experience handling chocolate confectionery, they had for six years been seeking a product line to round out their portfolio. They were currently each week supplying Frito-Lay type snacks directly to 450,000 retail stores and tiendas. (The trade referred to such extensive customer networks as "numeric distribution.") After listening to the initial proposal, Neilson agreed to give Sabritas three months to conduct research into the Mexican market.

Although the research revealed strong market potential for the Neilson products, Bateman felt that pricing at two pesos (at parity with other American style brands) would not provide any competitive advantage. Sabritas agreed that a one peso product, downsized to 40 grams (from a Canadian-U.S. standard of 43 to 65 grams), would provide an attractive strategy to offer "imported chocolate at Mexican prices."

Proposing a deal significantly different from the relationships offered by the two Mexican distributors, Sabritas intended to market the "Mr. Big," "Crispy Crunch" and "Malted Milk" bars as the first brands in the "Milch" product line. "Milch" was a fictitious word in Spanish, created and owned by Sabritas, and thought to denote goodness and health due to its similarity to the word "milk." Sabritas would offer Neilson 50 per cent ownership of the Milch name, in exchange for 50 per cent of Neilson's brand names, both of which would appear on each bar. As part of the joint branding agreement, Sabritas would assume all responsibility for advertising, promotion, distribution and merchandising.

The joint ownership of the brand names would provide Sabritas with brand equity in exchange for building brand awareness through heavy investments in marketing. By delegating responsibility for all marketing efforts to Sabritas, Neilson would be able to compete on a scale not affordable by Canadian standards.

Under the proposal, all "Milch" chocolate bars would be produced in Canada by Neilson. Neilson would be the exclusive supplier. Ownership of the bars would pass to Sabritas once the finished goods had been shipped. Sabritas in turn would be responsible for all sales to final consumers. Sabritas would be the exclusive distributor. Consumer prices could not be changed without the mutual agreement of Neilson and Sabritas.

Issues

Bateman reflected upon the decision he now faced for the Mexican market. The speed with which Sabritas could help them gain market penetration, their competitive advertising budget, and their "store door access" to nearly a half million retailers were attractive advantages offered by this joint venture proposal. But what were the implications of omitting the Neilson name from their popular chocolate bars? Would they be exposed to problems like those encountered in Taiwan with the "Bang Bang" launch, especially considering the strength and size of Pepsico Foods?

The alternative was to keep the Neilson name and to launch their brands independently, using one of the national distributors. Unfortunately, limited resources meant that Neilson would develop its presence much more slowly. With countline demand in Mexico growing at 30 per cent per year, could they afford to delay? Scott Begg had indicated that early entry was critical in burgeoning markets, since establishing market presence and gaining share were less difficult when undertaken before the major players had dominated the market and "defined the rules of play."

Bateman also questioned their traditional means of evaluating potential markets. Were the criteria considered in the market evaluation study really the key success factors, or were the competitive advantages offered through ventures with distributors more important? If partnerships were necessary, should Neilson continue to rely on independent, national distributors who were interested in adding Neilson brands to their portfolio, or should they pursue strategic partnerships similar to the Sabritas opportunity instead? No matter which distributor was chosen, product quality and handling were of paramount importance. Every chocolate bar reaching consumers, especially first time buyers, must be of the same freshness and quality as those distributed to Canadian consumers. How could this type of control best be achieved?

Case 22

eBay International

01/2004-5149

> *"If eBay is to achieve its ambitious goal of US3 billion revenues in 2005, it will have to replicate its US success around the world."*
>
> **—Thorold Barker, Financial Times, January 11, 2002.**

At the busy intersection in Paris of Rue de Flandre and Rue de Stalingrad, traffic was noisy and people were bustling about. Upstairs, on the fifth floor of a nondescript building, where a firm called iBazar operated, Michael van Swaaij, an INSEAD MBA, and now VP of eBay Europe, was huddling with his boss, Matt Bannick. Should eBay acquire rival iBazar in France or should it grow organically, as it had done successfully in the United Kingdom?

Bannick, a Harvard MBA, and now head of eBay's international operations, had his own quandaries. Japan had shaped up as a giant market in person-to-person auctions, second only to the United States. Yet, Yahoo!, in a joint venture with Softbank of Japan, had made deep inroads into Japan, and was now seemingly undisplaceable there. Should eBay cut its losses and pull out of the Japanese market?

van Swaaij was tantalized, not only by iBazar, but also by the possibility of cross-border person-to-person trade. eBay prided itself on "making impossible commerce possible, and on making inefficient commerce efficient." But commerce even on eBay was still largely national. In the future, would a Frenchman trade rare wine with an Austrian, and would the latter sell his violin to a buyer in Italy? The possibilities were inherent in the many-to-many technology that was the Internet. Indeed, the British and the Americans were already showing the way by trading collectibles and other items across the Atlantic. van Swaaij wondered to what extent the idea of a marketplace formed by a community of buyers and sellers could span national borders. Could cross-border trade develop into a growth engine for eBay in Europe?

Bannick, too, wondered about these possibilities. He had just received reports from Australia. The news was positive, but, to do even better, Australia wanted a site more customized to its local needs. The significant (approximately half-million dollar) expense of doing this aside, Bannick wondered what, if anything, in a "pure play" Internet business, was different in terms of global strategy. Ought eBay to become a "brand global, act local" player? What implications would that have for global cross-border trade?

INSEAD This case was written by Soumitra Dutta, The Roland Berger Chaired Professor of Business and Technology and Subramanian Rangan, Associate Professor of Strategy and Management, both at INSEAD as a basis for class discussion rather than to illustrate either effective or ineffective handling of an administrative situation.

eBay Background: 1995–2001

eBay was launched on Labor Day in 1995 in Campbell, California, by Pierre Omidyar, a software engineer. His (now) wife, Pam, a collector of candy dispensers, found it difficult to link up with others with a similar interest. Omidyar figured he could use the burgeoning technology of the Internet to create a marketplace for physical goods that would be as efficient as the stock exchanges were for trading stock. Thus, eBay (settled on as a domain name since Echo Bay, the name Omidyar had first requested, was taken) was born as an

Internet-based community where members, primarily collectors could list items for sale by auction, and interested others could make bids for those items. The auction closed when the seller was satisfied (on average, after one week), and the highest bidder won. eBay thus made it possible for thousands to indulge their hobbies and enjoy the thrill of the deal without leaving the comfort of their homes or offices.

The response was overwhelming. Within one year of starting, tens of thousands of individuals had posted their items for trade and had made purchases. The venture capital community spied an opportunity and eBay was transformed into a business venture. Incorporated in San Jose, California, in 1997, eBay spread nationally within the United States. Thanks to word of mouth and Internet marketing, listings from outside California had grown. The business' infrastructure (of servers and software) resided in California, but access was, of course, nationwide.

The model was simple and surprisingly successful. Unlike at other Internet firms, such as Amazon, at eBay customers performed most of the value added. They chose what to list and for how long, and they described and uploaded photos of the items. If a sale materialized, they packed, insured, and shipped items to the buyer. The buyer handled payment and verification. Importantly, customers monitored one another by rating their trading partners. The system policed itself. eBay neither took possession of the items, nor did it physically handle items, money, or documents. For these reasons, the model was truly "scalable" (i.e., expandable without proportional increase in cost).

For its part, eBay oversaw and optimized the entire process and user experience. It made listing items and uploading photos relatively simple. It made search intuitive and accurate. eBay managers, who created category directories (under which featured items were listed) were tuned-in to how people thought about and browsed for items. eBay also made auction bidding and notification interesting, yet efficient. It made feedback and rating simple, yet valuable. Also, working with "complementor" firms, such as iPix, Lloyds, and Billpoint, it facilitated photo-loading, insurance, and payments. If there was a problem, eBay was willing to step in, investigate, and sort out the matter. For this efficient, trust-efficient trade service, eBay charged a modest listing and transaction fee. (A car, for instance, could be sold on eBay for fees totaling around US$50).

eBay Goes International

By 1998, eBay was receiving hundreds of listings a day from Canadian residents. The major international markets, however, were turning out to be Germany and the United King-

dom. In both these markets, local imitators had emerged, and, indeed, eBay itself was witnessing bids and listings from the United Kingdom. The logic of critical mass appeared quite important. Because the probability of successful transactions was higher on a "thick" rather than a "thin" market, individuals would tend to tip to the more trafficked sites. eBay would have to get going in these international markets if it was not to be locked out.

Accordingly, in 1999, eBay ventured into the United Kingdom, Australia, and Germany. Through similar reasoning, in 2000, eBay launched sites in Japan, France, and Canada.

iBazar in France

Shortly thereafter, eBay became the leading auction site in Canada. (It was estimated that eBay was 50 times as large as the next auction site in Canada).[1] Success in the United States had certainly given the firm considerable publicity and credibility that had spilled over north of the border. More surprisingly, by the first quarter of 2000, eBay was pulling even in England with QXL (pronounced "quick sell"), the first mover there in person-to-person (p2p) auction-based trading.

In France, the country of birth of eBay's founder, Pierre Omidyar, the story was different. France was an important market in Internet commerce. By 2005, e-commerce revenues there were projected to be the fourth highest in the world (See Exhibit 1). Alas, eBay had entered France in October 2000, well after an upstart local firm, iBazar, had adapted the eBay model and launched an Internet auction site there in 1998.

As iBazar built traffic, eBay France languished. The problem, eBay felt, was actually worse than it appeared. iBazar was founded and run by a couple of "Net" entrepreneurs, Pierre-François Grimaldi and Marc Piquemal, but it was funded by a financial investor. At the time, building up traffic and registered users was considered critical. With the aim of maximizing this, iBazar offered free listings and charged relatively small fees for transactions, while promoting the site heavily through television advertising. Their revenues and profits were to come from advertising. Under this model, users flocked to the site and listed anything and everything. Critically, unlike eBay, iBazar focused on the trade of practicals. Collectors and hobbyists did not really warm to the site, and the users that came did not become repeat traders.

As listings and trades rose in France, van Swaaij at eBay Europe became increasingly apprehensive about the follow-

---

[1] eBay Analyst Day presentation, October 29, 2001.

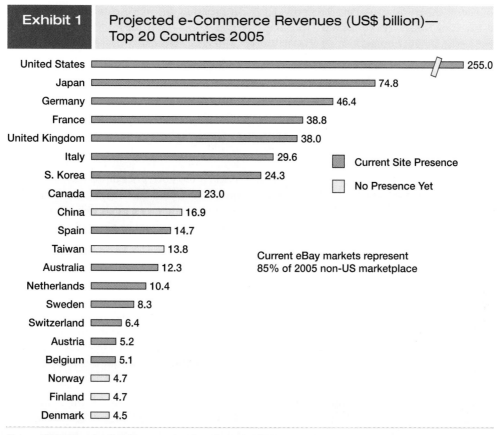

Exhibit 1 Projected e-Commerce Revenues (US$ billion)— Top 20 Countries 2005

Country	Revenue
United States	255.0
Japan	74.8
Germany	46.4
France	38.8
United Kingdom	38.0
Italy	29.6
S. Korea	24.3
Canada	23.0
China	16.9
Spain	14.7
Taiwan	13.8
Australia	12.3
Netherlands	10.4
Sweden	8.3
Switzerland	6.4
Austria	5.2
Belgium	5.1
Norway	4.7
Finland	4.7
Denmark	4.5

Current Site Presence
No Presence Yet

Current eBay markets represent 85% of 2005 non-US marketplace

Source: IDC; eBay Analyst Day presentation, Oct. 29, 2001.

ing. First, how could eBay build up listings on its own French site? Second, if iBazar attracted the good and the not so good (in terms of items listed), French users would have a poor experience, and the entire budding p2p market in France risked being compromised. Third, if users grew accustomed to listing without fees and to the "classifieds" model of iBazar, this could be detrimental to future "monetization" of traffic by eBay or, for that matter, others.

A Dutch national, van Swaaij, had previously worked at AOL in London. In the fairly new world of "e-business," he was relatively experienced. He had dealt with international expansion, with competition, and had lived and studied in France. Flying to France from his office in Switzerland, van Swaaij kept hovering between two major options. The first was to stick it out and wait for iBazar to self-destruct. After all, if he was right about the potential pitfalls in iBazar's approach to the business, the firm would run out of cash. (iBazar bad grown from 2 to a staff of 200; outside guesses put its "burn rate" at well over US$1 million per month; and it was taking in only 20–30% of that figure in revenues). The downside was that it was difficult to predict how long

this would take, and whether iBazar would take the whole French market down with it. Not to mention, iBazar was also already exporting its "weak model" into other southern European markets.

The second option was for eBay to acquire iBazar. Of course, in order to make this happen, van Swaaij would have to convince headquarters in San Jose, California, to fork out hard cash today to take out a bad player. (In 2000, before the Internet stock bubble collapsed, it was rumored that iBazar considered itself to be valued at over a billion dollars.) Headquarters was bound to ask why eBay France was not delivering in the face of competition, when eBay in England was. Further, given iBazar's different approach (that focused on practicals as opposed to collectibles, would the business evaporate once the television advertising stopped? Notwithstanding, the financial investor at iBazar was bound to put the squeeze on in terms of price. He was likely to perceive that eBay had more to gain than he had to lose. He could also be under the impression that iBazar, which, after all, had a couple of million registered users, would turn the corner any day and become a money-maker. Last but not least, Wanadoo, the leading Internet access provider in France (and a unit of France Télécom), was expressing interest in iBazar, as was Yahoo! Europe. Timing was vital; a smart acquirer would wait until the current owner was predisposed to selling, but would have to move before the others did.

It was for the purpose of discussing and deciding on this that van Swaaij had invited Bannick and eBay chief financial officer, Rajiv Dutta, to Paris to a meeting with François Grimaldi and the financial investor in iBazar.

Japan Calling

If France posed challenges for eBay, it was not the only foreign market to do so. Japan was, in some ways, an even more vexing case. Japan, the second largest economy in the world, was also the number two market in p2p e-commerce. Japanese city-dwellers were considered "tech savvy", and the younger population, in particular, was mobile phone and Internet friendly. By some estimates, p2p e-commerce in Japan was expected to reach US$75 billion by 2005.

The problem was that Yahoo!, the leading Internet portal firm, had also become aware of these trends and had entered not only the portal but also the auction business in Japan. Its joint venture with Softbank, at the time the leading Japanese venture capital firm, gave it considerable resources in Japan. In auctions, Yahoo! had torn a page from the eBay book. In Japan, it meticulously channeled its portal traffic to its auction site and built a business model similar to that of eBay. By the time eBay launched its site in Japan in 2000, Yahoo! was well under way.

The challenge of figuring out what to do in Japan fell to Matt Bannick, the head of eBay International. An American, and the youngest member of eBay's relatively young top management team, Bannick had worked in the U.S. State Department and traveled the world. Now entrusted with leading eBay's international operations, Bannick had to deliver profitable growth. On the US stock market, the firm was trading at extraordinary premiums (more than a hundred times earnings), which, without doubt, were premised on expectations of growth. International operations were expected to be a sure and significant contributor to this growth.

Unlike in France, in Japan, the option of acquiring the leader did not exist in any real sense. Yahoo! was already a giant in the United States and elsewhere (with a market capitalization that was sometimes as large as that of eBay, and often larger). Further, eBay did not see itself getting into the portal business. The problem, however, was that Yahoo! was

attracted by the p2p e-commerce and auction business. It offered auctions in the United States as well, although there, until now, eBay had dwarfed it.

Unappetizing as it was, one option was to pull out of Japan. Japan, being a major but distinct market, necessitated a customized site and local presence. Competition, however, was bruising. Consequently, the burn rate there for eBay was relatively high. Cash flows were interconnected and the firm would have to carefully consider to what extent the drain in Japan would cause financial analysts to mark down eBay's stock. If the stock price dipped, a key currency for other acquisitions would fall. Besides, the value of employee stock options would take a hit as well. Clearly, continued bad results in Japan would be harmful to the firm.

The other option in Japan was to stay and fight. If eBay could trump Yahoo! in auctions in the United States and other parts of the world, it should be able to vanquish it in Japan as well. Besides, by pulling out of Japan now, would eBay be conceding that market permanently to Yahoo!? Would Yahoo! use free cash flows generated there to attack eBay in other Asian markets (such as China and Taiwan, two potentially important e-commerce markets that eBay had not yet entered)?

Bannick, who worked out of the same building and same second floor as CEO, Meg Whitman, was to meet with her and brief her on an optimal course of action. At Whitman's next conference with analysts, she was certain to be asked about eBay's strategy in Japan.

Cross-Border Trade and the "Glocal" Model

Separately, in the background, there remained the question of cross-border person-to-person trade. The prospects for this were inherent in the Internet. It was clear that, at least in terms of the cost of the search for potential trading partners, the Internet shrank distance substantially. After all, local p2p markets (including garage sales, *vide greniers*, and flea markets) were, to some extent, being displaced by the electronic marketplace that eBay had pioneered and was perfecting. This electronic market, however, was still largely regional and national. Bigger opportunities for "arbitrage" lay in bridging greater distances and especially national borders.

The prospects of this cross-border p2p market intrigued van Swaaij. Europe, after all, was a continent of nations in the process of unifying further and further. How could he tap into this potential for cross-border trade? Already, certain categories, such as stamps, had shown promise in this area.

Rough estimates indicated that cross-border transactions accounted for close to 10% of total activity at eBay. There was also the question of the magnitude of resources to be devoted to the project. One person was already dedicating half time to keeping an eye on and fostering cross-border transactions. But a more fundamental question for van Swaaij was what could, and should, eBay do to actively promote global trade? Should eBay remain an "enabler," allowing global traders to figure out how and what to trade cross-border, or were there key barriers that eBay could help lower, but that individual traders were ill-equipped to tackle by themselves?

Of course, potential for cross-border trade would depend on the compatibility of the technological platform across various eBay markets. Bannick felt that it would be ideal if eBay looked like "Intel to us, but Unilever to our customers." That is, global on the inside but local on the outside. Indeed, in most international locations, eBay had a local site that listed items in the local currency and within local categories. In small, new markets (like Austria and New Zealand) eBay operated a "slimmed down" version, whereby it hosted a local home page that drew from the US site. In these cases, items would not be listed in local currency or within local categories. As and when trade grew, eBay would invest in developing a "full site" (as it had done in the UK and Germany). In all cases, however, the sites would be based and built on the same global platform.

Although this approach centralized and leveraged the costs of developing and upgrading the platform while maintaining the potential for cross-border trade, it raised the issue of whether concept and platform development, driven primarily outside the US, would be in eBay's best long-term interest. How, for instance, to ensure that innovative concepts from markets outside the US, would eBay find sufficient and timely expression in the common platform? On what aspects, beyond currency and categories, would it make sense to encourage local adaptation? Lastly, since the "glo-cal" approach was not very different from the centralized-but-adapted model that firms like McDonald's had used in their internationalization, the question arose as to what, if anything, was different about global strategy in a so-called "pure play" Internet company.

Decision Time

In 2001, over US$9 billion worth of transactions (gross merchandise sales) had been conducted on eBay. The firm reported revenues of US$750 million, and operating income and net profits of US$140 and US$90 million, respectively. eBay was the only Internet firm to be reporting steady and growing profits. The firm's market capitalization had hovered at between US$10 and US$20 billion. Outside the United States, eBay operated in some twenty countries. In 2001, international operations accounted for about 16% of eBay revenues. This proportion was expected to rise to one-third of the total by 2005. Although international listings generated lower revenues in terms of percentage of gross merchandise sales (5 to 6%, compared to more than 8% in the United States),[2] eBay reported that its operations in Canada, Germany, and the United Kingdom had turned profitable.

Now, it fell to Bannick, van Swaaij, and the others on the international team to take eBay's non-US revenues from US$114 million in 2001 to the over US$800 million projected for 2005. If 2005 seemed some time away, the dilemmas in France, Japan, and Europe were at hand now. Competition at home and abroad was not going to go away. The decisions were likely to have important implications for eBay's future.

[2]eBay Analyst Day presentation, October 29, 2001.

Exhibit 2	eBay Selected Financial Data

	Year Ended December 31			
	1997	1998	1999	2000
	(in thousands of US dollars)			
Net Revenues	US$ 41,370	US$ 86,129	US$ 224,724	US$ 431,424
Cost of net revenues	8,404	16,094	57,588	95,453
Gross profit	32,966	70,035	167,136	335,971
Operating expenses:				
Sales and marketing	15,618	35,976	96,239	166,767
Product development	831	4,640	24,847	55,863
General and administrative	6,534	15,849	43,919	73,027
Payroll expense on employee stock options	--	--	--	2,337
Amortization of acquired intangible assets	--	805	1,145	1,433
Merger related costs	--	--	4,359	1,550
Total operating expenses	22,983	57,270	170,509	300,977
Income (loss) from operations	9,983	12,765	(3,373)	34,994
Interest and other income (expense), net	(1,951)	(703)	21,412	46,025
Income before income taxes	8,032	12,062	12,062	81,019
Provision for income taxes	(971)	(4,789)	(8,472)	(32,725)
Net income	US$ 7,061	US$ 7,273	US$ 9,567	US$ 48,294
	(in millions)			
Supplemental Operating Data:				
Number of registered users at end of period	0.3	2.2	10.0	22.5
Number of items listed	4.4	33.7	129.6	264.7
Gross merchandise sales	US$95	US$745	US$95 2,805	US$ 5,422

Source: eBay Inc., 2001 Annual Report, p. 18.

Exhibit 3	eBay Revenue Breakdown

	1999	Percent Change	2000
	(in Thousands of US$, Except Percentage Changes)		
Online Net Revenues:			
Transactions	US$ 179,895	94%	US$ 348,174
Third-party advertising	2,030	541%	13,022
End-to end services and promotions	608	4,959%	30,756
Total online net revenues	182,533	115%	US$ 391,952
Butterfields	31,319	(6)%	29,405
Kruse	10,872	(7)%	10,067
Total offline net revenues	42,191	(6)%	39,472
Total net revenues	US$ 224,724	92%	US$ 431,424
US net revenues	US$ 222,130	81%	US$ 402,446
International net revenues	2,594	1,017%	28,978
Total net revenues	US$ 224,724	92%	US$ 431,424

Source: eBay Inc., 2001 Annual Report, p. 24.

Case 23

Renault-Volvo Strategic Alliance (A): March 1993

UVA-G-0480

In March 1993, the French elections turned the privatization of Régie Nationale des Usines Renault (Renault) from a hypothetical possibility into a likelihood. Louis Schweitzer, Renault's chief executive officer (CEO), regarded that exciting development as a challenge and an opportunity. The French government had a legacy of being fairly interventionist—would it give up control in Renault in one transaction or, instead, would it choose to relinquish control more slowly? More importantly, how would the privatization of Renault affect the strategic alliance between Renault and the Swedish AB Volvo—an alliance that had been in force since 1991?

The alliance had been based on the exchange of shares, the formation of an elaborate structure of coordinating committees, and the initiation of several strategic projects, including a jointly designed executive car targeted for sale by the year 2000. The long-run vision had been that the strategic alliance might one day culminate in a merger of the two automotive manufacturers. Whether the firms should combine would depend importantly on considerations of timing, the health of the strategic alliance, a careful assessment of the benefits to be gained, and the lessons Volvo and Re-

nault had learned through the alliance thus far. Volvo and Renault had discussed the possibility of merger for years—as recently as 1992. Should the two firms aim to consummate a merger before privatization or after?

Similar questions preoccupied Pehr Gyllenhammar, Volvo's CEO. The answers, however, seemed less problematic. As a small automobile manufacturer, Volvo would find it increasingly difficult to keep pace with the new model development and manufacturing initiatives of its competitors. Indeed, 1992 had been a disastrous year for Volvo's financial performance and lent strength to the industrial logic of combining with another automotive manufacturer. It seemed to Gyllenhammar that the alliance with Renault was working well. While the Swedes might be reluctant to dilute their control over Scandinavia's largest industrial group, Gyllenhammar had argued for years that fuller integration of Sweden—and Volvo—into the European community was the best path to national prosperity. The strategic alliance with Renault embodied that vision.

In short, Gyllenhammar and Schweitzer would need to develop a plan of action to respond to Renault's changing circumstances. One possibility would be to do nothing and simply continue indefinitely as strategic allies. Alternatively, the two firms could aim to merge, assuming this was even more beneficial than an alliance. If this was the preferred course, then questions of speed, timing, and form would need to be resolved.

DARDEN

This case was prepared from field interviews by Robert F. Bruner and Robert Spekman as a basis for class discussion rather than to illustrate effective or ineffective handling of an administrative situation. Copyright © 1995 by the University of Virginia Darden School Foundation, Charlottesville, VA. All rights reserved. *To order copies, send an e-mail to sales@dardenpublishing.com. No part of this publication may be reproduced, stored in a retrieval system, used in a spreadsheet, or transmitted in any form or by any means— electronic, mechanical, photocopying, recording, or otherwise— without the permission of the Darden School Foundation.* Rev. 2/97.

Renault S.A.

Renault had produced automobiles since 1898 and was, by 1993, the largest business enterprise in France, based on the number of employees (61,000 in France, 147,000 worldwide) and total revenues FRF170 billion (French francs) for the group. In 1993, the company sold 1,761,306 vehicles worldwide, ranking 9th in unit output in the industry. Over 80% of Renault's unit sales were in Europe, where it commanded 10.3% of the car and light commercial-vehicle market.[1] The company had been nationalized in 1945 by General Charles de Gaulle on charges that it collaborated with the enemy during the German occupation of France in the Second World War. The firm's "régie" status indicated that it was not simply a company, but a "state body" wholly owned by the government of France. The firm was headquartered in Boulogne Billancourt, a suburb of Paris.

Renault's financial performance had varied considerably in the postwar period—it nearly entered bankruptcy in the early 1980s. Renault recovered by the mid-1980s (Exhibit 1) and in 1992, reported an operating margin of 4.4%, ranking it among the most profitable automotive manufacturers in the world.[2] The engine of profitability was Renault's passenger car segment. In 1992, the truck and bus segment (Renault Véhicules Industriels S.A.) lost FRF1.59 billion in operating income as a result of declining demand for heavy trucks in Europe.

The turnaround in overall performance stemmed largely from the accession to power of a cadre of business-oriented

[1] Other leading competitors in the European new car market in 1993 were Opel (12.5% share of market), Ford (11.3%), Volkswagen (10.8%), Fiat (8.3%), Peugeot (7.4%), and Citroen (4.9%).

[2] Only Saab-Scania reported a higher operating margin (4.6%). The next highest were Suzuki (4.1%) and PSA (3.8%). By contrast, the largest manufacturers were substantially lower: GM (−2.5%), Ford (−2.1%), Volkswagen (−0.2%), Toyota (2.1%), Nissan (−0.1%), and Honda (−2.6%).

enterprise managers led by Raymond H. Lévy, a widely respected CEO who joined the firm in 1986. Lévy's management team implemented a broad-ranging restructuring of the firm, including substantial work-force reductions, changes in work rules, implementation of a total quality management program, introduction of a successful line of new products (including Clio [an inexpensive subcompact], Safrane [an expensive executive luxury car], and Espace [a van-style family car]), and a refocusing of the firm's activities toward Europe. Renault had entered North America in 1980 with a purchase of 46% of American Motors Corporation (AMC). In 1983, the AMC Alliance (designed in collaboration with Renault) won the Motor Trend Car of the Year Award. Yet AMC never attained the desired market position or profitability, so Renault sold its interest in 1987 to Chrysler and exited from the North American market. The refocus on Europe paid off with increases in market share and unit sales. A Renault executive told an interviewer:

> Even though Renault is a state-owned enterprise, we could not have recovered and achieved high profitability unless we had been run as if we were a private company. Renault is no longer the showcase for new social experiments by the French government. We cut the work force dramatically in the past seven years. The government accepts that Renault must become competitive.

The demand for new cars in Europe was relatively stable from 1989 to 1992, varying between 13.2 million and 13.5 million per year. But in 1993, as recession swept Eu-

Exhibit 1	Renault-Volvo Strategic Alliance (A)

Highlights of Renault's Financial History (in Millions of French Francs for Fiscal Years Ending 31 December)

	1985	1986	1987	1988	1989	1990	1991	1992
Turnover (revenues)	111,382	134,935	147,510	161,438	174,480	163,620	165,794	179,449
Operating profit (loss)	(4,398)	3,549	9,204	14,385	12,940	6,299	4,663	7,920
Pretax profit (loss)	(12,255)	(5,210)	3,562	8,975	9,730	1,380	4,109	6,549
Tax expense (tax credit)	(1,330)	648	(127)	62	910	516	963	(869)
Minority interests	28	176	433	79	48	(346)	68	236
Net profit (loss)	(10,953)	(6,034)	3,256	8,834	9,300	1,210	3,078	5,680
Total assets	42,003	45,988	43,489	46,648	49,780	119,451	127,098	132,081
Net debt	61,962	55,627	46,377	23,786	17,590	81,854	72,733	71,727
Capital expenditures	8,269	5,551	7,021	7,295	10,360	10,669	9,434	11,200
Total equity	(9,450)	(11,433)	(7,811)	14,012	16,770	20,513	31,331	33,965

Source: Renault annual reports. Note that Renault changed accounting policies in the early 1990s, and restated results only back to 1990. Thus, the figures for 1985–89 may not be directly comparable with those for 1990–92.

rope, new car sales fell 15%; and in France, demand for heavy trucks plummeted 21%.

AB Volvo

In 1993, Volvo was Scandinavia's largest industrial group, with headquarters in Gothenburg, Sweden. As a global competitor in several industries, AB Volvo was an object of Swedish national pride. Total sales in 1992 were (Swedish krona) SEK83 billion, on which the firm lost SEK3.3 billion in earnings. Volvo's assets amounted to SEK117 billion. Exhibit 2 presents a graph of the Volvo price per share since 1971. Exhibit 3 gives selected financial data for AB Volvo over recent years. (For comparative purposes, the exchange rate of Swedish krona to the French franc was about 1.3:1.)

In 1993, Volvo's business portfolio could be broken down into four main segments: (1) automobiles, (2) trucks and buses, (3) engines and aerospace, and (4) consumer products. Car production accounted for 54% of total revenues in 1992. The company held a 1.1% share of the world auto

market, producing 311,000 cars in 1993. Over 90% of Volvo's auto sales were outside Sweden, principally to North America and the United Kingdom. Volvo also owned 20% of Renault, as part of the strategic alliance formed in 1990. Volvo was second in world sales of heavy trucks and buses, with 51,300 units commanding a 10% share of market. Production of trucks and buses accounted for 37% of Volvo's total revenues in 1992. Over 95% of truck and bus sales were outside Sweden. As part of the Renault alliance, Volvo owned 45% of Renault Véhicules Industriels, the truck and bus manufacturing operation.

Volvo (which is Latin for "I roll") began operations in 1927 as a manufacturer of cars. Diversifying gradually into trucks, buses, and marine engines, the company grew steadily. Plants were established in Belgium, Peru, and Canada. In 1966, Volvo introduced its model 144, which was acclaimed, "Car of the Year"; thereafter, sales grew rapidly, especially in North America. In 1971, Volvo's CEO, Gunnar Engellau, designated Pehr G. Gyllenhammar (his 36-year-old son-in-law) as the new CEO, and Volvo entered a new phase of its

| Exhibit 2 | Renault-Volvo Strategic Alliance (A) |

Share Price Performance

Exhibit 3	Renault-Volvo Strategic Alliance (A)

Volvo's Recent Financial History
(Amounts in Millions of Swedish Krona, Unless Otherwise Stated)

The Volvo Group, 1988–92

Condensed Consolidated Statements of Income	1988	1989	1990	1991	1992
Sales	96,639	90,972	83,185	77,223	83,002
Operating income (loss)	7,028	4,817	567	(1,168)	(2,249)
Restructuring costs	–	–	(2,450)	–	(1,450)
Income from equity method investments	–	1,015	1,322	1,218	96
Financial income (expense)	1,039	822	234	1,478	(1,146)
Income (loss) after financial income (expense)	8,067	6,654	(327)	1,528	(4,749)
Extraordinary income (expense)	176	313	–	(725)	–
Minority interests in (income) loss	–	(56)	40	310	1,437
Taxes	(3,200)	(2,124)	(733)	(431)	(8)
Minority interests in (income) loss	(103)	–	–	–	–
Net income (loss)	4,940	4,787	(1,020)	682	(3,320)
Income (loss) per share, SEK	63.70	61.70	(13.10)	8.80	(42.80)
Condensed Consolidated Balance Sheets					
Liquid funds	15,632	18,470	17,585	18,779	21,760
Receivables and inventories	33,346	35,248	35,604	35,087	39,979
Investments in bonds	3,956	3,455	2,854	928	–
Restricted deposits in Bank of Sweden	4,034	5,293	2,072	41	2
Other assets	29,963	35,677	43,982	51,913	55,266
Total assets	86,951	98,143	102,097	106,748	117,007
Current liabilities	34,500	42,846	48,712	47,778	59,386
Long-term liabilities	18,727	17,244	17,794	20,120	23,981
Minority interests	484	414	300	4,986	3,919
Shareholders' equity	33,240	37,639	35,291	33,864	29,721
Total liabilities and shareholders' equity	86,951	98,143	102,097	106,748	117,007
Capital expenditures	3,948	6,281	4,598	2,874	2,915
Research and development costs	5,139	6,176	7,061	6,414	6,178
Number of employees, year-end	78,614	78,690	68,797	63,582	60,115
Wages, salaries, and social costs	15,434	16,875	17,865	17,654	16,857
Share capital	1,940	1,940	1,940	1,940	1,940
Dividends to shareholders	1,086	1,203	1,203	1,203	601
Dividend per share, SEK	14.00	15.50	15.50	15.50	7.75
Return on capital employed, percentage	17.2	13.8	4.4	6.8	0.7
Return on shareholders' equity, percentage	15.8	13.3	neg	2.0	neg
Shareholders' equity and minority interests to total assets, percentage	38.8	38.8	34.9	36.4	28.8

Source: AB Volvo annual reports.

Table 1	Results from Volvo's First Quarter Financial Report	
(in SEK Millions, Except Per-Share Figures)	*First Three Months 1993*	*First Three Months 1992*
Volvo Group sales	22,946	20,023
Operating loss	(189)	(347)
Income (loss) per share, most recent 12-month period	(44.10)	2.10
Return on capital employed during most recent 12-month period	0.9%	6.2%

history. Gyllenhammar's rise to power coincided with a shift in strategy toward reducing the firm's dependence on cars. Sweden itself offered little room for sales growth, so any car-based strategy would need to be export oriented.

But to compete in the export market meant regular style changes, which raised significant challenges because of the high cost of product development. Accordingly, Gyllenhammar undertook a series of investments and merger attempts aimed at diversifying Volvo's business base and attaining greater economies of scale and scope for Volvo cars. These moves included eight major transactions.[3]

Gyllenhammar retained the CEO title until 1990, when he appointed Christer Zetterberg to be CEO and himself "executive chairman"—a realignment that would allow Gyllenhammar to focus on larger strategic issues, especially those pertaining to the alliance. Zetterberg resigned in 1992, following disagreements with Gyllenhammar and in the midst of Volvo's cyclical decline. Gyllenhammar then

[3]The transactions included:

- Attempted merger with Saab-Scania, Sweden's other major car manufacturer. Plans for merger were announced in May 1977, but abandoned in August when opposition to the merger developed.
- Attempted investment in the Norwegian oil industry. In August 1977, Gyllenhammar initiated discussions with Norway's prime minister to exchange Volvo shares for a 40% interest in Norway's North Sea oil fields. The proposal was abandoned in January 1978, after a majority of Volvo shareholders opposed the plan.
- Acquisition of Beijerinvest Group in late 1981. Gyllenhammar was attracted by Beijerinvest's oil-trading firm, though the firm also operated food, engineering, and other businesses.
- In 1980, sale of a 9.9% share interest in Volvo to Renault. This took place in combination with a public share offering. Other issues of stock took place in 1981 and 1982.
- In the early 1980s, Volvo acquired a number of minority interests in consumer foods' manufacturers.
- In 1986, Gyllenhammar negotiated the sale of Volvo's pharmaceuticals' businesses to Fermenta AB, and the acquisition of 20% of Fermenta's shares. This deal broke down when it appeared that Fermenta's CEO had engaged in fraud.
- In 1986, Volvo acquired a 25% interest in a pharmaceuticals company, Pharmacia.
- In 1991, Volvo organized NedCar B. V. as a joint venture with Volvo, Mitsubishi, and the Dutch government. The object of this joint venture was to manufacture car models in the medium-size segment for sale under the Volvo and Mitsubishi names.

appointed Soren Gyll as CEO and gave him the mandate to turn the company around. Gyll had been president and CEO of Procordia, a large Swedish state-owned pharmaceuticals and consumer products company, and had proved to be a tough-minded and effective general manager. Before the year had ended, Gyll announced a profit improvement program for Volvo called Volvo 95. Under this plan, Volvo closed two car plants, reduced the cost basis of the firm by SEK4.5 million, lowered working capital by 25%, increased capital turnover by 25%, and reduced product development lead times by 50% throughout the organization. The program had an enormous financial impact, helping to deliver a rebound in profitability beginning in early 1993.

Volvo's financial outlook for 1993 was positive. The demand for automobiles in North America, Japan, and Southeast Asia was increasing. The 850-car model was well received. The Volvo 95 cost reduction program would deliver larger profit margins. Despite those positive trends, Volvo's financial report for the first quarter (ending March 31) included the following results (Table 1):

As the company explained:

> The business climate remained weak in nearly all of Volvo's markets. Sales of cars in Western Europe are estimated to decline slightly more than 10% during 1993. The fall in the European truck market is expected to be 25% to 30% during the year. Low domestic consumption is foreseen in Sweden, and car sales during the first months of the year were the lowest in over 30 years.[4]

Strategic Alliance between Volvo and Renault

In 1990, Volvo and Renault agreed to establish a strategic alliance through a complicated scheme of cross-shareholdings, joint production and research and

[4]AB Volvo, Volvo Interim Report: Three months ending March 31, 1993.

development (R&D) agreements, and supervisory boards. The alliance was the culmination of almost 20 years of industrial cooperation between the two firms. A components exchange agreement began in 1971. Renault invested in Volvo shares in 1980 (and sold them in 1985). Gyllenhammar and Raymond Levy (CEO of Renault at the time) believed that closer cooperation was necessary to exploit the opportunities that faced both companies. The European automotive industry had witnessed a number of combinations in recent years, including Ford/Jaguar, GM/Saab, and Peugeot/Citroen. Volvo estimated that the undiscounted value of economies available through the alliance would amount to SEK14 billion between the years 1991 and 2000. The alliance was consummated in January 1991, with an exchange of minority share interests in each company; the

structure of the resulting alliance is shown in Exhibit 4. The network of cross-shareholdings was accompanied by a "poison pill," which made unwinding the alliance difficult and costly. The official language of the alliance was to be English. The alliance would be headquartered in both Paris and Gothenburg.

The two companies began their alliance by targeting economies in several areas: purchasing, quality, components, and the introduction of a new range of executive cars in 1997, on the basis of a jointly developed platform known as the P4 Project. By early 1993, Volvo and Renault had created 21 coordinating committees. These committees were staffed equally from each firm. The understanding was that the two firms would share equally in decision-making (i.e., the power would be divided 50/50). By early 1993, Renault

Exhibit 4	Renault-Volvo Strategic Alliance (A)

Structure of the Strategic Alliance and Cross-Shareholdings
(Established January 1, 1991)

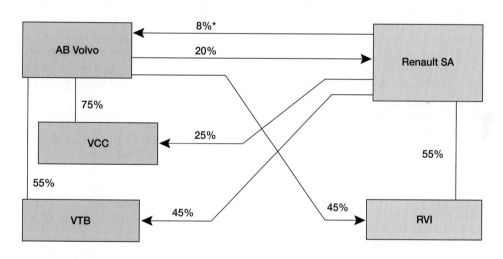

Abbreviations	Reference
VCC	Volvo's restructured car operations
VTB	Volvo's restructured truck and bus operations
Renault SA	Parent company of the Renault Group, following conversion to a capital stock company
RVI	Renault Véhicules Industriels SA

*Renault had acquired 8.24% of Volvo shares, and 10% of the votes.

Source of Information: AB Volvo, *"Information Prior to Extraordinary General Meeting of Shareholders in AB Volvo, November 9, 1993"*, p. 40.

was the larger partner in the alliance, almost five times larger in sales revenue and employees, six times larger in car units sold, and seven times larger in operating profit. Only in truck and bus units sold was Volvo slightly larger.

By most accounts, both partners perceived the alliance to be as healthy as could be expected. Components exchange had worked well. Purchasing had begun to realize economies, but would take more time to achieve the full potential. Quality efforts had made some headway. The two firms could look to such successes as the development of a new family of rear-axle drives and the establishment of a joint venture for manufacturing buses in France. The language difference was still a concern, although the French had made strides in mastering English for the alliance. Some newspaper accounts, however, reported that Renault engineers had reverted to speaking French and that some Swedes perceived that as a means of excluding them. Many observers believed that by 1993, the alliance had exploited the easy gains and that much more difficult challenges lay ahead. Two projects exemplified those challenges:

- **P4 project:** The effort to develop a new common platform for a high-end executive car occupied 200 to 300 engineers. For the French and the Swedes, the design of a flagship-model car summoned forth the strongest skills and feelings. The French were proud of the styling and cost-containment skills behind their successful new models of recent years. The Swedes were especially proud of the engineering and safety embedded in the Volvo cars— indeed, engineering was the "real heart of Volvo." Volvo's newest model, the 850, had taken seven years[5] and SEK7 billion to SEK8 billion[6] to launch. Models built on the P4 platform were to be launched in 1997. The French proposed that the P4 car be a front wheel drive. The Swedish engineers just as strongly wanted it to be rear wheel drive, similar to the Mercedes-Benz S class, and the BMW 500- and 700-series cars. A front wheel drive design would require the engine to be transverse-mounted, which raised other issues. For instance, Volvo had a modern six-cylinder, in-line engine that was powerful enough to drive an executive car and that met both European and U.S. emission standards, but was too long to be mounted transversely. Renault could supply its own V-6 engine, which was short enough to be mounted transversely but did not meet emission standards in the United States, where Volvo had a material market presence. One solution was to buy a

V-6 engine from Mitsubishi, but this idea was unpopular with the French. Finally, computer-simulated crash tests revealed the platform to be too light— the engine could be pushed into the passenger compartment. The safety-conscious Volvo engineers insisted on strengthening the platform (i.e., increasing its weight); Renault engineers were concerned about weight, cost, and development time. With a launch planned for 1997, the final commitment on the platform would be needed in six months.

- **Truck production:** Questions about truck production illustrated the need for making hard decisions to rationalize the efforts of the two firms. Should Volvo supply engines for sale in Renault trucks? Truck buyers were much more sophisticated than car buyers and perceived Volvo engines as being of higher quality than Renault engines. Because the price of Volvo trucks was higher than comparable Renault trucks, wouldn't it be possible to acquire a Volvo engine for less money by buying a Renault truck? Volvo's solution was to propose that Volvo assume responsibility for all production of heavy trucks—where Volvo was a major, if not dominant, producer—and that Renault assume responsibility for production of medium and light trucks, where it had good volume. Renault resisted, pointing out that it had a strong heavy-truck position in France. Observers sensed that Renault Véhicules Industriels was afraid of being swallowed by Volvo, and that Volvo feared losing or diluting part of its brand identity with the customer.

With a 50/50 control arrangement, both companies had the power to veto decisions. Many of those decisions were delicate. On the industrial side, they could affect the allocation of production—and jobs—between Sweden and France. Renault, a state-owned enterprise, was sensitive to the loss of jobs. In the area of new model development, the two firms were protective of their respective brand identities. But real cost savings lay with replacing a product completely; it would be difficult to obtain large savings with old products in the system. Compromises on product design would tend to erode savings. Volvo had a decentralized management structure; it was relatively easy to obtain and share information. Renault had a more centralized structure in place.

Gyllenhammar and Schweitzer believed that the two years of working together had proved the wisdom of the alliance, but they were impatient with the pace of joint work and integration. As Louis Schweitzer said, "If you want to win, you must go faster. Speed is of the essence. We must go beyond the limits of cooperation to date." He and Gyllenhammar viewed the merger as one obvious solution. Schweitzer added, "The advantage of a complete merger is simplicity and speed. Agreement between the two companies does not go as fast as managing a single group."

---

[5]The launch cycle for the 850 line took longer than normal, because the designers changed the specifications two years into the project.

[6]The development cost of SEK7 billion to SEK8 billion excluded the cost of a new engine plant built to produce gasoline engines for the 850 line. If the investment in the engine plant were included, the total launch cost would be SEK15 billion.

Louis Schweitzer

In 1993, Renault's CEO was Louis Schweitzer, grandson of Nobel Laureate Albert Schweitzer. Born in 1942, Louis Schweitzer was educated at École Nationale d'Administration, one of the elite French *grandes écoles*. He began his career as a civil servant and rose to the position of chief of staff to French Prime Minister Michel Rocard. In 1988, Schweitzer was recruited by Renault's CEO Raymond H. Lévy, to become a vice president at Renault. One of Schweitzer's prime assignments was to negotiate the terms of the strategic alliance with Volvo. In 1992, Schweitzer rose to become Lévy's successor as CEO of Renault. In 1993, he was a director of Renault, Institut Pasteur, Pechiney, Banque Nationale de Paris, and Union des Assurances de Paris.

Pehr G. Gyllenhammar

After 22 years at the helm of Volvo, Pehr Gyllenhammar was one of the most prominent businesspeople in Scandinavia. Born in 1935, he studied law in Sweden and other countries, after which he briefly practiced with a specialty in admiralty law. He joined Skandia Insurance Company (Sweden's largest insurer) in 1965 as an assistant manager and, by 1970, had risen to president and CEO, having been appointed by his father, who had headed the firm. In late 1970, he joined AB Volvo and was appointed managing director and CEO in 1971. He was prominently associated with the series of investment and merger transactions proposed by Volvo over the next 22 years, playing a personal role in their design and proposal. From 1983 to 1990, he served as the board chair and CEO; after 1990, his title was executive chairman of the board. He served on numerous boards of directors[7] and had received a number of honors.[8]

Gyllenhammar found time to cast his management ideas into numerous articles and four books: *Towards the Turn of the Century at Random* (1970), *I Believe in Sweden* (1973), *People at Work* (1977), and *Industrial Policy for Human Beings* (1979). This body of writing conveyed a humanistic orientation toward factory work, emphasizing a concern for worker safety, dignity, and fulfillment. Two prominent innovations associated with his early years as CEO were the construction of a revolutionary car assembly plant at Kalmar, Sweden (in which Volvo developed the team-based manufacturing techniques for which it became famous) and the invention of individual industrial carriers to move cars through the plant rather than using an assembly line—this technological innovation permitted the company to experiment with team-based manufacturing techniques.

Up to 1993, the business press used such words as, "outspoken," "visionary," "ambitious," "industrial statesman," and "strong advocate of Sweden's need to move closer to the rest of Europe," to describe Gyllenhammar. He was perceived as being a charismatic, popular leader. But the tone of his press treatment changed when Aktiespararna (the Swedish Small Shareholders' Association) petitioned the board of directors to disclose his salary. At the April 1993 annual meeting, Gyllenhammar revealed that he was paid SEK9.5 million, the highest individual compensation package in Scandinavia. Aktiespararna charged that Gyllenhammar had taken advantage of a board that had no compensation committee to pay himself an "excessive" salary at a time when the company was closing plants, cutting the dividend payouts, and losing money. Former business associates regarded Gyllenhammar as distant and even arrogant in his regard for the views of other senior managers at Volvo. One publication wrote that he was "a charming, gregarious autocrat whose nickname at the company was 'the emperor.' His critics say of him that he has used Volvo as a platform for his personal ambitions."[9] A Francophile, he spoke French fluently, sometimes reverting to French in his negotiations with Renault, to the consternation of his Volvo associates, who felt excluded.

Conclusion

Following the French elections in March 1993, the CEOs of Volvo and Renault needed to consider what modifications to their strategic alliance might be suggested by Renault's impending privatization. Was this the time to merge? What benefits would merger bring that were not already embodied in the alliance? How might a merger transform the alliance? If a merger was appropriate, then when should it be implemented? What controlling interests should the French and Swedish sides have?

[7]Gyllenhammar's board memberships included Skandinaviska Enskilda Banken (Sweden's largest bank), United Technologies Corporation (UTC), Kissinger Associates, Pearson PLC, Reuters Holdings PLC, NV Philips Gloeilampenfabrieken, and Renault.

[8]His honors included four honorary doctorates and the Legion d'Honneur (France), King's Medal (Sweden), Lion of Finland (Finland), and Order of Merit (Italy).

[9]Phyllis Berman, "Stretching the Platform," *Forbes* (19 December 1994): 198.

Case 24

Symbian Ltd. and Nokia: Building the Smart Phone Industry

05/2005-5274

What was Nokia up to? On 9 February 2004, the world's leading mobile handset maker announced its intention to buy the shares of its partner Psion Inc. in Symbian Ltd., a joint venture whose avowed purpose was to create a standard software platform for the next generation of "smart," data-enabled mobile phones. Such a deal could leave Nokia with an imposing 63.3% of the venture—unless Symbian's other partners, all major cellphone makers, exercised their rights to buy a portion of Psion's shares. But what were *they* up to? So far none of them seemed to be trying to stop Nokia.

As the news spread across the telecommunications industry, Nokia insisted that it had no desire to dominate mobile phone software, the way Microsoft dominated personal computer platforms. But not everyone was convinced. Was Nokia seeking control of Symbian? Could its promises that Symbian's platform would remain "open" to all players in the industry be trusted? Whether Symbian stayed open or not, would other players stay in the platform's network? The future—not only of Symbian but of the mobile phone industry—seemed to be at stake.

INSEAD — This case was written by Dr. Mark Hunter, Senior Research Fellow at INSEAD, under the supervision of Dr. Yves L. Doz, the Timken Chaired Professor of Global Technology and Innovation and Professor of Business Policy. It is based on public sources. The willingness of Nokia and Symbian Ltd. to review an earlier draft for factual errors is gratefully acknowledged. The case is intended to be used as a basis for class discussion rather than to illustrate either effective or ineffective handling of an administrative situation.

The Founding of Symbian

In 1992, U.K.-based Psion Inc. failed in its attempt to license an operating system from Microsoft for the handheld computing devices called "palmtops" or personal digital assistants (PDAs). In its stead, Psion chose to develop a new version of an existing operating system (OS), aiming at a "lighter" and more battery-friendly system than Microsoft could then deliver. Psion decided to license its software, called EPOC,[1] to competing PDA manufacturers in 1996.[2] However, the first three licensees included Nokia and another cellphone maker, Ericsson.

Their interest signified a major shift in cellphone technology. The devices required more and more software as they became rich in features and applications—ranging from games to text processing. Very soon, the manufacturers believed, cellphones would be used as much as personal computers (PCs) to access the Internet. A standard software platform for cellphones, like Microsoft's Windows for desktop computers, would hugely accelerate these developments.

Microsoft, too, was aiming at this market. But Nokia and Ericsson feared that if Microsoft could make Windows the standard OS for mobile devices, it would capture a large and practically permanent share of their value, as it had with personal computers. They believed EPOC could be developed more rapidly and effectively than a new OS, while

---

[1] The name stands for "electronic piece of cheese," an example of Psion founder David Potter's sense of humor. Psion is itself the acronym of "Potter scientific instruments or nothing."

[2] Palmtop devices were one of the few remaining computer sectors where small competitors like Palm, Psion and Handspring could control both hardware and OS of their products. Applications were designed primarily to be compatible with desktop office suites; content was essentially user-generated, like address books. The PDA industry was thus organized as relatively small and narrow competing vertical networks.

Psion's management agreed with them that PDAs would soon be displaced by "smart phones" offering some palmtop functions.[3] To survive, Psion must enter the new industry, and EPOC was the only wedge it possessed. It was far easier to build a smart phone (or "converged device") from the handset side than the PDA side.[4]

All the parties knew they must move quickly enough to encourage customers who were considering Microsoft solutions (like mobile network operators) to put off a decision until others were available for comparison. They must also ensure that Microsoft did not lock up partners needed to enrich the value of a new OS, such as software applications makers. Moreover, they must discourage other competitors from emerging. The worst case risk was an industry which developed as a series of incompatible solutions, each with different specifications and requirements. If it did, the "killer apps" that manufacturers and operators hoped would renew their markets, such as data-enabled cellphones, would be far less "killer." Who wants a handset that can't transmit or receive correctly across different networks?

A joint venture, Symbian Ltd. was founded as a private independent company in London on 24 June 1998. Its initial shareholders were Ericsson, Nokia, and Psion, while Motorola announced its intention to join. Symbian Ltd. promised an "open" operating system to its founders and the industry. Here, "openness" had four dimensions:

1. First came open *industry standards*. No company would own the specifications for the Symbian OS. All companies that licensed the OS would pay the same fees for the same software.

2. In *product design and manufacturing*, openness meant that third party software developers and device creators (such as video camera makers) could easily "plug in" their applications to the OS. Developers would thus be able to work with the same platform across different manufacturers' handsets. The advantage for manufacturers would be reduced time-to-market and lower costs (since third parties assumed some costs of development).

3. For *consumers*, openness would mean being able to download more, better and different software to add functions to their handsets.

4. *Operators* defined openness as the possibility of creating proprietary services, such as weather and stock news on demand, that could be ported across different phones.

Ruling Out Domination

The shareholder agreement foresaw the possibility that one or another of the founders might seek to dominate the venture, and sought to counter it in several ways. Licensing fees would be the same for shareholders and non-shareholders—a point that would be enforced by the European Commission, as Symbian's first CEO, Colly Myers, told an interviewer: "Being a monopoly isn't illegal, but leveraging it is—that's why we'll never become a Microsoft."[5]

To forestall even the appearance of monopolistic behavior, high firewalls were erected between owners and management. Owners were represented on a supervisory board, whose powers were to approve the budget—and thus the venture's cost base—its dividends, expenditures over £1 million, removal of directors or the CEO, major litigation, changes in auditors, and changes in licensing policy or the business model. Symbian's business model called for maximizing shareholder value instead of an R&D portfolio.

How the budget was spent was determined by Symbian's operations board. Only one person, Symbian's CEO, sat on both boards. Features of the company's software could not be discussed by the supervisory board. However, the operations board set up a technical committee to which customers, including both Symbian shareholders and non-owners, could send representatives to express the features they desired.

Major supervisory board decisions required the assent of shareholders owning more than 70% of Symbian's shares. Initially Psion held 40% of the shares, with the remaining 60% divided equally between Nokia and Ericsson. After the arrival of Motorola, Psion owned 30.7%, and the other 69.3% was divided equally among its three partners. Thus Psion retained a blocking minority, but only temporarily.

---

[3]Though the PDA market remained strong beyond Psion's expectation that it would be finished by 2001, at the beginning of 2004 it was in sharp and apparently irreversible decline, according to Tim Mui, senior analyst for mobile devices at IDC: "With retailers recognising that PDAs are no longer the 'in vogue' consumer electronic product, a growing number of handheld device models now vie for a dwindling amount of shelf space." Quoted in Matthew Clark, "Symbian, Nokia rule Europe but telcos loom", Electricnews.net, April 21 2004, http://www.enn.ie/news.html?code=9408827.

[4]Psion had considered building converged devices based on palmtops itself, but suffered what one executive called a "traumatic realization" of the profound differences between PDAs and handsets. For example, handsets are made to be dropped, PDAs are not; and unlike PDAs, handsets must be approved for use by separate operator networks.

[5]Microsoft would contest the notion that it is leveraging a monopoly; the quote nonetheless underlines Symbian's reliance on this argument. See Annie Kermath, "Symbian's Myers on Microsoft, antitrust and those memos," The Register, 1 June 2000. http://www.theregister.co.uk/2000/06/01/symbians myerson microsoft antitrust/

The admission of new shareholders to the venture required the agreement of all existing shareholders, who would ante up the holdings of new members from their own shares. It was in Psion's financial interest to encourage the entry of new shareholders who might become paying licensees of Symbian OS.

No shareholder could exit in the first five years after it joined. If a shareholder then chose to exit, it must offer its shares first to other members under a pre-emption process. Other members would have a chance to match the price set for the shares, and to pre-empt a number of shares proportional to their present holding in Symbian. However, there could not be open, winner-take-all bidding for a member's shares. If members did not exercise their rights, the original buyer could proceed with the purchase at the agreed-upon price. There was thus a possibility that one shareholder could amass a majority stake in Symbian, but only if other shareholders allowed it.

Initial Contributions and Technical Divergence

Besides capital,[6] each shareholder agreed to contribute key personnel to work on the development of the Symbian operating system. In all, several hundred employees were provided to Symbian by the partners, along with personnel recruited directly by Symbian. The shareholder agreement did not require that all Symbian-related development work conducted by partners take place within, or in direct collaboration with, the joint venture.

A key question for Symbian Ltd. was how its operating system would appear to handset owners, or in other words, what the user interface would be. Management thought that unlike the PC, where the user interfaces of keyboard, screen and mouse had become totally standard, there would be a variety of interfaces for smart phones, each tailored to different user needs. Initially the firm wanted to develop a set of nine interfaces. To further that project, on 14 January 1999, Ericsson Mobile Communications announced the sale to Symbian of its Mobile Applications Lab, based in Ronneby, Sweden. In 2000, however, it became apparent that Symbian Ltd.'s cost base wouldn't support development of even a few user interfaces. The project refocused mainly on a single interface called UIQ, which used a stylus and keyboard.

Nokia chose to create its own user interface for Symbian OS. Named Series 60, it was developed in the context of Nokia's groundbreaking "Calypso" project, a handset incorporating a digital camera. Series 60 maintained Nokia's existing product identity by offering "one-thumb" operation, using only a keyboard. By maintaining this approach, Nokia diverged from Symbian Ltd. on a key feature.

Using Global Standards to Create Partnerships

Twice in its first full year of operations Symbian Ltd. released technical specifications that could be used by any manufacturer to build devices that would run on the Symbian OS, in particular handsets and "communicators," which closely resemble PDAs. That opened the way to an accord on global standards for data-enabled devices with PDA manufacturer Palm, whose Palm OS platform competed mainly with Microsoft's software.

Meanwhile, other major players joined the Symbian venture. Matsushita Electric Co., the Japanese parent of handset maker Panasonic, became a new shareholder in May 1999. Following the merger of Sony's and Ericsson's handset operations in July 2001, Sony Ericsson joined Symbian Ltd. in January 2002. Siemens became a Symbian Ltd. shareholder on 23 April 2002. A Siemens executive said the decision to join Symbian was made only after much internal debate:[7]

> "We . . . asked what our vision was and how we could influence the emerging [smart phone] operating systems to ensure they contain the best features for our customers. Microsoft are setting the agenda for their products, we don't have much opportunity to influence the direction they are taking. Symbian, however, gives us the opportunity to have an influence over its development, to ensure the things that we believe are important to our customers are built-in."

Symbian Ltd. also pursued agreements with major operators and software firms on adapting its technological standards to allow better interoperation with existing systems. One significant early accord was reached with NTT DoCoMo, the Japanese operator who would soon introduce multimedia applications to mass mobile telephony.[8] It was interested in licensing Symbian as a platform for applica-

---

[6]The prices paid for Symbian shares were not disclosed prior to the admission of Siemens into the joint venture on 23 April 2002, when 5% of the shares were valued at £14.25 million, giving a value of £285 million to the entire venture. The value of Symbian had grown since its founding, but by how much is not known.

[7]Richard Bloor, "Dirk Hoffmans, Siemens," 2 October 2002, www.pmn. com. At the time Hoffmans was head of consumer marketing at Siemens.

[8]NTT DoCoMo eventually became the cornerstone of Symbian's "Operator Review Board," a very discrete council with 600 members, which helps Symbian to ensure phones based on its OS will meet differing network specifications.

tions layers, such as mobile commerce. NTT DoCoMo eventually became the cornerstone of Symbian Ltd.'s "Operator Review Board," a very discreet council with 600 members, which helped Symbian to ensure phones based on its OS would meet differing network specifications. Another milestone was an accord to ensure the compatibility of Symbian OS with applications developed for Sun's Java software platform, a de facto standard for mobile applications developers.

Later in 1999, Palm again joined a group composed of IBM, Oracle, Lotus—all firms that competed with Microsoft— plus Ericsson and Symbian Ltd., to propose standards for mobile applications. A separate partnership between Symbian and Oracle followed. The next year, Symbian's principal new partnership concerned an agreement with Toshiba, Matsushita and SanDisk to develop memory cards for cellphones, a prerequisite for multimedia applications.

The applications domain—games, utilities, office software, and so on—was where Symbian Ltd.'s progress was slowest, because there were hardly any handsets for developers to put them on yet. (The first Symbian OS phone, the Ericsson R380, came out in 2000; it would be nearly two years before there was another.) This amounted to a strategic risk on Symbian's part. Microsoft chairman Bill Gates publicly proclaimed that applications developers were the "catalyst" that would create a future of seamless interfacing between desktop PCs and smart phones.[9] But Symbian management believed that applications, though essential, would be less crucial for smart phones in the short term than they were for PCs. As they saw it, the physical properties of desktop computers were very similar, and applications were what differentiated them. In contrast, handsets offered other sources of value: they varied hugely in their features and could provide mobile services that were not available on desktops.

It was nonetheless "hugely important," said a Symbian manager, when Motorola's subsidiary, Metrowerks, announced the creation of the first full set of developer software tools for Symbian OS in January 2001. Developer tools enable makers of third-party applications to automate numerous tasks, from composing code to debugging a finished program. Their existence is thus a crucial factor in attracting applications developers to a new platform. Conversely, the absence of developer tools is an indication that an OS is not taken seriously, and raises the cost and risk of working with it for developers. Soon after Metrowerks, another leading software development tools firm, Borland, announced the creation of tools for Symbian OS.

Building Concentric Partner Rings

Symbian Ltd. management was determined to widen its "ecosystem." In the spring of 2001 the venture appointed a Business Development Manager whose responsibilities included recruitment to the venture network of partnerships. Over the next six months, three important applications firms—Opera, Real Networks, and Macromedia— announced applications for Symbian that were also enablers for future content providers. Real Networks' media player and Macromedia's Flash technology could facilitate music and animation on smart phones, while Opera's web browser, optimized for devices with small memories, brought far greater Internet capabilities. Both Opera and Real Networks were survivors of harsh competition with Microsoft.

Symbian structured its partnerships as a series of concentric rings. The first circle was composed of the so-called "Platinum Partners", defined as "companies with a technology or strategic position that is key to the success of Symbian OS phones in the market." Early members were mainly drawn from the anti-Microsoft front, though Symbian management later said this was "coincidental." Eight of the 150 Platinum Partner firms were also members of Microsoft's Mobile Partner Advisory Council, a roughly similar group.[10] As a group, the Platinum Partners represented leaders in sectors as different as Internet security, e-mail software and electronics manufacturing.

The second circle of Symbian's partnerships, the "Symbian Enterprise Advisory Council" (SEAC), founded in April 2003, served a much more focused strategic function with a far more restricted membership. The SEAC, Symbian hoped, would provide critical insight into how to make the OS viable for the enterprise market. It included a number of established Symbian partners (such as Borland, Metrowerks and Oracle) along with consulting firms like Accenture and Cap Gemini Ernst & Young, and IT solution providers (such as SAP). Seven of the SEAC's 11 members also belonged to Microsoft's council.[11]

The council was partly Symbian Ltd.'s way of assuring industry analysts that it was not neglecting the enterprise market. Many analysts believed that the massive installed

---

[9]See Matthew Broersma, "Microsoft Smartphone ships to developers," ZDNetUK (www.zdnet.co.uk), 5 June 2002.

[10]According to Microsoft, "The Mobility Partner Advisory Council (MPAC) was created to bring together companies and resources that will enable new mobile technologies, applications, and services for the future . . . they deliver a range of cutting-edge solutions for businesses worldwide."

[11]Shared members of the SEAC and MPAC included Accenture, Cap Gemini Ernst & Young, Certicom, Extended Systems, SAP, Synchrologic and XcelleNet.

base of Microsoft applications and operating systems in businesses constituted a profound strategic danger for Symbian. Bob Egan of the IT consulting group Gartner commented that gaining market share in smart phones would be "an enterprise fight, and it's Microsoft's to lose."[12] There were historical reasons for this viewpoint. Through the early 1990s, businesses were the lead and largest market for portable telephones, and the same pattern had applied to PDAs. If it was repeated for smart phones, and compatibility with Microsoft applications was a main criterion in purchase decisions, the enterprise market would be Microsoft's.

Microsoft was clearly playing that card. In March 2001, CEO Steve Ballmer promised that a Microsoft smart phone would be available by year-end, and would include applications like accessing e-mail through Outlook—a reminder to market analysts that there were already 68 million enterprise users of the program.

But Symbian Ltd. managers held a different view of the market: consumers, not enterprises, would be the lead and main users for smart phones, and consumers would not care if their phones ran on Windows. Siemens consumer marketing head Dirk Hoffmans explained:

> "A PDA buyer may look for a specific operating system to run specific software, particularly when you start looking at corporates, where the IT manager will decide what handheld or wireless device will be used so he can ensure the connectivity to back end systems. The phone buyer, on the other hand, will be looking at the features of the package, what they can do with the phone, and won't be considering the operating system as much."[13]

A Series 60 Network Emerges

In November 2001 Nokia launched its Series 60 user interface, optimized for the Symbian OS. Nokia presented Series 60 as a self-contained "platform" comprising "key telephony and personal information management applications, browser and messaging clients, [and] a complete and modifiable user interface." These were the basic applications necessary for a data-enabled handset.

The powerful attraction of such a package for manufacturers was evident. Almost immediately, Matsushita announced its intention to test Series 60 for use on its own smart phones. On the day that Siemens became a Symbian shareholder in April 2002, it announced a deal with Nokia to develop and implement applications around Series 60. Nokia licensed the source code for Series 60, allowing Siemens and other implementers to create proprietary extensions. A Siemens press release promised that "developers will enjoy significant benefits through easy access to both the Nokia and Siemens product platforms."[14]

Siemens' Dirk Hoffmans was frank about the strategy behind the partnership:

> "While Symbian OS provides a standard platform, we were conscious that there was a danger of it becoming fragmented if each licensee built their own smart phone user interface on top . . . we wanted to achieve the critical mass to drive the next generation of data services."[15]

Three layers of the developer community were directly targeted by Nokia and Siemens: makers of developer tools, followed by applications and content developers. Nokia's first partnership for Series 60 was with Texas Instruments to create developer tools, in the summer of 2001. Concurrently, Siemens and Nokia launched a series of workshops for applications and content developers, and each of them also created websites and contests to encourage developers. For example, games developers were courted through a contest called "Series 60 Challenge."

The critical mass sought by Nokia and Siemens began to emerge, not only in software applications, but in innovative hardware designs and development projects:

- In the summer of 2002 both Matsushita and Samsung licensed Series 60.
- In November 2002 Borland and Metrowerks announced developer tools for Series 60.
- Nokia introduced the first Symbian and Series 60-based handset—the Calypso, renamed the 7650—in September 2002. It represented a new product category, an "imaging" phone with a built-in camera.
- At the end of 2002 Matsushita announced a collaboration with Nokia aimed at creating data and content exchanges between smart phones and smart home appliances.
- The following February Nokia unveiled the "Series 60 Product Creation Community" of firms offering services

[12]See Bob Brewin, "Microsoft Touts Smart Phones, Wireless Plans," www.computerworld.com, 26 March 2001.

[13]Op. cit., Bloor.

[14]Siemens press release, "Nokia and Siemens to Collaborate on Mobile Software, Application Development and Implementation based on Open and Common Standards," 16 May 2002.

[15]Op. cit., Bloor.

for the design, manufacture and integration of hardware and software for Series 60-equipped phones. All but one of the 14 firms in Nokia's new community were also Symbian Platinum Partners.[16]

- Borland and Metrowerks released second-generation developer toolkits for Series 60 in the spring of 2003.
- Samsung's first Series 60-based smart phone was announced in March 2003.
- In the summer of 2003, both Opera and Real Networks announced new applications optimized for Series 60.
- Soon afterwards, Samsung announced that it would collaborate with Nokia on formulating standards for "push to talk" phones, handsets that function like walkie-talkies.

Alternatives to Series 60

While Nokia focused on Series 60 and Symbian OS, Motorola simultaneously developed handsets based on Windows, and embedded Linux and Symbian and proprietary software platforms. In principle, Motorola's strategy allowed it to maintain independence from any given OS, using its subsidiary Metrowerks to ensure close relationships with smart phone software innovators.[17] However, the strategy raised questions about Motorola's commitment to Symbian. In early 2003 analysts pointedly wondered if Motorola's failure to announce any forthcoming Symbian-based handset meant that it was abandoning the OS.[18]

Meanwhile, Sony-Ericsson launched its Symbian-based P800 handset in January 2003, soon followed by the more advanced P900. Both used Symbian Ltd.'s UIQ user interface. Borland announced its first developer toolkit for the UIQ interface in November 2003, a year after its first Series 60 toolkit had been available. Sony Ericsson launched its

own "Game Developers Challenge" in 2004, two years after Nokia had done so.

As of May 2004, this was the scorecard for the different user interfaces:

- Handset makers Sony Ericsson, Motorola and BenQ were using the UIQ interface on a total of six models, and another, Arima, had licensed UIQ.
- Only one manufacturer of Symbian phones, Japan-based FOMA, used neither UIQ nor Series 60. FOMA had released three Symbian OS-based handsets, two of which were designed specifically for NTT DoCoMo.
- Five manufacturers had shipped, or would soon ship, Series 60/Symbian OS handsets, including Samsung, Panasonic, Siemens and Sendo,[19] while China-based Lenovo and Korea's LG Electronics had licensed the interface but announced no products yet. Nokia said that manufacturers who had licensed Series 60 accounted for a total of 60% of world handset sales.[20]

Despite its apparent lead in the marketplace, Series 60 was still largely dependent on Nokia for its market presence. Nokia manufactured 12 of the 16 Series 60 devices that were either announced or present in the marketplace. Nokia also held the largest share of the smart phone market.[21]

Motorola Exits Symbian

Motorola announced on 29 August 2003 that, as provided under the shareholder agreement, it intended to exit the Symbian venture. A company spokesman insisted that it would maintain a close relationship to Symbian, offering as proof the simultaneous announcement of Motorola's first Symbian-based smart phone.[22]

Only Nokia and Psion exercised their rights to Motorola's 19% of Symbian shares. Nokia purchased an additional 13.2% of Symbian's shares, bringing its stake to 32.8% of the total. Though Psion's initial shareholding was larger than Nokia's, and thus in principle allowed it to purchase more shares, Psion purchased only sufficient shares to raise

[16]The exception was the software firm Freescale. The firms partnering with both Nokia and Symbian were ARM, Atelier, Digia, Elcoteq, Elektrobit, EMCC Software, Emuzed, Hampex, Kanrikogaku Kenkyusho, Samsung, TapRoot Systems, Teleca, and Texas Instruments.

[17]An astute observer reported: "Motorola joined its Metrowerks subsidiary in the OpenPDA project, with Metrowerks agreeing to ship Linux development tools for the Motorola variant of the ARM processor. In February [2003], the company announced its first Linux-based, third-generation super-phone, shipping into Europe . . . And it has an ordinary GSM phone that uses Linux for sale in the Far East, but that model isn't expected to be shown in Europe or America for some time." See Guy Kewney, "Symbian vs. Linux: Who Will Win in Wireless?" http://www.eweek.com/article2/0,1759,1238678,00.asp, 4 September 2003.

[18]See Anon., "NEWS FLASH: Motorola to make world's 1st Linux/Java handset", www.linuxdevices.com, 13 February 2003; and Anon., "Motorola Debuts 2003 Portfolio in Shanghai," Aberdeen Group Perspective, 22 January 2003. Via www.aberdeen.com.

[19]In 1999 Sendo had agreed to provide hardware and software for a smart phone in partnership with Micrososft. Three years later Sendo filed suit, alleging that Microsoft had failed to provide promised financing and software code, and had used Sendo's proprietary technology to create a device with another company. The case was eventually settled, but it did not contribute to improving Microsoft's image with potential partners.

[20]According to Nokia's Series 60 website, www.series60.com/index.html.

[21]See "Nokia in Ql 2004" athttp://www.nokia.com/nokia/0,1522,,00.html?orig=/2004/Ql/index.html.

[22]Peter Sayer, "Motorola Selling Stake in Symbian Consortium." IDG News Service, 29 August 2003.

its stake to 31.1%. Psion's directors said they wanted to regain "certain rights."[23] This was an allusion to the fact that owning more than 30% of Symbian's shares would give Psion a blocking minority holding again. Nokia and Psion were now each in a position to stop major decisions concerning Symbian's future which they did not approve.

Psion under Pressure

An apparent reason for Psion's move was that its position within Symbian was weakening. The OS could now develop without the inventors of EPOC. Moreover, Psion's board of directors acknowledged that "There is a growing divergence of interests between those shareholders who are customers of Symbian and those who are not."[24] Only Psion, which made no handsets, paid no license fees to Symbian Ltd.

Those fees were growing fast:

- The week before Motorola's exit, Symbian Ltd. reported that 2.68 million handsets running the OS had been shipped in the first half of 2003, more than ten times the number for the first half of 2002. License fees grew from $2.3 million to $16.5 million.
- By the end of the year, Symbian would claim shipments of 6.67 million handsets. In December 2003, for the first time, one million Symbian-based handsets were shipped in a month.[25]
- Royalty revenue for the fourth quarter of 2003 was £10.9 million (about $16 million), up 147% from the preceding quarter and 220% from the same quarter the preceding year.[26]

With the exception of Psion, it was in the interest of the shareholders to either reduce license fees,[27] or to reinvest Symbian Ltd.'s dividends in R&D. Raising R&D spending was the policy advocated by Nokia at supervisory board meetings in the months after Motorola's exit.

Psion could now resist that pressure through its blocking minority. But Psion founder and chairman David Potter was concerned that "Symbian still needs cash. It's idle to imagine that the cost base will remain the same. The cost base will need to go up in order to compete against Linux and Microsoft and the rest of the market that is there."[28] The best way to raise the necessary capital from Psion's point of view—an IPO—required the assent of all Symbian shareholders. It surprised few within Symbian Ltd. when Psion decided to exit in its turn in February 2004. But it surprised many when only Nokia appeared interested in Psion's shares.

Will Nokia Dominate?

Nokia immediately announced that by taking up Psion's shares it meant only to guarantee "that Symbian stays ahead of its competition."[29] But Jan Wareby, Sony Ericsson's head of sales and marketing, said that "if [Symbian] is made to be a proprietary Nokia OS, then it will immediately lose its value to us and to others."[30] And Sony Ericsson president Katsumi Ihara warned Nokia that it must not even appear that Symbian OS and the UIQ interface had become proprietary Nokia technologies. "As long as those two conditions are met," he promised, "we will have a continuing relationship with Symbian."

Carl-Henric Svanberg, Ericsson chief executive, argued that other shareholders must use their pre-emption rights—as Nokia, in fact, was urging them to do:

> "They [Nokia] must get below 50%, otherwise it becomes a Nokia platform. I don't think everybody would see that as a problem, but some people would do. If that happens there will be a gradual deterioration in the view of Symbian and other platforms could start to materialise."

Similar concerns were voiced across the Symbian partnership network. Games developer Cellsoft, Inc., a Symbian platinum partner, worried that "the market may well interpret this move by Nokia as an attempt . . . to make Symbian their own proprietary operating system."[31] Conversely, CEO David Nagel of Palmsource, a Symbian competitor founded by PDA manufacturer Palm, happily suggested that after Nokia's move, "other handset manufacturers may prefer to look at operating systems without that kind of

[23]Psion PLC, "Frequently Asked Questions." This document was posted on www.psion.co.uk by the firm's directors in February 2004, following the announcement of the forthcoming sale of Psion's stake to Nokia, and an ensuing shareholder protest.

[24]Psion PLC, "Statement regarding the disposal of Symbian Investment," 4 March 2004.

[25]Tony Hallett, "Investor Backs Symbian IPO over Sale to Nokia." www.silicon.com, 5 March 2004.

[26]Symbian Press Release, "Symbian Limited Q4 2003 Results." www.symbian.com, 23 February 2004.

[27]At the time Symbian Ltd.'s royalties on the OS were $7.25 per unit for the first 2 million units shipped by a licensee and $5 per unit thereafter.

[28]Gareth Vorster, "Symbian sale is £1bn mistake, shareholders claim." Seewww.netimperative.com, 10 March 2004.

[29]Quoted in Reuters, "Symbian Network Must be 'Vendor Neutral'," 10 March 2004.

[30]Quoted in Andy Reinhardt, "What's Nokia's Plan for Symbian?" www.technewsworld.com, 15 February 2004.

[31]Quoted in Chris Preimesberger, "Is Nokia trying to take over Symbian?" http://itmanagersjournal.com/, 9 February 2004.

alignment problem."[32] Likewise, Opera announced that it had created an interface for smart phones called the "Opera Platform," which could run on any OS.

Was Symbian OS indeed destined to become a Nokia platform only? What were Symbian Ltd.'s other partners likely to do—stay or go? Was Nokia's only real choice to take control, or should it try to avoid finding itself alone at the top of the Symbian ecosystem? Was Symbian OS still the open ecosystem it had set out to be, or was that vision dead?

Appendix One

Unlocking the Value in Smart Phones: Value Layer[33] of a New Industry and How They Interact

What the end user sees ("Top level")

Content Providers (What can we access?)

Games, news, information, services: Can be created by third-party providers or other, larger players, such as network operators seeking extra revenue. However, if operators or other big players seek too much control/revenue, they risk driving away smaller providers with innovative content!

Applications Software (How do we access it?)

Web browsers, calendars/agendas, news and mail readers, text capture and entry, taking pictures, recording sound, anti-virus . . . applications software allows you to perform specific functions with your phone. May be bundled with the operating system, as well as licensed from or created by a third-party provider.

User Interface (How do we get to the applications?)

Like Windows on the desktop, the user interface simplifies stopping and starting applications. In both Windows and MacIntosh computer, the manufacturer of the operating system creates the user interface and key applications, but a user interface may also be created by a third party, as is common with Linux on desktops.

Service Hardware ("Hard" platform and Plug-ins)

Without a hardware platform, there is no point in creating applications. The user interface affects the hardware: Do we want a stylus, or just a keyboard? So do applications: Does the phone take pictures? Components may be provided by EMS (electronic manufacturing services) firms or niche manufacturers, but generally overall design and specifications will be reserved to the OEM.

Service Software (Enable development)

These tools make writing applications for a device, or porting applications to it form other platforms, much faster and easier. They also make it easier to create and retain applications developer communities around a given platform.

System Software (The "soft" platform)

In the early days of PCs, and today in the PDA industry, virtually every hardware OEM had its own operating system. Today systems are increasingly open, to ensure larger ecosystems, and because creating a viable OS may be beyond any one firm.

Delivery Technologies/Channels (Network operators)

The network is more than wires and airwaves. It is a set of technical specifications that enable interoperability of hardware and software with other networks, which gives the operator a direct interest in and influence over software platforms. And, it is the commercial interface to the customer. That allows the operator to sell content directly to the end user, and to greatly influence applications built in to hardware.

Industry "backbone" (Infrastructure)

---

[32]Quoted in Anon., "Palm ups the stakes in the battle for smartphone share." www.computershopper.co.uk, 19 February 2004.

[33]This schematic is not intended to be definitive or complete, but to suggest the broad outlines of the necessary components of the smart phone ecosystem, where individual firms might fit into it, and how the layers influence one another.

Case 25

British Airways—USAir: Structuring a Global Strategic Alliance (A)

UVA-OB-0584

Within a week after having this whole alliance laid out, we were at it. At that point, I would say I was a little bit dazed. We basically had in front of us six weeks to engineer how we were going to go about this. What were the principles, what was the tone, how are we going to motivate people, how are we going to control the process, how are we going to get information to our respective officers—an awful lot of anticipating and engineering.

This would all lead up to the first senior officers meeting between the companies in March 1993. This was where we were going to be asked to lay out what we called the "blueprint" for the coordination effort: here's how it should work, here's how our management should be formed into teams to work together, here is how their recommendations and findings should be passed forward for review.

DARDEN This case was prepared by Theodore M. Forbes III, Lynn A. Isabella, Robert E. Spekman, and Thomas C. MacAvoy, of the Darden School. The authors gratefully acknowledge the financial support of the International Consortium for Executive Development Research (ICEDR) and the Darden School Foundation. The case was written as a basis for class discussion rather than to illustrate effective or ineffective handling of an administrative situation. Copyright © 1995 by the University of Virginia Darden School Foundation, Charlottesville, VA. All rights reserved. *To order copies, send an e-mail to sales@dardenpublishing.com. No part of this publication may be reproduced, stored in a retrieval system, used in a spreadsheet, or transmitted in any form or by any means— electronic, mechanical, photocopying, recording, or otherwise— without the permission of the Darden School Foundation.* Rev. 7/97.

This was how Rich Wilson of USAir, one of the four members of the team charged with implementing the recently initiated strategic alliance between British Airways and USAir, described the challenge that lay in front of him and his three colleagues on the BA–USAir Coordination Team. The team was scheduled to begin its work in January 1993 and would have just a few weeks to create the blueprint for how the alliance would be operationalized and governed. In March 1993, the team was expected to present its recommendations at a meeting of the senior officers of the two firms. Both sides had high expectations, but neither was quite clear how the two airlines would be brought together into a structure that would facilitate the business of the alliance. Yet Sir Colin Marshall, chair of British Airways, and Seth Schofield, chair, president, and chief executive officer (CEO) of USAir, would definitely expect an answer in six weeks.

British Airways PLC[1]

In 1923, the British Parliament asked the Civil Air Transport Subsidies Committee to form a national airline that would serve the various countries that constituted the British Empire. Imperial Air Transport, formed by combining and subsidizing a number of small, private companies, was formed in 1924, and by 1936, all the empire's countries were linked by air travel. In 1935, three small airlines merged to form British Airways. With a fleet of faster, longer-range Lockheed Electras, the upstart soon posed a major threat to Imperial. Parliament, seeking to protect Imperial, proposed that the two merge, and in 1939, British Overseas Airways Corporation (BOAC) was formed. BOAC grew quickly both during and after World War II, supplying

[1] *The International Director of Business Histories,* (ed.) (Thomas Derdak, Chicago, IL: St. James Press, 1988).

logistical support to the British war and later its reconstruction effort. The company became heavily loaded with debt through the 1950s and 1960s as it acquired new aircraft, experienced severe swings in capacity as passenger traffic ebbed and flowed, and began to compete internationally with the large U.S. airlines. The British government, unwilling to see its flagship airlines go under, continually subsidized the losses. By the late 1960s, the market turned around and BOAC became extremely profitable; by 1972, it had retired its debt to the government. Throughout the 1970s, the airline was reorganized several times by the government. In 1972, it was merged with its sister carrier, British European Airways, and in 1974, the two were renamed, creating the British Airways Group (BA). BA gained world renown as it launched service of the first supersonic transport (SST), the Concorde, in 1976.

In 1980, Prime Minister Margaret Thatcher began initiatives that would lead to privatization of the state-controlled airline. She installed a new chair, Lord King, who began to rationalize unprofitable routes and adopt aggressive marketing and management techniques. Lord King built strong relationships with the large, heavily unionized labor force, and by 1983, he had successfully reduced head counts from 60,000 to 38,000—without a strike. At the same time, then-CEO Sir Colin Marshall fired 50 top managers and replaced them with young executives who largely were from outside the industry. This corps of management launched an aggressive campaign to develop a new image for the airline, based on new colors and logo, new aircraft, and a focus on punctuality, reliability, and exceptional customer service. In 1985, the firm was made a public limited company, effectively privatizing the highly profitable airline completely. British Airways PLC (BA) used its healthy cash flow to grow and expand aggressively, and by the early 1990s, it had turned its eye toward the heavily traveled transatlantic market.

USAir Group, Inc.[2]

In 1953, All American Airways, which had been a regional carrier serving remote communities of Pennsylvania and West Virginia, changed its name to Allegheny Airlines. The firm grew rapidly under government regulation during the 1950s and 1960s, based on a network of routes assigned to it by the Civil Aeronautics Board. Allegheny subcontracted its less profitable routes to smaller, more efficient carriers; each of those, in turn, fed into Allegheny's route system that was expanding rapidly through a series of acquisitions. By

the mid-1970s, the company had become a major regional airline based out of Pittsburgh, Pennsylvania. Allegheny suffered, however, from a serious perception problem among its passengers. Because it faced no competition, it had little incentive to improve.

This all changed with the U.S. Airline Deregulation Act of 1978. Allegheny was suddenly free to offer routes to Arizona, Texas, or Florida. A 1978 survey of its passengers ranked Allegheny far behind a nonexistent airline, "USAir." Infuriated, Allegheny's CEO Edwin Colodny changed the name of the company to USAir and embarked on a program to upgrade the firm's image. He inaugurated routes to the southwest, bought new airplanes, and focused his competitive energy on the fact that two-thirds of U.S. domestic air travel covered fewer than 1,000 miles. Soon, USAir became a major force in the industry, and by the mid-1980s, it was the most profitable carrier in the United States. While the company's on-time and service statistics had improved dramatically, the focus on shorter routes was expensive, since turnaround times and maintenance costs were the same, regardless of trip length. Thus, the company was forced to live with a higher cost structure than its industry peers. In 1986, under CEO Seth Schofield, the predominantly East Coast firm acquired Pacific Southwest Airlines, and expanded to the West Coast market. In 1987, USAir absorbed Piedmont Airlines, which served the mid-Atlantic region, and in 1990–1992, the company launched international routes to Germany, France, and the United Kingdom. Yet all that expansion came at a high cost. Duplication of routes, hubs, personnel, high-priced union labor contracts, and expensive new long-range airplanes were part of the price USAir paid in its attempt to become a major player in the U.S. airline industry. By the late 1980s, the company began to lose money rapidly, and by the early 1990s, its financial viability had begun to be questioned. In 1991, Colodny retired, and Seth Schofield, former vice president of operations, took over the controls.

The Alliance Is Announced

Rumors of an alliance between the two airlines had been swirling for months. In July 1992, Sir Colin Marshall, chairperson of British Airways, and Seth Schofield, chairperson, president, and CEO of USAir Group, finally confirmed them. Both BA and USAir had experimented with strategic alliances before: BA had worked with KLM, United, and Northwest; USAir had been involved with Lufthansa and Air Canada. Yet, for a variety of reasons, ranging from unfavorable political conditions to cultural incompatibility to outright strategic differences, none of those efforts had survived. This alliance, however, promised to be different. It

[2]*The International Director of Business Histories,* (ed.) (Thomas Derdak, Chicago, IL: St. James Press, 1988).

involved firm commitments on both sides; moreover, BA had taken an equity position in its new partner.

The idea for an alliance had begun as the result of an informal discussion at a chance meeting in a New York investment banker's office, between USAir's vice president for marketing and British Air's director of corporate strategy. Following that conversation, Schofield and Marshall were introduced to one another. The two leaders quickly became friends. According to a senior BA executive:

> They have very strong common visions as to what proper business is all about, as well as getting on per-

sonally. There is a foundation for the personal relationship, not just that they like each other, but the way that they've lived their lives—the way they have practiced their business. Their beliefs have been very similar—moving toward the same point at the same time.

Once Marshall and Schofield realized the degree to which their views were parallel (Exhibit 1 provides their respective statements on the future of the industry), the idea of an alliance quickly followed. It was soon to become one of the most widely publicized, controversial ventures in corporate

---

Exhibit 1	British Airways—USAir: Structuring a Global Strategic Alliance (A)

Global Vision

Sir Colin Marshall Chairperson of British Airways Outlines His *Global Vision*

A world air transport network unhampered by the competitive constraints of political discrimination, and able to serve varied global markets with customized, but complementary range of services under the guarantee of one brand.

This is the vision of the future, which the contemporary business strategies of British Airways foresee and are geared to making reality.

To the casual observer and even the frequent airline user, the ways of the air transport business can seem complex in the extreme. In particular, the British Airways drive to invest in other airlines, and the publicly reported industry debates, which have attended them, can easily create confusion. It is the same with most innovations.

British Airways is at the forefront in breaking the mold of the traditional structure of the airline industry, which was arguably created for the benefit of aviation development, rather than the benefit of the customer.

For reasons which linger hazily in the mists of history, international airlines have operated to a commercial regime dictated by governments at either end of every single route of every single network in the world. Mostly, the airlines have been owned in the whole or in part by those same governments.

That is why the kind of competition in service, product and pricing, delivered as a matter of course in other industries, has been lacking in the field of international scheduled air services.

In recent years, however, there have been the stirrings of fundamental change in air transport. They have been brought about by two key factors: the sheer growth in volume and ambition of consumer demand; and the appetite of efficient airlines to respond to it.

The result is the process we call deregulation, or "open skies"— the lifting of government controls over our commercial activities to allow airlines the freedom to compete as freely as they and their customers desire.

Deregulation has occurred in the U.S. domestic market, in the United Kingdom and, more recently, in the EC with the emergence of the single market. The forces, which prompted these moves, are now swirling around the world.

A World of Service for Our Customers

We shall, therefore, see more open skies breaking out in more markets. Ultimately, there is no sound reason to believe that there will not be a single global market in air transport.

The old barriers which have contained even the biggest and strongest airlines within tight, national compartments are crashing down. The result is that growth, expansion, and investment across borders, in the way of most other major industries, is becoming available.

Instead of old, loosely connected national and regional networks of airlines with disparate products and varying standards, we are able to contemplate the building of integrated world transport systems offering consistency throughout.

They will emerge through international amalgamation of one kind or another; and, in the end, I believe there could be perhaps 10 or 12 such global systems, operating on a multinational basis from a range of geographically strategic hubs.

Against this exciting, but demanding, background of development, it is my objective that British Airways should form the core and motivating force of the first and most successful global combine.

Accordingly, we have set about seeking international partners who are like-minded in attitude to quality of product and

Exhibit 1	British Airways—USAir: Structuring a Global Strategic Alliance (A)—Continued

commitment to service. They must also offer network fit, in which route structures are complementary, to develop more choice and more competition for the consumer. In USAir, Quantas, Deutsche BA and TAT European Airlines, we have found them.

The overall world alliance produced through the catalyst of British Airways' investment and the British Airways brand will create a whole new set of air transport dynamics for the twenty-first century.

The most important one comes from recognition of the fact that airline regulations is [sic] rapidly passing from the restrictive grip of government to the free reign of the consumer.

The British Airways global alliance demonstrates the strength of our commitment to respond.

Not so long ago, Marshall McLuhan's "global village" was considered a radically new idea. Now, we see references to "globalization" and the "global economy" everywhere.

The notion of a "shrinking" world is hardly new. Bringing the world together through trade dates back to the Phoenicians. World trade flourished even when there were disagreements over the size and shape of the world itself, and when most people still believed that the Earth was the center of the universe.

Another not-so-new trend is foreign investment. Individuals and institutions have been investing their resources in foreign lands for many centuries. During the 18th and 19th centuries, erratic tariff wars did much to hinder the flow of goods, but had little effect on the flow of capital.

In the nineteenth century, for example, British investment contributed financing as well as foundation stock to the American cattle industry. The prospectors who broke open gold fields in California and the Yukon came from all over the world. So did much of the mining company investment and technology that followed them.

In this century, examples abound. You can drive an American-manufactured foreign car, fill it with foreign oil marketed by a U.S. oil company, then go home and watch an American movie produced by a foreign-owned entertainment company on your American-developed, foreign-built video recorder.

Our industry commercial aviation is behind the rest of U.S. business in capitalizing on the opportunities of foreign investment. While there has been foreign investment in the U.S. airlines, it has mostly been in the form of small minority stakes and debt financing.

This is because U.S. federal law bars foreigners from owning more than 25% of the voting stock of a U.S. airline (before the Civil Aeronautics Act of 1938, it was 49%). The reasons: national security concerns at the onset of World War II about possible foreign control of increasingly critical national assets and the fact that federal subsidy payments were then being made to U.S. airlines.

U.S. airlines no longer receive a federal subsidy, and there are no genuine foreign policy or defense reasons for prohibiting noncitizen investment in U.S. airlines. While the U.S. commercial airlines remain important to our national defense, increased foreign ownership will not affect the ability of the military to use the civil aircraft fleet in times of national emergency. Additional rules mandating the commitment of U.S.-registered aircraft to the military would solve any defense objection to increased foreign ownership.

Just as the 17th-century poet John Donne taught us, "No man is an island," we have learned that no country is *really* an island. In this modern age of jet transportation and satellite communications, economic isolation has become little more than an illusion.

In today's world economy, not to mention the hotly competitive airline industry, the most logical investors in U.S. airlines are foreign airlines. Investing in a U.S. carrier would give the foreign airline access to U.S. communities where individual access would be either impossible or too expensive. These communities would benefit by being linked to a worldwide transportation network. The U.S. carrier would benefit from the new source of investment capital, which would improve its economic well-being and enable it to compete more effectively.

Both parties would improve revenue from the coordination of their schedules and enjoy cost savings by combining their support services. Creating a stronger competitor with a wider selection of domestic and international routes on what would be viewed as a single airline would be very convenient for the traveling and shipping public. For the business traveler, global business would become local business.

This is exactly what USAir and British Airways, which together serve 339 destinations in 71 countries, had in mind when we announced our proposed alliance in late July. As this issue of *USAir Magazine* goes to press, we are seeking approval from regulatory authorities in the United States and the United Kingdom. Under the terms of the proposed transaction, British Airways would make an investment in USAir through new issues of convertible preferred stock. The British Airways holding would not exceed the 25% voting limit currently stipulated under U.S. law.

The proposed alliance ensures the viability and strength of USAir as a major U.S. carrier to the benefit of our millions of customers, our thousands of shareholders, our more than 47,000 employees, and the 260 cities that rely upon USAir and USAir Express for safe, high-quality service.

Our customers will benefit from increased opportunities for on-line service to the 339 worldwide destinations served by the two carriers and through coordinated schedules and related services. Further, with the dedication of both USAir and British Airways to be the best, this alliance will not only bring the world, but also a world of service, to our customers.

collaboration: widely publicized because it was the largest such venture ever attempted in an industry that literally spanned the globe, and controversial because it involved a foreign firm taking an equity position in a highly sensitive national industry. The "big three" U.S. airlines—American, United, and Delta—quickly went on the offensive. The transatlantic international route was the most profitable segment of the entire industry, and they were not about to let BA gain such a strategic advantage without a fight.

In fact, six months of legal wrangling involving the U.S. Congress and the U.S. Department of Transportation ensued; the alliance even became a topic in the 1992 U.S. presidential debates. At issue was whether BA's ownership of a minority interest in USAir ran counter to national security interests and constituted an unfair advantage (Exhibit 2 shows some of USAir's perspectives about the fight). Despite the fact that the initial deal conformed entirely to U.S. law, the "big three" were able to convince U.S. President George

Exhibit 2	British Airways—USAir: Structuring a Global Strategic Alliance (A)

Behind the Rhetoric

Perspective

- It is a global marketplace.
- There exists a worldwide capital shortage.
- For USAir to be an aggressive domestic and international competitor against the Big Three U.S. carriers—American, Delta, and United Airlines—it must improve its balance sheet. The British Airways investment of $750 million into USAir provides this strength.

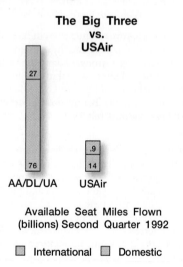

The Big Three vs. USAir

27

76

AA/DL/UA

.9

14

USAir

Available Seat Miles Flown (billions) Second Quarter 1992

☐ International ☐ Domestic

Summary

- The U.S. airline industry has become highly concentrated and dominated by three carriers, American, Delta, and United. Since deregulation of the U.S. airline industry in 1978, the number of airlines has shrunk from 23 to 10. The Big Three now account for about 60% of the domestic market and nearly 70% of U.S. carriers* international flights between the U.S. and Europe.
- For USAir to be a viable competitor with the Big Three, it needs a stronger balance sheet. This strength will come through the British Airways investment.
- British Airways gains absolutely no new route authority through its investment in USAir. The agreement is totally consistent with the current U.S.–U.K. bilateral.

- American, Delta, and United all have substantial rights to fly beyond the U.K. United has a hub in London with service to seven points beyond and Delta has a hub in Frankfurt with service to seven points beyond.
- USAir and British Airways are both major customers of the Boeing Company and neither has ever ordered an Airbus aircraft.
- Approval of this alliance promotes the attainment of global aviation liberalization and strengthens and broadens U.S. airline competition. Disapproval of this alliance would set back the movement of global aviation and create further U.S. consolidation and Big Three domination.

Economic Impact

Employment—USAir employs about 47,000 people across a route network that includes 160 cities in 38 states, Canada, the Bahamas, Puerto Rico, Bermuda, the United Kingdom, France, and Germany.

Geographic—USAir's economic contribution to these geographic areas includes billions of dollars paid for salaries, landing fees, airport space rentals, local goods and services, taxes, and other services. In addition, thousands of additional jobs exist with companies doing business with USAir.

Pittsburgh—USAir is the primary tenant at the new terminal complex at the Pittsburgh International Airport and has committed to about $ 1 billion in lease payments.

Aircraft industry—Both USAir and British Airways are major Boeing customers. Neither has ever ordered an Airbus aircraft. USAir operates a fleet of 268 Boeing-built planes and British Airways has 174. USAir has on order and option 183 additional Boeing aircraft and British Airways has orders and options for 151 more. British Airways is an initial customer for the new B777 and opted for U.S.-built GE engines to power its B777s. In the next two years, half of American Airlines' aircraft deliveries will be from foreign companies. The largest transatlantic carrier, Delta, performs 30% of its European departures with Airbus aircraft. United has announced 50 firm orders and 50 options for Airbus aircraft.

| Exhibit 2 | British Airways—USAir: Structuring a Global Strategic Alliance (A)—Continued |

Legality

Federal Aviation Act—The agreement between USAir and British Airways is perfectly legal. It fulfills every requirement of the U.S. Federal Aviation Act.

Straightforward investment—This is a straightforward investment in a U.S. business. It is not a merger, acquisition, or takeover. USAir will remain a company owned and operated by U.S. citizens.

Voting stock—Through its investment, British Airways will own 21% of the voting stock of USAir, well within the legal limit of 25% that can be owned by non-U.S. entities. British Airways will own 44% of USAir's total equity, also well within the legal maximum of 49%.

Board of director—U.S. law requires two-thirds of an airline's board of directors to be U.S. citizens. In fact, 75% of the USAir board will be U.S. citizens.

Business agreement—The agreement is totally consistent with existing aviation trade pacts. British Airways will receive absolutely no new route authority through this investment transaction. It represents a business agreement between two privately held companies and is not a political matter between two countries. The agreement should not be "politicized"

through linkage with on-going air bilateral negotiations between the U.S. and the U.K.

Competition

Consumer benefits—Competition benefits consumers and a stronger USAir will offer more travel options and competitive fares by challenging the Big Three market domination.

Domestic carriers—During the past 12 years the number of U.S. carriers dropped from 23 to 10 and the Big Three's domestic market share jumped from 38% to 60%.

Transatlantic service—Since 1979, the first year of airline industry deregulations, the Big Three share of U.S. carrier service between the United States and Europe has grown from 3% to nearly 70%.

The Big Three currently operate 644 nonstop transatlantic flights weekly, compared with USAir's 42 and British Airways' 177. United and American Airlines operate more nonstop flights to the U.S. from London's Heathrow Airport than British Airways.

Code-sharing—U.S. carriers have code-sharing rights within the U.K. and Europe, identical to that being proposed by USAir and British Airways within the U.S. United, for example, code-shares with British Midland Airlines from London to both Glasgow and Brussels.

Bush to block the alliance. Ultimately, the deal won approval from the Clinton administration when BA agreed to scale back its investment to a level of ownership of less than 25%.

When the dust finally settled in January 1993, the two airlines had agreed to enter into an unprecedented global alliance that would create seamless travel for a burgeoning customer base—the global traveler. The BA–USAir alliance would have access to more than 1,000 aircraft, flying more than 90 million passengers per year. Combined revenues would be in excess of $14 billion. In return for its $300 million investment in the ailing USAir, BA would receive approximately 19.9% of USAir's total equity. The deal contained a convertible stock mechanism that would increase BA's stake to 21.8% in the spring of 1993 and gave BA three seats on USAir's board of directors.

BA was the biggest, most profitable airline in the world (see Exhibit 3 for BA's financial data); with a far-flung route system serving 155 international destinations in 72 countries with 241 aircraft. BA was known for treating its passengers with the class and style that centuries of British service had raised to a fine art. USAir needed an alliance with a strong partner simply to survive. The company had lost $1 billion in the previous four years, and the infusion of capital was vital to its future (see Exhibit 4 for USAir's financial data).

Nevertheless, USAir and its USAir Shuttle, which ranked fourth in the U.S. market behind United, American, and Delta, dominated the populous eastern seaboard of the United States. This was of critical strategic importance to BA, because the domestic U.S. market represented 40% of the world's air passenger volume. USAir's complex web of commuter and main line routes (see Exhibit 5 for USAir system facts) demanded what was arguably the most sophisticated route planning and coordination skills in the world. Moreover, with more than 5,000 flights a day, USAir carried more than 54 million passengers per year, a great percentage of whom were business travelers paying full fare.

The potential to feed even a small percentage of those passengers into London's Heathrow, the gateway airport to Europe, and then into BA's extensive route system, could direct millions of British pounds in profits to BA. USAir's ability to directly link its U.S. domestic routes, through code sharing,[3] to BA's global network could boost USAir's image, its

---

[3]Code sharing was the practice of using a single flight number for a journey that might require several carriers. When a travel agent or passenger inquired about options, those flights that were linked by their "code" were the first to appear on the screen. Code sharing, for example, would allow a traveler flying from Albuquerque, New Mexico, to London, England, to book a single ticket for the entire trip. There would be one check-in, one rate quote and one tag on the baggage. The flight, however, would be on a USAir plane to New York and a BA plane to London.

Exhibit 3	British Airways—USAir: Structuring a Global Strategic Alliance (A)

BA Financial Data

Five-Year Summaries
For the five years ended 31 March 1994
Group Profit and Loss Account

	1990	1991	1992	1993	1994	1993	1994 US$million
$ million							
TURNOVER	4,838	4,937	5,224	5,566	**6,303**	8,405	**9,328**
Operating expenditure	(4,454)	(4,890)	(4,880)	(5,256)	**(5,807)**	(7,937)	**(8,594)**
OPERATING PROFIT	384	47	344	310	**496**	468	**734**
Income from interest in associated undertakings	(17)	6	(17)	**(11)**	(26)	**(16)**	
Other income and charges	(10)	6	(7)	(12)	**(32)**	**(18)**	**(48)**
(Loss)/profit on disposal of fixed assets	45	100	36	15	**(5)**	23	**(7)**
Profit on sale of engine overhaul business		149					
Net interest payable	(57)	(29)	(88)	(111)	**(147)**	**(168)**	**(218)**
Profit before taxation	345	130	434	185	**301**	279	**445**
Taxation and minority interests	(99)	(35)	(39)	(7)	**(15)**	**(10)**	**(22)**
Profit for the year	246	95	395	178	**286**	269	**423**
Dividends	(64)	(64)	(74)	(79)	**(106)**	**(119)**	**(157)**
Retained profit for the year	182	31	321	99	**180**	150	**266**

Translation rate =$1.51, $1 =$ 1.48

Following the adoption of Financial Reporting Standard 3 in 1993, amounts for prior years have been adjusted accordingly.

Geographical Analysis of Group
Turnover and Operating Profit

By area of destination

$ million	1990	1991	1992	1993	1994
TURNOVER					
Europe	1,825	1,950	2,064	2,238	**2,435**
The Americas	1,619	1,615	1,645	1,709	**2,029**
Africa	356				
Africa, Middle East, and Indian sub-continent		590	665	757	**900**
Middle East, Far East, and Australasia	1,038				
Far East and Australasia		782	850	862	**939**
	4,838	4,937	5,224	5,566	**6,303**
OPERATING PROFIT/(LOSS)					
Europe	3	(10)	20	30	**69**
The Americas	249	123	119	87	**129**
Africa	52				
Africa, Middle East, and Indian sub-continent		13	119	134	**203**
Middle East, Far East, and Australasia	80				
Far East and Australasia		41	86	59	**95**
	384	167*	344	310	**496**

In 1992, the directors changed the analysis of geographical segments to bring them into line with British Airways operational management structure, and the figures for 1991 were adjusted accordingly.
*In 1991, exceptional charges of $120 million (comprising costs associated with employee reductions of $93 million and the write down to estimated realizable value of TriStar aircraft surplus to requirements of $27 million) are not allocable by geographical region.

Exhibit 3	British Airways—USAir: Structuring a Global Strategic Alliance (A)—Continued

Operating Statistics
For the five years ended 31 March 1994

SCHEDULED SERVICES		1990	1991	1992	1993	**1994**
Traffic and capacity						
Revenue passenger km (RPK)	m	61,915	64,734	65,896	73,996	**81,907**
Available seat km (ASK)	m	86,601	92,399	93,877	104,507	**116,974**
Passenger load factor	%	71.5	70.1	70.2	70.8	**70.0**
Cargo tone km (CTK)	m	2,400	2,463	2,510	2,691	**2,991**
Total revenue ton km (RTK)	m	8,290	8,641	8,778	9,730	**10,792**
Total available ton km (ATK)	m	12,035	12,929	13,379	14,695	**16,240**
Overall load factor	%	68.9	66.8	65.6	66.2	**66.5**
Passengers carried	000	23,671	24,243	23,788	25,905	**28,656**
Tons of cargo carried	000	498	506	502	532	**607**
Financial						
Passenger revenue per RPK	p	6.37	6.27	6.50	6.13	**6.32**
Cargo revenue per CTK	p	16.21	15.27	15.78	14.72	**15.41**
Average fuel price (U.S. cents/U.S. gallon)		69.72	89.72	70.94	69.32	**63.64**
Operations						
Unduplicated route km	000	685	665	584	599	**643**
Punctuality within 15 minutes	%	72	73	79	81	**85**
Regularity	%	98.9	98.7	99.2	99.13	**99.3**
Total Group Operations						
Total revenue ton km (RTK)	m	8,627	8,979	9,111	10,313	**11,336**
Total available ton km (ATK)	m	12,445	13,351	13,818	15,424	**16,913**
Passengers carried	000	25,238	25,587	25,422	28,100	**30,595**
Average number of employees		52,054	54,427	50,409	48,960	**49,628**
RTK per employee	000	165.7	165.0	180.7	210.6	**228.4**
ATK per employee	000	239.1	245.3	274.1	315.0	**340.8**
Aircraft in service at year end		224	230	230	241	**253**
Aircraft utilization (average hours per aircraft per annum)		2,787	2,663	2,708	2,928	**3,051**
Revenue aircraft km	m	375	389	390	431	**476**
Revenue flights	000	274	271	261	268	**291**
Total traffic revenue per RTK	p	51.36	50.54	52.55	49.28	**51.03**
Total traffic revenue per ATK	p	35.60	33.99	34.65	32.95	**34.20**
Net operating expenditure per ATK	p	32.52	32.74	32.16	30.94	**31.27**
Breakeven overall load factor	%	63.3	64.8	61.2	62.8	**61.3**

Operating statistics do not include those of associated undertakings and franchises (CityFlyer Express and Maersk Air).

(continued)

Exhibit 3	British Airways—USAir: Structuring a Global Strategic Alliance (A)—Continued

Group Balance Sheet

$ million	1990	1991	1992	1993	**1994**
Fixed assets					
Tangible assets	2,464	3,134	3,472	4,230	**4,648**
Investments	108	108	93	546	**575**
	2,572	3,242	3,565	4,776	**5,223**
Current assets	1,295	1,057	1,687	1,577	**2,357**
Creditors: amounts falling due within one year	(1,816)	(1,600)	(1,706)	(1,851)	**(1,928)**
Net current assets/liabilities	(521)	(543)	(19)	(274)	**429**
Total assets less current liabilities	2,051	2,699	3,546	4,502	**5,652**
Creditors: amounts falling due after more than one year	(1,075)	(1,686)	(2,208)	(3,219)	**(3,759)**
Provisions for liabilities and charges	(64)	(55)	(54)	(69)	**(66)**
	912	958	1,284	1,214	**1,827**
Capital and reserves					
Called-up share capital	180	180	182	185	**293**
Reserves	732	778	1,102	1,029	**1,588**
	912	958	1,284	1,214	**1,827**

Following the adoption of Financial Reporting Standard 4 in 1994, the convertible capital bonds have been reclassified within creditors falling due after more than one year and corresponding amounts have been restated.

USAIR Financial Data

(Annual Report 11-Year Summary)
SELECTED FINANCIAL DATA

(in Millions, Except Per-Share Amounts)	1993	1992	1991	1990	1989	1988	1987	1986	1985	1984	1983
Statement of Operations:											
Operating revenues	$ 7,083	$ 6,686	$ 6,514	$ 6,559	$ 6,251	$ 5,707	$ 3,001	$ 1,835	$ 1,765	$ 1,630	$ 1,432
Operating expenses	7,159	7,017	6,682	7,052	6,224	5,273	2,682	1,666	1,597	1,438	1,304
Operating income (loss)	(75)	(331)	(168)	(493)	27	434	319	169	168	192	128
Income (loss) before accounting changes	(349)	(601)	(305)	(454)	(63)	165	195	98	117	122	81
Accounting changes[1]	(44)	(628)	—	—	—	—	—	—	—	—	—
Net income (loss)	(393)	(1,229)	(305)	(454)	(63)	165	195	98	117	122	81
Net income (loss) per share:											
Before accounting changes	(7.68)	(13.88)	(7.62)	(10.89)	(1.73)	3.81	5.27	3.33	3.98	4.46	3.22
Effect of accounting changes[1]	(0.80)	(13.35)	—	—	—	—	—	—	—	—	—
Income (loss) per common share	(8.48)	(27.23)	(7.62)	(10.89)	(1.73)	3.81	5.27	3.33	3.98	4.46	3.22
Dividends per common share	—	—	—	0.06	0.15	0.12	0.12	0.12	0.12	0.12	0.12
Balance Sheet:											
Total assets	6,878	6,595	6,454	6,574	6,069	5,349	5,257	2,147	1,951	1,621	1,318
Long-term obligations and redeemable preferred stock[2]	4,198	3,714	2,577	2,743	1,901	1,419	1,870	454	474	430	350
Stockholders' equity (deficit)	(213)	44	1,318	1,434	1,893	2,070	1,895	1,058	956	737	615
Shares of common stock outstanding	59.2	47.2	46.6	45.5	44.2	43.8	43.2	27.3	26.9	23.0	22.8
Book value per share	$ (7.19)	$ (3.58)	$ 23.69	$ 31.50	$ 42.86	$ 47.28	$ 43.90	$ 38.77	$ 35.44	$ 31.89	$ 26.77

[1]Cumulative effect of change in method of accounting for post-employment benefits in 1993 and postretirement benefits other than pensions (net of income tax benefit of $118) in 1992. See Note 11 of the USAir Group Consolidated Financial Statements for more information.

[2]Long-term obligations include long-term debt, capital, leases and postretirement benefits other than pensions, noncurrent.

(continued)

Exhibit 4 British Airways—USAir: Structuring a Global Strategic Alliance (A)—Continued

(Annual Report 11-Year Summary)
SELECTED FINANCIAL DATA

USAIR Financial Data

(in Millions, Except Per-Share Amounts)	1993	1992	1991	1990	1989[7]	1988[7]	1987	1986	1985	1984	1983
USAIR OPERATING STATISTICS											
Revenue passengers (millions)[3]	53.7	54.7	55.6	60.1	61.2	61.9	24.8	21.7	19.3	17.0	16.2
Average passenger journey (miles)[3]	656	642	614	592	551	505	528	514	505	481	447
Revenue passenger miles (millions)[3]	35,221	35,097	34,120	35,551	33,697	31,282	13,072	11,155	9,732	8,191	7,245
Available seat miles (millions)[3]	59,485	59,667	58,261	59,484	55,610	52,107	20,014	18,254	16,433	14,098	12,235
Passenger load factor[3]	59.2%	58.8%	58.6%	59.8%	60.6%	60.0%	65.3%	61.1%	59.2%	58.1%	59.2%
Revenue per revenue passenger mile (yield)[3]	17.274	16.494	16.674	16.184	16.504	16.184	14.914	14.934	16.714	18.574	18.424
Passenger revenue per available seat mile[3]	10.224	9.704	9.764	9.674	10.004	9.714	9.744	9.124	9.894	10.79	10.914
Total revenue per available seat mile[6]	11.044	10.384	10.334	10.194	10.484	10.164	10.194	9.634	10.454	11.324	10.544
Cost per available seat mile[4,6]	11.094	10.824	10.774	10.834	10.454	9.404	8.904	8.744	9.454	9.984	10.504
Average distance between stops (miles)[3]	536	516	495	469	440	407	425	406	395	374	355
Breakeven load factor[4,6]	61.7%	63.2%	62.7%	64.5%	60.6%	56.0%	57.3%	56.4%	54.2%	51.7%	54.6%
Gallons of fuel consumed (millions)	1,161	1,183	1,168	1,283	1,264	1,192	463	435	404	367	327
Cost per gallon of fuel	58.404	60.944	65.904	75.424	59.074	51.954	54.744	53.854	79.744	84.804	89.084
Number of employees at year-end[5]	45,400	46,200	45,300	49,200	49,900	44,670	16,509	14,976	13,789	12,524	11,899
Aircraft fleet at year-end[5]	441	440	436	454	441	421	162	149	143	133	127

[3]Scheduled service only.

[4]Adjusted to exclude nonrecurring and special items.

[5]Represents USAir, Inc., information only.

[6]Financial statistics for 1993 exclude revenue and expense generated under the BA wet lease arrangement.

[7]Statistics for 1988 and 1989 are set forth on a pro forma basis to include the jet operations of PSA and Piedmont as if both had merged into USAir effective January 1, 1988.

Note: Numbers may not add or calculate due to rounding.

Exhibit 5	British Airways—USAir: Structuring a Global Strategic Alliance (A)

USAIR System Fact Sheet[1]

Daily Departures

USAir: 2,548

USAir Express: 2,490

USAir Shuttle: 64

Combined USAir System: 5,102

Airports Served

USAir Jet service: 121

USAir Express service: 187

USAir Shuttle service: 3

Combined USAir System: 217

Daily Departures at Major Hub Airports

	USAir Jet	USAir Express	Total
Pittsburgh, PA	341	171	512
Charlotte, NC	371	146	517
Philadelphia, PA	187	128	315
Baltimore, MD	112	89	201

Destinations Served

Domestic:	International:	
40 U.S. states	Bahamas	Netherlands Antilles
District of Columbia	Bermuda	Cayman Islands
Puerto Rico	Canada	Germany
U.S. Virgin Islands	Mexico	France
	Jamaica	

USAir Fleet

Total jet aircraft	427
767–200ER (widebody)	12
757–200	27
727–200	6
737–400	54
737–300	100
737–200	66
MD–80	31
DC9–30	72
F–100	40
F28–4000	19

Passengers Boarded

1993	53,678,114
1992	54,654,575
1991	55,600,119

Employees

45,000 system wide

Corporate Headquarters

2345 Crystal Drive
Arlington, VA 22227

[1]December 15, 1994.

passenger count, and its profitability. Moreover, the alliance would represent a significant step in BA's plan to become a dominant player in what most observers expected to be a rapidly consolidating global industry. Increasingly, the costs and competitive dynamics of operating an airline business profitably had forced companies into one of two strategies: there were those who might survive by carving out and dominating niches, such as low-cost Southwest Airlines or ultra-luxury MGM Grand, and there were a few who might become strong global players. BA was determined to be one of the latter. According to one senior executive, BA got into the alliance, because it felt it had no other choice:

> If you believe the hypothesis that the airline industry is stabilizing in the way that many other industries have stabilized, there will be global players and there will be niche players. We were actually too large to shrink to become a niche player. Which meant that

the only option for long-term survival was to become a global player. So if you buy into that hypothesis, you need to find a way into becoming global. Alliances, for us, represented the best way to accomplish that.

Coordination

Build the premier global airline network by achieving superior levels of value for money, customer loyalty, and operational and financial performance through drawing on the complementary strengths and shared values of both airlines.

> —BA–USAir alliance mission statement

Numerous possible synergies, based on the core competencies of the two companies, had been identified (see Exhibit 6 for the alliance integration principles). There

---

Exhibit 6	British Airways—USAir: Structuring a Global Strategic Alliance (A)

Integration Principles

I. Mission and Goals

The aim is to create the first truly global airline group. The global airline group will seek to attain a presence in each of the major air transport markets of the world through establishing hubs and networks where there exists the economic conditions to support them. The airline group will strive to optimize long-term profitability as the best means to serve the interests of consumers, shareholders, and the communities in which the airline group operates. Consumers in each market segment are to be provided with value for money at a level of service delivery, which meets or exceeds those provided by the leading competitors and which consumers identify with the services provided elsewhere in the global airline group.

The integration and coordination of the functions and activities performed by the Company and the Investor constitute a central purpose of the transaction and will yield cost savings (from increased efficiency) and revenue enhancements (from improved service) that are necessary to fulfill the mission and goals of the airline group. It is the governing philosophy of the airline group to integrate and coordinate all functions and activities in as short a time as possible unless a sound commercial justification can be found not to do so.

It is intended that the integration described herein be undertaken in a manner that would not cause the airline group to be treated for any purpose as a partnership between the Company and the Investor.

This document represents the intentions of the Company and the Investor with respect to the coordination and integration of branding and certain airline functions. It is anticipated that the integration described herein shall be accomplished within five years.

II. Integration

The following is a list of the activities and functions which the Investor and the Company intend to integrate. The list reflects the preliminary identification by the parties of the core aspects of the airline business. To the extent that the airline business develops in ways which raise the commercial importance of other activities and functions, it is the intention of the Investor and the Company to seek the integration of such activities and functions.

1. *Brand.* Initially, there are to be three regional brands: Intercontinental (including all trans-Atlantic services), North American, and European. Within each of the regional brands, there will be sub-brands such as economy, business, and first class. Other regional brands may be added as the service coverage of the group expands. All regional brands will be closely associated with one another leading consumers to recognize the services provided in each region as part of the services provided by a unified airline system. The differences between regional brands will only reflect the special needs of the region in question. It is contemplated that within three years of the introduction of the regional brands, a global master brand will be introduced covering all operations of the global airline group.

   Harmonizing the brand identities of the Investor and the Company shall be an immediate priority. The Investor shall be responsible for specifying the intercontinental and European regional brands. The Company shall be responsible for developing the North American regional brand in a way that is consistent with the Investor-developed regional brands and with the mission and goals statement set forth above. The specification and market

Exhibit 6   British Airways—USAir: Structuring a Global Strategic Alliance (A)—(Continued)

research testing of the regional brands and their sub-brands should be completed within one year. The implementation of the new brands should take place as soon as possible thereafter. The Investor shall decide if and when the airline group shall adopt a global master brand and shall also develop its specifications.

A brand is defined to include not only the name and public identity, which lead to the expectation of service to the consumer, but also every aspect of the service, which affects the customer. In particular, a brand includes the following aspects:

A. Name

B. Public identity

C. Airline designator code (i.e., all flights operated within the group shall, to the extent feasible, carry the same airline designator code)

D. Product design, livery, and logo

   a. Aircraft exteriors, such as livery, paint work, logos, lettering, and temporary messages—e.g., World's Biggest Offer

   b. Aircraft interiors, such as seat covers and design, aircraft layout, carpets and other furnishings, bulkheads and wall coverings, storage space, galley specification and layout, toilet specification and layout

   c. Uniforms, including cabin crew, flight crew, customer service staff, engineering staff, and ramp staff

   d. Facilities and ground vehicles (signage, lounges, check-in desks, vehicle livery, city ticket offices, sales offices)

   e. Business cards and stationery

E. Service delivery standards covering

   a. In-flight service, including cabin crewing levels and training, catering, duty free and gifts, entertainment, publications

   b. Airport customer service, such as check-in facilities and check-in performance standards, waiting areas, lounge availability and qualifications, baggage handling, free or charged ground transportation, after baggage service).

   c. Sales, including telephone services, city, and airport sales offices

2. *Sales.* The integration of the sales function includes (for both cargo and passenger services): trade terms and incentives; sales-force manning levels and deployment (including primary/secondary role by account); management of national accounts; sales-force remuneration, benefits and incentives; below the line

promotional activities (trade or customer); telephone reservations facilities and procedures; city ticket office facilities and procedures.

The integration of the sales activities of the Company and the Investor shall be paced to preserve the existing relationships that are beneficial and strengths of each sales-force while seeking eventual full integration. The Company/Investor alliance shall be promoted and joint products sold as soon as they are in place.

3. *Pricing and inventory control* (including yield/capacity management). The immediate coordination and subsequent full integration of pricing and inventory control is a priority. The Company takes note of the Investor's expertise in this area and agrees to undertake changes to the organization and these functions as recommended by the Investor.

4. *Network planning* (including scheduling, analysis of commercial opportunities). The planning of the operations of the Company and the Investor shall be coordinated as a priority. After the first round of coordination of schedules has been achieved, the Company and the Investor will seek to bring this activity under an integrated management unit. The Company takes note of the Investor's expertise in this area and agrees to undertake changes to the organization of these functions as recommended by the Investor.

5. *Advertising and promotion.* The pace of coordination and integration of this activity shall be determined by progress in implementing the new brand structure described in (1) above. Both the Investor and the Company recognize the importance of assuring that the advertising and promotion of the airline group's services be consistent with the branding strategy as well as the mission and goals of the group.

6. *Frequent flyer programs.* A common frequent flyer program will be developed. The setting of accrual and redemption terms for frequent flyer program members and all other terms of the program shall be determined without regard for the carrier identity. All data and information, whether collected or generated by the Investor or the Company, shall be equally available to the Investor and the Company.

7. *Ground handling* (passenger and baggage handling, ramp services, local station maintenance/engineering station). The integration of ground handling at each location served by both the Investor and the Company provides an important element in the group's efforts to create a single identity and achieve cost savings. Each station faces unique circumstances and it is, therefore, agreed that the integration of the ground handling function shall be managed on a case-by-case basis.

8. *Cargo operations.* As with the carriage of passengers, the coordination and integration of the group's schedules shall open new commercial opportunities in the area of cargo. Cargo handling integration shall be managed on a

(continued)

station-by-station basis, while the administration of cargo operations will be integrated to best exploit the new opportunities that arise from the creation of the airline group.

9. *Catering* (including catering supplies, facilities). The administration of the catering function shall be integrated not only as a cost-saving measure, but also as a way to ensure that the delivery of catering is consistent with the branding strategy.

10. *Information management* (including systems development, computer reservations systems, inventory control systems, data networks, and management information systems). The integration of the information management functions of the Company and the Investor is a priority. Information management will provide much of the support base needed to bring about the overall integration of the Company and the Investor. In the first instance, an analysis of the relative strengths and weaknesses of the Company's and the Investor's systems and systems development capabilities shall be undertaken. Using the results of this analysis a unified information management function shall be created for the purpose of supporting the activities of the airline group. The Company takes note of the Investor's expertise in this area and agrees to undertake changes to the organization of these functions as recommended by the Investor.

11. *Training* (including customer service training, flight crew, and management). The coordination of customer service training is essential in bringing about the strategy agreed for branding. The management of such training should be integrated in the early stages of the new relationship. The coordination of the training of flight crew and others may yield cost savings.

12. *Financial reporting and systems.* The integration of systems development should give rise to opportunities to integrate many finance functions.

13. *Financing of capital equipment.* The pooling of joint expertise in aircraft and equipment financing is expected to yield benefits through such changes as economies of scale.

14. *Facilities* (including airport facilities, sales offices (city ticketing offices), and administration facilities). The integration of the Company and the Investor shall create a surplus of facility space in many cities. The airline group

will seek to make savings through the disposal of surplus facilities. As the circumstances and joint facility needs of the Company and the Investor will vary from city to city, decisions regarding changes to facility ownership/lease will be made on a case-by-case basis. The Company and the Investor agree that in no circumstance will duplicate facilities be opened in any city unless a compelling commercial reason can be found.

15. *Purchasing* (including fleet planning, acquisition and disposal of aircraft, fuel purchasing, spare parts, capital equipment, and general supplies). By combining the purchasing needs of the Company and the Investor, economies of scale should create cost savings. The Company and the Investor will seek the integration of the purchasing activity as a priority and in the meantime undertake not to seek the individual purchase of any goods or services, unless a compelling commercial justification can be found.

16. *Engineering.* The Company and the Investor recognize that at every level of engineering requirement, cost savings are possible by the coordination of engineering. An analysis of the engineering capability of the Company and the Investor shall be undertaken and it shall be compared to the engineering requirements of the airline group. Those changes that will achieve cost efficiencies will be made.

17. *Quality assurance.* In order to ensure that the branding strategy set forth above is proceeding as intended, an independent and wholly integrated quality assurance team will be created.

The development of time scales for each stage of coordination and integration shall be of critical importance in ensuring that the global airline group objective can be realized in the shortest possible period of time and for the most effective cost. Work on defining time scales and specific integration plans and objectives will begin prior to the transaction's closing. Those responsible for the planning of the integration should be clear that, unless a sound economic justification can be found to the contrary, it is the intention of the Company and the Investor to integrate all the core aspects of the airline business described above. It is envisioned that in many instances, to the extent consistent with the intention that the Company and the Investor not be treated for any purpose as a partnership, functions will be unified to the point where they operate under one management structure serving the needs of the entire airline group.

Exhibit 7 British Airways—USAir: Structuring a Global Strategic Alliance (A)

Organizing Ourselves

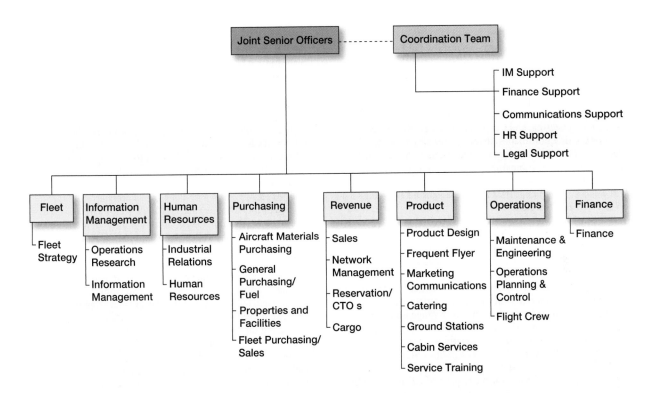

were obvious places to collaborate, such as linking flight schedules and gaining new economies in purchasing. There were also less obvious areas, such as financial reporting or catering. While the grand vision of the two CEOs was built on a combination of strategic vision, personal rapport, and gut feel, the reality of implementing the alliance would depend on the cold, hard facts of profitable business cases, operational viability, and the personal commitment of line managers. It was clear that sorting out *how* the two companies would take advantage of those opportunities was a daunting task.

In December 1992, BA and USAir agreed on the formation of a coordination team. This team, reporting directly to the senior officers of both partner companies, would be charged with actually creating the partnership between the BA and USAir organizations (Exhibit 7 provides an initial organizational chart). The coordination team would be guided by the integration principles and the mission statement of the alliance.

Coordination Team's Charge

The coordination team would consist of two senior executives from each company (Exhibit 8 presents background information on these four individuals). USAir chose Julie Roberts, whose background was in finance, and Rich Wilson, who came from operations. British Airways chose Paul Birch, who had a finance background, and John Wood, who had come up through the marketing ranks. The coordination team's mission was threefold: to champion the idea of two companies working together, to examine and define the scope of the alliance, and to manage the process for identifying cooperation opportunities. (Exhibit 9 provides the alliance's coordination principles.)

The Concorde climbed into the sky over northern Virginia and began its journey to London; aboard were Rich Wilson and Julie Roberts, on their way to the first meeting of the coordination team. They were about to begin a project for which they had little formal training, and the next six weeks

Exhibit 8	British Airways—USAir: Structuring a Global Strategic Alliance (A)

Biographical Sketches: The BA–USAir Alliance Coordination Team

- *Paul Birch, Head of USAir Coordination:* Paul Birch earned his BSc with honors in Sociology from Newcastle Polytechnic in 1978; in 1984, he earned a diploma in Management Studies from Slough Management Center, and in 1990, earned an MBA from Lancaster University. Birch started at British Airways in 1978, and worked in a variety of roles starting as a baggage handler through a series of clerical jobs and then into senior management posts. Birch worked in most of the departments at BA, including Ground Operations, Operational Research, Information Management, Marketing, Finance, Engineering, and Corporate Strategy. His job as Head of USAir Coordination involved ensuring that the alliance worked, and that it generated the maximum returns possible for the two companies, their shareholders, staff, and customers.

- *Julie Roberts, Vice President-Strategic & Financial Planning, USAir:* Julie Roberts earned her BBA at the University of Iowa in 1976; in 1980, she earned an MBA from the George Washington University. Roberts initially worked as a consultant at MACRO Systems, Inc., and then joined the staff of the Mitre Corporation. In 1980, she joined USAir as a systems analyst; she held a series of progressively responsible jobs in the finance area, rising to assistant vice president. In 1991, she was promoted to vice president. Roberts had direct responsibility for strategic planning, long-range financial forecasting, fleet planning, flight profitability, operating and capital budgets, statistics, investor relations, operations research, and the USAir/BA alliance activities. Her job as senior representative to establish the alliance was a one-year special assignment taken on at the request of Chair and CEO, Seth Schofield.

- *Richard Wilson, Director–Product Development, USAir:* Rich Wilson earned a BA from Stanford University in 1972, an MPhil (1976) and PhD (1981) from Yale University. Wilson joined USAir's Operations Research department in 1984, developing and supporting OR systems in support of crew planning, aircraft gate assignments, aircraft routing and inventory management. From 1988 to 1993, he served as Manager and Director of Budgets and Performance for the Operations division. In 1993, he was selected by the chair to be part of the BA–USAir Coordination Team. During his tenure with the team, Wilson helped to establish the framework for cooperation between British Airways and USAir. Wilson left the team in 1994 to head up USAir's Project Highground, which developed USAir's innovative short-haul product, Business Select.

- *John Wood, Vice President and General Manager, BA/USAir, Canada:* John Wood earned a BA with honors in classics from University of Reading (1970) and a Diploma in Management Studies from Ealing College of Technology. He joined BA in 1970 as a graduate trainee. His career involved a number of senior commercial positions both in the U.K. and overseas. Between 1986 and 1988, he was General Manager of BA's Capacity Management department, and from 1988 to 1990, he was General Manager of the World Sales Organization. In 1990, he moved to New York as Senior Vice President Marketing for the U.S. and returned to the U.K. in 1991 to become Head of Cabin Crew Operations. In 1993, he was appointed to the team that spearheaded the BA–USAir Alliance effort. In 1994, he left the team to become the first line manager to head up operations for both airlines in a global region.

Exhibit 9	British Airways—USAir: Structuring a Global Strategic Alliance (A)

Coordination Principles

Working together

- Create a true sense of partnership
- Build a "win/win" environment maximizing the shareholder value of both companies
- Ensure employee commitment through active communication

Scoping the effort

- Develop best practice throughout both organizations and implement where there is a business case to do so
- Encourage radical thinking—look beyond existing processes/practices for solutions
- Integrate where there is a business case to do so within legal constraints

Managing the process for identifying cooperation opportunities

- Lead by line management
- Coordinate centrally
- Dedicate resource
- Harness enthusiasm

would be critical to the success of the alliance. The "blue-print" that they were charged with creating would be a defining document that would set the tone and scope of the alliance. They wondered aloud what kinds of questions they would have to address and what kinds of answers they might propose. They had not yet met Paul Birch and John Wood, but had talked to them on the telephone. Birch and Wood had also indicated that there would be many questions to ask and many answers to consider. Roberts and Wilson looked at the fax from Paul Birch that read:

> We are also starting to think about the stage beyond all of this planning, because one of the issues that we have as a team is that—this is all very well for the moment: as a project management job, if you like. We know exactly what we have to do, we've got very clear

accountability, it's a great job from that point of view. Once this job finishes, however, something needs to happen so that the next stage of the process, which is actually the implementation of this thing, something needs to happen there. And it certainly isn't the same thing as the coordination team. It's actually lots of very small projects being implemented within each department, so we need to find a way of setting that up. We also need to talk about and have some understanding of what governance structures for the joint organization would be. So that when each department starts thinking about how we bring ourselves together, they don't develop local solutions to something that ought to be a consistent approach.

Case 26

Oracle: Growth by Acquisitions

© Jyoti Bachani
University of Redlands
Jyoti_Bachani@Redlands.edu
909 748 0545
909 748 8763

Oracle Corp. (ORCL) is the largest database company in the world, and according to the company's 2005 annual report, "it is the world's largest provider of enterprise software. The company is organized into two main businesses, software and services. Oracle's software products fall into two broad categories: database & middleware and application software." In 2005, new software license revenue from database and middleware products represented 81% of its revenue while the software license revenues from applications software provided the remaining 19%.

In 2005–2006 Oracle acquired over a dozen software companies, including some of its rivals in the applications business. "In January 2005, the company acquired PeopleSoft Inc., a provider of enterprise application software products, for approximately $11.1 billion. In April 2005, ORCL acquired Retek, Inc., a provider of software and services to the retail industry, for approximately $700 million. In January 2006, ORCL acquired Siebel Systems, a leading provider of customer relationship management software (CRM), for about $5.85 billion in cash and stock. ORCL believes these acquisitions support its long-term strategy, strengthen its competitive position within the enterprise applications market and expand its customer base."[1]

Oracle's applications, prior to these acquisitions, were integrated into a suite of Internet enabled applications. With these new products in its portfolio, Oracle has announced a two pronged technology strategy: (i) Applications Unlimited (AU) under which Oracle will maintain and continue to release newer versions of the software from the acquired companies, and (ii) Fusion Architecture, according to which Oracle will create a next generation Fusion Middleware, which is a set of industry standards based collection of tools and integration applications that can be deployed as middleware to enable a Service-Oriented-Architecture (SOA) based approach to allow any software application, whether owned by Oracle or its competitors, to be plugged into the Oracle Database infrastructure.[2]

The following extracts from the company's 2005 Annual Report provide further details of what this means:

"Fusion Middleware is the brand for the company's middleware software products, which include the Oracle Application Server, Oracle Collaboration Suite and Oracle Data Hub. These products enable users to integrate heterogeneous business applications and automate business processes. This class of software is built on industry standards such as J2EE and Business Process Execution Language, among others, thus allowing users to build and deploy Web-based applications, Web services, portals and Web sites.

Oracle's business applications software, Oracle E-Business Suite, PeopleSoft Enterprise, JD Edwards EnterpriseOne and JD Edwards World, etc, can be purchased both as an integrated suite of applications or on an individual component basis. The company's applications automate the performance of specific business data processing functions for

---

[1]Oracle Annual Report 2005

[2]See Appendix I for a glossary of technical terms, e.g. Middleware, Service-Oriented-Architecture, grid Computing, etc.

customer relationship management, supply chain management, financial management, procurement, project management, and human resources management. The company's applications can be customized to address the industry-specific need of its customers."[3]

With these acquisitions and technology moves, Oracle made a big move to rapidly grow its applications business, while solidifying its position as the database company of choice. According to Steve Miranda, Senior Vice President of Applications Development, Oracle was pursuing necessary innovation. He wrote: "Oracle is doing this because – No one else is both willing and able to make this investment in the next generation, everyone is holding the status quo, and Oracle has the wherewithal i.e. $2 billion in development spending, 14,000 developers, 275,000 customers, and 15,000 partners."[4]

In 2006, Oracle was a successful database company, headed by its founder Larry Ellison. It operated in over 140 countries and had over 65,000 employees worldwide. It had its head office in the heart of silicon valley at Redwood Shores, California. Oracle had a history of bold moves, being the first to bring innovations like a relational database and software that worked on many different kinds of hardware. In growing through acquisitions, Oracle was making some bold strategic moves again.

The Software Industry

In 2006, the software industry was still evolving. It was less than 40 years old and packaged software that was not custom-written for an organizations' mainframe computer had been around for even less time. As hardware and computing configurations evolved, software, as a complementary product, kept pace with these. The packaged software industry had three further sub-segments: (1) applications software, that end-users use, (2) applications development and deployment, which are the tools used by programmers and developers who write the applications code, and (3) system infrastructure, which is the software that the applications use to perform the functions they perform. In 2004, the applications segment was worth $92.1 billion, i.e. 47.7% of worldwide packaged software market, while applications development and deployment was worth $44.9 billion, approx 23.2%, and system infrastructure software was worth $56.2 billion, at 29.1% of market. The expected growth rates for these three segments are at CAGR of 5.6% for applications, leading to a $120.6 billion segment in 2009, applications development and deployment at 6.6% CAGR, growing to a $61.8 billion segment in 2009 and infrastructure growing at a CAGR of 8.3%, expected to be at $83.5 billion by 2009.[5] (Source: S&P report).

Enterprise applications are the software that automates business processes. It includes software applications for various business functions like accounting, budgeting, payroll, human resource planning, procurement, customer relationship management, and other management functions. "According to market researcher IDC, license and maintenance revenues for enterprise applications grew about 5.5% in 2004 to about $69.4 billion and are projected to rise to nearly $90 billion by 2009, for a compound annual growth rate of 5.4% over this period."[6]

Worldwide Enterprise Applications Revenue[7]

	MIL.$
E2009	90,585
E2008	86,158
E2007	81,788
E2006	77,417
2005	73,177
2004	69,389
CAGR*(%)	5

*CAGR- Compound annual growth rate 2004–2009.
E-Estimated. Source: IDC.

In 2004, Oracle, SAP and Microsoft were the three top revenue earners in the enterprise applications license and maintenance segment. According to a Standard and Poor's industry report, the $69.4 billion segment was divided up amongst the various players as shown in the following table.

---

[3]Oracle Annual Report 2005

[4]Fusion Development Process (Presentation by Steve Miranda, SVP, Applications Development) (2005).

[5]Standard and Poor's Industry Surveys, Computers: Software, April 27, 2006.

[6]Standard and Poor's Industry Surveys, Computers: Software, April 27, 2006, p 2.

[7]Standard and Poor's Industry Surveys, Computers: Software, April 27, 2006, p 2.

Worldwide Enterprise Applications License and Maintenance Revenue Leaders[8]

(Ranked by 2004 revenues, in millions of dollars)

Company	Revenues			
	2003	2004	%CHG.	2004 Mkt Share %
SAP AG	$4,870.4	$5,889.1	20.9%	8.5
Oracle Corp.	$3,144.2	$3,365.3	7%	4.8
Microsoft Corp.	$1,604.6	$1,680.2	4.7%	2.4
Sage Group plc	$853.4	$1,122.3	31.5%	1.6
Cadence Design Systems Inc.	$988.3	$1,060.5	7.3%	1.5
SunGard Data Systems Inc.	$997.1	$1,042.0	4.5%	1.5
Others	$53,338.9	$55,229.6	3.5%	79.6
Total	$65,797.0	$69.389.0	5.5%	100.0

SAP was the leader in the segment with an 8.5% market share while Oracle only managed a 4.85% share even after acquiring PeopleSoft, the human resource applications company. However, for the software industry as a whole, Microsoft was the clear leader with worldwide software revenues of $41.4 billion in 2005, while Oracle was in the second place with total revenues of $12.9 billion.[9] If we divided up the software industry by specific product categories, then for the market in Relational Data Base Management Systems (RDBMS), Oracle was the number one vendor over all, with 41.3% market share, with IBM at 30.6%, Microsoft at 13.4% and others at 14.7% share.[10]

Oracle, SAP and Microsoft were all competing for the entire technology stacks that align applications and middleware in the same architecture.

Oracle History

Oracle was created by its founder leader Larry Ellison and his two friends, Ed Oates and Bob Miner in 1977. At first it was a software services provider that soon became a product company when they realized they could race with IBM to create the first ever relational database. Oracle managed to beat IBM at creating the first relational database, and more importantly, to selling it to the CIA and other larger government customers who handled large quantities of data. IBM was the premiere computer company at the time with a formidable reputation. Oracle was an unknown company with

ambition, smart programmers under Ed Oates and a great salesman in Larry Ellison. Oracle's early software was bug-ridden but they managed to sell it to a handful of large government accounts, including the CIA and the Naval Office, who desperately needed better technology to manage the large amounts of data they handled. Oracle was small and nimble enough to rapidly fix bugs and send out newer versions promptly, almost using their first customers as beta-testers for the software. Having multiple large customers also forced Oracle to create a product that would run independent of the hardware. Oracle thus became the first company to offer portable software that could run on any hardware. This was a big novelty in an era when all software was written to be specific to some hardware. IBM could not match Oracle's strategy as it was tied to its own hardware and being a market leader, had a reputation to protect for quality products. While IBM was busy perfecting their relational database software, Oracle managed to rapidly install the Oracle database at several large and key customers. See Appendix II for a short timeline of Oracle's history.

The aggressive deployment of Oracle's database software led to rapid growth for the company. Oracle doubled in size every year for the first ten years of its life. It went public in 1986 at $15 a share, closing the day at over $20 to be valued at $270 million. Other newer companies that tried to create competing products were bought out or beaten by Oracle. Oracle also successfully navigated from the mainframe era to the client-server and pc era and then on to the Internet era, making suitable changes to the software and organization as it responded to the changing technologies of the times.

In the phase of rapid expansion, the company wanted to install the infrastructure and adopted methods suitable for that. For global expansion, it hired entrepreneurial country managers and rewarded them on the basis of revenue they generated. Decision making was decentralized to allow the

[8]Standard and Poor's Industry Surveys, Computers: Software, April 27, 2006, p 3.

[9]Standard and Poor's Industry Surveys, Computers: Software, April 27, 2006, p 8.

[10]IDC March 2005, Worldwide RDBMS Vendor Shares, as cited in presentation on Oracle 10g database by Andy Mendelsohn, SVP, Database Server Technologies, June 29, 2005.

country managers the freedom to cover the globe with Oracle as the database of choice for most large organizations in the public as well as the private sector. Oracle was able to continue its growth as it was able sell database support and related applications products to these organizations, after they had invested in installing the Oracle database. Oracle developed several applications in different areas of the business, starting with financials and enterprise resource management systems. Some managers left Oracle to start their own companies in order to develop software business applications that they considered to be important, but under-funded in the database dominated environment at Oracle. One such company was PeopleSoft, which created applications to handle the human resource aspects of business.

In the mid-1990s, when the Internet became a commercially deployed technology, Oracle was able to re-write their database and applications software to be integrated and compatible with the internet, called the e-business suite. During this phase, Larry promoted the integrated applications suite delivered over the Internet as a service, by saying: "If you need a car, you would not buy a dash board from one company, steering wheel from another, engine from a different company and then maintain engineers to patch together the car. That is what is happening with your software where you buy the so-called 'best-of-breed' software from different vendors to handle your enterprise's computing needs, and then patch it to work together. Instead, you need an integrated suite that is designed to work together to meet your needs." In early 2000s, Oracle was aggressively promoting all-Oracle solutions as a means to deliver optimal end-to-end interoperability and to cut escalating systems integration costs.

Oracle's primary product was a database, with applications business being a much smaller component of the overall revenues. Customers stored their enterprise data in Oracle's database. The Oracle software applications, like financials or human resources, provided a way to turn the data in the database into meaningful information. Applications offered analysis and reporting capabilities that allowed the data to be manipulated to meet the business needs. With the deployment of databases, companies stored more and more data leading to a greater need for more and more sophisticated applications.

Oracle Acquisitions

Oracle acquired almost twenty companies in the two years preceding November 2006. This was a radical departure from the past since Oracle had grown organically in the past with very few small acquisitions, if any. And these too were mostly aimed at eliminating potential threats to their in-house technologies.

The first major acquisition for Oracle was PeopleSoft. PeopleSoft was a competitor that was doing well. They sold applications for managing the human resource functions of a business. PeopleSoft was started by an ex-Oracle manager. In late 2003, when Oracle first made a bid for PeopleSoft, there was widespread opposition to the offer from PeopleSoft and the media. Oracle had a prior reputation for aggressively destroying its competition. This had convinced everyone that the PeopleSoft acquisition was primarily a way for Oracle to kill the competition since Oracle had competing applications in human resources segment that were not selling as well as the PeopleSoft products. PeopleSoft also received a competing offer from SAP, an Oracle competitor, which it considered more favorably. However, Oracle persisted in its pursuit and after a long and bitter eighteen month long battle, managed to acquire PeopleSoft in January of 2005. The long battle for control of PeopleSoft was bad for business. The uncertainty that prevailed during the takeover period caused PeopleSoft to lose key employees and customers. Customer companies were reluctant to invest in PeopleSoft's software as they expected Oracle to shut down the company and perhaps withdraw the product or at least withdraw the support for its products, should it succeed in the takeover battle.

The negative start to this acquisition and the prolonged battle for PeopleSoft presented an obstacle for Oracle to overcome. In an attempt to stop Oracle from targeting it, PeopleSoft management took several steps to make itself an unattractive target. One of these measures was to adopt a customer care program to reassure its customers that its products will be supported for at least five years after they invested in the products. This was offered as a guarantee to assure the customers that PeopleSoft will continue to exist as a product and a business. Oracle annual report estimates this to be an off balance-sheet liability to the tune of $4 billion, that was not uncovered in the due diligence process. After Oracle succeeded in acquiring PeopleSoft, it surprised everyone by shutting down its own human resources product development in favor of supporting and further developing the PeopleSoft product line. They also announced that the brand name PeopleSoft would be maintained as a separate brand within the Oracle portfolio of products and the sales force and development teams would also be allowed to continue under the Oracle umbrella. The employees that came over to Oracle with the acquisition were allowed to have hyphenated identities as Oracle-PeopleSoft teams, with no pressure to 'Oraclize' them in any way.

These steps dissipated most of the negativity surrounding Oracle's takeover of PeopleSoft, and won over the People-Soft employees who had now become part of Oracle, even though they had originally arrived in a state hostile to Oracle. This reception and similar measures allowed time for trust to be built over time and for the negativity built up during the hostile takeover process to be diffused. Having learnt several lessons in doing a take over, and having decided to keep the PeopleSoft product line, Oracle decided to acquire other applications companies to broaden its applications portfolio and widen its footprint in the customer-base. Oracle started on an acquisitions spree and set up periodic meetings amongst its managers to review the process for acquisitions, for dealing with post-merger integration and to learn from the mistakes made. This process helped Oracle learn from its mistakes and become good at integrating acquired companies in a smooth fashion.

Some of the other key acquisitions made by Oracle during this period are: J D Edwards, iFlex, Siebel, Retek, and others listed in the table and following paragraphs below.

TABLE: ORACLE ACQUISITIONS[11]   "On April 12th 2006 Oracle announced the agreement to acquire Portal Software, a leading global provider of billing and revenue management solutions for the communications and media industries. Oracle's Siebel Telecom applications have become the standard for telco call centers and customer care. Oracle currently supplies technology and applications to over 90% of communications companies worldwide, and 17 of the top 20 most profitable communications companies run Oracle Applications."[12]

"Oracle recently acquired the leading company in the BPEL server space, Collaxa, and has integrated its offering into Oracle Application Server. This acquisition, branded the Oracle Application Server BPEL Process Manager, complements the existing integration services available within Oracle Application Server, including data integration, data translation, data transformation, business activity monitoring, and support for business-to-business (B2B) protocols. . . . With this acquisition, Oracle becomes the first technology vendor to offer a fully Web-services-standards-based business process integration solution for service-oriented architectures.[13]

Industry Surveys Computer Software
Standard and Poor's

Recent Oracle Acquisition Activity

Company	Date Closed	Deal Size	Area of Focus
People Soft Inc.	1/5/2005	$11.1 billion	Enterprise applications: CRM ERP, supply chain management
Oblix Inc.	3/28/2005	Undisclosed	Identity-based security solutions
Retex Inc.	4/5/2005	$701M	Software for retail industry
TripleHop Technologies Inc. (cert)	6/14/2005	Undisclosed	Context-sensitive enterprise search products
Context Media Inc. (certain tech)	7/5/2005	Undisclosed	Enterprise content integration
Profit Logic Inc.	7/5/2005	Undisclosed	Software for retail industry
I-flex Solutions Inc. (43% stake)	12/14/2005	Aprx. $600M	Core banking software
TimesTen Inc.	6/10/2005	Undisclosed	Data management software
Global Logistics	11/2/2005	Undisclosed	Transportation management solutions
Technologies Inc.	10/7/2005	Undisclosed	Discrete transactional database technology
Thor Technologies Inc.	11/16/2005	Undisclosed	Identity and access management solutions
OctetString Inc.	11/16/2005	Undisclosed	Identity and access management solutions
TempSoft Inc. (IP assets)	December	Undisclosed	Retail workforce management
360Commerce Inc.	January	Undisclosed	Point of sales and other retail solutions
Siebel Systems Inc.	1/31/2006	$5.85 billion	CRM, business analytics software, on-demand CRM
Sleepycat Software Inc.	2/14/2006	Undisclosed	Embedded database software (open source)

[13]Author: Mike Lehmann (mike.lehmann@oracle.com) is a principal product manager for Oracle Application Server Containers for J2EE. Weaving Web Services Together

By Mike Lehmann

http://www.oracle.com/technology/oramag/oracle/04-jul/o44dev_web .html downloaded 12/12/06 at 10:50pm

[11]Standard and Poor's Industry Surveys: Computers: Software, April 27th, 2006, p 1.

[12]Oracle-press-release-from-web-page-22may06.

As Oracle acquired more companies, they were integrated in a systematic way. A number of processes involved in the take-over worked like smooth routines. Oracle had really learnt to manage the acquisition and post-acquisition integration process after the bad start with PeopleSoft and with the help of review meetings where the lessons from the process of acquisitions were formalized. Some of the routines that helped the other acquisitions go smoothly were: Oracle sent out timely letters to inform the shareholders and customers about any proposed takeover. Oracle made all personnel decisions related to acquisitions and integration in a quick and timely manner. This minimized the uncertainty and disruptions caused by people not knowing what to expect following the acquisitions. Whether it was personnel decisions about who would have to be let go and who got to remain with Oracle, it was effective and efficient to make and communicate these promptly. Similarly, the decisions about extent and kind of integration were made quickly, often within a matter of weeks. Several companies, specifically those with a large established customer base and with close ties between the sales teams and customers, were allowed to continue their brand as a hyphenated identity within Oracle. This minimized the disruption within the acquired companies and in the marketplace, which was well worth the extra cost of some duplication in the organizational functions within Oracle. Oracle's acquisition strategy and the competence to integrate acquired companies well offered it the opportunity to expand its operations in the business applications market.

Oracle was now able to offer applications that were 'best of breed'. They could reach a much larger customer base. The applications were sold to their traditional established database customers, as well as new customers who came with the acquired companies. When Oracle acquired a large company like Siebel or J D Edwards, they also acquired all the customers of these applications companies. These newly acquired customers had installed the applications from the acquired companies, but they did not necessarily run these applications on Oracle databases. They could have these applications running on and supported by other competing database companies, like SAP or IBM, but they still became Oracle customers for applications now. According to Oracle CEO, Charles Philips, 72% of SAP customers use Fusion Middleware, for example, EDS, BASF the Chemical Company, Lufthansa flight training, Burger King, etc.[14] These customers on non-Oracle databases with Oracle business applications were potential targets for cross-selling different Oracle products and services. Oracle offered them the convenience of dealing with a single vendor for both applications as well as the database. These ac-quisitions opened up a way for Oracle to make in-roads into the applications business as well as grow its traditional database business. This latter bonus was particularly valuable as the database market for the larger organizations of the world was becoming saturated by this time as most major organizations had made their choices in that arena.

Applications Unlimited

The post integration strategy was driven by three principles: (i) Protect—lifetime support, (ii) Extend—add new capabilities, and (iii) Evolve—Fusion applications built on Fusion middleware.[15] When Oracle realized that a number of customers were delaying their software investments in order to wait till Oracle had decided what it was doing in the post-acquisition world. These delayed software investments could have had a serious impact on Oracle's bottom line. Hence Oracle had to take a clear position now. The need for creating and communicating a clear strategy was evident. This is when Oracle announced these three guiding principles. As further follow up on these principles, the two pronged strategy of Applications Unlimited and Fusion were announced. Fusion middleware was to find a way to technologically assimilate the acquired company's software products into its own suite of products. In the meantime, the focus was to be on the Applications Unlimited initiative.

The Applications Unlimited initiative assured the customers that Oracle would continue to invest and improve the acquired products and release the next generation of these as planned and needed. The acquired technologies that were not being supported under the Applications Unlimited initiative or were to be discontinued were announced within weeks of the acquisition. If Oracle decided to keep the products and any of the acquired technologies, then it offered customers the assurance that they could expect these to be supported as before. Applications Unlimited also meant that Oracle would continue to invest in the development of the newer versions of these products, presumably, for an unlimited time or at least as long as there were customers who wanted to buy the products as stand alone products. Oracle even kept the same development teams working on the development of the acquired products and their newer versions as before, thus earning the trust of customers about how the seriousness of Applications Unlimited. Customers could have confidence that the products they were investing in were going to be developed and supported as before, so they could justify continuing to make their technology investments with the confidence they needed.

[14]Charles Philips, President, Oracle Corp. presentation online from Oracle Business Intelligence, Executive Briefing, March 22, 2006

[15]Charles Philips, President, Oracle Corp. presentation online from Oracle Business Intelligence, Executive Briefing, March 22, 2006

Most employees and customers from acquired companies were pleased with the post merger impact of being a part of Oracle. They had the same teams of people that they were used to working with before the acquisition, and they had the additional resources of a much larger Oracle corporation behind them. The number of people dedicated to support for any customer had gone up radically as the integrated suite of products meant cross-trained support personnel who were more in number and better trained. With the hyphenated-identities, the employees found none of the negativity and aggressiveness they had anticipated from being a part of Oracle. Oracle had worked patiently to earn the trust of the customers and the employees. In parallel, the Fusion middleware strategy was to be developed to make these products hot-pluggable into the integrated suite of Oracle applications.

Fusion

Every year in the fall Oracle hosted a conference attended by several thousand users, partners and other interested parties, called Oracle OpenWorld. At the Oracle OpenWorld in 2006, Oracle announced their Fusion Architecture strategy. "Oracle announced Oracle Fusion Architecture, a standards-based technology blueprint that details the linkage between enterprise applications, middleware and grid infrastructure technologies. Focusing on architectural integrity and openness for business applications and business information."[16]

According to John Wookey, senior vice president of Applications Development, at Oracle, "The Oracle Fusion Architecture provides the foundation for our vision of Information Age applications. Our singular mission is to help our customers drive business excellence through the blending of superior insight and adaptive processes. Oracle Fusion Architecture is both the architectural roadmap and the enabling technologies that allow us to do that." Fusion Architecture is the blue-print for SOA based enterprise solutions, while Fusion Middleware is the technology infrastructure for Fusion Architecture. Fusion Middleware enables Fusion applications and lowers technology and architecture risks.[17]

Fusion Middleware, as explained in the blog of Doug Kennedy, the VP of global alliances and channels, is "an open standards toolset, (that) provides rich, functional capabilities, and offers a viable strategy for extending and evolving to a Service Oriented Architecture (SOA)." He writes, "Fusion provides partners with well defined integration points – both to Oracle's applications and other third party apps." This layer of technology is driven by the prin-

ciple that the various software applications that Oracle, and Oracle customers have, ought to be integrated into a single suite of applications that use a single common data-base. Applications that are not integrated into a suite, maintain their own data that does not connect with the rest of the enterprise except at periodic intervals where the information between the different applications may by synchronized. Having a single suite of applications, drawing on a single repository of commonly used data, allows for all applications to be in-synch almost in real-time, and hence have better information. It is also economical as only a single database needs to be maintained and the synchronization tasks are not needed anymore. Another benefit from having a middleware layer that allows for different applications to be plugged into a core database on an as-needed basis is that the enterprise can expand their use of software as its needs rather than investing heavily up-front, and application vendors can update their applications independent of having to revamp the entire suite every time.

In a white paper, Oracle explains the Fusion Middleware as:

> "Fusion Middleware provides this capability by using open-sourced industry standards that allow not just Oracle applications to be usable on Oracle database but any applications from any vendor can be plugged into the Oracle core database, as an on-demand service. "... by supporting the open standards, Fusion middleware allows customers to substitute third-party components for any of the elements in the Oracle infrastructure portfolio in a 'hot-pluggable' fashion. Customers can deploy its middleware components within environments based on competitive platforms such as IBM WebSphere or BEA WebLogic."[18] Oracle Fusion Middleware (Integrated SOA standards-based Middleware Suite), and Oracle's Business Applications (Integrate, Extend, Evolve through Fusion Middleware).

Oracle has made this a priority and Fusion Middleware has become the second largest product, after Database, in terms of resources deployed on it. According to Thomas Kurian, there were 1200 engineers in 8 major product lines, and over 450 sales specialists and more than 275 support analysts working on Fusion Middleware. He called it "world's fastest growing middleware" and claimed to have over 27,000 customers, with 5,500 in the last year alone. Sixty percent of the customers are on release 10g. The License growth is expected to be over 30% towards a target of $1 billion. He also described it as an Ecosystem since at the end of 2005, 40–48% of license revenue came from partners. There were over 1500 new Independent Software Vendors in the

[16]Oracle: Annual Report 2005

[17]Source: executive slides on strategy

[18]Source:

last year, over 4,500 Value Added Distributors, over 28,000 System Integrators and consultants trained 49 countries.[19]

According to the company annual report:

> "In 2005, Oracle Fusion Middleware evolved as the fastest growing middleware suite with 35 of the 50 largest global companies (and more than 28,500 customers) using the proven software to solve a variety of IT challenges for departmental and enterprise deployment. Additionally, Oracle's network of independent software vendors (ISVs), value added resellers (VARs) and system integrators (SIs), who use Oracle Fusion Middleware to provide their customers the industry's most comprehensive, integrated middleware solutions grew to more than 7,500. For example, using Oracle BPEL Process Manager, a key component of Oracle Fusion Middleware, Oracle completed the integration between Oracle Financials, part of the Oracle E-Business Suite, and Oracle Retail Merchandising Systems less than six months following Oracle's acquisition of Retek. This integration provides customers with a complete retail and corporate administration application footprint. Oracle BPEL Process Manager enables organizations to orchestrate application integration and business processes in a standards-based manner. The product's strict adherence to the industry standard BPEL specification reduced the development time required to integrate the applications and will provide customers increased flexibility for extending and implementing the integrated products.[20]

Throughout the Fusion development process, important customers were kept involved by having a Fusion Strategy Council. This is an advisory board comprised of twenty customer Chief Information Officers, who have actively reviewed, validated and provided input to the evolving Fusion strategy. Amongst Oracle's Application and Fusion Middleware customers are Dell, Merrill Lynch, Virgin, Xerox, iHop, GE, Citigroup, Cisco Systems, McGraw Hill, etc.[21] The results, as presented by an Oracle executive in a presentation, are provided in the slides in appendix III.

THE INDUSTRY SUPPORTS ORACLE FUSION MIDDLEWARE

In addition to customer adoption, Fusion Middleware has also won industry accolades from industry analysts. Forrester

Research report on application platform wave for the second quarter of 2005 (April 2005) gives Fusion Middleware the best of breed middleware title.[22] According to the report: "Oracle is the leader." "We are surprised by (the high) degree of integration between components." Forrester Waves report on the state of the application server market also placed Oracle in the leader category in the areas of enterprise service buses, content services and records management.

Gartner Magic Quadrants also praised Oracle Fusion Middleware's vision, strategies, execution and performance. Oracle was included in the leader quadrant in all SOA related Gartner Magic Quadrants in 2005. This view is seconded by AS10gR2 Infoworld Review of April 2005 that also gave it an excellent rating. See appendix IV for how Oracle Fusion Middleware was in comparison to some of the competitor products.

CHALLENGES   With the Applications Unlimited strategy Oracle has addressed the needs of its current customers, particularly those customers who were acquired from the companies that Oracle has bought, and the employees who came with these companies. With the Fusion strategy, Oracle has laid out a roadmap for using technology as a way to integrate these varied products and services into a complete technology stack that can be available on-demand to the customers in the future. In creating this vision of the future of the software industry, Oracle has put itself at the forefront for becoming a company that can meet the complete IT needs of any enterprise. The challenge in this is the sheer scale of the enterprise. To create and deploy an entire stack of technologies, each with its own unique set of expertise for creating, selling, managing and supporting it, and to integrate it all on this large a scale is something that has not been attempted by any company yet. Some of the challenges involved in it are of building a complex technology, of having many different acquired companies under the Oracle umbrella, of maintaining the hyphenated identities for some of the companies and their employees, of driving integration using technology and of finding ways to continue to serve the customers as it works to realize the new vision. Oracle has the vision, the ambition and the resources to take on these challenges. It has promoted its end-to-end platform capabilities for several years now, and by embracing industry standards in its Fusion Middleware platform in 2006, it began to emphasize heterogeneous, grid-based commodity servers, virtualized into networked pools of virtualized resources that could be tapped as needed by applications, services, and automated business process. The verdict on the two pronged approach, with the current business being maintained and sustained by

---

[19]Thomas Kurian: Nov 30, 2005 presentation on Fusion: Oracle's Fusion Middleware
[20]Source: Oracle Annual Report 2005

[21]Charles Philips, President, Oracle Corp. presentation online from Oracle Business Intelligence, Executive Briefing, March 22, 2006

[22]Forrester Research—application platform wave—Q2 2005 (April 2005) as cited on Thomas Kurian's Nov 30, 2005 presentation.

the Applications Unlimited initiative and the future strategy be based on investments in Fusion, will be out soon.

Appendix I

1. **RDBMS:** Relational Database Management System, a database that stores information in a relational model, as opposed to simple tabular or hierarchical databases. These are the most common kinds of databases in use today. The theoretical possibility that such a database could be created was first published in 1970 by E F Codd in his seminal paper "A Relational Model of Data for Large Shared Data Banks". Oracle was amongst the first companies to create and commercialize this technology on a large scale.

2. **Middleware:** In the computer industry, middleware is a general term for any programming that serves to "glue together" or mediate between two separate and often already existing programs. A common application of middleware is to allow programs written for access to a particular database to access other databases. Typically, middleware programs provide messaging services so that different applications can communicate. The systematic tying together of disparate applications, often through the use of middleware, is known as enterprise application integration (EAI).

   Source: http://searchwebservices.techtarget.com/sDefinition/0,290660,sid26_gci212571,00.html contributed by Donald Bosset, LAST UPDATED: 22 Sep 2004. Downloaded on December 12, 2006.

3. **Grid Architecture:** "Oracle leads the market in grid computing, producing the world's first commercial, grid-ready database, Oracle Database 10g. Grid computing is computing as a utility—you request power and get it, as much as you want, whenever you want. Oracle grids connect networks of low cost PCs into a fault tolerant, reliable system that functions like a single computer. Grids enable more-efficient resource allocation, information sharing, and high availability. With an Oracle grid, if one machine fails, the grid keeps running. To expand a grid, simply add more PCs. It's fast, it's cheap, and it never breaks."[23]

4. **Service Oriented Architecture:** In computing, the term service-oriented architecture (SOA [pronounced "sō-uh" or "es-ō-ā"]) expresses a perspective of software architecture that defines the use of loosely coupled software services to support the requirements of the business processes and software users. In an SOA environment, resources on a network[1] are made available as independent services that can be accessed without knowledge of their underlying platform implementation.[1]

A service-oriented architecture is not tied to a specific technology. It may be implemented using a wide range of technologies, including REST, RPC, DCOM, CORBA or Web Services. SOA can be implemented without any of these protocols, and might, for example, use a file system mechanism to communicate data conforming to a defined interface specification between processes conforming to the SOA concept. The key is independent services with defined interfaces that can be called to perform their tasks in a standard way, without the service having pre-knowledge of the calling application, and without the application having or needing knowledge of how the service actually performs its tasks. SOA can support integration and consolidation activities within complex enterprise systems, but SOA does not specify or provide a methodology or framework for documenting capabilities or services . . .

High-level languages such as BPEL and specifications such as WS-CDL and WS-Coordination extend the service concept further by providing a method of defining and supporting orchestration of fine grained services into coarser grained business services, which in turn can be incorporated into workflows and business processes implemented in composite applications or portals [citation needed].

Source: http://en.wikipedia.org/wiki/Service-oriented_architecture downloaded on 12/12/06 at 1050pm

References

1. Standard and Poor's Industry Surveys, Computers: Software, April 27th, 2006
2. Bokhari, Zanieb, Applications and Systems Software Analyst

---

[23]Oracle Information Driven, p. 3.

Appendix II: Oracle History— Some Milestones

1979 Offers the first commercial SQL relational database management system (RDBMS)

1983 Offers a database written entirely in C for portability

1986 First client-server database

1995 First 64-bit relational database management system (RDBMS)

1996 Announces an open standards based, web-enabled architecture

Breaks the 30,000 tpc-c barrier

1997 First Web database. Moves client/server applications to the Web

1998 Launches Business Online, the first hosting service for enterprise applications designed to be run over the Web.

Offers full Web deployment of all applications.

Offers the first set of application modelling tools that generate 100 percent of the application.

Breaks the 100,000 tpc-c barrier

First database with Java support

1999 First to offer a full featured Internet database

Launches complete e-business initiative

Launches first industry exchange, AutoXchange, with Ford

First to integrate Java and XML into an application development tool

2000 Launches e-business network

Launches Oracle Mobile, wireless applications service provider

Launches Oracle technology Network Xchange, first online developers skills exchange

Industry's first developer Service Provider (DSP)

First to offer complete and simple software for information management, including the Oracle9i database, Oracle 9i Application Server and Oracle 9i Developer Suite

Revenue Growth: year ($): 1988 ($282 M), 1990 ($916 M), 1995 ($2967 M), 2000 ($10,100 M)

Appendix III: Fusion Adoption

Oracle Fusion Middleware

Global Customer Adoption

- 780+ of Top 1000 largest companies in the world
- 35 of top 50 largest companies in the world
- 9 of top 10 largest high-technology cos.
- 9 of top 10 largest automotive cos.
- 8 of top 10 largest manufacturing cos.
- 8 of top 10 largest financial services cos.
- 7 of top 10 largest financial services cos.
- 7 of top 10 largest pharma & health care cos.
- 6 of top 10 largest consumer retailing cos.

In Just 17 Quarters...

Revenues	0	→ $870 M/Year
Customers	0	→ 27,000+
Txns/Quarter	0	→ 3,000+
Sales Reps	0	→ 450+
ISVs	0	→ 1,500+
Consultants	0	→ 27,000+
VARs	0	→ 4,500+
Patents, Awards	0	→ 224,145+
Gartner, MQs	0	→ All 9

Appendix IV

Middleware Suite Proof Point

Forrester Research-June 2004

LEGEND:
⊞ View subattributes and scores
▽ Sort products by attribute and score
Scores are from 0 to 5.

Rank	Vendor & product	Overall score	Platform architecture	Availability and reliability	Administration and management	Development	Standards and interoperability	Market presence	Cost
1	Oracle Application Server 10q Enterprise Edition	4.1	4.0	4.4	4.6	4.1	4.3	3.9	3.4
2	Microsoft Windows Server System	3.5	3.6	3.1	3.5	4.4	3.7	2.8	3.2
3	IBM WebSphere software platform	3.3	3.8	3.0	3.3	3.4	3.6	4.5	1.4
4	BEA WebLogic Platform 8.1	3.2	4.4	2.4	3.9	3.5	3.9	3.5	1.0
5	SAP NetWeaver 04	2.8	3.7	2.1	4.0	3.3	3.4	3.1	0.0
5	Sun Sun Java System	2.8	3.1	1.5	3.5	2.4	3.1	2.8	3.2
7	Novell exteND Enterprise Suite 5.2	2.4	3.7	1.5	2.7	2.8	3.6	1.3	1.0
	Weightings		1.5%	1.5%	1.4%	1.4%	1.4%	1.4%	1.4%

Source: Forrester Research (November 2004)

Case 27

The Expansion of Vincor[*]

Noushi Rahman & Saima Prodhan,
Lubin School of Business, Pace University

Abstract

Within a decade since its inception, Vincor had become the tenth largest wine company of the world. Vincor's rapid growth was achieved through a series of acquisitions. Notwithstanding Vincor's impressive growth, by 2005 its stock was under-performing and the company started drawing the attention of various suitors. In 2006, under mounting pressures, Vincor's board agreed to be acquired by the spirit-giant Constellation Group. What happened to Vincor?

Vincor Background

In 1992, Canadian winemaker Cartier bought rival winemaker Inniskillin, and in 1993 merged with another Canadian winemaker T. G. Bright to form Vincor. After it acquired Dumont Vins et Spariteux in 1996, Vincor was the largest winery in Quebec. Also in 1996, Vincor listed its stocks on Toronto Stock Exchange. Vincor stocks soared in the following years as it engaged in numerous acquisitions and rapidly grew in size. Within a decade since its inception, Vincor was one of the largest wine companies of the world.

Vincor's rapid growth was through a series of acquisitions (see Table 1). The company acquired Okanagan Vineyards and London Winery (in 1996), R. J. Grape Inc. (in 1997), Spagnols Wine & Beer Making Supplies Ltd and Groupe Paul Masson Winery (in 1998), Sumac Ridge and Hawthorne Mountain Vineyards and R. H. Phillips (in 2000), Hogue Cellars (in 2001), Goundrey Wines (in 2002), Kim Crawford Wines (in 2003), and Western Wines (in 2004). With every acquisition, Vincor's debt increased. However, banks were willing to lend to Vincor, as its revenues also increased with each acquisition (see Table 2).

Simultaneous to its acquisitions, Vincor also made fresh investments to start new projects on its own. For example, Vincor started its first planting at Osoyoos Lake bench vineyards in BC (in 1998), established Les Clos Jordan Winery and Vineyards (in 1999), and opened Niagara Winery (in 2001). Namely, wherever there was impressive growth in the new world wine regions, Vincor entered the region through mechanistic growth (see Figure 1).

Vincor's main competitors were Andrew Peller, Constellation Group, Diageo, Gallo, Foster's, Kendall-Jackson, Magnotta Winery, and Sebastiani Vineyards. These companies exerted considerable pressure on Vincor's sales. Thus, despite its impressive growth, by 2005 Vincor's stock began to underperform and the company started drawing the attention of various suitors. Several credible offers were made to buyout Vincor, but the company was initially successful in staving off the buyout attempts. Vincor's competitors were keen on acquiring an undervalued Vincor to further their own consolidation efforts. Eventually, in 2006, Vincor's board agreed to be acquired by the spirit-giant Constellation Group.

Canadian Wine

HISTORY The history of the Canadian wine industry dates back nearly two hundred years. Wine entered Canada with Johann Schiller, a retired German corporal, who planted a small vineyard, made wine, and sold it to his neighbors. From the middle of the nineteenth century, small vineyards started to mushroom out along the Lake Erie coast up to the Niagara Peninsula. The first vineyards

---

[*]This case was compiled from public sources and is designed solely as a basis for classroom discussion of a management or company situation. A teaching note is associated with this case. It was funded by a grant from the Ford Motor Company.

Table 1	Vincor's Acquisitions and Associated Costs	
Year	Target Firm	Acquisition Costs
1996	Okanagan Vineyards (Canada)	$4.2 million
1996	London Winery (Canada)	$9.5 million
1997	R. J. Grape (Canada)	Undisclosed
1998	Spagnols Wine & Beer Making Supplies (Canada)	Undisclosed
1998	Groupe Paul Masson Winery (Canada)	$22 million + undisclosed deferred payments
2000	Sumac Ridge Vineyards (Canada)	$4.7 million (estimated)
2000	Hawthorne Mountain Vineyards (Canada)	Undisclosed
2000	R. H. Phillips (U.S.)	$92 million
2001	Hogue Cellars (U.S.)	$36.4 million
2002	Goundrey Wines (Australia)	$53.7 million
2003	Kim Crawford Wines (New Zealand)	$9 million + $2 million payout option
2004	Western Wines (U.K.)	$248 million (estimated)

Source: Allday, E. 2000. Canadian wine seller to buy R. H. Phillips. *Press Democrat.* August 29. *Food & Drink Weekly.* 2000. Vincor International, Inc. May 8. *Globe and Mail.* 1996. Profit to rise in 1996, Vincor says. September 18. Leong, M. 2002. Vincor buys Australian winemaker—Ontario firm uncorks $53.7 million deal for Goundrey Wines. *Toronto Star,* October 10: D3. *Market News Publishing.* 2001. Vincor International Inc—Acquisition of the Hogue Cellars. August 8. *Market News Publishing.* 2004. Vincor International Inc—Acquisition of UK-based Western Wines Ltd. July 29. Walker, L. 2003. Vincor International Inc. purchases Kim Crawford Wines. *Wines & Vines.* July 1. Walton, D. 1997. Vincor profit jumps 79%: Changing demographic tastes and new acquisitions boost earnings. *Globe and Mail.* August 7. *Gazette.* 1998. Masson sale closes. June 3.

Table 2	Vincor's Acquisitions, Revenue, Debt, and Shareholder's Equity			
Year	Acquisitions Affecting Performance	Revenue	Total Debt	Shareholders' Equity
2000	Spagnols; Groupe Paul Masson (1998)	269.7	80.5	130.6
2001	R. H. Phillips (2000)	294.9	254.4	145.3
2002	Hogue (2001)	376.6	195.1	396.8
2003	Goundrey (2002)	434.6	163.1	428.9
2004	Kim Crawford (2003)	476.1	152.1	640.9
2005	Western (2004)	653.9	293.4	660.7

Source: Vincor Annual Reports (2002, 2003, 2004, and 2005)

| Figure 1 | New World Wine: Growth Areas and Vincor's Presence |

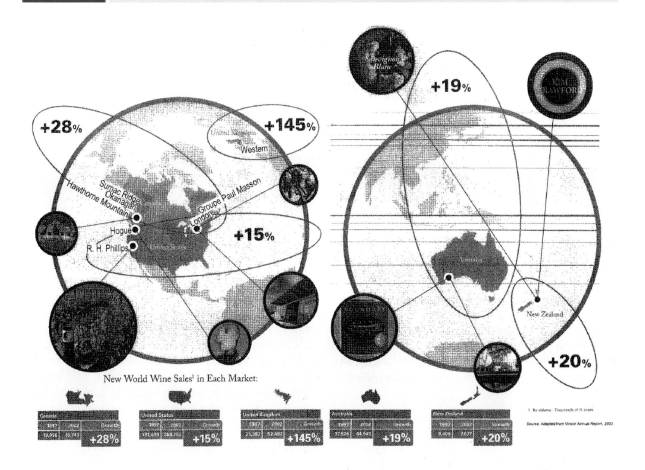

New World Wine Sales¹ in Each Market:

1. By volume - Thousands of 9L cases

Source: Adapted from Vincor Annual Report, 2002

in British Columbia were planted in the 1860s. In 1890, there were 41 commercial wineries in Canada; and most of them were in Ontario.

By 1997, Canada had over 110 licensed wineries. Presently, wine from locally grown grapes is made in four provinces: Ontario, British Columbia, Québec and Nova Scotia (small fruit wine operations exist in New Brunswick, Newfoundland and Prince Edward Island) (see Table 3).

CLIMATE Canada's climate is much colder than that of other wine growing countries. The quality of Canadian wines varies significantly from one vintage to another. The majority of plantings in Ontario have been the winter-hardy North American labrusca varieties and early-ripening, winter-resistant hybrids. Relatedly, Canada is also a major producer of icewine, made from grapes left to freeze on the vine and pressed in frozen state.

Table 3	Distribution of Canada's Wineries and Vineyards			
State	Number of Wineries	Acres under Vine (Acres)	Wine Grape Production (Tons)	Viticultural Areas
ONTARIO	33	16,000	29,000	1. Niagara Peninsula 2. Lake Erie North Shore 3. Pelee Island
BRITISH COLUMBIA	45	2,800	6,102	1. Okanagan Valley 2. Similkameen Valley 3. Fraser Valley 4. Vancouver Island
QUÉBEC	28	220	330	—Cottage wineries
NOVA SCOTIA	2	200	520	—Cottage wineries

ICEWINE Canada's climate affords the unique weather conditions to produce icewine. The basic ingredient of icewine is frozen grapes. According to VQA (Vintners Quality Alliance) regulations, icewine grapes must be left to freeze on the vine and cannot be artificially frozen later on. The naturally frozen grapes are painstakingly handpicked, ideally at temperatures of 7 to 13 degrees Fahrenheit (never warmer than 17 degrees Fahrenheit). To ensure the desired low temperatures, icewine grapes are sometimes picked at night (see Figure 2).

The frozen grapes are pressed in the extreme cold as well. Through this method, the water in the juice remains frozen as ice crystals, and only a few drops of sweet concentrated juice is extracted. The concentrated juice is then fermented slowly until the fermentation process stops naturally after several months. The natural freezing and thawing of the grapes intensify the flavors and add complexity to icewine. Since its inception, Vincor has been the principal producer of Canada's icewine, selling it under the name of Inniskillin (see Figure 3). In 1991, the '1989 Inniskillin' was awarded Bordeaux's Vinexpo Fair's highest prize, Le Grand Prix d'Honneur. Sold in over 50 countries, Inniskillin has become the premier icewine brand of the world (*Shareowner*, 2004).

Figure 2	Frozen Grapes and Harvesting Icewine at Night

Figure 3	Vincor's Inniskillin – Canada's Icewine

Vincor's Supply and Production

Vincor produced wines in various geographic regions; its supply and production processes were not integrated. In Ontario, the company owned approximately 119 acres of vineyard in the Niagara Peninsula. Here it could grow only a portion of the grape supplies it needed for its local wineries, such as Inniskillin and Jackson Triggs. Thus, Vincor also bought a large amount of grapes from other local vineyards. According to *Investors Digest* (2001), Vincor bought 30% of the Niagara wine-grape crop. Between in-house and outside supplies of grapes, Vincor used one third of the entire Niagara wine-grape crop (*Shareowner*, 2004).

In British Columbia, Vincor owned over one thousand acres of vineyard. Yet, the company still bought grapes through long-term supply agreements with almost two dozen local growers. According to *Investors Digest* (2001), Vincor bought 5% of the Okanagan crop in 2000. Between in-house and outside supplies of grapes, Vincor used one fourth of the entire Okanagan Valley wine crop (the most prominent wine-grape growing area of British Columbia) (*Shareowner*, 2004).

In 2000, Vincor effectively entered the U.S. through its acquisition of R. H. Phillips of California. A year later, Vincor acquired another U.S. winery—Hogue Cellars of Washington—to strengthen its foothold in the U.S. market (*Business Wire*, 2001). This represented Vincor's expansion beyond its core business of producing icewine. Both of these wineries came with vast vineyards: R. H. Phillips had 1600 acres and Hogue Cellars had 600 acres. Although

wine-grapes grown at R. H. Phillips and Hogue Cellars were used to produce their own existing brands of wines, the production capacity was not fully utilized (*Business Wire*, 2001). Dependent on local growers for its supply of grapes for its Canadian wineries, Vincor did not take advantage of its newly acquired supply capacities at R. H. Phillips and Hogue Cellars. Although grapes grown in the U.S. were not usable to make Vincor's prized icewine, the grapes could have been used for Vincor's various other brands coming out from the British Columbia region. Instead of shipping California and Washington wine-grapes to its British Columbia wineries, the company focused on increasing its in-house supply of Canadian grapes.

Distribution & Retailing

According to *Shareowner* (2004), Vincor had 149 professionals in its sales and marketing function, which was by far the largest in Canadian wine industry. Consumers could buy an array of Vincor wines belonging to three broad categories: popular-priced (under $8), premium ($8 to $10), and super-premium wines ($10 to $18).

Vincor primarily sold its wines in Canada, the U.S., the U.K., and Australia. In Canada, the company sold its wines through provincially regulated liquor stores. Also, in Ontario, it owned a chain of 165 wine boutiques, where it carried all of its Ontario wines. Given Vincor's low level of integration, it is not surprising that its Ontario chain did not carry its best selling wines from all around Canada or even the world, but rather from the Ontario region only.

In the U.S., Vincor sold wines from not only R. H. Phillips and Hogue Cellars (i.e., Vincor's U.S. wineries), but also Canada, Australia, New Zealand (*Shareowner*, 2004), and South Africa (*PR Newswire*, 2005). Vincor initially relied on R. H. Phillips' network of 90 distributors and a sales force of over 30 professionals to distribute and sell its wines in the U.S. from all around the world (*Canada NewsWire*, 2000). Acquisition of Hogue Cellars complemented its distribution network through R. H. Phillips. Vincor's U.S. sales soared in 2002, a year after its acquisition of Hogue Cellars. In addition to Canada and the U.S., Vincor also had its sales force working in the U.K. and Australia.

Export & Import

Although Vincor had been exporting Canadian wine to the U.S. since 1998 (*Canadian Press*, 2003), its U.S. presence increased in strides only after its acquisition of R. H. Phillips and Hogue Cellars. Vincor also imported some of its American wines back to Canada. However, given its significant presence in the U.S., Australia, and the U.K., Vincor was in a position to engage in exporting and importing at very high volumes. But, the company never took the initiative to take advantage of its uniquely diversified circumstances.

While Vincor produced scores of different wines through its various wineries, Inniskillin icewine was always its most famed wine. According to the *National Post* (2001), Vincor started exporting its icewine to the European Union, boosting its Inniskillin sales further. While Vincor positioned Inniskillin as a super premium brand, its retail price was mediocre (around $30 per bottle; whereas after being acquired by Constellation Group in 2006 the price jumped to around $90 per bottle), compromising Vincor's revenue stream. While sales revenue and market share ought to be synchronized, Vincor seemed to have focused excessively on market expansion, expecting revenue generation to be an automatic outcome.

Vincor—an Acquisition Target

Vincor's rapid expansion forced the company to take on additional debt with each new acquisition. The short-term positive reactions of the market may have partly fueled this acquisition frenzy. Prior to purchasing R. H. Phillips, Vincor's outstanding debt was $80.5 million. After it had completed its Hogue Cellars acquisition, Vincor's outstanding debt stood at a staggering $195.5 million. During this time, shareholder's equity also rose from $130.6 million to $396.8 million. Even then, Vincor continued in its acquisition

spree, making large acquisitions in Australia (Goundrey), Canada (Kim Crawford), and the U.K. (Western).

Beyond the general idea of international growth and expansion, Vincor's internationalizing strategy seems to be unclear. Since little effort was made to integrate its geographically dispersed operations, its very size became its biggest liability. Also, for several years, acquisition news seemed to have fuelled much of the upward movement in its stock price. But, as Vincor's debt burden climbed up to dizzying heights, the company was required to perform much better than before to prevent its stock price from sliding down a spiral. While a smaller-sized Vincor with smaller debt could have registered stronger performance, the larger-sized Vincor with a massive debt burden was overwhelmed by its debt and the accumulating interests. It was almost impossible by 2005 for Vincor to break out of its hapless conditions.

As Vincor started to underperform in 2005, Constellation Group became increasingly interested to acquire Vincor. Vincor management and board were not willing to sell their company, especially under such circumstances. However, after a year of resistance, Vincor's top brass agreed to sell off their prized company to the giant spirits company Constellation Group.

References

1. Allday, E. 2000. Canadian wine seller to buy R. H. Phillips. *Press Democrat*. August 29.

2. *Business Wire*. 2001. New Phillips-Hogue Wine Company shows how family farms succeed. August 10.

3. *Canadian NewsWire*. 2000. Vincor International Inc. completes tender offer for R. H. Phillips, Inc.: Vincor becomes fourth largest North American winery. October 5.

4. *Canadian NewsWire*. 2001. Vincor International announces record first quarter results: Quarter highlighted by strong contribution from R.H. Phillips acquisition and steady growth in all Canadian markets. August 8.

5. *Canadian Press*. 2003. Wine producer Vincor earns $9.5M in Q1, up from $8.2M as sales rise to $107M. August 7.

6. *Food & Drink Weekly*. 2000. Vincor International, Inc. May 8.

7. *Gazette*. 1998. Masson sale closes. June 3.

8. *Globe and Mail*. 1996. Profit to rise in 1996, Vincor says. September 18.

9. *Investors Digest*. 2001. Vincor captures Canada's premium wine market. June 15.

10. Leong, M. 2002. Vincor buys Australian winemaker—Ontario firm uncorks $53.7 million deal for Goundrey Wines. *Toronto Star*, October 10: D3.

11. *Market News Publishing*. 2001. Vincor International Inc—Acquisition of the Hogue Cellars. August 8.

12. *Market News Publishing*. 2004. Vincor International Inc—Acquisition of UK-based Western Wines Ltd. July 29.

13. *National Post* (Canada). 2001. Vincor soars as winemaker eyes foreign markets: Returns 62% since August: Company funds expansion with long-term debt. July 5.

14. *PR Newswire*. 2005. Vincor USA is ready to conquer another New World frontier with the upcoming launch of a South African wine called Kumala. April 25.

15. *Shareowner*. 2004. Vincor International Inc.: Good for you too. September/October. Retrieved from: <http://www.shareowner.com/index.html>.

16. *Vincor Annual Report*. 2002. Retrieved from <http://www.vincorinternational.com/base-module/level0.cfm?mainID=2&depth=2&mainNav=10>.

17. *Vincor Annual Report*. 2003. Retrieved from <http://www.vincorinternational.com/base-module/level0.cfm?mainID=2&depth=2&mainNav=10>.

18. *Vincor Annual Report*. 2004. Retrieved from <http://www.vincorinternational.com/base-module/level0.cfm?mainID=2&depth=2&mainNav=10>.

19. *Vincor Annual Report*. 2005. Retrieved from <http://www.vincorinternational.com/base-module/level0.cfm?mainID=2&depth=2&mainNav=10>.

20. Walker, L. 2003. Vincor International Inc. purchases Kim Crawford Wines. *Wines & Vines*. July 1.

21. Walton, D. 1997. Vincor profit jumps 79%: Changing demographic tastes and new acquisitions boost earnings. *Globe and Mail*. August 7.

Case 28

Cisco Systems, Inc.: Acquisition Integration for Manufacturing (A)

David Keller, vice president of manufacturing, new product introduction, and technology at Cisco Systems, Inc. (Cisco), hung up the phone and sat back to think about the challenges that lay ahead. He had just spent the last hour talking with Gary Wilder, director of manufacturing operations, and Dick Swee, vice president of engineering, at Summa Four Inc. (Summa Four)—a systems company which developed and manufactured programmable switches used in the development of telephony applications. Cisco had announced in July 1998 that it had reached an agreement to acquire publicly held Summa Four for $116 million in stock. The conversation had been about the major effort that lay ahead to integrate the two companies' manufacturing organizations. While the deal was not expected to officially close until November 1998, Keller had called Wilder and Swee to give them an overview of how Cisco managed these types of integration projects so that they could begin to prepare the Summa Four organization.

Keller had reviewed the due diligence report on Summa Four written by a team from his department and knew that the integration process would be complex. While Cisco had

made 25 acquisitions prior to the Summa Four acquisition, most had been of Silicon Valley–based software or pre-production hardware companies which had small (if any) manufacturing organizations. The Summa Four acquisition had the potential to be different. Summa Four was a 22-year-old hardware company with $42 million in revenues, over 200 employees, one manufacturing plant located in Manchester, New Hampshire, and a full line of products being shipped. Summa Four represented one of Cisco's largest acquisitions to date in terms of current revenues and employees.

Keller was concerned about just how difficult the acquisition integration process would be from a manufacturing standpoint. How would they treat Summa Four's legacy and next-generation products? Where would they be manufactured? How would Cisco deal with Summa Four's suppliers? Did it make sense to keep the Manchester plant operating? If so, for how long? What risks did Cisco face during the integration process and what could be done to help mitigate those risks?

Cisco Overview

Cisco Systems, founded in 1984 by Leonard Bosack and Sandy Lerner—a husband and wife team of computer specialists at Stanford University—grew out of a project to tie together disparate computer networks on campus. Bosack and Lerner developed the first "multi-protocol" router—a specialized microcomputer that sat between two or more networks (even those with different operating systems) and allowed those networks to "talk" to each other by deciphering, translating, and funneling data between them. As Bosack explained back then: "We network networks."[1] Cisco's technology opened up the potential for linking all of the world's disparate computer networks together in much

Nicole Tempest, Associate Director of the HBS California Research Center, and Dean's Research Fellow Christian G. Kasper prepared this case under the supervision of Professor Steven C. Wheelwright and Professor Charles A. Holloway, Kleiner Perkins Caufield and Byers Professor of Management at Stanford University's Graduate School of Business as the basis for class discussion rather than to illustrate either effective or ineffective handling of an administrative situation.

[1] *The San Francisco Chronicle*, February 17, 1990.

the same way as different telephone networks were linked around the world. Technology pioneered by Cisco provided the functionality for the World Wide Web.

As the global Internet and corporate Intranets grew in importance, so too did Cisco. With an early foothold in this rapidly growing industry, Cisco quickly became the leader in the data networking equipment market—the "plumbing" of the Internet. By 1998, most of the large-scale routers that powered the Internet were made by Cisco. While routers and switches continued to be Cisco's core products, the company's product line had expanded to include a broad range of other networking solutions, including Web site management tools, dial-up and other access solutions, Internet appliances, and network management software. (See Exhibit 1 for a list of Cisco's product categories.) Cisco's broad product line enabled it to offer customers an "end-to-end" network solution—an option which over 50% of *Fortune* 500 companies were actively considering, according to Cisco. By 1998 the company held the number one or number two position in 14 of the 15 markets in which it competed. As a result, Cisco had become a safe decision for large companies. As one industry analyst commented, "I have heard from a number of really large clients: 'It's like IBM in the old days—you won't get fired for choosing them.'"[2]

In 1996 Cisco entered the $250 billion telecom equipment market, which was undergoing significant change due to rapid advances in technology. Whereas historically there had been three separate types of networks—phone networks for transmitting voice, computer networks for transmitting data, and broadcast networks for transmitting video—advances in digitization had allowed voice, data, and video all to be translated into the ones and zeros of computer language. This, in turn, made it possible to transmit all three over *one* network in a more efficient and economical manner. As a result, phone companies were beginning to replace their century-old voice-only networks with new networks capable of carrying voice, data, and video. By positioning its products for this market, Cisco was competing with a far larger group of rivals than it had in the past—including Lucent Technologies and Nortel. In June 1998 Cisco scored a major victory against these rivals when Sprint selected Cisco to be the primary supplier of its new data and telephone network.

Having received its initial funding from the venture capital firm Sequoia Capital, Cisco went public in February 1990, closing its first day of trading with a market value of $222 million. Just 8 years later, Cisco's market value topped

[2]*Wired News*, March 1997.

Exhibit 1	Cisco Product Categories

Product Category	Description
High-end routers	Cisco's high-end platforms for the most mission-critical networks
WAN switches	Wide-area networking switching for Frame Relay and ATM, plus network access devices
LAN switches	Local area-networking switching for workgroup networks
Hubs	Devices to link small workgroups in local networks
Access products	Scalable products for remote access
Web scaling products and technologies	Products that provide Internet access, security, scalability, and management
Security products	Comprehensive solutions for network protection and enabling Internet business applications
InterWorks for SNA	Availability, scalability, performance, flexibility, and management for IBM/SNA networks
IOS software	Cisco's Internetworking Operating System software
Network management	Network management solutions that offer end-to-end network management for any Cisco-based network

Source: www.cisco.com.

the significant $100 billion mark, reaching that mark faster than any company in history and stripping Microsoft of the previous record of 11 years. Between 1989 and 1998 Cisco's revenues grew at a compound annual rate of 89%, from $28 million to $8.5 billion, and with traffic on the Internet doubling every four months, Cisco continued to have significant growth potential. (See Exhibit 2 for Cisco's financials.)

CISCO'S BUSINESS STRATEGY   Cisco's business strategy reflected the experience of CEO John Chambers and Chairman John Morgridge. Morgridge, who had been CEO of Cisco from 1988 to 1995, established many of Cisco's core business principles, including the importance of customer satisfaction, time-to-market, and frugality. Chambers, who took over as CEO in January 1995, spent most of his career at IBM and Wang, and watched both companies suffer crippling declines as a result of not adapting to changing market conditions quickly enough. Morgridge, Chambers, and Ed Kozel—then Cisco's chief technology officer—crafted a strategic plan for Cisco in 1993, which was still being executed in 1998. The plan consisted of four main components:

1. assemble a broad product line in order to provide customers one-stop-shopping for networking solutions,
2. systematize the acquisition process,

| Exhibit 2 | Cisco Financials |

Selected Financial Data

Five Years Ended July 25, 1998 (in Thousands, Except Per-Share Amounts)

	1998	1997	1996	1995	1994
Net sales	$8,458,777	$6,440,171	$4,096,007	$2,232,652	$1,334,436
Net income	$1,350,072[a]	$1,048,679[b]	$ 913,324	$ 456,489[c]	$ 322,981
Net income per common share—basic[d]	$ 0.88	$ 0.71	$ 0.64	$ 0.33	$ 0.25
Net income per share—diluted[d]	$ 0.84[a]	$ 0.68[b]	$ 0.61	$ 0.32[c]	$ 0.24
Shares used in per-share calculation—basic[d]	1,533,869	1,485,986	1,437,030	1,367,453	1,296,023
Shares used in per-share calculation—diluted[d]	1,608,173	1,551,039	1,490,078	1,425,247	1,342,213
Total assets	$8,916,705	$5,451,984	$3,630,232	$1,991,949	$1,129,034

[a]Net income and net income per share include purchased research and development expenses of $594 million and realized gains on the sale of a minority stock investment of $5 million. Pro forma net income and diluted net income per share, excluding these nonrecurring items net of tax, would have been $1,878,988 and $1.17, respectively.
[b]Net income and net income per share include purchased research and development expenses of $508 million and realized gains on the sale of a minority stock investment of $153 million. Pro forma net income and diluted net income per share, excluding these nonrecurring items net of tax, would have been $1,413,893 and $0.91, respectively.
[c]Net income and net income per share include purchased research and development expenses of $96 million. Pro forma net income and diluted net income per share, excluding these nonrecurring items net of tax, would have been $515,723 and $0.36, respectively.
[d]Reflects the three-for-two stock split effective September 1998.

3. define industry-wide software standards for networking equipment, and

4. pick the right strategic partners.

An inherent part of Cisco's strategy was using acquisitions and partnerships to gain access to new technologies. This strategy was relatively unique in the high-tech world, where many companies viewed looking to the outside for technological help as a sign of weakness. However, Chambers believed that this was just the sort of insular thinking that had led to IBM and Wang's downfall. He viewed partnerships and acquisitions as the most efficient means of offering customers an end-to-end networking solution and developing next-generation products. For example, Cisco's partnership with Microsoft enabled the company to develop a new technology for making networks more intelligent in just 18 months. Cisco insiders estimated that it would have taken Cisco four years to develop the product itself without the Microsoft partnership.

CISCO'S MANUFACTURING PHILOSOPHY AND ORGANIZATION   From its beginnings, Cisco was structured as a highly centralized organization. Morgridge believed that too many start-up companies decentralized too quickly, and therefore were unable to benefit from the advantages of scale and control associated with a centralized organization. However, in 1995 Cisco established three separate "lines of business"—Enterprise, Small/Medium Business, and Service Provider—each of which had two to nine sep-

arate "business units" reporting to them. Although Cisco had begun to move to a more decentralized structure, most of the company's functional areas still remained centralized as of mid-1998, including manufacturing, customer support, finance, information technology, human resources, and sales. Only engineering and marketing were decentralized at the business unit level.

Cisco operated three manufacturing facilities: two in San Jose, "Tasman" and "Walsh"; and a third in South San Jose, "Silver Creek." Tasman and Walsh were Cisco's first manufacturing plants and they produced most of Cisco's enterprise routers and LAN switches. The Silver Creek facility was inherited through the 1996 acquisition of StrataCom, Inc., and it produced most of Cisco's high-end Internet backbone products for service providers (e.g., Sprint, MCI). In addition to these three owned and operated manufacturing facilities, Cisco utilized "external factories" to outsource production of some of its high volume products. (See Exhibit 3 for Cisco's manufacturing department organization chart.)

Cisco's manufacturing strategy was heavily dependent on outsourcing. The company outsourced many manufacturing activities, such as board stuffing and board testing, to contract manufacturers since these activities required a significant investment in "bricks and mortar," were less scalable, and generated lower returns relative to Cisco's core business. For example, in the case of Cisco's higher-end,

Exhibit 3 Cisco's Manufacturing Organization (as of 7/98)

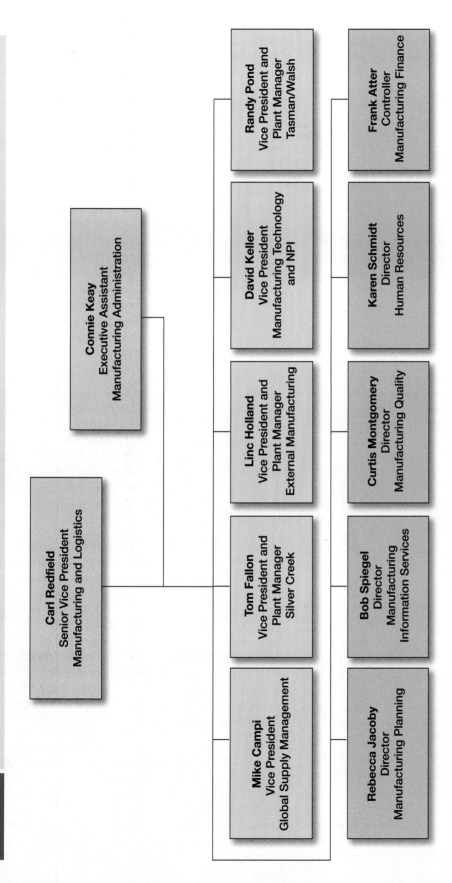

more highly configured products, Cisco would outsource subassembly, bring in completed subsystems, and conduct final testing and assembly in-house, in one of its three manufacturing facilities. At the other end of the spectrum, Cisco utilized external factories to build, test, and ship its less configured, high volume products, such as its low-end routers. Carl Redfield, senior vice president of manufacturing and logistics at Cisco, explained the strategy: "I want my people focusing on the intellectual portion, establishing the supply base, qualifying new suppliers, and developing better processes, not managing direct labor. We supply the intellect; they supply the labor."[3]

Tom Fallon, vice president and plant manager at Cisco, added: "If we can make it cheaper, we do. But even then, we look for suppliers who can match our costs. Strategically we want to outsource."[4]

Approximately 25% of Cisco's revenue and 50% of its unit volume was manufactured and shipped out of external factories. While external factories were not owned by Cisco, and their employees were not Cisco employees, Cisco did supply them with Cisco information systems and test systems to ensure that they met Cisco's standards for quality and customer satisfaction.

Cisco's Acquisition Strategy

Cisco regarded acquisitions primarily as a means to secure technology and scarce intellectual assets. As Chambers commented: "Most people forget that in a high-tech acquisition, you really are acquiring only people. That's why so many of them fail. At what we pay, $500,000 to $2 million an employee, we are not acquiring current market share. We are acquiring futures."[5]

Cisco had three primary goals for ensuring the success of its acquisitions. These were, in order of importance: 1) employee retention, 2) follow-up on new product development, and 3) return on investment.

EMPLOYEE RETENTION Since the employees of acquired companies were critical to the success of the acquisition, Cisco went to great efforts to retain them. Cisco itself was basically just the combination of 25 different organizations that had merged over time. Integration success was due in large part to the very organized, methodical approach that Cisco took toward managing the experience of acquired employees. In the words of a senior human re-

sources manager, "Our objective during the acquisition and transition is to make the employees whole." That is, their efforts were focused on ensuring that employees maintained comparable—if not better—financial consideration and benefits as they transitioned to Cisco's policies and plans.

The responsibilities of the human resources department (HR) began even before the acquisition was consummated. A team of HR professionals typically would spend several weeks at the acquisition candidate developing a transition plan. The plan would map the changes and time frame required to smoothly transfer the personnel, benefits, and compensation policies of the acquired company to Cisco. Based on a belief that people don't like change—especially change they can't predict—Cisco's HR professionals went to great lengths to tailor the specifics of the transition plan to the needs of the acquired company's employees. For example, Cisco added a new health care provider to its employee benefit options so that the acquired employees were able to keep their existing doctors.

After the acquisition closed, Cisco's HR team would spend another six to seven weeks on-site executing the transition plan. This would give them the opportunity to review the details of the plan with the acquired firm's management before rolling it out to all the employees. The rollout process typically centered on small group discussions with Cisco's HR team and employees from the acquired company. Furthermore, Cisco usually insisted that the acquired company's management team play an active role in educating their own employees.

For the employees of the acquired firm, working for Cisco required a number of significant changes to their compensation. One of the most significant issues was that Cisco required all employees to waive their rights to accelerated vesting on their existing stock options—an event usually triggered by an acquisition—before the deal closed. In return, employees would receive an equivalent value of Cisco options for all of their company's unvested options. In addition, they offered a retention bonus at the end of the first and second years. Given the historically strong performance of Cisco's stock, there was usually little resistance to the new compensation package.

The employees of the acquired companies also benefited from Cisco's history of explosive growth and need for skilled workers. Of its first 25 acquisitions, only two required layoffs, and every redundant person had the opportunity to apply for any Cisco job opening worldwide. Since Cisco typically had 300–600 job openings available at any one time, this represented an attractive option for redundant employees. Part of this policy stemmed from Chamber's

---

[3]Timothy Laseter, *Balanced Sourcing* (San Francisco: Jossey-Bass, 1998).
[4]Ibid.
[5]*BusinessWeek*, August 31, 1998.

experience as vice president of U.S. operations at Wang where he was given the unpopular and heart-wrenching task of laying off 4,000 of Wang's 10,000-person workforce. He vowed to never face this situation again.

These policies had met with great success in the past. The employee turnover rate for acquisitions was only 8%, the same level as for Cisco's long-term employees. Approximately one in five Cisco employees and one-third of Cisco's top management positions were filled by people who had come from acquired companies, and these individuals continued to promote an environment that welcomed acquired employees into its ranks.

NEW PRODUCT DEVELOPMENT Successful new product development required both technical expertise and management talent in order to understand the market, translate market needs into a product, and deliver that product to market quickly. Cisco's new product introduction (NPI) process required that input from marketing, engineering, and manufacturing was incorporated into the product design to ensure that products were designed for functionality, manufacturability, testability, and cost-effectiveness. Since Cisco viewed acquisitions as a means of introducing new products, it was important for Cisco to accelerate the acquired company's new product development efforts. Cisco had found that the most effective way to do this was for the acquired company to adopt Cisco's cross-functional, systematic NPI process. (See Exhibit 4 for a detailed description of Cisco's NPI process.)

More than simply adding to its list of offerings, Cisco saw product development as a high leverage item. Cisco's goal was to quickly convert newly acquired products to its own NPI process and hopefully reap significant sales volume improvements. This required Cisco to quickly assess where each of the company's products were in the development process. With this information, Cisco could make an informed decision about which products to convert to the NPI process, and which products were too far along in their development to benefit from the change. Although Cisco tried to convert as many new products as possible, typically only the early-stage development products would use the new process.

RETURN ON INVESTMENT Cisco also looked for acquisitions to generate a high return on investment. The key to accomplishing this was to quickly and effectively leverage Cisco's powerful sales organization and third party distributors (value added resellers, or "VARs") to sell the acquired company's products. Charles Giancarlo, vice president for global alliances at Cisco, reiterated Cisco's focus on generating results quickly following an acquisition: "If there are no results in three to six months, people begin to question

the acquisition. If you have good short-term results, it's a virtuous cycle."[6]

In order to generate results quickly, Cisco made every attempt to have the acquired company's products appear on Cisco's price list on the day the deal closed so that Cisco's sales force could immediately begin to sell the new products. The power of leveraging Cisco's sales and distribution channels, alone, could result in a two- to five-times ramp up in the acquired company's volume. Effectively leveraging its distribution channels in this manner was one of the key drivers behind the significant growth in Cisco's revenues.

TYPES OF ACQUISITIONS Cisco made its first acquisition in 1993, when it purchased Crescendo Communications—a LAN-switching company—for $97 million. By mid-1998, Cisco had announced 29 acquisitions worth about $7 billion and had made non-controlling investments in 40 companies—three of which Cisco later acquired.[7] (See Exhibit 5 for a list of Cisco's acquisitions.) Cisco's target was to have 30% of its revenue come from acquisition and development ("A&D") efforts and 70% from internal research and development (R&D) efforts. Proposals for specific acquisition candidates often came directly from Cisco's business units, based on feedback from customers. Cisco would then screen these potential candidates against a well-defined set of criteria (see Exhibit 6).

Cisco's acquisitions spanned a range of companies producing different types of products, at different points in their lifecycles. There were essentially four types of acquisitions: software companies, "pre-production" hardware companies, small hardware companies shipping product, and mature hardware companies. The complexity of the integration process, and the level of resources dedicated to the effort, varied depending on the type of acquisition. From a manufacturing standpoint, software companies and pre-production companies were the least complex to integrate into Cisco, since these types of companies typically did not have a manufacturing organization in place, nor an existing customer backlog to satisfy. At the other end of the spectrum, small hardware companies shipping product and mature hardware companies were the most complex to integrate. In fact, the complexity of the integration process had far more to do with the company's stage of development than with its acquisition price. For example, the manufacturing integration process for a $300 million acquisition of a pre-production company could be far easier than for a $100 million acquisition of a hardware company that was already shipping products. Keller compared

[6] *BusinessWeek*, August 31, 1998.
[7] *San Jose Mercury News*, October 12, 1998.

Exhibit 4	Cisco's New Product Introduction Process

Cisco's NPI process involved three phases: strategy and planning, execution, and deployment. The process also included a series of checkpoints between the "strategy and planning" and "deployment" stage to help instill rigor and discipline into the new product introduction process. The multiple checkpoints ensured that there was both a shared vision for the new product and a commitment to allocate sufficient resources to it.

The "concept commit checkpoint" came at the beginning of the strategy and planning phase. This checkpoint ensured that a cross-functional team had approved both the product requirement document (PRD) and the business plan attached to it, and was willing to commit resources sufficient to get to the product design point. By the end of the strategy and planning phase, designers would have developed a definitive design specification for the product.

Next the product had to clear the "execution checkpoint" which ensured that the cross-functional team agreed on both the design specifications and the revised PRD, and was committed to dedicating the resources required to ship the product on a particular date. In the execution phase, the engineering group worked with manufacturing to develop and test prototypes. Manufacturing would conduct a thorough design for manufacturability (DFM) review early in the prototype development process and would help the engineering group develop a product that was easily testable on the Autotest system.

Close to the end of the execution phase—about a month before the first product was shipped—the product had to pass the "orderability checkpoint." This was a manufacturing-driven checkpoint that ensured that the product had passed a rigorous set of [criteria] before being posted on Cisco's Web site. The manufacturing group used the test to ensure they could hit the ship date and meet the expected ramp-up in demand. The check list included questions such as:

Has the product completed and passed its development test?

Has the product been beta tested, and is the feedback good?

Are the results from the software tests positive?

Do we have suppliers lined up? Can they make the parts?

Do we have reasonable yields at the prototype stage?

Once the product passed the orderability check point, it was added to Cisco's price list, and it entered into the deployment phase where it was either slated for "unlimited release" or "controlled release." Products slated for unlimited release were typically those that were in high demand, had completed all the development milestones, and for which Cisco had significant capacity to build, test, ship, and service. Products slated for controlled release were typically those that still faced some degree of design risk. For example, the product could have received compliance approval in some, but not all geographic areas (i.e., approved for the U.S., but not yet for Europe). In these cases, Cisco would restrict output as a way of controlling the risk involved in the product launch.

Two to three months after the first product had been shipped, the product faced yet another manufacturing checkpoint, known as the "time to quality and volume" (TTQV) checkpoint. This checkpoint—which included analyses on yields and costs—was designed to ensure that the manufacturing group could make the product cost-effectively at high volumes. The TTQV checkpoint was conducted two to three months after production had begun so that sufficient run-rate data could be collected and used for analysis. Once the product had passed this checkpoint, it was produced according to its own roll-out plan and lifecycle.

Exhibit 5   Cisco's Acquisitions

Date[a]	Company	Business Description	Alignment with Cisco Line of Business	Approximate Acquisition Price ($MM)	Approximate Number of Employees
10/98	Selsius Systems	Supplier of network PBX systems for high-quality telephony over IP networks	Enterprise	$145 (stock + cash)	51
9/98	Clarity Wireless Corporation	Wireless communication technology for computer networking and the Internet service markets	Service Provider	$157 (stock)	39
8/98	American Internet Corporation	Software for IP address management and Internet access	Service Provider	$56 (stock)	50
7/98	Summa Four, Inc.	Open programmable digital switching systems	Service Provider	$116 (stock)	210
5/98	CLASS Data Systems	Network management software	Enterprise	$50 (stock + cash)	34
3/98	Precept Software, Inc.	Multimedia networking software	IOS Technologies[b]	$84 (stock)	50
3/98	NetSpeed, Inc.	Standards-based DSL technology	Service Provider	$236 (stock)	140
2/98	WheelGroup Corporation	Intrusion detection and security scanning software	IOS Technologies	$124 (stock)	75
12/97	LightSpeed International, Inc.	Voice signaling technologies	Service Provider	$160 (stock)	70
7/97	Dagaz (Integrated Network Corporation)	Broadband networking products	Service Provider	$126 (stock)	30
6/97	Ardent Communications Corp.	Combined communications support for compressed voice, LAN, data, and video traffic across public and private Frame Relay and Asynchronous Transfer Mode (ATM) networks	Service Provider	$156 (stock)	40
6/97	Global Internet Software Group	Windows NT security	Small/Medium Business	$40 (cash)	20
6/97	Skystone Systems Corp.	High-speed Synchronous Optical Networking/ Synchronous Digital Hierarchy (SONET/SDH) technology	Service Provider	$102 (stock + cash)	40
3/97	Telescend	Wide area network access products	Service Provider	Terms not disclosed	NA
12/96	Metaplex, Inc.	Network products for the IBM enterprise marketplace	Enterprise	Terms not disclosed	20
10/96	Netsys Technologies	Network infrastructure management and performance analysis software	Service Provider	$79 (stock)	50
9/[96]	Granite Systems, Inc.	Standard-based multi-layer Gigabit Ethernet switching technologies	Enterprise	$220 (stock)	50
8/96	Nashoba Networks, Inc.	Token Ring switching technologies	Enterprise	$100 (stock)	40
7/96	Telebit Corp's MICA Technologies	Modem ISDN Channel Aggregation (MICA) technologies	Service Provider	$200 (cash)	288
4/96	StrataCom, Inc.	ATM and Frame Relay high-speed wide area network switching equipment	Service Provider	$4,666 (stock)	625

(continued)

Exhibit 5   Cisco's Acquisitions—Continued

Date[a]	Company	Business Description	Alignment with Cisco Line of Business	Approximate Acquisition Price ($MM)	Approximate Number of Employees
1/96	TGV Software, Inc.	Internet software products for connecting disparate computer systems over local area, enterprise-wide and global computing networks	Small/Medium Business	$138 (stock)	130+
10/95	Network Translation, Inc.	Network address translation and Internet firewall hardware and software	Small/Medium Business	Terms not disclosed	10
9/95	Grand Junction, Inc.	Fast Ethernet (100Base-T) and Ethernet switching products	Small/Medium Business	$400 (stock)	85
9/95	Internet Junction, Inc.	Internet gateway software connecting desktop users with the Internet	Small/Medium Business	$5.5 (stock)	10
8/95	Combinet, Inc.	ISDN remote-access networking products	Small/Medium Business	$132 (stock)	100
12/94	LightStream, Corp.	Enterprise ATM switching, workgroup ATM switching, LAN switching and routing	Service Provider	$120 (cash)	60+
10/94	Kalpana, Inc.	LAN switching products	Enterprise	$240 (stock)	150
8/94	Newport Systems Solutions, Inc.	Software-based routers for remote network sites	Small/Medium Business	$91 (stock)	55
9/93	Crescendo Communications	High-performance workgroup networking products	Enterprise	$97 (stock)	60

Source: www.cisco.com, literature search.

[a]Date of announcement
[b]Internetworking Operating System

Exhibit 6	Screening Criteria for Potential Acquisition Candidates

Screening Criteria	Means of Achieving Criteria
Offer both short-term and long-term win-wins for Cisco and the acquired company	• Have a complementary technology that fills [. . .] a need in Cisco's core product space • Have a technology that can be delivered through Cisco's existing distribution channels • Have a technology and products which can be supported by Cisco's support organization • Is able to leverage Cisco's existing infrastructure and resource base to increase its overall value
Share a common vision and chemistry with Cisco	• Have a similar understanding and vision of the market • Have a similar culture • Have a similar risk-taking style
Be located (preferably) in Silicon Valley or near one of Cisco's remote sites	• Have company headquarters and most manufacturing facilities close to one of Cisco's main sites

the effort involved in integrating pre-production companies to companies already shipping product:

> The integration of pre-production companies tends to be less difficult than integrating companies that are already shipping product, since we can have more influence and add more value on the manufacturing side, and there isn't a lot we have to "undo." We can integrate the company into our operations and set them up on our systems right from the start.

While Cisco had made several acquisitions of software, pre-production hardware, and small hardware companies already shipping product, as of 1998 Cisco had made only one acquisition of a mature hardware company—the acquisition of StrataCom in 1996. (See Exhibit 7 for examples of acquisitions by type.)

Cisco's Acquisition Integration Process

Before agreeing to the terms of an acquisition, Cisco conducted thorough due diligence on the company. A project manager from Cisco's business development group would coordinate the overall due diligence process, in which a cross-functional team—comprised of representatives from marketing and engineering within Cisco's business units and representatives from Cisco's centralized manufacturing organization—conducted a detailed assessment of the acquisition candidate's business processes. For example, the manufacturing due diligence team reviewed the company's manufacturing processes, identified risks, provided input to valuation discussions, and scoped the work that would be required to integrate the two companies, if the deal were to close. The manufacturing due diligence process centered around a 1 to 2 day visit to the company to see and discuss a number of details regarding their technology, manufacturing and engineering processes, and organization. Prior to the due diligence session, Cisco would send an outline of issues for discussion to the heads of the manufacturing and engineering groups at the company to help prepare for the visit. (See Exhibit 8 for a sample list of manufacturing due diligence issues.)

After the acquisition had closed, Cisco would move forward with its post-acquisition integration process. Although each of Cisco's acquisitions was unique and required a customized integration approach based on a comprehensive understanding of the company, there were ten common steps that were mandatory. The mandatory steps centered on converting the acquired company to Cisco's manufacturing systems, processes, and methodologies. While the time allotted for completing these steps could vary, ultimately the "Cisco way" would be put into place. Cisco described these steps as "stakes in the ground." On the other hand, certain decisions—such as how to handle the integration of an acquired company's employees and manufacturing plants—varied from acquisition to acquisition and required significant management judgment. (See Exhibit 9 for a diagram of the integration process.)

In both cases, Cisco utilized a "scenario planning" approach to make decisions about what to do and how fast to do it. The scenario planning approach took into account Cisco's business objectives for the acquisition, information on the company gathered from the due diligence effort, and projected outcomes under various integration scenarios (e.g., higher volumes, merging plants). The approach was used to help outline alternatives and generate consensus regarding recommendations.

MANUFACTURING INTEGRATION TEAM Cisco organized a manufacturing integration team to manage the post-acquisition process. Cisco's approach was to appoint one of the senior managers within the *acquired* company as the integration team leader. Tony Crabb, previously the vice president of manufacturing for StrataCom (before becoming director of manufacturing at Cisco), was chosen to lead

Exhibit 7	Examples of Acquisitions by Type	
Acquisition Type	Description	Examples of Acquisitions by Type
Software Companies	These were companies that designed and sold software—primarily engineering companies. Since they were not involved in the hardware side of the business, they did not have a manufacturing organization. As a result, this type of acquisition required the least amount of involvement from the Cisco manufacturing organization during the integration process.	American Internet Corporation CLASS Data Systems Precept Software, Inc. WheelGroup Corporation LightSpeed International, Inc. Global Internet Software Group Netsys Technologies TGV Software, Inc. Internet Junction, Inc.
Pre-production Hardware Companies	These were companies that had a technology that Cisco wanted, but they were not yet shipping any product. Frequently these companies had developed a prototype, but the product was not yet designed for manufacturability. This type of acquisition was relatively straightforward from a manufacturing integration standpoint, since there was no existing infrastructure with which to contend and no existing customer order backlog to satisfy.	Clarity Wireless Corporation Dagaz Ardent Communications Corp. Skystone Systems Corp. Telescend Granite Systems, Inc. Nashoba Networks, Inc. Telebit Corp's MICA Technologies
Small Hardware Companies Shipping Product	These were small companies—sometimes private, sometimes public—that were shipping products to a limited installed base of customers. Cisco would typically acquire these companies for their engineering team and the potential they offered for developing next generation products. These companies typically had some sort of enterprise resource planning (ERP) system in place, but often would not have the manufacturing quality standards of a mature company. This type of acquisition proved to be more complex than pre-production companies since the integration process had to proceed without impacting the continuity of supply to existing customers.	Summa Four, Inc. NetSpeed Inc. Network Translation, Inc. Grand Junction, Inc. Combinet, Inc. Kalpana, Inc. LightStream Corp. Newport Systems Solutions, Inc. Crescendo Communications
Mature Hardware Companies	These were large, mature companies that had a substantial customer base. They typically had established manufacturing processes in place and were ISO-certified (International Organization for Standardization). This type of acquisition typically took far longer to integrate due to the complexity of decisions that had to be made. However, in this type of acquisition both companies would typically have significant resources to dedicate to the integration process, thereby facilitating the effort.	StrataCom, Inc.

the StrataCom integration team. Crabb reflected on the impact of Cisco's approach to leading the integration process:

> From the perspective of employees within the acquired company, it's pretty important to see someone they know and trust leading the integration effort. If it were a Cisco person leading the process, they would feel as if it were being imposed upon them, and therefore resent the process. On the other hand, if it's someone they know, it's easier for them to ask questions and feel a part of the process.

The balance of the integration team was comprised of experienced members of both organizations. The overall team was then divided into subteams that were responsible for leading key business process conversion tasks.

Based on experience from several acquisitions, Cisco also had developed an approach called the "buddy system." The buddy system involved appointing an experienced Cisco employee to be the "manager of the intangibles" within both the acquired company's engineering and manufacturing organizations, and swapping a handful of Cisco employees with employees from the acquired company. Both the "managers of intangibles" and the on-site Cisco staff would assist employees from the acquired company with questions regarding how to access information and get things done within the Cisco organization. While the "manager of intangibles" position had no official reporting structure beneath it, the role was considered a critical part of the integration process and was reserved for strong performers

Exhibit 8	Sample List of Manufacturing Due Diligence Issues
Issues	Sample Questions
Target market dynamics	• What was the demand forecast? • What were the gross margin targets?
Product portfolio	• What was the product set? • What was the development status on new products?
Manufacturing technology	• What was their process for designing products for manufacturability, testability, cost, cycle time, and volume?
Verification process	• How did they conduct internal and external design verification?
Supply base and order fulfillment	• Who was on their approved vendor and subcontractor list? • How did they manage their material pipeline and inventory?
Development, release, and manufacturing process	• What was their philosophy on design? • How much were they influenced by sales versus engineering? • Did they utilize cross-functional teams in the development process?
Manufacturing process competencies	• Did they have any specific manufacturing core competencies that should be taken into consideration?
Organizational structure	• How were they organized? • How many people were in each area?
Leadership/management competencies	• What was the skill level of the work force as a whole? • What were the leadership capabilities of the management team?

within the Cisco organization. Crabb described how the buddy system worked in the StrataCom acquisition:

> One of the keys to success in the StrataCom integration process was to have Cisco people within the StrataCom organization, so that we had people on site who knew how to get information from the big Cisco organization. As an outsider you don't know how to get even the most basic things done—like how to get a new ID badge. But, by having a Cisco person sitting in the cube right next to you, he or she can immediately tell you who to call and even give you the person's number. The buddy system de-stresses a lot of angst about how to do things and how to be productive within the Cisco organization. As Cisco does

more remote acquisitions, the buddy system will become even more important because you won't have the opportunity to walk down the hall and talk to someone.

MANDATORY INTEGRATION STEPS As soon as the manufacturing integration team was created, work began on the mandatory components of the integration process. The mandatory steps provided a clearly articulated plan for achieving fast and seamless integration. From the customer's perspective, Cisco wanted to make it appear that the acquired company was a part of Cisco from the day the deal closed. Yet, Cisco was very aware that massive and unilateral changes could potentially have enormous disruptive effects. Cisco's mandatory steps drew on the experience gained from numerous previous acquisitions and provided a framework and timeline for the integration team to tackle their job (see Exhibit 10 for more details on the mandatory integration steps).

The mandatory steps effectively broke down into three primary categories: merging information systems, aligning current processes, and implementing ongoing methodologies. The merging of information systems involved both the materials resource planning system (MRP) and the product testing system (Autotest). Due to the large number of acquisitions undertaken, it would have been incredibly complex and redundant for Cisco to maintain multiple systems. Thus, the integration team was tasked with transitioning the acquired company to Cisco's MRP and Autotest systems in a staged process that typically achieved full integration within 90 days. Although an aggressive timeline, the rapid implementation of the Autotest system ensured that the product quality would meet Cisco's standards. The move to Cisco's MRP system not only aided the sales staff in placing orders for the new product, but also helped identify opportunities for part consolidation and supplier rationalization.

In aligning the acquired company's current processes with Cisco's, the integration team focused on three areas: evaluating suppliers, assessing outsourcing options, and determining product lifecycles. In the first area, the integration team reviewed the suppliers of the acquired company, with the ultimate goal of transitioning them to Cisco's vendors. Supplier choice was a difficult decision, and factors such as continuity of supply, on-time delivery, quality, customer support, and cost were all taken into consideration. The second area, assessing outsourcing options, examined the role that outsourced manufacturing could play in the acquired company. Cisco relied heavily upon outsourcing, and mandated that all piece part assembly and board level testing be outsourced. A comprehensive outsourcing plan was crafted

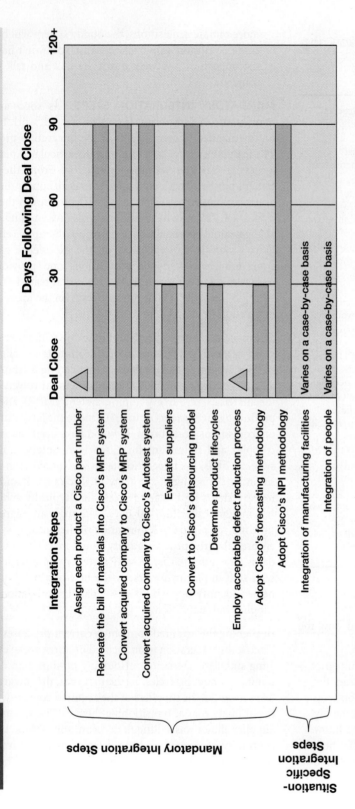

Exhibit 9   Post-Acquisition Integration Steps

Days Following Deal Close

Integration Steps	Deal Close	30	60	90	120+

Mandatory Integration Steps
- Assign each product a Cisco part number
- Recreate the bill of materials into Cisco's MRP system
- Convert acquired company to Cisco's MRP system
- Convert acquired company to Cisco's Autotest system
- Evaluate suppliers
- Convert to Cisco's outsourcing model
- Determine product lifecycles
- Employ acceptable defect reduction process
- Adopt Cisco's forecasting methodology
- Adopt Cisco's NPI methodology

Situation-Specific Integration Steps
- Integration of manufacturing facilities — Varies on a case-by-case basis
- Integration of people — Varies on a case-by-case basis

Source: Casewriter interviews.

Exhibit 10	Mandatory Manufacturing Integration Steps

Assign Each of the Acquired Company's Products a New Cisco Product Number

Cisco assigned a new product number to each of the acquired company's products that would be entered into Cisco's MRP (manufacturing resource planning) database. At the initial phase, there would be no other details on the product (e.g., parts, cost data) in the database, so a transaction could not be fully conducted electronically through Cisco's MRP database. Instead, if a customer placed an order for one of the acquired company's products, Cisco would transfer the order internally (by phone, email, or fax) to the acquired company's order desk for fulfillment. The acquired company would then make, test, and ship the product from its facilities. However, all of this was done behind the scenes; from the customer's perspective, they were dealing directly with Cisco. (See **Table 2** below.)

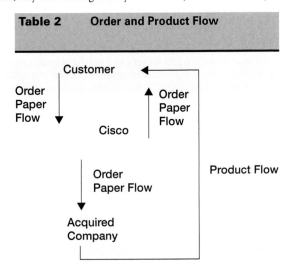

Table 2	Order and Product Flow

Recreate the Bill of Materials into Cisco's MRP Database

The next step was to recreate the bill of materials for each of the acquired company's products into Cisco's MRP database. This involved a detailed part-mapping process whereby a team from Cisco's component engineering group would analyze each specific part that went into each product to determine if an identical part was already used by Cisco—and therefore, already in the MRP database. The process involved an extensive review of each part's data sheet, since parts that seemed identical on the surface could be ever-so-slightly different in reality. If an exact match were found, then the part would be given the existing Cisco part's number. If no match were found, then the part would be given a new part number. Since it was a detailed and time-consuming process, often taking up to 90 days to complete, the detailed part-by-part mapping would not be done for those products that were slated for short-term production or end of life.

While the primary goal of the part-mapping process was to "get it done," a secondary goal was to identify opportunities to consolidate parts and vendors. Cisco's goal was to utilize existing, pre-approved vendors where possible and minimize the growth of its parts database. In other words, if the acquired company was buying a part that was almost identical to one that Cisco was already buying from another vendor, the team would flag it as an opportunity for near-term substitution. However, since the overarching goal was to integrate the parts data into Cisco's MRP database, only the obvious substitution opportunities were identified during this process. As Crabb described it: "We'll take all the low hanging fruit, but we don't try to do everything at this point."

Convert the Acquired Company to Cisco's MRP System

Once all the parts had been given Cisco part numbers, Cisco would convert the company over to Cisco's MRP system. Unlike some of its competitors, Cisco did not believe in running multiple MRP systems in parallel; instead, Cisco made it mandatory for acquired companies to convert to Cisco's MRP system. However, in some cases, Cisco would recommend that the acquired company keep its own MRP system in place for its short-term production products or end of life products. Once the company had converted to Cisco's MRP system, Cisco had all the necessary infrastructure required to plan, build, and ship the acquired company's products. Typically conversion to Cisco's MRP system would take place within 90 days of close.

Convert the Acquired Company to Cisco's Autotest System

Cisco considered its Autotest system—a software-based automated testing system that measured the functionality and configuration of products—to be an essential component of its overall quality control process. The system worked by running data from the manufacturing process through a set of test "scripts." The Autotest system analyzed the data and determined whether the product passed or failed the tests, and under what conditions. The Autotest system was networked to Cisco's MRP system, enabling it also to test final product configuration to ensure that it matched the customer's order. Since Cisco sold many built-to-order, highly configurable

| Exhibit 10 | Mandatory Manufacturing Integration Steps—Continued |

products, there were numerous opportunities to make mistakes. The Autotest system gave the operator an almost foolproof way to ensure that the right product was being shipped to the customer. Cisco's external factories and sub-assembly contractors were also networked into the Autotest system.

If Cisco decided to continue operating an acquired company's plant for an extended period of time, then Cisco would require that the Autotest system be implemented in the acquired company's manufacturing facility. To set up the Autotest system, the integration team had to first determine whether the company had a set of written diagnostics for each product, since diagnostics were needed to write the test scripts. If the company did not have written diagnostics—which was typically the case—then development engineers from the relevant Cisco business unit would work with engineers from the acquired company to write diagnostics for the Autotest system.

On average it took three months to get the Autotest system up and running in an acquired company; however, it could take longer in cases where the engineering department was making significant changes to product design. During the period in which the Autotest system was being set up, Cisco depended on the acquired company's existing test processes for quality control—usually a set of PC-driven tests that required an operator to enter the script coding, run the test, and watch the results on the computer screen. While these types of tests were adequate for a small company, they were prone to human error, which was why Cisco mandated conversion to the Autotest system. In the best case scenario, the implementation of the Autotest system would coincide with the ramp-up in the acquired company's production volume.

Evaluate Suppliers

Cisco's supply operations (supply ops) group evaluated, approved, and managed suppliers for both Cisco and its acquired companies. To qualify as an approved Cisco vendor, the vendor had to meet pre-determined financial and business criteria, such as:

> Cisco could represent no more than 20% of the supplier's business, so that fluctuations in Cisco's demand did not threaten continuity of supply,
>
> The vendor had to be in solid financial standing, and
>
> The vendor had to rate highly on a quarterly scorecard administered by Cisco which measured performance against a series of [criteria], including on-time delivery, lead time, quality level, customer support, and cost.

Cisco's supply ops group began to evaluate an acquired company's suppliers during the due diligence process to identify any risks to continuity of supply following the acquisition. Within 30 days of close the supply ops group was expected to have developed a plan for how to handle the supplier base. The goal was to convert the acquired companies to Cisco suppliers over time. However, the desire to use Cisco vendors had to be weighed against the impact the conversion would have on the continuity of supply and the development time for new products—in addition to the cost of the effort. As a result, Cisco rarely made supplier changes for products slated for short term production or end of life. For products slated for long term production and new products, Cisco's supply ops group evaluated new suppliers using the same criteria used to add suppliers to Cisco's approved vendor list. Marc Beckman, senior manager of global supply management for electronic components at Cisco, explained:

> We want to be able to influence supplier selection decisions just like we do here at Cisco. On the other hand, we don't want to impact the acquired company's business in a negative way. If we can switch to an existing Cisco supplier without having an adverse impact on their business, then we do. If we think it will have a real adverse impact, then we won't make the switch; we'll approve the vendor, but only for that *particular* product. If it's a critical supplier for a new product and we're too far down the road on development to switch, then we'll evaluate the proposed supplier and analyze the risks on a case by case basis.
>
> One thing we are sensitive about is the effect our decisions have on suppliers who have been supporting the acquired company over a period of time. We will often evaluate the impact of switching suppliers on the existing suppliers, and if the impact appears severe, we will try to work out an arrangement whereby they can support the product for a period of time until they can re-address their customer base.

Convert to Cisco's Outsourcing Model

Cisco required that the companies that it acquired convert to its outsourced manufacturing model as well. There were essentially three levels of outsourcing: piece part assembly, board level testing, and final assembly and testing. As a rule, Cisco always outsourced the first two to contract manufacturers. They also outsourced the third—final assembly and testing—in the case of products fulfilled by external factories. If the acquired company were operating under a highly vertically-integrated production model, Cisco developed a transition plan for outsourcing the piece part assembly and intermediate testing activities, at a minimum. However, for products slated for short-term production or end of life, Cisco would often leave their in-house manufacturing processes in place. Cisco had also explored the possibility of leveraging its contract manufacturers to produce, fulfill, and provide after-sale support for products slated for end of life—but had not yet tested this option. Cisco's goal was to have a comprehensive outsourcing plan in place within 90 days of the close.

Determine Product Lifecycles

In order to determine how to treat each of the acquired company's products, the manufacturing group first needed to determine how long Cisco planned to manufacture and support each product. Due to their importance, a first pass at these decisions was typically made within

Exhibit 10	Mandatory Manufacturing Integration Steps—Continued

30 days of the close. In order to make these decisions, the manufacturing team carefully reviewed the business case underlying the acquisition. In some cases Cisco acquired a company for its current line of products—meaning that most of its products would be slated for long-term production. In other cases, Cisco acquired the company for its potential to develop next generation products, rather than for its existing products—meaning that many of the existing products would be slated for short-term production or positioned for end of life. However, even if a product were slated for end of life, it would be phased out over time, rather than eliminated outright, since Cisco's goal was to assure continuity of supply to the acquired company's customers immediately following the acquisition.

Employ an Acceptable Defect Reduction Process

Cisco required that a basic statistical process control [mechanism] be put in place to track yield and failure data on a daily and weekly basis. While the Autotest system would ultimately produce these data, Cisco mandated that the acquired company have an acceptable process in place at the time of the close for charting the data—even if it were a manual process.

Adopt Cisco's Forecasting Methodology

Following an acquisition, Cisco continued to depend on the acquired company to provide product booking forecasts, since Cisco believed that the acquired company was most familiar with the demands of its own customers and marketplace. However, the acquired company would submit its forecasts to Cisco's business-unit level marketing group to discuss and revise, if needed. Input from Cisco's business-level marketing group was essential since they had the experience to project the implications of leveraging Cisco's sales and distribution channels on an acquired company's production volume. Since the forecast would ultimately be entered into Cisco's MRP system and drive production decisions, it was important to reach consensus on it. As a result, Cisco required that acquired companies adopt Cisco's approach to forecasting within 30 days of the close.

Cisco required both a monthly review as well as a transaction-level forecast, and was just as interested in the assumptions that were used to develop the forecasts as in the forecasts themselves. Cisco required that acquired companies adopt Cisco's "envelope of demand" methodology of monthly forecasting, which entailed providing a set of quantified upside and downside ranges to the forecast. As part of the forecast, the marketing group included detailed assumptions about what would need to happen to achieve the upside and downside forecasts (e.g., three accounts would need to sign contracts to meet the upside forecast) and they provided probability assessments for these scenarios. By providing analytical rigor behind a set of ranges to the forecast, the marketing group helped the manufacturing group determine the types and levels of buffers to set up in manufacturing.

Adopt Cisco's New Product Introduction (NPI) Methodology

Cisco required that the companies it acquired adopt Cisco's NPI process for its new product development where feasible (sometimes new products were too far along the development process to convert to Cisco's NPI process). On the day the deal closed, Cisco would make a determination as to which new products were early enough in their development cycle to convert to Cisco's NPI process, and within 90 days of the close, the NPI process would be implemented.

---

to move the acquired company toward optimal use of outsourcing. The third area, determining product lifecycle, was one of the most important tasks of the integration team. The acquired company's products needed to be segmented by development phase so that appropriate decisions could be made about their integration into Cisco's organization. In all, these steps were usually completed within 90 days of the time of the merger.

The last category of mandatory integration steps was the implementation of ongoing methodologies, including defect reduction, forecasting, and new product introductions. To reduce defects, Cisco required the acquired company to immediately implement statistical process controls. While this functionality would later be provided by the Autotest system, quickly reducing and maintaining low defect rates was a crucial driver of financial performance. Cisco also required that the acquired company adopt its forecasting methodology within 30 days of the close of the deal. Forecasting at Cisco stressed joint development of production and sales volume predictions between Cisco's business-unit level marketing group and the management of the acquired company. Cisco believed there was great value in the analytical rigor of a detailed plan with clearly articulated assumptions. Finally, the integration team implemented Cisco's new product introduction methodology. Within 90 days of purchase, the new company would use Cisco's NPI model—including cross-functional teams—on all products that were early enough in their development cycle to benefit.

SITUATION-SPECIFIC INTEGRATION STEPS While Cisco had a number of mandatory integration steps, it handled manufacturing facility and employee integration issues on a situation-specific basis. On the manufacturing facility side, the preliminary question was whether to leave the acquired facilities essentially intact, fully integrate them into Cisco's facilities, or any one of many options in between. The time required to reach decisions on these issues and implement a transition plan also varied widely from acquisition to acquisition. A team, made up of staff from Cisco's new product introduction group, considered a number of factors in making their recommendations on how to treat an acquired company's production facilities. These factors included the business plan for the acquired company (e.g., projected volumes, ramp-up timing, product lifecycles), the competencies of the acquired company's production facilities (e.g., quality controls, production processes), an affordability assessment (e.g., how can we maximize the value of the company's products?), and an assessment of other intangibles (e.g., how would a plant closure affect the R&D and engineering effort?).

During the period the team was developing the recommendation on whether and when to merge plants, Cisco would continue to operate out of the acquired company's production facility. However, since Cisco was ultimately accountable for the quality of the products coming out of the acquired company's plants, the team would frequently audit the company's quality control processes to ensure that they met Cisco's standards. In addition, Cisco mandated that its acquired companies implement certain of its engineering and manufacturing procedures in their production facilities and go through an ISO (International Organization for Standardization) audit of those procedures within six to twelve months.

In terms of employee integration, Cisco would customize a plan to meet the needs of the acquired company's labor force. Cisco would offer employees flexibility around the transition process (e.g., timing of geographic moves), in addition to the traditional economic incentives. For example, they might be given the option to continue working at the acquired company's plant for as long as the facility was maintained; move to one of Cisco's production facilities in California; or move into another part of the Cisco organization (e.g., quality control, field service). Cisco believed in being open, honest, sensitive, and flexible with the employees of the acquired company during the post-acquisition integration process.

The Summa Four Acquisition

Founded in 1976, Summa Four had become a leading provider of open programmable digital switching systems, sold primarily to telecommunications service providers worldwide (i.e., AT&T, MCI, Sprint, British Telecom). By 1998, Summa Four had installed over 2,000 switches in over 30 countries. Approximately 50% of its systems were installed outside the United States. Customers used Summa Four's open programmable switching platforms for basic call switching as well as for delivering value-added services, such as voice mail, calling card applications, voice-activated dialing, intelligent 800-call routing, and voice and fax messaging. Summa Four was also developing a next-generation product—code-named Project Alpha[8]—that represented the industry's first standards-based open programmable switch.

Due to the deregulation of the telecommunications industry, service providers were in a fierce, competitive race to develop and deliver these types of enhanced services to their customers. Prior to the advent of open programmable switching technology, service providers typically used large-scale proprietary central office switches. The proprietary nature of these switches made service providers dependent on their switching equipment vendors to help develop new services. However, open programmable switches allowed service providers to develop or purchase their own applications, which reduced development costs and accelerated time to market. Summa Four's company vision was to "provide open, intelligent, standards-based switches to telecom service providers worldwide, fundamentally changing the cost and time-to-market for deploying new networks and services."

Cisco announced it would acquire the Manchester, New Hampshire–based company in July 1998. The acquisition was intended to enable Cisco to offer value-added telephony applications to telecommunication service providers, and extend these services to IP (Internet Protocol) networks, which were able to transmit voice, data, and video.

SUMMA FOUR PRODUCT LINE Summa Four's product line included the VCO Series/20, the VCO Series/80, and the VCO/4K—all of which were highly configurable and built-to-order. While Project Alpha was still in the development phase at the time of the acquisition, and over a year away from product launch, it was a key reason behind Cisco's interest in Summa Four.

All products in the VCO family shared a similar architecture and many of the same features. (See Exhibit 11 for an overview of Summa Four's products.) The key distinguish-

---

[8]Name has been disguised.

Exhibit 11	Summa Four's Product Line		
Product Name	VCO/Series 80	VCO/Series 20	VCO/4K
Introduction Date	February 1995	September 1996	March 1998
Description	High-density open-programmable switch used for application development, highly distributed intelligent peripheral implementations, and scaleable transport deployments in both wireline and wireless networks	Same functionality as VCO/Series 80, but offers a smaller footprint and rack-mountable design, which makes it suitable for turnkey integration with other application systems	World's highest density open-programmable switch
Density	2,048 timeslots	2,048 timeslots	4,096 timeslots
Fully-NEBS Compliant	Yes	No	Yes

Source: www.summafour.com, casewriter interview.

ing feature among them was their time slot density (the greater the time slots, the more lines could run in and out of the switch). The VCO Series/80—introduced in February 1995—offered a non-blocking switching matrix of 2,048 time slots. In addition, the Series/80 was fully NEBS (Network Equipment Building Systems) compliant—meaning that it conformed to a specific set of environmental compatibility criteria (e.g., physical protection, electromagnetic compatibility, and electrical safety) that most of the large telecommunication service providers required. Smaller telecommunication service providers were often willing to work with products that were not fully NEBS compliant in order to gain a particular design advantage or reduce costs.

The VCO Series/20—introduced in September 1996—offered the same number of time slots as the Series/80, but was a far smaller unit than the Series/80. Its small footprint and rack-mountable design made it well-suited for turnkey integration with other application subsystems. However, the Series/20 was not fully NEBS compliant, due to tradeoffs in design that would have been required to comply with NEBS standards. Both the VCO Series/20 and VCO Series/80 were considered mature products and the plan was to migrate customers to the VCO/4K over time.

The VCO/4K was Summa Four's newest and most advanced product. Introduced in March 1998, the VCO/4K was the world's highest density programmable switch. It offered a non-blocking switching matrix of 4,096 time slots, was fully NEBS compliant, and included all of the other features common to the Series/20 and Series/80. While the VCO/4K was still in field trial deployment, it was ramping up faster than expected. While the initial signs were positive, Cisco would have to wait to see the market's reaction to the 4K before it could make a determination about its potential lifespan. If the 4K turned out to be a highly successful product and the decision was made to keep its production in Manchester, Cisco would need to invest in both equipment and labor in order to

increase the capacity of the Manchester manufacturing facility. Given that Cisco's California manufacturing facilities had additional capacity and had all the key testing infrastructure in place, Cisco was unsure of whether this type of investment into Summa Four's Manchester facility was prudent.

SUMMA FOUR ORGANIZATION In September of 1998, the idea of being acquired by Cisco was still very new to Summa Four's employees. At the time of the acquisition announcement, Summa Four had 210 employees, including 65 development engineers and 23 employees in the manufacturing organization. While there was a good deal of excitement about the prospect of working for Cisco, a number of employees voiced reservations. One manager said, "This is an exciting time, but I worry that a number of changes are going to be forced down our throats."

One of the areas that attracted the most concern was the cultural implications of being acquired by a much larger firm. Summa Four's management knew that they were just one of many in a long line of Cisco acquisitions. They had built their business in a simple functional organization, where personal connections and informal processes allowed for quick action. In a larger organization, effective problem solving would likely require a host of specialists and multiple organizational units, resulting in a far more complex process. Some employees worried that the feel of working in the high-energy world of a small business would be lost. Dick Swee captured much of this sentiment when he said, "There is a big difference between a $10 billion organization and a $50 million organization. We've been used to the feel of a small company, and that is certainly going to change."

There was also concern about the level of influence that Summa Four employees would be able to exert within Cisco. It was unclear what [role] their current products would play among the Cisco offerings, and their ability to guide the integration process might be severely limited. With well over 10,000 people working for Cisco, Summa Four employees worried that Cisco would not be very receptive to their input. However, with the New England job market so hot, at least there would be attractive alternatives for most of the experienced engineers if things didn't work out.

SUMMA FOUR MANUFACTURING Summa Four's headquarters and manufacturing plant shared the same facility in Manchester, which was less than an hour away from one of Cisco's remote R&D facilities, located in Chelmsford, Massachusetts. Cisco's due diligence team found Summa Four's plant to be clean, orderly, and efficient. Summa Four's plant compared favorably to many of the other plants that Cisco had acquired. However, the plant used a homegrown, PC-based test system that was far less automated than Cisco's Autotest system. Summa Four's MRP system was from Symix, a supplier of systems for midrange manufacturers of discrete, configurable products. It did not appear that the Symix software was compatible with Cisco's MRP system.

As for its manufacturing processes, Summa Four had moved toward more and more outsourcing with each generation of products. For example, almost all of the assembly and testing for Summa Four's early VCO Series/20 and Series/80 products was conducted in-house, including power supply assembly and board testing. On the other hand, in the case of its newer VCO/4K product, Summa Four had outsourced most of the piece part assembly.

SUPPLIERS Summa Four purchased approximately 5,000 individual parts from 250 suppliers, 85 of whom were new to Cisco. While the Summa Four acquisition was far smaller than the $4.6 billion acquisition of StrataCom in 1996, Summa Four had a comparable number of parts and suppliers to StrataCom, reflecting the complexity of the Summa Four integration process. Of some concern was the fact that approximately 200 of Summa Four's parts were sole-sourced, meaning that only one vendor supplied each of those parts, which created a pricing and continuity of supply risk.

Fortuitously, Summa Four had recently contracted with Sanmina—a Cisco approved back-plane and chassis integration company—to do sub-assembly for its VCO/4K product. Sanmina had quickly become one of Summa Four's major suppliers. Cisco considered Sanmina to be a potential candidate for testing the idea of leveraging a contract manufacturer to handle the production, fulfillment, and after-sale support of mature products in the future.

Decisions Ahead

Keller anticipated that the post-acquisition integration of Summa Four would be relatively complex given the company's remote location, its line of legacy products, and its number of employees. In a week's time he would have to present his recommendations on how to integrate Summa Four's products, plant, and people. His initial thoughts were that it would make the most sense to transfer the Alpha generation to the main Cisco facility and leave the other products where they were, to eventually be phased out. While this appeared to be the easiest route to take, would it deliver the type of [. . .] returns that Cisco had come to expect? What would he do with the Manchester plant if expected demand were to increase dramatically? What were the risks inherent in these choices? What would be the impact on retaining Summa Four's key employees?

As Keller sat back to consider these issues, he received a phone call informing him of yet another Cisco acquisition on the horizon, this time of Selsius Systems of Texas—a maker of products which allowed companies to combine voice and data communications on their corporate networks. Keller knew that Summa Four would likely serve as a role model for the Selsius acquisition integration process and potentially many more to come. He knew that he would have to think very carefully about the myriad of integration issues facing Cisco with the Summa Four acquisition.

Case 29

Implementation of the Balanced Scorecard as a Means of Corporate Learning: The Porsche Case

903-030-1

"We will endeavor to maintain this top position in the future as well. The basic requirement is a continuous increase in the efficiency of all processes and the streamlining of structures."

—Dr. Wendelin Wiedeking, President and CEO of the Porsche AG[1]

An innovative modernization process allowed Porsche to turn around and reconquer its position as one of the world's leading sports car manufacturers, thus recovering from the crisis it had faced in the early 1980s. Since the memory of the past problems was still fresh, there was a general awareness in the company that they could not afford to rest on their laurels if they wanted to stay ahead of the competition. In this spirit of continually striving to hone every single element of the business to perfection, the International Dealer Network Development team at the headquarters in Germany convened with some market representatives in 2000 to discuss new ideas on how to secure Porsche's success story for the future.

At this meeting, project manager for the international dealer development, Andreas Schlegel, presented his idea of implementing a balanced scorecard to measure performance. After long discussions, the participants finally arrived at a common understanding of how to implement this business tool as a means to turn the international dealer network into a learn-

ing organization. The goal was to make efficient use of the vast store of knowledge that lay dormant in the different dealerships and subsidiaries of the major markets around the world, and, eventually, to turn this knowledge into profit. Another significant benefit would be the mass of data on the individual dealerships that the headquarters would acquire in the course of generating the balanced scorecard figures in each reporting cycle. After the senior representatives of the Sales Operations department had been convinced of the idea, a decision was taken in favor of the balanced scorecard and work began in the autumn of 2001.

However, soon after, resistance to the idea began to arise within the company itself. Dr. Andreas Offermann, the director [of] sales, was quick to comprehend the peril of the situation. Knowing that a previous attempt to introduce a balanced scorecard in another department had failed, which meant that the new effort would be met with resistance at all stages, he had the project renamed "Porsche Key Performance Indicators" (KPI).

Andreas Schlegel, who had focused on balanced scorecard research during most of his studies, became the project manager. Together with a capable team of assistants, he accepted the challenge to revolutionize the international Porsche Sales Organization.[2]

This case was written by **Professor Gilbert Probst**, HEC, University of Geneva, and **Jan Dominik Gunkel**, WHU, Otto Beisheim Graduate School of Management. It is intended to be used as the basis for class discussion rather than to illustrate either effective or ineffective handling of a management situation.

The case was made possible by the co-operation of Porsche AG.

[1]Porsche AG, *Annual Report 1999/2000.*

[2]The Porsche Sales Organization includes the Sales Operations department at the headquarters, the subsidiaries in the markets and the dealerships.

Exhibit 1   The Balanced Scorecard[3]

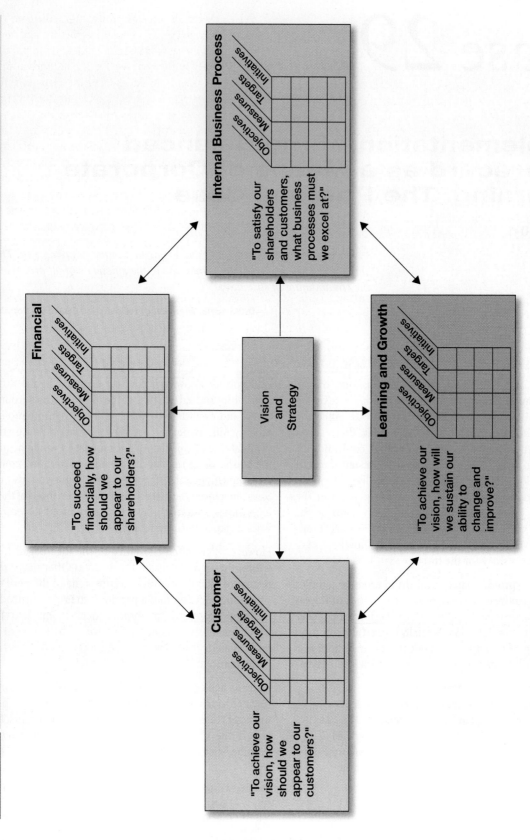

[3]Robert S. Kaplan, David P. Norton, "Using the Balanced Scorecard as a Strategic Management System," *Harvard Business Review*, January–February 1996, p. 76.

Design Phase

Everyone was aware of the heavy burden they had to bear to make a success of this huge project. Sun-Tzu, the ancient Chinese strategist, once suggested that large enemy armies should be maneuvered and split into small, vincible units. In this spirit, the project team decided on a step-by-step approach and started by selecting a few pilot markets in which to kick off the project.

First the members of the project team familiarized themselves with balanced scorecard theory by reading everything they could lay their hands on. After a careful study of all major Porsche markets, the markets in France (POF), Italy (PIT) and the UK (PCGB) were chosen for their proximity to the headquarters. The [German] market was specifically excluded to prevent the impression of a home market bias. In addition, the three markets were on different levels of dealership sophistication, with PIT at the lower and PCGB at the upper end of the scale. But all of them had basic IT infrastructure in their accounting as well as in their communication technologies. PCGB's highly developed internal reporting system was considered the benchmark with which the others had to comply. For instance, PCGB's reports provided almost twice the number of figures than those of Porsche Italia. The project team therefore organized several workshops with representatives of the three markets to discuss their various reporting systems in order to compile a comprehensive list of key issues. It was clear that PIT, which had the largest gap to close in its reporting system, would benefit most, but even PCGB was able to learn from the interesting reporting methods that the PIT management had devised. After all, the Italians invented accounting centuries ago.

By including the markets in the creation process, their full acceptance of the balanced scorecard as part of themselves was ensured.

With extensive input from the markets guaranteed, the project team started to outline its ideas. Once they had a common understanding of their goals, they sought the assistance of an experienced automotive IT consultancy. After a long selection process, a European-based British provider that specialized in complete solutions in respect [to] reporting systems for the automobile industry was chosen. This project was, however, the consultancy's first contract with the headquarters of an automobile group, since it had previously only dealt with national subsidiaries of other renowned car manufacturers. The consultancy appeared highly motivated, presumably because of the chance to add Porsche's good name to its list of clients. It was, furthermore, the company's first balanced scorecard project; therefore its strategic importance was considerable.

In a challenging process, the project team, the consultancy and the markets agreed upon the structure and the content of the balanced scorecard. The idea was to publish the KPIs as a PDF report adapted for the individual markets and thus only showing the data of the respective dealership. [The reports] would contain almost 40 front-page indicators distributed across four categories: "Financial," "Customer/Market," "Internal Processes," and "Staff and Learning." The dealers would be able to retrieve the underlying detailed data on the following pages through a simple drill-down approach by clicking on a figure. On the first pages the figures would be marked according to a traffic-light scheme, with red lights indicating that urgent action was required. POF and PIT were to receive quarterly reports reflecting fewer figures than the monthly report that PCGB would receive. Yet the goal was to have a common report for the participating markets in the long run.

During the development phase, close contact was maintained with the area sales manager in charge of the communication with the American market (PCNA), whose office was next to that of the project team. PCNA had independently developed a similar, but less evolved system several years previously and had thus acquired a plethora of valuable experiences.

A tool, such as the balanced scorecard, that evaluates several [thousands] . . . figures per dealer has to first retrieve the data from somewhere. Luckily, most of the values could be derived from the multitude of figures already available in every dealership. The consultants therefore developed a software client to retrieve these data from the existing dealer management system on site. The additionally required data were entered by hand. Via the secure Porsche Partner Network phone lines, the data were then transferred to the server that generated the reports. The latter process was supervised by the consultants, who also notified the dealerships once [the reports] were available. The reports were then downloaded via a web-based interface. All the data available on the server could also be accessed by the regional managers—the people in charge of several dealerships. The concept even included a high-end profiling tool to compare dealerships, their performance and development.

The result was a unique system of such sophistication that it had no competitor. The Key Performance Indicator System was recommended to the dealers as a tool with many advantages:

- It focused on long-term strategic action, leading to lasting success instead of invoking shortsighted decisions to improve the annual accounts. Each dealership could evaluate its performance beyond that indicated by financial figures. Values such as customer satisfaction could be monitored constantly. And the KPI could even reveal specific potential for future improvement. Moreover, since warnings regarding critical developments were generated automatically, this allowed countermeasures to be taken to prevent these problems before they arose. All the KPI of the dealership were benchmarked to the national average and averages of groups of selected dealerships. These groups were determined by each of the markets.

- A two-way communication between the dealership and the headquarters during all stages allowed everyone to understand one another and to adapt to the overall strategic objectives of the organization and to adapt these objectives as well.
- In the long run the profitability of the entire sales network would improve.

Rolling Out—Hitting the Road

After the development of this revolutionary tool, it was necessary to ensure that the dealerships could and would make appropriate use of it. Unfortunately, a new tool initially always means additional work, and there are rarely immediate payoffs. During the development phase the project team had already laid the foundation for the dealerships' acceptance of the KPI by constantly keeping them informed and included in the process. The early pilot dealerships were proud of their participation and therefore put considerable effort into the system. The project team anticipated that after word about the first positive results had spread, further successes would be ensured.

The project team was fortunate to be able to draw on the previous experiences of either team members or colleagues in the same department, since many other innovations had been rolled out before. The most closely related example was the dealer web platform for pre-owned Porsche cars, whose schedule was only [a] few months ahead of the KPI. The tool itself could not be compared to a balanced scorecard, but it too was a web-based application on the Porsche Partner Network that was distributed to all dealerships and that depended on the active participation of every single dealership to be a success. With its similar structure, much of this innovation's incoming feedback could be directly applied to the KPI rollout process as well.

Another source of experience was the Porsche training department. Here manuals are written and trainings in respect [to] technical issues and sales techniques are provided for dealership employees. As the dealers participating in the project were used to their way of communication, the project team tried to understand the working style of the train-

ing department in order to emulate their approach, which would expedite the chances of acceptance by the dealerships. The knowledge transfer between the two departments was arduous at times since the training department had a natural desire to take charge of the training. It was, however, short of training resources due to the introduction of the new SUV: the Cayenne. In addition, knowledge of the KPI was almost exclusively limited to the project team. It was finally agreed to leave the team in charge of training, while continuous communication with the training department would allow the latter to monitor conformity to the Porsche training spirit.

One of the assistants [to] the project team wrote a handbook for the Key Performance Indicator System. This includes an introductory chapter on the motivation behind the KPI, its purposes, background and underlying theories, plus a description of the implementation and installation steps of the system, as well as instructions for its use. The manual moreover includes descriptions of and tips on approximately fifty main indicators. Restricted to the essence, this manual is targeted at general managers, dealership accountants and, in an extended version, at regional managers. The project team furthermore developed initial training sessions for accountants, which were to be conducted by the staff of the external agency and the project manager.

As the project took shape, contact between the headquarters, the external agency, and the markets was maintained. The initial version of the software system itself was basically completed, so process details and roll-out issues became more urgent. In a discussion with the market managers, the well-organized German project team learned that there was a strong tendency by the Italian dealers not to submit their data on time, while the British dealerships, conversely, would most likely submit their data without being reminded at all. This information led to a submission schedule being issued for each market: the official closing dates for PIT were brought forward to several days before the official internal closing date, with the real closing date being made known to PCGB. A series of reminders were also initiated to ensure submissions in a timely fashion, since the generation of the report would be delayed until all data had been collected.

It was very obvious that flawed submissions would disrupt the whole system and, due to the sheer size of the eighty-page report, the submissions were prone to errors. Before submission of the data, the client system would therefore validate it automatically and issue warnings and errors that would have to be removed by the dealer. Dealers were also asked to update their data if they discovered faulty submissions after the submission date. This kept the database accurate and long-term development could be monitored more precisely. If such an update were to occur, new reports would not be issued—neither for all dealerships, nor for the relevant dealership.

The roll-out was planned to start with a connection time of approximately one to 1.5 days per dealer and to arrive at five dealers per week in the long run. On these days a representative of the consultancy would visit the particular dealership and configure the KPI client application to fit the dealer management system. Prior to the roll-out, one of the assistants developed checklists of what would have to be done before and during a dealership's roll-out day. There were checklists for the consultancy, for the project team and for the dealership itself. The consultancy and the dealership had to evaluate each other's performance and suggest improvements. This feedback, which was initially copious, helped to improve the roll-out process dramatically.

In the first dealerships, the roll-out was supervised by the project manager and one of his assistants as well as the market manager in order to have an immediate on-site evaluation of the performance. During these first roll-out sessions many questions were answered and open issues resolved, which were then compiled into an information sheet that could be distributed to the dealerships beforehand. The dealership accountant, or whoever else was responsible for the KPI, had to be present at the roll-out. He was shown how to [set up] the system if a reinstallation or adaptation were ever necessary. In addition, he received a quick introductory training by the consultancy's representative and was given the KPI System Handbook.

On each roll-out day the consultant compiled a list of what had to be done for the dealership to fully comply with the requirements of the KPI System. Many dealerships had to create new accounts and start keeping track of previously ignored figures. These action lists were also passed on to the project team, who then monitored the course of their implementation according to a schedule that had been agreed upon with the dealerships. In general, the headquarters always endeavored to maintain their relationship with the dealerships as one of equal partners, but from time to time decisions had to be taken and thereafter enforced.

Since, despite the comprehensive documentation available, questions were sure to arise when the accountants entered data into the system, or when a general manager analyzed a report, the consultancy set up a hotline in each market. The dealerships were also provided with a small flowchart as a decision aid on when to contact the consultants' support network, or when to contact their particular regional man-

ager. At this stage the dealerships were truly equipped for the first phase.

Approximately a month after the first dealerships had been piloted through the system, data had to be submitted for the first time. Everything went well, although some minor delays occurred on the server generating the reports. Everyone involved was proud to see that things had worked out well and Dr. Offermann was pleased to receive the first report.

Hot Phase

When the reports were sent to the first dealerships, it became increasingly clear that the planned dedicated training was necessary. The training, which was already in the pipeline, targeted general managers and dealership accountants who had to deal with the tool in their daily business. Regional managers too had to be trained to provide their dealerships with consultation in respect [to] KPI issues. The first training sessions were therefore scheduled as soon as enough dealerships had been connected, which was about two months after the first dealership had been piloted. In order to carry out the trainings, the trainees were summoned to a regional training facility—Porsche-owned or independent—and [...] the capabilities and the features of the system [were explained]. Questions were encouraged, and first experiences were exchanged amongst participants from the various dealerships. As many dealerships also handled other automobile brands, they could make use of previous experiences with other, interior, reporting systems. Porsche was utterly convinced that it was the first manufacturer to introduce this type of balanced scorecard in automotive retailing.

In its handbook, the project team suggests a way of dealing with the reports, although the dealerships are not bound to this suggestion. They suggest that on receiving the report, the accountant should analyze it and create a memo of points that require attention. The report and the memo are then to be passed on to the general manager, who should study them and decide which actions to take. A print function allows a selection of pages that refer to a specific job position to be printed for these specific employees. With this personal printout everyone has access to information on issues in his sphere of influence without the inconvenience of receiving data related to other domains. This is thought to raise the awareness of the key factors that really matter for continuous improvement. The project team also stresses that simply handing out the sheets may not suffice—explicit encouragement to review them and information regarding their meaning may be required as well. Conducting a KPI meeting with managers, or putting KPI on the agenda of regular management meetings may further improve the success of the KPI System. During these meetings, all upcoming dangers, obstacles and progress should be examined to decide on how to handle the consequences. The meetings are promoted to focus on strategic questions—not tactical ones.

A regional manager's job is to visit and to provide all the dealers of a region with consultation. In order to facilitate their work, they, too, receive their dealerships' reports. They can analyze the performance with the profiling application and benchmark it to any other dealership, which might help to find the source of problems quicker than with the report alone. This unique profiling tool accelerates many of the regional managers' tasks that they would have to do by hand otherwise. Previously, i.e., before the balanced scorecard, these could only be done on the basis of information that the dealerships wished to provide. However, this profiling tool was not directly given to the dealerships, since the detailed data of other dealerships were kept strictly confidential.

Outlook

For the future, annual or semi-annual meetings, so-called Corporate KPI Conferences with representatives of all connected markets, are planned. The goal of these conferences, which nurture mutual exchange among markets, is to discuss ideas about improvement and future development of the KPI system. A further plan, suggested by the team, is to offer an award for the dealership of the quarter, which would then be presented as a best practice example in a circular. To improve the acceptance and the usage of the Key Performance Indicators by dealership employees, a KPI flyer was also introduced. This flyer summarizes all generally important information on the project plus information specific to various job positions. Employees will accordingly always know to which KPIs they primarily contribute.

Porsche has been committed to *Kaizen*—the Japanese expression for continuous improvement—since Dr. Wiedeking requested Japanese consultants to review all processes. It is therefore clear to everyone that a business tool such as the KPI System cannot be static. It has to keep track of the changes in its environment that can occur in very many ways to undermine core assumptions. For instance, competitors might take unexpected actions, new ones might emerge, major technological innovations could arise, government regulatory or deregulatory actions could change the competitive circumstances, and macroeconomic conditions could alter. Consequently, the project team emphasized the need for a regular review of the KPI System right from the beginning. The idea is to initiate a process of bilateral exchange in order to develop and improve the KPI System constantly. To keep the participants up to date with the development of the system, dealerships and regional managers will receive a regular circular that will also contain the best practice example mentioned above. It is planned to keep them informed about the news, exceptional successes, problem-solving strategies, and future plans. A questionnaire through which they can provide feedback will also be attached to the circular. Dealerships are also encouraged to let all levels participate in the feedback process, since many important ideas come from front-line employees and not only from general managers. Sufficient feedback could result in the removal or addition of key figures to the balanced scorecard. Additionally, a whole development cycle around the Corporate KPI Conferences, comparable to the initial planning workshops, is under way and will take place in November 2003 to continuously improve the KPI System.

Despite the satisfying initial results in the piloting markets and the promising future, only the first steps of a long [journey] have been taken.

Exhibit 2

Porsche Group Highlights

		1992/93	1993/94	1994/95	1995/96	1996/97	1997/98	1998/99	1999/00	2000/01	2001/02
Sales	€ million	978.1	1,194.2	1,332.9	1,437.7	2,093.3	2,519.4	3,161.3	3,647.7	4,441.6	4,857.3
Domestic	€ million	447.6	554.1	569.7	527.7	671.9	735.5	955.6	893.2	1,001.3	1,121.0
Export	€ million	530.5	640.1	763.2	910.0	1,421.4	1,783.9	2,205.7	2,754.5	3,440.2	3,736.3
Vehicle sales (new cars)	units	14,362	18,402	21,124	19,262	32,383	36,688	43,982	48,797	54,586	54,234
Domestic Porsche	units	3,544	5,574	6,420	5,873	9,670	9,174	10,607	11,754	12,401	12,825
Export Porsche	units	8,219	10,269	11,992	13,346	22,713	27,512	33,375	37,043	42,185	41,409
Other Models	units	2,599	2,559	2,712	43	—	—	—	—	—	—
Vehicle Sales Porsche	units	11,763	15,843	18,412	19,219	32,383	36,686	43,982	48,797	54,586	54,234
911	units	7,702	13,010	17,407	19,096	16,507	17,869	23,090	23,050	26,721	32,337
928	units	672	509	510	104	—	—	—	—	—	—
944/968	units	3,389	2,324	495	19	—	—	—	—	—	—
Boxster	units	—	—	—	—	15,876	18,817	20,892	25,747	27,865	21,897
Production	units	15,082	19,348	20,791	20,242	32,390	38,007	45,119	48,815	55,782	55,050
Porsche total	units	12,483	16,789	18,079	20,242	32,390	38,007	45,119	48,815	55,782	55,050
911	units	7,950	13,771	17,293	20,132	16,488	19,120	23,056	22,950	27,325	33,061
928	units	730	633	470	28	—	—	—	—	—	—
944/968	units	3,803	2,385	316	82	—	—	—	—	—	—
Boxster	units	—	—	—	—	15,902	18,887	22,063	25,865	28,467	21,989
Other models	units	2,599	2,559	2,712	—	—	—	—	—	—	—
Employees	at year-end	7,133	6,970	6,847	7,107	7,959	8,151	8,712	9,320	9,752	10,143
Personnel expenses	€ million	357.4	343.6	363.7	392.1	464.4	528.2	574.9	631.3	709.9	799.4
Balance Sheet											
Total Assets	€ million	769.7	795.6	836.7	951.4	1,249.7	1,490.9	1,916.1	2,205.4	2,891.6	5,408.7
Shareholders' Equity	€ million	197.2	218.2	210.5	239.1	298.1	415.8	587.4	782.0	1,053.3	1,466.8
Fixed Assets	€ million	382.8	351.4	353.2	482.5	565.3	579.6	525.6	577.7	731.8	2,207.7
Capital Expenditures	€ million	90.6	63.0	83.9	213.6	234.8	175.8	155.0	243.7	293.8	1,739.5[3]
Depreciation	€ million	78.2	76.6	55.2	67.7	107.6	157.1	183.7	196.6	132.7	278.8
Cash Flow	€ million	−17.9	17.6	94.8	123.6	205.5	305.0	407.8	424.7	418.4	781.5
Extended Cash Flow	€ million						413.1	592.5	506.5	764.4	1,067.3
Net income/loss before taxes	€ million	−122.3	−73.9	5.8	27.9	84.5	165.9	357.0	433.8	592.4	628.9
Net income/loss after taxes	€ million	−122.1	−76.8	1.1	24.6	71.3	141.6	190.9	210.0	270.5	462.0
Dividends	€ million	—	1.0	1.1	1.8	13.0	21.9	21.9	26.4	46.0	297.0[4]
Dividends per share[1]											
Common stock	€	—	—	—	0.08	0.72	1.23	1.23	1.48	2.54	16.94[5]
Preferred stock	€	—	0.13	0.13	0.13	0.77	1.28	1.28	1.53	2.60	17.00[5]
DVFA/SG earnings per share[2]	€	−8.90	−5.30	0.10	1.10	4.10	4.80	13.00	13.70	17.20	27.80

[1] Fiscal years up to 1999/00 have been retroactively recognized according to the stock split in fiscal year 2000/01.
[2] Deutsche Vereinigung für Finanzanalyse und Anlageberatung/Schmalenbach-Gesellschaft, fiscal years up to 1999/00 have been retroactively recognized according to the stock split in fiscal year 2000/01.
[3] Excluding additions related to initial consolidations.
[4] Thereof special dividend of 245 million Euros.
[5] Thereof special dividend of 14 Euros.

Source: Porsche AG, Online Annual Report, December 1, 2002

Case 30

Google in China

Case: P-54
DATE: 11/15/06

"It's an imperfect world, we had to make an imperfect choice."

—Elliot Schrage, Google vice president for global communications and public affairs.

Introduction

Using servers located in the United States, Google began offering a Chinese-language version of Google.com in 2000. The site, however, was frequently unavailable or slow because of censoring by the Chinese government. Google obtained a significant share of searches in China but lagged behind market leader Baidu.com. To achieve commercial success, Google concluded that it was imperative to host a website from within China. Given its motto, "Don't Be Evil," Google had to decide whether to operate from within China or to continue to rely on Google.com. If it decided to establish operations in China, the company had to decide how to deal with the censorship imposed by the Chinese government.

As a result of an extensive debate within the company, co-founder Serge Brin explained their decision: "We gradually

STANFORD Professor David P. Baron prepared this case from public sources as the basis for class discussion rather than to illustrate either effective or ineffective handling of an administrative situation.

came to the realization that we were hurting not just ourselves but the Chinese people."[1] Google decided to establish the site Google.cn, but without features that allowed users to provide content. To avoid putting individuals in jeopardy of being arrested, Google offered neither e-mail nor the ability to create blogs, since user-generated material could be seized by the Chinese government. This allowed Google to avoid putting individuals in jeopardy of being arrested. Because it would be required by Chinese law to censor search results associated with sensitive issues, Google decided to place a brief notice at the bottom of a search page when material had been censored, as it did in other countries such as France and Germany which banned the sale of Nazi items. Google planned to exercise self-censorship and developed a list of sensitive items by consulting with third parties and by studying the results of the Chinese government's Internet filtering. Senior policy counsel Andrew McLaughlin stated, "Google is mindful that governments around the world impose restriction on access to information. In order to operate from China, we have removed some content from the search results available on Google.cn, in response to local law, regulation or policy. While removing search results is inconsistent with Google's mission, providing no information (or a heavily degraded user experience that amounts to no information) is more inconsistent with our mission."[2]

Within a month of offering Google.cn, Google came under criticism from two government-run newspapers in China. The *Beijing News* criticized the company for not doing enough to block "harmful information." Referring to Google's practice of informing users when search results

[1] *San Jose Mercury News*, March 3, 2006.
[2] *The New York Times*, January 25, 2006.

had been censored, the *China Business Times* wrote in an editorial, "Is it necessary for an enterprise that is operating within the borders of China to constantly tell your customers you are following domestic law?" Both publications claimed that Google was operating as an Internet content provider without a proper license.[3]

Reporters Without Borders, a Paris-based organization campaigning for freedom of expression, called the establishment of Google.cn "a black day for freedom of expression in China." It stated:

> The firm defends the rights of U.S. Internet users before the U.S. government, but fails to defend its Chinese users against theirs. United States companies are now bending to the same censorship rules as their Chinese competitors, but they continue to justify themselves by saying their presence has a long-term benefit. Yet the Internet in China is becoming more and more isolated from the outside world.[4]

Other activists demanded that Google publish its censorship blacklist in the United States.

INTERNET CENSORSHIP IN CHINA According to the U.S. State Department, companies offering Internet services were "pressured to sign the Chinese government's 'Public Pledge on Self-Discipline for the Chinese Internet Industry.'" Under the agreement, they promised not to disseminate information that "breaks laws or spreads superstition or obscenity" or that "may jeopardize state security and disrupt social stability."[5] Providing Internet services required a license which in turn required not circulating information that "damages the honor or interests of the state" or "disturbs the public order or destroys public stability . . ."[6]

Censorship in China involved self-regulation by Internet companies as well as government actions. The government did not provide a list of objectionable subjects—instead companies inferred which topics were out of bounds by observing what the government censors removed. The State Council Information Office also convened weekly meetings with Internet service providers. An American executive explained, "It's known informally as the 'wind-blowing meeting'—in other words, which way is the wind blowing. They say: 'There's this party conference going on this week. There are some foreign

dignitaries here on this trip.'"[7] Xin Ye, a founder of Sohu.com, a Chinese value-added Internet services firm, was asked how hard it was to navigate the censorship system. He said, "I'll tell you this, it's not more hard than dealing with Sarbanes and Oxley."[8]

Zhao Jing, a political blogger in China, "explained that he knew where the government drew the line. 'If you talk every day online and criticize the government, they don't care. Because it's just talk. But if you organize—even if it's just three or four people—that's what they crack down on. It's not speech; it's organizing.'"[9] In December 2005 Zhao called for a boycott of a newspaper because it had fired an editor. In response, the Chinese government asked Microsoft's MSN to close Zhao's blog and Microsoft complied.[10] Brooke Richardson of MSN said, "We only remove content if the order comes from the appropriate regulatory authority."[11]

Yahoo and MSN, as well as other sites, complied with Chinese law as well as exercising self-censorship.[12] Robin Li, chairman of the Chinese search company Baidu.com, said, "We are trying to provide as much information as possible. But we need to obey Chinese law."[13] Baidu had reached an agreement that allowed the Chinese government to oversee its website and in exchange it avoided the disruptions of service and strict operating rules that plagued foreign Internet companies.[14]

In 2004 Yahoo provided information to the Chinese government that led to the arrest of the journalist Shi Tao. Shi was subsequently sentenced to 10 years in prison for releasing state secrets on a foreign website. Shi had provided information by e-mail about a Communist party decision. Yahoo general counsel Michael Callahan said the company regretted the action but had no alternative since its Chinese employees could have been arrested on criminal charges for

---

[3] *Washington Post*, February 22, 2006. Google shared a license with a Chinese company Ganji.com. This practice was common among foreign Internet firms.

[4] *The New York Times*, January 25, 2006, op. cit.

[5] *Business Week*, January 23, 2006.

[6] Clive Thompson, "Google's China Problem (and China's Google Problem)," *The New York Times Magazine*, April 23, 2006.

[7] Clive Thompson, "Google's China Problem (and China's Google Problem)," *The New York Times Magazine*, April 23, 2006.

[8] Ibid.

[9] Ibid.

[10] Microsoft's blogging servers are located in the United States. Clive Thompson, "Google's China Problem (and China's Google Problem)," *The New York Times Magazine*, April 23, 2006.

[11] *Business Week*, January 23, 2006, op. cit.

[12] Yahoo lagged behind other Internet companies in China and in 2005 invested $ 1 billion for a 40 percent interest in the Chinese company Alibaba.com. Yahoo then turned operating control of Yahoo China over to Alibaba.com.

[13] *Business Week*, January 23, 2006, op. cit. Baidu had a 46.5 percent share of Internet searches in China; Google was second with 26.9 percent. Google had a small stake in Baidu but sold it in June 2006.

[14] *The New York Times*, September 17, 2006.

not providing the information to the government. Callahan also said that Chinese law prohibited disclosing how many times the company had provided information on users to the government.[15]

The agencies that regulated the Internet employed 30,000 people who monitored e-mail, websites, blogs, and chat rooms. Internet cafes were required to use software that stored data on all users. Anyone establishing a blog was required to register with the government. Telephone companies were required to incorporate software that censored text messaging.

A key part of the censorship system was the control by the government of all gateways into China. This allowed the censors to block undesired content on websites and restrict Internet search results. Referred to as the Great Firewall of China, routers at China's nine Internet gateways examined messages and search requests and were programmed to block or censor information. It was this firewall that made accessing Google.com slow or at times unavailable from China.

China also blocked certain news sites including the BBC News, Voice of America, Amnesty International, Human Rights in China, and Wikipedia, in addition to any information on the spiritual movement Falun Gong which was banned in China. Search results on terms such as Tiananmen Massacre, Tibet, and Dalai Lama were also suppressed.

Censorship was also practiced elsewhere, including at universities. University computer systems and bulletin boards banned certain subjects such as politics, and student monitors directed chatroom conversation away from sensitive subjects to those that helped build a "harmonious society." Student monitor Hu Yingying said, "We don't control things, but we don't want bad or wrong things to appear on the websites. According to our social and educational systems, we should judge what is right and wrong. And as I'm a student cadre, I need to play a pioneering role among other students, to express my opinion, to make stronger my belief in Communism." Another student, Tang Guochao, said, "A bulletin board is like a family, and in a family, I want my room to be clean and well-lighted, without dirty or dangerous things in it."[16]

The censorship system was in a technology race with those attempting to evade it. Bill Xia, who arrived in the United States as a student in the 1990s and subsequently founded Dynamic Internet Technology (DIT), developed software called FreeGate that masks the websites that users visit.[17] Companies such as DIT and UltraReach also used software

to create new websites to elude the Chinese censors.[18] For Voice of America, for example, DIT established uncensored proxy sites that directed users to the real site. DIT and UltraReach sent millions of e-mails a day alerting users to the uncensored sites. The Chinese censors worked to shut down the proxy sites and were often able to close the sites within a few days. The companies then would develop new software to evade the censors.

The Chinese government sought to justify its practices. Liu Zhengrong, deputy director of the State Council Information Office's Internet Affairs Bureau, argued that China's efforts to keep out "harmful" and "illegal" information were similar to those in Western countries. He said, "If you study the main international practices in this regard you will find that China is basically in compliance. The main purposes and methods of implementing our laws are basically the same."[19] He observed that the *New York Times* and *Washington Post* websites deleted content that was illegal or in bad taste. He added, "Our practices are completely consistent with international practices." He continued, "Many of our practices we got from studying the U.S. experience."[20] He noted, "It is clear that any country's legal authorities closely monitor the spread of illegal information. We have noted that the U.S. is doing a good job on this front."[21]

Liu commented, "No one in China has been arrested simply because he or she said something on the Internet."[22] Reporters Without Borders claimed that 62 Chinese were in prison for "Posting on the Internet articles and criticism of the authorities."[23]

Despite the international criticism of Internet censorship in China, it was not clear that the Chinese people were concerned. Kai-Fu Lee, who headed operations for Google in China said, "People are actually quite free to talk about [democracy and human rights in China]. I don't think they care that much. I think people would say: 'Hey, U.S. democracy, *that's* a good form of government. Chinese government, good and stable, *that's* a good form of government. Whatever, as long as I get to go to my favorite website, see my friends, live happily.'"[24]

Ji Xiaoyin, a junior at Shanghai Normal University, commented, "I don't think anybody can possibly control any information in the Internet. If you're not allowed to talk here

---

[15] *San Jose Mercury News*, February 20, 2006.

[16] *The New York Times*, May 9, 2006.

[17] Human Rights in China and Radio Free Asia were also DIT clients.

[18] Both DIT and UltraReach were said to be connected to the Falun Gong movement. *San Jose Mercury News*, July 2, 2006.

[19] *The New York Times*, February, 15, 2006.

[20] *Wall Street Journal*, February 15, 2006.

[21] *The New York Times*, February, 15, 2006, op. cit.

[22] *San Jose Mercury News*, February 20, 2006, op. cit.

[23] *San Jose Mercury News*, July 2, 2006.

[24] Clive Thompson, op. cit.

you just go to another place to talk, and there are countless places for your opinions. It's easy to bypass the firewalls, and anybody who spends a little time researching it can figure it out."[25]

GOOGLE'S PERSPECTIVE In response to criticism that Google should lobby the Chinese government to change its censorship system, CEO Eric E. Schmidt said during a visit to China, "I think it's arrogant for us to walk into a country where we are just beginning operations and tell that country how to run itself." He also explained, "We had a choice to enter the county and follow the law. Or we had a choice not to enter the country." Earlier he had said, "We believe the decision that we made to follow the law in China was absolutely the right one."[26]

Speaking at an ethics conference on Internet search at Santa Clara University, Peter Norvig, director of research at Google, commented on the decision not to offer services such as e-mail and blogging in China. "We didn't want to be in a position to hand over users' information. . . .We thought that was just too dangerous. . . .We thought it was very important to keep our users out of jail."[27]

Norvig justified Google's policies in China. "Yes, it's important to get information about democracy and Falun Gong. They also want to know about outbreaks of bird flu. We thought it was more important to give them this information that they can use even if we have to compromise."[28]

Google continued to debate internally whether and how it should operate in China. It also hoped for guidance from the U.S. government and the industry. Norvig said, "We feel that the U.S. government can stand up and make stronger laws, and we feel that corporate America can get together and have stronger principles. We're supporting efforts on both those fronts. We feel we can't do it alone."[29]

Norvig disclosed that Google was not keeping search logs in China. "They don't have personally identifiable information but they do have IP addresses that are potentially identifiable with an individual."[30] That information was kept in the United States, and China could request that information through the U.S. State Department.

POLITICAL PRESSURE IN THE UNITED STATES In advance of congressional hearings on China and censorship, the State Department announced the creation of a Global Internet Task Force to decrease censorship and encourage change in other countries. Paula Dobriansky, undersecretary of state for democracy, human rights, and labor, said, "The Internet, especially, can be a liberating force. Topics once politically taboo can become freely discussed, and people can communicate anonymously. We must ensure it does not become a tool of repression."[31]

Representative Chris Smith (R-NJ), chairman of the House Subcommittee on Africa, Global Human Rights, and International Operations, introduced the Global Internet Freedom Act that would impose restrictions on U.S. companies operating in China. It included a code of conduct, requiring that e-mail servers be located outside the country, and licensing requirements for the export of technologies that could be used for censorship. Smith held a hearing in which Cisco Systems, Google, Microsoft, and Yahoo testified and were grilled by subcommittee members. Commenting on China's sophisticated censorship system, Smith said, "It's an active partnership with both the disinformation campaign and . . . , and the secret police in China are among the most brutal on the planet. I don't know if these companies understand that or they're naïve about it, whether they're witting or unwitting. But it's been a tragic collaboration. There are people in China being tortured courtesy of these corporations."[32] The bill was passed by the subcommittee and was sent to full committee for consideration.

Representative Tom Lantos (D-CA), leader of the Congressional Human Rights Caucus and a survivor of the Holocaust, said, "These captains of industry should have been developing new technologies to bypass the sickening censorship of government and repugnant barriers to the Internet. Instead, they enthusiastically volunteered for the censorship brigade."[33]

In congressional testimony Elliot Schrage, vice president of global communications and public affairs at Google, explained that China was an important market for the company. He said, "It would be disingenuous to say that we don't care about that because, of course, we do. We are a business with stockholders, and we want to prosper and grow in a highly competitive world. At the same time, acting ethically is a core value for our company, and an integral part of our business culture."[34]

Earlier in 2006 Google had refused to comply with a request from the U.S. government to provide information on

[25] *The New York Times*, May 9, 2006, op. cit.

[26] *The New York Times*, April 13, 2006.

[27] *San Jose Mercury News*, March 1, 2006, and March 3, 2006, op. cit.

[28] *San Jose Mercury News*, March 1, 2006, op. cit.

[29] *San Jose Mercury News*, March 1, 2006, op. cit.

[30] *San Jose Mercury News*, March 3, 2006, op. cit.

[31] *San Jose Mercury News*, February 15, 2006, op. cit.

[32] Ibid.

[33] *San Jose Mercury News*, February 19, 2006.

[34] *Wall Street Journal*, March 10, 2006.

Internet search requests.[35] The government had asked Google for a random sample of 1 million web addresses and a week's search requests with any information that could identify the user removed. The information was to be used for a study to show that Internet filters were not sufficient to prevent children from accessing pornographic websites. The Department of Justice sought the information to help revive the 1998 Child Online Protection Act that had been blocked by the Supreme Court and sent to the Court of Appeals for reconsideration. Google strongly objected to the request on privacy grounds and refused to provide the information. The Department of Justice then took Google to court to force it to provide the information. In the court hearing the government substantially scaled back its request, and the judge ordered Google to provide 50,000 random web addresses. The judge also ruled that providing the requested 50,000 random search queries could harm Google through a loss of goodwill among its users.[36]

In June Brin commented on the criticism Google had received. He said, "We felt that perhaps we could compromise our principles but provide ultimately more information for the Chinese and be a more effective service and perhaps make more of a difference. . . . Perhaps now the principled approach makes more sense."[37]

In July Amnesty International launched a campaign against Internet oppression, mentioning Sun Microsystems, Nortel, Cisco, Yahoo, Google, and Microsoft. Amnesty stated, "Internet companies often claim to be ethically responsible—these pledges will highlight how their cooperation in repression risks making them complicit in human rights abuses and damages their credibility."[38]

Preparation Questions

1. What principles are relevant for Google's decision to enter China? Is censorship consistent with Google's core values? Should compromises be made?

2. Why does the Chinese government censor information so aggressively?

3. Should Google have entered China?

4. Given that Google decided to enter China, should it have offered e-mail and hosted blogs? Should it have restricted its offerings more than it actually did?

5. Are Google's practices sufficient? What else should it do?

6. Should Google lobby the Chinese government to change its censorship policies?

7. Should Google lobby the U.S. government to develop a policy to guide U.S. Internet companies in China?

---

[35]The government also sought similar data from AOL, Microsoft's MSN, and Yahoo, all of which complied with the request.

[36]The judge also stated that the search queries could be within the scope of a subpoena. *San Francisco Chronicle*, March 18, 2006.

[37]*San Jose Mercury News*, June 7, 2006.

[38]Amnesty International, press release, July 20, 2006, www.amnesty.org.

Case 31

Green Room Productions, LLC

UVA-ENT-0080

In November 1995, Trip Davis sat facing his two business partners and fellow Dartmouth alums, Greg Waldbaum and Eric Butz, at the table in the conference room of their Charlottesville, Virginia, office. The three old friends and new business partners had reached a crucial point in their startup business, Green Room Productions. Just five months earlier, they had combined their talents to provide professional and technology services to companies in the travel industry seeking to do business via the burgeoning Internet commerce sector. Since then, the firm had been unable to find sufficient human resources to staff its technology projects. As the weeks dragged on, the partners realized that their business would not succeed in its current location. Now, in the cramped conference room of their fledgling company, the partners considered two options: close the business down or move to another city for the second time in five months.

The current conversation focused on the business itself, but each partner knew that the ultimate decision would have a profound impact not only on their business, but also their professional careers and personal lives. Closing the business

meant that each would have to seek new employment—and perhaps relocate. Moving the business meant personal relocation was a certainty—but to where? Where could Green Room Productions move to find the human resources it needed to be a viable business? The partners realized that even if they found an appropriate location and decided to move rather than shut down the business, they also needed to consider a new division of the firm's equity stakes. A related consideration was whether it was time to reallocate roles and titles as potential new employees joined the firm? As he listened to the other young men debate the options with rising tension, Davis wondered if Green Room Productions could survive. Above all, he didn't want to "screw up our friendships over the business."

The Rise of Internet Commerce and the Travel Industry

In 1994, as the Internet flourished, consumers and businesses alike were exploring the benefits and limitations of conducting business via the World Wide Web (See Exhibit 1 for a chart of growth in websites and trends in server efficiencies. See Exhibit 2 for a chart of growth in the World Wide Web commerce sites). Travelers who had previously relied on intermediary agencies for information could increasingly gather data on flight schedules, hotels, automobile rentals, and destinations by logging on via dial-up services such as Prodigy. *The New York Times* Practical Traveler suggested that "People with computers, modems, and memberships in one or more of the on-line services can act as their own travel agents. It isn't always easy, and it isn't free, but it can be rewarding."[1]

DARDEN

This case was prepared by Dorothy Kelly, CFA (MBA '92), and Susan Singer (MBA '06), under the supervision of Gregory B. Fairchild, Assistant Professor of Business Administration. It was written as a basis for class discussion rather than to illustrate effective or ineffective handling of an administrative situation.

[1] L.R. Shannon, "Practical Traveler; Getting on Line Before You Go," *New York Times*, 30 January 1994.

Exhibit 1 Green Room Productions, LLC

Growth of the World Wide Web and Server Efficiency Increases

Growth of WWW, .Com Sites and Server Efficiency

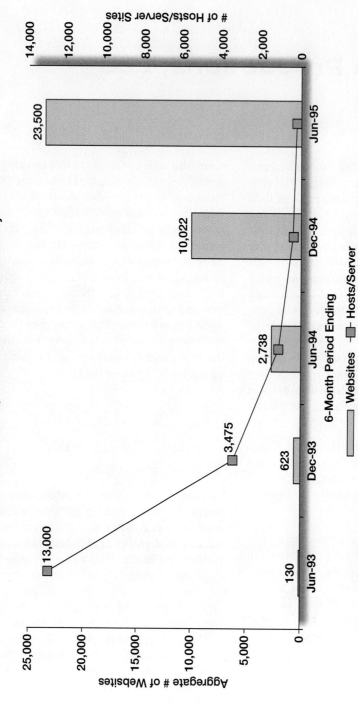

Source: Matthew Gray, "Measuring the Growth of the Web," 1995, http://www.mit.edu/people/mkgray/net/web-growth-summary.html (accessed 28 July 2006).

Exhibit 2

Green Room Productions, LLC

Growth of the World Wide Web and Server Efficiency Increases

Growth of WWW, .Com Sites and Server Efficiency

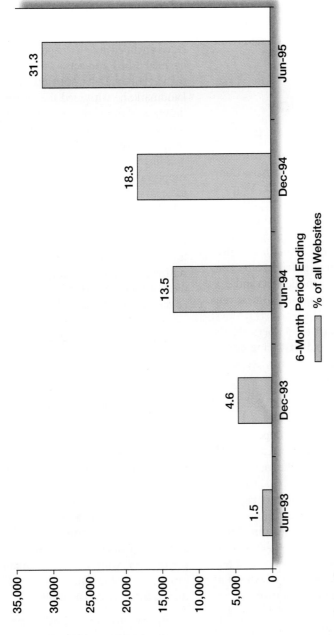

Source: Gray.

Booking travel via the Internet was not as easy as collecting travel information, however. Many sites lacked the proper interfaces necessary to link existing computer reservation systems to the Internet and thus did not offer on-line reservations systems. Walt Disney World's site, for example, collected information via a "reservation request" form and passed it on to a travel agent to complete the booking via telephone. Other sites simply provided the same information provided by the business's glossy brochures, including a telephone number to call for more information and booking reservations.

An Influential Experience: The Travel Channel

After graduating from business school in 1994, Trip Davis had accepted a position as an analyst at Landmark Communications, a media conglomerate in Norfolk, Virginia. Landmark, which held interests in newspapers (the *Virginian-Pilot* and the *Roanoke Times*), television broadcasting (KLAS-TV, based in Las Vegas), cable programming (the Weather Channel and the Travel Channel), and electronic publishing (weather.com and goTriad.com), was among the many businesses exploring the benefits and limitations of the Web. Davis's position focused on new ventures for the Travel Channel, a cable channel offering travel information to 15 million individual subscribers. At the time, the channel operated at a loss and was losing money daily. To become profitable, the cable channel needed to double its audience to 30 million subscribers.

Davis was tasked with finding ways to extend the Travel Channel's distribution and work toward break-even. He expended considerable time learning about the opportunities the Internet was creating. From his office in Landmark's headquarters, Davis witnessed the changes the Internet was causing in the media and publication industries. He came to understand the struggles many industries were facing as unique opportunities that the breadth, reach, and cost-effectiveness of the Internet offered as a medium. Landmark, for example, owned the content provided on the Weather Channel, and thus found it easy to set up and register the domain name for www.weather.com to expand its reach. The Travel Channel, however, did not own its content. Consequently Landmark found it difficult to translate the Travel Channel offerings to the Internet.

Davis investigated the travel industry in an effort to determine how to position the Travel Channel in this new medium. He analyzed the changes in the industry and looked at ways the Travel Channel could capitalize on the changing landscape. His efforts led to meetings with Internet Service Providers (ISPs) such as AOL, Prodigy, and CompuServe. Those ISPs already provided limited travel information on their Web sites and expected travel to be an increasingly significant draw for their clients. The rising consumer demand for access to information, paired with a limited supply of content, created an anxiety among ISPs, however. They had created the channel, and now needed to fill it. Many were eager to partner with companies that could provide additional travel content.

Davis attended and participated in many conferences, where he established contacts with mainstream travel suppliers such as Hilton, Delta, Marriott, and Disney. As an analyst for Landmark, he witnessed the excitement in the nascent industry as a front-row spectator. Davis, however, felt "frustrated as a spectator—I wanted to be in the game." He regularly received calls from travel suppliers who needed help deciding whether to build, buy, or partner with an ISP. The suppliers needed Web sites, but did not know how or where to begin to develop them. They lacked understanding of how a Web site would relate to their current business. Smaller companies were turning to ISPs and getting help from them. Larger firms, however, could not rely on ISPs, which at the time lacked the nationwide reach of the larger players. Consulting groups, system integrators, and advertising agencies did not fully understand the technology yet and had yet to educate their own staffs about the emerging technology.

A Conference Creates a Reunion

In early 1995, Davis coincidentally ran into longtime friend and former university classmate Greg Waldbaum at a travel conference in Washington, D.C. The two had been friends since they met during the winter of 1986 at a fraternity house near Dartmouth College. Throughout their friendship, they had often discussed the idea of starting their own business together. Waldbaum had grown up in Denver and watched his father, a lawyer, participate in many varied business deals. According to Waldbaum, his father "owned a little piece of everything." And he himself had already experimented with entrepreneurship, securing the campuswide distributorship for the Miller Brewing Company during his time at Dartmouth.

Newly reunited, the friends explored the travel business idea with commensurate vigor. Waldbaum, like Davis, had recently completed his MBA. He worked in Breckenridge, Colorado, as a senior marketing manager for Ralston Resorts, the resort division of Ralston-Purina. Still, he was eager to start his own business. Each night during the travel conference, the two met in the hotel and brainstormed various business ideas. They made the fundamental decision to start a company together. For the next several evenings, they debated what kind of company it would be.

Through their discussions, Davis and Waldbaum concluded they had a central advantage, a "natural synergy." with Davis's experience in travel marketing and Waldbaum's experience in distribution. Both had been working to incorporate the Internet into their companies' respective marketing strategies. With their interests in travel and technology, they focused on two ideas: (1) provide technology services to help travel companies develop their Internet presence, and (2) develop original on-line content such as sightseeing guides to resorts and travel destinations.

At the time, only two online travel Web sites existed: pctravel.com and Mountain Travel*Sobek (MTS). Pctravel.com was a service offered by American Travel Corp. (ATC) in North Carolina, a regional travel agency. The service allowed consumers to book airline flights over the Internet at no cost. Pctravel.com connected users through ATC's computers to the Apollo Computer Reservation Systems (CRS), translating complex codes and commands into a simpler interface. The agency collected its normal commissions for issuing tickets booked through the system. MTS, a leader in adventure travel, had, according to Davis, an "eye-popping Web site with gorgeous content" showcasing the company's trips to Europe, Nepal, and other destinations.

Waldbaum and Davis knew that the development and rapid growth of the Internet presented a unique opportunity for them. Venture capitalists were furiously funding technology and Internet-related companies. They were certain that travel on the Internet would be "huge." (See Exhibits 3 and 4 for information regarding the growth of airline travel as well as the productivity and labor costs of travel agents.) Both had witnessed the demand and frustrations of travel companies that wanted technical help but could not find it readily available. One issue they needed to ponder was their relationships with their current employers, both legal and otherwise. They wondered how they could position themselves with their current employers so that they would be seen as viable vendors in the future.

Location, Location, Location

Davis and Waldbaum's next major decision was to decide where to locate the business. Because of the nature of the Internet and technology business, their venture did not need to be in the same location as potential clients. Face-to-face interaction was not necessary outside of organized

meetings and conference calls. Said Davis, "We can do it wherever we want to do it. We just need the resources."

Waldbaum, who was living in his hometown of Denver, believed that his city would be a great place to locate the business. Davis and his wife, Nicol, lived in Norfolk, Virginia, and preferred to live in either Charlottesville, where Davis had attended graduate school, or Hanover, New Hampshire, home of his and Waldbaum's undergraduate alma mater.

Charlottesville, home to the University of Virginia (U.Va.), was a college town with total population, city and county, of approximately 100,000.[2] The area boasted a well-educated work force, excellent medical facilities, and a relaxed lifestyle just two hours' drive from Washington, D.C. With a reputation as a writers' and readers' paradise, the area had more newspaper readers per capita than any other locale in the nation.[3] In 1993, Charlottesville ranked 37th on *Money* magazine's list of the nation's most livable cities. Davis had fallen in love with the locale during his two years of graduate school. He and Nicol thought it would be a "fantastic place to raise a family."

In the spring of 1995, Davis, with the help of colleagues, established contacts in U.Va.'s Computer Science department. Faculty members there were enthusiastic, energetic, and helpful. Davis believed that such contacts would be useful in finding and identifying talented people for their new venture. He felt confident that with the help of that department's faculty, he and Waldbaum could obtain staffing resources from U.Va. If necessary, he thought they might attract talent from nearby Richmond, Washington, D.C., and even the Research Triangle in neighboring North Carolina. With those strong connections and idyllic lifestyle, Charlottesville looked like a terrific place to locate the business. Although Waldbaum believed that Denver, too, would be a great place to be, he was eager to start a company and was mobile—unmarried, though with a girlfriend. So Waldbaum agreed to move to Charlottesville.

Yet Another Hanover Acquaintance

Before moving to Charlottesville, the partners realized they needed to fill a significant gap in their partnership—technical skills. On his first visit to U.Va.'s Computer Science department in the spring of 1995, Davis

[2]http://www.census.gov/prod/cen1990/cp-1-48.pdf (accessed 17 July 2006)

[3]"Best Place to Get Found," *Outside* magazine, May 1999.

Exhibit 3 Green Room Productions, LLC

Airline Data

Passengers Carried and Revenue per Passenger Mile (in 1982 cents): 1960–94

Travel Passenger and Revenue Trends

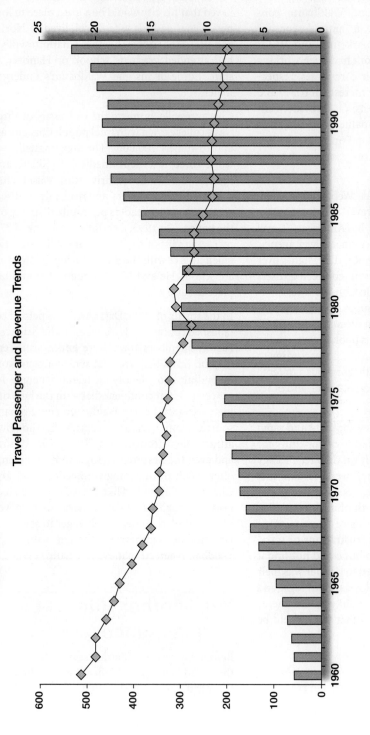

▬ Millions of passengers   ◇ $/passenger mile (1982 $s)

Source: Air Transport Association, http://www.airlines.org/econ/Exhibit 3 (accessed 20 July 2006).

Exhibit 4

Green Room Productions, LLC

Travel Agent Cost and Productivity: 1987–94

Travel Agent Productivity and Costs

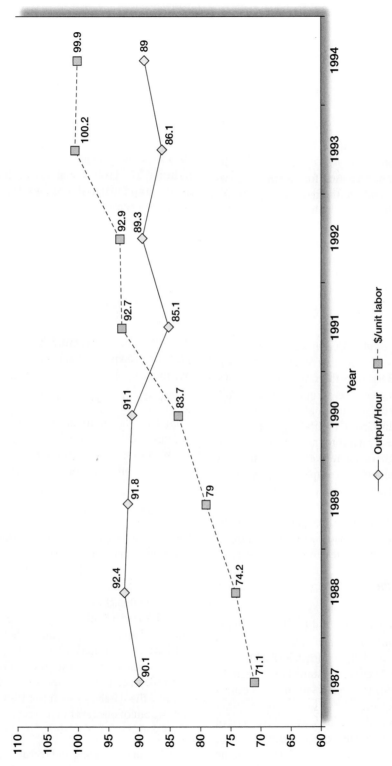

Source: "New Service Industry Productivity Measures, Report 979." U.S. Department of Labor Bureau of Labor Statistics, September 2004.

encountered a Dartmouth classmate who informed him that yet another classmate, Eric Butz, would soon move to Charlottesville.

Butz, who also had been raised in Denver, had just completed his master's degree in computer science, with a focus on artificial intelligence. He was moving from Boulder, Colorado, with his wife, Lucinda, who would soon begin her first year at U.Va.'s School of Architecture. Butz had been in the process of looking for technical work in Charlottesville and was finding limited opportunities.

Through a series of conference calls in May and June 2005, Davis, Waldbaum, and Butz discussed the business opportunity. Butz, who already had a reason for moving to Charlottesville, was intrigued and considered the opportunity appealing. Growing up in Denver, he had watched his father, a lawyer by training, invest in many different types of ventures ranging from an ice cream store to local filmmakers. According to Butz, that upbringing built "a tolerance for turbulence and living with risk." Given the early stage of the opportunity, Butz told himself, "even if it doesn't succeed, at least I'll get a great experience and learn something."

The threesome turned their attention to finding a name for their venture. All agreed that including "green" in the name made an appropriate allusion to their alma mater, Dartmouth (a shade of forest green was adopted as the school's official color in 1866, and Dartmouth athletic teams were unofficially known as "the Green" or "the Big Green"). Although they wanted to tie the name to the Web in some way, they wanted to avoid a generic name like "travel technology company" or "Web development company." The solution came to them from an unexpected source. Butz's brother, an avid surfer, explained that surfers entering the tube of a wave call it the "Green Room." The three partners loved the analogy, as "surfing the Internet" had become part of Internet lingo. Because they hoped they might eventually expand the business into producing original content and programs for the Web, they added the word "productions" and Green Room Productions was born.

With the financial backing of their families, the three partners each made a contribution to startup capital. Davis and Waldbaum each contributed approximately $4,000, and Butz contributed $1,500. They each assumed the title of director. Within 60 days, they received a $40,000 loan from a local bank. Each partner signed the loan; Davis's father cosigned. The partners leased an office on the third floor of an historic building near downtown Charlottesville and equipped it with used office furniture and a leased phone system. They agreed not to use the entire $40,000 loan to buy computers and servers during the first few weeks of the business. Instead they found a local entrepreneur and real estate agent with a leasing company who leased them $20,000 in computer equipment. Like the bank loan, the leasing agreement was personally guaranteed by the three.

Green Room Productions, LLC

With an office, phones, and a computer network, Green Room Productions, LLC, opened for business. The firm followed a dual business model: develop proprietary travel Web sites and provide technology solutions for the travel industry. The professional services business was structured as a time and materials business. Davis felt it was an attractive business model—especially for a first business. "If you have employees that are working at 80%, the business just works." Within weeks, the partners had hired two technical employees including a boyish-looking 18-year-old high school graduate with a morning paper route. He lacked formal training and education but was an avid gamer and occasional hacker with adequate technical skills who was able to quickly learn the skills they needed.

While Butz and the technical hires worked on developing the Web sites, Davis and Waldbaum focused on developing new business. In sales pitches, they offered clients the "three S":

Site: Set up and create Web site infrastructure;

Systems: Create applications connected to the client's existing information infrastructure with systems that enabled customers to make reservations, book tickets, or transact other business on the client's Web site;

Strategy: Assist clients with Internet strategy and maintain a focus on their brand.

Demand from clients, including the Travel Channel and other industry participants such as Mountain Travel* Sobek, Disney, and ITT Sheraton, was instant. Whereas smaller HTML projects brought gross revenues of $10,000 to $100,000 each, the larger more code-intensive projects ranged from $0.5 million to $1.0 million. Green Room Productions had a handful of other clients ready to go, but did not have the technical resources to staff the projects. They needed designers to create the professional look and feel, and infrastructure developers to code the applications to connect the databases with the Web sites. "We had clients coming out of our ears but no resources in terms of people," Davis said.

They began advertising and recruiting for additional staff in local papers in Charlottesville, Washington D.C., Richmond, and Raleigh/Durham. They also posted notices on bulletin boards around the university, with particular focus on the Computer Science and Engineering departments. Davis reflected on the early period:

> We very quickly discovered that we were way ahead of the curve. There were very few people who understood the Internet; who understood how to program for the Internet; who knew how to design for the Internet. We had an instant business where we could have 100 full time employees cranking away for paying clients. But we couldn't get the people . . . I'd open my e-mail box and there was nothing there in terms of the recruits . . . And go down to the PO Box and there was just air . . . Those were very disappointing moments in August and September.

Some of the partners encountered comparable disappointments at home. Davis and his wife had a relatively easy transition to Charlottesville. Nicol, a grade school teacher, quickly found a position in the local school system. They lived rent-free in a condominium owned by Davis's mother and were able to manage on Nicol's salary.

Waldbaum had a more difficult time. He had moved into "a dinky little shack behind a mansion" with his girlfriend Abby English. After dating for a year in Denver, English had decided to follow Waldbaum to Charlottesville. Waldbaum's invitation was simply, "If you want to come, great—that's cool." During the height of the hot and humid Virginia summer, the couple and their large, energetic golden retriever moved into a tiny studio apartment that lacked air-conditioning. Accustomed to Colorado's dry summer climate, English complained the air in Charlottesville was like "soup." Compounding the problems, English had a difficult time finding a job that suited her skills. She had been happily employed as an event planner in Denver, where she coordinated large-scale events for corporate clients such as Anheuser-Busch. In Charlottesville, English coordinated much smaller events such as the two-day MS 150 (a 150 km bike ride to raise funds for multiple sclerosis, which attracted 500 cyclists). It was, according to Davis, "junior varsity compared to her varsity." Within two months, English abandoned the "idyllic" Charlottesville life and moved back to Denver.

Butz and his wife, having lived as students in Colorado, continued the lifestyle to which they had become accustomed. While Butz toiled for hours at Green Room Productions' office, his wife struggled with the demands of a rigorous courseload.

The Other Business Dilemma: Where to Locate?

August and September passed with no new prospects of employees. The three partners asked themselves, "what are we going to do? We have a business that we know categorically can work. We have demand. We have real clients. We can't deliver."

In October 1995, they began a partnership debate. They brainstormed a number of different scenarios before focusing on two choices: shut the business down or move. Each option introduced new problems and each partner had to consider his personal and professional interests. If they closed the business, each would have to seek new employment. If they decided to move the business, they would again have to determine a location.

The partners discussed different cities that were technology centers, had resource availability, and offered reasonable costs of living (see Exhibits 5 and 6 for demographic and cost-of-living estimates for various areas). They focused on concepts, instincts, experience, personal preferences, and prior knowledge of the cities, creating a grid of the different options. They considered the following cities:

- Austin, Texas: Home to Motorola and Dell Computing, Austin had developed a reputation as an up-and-coming new technology hub. With the University of Texas at Austin, the city had a young, educated work force.
- Denver: Home to technology companies and telecommunications giant US West; Waldbaum and Butz believed that Denver was a great city in which to live and work.
- San Francisco: A known technology center with the necessary technical and design talent base and successful companies such as Intel, Apple, and Hewlett-Packard as well as technology startups such as Netscape.
- Seattle: Home to Microsoft, the city attracted and offered significant talent. Well-funded former Microsoft employees left the software giant to start other technology companies including Progressive Networks (later Real Networks).
- Washington, D.C.: Home to AOL and telecommunications providers, D.C. offered both a strong talent pool and proximity to Charlottesville.

In addition, they considered the perspectives of their significant others. Each couple talked extensively about the challenges the partnership was facing and discussed the different scenarios as couples. As an elementary school teacher, Nicol Davis was unable to leave Charlottesville

Exhibit 5 Green Room Productions, LLC

1990 Demographics for
Austin, Denver, San Francisco, Seattle, and Washington, D.C.

	Total Population	% of Population 18 to 64 Years	People 25 Years & Older	Education of People 25 Years & Older		Number of Technology Companies**	Number of Paid Employees in Technology Companies**
				% with High School Degree or Higher	% with Bachelor's Degree or Higher		
Austin	576,407*	69.5%	349,209	83.4%	34.7%	1,300	16,250
Denver	467,610	64.1%	321,186	79.2%	29%	3,720	23,200
San Francisco	723,959	69.3%	536,015	78%	35%	4,230	40,700
Seattle	1,507,319*	68.4%	1,017,973	88.2%	32.8%	2,880	28,400
Washington, D.C.	606,900	67.9%	409,131	73.1%	33.3%	710	10,080

* Includes surrounding county (Seattle = King County, Austin = Travis County)
** Estimated numbers

Source: 1990 Census, U.S. Census Bureau *American FactFinder,* http://factfinder.census.gov/ (accessed 20 July 2006).

Exhibit 6 Green Room Productions, LLC

Weighted Average of Office Rental Rates in 1994 (dollars per square foot):
Austin, Denver, San Francisco, Seattle, Washington, D.C., and Northern Virginia (NOVA)/Metro D.C.

Office Space Pricing by City, 1994

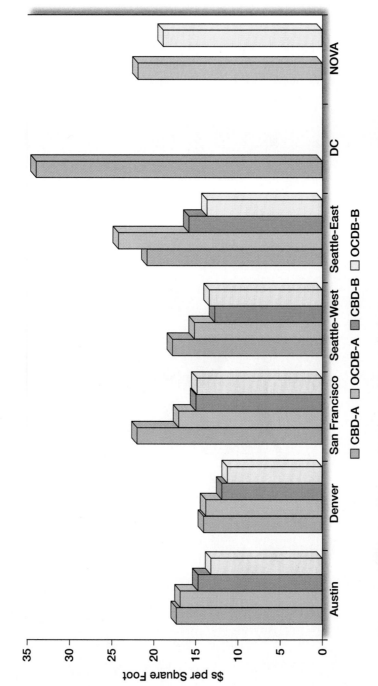

(CBD = Central Business District, OCDB = Outside Central Business District, A = Best Areas, B = Better Areas)

Source: Comparative Statistics of Industrial and Office Real Estate Markets, Society of Industry and Office REALTORS®, 1995.

807

until the following June. Abby English had already returned to Denver. Lucinda Butz was stressed by the demands of her study program but would not consider leaving before May if she would consider it at all.

The Decision

Davis, Waldbaum, and Butz reconvened in the conference room of their downtown office. The sense of urgency was palpable as they debated moving the business. Each was feeling the stress both at home and at work. The partners asked each other, "What do you think about Seattle? How about San Francisco? Austin? Denver? D.C.?" They agreed that they could not risk being in the wrong place again, but they wondered if the decision to move would submit the nascent firm to multiple known and unknown risks. Should they go, and if so, where? If they moved, how would they deal with the issue of assigning equity stakes between themselves and allocating an additional amount for new employees?

Case 32

Blue Whale Moving Company, Inc. (A)

9-496-001

It was a late evening in September 1988 when Blake Miller sat alone pondering the events that had taken place that afternoon. Earlier in the day, Blake met with Brad Armstrong, a local attorney and entrepreneur. The pair discussed the possibility of starting a new business together and Brad wanted to have a firm answer by the next day. Faced with what was undoubtedly the most important decision of his young life, Blake stared into space trying to imagine what success, or failure, would be like. Maybe he would become famous, or rich, or both. Or perhaps he would fail miserably and waste the most important years of his life. Either way, he had 14 hours to decide whether the business concept would work at all and whether Brad Armstrong was the individual with whom he wanted to develop the idea. Two weeks earlier, he never would have imagined the possibilities that lay ahead.

Blake Miller and Brad Armstrong

Having just graduated from the University of Texas, Blake Miller, 23, was sure that he wanted to enter a challenging and rewarding career. He had put himself through college by working for Advanced Moving, a local moving company in Austin, and had continued to work there since graduation. He was hard working and motivated, but disliked his current job. He was applying for entry into an MBA program and looked forward to an exciting business career.

Research Associate Adam Friedman and PhD Student Chris Long prepared this case under the supervision of Professors Laura Cardinal and Sim Sitkin as a basis for class discussion rather than to illustrate either an effective or ineffective handling of an administrative situation. Laura Cardinal was at the Fuqua School of Business, Duke University at the time the case was developed. She is currently at Tulane University.

At the age of 29, Brad Armstrong was a successful attorney looking to diversify into different types of businesses. He was passionate about business and had already initiated ventures in a few different industries: a clothing manufacturer that created doctor style scrub shirts out of Hawaiian prints, a federal firearms importing business, and a media company that published a local business newsletter. None of the businesses became an overwhelming financial success, but each turned a small profit.

A few days earlier, Blake had given Brad Armstrong a phone call. Blake thought Brad would be an excellent business reference for his MBA application and planned to ask him for his consent. The two had met a year earlier when Brad hired Advanced Moving for an office move. Brad had been impressed with Blake's energy and requested him by name when he hired Advanced Moving for a residential move a few months later. This time, even more delighted by Blake's commitment to the move, Brad asked Blake to give him a call upon graduation.

The Meeting

When Brad agreed to have lunch with Blake, he was clearly approaching the meeting as a business opportunity. Blake, on the other hand, saw Brad simply as a business contact. The discussion quickly moved toward Brad's agenda. Brad posed the idea of Blake's expanding some of his already established businesses, but Blake was not very excited by any of them. As the empty appetizer plates were removed and the main course was served, conversation turned more toward Blake's current job as a mover.

Blake explained to Brad some of the intricacies of the local moving industry in Austin. The rivalry among firms was fierce. He described how both customers and movers alike were treated as disposable commodities by moving companies. Furthermore, the movers felt a level of dissatisfaction that created a negative experience for the customers and, in turn, for the movers themselves. The vicious circle was made even worse by the financial situation of the industry as a whole. Competitors understood that price was the determining factor in the customer decision, so sales representatives with the responsibility for quoting prices would do anything possible to cut the price of a potential move, which eventually affected how much the movers earned. Morale in the industry was low and customer perceptions were negative.

Blake continued to explain how most of the competitors knew each other because they had worked together at some time in the past. It was common for employees to break away from their old employers and start up competing companies. The capital costs could be kept to a minimum and the necessary know-how was minimal. For this reason alone, new competitors were constantly entering the Austin market. As the competitive situation became more intense, though, competitors would leave as quickly as they entered. The only thing that could be said definitively about the Austin market was that it was in a constant state of turmoil.

As Blake discussed the situation, he found himself getting increasingly excited. He had worked in the industry for four years and had his own personal solutions for each of the problems he had encountered. Brad, too, was intrigued by the vivid description. As the two continued to talk, they began to form the idea for a new company that would do everything "right." At first, it was no more than a chat about a problematic industry, but it soon turned into a discussion of a possible business opportunity.

The pair analyzed the concept by calculating gross profits for a theoretical company. They used the $25,000 that Blake had made the previous year on 18 percent of the price of his moves to estimate the possible revenue for one moving crew. Multiplying by the number of crews at an average local moving company, Advanced Moving for example, Brad and Blake were able to calculate the total possible revenue they could anticipate. Furthermore, they calculated some of the expenses necessary to get the business started: a phone, business cards and stationery, a trailer for Blake's truck and a paint job for the trailer. Based on this set of assumptions, they soon agreed that a new moving company would not only be feasible but also profitable.

The company they envisioned would provide customers with unparalleled service and empower movers to provide that service. Furthermore, the company would compete in the high-end market and differentiate itself not on price but on superior customer service. While this was a far cry from the industry norms, the pair was convinced that a substantial segment of the rapidly growing Austin market of about 1 million people would be willing to pay a premium for the confidence that they and their possessions were being treated with the utmost respect.

By the end of a 90-minute lunch, Blake and Brad had tentatively agreed to form a new local moving company in Austin. Brad would provide the needed capital and Blake would run the moving operation. Each man decided that he needed to think about the decision overnight, so the pair agreed to talk the next afternoon to confirm the decision to form a partnership.

The Local Moving Industry

The United States has the world's most mobile society. More than 42 million Americans—almost 20 percent of the U.S. population—move each year at an average cost per household of more than $3,200. These moves can be classified as either long-haul or short-haul. Long-haul moves are generally between states and are handled by large van-line companies such as Allied Van Lines, Atlas Van Lines, Mayflower Transit Co., and United Van Lines. Short-haul moves, or local moves, are generally within the same city, or at least the same state. While some people choose to move themselves, the majority of these moves are handled by local moving companies in the area. The van-line industry is controlled by a few major carriers and is monitored by national moving associations. Conversely, the local moving industry, while deeply entrenched in every city across the country, is made up of thousands of different players. There are no nationwide local moving companies and no sources of precise competitive information on the industry.

A small metropolitan area of 1 million people may have as many as 80 local moving companies. The smallest of these companies may be a two-person operation where each person has a career other than moving. This company may post advertisements around town, rent a truck and trailer on the weekend, and perform one or two moves a week. On the other hand, the largest of these companies has a well-placed advertisement in the yellow pages, owns their own trucks and trailers, and can perform as many as 200 moves a week. The local moving industry is profitable for both types of movers.

A large moving job may take three or four movers one complete day to finish. An example might be a family moving from a five-bedroom house on one end of town to a larger house on the other. Depending on the number of items, the move may cost anywhere from $2,000 to $5,000. A smaller move, on the other hand, may involve a single person living in an apartment who is moving down the street. This move requires only a few hours and may cost as little as $200. A two-person moving team may perform as many as six apartment moves in one day. The larger move is obviously most preferable to both moving companies and the movers themselves due to higher profit margins and the easier moving situation. One additional type of move is an office relocation. Due to the logistical complexities of these moves, these are low-profit, difficult moves that require many movers. In addition, these relocations almost always need to be performed on the weekends, when higher profit residential moves are most frequent.

The decision to hire a moving company is made almost exclusively on price. Customers will inevitably call, or be visited by, multiple moving companies to obtain and compare price quotes. The key in the moving industry, therefore, is getting the phone to ring. Prospective customers can be brought in through a variety of means. They may have used the company previously and been happy with the results, been referred by a friend or colleague, seen an advertisement in the yellow pages, or noticed one of the company's trucks around town. In addition, moving companies sometimes establish contracts with a large business in the local area, a real estate agency, a housing subdivision, or an apartment complex. Although this generates greater volumes, profits can be undermined because people moving in association with one of these groups are always given a discount.

EQUIPMENT

Because the cost of acquiring a new truck or trailer is significant (as high as $60,000), many companies try to buy used equipment. Most of the distances driven are fairly short, so a used vehicle can be driven with relative security. Alternatively, in order to minimize the fixed cost of owning trucks and trailers, many local moving companies have established relationships with truck rental companies like U-Haul and Ryder. The moving companies will enter into a lease agreement for a used truck or trailer in which the maintenance (and sometimes storage) of the vehicle is the responsibility of the rental company.

MOVERS

Movers are generally treated as independent contractors to keep labor costs as low as possible. In addition, their low salaries are reflective of their respective education and work experiences. Often the only job qualification is physical strength. Most moving companies will have at least one ex-convict or parolee in their ranks. Some movers have attended college and some are not as strong, but these are definitely the exceptions, not the rule. This fact spurred one mover to comment that "Education doesn't mean anything in this business. It's all strength." Although working conditions are good and movers are paid more than they would earn performing similar manual labor elsewhere, turnover in the industry is as high as 50 percent a year. The cited reason is predominantly job dissatisfaction. Movers generally become frustrated by their managers or customers or are simply worn down by the constant strain on their bodies.

CUSTOMER PERCEPTIONS

Customers generally have negative perceptions of the moving industry. Customers expect the service to be substandard, their goods to be damaged, and their nerves to be frayed. Like a nuclear power plant that avoids accidents or a prison that avoids escapes, customers consider a good move to be one that minimizes damage—positive outcomes are never cited. People generally have these expectations regardless of whether they previously had a good or bad encounter with a moving company. Although some of this bad sentiment may be well-founded, moving company personnel are quick to comment that customers are extremely sensitive to even the most minor errors during a move due to the other stress that they may be feeling at the time. This stress might be caused by the selling or purchase of a home, career changes, marriage, divorce, or other life events. Regardless of the cause, however, negative customer perceptions are prevalent.

The Decision

Blake returned home the evening of the meeting to find himself plagued by unanswered questions. Although Blake's concept of a new strategy in the moving industry seemed to make sense, he was unsure whether it was realistic given the harsh industry norms. He worried about alienating his current employer, as well as his peers. Maybe they would ridicule his new concept or, worse yet, exploit him in a competitive situation. In addition, because this new concept was a serious departure from the traditional method of business in the industry, he knew that it would be difficult to both implement and maintain.

In addition, he wondered whether Brad was really the best partner for such a venture. With no experience in the industry, would their visions of the company be the same or would they be destined to split? He thought that Brad, too, must have had some reservations about the venture. Maybe Brad felt uneasy putting his money into an unknown industry with a partner he barely knew. Perhaps he was not committed to the success of the company and would leave Blake without a job if at any time he decided to divest his capital. Blake knew he could make a profit, but was unsure whether it would be enough to justify the financial investment.

Blake called his parents and then his sister to ask their advice. Each of them thought he was crazy for even thinking of the idea. Not only did he know nothing about running his own company, but he also knew nothing of his new "partner." The combination, they felt, was cause for serious concern. Blake hesitantly agreed, thanked them for their advice, and hung up the phone. He truly wanted to join Brad in the venture, but there were so many issues that were either unclear or unknown. As midnight approached, Blake was as uneasy as ever, but he was determined to make a decision before drifting off to sleep.

The Early Years

Blue Whale Moving Company was cofounded by Brad Armstrong and Blake Miller in September 1988. Faced with a fast approaching deadline for submission of an advertisement in the yellow pages, the pair was challenged with creating, trademarking, and incorporating a business all within a week of their initial discussion of the business concept. But the first hurdle to climb was deciding on a name. The two founders thought endlessly of names before one of

Brad's law partners inspired them to think of a somewhat fanciful name, one that conveyed trust and courage. This spurred the pair to think about animals and when they imagined the biggest animal of them all, the blue whale, the name stuck. They felt that it not only conjured a pleasant image in one's mind but also instilled a feeling of strength and confidence. Later advertisements often referred to the company as the "Gentle Giant," supporting the idea of a large and powerful company that can move household goods safely and effortlessly. Additionally, each truck was painted with a lifelike image of a blue whale (see Exhibit 1). While this was a fairly high-cost proposition, they later found that much of their business stemmed from potential customers seeing their trailers on the street and remembering them vividly.

In a market where moving companies are named Advanced Moving, Apartment Movers, AAA Moving, and Discount Moving, the moniker Blue Whale Moving is a far cry from the norm. But while its competitors assumed a nondescript profile, Blue Whale emphasized that its service, and therefore the company, was discernible from the rest of the competition. Although their competitors often used sub-standard equipment and labor, Blue Whale stressed the importance of spotless trucks, tidy equipment, and clean-cut personnel—reasoning that if their customers saw Blue Whale take care of its business, they would certainly feel that Blue Whale could

| Exhibit 1 | Blue Whale Moving Truck and Trailer |

Exhibit 2	Blue Whale Moving Co. (Austin) Statement of Earnings (Years Ended December 31, 1989 to 1993)				
	1989[A]	1990[A]	1991	1992	1993
Revenue					
Sales	181,971	388,396	587,708	1,106,586	1,659,108
Less: Refunds/Discounts	0	0	0	453	6,660
Net Sales	181,971	388,396	587,708	1,106,133	1,652,448
Cost of Sales	0	319,309	515,667	489,283	671,624
Gross Profit	181,971	69,087	72,041	616,850	980,824
Expenses					
Operating Expenses	181,840	20,805	43,326	572,972	992,261
Other Income/(Expenses)		(567)	(6)	(27,368)	(33,239)
Total Expenses	181,840	21,372	43,332	600,339	1,025,500
Net Earnings	131	47,714	28,709	16,510	(44,677)

[A]There was an accounting change in 1990. Much of the information for 1989 was either incomparable or incomplete.

take care of their valuables.[1] With the initial investment of $10,000, the company purchased a used trailer (Blake already owned a truck), a cellular phone, and some miscellaneous supplies. Before the yellow pages ad was published, Blake posted fliers around the city and made endless phone calls to drum up business. Blake and one other employee formed the first moving crew. They would perform as many moves as possible, seven days a week, and take calls on the cellular phone to quote or book new moves. In a sense, Blake *was* the business; Brad was not involved in the daily operations of Blue Whale. Eight weeks later, the yellow pages advertisement was published and revenues started to take off. By April 1989, Blue Whale was able to purchase another trailer and hire a second crew with its cash flow from the first seven months of operations. By 1993, revenue soared to $1.7 million (see Exhibits 2 and 3 for specific financial data).

Blue Whale's Vision and Growth

The local moving business that Brad and Blake established was different than other moving companies. The two entrepreneurs constantly stressed the importance of customer service in their organization. While the mainstream attempted to undercut their competition in price wars, Blue Whale targeted the subset of customers who felt that a professional, stress-free move had an intangible value for which they would pay a premium.[2] Brad and Blake recognized that moving meant a transition for most people. As a result, customers were particularly sensitive and responsive to the perceived quality of the move. The entrepreneurs summed up their key notion:

> Moving . . . is a stressful time for most customers. You have the potential to ruin this person's day or make it the best day they've ever had.[3]

Blue Whale's vision statement, which every employee recited to each potential customer, further emphasized the importance of customer service:

> By 31 December 2000, Blue Whale will have become preeminent in the moving and storage industry, with locations in 100 cities worldwide.

> Marked by complete commitment and dedication to the highest standards of moral and ethical excellence, Blue Whale will be delivering an exceptional service experience created uniquely for each customer, by radiating positive energy throughout our team, and reflecting this love and respect upon our customers and all those we serve.

> Only then will our successful evolution into other markets, products and services be guaranteed.

[1]"Austin's Gentle Giant: The Blue Whale Moving Company," *Moving and Storage Times*, March 15, 1993.

[2]"Austin's Gentle Giant."

[3]"This Blue Whale Is on the Move," *Austin-American Statesman*, January 1, 1993, p. E1.

| Exhibit 3 | Blue Whale Moving Co. (Austin) Balance Sheet (Years Ended December, 31, 1989 to 1993) |

	1989[A]	1990[A]	1991	1992	1993
Assets					
Cash		3,763	19,133	(4,095)	22,485
Accounts Receivable		1,131	6,356	13,355	25,140
Other Current Assets		775	1,130	776	5,063
Total Current Assets		5,669	26,619	10,036	52,688
Net Fixed Assets		28,083	76,937	90,431	188,932
Other Assets		0	0	4,032	4,307
Total Assets		33,753	103,556	104,500	245,927
Liabilities					
Current Liabilities		14,930	62,523	34,500	133,356
Long-Term Liabilities		9,753	7,753	20,209	107,457
Total Liabilities		24,683	70,276	54,709	240,813
Shareholder's Equity					
Capital Stock		1,000	1,000	1,000	1,000
Retained Earnings		(39,645)	3,570	32,280	48,790
Profit (Loss) for Year		47,714	28,710	16,510	(44,677)
Total SE		9,070	33,280	49,790	5,114
Total Liabilities and SE		33,753	103,556	104,500	245,927

[A] There was an accounting change in 1990. Much of the information for 1989 was either incomparable or incomplete.

Brad believed that the Blue Whale vision was the most important thing his customers should know about the company. He remarked,

> If a customer just wants a price, I can give him the name of several other companies. We're offering something different.

> Our vision statement was built from the bottom up. We all developed it together and we've never known any other way. Then we created a training program for incoming employees so everyone knows right from the start what Blue Whale is all about.[4]

Brad and Blake required that all employees know the vision and demonstrate Blue Whale's values to the customer. This was extremely unusual in an industry best known for rude, belligerent movers and managers. Brad felt that even though the initial investment in developing character was significant, so were the long-term payoffs. He felt that if employees were able to internalize Blue Whale's principles, it would instill pride in the organization and teach employees how to behave when no one was looking over their shoulder.[5] Blue Whale's customers would frequently comment about how professional the Blue Whale movers were compared with their competitors. In addition, movers were given the ability to make discretionary decisions regarding certain aspects of the move, such as the application of additional charges or discounts. Other than reinforcing the concept of customer service, Brad and Blake exercised little formal control over their movers.

Brad and Blake's strategy worked. Revenues grew exponentially and the number of employees in the firm swelled. While competitors initially mocked the company for its fanciful name and vision, these companies were soon copying Blue Whale both in service delivery and style. Some of them began using mission statements in their advertisements that stressed customer service. New competitors began using more imaginative names like Aardvark, American Eagle, and Unicorn. Both Brad and Blake were heralded for the entrepreneurial spirit in the local and national press, and they were soon the recipients of many esteemed entrepreneurial awards (see Exhibit 4 for a list of Blue Whale honors and awards).

[4] "A Whale of an Idea," *AdInfinitum*, March 1994.

[5] Ibid.

Exhibit 4	Blue Whale Awards and Honors During the First Six Years of Operation

1992 **Best of Austin—"Best Way to Get from Point A to Point B"**
Recipient: Blue Whale Moving Company, Inc.
Sponsor: *Austin Chronicle*

1993 **Austin Entrepreneurs of the Year—Service Category**
Recipients: Blake Miller, CEO, President /
Brad Armstrong, CFO, Secretary, Treasurer
Sponsors: Ernst & Young, *Inc.* Magazine, Merrill Lynch

1993 **Best of Austin—"Best Moving Day Companions"**
Recipient: Blue Whale Moving Company, Inc.
Sponsor: *Austin Chronicle*

1994 **Blue Chip Enterprise/Blue Chip Initiative State Designee—Service Category**
Recipient: Blue Whale Moving Company, Inc.
Sponsors: Connecticut Mutual Life Insurance Company, United States Chamber of Commerce, *Nation's Business* Magazine

1994 ***Inc.* 500 Listing**
Recipient: Blue Whale Moving Company, Inc.
Sponsor: *Inc.* Magazine

CUSTOMERS Blue Whale was devoted to customer service but not only in a traditional sense. A Blue Whale brochure clarifies this by stating, "We don't sell moving services. We sell 'peace of mind.'" According to Brad and Blake, the most important quality that a Blue Whale employee could possess was the ability to make customers relax. This concept was manifest throughout the organization, from the first inquiry to the final payment. Sales representatives were supposed to continuously remind potential customers that "Blue Whale will take care of everything" and it was an explicit goal to have customers "breathe a sigh of relief" when Blue Whale movers arrived at their door. Additionally, each move was followed up with a phone call from a Blue Whale employee during which he/she asked the following questions:

1. Do you feel that the movers on your job fully executed the Blue Whale vision statement?

2. Were you treated with respect and made aware of all the events that occurred on your move?

3. Can Blue Whale do anything further for you at this time?

Customers were then asked to rate Blue Whale on a scale of 1 to 10. On average, customers rated Blue Whale a 9.5. Brad stated, "As we continue to grow and expand, we take pride in the high customer satisfaction ratings we consistently re-

ceive."[6] Each of these scores and comments was recorded and followed up on with managers and movers alike. Brad and Blake reinforced that negative experiences were to be eliminated and positive experiences were to be duplicated. The idea was that this feedback would help produce a positive experience for each and every customer. One clear sign that customers found value in the service they received was that 25 percent of Blue Whale's business was from repeat customers and 41 percent came from personal referrals,[7] far greater than the industry average. Customers became an unpaid but highly credible sales force, reducing Blue Whale's expenses for promoting itself.[8]

Blue Whale often received letters from customers thanking them for the care with which they transported their goods or just commending them for the overall moving experience (see Exhibit 5 for excerpts from customer satisfaction letters). These letters were promptly posted where all employees could see for themselves the difference they could make in a person's life.

EMPLOYEES Blue Whale had only 49 employees in 1993 and almost 75 percent of these were movers. The administrative side of the company was very small and could be loosely[9] broken down into operations, sales, accounting, and support staff, all of whom reported to the company vice-president, Jim Traynor. All movers reported to the operations manager, B. "Bernie" Bernard (see Exhibit 6 for the Blue Whale organizational structure), who also reported to Traynor.

BRAD ARMSTRONG As one of the cofounders of the business, Brad Armstrong was the guiding force behind Blue Whale's customer service orientation. While originally having only a small role in the business in 1988, he became increasingly involved as Blue Whale's revenues grew. When he would visit potential customers on his marketing rounds, he would jovially recite the Blue Whale vision and then proceed to impress them with his many tales of customer service. He built relationships with past and potential customers so they felt as if they were part of the Blue Whale "family." Whether at a social or business gathering, he would never fail to discuss the merits of Blue Whale moving. Brad felt that the Blue Whale approach was new and innovative, and was proud of it. In many cases, he made business decisions that sharply contradicted industry

---

[6]"Blue Whale Moving Company, Update" *Moving and Storage Times,* July 15, 1994.

[7]Blue Whale International, Inc., franchise proposal, 1995.

[8]"A Whale of an Idea."

[9]The term "loosely" is used because employees often covered each other's positions, as necessary.

Exhibit 5	Excerpts from Customer Satisfaction Letters

"I want to extend my thanks to your company's assistance with my grandmother's recent move. Your tremendous capabilities in aiding her during a busy time of the year and on short notice, proved to be very helpful. Your responsiveness and reliability are to be commended. I would be happy to recommend your company to anyone. Thank you again for all your help."

"This team of movers was professional, courteous, careful, and fast."

"The movers were professional, efficient, and sensitive to our concerns, especially with regard to several large and delicate antique pieces. The fellows were very patient, and they had a wonderful attitude, not only toward us but with each other as well. We can say that this was the most stress-free moving experience we have ever had! We would heartily recommend your company to our friends and neighbors. Thanks again."

"You run a business that is second to none. The entire moving event was actually pleasant due to your superior employees."

"The guys were courteous and attentive. I felt like we were friends!"

"The movers' careful handling of all of our furniture made the move a lot less stressful."

"I would definitely recommend Blue Whale to my personal friends and business colleagues."

"Moving is never pleasant especially right before Christmas and on a drizzly day, however, due to two of your employees my move was most pleasant. The movers were hardworking, punctual, polite, and just enjoyable. They should get high marks. I will highly recommend your company anytime due to their service. Blue Whale was recommended to me by several friends and now I can see why. Your company is run extremely efficiently. Keep up the good work."

norms because he wanted Blue Whale to be built with completely original ideas. He noted,

> . . . if it has been done before by someone else, I tend to reject it. . . .

In addition to the customer focus, he also continuously stressed the importance of employee satisfaction. He talked with managers about employee needs and often asked new employees what they were hoping to achieve both as a part of Blue Whale as well as in their personal life. He tried to build a relationship with each employee and empower him/her to act in the best interest of the customer and, therefore, the company. The idea was that a happy mover was a good mover. While this was extremely uncommon in the industry, Brad felt that it was one of the most important elements of the business.

Most employees, however, felt that Brad was rather unapproachable. Instead of consulting with him on a business or personal issue, they would instead seek out Blake or employ a different approach to solving the problem.

BLAKE MILLER　Because Blake had worked as a mover prior to starting Blue Whale, he was responsible for the general operations of the firm. As profits grew, he shifted out of the "mover" role and into the "manager" role, but still maintained an inseparable tie to the day-to-day operations of the business. He was extremely driven, due in part to a strict upbringing by his father, and worked as many as 110 hours per week making the business run.

To some extent, Blake fit the stereotypical image of a tall, easygoing, friendly Texan. He frequently "visited with" customers during a move and talked with both them and the movers to see how things were going. At the end of a long moving day, when the movers congregated back at the office, he would join them for a beer or a good story. Movers respected him as "one of us" and often sought his help solving personal and professional problems. He established professional relationships with equipment leasing companies, gas stations, mechanics, advertising agents, the phone company, and any other source of external contact. When Brad was asked by a reporter to comment on one of Blue Whale's many awards, he said, "We're thrilled about it . . . but I really give all the credit to Blake."[10] His comment reflected the general feeling throughout the organization.

OTHER MANAGERS　Jim Traynor joined Blue Whale in 1992 and was named vice-president of Blue Whale in January 1994. Brad and Blake established the position in order to delegate some of the day-to-day operations of the business. Jim, an ex-mover in his late twenties, was responsible for the bottom line of the Austin office. He was given full authority to act in the best interest of the firm, with the exception of hiring employees, a responsibility that was retained by Brad and Blake. Although Jim was diligent, many employees felt that Brad and Blake still maintained full control of the organization and that Jim was no more than a puppet for the owners.

B. "Bernie" Bernard joined Blue Whale in 1991 as a mover and by 1994 had worked his way up to become the operations manager of the company. Bernie was responsible for managing all of the movers and scheduling jobs and equipment. Additionally, he often went out on moves on the weekends, when the administrative office was closed. There was no doubt in any employee's mind that Bernie was completely committed to Blue Whale and its values. Movers felt comfortable with him and trusted his ability to communicate their issues and concerns to both Jim and the owners. Where many employees felt that Jim was committed to Brad and Blake, the same individuals agreed that Bernie was committed to helping them.

[10]"Austin's Finalists for the 1993 Entrepreneur of the Year Award," *Austin Business Journal*, May 1993.

Exhibit 6	Blue Whale Moving Co. Organization Chart, 1994

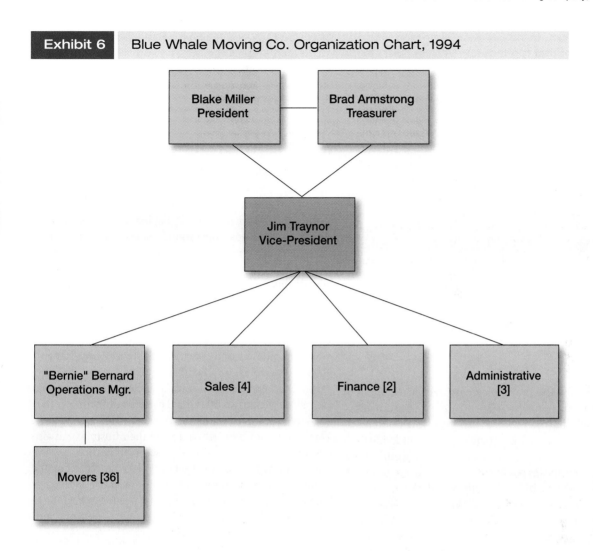

Control Issues
MOVERS

Blue Whale movers were called *associates* in all of the company's brochures. Brad and Blake felt this more accurately highlighted the caring relationship that the movers were supposed to develop with customers. Within the company, though, movers were called *movers*. Typical for the industry, they were not highly educated, some of them had spent time in jail, and all of them were strong. Movers generally stuck together and had little contact with the administrative office. They were happy just to show up in the morning to pick up a truck and a schedule, work hard all day, and get a paycheck at the end of the week.

Blue Whale movers were all hired as employees, while movers in the rest of the industry were typically hired as contract labor and bonded[11] by the firm. This was an expensive proposition (movers' pay represented about 45 percent of the total revenue of the firm), but Brad was adamant that Blue Whale not engage in a potentially damaging practice. Not only was the industry norm illegal, but it also encouraged movers to "cheat" on their taxes. Since income tax was not deducted from their paychecks, they frequently had no money saved up to pay the IRS when taxes came due. For this reason alone, Blue Whale movers had much more job security than movers employed with other companies.

The movers were paid on a commission (percentage per move) basis. Each mover on a two-man team typically received between 12 percent and 26 percent of the price of a

[11]"Bonded" refers to the insurance that a moving company purchases to cover its contract employees for the damage or theft of goods.

move. If a third man was necessary, each mover would receive two-thirds of their two-man rate. Brad and Blake believed the commission basis created a disincentive for the low productivity typically seen with an hourly pay scheme. Movers under this compensation system were motivated to finish a job as quickly and efficiently as possible. The compensation for a hard working mover at Blue Whale was a little higher than at other companies in the industry. This was a critical factor because money was the most important element of the movers' motivation. When asked for the primary reason they enjoyed working at Blue Whale, each and every mover responded, "The money." One mover made $52,000 in 1993. While this was extremely unusual (annual mover earnings averaged $25,000 to $30,000), compensation was clearly one of the benefits of working at Blue Whale. As was the case for other moving companies, movers were responsible for the payment of damages out of their own pocket. Although this rarely occurred, it was quite a bone of contention when it did.

SALES

Anywhere from three to five employees worked in a sales capacity. Most of their time was spent providing estimates over the phone, but they would also visit potential customers if the move was large enough or if the individuals wanted a written estimate. Their goal was to secure the move by whatever means possible. Often, this meant reducing the price of a move to be competitive with the industry. As one salesperson commented, ". . . some customers just don't understand our concept of customer service." This often created friction between the movers and the salespeople because the movers' pay was based upon the total dollar value of the job. The salespeople did their best to keep the movers happy, but they were primarily driven by their own needs, which were to book as many moves as possible and earn the small commission (between 3% and 5%) that came with each one. Salespeople earned between $24,000 and $28,000 per year, of which approximately 75 percent was salary-based.

FINANCE

One part-time clerk performed most of the financial functions within the firm. The clerk was not an accountant but rather an individual who was just "good with numbers." She spent most of her time processing payroll, depositing checks, and keeping the checkbooks balanced. One day a week, a CPA would come to Blue Whale and perform all of the "official"[12] accounting duties like budgeting and financial statement preparation.

Brad and Blake's Challenge

The two founders had tried a variety of management structures and controls over the preceding years, yet they remained unsure about which was the most effective. Even though they liked the idea of having a vice-president in charge of day-to-day operations, they wondered whether their direct involvement was essential to the functioning of the firm and were concerned that a vice-president might impede this contact.

Everything seemed to go so smoothly when the business was smaller and people were guided solely by the Blue Whale vision of customer service. Now the business was more complicated, and control of the business and its employees was much more difficult. Despite the "growing pains," Brad Armstrong and Blake Miller were as excited as ever about the possibilities that lay ahead of them, but they knew one thing for sure, the journey would not be easy. They had to not only get control of their business but also reach the goal of expansion they set forth in their mission statement. As they planned their discussions regarding the actions to be taken on some of the specific labor issues, they each thought individually about what needed to be done to get the entire business moving in the right direction again.

It was important to Blake and Brad that Blue Whale expand in its current markets, as well as in new markets. In the Blue Whale vision statement, they established an aggressive goal of opening 100 Blue Affiliates in different cities by the year 2000. As a first step along this path, they made a concerted effort to expand by opening offices in other Texas cities. Although they were optimistic about their plans, they questioned the timing and implementation of their expansion efforts. They also wondered if they could continue to use the management approach that had made their initial efforts so successful.

---

[12]The term *official* is what the part-time clerk used to refer to the accountant's work.

Case 33

AtomShockwave (A): A Venture Rollercoaster in the Online Entertainment Industry

06/2006-5356

Mika Salmi was immersed in his thoughts as he enjoyed the sunset over the Pacific Ocean on a balmy Sunday afternoon in November 2003. The entrepreneurial road had been bumpy for Salmi since the founding of his online film distribution enterprise in 1998. AtomFilms was the first step in Salmi's vision of bringing short-format entertainment to the masses. After struggling to raise funds for more than a year, AtomFilms became the darling of online media companies in 2000. However, despite increasing audiences for short-format content, Salmi saw his venture's revenue and investors' appetite plummet late that year, accompanied by the meltdown of the internet advertising market. To strengthen the venture's position, Salmi agreed to merge AtomFilms with the online entertainment company Shockwave.com in December 2000. Salmi became CEO of the merged entity—AtomShockwave—just in time to witness the worsening of economic conditions for internet companies. After a brush with bankruptcy in December 2001, which was only avoided through deep cost-cutting and painful restructuring, Atomshockwave finally reached financial break-even at the end of 2002 with a bare bones organization of 40 employees and revenue close to $10M.

Hundreds of online content distribution ventures had folded between 2000 and 2002. AtomShockwave was one of the few that survived the bloodbath.

Nevertheless, there were tough challenges ahead. In mid-2003, after two stellar quarters, AtomShockwave's growth stalled due to increasing competition for content, audiences, and advertising dollars. Although the venture was the leading player in the short films niche market, AtomShockwave competed in the larger market for online mass-market games with some of the most powerful internet companies, including Yahoo, Microsoft, AOL, and Real Networks. Could a small start-up operating in two market niches survive and thrive in the face of these giant competitors?

In the November sunset, towards the end of a day's surfing, Salmi pondered his options as he prepared for the meeting with AtomShockwave's board. What should be his next moves? In which business and initiatives should he invest the cash flow that his company was starting to generate?

An Entrepreneur Meets a Venture Capitalist

In 1997, Mika Salmi and Thomas Hoegh were on a collision course with one another, although neither knew it. Salmi had left Real Networks that August to work on a project at Getty Images, while developing a plan for a short films business that he hoped his employer would help him launch. Hoegh had launched a venture capital firm, Arts Alliance, based on his track record as a successful early investor in Internet-based "new media" companies. After exiting a few investments in the online music industry,

INSEAD This case was written by Philip Anderson, the IAF Chaired Professor of Entrepreneurship, and Filipe Santos, Assistant Professor of Entrepreneurship, both at INSEAD. It is intended to be used as a basis for class discussion rather than to illustrate either effective or ineffective handling of an administrative situation.

Hoegh and his partners looked for the most under-valued asset bases in the media sector. They identified short films, which, according to Hoegh, "had never generated any value, because the market is completely fragmented. It had intrinsic value for the people who make them, but they used them primarily as a calling card into the film industry." What intrigued the Arts Alliance team was the audience for short films:

> "Our research indicated the market was perhaps $100 million, but it had much larger potential, because the same customers who see short films are the audience in mainstream cinemas the first weekend a feature film is released. That first weekend audience, maybe five million people in America, influences others. We thought we could monetize that market if we could reach them."

Salmi had identified short films as an attractive target through a different process. During his time as an MBA student at INSEAD's campus in Fontainebleau, France, in 1992, Salmi became fascinated by the innovative French television channel M6, which showed music and video clips, as well as short animations and films. Later, as Director of Business Development for Real Networks' entertainment division, Salmi participated in the launch of their streaming video product, RealVideo in February 1997. At the time, Salmi did a lot of research for the launch, investigating what people wanted to watch on the internet:

> "It had to be unique and short, since the quality of the first streaming video was poor and you had to buffer it. It could be news, but it could not be sports, since the action was too fast and would blur. We came up with short films and animation, and I thought it would be a great spot for my idea of starting a business. I wrote a business plan focused on short films for the internet, and pitched it to some people during the summer."

Among those who heard Salmi's RealVideo presentation were Mark Torrance and Tom Hughes, founders of Photodisc, part of Getty Images, who were building a business digitizing images for internet sales. "I was looking for investors or help," Salmi says, "and they said they liked my idea. They needed help with one project right away, and said that if I came to work for them, they would help me get my company off the ground. I thought that was a great offer, since they were going public." Salmi joined the company in August 1997, and worked there until June 1998, when he officially launched AtomFilms.

With his former employers' permission, Salmi worked out of Getty Images' offices for the next four months. He was pessimistic about the fund-raising environment for his venture: "The venture capital market was not that great for online content business in 1997–98. People had been burned by investing in content companies. AOL's Greenhouse Studios had sponsored a lot of content providers, but they were all bombs. Nobody watched it, and nobody cared."

Consequently, when AtomFilms launched its website in November 1998, the idea was to use the internet to display the firm's wares, but make money selling short-film content offline. Salmi explains:

> "Short film has a market: television stations buy it and airlines buy it. Our idea was to acquire rights to short-form content and resell the films, using the internet as an efficient marketing brochure. There was no big player selling entertainment in this category. I thought I could aggregate the market, become the big kahuna, license content, and syndicate it."

AtomFilms moved aggressively to acquire content, building awareness by establishing a strong presence at film festivals. In December 1998, Air Canada licensed five films to be shown on flights, and a handful of sales to other airlines and to television stations followed. By early 1999, AtomFilms' distribution partners and customers included the cable television channels HBO and the Sundance Channel, the high-speed internet service @Home, and a host of online properties such as Reelcom, Film.com and Warner Brothers Online.

It was still a difficult economic climate to find investors, but Salmi was trying. In mid-February 1999, he and Matt Hulett (who had been a group product manager at Real Networks before joining AtomFilms) flew to New York to meet prospective investors Thomas Hoegh and Tori Hackett of Arts Alliance. Salmi recalls:

> "Thomas asked questions, and then said, 'I have been thinking about this for a while, and I can't believe you guys are doing it.' He took us that night to meet Stan Shuman of Allen and Company in a wood-paneled conference room that had original Norman Rockwell paintings. We were exhausted when this distinguished-looking older gentleman with a serious demeanor and a firm handshake met us. He said that Thomas had done well by him, and that he trusted Thomas. After that, a lot of people called us. We went from no interest to a lot of interest."

However, by early 1999 Salmi had become increasingly disappointed with the quality of video streaming on the internet. He felt he needed to offer a better-quality streaming experience in order to increase audiences. AtomFilms then developed one of the first websites to make extensive use of Macromedia's Flash technology, which made it possible to deliver full-screen, interactive content via the internet. AtomFilms conducted a strong press campaign to promote the site and, on the same day it launched the newly revamped AtomFilms.com in March 1999, the newspaper *USA Today* featured the site in its lifestyle section. According to Salmi, "100,000 people came all of a sudden, and it just exploded from that. Suddenly, there were articles everywhere about us."

At this time, Arts Alliance was investigating the AtomFilms business model. Hoegh and Hackett concluded the company had shown it could acquire assets inexpensively and generate licensing revenues from other media companies and distribution companies: "We thought the market for syndicating content offline was probably premature, but we thought their plans were reasonably sound." Heogh and Hackett believed the company might be able to gain access to enough exclusive, high-quality content to corner the market. Basing analysis on the number of short film festivals, amateur film-makers, applicants to film schools, and film-fan websites, Hoegh thought the worldwide audience for short films was large enough to support a successful media company. He also believed the company could distribute films via the internet and build significant profits from advertising. The start-up's business model, however, was not the primary driver of the investment decision: it was the management team.

> "You get a sense about people when their arguments are well-constructed. They say they can attract talent, and they have the experience to back up the argument. When we met Mika, the content he chose to acquire first showed the team had taste. We go after things that definitely have a creative component. If the taste is off, it is hopeless."

The Darling of Online Media Companies

The online audience for Atomfilms grew at a very fast pace in 1999. Eight hundred thousand unique visitors visited the AtomFilms website in the second quarter. Suddenly, many prospective investors were contacting AtomFilms. Salmi remembers, "We went with those who were originally interested because I appreciated their sincere interest." In May, AtomFilms closed its first round of professional funding, raising $5M. Investors included Arts Alliance, Allen & Company and Warner Brothers Online.

More than three million more unique visitors came to AtomFilms.com in the third and fourth quarters of 1999, nearly 30% of them in the 18–24 age demographic that web

advertisers valued. Several other short film sites had appeared, but AtomFilms generated far and away the most traffic in its category. On the strength of its growth, a $20M round of financing was raised from the original investors, plus Chase Capital Partners, Intel, and Trans Cosmos. In early 2000, AtomFilms debuted the first animated character ever introduced on the web, *Angry Kid,* and within two months over a million viewers had watched at least one film featuring the character. Hoegh recalls this heady period:

> "The company was the hottest thing around. A lot of A-class investors and Hollywood figures were making offers. We signed an agreement with Morgan Stanley to represent the company in its forthcoming IPO. We were going to raise a strategic round that would eliminate any doubt that we had lots of cash, and we were going to go for bust."

From AtomFilms to AtomShockwave

The situation changed radically when the NASDAQ swooned in the early spring of 2000 and the advertising market started collapsing later that year. Hoegh describes the situation:

> "The market deteriorated very quickly, and suddenly we understood that not only did we not have a lot of cash, but we were not able to raise any cash at the kinds of prices that would keep the current investment group somewhat intact. The speed at which the market and the appetite for investment deteriorated was such that by early fall, it was clear we would not only have a hard time going for the IPO, we would have a hard time pursuing any high-growth, high-spend strategy. We started to look for opportunities to have a broader base, with more solid revenues coming from a number of different arenas."

AtomFilms' search quickly led to Shockwave, a private company controlled by software company Macromedia. Macromedia produced Director, one of the best-selling tools for authoring interactive multimedia. Shockwave was a tool that allowed Director to run on websites. Macromedia gave away a downloadable browser plug-in, the Shockwave Player, and earned revenues from selling its Director software to website designers, allowing them to create "shocked" websites. To view Shockwave content (animated clips or interactive 3D games), users had to download the Shockwave player at http://www.shockwave.com. The Shockwave site was a showcase illustrating what could be done with Shockwave animation, and it rapidly became a destination site, because people had to visit it to get the player. By the end of 2000, the Shockwave site was one of the most popular on the web, with roughly 10 times the traffic of AtomFilms.

Although Shockwave had roughly three times the revenue of AtomFilms, Hoegh thought Shockwave's business model was sorely in need of rationalization:

> "They sold mostly banner advertising through a third party, Doubleclick, and they had not built up a relationship with customers in a meaningful way. There was not much of a community, no sense that there was something that mattered to people. The site was bland and uninteresting . . . They had struck deals with content producers that we thought were ridiculous; they paid a lot up front, as if they were a seasoned media company. They had a key technology and were clearly good at some elements related to hardcore gamers, and they had massive traffic. We thought AtomFilms had a more effective advertising force that were selling out our inventory and could fill out their empty ad space."

The presence of respected venture industry professionals, such as Michael Moritz from Sequoia Capital, on Shockwave's board of directors was a positive factor for AtomFilms' backers. These investors agreed to put more capital into the combined entity, to be headed by Salmi, and a merger was concluded on 15 December 2000. AtomFilms shareholders received 30% of the merged entity. Hoegh comments, "It gave us a relatively secure future in a market that people at that time expected to rebound. It was not an ideal merger, but under the circumstances, it was better than the alternatives."

Salmi and his new team worked to redesign the Shockwave site, aiming to make it the most compelling place on the internet for interactive online games. The new AtomShockwave had a tremendous asset: the growing popularity of the Shockwave player, installed in 70% of the computers connected to the web around the world. Traffic continued to build on both the AtomFilms and Shockwave sites, which were independent but linked to one another. However, internet advertising rates plummeted throughout 2001 and 2002, as click-through rates dropped below 1%. The banner advertising market was caught in a vicious circle. Many of the heaviest online advertisers were dotcoms, and as funding dried up, hundreds went out of business. This decreased the volume of advertising, leaving online sites with unsold inventory, which fueled a further decline in advertising rates. AtomShockwave's revenue evaporated in 2001, generating heavy losses and a fast cash burn-rate. The situation required extreme measures to downsize the merged company and reach financial break-even.

Rationalizing AtomShockwave's Structure

Salmi hired a new chief financial officer from Macromedia, Margaret McCarthy. They were forced to slash costs dramatically during 2001 and 2002. Salmi explains:

> "When the two companies merged, AtomFilms had 170 employees and Shockwave had 190. We had lots of offices in different parts of the world, obligations to Oracle, MCI, and an amazing amount of stuff on the books we were paying for. Since then, we have been falling off our expense line slowly, getting leaner and leaner."

The largest expense item of the company was salaries. In the two years following the merger, the company eliminated nearly 90% of its staff. From 360 people at the time of the merger, the venture was reduced to 42 people in 2002 (see Table 1 for a breakdown of employees).

Salmi recalls, "We could not cut more; we were on the edge." According to McCarthy, "We were lean in head count in a lot of areas. Everyone was running way over capacity, and at peaks, nobody slept." The legal and accounting areas represented a disproportionate fraction of employee expenses, and McCarthy found that exceptionally difficult to shrink: "We have more general and administrative expenses than you would like, but we have thousands of pieces of content that need royalty statements each quarter."

Infrastructure costs were the second-largest category of expenses. The venture moved to less expensive offices in South San Francisco in 2002, where rental cost $18 per square foot,

Table 1 AtomShockwave Employee Count by Area in 2002

	42
Salespeople	10
Web Group (engineering and creative)	10
HR/admin/legal/accounting	10
E-commerce/business development	2
Customer support	2
Game acquisition and engineering	3
Film acquisition	1
Information technology	2
CEO and CFO	2

as opposed to $45 per square foot. In January 2003, Atom-Shockwave moved again to even less expensive (but more comfortable) quarters. The company also re-negotiated its long-term commitments and signed shorter-term contracts with telecommunications and infrastructure providers, taking advantage of overcapacity to win steep price cuts from suppliers of bandwidth and streaming services.

The third-largest expense category was royalties. Atom-Shockwave had reduced its payments to game developers considerably, mainly by re-negotiating deals that had been struck during the internet boom. Acquisition costs for short-form content had also been driven down, because film-makers look for exposure to enhance their reputation, and AtomFilms was clearly the most popular outlet in the genre. On the Shockwave side, AtomShockwave paid Macromedia two cents per email address captured and had built a database of 40 million addresses.

Despite a near-bankruptcy in December 2001, the situation improved in 2002 due to increased revenue in the last quarter of 2001 and tight cost controls during the year. The company closed the year 2002 with $10M in revenue and achieved a positive EBITDA in the last quarter. Yet the company was still not profitable, despite cutting costs to the bone. Salmi started to focus all his energies on increasing his company's audience and revenues.

Exploring Different Business Models

At the start of 2003, The Shockwave site was averaging 15 million unique visitors per month, ranging from 700,000 to 1 million per day. The AtomFilms site averaged between 1.5 million and 2 million unique visitors per month, ranging from 50,000 to 80,000 per day. The demographics of the two sites were quite different. About 80% of AtomFilms' visitors were male and in the 18–24 age range. In contrast, Shockwave's was more diverse, evenly split between male and female audiences with a third of its audience under 15, a third aged 16–30, and a third over 30.

Although AtomFilms's content is mostly exclusive, relatively few of Shockwave's games are exclusive. The site's model is to attract users who need to download the Shockwave player, get them interested in a game, and rely on comfort and familiarity to persuade them to return. McCarthy says: "The mass market is for games that are light and not hard to learn. That's our market, not serious gamers, which is a much smaller segment. . . . Shockwave is the online equivalent of family game night."

Table 2	Revenue Sources for AtomShockwave, Q4 2002
Advertising (including sponsorships)	50%
Electronic Commerce (including downloads and subscriptions)	37%
Syndication	8%
International (Licensing fees from Japan)	5%

The revenue mix of AtomShockwave at the end of 2002 was mostly based on advertising and e-commerce revenues (see Table 2 for the revenue breakdown).

Salmi describes his two main revenue sources, "The interesting thing we discovered in early 2002 was that 70–80% of the people buying our downloadable games were women over 30; they are willing to spend money online for games as opposed to teenage boys or the Playstation crowd. The diverse and large traffic supported our advertising business model, but this particular demographic supported our e-commerce business."

ADVERTISING Advertising remained the principal source of revenue for both AtomFilms and Shockwave. Atom-Shockwave sold most of its advertising directly. Says McCarthy, "We sell higher value-added units like interstitials[1] at a cost per thousand viewings (CPMs) of $5 to $25, depending on how much rich media are used. We have a cost of between 35 cents and $5 to serve them up, plus we need our own staff of four people who receive the content, ensure it is up on our website, track it, and ensure we don't oversell our inventory." Salmi adds, "E-commerce is very scalable because it is a digital business. Advertising is not. To service more clients, you need more people."

Another advertising revenue stream was direct sponsorship: a sponsor's brand could be integrated into a game or a section of either website. Salmi says, "Sponsoring is great business, but it's hard to land." Each sponsorship deal was a customized arrangement. For example, AtomFilms had run a fan film contest for Stars Wars/LucasFilm, and a "Make Your Mark" movie contest for Sony. Games were developed with products from sponsors embedded in them, like the Nissan Xterra Snowboarding game. McCarthy summarizes, "Some of these have been a borderline pain in the neck, where you put in a lot of time and energy, but once people have seen a movie, they don't come back to watch again.

[1] Unlike a banner advertisement, an interstitial ad occupies the full screen. It is shown between views of two web pages, for example while a game is loading.

Games are more intriguing, because the sponsor pays for the game. You can get valuable intellectual property through game deals."

A third source of advertising revenues stemmed from the firm's database of e-mail addresses. "We get an immediate, measurable, valuable response to an e-mail blast," says McCarthy. "We are trying to get a lot smarter about creating e-mail marketing campaigns that attract a market willing to buy."

ELECTRONIC COMMERCE   From the start, both Atom-Films and Shockwave had experimented with selling related goods on their site, but neither had been successful.

> "[At AtomFilms] we sold DVDs and VHS tapes. We tried selling T-shirts, and I hate that business. We were negotiating a deal to put short-film compilations in retail stores, but decided not to do that at the time. Shockwave experimented with other kinds of consumer products, but they have sold limited amounts."

However, Shockwave had considerable success selling premium versions of some of the games on its site for download.

> "The games on our site are not crippled, but they are limited versions. You may want to play longer or have more features, and that is why you would buy a game. The games people buy are mainly puzzles, or games that are easy to play, but hard to master. When you are addicted, you want to play more, so you put your credit card in . . ."

McCarthy notes:

> "People get addicted to puzzle games and love to buy them. The mass audience, mostly women between the ages of 25–45, is driving e-commerce. Advertisers want the 18–35 year-old game players, but they do not spend money to download games."

On the AtomFilms side, few people appeared eager to purchase short subjects online. AtomFilms had licensed Wallace and Gromit, a popular animation feature developed in the United Kingdom, offering a free episode and charging customers to download 10 more. "It was going up, but it was not going through the roof. We hadn't sold as many as we thought we would; people watch the free episode, but they don't want to pay. We've sold closer to 10,000 than 100,000, even though four million Wallace and Gromit DVDs have been sold."

E-commerce revenues climbed steadily throughout 2002, partially replacing declining advertising revenues. This trend heartened Salmi, because he felt the underlying eco-

nomics were better for e-commerce than for advertising: "A dollar of revenue from advertisements costs us more than a dollar from digital e-commerce. The costs of serving an advertisement are higher, and so are the royalty costs." Furthermore, streaming ad-supported content to customers was much more expensive than serving up files to be downloaded. It appeared, however, that growing e-commerce income would tilt the revenue balance of the company even more toward the Shockwave side. Salmi concludes, "It seems that people will pay for games, but not for linear film or animation content."

In late 2002, Shockwave.com introduced Gameblast, a service intended to add a significant subscription revenue stream to the mix. For $9.95 per month, Gameblast subscribers were granted round-the-clock access to more than 30 premium games, some exclusive to Gameblast and others enhanced versions of popular games available on Shockwave. If Gameblast succeeded, AtomShockwave intended to market it to Internet Service Providers and portals, who could offer it under their own brands. These companies could charge their customers subscription fees, and pay AtomShockwave to run the service for them.

Charging AtomFilms subscribers for access to premium content seemed less promising. Digital services that offered movies, music, and television to subscribers via broadband connections were failing. One high-profile example was Intertainer, launched in 1996 and shuttered in the fall of 2002. Intertainer had offered pay-per-view feature films for prices similar to video rentals. However, as Salmi says, "Short clips are what works on the Internet. If we had short clips the quality of *The Sopranos,* we could sell subscriptions, but no one is making them and we can't pay for them." AtomFilms did have a number of ongoing series, but nothing of sufficiently high quality. Says McCarthy, "If we could find a killer series that brought people back every day, it would be awesome, but we would have to find someone else who has it."

SYNDICATION   AtomFilms continued working to sell short-film content to distributors, such as cable channels, airlines, and other websites. McCarthy says: "We thought the revenue would be millions of dollars per quarter, but it turned out to be a couple of hundred thousand per quarter. Offline, airlines are cost-constrained, and are not worried about entertaining you on a short flight. Online, the market is declining, as people find that putting content on their site doesn't do anything for them". At one point, Salmi had thought syndication of short-film content to wireless devices would be a major business, but he was disappointed with the results: "AtomFilms did a syndication deal with Nokia, but the returns on that were not good."

AtomFilms was also a partner in a joint venture with Global Media. Atom Television was a digital cable channel offering short films and animations (under 10 minutes' length) around the clock. AtomFilms was to provide the content, marketing and the brand, with the channel paying Atom-Films for access to its library of content. Salmi comments, "Atom Television gave us a little broader outlet, and that helped, but it is very hard to start a TV channel." Atom Television had more interest from video-on-demand programming than for a round-the-clock cable channel.

Syndication was not a large source of revenue for Shockwave, as few online sites wanted to license games. One promising path was syndicating games to other online sites for the purpose of selling upgraded versions of the games themselves. However, as McCarthy notes:

"Content syndication rode the bubble and pretty much evaporated. One potential market is to let other sites put games on their website with some build-in limitations and messages that drive purchase of the game. A limited revenue share goes back to the partner who distributed the game. Our content on other sites gets our name out there, and gives them content that is valuable to their users. Only e-commerce justifies the expense of serving it on their site. People want to know how they make money by syndicating our content, and stickiness isn't good enough."

INTERNATIONAL Shockwave was a minority owner of an independent subsidiary that had been established in Japan at the peak of the bubble. Cash had been raised for the venture independently, and Shockwave had never had to put money into it. The Japanese organization paid AtomShockwave to license its name and syndicate content from the American organization. Over time, it was expected to source its own content locally. AtomShockwave decided to maintain the link with the Japanese subsidiary.

Before the collapse of the technology market in 2000 Shockwave's strategy had been to establish a web of local companies in the same mold as this Japanese subsidiary. A Swiss organization was created whose aim was to penetrate a host of countries one by one. In each nation, it was to find the right strategic partners, set up a local team to run the business, and motivate them via incentives to find local content and run a profitable business. If a game became a hit in one country, it would be possible to roll it out to many others. The strategy foundered because Shockwave was unable to find enough people to replicate its model successfully, and prospective local partners became difficult to find as the market for technology stocks spiraled downward. Salmi then decided to put the internationalization strategy on hold.

In addition, AtomFilms had set up a sales organization in the UK to syndicate short-form content in Europe. "It tended to generate a lot of $2000–3000 sales that were hard to collect," McCarthy says. The operation was shut down in 2002, and all content syndication worldwide was managed from the US headquarters

OTHER REVENUE STREAMS Salmi did not think new revenue streams would change the business equation:

"Coming up with new revenue streams is easy; the reality is that executing them is difficult. I am averse to listening to them at this stage. We have chosen our path: e-commerce and subscriptions. We can refine them or veer from them, but I think we need to make them work. Our gross margins are good and getting better. We clearly have a real business on our hands. However, I need to see some real growth. If the subscription story works and selling content directly to consumers takes off, I can stand behind the company and say this is going to happen."

A Tale of Two Businesses: Strategic Challenges in November 2003

AtomShockwave revenues grew at a rapid pace in the first semester of 2003 and for the first time in its short history, the company was cash-flow positive. Surprisingly, the main engine for growth was the advertising market. TV-style ads, played prior to the games and films, and sponsorship deals became very popular with advertisers. On the commerce side, while revenues from game downloads were strong, customer adoption of the new GameBlast subscription service was slower than expected.

Unfortunately, the advertising market cooled-off in the second semester and AtomShockwave's growth stalled again. At the same time, each of the businesses was facing distinct strategic challenges: the AtomFilms business was too small to be profitable by itself, while the games business was facing increasing competition from large internet players.

ATOMFILMS AtomFilms' revenue was small compared to Shockwave but attracted advertisers and added an intangible value to the brand. Advertising from the large movie studios and gaming houses was particularly strong. Salmi ponders:

". . . the question is still what to do with AtomFilms. AtomFilms is sexy for advertisers, but it is only 15% of the revenue, and it is hard for us to grow it much larger. On the web, AtomFilms often can't deliver what advertisers want, because it doesn't have enough inventory or the right market segment, and in those cases, we try to convince them to go to Shockwave. It is focused on the short films area, where there is a lot of interest but not huge interest. Its costs are very low, and it kind of works, but where do we take it?

Having initially relied on publicity and word-of-mouth to attract the best short-form content, by 2003, the Atom-Films brand was so strong that film-makers sought it out. AtomFilms looked at building a network to facilitate amateur submissions and held sponsored contests for amateur short-subject makers. McCarthy comments, "You end up with a lot of mediocre stuff that people don't want to see. Streaming is expensive, and it's not a great business model unless people enjoy what is being streamed. People don't want to pay you to put their works on the web, but you end up with operating costs when you show amateur submissions."

The central strategic challenge for the AtomFilms business was that while they were the number one short films site, the market was small and had not reached a critical mass that could support a profitable venture. Also, despite many experiments, the only viable distribution channel seemed to be the Atomfilms website. Hoegh's doubt was whether AtomFilms could survive, as it was so dependent on the advertising market and sponsorship opportunities:

> "They are too small to make enough money from the traffic they generate. They need to double their size; if they could fill that much inventory, it would make money on its own. For a while, they had serialized content that gave people reasons to return. They must develop that further and develop some hits–media is a hit-driven business."

AtomFilms' attempts at leveraging their assets in short films by tapping the emerging mobile content market had come to nothing. They didn't have the rights for mobile distribution of some of their biggest hits and the wireless carriers offered deals that were not attractive for the content providers. Several deals they were negotiating provided very little revenue compared to the implementation costs and the initiatives were dropped. Salmi was frustrated with the lack of success of these experiments. Could he grow AtomFilms and make it profitable? Should he sell the business and focus resources and attention on the growing games market?

Exhibit 1	**Biography of Mika Salmi**

Mika Salmi was born in Helsinki in 1965 and lived in Finland until the age of two. The only child of two Finns, he grew up in the United States, where his father worked for Finnair. The family moved frequently, but always returned to their home in Rovaniemi, Finland for 2–4 months per year. By the age of 10, Mika Salmi had lived in New York, Detroit, and Washington DC. In 1975, they moved to Chicago, where Mika lived until he went to college. He retained his Finnish passport until 1995, and has been a citizen of the United States since then. "I hope to be a Finnish citizen again," he says, "and I'd like dual citizenship if the law changes."

After graduating from high school, Salmi knew he would have to pay his own way through college, as his parents could not afford the expense. He had been working since the age of 15, teaching windsurfing on Lake Michigan and selling skis at a sporting goods store, and his savings allowed him to start at the University of Vermont on a partial skiing scholarship. "I wasn't quite good enough to make the ski team, and the university was very expensive; my student loan wasn't enough," he recalls. Consequently, he moved to the University of Wisconsin after his freshman year. "It was cheaper, and they needed a ski coach, which helped with tuition," he says. "My windsurfing business partners had a store in Madison [where the university is located], so I could work there too." Salmi chose a finance and international business double major, with a specialization in computer science. Salmi was something of a contradiction at university. On the one hand, he found finance exciting and interesting, particularly after spending the summer of his junior year working for a bank in Luxemburg. On the other hand, he was a punk rocker who "worked as a disc jockey and played in some bad bands," he reminisces. "I was the guy in the business classes with spiked hair who wore army fatigues and came to class on a skate board," he laughs.

"Music has been really important to me since I was six," Salmi says. "When I graduated without a job in 1987, I sent out about 100 letters to entertainment companies, but got nowhere. I landed a sort of job in New York, went there, and found a 'real' job at Bankers Trust. I hated it once I got in—what I believed in and my punk-rock social orientation did not fit in with the banking world."

In New York, Salmi kept moonlighting as a disc jockey after his work-day as a banker was finished. About a year after, he happened to be DJ for a Finnish May Day party. "A guy saw me and said I was a good DJ," Salmi recalls. "He asked me what my day job was, and he couldn't believe it when I told him. It turns out he was a music lawyer, and he made it his mission to get me a job in the music business." Through this contact, Salmi landed a sales job with a smaller label, TVT Records. "I handled the Tower Records account; they had small bands, so my job was asking Tower Records to buy, maybe, five copies of a record," he says. Additionally, Salmi ran TVT's computer systems, which were based on the DBASE III database program for personal

Exhibit 1   Biography of Mika Salmi—Continued

computers. Because TVT only paid him $20,000 per year, Salmi also worked for Bankers Trust during the evenings. "Although I had wanted to trade currencies, my job was tracking how much money currency traders in Bankers Trust offices around the world made," he says. "We kept the figures in a database and tracked them relative to the salary and bonus scheme. I was the only guy who knew how to run the database, so they let me do it at home, working for them at night."

Salmi's career at TVT lasted all of seven months. "Big labels loved to pick up people from the company, because it was intense; you learned a lot; and you didn't last long," he says. "I started there in June, and in October, I went to a concert and fell in love with the opening band, a group nobody had then heard of called Nine-Inch Nails. I pursued them, and convinced my boss to sign them, even though he hated them. I thought I would become the A&R guy if I signed them, but they wouldn't let me, so I quit in December," he says.

For three months, Salmi moved to Vail, Colorado, working as a waiter and the coach of a local ski team. In the spring, he moved to Seattle, Washington, where his parents had relocated while Mika was at University. "I met somebody who helped me get a job selling commercial real estate," he recalls. "It was 100% commission, and it sounded like I could do the job at the same time I was doing other stuff." Salmi's firm focused on apartment building and shopping centers, and his biggest sale was a $10.5 million shopping center. Meanwhile, he coached a local ski team, managed bands, and kept disk jockeying. "My friend and I threw the first rave party in Seattle," he notes.

After two years in Seattle, Salmi was looking for something else to do. "I had been in the US for a while and I was hankering to get back to Europe," he says. "I was missing my roots and the lifestyle, and I wanted to challenge myself a bit more intellectually." In January, 1992, he started the MBA program at INSEAD. "I applied to IMD and LBS, but I liked the one year program," he says. "INSEAD was broader, and the diversity of the students was the important thing for me."

"When I first got to INSEAD, I was very serious in Period 1," he reminisces. "I thought I should look at finance or consulting, and ensure I came out of business school with something interesting. I got to know people in those industries and went to presentations, and I found it way too boring. I decided to get a higher-level job in the entertainment business, and I became the music guy of my promotion. Whenever there were parties, I was the DJ. I was social and part of the group, but I plowed my own road at school, because very few of my classmates wanted to be in the entertainment business."

Then, Salmi took a marketing class that set him on the right path. He explains: "We had to pick a product or market for a real company and do research for them. I got the chance to research the Polish music market. An INSEAD alumnus was head of Eastern

Europe for EMI, and they wanted to know what to do with Poland—enter it by themselves, buy a record company, form a joint venture, or export to Poland. It was a fantastic six-week project. I got to know the alumnus, spent time in Warsaw, analyzed artists, and learned all about radio stations and piracy."

The project led to a summer job with EMI in Budapest, where Salmi studied the Hungarian, Czech, and Romanian market. After graduating in December, 1992, he took a job with EMI in Paris as a business planner, working as an internal consultant for the CEO who ran France and the Benelux region. "I did a weekly analysis of each market's performance, and he sent me off on little missions, for example to find out why someone's marketing budget was out of line," Salmi says. "I did not have day-to-day responsibility and I really wanted to sink my teeth into something."

In the spring of 1994, Salmi joined Sony Music in New York. "I had met them while I was at INSEAD, and they asked me to take US-based artists and craft international marketing plans for them in 51 countries," he explains. "There was tons of travel and it was internationally focused. It was a great job, and I loved it. While he was at Sony, Salmi wrote his first entrepreneurial business plan, which was not a success. He elaborates: "I started going to film festivals in the 1980s, and I used video content at raves. I got really enamored with short-form content early on. When I was in Paris, I loved the channel M6, which showed music videos, animation, and short film. When I moved to New York, I hated MTV, so I wrote a business plan in 1994 for a cable channel around short-form content. It was a poorly-written, eight-page plan, and I didn't known how to start a company or launch a channel; I didn't know who to go to."

Salmi's girlfriend decided to move to Seattle in 1995, and he decided to move there to be with her. "I had started using the Internet in 1994 with a Mosaic browser and it was really starting to take off in 1995," he comments. "I had a computer background, so I thought I could do something in that new world. I had offers to start my own small record label, because I had shown I could find good music–I signed Presidents of the USA and co-signed 311 for Sony. I had some discussions about starting my own record business, but it didn't ring true for me. The Internet was really interesting and Seattle was a hotbed for it, so I decided to focus on it and learn more about it."

In January, 1996, Salmi took a job at Real Networks in Seattle, as Director of Business Development for the entertainment business. Principally, he worked with artists, labels, and radio stations, to ensure that content was being placed on the Internet using the Real Audio streaming format. He ran many promotions, including one of the first live Netcast concerts, featuring Ozzy Osbourne. In February, 1997, Real Networks introduced its first streaming video product, RealVideo. Salmi's involvement with this product caused him to return to the idea that had seized him in 1994, but focused on the Internet. The rewritten plan became the basis for what would become AtomFilms.

Exhibit 2	Main Players in the US Market for Online Casual Games

The market leader in 2003 was Real Networks (http://www.realarcade.com/). The company had about 25% of the US market share, following a series of acquisitions of smaller sites. Its business model was supported by e-commerce revenues from game downloads, although the company was starting to focus more on advertising. Real Networks was implementing an aggressive strategy of US and International acquisitions.

The other key players, like AtomShackwave, had a market share of between 10–15%.

- Electronic Arts/ Pogo.com: http://ea.pogo.com
- Yahoo Games: http://games.yahoo.com/
- MSN Games: http://zone.msn.com/
- AOL Games: http://onlinegames.channel.aol.com/

All of these players were financially strong and three of them had a huge user base. Their business model was mainly based on advertising with a small but growing e-commerce revenue base from game downloads.

SHOCKWAVE.COM The strategic challenges of Shockwave's business at this time were very different. The market for casual games was large and growing at a fast pace, being expected to reach $200M worldwide by 2005. While Shockwave.com was one of the top six companies in 2003, all its competitors were much larger players with deep pockets. Real Networks, the market leader, had launched an aggressive series of acquisitions of smaller sites. Other key players included Yahoo, Microsoft, AOL, and Electronic Arts (see Exhibit 2). Competitive pressure was increasing, leading to higher costs of acquiring rights to games, more competition for audience, and less pricing power in advertising and e-commerce.

Shockwave was relying on close, fraternal relationships with game developers to ensure it could continue to attract the best new games:

"We defined game developers as a key resource. E-commerce is giving developers a revenue opportunity, and we spend a lot of time working with them, sharing our knowledge about what makes games sell. There is a big migration to selling games to consumers instead of seeing them as content for a website . . . (McCarthy)

"We want to have the best games, not just the ones you see everywhere, but also exclusive games you won't find on other sites. That is where having money is helpful: either you have to develop a game yourself or buy it. It's necessary for people to say we have the best stuff." (Salmi)

For Salmi, the issue was whether Shockwave could survive as an independent player:

"I want to remain independent, but I don't want to be an also-ran. I want to go head-to-head with larger companies—is that possible, or is it just a pipe dream? Will we end up a third-tier player if we don't sell the business to a bigger player? Will the

big players focus more on what we are doing and cut off our supply of content by spending more money than we can?"

McCarthy, however, was sanguine about Shockwave's ability to compete:

"Developers like us. They don't want to be in a position where Real Networks, Microsoft, and Yahoo have too much power. They are very free-spirited people who could get jobs anywhere, and big players could drive them out of the market if they aren't careful."

Shockwave had been developing a capability to support more multiplayer games. It relied on chat tools and synchronization technology allowing people to interact with one another. McCarthy believed this was the feature that made multiplayer games compelling. "There is a market for community and chat, but not for games where you make up a new character for yourself. Women between the ages of 25 and 45 are not looking for an alternate universe." McCarthy also believed that a focused strategy would allow Atom-Shockwave to succeed against much larger competitors for the games mass market:

"In our sector, we are not much smaller in revenue than Microsoft or Yahoo, but we are focused on this area while they have many priorities. I think we have a window to do interesting things and become the supplier of this kind of content."

It was clear that new growth initiatives would be needed if Shockwave was to remain a viable contender. The Game-Blaster subscription service was growing slowly but steadily and the downloading of games continued to be profitable. Although the advertising market had stalled, with a larger audience it would be possible to increase revenue. The key questions were how to secure the best content and increase audience in such a competitive environment? Would self-funded growth be enough to sustain the company? Could they survive as an independent player?

Crafting a Strategy for AtomShockwave

For the previous three years, Salmi had just been focused on making his venture survive and reach financial break-even. Now, he realized he might need to make some tough strategic choices about his business portfolio and growth priorities. One tempting path was selling one of the businesses to focus on the other. The improved results in 2003 and the fact that AtomShockwave was now cash-flow positive increased the attractiveness of the company as an acquisition target. AtomShockwave's board had already received several inquiries from large media companies about selling the whole company or one of the two businesses. The valuation was up to four times the revenue. The board was looking to Salmi to provide a clear strategic direction in their November 2003 meeting.

Salmi had some crucial issues to consider. Could he survive as an independent player or should he sell now? Was the potential of the company greater with the two businesses together? In which business and initiatives should he invest his cash flow? How best could he pursue his long-time vision of becoming the market leader for short-format entertainment? As the sun sank towards the horizon, Salmi picked up his surfboard to ride one last wave. The answers could wait until Monday morning . . .

Case 34

David Walentas' Two Trees Management Company: A Case of Deliberate Entrepreneurship

Noushi Rahman, Pace University
Department of Management and Management Science
Lubin School of Business, Pace University
One Pace Plaza, W-414
New York, NY 10038

Voice: (212) 618-6446
Fax: (212) 618-6482
E-mail: nrahman@pace.edu

Fabiha Naumi, Katalyst, Bangladesh
Business Environment Division
Katalyst, Bangladesh
House#20, Road#6, Baridhara
Dhaka-1212 Bangladesh

Voice: +88(017)2001-5690
E-mail: fabiha.naumi@swisscontact-bd.org

Case Synopsis

DUMBO is one of the most chic neighborhoods in the New York City borough of Brooklyn, and the revitalization has been a "planned gentrification" as opposed to a "natural gentrification" process.

Real estate entrepreneur-turned-mogul David Walentas has deliberately transformed Brooklyn's DUMBO neighborhood, where he holds about 3 million square feet of building space. Walentas has worked methodically to give the deserted area of DUMBO a neighborhood feel. Initially, he allowed artists to move in his properties for very low rent. As artists moved in, so did culture, sophistication, and the need for art-related things. This gave rise to multiple galleries, design studios, and printing services firms in DUMBO. With an increasing population in the neighborhood, the government was more willing to invest in redeveloping State-owned properties in the area. This had strong positive spill over for Walentas' Two Trees Management Company.

In 2005, at an estimated going price of $700 per square foot, Walentas' 3 million square feet real estate holdings are worth about $2.1 billion. With development work in DUMBO facing buildings going full-steam, however, Walentas now faces a dilemma concerning his growth strategy. Once these buildings are all fully leased or sold, the growth of Two Trees Management will stagnate. Thus, despite tremendous success, what the future holds for Two Trees is anyone's guess.

Situation

By 2001, DUMBO (acronym for Down Under the Manhattan Bridge Overpass) was dubbed the most chic and up-and-coming neighborhood of Brooklyn. Comparing DUMBO's chic-ness to the most art-focused neighborhoods of Manhattan, *New York Times* quipped, "DUMBO is the new SoHo." Under the careful strategizing of real estate entrepreneur David Walentas, DUMBO has changed from a dilapidated graveyard of desolate buildings to a vibrant and happening residential-commercial hotspot.

Gentrification of DUMBO has been focused and quick. While urban scholars recognize gentrification as a gradual and slow process of neighborhood reversal through a variety of contributions from developers, real estate business-people, landlords, and the upper-middle class (Smith, 1982), such is not the development path in DUMBO. Control of a large portion of the DUMBO real estate allowed David Walentas the ability to act as a catalyst to speed up the gentrification of the neighborhood.

An earlier version of this case appears in the *Journal of the International Academy for Case Studies.*

Through his company Two Trees Management, Walentas has reaped returns of almost one-hundred times that of his initial investments! As great as it sounds, Walentas is faced with a major dilemma choosing among rent-now, sell-now, and sell-later options.

Walentas converted his third building to condominiums in 2005. He owns 15 buildings in DUMBO. Prices keep increasing in the area, with the latest offering being in the range of $700–900 per square foot. So, converting all of the buildings now would mean earning less than what may be possible in the future (assuming prices will increase further). However, prices keep increasing partly because of record-low interest rates, enabling many people to afford homes that they previously could not. Industry experts keep warning that mortgage interest rates will start going up (this has already started, although very modestly). So, when the mortgage interest rates go up, fewer buyers will be able to afford Walentas' highly priced luxury condos. Waiting for the economic cycle to come around 360 degrees (i.e., back to low interest rates) to sell his remaining housing stock at high prices is a huge gamble!

So what comes next for Walentas? His core competence is in real estate development. There are, however, several possibilities that lay ahead. Walentas can start working on another dilapidated neighborhood (perhaps Red Hook, which looks eerily similar to what DUMBO looked like 25 years ago). Or he could consider interior design, cleaning and maintenance, and other lines of businesses that will give him greater control over the real estate development business. He can continue to cater to the needs of his customers. Bringing in dry cleaning, bookstores, salons, spas, and a sports arcade could all add tremendous value to DUMBO. Walentas is torn between two options—starting full-fledged real estate development in some other area or starting other lines of business that will complement his existing DUMBO project. Looking out the window of his office, Walentas saw two iconic bridges (i.e., Brooklyn and Manhattan winged out) symbolically showing him the different paths to the future. A mistake here could seriously jeopardize his greatest achievement thus far. What should be his strategic path from here on?

Background

Walentas grew up amidst poverty in Rochester; he describes himself as "an indentured orphan." He went to the University of Virginia and while there he decided he wanted to be a developer. Determined and confident, Walentas got established as a developer relatively early in his life (Finn,

2003). It was, however, his project in DUMBO that turned him from an established developer to a real estate legend. It all started in 1979 when Walentas drove through the Fulton Ferry Landings, a several square block river-side area between the Brooklyn Bridge and the Manhattan Bridge. With the greatest skyline of the world as the background scenery, Walentas envisioned tremendous investment potentials in DUMBO.

Walentas himself described his career as being constantly "on the edge." His shirt sleeves have the embroidered phrase: "No guts, no glory." His philosophy complements two of Winston Churchill's much renowned quotes that Walentas deeply believes in—"Fortune favors the brave" and "Never, never, never give up." While growing up, Walentas was always a smart straight-talker—never hesitant to pursue what he believed in. Walentas describes his younger-self as 'fresh.' Reinforced with his spectacular success in DUMBO, he proclaimed that "perseverance beats inspiration any day" and one should "never take 'no' for an answer" (Schmid, 2004).

In 1982, Two Trees Management Co. purchased 9 buildings from Harry Helmsley for $16.5 million (*Beyer Blinder Belle*, 1990). The purchase price for 2.5 million square feet of space was at the rate of $6.6 per square foot (Schmid, 2004). Two Trees later acquired other buildings, thus increasing its holdings to roughly 3 million square feet of space.

Soon after the purchase of these factory buildings in a completely dilapidated neighborhood, Walentas applied to the City government for a rezoning of the area. In 1984, the City and State governments conditionally designated Two Trees Management to develop the Empire Stores along with a number of city-owned sites in DUMBO (*Beyer Blinder Belle*, 1990). Walentas saw tremendous prospects in DUMBO and 'seized the opportunity' to bring about his plans. He proposed an elaborate rejuvenation plan for DUMBO. His grand plan was 'too heavy' to fly and needed revision.

Prior to his DUMBO investment, Walentas' strategy has been simple: buy space, add value, and sell at high margin. The DUMBO investment, being Walentas' largest holdings, did not fit into this traditional mold. Adding value to DUMBO seemed like an extremely challenging task. First, Walentas' proposed long-term plans of rejuvenation were plagued by political problems. The deputy Mayor at that time, Kenneth Lipper put many obstacles in Walentas' way with the DUMBO project for what have been described as some personal reasons (Finn, 2003). Then, in 1987, the stock market crashed. This had trickling effects on the real estate market. During 1989–1993, the New York real estate market was a total buyers market. So, one decade after acquiring roughly 3 million square feet of space, Walentas realized no gain. Worse yet, a significant portion of Walentas' wealth remained stuck in the gutters. At times, he considered selling the properties; but could not do so as there was not a single buyer who would buy his vast building space.

During his continued financial hard-times, Walentas was patient. He survived through his other businesses—other revenue generating activities. Amidst all the financial woes, Walentas was unwavering about his vision. He sent his son to the University of Pennsylvania. His son, Jed Walentas, apprenticed under Donald Trump (successfully, without being fired). And, the real estate boom beginning in the late 1990s set the stage for Walentas to realize his vision. Jed Walentas' solid education and excellent training made him his father's most reliable partner. Two Trees Management got a break in 1997 when the State Office of Parks, Recreation, and Historic Preservation solicited proposals for the redevelopment of the Empire–Fulton Ferry State Park. It was 'carpe diem' for Walentas, who was the only one to submit a proposal (on behalf of Two Trees). The State Office of Parks, Recreation, and Historic Preservation granted the proposal in 1998.

With great hopes and high spirits, Walentas engaged in detailed planning for the Fulton Ferry Park. The park was on the far-west side of DUMBO, just by the East River. Walentas' development plans of the State Park would provide a much needed green recreation area for DUMBO residents. The proposed redevelopment plan was very grand and expensive, costing the government $300 million. By 2000, the government withdrew its support for redeveloping the Park.

The Functioning of Two Trees Management Corporation

Two Trees adds value to the properties it owns by converting factory buildings to posh offices and residential apartments. These offices and apartments have new fittings, large windows, and concealed electric, phone, and cable wirings. An excited Walentas exclaims: "We are thrilled to offer the finest move-in ready office suites in Brooklyn. DUMBO has Manhattan quality at one-tenth of the price" (*Hagerdon Publication*, 2001).

Two Trees Management caters to businesses that are looking for a great deal of convenience in their daily operations. To facilitate in-coming business tenants, Two Trees offers four steps: visit space, sign lease, move-in, and get-to-work. In other words, all amenities, such as electrical wirings, telephone connections, and internet facilities are inclusive in the lease package.

The City and State governments' actions have had mixed effects on Two Trees. On the positive side, the rerouting of

Bus 25 through DUMBO has added convenience for the residents. In contrast, the State and City governments' on-and-off approach toward Empire–Fulton Ferry Park has caused much grief for Two Trees Management.

Governmental tax-breaks have made leasing prices in DUMBO and other Brooklyn neighborhoods relatively attractive. For example, through the Relocation and Employment Assistance Program (REAP) program, businesses moving to Brooklyn can potentially save $13–15 per square foot over the price in Manhattan. Another tax-break is in the form of annual tax credits. Small businesses meeting certain specifications become eligible for $3000 per employee tax credits. Also, real estate tax abatement of up to $2.50 per square foot is available to these new business tenants (Grassi, 2001). Lastly, many businesses qualify for reduced energy rates. Two Trees Management has definitely benefited from these government-induced benefits, for these benefits have made DUMBO office space even more attractive than what Two Trees can claim credit for.

Beyond Real Estate—the Making of a Neighborhood

Two Trees' approach to DUMBO has largely been way beyond real estate development. Walentas has always given much attention to bringing in businesses of 'certain types,' particularly businesses that add cultural character to the neighborhood (see Table 1). In the 1980s, Walentas offered a great deal of space for zero or very little rent to artists who would come and make DUMBO their workplace and home. It is not surprising that over the years many galleries, printing services, design studios, and software businesses have leased offices in DUMBO. Boutique galleries include M3 Projects, 5 + 5 Gallery, Metaphor Contemporary Art, Howard Schickler Fine Art, Paint Gallery, Gale Gates et al., Smack Mellon Studios, and d.u.m.b.o. Arts Center (DAC). More than a dozen printing services firms are also DUMBO tenants. Design studios, such as Four Eyes Production and Sceptre Consulting have added to the artistic or cultural character of the neighborhood. In recent months, several software firms and a couple of business consulting firms have also moved into the neighborhood.

Bringing in culturally linked firms as business tenants, Walentas has created an environment that facilitates trade. The design studios can get access to the best and most competitively priced printing facilities. The galleries serve as an important channel to display and sell artworks and new designs to the public. Business consulting and software firms may contribute to all of these businesses in more spe-

Table 1	Esteemed Artists and Arts Organizations Working in DUMBO	
Artists and Arts Organization	Genre	Critical Acclaim
Vito Acconci	Film, video, photographs, & sculptures	MoMA
Art at St. Anns	Concert, music theater, puppet theater	
Brooklyn Front	Miscellaneous (art gallery)	
Creative Time	Miscellaneous (public arts projects)	Installations: "Consuming Places"
DUMBO Arts Center	Miscellaneous (annual d.u.m.b.o. art under the bridge festival)	
Tom Fruin	Sculptures (made of 'found objects')	
GAle GAtes et al.	Theater	
Howard Schickler Fine Art	Photographs, paintings, drawings, and rare books (19th and 20th century)	
J. Mandle Performance	Miscellaneous (experimental arts using performances and installations)	
Lunatarium	Music, dance, film, video, installation, and performance art	
Mastel + Mastel	Digital art	
Sheila Metzner	Fine art, photography	Metropolitan Museum of Art; International Center for Photography; MoMA
One Arm Red	Meeting place for artists to mingle, establishing a sense of community	

Source: http://www.dumbolofts.com

cialized and/or technical ways. Overall, Walentas' neighborhood design has converted DUMBO into a trade-friendly neighborhood.

Walentas's goal is not merely to facilitate his business tenants. The primary goal is to make DUMBO a vibrant and lively community where employment and entertainment create a synergy. He has been actively involved in organizing a variety of festive events, such as the Egg Hunt & Spring Fling, BARGEMUSIC, Summer Film Series, and It's My Park Day (see Table 2). Since DUMBO's buildings are mostly old factory-buildings, adding a residential feeling to the neighborhood is critical.

Another telling example of neighborhood gentrification comes from Walentas' search for a bakery. When some 2400 square feet of store space became available at 85 Water Street, Walentas decided to find a specific baker. While various businesses wanted to rent the space, Walentas would only rent the space to a baker. This choice prevented Two Trees Management from securing several confirmed tenants for the space, but it enabled Walentas to add a critical neighborhood-element to DUMBO. After much searching, Walentas found Almondine—a French-style bakery with

surprisingly affordable fancy delicacies (Croghan, 2004). This was a significant step in DUMBO's transformation, because, as home improvement guru Bob Vila says, "what's a neighborhood without a bakery" (Croghan, 2004). Adding a high-end bakery and other gourmet shops added an upper-middle class aura to the neighborhood.

As DUMBO picks up momentum as a neighborhood, both residential and business tenants keep flocking in to get some space of their own. Upper-middle class buying power, coupled with a degree of sophistication, has attracted fine restaurants to the neighborhood. DUMBO residents can now go to *Pete's Downtown* for Italian, *Superfine* for Mediterranean, *Grimaldis* for Pizza, *Rice* for eclectic dishes, *Bubby's* for traditional American food, and *Five Front* and *River Café* for new American dishes (*Zagat Survey*, 2005). All of these restaurants are medium to high end. Grimaldis' coal oven pizzas are the highest rated New York pizzas by Zagat (food score 27 out of 30) (*Zagat Survey*, 2005). The River Café, which is very expensive, is one of the foremost all-round restaurants of greater New York City (food score 25, decoration score 28, service score 24—each score is out of 30) (*Zagat Survey*, 2005).

Table 2	Organized Cultural Events in DUMBO, April 2002—October 2004

Dates	Events
April 10, 2002	Egg Hunt & Spring Fling at Brooklyn Bridge Park
September 2002–May 2003	BARGEMUSIC
November 2003–December 2003	Snapshot Fashions: Dressing in the 20th Century Exhibition at the MF Adams Gallery
January 29, 2004	Brooklyn Underground's Moonshine Theater presentation: "The Holy Mountain"
January 2004–March 2004	MULTIPLEX at Smack Mellon
March 2004–April 2004	MULTIPLEX at Smack Mellon
March 2004–May 2004	Ricoh Gerbl and Robert Taplin and Smack Mellon
April 1, 2004	Jen Ferguson April Fool's Day at Superfine
July 2004–August 2004	The Brooklyn Bridge Park Summer Film Series
August 2004–August 2005	Family Concert—The Persuasions
October 2004	Good Samaritans
October 23, 2004	"It's My Park" Day

Source: http://www.dumbo-newyork.com

Financial Status and the Future

The real estate development project of DUMBO has been extremely profitable for Walentas. From $6.6 per square foot to an average of $700 per square foot is indeed a long stretch. Nevertheless, now is a crucial time for Walentas because once his renovated buildings are fully leased and/or sold, the growth of Two Trees will stand still. Anticipating this impending slowdown, Walentas has been trying hard to construct new high-rise buildings in DUMBO. However, political opposition has made such vertical expansion remote. Growing in other neighborhoods in a manner similar to DUMBO remains another alternative for Walentas' Two Trees. Besides growth through real estate development, Two Trees Management may consider venturing into other supporting businesses. For example, a household appliance store, a grocery, a salon and a barber shop can contribute to completing the neighborhood feel and convenience. Whatever path Walentas chooses to pursue now will be crucial to the continued success (or failure) of Two Trees Management Corporation.

References

Beyer Blinder Belle. Empire–Fulton Ferry State Park Feasibility Study. (1990). "Historical Chronology, 1642–2000: Post–War Decline, and Rebirth," Retrieved from: <http://www.placeinhistory.org/Projects/Dumbo/DumboChron4.htm>.

Croghan, Lore. "Baking in Dumbo," *New York Daily News,* 21 May 2004. Retrieved from: <http://www.nydailynews.com/business/v-pfriendly/story/195380p-168826c.html>.

DUMBO Brooklyn: Culture. (2004). Retrieved from: <http://www.dumbolofts.com>.

Finn, Robin. "PUBLIC LIVES; One Name He Can Remember. It Was an Elephant's." New York Times, 16 July 2003. Retrieved from: <http://www.query.nytimes.com/search/article-printpage.html>.

Grassi, Joseph P. "There's Nothing Dumb About Brooklyn's DUMBO; Revitalized District Clearly Is Poised To Take Off," *Printing News,* 23 July 2001. Retrieved from: <http://www.printingnews.com/pages/issues/2001/72301/dumbo.shtml>.

Hagedorn Publication. "Pre-built offices at DUMBO deliver space, tech & amenities–Two Trees Management Co-Brief Article," (2001). *Real Estate Weekly,* 23 May 2001.

Kim, Janet. "Close-Up on DUMBO, Brooklyn," *Village Voice,* 18 April 2003. Retrieved from: <http://www.villagevoice.com/print/issues/0317/kim.php>.

Mapquest. (2004) Retrieved from: <http://www.mapquest.com>.

Schmid, Elizabeth V. "David C. Walentas: Making DUMBO Fly," *U. Va. Top News Daily,* 13 July 2004.

Retrieved from: <http://www.virginia.edu/topnews/david_walentas.html>.

Smith, Neil. (1982). "Gentrification and uneven development," *Economic Geography,* 58: 139–155.

Two Trees website. (2004). Retrieved from: <http://www.dumbolofts.com/>.

Zagat Survey. (2005). Retrieved from: <http://www.zagat.com>.

Zukin, Sharon. (1982). "*Loft living: Culture and Capital in change,*" Baltimore, MD: Johns Hopkins University Press.

Case 35

DaimlerChrysler: Corporate Governance Dynamics in a Global Company

"We need a new, dynamic global partnership of business and politics. The dust of the trust crisis has settled somewhat. And many national governments have demonstrated their ability to act swiftly within their own territories. Now we should join forces in leading the way towards a wider, increasingly multilateral approach to Corporate Governance rules."

—Jürgen Schrempp, CEO, DaimlerChrysler AG, 2003

Ever since the announcement of the merger between Daimler-Benz AG and Chrysler Corporation in May 1998, the company had been in the spotlight. The merged company, DaimlerChrysler (DC) was a full-range provider controlling six car brands and eight truck brands. In addition, DC acquired strategic holdings in Mitsubishi Motors of Japan (37% stake) and Hyundai Motors of Korea (10% stake). Besides this global push, DC divested many of its non-core businesses as recommended by the financial community. Nevertheless, the dividend dropped from € 2.35 in the first three years to € 1.00 in 2001. By 2002 the turnarounds at Chrysler and Mitsubishi had led to profitability, and the dividend was raised by 50%. However, by 2003, an ongoing price war in North America, with average rebates of $4,500 per vehicle, was proving costly and the outcome was uncertain.

Over the years, DC became an international benchmark for global operations and management. As for all corporations, corporate governance was of special importance. New regulations, a lack of shareholder and public confidence in big business, and general uncertainty increased the pressure on companies to consider their governance structures. How could a company such as DC reconcile regulatory differences and the diverse expectations of various stakeholders around the globe? There was agreement that corporate governance "had to be lived," but how?

Background: Understanding the DaimlerChrysler Merger

When the merger of Daimler-Benz AG and Chrysler Corporation was announced on May 6, 1998, this "merger in heaven" came as a total surprise to everyone in the industry. Both companies seemed to complement each other well on geographic and product dimensions[1] and both had outstanding reputations. *Forbes* had even selected Chrysler as "company of the year 1996":

> You may think of Chrysler as an old-fashioned metal bender in a mature industry, cyclical as hell. You may think it's just lucky with all those Jeeps and minivans when everyone happens to want a Jeep or minivan. Jeeps and vans go out of fad, Chrysler flops. That's the perception—which is why Chrysler stock sells at less than seven times earnings. But perceptions notoriously lag reality, and we think the reality here is that Chrysler's good luck is being leveraged by a superb

[1]See Radler, Neubauer and Steger, *The DaimlerChrysler Merger: The Involvement of the Boards,* Case no. IMD-3–0771, for detailed corporate governance issues during the merger negotiations in 1998. The present case only covers the developments after the deal had taken place.

Figure 1	Overview of Phases

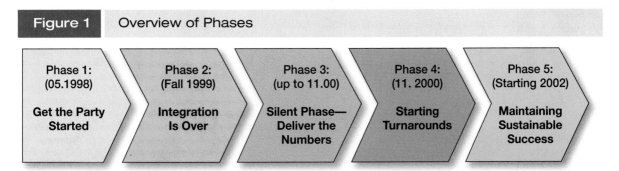

Note: While reading this case, please keep on referring to Exhibit 1 for the representation of the phases and the creation/elimination of various committees.

management team that has made smart, disciplined decisions.[i]

Chrysler was perceived as a very efficient producer and thereby earning more cash than any other major carmaker. Daimler-Benz's luxury car division (Mercedes-Benz) was the envy of the industry. This was a "merger of equals" with anticipated synergies of $1.4 billion for a combined revenue of $132 billion in its first year of operation. The merger of these two icons also caught the attention of the public right from the beginning. This $36 billion merger became a symbol for what is generally described as a complex business environment for global players: total transparency, Wall Street formulating earnings growth, and immense scrutiny of all stakeholders involved.

With hindsight, the merger developments between 1998 and 2003 can be split into five phases. Figure 1 gives an overview of the five phases.

Revenues increased from €132 billion in 1998 to €162 billion in 2000, before falling to €150 for 2002 (*refer to* Exhibit 2 for a fact sheet on DaimlerChrysler for the five years up to 2002).

PHASE 1: MERGER ANNOUNCEMENT 1998—"GET THE PARTY STARTED"
Initially, the rationale for the deal was clear. In an interview on October 5, 1998 Dieter Zetsche, board member of Daimler-Benz AG, explained:

> Our problem has been that costs are high for these new technologies because of our low volume. We always lost the technology to competitors. (. . .) Like with ESP (electronic stability program) we wanted one year of exclusivity [from our suppliers]; but they gave us three months, and we had to fight for it. Chrysler will give us the volume. We can stay No. 1 in

developing technology—and take it as soon as possible to Chrysler.[ii]

The synergy target of $1.4 billion (around 1% of gross revenue) was generally seen as low, but there was only a limited overlap of products. Helmut Petri, executive VP Production for Mercedes cars, explained at the time: "There will be no platform sharing. We can share parts and components, but we won't share platforms." However, competitors in the industry considered platforms as the "holy grail" for reaping synergies.

November 17, 1998 marked the first day of stock-trading for the DC share, which rose by around 30% to the high €90s in the spring of 1999. Executives and board members were trying to turn DC into one company, not just a company name. The integration was organized around 17 clusters (Issue Resolution Teams, or IRTs) and dealt with both automotive and non-automotive issues (*refer to* Exhibit 3 *for an overview of the integration structure and IRT cluster*). A corporate airline was set up to shuttle executives between Stuttgart (home of Daimler-Benz) and Auburn Hills (Chrysler), with video or telephone conferences complementing the integration efforts.

As part of the strategy to become a truly global company, managers at DC continued to develop strategies for Asia. Asia was going to be *the* growth market for automobiles, but it was a missing link for DC. DC identified two possible partners and even performed due diligence for acquiring a stake in Nissan Motors. However, after a lively discussion among the management board, this idea was dropped.

As integration got off the ground, second quarter earnings (1999) failed to meet Wall Street expectations and the

[i]Flint, Jerry. "Company of the Year: Chrysler." *Forbes*, January 13, 1997, p. 82 ff.

[ii]"Merger Details, from 'Autonomy' to 'Zetsche.'" *Automotive News*, October 5, 1998, Vol. 73, Issue 5787, p. 41 ff.

| Exhibit 1 | Overview of Phases and the Creation/Elimination of Various Committees |

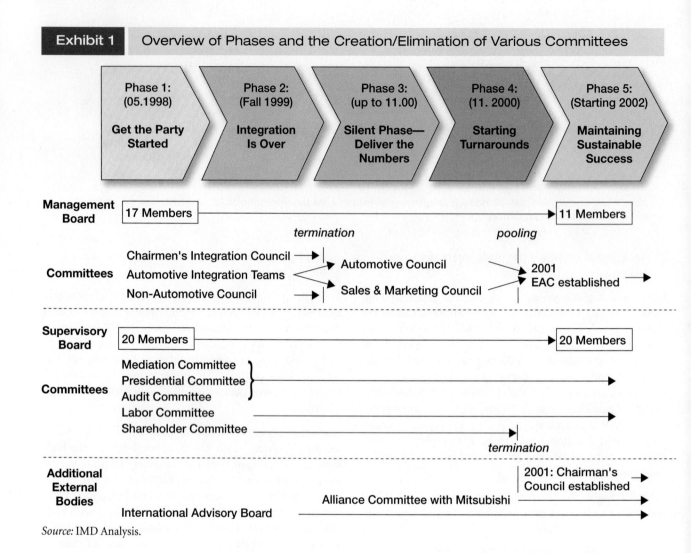

Source: IMD Analysis.

stock started to fall. In addition, the share was refused from the American S&P 500 index, a move which took the stock off the shopping list of many funds. By July, the company had to reduce its earnings growth expectations and suddenly synergies became very important. *Automotive News,* an industry journal, stated: "Meanwhile, Wall Street, underwhelmed by the company's performance to date, is expecting much more from DaimlerChrysler."[iii]

PHASE 2: SEPTEMBER 1999 "INTEGRATION IS OVER!"
On September 27, 1999 Jürgen Schrempp announced the completion of the integration of both companies. The formal integration with its 17 IRTs was concluded and the Chairmen's Integration Council was abandoned (after two of its eight members left the company). One of them, Tom

Stallkamp, the president of North American Chrysler operations and the executive in charge of integrating the company, was replaced by James Holden. Holden was previously executive VP Sales & Marketing.

Following its earlier decision to focus its business lines, DC decided to concentrate on the automotive and trucking business. Non-core activities (Adtranz trains, Debitel telecommunications, European Aeronautic Defense and Space Company [EADS, maker of Airbus]) were either sold, prepared for sell-off or merged with other companies. Selling some of the non-core businesses added financial flexibility for possible acquisitions.

But the geographic expansion continued. Schrempp and his team were convinced that they needed a local partner in Asia in order to participate in the forecasted growth there. In the summer of 2000 DC ultimately bought:

[iii]Kisiel, Ralph. "Gale: D/C Won't Share Platforms." *Automotive News,* October 4, 1999, Vol. 74, Issue 5841, p. 1.

Exhibit 2	DaimlerChrysler Fact Sheet 1998–2002 (in € billion)				
	1998	1999	2000	2001	2002
Revenues	131.782	149.985	162.384	152.873	149.583
Operating Profit	8.593	11.012	9.752	(1.318)	6.854
Operating Margin	6.5%	7.3%	6.0%	(0.9%)	4.6%
Net Operating Income	6.359	7.032	4.383	1.647	4.335
Net Operating Income as % of Net Assets (RONA)	12.7%	13.2%	7.4%	2.5%	6.7%
Net income (loss)	4.820	5.746	7.894	(662)	4.718
Cash Dividend per Share in €	2.35	2.35	2.35	1.00	1.50
Employees (in 000s)	442	467	416	372	366

Sales and Operating Profit by Division 2002 (in € billion)

	Sales	Operating Profit
Mercedes Car Group	50.170	3.020
Chrysler Group	60.181	0.609
Commercial Vehicles	28.401	(0.343)
Services	15.699	3.060
Other Activities	2.723	0.903

Regional Sales Distribution 2001

	DaimlerChrysler	Global GDP Distribution
NAFTA	53%	36%
Western Europe	31%	27%
Asia	11%	27%
ROW	5%	10%

Source: DaimlerChrysler.

- A 34% equity stake in Mitsubishi Motors of Japan, and later raised it to 37%.
- A 10% equity stake in Hyundai Motors of South Korea.

With this set-up, DC did not need to consolidate these minority stakes, which was an issue given Mitsubishi Motors' debt.

PHASE 3: UP TO NOVEMBER 2000 "SILENT PHASE—DELIVER THE NUMBERS" The year 2000 was actually a good year for the car industry. Mercedes-Benz cars benefited from its product line extension and maintained strong financial results. The American market was performing very well and a new record was expected for the whole year. However, Chrysler was no longer able to grow with the market. A flood of new competitive models was expected in the minivan segment for which Chrysler had up to 55% share (in the U.S.). As a result, Chrysler loaded its new minivan with expensive options and prices rose accordingly. However, sales of the new minivan were below expectations and the vehicles needed sales incentives/price reductions early on. For Chrysler's other pillar of profitability, SUVs, a wide range of competitive products was suddenly eating into Chrysler's market, too.

The results soon became visible: Chrysler's U.S. market share fell from over 16.2% in 1998 to 13.5% in 2000 and no miracle cure was to be expected from international demand. In order to move the vehicles, cash rebates/incentives of up to $3,000 had to be paid. At the same time, production costs spiraled out of control, as production capacity could not be

Exhibit 3 Integration Structure and IRT Clusters

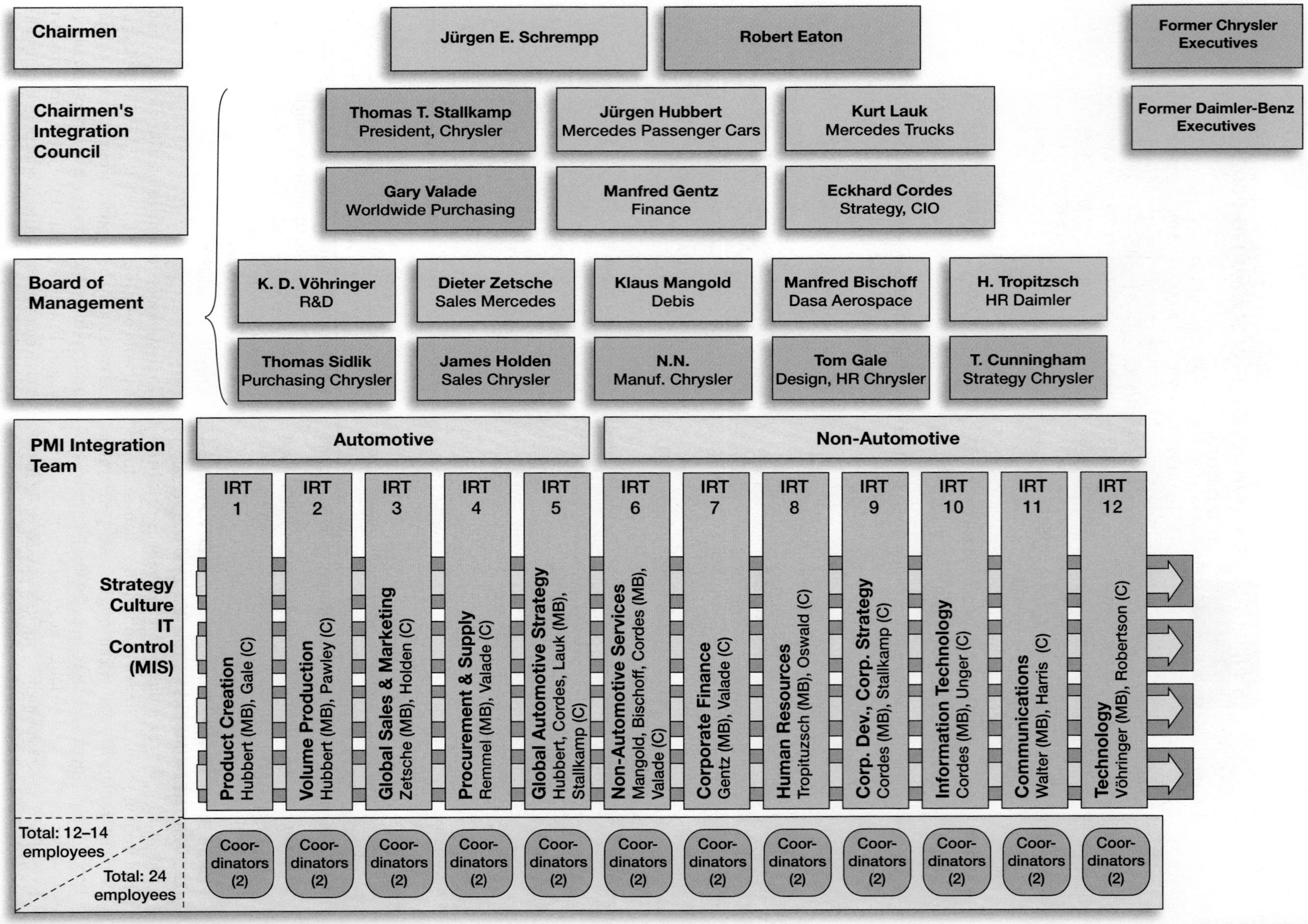

Chairmen

Jürgen E. Schrempp   Robert Eaton

Chairmen's Integration Council

Thomas T. Stallkamp
President, Chrysler

Jürgen Hubbert
Mercedes Passenger Cars

Kurt Lauk
Mercedes Trucks

Gary Valade
Worldwide Purchasing

Manfred Gentz
Finance

Eckhard Cordes
Strategy, CIO

Board of Management

K. D. Vöhringer
R&D

Dieter Zetsche
Sales Mercedes

Klaus Mangold
Debis

Manfred Bischoff
Dasa Aerospace

Thomas Sidlik
Purchasing Chrysler

James Holden
Sales Chrysler

N.N.
Manuf. Chrysler

Tom Gale
Design, HR Chrysler

H. Tropitzsch
HR Daimler

T. Cunningham
Strategy Chrysler

PMI Integration Team

Strategy
Culture
IT
Control (MIS)

Former Chrysler Executives

Former Daimler-Benz Executives

Automotive

Non-Automotive

IRT 1	IRT 2	IRT 3	IRT 4	IRT 5	IRT 6	

IRT 1 — Product Creation
Hubbert (MB), Gale (C)

IRT 2 — Volume Production
Hubbert (MB), Pawley (C)

IRT 3 — Global Sales & Marketing
Zetsche (MB), Holden (C)

IRT 4 — Procurement & Supply
Remmel (MB), Valade (C)

IRT 5 — Global Automotive Strategy
Hubbert, Cordes, Lauk (MB), Stallkamp (C)

IRT 6 — Non-Automotive Services
Mangold, Bischoff, Cordes (MB), Valade (C)

IRT 7 — Corporate Finance
Gentz (MB), Valade (C)

IRT 8 — Human Resources
Tropitzsch (MB), Oswald (C)

IRT 9 — Corp. Dev., Corp. Strategy
Cordes (MB), Stallkamp (C)

IRT 10 — Information Technology
Cordes (MB), Unger (C)

IRT 11 — Communications
Walter (MB), Harris (C)

IRT 12 — Technology
Vöhringer (MB), Robertson (C)

Coordinators (2) — (one for each IRT 1–12)

Total: 12–14 employees

Total: 24 employees

| Exhibit 4 | Perception vs. Reality at Chrysler |

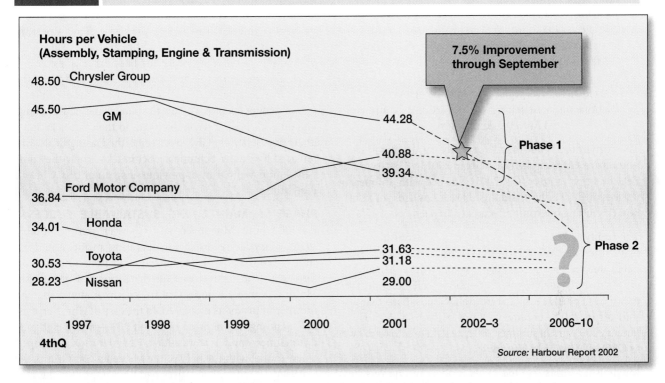

Source: Wolfgang Bernhard, presentation at JP Morgan/Harbour Auto Conference, August 7, 2002.

reduced fast enough *(refer to* Exhibit 4 *for a comparison of manufacturing hours by make).* In late 2000 *Fortune* reported:

> (...) after its merger with Daimler-Benz, Chrysler was in the midst of one of its once-a-decade swoons. Having ridden the crest of the 1990s boom with popular minivans and sport-utility vehicles, the company's American managers had allowed costs to career out of control and big gaps to open in Chrysler's new-product program. Despite record U.S. auto sales, the company reported an operating loss.[iv]

Within DC, divisions had to meet prearranged profit and sales targets ("deliver the numbers"). This approach made it relatively easy to compare different divisions and several executives hoped it "would bring back the Chrysler spirit." Holden argued that Chrysler could not make money because of the huge incentives that were bringing down transaction prices. When the Chrysler Group missed a set of prearranged goals (and profit levels), a supervisory board meeting was held on November 17, 2000 and the decision taken to dismiss Holden—after only one year. DC brought

in Dieter Zetsche, who had been running the commercial vehicles division, and he started three days later. However, in the fall of 2000, the share price fell below €50.

PHASE 4: NOVEMBER 2000 "STARTING TURN-AROUNDS AT CHRYSLER, MITSUBISHI AND FREIGHT-LINER" The situation facing Zetsche when he arrived was complicated. According to Ward's *Autoworld,* "to say that Zetsche inherited a mess is an understatement." He arrived in Detroit with only his chief operating officer (COO), Wolfgang Bernhard, to a welcome that was anything but friendly. During a press conference, Zetsche was asked how many more Germans they should expect in Detroit. He replied: "Four. My wife and three kids."

Excluding one-time write-offs, Chrysler Group lost $1.8 billion in the last two quarters of 2000. Within DC, the Mercedes Car Group was producing strong cash flows and in Stuttgart, the public opinion was that Mercedes was financing the rest of the Group. After three months, Zetsche presented his turnaround plan. *The Economist* reported on February 3, 2001:

> Chrysler's German overlords this week mounted a dramatic assault on the growing losses at Daimler-Chrysler's ailing American subsidiary. At least 26,000

[iv]Taylor, Alex. "Just Another Sexy Sports Car." *Fortune,* March 17, 2003: 32.

jobs will go [equivalent to 20% of the total work-force] in a reorganization that will close six plants and trim production at seven more. (. . .) Analysts (. . .) noted the absence of any American assembly plants on the list. The plant in Belvidere, Illinois, which produces the slow-selling Neon, seemed a sure bet to be shuttered, but Chrysler inadvertently out-smarted itself two years ago, when it agreed to re-strictions on plant shutdowns as part of its contract with the United Auto Workers union.

The turnaround plan called for lowering the break even point from 113% of plant capacity in 2001 to 83% in 2003.[v] Zetsche's first quarter (Q1, 2001) finished with an operating loss of €1.4 billion, and the full year saw a loss of $5 billion (including one-time effects) at Chrysler.

The equity stakes in Asia (Hyundai and Mitsubishi) developed differently. While Hyundai was becoming highly profitable due to very successful cars and trucks, Mitsubishi required more management attention. Rolf Eckrodt, formerly CEO of ADTRANZ trains [a DC subsidiary that was sold off in 2001], became COO of Mitsubishi Motors in January 2001 and in summer 2002, he left DC and took over as CEO of Mitsubishi Motors.

Mitsubishi Motors had too many models and no real success. The company was plagued by a set of issues. *Manager Magazin,* a German publication, commented:

> No controlling, inefficient structures and processes, which killed the company due to excessive harmony. After two failed turnaround attempts, the company was unable to reform itself.[vi]

The turnaround plan at Mitsubishi was drastic. Within three years, the production capacity was going to be cut by 28% and material cost by 15%. The turnaround was also a test for the DC merger, as it dispatched a group of 35 executives from both companies to Japan. The financial year 2000 ended with a loss of $750 million at Mitsubishi.

Neither of the equity stakes in Asia were limited to cars. In 2002 both Mitsubishi and Hyundai spun off their truck and bus divisions. Soon afterwards, DC announced the acquisition of a 43% share in Mitsubishi Fuso Truck and Bus Corporation for €760 million. In Korea, the "Daimler Hyundai Truck Corporation" was expected to be founded in 2003 with both companies holding equal shares.

DC's truck division, with revenues of €28 billion in 2002, also saw considerable changes. In 2000 DC acquired Detroit

Diesel, a highly regarded supplier of heavy-duty engines, and Western Star Trucks of Canada for $877 million. But around the same time, Freightliner, DC's trucking division in North America, was facing problems. The American market for new trucks decreased by 50%. This slump hit Freightliner, as market leader for heavy trucks, especially hard. The demand for new trucks collapsed, and at the same time, leasing models were returned. "Easy credit" and market values dropping below the book values led to a huge loss on each leasing truck returned. In the case of Freightliner, Jim Hebe, the CEO overseeing the leasing deals, was replaced by Rainer Schmückle. Schmückle knew the company quite well from a previous assignment as CFO of Freightliner.

PHASE 5: "MAINTAINING SUSTAINABLE SUCCESS"
By 2002 both Mitsubishi and Chrysler were profitable again. Chrysler recorded an operating profit, and Mitsubishi Motors recorded an after-tax profit of $290 million for 2002—the highest ever in the history of Mitsubishi Motors! Although budgets were cut in many cases, the number of products increased. In the case of Chrysler, capital spending was reduced by about 30%—while eight additional new models were added. Chrysler even developed a new model with the help of the Mercedes Car Group, the Chrysler Crossfire. Executives had high hopes for the new vehicles, as sales of Chrysler had fallen from 3.2 million units in 1999 to 2.8 million in 2002. Nevertheless, Chrysler set a growth target of one million additional units by 2011.[vii] Table 1 summarizes the results between 1998 and 2002.

However, 2003 remained a challenging year. The *Financial Times* reported on June 5, 2003:

> Chrysler's incentives for buyers have reached $4,500 per vehicle, almost doubling in a year. . . . The company said Chrysler's second-quarter operating loss would be about €1 billion—against analyst forecasts of a €500 million profit. Most of the difference was accounted for by an estimated $400m–$500m write-down in the value of 500,000 cars in dealers' lots and by a cut in the second-hand value of cars held by rental companies.

By Q3, 2003, Chrysler was able to rebound into profit, but the focus on controlling cost continued. The share price remained at around €30.

In order to reap the synergies, Chrysler and Mitsubishi also evaluated the development of a joint platform with an annual volume of one million cars. This was expected to enter

[v]Taylor, Alex. "Can the Germans Rescue Chrysler?" *Fortune,* April 30, 2001: 47.

[vi]Hirn, Wolfgang. "Die Revolution von Tokio." *Manager Magazin,* November 2002: 88ff.

[vii]Smith, David C. "Is This the Next Chairman?" *Ward's AutoWorld,* November 2002: 48.

Table 1	Financial Summary in € billion (at year-end)			
	1998		2002	
	Sales	Operating Profit	Sales	Operating Profit
Mercedes Car Group	32.6	1.9	50.2	3.0
Chrysler Group	56.4	4.2	60.2	0.6

Source: Der Spiegel, September 8, 2003: 117.

the market by 2005. For the same year an annual capacity of 1.5 million units was expected from a "global four cylinder engine." Of this, 600,000 units would be made in a new factory that would be jointly owned by Chrysler, Mitsubishi and Hyundai. The engine would also be built in a Hyundai factory in Korea and at Mitsubishi in Japan.

In summary, DC had considerably streamlined its portfolio. Table 2 outlines major acquisitions and divestitures since 2000.

Corporate Governance at Global Corporations Post-Enron

Manfred Gentz, DC's chief financial officer, commented as early as 1999 on the corporate governance challenges:

> The merger of the former Chrysler Corporation and the Daimler-Benz Aktiengesellschaft presented us with a number of integration challenges, including how to combine two different legal systems in such a way as to meet the differing expectations of each company's shareholders and management. With DaimlerChrysler AG's corporate governance, which was already finalized in the Business Combination Agreement of May 6, 1998, we tried to find a solution that combines German and U.S. forms of corporate management.

While the merger was taking place and requiring considerable management attention, the external environment for corporate governance changed dramatically. Although DC was legally based in Germany, it was traded on the New York Stock Exchange (NYSE) and hence had to adhere to many rules and regulations: [the] Sarbanes-Oxley Act, SEC regulations and the German Corporate Governance Code. On top of that, DC had to comply with German codetermination rules and other peculiarities in the different countries where DC operated. The effort and bureaucracy involved were considerable:

- **The Sarbanes-Oxley Act (SOA)** aimed to improve investor confidence and the accuracy of financial statements. It stated that CEOs and CFOs should certify the "appropriateness of the financial statements..." and that the audit committee should be totally independent.

- **[The] American Securities and Exchange Commission (SEC)** stipulated more detailed requirements for audit committees, e.g., committee members had to prove their familiarity with US-GAAP accounting rules. The chief regulators also wanted a better power balance between managers, board members and shareholders.

- **The German Corporate Governance Code** (Cromme Code) provided an overview of various existing laws and regulations in order to create transparency for foreign investors (as opposed to creating new laws). This resulted in about 50 recommendations (e.g., deductible of liability insurance for directors and officers, or the need to disclose financial reports within 90 days). By law, publicly traded companies had to state whether they complied with each recommendation (*refer to* Exhibit 5 *for the main headings of the code*). If not, management was requested to publish reasons for not doing so. In addition, there were several suggestions covering items such as individual salaries of management board members.

  Generally, the code was seen as an opportunity to evaluate control and management structures. Moreover, according to the code, members of the management board could be on a maximum of five different supervisory boards of listed companies if they held executive

Table 2	Acquisitions and Divestitures (Year, Company, Value)					
	Acquisitions			Divestitures		
2000	Mitsubishi Motors (34%, later 37%)	€2 billion	2000 and 2002	Debis Systemhaus (IT Services)	€5.5 billion
2000	Hyundai (10%)	$428 million	2001	Debitel (mobile phone operator)	€300 million
2000	Detroit Diesel and Western Star	$877 million	2001	ADTRANZ trains	$725 million
2003	Mitsubishi Trucks	€760 million			

Note: DC owns 33% of EADS. This stake was estimated at around €5 billion at the time of the IPO in 2000.

Exhibit 5	German Code for Corporate Governance

Source: Government Commission, German Corporate Governance Code, version May 21, 2003; www.corporate-governance-code.de.

functions in [other] listed companies. The code also suggested more personal liability (including personal assets) and a maximum of two members could immediately transfer from the management board to the supervisory board. The code also strongly encouraged the creation of different committees. The chairman of the commission, Gerhard Cromme, explained: "[After

all], an efficient and confidential discussion is not possible at regular supervisory board meetings."[viii]

- **Intricacies of the German Corporate Governance System:** The German system had some special features:
- The size of board meetings in this two-tier system was considerable. With 20 members of the supervisory board, plus the board of management, plus staff, there could easily be up to 40 people at the table. As an American board member put it, "A German supervisory board meeting is like an opera."
- Increasingly, the salaries of German supervisory board members were heavily debated among the general public. The lowest paid head of a supervisory board (Lufthansa Airlines) earned €21,000[2]—the highest paid (Schering Pharmaceuticals) received €343,000. Kari-Hermann Baumann, former CFO of Siemens and now on the supervisory boards of six big German companies (Siemens, Deutsche Bank, Eon, Linde, Schering, Thyssen-Krupp), earned a total salary of €589,000. In comparison, a board member at Nestlé earned on average €371,000 in 2002 (for one seat). At DC, the 2003 annual assembly voted for an increase from €51,000 to €75,000 for regular members of the supervisory board and from €102,000 to €225,000 for the chairman.
- German corporate law was written with the aim of protecting creditors and thereby allowed companies to accumulate hidden reserves, using book values rather than market values in accounting, etc. This was in sharp contrast to the American system, where corporate laws were aimed at creating transparency for the shareholders, allowing them to control management, and thereby limiting principal–agent conflicts.

Corporate Governance At DaimlerChrysler

At DC, trying to adhere to the different codes caused regulatory conflicts. While Sarbanes-Oxley increased the personal responsibilities of CEOs and CFOs, in Germany the members of the management board had collective responsibility (*refer to* Exhibit 6 *for more conflicts*). As part of this collective responsibility, the board met as a "legal entity" rather than as a set of individuals. At the same time, Sarbanes-Oxley also led to considerable organizational adjustments, in order to comply with the comprehensive requirements. Schrempp explained:

[viii]Wiskow, Jobst-Hinrich. "Beschränkter Durchblick." *Capital*, March 6, 2003.
[2]Salary levels are for 2001 or 2002.

Exhibit 6	Managing Conflicts	
	Germany	USA
CEO/CFO Certification (Sarbanes-Oxley Act)	Collective responsibility of the board of management	Personal responsibility of CEO and CFO
Disclosure of Deviation to Regulation (German Code, NYSE)	Disclosure of deviation from German Code	Disclosure of significant differences to CG practices*
Audit Committee Appointment of Auditors (Sarbanes-Oxley Act, NYSE)	Annual general meeting of shareholders	Audit committee
Public Company Accounting Oversight Board Inspections	Secrecy agreement between company and auditor	Right to request confidential records from auditor
D&O Insurance Policy	Introduce suitable deductible/excess	Deductible/excess not common

*Not yet in effect.

Source: DaimlerChrysler.

In this context, several international initiatives designed to improve corporate governance and restore public confidence in the corporate sector have been undertaken. (...) I can tell you:

1. There can be no barriers to information.

2. The whole company has to be as committed to DaimlerChrysler's balance sheet as Manfred Gentz [CFO] and I are. It is obvious that with their signature on those documents, the chairman and the CFO are accepting certain obligations for the company. Therefore, it is also clear that every senior executive must feel this obligation as well.

3. This means that we will install a cascade signing system. Starting with every General Manager and CFO of every business entity within DC and going to the top via every principal.

Due to the changes in the corporate governance landscape, considerable challenges lay ahead. As Dr. Manfred Schneider, member of the supervisory board at DC, explained: "We have to anticipate that in the future less people will be willing to become members of the supervisory board or even head of the supervisory board."[ix]

For a global company like DaimlerChrysler, corporate governance was centerstage. But corporate governance went far beyond the newly introduced six-page special in the 2002 annual report. This special feature covered the functioning of the annual meeting, a short explanation of the two-tier system and some of the legally non-binding arrangements: Executive Automotive Council (EAC), Chairman's Council and the International Advisory Board (IAB). The implications of the new corporate governance system were far-reaching, as can be seen by the developments on both boards and within various committees.

The Management Board: Running DaimlerChrysler

DEVELOPMENTS Strong leaders, such as Lee Iacocca, often dominated the board of [the] former Chrysler Corp. Their ability was to get designers to "think outside the box" while getting their managers to meet budgets and cost targets. In 1999 key executives of [the] former Chrysler Corp. left the DC management board, including Stallkamp (President), Gale (Design), Cunningham (Strategy), and co-chairman Bob Eaton followed in March 2000. On the former Daimler-Benz side, two members had left the board: Lauk (Trucks) and Tropitzsch (HR). After Holden's dismissal in November 2000, two former Chrysler executives remained on the board (both in purchasing functions).

Between 1998 and 2003 the board shrank from 17 members to 11, and by 2003 only two members retained their original positions (Hubbert, Mercedes Car Group, and Gentz, CFO). In the process, the structure of the board was also changed. The organizational chart showed clear separations between operating and functional divisions (*refer to* Exhibit 7 *for the evolution of the organizational chart*). Several former board members remained as advisors to the company (Mangold, Bischoff, Valade). Interestingly, new board members appointed were only "deputy board members," with a three-year contract rather than the usual five-year contract for regular board members (the norm in Germany). Company policy generally required board members over the age of 60 to have their contracts renewed on an annual basis.

[ix]"Neue Aufsichtsräte sind nur noch schwer zu finden." *Handelsblatt*, April 1, 2003.

Exhibit 7 Evolution of the Board of Management (1998–2003)

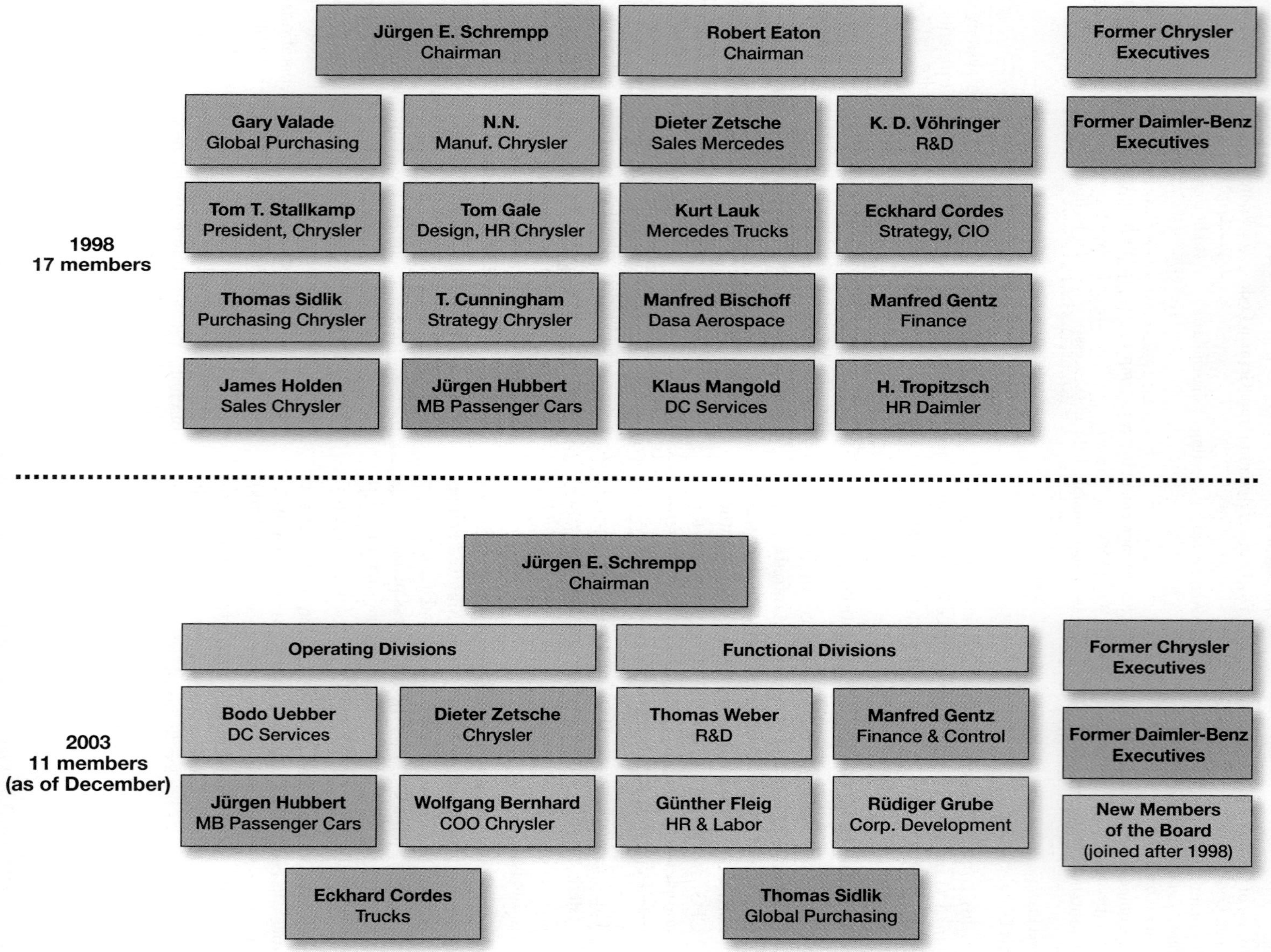
1998
17 members
Jürgen E. Schrempp
Chairman
Robert Eaton
Chairman
Former Chrysler Executives
Former Daimler-Benz Executives
Gary Valade
Global Purchasing
N.N.
Manuf. Chrysler
Dieter Zetsche
Sales Mercedes
K. D. Vöhringer
R&D
Tom T. Stallkamp
President, Chrysler
Tom Gale
Design, HR Chrysler
Kurt Lauk
Mercedes Trucks
Eckhard Cordes
Strategy, CIO
Thomas Sidlik
Purchasing Chrysler
T. Cunningham
Strategy Chrysler
Manfred Bischoff
Dasa Aerospace
Manfred Gentz
Finance
James Holden
Sales Chrysler
Jürgen Hubbert
MB Passenger Cars
Klaus Mangold
DC Services
H. Tropitzsch
HR Daimler
2003
11 members
(as of December)
Jürgen E. Schrempp
Chairman
Operating Divisions
Functional Divisions
Former Chrysler Executives
Former Daimler-Benz Executives
New Members of the Board
(joined after 1998)
Bodo Uebber
DC Services
Dieter Zetsche
Chrysler
Thomas Weber
R&D
Manfred Gentz
Finance & Control
Jürgen Hubbert
MB Passenger Cars
Wolfgang Bernhard
COO Chrysler
Günther Fleig
HR & Labor
Rüdiger Grube
Corp. Development
Eckhard Cordes
Trucks
Thomas Sidlik
Global Purchasing

Source: Company information.

Exhibit 8	Frequency and Location of Management Board Meetings				
	1999	2000	2001	2002	2003*
Germany	11	13	17	16	16
USA	17	18	9	7	6
Other	1	4	1	1	—
Total	**29**	**35**	**27**	**24**	**22**

*planned

Note: Some of these board meetings lasted for two days. In this case, they were counted twice. This list also includes meetings of the strategic and planning process.

Source: Company information.

WORKING STYLE Initially the meetings were held in Stuttgart and Auburn Hills, but most American meetings were soon moved to New York (for travel reasons). English was the management language. Annually, there were between 22—in 2003—and 35—in 2000—meetings (*refer to* Exhibit 8 *for the frequency and location of meetings*).

CREATION OF NEW COMMITTEES In the first year of the merger, the Chairmen's Integration Council (CIC) was a central point of the integration. However, the overlap between the CIC and the board of management could not be avoided (*refer to* Exhibit 3) and all members of the management board were also allowed to join the meetings of the CIC. On the CIC, votes had to be unanimous, while on the management board they could be majority-based. The CIC ceased to exist in September 1999, as the integration was officially completed. Instead, two councils (Automotive, and Sales & Marketing) were set up to coordinate possible component sharing, etc. However, both councils were abandoned.

The potential for sharing components and parts increased fundamentally with the addition of partners in Asia. In order to reap "potentially huge synergies" (*Wall Street Journal Europe*) from economies of scale and to improve the decision-making procedure, the Executive Automotive Committee (EAC) was set up. This committee, co-chaired by Schrempp and Hubbert, normally met before each board meeting and prepared recommendations regarding the product portfolio, technology, production capacity, and sales and marketing. The EAC's recommendations were then taken to the board (*refer to* Exhibit 9 *for an overview of the EAC*). Besides Hubbert and Schrempp, EAC members included Zetsche (Chrysler), Cordes (Trucks), Bischoff (Head of the Alliance Committee with Mitsubishi) and Grube (corporate development). All of them were board members, too.

Grube's staff members prepared the materials for the EAC. Early on in the process, the team considered corporate governance implications. Grube explained:

> Strategic initiatives, e.g., our new efforts in China, are discussed on every aspect of our corporate governance system. Strategy depends on feedback and consensus in our governance structure.

For cultural and legal reasons, a similar EAC structure was set up for the minority stakes in Asia. The "Alliance Committee" functioned in [a] similar way to the EAC. In 2002 a similar structure to the EAC was also created for trucks (Truck Product and Decision Committee).

Supervisory Board: Keeping Up in a Changing Industry

In the German two-tier system, the main function of the supervisory board was to supervise, advise on and monitor business developments. At the same time, this board was also responsible for hiring board members (for which a two-thirds majority was required). The spoken language was German, but all documents were prepared in both German and English, with simultaneous translation at the meetings. The meetings remained driven by the issues. Lynton Wilson, former board member of Chrysler and current board member of DC, explained the style of these meetings:

> Schrempp is a very American-style leader. He is open and [knows] he has to make sure to have relationships and support in the company. So the discussions are matter of fact, issue-related and [end with a decision] on what to do.

The DC supervisory board was led by Hilmar Kopper, former CEO and chairman of Deutsche Bank, who also sat on the boards of Akzo Nobel, Xerox, Solvay and Unilever. The media reported on the close working relationship between Kopper and Schrempp.

The supervisory board had seen few membership changes on the capital side over the years (*refer to* Exhibit 10 *for the evolution of the supervisory board*). The supervisory board met six times in 2003, both in the U.S. and in Germany.

Corporate Governance in Action

DC, like any other global company, had to deal with increasing complexity. However, its corporate governance system had to combine both the American and German governance systems. Wilson explained:

> We are talking here about two very different systems. In North America, non-executive directors are much

Exhibit 9	Role of the Executive Automotive Committee

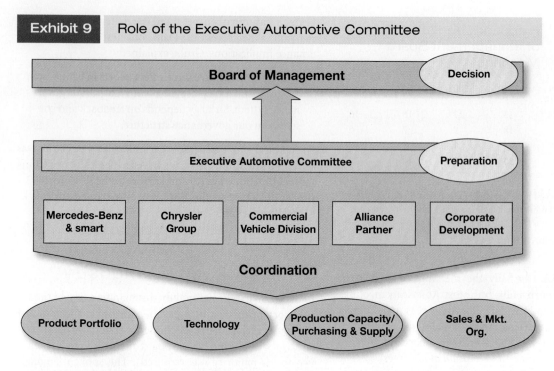

Source: Company information.

Exhibit 10	Evolution of the Supervisory Board (1998–2002)

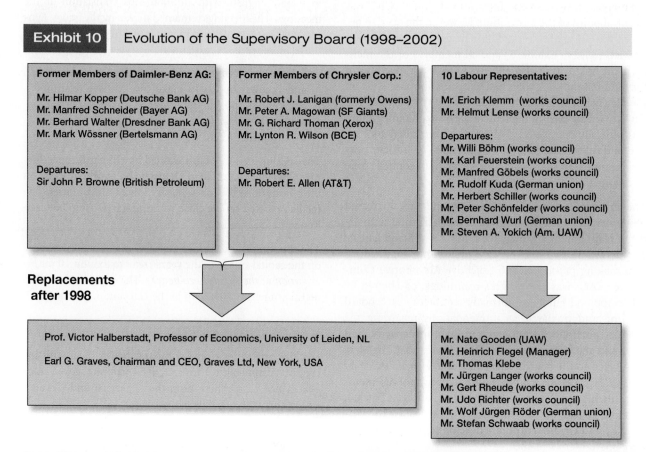

Source: Company information.

more involved and have certain responsibilities. In the German system, you have co-determination. Nevertheless, both systems work.

Three committees were established, each consisting of two shareholder and two employee representatives.

1. Committee: Employment terms and remuneration for board members. It also conducted "preliminary discussions on key decisions to be taken by the supervisory board."

2. Committee: Examination of annual and semi-annual statements of accounts. This committee also ensured the independence of the auditors. The committee's work became a lot more important due to Sarbanes-Oxley.

3. Committee: In case of disagreement between supervisory board members with regard to the nomination of the new board (this was required by law).

Over the years, however, DC developed several legally nonbinding committees:

SHAREHOLDER COMMITTEE AND LABOR COMMITTEE

The shareholder committee was a big change for the German establishment. CFO Gentz explained:

A shareholder committee modeled on the U.S.-style board of directors was set up alongside the supervisory board. The committee included the two chairmen, all ten shareholder representatives as well as four prominent outsiders. [This committee] has no decision-making powers, which rest solely with the supervisory board, but instead restricts itself to debate and counseling and provides fact-based recommendations to support opinion-forming among the shareholder representatives.

The committee met six times a year and had two subcommittees. The audit sub-committee dealt with the examination of financial accounts and dividend policy, while the nomination & compensation sub-committee dealt with remuneration of board members and senior executives. The aim was to ensure competitive packages on a global scale, for which outside advisors were hired. However, the issues discussed in the shareholder committee were too similar to those discussed in the supervisory board—it was seen as a duplication, and the committee ceased to exist in January 2001.

Members of the workforce formed the labor committee to accommodate the needs of American and Canadian labor unions, which had only one seat on DC's supervisory board. In addition, employees formed various international

committees that were independent of the supervisory board; they met around five times in 2003.

Additional Committees

CHAIRMAN'S COUNCIL   A new council was started in the fall of 2001. The *Financial Times* reported in September 2001:

DaimlerChrysler, the international automotive group, is to become the first German-based company to embrace Anglo-Saxon corporate governance rules by forming an independent chairman's council of non-executive directors. (. . .) Officials describe the project as a "unique hybrid" between Anglo-Saxon corporate governance and the co-determination preferred by most German companies.[x]

The Chairman's Council consisted of six selected members of the capital side of the supervisory board and selected external members, including CEOs from blue chip companies. In a press statement, DC formalized the council:

The council will provide advice to management on global business strategy issues. Elements of American and European corporate governance structures are combined to meet the specific requirements of a truly global company and the interests of the different stakeholders. The legal rights and responsibilities of the supervisory board will remain untouched. The Chairman's Council is complementary to the current governance structure.

INTERNATIONAL ADVISORY BOARD (IAB)   The IAB replaced the Daimler-Benz International Advisory Board, which was started in 1995. It usually met once a year. The IAB's activities were outlined in the annual report:

The IAB of DaimlerChrysler advises the DaimlerChrysler Group on questions relating to global economic, technological, and political developments and their effect on the business activities of the group. It supports the DaimlerChrysler Board of Management but is not responsible for making business decisions. The meetings are private to encourage frank and open discussion.

(*Refer to* Exhibit 11 *for members of the Chairman's Council and IAB.*) Figure 2 summarizes the various levels of supervision and management in DC.

---

[x]Burt, Tim. "First German-Based Firm to Adopt Anglo-Saxon Corporate Governance Rules." *Financial Times*, September 28, 2001.

Exhibit 11	Members of the Chairman's Council and International Advisory Board

Chairman's Council

Jürgen E. Schrempp	Chairman

Internal Members

Victor Halberstadt	Prof. of Economics, Leiden University
Hilmar Kopper	Chairman of the Supervisory Board DCX
Robert J. Lanigan	Chairman Emeritus of Owens-Illinois
Dr. Manfred Schneider	Chairman of the Supervisory Board of Bayer AG
Lynton R. Wilson	Chairman of the Board of Nortel Networks
Dr. Mark Wössner	Former CEO and Chairman of Bertelsmann

External Members

The Lord Browne	Group CEO of BP Amoco
Louis V. Gerstner, Jr.	Former Chairman and CEO of IBM
Minoru Makihara	Chairman of Mitsubishi Corp.
Dr. Daniel Vasella	Chairman & CEO of Novartis AG
Lorenzo H. Zambrano	Chairman and CEO of Cemex

International Advisory Board (IAB)

Internal Members

DC Board of Management

External Members

12 members with various backgrounds in academia, politics and business.

The members are based in Asia, Europe and the Americas.

Source: Company information.

Outside View: Financial Markets

Right from the beginning, there was a strong focus on pleasing the financial markets. DC tried to create awareness about the stock price and installed TV screens showing stock prices around HQ. DC had done a lot to cater to the needs of institutional investors. Even before the merger, both companies had used U.S. GAAP accounting rules; afterwards DC added detailed reporting according to business segments, value-based stock options plans and employee profit sharing based on operating profits. Nevertheless, the base of American shareholders was rapidly decreasing. By December 31, 2002 American shareholders accounted for only 14% of total DC shareholders (down from 44% in 1998). Most shareholders were based in Germany (57%), with 21% in the rest of Europe and 8% in the rest of the world, other than the U.S. The reduction in the number of American shareholders could have been the result of DC's removal from the S&P 500 Index or, as an industry expert explained, "Americans don't trust the two-tier boards." The stock price development was unsatisfactory, but it was in line with that of major competitors (*refer to* Exhibit 12 *for the share price development of DC and some competitors*).

Deutsche Bank remained the largest shareholder, owning 12%, followed by the Emirate of Kuwait, with 7%. Institutional investors held 54%, private investors 27%.

Understanding Risks

The globalization of DC created many opportunities. However, for corporate governance purposes, it was also essential to understand the business risk. Besides risks originating from *off-balance sheet activities* or *bad debt*, DC and other car companies faced considerable industry-specific risks: Being a global player and consolidating in euros, any drastic *exchange rate fluctuations* could severely impact the financial results. At the same time, large parts of the operating income resulted from *financial services* (e.g., car leasing), a business dependent on many "outside" forces. DC also faced considerable *technology risks* (e.g., fuel cells, fuel efficiency, lightweight materials). Missing one trend could mean suffering for half a decade. The increasing number of brands brought with it the risk of wrong *brand positioning*. Also, because the factory assets were so specific to the industry, the *exit risk* was considerable. And since the merger, the company was also increasingly subject to North American risks such as *product liability* issues or court cases from *disgruntled shareholders*.

In 2003 Schrempp commented on the merger and corporate governance:

> When Daimler-Benz and Chrysler merged, there was no textbook written on how to do it. I admit, we were not as efficient from day one as we could have [been]. But now the international cooperation and the implementation of the strategy work very well.[xi]

And they broke new ground in corporate governance, too.

[xi]"Ein hartes Stück Arbeit," Interview with Jürgen Schrempp. *Der Spiegel*, September 8, 2003: 120.

Figure 2	Levels of Supervision and Management (scheduled number of meetings in 2003)

Controlling the Management...	Managing the Company...	Advising the Management...
Supervisory Board 6 meetings p.a.	Board of Management 22 meetings p.a.	Chairman's Council 5 meetings p.a.
International Employee Committees 5 meetings p.a.	Executive Automotive Committee 10 meetings p.a.	International Advisory Board 1 meeting p.a.
...according to German Law & Co-Determination Principles	...combining German legal requirements and global business needs	...combining elements of U.S. and European Corporate Governance

Exhibit 12	Share Price Developments of DaimlerChrysler vs. Major Competitors

Source: www.comdirect.de.

Case 36

Trouble in the "Magic Kingdom"— Governance Problems at Disney

BECG-038

"I spend my life being Odysseus. I tie myself to the mast, and I don't listen to the Sirens."

—Michael Eisner, chairman and CEO of Disney in 2002[1]

"Michael has used the shield of corporate governance to get rid of people who were not in his pocket."

—Andrea Van de Kamp, an ex-director of Disney in 2003[2]

"It's almost a religious view, fervently held, that directors (at Disney) don't talk. They don't talk to the press. They don't talk to investors. They don't talk about what goes on in the boardroom. I think that's got to change. They were elected by the shareholders, and they ought to be accountable. As it stands now, the owners have no clue as to who's effective or what's going on."

—Richard Koppes, a corporate governance lawyer with Jones Day in 2003[3]

Disney Directors Resign

At the end of November 2003, Roy Disney (Roy), the vice chairman of the Walt Disney Company (Disney) and the chairman of its animation department, resigned from the company. Roy was the nephew of Walt Disney (Walt), the founder of Disney, and last surviving member of the Disney family to work at the company. Holding over 17 million shares, he was the company's largest individual stockholder and served on the board of directors. Roy's resignation was said to be prompted by the information that he would not be nominated to the board in the following year. This was because according to the new corporate governance norms adopted by Disney in 2002, he was past the maximum age limit to be a director of the company. Roy, who had served the company throughout his life in various capacities, preferred to avoid such an ignominious exit and chose to resign voluntarily.

Close on the heels of Roy's resignation came the resignation of Stanley Gold (Gold), an investment banker, who was also a director at Disney. Both men wrote lengthy resignation letters outlining their reasons for leaving the company. They laid the major portion of the blame on Disney's CEO

ICFAI This case was written by **Sirisha Regani,** under the direction of **Sanjib Dutta,** ICFAI Center for Management Research (ICMR). It is intended to be used as a basis for class discussion rather than to illustrate either effective or ineffective handling of a management situation.

The case was compiled from published sources.

© 2004, ICFAI Center for Management Research. All rights reserved. No part of this publication may be reproduced, stored in a retrieval system, used in a spreadsheet, or transmitted in any form or by any means—electronic or mechanical, without permission.

To order copies, call 0091-40-2343-0462/63 or write to ICFAI Center for Management Research, Plot # 49, Nagarjuna Hills, Hyderabad 500 082, India or email icmr@icfai.org. Website: www.icmrindia.org.

[1]Marc Gunther, "Has Eisner Lost the Disney Magic?" *Fortune,* January 7, 2002.

[2]Marc Gunther, "Disney's Loss Is Eisner's Gain," *Fortune,* December 22, 2003.

[3]Marc Gunther, "The Directors," *Fortune,* December 27, 2003.

and chairman[4] Michael Eisner (Eisner) who, they alleged, did not run the company in accordance with the principles of good governance. They also expressed concern that bad governance would put the future of the company at risk, unless drastic changes were made. They believed that Eisner was the root of all troubles at Disney and that the company would benefit from his departure. In his resignation letter to Eisner, Roy wrote, "It is my sincere belief that it is you that should be leaving and not me."[5]

The company's board was also criticized for being a rubber-stamp to the decisions of Eisner and for not giving sufficient consideration to the benefit of the shareholders. Criticizing the board, Gold wrote, "It is clear to me that this board is unwilling to tackle the difficult issues I believe this company continues to face—management failures and accountability for those failures, operational deficiencies, imprudent capital allocations, the cannibalization of certain company icons for short-term gain, the enormous loss of creative talent over the last years, the absence of succession planning and the lack of strategic focus."[6]

After leaving the company, both men launched a public campaign to oust Eisner ([whom] they had helped appoint in 1984). They said that he held sway over the board and ran the company like a "personal fiefdom." Both were considering meeting with the company's major shareholders to muster support in their campaign.

Well known for its animated films and theme parks, Disney was popularly known as the "Magic Kingdom," because of the entertainment and pleasure it provided to children and adults alike. However, the resignation of two of the company's directors and their bid to oust the CEO made analysts wonder if the Magic Kingdom was losing its magic.

Background Note

Disney was first set up by Walt and his brother Roy O. Disney (the father of the present Roy Disney) in 1923, as a small studio. The studio was moderately successful, making and selling short animated films and commercials. In 1927, during a train journey from New York to Los Angeles (where the studio was based), Walt created the character of Mickey Mouse. In November 1927, the Disney studio made "Steamboat Willie," the first Mickey Mouse animated film.

It was also the first animated film synchronized to sound. The movie was very successful and Mickey Mouse soon became the world's most loved cartoon character.

Over the years, the Disney studio grew and started making several other animated films apart from Mickey Mouse cartoons. In the late 1920s, Disney animators started working on an animation series called "Silly Symphonies." This series featured animation pieces that were set to classical music. One of this series, "Flowers and Trees," won Disney its first Academy Award. In the late 1930s, [the] Disney studio made "Snow White," which was the first ever full length animation film. "Snow White" was extremely successful, receiving critical acclaim as well as commercial success. Gradually, the studio began making live action movies [without] animation. The first live action movie made by Disney was "Treasure Island."

In the early 1940s, Walt conceptualized Disneyland, which was to be a theme park that would provide entertainment facilities for children as well as their adult companions. To raise money for the development of the park, Walt decided to make a television show, which would yield additional revenues [for] the studio. The first Disney television show, also called "Disneyland," debuted on [the] ABC network[7] in 1954. [The] Disneyland park was opened in 1955 and soon became very popular, attracting millions of visitors every year from all around the world.

In the 1960s, [the] Disney [studio] made films like "Sleeping Beauty," "101 Dalmatians," and "Pollyanna," which did reasonably well, but were not successful enough to make huge profits for the studio. In the mid-1960s, the studio made "Mary Poppins,"[8] a movie that Walt had been trying to make since the 1950s. The movie was a huge success and received 13 Academy Award nominations. In 1966, Walt died of lung cancer. After Walt's death, the company was managed by his brother Roy Disney. Under him, the company opened Walt Disney World, a new theme park in Florida, which was Walt's unrealized dream. (The concept for the park was initially called Experimental Prototype Community of Tomorrow [EPCOT], and was later renamed Walt Disney World.)

Roy Disney died in 1971, and after his death Don Tatum (Tatum) became the chairman and Card Walker (Walker), the president of the company. Ron Miller (Miller), Walt's son-in-law, became the executive producer. According to

---

[4] In early March 2004, Eisner was replaced by former U.S. Senator George Mitchell as the chairman of Disney after 43% of shareholders gave him a no-confidence vote.

[5] *Corporate Conflict*, www.cbsnews.com, December 1, 2003.

[6] *Corporate Conflict*, www.cbsnews.com, December 1, 2003.

[7] American Broadcasting Corporation. One of the biggest television networks in the U.S. It was taken over by the Disney conglomerate in 1995.

[8] *Mary Poppins* was a book written by Pamela L. Travers, published in 1934. "Mary Poppins" is also the name of the lead character in the book and its sequels.

analysts, the successors lacked the vision of Walt and Roy Disney and almost led the company to bankruptcy. Initially, the company had planned to fund the EPCOT project completely with outside sponsorship. However, as the work progressed, a part of the company's internal surpluses had to be ploughed into the project. This led to a severe resource crunch. Another major problem cropped up in 1979 when 14 of the company's best animators left it. In 1980, after Tatum retired, Walker became the chairman and CEO of the company. In 1982, the EPCOT center was finally opened and plans were made for a new Disney channel on television. The channel was launched in 1983, the same year in which Tokyo Disneyland was opened.

In 1983, Walker resigned from his post and Miller became the CEO. Just a month later, Miller gave up his post to Ray Watson (who was his [right-hand] man in the company). These constant changes in leadership led to a steep fall in the company's share price. The share price fell from $84 in 1983 to $45 in 1984. The lowered share prices and the lack of stability in the top management resulted in a number of corporate houses attempting to take over Disney in the early 1980s.

One of the most serious takeover bids faced by Disney was from Saul Steinberg (Steinberg), the chairman of Reliance Group Holdings Inc.[9] Steinberg started making serious bids to acquire stock in Disney. By April 1984, he had acquired 8.3% of the stock and announced his intention to acquire 25% of the company before long. Recognizing the threat, Disney management started making defensive moves. It announced its decision to buy back shares at a premium. Roy and Gold played a very important role at this stage and helped muster shareholder support to prevent Disney from being taken over.[10] They enlisted the support of the Bass family, who were the largest shareholders in Disney, to regain a majority. Steinberg finally agreed to re-sell his stock to the company at a premium of $32 million and an additional $28 million for his expenses. All this added to the huge debt of the company. By the mid-1980s, what was needed was a change in leadership to bring about a turnaround.

Disney's board, led by Roy and Gold, installed Eisner as the chairman and CEO of Disney and Frank Wells (Wells) as its president in 1984. The decision to bring in Eisner proved to be a good one as Eisner and Wells helped Disney reestablish its position in the entertainment industry. They began by

revamping the entire internal structure of the company. They brought in 60 executives from Warner Bros. and Paramount Studios, two of the major movie studios in Hollywood, and retrenched over 1000 Disney employees. They developed a new culture among the employees, of complete commitment to the company. The employees were expected to stay late every night and work seven days a week. A new strategic planning department was set up, and focus was on strategic alliances and acquisitions that would help the company move forward.

By the early 1990s, Disney established itself as a diversified media company. It opened another theme park in Paris, called Euro Disney. Disney Stores, which sold Disney [merchandise] exclusively, were opened across the U.S. The company also set up or acquired film studios, which helped it make a foray into adult entertainment. Further, it acquired ABC networks in the mid-1990s and started an Internet portal called Disney.Go.com. In the first thirteen years under Eisner (between 1984 and 1997), Disney's revenues rose from $1.65 billion to $22 billion.

Things began to change after the tragic death of Wells in a helicopter crash in 1994. Analysts had often felt that the success of Disney was primarily due to the fact that Eisner and Wells made a good team. Eisner was an aggressive person who tended to dominate people to get his own way. Wells, on the other hand, was people oriented and could tackle people and situations in more subtle ways. "When people came out of Michael's office wounded, Frank was the emergency room," said a Disney insider.[11] The leadership style of one complemented that of the other and together, the two of them were able to get people to work for the company's growth.

After Wells died however, Eisner's working style reportedly began to fail. He was often criticized for being too aggressive and for not giving people enough importance. Unable to put up with Eisner's overbearing attitude, several key people like Jeffrey Katzenberg (Katzenberg, a former studio chief), Steven Bollenbach (the Chief Financial Officer), and Paul Pressler (the head of Disney's theme parks and resorts) left the company. A series of wrong decisions in the 1990s also increased the strength of Eisner's opposition. The appointment of Michael Ovitz (Ovitz) as the company's president in 1995, the failure of the company's Internet venture, a long-drawn lawsuit with Katzenberg, and the acquisition of the Fox Family Network[12] were counted among the major mistakes made by Eisner. In the early 2000s, ABC began to experience a de-

---

[9]Reliance Group Holdings Inc. is a New York–based company, which underwrites a broad range of commercial property and provides personal-casualty and automobile insurance. It also provided information technology consulting services.

[10]Roy joined the company in 1954 as an assistant film editor and took over as the chairman of the animation department in 1984. He became a member of the board in 1967. He met Gold in the late 1970s and made him his financial adviser. Gold was later nominated to the Disney board.

[11]Marc Gunther, "Has Eisner Lost the Disney Magic?" *Fortune,* January 7, 2002.

[12]The television channels of Rupert Murdoch's NewsCorp.

cline in viewership, due to a rut in the programs and the overexposure of its most popular show, 'Who Wants to Be a Millionaire?'[13]

Problems intensified after the terrorist attacks on the U.S. in September 2001. The attacks led to a drastic fall in theme park attendance due to people's fear of travel. The recession that gripped the U.S. in the late 1990s and early 2000s also affected Disney. The consumer-products division, which had been struggling for years, had to be revamped and Disney closed 50 of its 530 American stores in 2001. In the same year, Disney also closed its web portal, which had been losing money since it was launched in the late 1990s. The closure had cost the company an estimated $900 million. Disney's net result for 2001 was a loss of $158 million, on revenues of $25.2 billion. To meet the requirements of the new situation, the company laid off 400 people in 2001. Disney's share price also began to drop precipitously and was trading around $14 in 2002, as against $40 in 2000. Although the company returned to profit in 2002 with a net income of $1.2 billion, it was a third lower than the profit of $1.8 billion in 1997.

In 2002, Eisner developed a new plan for turning around the company and obtained approval from the board. By 2003, the company started showing signs of a turnaround and during 2003, the company's share price rose by about 34%. Disney also made a profit of $1.26 billion on revenues of $27 billion (Refer [to] Exhibit 1 for Disney's Income Statement and Exhibit 2 for Disney's performance in relation to the Standard & Poor's Index).

New Governance Norms

According to analysts, by the early 2000s, the Disney board had acquired the dubious distinction of being one of the worst boards in the U.S. Analysts believed that the board was not powerful enough to oppose Eisner on any matter and that it allowed him to bulldoze all the decisions. In January 2002, the board appointed Ira Millstein (Millstein), a leading corporate governance lawyer, to suggest changes that would improve the governance of the company. Some of Millstein's recommendations included: the expansion of the company's corporate governance committee, the shrinking of the board from 16 to 12 directors and not using the company's auditor for non-auditing consulting work. By the end of 2002, the company had formally adopted the new governance norms [that] were based on Millstein's recommendations.

By early 2003, the company had stopped using its auditor, PricewaterhouseCoopers, for non-auditing consulting

[13]A popular game show on which a contestant could win a million dollars by answering certain questions correctly.

Exhibit 1	Income Statement

Income Statement (All Numbers in Thousands)

Period Ending	30-Sep-03	30-Sep-02	30-Sep-01
Total Revenue	27,061,000	25,329,000	25,269,00
Cost of Revenue	—	—	—
Gross Profit	27,061,000	25,329,000	25,269,00
Operating Expenses			
Research Development	—	—	—
Selling General and Administrative	24,330,000	22,924,000	21,670,00
Non Recurring	—	(34,000)	1,454,000
Others	18,000	21,000	767,000
Total Operating Expenses	—	—	—
Operating Income or Loss	2,713,000	2,418,000	1,378,000
Income from Continuing Operations			
Total Other Income/Expenses Net	334,000	495,000	322,000
Earnings Before Interest and Taxes	3,047,000	2,913,000	1,700,000
Interest Expense	793,000	723,000	417,000
Income Before Tax	2,254,000	2,190,000	1,283,000
Income Tax Expense	789,000	853,000	1,059,000
Minority Interest	(127,000)	(101,000)	(104,000)
Net Income from Continuing Ops	1,338,000	1,236,000	120,000
Non-recurring Events			
Discontinued Operations	—	—	—
Extraordinary Items	—	—	—
Effect of Accounting Changes	(71,000)	—	(278,000)
Other Items	—	—	—
Net Income	1,267,000	1,236,000	(158,000)
Preferred Stock and Other Adjustments	—	—	—
Net Income Applicable to Common Shares	**$1,267,000**	**$1,236,000**	**($158,000)**

Source: finance.yahoo.com.

work. Disney adopted a policy that two-thirds of the directors be independent, and that all of them hold at least $100,000 in company stock. The size of the board was reduced and the company began making moves towards cutting all business relationships between board members and the company. However, the resignations of Roy and Gold in protest against bad governance raised doubts in the minds of observers about whether the moves towards good governance at the company were just an eyewash.

Exhibit 2	Disney's Performance

Disney's Performance in Relation to the Standard and Poor Index

Period Between		Compounded Annual Growth
1984–1995	S&P 500	15.4%
	Disney	28.1%
1995–2003	S&P 500	8.8%
	Disney	2.8%

Adapted from Marc Gunter, "Mouse Hunt," *Fortune*, January 12, 2004.

Exhibit 3	Attributes of a Good Board

INDEPENDENCE

Friends and cronies of the CEO are out. Crucial panels like audit should contain no insiders. Cross-directorships are taboo.

QUALITY

Board meetings should include real, open debate. Directors need to be familiar with managers and conditions in the field.

ACCOUNTABILITY

Directors ought to hold serious stakes in the company. They should also be prepared to challenge under-performing CEOs.

Source: "Attributes of a Good Board," *BusinessWeek*, January 24, 2000.

Instances of Bad Governance

Although it was generally acknowledged that Eisner was responsible for making Disney (which was until then known for its children's films and theme parks) into a well recognized and successful global media conglomerate, it was felt that he was assuming too much power in the organization. In the first thirteen years under Eisner, the market value of Disney rose from $2 billion to $67 billion. However, by the late 1990s, analysts began noticing that the company was hinging too much on Eisner.

In 1999 and 2000, Disney [was] featured in *BusinessWeek*'s[14] annual survey of corporate boards [as] among the worst boards in the U.S. Ever since Eisner took over as chairman and CEO, analysts felt that he exercised an undesirable level of control over the board at Disney. It was alleged that he resorted to nepotism in appointing board members, and tried to make most of the appointments from among his personal friends and acquaintances. This seemed to have increased his clout in the company and the board became a rubber stamp to his decisions. It was alleged that dissenting members on the board were often victimized and prevented from serving on important committees on some pretext. The instances of bad governance at Disney are outlined below (Refer [to] Exhibit 3 for attributes of a good board).

Appointments at Disney

While the principles of good corporate governance required that the CEO be accountable to the board, analysts felt that this was not the case at Disney. Eisner was known to appoint his personal friends and acquaintances on the board, whether or not they were Disney shareholders at the time of appointment. As a result, the board ceased to be independent and Eisner held sway over the directors of the company.

The composition of the board also came under criticism. Of the 16 board members in 2002, half were either current or former executives at Disney, or people who did business with the company. Some of the others were the headmistress of an elementary school where one of Eisner's children had studied, Eisner's personal lawyer, his architect and a Hollywood actor. Therefore, the directors were either not independent (working, or having worked at Disney, or doing business with the company), or were dummy appointments. Nell Minnow (Minnow), a corporate governance expert based in the U.S., said that the Disney board was "About as bad a board as we've seen."[15] What was even more objectionable was that some of these members were serving on critical committees like the compensation committee or the nomination committee.

The method of determining a member's independence was also largely arbitrary. Gold was judged as not independent because he was the financial adviser of Roy, who was a company executive. On this basis he was deprived of the chairmanship of the governance committee. On the other hand, another director, John Bryson, whose wife held a high and well paid position in Lifetime Entertainment cable channel (which was 50% owned by Disney) was judged independent and was appointed as the chairman of the same committee. Patrick McGurn, an analyst with Institutional Shareholder Services, a Rockville-based organization, which advises investors on corporate-governance issues, believed that Bryson could not be judged as independent because of the strong financial links that his family had with Disney (Bryson was later judged as non-independent and replaced on the committee). He also questioned the independence of former Senator George Mitchell (Mitchell), whose law firm

---

[14]A leading business magazine.

[15]Marc Gunther, "Has Eisner Lost the Disney Magic?" *Fortune*, January 7, 2002.

used to work for Disney (the firm severed its ties with Disney prior to Mitchell's becoming the board's presiding director). Mitchell was appointed to the governance and nomination committee. Another important issue was that Mitchell was appointed although he was a member of four other boards, when good governance principles mandated that a person should not sit on more than three or four boards in all.

The most controversial appointment made by Eisner, however, was that of Ovitz, who was a personal friend of Eisner. He was brought in as the president of Disney in 1995. By 1996, it was clear that Ovitz was a failure. He himself was not satisfied with his work and wanted to leave. Eisner wanted his friend to leave the company on good terms and, under Eisner's influence, the board approved of a severance package of $38 million in cash as well as stock options valued at $101 million. Analysts felt that this package (which represented 10% of Disney's revenues in 1996) was far too generous. It was also far greater than the amount Ovitz would have made, had he continued to work at Disney for the full five-year period of his contract. The package caused great uproar and triggered a lawsuit by Disney shareholders, demanding that the money be returned to the company.

It was also alleged in the [lawsuit] that Eisner was advised by at least three members of the board that Ovitz was not suitable for the post. Eisner, however, chose to disregard their advice. He also appointed Irwin Russell, his personal lawyer who was also a board member, to negotiate the contract with Ovitz. Russell then sat on the compensation committee that approved Ovitz's hiring based on a summary of the deal. No written contract went before the board for approval and Ovitz's contract was later altered in his favor without board approval. It was said that the board did not try to negotiate with Ovitz to obtain better terms for the company and the shareholders. It simply approved the amount that Ovitz demanded.

Eisner's Compensation

Corporate governance experts believe that the compensation made to CEOs should be linked to the performance of the company. Under this consideration, the compensation made to Eisner was also severely criticized by analysts. At the time of his appointment in 1984, Eisner was granted a base salary of $75,000 per year and some stock options. Many analysts found this amount a fair one. However, in 1996, when he renegotiated his contract, he was granted 24 million options at the then-current price of $21.10, meaning that if Disney's stock climbed $1 a year, or less than 5%, for

the seven years until they vested, Eisner would collect $105 million. Of the 24 million options granted, 19 million were not indexed.[16] During the mid-1990s, when Disney shares were trading at around $40, Eisner had cashed in more than $750 million worth of options, which was one of the highest payments ever made in American corporate history.

The performance of the company also left a lot to be desired. After the performance peaked in 1997, the journey [had] been downhill. Earnings per share fell from 92 cents in 1997 to about 55 cents in 2003. Operating income also fell from $4.3 billion in 1997 to $2.7 billion in 2003. Although Eisner did not receive any bonus in 2002 (because of the loss in 2001), he still had a huge number of options which he could [cash]. Another important reason for criticism was that the compensation committee at Disney was made up largely of Eisner's friends, whom he could manipulate to suit his interests.

Lack of Succession Planning

The Disney board was further criticized for not making an effort to develop a formal succession plan. Eisner had been the chairman and CEO of Disney since 1984 and analysts believed that it was time he made way for a new person. However, Eisner showed no inclination to leave. It was said that when he underwent a risky bypass surgery in 1994, he called his family to the hospital bed and suggested a few names of those he thought could succeed him in case of [a bad outcome].

Analysts felt that it was not healthy for the company to be overly dependent on a particular person. They expressed concern that if something happened to Eisner, the company would suffer from a lack of leadership. It was said that Eisner had the name of a possible successor in a closed envelope in his desk. This was to be opened in case something happened to prevent him from continuing with his duty. But analysts felt that this was not a good method and did not constitute succession planning. "This is not an Oscar Award winner. This is the next leader of the company. It's not supposed to be a surprise to the board," said Minnow.[17] Grooming a possible successor was [an] important function of a CEO and not doing so could be risky for the future of the company. Besides, analysts said

---

[16]Indexed options are those [that] are linked to performance. They reward only those executives who outperform their peers. For instance, if a company's stock goes up by 10%, when the rest of the stocks in the industry go up by 12%, the options are not paid. They are usually linked to an industry index.

[17]Richard Verrier and James Bates, "No Succession Plan at Disney," *The Herald*, December 10, 2003.

that it was the duty of the board to select a CEO, and that the current CEO would be exceeding his powers if he chose his successor arbitrarily. They compared the situation at Disney to that at GE,[18] where [long-standing] CEO Jack Welch identified three possible successors and encouraged the board to interact with them long before he was due to retire.

The Future of the Magic Kingdom

Soon after their well publicized resignations, Roy and Gold announced that they would launch a campaign to oust Eisner. Both men were planning to meet major shareholders in the company as well as institutional investors and governance bodies to seek their help in ousting Eisner from Disney. In addition to removing Eisner, they also hoped to get the shareholders to nominate a new body of independent directors at an upcoming board meeting in March 2004.

Their efforts began to yield results when, in December 2003, the corporate governance wing of a major investment firm asked Disney's independent directors to respond to some of the issues raised by Roy and Gold. At the end of December 2003, Herbert Denton (Denton), who ran a firm called Providence Capital and specialized in leading shareholder campaigns, organized a meeting of about 50 investment firms and sent a letter to the Disney board outlining some of their demands.

The letter demanded that the post of chairman be separated from that of CEO, director nominees be solicited from major investors, financial benchmarks and timetables be set, the board develop a succession plan, and make it easier for shareholders to vote changes to company by-laws. "It's our way of seeing whether Michael Eisner's embrace of good governance is for real or for show," said Denton.[19] Several other analysts also favored splitting the positions of chairman and CEO. "It basically provides checks and balances," said Kathy Styponias, an analyst at Prudential Securities.[20]

There was also some speculation that Disney could become a target of takeover bids, considering the vulnerable condition it was in following the threats to remove the CEO. Comcast (a cable firm), Yahoo (a major Internet company) and InterActiveCorp (a multibrand interactive commerce company) were thought to be some of the likely suitors of Disney.[21] There was considerable speculation as well, on who would replace Eisner if the dissidents were successful in overthrowing him. Even if they were not, Eisner's term was due to expire in 2006, and analysts felt that it was time some potential successors were considered.

However, analysts felt that Roy and Gold would require a fair amount of luck to be able to succeed in their intentions to remove Eisner. They felt that it would not be very easy to obtain unconditional support from Disney shareholders, especially in [. . .] light of the company's improved performance in 2003. In 2003, stock [prices] grew by about 35% and analysts expected the earnings per share to increase simultaneously by more than 30%. Another reason for the skepticism was that, when Roy and Gold were not able to convince the board of the need to remove Eisner when they were board members themselves, it would be even more difficult to do so as outsiders. Their [resignations were] perceived by many as an admission of defeat, and the future of the "Magic Kingdom" was in the hands of the shareholders.

Questions for Discussion

1. Roy and Gold alleged that most of the governance problems at Disney could be traced to Eisner. What were the major governance problems at Disney? Is it true that Eisner was responsible for the company's governance problems? Do you think that the new governance norms adopted by the company were an eyewash?

2. Not identifying a successor has been one of the major complaints against Eisner. What could be the reason for this? What are the possible repercussions to the company in case of an emergency? Comment also on the independence issue of the Disney board.

3. Governance problems at Disney were forcefully brought to notice with the resignation of Roy and Gold. Do you think that their resignation from the board was a good move? Discuss the future of Disney in [. . .] light of the criticism it faced regarding governance.

[18]General Electric was the largest and most successful [company] in the world. GE was a conglomerate comprising several mature businesses, from aircraft engines to household and electric appliances.

[19]Marc Gunther, "The Directors," *Fortune*, December 27, 2003.

[20]Marc Gunther, "The Directors," *Fortune*, December 27, 2003.

[21]In February 2004, Comcast Corp., the No. 1 cable operator in the U.S., made an offer to buy Disney for $54 billion.

Additional Readings & References

1. **"Elbow Power,"** *The Economist*, November 19, 1998.
2. **"Attributes of a Good Board,"** *BusinessWeek*, January 24, 2000.
3. **"The Best and Worst Corporate Boards,"** *BusinessWeek*, January 24, 2000.
4. Marc Gunther, **"The Wary World of Disney,"** *Fortune*, October 15, 2001.
5. Marc Gunther, **"Has Eisner Lost the Disney Magic?"** *Fortune*, January 7, 2002.
6. **"Disney or Doesn't He?"** *The Economist*, January 10, 2002.
7. Ronald Grover, **"Eisner's Challenge: Beat the Buzz,"** *BusinessWeek*, August 16, 2002.
8. Frank Ahrens, **"At AOL and Disney, Uneasy Chairs,"** *Washington Post*, September 18, 2002.
9. **"Disney Top Shareholders Urged to Meet,"** money.cnn.com, September 11, 2002.
10. Dan Milmo, **"Eisner Survives as Disney Board Backs Recovery Plan,"** *The Guardian*, September 25, 2002.
11. David Teather, **"Magic Kingdom May Expel Eisner,"** *The Guardian*, September 25, 2002.
12. **"Peacemaker to Aid Disney Shake-Up,"** news.bbc.co.uk, September 25, 2002.
13. **"Disney Board Backs Eisner's Plan for Growth,"** www.telegraph.co.uk, September 26, 2002.
14. **"Wobbly Kingdom,"** *The Economist*, September 26, 2002.
15. **"The Tragic Kingdom,"** *The Economist*, July 24, 2003.
16. Marc Gunther, **"Boards Beware,"** *Fortune*, November 10, 2003.
17. Ronald Grover and Gerry Khermouch, **"Renovating This Old Mouse,"** *BusinessWeek*, November 10, 2003.
18. Ronald Grover, **"Stalking a Wily Prey at Disney,"** *BusinessWeek*, December 2, 2003.
19. Gary Gentile, **"Gold 2nd to Quit Disney Board,"** *Newsday*, December 2, 2003.
20. **"Wishing Upon a Star,"** *The Economist*, December 4, 2003.
21. **"A Tale of Two Boards,"** *The Economist*, December 4, 2003.
22. Ronald Grover, **"Eisner's Very Repressive Regime,"** *BusinessWeek*, December 4, 2003.
23. Richard Verrier and James Bates, **"No Succession Plan at Disney,"** *The Herald*, December 10, 2003.
24. **"Succession Planning,"** *The Economist*, December 11, 2003.
25. Marc Gunther **"Disney's Loss is Eisner's Gain,"** *Fortune*, December 22, 2003.
26. Marc Gunther, **"The Directors,"** *Fortune*, December 27, 2003.
27. Marc Gunther, **"Mouse Hunt,"** *Fortune*, January 12, 2004.
28. **"Corporate Conflict,"** www.cbsnews.com, December 1, 2003.
29. **"Disney Corporate's Mouse Droppings,"** www.cbsnews.com, December 1, 2003.
30. **"Disney Heir Quits; Blasts Eisner,"** www.cbsnews.com, December 1, 2003.
31. finance.yahoo.com.
32. www.disney.com.

Case 37

VNU's Strategy Derailed by Active Investors

04/2007-5433

On July 12th 2005, Mr. Robert van den Bergh, CEO of VNU, and Mr. Aad Jacobs, Chairman of the Supervisory Board, announced the acquisition of IMS, a leading provider of information solutions to the pharmaceutical and healthcare industries for €5.8 billion. Van den Bergh and Jacobs would need to persuade shareholders that this new venture would create a much stronger company.

The timing of the deal was not surprising, since VNU had sold their World Directories business for €2.1 billion in late 2004, and had announced that half of the cash would be used in acquisitions. But the size of the transaction did take the market by surprise. Expectations were for a medium-sized acquisition in combination with cash return to shareholders—IMS, in contrast, would be VNU's largest acquisition in its history. The very same day of the announcement, VNU shares fell 3.7% to close at €22.49 in Amsterdam.[1]

The move was expected to be approved by the shareholders of both companies early in 2006. A simple majority of shares was needed to pass it.

INSEAD This case was written by Sylvie Bergeron and Justin Brodie-Smith, Research Associates at INSEAD, under the supervision of Philippe Haspeslagh, the Paul Desmarais Chaired Professor of Partnership and Active Ownership at INSEAD. It is intended to be used as a basis for class discussion rather than to illustrate either effective or ineffective handling of an administrative situation.

[1] International Herald Tribune 17 July 2005.

History of VNU

VNU was founded in 1964, through the merger of two Dutch publishing companies, Cebema ('sHertogenbosch) and De Spaarnestad (Haarlem). In the 1960s, the company operated mainly in the Netherlands and Belgium, publishing, printing and distributing consumer magazines, newspapers and books. During the 1980s, the company's activities were strengthened by expanding into other European countries and the US. VNU went on an expansion drive, acquiring assets in both the publishing and printing sectors.

In the early 1990s, VNU management decided to focus on publishing only. The company gave various reasons for selling its printing facilities. The most important one was the level of investment required to stay competitive: "The printing industry requires more and more investment in updating machinery."[2]

In the years that followed, through acquisitions, the company entered the publishing of telephone directories and providing information about the media and consumers for use by advertisers. These supplemented its consumer magazines, newspapers, and professional and educational publications.

Its leading Dutch rivals, Elsevier and Wolters Kluwer, embarked on global expansion programmes, and VNU worried that it would fall far behind. "We were not as advanced as they were," VNU's chief financial officer, Frans Cremers, recalled.[3]

Thus, in 1999, the company bought television and Web-ratings source Nielsen Media Research for US$2.7 billion,

[2] Het Financieele Dagblad 13 April 1991.
[3] The New York Times 13 August 2001.

VNU's largest-ever purchase. The acquisition underlined a strategy to focus on high growth, high margin business and was seen as a big step to strengthening its position in global markets.

A NEW CEO ROBERT VAN DEN BERGH On April 18th 2000, Robert van den Bergh Succeeded Joep Brentjens as the new Chief Executive for the company. "My style is different," he admitted in an interview. "I'm not much of a diplomat, while Brentjens' ability to stay patient was also considerably greater than mine . . . Brentjens gave me plenty of room, which was logical. If you are smart, you give the man under you the room to prove himself when you reach your final years, to allow him prove that he may be a candidate to succeed you."[4]

Van den Bergh, then 49, had been Vice-Chairman of VNU since 1998 and a member of the company's Executive Board since 1992. After 19 years in the company, van den Bergh had gained experience, ultimately as head of its business publications and magazines divisions. "I keep a low profile. That feels best to me. That's how people in the company know me too . . . The point is to keep good connections on an internal level. And that may well change somewhat over the years. . . ."[5]

From 1992, the management had been very focused on doubling the size of VNU and becoming stronger in the US, where van den Bergh had become famous as the head of the US publishing unit. "I was the American spearhead," he said. "When I got to the US as the person in charge of the US division, I realised that VNU didn't mean much in the US. But I had to make the best of it. The Netherlands was much more a culture of newspapers and magazines back then. Without my US experience, my present job would have been more difficult," he reckoned.[6]

In order to boost the US share of the business, the new top man did not hesitate to jet around the world: "I am trying to build a really, truly international company, a company that has its people spread around the world," he said.[7] "I am not afraid to say loudly that it is a challenge," he emphasized, remaining confident about making the many deals work and integrating the different companies. This, according to insiders, made him uniquely suitable for organizing the different activities into one company.

CONTINUING TRANSFORMATION THROUGH ACQUISITION On appointment as CEO, van den Bergh was quick to announce new acquisitions. Convinced that demand from advertisers for accurate Internet-usage data would

soar, he convened an emergency Board meeting by telephone, and three days later acquired 54% of Nasdaq-listed NetRatings. "We are keen to play a leading role on the Net, and we know that we have to be quick."[8]

In July 2000, he agreed to pay US$650 million for Miller Freeman USA, which specialized in trade shows and business publications. "VNU has tapped into the hottest US media sectors,"[9] commented a Forbes journalist. That deal pushed the US part of the Dutch company's business to more than 50%. At that time, van den Bergh commented, "The US is our key area of growth, and it is possible that it could account for 70% to 80% of VNU's revenue in the next five years or so."[10]

Shortly afterwards in 2001, VNU acquired ACNielsen Corp., the market research firm, for US$2.3 billion, furthering the company's metamorphosis into business information and away from newspapers. The deal reunited ACNielsen, best known for tracking consumer shopping habits and box-office data, and Nielsen Media Research, the television-ratings service, as both had once been part of Dun & Bradstreet.

In only a few years, the company had made three major acquisitions and divested two traditional core businesses, its Dutch regional newspapers and its Consumer and Educational Information businesses. The latest major steps, the acquisition of ACNielsen and the announcement of the intended sale of the magazine division, were a clear indication of how VNU was moving its business into a new field of activities. "You won't find many examples of a transformation process as major as that which we've been through in the last five to six years," van den Bergh remarked. He added, "We are very well regarded by the analyst community because we are straightforward and open in what we do. Analysts like our transparency and clear focus."[11]

Late in 2003, van den Bergh announced another dramatic change in strategy, stating that World Directories was "a bit far away from the core of the company and slow-growing". VNU went on to sell the business for €2.1 billion in late 2004.

VNU in 2004

VNU at the end of 2004 consisted of three business groups, Marketing Information, Media Measurement and Information, and Business Information. At the same time, VNU

[4]www.7d-culture.n1/SpSt%20book/chapter13.htm
[5]www.7d-culture.n1/SpSt%20book/chapter13.htm
[6]www.7d-culture.n1/SpSt%20book/chapter13.htm
[7]NYT 13 August 2001.

[8]WSJ 28 February 2000.
[9]Forbes 7 July 2000.
[10]WSJ 28 February 2000.
[11]WSJ 28 February 2000.

Exhibit 1	VNU—Key Financial Indicators			
€ *millions*	2001	2002	2003	2004
Total revenues*	4,825	4,275	3,882	3,781
Operating income**	806	746	643	688
Cash earnings	416	452	382	454
Net earnings	1,004	170	130	163
Dividends	129	142	143	140
Shareholders' equity	4,900	4,600	4,066	3,957
Guarantee capital	5,678	5,330	4,653	4,398
Number of common shares outstanding (millions)	238	248	250	254
Ratios	2001	2002	2003	2004
Operating income: total revenues (%)	16.7	17.4	16.6	18.2
EBITDA: Net Interest	4.1	5.6	5.7	6.6
Net earnings: Shareholders' equity (%)	23.0	3.5	3.0	4.1

Source: VNU Annual Reports.

reported revenues of €3.78 billion, representing organic growth of 5% after accounting for acquisitions, divestitures and currency effects (See Exhibit 1).

Marketing Information accounted for 54% of VNU's total revenues. It consisted of two businesses, ACNielsen and VNU Advisory Services. The major business ACNielsen (45% of VNU's total revenues) provided market and consumer information to manufacturers and retailers of fast-moving consumer goods. Its activities included Retail Measurement, with data on purchases collected at point of sale, Consumer Panel, with panel data available in 24 countries, and Customized Research, available in 60 countries. The second business, VNU Advisory Services, advised clients regarding complex sales and marketing issues.

Media Measurement and Information comprised Nielsen Media Research, Nielsen//NetRatings, Entertainment Information Services, and Media Solutions. Nielsen Media Research, accounting for 28% of VNU's revenues, measured TV viewing habits across the world. Nielsen//NetRatings collected data on over 70% of global Internet activity. Entertainment Information Services provided measurement and other services for the motion picture, home entertainment, music and publishing industries. Finally, Media Solutions offered a complete range of software, systems and tools for analyzing advertising data and planning media campaigns in the US.

VNU's third division, Business Information, consisted of two main businesses, Publications and Trade Shows. Publications in the US included titles like The Hollywood Reporter, Commercial Property News and National Jeweler, with a circulation of 1.8 million. In Europe, VNU was active

in the Netherlands, the United Kingdom, Belgium, France, Germany, Italy and Spain, publishing approximately 70 trade magazines with some 70 million copies per year. Leading titles included Intermediair (career development), Computable and Management Team in The Netherlands, Computing, Accountancy Age and Computeractive in the United Kingdom, and PC Professional in Germany. The second business, Trade Shows, consisted of trade events and exhibitions in the US, Europe and Asia.

MARKETING INFORMATION: ONGOING STRUCTURAL CONCERNS Marketing Information had become the black sheep of VNU's portfolio. In terms of profitability trends, as measured by return on sales, Marketing Information had declined since 2001 with ROS dropping from 14.4% to 11.7% in 2004 (See Exhibit 2). In contrast, the two other business groups had improved. Media Measurement had gone from 16.9% to 22.8%, and Business Information from 12.1% to 16.1%. At ACNielsen, the biggest unit by sales, margins had repeatedly decreased since its acquisition in 2001.[12] Management had stayed away from margin guidance because as CFO Ruijter explained, "I can't predict future price pressure."[13] "The company rightly identified market research as one of the highest growth sub-sectors of media" said one analyst,[14] "but the management has underestimated the cost of securing this growth."

While the Nielsen Businesses were well positioned competitively, they faced increasingly sophisticated and demand-

[12]Reuters 18 August 2005.

[13]Conference Call Streetevens.com November 2005.

[14]JM Morgan 10 October 2005.

Exhibit 2	Key Figures by Business 2001/2004 of VNU			
In € Million	2001	2002	2003	2004
Marketing Information				
Revenues	1,664	1,881	1,765	1,818
Operating Income	240	258	193	213
Book Assets	3414	3036	2960	
ROS	14.4%	13.7%	10.9%	11.7%
ROBA		7.6%	6.4%	7.2%

Source: VNU Annual Reports.

In € Million				
Media Measurement and Information				
Revenues	992	1032	929	939
Operating Income	168	188	197	214
Book Assets	5,372	3,411	2,806	2,583
ROS	16.9%	18.2%	21.2%	22.8%
ROBA	NA	5.5%	7.0%	8.3%

VNU Annual Reports

In € Million				
Business Information				
Revenue	926	775	636	610
Operating Income	112	107	95	98
Book Assets	NA	NA	972	873
ROS	12.1%	13.8%	14.9%	16.1%
ROBA*	NA	NA	9.8%	11.2%

Source: VNU Annual Reports.

*Return on Book Assets.

ing clients, looking for more targeted ways to drive volume growth with better ROI. Retailers exerted greater power over time either by withdrawing access to data, such as Wal-Mart, or increasing the cost of the data to VNU. As a result, cost pressure was growing. In response, the management was attempting to reposition its broad and global market research offering focusing on higher growth higher value areas of analytics and advisory services.

For the first time in several years, in 2004 revenue growth in Marketing Information was better than expected and VNU achieved the upper part of its forecasts.[15] As a result, van den Bergh received 11% higher compensation in 2004, an increase of US$4.4 million on the year before. Meanwhile, the company was considering a US listing in 2006 as a way of increasing the exposure of the company to US investors,

although US ownership had already risen to around 50% of shares.

IMS

IMS was a financially solid company with revenues of $1.6 billion in 2005 and net profit of $285 million. Founded in 1954, the company had built a business around syndicated market research studies for the drug industry. IMS now had almost every pharmaceutical and biotech company as a customer. It offered data, applications, advisory services and consulting, enabling it to create tailored offerings designed to match the core activities of pharmaceutical companies.

IMS collected pharmaceutical data from 29,000 data suppliers at 225,000 supplier sites worldwide. It monitored 75% of prescription drug sales in over 100 countries, and 90% of US sales, tracking 1 million products from more

[15]Reuters 15 December 2005.

than 3,000 active drug manufacturers. Through refining this data, IMS examined market share, sales volumes, pricing patterns, and promotional effectiveness. From this, the company provided customized offerings, assisting customers with insights and advice about their business and market position.

IMS's history was intertwined with that of Dun & Bradstreet. D&B had acquired IMS for nearly US$1.8 billion in 1988, bringing ACNielsen and IMS together in the same group. D&B regarded IMS as the "jewel in its crown" and invested heavily in the company to preserve its leadership position. The company also sought to leverage competences between IMS and ACNielsen.

In 1996, D&B split into three independent public companies one of which was Cognizant, consisting primarily of IMS and Nielsen Media Research. IMS became a separate independent company in 1998 with its own listing on the New York Stock Exchange. IMS spun off Gartner Group the following year, and several other companies in 2000 to become a pure-play healthcare information provider.

Like VNU, IMS had undergone its own significant business transformation in recent years, beginning the process in 2001, laying out a strategy to invest in its strengths of data and analytics, accelerate its growth through services and consulting and expand into new markets. In addition, it had taken 100 country affiliates and turned them into an integrated global company. Global Account Managers had been appointed and it had created a global customer delivery organization to serve its global customers.

IMS had also acquired 26 companies since 2001. Nancy Cooper, CFO of IMS, commented: "We've developed a structured approach to integration. We have built a core competency in this area by applying focus and discipline in how we buy, integrate and manage acquisitions."[16]

Since becoming independent, IMS had ridden the rapid growth of the pharmaceutical business. IMS had, however, witnessed significant pressure on its margins. Operating margins had fallen from 33% in 2002 to 27% in 2004 as a result of data disruption in Japan and investment in data assets.[17] Nevertheless, commenting on the financial performance at the time of the merger announcement, David Carlucci, CEO stated: "We have strong revenue growth, high free cash flows, outstanding return on invested capital and strong EBITDA margins of 33%. For the full year 2004, we achieved double-digit growth in all key metrics of our business – 14% reported revenue growth, 11% growth in

adjusted net income, 17% adjusted earnings per share growth, and 22% growth in free cash flow. And our business has momentum."[18]

A Potential Acquisition

On January 10th 2005, following the sale of World Directories, van den Bergh announced that he was considering spending around €1 billion on acquisitions in market research. Likely candidates included researchers Aprovia and Arbitron Inc.[19]

"Sixty percent of VNU's sales are in America, 25% to 30% in Europe and the remainder in Asia," said van den Bergh.[20] Yet, Europe was comparatively more profitable (See Exhibit 3). "We would like to expand in Europe, but unfortunately the best candidates are in America, he added.

Observers were sceptical about some ongoing activities, including major restructuring programmes at ACNielsen. "Van den Bergh's longer-term vision for Marketing Information is not going down well with investors," an analyst warned.[21]

Van den Bergh was aware of analysts' concerns and made an attempt to dispel some of these fears by comparing the current situation to previous acquisitions, stating that historically the "return on all acquisitions had met VNU's WACC (8%) within 3–4 years."[22] On March 9 2005, VNU announced it would use "at least half" of the proceeds of the directories sale to repay debt, with the remainder being earmarked by the company for acquisitions.

That same month two private-equity firms approached VNU. The private-equity firms, Kohlberg Kravis Roberts & Co. and Blackstone Group, said they were interested in buying the whole company. "We didn't receive any bids. I only had a phone call in March from KKR. They showed some interest, and it stopped after that call," said van den Bergh.[23]

At the general meeting of shareholders in April, the representative of the Dutch Association of Shareholders, the VEB, asked for further explanation. To allay investor fears, van den Bergh responded that if suitable acquisitions could not be identified at the right price, debt would be paid down

[16]IMS Merger Conference Call Transcript 11 July 2005.

[17]JP Morgan October 2005.

[18]IMS Merger Conference Call Transcript 11 July 2005.

[19]JP Morgan 10 March 2005.

[20]De Brauw Blackstone Westbroek General Meeting of Shareholders 19 April 2005.

[21]Reuters 15 December 2005.

[22]JP Morgan 10 March 2005.

[23]Thomson Financial www.streetevents.com 17 November 2005.

| Exhibit 3 | Financial Performance by Regions (2004) |

(in € Million)

Geography	Revenues	%	Operating Income	%	ROS
Americas	2,040	54	234	34	11%
Europe, Middle East and Africa	1,447	38	420	61	29%
Asia Pacific	294	8	34	5	12%

Source: VNU Annual Reports.

and cash returned to shareholders. Meanwhile, van den Bergh admitted that the growth rate in the US had been affected along with Europe, highlighting the apprehension that it would be "difficult for Marketing Information to achieve its revenue growth target of 5% in 2005."[24]

Eric Knight Enters the Picture

On June 27th 2005, Eric Knight, founder of Knight Vinke Asset Management (KVAM), wrote to van den Bergh and Jacobs voicing concern at the damage to shareholders from a further acquisition.

KVAM was the managing general partner of Knight Vinke Institutional Partners (KVIP), a fund established in 2003 with $200 million of seed capital from CalPERS, and partly owned by CalPERS. The fund had grown to €500 million under management in 2005, and invested in underperforming large cap public companies highlighting inefficiencies with respect to structure or corporate governance. Following investment, it sought to build consensus among institutional shareholders, analysts, Board members and management as to the remedies, and subsequently to convince the controlling shareholder or Board of directors to adopt these remedies, creating value for all shareholders. Knight Vinke adopted a highly focused approach concentrating on no more than two or three "active" investments at any one time.

KVAM collected 1% to 1.5% in management fees from investors and reaped 20% performance fees on any profits earned. Eric Knight had previously worked at Merrill Lynch & Co. and the Virgin Islands-based Sterling Investment Group—which also targeted underperforming companies—building up a decade of experience in this area.

KVAM had already had considerable success with major European corporates. At Shell, where Aad Jacobs was Non-Executive Chairman, the dual management and committee structure of Royal Dutch Shell and Shell Transport and Trading had been challenged, and on October 28th 2004, Shell had adopted a new unitary management structure. On December 8th 2004, Knight Vinke had turned its attention to Suez, calling for Suez to divest its 50.1% holding in Electrabel, a major Belgian-based electric utility, removing the Suez control discount. Suez announced that it would acquire 100% of Electrabel on August 9th 2005, effectively also removing the discount. Knight's fund gained 20% in its first 18 months.

Eric Knight's style was distinctive: "We are not launching personal crusades," he said. In fact, in the midst of the Shell battle, Jeroen van der Veer, the CEO, thanked Knight for being so polite. Investors also noted that he had found the right formula to rally shareholders, tirelessly making the rounds of institutions in London, Frankfurt, Amsterdam, and elsewhere, keeping the names of other fund managers out of the newspapers. "Eric is finding the right balance between aggression and being part of the investment mainstream," said one. *BusinessWeek* called him "The Polite Agitator".[25]

Following Shell and Suez, VNU had now attracted Knight's attention. KVIP owned about 2 percent of VNU. Knight's letter noted the possibility of VNU undertaking a €1 billion acquisition, and warned:

"We are shareholders of VNU and plan to increase our position substantially over the next few months. We believe that the current share price of the company does not reflect its true value . . . We are also concerned that the company will embark on further transforming acquisitions prior to having fully integrated and rationalised what has been acquired over the past five years." He added, "From a financial point of view, we believe that a share buyback or capital reduction would create more value for shareholders with lower risk and would go a long way towards restoring the market's confidence in the company. . . . We

[24]JP Morgan 10 March 2005.

[25]Business Week, 24 January 2005.

believe that these concerns are shared by other institutional shareholders."[26]

The IMS Merger

Such comments did not seem to influence van den Bergh. On July 11th 2005, about two weeks later, he announced the acquisition of IMS Health for €5.8 billion, the largest acquisition in VNU's history. The company would make a buy-back of up to €500 million of its own shares and, in order to finance the deal, borrow €2.5 billion in a bridge loan from the banks.[27]

On paper, the deal was strategically justified by making information on broad consumer trends, tracked by VNU subsidiaries, more valuable in combination with more specialized information on drug products, provided by IMS. It would also offer the prospect of €85 million in annual cost savings by 2008, according to VNU.[28]

The transaction was expected to close in the first quarter of 2006. IMS shareholders would receive US$11.25 per share in cash and 0.6 shares of VNU stock for every IMS share they held. That valued IMS shares at US$28.10, a premium of about 9% to the closing price of US$25.89.[29] The shares would be listed on the Amsterdam and New York stock exchanges. Rob van den Bergh would remain CEO of the merged group, and Rob Ruitjer would maintain the CFO position. David Carlucci, the CEO of IMS, would become Deputy CEO and COO, and take responsibility for the vast majority of the businesses, namely, ACNielsen, VNU's largest division, Nielsen Media Research and IMS. Nancy Cooper, CFO of IMS, would become Chief Transformation Officer, dealing with IT, Corporate Development and Integration. IMS and VNU had been working together for two years prior to the merger announcement on multiple initiatives including an Indian joint venture, Medicine Cabinet in the US, and OTC activities in Germany and the U.K.

Regarding the rationale for the merger, Rob van den Bergh commented: "The strategic logic to the deal is compelling, and there are meaningful synergies that will allow us to accelerate earnings growth. The key benefits of the deal: merging two strong global, high growth, high margin businesses; bringing together complementary management teams that have already worked together during this time;

combining our capabilities and accelerating, very importantly, our advisory services; building on our geographic reach and global skill to serve our international clients; creating a very focused company, an almost pure play marketing information company, serving three very interesting and key industries."[30] He noted that five of the ten largest fast-moving consumer goods companies were also pharmaceutical companies.

He also remarked on a couple of key trends behind putting the businesses together:

"Clients are nowadays, especially in the last few years, facing increasing challenges in their industries, e.g., retailer consolidation in pharmaceuticals and CPG, which has driven the growth in both companies of our advisory and consulting services."

"The second trend that is very important is global reach. We will strengthen our position in Europe and in America, especially with our panel business. In Asia and Latin America, we will combine our infrastructure and leverage our assets, so that we will grow more quickly."

VNU and IMS had identified annual revenue synergies of €125 million realizable in 2008 based on exploiting data across the three information businesses, expansion of advisory and consulting services, new consumer opportunities and geographic depth. On the cost side, synergies of €85 million had been identified at the corporate level, in the regions and for IT and production. The net impact on EBITDA was expected to be €110 million. This represented, in the eyes of the two management teams, a conservative provisional assessment.

The Supervisory Board would consist of six members from VNU and four from IMS. "It will be a more international board, better reflecting the businesses," said van den Bergh (See Exhibits 4 and 5 for the boards of each company).

David Carlucci, the CEO of IMS, would become Deputy CEO and COO. At the announcement meeting, he gave some examples of how, in the eyes of customers, the combination could create enhanced product offerings. In the case of a product manager of OTC Antihistamine, VNU and IMS together would be able to give a much better view of the market shares, consumer perception, promotional spending for the product within the OTC and the prescription market as a whole. Similarly, for a pharmaceutical brand executive, launching a new chronic-care patented

---

[26]Knight Vinke Press Release, 27 June 2005.

[27]International Herald Tribune 12 July 2005.

[28]International Herald Tribune 12 July 2005.

[29]International Herald Tribune 12 July 2005.

[30]IMS Merger Conference Call Transcript 11 July 2005.

Exhibit 4	Supervisory Board—VNU

Aad G. Jacobs (1936), Chairman

1. Former Chairman of the Executive Board of ING Groep nv
2. Other important positions:
3. Supervisory Director of: Imtech nv (Chairman); Joh. Enschedé bv (Chairman); Koninklijke Nederlandsche Petroleum Maatschapij nv (Chairman); Buhrmann nv (Vice Chairman); IHC Caland nv (Vice Chairman) and ING Groep nv
4. Nationality: Dutch, Residing in The Netherlands
5. First appointment: 1998, Term expires: 2006
6. Member of the Audit Committee and the Remuneration and Nomination Committee

Frank L. V. Meysman (1952), Vice Chairman

1. Former Chairman of the Board of Management of Sara Lee/DE International bv and Executive Vice President and Director of Sara Lee Corporation
2. Other important positions: Supervisory Director of Grontmij nv and Member of the Board of GIMV nv
3. Nationality: Belgian, Residing in Belgium
4. First appointment: 1995, Term expires: 2007
5. Chairman of the Remuncration and Nomination Committee

Joep L. Brentjens (1940)

1. Former Chairman of the Executive Board of VNU nv
2. Other important positions:

   Supervisory Director of: Heijmans nv (Chairman); Oce nv (Chairman); ArboNed nv (Chairman); Roto Smeets De Boer nv (Vice Chairman); Fortis Obam nv and P. Bakker Hillegom bv; Governor of Van Leer Group Foundation (Vice chairman); Stichtingsbestuur Radbout Universiteit Nijmegen (Chairman) and board member of several foundations.
3. Nationality: Dutch, Residing in The Netherlands
4. First appointment: 2000, Term expires: 2008
5. Member of the Audit Committee

René Dahan (1941)

1. Former Executive Vice President and Director of Exxon Mobil Corporation
2. Other important positions

   Interim Chairman of the Supervisory Board of Koninkijke Ahold nv; Supervisory Director of TPG nv and Aegon nv; Member of the International Advisory Board of: Institudo dc Empresa; CvC Capital Partners and Guggenheim Group

3. Nationality: Dutch, Residing in the United States
4. First appointment: 2003, Term expires: 2007
5. Member of the Remuneration and Nomination Committee

Peter A.F.W. Elverding (1948)

1. Chairman of the Managing Board of Directors of Koninklijke DSM nv
2. Other important position:

   Chairman of the European Chemical Industry Council (CEFIC); member of the Board of the American Chemical Council (ACC); member of the Supervisory Board of nv Nederlandse Gasunie and Chairman of the Committee of Delegate Members of the Supervisory Board of nv Nederlandse Gasunie; Vice Chairman of the Supervisory Board of De nederlandsche Bank nv; member of the General Council of Association VNO NCW;
3. Nationality: Dutch, Residing in The Netherlands
4. First appointment: 2000, Term expires: 2008
5. Chairman of the Audit Committee

Gerald S. Hobbs (1941)

1. Former Vice Chairman of the Executive Board of VNU nv
2. Other important positions

   Director of: The Advertising Council; Jobson Publishing, inc; Bureau of National Affairs and Governor of The Sky Club, inc; Partner Boston Ventures inc (private equity fund)
3. Nationality: American/Irish, Residing in the United States
4. First appointment: 2004, Term expires: 2008

Anton van Rossum (1945)

1. Former Chief Executive Officer of Fortis
2. Other important positions

   Member European Roundtable of Financial Services; member of the Board of Trustees of the Conference Board; member of the Advisory Board of the American European Community Association; member of the Philharmonic Association in Brussels; member of the Advisory Board of the Solvay business School; member of the management board of the Belgian employers' federation.
3. Nationality: Dutch, Residing in Belgium
4. First appointment: 2005, Term expires: 2009

---

ethical drug, VNU would provide the consumer perspective and IMS that of the physician. Nancy Cooper, the CFO of IMS and Chief Transformation Officer of the new company, commented: "We are taking a disciplined approach towards integration, because we believe there are process synergies across the organization. We understand each other's businesses and the opportunities that the merger will create."[31] The approach to integration would involve creating common global processes for six areas: data assets, IT and production, acquisitions, advisory and consulting services, client coverage and infrastructure. To deliver revenue and cost synergies, assets would be integrated across

[31]IMS Merger Conference Call Transcript 11 July 2005.

David R. Carlucci is chief executive officer and president of IMS. He was elected to the IMS board in 2005.

Constantine L. Clemente is retired executive vice president, Corporate Affairs, secretary and corporate counsel of Pfizer Inc., a global pharmaceutical company. He was elected to the IMS board in 2001 and serves on the Nominating and Governance Committee and the Compensation and Benefits Committee.

James D. Edwards is former managing partner-Global Markets for Andersen the public accounting firm. He was elected to the IMS board in 2002 and is a member of the Audit Committee.

Kathryn E. Giusti is president of the Multiple Myeloma Research Foundation, a non-profit organization aimed at funding research and advancing awareness of multiple myeloma. She joined the IMS board in 2002, and is a member of the Nominating and Governance Committee.

John P. Imlay, Jr. is chairman, Imlay Investments, Inc., a private venture capital investment firm. He has been a director since 1998 and is a member of the Compensation and Benefits Committee.

Robert J. Kamerschen is former chairman and chief executive officer of ADVO, Inc., and former chairman and chief executive officer of DIMAC Marketing Corporation, both direct marketing services firms. He was elected to the IMS board in 1998, serves on the Compensation and Benefits Committee, and chairs the Nominating and Governance Committee.

H. Eugene Lockhart is a venture partner for Oak Investment Partners, a private equity investment firm. He has been an IMS director since 1998 and serves on the Audit Committee and Nominating and Governance Committee.

M. Bernard Puckett is a private investor who has served on the IMS board since 1998. He chairs the Compensation and Benefits Committee.

David M. Thomas is executive chairman of IMS. An IMS director since 2000, he served as chairman and chief executive officer of IMS until December 2004.

William C. Van Faasen is chairman and chief executive officer of Blue Cross & Blue Shield of Massachusetts, a health insurance firm. He was elected to the IMS board in 1998 and chairs the Audit Committee.

---

all businesses, and in consulting the emphasis would be on building repeatable consulting and services capabilities.

Investors' Reaction

Soon after the announcement, investors, including Templeton Global Advisors, Fidelity Management & Research and Fidelity Investments voiced scepticism. At that time, Templeton, Fidelity, ING Groep NV, Norges Bank, Barclays Global and Robeco were among VNU's biggest shareholders, according to data from Thomson Financial.

"I wouldn't say 'no' upfront having seen the IMS management, but I'm not 100% confident either," said a portfolio manager at the Dutch investment firm, Robeco.[32]

On August 18th, VNU explained in a prepared statement: "While some shareholders have expressed a negative reaction initially, this is less of an issue than how those shareholders may view the transaction at the time of the shareholder vote, which is many months from now."[33]

Equally an IMS spokesman announced in September: "I can't speak specifically for VNU shareholders, but the people that we're talking to, and we've talked to more than 300 people from both sides, have been very positive (. . .)." He concluded, "We think that everything will work out, and again, we're on track."[34]

Yet, one of the large IMS shareholders noted, "We don't like the price. It is a very low premium, and so we are very disappointed." Regarding the fact that IMS shareholders were going to get VNU stock, he added: "We can't own foreign stocks and we don't want to own VNU."[35]

Another large holder was Templeton Global Advisors, which controlled about 10% of VNU's shares and had an affiliate controlling a further 4%. On September 29th 2005, Mr. Murdo Murchison of Templeton's Growth Fund spoke out against the merger:

"The projected benefits do not appear to warrant the risk associated with a transaction of this size. In addition, we believe the scale and timing of the projected synergies of this merger appear to be less attractive than alternative uses of shareholder capital."[36]

The following day, Fidelity International and Fidelity Management Research said they wished "to go on record to express their opposition to the proposed purchase" of IMS. Fidelity's funds held 14.99% of VNU's ordinary shares.[37]

---

[32]Reuters News 18 August 2005.

[33]Reuters News 18 August 2005.

[34]Mergers and Acquisitions Report 19 September 2005.

[35]Mergers and Acquisitions Report 19 September 2005.

[36]Financial Times 30 September 2005.

[37]Financial Times 30 September 2005.

Knight Vinke's Stance

Then on October 3rd, Knight Vinke Asset Management, following a meeting with VNU management, issued a press statement concerning its opposition to the IMS acquisition and appointing a proxy solicitor to coordinate shareholder opposition. It urged the Boards of VNU and IMS "to seek an early consensual solution involving shareholders to avoid unnecessary expense."[38] Contractually, the transaction could not be broken without IMS's approval unless VNU received a takeover bid or shareholders voted against it. VNU only had the option of walking away by paying a large termination fee.

Knight Vinke laid out detailed reasons for its opposition to the bid. VNU's financial performance was one element. Eric Knight noted that VNU shares had underperformed every one of its peers over the previous two years, and that: "free cash flow was higher in 1998 than it is today. Since the beginning of 1999, VNU had shown a negative total return of −18%" (See Exhibit 6).

According to Knight, the reasons for this lay in the acquisition strategy and subsequent execution. "VNU top management was more interested in transactions than operations." ACNielsen had repeatedly failed to reach stated margin targets, and the European data factory roll-out had been delayed. "Other acquisitions have also failed to fulfil initial expectations."

Knight summarized: "The market remains unconvinced as to the validity of the VNU business model. Do the benefits of integrating heterogeneous providers of data under one roof truly outweigh the execution risks? Each of VNU's divisions appears still to operate very independently and the market needs to be convinced that this is not the case."

Execution risk was seen as a critical issue with the IMS acquisition. "Integrating a global business such as IMS—present in over 100 countries—will add substantially to VNU's complexity. The potential for massive value destruction from poorly executed large-scale IT projects is well-known."

VNU Attempts to Ameliorate

"We've met with literally hundreds of investors," claimed a spokesman of VNU.[39] To appease unhappy investors, possible measures included a stock buyback, the sale of the business unit publishing trade magazines and organizing trade fairs, or even a change in CEO.

[38]Knight Vinke Press Release 3 October 2005.

[39]WSJ 29 September 2005.

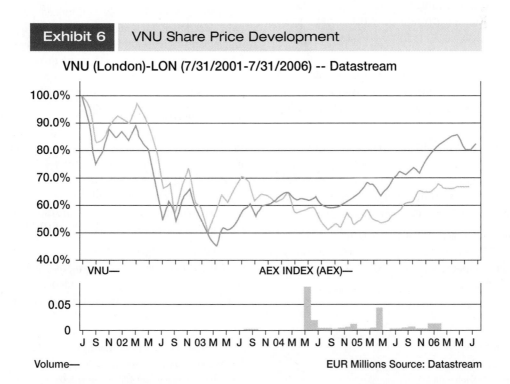

| Exhibit 6 | VNU Share Price Development |

VNU (London)-LON (7/31/2001-7/31/2006) -- Datastream

VNU—   AEX INDEX (AEX)—

Volume—   EUR Millions Source: Datastream

In a statement, VNU said that "it would continue to meet with shareholders to address their concerns."[40]

INVESTOR OPPOSITION CONTINUES

On October 5th 2005, KVAM won backing for its stance over VNU winning "six or seven" institutional investors to the rebel shareholders' camp. Claiming support from at least 42% of the shareholder base, Knight pushed for alternatives, including a break-up of the Dutch information group.[41]

On October 12th, the Dutch Shareholders Association, the VEB, opposed the IMS deal. This organisation, representing the interests of minority shareholders in companies, said VNU's proposal to buy IMS was overpriced, strategically weak and risky.

A week later, on October 19th, a meeting took place between the Chairman of VNU's Supervisory Board, Jacobs, and shareholders representing approximately 40% of the outstanding share capital.[42]

On October 26th as VNU received approval in the United States for the IMS takeover, VNU shareholders told the Dutch publishing and market-research firm that the acquisition of IMS was likely to lead to VNU itself being taken over or broken up.

PRIVATE EQUITY ENTERS THE FRAY

Meanwhile, a consortium of four private-equity firms, including New York-based Kohlberg Kravis Roberts & Co. and The Blackstone Group, was already weighing a possible bid for VNU. This was the same group of private-equity firms that had first approached VNU in March before VNU announced plans to buy IMS.

As VNU was becoming a bid target, it was a strenuous time for van den Bergh, the architect of the takeover, and there were signs that his normally laid back style was increasingly giving way.

In the light of strong shareholder opposition, on October 27th 2005, VNU and IMS started discussing whether to reduce the price of the deal and change the terms, offering IMS shareholders less equity in the merged group, or whether to give up on the plan altogether.

One sticking point was that both sides were eager to avoid paying a US$125 million break-up fee, which could be triggered if either company decided to walk away or if a third party bid for VNU or IMS.[43]

VNU ABANDONS THE DEAL

On November 17th 2005, VNU abandoned the deal and Rob van den Bergh quit. The company said it would also return €1 billion to shareholders in March 2006. Aad Jacobs, VNU's Chairman, would have to stand for re-election in April of the following year.

After weeks of talks on how to rescue or restructure the deal, it had proved impossible to find an acceptable formula to satisfy major shareholders like Templeton Global Advisors, Fidelity and Knight Vinke Asset Management.

"Having heard the views of our shareholders, it became clear that it would not be possible for us to proceed with the proposed merger," van den Bergh said. He said that he had tendered his resignation but would stay until a new CEO was found. "I am not bitter," he told journalists. "I accept that shareholders have the last word."[44]

The same day, VNU announced it had agreed to reimburse IMS US$15 million for out-of-pocket costs related to the failed merger and to pay an additional US$45 million if VNU agreed to be acquired over the next 12 months. IMS agreed to pay VNU US$15 million should it reach a deal to be bought in the next 12 months. The two companies would still pursue their partnership as they had prior to the merger. Van den Bergh commented. "Dave Carlucci and I are very committed to having our companies work together to develop the many joint revenue initiatives that came out of our planning process."[45]

Meanwhile, VNU had also announced plans to pursue a New York Stock Exchange listing to raise its public profile and expand its shareholder base. At that stage, a break-up of VNU could not be ruled out as the group was reported to be "evaluating" its portfolio and potentially considering selling its Business Information Division.[46]

The €1 billion cash return to shareholders "may be a little disappointing in its absolute size," analysts commented, noting that World Directories was sold for over €2 billion "But even if they were forced into it, it represents a positive, more shareholder-friendly change for VNU," they added. "A new CEO and any cost savings will also be a positive in the short term, as further out the potential for restructuring and pressures at ACNielsen should drive the stock."[47]

On December 9th, it became apparent that two private-equity consortia were considering bids for VNU. One consortium of seven partners included Apax Partners, The Blackstone Group, Carlyle Group, Kohlberg Kravis Roberts

[40]WSJ 1 October 2005.

[41]FT 5 October 2005.

[42]KVAM Press Release 19 October 2005.

[43]Financial Times 27 October 2005.

[44]Reuters 17 November 2005.

[45]IMS Merger Conference Call Transcript 17 November 2005.

[46]AFX International 17 November 2005.

[47]AFX International Focus 17 November 2005.

& Co., Permira Advisers, Thomas H. Lee Partners and Alpinvest Partners NV, which invested on behalf of two Dutch pension funds. Another group of private-equity firms, including Bain Capital, Texas Pacific Group and Warburg Pincus, was considering a separate bid, although it was judged not to be so far along in its evaluation.[48]

VNU had gone from being predator to prey.

A BID OF €7.3 BILLION FOR VNU   On Monday, January 16th 2006, VNU received a bid of up to €7.3 billion from the seven-partner group, consisting of the same private equity groups as in December with the addition of Hellman & Friendman but excluding Apax Partners.

The bid was priced at €28 to €28.50 a share. On the Friday before, VNU had closed at €28.25, and the offer was thus pitched at VNU's share price, representing at best a 1% premium. VNU shares had, however, risen around 35% since hitting a low in May 2005. VNU announced that "While this bid is on the table, it is not continuing discussions with any other party. With seven members, the large size of the bidding group made it less obvious that other groups could be invited in later, and left limited possibility for a broader auction that could drive the price higher.

Many analysts believed the bid would not be enough to satisfy VNU's key shareholders. An analyst at Rabo Securities, who rated VNU neutral, said that he doubted whether VNU shareholders Fidelity, Templeton and Knight Vinke would bite.

A SNS Securities analyst agreed: "I doubt the major investors will tender their shares at this bid price," he said, adding, "And with this bid price, it is likely another consortium could come up with a higher offer." SNS rated VNU as add and estimated a leveraged buyout price of €32 per share.[49]

In November prior to the bid, VNU had said that it would return €1 billion to shareholders in March 2006. But on the announcement of the bid, VNU spokesman, Will Thoretz, declined to confirm whether the €1 billion share buyback plans were on track. Thoretz did confirm that the consortium was "getting full access to the most current financial results" and that "the formal process of due diligence had begun". VNU expected to be in a position to provide an update on the ongoing discussions within three to four weeks. He also stated that both the supervisory and executive boards "believe it's in the best interest of the stakeholders to proceed with the discussions but this doesn't imply an acceptance or recommendation to accept the bid."

VNU intended to meet with its shareholders to discuss the offer over the coming weeks. The same day of the bid, van den Bergh sent a letter to all VNU employees stressing that VNU was working towards a "prompt resolution" regarding the VNU takeover bid.[50]

Knight Vinke continued to keep up the pressure. In December, KVAM had appointed the Boston Consulting Group to conduct an operating and strategic review of VNU and its constituent businesses based on public information only. KVAM believed that shareholders required a better understanding as to what VNU's individual businesses are truly capable of earning prior to reaching a conclusion as to what the separate divisions might be worth. KVAM presented its findings to the board of VNU at the beginning of February.

VNU ACCEPTS THE PRIVATE EQUITY OFFER   On March 8th 2006, VNU announced that they had agreed to the public offer by the equity group, except Permira who had dropped out. VNU clarified that the offer price of €28.75 per common share represented a multiple of 13.4 times the 2005 normalized EBITDA, "an attractive valuation compared to the recent trading of peer company stocks",[51] as well as to the recent history of trading of VNU's stock, and a 23% premium over the closing price on July 8, 2005, the last trading day prior to VNU's announcement of its planned merger with IMS Health.

The closing of the transaction was conditional upon 95% of VNU shareholders in each class, common and preferred, tendering their shares, as well as regulatory approval on both sides. Rob van den Bergh, CEO of VNU, said, "This transaction brings VNU new owners who support our long-term strategy of growth through expanded market coverage; expansion into developing markets; technology and service innovation; and development of integrated business solutions for our clients. It gives the company the added operational flexibility of private ownership."

In a statement, the group of private equity companies said: "We intend to keep VNU substantially together as an integrated company and continue to pursue its long-term strategy of improving operational efficiency and investing in product development and innovation. VNU's businesses bring together a unique combination of market intelligence, analysis, advice and service."[52]

Over the previous six months, VNU had worked on a standalone operating plan that included Project Forward, a three-year programme targeting annualized cost savings of

---

[48]WSJ 9 December 2005.

[49]Dow Jones Newswire 16 Monday 2006.

[50]Dow Jones Newswire 16 Monday 2006.

[51]VNU Press Release 8 March 2006.

[52]VNU Press Release 8 March 2006.

€125 million incremental to the current operating plans of VNU's business units.

Before committing to the private-equity offer, VNU had also analysed the risk-reward benefits of breaking up the company. VNU had determined that pursuing a break-up would not be as attractive to shareholders as a sale of VNU in a single transaction, particularly after taking into account the time value of money and substantial valuation and execution risks, including:

Uncertain completion: No other offers currently exist for the businesses, and there would be both timing and achievability risks to obtain such offers at reasonable valuations.

Adverse tax effects: There would be adverse tax effects on a sale or potential spin-off of VNU's businesses. Additionally, the company enjoyed certain tax advantages as a Dutch company that would not be available to spin-off companies based in the US.

Negative client reaction: VNU had been working with major clients to create unique combinations of its marketing, media and consumer information.

Distraction cost: A break-up of the company could take an extended period of time to complete, disrupting management and employees and potentially damaging client relationships.

KVAM AGAINST THE OFFER   Despite VNU's seemingly careful and thorough analysis of its situation, not all were happy. Knight Vinke rejected the offer for VNU on the same day and submitted resolutions to the AGM including modification of the sale process and appointment of Eric Knight to the Supervisory Board. Fidelity International, which owned 15% of VNU, said it was also unlikely to support the deal.

As KVAM had previously indicated to VNU's boards, KVAM believed that a higher value could be obtained by VNU's shareholders if the boards were to open up the sale process publicly. KVAM's preferred option would involve selling the Media Measurement and Information and Business Information divisions and allowing shareholders to benefit from a more ambitious restructuring of the Marketing Information division. KVAM's AGM resolution calling for a modification of the VNU sale process, asked that the Executive and Supervisory Boards, besides considering potential offers for VNU as a whole, give equal consideration to a wider range of alternatives."[53]

The Shareholders Meeting on April 16th looked set to be an interesting event.

[53]KVAM Press Release 8 March 2006.

Glossary

acquisition Strategy by which one firm acquires another through stock purchase or exchange.

acquisition premium Difference between current market value of a target firm and purchase price paid to induce its shareholders to turn its control over to new owners.

agency problem Separation of its ownership from managerial control of a firm.

agent Party, such as a manager, who acts on behalf of another party.

ambidextrous structure Organizational structure for dynamic contexts in which project teams are organized as structurally independent units and encouraged to develop their own structures, systems, and processes.

arena Area (product, service, distribution channels, geographic markets, technology, etc.) in which a firm participates.

balanced scorecard Strategic management support system for measuring vision and strategy against business- and operating-unit-level performance.

barrier to entry Condition under which it is more difficult to join or compete in an industry.

behavioral controls Practice of tying rewards to criteria other than simply financial performance, such as those broadly identified in the balanced scorecard.

board of directors Group of individuals that formally represents the firm's shareholders and oversees the work of top executives.

bootstrapping Process of finding creative ways to support a startup business financially until it turns profitable.

business strategy Strategy for competing against rivals within a particular industry or industry segment.

buyer power Degree to which firms in the buying industry are able to dictate terms on purchase agreements that extract some of the profit that would otherwise go to competitors in the focal industry.

CAGE framework Tool that considers the dimensions of culture, administration, geography, and economics to assess the distance created by global expansion.

capabilities A firm's skill at using its resources to create goods and services; combination of procedures and expertise on which a firm relies to produce goods and services.

causal ambiguity Condition whereby the difficulty of identifying or understanding a resource or capability makes it valuable, rare, and inimitable.

codes of governance Ideal governance standards formulated by regulatory, market, and government institutions.

coevolution Process by which diversification causes two or more interdependent businesses to adapt not only to their environment, but to each other.

commoditization Process during industry evolution by which sales eventually come to depend less on unique product features and more on price.

competitive advantage A firm's ability to create value in a way that its rivals cannot

complementor Firm in one industry that provides products or services which tend to increase sales in another industry.

conglomerate Corporation consisting of many companies in different businesses or industries.

consortia Association of several companies and/or governments for some definite strategic purpose.

contractual agreements An exchange of promises or agreement between parties that is often enforceable by the law.

co-opetition Situation in which firms are simultaneously competitors in one market and collaborators in another.

core competence Capability which is central to a firm's main business operations and which allow it to generate new products and services.

corporate governance The system by which owners of firms direct and control the affairs of the firm.

corporate new-venturing New-venture creation by established firms.

corporate renewal Outcome of successful strategic change in the context of an established business.

corporate strategy Strategy for guiding a firm's entry and exit from different businesses, for determining how a parent company adds value to and manages its portfolio of businesses, and for creating value through diversification.

cross-subsidizing Practice by which a firm uses profits from one aspect of a product, service, or region to support other aspects of competitive activity.

culture Core organizational values widely held and shared by an organization's members.

differentiation Strategic position based on products or offers services with quality, reliability, or prestige that is discernibly higher than that of competitors and for which customers are willing to pay.

differentiator Feature or attribute of a company's product or service (e.g., image, customization, technical superiority, price, quality, and reliability) that helps it beat its competitors in the marketplace.

diseconomies of scope Condition under which the joint output of two or more products within a single firm results in increased average costs.

diseconomy of scale Condition under which average total costs per unit of production increases at higher levels of input.

disruptive technology Breakthrough product- or process-related technology that destroys the competencies of incumbent firms in an industry.

distinctive competence Capability that sets a firm apart from other firms; something that a firm can do which competitors cannot.

diversification Degree to which a firm conducts business in more than one arena.

divestiture Strategy whereby a company sells off a business or division.

due diligence Initial pre-closing screening, analysis, and negotiations for an acquisition.

dynamic capabilities A firm's ability to modify, reconfigure, and upgrade resources and capabilities in order to strategically respond to or generate environmental changes.

economic logic Means by which a firm will earn a profit by implementing a strategy.

economy of scale Condition under which average total cost for a unit of production is lower at higher levels of output.

economy of scope Condition under which lower total average costs result from sharing resources to produce more than one product or service.

entrepreneurial process Integration of opportunity recognition, key resources and capabilities, and an entrepreneur and entrepreneurial team to create a new venture.

entrepreneurship Recognition of opportunities and the use of resources and capabilities to implement innovative ideas for new ventures.

equity alliance Alliance in which one or more partners assumes a greater ownership interest in either the alliance or another partner.

escalation of commitment Decision-making bias under which people are willing to commit additional resources to a failing course of action.

ethnocentrism Belief in the superiority of one's own ethnic group or, more broadly, the conviction that one's own national, group, or cultural characteristics are "normal."

exit barriers Barriers that impose a high cost on the abandonment of a market or product.

exporting Foreign-country entry vehicle in which a firm uses an intermediary to perform most foreign marketing functions.

first mover The firm that is first to offer a new product or service a market.

five-forces model Framework for evaluating industry structure according to the effects of rivalry, threat of entry, supplier power, buyer power, and the threat of substitutes.

focused cost leadership Strategic position based on being a low-cost leader in a narrow market segment.

focused differentiation Strategic position based on targeting products to relatively small segments.

foreign direct investment (FDI) Foreign-country entry vehicle by which a firm commits to the direct ownership of a foreign subsidiary or division.

functional structure Form of organization revolving around specific value-chain functions.

general resources Resource that can be exploited across a wide range of activities.

generic strategies Strategic position designed to reduce the effects of rivalry, including *low-cost, differentiation, focused cost leadership, focused differentiation, and integrated positions.*

geographic roll-up Strategy whereby a firm acquires many other firms in the same industry segment by in different geographic arenas in an attempt to create significant scale and scope advantages.

geographic scope Breadth and diversity of geographic arenas in which a firm operates.

globalization Evolution of distinct geographic product markets into a state of globally interdependent product markets.

goals and objectives Combination of a broad indication of organizational intentions (goals) and specific, measurable steps (objectives) for reaching them.

greenfield investment Form of FDI in which a firm starts a new foreign business from the ground up.

high-end disruption Strategy that may result in huge new markets in which new players redefine industry rules to unseat the largest incumbents.

horizontal alliance Alliance involving a focal firm and another firm in the same industry.

horizontal scope Extent to which firm participates in related market segments or industries outside its existing value-chain activities.

hubris Exaggerated self-confidence that can result in managers' overestimating the value of a potential acquisition, having unrealistic assumptions about the ability to create synergies, and a willingness to pay too much for a transaction.

implementation levers Mechanisms used by strategic leaders to help execute a firm's strategy.

importing Internationalization strategy by which a firm brings a good, service, or capital into the home country from abroad.

incentive alignment Use of incentives to align managerial self-interest with shareholders'.

industry life cycle Pattern of evolution followed by an industry inception to current and future states.

initial public offering (IPO) First sale of a company's stock to the public market.

innovator's dilemma When incumbents avoid investing in innovative and disruptive technologies because those innovations do not satisfy the needs of their mainstream and most profitable clients.

institutional investors Pension or mutual fund that manages large sums of money for third-party investors.

integrated position Strategic position in which elements of one position support strong standing in another.

international strategy Process by which a firm approaches its cross-border activities and those of competitors and plans to approach them in the future.

intrinsic value Present value of a company's future cash flows from existing assets and businesses.

joint venture Alliance in which two firms make equity investments in a third legal entity.

key success factor (KSF) Key asset or requisite skill that all firms in an industry must possess in order to be a viable competitor.

knowing-doing gap Phenomenon whereby firms tend to be better at generating new knowledge than at creating new products based on that knowledge.

learning curve Incremental production costs decline at a constant rate as production experience is gained; the steeper the learning curve, the more rapidly costs decline.

Level 5 Hierarchy Model of leadership skills calling for a wide range of abilities, some of which are hierarchical in natures.

long-tail When the selling of individual products that each have low sales volume add up to huge revenues.

low-cost leadership Strategic position based on producing a good or offering a service while maintaining total costs that are lower than what it takes competitors to offer the same product or service.

low-end disruption Strategy that appears at the low end of industry offerings, targeting the lest desirable of incumbents' customers.

managerialism Tendency of managers to make decisions based on personal self-interest rather than the best interests of shareholders.

market for corporate control Control over public corporations is traded, and this theoretically puts some pressure on managers to perform, otherwise their corporation can be taken over.

market value Current market capitalization of a firm.

matrix structure Form of organization in which specialists from functional departments are assigned to work for one or more product or geographic units.

merger Consolidation or combination of two or more firms.

minimum efficient scale (MES) The output level that delivers the lowest total average cost.

mission Declaration of what a firm is and what it stands for—its fundamental values and purpose.

monitoring Functioning of the board in exercising its legal and fiduciary responsibility to oversee executives' behavior and performance and to take action when it's necessary to replace management.

multidivisional structure Form of organization in which divisions are organized around product or geographic markets and are often self-sufficient in terms of functional expertise.

multipoint competition When a firm competes against another firm in multiple product markets or multiple geographic markets (or both).

network structure Form of organization in which small, semiautonomous, and potentially temporary groups are brought together for specific purposes.

new-venture creation Entrepreneurship and the creation of a new business from scratch.

nonequity alliance Alliance that involves neither the assumption of equity interest nor the creation of separate organizations.

offshoring Moving a value chain activity or set of activities to another country, typically where key costs are lower.

organizational structure Relatively stable arrangement of responsibilities, tasks, and people within an organization.

outcome controls Practice of tying rewards to narrowly defined financial criteria.

outsourcing Activity performed for a company by people other than its full-time employees.

patching Process of remapping businesses in accordance with changing market conditions and restitches them into new internal business structures.

peer-to-peer Where individual network members can engage in exchange with any other member of the network.

PESTEL analysis Tool for assessing the political, economic, sociocultural, technological, environmental, and legal contexts in which a firm operates.

portfolio planning Practice of mapping diversified businesses or products based on their relative strengths and market attractiveness.

principal Party, such as a shareholder, who hires an agent to act on his or her behalf.

profit pool Analytical tool that enables managers to calculate profits at various points along an industry value chain.

purchase price Final price actually paid to the target firm's shareholders of an acquired company.

real-options Process of maximizing the upside or limiting the downside of an investment opportunity by uncovering and quantifying the options and discussion points embedded within it.

related diversification Form of diversification in which the business units operated by a firm are highly related.

relational quality Principle identifying four key elements (initial conditions, negotiation process, reciprocal experiences, outside behavior) in establishing and maintaining interorganizational trust.

required performance improvements The increases in combined cash flow of the acquiror and target that are necessary to justify the acquisition premium.

resources Inputs used by firms to create products and services.

return on invested capital (ROIC) How effectively a company uses the money (borrowed or owned) invested in its operations.

revenue-enhancement synergy When total sales are greater if two products are sold and distributed within one company than when they are owned by separate companies.

reward system Bases on which employees are compensated and promoted.

rivalry Intensity of competition within an industry.

road show Series of presentations in which top management promotes an IPO to interested investors and analysts.

S-1 statement Legal document outlining a firm's financial position in preparation for an initial public stock offering.

second mover (often fast follower) Second significant company to move into a market, quickly following the first mover.

serial acquirers Company that engages in frequent acquisitions.

social capital The advantage created through the characteristics of a person's network

social network The collection of ties between people and the strength of those ties.

specialized resources Resource with a narrow range of applicability.

staging Timing and pace of strategic moves.

stakeholder Individual or group with an interest in an organization's ability to deliver intended results and maintain the viability of its products and services.

stereotyping Relying on a conventional or formulaic conception of another group based on some common characteristic.

stock options Incentive device giving an employee the right to buy a share of company stock at a later date for a predetermined price.

straddling Unsuccessful attempt to integrate both low-cost and differentiation positions.

strategic alliance Relationship in which two or more firms combine resources and capabilities in order to enhance the competitive advantage of all parties.

strategic change Significant changes in resource allocation choices, in the business and implementation activities that align the firm's strategy with its vision, or in its vision.

strategic coherence Symmetric coalignment of the five elements of the firm's strategy, the congruence of functional-area policies with these elements, and the overarching fit of various businesses under the corporate umbrella.

strategic group Subset of firms which, because of similar strategies, resources, and capabilities, compete against each other more intensely than with other firms in an industry.

strategic leadership Task of managing an overall enterprise and influencing key organizational outcomes.

strategic management Process by which a firm manages the formulation and implementation of a strategy.

strategic positioning Means by which managers situate a firm relative to its rivals.

strategic purpose Simplified, widely shared mental model of the organization and its future, including anticipated changes in its environment.

strategy The coordinated means by which an organization pursues its goals and objectives.

strategy formulation Process of developing a strategy.

strategy implementation Process of executing a strategy.

succession planning Process of managing a well-planned and well-executed transition from one CEO to the next with positive outcomes for all key stakeholders.

superordinate goal Overarching reference point for a host of hierarchical subgoals.

supplier power Degree to which firms in the supply industry are able to dictate terms to contracts and thereby extract some of the profit that would otherwise by available to competitors in the focal industry.

synergy Condition under which the combined benefits of activities in two or more arenas are greater than the simple sum of those benefits.

takeoff period Period during which a new product generates rapid growth and huge sales increases.

threat of new entry Degree to which new competitors can enter an industry and intensify rivalry.

threat of substitutes Degree to which products of one industry can satisfy the same demand as those of another.

unrelated diversification Form of diversification in which the business units that a firm operates are highly dissimilar.

value chain Total of primary and support value-adding activities by which a firm produces, distributes, and markets a product.

value curve A graphical depiction of how a firm and major groups of its competitors are competing across its industry's factors of completion.

value net model Map of a firm's existing and potential exchange relationships.

vertical alliance Alliance involving a focal firm and a supplier or customer.

vertical integration Diversification into upstream and/or downstream industries.

vertical scope The extent to which a firm is vertically integrated.

vision Simple statement or understanding of what the firm will be in the future.

VRINE model Analytical framework suggesting that a firm with resources and capabilities which are valuable, rare, inimitable, nonsubstitutable, and exploitable will gain a competitive advantage.

willingness to pay Principle of differentiation strategy by which customers are willing to pay more for certain product features.

winner's curse Situation in which a winning M&A bidder must live with the consequences of paying too much for the target.

Index

Photo Credits